Henry D. Thoreau

Dylan Thomas

D1591694

Countee Cullen

Charles Dickens

Jonathan Swift

Daniel DeFoe

G. Bernard Shaw

Phillis Wheatley

Stephen Crane

Langston

Bret Harte

Henry W. Longfellow

Oscar Wilde

Thornton Wilder

Edgar A Poe

Ernest Hemingway

J. Austen

Sinclair Lewis

Herman Melville

Ivan Turgenev

A Bradstreet

T. S. Eliot

Jack London

Thomas Hardy

MACMILLAN LITERATURE SERIES

UNDERSTANDING LITERATURE

SIGNATURE EDITION

TEACHER'S ANNOTATED EDITION

GLENCOE/McGRAW-HILL
A Macmillan/McGraw-Hill Company
Mission Hills, California

Copyright © 1991, 1989 by Glencoe/McGraw-Hill Educational Division.

All rights reserved. Printed in the United States of America.
Except as permitted under the United States Copyright Act of 1976, no part of this publication may be reproduced or distributed in any form or by any means, or stored in a database or retrieval system, without prior permission of the publisher.

Send all inquiries to:
Glencoe/McGraw-Hill
15319 Chatsworth Street
P.O. Box 9509
Mission Hills, CA 91395-9509

ISBN 0-02-635062-9 / 9

1 2 3 4 5 6 7 8 9 97 96 95 94 93 92 91

Macmillan Literature Series

SIGNATURE EDITION

TABLE OF CONTENTS

Student's Edition

PREREADING STRATEGIES CAPTIVATE STUDENTS' MINDS AND PROMOTE LITERARY APPRECIATION.

ake literature the heart of your Language Arts program with *Macmillan Literature Series,* Signature Edition.

The Unit Preview

1 provides a frame of reference for the selection
2 offers a springboard for classroom discussion
3 opens students' minds to learning about themselves through the experiences of others

Before each selection, students will find

1 a brief biography of the author and notes on the author's contributions to literature
2 a purpose-setting question that links the students' experiences to concepts in the selection

PEARL BUCK

1892–1973

•

Buck was born in West Virginia but grew up in China. Many of her works, such as *The Good Earth,* take place in China. The stories by this Nobel Prize recipient create better understanding among people.

Student's Edition

GUIDE STUDENTS THROUGH EXCITING LITERATURE.

rom Beowulf to James Michener, from Emily Dickinson to Dante, *Macmillan Literature Series* presents the most thought-provoking classic and contemporary selections, crossing periods, cultures, and genres. Selections were chosen and organized in response to surveys of 5,200 English teachers.

STUDENTS BECOME ACTIVE READERS THROUGH STUDY AND RESPONSE ACTIVITIES.

After each selection, a three-part questioning strategy leads students through various levels of thinking:

1 Recalling: students recall literal facts.
2 Interpreting: students apply critical thinking skills.
3 Extending: students explore selection ideas.

Challenge and Viewpoint activities encourage different types of response.

Comparing Activities encourage students to look at literature in new ways.

SPEAKING AND LISTENING HANDBOOK *Grades 7–12*

Includes lessons on how to present orally, listen effectively, and interact in collaborative learning activities.

THINKING SKILLS HANDBOOK *Grades 7–12*

Provides lessons on how to apply higher order thinking skills.

READING AND STUDY SKILLS HANDBOOK *Grades 7–10*

Lessons reinforce the skills essential to demonstrating comprehension.

BENJAMIN
FRANKLIN

1706–1790

•

Franklin educated himself by reading widely. He published his first essay as a teenager. He moved penniless from Boston to Philadelphia, where he became a civic leader.

Student's Edition

BY WRITING ABOUT LITERATURE, READERS BECOME GOOD WRITERS.

Writing assignments challenge students at different levels. At the end of selections, students have a choice of two different writing assignments—an analytical composition about the selection or a creative writing project.

The *Writing About Literature Handbook* encourages writing about the selections.

The Research Paper Casebook

Grades 11–12

Guides students through the specific steps needed to produce a successful research paper.

EVALUATE STUDENT PROGRESS WITH UNIT REVIEWS AND ACTIVITIES TO ENSURE COMPREHENSION.

The *Model for Active Reading* and follow-up activities help students extract meaning and enjoyment from the selections in each unit.

Literary Skills Reviews and *Themes Reviews* reinforce the unit lessons.

Student's Resources
Lessons in Active Learning

In the Student Resources handbooks at the back of the Student's Edition are guides for independent learning and evaluation.

ROBERT FROST

1874–1963

Frost is closely identified with New England even though he was born in San Francisco and moved to New Hampshire as a child. He received many honors, including four Pulitzer Prizes.

Teacher's Annotated Edition

IT IS MORE THAN JUST A PLANNING TOOL!
IT IS A PRACTICAL GUIDE WITH
TIME-SAVING FEATURES.

Every feature in the Teacher's Annotated Edition can be immediately used and applied in the classroom.

On-the-page annotations

1 provide on-the-spot help in directing class discussion
2 include ideas that can be shared with students of various abilities
3 save time for busy teachers rather than demand more time

INTRODUCE STUDENTS TO GREAT LITERATURE WITH EFFECTIVE PREREADING STRATEGIES.

Lead students into the literature with the help of these prereading features:

1 *At a Glance* summarizes major developments on the page; teachers can see "what happens where" without having to read the entire selection.
2 *Literary Options* lists the most obvious literary elements associated with the selection allowing teachers to focus on one or more dominant elements or techniques.
3 *Thematic Options* lets teachers select one or more themes to focus on in the teaching of the selection.

GWENDOLYN
BROOKS

1917–

•

Brooks was the first black woman to win a Pulitzer Prize. She began writing poetry that was quite traditional, but in her later work she often uses free verse and open forms.

Teacher's Annotated Edition

THE HELPFUL ANNOTATIONS ARE EASY TO FIND AND USE.

Keyed-to-text annotations highlight passages in the selection for the teacher. Similar to marginal notes that any teacher keeps, these annotations

1 give insight about the passage and its relation to the selection as a whole
2 enrich class discussion
3 are brief enough to be used while teaching

These keyed-to-text annotations include literary elements, background, vocabulary, paraphrases, reading skills, and response journal.

Response Journal offers suggestions for student writing about a specific passage in a selection.
Reflecting on the Selection suggests overview questions that allow students to respond in general before beginning a detailed post-selection analysis.
Guided Reading questions address thinking skills and check students' comprehension page by page, helping prepare them for end-of-selection study questions.

CHALLENGE STUDENTS WITH ACTIVITIES AND REVIEWS THAT DEVELOP THEIR THINKING SKILLS AS THEY RESPOND TO LITERATURE.

Unit teaching notes offer activities for the *Model for Active Reading* feature in the student text.

Answers to themes review help to encourage class discussion.
Answers to end-of-selection questions appear on the Teacher's Annotated Edition page, so there's no more juggling separate answer keys.
Annotations at the beginning of each Student's Resources handbook explain the philosophy, structure, or application of the lessons.

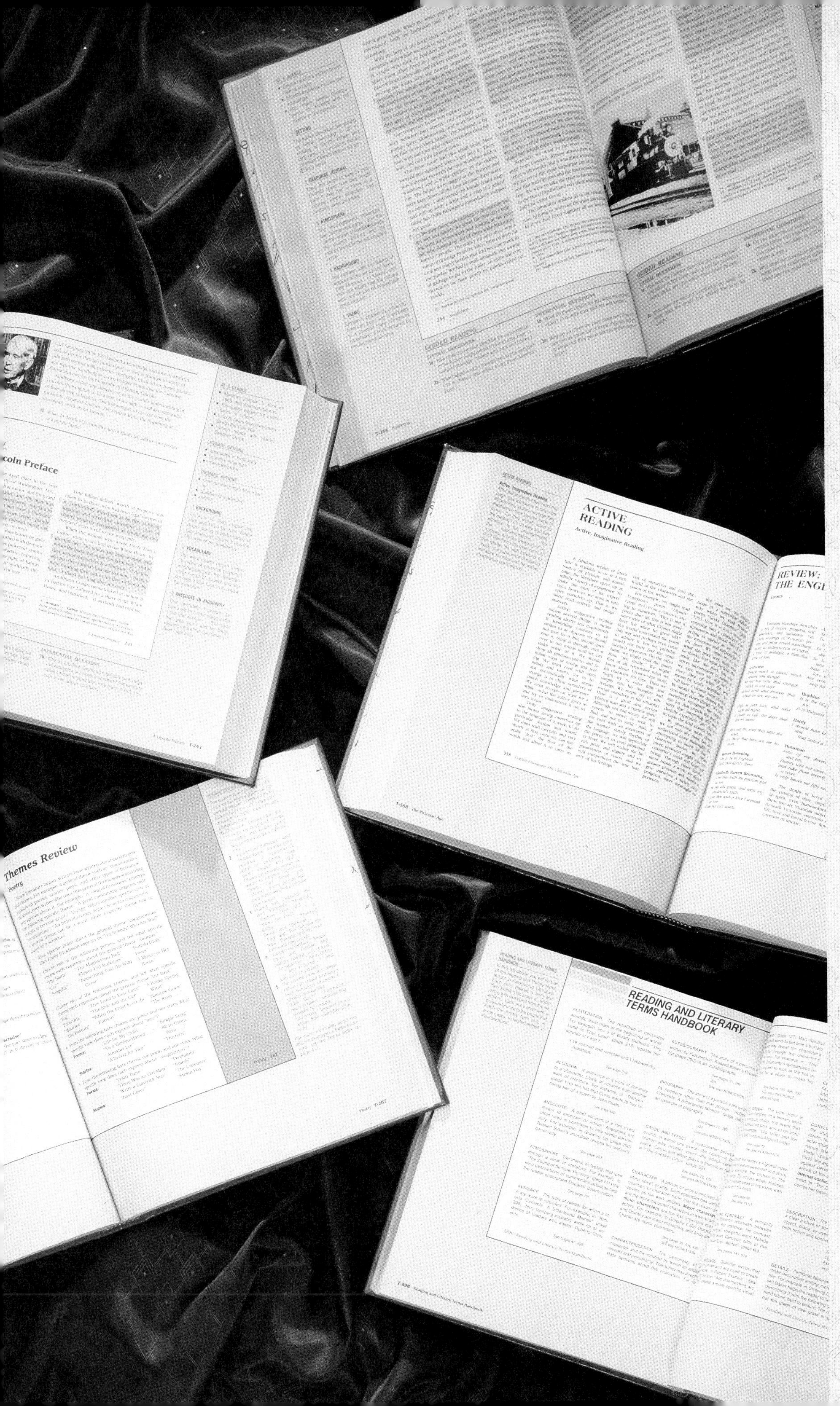

ANTON CHEKHOV

1860–1904

•

Chekhov was the grandson of a Russian serf. While at medical school he began to write, launching a brilliant literary career.

Teacher's Annotated Edition

PROVISION FOR EVALUATION AND WRITING ABOUT LITERATURE TEACH STUDENTS SKILLS TO HELP THEM IN ALL CURRICULUM AREAS.

n-the-page *Suggestions for Critiques* of the two-part composition assignments suggested in the student text save you time in assessing student writing.

It is easy to assess student achievement with a variety of reviews and checkpoints:

1. Selection End: three-level study questions feature recall, interpretation, and extension.
2. Unit End: Literary Skills Review encourages students to look at literature in a broad context.

WILLIAM SHAKESPEARE

1564–1616

•

Shakespeare, poet and playwright, is said to be the world's favorite author. No other writer's plays have been produced so often and read so widely all over the world.

Teacher's Classroom Resources

THE LESSON PLAN BOOKLETS—PREREADING, READING, RESPONDING, AND EVALUATING—BRING IT ALL TOGETHER.

These booklets in the Teacher's Classroom Resources specify when to use each component while teaching a selection.

1 One-page lesson plans begin with clearly stated objectives.
2 Each lesson plan lists materials and activities by lesson elements: *Prereading, Reading and Response, Composition, Closure and Transfer, Reteaching, Enrichment and Extension, and Evaluation.*

The *Macmillan Literature Series* Lesson Plans make teaching manageable by providing step-by-step management of each and every component.

UNIT BOOKLETS HELP STUDENTS BECOME ACTIVE READERS AND IN-DEPTH THINKERS.

For teaching each selection, teachers will find in the Unit Booklets:

A Teaching Chart to identify features in the Student's Edition, Teacher's Annotated Edition, and Teacher's Classroom Resources (including Overhead Transparencies) for use before, during, and after reading a selection.

Teaching Notes

1 Author notes to help teachers provide additional background and context for the selection.
2 A Statement of Theme or Main Idea and Synopsis.
3 Motivation suggestions to engage students' interest before reading.
4 Words in Glossary to show teachers the selection words that appear in the Glossary in the Student's Edition.
5 Additional Projects to help students work in a novel, often nonverbal, way to further explore the selection.

A Prereading Vocabulary blackline master to introduce and provide practice with difficult words from the selection using various strategies.

A Reading Guide blackline master to keep less-able readers focused on the selection and help them note key points as they read.

A Check Test blackline master to give teachers a quick sense of students' grasp of the selection on a literal level.

A Writing Process Guide blackline master to help students complete the analytical composition assignments in the Student's Edition.

A Selection Test blackline master including vocabulary test items to help teachers evaluate the students' understanding.

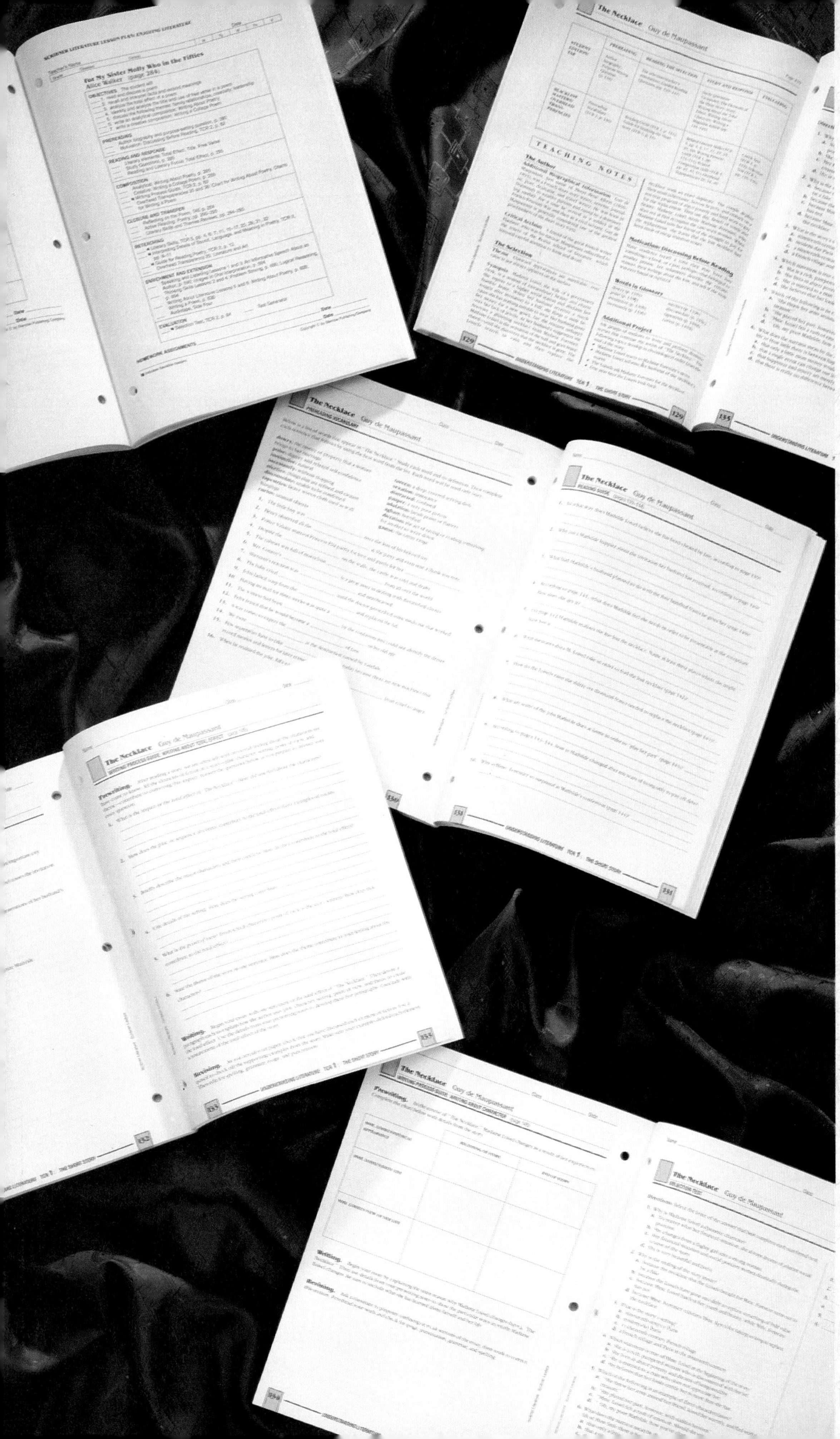

TEACHER'S CLASSROOM RESOURCES

These resources offer everything a teacher needs for planning and teaching lessons for Grades 6–12.

Teacher's Classroom Resources

THE LITERATURE IS MADE ACCESSIBLE TO ALL THE STUDENTS.

Literary Skills and *Active-Learning Guides* provide opportunities for students to become actively involved with literary terms and elements as well as reinforcement of *Student's Resources Lessons in Active Learning*.

An *Answer Key booklet* is a quick reference that provides answers and guidelines for evaluation.

Overhead Transparencies provide an alternative medium for instruction while students are actively involved with great literature.

Teacher's Professional Resources booklet contains helpful articles about the teaching of literature.

Models of Student Writing cover twelve types of writing and exemplify the writing process and the teacher's evaluation of that process.

Additional Teaching Materials complete a comprehensive literature program.

Macmillan Literature Series Test Generator provides individual test items that can be selected from the computer data bank so that tests can be customized.

Macmillan Literature Novel and Drama Guides enable students to apply independently their literary and vocabulary skills.

The Macmillan Literature Series Video Library supports classroom instruction and brings literature to life by showing how to integrate videotapes with reading.

The Macmillan Literature Series Audiotapes expand students' literary experiences with outstanding presentations and active reader comments.

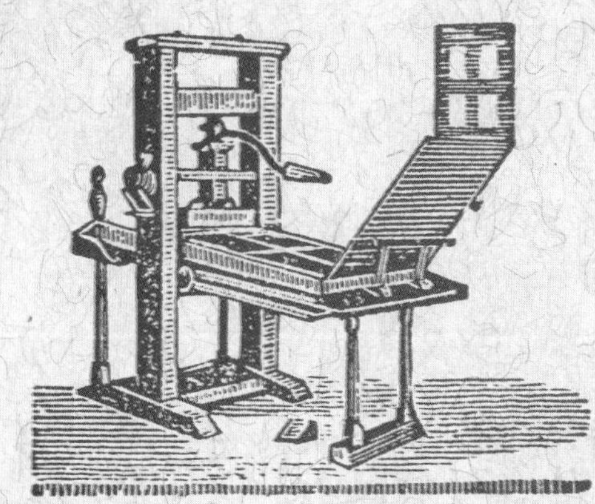

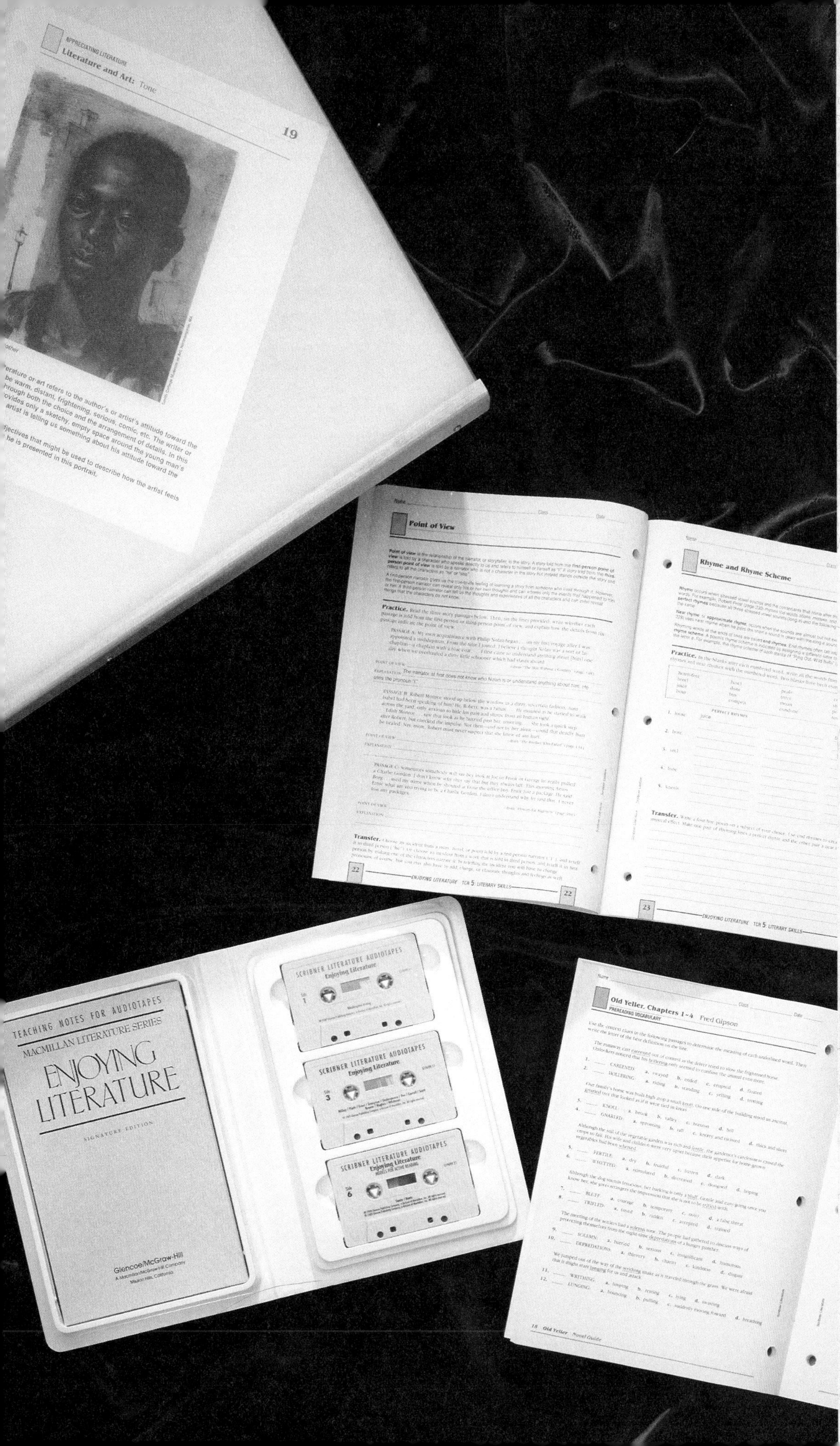

MARK TWAIN

1835–1910

Mark Twain, who was born Samuel Clemens, did not just write a story. He told it. His mastery of American speech and his ability to spin a yarn are unsurpassed.

Scope and Sequence

MACMILLAN LITERATURE SERIES

All the components fit together to make MACMILLAN LITERATURE SERIES, Signature Edition, a comprehensive language arts program.

Reading and Literary Skills	Discovering Literature	Introducing Literature	Enjoying Literature	Understanding Literature	Appreciating Literature	American Literature	English Literature with World Masterpieces	World Literature
allegory						181, 936	56, 120, 287, 290, 893	
alliteration		219, 274, 598	224, 282, 628, 630, 646	195, 720, 724, 730	200, 788, 792	131, 936	18, 26, 430, 996, 1020	
allusion		430, 598	453, 646	487, 724	200, 792	29, 936	276, 285, 286, 656, 1020	
analogy					332, 792	39, 936	1020	
antagonist					792	665, 936	1020	
assonance			227, 646	195, 720, 724	192, 788, 792	131, 937	430, 996, 1020	
atmosphere		131, 172, 598	92, 165, 646	75, 304, 724	58, 792	148–149	225, 756, 1020	
audience		47, 289, 322, 598	25, 297, 330, 486, 646	233, 261, 327	263, 353	68	236	
autobiography, biography		21, 289, 295, 303, 333, 598	11, 297, 304, 312, 646	234, 240, 245, 251, 716, 724	264, 270, 277, 346, 792	58, 244, 937	365, 498, 1021	
ballad, song				171, 724	225, 792	7, 12–14, 170–171, 236–238, 286	5, 49, 52, 55, 141, 143, 266, 313, 366, 372, 394–395, 554, 651, 804, 1021	
blank verse				356, 724	196, 491, 793	123, 937	165, 277, 285, 286, 1021	
cause and effect		72, 479, 598	47, 318, 341, 494, 646					
character		105, 171, 368, 404, 434, 447, 498, 574, 598	67, 77, 430, 462, 468, 496, 566, 622, 624, 646	53, 63, 145, 157, 326–327, 374, 428, 613, 708, 724	44, 134, 432, 512, 612, 772, 793	114, 323, 339, 710, 937	78, 225, 502, 510, 640, 701, 712, 724, 731, 904, 913, 1021	
characterization		95, 109, 170, 404, 434, 498, 532, 574, 598	67, 85, 160, 406, 430, 622, 624, 646, 647	40, 47, 613, 725	39, 793	323, 512, 600–601, 937	78, 79, 104, 698, 712, 724, 819, 1021–1022	
chronological order		72, 308, 599	47, 159, 318, 332, 647					
Classicism						101, 937	311–313, 1022	
climax		65, 172, 308, 332, 404, 599	41, 166, 430, 647	10, 273, 326, 427, 725	20, 448, 793	323, 711, 937	224, 711, 1022, 1028	
comedy			349, 350, 647	293, 725	353, 384, 793	665, 667	132–133, 242–243, 313, 569, 913, 1022	
comparison/contrast		143, 519, 599	211, 647	708	345, 346	92, 896–897	986	
concrete language		235, 599	238, 647	277, 725	320			
conflict		79, 85, 170, 308, 330, 404, 451, 508, 599	52, 165, 430, 647	26, 33, 273, 326, 427, 458, 592, 725	28, 134, 448, 491, 793	323, 365–366, 938	224, 701, 1022, 1028	
consonance				720	192, 788	131, 938	430, 996, 1022	
description		289, 312, 327, 599	297, 323, 333, 648	240, 725	794	92, 311, 938	1023	
details		100, 138, 202, 282, 312, 406, 599	73, 96, 212, 290, 291, 292, 323, 432, 434, 618, 648	69, 158, 240	58, 103, 174, 296, 320	92, 150	42, 78, 79, 104	
dialogue		45, 161, 171, 341, 355, 600	22, 189, 344, 349, 364, 642, 648	33, 273, 293, 326, 726	309, 354, 382, 794	665, 939	52, 476, 933, 1023	
drama		44, 341, 404, 592, 594, 600	22, 349, 364, 430, 432, 433, 640, 642, 648	293, 726	353, 354, 794	665, 710–711, 753, 939	144–145, 236, 242, 391, 826, 1023	
dramatic monologue					235, 794	414, 419, 939	502, 507, 1023	
elegy						261	38, 274, 366, 371, 498, 1024	
epic				433, 726	225, 576, 794	939	5, 8, 120, 277, 285, 351, 786, 820, 1024, 1027	
essay		21, 289, 317, 600	11, 297, 318, 323, 327, 331, 648	263, 273, 277, 280, 285, 726	290, 296, 309, 313, 319, 325, 339, 346, 794	664, 939	228, 332, 339, 461, 466, 1024	
exposition (in plot)				10, 273, 326, 427, 726	20, 296, 448, 794	323, 710, 848, 939	224, 711, 1024, 1028	
fable		145, 455, 600	471, 649	114, 727	90, 795	303, 939–940	732, 1024	

Scope and Sequence

MACMILLAN LITERATURE SERIES

The heart of your language arts program.

Reading and Literary Skills	Discovering Literature	Introducing Literature	Enjoying Literature	Understanding Literature	Appreciating Literature	American Literature	English Literature with World Masterpieces	World Literature
fact vs. opinion		334	342, 343, 651					
falling action				10, 273, 326, 427, 727	20, 448, 795	323, 711	224, 711, 1024, 1028	
figurative language		273, 601	245, 247, 248, 282, 628, 630, 649, 650, 651, 654	63, 196, 727	201, 289, 346, 788, 795	164, 940	140, 177, 448, 1024–1025	
figure of speech		601	649	196, 727	177, 201, 209, 211, 213, 219, 249, 795	164, 220, 940	140, 448, 1025	
foil					795	600–601, 940	903	
folk literature		413, 461, 601	469, 471, 486, 649	75	575, 644	7, 12–14, 70, 170, 236, 426	49, 52, 55, 103, 554, 641, 651, 804, 827, 1025, 1027	
foot				185, 727	795	123, 940	119, 165, 540, 940, 1025	
foreshadowing		91, 172, 369, 508, 601	57, 130, 160, 458, 566, 649	26, 639, 727	20, 795	810, 940	18, 1025	
frame				126, 727	90, 664, 795	298, 613, 940	57, 1025	
free verse			260, 649	727	198, 246, 260, 795	260–261, 265, 404, 413, 426, 940	232, 563, 656, 1025	
hero, protagonist		466, 601	449, 650	433, 467, 726	460, 568, 576, 606, 794, 798	323, 665, 711, 944	5, 146, 224, 351, 433, 436, 861, 1029, 1031	
heroic couplet						87, 170, 941	291, 352, 438, 1025	
imagery, sensory language		16, 233, 274, 498, 601	7, 238, 282, 628, 650	196, 199, 277, 399, 428, 728, 731	75, 205, 249, 320, 346, 796	32, 34, 92, 132, 164, 227, 274, 404, 413, 426, 574, 941	177, 246, 286, 652, 687, 1025–1026	
Imagism						401–402, 404, 409, 413, 427, 450, 783, 941		
inferring		100, 138, 170, 203, 283, 472, 601	73, 96, 213, 292, 406, 650	290	350	536	384	
irony		178, 602	189, 650	145, 428, 728	129, 133, 416, 612, 784, 796	391, 474, 496, 941	225, 640, 1026	
literal language				63, 196, 728	796	164, 942	177	
local color				40, 728	167, 796	311, 315, 334, 340, 395		
lyric poetry		271, 602	275, 650	208, 222, 730	177, 222, 231, 249, 796	286–287, 942	8, 38, 110, 557, 1026	
main idea		317, 324	327, 335, 634	114, 285	90, 780	323, 534, 947	698, 764, 1031	
metaphor		243, 602	247, 628, 630, 650	63, 203, 720, 728	213, 215, 217, 289, 788, 796	39, 164, 942	140, 242, 448, 893, 996, 1026	
meter				185, 728	192, 796	122–123, 215, 942	119, 165, 501, 540, 563, 1026	
Middle English							40, 56–57, 96–97, 1026	
mock-epic						286	351, 439, 1026	
Modernism						401–405, 409, 421, 429, 442, 446, 450, 459, 464, 489, 540, 545, 575, 666–667, 758, 767, 942	563–565, 651, 655, 683	
mood		131	92	729	58, 383, 774, 797	148–149, 621	165, 177, 225, 756, 1027	
myth/legend		413, 422, 602	439, 440, 650–651	439	575–580, 794	7	103, 827, 877, 1026, 1027	
narration		169, 209, 308, 324, 602	297, 318, 332, 651	729	225, 296, 797	113, 844, 942	1027	
narrative poetry		258, 264, 602	273, 651	162, 222, 730	177, 222, 225, 249, 797	286, 942	38, 553, 557, 1027	
narrator		115, 126, 532, 602	107, 120, 550, 651	85, 729	75, 612, 797	319, 333, 753, 942	553, 689, 716, 1027	
Naturalism						311, 396, 399, 942	487, 541, 545, 1027	
nonfiction		21, 289, 308, 312, 317, 322, 586, 588, 603	10, 297, 318, 323, 327, 330, 634, 636, 651	233, 729	263, 346, 786, 797	58, 244, 664	228, 332, 339, 365, 461, 498	
novel		91, 485, 603	501, 651	491, 729	611, 612, 797	114, 156, 395, 943	313, 321, 391, 514, 665, 894, 1027–1028	
Old English							3, 5, 40–41, 1028	
onomatopoeia		228, 603	234, 628, 630, 651	188, 720, 729	200, 788, 797	131, 436, 943	431, 996, 1028	

Scope and Sequence

MACMILLAN LITERATURE SERIES

The heart of your language arts program.

Reading and Literary Skills	Discovering Literature	Introducing Literature	Enjoying Literature	Understanding Literature	Appreciating Literature	American Literature	English Literature with World Masterpieces	World Literature
oral tradition		216, 341, 418, 603	349	433	579	7, 14, 943	5, 18, 49, 52, 55, 804, 820, 862, 1028	
oratory					331	65, 68–69, 96, 255, 943	225	
parallelism				195, 729	194, 331, 346, 797	84, 943	1028	
parody						566, 943	323, 338, 1028	
personification			248, 628, 630, 651	201, 720, 729	209, 788, 798	220, 943	448, 996, 1028	
persuasion		322, 336, 603	297, 330, 344, 652	263, 280, 729	326, 798	84, 943	1028	
plot		57, 65, 404, 532, 572, 603	41, 47, 52, 57, 63, 157, 430, 458, 501, 566, 581, 620, 624, 652	10, 26, 138, 145, 151, 273, 427, 592, 704, 729–730	20, 104, 134, 448, 612, 770, 798	323, 794, 943	224, 391, 514, 639–640, 698, 711, 725, 731, 750, 827, 1028	
point of view		115, 126	107, 120, 157, 550, 652	85, 94, 109, 145, 151, 509, 565, 712, 730	75, 82, 86, 134, 612, 776, 798	333, 384, 613, 943–944	689, 698, 716, 731, 1029	
predicting outcomes		91, 204, 369, 508	57, 214, 566, 620	26, 639, 727	20, 795	810, 940	1025	
purpose		47, 289, 295, 322, 604	25, 297, 305, 652	233, 273, 277, 280, 285, 718	263, 277, 290, 313, 346, 786	69, 83	990	
Realism						310–311, 367, 388, 395–396, 399, 666, 669, 944	487, 488, 545, 563, 1029	
resolution		65, 172, 604	41, 167, 620, 653	10, 273, 326, 427, 730	20, 798	323, 711	224, 711, 1028, 1029	
rhyme		16, 221, 604	7, 228, 628, 653	187, 356, 720, 725, 730	192, 239, 250, 260, 261, 798, 799	131, 170, 286, 552, 944	119, 430, 996, 1029	
rhyme scheme			228, 653	187, 730	239, 241, 799	170, 945	119, 458	
rhythm		16, 225, 274, 604	7, 231, 282, 628, 630, 653	185, 356, 720	177, 192, 196, 260, 261, 491, 788, 799	87, 122–123, 170, 215, 228, 265, 426, 436, 758, 945	57, 119, 165, 258, 327, 352, 439, 501, 540, 554, 563, 684, 996, 1029, 1030	
rising action				10, 273, 326, 427, 730	20, 799	323, 711, 945	224, 711, 1028	
romance					579, 799	156, 945	49, 353, 441, 894	
Romanticism						101, 119, 132, 437, 567, 570, 628, 666, 945	366, 372, 376, 387, 389–391, 394–395, 408, 432–433, 442, 487, 1029	
satire					663, 722, 799	483, 548, 945	242, 243, 295, 312, 331, 340, 732, 894, 903, 1030	
setting		131, 169, 186, 404, 532, 605	92, 101, 157, 164, 349, 430, 502, 581, 624, 653	69, 75, 145, 304, 428, 509, 710, 731	58, 68, 134, 383, 612, 774, 799	148–149, 323, 945	225, 514, 640, 698, 756, 1030	
short story		13, 53, 576, 605	4, 31, 624, 653	1, 145, 158, 159, 731	1, 149, 153, 166, 174, 799	323, 945–946	565, 698, 1030	
simile		240, 605	245, 628, 630, 654	63, 202, 487, 720, 727, 731	211, 289, 788, 799	39, 164, 946	140, 820, 996, 1024, 1025, 1030	
skimming and scanning		49, 604, 605	27, 653, 654	185		123, 945		
soliloquy				399, 731	512, 799	946	145, 165, 612, 1030	
sonnet					236, 239, 241, 799, 800	392, 394, 946	114, 119, 139, 251, 274, 396, 442, 1030	
speaker			279, 654	175, 177, 720, 731	178, 181, 249, 788, 800	946	116, 165, 557, 996	
stage directions and staging		45, 341, 385, 605	22, 349, 365, 642, 654	293, 304, 326–327, 430, 731	354, 383, 432, 465, 536, 800	665, 669, 710, 946	236, 1030	
stanza		16, 252, 605	7, 258, 654	161, 171, 731	177, 239, 241, 800	170–171, 552, 946	55, 127, 371, 406, 438, 439, 458, 883, 1021, 1031	
stream of consciousness						403–404, 575, 582–583, 639, 946	563, 565, 725, 731, 1028, 1031	

Scope and Sequence

MACMILLAN LITERATURE SERIES

The heart of your language arts program.

Reading and Literary Skills	Discovering Literature	Introducing Literature	Enjoying Literature	Understanding Literature	Appreciating Literature	American Literature	English Literature with World Masterpieces	World Literature
style		47	25	233, 277, 731	263, 800	3, 23, 384, 464, 496, 772–773, 946	243, 246, 277, 285, 286, 653, 683, 752, 1031	
symbol			287	436	114, 134, 173, 219, 782, 800	190–191, 650–651, 902–903, 947	376, 382, 383, 640, 650, 717, 992, 1031	
theme		145, 156, 174, 178, 186, 200, 209, 267, 269, 342, 368, 371, 404, 605	4, 7, 139, 145, 157, 276, 277, 279, 282, 287, 350, 366, 430, 502, 654	114, 118, 126, 145, 157, 188, 327, 428, 540, 714, 731	90, 98, 134, 536, 612, 780, 800	323, 384, 534, 650–651, 710–711, 904–905, 947	225, 514, 698, 764, 994, 1031	
thesis statement		317, 324, 606	327, 335, 618, 654	285, 702	339, 769, 800	894	984	
tone					82, 134, 178, 186, 263, 778, 800	474, 870, 947	246, 265, 285, 312, 640, 658, 676, 756, 1002, 1031	
topic sentence		322, 331, 606	305, 335, 655	285, 703	769			
total effect		178, 186, 200, 277, 323, 404, 532	157, 178, 211, 285, 331, 430, 581, 628	127, 220, 222, 227, 286, 427, 540, 668	134, 247, 253, 346, 459, 569, 605, 661, 734, 790	306, 908–909	224–225, 639, 998	
tragedy			350, 655	293, 331, 731	353, 462, 568, 800	665	133, 146, 224, 313, 826, 861, 1031	
Transcendentalism						154–155, 260, 947		
word choice		47, 238	25, 243, 655	181, 728, 731	178, 181, 249, 800	211	395, 502, 554, 569, 651, 663, 679, 683, 756	

Composition Skills	Discovering Literature	Introducing Literature	Enjoying Literature	Understanding Literature	Appreciating Literature	American Literature	English Literature with World Masterpieces	World Literature
ANALYTICAL (Students are asked to write about the following literary genres, techniques, elements, and terms.)								
autobiography, biography		295, 586	305, 634	240, 245, 251, 257, 716	270, 277, 281	64		
character		105, 115, 156, 174, 369, 447, 472, 574	67, 77, 107, 270, 365, 468, 622	40, 47, 53, 63, 109, 126, 145, 157, 429, 669, 706, 708	39, 44, 52, 154, 460, 570, 662, 772	211, 339, 441, 512	41, 79, 103, 726, 731	
comparison/contrast		265, 369	67	63, 669, 708	52, 570, 662, 772	29, 39, 95, 391, 496, 588, 605, 621, 632, 896–897	127, 269, 507, 650, 701, 893, 913, 937, 951, 986	
diction and sentence structure						171, 827	249	
drama		45, 405, 592	23, 431, 640		383	711	225, 640	
figures of speech				205	114, 117	220		
imagery		233, 240	238, 247, 628	216	207, 213, 251	227	143	
irony					129, 784	391	351	
nonfiction		295, 312, 586	305, 323, 328, 634	262, 273, 277, 280, 285, 289, 718	296, 309, 320, 323, 326, 332, 339, 349, 786	180, 244, 844, 853, 900–901	231, 339, 465, 705, 990	
plot		57, 72, 85, 126, 167, 279, 443, 461, 572	41, 52, 243, 273, 620	26, 138, 151, 704	28, 770	113, 583	764	
poetry		218, 269, 277, 281, 580	225, 234, 285, 289, 628	167, 173, 178, 205, 212, 215, 217, 225, 226, 720	181, 194, 198, 206, 215, 217, 227, 230, 233, 235, 239, 255, 788	134, 273, 287, 387, 413, 420, 426, 449, 463, 779, 906–907	452, 527, 537, 545, 646, 671, 679, 685, 996	
point of view				85, 94 ,151, 178, 712	75, 776	801		
purpose				245, 257, 280, 285	270	653, 660, 853	339, 990	
review of a book or drama		45, 405, 533, 592	23, 431, 582, 640					
setting		131, 182	92, 167, 482	69, 75, 80, 710	58, 68, 774	324		
symbol					114, 117, 345, 782	333, 627, 832, 840, 902–903	431, 501, 667, 688, 724, 992	
theme		145	189	114, 118, 157, 540, 714	90, 99, 108, 780	124, 475, 535, 810, 904–905	285, 756, 803, 873, 994	
tone					86, 154, 289, 778	305	656	
total effect			189, 628	145, 429, 540, 669, 722	141, 167, 259, 570, 735, 790	149, 637, 651, 908–909	225, 640, 998	

Scope and Sequence

MACMILLAN LITERATURE SERIES

The heart of your language arts program.

Composition Skills	Discovering Literature	Introducing Literature	Enjoying Literature	Understanding Literature	Appreciating Literature	American Literature	English Literature with World Masterpieces	World Literature
CREATIVE (Students are asked to create the following kinds of written materials.)								
anecdote				126	270	588		
aphorisms						64		
article				145	108, 114, 606			
description		156, 182, 216, 265, 269, 312, 447, 466, 472, 477	67, 77, 92, 273, 323, 462, 482, 493	69, 75, 94, 151, 205, 216, 277, 289	58, 68, 99, 117, 141, 192, 206, 207, 251, 320, 323, 383	45, 92, 118, 149, 191, 339, 366, 463, 475, 512, 621, 660	41, 103, 294, 406, 431, 527, 545	
dialogue		150, 423, 443	243, 468	109	20, 52, 570	711	933	
diary, journal entry		105	52, 582	33, 47, 262	133	29, 252, 651	305, 711, 756	
drama		45, 126, 369, 594	23, 189, 431, 468, 642	138, 304	75	420, 711	507, 861, 877, 913	
essay		295, 312, 322	305, 323, 328	273, 280, 285	296, 309, 326, 339, 349	171, 180, 844, 869	231, 339, 705	
fable		145, 455	139	118	90	305		
figurative language, imagery			238	63	213, 217	220, 387	143, 342, 667	
narrative, story		14, 72, 115, 174, 279, 308, 451, 461, 576	5, 107, 167, 624	53, 80, 85, 151, 157, 225, 429, 540	150, 281, 309	449, 482, 496, 613	286, 514, 724, 893	
opinion				245, 280	129	69, 353, 653		
persuasion		238, 322	365	280	44, 167, 326, 332	39, 84, 605		
poem		131, 218, 226, 233, 240, 257, 277, 281, 582	229, 265, 275, 279, 285, 630	167, 215, 217, 226, 327	181, 183, 186, 194, 198, 213, 215, 227, 230, 233, 235, 239, 244, 251, 255, 259	273, 413, 426, 459, 552, 765	127, 646, 650, 656, 662, 671, 679, 683, 825, 937	
point of view				173, 178, 669	309	113	685, 873	
setting			92, 487	304	68, 320	333, 637		
sketch				240, 251, 487	270	118, 211, 324	365, 701	
speech				114	44, 332, 460	257, 420, 827	225, 507	

Vocabulary Skills	Discovering Literature	Introducing Literature	Enjoying Literature	Understanding Literature	Appreciating Literature	American Literature	English Literature with World Masterpieces	World Literature
analogies		182, 317	73, 328	262	154, 309, 662	287, 560, 660	469, 501, 925, 937, 961	
antonyms		135, 150, 447	156, 232, 449	26, 114, 157	114, 296, 332	39, 124, 366, 601, 711	286, 358, 540, 764, 913, 955	
connotation/denotation			453	213	200	149, 211		
context clues		22, 95, 201	11, 86, 365, 458, 581	85	99, 150, 320			
dialect		238	102	126, 210	606	324	640	
dictionary		80	58, 482					
etymology		267, 385, 477	260, 318	75, 151, 487	39, 270, 339, 460	14, 92, 420, 773, 785	97, 305, 873	
glossary		138	96					
jargon, technical words, slang		369	305	181, 728	735	512		
pronunciation key		303	393					
sentence completions		65, 115, 161, 186, 265, 279, 461	47, 227	273	44, 133, 326	29, 87, 535, 651	861	
synonyms		14, 58, 107, 221, 295	5, 41, 130, 312	10, 40, 245	20, 75, 345	22, 64, 455, 832	89, 231, 331, 481, 650, 929	
thesaurus		252	179					
word choice		252	179	185, 251, 280	129, 188, 200, 227, 232, 289, 735	80, 171, 227, 257, 366, 512, 563	371, 431, 679	
word development, invention				190	167, 246, 270, 339	273	903	

Glencoe/McGraw-Hill
A Macmillan/McGraw-Hill Company
15319 Chatsworth Street
Mission Hills, California 91345

MACMILLAN LITERATURE SERIES

SIGNATURE EDITION

DISCOVERING LITERATURE

INTRODUCING LITERATURE

ENJOYING LITERATURE

UNDERSTANDING LITERATURE

APPRECIATING LITERATURE

AMERICAN LITERATURE

ENGLISH LITERATURE
WITH WORLD MASTERPIECES

WORLD LITERATURE

FRONT COVER, detail, and BACK COVER: *Waterlilies and Japanese Bridge,* 1899, oil on canvas, Claude Monet, French (1840–1926).
The Art Museum, Princeton University. From the Collection of William Church Osborn, Class of 1883, Trustee of Princeton University (1914–1951), President of the Metropolitan Museum of Art (1941–1947); gift of his family.

GENERAL ADVISERS

READING AND INSTRUCTIONAL METHODS
Jack Cassidy
Professor of Education
Millersville University
Millersville, Pennsylvania

TEACHER'S PROFESSIONAL RESOURCES
Robert DiYanni
Professor of English
Pace University
Pleasantville, New York

SPEAKING AND LISTENING SKILLS
R. Brian Loxley
Communications Consultant
New York, New York

THINKING SKILLS
Eric Cooper
Former Director, Comprehension and Cognition Project, The College Board
New York, New York

LITERATURE AND CURRICULUM
George Kearns
Associate Professor of English
Rutgers University
New Brunswick, New Jersey

CONSULTANTS

Paula A. Calabrese, Principal, Espe School, North Allegheny School District, Pennsylvania

Sandra A. Cavender, English Teacher and Former Chairperson, Nathan Hale High School, West Allis, Wisconsin

Cathy Y. Lynn, Judson High School, Judson Independent School District, Texas

Judi Purvis, Secondary Language Arts Appraiser, Carrollton–Farmers Branch Independent School District, Texas

Robert S. Ranta, Supervisor of Languages, Lacey Township High School, Lanoka Harbor, New Jersey

Marjory Carter Willis, Teacher, Midlothian High School, Midlothian, Virginia

WRITERS

Instructional Text

Elizabeth Ackley, English Teacher

Cosmo F. Ferrara, Writer and Consultant, Former Department Chair

Gale Cornelia Flynn, Poet and Writer, Former English Teacher

Brian McLaughlin, Educational Writer

Patricia Dodge Posephney, English Teacher

Barbara King-Shaver, Writer

Marilyn Sulsky, English Teacher

Thinking Skills Handbook

Beau F. Jones-Davis, North Central Regional Educational Laboratory, Elmhurst, Illinois

Susan Sardy, Yeshiva University, New York, New York

John Sherk, University of Missouri, Kansas City, Missouri

Writing About Literature Handbook

Catherine Sagan, English Department Chair

WRITERS

Teacher's Classroom Resources

Stanlee Brimberg, Bank Street School for Children, New York, New York

Ellen Davis, Friendswood Independent School District, Texas

Judith H. McGee, Coordinator of Secondary Education, Athens Independent School District, Texas

Robin Messing, Teachers and Writers Collaborative, New York, New York

David Nicholson, Riverdale Country School, Bronx, New York

The publisher is grateful for assistance and comments from the following people:

Jack V. Booch, Theatre Guild, New York, New York

Mrs. Rosalie Clark, Austin High School, Decatur, Alabama

Mr. Albert G. Craz, Northport–East Northport High School, Northport, New York

Gerald Dwight, Cherry Hill High School West, Cherry Hill, New Jersey

José Flores, Center for Mexican American Studies, University of Texas, Austin

Mrs. Doris E. R. Gilbert, Syracuse City Schools, Syracuse, New York

William Ince, Stuyvesant High School, New York, New York

Francisco Jiménez, Santa Clara University, Santa Clara, California

Mr. William C. Johanson, Mountain View High School, Orem, Utah

Iris Gates McAnear, Austin High School, Decatur, Alabama

Mr. Martin Moldenhauer, Northwestern Preparatory School, Watertown, Wisconsin

Nancy Murvine, Tatnall Middle School, Wilmington, Delaware

Margaret McCardell Ruska, Austin Public Schools, Austin, Texas

Richard E. Stebbins, Principal, Howard Elementary School, Medford, Oregon

Mrs. Edward M. Strieber, (Formerly) Austin Public Schools, Austin, Texas

MACMILLAN LITERATURE SERIES

UNDERSTANDING LITERATURE

SIGNATURE EDITION

GLENCOE/McGRAW-HILL
A Macmillan/McGraw-Hill Company
Mission Hills, California

Copyright © 1991, 1989, 1987, 1984 by Glencoe/McGraw-Hill Educational Division.

All rights reserved. Printed in the United States of America. Except as permitted under the United States Copyright Act of 1976, no part of this publication may be reproduced or distributed in any form or by any means, or stored in a database or retrieval system, without prior permission of the publisher.

Send all inquiries to:
Glencoe/McGraw-Hill
15319 Chatsworth Street
P.O. Box 9509
Mission Hills, CA 91395-9509

Pupil's Edition ISBN 0-02-635061-0 / 9

Teacher's Annotated Edition ISBN 0-02-635062-9 / 9

1 2 3 4 5 6 7 8 9   97 96 95 94 93 92 91

ACKNOWLEDGMENTS

Grateful acknowledgment is given authors, publishers, and agents for permission to reprint the following copyrighted material. Every effort has been made to determine copyright owners. In the case of any omissions, the Publisher will be pleased to make suitable acknowledgments in future editions.

Arte Público Press
EVANGELINA VIGIL-PIÑÓN: "space." First published in *The Computer Is Down.* Copyright © 1987 by University of Houston Arte Público Press. Reprinted by permission of Arte Público Press.

Elizabeth Barnett
EDNA ST. VINCENT MILLAY: "The Courage That My Mother Had" from *Collected Poems,* Harper & Row. Copyright © 1954, 1982 by Norma Millay Ellis. Reprinted by permission of Elizabeth Barnett.

Branden Press, Inc.
MATSUO BASHŌ: "The moon glows the same," "Within plum orchard," and "Yellow rose petals" from *Full Moon Is Rising,* translated by James David Andrews. Reprinted courtesy of Branden Press, Inc., 21 Station Street, Brookline Village, MA 02147.

Brandt & Brandt Literary Agents, Inc.
ERNLE BRADFORD: Much of the information on the map of the Mediterranean that appears in the introduction of the *Odyssey* was taken from *Ulysses Found.*
RICHARD CONNELL: "The Most Dangerous Game." Copyright, 1924 by Richard Connell, copyright renewed, 1952 by Louise Fox Connell.
SHIRLEY JACKSON: "About Two Nice People." First published in *Ladies Home Journal.* Copyright © 1951 by Shirley Jackson.
The preceding selections were reprinted by permission of Brandt & Brandt Literary Agents, Inc.

Doubleday & Company, Inc.
ANNE FRANK: Excerpts from *The Diary of a Young Girl.* Copyright 1952 by Otto H. Frank.
HOMER: From Homer, *The Odyssey,* translated by Robert Fitzgerald. Copyright © 1961 by Robert Fitzgerald.
THEODORE ROETHKE: "Child on Top of a Greenhouse" from *The Collected Poems of Theodore Roethke.* Copyright 1946 by Editorial Publications, Inc.
The preceding selections were reprinted by permission of Doubleday, a division of Bantam, Doubleday, Dell Publishing Group, Inc.

E. P. Dutton & Company, Inc.
MARCHETTE CHUTE: From *Shakespeare of London.* Copyright © 1949 by E. P. Dutton & Co., Inc. Renewal 1977, by Marchette Chute. Reprinted by permission of the publisher, E. P. Dutton, a division of NAL Penguin.

Farrar, Straus and Giroux, Inc.
ISAAC BASHEVIS SINGER: "The Son from America" from *A Crown of Feathers.* Copyright © 1970, 1971, 1972, 1973 by Isaac Bashevis Singer. Reprinted by permission of Farrar, Straus and Giroux, Inc.

Samuel French, Inc.

SERAFIN AND JOAQUIN ALVAREZ QUINTERO: *A Sunny Morning*, translated by Lucretia Xavier Floyd. Copyright, 1920, by Lucretia Xavier Floyd. Copyright, 1947 (In Renewal), by Mrs. Geneva Floyd.

The preceding selection was reprinted by permission of Samuel French, Inc. *Caution:* Professionals and amateurs are hereby warned that the preceding selection, being fully protected under the copyright laws of the United States of America, the former British Empire and Commonwealth countries, and all other countries of the Copyright Union, is subject to a royalty. All rights, including professional, amateur, motion pictures, recitation, public reading, radio, television and cablevision broadcasting and the rights of translation into foreign languages are strictly reserved. Amateurs may give *stage* production of "A Sunny Morning" upon payment of a royalty of Ten Dollars ($10.00) for each performance, one week before the play is given. For all other rights contact Samuel French, Inc., at 45 West 25th Street, New York, N.Y. 10010. Copies of this play, in individual paper covered acting editions, are available from Samuel French, Inc., 45 West 25th St., New York, N.Y. 10010 or 7632 Sunset Blvd., Hollywood, Calif. 90046 or in Canada Samuel French, (Canada) Ltd., 80 Richmond Street East, Toronto M5C 1P1, Canada.

Harcourt Brace Jovanovich, Inc.

ANTON CHEKHOV: "A Slander" translated by Natalie Wollard. Copyright © 1970 by Harcourt Brace Jovanovich, Inc.

E. E. CUMMINGS: "maggie and milly and molly and may" from *E. E. Cummings Complete Poems 1913–1962.* Copyright © 1956 by E. E. Cummings.

ANNE MORROW LINDBERGH: "Sayonara" from *North to the Orient.* Copyright 1935, 1963 by Anne Morrow Lindbergh.

GUY DE MAUPASSANT: "The Necklace" translated by Newbury LeB. Morse from *Adventures in Reading*, Olympic Edition. Copyright © 1958 by Harcourt Brace Jovanovich, Inc.

CARL SANDBURG: Abridged from *A Lincoln Preface.* Copyright 1953 by Carl Sandburg; renewed 1981 by Margaret Sandburg, Janet Sandburg, and Helga Sandburg Crile. "Lost" from *Chicago Poems* by Carl Sandburg. Copyright 1916 by Holt, Rinehart and Winston, Inc.; renewed 1944 by Carl Sandburg.

ALICE WALKER: "Women" from *Revolutionary Petunias and Other Poems.* Copyright © 1970 by Alice Walker.

JESSAMYN WEST: "Sixteen" from *Cress Delahanty.* Copyright 1946, 1974 by Jessamyn West.

The preceding selections were reprinted by permission of Harcourt Brace Jovanovich, Inc.

Harper & Row, Publishers, Inc.

PEARL S. BUCK: "The Good Deed" from *The Good Deed and Other Stories of Asia, Past and Present.* Copyright, 1953 by Pearl S. Buck.

The preceding selection was reprinted by permission of Harper & Row, Publishers, Inc.

Harvard University Press

EMILY DICKINSON: "A Narrow Fellow in the Grass" and "A Word is Dead" from *The Poems of Emily Dickinson*, edited by Thomas H. Johnson, Cambridge, Mass.: The Belknap Press of Harvard University Press. Copyright 1951, © 1955, 1979, 1983 by the President and Fellows of Harvard College. Reprinted by permission of the publishers and the Trustees of Amherst College.

John Hawkins & Associates, Inc.

RICHARD WRIGHT: Seven Hokku Poems. Copyright by Richard Wright. Reprinted by permission of John Hawkins & Associates, Inc.

Henry Holt & Company

DOROTHY CANFIELD FISHER: "The Heyday of the Blood" from *Hillsboro People.* Copyright 1915 by Holt, Rinehart and Winston. Copyright 1943 by Dorothy Canfield Fisher.

ROBERT FROST: "The Runaway" from *The Poetry of Robert Frost,* edited by Edward Connery Lathem. Copyright 1923, © 1969 by Holt, Rinehart and Winston. Copyright 1951 by Robert Frost.

The preceding selections were reprinted by permission of Henry Holt & Company.

Lucy Kroll Agency

HORTON FOOTE: *The Dancers.* Copyright © 1955 by Horton Foote. By permission of Lucy Kroll Agency.

Caution: Professionals and amateurs are hereby warned that all of the plays in this volume, being fully protected under the copyright laws of the United States of America, the British Empire, including the Dominion of Canada, and all other countries of the Copyright Union, are subject to royalty. All rights, including professional, amateur, motion picture, recitation, lecturing, public reading, radio broadcasting, television, and the rights of translation into foreign languages, are strictly reserved. All inquiries (except for amateur rights) should be addressed to the author's representative, Lucy Kroll, 119 West 57th Street, New York, N.Y. 10019.

The amateur acting rights of all the plays in this volume are controlled exclusively by DRAMATISTS PLAY SERVICE, INC., 440 Park Avenue South, New York, N.Y. 10016, without whose permission in writing no amateur performance of them may be made.

SOUND EFFECT RECORD

The Play Service can furnish the following sound effect record, which may be used in connection with producing this play. The *The Dancers*—Record No. 5003, Car horn record sells for $2.95, which price includes packing and shipping.

NOTE BY THE PUBLISHER

The Play Service reminds all persons that it cannot authorize the use of any of the plays in this volume for radio or television broadcasting. All groups, amateur or professional, interested in using any of these plays over the radio or on television must secure permission from the author's agent, Lucy Kroll Agency, 119 West 57th Street, New York, N.Y. 10019.

This play has been adapted for production on the living stage.

Copyrights and Acknowledgments continue on pages 748–750, which represent a continuation of the copyright page.

A LETTER TO THE STUDENT

Understanding Literature is an anthology, or collection, of stories, poems, plays, novels, and other works of literature written by many different authors. All authors, no matter what they write, want their readers to understand them. As you may have guessed from its title, the goal of this book is to help you gain that understanding.

The best way to understand literature is to *think* about what you read. Just as you learn to throw a baseball only by throwing a baseball, you develop the skills you need to think about literature by thinking about literature. This is just what *Understanding Literature* is designed to help you do.

You have, of course, been doing this kind of thinking for many years. You have asked yourself questions like "What makes this character act this way?" and "What idea is this poet trying to communicate?"

Now, to help you think about each selection in an organized way, this anthology provides you with three different types of Study Questions. These questions are designed to help you focus your thoughts as you *recall* the details of a selection, *interpret* the meaning of those details, and *extend* those details into your own experience. Special features in this book direct your attention to the language of the selection and the specific literary skills the author used to write it.

Near the back of this book you will find a special section called "Student's Resources: Lessons in Active Learning." The handbooks that make up this section are practical guides for responding to literature by speaking, thinking, reading and studying, and writing. Each handbook lesson is designed to help you grow as an active, independent reader and thinker, to help you take charge of your own learning.

The British writer Richard Steele once said, "Reading is to the mind what exercise is to the body." This anthology will help you exercise both your mind and your imagination. As you have already begun to find out, the rewards of this kind of exercise are great. Those rewards include the enjoyment of what you read and the sense of discovery that all great literature provides.

CONTENTS

THE SHORT STORY

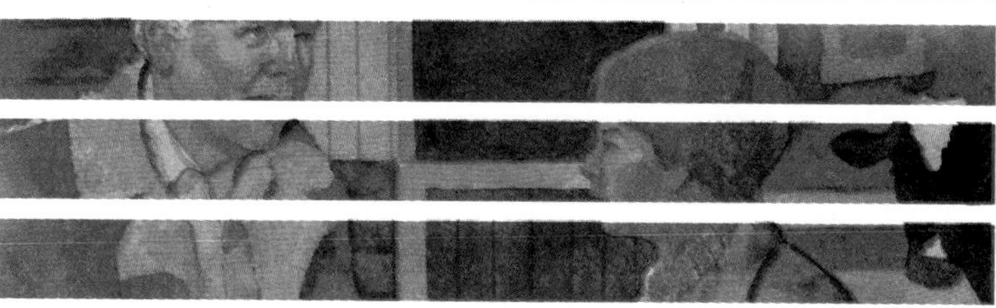

PREVIEW: THE SHORT STORY *1*

The selections in Understanding Literature *were carefully chosen. The annotations in this column indicate the literary skill or element that each selection illustrates.*

POETRY

NONFICTION

DRAMA

THE EPIC

THE NOVEL

STUDENT'S RESOURCES

Related blackline masters in *Teacher's Classroom Resources*.

Instruction and literature-based activities for oral/aural skills. Students may use lessons with *any* selection.

Definition, example, explanation for each skill plus procedures for application to literature. Students may use lessons with *any* selection.

Focused instruction on skills most essential to extracting meaning and demonstrating mastery. Students may use handbook as *constant* reference.

Composition assignments throughout the text refer to these lessons, which reinforce prewriting, writing, and revising skills.

The Short Story

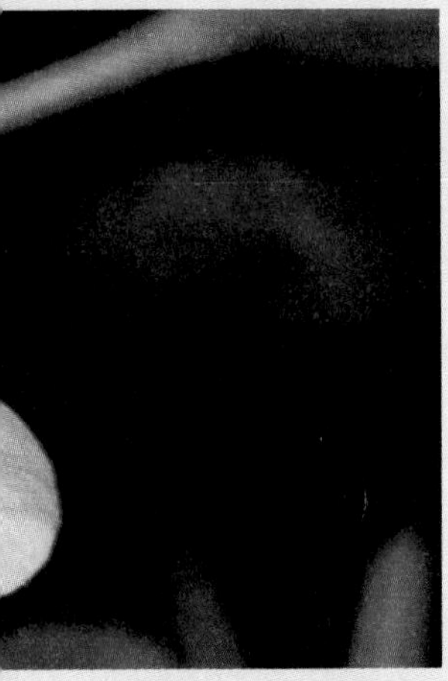

PREVIEW: THE SHORT STORY

Why do we read fiction? The answer is simple. We read it because we like it. And we like it because fiction, as an image of life, stimulates and gratifies our interest in life.

—Robert Penn Warren

A short story, like any work of fiction, is not a real-life account but the product of an author's imagination. As such, stories can be written on a wide range of subjects. The only limit on a story is its length—a short story should be readable in one sitting. A good short story, however, presents enough lifelike qualities to help us better understand ourselves and our world.

The following stories illustrate the enormous range and wealth of short stories. Some stories are great adventure tales that make us read on, eager to find out what will happen next. Some stories present quiet, ordinary-sounding events. Other stories carry us to faraway places or times. Always, a story presents us with a world of the author's imagination. The author artfully combines people, places, events, and ideas to create a unique, fictional world. In putting these parts together to form a story, the author always has at least one important purpose in mind: to illustrate a truth—a generalization—about life.

The stories on the following pages are grouped according to some of the basic elements that an author works with when writing a story: plot, character, setting, point of view, and theme. The last group of stories illustrates the total effect achieved from skillfully varying and intermingling these basic ingredients. These elements contain the key to approaching any story with deeper understanding and greater pleasure.

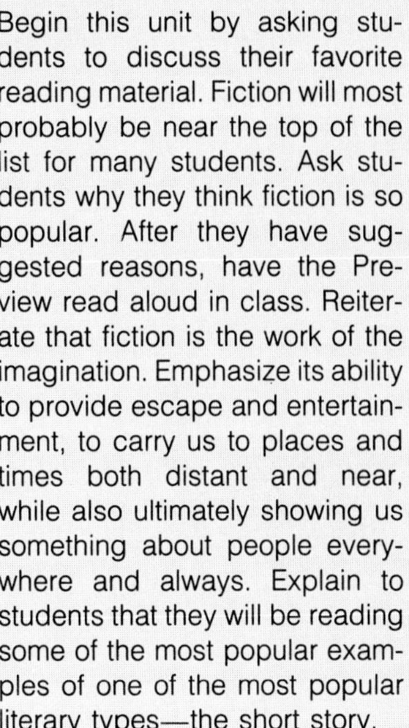

PREVIEW

Begin this unit by asking students to discuss their favorite reading material. Fiction will most probably be near the top of the list for many students. Ask students why they think fiction is so popular. After they have suggested reasons, have the Preview read aloud in class. Reiterate that fiction is the work of the imagination. Emphasize its ability to provide escape and entertainment, to carry us to places and times both distant and near, while also ultimately showing us something about people everywhere and always. Explain to students that they will be reading some of the most popular examples of one of the most popular literary types—the short story.

AT A GLANCE

- Mr. White plays chess with his son as his wife knits by the fire on a cold, stormy night.
- A visitor comes to their door, and Mr. White greets him.

LITERARY OPTIONS

- plot development
- setting
- irony

THEMATIC OPTIONS

- fate
- mystery and suspense

1 SETTING

The bright fire and drawn blinds of the home contrast with the cold and wet world outside.

2 CHARACTERIZATION

A strong bond of love and understanding exists among the members of the family.

LITERARY FOCUS: Plot

Although W. W. Jacobs (1863–1943) worked as a civil servant in England, he devoted his spare time to what he enjoyed doing most—writing fiction. Jacobs' most famous story is "The Monkey's Paw," which has also been dramatized as a one-act play.

- As you read, think about how this story may end. Are you surprised by the actual ending?

W. W. Jacobs

The Monkey's Paw

I

1 Without, the night was cold and wet, but in the small parlor of Lakesnam Villa the blinds were drawn and the fire burned brightly. Father and son were at chess, the former, who possessed ideas about the game involving radical changes, putting his king into such sharp and unnecessary perils that it even provoked comment from the white-haired old lady knitting placidly by the fire.

"Hark at the wind," said Mr. White, who, having seen a fatal mistake after it was too late, was amiably desirous of preventing his son from seeing it.

"I'm listening," said the latter, grimly surveying the board as he stretched out his hand. "Check."[1]

"I should hardly think that he'd come tonight," said his father, with his hand poised over the board.

"Mate," replied the son.

"That's the worst of living so far out," bawled Mr. White, with sudden and unlooked-for violence; "of all the beastly, slushy, out-of-the-way places to live in, this is the worst. Pathway's a bog, and the road's a torrent. I don't know what people are thinking about. I suppose because only two houses on the road are let, they think it doesn't matter."

"Never mind, dear," said his wife soothingly; "perhaps you'll win the next one."

2 Mr. White looked up sharply, just in time to intercept a knowing glance between mother and son. The words died away on his lips, and he hid a guilty grin in his thin gray beard.

"There he is," said Herbert White, as the gate banged to loudly and heavy footsteps came toward the door.

The old man rose with hospitable haste, and, opening the door, was heard condoling with the

1. **check:** chess move that places the opponent's king in danger. If the opponent fails to protect the king, the result is "checkmate" and the end of the game.

GUIDED READING

LITERAL QUESTION

1a. What is the setting at the beginning of the story? (the parlor of the Whites' isolated home on a cold and stormy night)

INFERENTIAL QUESTION

1b. What kind of mood does the setting suggest? (The setting suggests an oasis of family warmth surrounded by an unpleasant, possibly threatening, outside world.)

new arrival. The new arrival also condoled with himself, so that Mrs. White said, "Tut, tut!" and coughed gently as her husband entered the room, followed by a tall burly man, beady of eye and rubicund of visage.[2]

"Sergeant Major Morris," he said, introducing him.

The sergeant major shook hands, and, taking the proffered seat by the fire, watched contentedly while his host got out whiskey and tumblers and stood a small copper kettle on the fire.

At the third glass his eyes got brighter, and he began to talk, the little family circle regarding
1 with eager interest this visitor from distant parts, as he squared his broad shoulders in the chair and spoke of strange scenes and doughty[3] deeds, of wars and plagues and strange peoples.

"Twenty-one years of it," said Mr. White, nodding at his wife and son. "When he went away he was a slip of a youth in the warehouse. Now look at him."

"He don't look to have taken much harm," said Mrs. White politely.

"I'd like to go to India myself," said the old man, "just to look around a bit, you know."

"Better where you are," said the sergeant major, shaking his head. He put down the empty glass and, sighing softly, shook it again.

"I should like to see those old temples and fakirs[4] and jugglers," said the old man. "What was that you started telling me the other day about the monkey's paw or something, Morris?"

"Nothing," said the soldier hastily. "Leastways, nothing worth hearing."

"Monkey's paw?" said Mrs. White curiously.

2 "Well, it's just a bit of what you might call magic, perhaps," said the sergeant major offhandedly.

His three listeners leaned forward eagerly.

2. **rubicund** [ro͞o'bə kənd] **of visage** [viz'ij]: red-faced.
3. **doughty:** courageous.
4. **fakirs** [fə kērz']: Hindu or Moslem holy men thought to have magical powers.

The visitor absent-mindedly put his empty glass to his lips and then set it down again. His host filled it for him.

"To look at," said the sergeant major, fumbling in his pocket, "it's just an ordinary little paw, dried to a mummy."

He took something out of his pocket and proffered it. Mrs. White drew back with a grimace, but her son, taking it, examined it curiously.

"And what is there special about it?" inquired Mr. White as he took it from his son and, having examined it, placed it upon the table.

3 "It had a spell put on it by an old fakir," said the sergeant major, "a very holy man. He wanted to show that fate ruled people's lives, and that those who interfered with it did so to their sorrow. He put a spell on it so that three separate men could each have three wishes from it."

His manner was so impressive that his hearers were conscious that their light laughter jarred somewhat.

"Well, why don't you have three, sir?" said Herbert White cleverly.

The soldier regarded him in the way that middle age is wont to regard presumptuous youth. "I have," he said quietly, and his blotchy face whitened.

"And did you really have the three wishes granted?" asked Mrs. White.

"I did," said the sergeant major, and his glass tapped against his strong teeth.

"And has anybody else wished?" inquired the old lady.

"The first man had his three wishes, yes,"
4 was the reply. "I don't know what the first two were, but the third was for death. That's how I got the paw."

His tones were so grave that a hush fell upon the group.

"If you've had your three wishes, it's no good to you now, then, Morris," said the old man at last. "What do you keep it for?"

The soldier shook his head. "Fancy, I suppose," he said slowly. "I did have some idea of

AT A GLANCE

- Sergeant Major Morris talks about India and shows the Whites a monkey's paw.
- A fakir put a spell on the paw, allowing three people three wishes each.
- Morris says the first owner chose death as his third wish.
- Morris also has made three wishes, but he does not discuss them.

1 CHARACTERIZATION

The strange and mysterious enter this simple home through the stories of the old soldier.

2 STYLE: DIALOGUE

Morris' understated use of the word *magic* arouses the curiosity of his listeners.

3 PLOT: EXPOSITION

Morris tells of the spell placed on the monkey's paw and the fakir's intention in granting three men three wishes.

4 IRONY

One expects people to wish for good things, not death. This unusual wish causes the reader to begin to wonder about the value and power of the monkey's paw.

GUIDED READING

LITERAL QUESTIONS

1a. What question does Mr. White pose after he tells Morris that the paw is no good to him any longer? ("What do you keep it for?")

2a. What was the third wish of the first owner of the paw? (death)

INFERENTIAL QUESTIONS

1b. What do you think Mr. White has in mind? (He would like to be the next owner of the paw and to make three wishes.)

2b. What does this wish tell you about the paw? (The three wishes may not bring good fortune. Something mysterious and evil is connected with the paw.)

AT A GLANCE

- Morris throws the monkey's paw on the fire.
- Mr. White snatches it off the fire.
- Morris tells White how to make a wish with the paw; he disclaims responsibility for the consequences if White keeps it.

1 PLOT: NARRATIVE HOOK

White's snatching the paw from the fire is an arresting moment that heightens the story's suspense and bodes ill.

2 FORESHADOWING

Many warnings have been provided by the soldier, but White is not thinking about the possible evil consequences connected with the paw.

selling it, but I don't think I will. It has caused enough mischief already. Besides, people won't buy. They think it's a fairy tale, some of them, and those who do think anything of it want to try it first and pay me afterward."

"If you could have another three wishes," said the old man, eyeing him keenly, "would you have them?"

"I don't know," said the other. "I don't know."

1 He took the paw, and dangling it between his front finger and thumb, suddenly threw it upon the fire. White, with a slight cry, stooped down and snatched it off.

"Better let it burn," said the soldier solemnly.

"If you don't want it, Morris," said the old man, "give it to me."

"I won't," said his friend doggedly. "I threw it on the fire. If you keep it, don't blame me for what happens. Pitch it on the fire again, like a sensible man."

The other shook his head and examined his new possession closely. "How do you do it?" he inquired.

2 "Hold it up in your right hand and wish aloud," said the sergeant major, "but I warn you of the consequences."

"Sounds like the *Arabian Nights,*"[5] said Mrs.

---

5. ***Arabian Nights:*** also called *A Thousand and One Nights,* a collection of adventure tales from Arabia, Persia, and India gathered in the tenth century.

GUIDED READING

LITERAL QUESTION

1a. What does Sergeant Major Morris do with the paw? (He throws it in the fire.)

INFERENTIAL QUESTION

1b. Why do you think he does this? (He wants to destroy it, perhaps so that no one else will suffer from its evil spell.)

White, as she rose and began to set the supper. "Don't you think you might wish for four pairs of hands for me?"

Her husband drew the talisman[6] from his
1 pocket and then all three burst into laughter as the sergeant major, with a look of alarm on his face, caught him by the arm. "If you must wish," he said gruffly, "wish for something sensible."

Mr. White dropped it back into his pocket, and placing chairs, motioned his friend to the table. In the business of supper the talisman was partly forgotten, and afterward the three sat listening in an enthralled fashion to a second installment of the soldier's adventures in India.

"If the tale about the monkey paw is not more truthful than those he has been telling us," said Herbert, as the door closed behind their guest, just in time for him to catch the last train, "we shan't make much out of it."

"Did you give him anything for it, Father?" inquired Mrs. White, regarding her husband closely.

"A trifle," said he, coloring slightly. "He didn't want it, but I made him take it. And he pressed me again to throw it away."

"Likely," said Herbert, with pretended horror. "Why, we're going to be rich, and famous, and happy. Wish to be an emperor, Father, to begin with: then you can't be bossed around."

He darted round the table, pursued by the maligned Mrs. White armed with an antimacassar.[7]

Mr. White took the paw from his pocket and eyed it dubiously. "I don't know what to wish for, and that's a fact," he said slowly. "It seems to me I've got all I want."

2 "If you only cleared the house, you'd be quite happy, wouldn't you?" said Herbert, with his hand on his shoulder. "Well, wish for two hundred pounds,[8] then; that'll just do it."

His father, smiling shamefacedly at his own credulity, held up the talisman, as his son, with a solemn face somewhat marred by a wink at his mother, sat down at the piano and struck a few impressive chords.

3 "I wish for two hundred pounds," said the old man distinctly.

A fine crash from the piano greeted the words, interrupted by a shuddering cry from the old man. His wife and son ran toward him.

"It moved," he cried, with a glance of disgust at the object as it lay on the floor. "As I wished it twisted in my hands like a snake."

"Well, I don't see the money," said his son, as he picked it up and placed it on the table, "and I bet I never shall."

"It must have been your fancy, Father," said his wife, regarding him anxiously.

He shook his head. "Never mind, though; there's no harm done, but it gave me a shock all the same."

They sat down by the fire again while the two men finished their pipes. Outside, the wind was higher than ever, and the old man started nervously at the sound of a door banging upstairs. A silence unusual and depressing settled upon all three, which lasted until the old couple rose to retire for the night.

"I expect you'll find the cash tied up in a big bag in the middle of your bed," said Herbert, as he bade them good night, "and something horrible squatting up on top of the wardrobe watching you as you pocket your ill-gotten gains."

II

4 In the brightness of the wintry sun next morning as it streamed over the breakfast table Herbert laughed at his fears. There was an air of prosaic wholesomeness about the room which it had lacked on the previous night, and the dirty, shriveled little paw was pitched on the sideboard with a carelessness which betokened no great belief in its virtues.

"I suppose all old soldiers are the same," said Mrs. White. "The idea of our listening to such

---

6. **talisman** [tal′is mən]: magical charm.
7. **antimacassar** [an′ti mə kas′ər]: ornamental, protective cloth covering for the back or arms of a chair.
8. **two hundred pounds:** British currency, one thousand dollars at the time the story was written.

AT A GLANCE

- Morris leaves after warning the Whites to avoid frivolous wishes.
- Herbert jokes about the paw.
- Half-seriously, White wishes for two hundred pounds; the paw moves in response, and the family becomes subdued.
- By the next morning Herbert is again cheerful.

1 FORESHADOWING

Morris' warning suggests that Mr. White, in fact, may not wish sensibly and thereby may cause misfortune.

2 CHARACTERIZATION

Herbert's concern with his father's happiness and peace of mind indicates a strong tie between father and son.

3 PLOT: RISING ACTION

The announcement of the first wish is immediately followed by a frightening cry that heightens the reader's interest.

4 SETTING

The next morning, sunshine dispels both the darkness and cold of the previous night as it dispels Herbert's fears.

GUIDED READING

LITERAL QUESTIONS

1a. How does the family react after Mr. White makes his first wish? (Herbert doesn't believe anything will happen. Mr. White is frightened when the paw moves but then joins his wife in dismissing the incident.)

2a. How does the author describe the atmosphere as the family sits down by the fire before going to bed? ("A silence unusual and depressing [has] settled upon all three. . . . ")

INFERENTIAL QUESTIONS

1b. What can you infer from their behavior? (They seem unaffected by all the warnings given by Sergeant Major Morris.)

2b. Why do you think they are so unusually quiet and solemn? (They may sense that something serious has happened to them: The strange monkey's paw has invaded their safe oasis.)

AT A GLANCE

- The Whites joke about the first wish.
- Herbert leaves for work.
- Later a mysterious man comes to the house and tells of Herbert's accidental death.

1 THEME

We learn that when the wishes are granted it may seem more like coincidence than fate.

2 FORESHADOWING

The "mysterious movements" of a stranger outside suggest that something unusual and unpleasant is about to happen.

3 PLOT: RISING ACTION

The death of the son is an additional, crucial complication of the plot, and the reader follows the story with increasing interest.

nonsense! How could wishes be granted in these days? And if they could, how could two hundred pounds hurt you, Father?"

"Might drop on his head from the sky," said the frivolous Herbert.

1 "Morris said the things happened so naturally," said his father, "that you might if you so wished attribute it to coincidence."

"Well, don't break into the money before I come back," said Herbert, as he rose from the table. "I'm afraid it'll turn you into a mean, avaricious man, and we shall have to disown you."

His mother laughed, and followed him to the door, watched him down the road, and, returning to the breakfast table, was very happy at the expense of her husband's credulity. All of which did not prevent her from scurrying to the door at the postman's knock, nor prevent her from referring somewhat shortly to retired sergeant majors of bibulous[9] habits when she found that the post brought a tailor's bill.

"Herbert will have some more of his funny remarks, I expect, when he comes home," she said, as they sat at dinner.

"I dare say," said Mr. White, pouring himself out some beer; "but for all that, the thing moved in my hand; that I'll swear to."

"You thought it did," said the old lady soothingly.

"I say it did," replied the other. "There was no thought about it. I had just—What's the matter?"

2 His wife made no reply. She was watching the mysterious movements of a man outside, who, peering in an undecided fashion at the house, appeared to be trying to make up his mind to enter. In mental connection with the two hundred pounds, she noticed that the stranger was well dressed and wore a silk hat of glossy newness. Three times he paused at the gate, and then walked on again. The fourth time he stood with his hand upon it, and then with sudden resolution flung it open and walked up the path. Mrs. White at the same moment placed her hands behind her, and hurriedly unfastening the strings of her apron, put that useful article of apparel beneath the cushion of her chair.

She brought the stranger, who seemed ill at ease, into the room. He gazed furtively at Mrs. White, and listened in a preoccupied fashion as the old lady apologized for the appearance of the room, and her husband's coat, a garment which he usually reserved for the garden. She then waited patiently for him to broach his business, but he was at first strangely silent.

"I—was asked to call," he said at last, and stooped and picked a piece of cotton from his trousers. "I came from Maw and Meggins."

The old lady started. "Is anything the matter?" she asked breathlessly. "Has anything happened to Herbert? What is it? What is it?"

Her husband interposed. "There, there, Mother," he said hastily. "Sit down and don't jump to conclusions. You've not brought bad news, I'm sure, sir," and he eyed the other wistfully.

"I'm sorry—" began the visitor.

"Is he hurt?" demanded the mother.

The visitor bowed in assent. "Badly hurt," he said quietly, "but he is not in any pain."

"Oh, thank God!" said the old woman, clasping her hands. "Thank God for that! Thank—"

3 She broke off suddenly as the sinister meaning of the assurance dawned upon her and she saw the awful confirmation of her fears in the other's averted face. She caught her breath, and turning to her husband, laid her trembling old hand upon his. There was a long silence.

"He was caught in the machinery," said the visitor at length, in a low voice.

"Caught in the machinery," repeated Mr. White, in a dazed fashion, "yes."

He sat staring blankly out at the window, and taking his wife's hand between his own, pressed it as he had been wont to do in their old courting days nearly forty years before.

9. **bibulous** [bib′yə ləs]: fond of drinking.

GUIDED READING

LITERAL QUESTIONS

1a. Whom does Mrs. White see outside? (a mysterious man who cannot decide whether or not to enter the house)

2a. What does the mysterious man tell Mrs. White? (Her son is badly hurt but is not in any pain.)

INFERENTIAL QUESTIONS

1b. Why do you think the man is described in this way? (It lends an air of uncertainty and foreboding to the story.)

2b. What does the man mean when he says Mrs. White's son "is not in any pain"? (He means Herbert is dead.)

"He was the only one left to us," he said, turning gently to the visitor. "It is hard."

The other coughed, and, rising, walked slowly to the window. "The firm wished me to convey their sincere sympathy with you in your great loss," he said, without looking around. "I beg that you will understand I am only their servant and merely obeying orders."

There was no reply; the old woman's face was white, her eyes staring, and her breath inaudible; on the husband's face was a look such as his friend the sergeant might have carried into his first action.

"I was to say that Maw and Meggins disclaim all responsibility," continued the other. "They admit no liability at all, but in consideration of your son's services they wish to present you with a certain sum as compensation."

Mr. White dropped his wife's hand, and rising to his feet, gazed with a look of horror at his visitor. His dry lips shaped the words, "How much?"

"Two hundred pounds," was the answer.

Unconscious of his wife's shriek, the old man smiled faintly, put out his hands like a sightless man, and dropped, a senseless heap, to the floor.

III

In the huge new cemetery, some two miles distant, the old people buried their dead, and came back to a house steeped in shadow and si-
2 lence. It was all over so quickly that at first they could hardly realize it, and remained in a state of expectation as though of something else to happen—something else which was to lighten this load, too heavy for old hearts to bear. But the days passed, and expectations gave place to resignation—the hopeless resignation of the old, sometimes miscalled apathy. Sometimes they hardly exchanged a word, for now they had nothing to talk about, and their days were long to weariness.

It was about a week after that that the old man, waking suddenly in the night, stretched out his hand and found himself alone. The room was in darkness, and the sound of subdued weeping came from the window. He raised himself in bed and listened.

3 "Come back," he said tenderly. "You will be cold."

"It is colder for my son," said the old woman, and wept afresh.

The sound of her sobs died away on his ears. The bed was warm, and his eyes heavy with sleep. He dozed fitfully, and then slept until a sudden wild cry from his wife awoke him with a start.

"The monkey's paw!" she cried wildly. "The monkey's paw!"

He started up in alarm. "Where? Where is it? What's the matter?"

She came stumbling across the room toward him. "I want it," she said quietly. "You've not destroyed it?"

"It's in the parlor, on the bracket,"[10] he replied, marveling. "Why?"

She cried and laughed together, and bending over, kissed his cheek.

"I only just thought of it," she said hysterically. "Why didn't I think of it before? Why didn't you think of it?"

"Think of what?" he questioned.

"The other two wishes," she replied rapidly. "We've only had one."

"Was not that enough?" he demanded fiercely.

4 "No," she cried triumphantly; "we'll have one more. Go down and get it quickly, and wish our boy alive again."

The man sat up in bed and flung the bedclothes from his quaking limbs. "You are mad!" he cried, aghast.

"Get it," she panted; "get it quickly, and wish—Oh, my boy, my boy!"

Her husband struck a match and lit the candle. "Get back to bed," he said unsteadily. "You don't know what you are saying."

---

10. **bracket:** shelf.

AT A GLANCE

- The man offers the Whites two hundred pounds as compensation for the loss of their son.
- Mrs. White screams, and Mr. White faints.
- The parents bury their son and mourn his loss.
- Mrs. White wants to use the monkey's paw to wish her son alive again.

1 IRONY

Mr. White's first wish has been granted in the most gruesome way possible.

2 POINT OF VIEW

By using the omniscient third-person point of view, Jacobs is able to describe what both characters are thinking.

3 STYLE: DIALOGUE

Mr. White's words show his concern and affection for his wife; her twist of the word *cold* shows that she is devastated by the death of her son.

4 THEME

Mrs. White wants to use a second wish to undo the damage caused by the first wish; she is still willing to tamper with fate.

GUIDED READING

LITERAL QUESTIONS

1a. What does the mysterious man offer the Whites? (two hundred pounds)

2a. What does Mrs. White want her husband to do? (She wants him to use the monkey's paw to wish their son alive again.)

INFERENTIAL QUESTIONS

1b. Why is this significant? (It shows that the wish is fulfilled as a result of a tragedy.)

2b. What does this desire tell you about her? (Her grief over her son's death has obscured the gravity of the fakir's lesson.)

AT A GLANCE

- Mrs. White continues to insist that her husband use the paw to wish their son alive again.
- Reluctantly, Mr. White does so.
- There is a knocking at the door; Mrs. White runs to it.
- Mr. White begs her not to let "it" in.

1 CHARACTERIZATION

Though Mr. White insists the first wish was merely a coincidence, his nervousness implies he fervently believes in the power of the monkey's paw.

2 PLOT: RISING ACTION

Mr. White's dramatic second wish, an attempt to undo the first, continues to fuel the reader's interest in the story's outcome.

3 SETTING

This domestic scene contrasts with the earlier description of the home: Now a cold, eerie feeling pervades the interior.

1 "We had the first wish granted," said the old woman feverishly; "why not the second?"

"A coincidence," stammered the old man.

"Go and get it and wish," cried his wife, quivering with excitement.

The old man turned and regarded her, and his voice shook. "He has been dead ten days, and besides he—I would not tell you else, but—I could only recognize him by his clothing. If he was too terrible for you to see then, how now?"

"Bring him back," cried the old woman, and dragged him toward the door. "Do you think I fear the child I have nursed?"

He went down in the darkness, and felt his way to the parlor, and then to the mantelpiece. The talisman was in its place, and a horrible fear that the unspoken wish might bring his mutilated son before him ere he could escape from the room seized upon him, and he caught his breath as he found that he had lost the direction of the door. His brow cold with sweat, he felt his way round the table, and groped along the wall until he found himself in the small passage with the unwholesome thing in his hand.

Even his wife's face seemed changed as he entered the room. It was white and expectant, and to his fears seemed to have an unnatural look upon it. He was afraid of her.

2 "Wish!" she cried, in a strong voice.

"It is foolish and wicked," he faltered.

"Wish!" repeated his wife.

He raised his hand. "I wish my son alive again."

The talisman fell to the floor, and he regarded it shudderingly. Then he sank trembling into a chair as the old woman, with burning eyes, walked to the window and raised the blind.

3 He sat until he was chilled with the cold, glancing occasionally at the figure of the old woman peering through the window. The candle end, which had burned below the rim of the china candlestick, was throwing pulsating shadows on the ceiling and walls, until, with a flicker larger than the rest, it expired. The old man, with an unspeakable sense of relief at the failure of the talisman, crept back to his bed, and a minute or two afterward the old woman came silently and apathetically beside him.

Neither spoke, but both lay silently listening to the ticking of the clock. A stair creaked, and a squeaky mouse scurried noisily through the wall. The darkness was oppressive, and after lying for some time screwing up his courage, the husband took the box of matches, and striking one, went downstairs for a candle.

At the foot of the stairs the match went out, and he paused to strike another, and at the same moment a knock, so quiet and stealthy as to be scarcely audible, sounded on the front door.

The matches fell from his hand. He stood motionless, his breath suspended until the knock was repeated. Then he turned and fled swiftly back to his room, and closed the door behind him. A third knock sounded through the house.

"What's that?" cried the old woman, starting up.

"A rat," said the old man, in shaking tones—"a rat. It passed me on the stairs."

His wife sat up in bed listening. A loud knock resounded through the house.

"It's Herbert!" she screamed. "It's Herbert!"

She ran to the door, but her husband was before her, and catching her by the arm, held her tightly.

"What are you going to do?" he whispered hoarsely.

"It's my boy; it's Herbert!" she cried, struggling mechanically. "I forgot it was two miles away. What are you holding me for? Let's go. I must open the door."

"Don't let it in," cried the old man, trembling.

"You're afraid of your own son," she cried, struggling. "Let me go. I'm coming, Herbert; I'm coming."

There was another knock, and another. The old woman with a sudden wrench broke free and ran from the room. Her husband followed to

GUIDED READING

LITERAL QUESTIONS

1a. What is the second wish? (Mr. White wishes his son alive again.)

2a. What does Mr. White tell his wife when she insists she must open the door? ("Don't let it in.")

INFERENTIAL QUESTIONS

1b. Do you think making this wish is a good idea? (Jacobs hints repeatedly that any wish will be surrounded by sorrow and pain.)

2b. Why is Mr. White so insistent on keeping the door closed? (He believes his son will return in a mutilated form; also, he now understands that whatever he wishes for will have tragic consequences.)

the landing, and called after her appealingly as she hurried downstairs. He heard the chain rattle back and the bottom bolt drawn slowly and stiffly from the socket. Then the old woman's voice, strained and panting.

"The bolt," she cried loudly. "Come down. I can't reach it."

But her husband was on his hands and knees groping wildly on the floor in search of the paw. If he could only find it before the thing outside got in. A perfect fusillade[11] of knocks reverberated through the house, and he heard the scraping of a chair as his wife put it down in the passage against the door. He heard the creaking of the bolt as it came slowly back, and at the same moment he found the monkey's paw, and frantically breathed his third and last wish.

2 The knocking ceased suddenly, although the echoes of it were still in the house. He heard the chair drawn back and the door opened. A cold wind rushed up the staircase, and a long loud wail of disappointment and misery from his wife gave him courage to run down to her side, and then to the gate beyond. The street lamp flickering opposite shone on a quiet and deserted road.

11. **fusillade** [fū'sə lād']: firing of many guns; here, repeated knocking.

STUDY QUESTIONS

Recalling

1. What was the fakir's purpose in placing the spell on the paw?
2. What are Mr. White's three wishes?
3. Briefly describe the way in which each of Mr. White's wishes seems to be granted.
4. Describe Mrs. White's actions while her husband is searching for the paw and making his last wish.

Interpreting

5. Find two clues during the first evening of the story that hint that the paw is not necessarily a desirable gift.
6. Morris says that his wishes were granted so naturally "that you might . . . attribute it to coincidence." In what way can the events that the Whites experience be explained as coincidence?
7. Could Mr. White have worded his first two wishes more carefully in order to have prevented any possible misfortune? If so, how? If not, why not?

Extending

8. Based on what happens in the story, do you think the old fakir's attitude toward fate was correct? Why or why not?

VIEWPOINT

We can often increase our pleasure in a piece of literature by consulting the opinion of an expert on the author's writing. Throughout this book in each section titled "Viewpoint," you will find a quotation by a literary critic about the author and selection just read. Each quotation is followed by one or more questions that will ask you to consider the critic's opinion in light of your own reaction to the literature.

"The Monkey's Paw" is one of many stories in which a person is given three wishes. Many such stories have similar plots. Two writers note that this story

> is the best ever written on the theme of the three wishes. . . . In a typical story, the first wish is . . . granted in an unexpected manner. The second is a reckless response . . . to the first; and the third has to be wasted to undo the second.
>
> —H. A. Wise and P. Fraser

■ In what way do the Whites' three wishes fit the pattern described above? What other stories or films that you know have similar plots?

AT A GLANCE

- Mrs. White struggles to open the door as Mr. White makes his third wish.
- The knocking ceases, and Mr. White joins his wife at the door; they stare at a deserted road.

1 PLOT: CLIMAX

Both Mr. White and the reader now know that the third wish must be used to negate the second.

2 PLOT: FALLING ACTION AND RESOLUTION

The open door and deserted road reveal that Mr. White's third wish has been granted.

REFLECTING ON THE STORY

Do you think that the monkey's paw has magical powers? (The death of the son and the knocking at the door could be coincidence, or they could be the effect of the paw's magic.)

STUDY QUESTIONS

1. to show tampering with fate leads to grief
2. two hundred pounds; son's return; to withdraw second wish
3. receives two hundred pounds as compensation for son's death; knock at door; no one at door
4. hurries downstairs; unchains door; draws back bolts
5. Visitor is reluctant to speak of his own wishes; he throws paw into the fire.
6. Son's death was accident, amount of compensation coincidental; noise at door was wind.
7. Students may try to reword; if paw has spell, though, there is no avoiding misfortune.
8. only if we believe paw had magic powers

VIEWPOINT

First wish is careless; second is reckless; third is wasted on withdrawing second; *Arabian Nights*

LITERARY FOCUS

1. exposition: chess game, tale of paw
2. hook: when White grabs paw from fire
3. rising action: first wish, death of son, second wish
4. climax: knock on door, search for paw, third wish
5. falling action: opening door
6. resolution: final sentence

VOCABULARY

1. (c) extreme
2. (d) comforting
3. (b) daring
4. (c) insulted
5. (c) belief

LITERARY FOCUS

Plot Development

The **plot** is the sequence of events in a story, each event causing or leading to the next. The plot of a good story usually proceeds according to the following pattern:

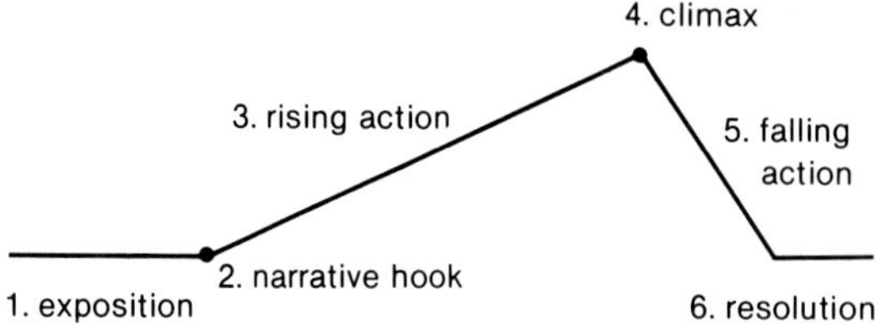

In the beginning of the story, the **exposition,** the author introduces us to the people, places, and situations we will need to know in order to enjoy the story. The **narrative hook** is the point at which the author catches our attention. It is the beginning of the rising action of the plot. We become aware of the character's problems, and, from this point on, we are in suspense about what will happen next. The **rising action** adds complications to the problems and increases our interest in the story. The **climax** is the point of our highest interest and greatest emotional involvement in the story. It is the point in the story when we know for certain how the problems are going to be resolved. The **falling action** relates the events that are the result of the climax. The **resolution** ends the falling action of a story by telling or implying the final outcome.

Thinking About Plot

■ Draw a diagram to represent the plot of "The Monkey's Paw." On your diagram identify the events of the story that are its (1) exposition, (2) narrative hook (At what point in the story does the Whites' involvement with the paw actually begin?), (3) rising action, (4) climax (At what point in the story do we know the outcome of the Whites' three wishes?), (5) falling action, and (6) resolution. For example, the last item on your chart will note that the resolution is the final sentence of the story.

VOCABULARY

Synonyms

A **synonym** is a word that has the same or nearly the same meaning as another word. *Begin* and *start* are synonyms. The words in capitals are from "The Monkey's Paw." Choose the word that is *nearest* the meaning of each word in capitals, *as the word is used in the story.* Write the number of each item and the letter of your choice on a separate sheet.

1. RADICAL: (a) normal (b) conservative (c) extreme (d) stupid
2. CONDOLING: (a) mourning (b) welcoming (c) mocking (d) comforting
3. PRESUMPTUOUS: (a) timid (b) daring (c) ignorant (d) boasting
4. MALIGNED: (a) flustered (b) praised (c) insulted (d) informed
5. CREDULITY: (a) security (b) skepticism (c) belief (d) fearfulness

COMPOSITION

Writing About Your Reaction to a Story

■ Did you consider "The Monkey's Paw" predictable, or did you keep wondering what would happen next? Begin your brief essay answer by stating your general reaction. Then as you explain your reaction to the story, keep in mind these questions: What was your reaction to Morris' story about the paw? Were you surprised by the result of each of the Whites' wishes? Be sure to use examples from the story to support your opinion. *For general advice on writing an essay about literature, see Lesson 1 in the Writing About Literature Handbook at the back of this book.*

Writing a Letter

■ Imagine that you are Mr. White, and you have found out that someone else now has the monkey's paw. Write a personal letter to that person explaining why it would be dangerous to ask for any wishes. Include in your letter (a) a brief summary of the pain you suffered because of the paw, (b) a warning about the power of the charm and the risk involved, and (c) an offer to help dispose of the paw.

COMPOSITION: GUIDELINES FOR EVALUATION

WRITING ABOUT YOUR REACTION TO A STORY

Objective

To state a reaction and support it with specific references to story

Guidelines for Evaluation

- suggested length: one to three paragraphs
- should clearly state writer's reaction to story
- should support statement with references to story and examples from text

WRITING A LETTER

Objective

To write a persuasive letter

Guidelines for Evaluation

- suggested length: three to four paragraphs
- should summarize White's experiences
- should explain how paw subverts intent of wish
- should include ideas for paw's disposal

Richard Connell (1893–1949) was born in Poughkeepsie, New York, and was educated at Harvard University. Although he wrote more than three hundred short stories, several novels, and many screenplays, he is best known for "The Most Dangerous Game."

■ An old saying claims, "It's not whether you win or lose. It's how you play the game." How much do you agree with that statement?

Richard Connell

The Most Dangerous Game

"Off there to the right—somewhere—is a large island," said Whitney. "It's rather a mystery—"

"What island is it?" Rainsford asked.

"The old charts call it 'Ship-Trap Island,'" Whitney replied. "A suggestive name, isn't it? Sailors have a curious dread of the place. I don't know why. Some superstition—"

"Can't see it," remarked Rainsford, trying to peer through the dank tropical night that was palpable as it pressed its thick warm blackness in upon the yacht.

"You've good eyes," said Whitney, with a laugh, "and I've seen you pick off a moose moving in the brown fall bush at four hundred yards, but even you can't see four miles or so through a moonless Caribbean night."

"Nor four yards," admitted Rainsford. "Ugh! It's like moist black velvet."

"It will be light in Rio," promised Whitney. "We should make it in a few days. I hope the jaguar guns have come from Purdey's.[1] We should
2 have some good hunting up the Amazon.[2] Great sport, hunting."

"The best sport in the world," agreed Rainsford.

"For the hunter," amended Whitney. "Not for the jaguar."

"Don't talk rot, Whitney," said Rainsford. "You're a big-game hunter, not a philosopher. Who cares how a jaguar feels?"

"Perhaps the jaguar does," observed Whitney.

"Bah! They've no understanding."

"Even so, I rather think they understand one thing—fear. The fear of pain and the fear of death."

"Nonsense," laughed Rainsford. "This hot weather is making you soft, Whitney. Be a real-
3 ist. The world is made up of two classes—the hunters and the huntees. Luckily, you and I are hunters. Do you think we've passed that island yet?"

"I can't tell in the dark. I hope so."

1. **Purdey's:** well-known British manufacturer of hunting guns and supplies.

2. **Amazon** [am′ə zon′]: longest river in South America, flowing through Brazil.

AT A GLANCE

- Rainsford, a famous hunter, and Whitney discuss Ship-Trap Island, which they are passing aboard their yacht bound for South America.
- Rainsford indicates that he feels no compassion for hunted animals.

LITERARY OPTIONS

- external conflict
- foreshadowing
- style

THEMATIC OPTIONS

- understanding through experience
- adventure and suspense
- man vs. nature and vs. man

1 STYLE: DIALOGUE

At the outset of the story, Whitney's remarks establish that an atmosphere of mystery and suspense is associated with this island.

2 CONFLICT

This exchange introduces the story's conflict between the hunter and the hunted.

3 CHARACTERIZATION

The irony of Rainsford's self-assured, arrogant response to Whitney's defense of animals' feelings will become central as the story unfolds.

GUIDED READING

LITERAL QUESTION

1a. What does Rainsford think about what hunted animals feel? (He doesn't care how hunted animals feel; he thinks they have no understanding.)

INFERENTIAL QUESTION

1b. What does this tell you about Rainsford? (He seems to lack compassion for the pain and fear that any hunted creature can suffer.)

AT A GLANCE

- Captain Nielsen and the sailors seem nervous about the island.
- Rainsford, on deck alone, hears gunshots from the island and falls off the boat while investigating the sound.
- He shouts for help; the yacht disappears from sight, and he begins to swim.

1 FORESHADOWING

The island's aura of danger increases as the reader learns that a tough old captain and the entire crew are afraid.

2 STYLE: DIALOGUE

Whitney's conversation continues to convey background information about Ship-Trap Island and reinforces the idea that mystery and evil are associated with the place.

3 FORESHADOWING

The threat of evil on the island becomes vividly real as Rainsford hears actual gunshots.

4 CONFLICT

In this person-against-nature conflict Rainsford realizes that he might be able to overcome the forces of nature by referring to his experience and employing his mind.

"Why?" asked Rainsford.

"The place has a reputation—a bad one."

"Cannibals?" suggested Rainsford.

"Hardly. Even cannibals wouldn't live in such a Godforsaken place. But it's gotten into sailor lore, somehow. Didn't you notice that the crew's nerves seemed a bit jumpy today?"

"They were a bit strange, now you mention it. Even Captain Nielsen—"

1 "Yes, even that tough-minded old Swede, who'd go up to the devil himself and ask him for a light. Those fishy blue eyes held a look I never saw there before. All I could get out of him was: 'This place has an evil name among seafaring men, sir.' Then he said to me, very gravely: 'Don't you feel anything?'—as if the air about us was actually poisonous. Now, you mustn't laugh when I tell you this—I did feel something like a sudden chill.

"There was no breeze. The sea was as flat as a plate-glass window. We were drawing near the island then. What I felt was a—a mental chill; a sort of sudden dread."

"Pure imagination," said Rainsford. "One superstitious sailor can taint the whole ship's company with his fear."

"Maybe. But sometimes I think sailors have an extra sense that tells them when they are in
2 danger. Sometimes I think evil is a tangible thing—with wavelengths, just as sound and light have. An evil place can, so to speak, broadcast vibrations of evil. Anyhow, I'm glad we're getting out of this zone. Well, I think I'll turn in now, Rainsford."

"I'm not sleepy," said Rainsford. "I'm going to smoke another pipe up on the afterdeck."

"Good night, then, Rainsford. See you at breakfast."

"Right. Good night, Whitney."

There was no sound in the night as Rainsford sat there, but the muffled throb of the engine that drove the yacht swiftly through the darkness, and the swish and ripple of the wash of the propeller.

Rainsford, reclining in a steamer chair, indolently puffed on his favorite brier.[3] The sensuous drowsiness of the night was on him. "It's so dark," he thought, "that I could sleep without closing my eyes; the night would be my eyelids—"

An abrupt sound startled him. Off to the right he heard it, and his ears, expert in such matters,
3 could not be mistaken. Again he heard the sound, and again. Somewhere, off in the blackness, someone had fired a gun three times.

Rainsford sprang up and moved quickly to the rail, mystified. He strained his eyes in the direction from which the reports had come, but it was like trying to see through a blanket. He leaped upon the rail and balanced himself there, to get greater elevation; his pipe, striking a rope, was knocked from his mouth. He lunged for it; a short, hoarse cry came from his lips as he realized he had reached too far and had lost his balance. The cry was pinched off short as the blood-warm waters of the Caribbean Sea closed over his head.

He struggled up to the surface and tried to cry out, but the wash from the speeding yacht slapped him in the face and the salt water in his
4 open mouth made him gag and strangle. Desperately he struck out with strong strokes after the receding lights of the yacht, but he stopped before he had swum fifty feet. A certain coolheadedness had come to him; it was not the first time he had been in a tight place. There was a chance that his cries could be heard by someone aboard the yacht, but that chance was slender, and grew more slender as the yacht raced on. He wrestled himself out of his clothes, and shouted with all his power. The lights of the yacht became faint and ever-vanishing fireflies; then they were blotted out entirely by the night.

Rainsford remembered the shots. They had come from the right, and doggedly he swam in

3. **brier** [brī′ər]: pipe made from the root of the brier, a heather plant.

GUIDED READING

LITERAL QUESTIONS

1a. What does Whitney tell Rainsford about the captain and the sailors? (They are afraid and nervous about Ship-Trap Island.)

2a. How does Rainsford react after he falls off the yacht? (At first he panics, but then he calms down and starts to save himself.)

INFERENTIAL QUESTIONS

1b. What does this suggest about the island? (Something mysterious—and possibly evil—is associated with the island.)

2b. What does this tell you about him? (He possesses an ability to remain calm when in danger; he is able to think out a solution to his problem.)

that direction swimming with slow, deliberate strokes, conserving his strength. For a seemingly endless time he fought the sea. He began to count his strokes; he could do possibly a hundred more and then—

Rainsford heard a sound. It came out of the darkness, a high screaming sound, the sound of an animal in an extremity of anguish and terror.

He did not recognize the animal that made the sound; he did not try to; with fresh vitality he swam toward the sound. He heard it again; then it was cut short by another noise, crisp, staccato.

"Pistol shot," muttered Rainsford, swimming on.

Ten minutes of determined effort brought another sound to his ears—the most welcome he had ever heard—the muttering and growling of the sea breaking on a rocky shore. He was almost on the rocks before he saw them; on a night less calm he would have been shattered against them. With his remaining strength he dragged himself from the swirling waters. Jagged crags appeared to jut up into the opaqueness; he forced himself upward, hand over hand. Gasping, his hands raw, he reached a flat place at the top. Dense jungle came down to the very edge of the cliffs. What perils that tangle of trees and underbrush might hold for him did not concern Rainsford just
3 then. All he knew was that he was safe from his enemy, the sea, and that utter weariness was on him. He flung himself down at the jungle edge and tumbled headlong into the deepest sleep of his life.

When he opened his eyes he knew from the position of the sun that it was late in the afternoon. Sleep had given him new vigor; a sharp hunger was picking at him. He looked about him, almost cheerfully.

"Where there are pistol shots, there are men. Where there are men, there is food," he thought. But what kind of men, he wondered, in so forbidding a place? An unbroken front of snarled and ragged jungle fringed the shore.

He saw no sign of a trail through the closely knit web of weeds and trees; it was easier to go along the shore, and Rainsford floundered along by the water. Not far from where he had landed, he stopped.

Some wounded thing, by the evidence a large

AT A GLANCE

- Rainsford hears a scream from the island and swims toward the sound.
- After a rough swim he reaches the island and falls asleep; upon waking he begins to look for the hunters.

1 POINT OF VIEW

The omniscient third-person narrator is a detached observer of the dangers and terrors he relates.

2 READING SKILLS: SEQUENCE OF EVENTS

Here the author establishes Rainsford's progression from the water to the jagged rocks to a flat place where he is safe.

3 CONFLICT

Although the sea is truly dangerous and is Rainsford's "enemy," it is entirely impersonal and does not "want" to harm Rainsford.

GUIDED READING

LITERAL QUESTION

1a. How does Rainsford think of the sea after he reaches land? (He thinks of it as his enemy.)

INFERENTIAL QUESTION

1b. What kind of enemy is the sea, and how can it be overcome? (It is a dangerous but impersonal enemy; it can sometimes be overcome by brute strength, intelligence, and will.)

AT A GLANCE

- Rainsford finds a spot where "a fairly large animal" was killed with a light gun.
- He follows the hunter's tracks to a palatial mansion and is greeted by a gigantic man aiming a long-barreled revolver at him.

1 FORESHADOWING

The apparent hunting of a large "brute" is another warning that something unusual will occur on this island.

2 SETTING

An enormous lighted chateau, set ominously on steep cliffs in the midst of this island jungle, enhances the eerie atmosphere already established.

3 CHARACTERIZATION

The huge, threatening man does not respond to Rainsford's simple and straightforward words; the gigantic creature seems hostile and impenetrable.

animal, had thrashed about in the underbrush; the jungle weeds were crushed down and the moss was lacerated; one patch of weeds was stained crimson. A small, glittering object not far away caught Rainsford's eye and he picked it up. It was an empty cartridge.

1 "A twenty-two," he remarked. "That's odd. It must have been a fairly large animal too. The hunter had his nerve to tackle it with a light gun. It's clear that the brute put up a fight. I suppose the first three shots I heard was when the hunter flushed his quarry[4] and wounded it. The last shot was when he trailed it here and finished it."

He examined the ground closely and found what he had hoped to find—the print of hunting boots. They pointed along the cliff in the direction he had been going. Eagerly he hurried along, now slipping on a rotten log or a loose stone, but making headway; night was beginning to settle down on the island.

Bleak darkness was blacking out the sea and jungle when Rainsford sighted the lights. He came upon them as he turned a crook in the coastline, and his first thought was that he had come upon a village, for there were many lights. But as he forged along he saw to his great astonishment
2 that all the lights were in one enormous building—a lofty structure with pointed towers plunging upward into the gloom. His eyes made out the shadowy outlines of a palatial château;[5] it was set on a high bluff, and on three sides of it cliffs dived down to where the sea licked greedy lips in the shadows.

"Mirage," thought Rainsford. But it was no mirage, he found, when he opened the tall spiked iron gate. The stone steps were real enough; the massive door with a leering gargoyle[6] for a knocker was real enough; yet about it all hung an air of unreality.

He lifted the knocker, and it creaked up stiffly, as if it had never before been used. He let it fall, and it startled him with its booming loudness. He thought he heard steps within; the door remained closed. Again Rainsford lifted the heavy knocker, and let it fall. The door opened then, opened as suddenly as if it were on a spring, and Rainsford stood blinking in the river of glaring gold light that poured out. The first thing Rainsford's eyes discerned was the largest man Rainsford had ever seen—a gigantic creature, solidly made and black-bearded to the waist. In his hand the man held a long-barreled revolver, and he was pointing it straight at Rainsford's heart.

Out of the snarl of beard two small eyes regarded Rainsford.

"Don't be alarmed," said Rainsford, with a smile which he hoped was disarming. "I'm no robber. I fell off a yacht. My name is Sanger Rainsford of New York City."

3 The menacing look in his eyes did not change. The revolver pointed as rigidly as if the giant were a statue. He gave no sign that he understood

4. **flushed his quarry:** frightened his prey out of hiding.

5. **château** [sha tō′]: castle or mansion.

6. **gargoyle** [gär′goil]: grotesque animal or human form carved in stone as a decoration for a building.

GUIDED READING

LITERAL QUESTION

1a. Who is the first person to greet Rainsford at the door of the chateau? (a gigantic man pointing a gun at Rainsford's heart)

INFERENTIAL QUESTION

1b. What does this suggest about the inhabitants of the chateau? (They do not trust strangers, or they simply do not want anyone from the outside world visiting them.)

Rainsford's words, or that he had even heard them. He was dressed in uniform, a black uniform trimmed with gray astrakhan.[7]

"I'm Sanger Rainsford of New York," Rainsford began again. "I fell off a yacht. I am hungry."

The man's only answer was to raise with his thumb the hammer of his revolver. Then Rainsford saw the man's free hand go to his forehead in a military salute, and he saw him click his heels together and stand at attention. Another man was coming down the broad marble steps, an erect, slender man in evening clothes. He advanced to Rainsford and held out his hand.

In a cultivated voice marked by a slight accent that gave it added precision and deliberateness, he said: "It is a very great pleasure and honor to welcome Mr. Sanger Rainsford, the celebrated hunter, to my home."

Automatically Rainsford shook the man's hand.

"I've read your book about hunting snow leopards in Tibet, you see," explained the man. "I am General Zaroff."

Rainsford's first impression was that the man was singularly handsome; his second was that there was an original, almost bizarre quality about the general's face. He was a tall man past middle age, for his hair was a vivid white; but his thick eyebrows and pointed military mustache were as black as the night from which Rainsford had come. His eyes, too, were black and very bright. He had high cheek bones, a sharp-cut nose, a spare, dark face, the face of a man used to giving orders, the face of an aristocrat. Turning to the giant in uniform, the general made a sign. The giant put away his pistol, saluted, withdrew.

"Ivan is an incredibly strong fellow," remarked the general, "but he has the misfortune to be deaf and dumb. A simple fellow, but, I'm afraid, like all his race, a bit of a savage."

"Is he Russian?"

"He is a Cossack,"[8] said the general, and his smile showed red lips and pointed teeth. "So am I."

"Come," he said, "we shouldn't be chatting here. We can talk later. Now you want clothes, food, rest. You shall have them. This is a most restful spot."

Ivan had reappeared, and the general spoke to him with lips that moved but gave forth no sound.

"Follow Ivan, if you please, Mr. Rainsford," said the general. "I was about to have my dinner when you came. I'll wait for you. You'll find that my clothes will fit you, I think."

3 It was to a huge, beam-ceilinged bedroom with a canopied bed big enough for six men that Rainsford followed the silent giant. Ivan laid out an evening suit, and Rainsford, as he put it on, noticed that it came from a London tailor who ordinarily cut and sewed for none below the rank of duke.

The dining room to which Ivan conducted him was in many ways remarkable. There was a medieval magnificence about it; it suggested a baronial hall of feudal times with its oaken panels, its high ceiling, its vast refectory table where twoscore men could sit down to eat.
4 About the hall were the mounted heads of many animals—lions, tigers, elephants, moose, bears; larger or more perfect specimens Rainsford had never seen. At the great table the general was sitting, alone.

"You'll have a cocktail, Mr. Rainsford," he suggested. The cocktail was surpassingly good; and, Rainsford noted, the table appointments were of the finest—the linen, the crystal, the silver, the china.

They were eating borsch, the rich, red soup with sour cream so dear to Russian palates. Half apologetically General Zaroff said: "We do our best to preserve the amenities of civilization here. Please forgive any lapses. We are well off

---

7. **astrakhan** [as′trə kən]: fur of young lambs, often worn as a collar.

8. **Cossack** [kos′ak]: native of southeastern Russia.

AT A GLANCE

- Rainsford introduces himself, but the large man gives no indication that he understands him.
- As the large man seems about to shoot, General Zaroff enters and introduces Ivan and himself.
- Rainsford is given clothes and dinner.

1 PLOT: EXPOSITION

General Zaroff's timely entrance introduces the other main character in the story.

2 CHARACTERIZATION

Rainsford's—and the reader's—initial impression of General Zaroff is of a cultured, civilized, and intelligent person.

3 SETTING

The opulence of the chateau and the high quality of the general's clothes are at once apparent to Rainsford, who is still practically naked after his struggle in the ocean.

4 THEME

The results of man's conquests over nature surround Rainsford in Zaroff's dining room.

GUIDED READING

LITERAL QUESTIONS

1a. How does Zaroff know who Rainsford is? (He has read Rainsford's book on hunting snow leopards in Tibet.)

2a. What is mounted around General Zaroff's dining room? (the heads of many large and perfect animals)

INFERENTIAL QUESTIONS

1b. What does this suggest about Zaroff? (He is interested in hunters and in the sport of hunting.)

2b. Why do you think the author mentions this detail? (It shows in a concrete and vivid way Zaroff's ability to hunt and kill any prey; it illustrates that Zaroff likes to be surrounded by evidence of his skill.)

AT A GLANCE

- Zaroff appears to be a cultured man; he professes his passion for hunting.
- He says that on his island he hunts the most dangerous game.
- Rainsford wonders what game Zaroff hunts; the general talks about his hunting career.

1 CHARACTERIZATION

Zaroff is presented as a cultured and well-read person, and he professes his passionate interest in hunting.

2 PLOT: SUSPENSE

Zaroff's teasing about what constitutes the most dangerous game keeps the reader interested in the general's opinion.

3 STYLE: DIALOGUE

Zaroff's one-sided conversation with Rainsford sets the stage for the conflict between the two main characters.

4 CHARACTERIZATION

The matter-of-fact tone Zaroff uses when speaking of the deaths of so many animals suggests his lack of feeling and compassion.

the beaten track, you know. Do you think the champagne has suffered from its long ocean trip?"

"Not in the least," declared Rainsford. He was finding the general a most thoughtful and affable host, a true cosmopolite.[9] But there was one small trait of the general's that made Rainsford uncomfortable. Whenever he looked up from his plate he found the general studying him, appraising him narrowly.

"Perhaps," said General Zaroff, "you were sur-
1 prised that I recognized your name. You see, I read all books on hunting published in English, French, and Russian. I have but one passion in my life, Mr. Rainsford, and it is the hunt."

"You have some wonderful heads here," said Rainsford as he ate a particularly well-cooked filet mignon. "That Cape buffalo is the largest I ever saw."

"Oh, that fellow. Yes, he was a monster."

"Did he charge you?"

"Hurled me against a tree," said the general. "Fractured my skull. But I got the brute."

"I've always thought," said Rainsford, "that the Cape buffalo is the most dangerous of all big game."

2 For a moment the general did not reply; he was smiling his curious red-lipped smile. Then he said slowly; "No. You are wrong, sir. The Cape buffalo is not the most dangerous big game." He sipped his wine. "Here in my preserve on this island," he said in the same slow tone, "I hunt more dangerous game."

Rainsford expressed his surprise. "Is there big game on this island?"

The general nodded. "The biggest."

"Really?"

"Oh, it isn't here naturally, of course. I have to stock the island."

"What have you imported, general?" Rainsford asked. "Tigers?"

The general smiled. "No," he said. "Hunting tigers ceased to interest me some years ago. I exhausted their possibilities, you see. No thrill left in tigers, no real danger. I live for danger, Mr. Rainsford."

The general took from his pocket a gold cigarette case and offered his guest a long black cigarette with a silver tip; it was perfumed and gave off a smell like incense.

3 "We will have some capital hunting, you and I," said the general. "I shall be most glad to have your society."

"But what game—" began Rainsford.

"I'll tell you," said the general. "You will be amused, I know. I think I may say, in all modesty, that I have done a rare thing. I have invented a new sensation. May I pour you another glass of port, Mr. Rainsford?"

"Thank you, general."

The general filled both glasses, and said: "God makes some men poets. Some He makes kings, some beggars. Me He made a hunter. My hand was made for the trigger, my father said. He was a very rich man with a quarter of a million acres in the Crimea,[10] and he was an ardent sportsman. When I was only five years old he gave me a little gun, specially made in Moscow for me, to shoot sparrows with. When I shot some of his prize turkeys with it, he did not punish me; he complimented me on my marksmanship. I killed my first bear in the Caucasus[11] when I was ten. My whole life has been one prolonged hunt. I went into the army—it was expected of noblemen's sons—and for a time commanded a division of Cossack cavalry, but my
4 real interest was always the hunt. I have hunted every kind of game in every land. It would be impossible for me to tell you how many animals I have killed."

The general puffed at his cigarette.

---

9. **cosmopolite** [koz mop′ə līt′]: sophisticated world-traveler.

10. **Crimea** [krī mē′ə]: area in southern Russia bordering the Black Sea.

11. **Caucasus** [kô′kə səs]: mountain range in southern Russia.

GUIDED READING

LITERAL QUESTIONS

1a. In what languages does Zaroff read about hunting? (English, French, and Russian)

2a. What is Zaroff's "one passion in life"? (the hunt)

INFERENTIAL QUESTIONS

1b. What does this tell you about him? (He is well-educated and intelligent.)

2b. What does Zaroff's lengthy speech about his hunting experiences indicate? (He is convinced that there are good reasons for his obsession with hunting.)

"After the debacle[12] in Russia I left the country, for it was imprudent for an officer of the Czar to stay there. Many noble Russians lost everything. I, luckily, had invested heavily in American securities, so I shall never have to open a tearoom in Monte Carlo[13] or drive a taxi in Paris. Naturally, I continued to hunt—grizzlies in your Rockies, crocodiles in the Ganges,[14] rhinoceroses in East Africa. It was in Africa that the Cape buffalo hit me and laid me up for six months. As soon as I recovered I started for the Amazon to hunt jaguars, for I had heard they were unusually cunning. They weren't." The Cossack sighed. "They were no match at all for a hunter with his wits about him, and a high-powered rifle. I was bitterly disappointed. I was lying in my tent with a splitting headache one night when a terrible thought pushed its way into my mind. Hunting was beginning to bore me! And hunting, remember, had been my life. I have heard that in America businessmen often go to pieces when they give up the business that has been their life."

"Yes, that's so," said Rainsford.

The general smiled. "I had no wish to go to pieces," he said. "I must do something. Now, mine is an analytical mind, Mr. Rainsford. Doubtless that is why I enjoy the problems of the chase."

"No doubt, General Zaroff."

"So," continued the general, "I asked myself why the hunt no longer fascinated me. You are much younger than I am, Mr. Rainsford, and have not hunted as much, but you perhaps can guess the answer."

"What was it?"

"Simply this: hunting had ceased to be what you call 'a sporting proposition.' It had become too easy. I always got my quarry. Always. There is no greater bore than perfection."

The general lit a fresh cigarette.

"No animal had a chance with me any more.
3 That is no boast; it is a mathematical certainty. The animal had nothing but his legs and his instinct. Instinct is no match for reason. When I thought of this it was a tragic moment for me, I can tell you."

Rainsford leaned across the table, absorbed in what his host was saying.

"It came to me as an inspiration what I must do," the general went on.

"And that was?"

The general smiled the quiet smile of one who has faced an obstacle and surmounted it with success. "I had to invent a new animal to hunt," he said.

"A new animal? You're joking."

"Not at all," said the general. "I never joke about hunting. I needed a new animal. I found one. So I bought this island, built this house, and here I do my hunting. The island is perfect for my purposes—there are jungles with a maze of trails in them, hills, swamps—"

"But the animal, General Zaroff?"

"Oh," said the general, "it supplies me with the most exciting hunting in the world. No other hunting compares with it for an instant. Every day I hunt, and I never grow bored now, for I have a quarry with which I can match my wits."

Rainsford's bewilderment showed in his face.

"I wanted the ideal animal to hunt," explained the general. "So, I said: 'What are the attributes of an ideal quarry?' And the answer was,
4 of course: 'It must have courage, cunning, and, above all, it must be able to reason.' "

"But no animal can reason," objected Rainsford.

"My dear fellow," said the general, "there is one that can."

"But you can't mean—" gasped Rainsford.

"And why not?"

12. **debacle** [di bä'kəl]: sudden collapse; here, the fall of the czar, or emperor, in 1917. To Zaroff the revolution was a disaster because he lost his position as an officer of the czar and had to leave Russia.
13. **Monte Carlo** [mon'tē kär'lō]: resort city in Monaco on the Mediterranean Sea.
14. **Ganges** [gan'jēz]: river that flows through northeastern India and Bangladesh.

AT A GLANCE

- Zaroff is an aristocrat who fled from Russia after the revolution.
- He tells of recuperating from a Cape buffalo's attack and of realizing that hunting had begun to bore him.
- He says he has devised a way to keep the hunt exciting.
- Rainsford realizes that Zaroff hunts humans.

1 BACKGROUND

Zaroff is better off economically than most of the expatriate Russian aristocracy, many of whom lost everything in the Russian Revolution.

2 CHARACTERIZATION

Zaroff's exaggerated concern for his own sanity and his insistence on his analytical powers are warnings that he may be unbalanced.

3 THEME

While nature is predictable and animals follow their instincts, only man has the superior power of reason.

4 STYLE: DIALOGUE

Zaroff's conversation with Rainsford advances the plot and finally reveals that Zaroff is hunting humans.

GUIDED READING

LITERAL QUESTIONS

1a. What reason does Zaroff give for losing interest in hunting? (He became bored because he always got his prey.)

2a. According to Zaroff, what are the attributes of an ideal quarry? ("'It must have courage, cunning, and, above all, it must be able to reason.'")

INFERENTIAL QUESTIONS

1b. What does Zaroff's loss of interest in hunting even the most difficult quarry suggest about him? (He must be an unusually accomplished hunter.)

2b. How does Rainsford react to Zaroff's implication that he hunts human beings? (with shock and horror)

AT A GLANCE

- Rainsford characterizes Zaroff's hunting as "cold-blooded murder" and declines his offer to join in a hunt.
- Zaroff tries to convince Rainsford to join him by saying that the weak exist to give the strong pleasure.
- Zaroff explains that he gets his victims by indicating a channel for ships where there is none.
- Zaroff continues to justify his activity as civilized.

1 CONFLICT

The dialogue presents a basis for conflict between Rainsford and Zaroff: What Zaroff calls "hunting" Rainsford calls "murder."

2 THEME

Zaroff's philosophy betrays his lack of understanding and compassion for lives other than his own.

3 STYLE: DIALOGUE

Through Zaroff's words the reader learns the meaning behind the name "Ship-Trap Island," which was introduced in the story's exposition.

4 IRONY

That Zaroff considers himself a civilized man and does not recognize the barbarity of his behavior betrays his unbalanced mind.

"I can't believe you are serious, General Zaroff. This is a grisly joke."

1 "Why should I not be serious? I am speaking of hunting."

"Hunting? General Zaroff, what you speak of is murder."

The general laughed with entire good nature. He regarded Rainsford quizzically. "I refuse to believe that so modern and civilized a young man as you seem to be harbors romantic ideas about the value of human life. Surely your experiences in the war—"

"Did not make me condone cold-blooded murder," finished Rainsford stiffly.

Laughter shook the general. "How extraordinarily droll you are!" he said. "One does not expect nowadays to find a young man of the educated class, even in America, with such a naive, and, if I may say so, mid-Victorian point of view. It's like finding a snuffbox in a limousine. Ah, well, doubtless you had Puritan ancestors. So many Americans appear to have had. I'll wager you'll forget your notions when you go hunting with me. You've a genuine new thrill in store for you, Mr. Rainsford."

"Thank you, I'm a hunter, not a murderer."

"Dear me," said the general, quite unruffled. "Again that unpleasant word. But I think I can show you that your scruples are quite ill-founded."

"Yes?"

2 "Life is for the strong, to be lived by the strong, and, if need be, taken by the strong. The weak of the world were put here to give the strong pleasure. I am strong. Why should I not use my gift? If I wish to hunt, why should I not? I hunt the scum of the earth—sailors from tramp ships—lascars,[15] blacks, Chinese, whites, mongrels—a thoroughbred horse or hound is worth more than a score of them."

"But they are men," said Rainsford hotly.

"Precisely," said the general. "That is why I use them. It gives me pleasure. They can reason, after a fashion. So they are dangerous."

"But where do you get them?"

The general's left eyelid fluttered down in a wink. "This island is called Ship-Trap," he answered. "Sometimes an angry god of the high seas sends them to me. Sometimes, when Providence is not so kind, I help Providence a bit. Come to the window with me."

Rainsford went to the window and looked out toward the sea.

"Watch! Out there!" exclaimed the general, pointing into the night. Rainsford's eyes saw only blackness, and then, as the general pressed a button, far out to sea Rainsford saw the flash of lights.

3 The general chuckled. "They indicate a channel," he said, "where there's none: giant rocks with razor edges crouch like a sea monster with wide-open jaws. They can crush a ship as easily as I crush this nut." He dropped a walnut on the hardwood floor and brought his heel grinding down on it. "Oh, yes," he said, casually, as if in answer to a question, "I have electricity. We try to be civilized here."

"Civilized? And you shoot down men?"

A trace of anger was in the general's black eyes, but it was there for but a second, and he
4 said, in his most pleasant manner: "Dear me, what a righteous young man you are! I assure you I do not do the thing you suggest. That would be barbarous. I treat these visitors with every consideration. They get plenty of good food and exercise. They get into splendid physical condition. You shall see for yourself tomorrow."

"What do you mean?"

"We'll visit my training school," smiled the general. "It's in the cellar. I have about a dozen pupils down there now. They're from the Spanish bark *San Lucar* that had the bad luck to go on the rocks out there. A very inferior lot, I regret to say. Poor specimens and more accustomed to the deck than to the jungle."

15. **lascars** [las′kərz]: Oriental sailors, especially merchant sailors from India.

GUIDED READING

LITERAL QUESTIONS

1a. According to Zaroff, what is the purpose of the weak of the world? (He says the weak exist only to give the strong pleasure.)

2a. How does Zaroff lure his victims? (He lures ships through a nonexistent channel filled with giant rocks that crush ships.)

INFERENTIAL QUESTIONS

1b. What does this imply about Zaroff? (He has no compassion for the world's weak; his way of life is not civilized, but barbaric.)

2b. What does this indicate about Zaroff's sportsmanship? (He is not really a sportsman. He will use any trick or deception.)

He raised his hand, and Ivan, who served as waiter, brought thick Turkish coffee. Rainsford, with an effort, held his tongue in check.

"It's a game, you see," pursued the general blandly. "I suggest to one of them that we go hunting. I give him a supply of food and an excellent hunting knife. I give him three hours' start. I am to follow, armed only with a pistol of the smallest caliber and range. If my quarry eludes me for three whole days, he wins the game. If I find him"—the general smiled—"he loses."

"Suppose he refuses to be hunted?"

"Oh," said the general, "I give him his option, of course. He need not play that game if he doesn't wish to. If he does not wish to hunt, I turn him over to Ivan. Ivan once had the honor of serving as official knouter[16] to the Great White Czar, and he has his own ideas of sport. Invariably, Mr. Rainsford, invariably they choose the hunt."

"And if they win?"

The smile on the general's face widened. "To date I have not lost," he said.

Then he added, hastily: "I don't wish you to think me a braggart, Mr. Rainsford. Many of them afford only the most elementary sort of
3 problem. Occasionally I strike a tartar.[17] One almost did win. I eventually had to use the dogs."

"The dogs?"

"This way, please. I'll show you."

The general steered Rainsford to a window. The lights from the windows sent a flickering illumination that made grotesque patterns on the courtyard below, and Rainsford could see moving about there a dozen or so huge black shapes;

16. **knouter** [nout′ər]: person who flogs criminals with a leather whip, or knout.

17. **tartar** [tär′tər]: person who stubbornly refuses to cooperate.

AT A GLANCE

- Zaroff explains the rules of his "game" and says he is armed only with a small pistol.
- The victim must elude Zaroff for three days to win, but so far Zaroff has not lost.
- The alternative is to be tortured by Ivan.
- Zaroff offhandedly announces that he also uses his dogs to hunt men.

1 PLOT: EXPOSITION

Zaroff explains to Rainsford the basic rules of the hunt as he has established them.

2 THEME

There is little chance of escape from death or of victory in the conflict established by Zaroff, whereas in the earlier person-against-nature conflict the ocean could be conquered by sheer force and determination.

3 CHARACTERIZATION

By giving himself this final advantage, Zaroff makes sure that no one else can win his "game."

GUIDED READING

LITERAL QUESTION

1a. What must the hunted do to win Zaroff's "game"? (Supplied only with a hunting knife, he must elude the armed Zaroff for three days.)

INFERENTIAL QUESTION

1b. Do you think the hunted man has a real chance of winning? (Seemingly not, as Zaroff is a highly skilled hunter and has a gun and dogs, and the hunted man has only a knife.)

AT A GLANCE

- Zaroff mentions the viciousness of his dogs and invites Rainsford to view his new collection of heads in the library.
- Rainsford declines and retires for the night.
- Unable to sleep, Rainsford looks at the dogs in the courtyard below and, toward dawn, hears a pistol shot.
- At lunch, Rainsford tells Zaroff he must leave the island, and Zaroff protests, saying they must hunt.

1 CHARACTERIZATION

Zaroff's menacing reference to his dogs followed by his humming a light song reinforces the notion of an unbalanced man.

2 STYLE

The worlds *softest, quiet,* and *opiate* contrast with the terribly dangerous situation Rainsford is in.

3 CONFLICT

This conversation indicates the approach of actual physical conflict.

as they turned toward him, their eyes glittered greenly.

"A rather good lot, I think," observed the general. "They are let out at seven every night.
1 If anyone should try to get into my house—or out of it—something extremely regrettable would occur to him." He hummed a snatch of song from the Folies Bergère.[18]

"And now," said the general, "I want to show you my new collection of heads. Will you come with me to the library?"

"I hope," said Rainsford, "that you will excuse me tonight, General Zaroff. I'm really not feeling at all well."

"Ah, indeed?" the general inquired solicitously. "Well, I suppose that's only natural, after your long swim. You need a good, restful night's sleep. Tomorrow you'll feel like a new man, I'll wager. Then we'll hunt, eh? I've one rather promising prospect—"

Rainsford was hurrying from the room.

"Sorry you can't go with me tonight," called the general. "I expect rather fair sport—a big, strong fellow. He looks resourceful—Well, good night, Mr. Rainsford; I hope you have a good night's rest."

2 The bed was good, and the pajamas of the softest silk, and he was tired in every fiber of his being, but nevertheless Rainsford could not quiet his brain with the opiate of sleep. He lay, eyes wide open. Once he thought he heard stealthy steps in the corridor outside his room. He sought to throw open the door; it would not open. He went to the window and looked out. His room was high up in one of the towers. The lights of the château were out now, and it was dark and silent, but there was a fragment of sallow moon, and by its wan light he could see, dimly, the courtyard; there, weaving in and out in the pattern of shadow, were black, noiseless forms; the hounds heard him at the window and looked up, expectantly, with their green eyes. Rainsford went back to the bed and lay down. By many methods he tried to put himself to sleep. He had achieved a doze when, just as morning began to come, he heard, far off in the jungle, the faint report of a pistol.

General Zaroff did not appear until luncheon. He was dressed faultlessly in the tweeds of a country squire. He was solicitous about the state of Rainsford's health.

"As for me," sighed the general, "I do not feel so well. I am worried, Mr. Rainsford. Last night I detected traces of my old complaint."

To Rainsford's questioning glance the general said: "Ennui. Boredom."

Then, taking a second helping of crêpes suzette, the general explained: "The hunting was not good last night. The fellow lost his head. He made a straight trail that offered no problems at all. That's the trouble with these sailors; they have dull brains to begin with, and they do not know how to get about in the woods. They do excessively stupid and obvious things. It's most annoying. Will you have another glass of Chablis, Mr. Rainsford?"

3 "General," said Rainsford firmly, "I wish to leave this island at once."

The general raised his thickets of eyebrows; he seemed hurt. "But, my dear fellow," the general protested, "you've only just come. You've had no hunting—"

"I wish to go today," said Rainsford. He saw the dead black eyes of the general on him, studying him. General Zaroff's face suddenly brightened.

He filled Rainsford's glass with venerable Chablis from a dusty bottle.

"Tonight," said the general, "we will hunt—you and I."

Rainsford shook his head. "No, general," he said. "I will not hunt."

The general shrugged his shoulders and delicately ate a hothouse grape. "As you wish, my friend," he said. "The choice rests entirely with

18. **Folies Bergère** [fô′lē ber zhār′]: musical theater and nightclub in Paris.

GUIDED READING

LITERAL QUESTIONS

1a. What does Rainsford hear just before dawn? (the faint report of a pistol)

2a. What does Rainsford say to Zaroff the next day? (He wants to leave the island at once.)

INFERENTIAL QUESTIONS

1b. What can you tell from the sound of the gunshot? (Another victim has died at the hands of Zaroff. He is not telling a crazed story; he is really killing people.)

2b. Why do you think Rainsford is so insistent about wanting to leave the island? (He now knows that Zaroff truly murders people. Rainsford wants to escape the mad general before it is too late.)

you. But may I not venture to suggest that you will find my idea of sport more diverting than Ivan's?"

He nodded toward the corner to where the giant stood, scowling, his thick arms crossed on his hogshead of chest.

"You don't mean—" cried Rainsford.

"My dear fellow," said the general, "have I not told you I always mean what I say about hunting? This is really an inspiration. I drink to a foeman worthy of my steel—at last."

The general raised his glass, but Rainsford sat staring at him.

"You'll find this game worth playing," the general said enthusiastically. "Your brain against mine. Your woodcraft against mine. Your strength and stamina against mine. Outdoor chess! And the stake is not without value, eh?"

"And if I win—" began Rainsford huskily.

"I'll cheerfully acknowledge myself defeated if I do not find you by midnight of the third day," said General Zaroff. "My sloop will place you on the mainland near a town."

The general read what Rainsford was thinking.

"Oh, you can trust me," said the Cossack. "I will give you my word as a gentleman and a sportsman. Of course you, in turn, must agree to say nothing of your visit here."

"I'll agree to nothing of the kind," said Rainsford.

"Oh," said the general, "in that case—But why discuss that now? Three days hence we can discuss it over a bottle of Veuve Cliquot, unless—"

The general sipped his wine.

Then a businesslike air animated him. "Ivan," he said to Rainsford, "will supply you with hunting clothes, food, a knife. I suggest you wear moccasins; they leave a poorer trail. I suggest too that you avoid a big swamp in the southeast corner of the island. We call it Death Swamp. There's quicksand there. One foolish fellow tried it. The deplorable part of it was that

3 Lazarus followed him. You can imagine my feelings, Mr. Rainsford. I loved Lazarus; he was the finest hound in my pack. Well, I must beg you to excuse me now. I always take a siesta after lunch. You'll hardly have time for a nap, I fear. You'll want to start, no doubt. I shall not follow till dusk. Hunting at night is so much more exciting than by day, don't you think? Au revoir,[19] Mr. Rainsford, au revoir."

General Zaroff, with a deep, courtly bow, strolled from the room.

From another door came Ivan. Under one arm he carried khaki hunting clothes, a haversack of food, a leather sheath containing a long-bladed hunting knife; his right hand rested on a cocked revolver thrust in the crimson sash about his waist. . . .

Rainsford had fought his way through the bush for two hours. "I must keep my nerve. I must keep my nerve," he said through tight teeth.

He had not been entirely clearheaded when the chateau gates snapped shut behind him. His whole idea at first was to put distance between himself and General Zaroff, and, to this end, he had plunged along, spurred on by the sharp row-
4 els of something very like panic. Now he had got a grip on himself, had stopped, and was taking stock of himself and the situation.

He saw that straight flight was futile; inevitably it would bring him face to face with the sea. He was in a picture with a frame of water, and his operations, clearly, must take place within that frame.

5 "I'll give him a trail to follow," muttered Rainsford, and he struck off from the rude paths he had been following into the trackless wilderness. He executed a series of intricate loops; he doubled on his trail again and again, recalling all the lore of the fox hunt, and all the dodges of the fox. Night found him leg-weary, with hands and

19. **Au revoir** [ō'rə vwär]: French for "until we meet again."

AT A GLANCE

- Rainsford learns that he will be Zaroff's next quarry.
- Ivan supplies Rainsford with hunting clothes, food, and a knife.
- Rainsford starts out in panic but then tries to hide his trail.

1 PLOT: NARRATIVE HOOK

Rainsford learns he will be Zaroff's next quarry, and the reader's concern for his welfare escalates.

2 CHARACTERIZATION

Zaroff considers himself a trustworthy gentleman and a sportsman, though Rainsford now knows that the savage arrangement is a result of Zaroff's chilling madness.

3 IRONY

Zaroff is capable of loving one of his dogs, but he is unable to feel compassion for the suffering of a fellow human being.

4 CONFLICT

Just as he had to stay calm in the person-against-nature conflict with the ocean, so Rainsford must keep his head in the present person-against-person conflict in order to outwit his adversary and survive.

5 PLOT: RISING ACTION

Rainsford embarks on his first ploy in the hunt: the creation of a trail sufficiently intricate to challenge Zaroff.

GUIDED READING

LITERAL QUESTIONS

1a. What choice does Zaroff give Rainsford? (He can be hunted by Zaroff or be tortured by Ivan.)

2a. What does Rainsford realize after his initial panic in the jungle? (Straight flight will not help; he must stay calm and think of a plan.)

INFERENTIAL QUESTIONS

1b. What kind of choice is this? (It appears to be no real choice at all. It is merely choosing which way he will die.)

2b. Why is thinking things through so important in this story? (The ability to think things through is what separates man from other animals. Rainsford can survive only by outsmarting Zaroff.)

AT A GLANCE

- Rainsford hides in a tree after creating a trail he thinks cannot be followed.
- Nonetheless Zaroff follows the trail in the dark.

1 PLOT: RISING ACTION

Rainsford's second ploy in the hunt is to hide in a tree, once he feels sure that Zaroff will not be able to track him.

2 STYLE: IMAGERY

The words *apprehensive, wounded,* and *dead* refer both to the night surrounding Rainsford and to his thoughts.

3 CONFLICT

In the battle between the two expert hunters, Zaroff proves himself a much better hunter than Rainsford has given him credit for being.

face lashed by the branches, on a thickly wooded ridge. He knew it would be insane to blunder on through the dark, even if he had the strength. His need for rest was imperative and he thought: "I have played the fox, now I must play the cat of the fable." A big tree with a thick trunk and
1 outspread branches was nearby, and, taking care to leave not the slightest mark, he climbed up into the crotch, and stretching out on one of the broad limbs, after a fashion, rested. Rest brought him new confidence and almost a feeling of security. Even so zealous a hunter as General Zaroff could not trace him there, he told himself; only the devil himself could follow that complicated trail through the jungle after dark. But, perhaps, the general was a devil—

2 An apprehensive night crawled slowly by like a wounded snake, and sleep did not visit Rainsford, although the silence of a dead world was on the jungle. Toward morning when a dingy gray was varnishing the sky, the cry of some startled bird focused Rainsford's attention in that direction. Something was coming through the bush, coming slowly, carefully, coming by the same winding way Rainsford had come. He flattened himself down on the limb, and through a screen of leaves almost as thick as tapestry, he watched. The thing that was approaching was a man.

3 It was General Zaroff. He made his way along with his eyes fixed in utmost concentration on the ground before him. He paused, almost beneath the tree, dropped to his knees and studied the ground. Rainsford's impulse was to hurl himself down like a panther, but he saw that the general's right hand held something metallic—a small automatic pistol.

The hunter shook his head several times, as if he were puzzled. Then he straightened up and took from his case one of his black cigarettes; its pungent incenselike smoke floated up to Rainsford's nostrils.

GUIDED READING

LITERAL QUESTION

1a. Where does Rainsford hide? (in a tree)

INFERENTIAL QUESTION

1b. What does this tell you about Rainsford's state of mind? (Rainsford is thinking like a hunted animal would.)

Rainsford held his breath. The general's eyes had left the ground and were traveling inch by inch up the tree. Rainsford froze there, every muscle tensed for a spring. But the sharp eyes of the hunter stopped before they reached the limb where Rainsford lay; a smile spread over his brown face. Very deliberately he blew a smoke ring into the air; then he turned his back on the tree and walked carelessly away, back along the trail he had come. The swish of the underbrush against his hunting boots grew fainter and fainter.

The pent-up air burst hotly from Rainsford's lungs. His first thought made him feel sick and numb. The general could follow a trail through the woods at night; he could follow an extremely difficult trail; he must have uncanny powers; only by the merest chance had the Cossack failed to see his quarry.

Rainsford's second thought was even more terrible. It sent a shudder of cold horror through his whole being. Why had the general smiled? Why had he turned back?

Rainsford did not want to believe what his reason told him was true, but the truth was as evident as the sun that had by now pushed through the morning mists. The general was playing with him! The general was saving him for another day's sport! The Cossack was the cat; he was the mouse. Then it was that Rainsford knew the full meaning of terror.

"I will not lose my nerve. I will not."

He slid down from the tree, and struck off again into the woods. His face was set and he forced the machinery of his mind to function. Three hundred yards from his hiding place he stopped where a huge dead tree leaned precariously on a smaller, living one. Throwing off his sack of food, Rainsford took his knife from its sheath and began to work with all his energy.

The job was finished at last, and he threw himself down behind a fallen log a hundred feet away. He did not have to wait long. The cat was coming again to play with the mouse.

Following the trail with the sureness of a bloodhound came General Zaroff. Nothing escaped those searching black eyes, no crushed blade of grass, no bent twig, no mark, no matter how faint, in the moss. So intent was the Cossack on his stalking that he was upon the thing Rainsford had made before he saw it. His foot touched the protruding bough that was the trigger. Even as he touched it, the general sensed his danger and leaped back with the agility of an
4 ape. But he was not quite quick enough; the dead tree, delicately adjusted to rest on the cut living one, crashed down and struck the general a glancing blow on the shoulder as it fell; but for his alertness, he must have been smashed beneath it. He staggered, but he did not fall; nor did he drop his revolver. He stood there, rubbing his injured shoulder, and Rainsford, with fear again gripping his heart, heard the general's mocking laugh ring through the jungle.

"Rainsford," called the general, "if you are within sound of my voice, as I suppose you are, let me congratulate you. Not many men know how to make a Malay man-catcher. Luckily, for me, I too have hunted in Malacca.[20] You are proving interesting, Mr. Rainsford. I am going now to have my wound dressed; it's only a slight one. But I shall be back. I shall be back."

When the general, nursing his bruised shoulder, had gone, Rainsford took up his flight again. It was flight now, a desperate, hopeless flight, that carried him on for some hours. Dusk came, then darkness, and still he pressed on. The ground grew softer under his moccasins; the vegetation grew ranker, denser; insects bit him
5 savagely. Then, as he stepped forward, his foot sank into the ooze. He tried to wrench it back, but the muck sucked viciously at his foot as if it were a giant leech. With a violent effort, he tore his foot loose. He knew where he was now. Death Swamp and its quicksand.

---

20. **Malacca** [mə lak′ə]: province of Malaysia in southeastern Asia.

AT A GLANCE

- Zaroff scans the tree Rainsford is hiding in and walks away; Rainsford realizes that Zaroff is toying with him.
- Rainsford tries to kill Zaroff with a Malay man-catcher, but he only wounds him.
- Zaroff leaves to have his wound dressed, and Rainsford continues his flight, reaching Death Swamp.

1 CONFLICT

Zaroff the hunter toys with Rainsford, who is like a hunted animal "tensed for a spring."

2 CHARACTERIZATION

Zaroff is so excellent a hunter that his abilities strike Rainsford, a superb hunter himself, as sickeningly uncanny.

3 THEME

The brutal awareness of the terror the hunted animal feels finally strikes the man who earlier had said to Whitney: "Who cares how a jaguar feels?"

4 PLOT: RISING ACTION

Rainsford's first trap, which would certainly have killed most men, merely wounds Zaroff.

5 CONFLICT

Rainsford's confrontation with danger continues as nature again threatens him with death.

GUIDED READING

LITERAL QUESTIONS

1a. What does Zaroff do after he begins looking at the tree? (He stops, smiles, deliberately blows a smoke ring, and walks away.)

2a. What is the first trap Rainsford constructs? (a Malay man-catcher)

INFERENTIAL QUESTIONS

1b. What do Zaroff's actions at the tree indicate to Rainsford? (Zaroff knows where he is and is toying with him.)

2b. What does this suggest Rainsford is trying to do? (He is now trying to use his head in an attempt to outsmart Zaroff.)

AT A GLANCE

- Rainsford tries to kill Zaroff with a Burmese tiger pit but only kills one of Zaroff's dogs.
- At daybreak Rainsford hears a sound that terrifies him: the distant baying of a pack of hounds.
- As the hounds, held by Ivan, draw nearer, Rainsford frantically builds a third trap.

1 STYLE: IMAGERY

Rainsford's mind, capable of formulating an idea, is contrasted with his actions, which are like those of a "huge prehistoric beaver."

2 PLOT: RISING ACTION

Rainsford is again unsuccessful: though his second trap kills one of the general's dogs, Zaroff himself remains alive.

3 RESPONSE JOURNAL

Have students write their own idea about ways Rainsford could escape Zaroff, or how they would try to do so if they were in such a predicament.

4 PLOT: RISING ACTION

Rainsford frantically recalls another type of trap.

5 THEME

Finding himself in the position of an animal at bay, Rainsford learns to have empathy for a hunted animal.

His hands were tight closed as if his nerve were something tangible that someone in the darkness was trying to tear from his grip. The
1 softness of the earth had given him an idea. He stepped back from the quicksand a dozen feet or so and, like some huge prehistoric beaver, he began to dig.

Rainsford had dug himself in in France[21] when a second's delay meant death. That had been a placid pastime compared to his digging now. The pit grew deeper; when it was above his shoulders, he climbed out and from some hard saplings cut stakes and sharpened them to a fine point. These stakes he planted in the bottom of the pit with the points sticking up. With flying fingers he wove a rough carpet of weeds and branches and with it he covered the mouth of the pit. Then, wet with sweat and aching with tiredness, he crouched behind the stump of a lightning-charred tree.

He knew his pursuer was coming; he heard the padding sound of feet on the soft earth, and the night breeze brought him the perfume of the general's cigarette. It seemed to Rainsford that the general was coming with unusual swiftness; he was not feeling his way along, foot by foot. Rainsford, crouching there, could not see the general, nor could he see the pit. He lived a year in a minute. Then he felt an impulse to cry aloud with joy, for he heard the sharp crackle of the breaking branches as the cover of the pit gave way; he heard the sharp scream of pain as the pointed stakes found their mark. He leaped up from his place of concealment. Then he cowered back. Three feet from the pit a man was standing, with an electric torch in his hand.

2 "You've done well, Rainsford," the voice of the general called. "Your Burmese[22] tiger pit has claimed one of my best dogs. Again you score. I think, Mr. Rainsford, I'll see what you can do against my whole pack. I'm going home for a rest now. Thank you for a most amusing evening."

At daybreak Rainsford, lying near the swamp, was awakened by a sound that made him know that he had new things to learn about fear. It was a distant sound, faint and wavering, but he knew it. It was the baying of a pack of hounds.

Rainsford knew he could do one of two things. He could stay where he was and wait. That was suicide. He could flee. That was postponing the inevitable. For a moment he stood
3 there, thinking. An idea that held a wild chance came to him, and tightening his belt, he headed away from the swamp.

The baying of the hounds drew nearer, then still nearer, nearer, ever nearer. On a ridge Rainsford climbed a tree. Down a watercourse, not a quarter of a mile away, he could see the bush moving. Straining his eyes, he saw the lean figure of General Zaroff; just ahead of him Rainsford made out another figure whose wide shoulders surged through the tall jungle weeds; it was the giant Ivan, and he seemed pulled forward by some unseen force; Rainsford knew that Ivan must be holding the pack in leash.

4 They would be on him any minute now. His mind worked frantically. He thought of a native trick he had learned in Uganda.[23] He slid down the tree. He caught hold of a springy young sapling and to it he fastened his hunting knife, with the blade pointing down the trail; with a bit of
5 wild grapevine he tied back the sapling. Then he ran for his life. The hounds raised their voices as they hit the fresh scent. Rainsford knew now how an animal at bay feels.

He had to stop to get his breath. The baying of the hounds stopped abruptly, and Rainsford's heart stopped too. They must have reached the knife.

He shinnied excitedly up a tree and looked

21. **dug himself in in France:** dug a foxhole on the front during World War I.
22. **Burmese** [bər mēz′]: of Burma, a country of Indochina, in southeastern Asia.
23. **Uganda** [ū gan′də]: country in east central Africa.

GUIDED READING

LITERAL QUESTIONS

1a. Who or what is killed by Rainsford's second trap? (one of Zaroff's dogs)

2a. What sound does Rainsford hear in the morning? (the baying of hounds)

INFERENTIAL QUESTIONS

1b. What does Zaroff's use of his dogs indicate about the fairness of this match of wits? (This is not an even match between Rainsford and Zaroff; this is an unfair contest.)

2b. Why is Rainsford's reaction to this sound so important in the story? (Rainsford's reaction shows that he now knows what an animal feels; he knows that the feelings of a hunted animal are legitimate and real.)

back. His pursuers had stopped. But the hope that was in Rainsford's brain when he climbed died, for he saw in the shallow valley that General Zaroff was still on his feet. But Ivan was not. The knife, driven by the recoil of the springing tree, had not wholly failed.

Rainsford had hardly tumbled to the ground when the pack took up the cry again.

"Nerve, nerve, nerve!" he panted, as he dashed along. A blue gap showed between the trees dead ahead. Ever nearer drew the hounds. Rainsford forced himself on toward that gap. He reached it. It was the shore of the sea. Across a cove he could see the gloomy gray stone of the château. Twenty feet below him the sea rumbled and hissed. Rainsford hesitated. He heard the hounds. Then he leaped far out into the sea. . . .

When the general and his pack reached the place by the sea, the Cossack stopped. For some minutes he stood regarding the blue-green expanse of water. He shrugged his shoulders. Then he sat down, took a drink of brandy from a silver flask, lit a perfumed cigarette, and hummed a bit from *Madame Butterfly*.[24]

General Zaroff had an exceedingly good dinner in his great paneled dining hall that evening. With it he had a bottle of Pol Roger and half a bottle of Chambertin. Two slight annoyances kept him from perfect enjoyment. One was the thought that it would be difficult to replace Ivan; the other was that his quarry escaped him; of course the American hadn't played the game—so thought the general as he tasted his after-dinner liqueur. In his library he read, to soothe himself, from the works of Marcus Aurelius.[25] At ten he went up to his bedroom. He was deliciously tired, he said to himself, as he locked himself in. There was a little moonlight, so, before turning on his light, he went to the window and looked down at the courtyard. He could see the great hounds, and he called: "Better luck another time," to them. Then he switched on the light.

2 A man, who had been hiding in the curtains of the bed, was standing there.

"Rainsford!" screamed the general. "How did you get here?"

"Swam," said Rainsford. "I found it quicker than walking through the jungle."

The general sucked in his breath and smiled. "I congratulate you," he said. "You have won the game."

Rainsford did not smile. "I am still a beast at bay," he said, in a low, hoarse voice. "Get ready, General Zaroff."

The general made one of his deepest bows. "I see," he said. "Splendid! One of us is to furnish a repast for the hounds. The other will sleep in this very excellent bed. On guard, Rainsford. . . ."

3 He had never slept in a better bed, Rainsford decided.

24. ***Madame Butterfly:*** opera by Giacomo Puccini.

25. **Marcus Aurelius** [ô rē′lē əs]: Roman philosopher and emperor of the second century.

STUDY QUESTIONS

Recalling

1. Explain how Rainsford gets to Ship-Trap Island.
2. In what way has Zaroff changed the sport of hunting? Why?
3. Describe three methods that Rainsford uses to keep from being found by Zaroff during the hunt.
4. Briefly describe Zaroff's activities after he returns from the hunt at the end of the story.

Interpreting

5. Consider Zaroff's daily life, and give three details that are in sharp contrast to the savagery of his hunting. What does this contrast tell us about Zaroff's personality?

AT A GLANCE

- Ivan is killed by Rainsford's Ugandan trap.
- Pursued by the hounds, Rainsford leaps into the sea.
- Later that evening Zaroff is surprised by Rainsford, who is hiding in his bedroom.
- The men confront each other and Rainsford, victorious, sleeps in Zaroff's bed.

1 THEME

Rainsford realizes that the ocean, which had been his first "enemy," offers the only possible escape route from his present adversary, who is a far more threatening foe.

2 VOCABULARY: CONNOTATION

The application of the word *man* to Rainsford after the many references to him as a hunted animal indicates that Rainsford has finally outsmarted Zaroff.

3 PLOT: CLIMAX, FALLING ACTION, RESOLUTION

All three plot elements are contained in this final sentence, which concludes the battle between Rainsford and Zaroff.

REFLECTING ON THE STORY

Do you think Rainsford will ever hunt again? (Since he has learned firsthand what a hunted animal feels, perhaps it is unlikely that Rainsford would ever hunt again.)

STUDY QUESTIONS

1. falls overboard, swims to island
2. hunts humans; more challenging
3. moves in circles; hides at night in tree; makes traps
4. eats dinner, reads, goes to bedroom, finds Rainsford
5. - He is refined, cultured, and educated.
   - complex personality; contrast suggests insanity

STUDY QUESTIONS

6. It would detract from the main idea.

7. He has learned how it feels to be hunted; he may not hunt again.

VIEWPOINT

Zaroff might disagree, believing the nobler the prey, the better the hunt; Rainsford, after learning empathy for animals, would agree.

LITERARY FOCUS

Thinking About Conflict

1. Rainsford vs. Zaroff; Rainsford's life; Zaroff's death

2. Rainsford vs. ocean; nature impersonal, requiring Rainsford's strength, not cunning

Thinking About Foreshadowing

- crew uncomfortable; captain afraid; shots and scream heard; beast killed

VOCABULARY

1. (d) advancing
2. (d) praiseworthy
3. (d) seldom
4. (a) safely
5. (b) forbid

6. The author does not show us Rainsford's final fight with Zaroff. Why?

Extending

7. Do you think Rainsford's ideas about hunting have changed by the end of the story? Why or why not?

VIEWPOINT

The great American novelist Ernest Hemingway was also a noted big game hunter. Hemingway once said that he would never hunt elephants because they are

Too big, too important, too noble. . . .

■ Would Rainsford or Zaroff agree with Hemingway? Why?

LITERARY FOCUS

External Conflict

The action at the core of a good plot usually centers on a **conflict,** a struggle between two opposing forces. Conflicts can be internal or external. An **external conflict** exists when a person struggles against some outside force, such as another person, nature, society, or fate. For example, a person-against-person conflict exists in a bicycle race between rivals or in a battle of wills between two stubborn people. A person-against-nature conflict exists when a character flees from a wild bear or tries to get home before a terrible storm.

Thinking About Conflict

1. What is the person-against-person conflict in "The Most Dangerous Game"? What is at stake? What is the outcome?
2. Identify a person-against-nature conflict in the story. What is different about this conflict compared to the story's person-against-person conflict?

Foreshadowing

Foreshadowing is the use of clues by the author to prepare readers for events that will happen later in a story. These clues add to reading pleasure. They appeal to our curiosity, increase our interest, and often build suspense.

Thinking About Foreshadowing

■ Find four hints that something unusual is happening on the island. Go back to Rainsford's conversation with Whitney on shipboard and to Rainsford's first exploration of the island.

VOCABULARY

Antonyms

Antonyms are words that have opposite or nearly opposite meanings. *Light* and *dark* are antonyms. The words in capitals are from "The Most Dangerous Game." Choose the word that is *most nearly the opposite* of each word in capitals, *as the word is used in the story.* Write the number of each item and the letter of your choice on a separate sheet.

1. RECEDING: (a) giving (b) admitting (c) retreating (d) advancing
2. DEPLORABLE: (a) awful (b) clear (c) expensive (d) praiseworthy
3. INVARIABLY: (a) frequently (b) often (c) always (d) seldom
4. PRECARIOUSLY: (a) safely (b) gently (c) insecurely (d) intensely
5. CONDONE: (a) forgo (b) forbid (c) forget (d) forgive

COMPOSITION

Writing About Plot

■ State the key, underlying conflict that Rainsford experiences on Ship-Trap Island. Defend your generalization by identifying the specific problems that Rainsford experiences once he arrives on the island and throughout the story. *For help with this assignment, see Lesson 2 in the Writing About Literature Handbook at the back of this book.*

Writing a Magazine Article

■ Imagine that you are Rainsford and have just returned home from Ship-Trap Island. A magazine has asked you to write an article explaining how you now feel about hunting. Write the article as Rainsford might have written it after his experience with General Zaroff. Give a general opinion, and explain the reason for that opinion.

COMPOSITION: GUIDELINES FOR EVALUATION

WRITING ABOUT PLOT

Objective:

To write a paragraph in which the topic sentence states the conflict and is supported by examples

Guidelines for Evaluation:

- suggested length: one paragraph
- should include a clear topic sentence
- should make at least three references to problems confronting Rainsford
- should make a final statement about resolution

WRITING A MAGAZINE ARTICLE

Objective:

To express an opinion and support it with examples and reasons

Guidelines for Evaluation:

- suggested length: three to four paragraphs
- should assume the persona of Rainsford
- should state an opinion about hunting in first paragraph
- should cite examples from story

As a young girl Jessamyn West (1907–1984) kept a journal to record her thoughts. The journal provided inspiration for *Cress Delahanty,* a collection of stories about the passage to maturity of an adolescent girl in California. The events portrayed in "Sixteen" represent a major step on that road to adulthood for Cress.

■ Which event, if any, in this story reminds you of grandparent-grandchild relationships you may know?

Jessamyn West

Sixteen

The steam from the kettle had condensed on the cold window and was running down the glass in tear-like trickles. Outside in the orchard the man from the smudge company was refilling the pots with oil. The greasy smell from last night's burning was still in the air. Mr. Delahanty gazed out at the bleak darkening orange grove; Mrs. Delahanty watched her husband eat, nibbling up to the edges of the toast, then stacking the crusts about his tea cup in a neat fence-like arrangement.

"We'll have to call Cress," Mr. Delahanty said finally. "Your father's likely not to last out the night. She's his only grandchild. She ought to be here."

Mrs. Delahanty pressed her hands to the bones above her eyes. "Cress isn't going to like being called away from college," she said.

"We'll have to call her anyway. It's the only thing to do." Mr. Delahanty swirled the last of his tea around in his cup so as not to miss any sugar.

"Father's liable to lapse into unconsciousness any time," Mrs. Delahanty argued. "Cress'll hate coming and Father won't know whether she's here or not. Why not let her stay at Woolman?"

Neither wanted, in the midst of their sorrow for the good man whose life was ending, to enter into any discussion of Cress. What was the mat-
3 ter with Cress? What had happened to her since she went away to college? She, who had been open and loving? And who now lived inside a world so absolutely fitted to her own size and shape that she felt any intrusion, even that of the death of her own grandfather, to be an unmerited invasion of her privacy. Black magic could not have changed her more quickly and unpleasantly and nothing except magic, it seemed, would give them back their lost daughter.

Mr. Delahanty pushed back his cup and saucer. "Her place is here, Gertrude. I'm going to call her long distance now. She's a bright girl and it's not going to hurt her to miss a few days from classes. What's the dormitory number?"

"I know it as well as our number," Mrs.

AT A GLANCE

- Cress's grandfather is dying.
- Her parents decide to call her home, but they worry about her reaction.
- Cress is like a different person since going to college; she has begun to seem selfish.

LITERARY OPTIONS

- internal conflict
- characterization
- style

THEMATIC OPTIONS

- relationships between generations
- family love
- death and dying

1 SETTING

The "cold window" and the smudge pots suggest a recent freeze. Nature mirrors the cold presence of death.

2 PLOT: EXPOSITION

The imminent death of Cress's grandfather demands her presence at home.

3 THEME

Cress's parents cannot understand the change in her personality. Cress wants only to live in her own world, and they expect her to see her grandfather's death as an intrusion on her privacy.

GUIDED READING

LITERAL QUESTION

1a. Why are Cress's parents worried about having to call Cress home? (They expect resistance.)

INFERENTIAL QUESTION

1b. What do you think the relationship of Cress and her parents is like? (It is probably strained. Cress's parents cannot understand what has happened to her since she went off to college; she wants only to be left alone.)

AT A GLANCE

- Mr. Delahanty goes to telephone Cress.
- Cress and her boyfriend, Edwin, banter about nature.
- Cress wonders if she has matured as much as Edwin.

1 POINT OF VIEW

As the narrator shares Cress's thoughts for the first time, the reader is able to see the world from Cress's perspective.

2 CHARACTERIZATION

Cress first appears in the story as a person in love with nature. This characterization suggests a certain sensitivity.

3 STYLE: DIALOGUE

Cress tries to act mature, but her words betray her childishness. Edwin's calm and direct words are more mature.

4 THEME

The self-assurance of a moment ago is placed in sharp contrast to the inner confusion of a young girl reaching adolescence.

5 CHARACTERIZATION

Cress's insistent and exaggerated love of nature is demonstrated when she "capers" in the leaves.

Delahanty said. "But at the minute it's gone. It's a sign of my reluctance, I suppose. Wait a minute and I'll look it up."

Mr. Delahanty squeezed out from behind the table. "Don't bother. I can get it."

Mrs. Delahanty watched her husband, his usually square shoulders sagging with weariness, wipe a clear place on the steamy windowpane with his napkin. Some of the green twilight appeared to seep into the warm dingy little kitchen. "I can't ever remember having to smudge before in February. I expect you're right," he added as he went toward the phone. "Cress isn't going to like it."

1 Cress didn't like it. It was February, the rains had been late and the world was burning with a green fire; a green smoke rolled down the hills and burst shoulder-high in the cover crops that filled the spaces between the trees in the orange orchards. There had been rain earlier in the day and drops still hung from the grass blades, sickle-shaped with their weight. Cress, walking across the campus with Edwin, squatted to look into one of these crystal globes.

2 "Green from the grass and red from the sun," she told him. "The whole world right there in one raindrop."

"As Blake[1] observed earlier about a grain of sand," said Edwin.

"O.K., show off," Cress told him. "You know it—but I saw it." She took his hand and he pulled her up, swinging her in a semicircle in front of him. "Down there in the grass the world winked at me."

3 "Don't be precious, Cress," Edwin said.

"I will," Cress said, "just to tease you. I love to tease you, Edwin."

"Why?" Edwin asked.

"Because you love to have me," Cress said confidently, taking his hand. Being older suited Edwin. She remembered when she had liked him in spite of his looks; but now spindly had become spare, and the dark shadow of his beard—Edwin had to shave every day while other boys were still just fuzzy—lay under his pale skin; and the opinions, which had once been so embarrassingly unlike anyone else's, were now celebrated at Woolman as being "Edwinian." Yes, Edwin had changed since that day when she had knocked his tooth out trying to rescue him
4 from the mush pot. And had she changed? Did she also look better to Edwin, almost slender now and the freckles not noticeable except at the height of summer? And with her new-found ability for light talk? They were passing beneath the eucalyptus trees and the silver drops, falling as the wind shook the leaves, stung her face, feeling at once both cool and burning. Meadow larks in the fields which edged the campus sang in the quiet way they have after the rain has stopped.

"Oh, Edwin," Cress said, "no one in the world loves the meadow lark's song the way I do!"

"It's not a competition," Edwin said, "you against the world in an 'I-love-meadow-larks' contest. Take it easy, kid. Love 'em as much as in you lieth, and let it go at that."

"No," she said. "I'm determined to overdo it. Listen," she exclaimed, as two birds sang together. "Not grieving, nor amorous, nor lost. Nothing to read into it. Simply music. Like Mozart.[2] Complete. Finished. Oh, it is rain to
5 listening ears." She glanced at Edwin to see how he took this rhetoric. He took it calmly. She let go his hand and capered amidst the fallen eucalyptus leaves.

---

1. **Blake:** William Blake (1757–1827), an English poet. Edwin refers to the following poem:

> To see a World in a grain of sand,
>   And Heaven in a wild flower;
> Hold Infinity in the palm of your hand,
>   And Eternity in an hour.

2. **Mozart** [mōt′särt]: Wolfgang [woolf′gang′] Amadeus [ä′mə dā əs] Mozart (1756–1791), great classical composer from Austria.

GUIDED READING

LITERAL QUESTIONS

1a. In what ways does Cress wonder if she has changed? (She wonders if she looks better, thinner, less freckled; she wonders if she is a good conversationalist.)

2a. What does Cress say about the song of the meadow lark? ("No one in the world loves the meadow lark's song the way I do!")

INFERENTIAL QUESTIONS

1b. What do these concerns tell you about Cress? (She is not very self-assured. She worries about her looks and ability to please others.)

2b. What does this tell you about Cress? (Cress's exaggerated reactions to everything show her immaturity.)

AT A GLANCE

- Cress says Old Boat Swain doesn't exist.
- Cress returns to the dorm and prepares for her date with Edwin.
- She is called home but feels no sympathy for her grandfather.
- Her friends console her about her grandfather; in fact, Cress is angry, and she decides not to go home.

1 INTERNAL CONFLICT

Cress's words betray her selfishness and immaturity. This is a very different Cress from the earlier lover of nature.

2 STYLE: IMAGERY

Images of dressing up like an adult contrast with Cress's childish ways.

3 DIALOGUE

Cress's affected speech is contrasted with Edwin's direct and down-to-earth words.

4 PLOT: NARRATIVE HOOK

When Cress is called home, the reader's interest in how she will respond to the news and interact with her parents is heightened.

5 CHARACTERIZATION

Cress does not think of her grandfather as a whole person; rather, she recalls what she saw as a child: "a rough, hot hand, a scraggly mustache that repelled her."

"The gardener thinks you've got St. Vitus' dance,"[3] Edwin said.

Old Boat Swain, the college gardener whose name was really Swain, was leaning on his hoe, watching her hopping and strutting. She didn't give a hoot about him or what he thought.

1 "He's old," she told Edwin. "He doesn't exist." She felt less akin to him than to a bird or toad.

There were lights already burning in the dorm windows. Cress could see Ardis and Nina still at their tables, finishing their Ovid[4] or looking up a final logarithm.[5] But between five and six most of the girls stopped trying to remember which form of the sonnet Milton[6] had used or when the Congress of Vienna[7] had met, and
2 dressed for dinner. They got out of their sweaters and jackets and into their soft bright dresses. She knew just what she was going to wear when she came downstairs at six to meet Edwin—green silk like the merman's wife. They were going to the Poinsettia for dinner, escaping salmon-wiggle night in the college dining room.

3 "At six," she told him, "I'll fly down the stairs to meet you like a green wave."

"See you in thirty minutes," Edwin said, leaving her at the dorm steps.

The minute she opened the door, she began to hear the dorm sounds and smell the dorm smells—the hiss and rush of the showers, the thud of the iron, a voice singing, "Dear old Woolman we love so well," the slap of bare feet down the hall, the telephone ringing.

And the smells! Elizabeth Arden and Cashmere Bouquet[8] frothing in the showers; talcum powder falling like snow; *Intoxication* and *Love Me* and *Devon Violet*; rubber-soled sneakers, too, and gym T-shirts still wet with sweat after basketball practice, and the smell of the hot iron on damp wool.

But while she was still listening and smelling, Edith shouted from the top of the stairs, "Long distance for you, Cress. Make it snappy."

Cress took the stairs three at a time, picked up the dangling receiver, pressed it to her ear.

4 "Tenant calling Crescent Delahanty," the operator said. It was her father: "Grandfather is dying, Cress. Catch the 7:30 home. I'll meet you at the depot."

"What's the matter—Cressie?" Edith asked.

"I have to catch the 7:30 Pacific Electric. Grandfather's dying."

"Oh, poor Cress," Edith cried and pressed her arm about her.

Cress scarcely heard her. Why were they calling her home to watch Grandpa die, she
5 thought, angrily and rebelliously. An old man, past eighty. He'd never been truly alive for her, never more than a rough, hot hand, a scraggly mustache that repelled her when he kissed her, an old fellow who gathered what he called "likely-looking" stones and kept them washed and polished, to turn over and admire. It was silly and unfair to make so much of his dying.

But before she could say a word, Edith was telling the girls. They were crowding about her. "Don't cry," they said. "We'll pack for you. Be brave, darling Cress. Remember your grandfather has had a long happy life. He wouldn't want you to cry."

"Brave Cress—brave Cress," they said. "Just frozen."

She wasn't frozen. She was determined. She was not going to go. It did not make sense. She

3. **Saint Vitus' dance:** nervous disease that causes involuntary muscle movement.
4. **Ovid** [ov′id]: Roman poet of the first century whose work is often translated in college Latin classes.
5. **logarithm** [lo′gə rith′əm]: mathematical term associated with trigonometry.
6. **Milton:** John Milton (1608–1674), an English poet, author of *Paradise Lost.*
7. **Congress of Vienna:** meeting of statesmen from England, Russia, Austria, and Prussia in 1814.
8. **Elizabeth Arden and Cashmere Bouquet:** popular brands of soap and toiletries.

GUIDED READING

LITERAL QUESTIONS

1a. How does Cress describe Old Boat Swain? (He is old; he doesn't exist.)

2a. How do the other girls react to Cress's misfortune? (They console her and help her pack.)

INFERENTIAL QUESTIONS

1b. What does this description suggest about Cress? (She is selfish and indifferent to others unlike herself. Old age does not even exist for her.)

2b. Why does West mention the reaction of the other girls? (Their reaction contrasts with Cress's lack of emotion. Also, it is ironic that they think she is being brave.)

went downstairs to meet Edwin as she had planned, in her green silk, ready for dinner at the Poinsettia. The girls had told him.

"Are you wearing that home?" he asked.

"I'm not going home," she said. "It's silly and useless. I can't help Grandfather. It's just a
1 convention. What *good* can I do him, sitting there at home?"

"He might do you some good," Edwin said. "Had you thought about that?"

"Why, Edwin!" Cress said. "Why, Edwin!" She had the girls tamed, eating out of her hand, and here was Edwin who loved her—he said so, anyway—cold and disapproving. Looking at herself through Edwin's eyes, she hesitated.

"Go on," Edwin said. "Get what you need and I'll drive you to the station."

2 She packed her overnight bag and went with him; there didn't seem—once she'd had Edwin's view of herself—anything else to do. But once on the train her resentment returned. The Pacific Electric was hot and smelled of metal and dusty plush. It clicked past a rickety Mexican settlement, through La Habra and Brea, where the pool hall signs swung in the night wind off the
3 ocean. An old man in a spotted corduroy jacket, and his wife, with her hair straggling through the holes in her broken net, sat in front of her.

Neat, thought Cress, anyone can be neat, if he wants to.

Her father, bareheaded, but in his big sheepskin jacket, met her at the depot. It was after nine, cold and raw.

"This is a sorry time, Cress," he said. He put her suitcase in the back of the car and climbed into the driver's seat without opening the door for her.

Cress got in, wrapped her coat tightly about herself. The sky was clear, the wind had died down.

"I don't see any sense in my having to come home," she said at last. "What good can I do Grandpa? If he's dying, how can I help?"

"I was afraid that was the way you might feel about it. So was your mother."

"Oh, Mother," Cress burst out. "Recently she's always trying to put me. . ."

Her father cut her off. "That'll be about enough, Cress. Your place is at home and you're coming home and keeping your mouth shut, whatever you think. I don't know what's happened to you recently. If college does this to you, you'd better stay home permanently."

There was nothing more said until they turned up the palm-lined driveway that led to the house. "Here we are," Mr. Delahanty told her.

Mrs. Delahanty met them at the door, tired and haggard in her Indian design bathrobe.

"Cress," she said, "Grandfather's conscious now. I told him you were coming and he's anxious to see you. You'd better go in right away—this might be the last time he'd know you."

Cress was standing by the fireplace holding first one foot then the other toward the fire.
4 "Oh, Mother, what am I to say?" she asked. "What can I say? Or does Grandfather just want to see me?"

Her father shook his head as if with pain. "Aren't you sorry your grandfather's dying, Cress? Haven't you any pity in your heart? Don't you understand what death means?"

5 "He's an old man," Cress said obstinately. "It's what we must expect when we grow old," though she, of course, would never grow old.

"Warm your hands, Cress," her mother said. "Grandfather's throat bothers him and it eases him to have it rubbed. I'll give you the ointment and you can rub it in. You won't need to say anything."

Cress slid out of her coat and went across the hall with her mother to visit her grandfather's room. His thin old body was hardly visible beneath the covers; his head, with its gray skin and sunken eyes, lay upon the pillow as if

AT A GLANCE

- Edwin shames Cress into going home.
- Cress distresses her parents by not wanting to help her grandfather.
- She enters her grandfather's room.

1 THEME

Edwin tells Cress that her grandfather's life might have some important meaning for her.

2 CHARACTERIZATION

Cress is not a person of strong convictions. She is easily persuaded to change her mind by Edwin's disapproval.

3 STYLE: IMAGERY

The images of two disheveled old people underscore Cress's immature view that old people are only a nuisance.

4 INTERNAL CONFLICT

Cress's true fear of death surfaces in sharp contrast to her earlier professed love of life.

5 THEME

Cress reveals her naiveté and immaturity in thinking that she will never grow old and die.

GUIDED READING

LITERAL QUESTIONS

1a. What does Edwin say to make Cress decide to go home? (He says her grandfather might do her some good.)

2a. What is Cress's response to her mother's urging her to see her grandfather? ("What can I say?")

INFERENTIAL QUESTIONS

1b. What does Cress stand to learn from involving herself in her grandfather's death? (She will discover that any life can be filled with love and enjoyment and that such things continue into old age.)

2b. What does this response tell us about Cress? (She is afraid to confront her dying grandfather. She is not merely being selfish; she is truly afraid of death and is unsure how to respond to it.)

AT A GLANCE

- Cress rubs ointment on her grandfather's throat.
- She gives her grandfather her violets, which remind him of her grandmother.
- She cries as she realizes that he too loves nature and life.

1 PLOT: RISING ACTION

Cress's mother makes her confront death in a real and concrete way, thereby giving her daughter something to do.

2 STYLE: IMAGERY

The image of an awkward and trembling finger shows the debilitating power of death and contrasts with the vibrant life of the yellow violets.

3 THEME

Cress's grandfather shares her love of nature and living things; by comparing Cress and her grandmother, he links the generations.

REFLECTING ON THE STORY

What does the last line of the story indicate that Cress has learned? (Cress has learned that the need for love is the same for all people—no matter what their age.)

STUDY QUESTIONS

1. her independence, rebelliousness; grandfather may lapse into coma and not recognize her
2.
   - He is old and ready for death; she feels useless to help him, resents social convention.
   - "He might do you some good."
3. says Old Boat Swain doesn't matter; resents old couple on train; says death is "what we must expect when we grow old"

bodiless. The night light frosted his white hair but made black caverns of his closed eyes.

"Father," Mrs. Delahanty said. "Father." But the old man didn't move. There was nothing except the occasional hoarse rasp of an indrawn breath to show that he was alive.

Mrs. Delahanty pulled the cane-bottomed
1 chair a little closer to the bed. "Sit here," she said to Cress, "and rub this into his throat and chest." She opened her father's nightshirt so that an inch or two of bony grizzled chest was bared. "He says that this rubbing relieves him, even if he's asleep or too tired to speak. Rub it in with a slow steady movement." She went out to the living room leaving the door a little ajar.

Cress sat down on the chair and put two squeamish fingers into the jar of gray ointment; but she could see far more sense to this than to any talking or being talked to. If they had brought her home from school because she was needed in helping to care for Grandpa, that she could understand—but not simply to be present at his death. What had death to do with her?

She leaned over him, rubbing, but with eyes shut, dipping her fingers often into the gray grease. The rhythm of the rubbing, the warmth and closeness of the room, after the cold drive, had almost put her to sleep when the old man
2 startled her by lifting a shaking hand to the bunch of yellow violets Edith had pinned to the shoulder of her dress before she left Woolman. She opened her eyes suddenly at his touch, but the old man said nothing, only stroked the violets awkwardly with a trembling forefinger.

Cress unpinned the violets and put them in his hand. "There, Grandpa," she said, "there. They're for you."

The old man's voice was a harsh and faltering whisper and to hear what he said Cress had to lean very close.

3 "I used to—pick them—on Reservoir Hill. I was always sorry to—plow them up. Still—so sweet. Thanks," he said, "to bring them. To remember. You're like her. Your grandmother," he added after a pause. He closed his eyes, holding the bouquet against his face, letting the wilting blossoms spray across one cheek like a pulled-up sheet of flowering earth. He said one more word, not her name but her grandmother's.

The dikes about Cress's heart broke. "Oh, Grandpa. I love you," she said. He heard her. He knew what she said, his fingers returned the pressure of her hand. "You were always so good to me. You were young and you loved flowers." Then she said what was her great discovery. "And you still do. You still love yellow violets, Grandpa, just like me."

At the sound of her uncontrolled crying, Mr. and Mrs. Delahanty came to the door. "What's the matter, Cress?"

Cress turned, lifted a hand toward them. "Why didn't you tell me?" she demanded. And when they didn't answer, she said, "Edwin knew."

Then she dropped her head on to her grandfather's outstretched hand and said something, evidently to him, which neither her father nor her mother understood.

"It's just the same."

STUDY QUESTIONS

Recalling

1. Give two reasons that Cress's parents are reluctant to call her away from college.
2. What reasons does Cress give for not going home? What does Edwin say to change her mind?
3. Find three examples of Cress's lack of sympathy for the elderly before she sees her grandfather.

4. What does Cress do for her grandfather while he is asleep?
5. Describe how the grandfather reacts when he notices Cress's yellow violets.

Interpreting
6. Why does Cress feel that death has nothing to do with her? In what ways does that feeling change by the end of the story?
7. What does her grandfather actually do for Cress?
8. What attitude toward life unites Cress and her grandfather? What does Cress learn that she has in common with him?

Extending
9. Why do you think the author called this story "Sixteen"? What might she be saying about some people of that age?

VIEWPOINT

Once an author has described a character's personality, that character must act accordingly. As a result, the personality dictates the character's actions to the author. Jessamyn West enjoys being startled by the actions of her characters. West, herself, has said:

> I expect my characters to reveal more of themselves to me as the story progresses. I think the writer, as well as the reader, deserves a few surprises in the story.

■ In what ways are Cress's actions surprising? Explain how Cress is true to her own personality throughout the story.

LITERARY FOCUS

Internal Conflict

An **internal conflict,** a conflict of person against self, takes place within a character. Internal conflicts are often more subtle than external conflicts, which set a person against another person or against society, nature, or fate (see page 26). In an internal conflict a character may struggle to reach a decision, to make a moral choice, or to attain a personal goal. For example, a character may have to decide between two courses or may have to struggle with a conscience over some action.

Thinking About Internal Conflict

■ Name two different desires within Cress that are in conflict in the story. Give one or two actions that illustrate each desire.

Dialogue

Dialogue is conversation between characters in any form of writing. Dialogue makes a story more interesting by enabling us to feel like eyewitnesses to what happens. From what a character says we learn about the character's thoughts and feelings and are able to form our own impression of that character's personality.

Thinking About Dialogue

■ Explain how dialogue helps us to understand the internal conflict in this story. That is, give examples of conversation in the story that show Cress's conflict.

COMPOSITION

Writing About Conflict

■ Using specific examples from the story, explain how West presents the conflict within Cress. First identify the conflict. Then point out the climax of the story, and explain the resolution of the conflict.

Writing a Journal Entry

■ Imagine that you are drawn into a conversation with an elderly man or woman while sitting on a park bench. Write a journal entry that tells of this meeting. Explain something important that you realize for the first time because of the encounter.

COMPARING STORIES

1. The plots of "The Monkey's Paw" and "The Most Dangerous Game" have more outward adventure than the plot of "Sixteen." Compare two or more of these stories by explaining how the type of conflict in the story determines the type and amount of adventure in each story.
2. In "The Monkey's Paw," "The Most Dangerous Game," and "Sixteen" a main character learns an important lesson from a conflict. For two or more of the stories, compare the kind of lesson the character learns as a result of the conflict.

COMPOSITION: GUIDELINES FOR EVALUATION

WRITING ABOUT CONFLICT

Objective

To explain how West presents conflict within Cress

Guidelines for Evaluation

- suggested length: three to five paragraphs
- should clearly describe an internal conflict with examples
- should explain the climax and resolution

WRITING A JOURNAL ENTRY

Objective

To write a journal entry about encounter with elderly person

Guidelines for Evaluation

- suggested length: 150–300 words
- should clearly report encounter and realization
- should relate incident to realization
- should use first-person narration

STUDY QUESTIONS

4. rubs ointment on throat, chest
5. strokes them, remembers wife's love of flowers, compares Cress to her
6. denial of own mortality; realizes death is inevitable
7. helps her regain "open, loving nature"; shows her all share her enthusiasm for life and all must face death
8. love of life; memories of grandmother, need for—and ability to—love
9. self-involvement of teens; can be age of revising judgments

VIEWPOINT

Surprising: refuses to go home, then follows Edwin's advice; angers father; weeps at grandfather's bed
Personality: Cress's personality battles itself; she is loving/selfish, rebellious/obedient, confused/self-assured.

LITERARY FOCUS

Internal conflict: desire for independence (not wanting to go home); desire to be caring (final sympathy for grandfather)
Dialogue: first conversation with Edwin shows her love of life in conflict with selfishness; conversation with grandfather changes perception of aging and death

COMPARING STORIES

1. In general, the more overt the conflict the more adventurous the story; "Paw": person vs. fate leads to dramatic mystery; "Game": person vs. person leads to life and death competition; "Sixteen": internal conflict leads to little overt action.
2. "Paw": Whites learn not to meddle with fate; "Game": Rainsford learns empathy for hunted animals; "Sixteen": Cress gains greater understanding of herself and life.

AT A GLANCE

- Markham, a farmer, tells his wife he is going to town the next day.
- She says she will accompany him with their baby, since she hasn't been off the farm for six months.
- They put their wheat into sacks that night.

LITERARY OPTIONS

- characterization
- theme
- setting

THEMATIC OPTIONS

- the power of human sympathy
- friendship
- understanding different life-styles

1 CHARACTERIZATION

At the outset of the story, Garland calls Mrs. Markham "a tired and sullen woman," thereby directly presenting the reader with an impression of her appearance and personality.

2 VOCABULARY: DIALECT

The authenticity of this portrayal of the American midwestern farmer is enhanced by the use of regional language, including words such as *git*.

LITERARY FOCUS: Character

Because Hamlin Garland (1860–1940) was raised on farms throughout the Middle West, he vowed to bring the hard life of the prairie farmer to the eyes of the public. Like many of his short stories, "A Day's Pleasure" takes place on the American plains and describes the spirit of pioneer men and women.

- Does the main character of this story have anything in common with actual people living today?

Hamlin Garland

A Day's Pleasure

I

1 When Markham came in from shoveling his last wagonload of corn into the crib he found that his wife had put the children to bed, and was kneading a batch of dough with the dogged action of a tired and sullen woman.

He slipped his soggy boots off his feet, and having laid a piece of wood on top of the stove, put his heels on it comfortably. His chair squeaked as he leaned back on its hinder legs, but he paid no attention; he was used to it, exactly as he was used to his wife's lameness and ceaseless toil.

2 "That closes up my corn," he said after a silence. "I guess I'll go to town tomorrow to git my horses shod."

"I guess I'll git ready and go along," said his wife, in a sorry attempt to be firm and confident of tone.

"What do you want to go to town fer?" he grumbled.

"What does anybody want to go to town fer?" she burst out, facing him. "I ain't been out o' this house fer six months, while you go an' go!"

"Oh, it ain't six months. You went down that day I got the mower."

"When was that? The tenth of July, and you know it."

"Well, mebbe 'twas. I didn't think it was so long ago. I ain't no objection to your goin', only I'm goin' to take a load of wheat."

"Well, jest leave off a sack, an' that'll balance me an' the baby," she said spiritedly.

"All right," he replied good-naturedly, seeing she was roused. "Only that wheat ought to be put up tonight if you're goin'. You won't have any time to hold sacks for me in the morning with them young ones to get off to school."

"Well, let's go do it then," she said, sullenly resolute.

"I hate to go out agin; but I s'pose we'd better."

He yawned dismally and began pulling his

GUIDED READING

LITERAL QUESTION

1a. Why does Mrs. Markham want to go to town? (She has not been away from the house for six months.)

INFERENTIAL QUESTION

1b. What does this tell you about her way of life? (She has much work at home and has little opportunity for relaxation or change of scene.)

boots on again, stamping his swollen feet into them with grunts of pain. She put on his coat and one of the boy's caps, and they went out to the granary. The night was cold and clear.

"Don't look so much like snow as it did last night," said Sam. "It may turn warm."

Laying out the sacks in the light of the lantern, they sorted out those which were whole, and Sam climbed into the bin with a tin pail in his hand, and the work began.

1 He was a sturdy fellow, and he worked desperately fast; the shining tin pail dived deep into the cold wheat and dragged heavily on the woman's tired hands as it came to the mouth of the sack, and she trembled with fatigue, but held on and dragged the sacks away when filled, and brought others, till at last Sam climbed out, puffing and wheezing, to tie them up.

"I guess I'll load 'em in the morning," he said. "You needn't wait fer me. I'll tie 'em up alone."

"Oh, I don't mind," she replied, feeling a little touched by his unexpectedly easy acquiescence to her request. When they went back to the house the moon had risen.

It had scarcely set when they were wakened by the crowing roosters. The man rolled stiffly out of bed and began rattling at the stove in the dark, cold kitchen.

His wife arose lamer and stiffer than usual, and began twisting her thin hair into a knot.

Sam did not stop to wash, but went out to the barn. The woman, however, hastily soused her face into the hard limestone water at the sink, and put the kettle on. Then she called the children. She knew it was early, and they would
2 need several callings. She pushed breakfast forward, running over in her mind the things she must have: two spools of thread, six yards of cotton flannel, a can of coffee, and mittens for Kitty. These she must have—there were oceans of things she needed.

The children soon came scudding down out of the darkness of the upstairs to dress tumul-
3 tuously at the kitchen stove. They humped and shivered, holding up their bare feet from the cold floor, like chickens in new-fallen snow. They were irritable, and snarled and snapped and struck like cats and dogs. Mrs. Markham stood it for a while with mere commands to "hush up," but at last her patience gave out, and she charged down on the struggling mob and cuffed them right and left.

They ate their breakfast by lamplight, and when Sam went back to his work around the barnyard it was scarcely dawn. The children, left alone with their mother, began to tease her to let them go to town also.

"No, sir—nobody goes but baby. Your father's goin' to take a load of wheat."

She was weak with the worry of it all when she had sent the older children away to school and the kitchen work was finished. She went into the cold bedroom off the little sitting room
4 and put on her best dress. It had never been a good fit, and now she was getting so thin it hung in wrinkled folds everywhere about the shoulders and waist. She lay down on the bed a moment to ease that dull pain in her back. She had a moment's distaste for going out at all. The thought of sleep was more alluring. The thought of the long, long day, and the sickening sameness of her life, swept over her again, and she rose and prepared the baby for the journey.

It was but little after sunrise when Sam drove out into the road and started for Belleplain. His wife sat perched upon the wheat sacks behind him, holding the baby in her lap, a cotton quilt under her, and a cotton horse-blanket over her knees.

Sam was disposed to be very good-natured, and he talked back at her occasionally, though she could only understand him when he turned his face toward her. The baby stared out at the passing fence posts, and wiggled his hands out of his mittens at every opportunity. He was merry at least.

It grew warmer as they went on, and a strong

AT A GLANCE

- Markham and his wife fill sacks with wheat in the granary.
- In the morning she makes breakfast and sends the children to school.
- She changes her clothes and rests briefly before she, her husband, and the baby set out for town.

1 SETTING

The hard life of a farmer and his wife is presented in vivid detail as they perform an exhausting task in the cold granary.

2 THEME

Mrs. Markham's concerns indicate that she can afford only the barest essentials; the life style of a midwestern farm family is shaped by financial constraints.

3 POINT OF VIEW

Garland uses a third-person narrator to report information about the characters (they were *irritable*, her *patience gave out*) and their surroundings.

4 CHARACTERIZATION

The reader learns several significant facts about Mrs. Markham: She is undernourished, overworked, and exhausted.

GUIDED READING

LITERAL QUESTIONS

1a. What must Mrs. Markham buy in town? (thread, cloth, coffee, mittens)

2a. What does Mrs. Markham do after the children go to school? (puts on her best dress, lies down, considers going to sleep, remembers the "sickening sameness of her life," prepares the baby for the journey)

INFERENTIAL QUESTIONS

1b. Why is this list significant? (It shows that the Markhams can afford only the bare necessities of life.)

2b. What do these details tell us about her character? (She is undernourished and physically tired, but she is much more tired of her life's boring routine.)

AT A GLANCE

- Mrs. Markham's physical discomfort increases.
- Markham leaves his wife at the grocery store and goes to sell his wheat.
- Mrs. Markham asks Markham for money for necessities.

1 SETTING

The dry spareness of this prairie town makes a mockery of its fancy name, Belleplain; it is hardly a beautiful place.

2 THEME

The kindness and decency of the grocer makes life a little easier for Mrs. Markham.

3 STYLE: DIALOGUE

Despite their clipped exchange, Markham loves his wife and knows when he must give in to her requests.

south wind arose. The dust settled upon the woman's shawl and hat. Her hair loosened and blew unkemptly about her face. The road which led across the high, level prairie was quite smooth and dry, but still it jolted her, and the pain in her back increased. She had nothing to lean against, and the weight of the child grew greater, till she was forced to place him on the sacks beside her, though she could not loose her hold for a moment.

1 The town drew in sight—a cluster of small frame houses and stores on the dry prairie beside a railway station. There were no trees yet which could be called shade trees. The pitilessly severe light of the sun flooded everything. A few teams were hitched about, and in the lee of the stores a few men could be seen seated comfortably, their broad hat-rims flopping up and down, their faces brown as leather.

Markham put his wife out at one of the grocery stores, and drove off down toward the elevators to sell his wheat.

2 The grocer greeted Mrs. Markham in a perfunctorily kind manner, and offered her a chair, which she took gratefully. She sat for a quarter of an hour almost without moving, leaning against the back of the high chair. At last the child began to get restless and troublesome, and she spent half an hour helping him amuse himself around the nail-kegs.

At length she rose and went out on the walk, carrying the baby. She went into the dry-goods store and took a seat on one of the little revolving stools. A woman was buying some woolen goods for a dress. It was worth twenty-seven cents a yard, the clerk said, but he would knock off two cents if she took ten yards. It looked warm, and Mrs. Markham wished she could afford it for Mary.

A pretty young girl came in and laughed and chatted with the clerk, and bought a pair of gloves. She was the daughter of the grocer. Her happiness made the wife and mother sad. When Sam came back she asked him for some money.

3 "What you want to do with it?" he asked.

"I want to spend it," she said.

She was not to be trifled with, so he gave her a dollar.

"I need a dollar more."

"Well, I've got to go take up that note at the bank."

"Well, the children's got to have some new underclo'es," she said.

GUIDED READING

LITERAL QUESTION

1a. How is Belleplain described? (as a cluster of small frame houses and stores on a glaring, dry prairie with no shade trees)

INFERENTIAL QUESTION

1b. Why do you think the town's unexciting setting might be significant? (The dry, desolate town seems to offer Mrs. Markham little opportunity for excitement or relief from the boredom and loneliness of her harsh life.)

He handed her a two-dollar bill and then went out to pay his note.

She bought her cotton flannel and mittens and thread, and then sat leaning against the counter. It was noon, and she was hungry. She went out to the wagon, got the lunch she had brought, and took it into the grocery to eat it—where she could get a drink of water.

The grocer gave the baby a stick of candy and handed the mother an apple.

"It'll kind o' go down with your doughnuts," he said.

After eating her lunch she got up and went out. She felt ashamed to sit there any longer. She entered another dry-goods store, but when the clerk came toward her saying, "Anything to-day, Mrs. ——?" she answered, "No, I guess not," and turned away with foolish face.

1 She walked up and down the street, desolately homeless. She did not know what to do with herself. She knew no one except the grocer. She grew bitter as she saw a couple of ladies pass, holding their demi-trains[1] in the latest city fashion. Another woman went by pushing a baby carriage, in which sat a child just about as big as her own. It was bouncing itself up and down on the long slender springs, and laughing and shouting. Its clean round face glowed from its pretty fringed hood. She looked down at the dusty clothes and grimy face of her own little one, and walked on savagely.

She went into the drugstore where the soda fountain was, but it made her thirsty to sit there
2 and she went out on the street again. She heard Sam laugh, and saw him in a group of men over by the blacksmith shop. He was having a good time and had forgotten her.

Her back ached so intolerably that she concluded to go in and rest once more in the grocer's chair. The baby was growing cross and fretful. She bought five cents' worth of candy to take home to the children, and gave baby a little piece to keep him quiet. She wished Sam would come. It must be getting late. The grocer said it was not much after one. Time seemed terribly long. She felt that she ought to do something while she was in town. She ran over her purchases—yes, that was all she had planned to buy. She fell to figuring on the things she needed. It was terrible. It ran away up into twenty or thirty dollars at the least. Sam, as well as she, needed underwear for the cold winter, but they would have to wear the old ones, even if they were thin
3 and ragged. She would not need a dress, she thought bitterly, because she never went anywhere. She rose and went out on the street once more, and wandered up and down, looking at everything in the hope of enjoying something.

A man from Boon Creek backed a load of apples up to the sidewalk, and as he stood waiting for the grocer he noticed Mrs. Markham and the baby, and gave the baby an apple. This was a pleasure. He had such a hearty way about him.
4 He on his part saw an ordinary farmer's wife with dusty dress, unkempt hair, and tired face. He did not know exactly why she appealed to him, but he tried to cheer her up.

The grocer was familiar with these bedraggled and weary wives. He was accustomed to see them sit for hours in his big wooden chair, and nurse tired and fretful children. Their forlorn, aimless, pathetic wandering up and down the street was a daily occurrence, and had never possessed any special meaning to him.

II

In a cottage around the corner from the grocery store two men and a woman were finish-
5 ing a dainty luncheon. The woman was dressed in cool, white garments, and she seemed to make the day one of perfect comfort.

The home of the Honorable Mr. Hall was by no means the costliest in town, but his wife made it the most attractive. He was one of the leading lawyers of the county, and a man of

1. **demi-trains** [dem'ē trānz]: small part of a woman's dress that trails in back, a popular fashion during the early twentieth century.

AT A GLANCE

- Mrs. Markham buys what she needs, eats lunch, and wanders around town.
- Sam talks with a group of men, apparently unconcerned about her.
- In a charming cottage around the corner from the grocer's, the Halls finish lunch.

1 CHARACTERIZATION

Mrs. Markham's exhaustion turns to bitterness in town: She resents her situation and envies the luxuries of other women.

2 CONFLICT

Mrs. Markham's anger is caused partly by her husband's lack of concern for her loneliness in a strange place.

3 CHARACTERIZATION

Mrs. Markham reflects bitterly on the harshness of her life: She can visit only this dismal town, where she has little hope of finding diversion or enjoyment.

4 THEME

Through the sympathetic eyes of another character, the reader sees the reality of a poor and worn-out farmer's wife.

5 STYLE: IMAGERY

The "cool, white garments" of Mrs. Hall contrast with Mrs. Markham's appearance, described earlier.

GUIDED READING

LITERAL QUESTIONS

1a. What makes Mrs. Markham bitter? (seeing other women's fine clothes and clean children; realizing she cannot go anywhere)

2a. What does the apple farmer do? (He gives the baby an apple.)

INFERENTIAL QUESTIONS

1b. What does this tell you about Mrs. Markham? (She has a difficult life with few opportunities for pleasure, self-indulgence, or enjoyment.)

2b. Why is his action significant? (It shows that Mrs. Markham appears depressed and needy and indicates his desire to help.)

AT A GLANCE

- Otis, a friend of the Halls, observes Mrs. Markham's forlorn appearance and says that no one is sympathetic to the plight of farmers' wives.
- Otis and Hall leave as Mrs. Hall invites Delia Markham into her home.

1 CHARACTERIZATION

Mrs. Markham is described by Otis as "a forlorn, weary woman" and by the narrator as one in whom there was "hopeless tragedy in her shambling walk and weak back."

2 THEME

In stark, certain terms, Otis describes Mrs. Markham's difficult way of life and her need for sympathy and kindness.

3 VOCABULARY: CONNOTATION

The author first chooses to call Mrs. Markham "Delia" when another character approaches her as an individual.

culture and progressive views. He was entertaining a friend who had lectured the night before in the Congregational church.

They were by no means in serious discussion. The talk was rather frivolous. Hall had the ability to caricature men with a few gestures and attitudes, and was giving to his Eastern friend some descriptions of the old-fashioned Western lawyers he had met in his practice. He was very amusing, and his guest laughed heartily for a time.

But suddenly Hall became aware that Otis was not listening. Then he perceived that he was peering out of the window at someone, and that on his face a look of bitter sadness was falling.

Hall stopped. "What do you see, Otis?"

1 Otis replied, "I see a forlorn, weary woman."

Mrs. Hall rose and went to the window. Mrs. Markham was walking by the house, her baby in her arms. Savage anger and weeping were in her eyes and on her lips, and there was hopeless tragedy in her shambling walk and weak back.

In the silence Otis went on: "I saw the poor, dejected creature twice this morning. I couldn't forget her."

"Who is she?" asked Mrs. Hall, very softly.

"Her name is Markham; she's Sam Markham's wife," said Hall.

The young wife led the way into the sitting room, and the men took seats and lit their cigars. Hall was meditating a diversion[2] when Otis resumed suddenly:

"That woman came to town today to get a change, to have a little playspell, and she's
2 wandering around like a starved and weary cat. I wonder if there is a woman in this town with sympathy enough and courage enough to go out and help that woman? The saloonkeepers, the politicians, and the grocers make it pleasant for the man—so pleasant that he forgets his wife. But the wife is left without a word."

Mrs. Hall's work dropped, and on her pretty face was a look of pain. The man's harsh words had wounded her—and wakened her. She took up her hat and hurried out on the walk. The men looked at each other, and then the husband said:

"It's going to be a little sultry for the men around these diggings. Suppose we go out for a walk."

3 Delia felt a hand on her arm as she stood at the corner.

"You look tired, Mrs. Markham; won't you come in a little while? I'm Mrs. Hall."

Mrs. Markham turned with a scowl on her face and a biting word on her tongue, but something in the sweet round little face of

2. **meditating a diversion:** planning something to pass the time.

GUIDED READING

LITERAL QUESTION

1a. When does the author reveal Mrs. Markham's first name? (when Mrs. Hall touches her arm)

INFERENTIAL QUESTION

1b. Why do you think he chooses this occasion to reveal Mrs. Markham's first name? (It emphasizes that this is the first time anyone has treated Mrs. Markham as an individual.)

the other woman silenced her, and her brow smoothed out.

"Thank you kindly, but it's most time to go home. I'm looking fer Mr. Markham now."

"Oh, come in a little while; the baby is cross and tired out; please do."

Mrs. Markham yielded to the friendly voice, and together the two women reached the gate just as two men hurriedly turned the other corner.

"Let me relieve you," said Mrs. Hall.

The mother hesitated: "He's so dusty."

"Oh, that won't matter. Oh, what a big fellow he is! I haven't any of my own," said Mrs. Hall, and a look passed like an electric spark between the two women, and Delia was her willing guest from that moment.

They went into the little sitting room, so dainty and lovely to the farmer's wife, and as she sank into an easy chair she was faint and drowsy with the pleasure of it. She submitted to being brushed. She gave the baby into the hands of the Swedish girl, who washed its face and hands and sang it to sleep, while its mother sipped some tea. Through it all she lay back in her easy chair, not speaking a word, while the ache passed out of her back, and her hot, swollen head ceased to throb.

2 But she saw everything—the piano, the pictures, the curtains, the wallpaper, the little tea stand. They were almost as grateful to her as the food and fragrant tea. Such housekeeping as this she had never seen. Her mother had worn her kitchen floor thin as brown paper in keeping a speckless house, and she had been in houses that were larger and costlier, but something of the charm of her hostess was in the arrangement of vases, chairs, or pictures. It was tasteful.

Mrs. Hall did not ask about her affairs. She talked to her about the sturdy little baby, and about the things upon which Delia's eyes dwelt. If she seemed interested in a vase she was told what it was and where it was made. She was shown all the pictures and books. Mrs. Hall
3 seemed to read her visitor's mind. She kept as far from the farm and her guest's affairs as possible, and at last she opened the piano and sang to her—not slow-moving hymns, but catchy love songs full of sentiment, and then played some simple melodies, knowing that Mrs. Markham's eyes were studying her hands, her rings, and the flash of her fingers on the keys—seeing more than she heard—and through it all Mrs. Hall conveyed the impression that she, too, was having a good time.

The rattle of the wagon outside roused them both. Sam was at the gate for her. Mrs. Markham rose hastily. "Oh, it's almost sundown!" she gasped in astonishment as she looked out of the window.

"Oh, that won't kill anybody," replied her hostess. "Don't hurry. Carrie, take the baby out to the wagon for Mrs. Markham while I help her with her things."

4 "Oh, I've had such a good time," Mrs. Markham said as they went down the little walk.

"So have I," replied Mrs. Hall. She took the baby a moment as her guest climbed in. "Oh, you big, fat fellow!" she cried as she gave him a squeeze. "You must bring your wife in oftener, Mr. Markham," she said, as she handed the baby up.

Sam was staring with amazement.

"Thank you, I will," he finally managed to say.

"Good night," said Mrs. Markham.

"Good night, dear," called Mrs. Hall, and the wagon began to rattle off.

The tenderness and sympathy in her voice brought the tears to Delia's eyes—not hot or bitter tears, but tears that cooled her eyes and cleared her mind.

The wind had gone down, and the red sunlight fell mistily over the world of corn and stubble. The crickets were still chirping and the feeding cattle were drifting toward the farmyards. The day had been made beautiful by human sympathy.

AT A GLANCE

- Mrs. Hall convinces Mrs. Markham to come into her home and reveals she has no children.
- Mrs. Hall entertains Delia, who admires the pretty home.
- Sam arrives to take Delia home.
- As the women part, Delia feels pleasure because of Mrs. Hall's kindness.

1 THEME

Delia's acceptance of the invitation is eased by her realization of Mrs. Hall's situation: She is childless and wants to hold the baby.

2 SETTING

The tasteful, well-maintained furnishings and decorations of this room contrast with the earlier description of the Markhams' kitchen.

3 CHARACTERIZATION

Understanding that Delia needs some escape from her life on the farm, Mrs. Hall truly diverts her.

4 THEME

The new friendship of the women is based in part on an understanding that each has something the other lacks: a baby, a nice home.

REFLECTING ON THE STORY

Do you think the two women will remain friends? (Since there is not much opportunity for them to get together, the friendship may not last. However, Mrs. Hall's desire to play with the baby and her sympathy for Delia's plight might motivate them to meet now and then.)

GUIDED READING

LITERAL QUESTIONS

1a. What is Mrs. Hall's home like? (It is tasteful and charming and has a piano, curtains, wallpaper, pictures, books, and vases.)

2a. How is Mrs. Markham's day described at the end of the story? ("The day had been made beautiful by human sympathy.")

INFERENTIAL QUESTIONS

1b. Why do you think this description is so important? (It contrasts the life styles of the two women.)

2b. How do you think Mrs. Hall's human sympathy has made the day beautiful? (Mrs. Hall's actions have renewed Delia's acceptance of her family, revived her spirits, and changed her attitude about potential excursions to town.)

STUDY QUESTIONS

1. wants a change of scene; needs to buy a few things
2. shops; eats lunch; wanders the streets; visits drugstore
3. She is weary and has nowhere to rest; the town welcomes farmers.
4. takes care of her baby; serves tea; plays piano and sings
5. amazement
6. They work together; although he is pleasant to her en route, he doesn't notice her loneliness in town.
7. It is the first time in story she is treated as an individual.
8. She has something Mrs. Hall does not have, and feels some worth in her own situation.
9. She knows Mrs. Markham is embarrassed by her poverty.
10. The experience renews her appreciation for her family; the friendship may last, but the women live far apart and Delia faces hard work on farm.

VIEWPOINT

depicts farm life realistically; uses dialect; describes typical town and its inhabitants

LITERARY FOCUS

Mrs. Markham: "not to be trifled with"; "desolately homeless"; "bitter"; "hopeless tragedy"
Sam: "good-natured", "grumbling"
Mr. Hall: "man of culture"; "amusing"
Mrs. Hall: "seemed to read her visitor's mind"; "the charm of her hostess"

VOCABULARY

1. (c) tempting
2. (a) miserably
3. (a) stubborn
4. (d) agreement
5. (b) steadfast

STUDY QUESTIONS

Recalling

1. Give two reasons that Mrs. Markam wants to go to town.
2. Find three things Mrs. Markham does in town before meeting Mrs. Hall.
3. Why does Mr. Otis say that someone should have sympathy for Mrs. Markham?
4. Give three examples of how Mrs. Hall makes Mrs. Markham feel comfortable.
5. What is Mr. Markham's reaction to his wife's new friendship?

Interpreting

6. Describe the relationship between Mr. and Mrs. Markham. Give examples from the story.
7. Why do you think the author first calls Mrs. Markham "Delia" when she meets Mrs. Hall?
8. Mrs. Hall says that she has no children. Why does this make Mrs. Markham more friendly?
9. Why does Mrs. Hall avoid talking about Mrs. Markham's life?

Extending

10. Mrs. Markham's day is brightened by her afternoon with Mrs. Hall. Do you think the experience will cause a more lasting improvement in Mrs. Markham's life? Why or why not?

VIEWPOINT

Proud to write about American topics, Garland considered himself a writer of **local color,** literature that is tied in location and topic to one section of the country. He described local color as having

> such a quality of texture and background that it could not have been written in any other place or by any one else than a native.

■ Explain how the background of "A Day's Pleasure" shows that the author was very familiar with the American Midwest.

LITERARY FOCUS

Direct Characterization

When an author directly states facts about a character's personality, the story is said to have **direct characterization.** We can trust a direct statement from the author that a character is honest or has a wonderful sense of humor. Direct characterization is the easiest way for an author to reveal the personality of a character.

Thinking About Direct Characterization

■ Garland directly calls Mrs. Markham "a tired and sullen woman." Find three other direct statements by the author about Mrs. Markham. Find one direct statement each about Sam, Mr. Hall, and Mrs. Hall.

VOCABULARY

Synonyms

A **synonym** is a word that has the same or nearly the same meaning as another word. *Happy* and *glad* are synonyms. The words in capital letters are from "A Day's Pleasure." Choose the word that is *nearest* the meaning of each word in capitals, *as the word is used in the story.* Write the number of each item and the letter of your choice on a separate sheet.

1. ALLURING: (a) looming (b) alarming (c) tempting (d) elusive
2. DESOLATELY: (a) miserably (b) restlessly (c) unconsciously (d) gloriously
3. DOGGED: (a) stubborn (b) willing (c) afraid (d) exhausted
4. ACQUIESCENCE: (a) essence (b) protest (c) indifference (d) agreement
5. RESOLUTE: (a) weary (b) steadfast (c) spirited (d) aimless

COMPOSITION

Writing About Character

■ Explain how Garland creates sympathy for Mrs. Markham. You may want to consider the following: (a) her work on the farm and (b) contrasts between her and women she sees in town.

Writing a Letter to the Editor

■ Imagine that you are Mr. or Mrs. Hall. Write a letter to the editor of the local newspaper about people like Mrs. Markham and the ways in which townspeople can brighten their lives. Point out also what people in town can gain from associating with farmers.

COMPOSITION: GUIDELINES FOR EVALUATION

WRITING ABOUT CHARACTER

Objective

To make clear at least two ways author elicits sympathy for Mrs. Markham

Guidelines for Evaluation

- suggested length: two to three paragraphs
- should contain clear thesis statement
- should include clear explanation of author's methods for creating sympathy

WRITING A LETTER TO THE EDITOR

Objective

To write a brief descriptive and persuasive letter that could be printed in the newspaper

Guidelines for Evaluation

- suggested length: maximum of three paragraphs
- should contain an account of the plight of people like Mrs. Markham
- should offer suggestions for helping them
- should assume the role of Mr. or Mrs. Hall

Toni Cade Bambara (born 1939) is from New York City. She took her last name from the name of a people of northwest Africa who are noted for their delicate wood carvings. The name seems particularly appropriate for her because of the sensitive and finely carved characters in her stories.

■ What do you think you would like or not like about the main character of this story if she were your acquaintance?

Toni Cade Bambara

Raymond's Run

I don't have much work to do around the house like some girls. My mother does that. And I don't have to earn my pocket money. George runs errands for the big boys and sells Christmas cards. And anything else that's got to get done, my father does. All I have to do in life is mind my brother Raymond, which is enough.

Sometimes I slip and say my little brother Raymond. But as any fool can see, he's much bigger and he's older too. But a lot of people call him my little brother cause he needs looking after cause he's not quite right. And a lot of smart mouths got lots to say about that too, especially when George was minding him. But now, if anybody has anything to say to Raymond, anything to say about his big head, they have to come by me. And I don't play the dozens[1] or believe in standing around with somebody in my face doing a lot of talking. I much rather just knock you down and take my chances even if I am a little girl with skinny arms and a squeaky voice, which is how I got the name Squeaky. And if things get too rough, I run. And as anybody can tell you, I'm the fastest thing on two feet.

There is no track meet that I don't win the first-place medal. I used to win the twenty-yard dash when I was a little kid in kindergarten. 3 Nowadays, it's the fifty-yard dash. And tomorrow I'm subject to run the quarter-meter relay all by myself and come in first, second, and third. The big kids call me Mercury[2] cause I'm the swiftest thing in the neighborhood. Everybody knows that—except two people who know better, my father and me. He can beat me to Amsterdam Avenue with me having a two-fire-hydrant head start and him running with his hands in his pockets and whistling. But that's private information. Cause can you imagine some thirty-five-year-old man stuffing himself into PAL[3] shorts to race little kids? So as far as everyone's concerned, I'm the fastest and that goes for Gretchen, too, who has put out the tale that she is

1. **the dozens:** game in which people try to remain calm while trading insults.

2. **Mercury** [mur′kyər ē]: Roman mythological messenger of the gods. He is pictured with wings on his heels to show his speed.

3. **PAL:** Police Athletic League, an organization in New York City that promotes educational, athletic, and social activities for young people.

AT A GLANCE

- Squeaky has to look after her brother Raymond, who is "not quite right."
- She explains how she got the nickname *Squeaky* and tells of her love for running and winning races.
- She says she'll win the fifty-yard dash tomorrow.

LITERARY OPTIONS

- characterization
- conflict
- tone

THEMATIC OPTIONS

- identity and self-respect
- hopes and ideals
- communication

1 POINT OF VIEW

The story unfolds in a continuous monologue. The narrator, Squeaky, is a young city girl whose voice is clear and direct.

2 CHARACTERIZATION

Squeaky is tough and straightforward with others. These streetwise traits contrast with her caring feelings for her brother.

3 THEME

Squeaky knows who she is and where she is going; she has no illusions about herself. She knows she is the best runner in the neighborhood.

GUIDED READING

LITERAL QUESTION

1a. How does Squeaky describe her appearance? ("a little girl with skinny arms and a squeaky voice")

INFERENTIAL QUESTION

1b. Why might this description be surprising? (Her strong sense of identity implies an older girl.)

AT A GLANCE

- Squeaky walks down Broadway with Raymond and keeps him out of trouble.
- She practices running and cannot stand people who pretend they don't practice.
- She notes that Raymond keeps up with her when she runs.

1 PLOT: NARRATIVE HOOK

Squeaky dismisses Gretchen and is sure that she, Squeaky, will win the race. The reader wonders if Squeaky is just boasting or if she will actually win.

2 CHARACTERIZATION

Squeaky's responsibility for caring for Raymond is a serious task for a young girl.

3 THEME

Squeaky admits she has to practice to be good, and she announces that she cannot stand people who pretend to be something they are not.

4 PLOT: FORESHADOWING

This brief, offhand statement about Raymond's running will figure crucially later in the story.

going to win the first-place medal this year.
1 Ridiculous. In the second place, she's got short legs. In the third place, she's got freckles. In the first place, no one can beat me and that's all there is to it.

I'm standing on the corner admiring the weather and about to take a stroll down Broadway so I can practice my breathing exercises, and I've got Raymond walking on the inside close to the buildings, cause he's subject to fits of fantasy and starts thinking he's a circus performer and that the curb is a tightrope strung
2 high in the air. And sometimes after a rain he likes to step down off his tightrope right into the gutter and slosh around getting his shoes and cuffs wet. Then I get hit when I get home. Or sometimes if you don't watch him he'll dash across traffic to the island in the middle of Broadway and give the pigeons a fit. Then I have to go behind him apologizing to all the old people sitting around trying to get some sun and getting all upset with the pigeons fluttering around them, scattering their newspapers and upsetting the wax-paper lunches in their laps. So I keep Raymond on the inside of me, and he plays like he's driving a stagecoach, which is OK by me so long as he doesn't run me over or interrupt my breathing exercises, which I have to do on account of I'm serious about my running, and I don't care who knows it.

3 Now some people like to act like things come easy to them, won't let on that they practice. Not me. I'll high-prance down 34th Street like a rodeo pony to keep my knees strong even if it does get my mother uptight so that she walks ahead like she's not with me, don't know me, is all by herself on a shopping trip, and I am somebody else's crazy child. Now you take Cynthia Procter for instance. She's just the opposite. If there's a test tomorrow, she'll say something like, "Oh, I guess I'll play handball this afternoon and watch television tonight," just to let you know she ain't thinking about the test. Or like last week when she won the spelling bee for the millionth time, "A good thing you got *receive*, Squeaky, cause I would have got it wrong. I completely forgot about the spelling bee." And she'll clutch the lace on her blouse like it was a narrow escape. Oh, brother. But of course when I pass her house on my early morning trots around the block, she is practicing the scales on the piano over and over and over and over. Then in music class she always lets herself get bumped around so she falls accidentally on purpose onto the piano stool and is so surprised to find herself sitting there that she decides just for fun to try out the ole keys. And what do you know—Chopin's[4] waltzes just spring out of her fingertips and she's the most surprised thing in the world. A regular prodigy. I could kill people like that. I stay up all night studying the words for the spell-
4 ing bee. And you can see me any time of day practicing running. I never walk if I can trot, and shame on Raymond if he can't keep up. But of course he does, cause if he hangs back someone's liable to walk up to him and get smart, or take his allowance from him, or ask him where he got that great big pumpkin head. People are so stupid sometimes.

---

4. **Chopin** [shō′pan]: (1810–1849) Polish pianist and composer.

GUIDED READING

LITERAL QUESTION

1a. Why doesn't Squeaky like Cynthia Procter? (Cynthia says she doesn't practice, but then Squeaky finds out that Cynthia really does have to practice.)

INFERENTIAL QUESTION

1b. What does Squeaky's reaction to people like Cynthia tell you about Squeaky? (She cannot stand pretense on the part of others and is very straightforward about herself.)

So I'm strolling down Broadway breathing out and breathing in on counts of seven, which is my lucky number, and here comes Gretchen and her sidekicks: Mary Louise, who used to be a friend of mine when she first moved to Harlem from Baltimore and got beat up by everybody till I took up for her on account of her mother and my mother used to sing in the same choir when they were young girls, but people ain't grateful, so now she hangs out with the new girl Gretchen and talks about me like a dog; and Rosie, who is as fat as I am skinny and has a big mouth where Raymond is concerned and is too stupid to know that there is not a big deal of difference between herself and Raymond and that she can't afford to throw stones. So they are steady coming up Broadway and I see right away that it's going to be one of those Dodge City[5] scenes cause the street ain't that big and they're close to the buildings just as we are. First I think I'll step into the candy store and look over the new comics and let them pass. But that's chicken and I've got a reputation to consider. So then I think I'll just walk straight on through them or even over them if necessary. But as they get to me, they slow down. I'm ready to fight, cause like I said I don't feature a whole lot of chitchat, I much prefer to just knock you down right from the jump and save everybody a lotta precious time.

"You signing up for the May Day races?" smiles Mary Louise, only it's not a smile at all. A dumb question like that doesn't deserve an answer. Besides, there's just me and Gretchen standing there really, so no use wasting my breath talking to shadows.

2 "I don't think you're going to win this time," says Rosie, trying to signify with her hands on her hips all salty, completely forgetting that I have whupped her many times for less salt than that.

"I always win cause I'm the best," I say straight at Gretchen, who is, as far as I'm concerned, the only one talking in this ventriloquist-dummy routine. Gretchen smiles, but it's not a
3 smile, and I'm thinking that girls never really smile at each other because they don't know how and don't want to know how and there's probably no one to teach us how, cause grown-up girls don't know either. Then they all look at Raymond, who has just brought his mule team to a standstill. And they're about to see what trouble they can get into through him.

"What grade you in now, Raymond?"

5. **Dodge City:** frontier town in Kansas famous for lawlessness.

AT A GLANCE

- Squeaky meets Gretchen and her friends and decides to confront them.
- Squeaky tells Gretchen she will win the upcoming race.
- The girls look at Raymond, and Squeaky anticipates trouble.

1 STYLE: HUMOR

Squeaky's comparison of the impending confrontation with "Dodge City scenes" accurately conveys her barbed, sarcastic tone of voice and her penchant for hyperbole.

2 CONFLICT

The girls' external conflict over who will win the race is vividly portrayed through dialogue and the narrator's haughty scrutiny.

3 THEME

Squeaky says that there is no respect between girls because grown women don't show mutual respect either.

GUIDED READING

LITERAL QUESTION

1a. Why does Squeaky decide not to enter the candy store as the girls approach? (To do so would be "chicken"; she has a reputation to maintain.)

INFERENTIAL QUESTION

1b. What does this decision tell you about her? (She stands her ground and confronts trouble head-on.)

AT A GLANCE

- She confronts the other girls, who keep on walking up Broadway.
- Squeaky has refused to dress up and dance around the Maypole.
- She puts Raymond in a swing and looks for the race official.

1 CONFLICT

In an external conflict Squeaky seems able to assert herself and stand her ground.

2 THEME

Squeaky realizes that the most important thing in life is to "be yourself," even if that self is not the most fortunate in the world.

3 CHARACTERIZATION

Squeaky claims to be more aware of her identity than are the grown-ups who try to encourage children to participate in "nonsense."

4 SETTING

The world of an inner-city park comes alive in these images of people enjoying the day.

"You got anything to say to my brother, you say it to me, Mary Louise Williams of Raggedy Town, Baltimore."

1 "What are you, his mother?" sasses Rosie.

"That's right, Fatso. And the next word out of anybody and I'll be *their* mother too." So they just stand there and Gretchen shifts from one leg to the other and so do they. Then Gretchen puts her hands on her hips and is about to say something with her freckle-face self but doesn't. Then she walks around me looking me up and down but keeps walking up Broadway, and her sidekicks follow her. So me and Raymond smile at each other and he says, "Gidyap" to his team and I continue with my breathing exercises, strolling down Broadway toward the ice man on 145th with not a care in the world cause I am Miss Quicksilver[6] herself.

I take my time getting to the park on May Day because the track meet is the last thing on the program. The biggest thing on the program is the Maypole dancing, which I can do without, thank you, even if my mother thinks it's a shame I don't take part and act like a girl for a change. You'd think my mother'd be grateful not to have to make me a white organdy dress with a big satin sash and buy me new white baby-doll shoes that can't be taken out of the box till the big day. You'd think she'd be glad her daughter ain't out there prancing around a Maypole getting the new clothes all dirty and sweaty and trying to act like a fairy or a flower or whatever you're
2 supposed to be when you should be trying to be yourself, whatever that is, which is, as far as I am concerned, a poor black girl who really can't afford to buy shoes and a new dress you only wear once a lifetime cause it won't fit next year.

I was once a strawberry in a Hansel and Gretel pageant when I was in nursery school and didn't have no better sense than to dance on tiptoe with my arms in a circle over my head doing umbrella steps and being a perfect fool just so my mother and father could come dressed up
3 and clap. You'd think they'd know better than to encourage that kind of nonsense. I am not a strawberry. I do not dance on my toes. I run. That is what I am all about. So I always come late to the May Day program, just in time to get my number pinned on and lay in the grass till they announce the fifty-yard dash.

I put Raymond in the little swings, which is a tight squeeze this year and will be impossible next year. Then I look around for Mr. Pearson, who pins the numbers on. I'm really looking for Gretchen if you want to know the truth, but she's not around. The park is jam-packed. Parents in hats and corsages and breast-pocket handkerchiefs peeking up. Kids in white dresses
4 and light-blue suits. The parkees unfolding chairs and chasing the rowdy kids from Lenox as if they had no right to be there. The big guys with their caps on backwards, leaning against the fence swirling the basketballs on the tips of their fingers, waiting for all these crazy people to clear out the park so they can play. Most of the kids in my class are carrying bass drums and glockenspiels[7] and flutes. You'd think they'd put in a few bongos or something for real like that.

Then here comes Mr. Pearson with his clipboard and his cards and pencils and whistles and safety pins and fifty million other things he's always dropping all over the place with his clumsy self. He sticks out in a crowd because he's on stilts. We used to call him Jack and the Beanstalk to get him mad. But I'm the only one that can outrun him and get away, and I'm too grown for that silliness now.

"Well, Squeaky," he says, checking my name off the list and handing me number seven and two pins. And I'm thinking he's got no right to call me Squeaky, if I can't call him Beanstalk.

---

6. **Quicksilver:** another name for mercury, the liquid metal that dashes about rapidly if spilled.

7. **glockenspiel** [glok′ən spēl′]: musical instrument that resembles a xylophone but can be carried and is usually played in school bands.

GUIDED READING

LITERAL QUESTION

1a. Why does Squeaky come to the park late? (She wants no part of the Maypole dancing.)

INFERENTIAL QUESTION

1b. What does this tell you about her? (She places the most value on those activities that she views as real and worthwhile.)

"Hazel Elizabeth Deborah Parker," I correct him and tell him to write it down on his board.

"Well, Hazel Elizabeth Deborah Parker, going to give someone else a break this year?" I squint at him real hard to see if he is seriously thinking I should lose the race on purpose just to give someone else a break. "Only six girls running this time," he continues, shaking his head sadly like it's my fault all of New York didn't turn out in sneakers. "That new girl should give you a run for your money." He looks around the park for Gretchen like a periscope in a submarine movie. "Wouldn't it be a nice gesture if you were . . . to ahhh . . ."

I give him such a look he couldn't finish putting that idea into words. Grown-ups got a lot of nerve sometimes. I pin number seven to myself and stomp away, I'm so burnt. And I go straight for the track and stretch out on the grass while the band winds up with "Oh, the Monkey Wrapped His Tail Around the Flagpole," which my teacher calls by some other name. The man on the loudspeaker is calling everyone over to the track and I'm on my back looking at the sky, trying to pretend I'm in the country, but I can't, because even grass in the city feels hard as sidewalk, and there's just no pretending you are anywhere but in a "concrete jungle" as my grandfather says.

The twenty-yard dash takes all of two minutes cause most of the little kids don't know no better than to run off the track or run the wrong way or run smack into the fence and fall down and cry. One little kid, though, has got the good sense to run straight for the white ribbon up ahead so he wins. Then the second-graders line up for the thirty-yard dash and I don't even bother to turn my head to watch cause Raphael Perez always wins. He wins before he even begins by psyching the runners,[8] telling them they're going to trip on their shoelaces and fall on their faces or lose their shorts or something, which he doesn't really have to do since he is very fast, almost as fast as I am. After that is the forty-yard dash, which I used to run when I was in first grade. Raymond is hollering from the swings cause he knows I'm about to do my thing cause the man on the loudspeaker has just announced the fifty-yard dash, although he might just as well be giving a recipe for angel food cake cause you can hardly make out what he's saying
4 for the static. I get up and slip off my sweat pants and then I see Gretchen standing at the starting line, kicking her legs out like a pro. Then as I get into place I see that ole Raymond is on line on the other side of the fence, bending down with his fingers on the ground just like he knew what he was doing. I was going to yell at him but then I didn't. It burns up your energy to holler.

5 Every time, just before I take off in a race, I always feel like I'm in a dream, the kind of dream you have when you're sick with fever and feel all hot and weightless. I dream I'm flying over a sandy beach in the early morning sun, kissing the leaves of the trees as I fly by. And there's always the smell of apples, just like in the country when I was little and used to think I was a choo-choo train, running through the fields of corn and chugging up the hill to the orchard. And all the time I'm dreaming this, I get lighter and lighter until I'm flying over the beach again, getting blown through the sky like a feather that weighs nothing at all. But once I spread my fingers in the dirt and crouch over the Get on Your Mark, the dream goes and I am solid again and am telling myself, Squeaky you must win, you must win, you are the fastest thing in the world, you can even beat your father up Amsterdam if you really try. And then I feel my weight coming back just behind my knees then down to my feet then into the earth and the pistol shot explodes in my blood and I am off and weightless again, flying past the other runners, my arms pumping up and down and the whole world is quiet except for the crunch as I zoom over the

8. **psyching** [sī′king] **the runners:** upsetting the competition by making them mentally uneasy and therefore unable to perform well.

AT A GLANCE

- Squeaky tells the race official her real name is Hazel Elizabeth Deborah Parker.
- She waits for the fifty-yard dash.
- She describes how she prepares for a race.

1 THEME

Squeaky reveals her real name, Hazel, for the first time; it is clear she wants to be respected as a person.

2 STYLE: DIALOGUE

The tough, no-nonsense stance of a person who knows exactly what she wants in life stops the official in midsentence.

3 SETTING

The inner city comes alive with one brilliant image, "even grass in the city feels hard as sidewalk."

4 PLOT: RISING ACTION

Gretchen is a worthy competitor. The image of Gretchen "kicking her legs out like a pro" suggests that perhaps she can win the race.

5 CHARACTERIZATION

Hazel's dream images contrast with the reality of the concrete jungle. These prerace dreams (which suggest that she sometimes yearns to be elsewhere) allow her to visualize her own power, grace, and speed.

GUIDED READING

LITERAL QUESTIONS

1a. What is Squeaky's real first name? (Hazel)

2a. What does she imagine before the race? (that she is flying over a beach)

INFERENTIAL QUESTIONS

1b. Why does she announce this? (She wants Mr. Pearson to treat her with respect.)

2b. Why do you think she visualizes this? (It prepares her for the race by making her think she is light and swift.)

AT A GLANCE

- During the race Hazel sees Raymond running for the first time.
- She wins but is more interested in Raymond's potential as a runner.
- She and Gretchen exchange smiles of respect.

1 PLOT: CLIMAX

For the first time Squeaky realizes that Raymond can be a great runner.

2 STYLE: SIMILE

Bambara uses two similes to underscore Hazel's new appreciation of Raymond. Her vision of him as "a gorilla in a cage" is immediately supplanted by one in which he is "like a dancer."

3 THEME

The smiles of the two girls show that they have achieved an authentic respect for each other and a new awareness of who the other is.

REFLECTING ON THE STORY

Do you think the story would have ended differently if Hazel had lost the race? (no, because her realization about Raymond has become more important to her)

gravel in the track. I glance to my left and there is no one. To the right, a blurred Gretchen, who's got her chin jutting out as if it would win
1 the race all by itself. And on the other side of the fence is Raymond with his arms down to his side and the palms tucked up behind him, running in his very own style, and it's the first time I ever saw that and I almost stop to watch my brother Raymond on his first run. But the white ribbon is bouncing toward me and I tear past it, racing into the distance till my feet with a mind of their own start digging up footfuls of dirt and brake me short. Then all the kids standing on the side pile on me, banging me on the back and slapping my head with their May Day programs, for I have won again and everybody on 151st Street can walk tall for another year.

"In first place . . ." the man on the loudspeaker is clear as a bell now. But then he pauses and the loudspeaker starts to whine. Then static. And I lean down to catch my breath and here comes Gretchen walking back, for she's overshot the finish line too, huffing and puffing with her hands on her hips taking it slow, breathing in steady time like a real pro and I sort of like her a little for the first time. "In first place . . ." and then three or four voices get all mixed up on the loudspeaker and I dig my sneaker into the grass and stare at Gretchen, who's staring back, we both wondering just who did win. I can hear old Beanstalk arguing with the man on the loudspeaker and then a few others running their mouths about what the stopwatches say. Then I hear Raymond yanking at the fence to call me and I wave to shush him, but he keeps rattling
2 the fence like a gorilla in a cage like in them gorilla movies, but then like a dancer or something he starts climbing up nice and easy but very fast. And it occurs to me, watching how smoothly he climbs hand over hand and remembering how he looked running with his arms down to his side and with the wind pulling his mouth back and his teeth showing and all, it occurred to me that Raymond would make a very fine runner. Doesn't he always keep up with me on my trots? And he surely knows how to breathe in counts of seven cause he's always doing it at the dinner table, which drives my brother George up the wall. And I'm smiling to beat the band cause if I've lost this race, or if me and Grethcen tied, or even if I've won, I can always retire as a runner and begin a whole new career as a coach with Raymond as my champion. After all, with a little more study I can beat Cynthia and her phony self at the spelling bee. And if I bugged my mother, I could get piano lessons and become a star. And I have a big rep as the baddest thing around. And I've got a roomful of ribbons and medals and awards. But what has Raymond got to call his own?

So I stand there with my new plans, laughing out loud by this time as Raymond jumps down from the fence and runs over with his teeth showing and his arms down to the side, which no one before him has quite mastered as a running style. And by the time he comes over I'm jumping up and down so glad to see him—my brother Raymond, a great runner in the family tradition. But of course everyone thinks I'm jumping up and down because the men on the loudspeaker have finally gotten themselves together and compared notes and are announcing "In first place—Miss Hazel Elizabeth Deborah Parker." (Dig that.) "In second place—Miss Gretchen P. Lewis.' And I look over at Gretchen wondering what the *P* stands for.
3 And I smile. Cause she's good, no doubt about it. Maybe she'd like to help me coach Raymond; she obviously is serious about running, as any fool can see. And she nods to congratulate me and then she smiles. And I smile. We stand there with this big smile of respect between us. It's about as real a smile as girls can do for each other, considering we don't practice real smiling every day, you know, cause maybe we too busy being flowers or fairies or strawberries instead of something honest and worthy of respect . . . you know . . . like being people.

GUIDED READING

LITERAL QUESTION

1a. Who wins the race? (Hazel)

INFERENTIAL QUESTION

1b. Is the identity of the winner of central importance in the story? Why? (No; Hazel's compassion for her brother and her awareness that he too needs something to be proud of is of central importance.)

STUDY QUESTIONS

Recalling

1. Find two or three details to show that Squeaky's responsibility to mind her handicapped brother is a difficult job.
2. In what ways does Squeaky claim to be different from Cynthia Procter?
3. Why does Squeaky not want to participate in the May Day activities?
4. Describe Raymond's behavior during Squeaky's race.
5. Who wins the race? What does Squeaky say she will do if she gives up running?

Interpreting

6. What do you know about Squeaky from her manner of controlling, defending, and encouraging Raymond?
7. On the street Squeaky confronts Gretchen, Mary Louise, and Rosie rather than avoid them. What does this action tell us about Squeaky's personality?
8. Why do you think the author titled the story "Raymond's Run"?

Extending

9. Why would Squeaky have had good reason to be proud even if she had lost the race? Why is winning not the only cause for pride in an athletic competition?

VIEWPOINT

Speaking of another Bambara character in words that also fit Squeaky perfectly, the *New York Times* said:

> [She] is so full of life she almost bursts from the page. Shrewd, tough, cat-smart and, at the same time, both sentimental and humane, she's an original.

■ Show how this quotation applies to Squeaky. Give examples from the story of both sides of Squeaky's personality, her toughness and her humaneness.

LITERARY FOCUS

Indirect Characterization

When an author reveals a character's personality indirectly, through the character's words and actions or through what other characters say about that character, the story is said to have **indirect characterization.** In everyday life people do not carry labels with direct descriptions of their personalities. Instead, people reveal their personalities to each other in a variety of indirect ways, including what they say about themselves and what they do. We judge that a person is intelligent or funny based on the evidence available. The same is true with indirect characterization in stories. We must judge a character's personality based on the character's own words and actions.

In "Raymond's Run" Squeaky tells us her own story. She describes herself to us, but she is a character, not the author. We need to match her words to her actions in order to understand her personality. The story has indirect characterization.

Thinking About Indirect Characterization

■ Choose one statement that Squeaky makes about herself. Then describe one thing she does that proves her statement to be true.

COMPOSITION

Writing About Character

■ Describe the key traits of Squeaky's personality as they are revealed in what she does, says, and thinks. *For help with this assignment, see Lesson 3 in the Writing About Literature Handbook at the back of this book.*

Writing a Journal Entry

■ On page 45 reread the paragraph beginning, "Every time, just before I take off in a race. . . ." Squeaky is describing her emotions at the moment of tension just before her race. Imagine or recall a time when you were competing in a specific sporting event. Write a journal entry describing the event and what went through your mind at your moment of tension.

STUDY QUESTIONS

1. She protects him when he is teased; she has to watch him all the time; he gets wet in the gutter, and she "gets hit."
2. She admits she works hard, whereas Cynthia pretends to be naturally gifted.
3. She thinks Maypole dancing is silly.
4. He runs beside her, mimicking her "in his very own style."
5. Squeaky; coach Raymond, win spelling bee, study piano, and "become a star"
6. She's loyal, tolerant, and responsible.
7. She's straightforward; she faces her problems.
8. Raymond's participation teaches her about human needs.
9. She had done her best; skill, practice, and participation are also important.

VIEWPOINT

Her rapid monologue and constant activity show she is full of life; her handling of her rivals shows shrewdness;

- *toughness:* "I much rather knock you down and take my chances," confrontation with three classmates
- *humaneness:* compassion for Raymond, concern for old people, final sentence

LITERARY FOCUS

Example: "I always win cause I'm the best"; she wins the race.

COMPOSITION: GUIDELINES FOR EVALUATION

WRITING ABOUT CHARACTER

Objective

To write about at least two of Squeaky's traits

Guidelines for Evaluation

- suggested length: three to four paragraphs
- should contain a thesis statement declaring key traits
- should develop the essay in order from thesis
- should prove each trait by examples from story
- should maintain coherence between paragraphs

WRITING A JOURNAL ENTRY

Objective

To write a brief, informal journal entry describing a sporting event and the writer's thoughts

Guidelines for Evaluation

- suggested length: 150–300 words
- should give the time, place and type of event
- should express writer's thoughts
- should use first-person narration

AT A GLANCE

- The narrator rents a cabin near an orphanage in the North Carolina mountains in order to write.
- A twelve-year-old boy from the orphanage will chop wood for her.

LITERARY OPTIONS

- characterization
- conflict
- setting

THEMATIC OPTIONS

- integrity and self-respect
- methods of communication
- coping with isolation and loss

1 SETTING

The story begins with images of cold and isolation: In the winter the orphanage is "cut off . . . from all the world" by fog, snow, and bitter winds.

2 POINT OF VIEW

The narrator is a writer who seems both forthright and sensitive: She knows precisely why she has come to the Carolina hills and approaches her surroundings with an eye for details and gentle irony ("He called it laurel").

3 CHARACTERIZATION

Although the boy from the orphanage is described as "undersized," he is confident of his abilities.

Marjorie Kinnan Rawlings (1896–1953) was in North Carolina working on her Pulitzer Prize–winning novel, *The Yearling,* when she met a young orphan boy who became the model for Jerry in the following story.

■ Both loneliness and aloneness figure in this story. How do loneliness and aloneness differ?

Marjorie Kinnan Rawlings

A Mother in Mannville

1 The orphanage is high in the Carolina mountains. Sometimes in winter the snowdrifts are so deep that the institution is cut off from the village below, from all the world. Fog hides the mountain peaks, the snow swirls down the valleys, and a wind blows so bitterly that the orphanage boys who take the milk twice daily to the baby cottage reach the door with fingers stiff in an agony of numbness.

"Or when we carry trays from the cookhouse for the ones that are sick," Jerry said, "we get our faces frostbit, because we can't put our hands over them. I have gloves," he added. "Some of the boys don't have any."

He liked the late spring, he said. The rhododendron was in bloom, a carpet of color, across the mountainsides, soft as the May winds that stirred the hemlocks. He called it laurel.

"It's pretty when the laurel blooms," he said. "Some of it's pink and some of it's white."

2 I was there in the autumn. I wanted quiet, isolation, to do some troublesome writing. I wanted mountain air to blow out the malaria[1] from too long a time in the subtropics. I was homesick, too, for the flaming of maples in October, and for corn shocks[2] and pumpkins and black-walnut trees and the lift of hills. I found them all, living in a cabin that belonged to the orphanage, half a mile beyond the orphanage farm. When I took the cabin, I asked for a boy or man to come and chop wood for the fireplace. The first few days were warm, I found what wood I needed about the cabin, no one came, and I forgot the order.

I looked up from my typewriter one late afternoon, a little startled. A boy stood at the door, and my pointer dog, my companion, was at his side and had not barked to warn me. The boy was probably twelve years old, but undersized. He wore overalls and a torn shirt, and was barefooted.

3 He said, "I can chop some wood today."

I said, "But I have a boy coming from the orphanage."

"I'm the boy."

"You? But you're small."

"Size don't matter, chopping wood," he said. "Some of the big boys don't chop good. I've

1. **malaria** [mə lãr′ē ə]: disease which is contracted in warm climates and which causes extreme tiredness. Here, the woman is not actually ill; she hopes the mountain air will cure her laziness.

2. **corn shocks:** corn plants, stacked together to dry.

GUIDED READING

LITERAL QUESTION

1a. What does the boy say he likes about the late spring? (He says he likes the pink and white laurel.)

INFERENTIAL QUESTION

1b. What does this tell you about him? (It shows that he is sensitive and appreciates nature.)

been chopping wood at the orphanage a long time."

I visualized mangled and inadequate branches for my fires. I was well into my work and not inclined to conversation. I was a little blunt.

"Very well. There's the ax. Go ahead and see what you can do."

I went back to work, closing the door. At first the sound of the boy dragging brush annoyed me. Then he began to chop. The blows were rhythmic and steady, and shortly I had forgotten him, the sound no more of an interruption than a consistent rain. I suppose an hour and a half passed, for when I stopped and stretched, and heard the boy's steps on the cabin stoop, the sun was dropping behind the farthest mountain, and the valleys were purple with something deeper than the asters.[3]

The boy said, "I have to go to supper now. I can come again tomorrow evening."

I said, "I'll pay you now for what you've done," thinking I should probably have to insist on an older boy. "Ten cents an hour?"

"Anything is all right."

We went together back of the cabin. An astonishing amount of solid wood had been cut. There were cherry logs and heavy roots of rhododendron, and blocks from the waste pine and oak left from the building of the cabin.

"But you've done as much as a man," I said. "This is a splendid pile."

I looked at him, actually, for the first time. His hair was the color of the corn shocks and his eyes, very direct, were like the mountain sky when rain is pending—gray, with a shadowing of that miraculous blue. As I spoke, a light came over him, as though the setting sun had touched him with the same suffused glory with which it touched the mountains. I gave him a quarter.

"You may come tomorrow," I said, "and thank you very much."

He looked at me, and at the coin, and seemed to want to speak, but could not, and turned away.

"I'll split kindling tomorrow," he said over his thin ragged shoulder. "You'll need kindling and medium wood and logs and backlogs."

At daylight I was half wakened by the sound of chopping. Again it was so even in texture that I went back to sleep. When I left my bed in the cool morning, the boy had come and gone, and a stack of kindling was neat against the cabin wall. He came again after school in the afternoon and worked until time to return to the orphanage. His name was Jerry; he was twelve years old, and he had been at the orphanage since he was four. I could picture him at four, with the same grave gray-blue eyes and the same—independence?
3 No, the word that comes to me is "integrity."

The word means something very special to me, and the quality for which I use it is a rare one. My father had it—there is another of whom I am almost sure—but almost no man of my acquaintance possesses it with the clarity, the purity, the simplicity of a mountain stream. But the boy Jerry had it. It is bedded on courage, but it is more than brave. It is honest, but it is more than honesty. The ax handle broke one day. Jerry said the woodshop at the orphanage would repair it. I brought money to pay for the job and he refused it.

"I'll pay for it," he said. "I broke it. I brought the ax down careless."

"But no one hits accurately every time," I told him. "The fault was in the wood of the handle. I'll see the man from whom I bought it."

It was only then that he would take the money. He was standing back of his own care-
4 lessness. He was a free-will agent and he chose to do careful work, and if he failed, he took the responsibility without subterfuge.

And he did for me the unnecessary thing, the gracious thing, that we find done only by the great of heart. Things no training can teach, for they are done on the instant, with no predicated experience. He found a cubbyhole beside the

3. **asters:** deeply colored flowers.

AT A GLANCE

- The narrator is skeptical about the boy's ability to chop wood but allows him to try.
- He impresses the narrator with his ability and integrity.

1 PLOT: NARRATIVE HOOK

In the face of the narrator's skepticism, the boy insists he can chop wood, and the reader wonders how well he will do.

2 STYLE: IMAGERY

Jerry is described in natural images that emphasize both the Carolina mountain setting and Jerry's lack of pretense.

3 THEME

The narrator realizes that Jerry possesses integrity, a trait that she believes combines and surpasses both honesty and bravery.

4 CHARACTERIZATION

By taking responsibility for the broken ax handle, Jerry demonstrates his integrity; by performing services beyond those required he shows that he is "gracious" and "great of heart."

GUIDED READING

LITERAL QUESTION

1a. What does Jerry do when he receives the quarter? (He looks at the narrator but cannot speak.)

INFERENTIAL QUESTION

1b. What does this suggest about Jerry's personality? (His shyness complicates his ability to express gratitude.)

AT A GLANCE

- Jerry helps and visits with the narrator.
- He cares for her dog one weekend.
- He arrives at her cabin at night.

1 CHARACTERIZATION

Jerry is a complex person: He exhibits courtesy, gratitude, and affection while, at the same time, displaying aspects of a "granite" character.

2 THEME

Jerry's need for companionship—portrayed by his waiting to visit with the narrator—is contrasted with the fact that he is isolated from her by her work.

3 SETTING

The isolation of the orphanage from the rest of the world is emphasized by the imagery of treacherous fog-filled mountain passes.

4 CHARACTERIZATION

Jerry's integrity and selflessness are evident as he cares for the narrator's dog beyond the time agreed upon; he even shares his food with the animal.

fireplace that I had not noticed. There, of his own accord, he put kindling and "medium" wood, so that I might always have dry fire material ready in case of sudden wet weather. A stone was loose in the rough walk to the cabin. He dug a deeper hole and steadied it, although he came, himself, by a short cut over the bank. I found that when I tried to return his thoughtfulness with such things as candy and apples, he
1 was wordless. "Thank you" was, perhaps, an expression for which he had had no use, for his courtesy was instinctive. He only looked at the gift and at me, and a curtain lifted, so that I saw deep into the clear well of his eyes, and gratitude was there, and affection, soft over the firm granite of his character.

He made simple excuses to come and sit with me. I could no more have turned him away than if he had been physically hungry. I suggested once that the best time for us to visit was just before supper, when I left off my writing. After that, he waited always until my typewriter had
2 been some time quiet. One day I worked until nearly dark. I went outside the cabin, having forgotten him. I saw him going up over the hill in the twilight toward the orphanage. When I sat down on my stoop, a place was warm from his body where he had been sitting.

He became intimate, of course, with my pointer, Pat. There is a strange communion between a boy and a dog. Perhaps they possess the same singleness of spirit, the same kind of wisdom. It is difficult to explain, but it exists. When I went across the state for a week end, I left the dog in Jerry's charge. I gave him the dog whistle and the key to the cabin, and left sufficient food. He was to come two or three times a day and let out the dog, and feed and exercise him. I should return Sunday night, and Jerry would take out the dog for the last time Sunday afternoon and then leave the key under an agreed hiding place.

3 My return was belated and fog filled the mountain passes so treacherously that I dared not drive at night. The fog held the next morning, and it was Monday noon before I reached

Nicholas, Andrew Wyeth. Private Collection.

the cabin. The dog had been fed and cared fo that morning. Jerry came early in the afternoon anxious.

4 "The superintendent said nobody woul drive in the fog," he said. "I came just befor bedtime last night and you hadn't come. So brought Pat some of my breakfast this morning. wouldn't have let anything happen to him."

"I was sure of that. I didn't worry."

"When I heard about the fog, I though you'd know."

He was needed for work at the orphanag and he had to return at once. I gave him a dolla in payment, and he looked at it and went away But that night he came in the darkness an knocked at the door.

"Come in, Jerry," I said, "if you're allowe to be away this late."

"I told maybe a story," he said. "I told them I thought you would want to see me."

"That's true," I assured him, and I saw his relief. "I want to hear about how you managed with the dog."

GUIDED READING

LITERAL QUESTIONS

1a. What does Jerry make "simple excuses" to do? (visit with the narrator)

2a. How does the narrator describe the relationship between Jerry and her dog? (She says they became intimate, and she observes the "strange communion between a boy and a dog.")

INFERENTIAL QUESTIONS

1b. Why do you think he does this? (He is lonely and needs companionship and affection.)

2b. What does this relationship tell you about Jerry? (He is a regular boy who appreciates a dog's companionship.)

He sat by the fire with me, with no other ight, and told me of their two days together. The dog lay close to him, and found a comfort here that I did not have for him. And it seemed o me that being with my dog, and caring for im, had brought the boy and me, too, together, o that he felt that he belonged to me as well as o the animal.

"He stayed right with me," he told me, "ex- ept when he ran in the laurel. He likes the aurel. I took him up over the hill and we both an fast. There was a place where the grass was igh and I lay down in it and hid. I could hear at hunting for me. He found my trail and he arked. When he found me, he acted crazy, and e ran around and around me, in circles."

We watched the flames.

"That's an apple log," he said. "It burns the rettiest of any wood."

We were very close.

He was suddenly impelled to speak of things e had not spoken of before, nor had I cared to sk him.

"You look a little bit like my mother," he aid "Especially in the dark, by the fire."

"But you were only four, Jerry, when you ame here. You have remembered how she ooked, all these years?"

"My mother lives in Mannville," he said.

For a moment, finding that he had a mother hocked me as greatly as anything in my life has ver done, and I did not know why it disturbed ne. Then I understood my distress. I was filled vith a passionate resentment that any woman hould go away and leave her son. A fresh anger dded itself. A son like this one— The orphanage was a wholesome place, the executives were kind, good people, the food was more than ade- quate, the boys were healthy, a ragged shirt was o hardship, nor the doing of clean labor. Granted, perhaps, that the boy felt no lack, what lood fed the bowels of a woman who did not earn over this child's lean body that had come n parturition out of her own? At four he would ave looked the same as now. Nothing, I

3 thought, nothing in life could change those eyes. His quality must be apparent to an idiot, a fool. I burned with questions I could not ask. In any, I was afraid, there would be pain.

"Have you seen her, Jerry—lately?"

"I see her every summer. She sends for me."

I wanted to cry out, "Why are you not with her? How can she let you go away again?"

He said, "She comes up here from Mannville whenever she can. She doesn't have a job now."

His face shone in the firelight.

"She wanted to give me a puppy, but they can't let any one boy keep a puppy. You remem- ber the suit I had on last Sunday?" He was plainly proud. "She sent me that for Christmas. The Christmas before that"—he drew a long breath, savoring the memory—"she sent me a pair of skates."

"Roller skates?"

My mind was busy, making pictures of her, trying to understand her. She had not, then, en- tirely deserted or forgotten him. But why, then—I thought, "I must not condemn her without knowing."

"Roller skates. I let the other boys use them. They're always borrowing them. But they're careful of them."

What circumstance other than poverty—

"I'm going to take the dollar you gave me for taking care of Pat," he said, "and buy her a pair of gloves."

I could only say, "That will be nice. Do you know her size?"

"I think it's 8½," he said.

He looked at my hands.

"Do you wear 8½?" he asked.

"No, I wear a smaller size, a 6."

"Oh! Then I guess her hands are bigger than yours."

4 I hated her. Poverty or no, there was other food than bread, and the soul could starve as quickly as the body. He was taking his dollar to buy gloves for her big stupid hands, and she lived away from him, in Mannville, and contented her- self with sending him skates.

AT A GLANCE

- Jerry tells the narrator of his experiences caring for her dog.
- He shocks the narrator by saying that his mother lives in Mannville and sends him gifts.
- The narrator is angry at the mother's disregard for such a fine son.

1 SETTING

The scene of comfort around the fire contrasts with the isolation of the orphanage and the fog.

2 CONFLICT

The shock of discovery and the resulting anger spark a conflict within the narrator: She wants to help Jerry but is also committed to her work and personal life.

3 POINT OF VIEW

The first-person point of view allows Rawlings to proceed without answering certain questions for the reader.

4 THEME

The theme of isolation and loss is highlighted by the narrator's anger, which results from her recognition that a child needs to be nurtured.

GUIDED READING

LITERAL QUESTION

1a. What does Jerry tell the narrator that shocks her? (that he has a mother who lives in Mannville.)

INFERENTIAL QUESTION

1b. Why is the narrator's reaction so important? (It shows that the narrator is starting to feel close to Jerry and perhaps even responsible for him.)

"She likes white gloves," he said. "Do you think I can get them for a dollar?"

"I think so," I said.

I decided that I should not leave the mountains without seeing her and knowing for myself why she had done this thing.

The human mind scatters its interests as though made of thistledown,[4] and every wind stirs and moves it. I finished my work. It did not please me, and I gave my thoughts to another field. I should need some Mexican material.

I made arrangements to close my Florida place. Mexico immediately, and doing the writing there, if conditions were favorable. Then, Alaska with my brother. After that, heaven knew what or where.

I did not take time to go to Mannville to see Jerry's mother, nor even to talk with the orphanage officials about her. I was a trifle abstracted
1 about the boy, because of my work and plans. And after my first fury at her—we did not speak of her again—his having a mother, any sort at all, not far away, in Mannville, relieved me of the ache I had had about him. He did not question the anomalous[5] relation. He was not lonely. It was none of my concern.

He came every day and cut my wood and did small helpful favors and stayed to talk. The days had become cold, and often I let him come inside the cabin. He would lie on the floor in front of the fire, with one arm across the pointer, and they would both doze and wait quietly for me. Other days they ran with a common ecstasy through the laurel, and since the asters were now gone, he brought me back vermilion maple leaves, and chestnut boughs dripping with imperial yellow. I was ready to go.

I said to him, "You have been my good friend, Jerry. I shall often think of you and miss you. Pat will miss you too. I am leaving tomorrow."

2 He did not answer. When he went away, I remember that a new moon hung over the mountains, and I watched him go in silence up the hill I expected him the next day, but he did no come. The details of packing my personal belongings, loading my car, arranging the bed ove the seat, where the dog would ride, occupied m until late in the day. I closed the cabin an started the car, noticing that the sun was in th west and I should do well to be out of the mountains by nightfall. I stopped by the orphanag and left the cabin key and money for my ligh bill with Miss Clark.

"And will you call Jerry for me to say good-by to him?"

"I don't know where he is," she said. "I'm afraid he's not well. He didn't eat his dinner thi noon. One of the other boys saw him going ove the hill into the laurel. He was supposed to fir the boiler this afternoon. It's not like him; he's unusually reliable."

3 I was almost relieved, for I knew I shoul never see him again, and it would be easier no to say good-by to him.

I said, "I wanted to talk with you about hi mother—why he's here—but I'm in more of a hurry than I expected to be. It's out of the question for me to see her now too. But here's som money I'd like to leave with you to buy thing for him at Christmas and on his birthday. It wil be better than for me to try to send him things. I could so easily duplicate—skates, for instance."

She blinked her honest spinster's eyes.

"There's not much use for skates here," sh said.

Her stupidity annoyed me.

"What I mean," I said, "is that I don't wan to duplicate things his mother sends him. I migh have chosen skates if I didn't know she ha already given them to him."

4 She stared at me.

"I don't understand," she said. "He has no mother. He has no skates."

---

4. **thistledown** [this′əl doun′]: feathery seed that floats in the air.
5. **anomalous** [ə nom′ə ləs]: abnormal, unusual.

AT A GLANCE

- The narrator decides she should see Jerry's mother but is caught up in work and plans.
- As the narrator prepares to leave, Jerry hides to avoid a parting scene.
- She learns that Jerry has no mother.

1 CONFLICT

The narrator's professional obligations lessen her resolve to visit Jerry's mother. Her initial desire to help him fades into the feeling she expresses as "none of my concern."

2 CHARACTERIZATION

Jerry's isolation becomes more pronounced as he flees without a word. He cannot communicate his distress at the prospect of being alone again.

3 THEME

The narrator's relief at not having to communicate her feelings contrasts with Jerry's having done the "unnecessary thing, the gracious thing" for her.

4 PLOT: CLIMAX, FALLING ACTION, RESOLUTION

The reader learns the true extent of Jerry's isolation. An internal conflict plays a central part in his character: His self-respect is maintained by promoting a fantasy.

REFLECTING ON THE STORY

How does the ending of the story help you understand Jerry? (It may allow you to realize that some of Jerry's strength of character may come from a story he has to tell *himself*.)

GUIDED READING

LITERAL QUESTION

1a. Why doesn't the narrator visit Jerry's mother? (She is distracted by her work and plans.)

INFERENTIAL QUESTION

1b. What does this tell you about the narrator? (Her desire to help Jerry fades as other commitments take her attention.)

STUDY QUESTIONS

Recalling

1. What is the woman's first impression of Jerry? What action by Jerry changes that impression?
2. Find two incidents that show that Jerry has integrity.
3. What is the woman's reaction to Jerry's statement that he has a mother who visits him occasionally?
4. What does the woman learn about Jerry's mother just before leaving?

Interpreting

5. What does the fact that Jerry makes frequent excuses to visit the woman tell us about Jerry's life?
6. Give two or three examples of Jerry's self-respect. Explain how his self-respect is the reason he pretends to have a mother.
7. Why do you think Jerry responds to the woman's news that she is leaving by remaining silent and by neglecting his duties?

Extending

8. Why do you think Rawlings ended the story immediately after revealing the truth about Jerry's mother? What do you think the woman's reaction was?

LITERARY FOCUS

Flat and Round Characters

People have many different character traits that make up their personalities; some of these traits may actually seem to contradict one another. For example, it is possible for a person to be both popular and lonely.

The author of a story may use one trait or many traits to describe a character. Characters who reveal only one trait are called **flat**. Peter Pan has a flat character because we know only one aspect of his personality, his refusal to grow up. Characters who show varied and sometimes contradictory traits are called **round**. Round characters are **complex characters**, and they can surprise us with an action or a statement. They are more like real people than flat characters are.

Thinking About Characterization

■ Prove that Jerry is a round character by listing six of his personality traits. Explain how some of these traits seem to contradict one another.

COMPOSITION

Writing About Character

■ The woman in the story says, "I saw deep into the clear well of his eyes, and gratitude was there, and affection, soft over the firm granite of his character." Using specific references to Jerry's words and actions, explain how this quotation illustrates his personality. Include examples of Jerry's (a) gratitude, (b) affection, (c) sensitivity, and (d) strength.

Writing a Sequel to a Story

■ Suppose it is now one year after the end of the story. Using one of the following situations, write a dialogue in which Jerry and the woman discuss what has happened during the preceding year: (a) The woman comes back to visit Jerry. (b) The woman has adopted Jerry, and they have remained in North Carolina. (c) The woman has adopted Jerry and taken him to her home.

STUDY QUESTIONS

1. He is too small to do the work; he produces "a splendid pile" of wood.
2. He offers to pay for broken axe; he does services that are not asked for; he feeds the dog part of his own breakfast.
3. She is "filled with a passionate resentment that any woman should go away and leave . . . a son like this one"; "I hated her."
4. Jerry has no mother.
5. He is lonely and hungry for affection.
6. ■ Except with his eyes he never thanks narrator for her kindnesses; wants to pay for axe; works hard and responsibly; makes excuses to visit her.
   ■ Because of his self-respect, he does not want narrator to consider him weak or disadvantaged and so pretends to have a mother.
7. He is too proud to communicate his distress and neglects his duties to avoid seeing the narrator. Such uncharacteristic actions show that he is upset at her leaving.
8. Since we expect that the woman is shocked and sympathetic, there is no need to continue the story beyond the revelation of the truth; the ending emphasizes the discovery.

LITERARY FOCUS

- He is strong (works hard), yet dependent (relies on her company).
- He is responsible (wants to pay for axe), yet neglects duties at end of story.
- He is boyish (plays with dog), yet mature (accepts responsibility).
- He has integrity, yet lies about having a mother.

COMPOSITION: GUIDELINES FOR EVALUATION

WRITING ABOUT CHARACTER

Objective

To illustrate four of Jerry's personality traits

Guidelines for Evaluation

- suggested length: four to six paragraphs
- should offer a thesis statement in the first paragraph
- should include a paragraph for each trait or every two traits

WRITING A SEQUEL TO A STORY

Objective

To write a short sequel in dialogue form

Guidelines for Evaluation

- suggested length: 150–400 words
- should be in dialogue form
- should demonstrate understanding of character's personality traits

AT A GLANCE

- Professor Herbert makes the narrator stay after school to help pay for a broken cherry tree.
- As the narrator sweeps the floor, he worries about how his father will react to his lateness.

LITERARY OPTIONS

- characterization
- theme
- plot

THEMATIC OPTIONS

- the nature of education
- understanding different life styles
- identity and self-respect

1 CHARACTERIZATION

The reader learns indirectly about the narrator's father through the narrator's words.

2 THEME

Professor Herbert instills a sense of discipline and responsibility as part of the educational process.

3 POINT OF VIEW

The first-person narrator's anxious mind jumps from question to question, and the reader gets a sense of a young man who is reflective, excitable, intelligent, and ultimately honest.

In a distant corner of the Kentucky hills at Lonesome Valley School, Jesse Stuart (1907–1984) began teaching at the age of seventeen. Stuart's most famous book, *The Thread That Runs So True,* concerns his career in education. The following story is about a rural school similar to the one where Stuart taught.

■ "You can't teach an old dog new tricks." Or can you?

Jesse Stuart

Split Cherry Tree

"I don't mind staying after school," I says to Professor Herbert, "but I'd rather you'd whip me with a switch and let me go home early. Pa will whip me anyway for getting home two hours late."

"You are too big to whip," says Professor Herbert, "and I have to punish you for climbing up in that cherry tree. You boys knew better than that! The other five boys have paid their dollar each. You have been the only one who has not helped pay for the tree. Can't you borrow a dollar?"

"I can't," I says. "I'll have to take the punishment. I wish it would be quicker punishment. I wouldn't mind."

Professor Herbert stood and looked at me. He was a big man. He wore a gray suit of clothes. The suit matched his gray hair.

1 "You don't know my father," I says to Professor Herbert. "He might be called a little old-fashioned. He makes us mind him until we're twenty-one years old. He believes if you spare the rod you spoil the child.[1] I'll never be able to make him understand about the cherry tree. I'm the first of my people to go to high school."

2 "You must take the punishment," says Professor Herbert. "You must stay two hours after school today and two hours after school tomorrow. I am allowing you twenty-five cents an hour. That is good money for a high school student. You can sweep the schoolhouse floor, wash the blackboards, and clean windows. I'll pay the dollar for you."

I couldn't ask Professor Herbert to loan me a dollar. He never offered to loan it to me. I had to stay and help the janitor and work out my fine at a quarter an hour.

3 I thought as I swept the floor, "What will Pa do to me? What lie can I tell him when I go home? Why did we ever climb that cherry tree and break it down for anyway? Why did we run crazy over the hills away from the crowd? Why did we do all of this? Six of us climbed up in a little cherry tree after one little lizard! Why did the tree split and fall with us? It should have been a stronger tree! Why did Eif Crabtree just happen to be below us plowing and catch us in his cherry tree? Why wasn't he a better man than to charge us six dollars for the tree?"

---

1. **spare . . . child:** old proverb that warned parents that a lack of physical discipline would spoil children.

GUIDED READING

LITERAL QUESTION

1a. Why does the narrator have to stay after school while the other boys can go home? (He and five other boys broke a cherry tree; since he doesn't have a dollar, he must earn money to pay for his share.)

INFERENTIAL QUESTION

1b. What does this tell you about the narrator in relation to the other boys? (He is poorer than they are.)

It was six o'clock when I left the schoolhouse. I had six miles to walk home. It would be after seven when I got home. I had all my work to do when I got home. It took Pa and me both to do the work. Seven cows to milk. Nineteen head of cattle to feed, four mules, twenty-five hogs, firewood and stovewood to cut, and water to draw from the well. He would be doing it when I got home. He would be mad and wondering what was keeping me!

I hurried home. I would run under the dark, leafless trees. I would walk fast uphill. I would run down the hill. The ground was freezing. I had to hurry. I had to run. I reached the long ridge that led to our cow pasture. I ran along this ridge. The wind dried the sweat on my face. I ran across the pasture to the house.

I threw down my books in the chipyard.[2] I ran to the barn to spread fodder[3] on the ground for the cattle. I didn't take time to change my clean school clothes for my old work clothes. I ran out to the barn. I saw Pa spreading fodder on the ground to the cattle. That was my job. I ran up to the fence. I says, "Leave that for me, Pa. I'll do it, I'm just a little late."

"I see you are," says Pa. He turned and looked at me. His eyes danced fire. "What in th' world has kept you so? Why ain't you been here to help me with this work? Make a gentleman out'n one boy in th' family and this is what you get! Send you to high school and you get too onery fer th' buzzards to smell!"

I never said anything. I didn't want to tell why I was late from school. Pa stopped scattering the bundles of fodder. He looked at me. He says, "Why are you gettin' in here this time o' night? You tell me or I'll take a hickory withe[4] to you right here on th' spot!"

I says, "I had to stay after school." I couldn't lie to Pa. He'd go to school and find out why I had to stay. If I lied to him it would be too bad for me.

"Why did you haf to stay atter school?" says Pa.

3 I says, "Our biology class went on a field trip today. Six of us boys broke down a cherry tree. We had to give a dollar apiece to pay for the tree. I didn't have the dollar. Professor Herbert is making me work out my dollar. He gives me twenty-five cents an hour. I had to stay in this afternoon. I'll have to stay in tomorrow afternoon!"

"Are you telling me th' truth?" says Pa.

"I'm telling you the truth," I says. "Go and see for yourself."

"That's jist what I'll do in th' mornin'," says Pa. "Jist whose cherry tree did you break down?"

"Eif Crabtree's cherry tree!"

"What was you doin' clear out in Eif Crabtree's place?" says Pa. "He lives four miles from
4 th' county high school. Don't they teach you no books at that high school? Do they jist let you get out and gad over th' hillsides? If that's all they do I'll keep you at home, Dave. I've got work here fer you to do!"

"Pa," I says, "spring is just getting here. We take a subject in school where we have to have bugs, snakes, flowers, lizards, frogs, and plants. It is biology. It was a pretty day today. We went out to find a few of these. Six of us boys saw a lizard at the same time sunning on a cherry tree. We all went up the tree to get it. We broke the tree down. It split at the forks. Eif Crabtree was plowing down below us. He ran up the hill and got our names. The other boys gave their dollar apiece. I didn't have mine. Professor Herbert put mine in for me. I have to work it out at school."

5 "Poor man's son, huh," says Pa. "I'll attend to that myself in th' mornin'. I'll take keer o' 'im. He ain't from this county nohow. I'll go down there in th' mornin' and see 'im. Lettin' you leave your books and gallivant all over th' hills. What kind of a school is it nohow! Didn't

2. **chipyard:** area where wood is chopped for fuel.
3. **fodder** [fod′ər]: food for livestock.
4. **hickory withe** [with]: a tough but flexible twig, often used for tying bales of fodder.

AT A GLANCE

- At six o'clock the narrator hurries home to do his chores.
- He tells his father about his punishment.
- His father decides to see the teacher the next morning.

1 THEME

The list of farm chores the narrator must perform after school gives the reader some idea of the difficult life style of a poor Appalachian farm family.

2 STYLE: METAPHOR

Pa's eyes are compared to a flickering fire. This simple image concisely communicates the father's anger.

3 CHARACTERIZATION

The narrator states the facts of the situation completely and honestly. Our appreciation of his honesty is grounded in our awareness of his remorse and fear of his father's response.

4 THEME

Pa's ideas on education have not changed since he was a boy. He does not realize how and why educational ideas have changed.

5 CONFLICT

The external conflict between Pa and the professor is based on Pa's pride and his lack of open-mindedness to different ways of doing things.

GUIDED READING

LITERAL QUESTIONS

1a. What does the narrator have to do when he gets home? (He has to milk the cows, feed the farm animals, cut wood, and draw water.)

2a. Why does Pa decide to see Professor Herbert in the morning? (to protest that his son had to stay after school because he could not pay the dollar)

INFERENTIAL QUESTIONS

1b. What do these activities tell you about the narrator? (He works hard out of school.)

2b. What does this decision tell you about Pa? (He is angry his son is being punished because he is poor.)

AT A GLANCE

- Dave worries that his father might make trouble.
- He wishes he could explain that school has changed since his father was a boy.

1 CHARACTERIZATION

Pa is shown as a tough, self-reliant person who believes in confrontation: His pride has been hurt because he cannot afford to give his son money.

do that, my son, when I's a little shaver in school. All fared alike, too."

"Pa, please don't go down there," I says, "just let me have fifty cents and pay the rest of my fine! I don't want you to go down there! I don't want you to start anything with Professor Herbert!"

"Ashamed of your old Pap, are you, Dave," says Pa, "atter th' way I've worked to raise you! Tryin' to send you to school so you can make a better livin' than I've made.

1 "I'll straighten this thing out myself! I'll take keer o' Professor Herbert myself! He ain't got no right to keep you in and let the other boys off jist because they've got th' money! I'm a poor man. A bullet will go in a professor same as it will any man. It will go in a rich man same as it will a poor man. Now you get into this work before I take one o' these withes and cut the shirt off'n your back!"

I thought once I'd run through the woods above the barn just as hard as I could go. I thought I'd leave high school and home forever! Pa could not catch me! I'd get away! I couldn't go back to school with him. He'd have a gun and maybe he'd shoot Professor Herbert. It was hard to tell what he would do. I could tell Pa that school had changed in the hills from the way it was when he was a boy, but he wouldn't understand. I could tell him we studied frogs, birds, snakes, lizards, flowers, insects. But Pa wouldn't understand. If I did run away from home it wouldn't matter to Pa. He would see Professor Herbert anyway. He would think that high school and Professor Herbert had run me away from home. There was no need to run away. I'd just have to stay, finish foddering the cattle, and go to school with Pa the next morning.

I would take a bundle of fodder, remove the hickory-withe band from around it, and scatter it on rocks, clumps of green briers, and brush, so the cattle wouldn't tramp it under their feet. I would lean it up against the oak trees and the

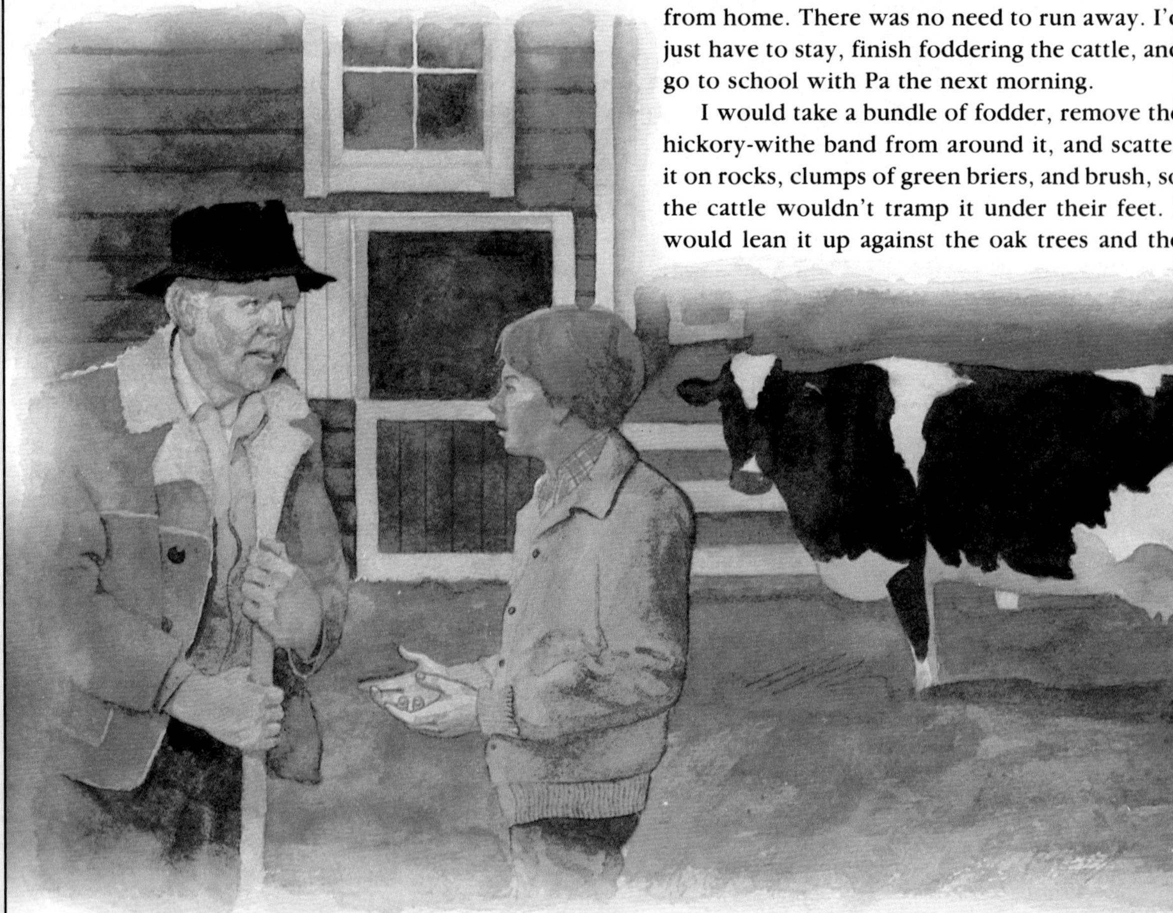

GUIDED READING

LITERAL QUESTION

1a. Why doesn't Dave tell his father that school has changed since his father was a boy? (He thinks his father won't understand.)

INFERENTIAL QUESTION

1b. What does Dave's opinion tell you about Pa? (Since Pa doesn't understand why the educational process now includes "field work," it seems Pa would not be open to new ideas.)

ocks in the pasture just above our pigpen on the ill. The fodder was cold and frosty where it had et out in the stacks. I would carry bundles of the odder from the stack until I had spread out a undle for each steer. Pa went to the barn to eed the mules and throw corn in the pen to the ogs.

The moon shone bright in the cold March ky. I finished my work by moonlight. Professor Ierbert really didn't know how much work I ad to do at home. If he had known he would ot have kept me after school. He would have oaned me a dollar to have paid my part on the herry tree. He had never lived in the hills. He idn't know the way the hill boys had to work o that they could go to school. Now he was eaching in a county high school where all the oys who attended were from hill farms.

After I'd finished doing my work I went to the ouse and ate my supper. Pa and Mom had eaten. Iy supper was getting cold. I heard Pa and Mom alking in the front room. Pa was telling Mom bout me staying in after school.

"I had to do all th' milkin' tonight, chop h' wood myself. It's too hard on me atter I've urned ground all day. I'm goin' to take a day off omorrow and see if I can't remedy things a lit-le. I'll go down to that high school tomorrow. I von't be a very good scholar fer Professor Her-ert nohow. He won't keep me in atter school. 'll take a different kind of lesson down there nd make 'im acquainted with it."

"Now, Luster," says Mom, "you jist stay away rom there. Don't cause a lot o' trouble. You can e jailed fer a trick like that. You'll get th' Law tter you. You'll just go down there and show ff and plague your own boy Dave to death in ront o' all th' scholars!"

"Plague or no plague," says Pa, "he don't take nto consideration what all I haf to do here, does e? I'll show 'im it ain't right to keep one boy in nd let the rest go scot-free. My boy is good as h' rest, ain't he? A bullet will make a hole in a choolteacher same as it will anybody else. He can't do me that way and get by with it. I'll plug 'im first. I aim to go down there bright and early in the mornin' and get all this straight! I aim to see about bug larnin' and this runnin' all over God's creation huntin' snakes, lizards, and frogs.
2 Ransackin' th' country and goin' through cherry orchards and breakin' th' trees down atter lizards! Old Eif Crabtree ought to a-poured th' hot lead to 'em instead o' chargin' six dollars fer th' tree! He ought to a-got old Herbert th' first one!"

I ate my supper. I slipped upstairs and lit the lamp. I tried to forget the whole thing. I studied plane geometry. Then I studied my biology lesson. I could hardly study for thinking about Pa. "He'll go to school with me in the morning. He'll take a gun for Professor Herbert! What will Professor Herbert think of me! I'll tell him when Pa leaves that I couldn't help it. But Pa might shoot him. I hate to go with Pa. Maybe he'll cool off about it tonight and not go in the morning."

Pa got up at four o'clock. He built a fire in the stove. Then he built a fire in the fireplace. He got Mom up to get breakfast. Then he got me up to help feed and milk. By the time we had our work done at the barn, Mom had breakfast ready for us. We ate our breakfast. Daylight came and we could see the bare oak trees covered white with frost. The hills were white with frost. A cold wind was blowing. The sky was clear. The sun would soon come out and melt the frost. The afternoon would be warm with sunshine and the frozen ground would thaw. There would be mud on the hills again. Muddy water would then run down the little ditches on the hills.

3 "Now, Dave," says Pa, "let's get ready fer school. I aim to go with you this mornin' and look into bug larnin', frog larnin', lizard and snake larnin', and breakin' down cherry trees! I don't like no sicha foolish way o' larnin' myself!"

Pa hadn't forgot. I'd have to take him to school with me. He would take me to school with him. We were going early. I was glad we

AT A GLANCE

- Dave finishes his chores by moonlight.
- Pa plans to visit the school.
- Dave studies and hopes his father will change his mind.
- Pa sticks to his decision to see Professor Herbert in the morning.

1 THEME

Dave is aware that Professor Herbert lacks understanding of the hardships faced by the hill farm students that he teaches.

2 VOCABULARY: DIALECT

The local dialect of the Appalachian farmer is revealed in Pa's colorful language. The dialect seems most intense when he is emotionally upset.

3 PLOT: NARRATIVE HOOK

As Pa insists on visiting the school, the reader's sense of impending conflict grows stronger. Dave seems caught between two clashing views of life.

GUIDED READING

LITERAL QUESTIONS

1a. What does Dave think Professor Herbert would have done if he had known how much work Dave had to do at home? (loaned him the dollar and excused him from staying after school)

2a. What does Pa tell Dave the next morning? (He is going to school to find out why the students must learn things outside the classroom.)

INFERENTIAL QUESTIONS

1b. How do you think Dave feels about having a teacher who does not know how hard hill farm boys must work? (He tries to excuse the professor's lack of knowledge but may feel somewhat annoyed or resentful.)

2b. What does this action suggest about Pa's views on education? (His views are outdated: He doesn't understand that formal education can include experiences beyond books and the classroom.)

AT A GLANCE

- Pa takes his gun and sets off for school with Dave.
- Pa argues with Professor Herbert.
- Pa asks why students must leave the schoolroom to learn.

1 CONFLICT

The description of Pa's work clothes emphasizes the gap between Dave's life on the farm and at school.

2 THEME

Dave realizes that knowledge results from exposure to new ideas and situations. He remembers his experience with the Lambert boys and draws a potential parallel.

3 PLOT: RISING ACTION

Pa's gun adds suspense to his initial confrontation with Professor Herbert.

4 CHARACTERIZATION

Comparing the two men makes Dave aware of his father's toughness and considerable physical stature for the first time.

were going early. If Pa pulled a gun on Professor Herbert there wouldn't be so many of my classmates there to see him.

1 I knew that Pa wouldn't be at home in the high school. He wore overalls, big boots, a blue shirt and a sheepskin coat, and a slouched black hat gone to seed[5] at the top. He put his gun in its holster. We started trudging toward the high school across the hill.

It was early when we got to the county high school. Professor Herbert had just got there. I just thought as we walked up the steps into the
2 schoolhouse, "Maybe Pa will find out Professor Herbert is a good man. He just doesn't know him. Just like I felt toward the Lambert boys across the hill. I didn't like them until I'd seen them and talked to them. After I went to school with them and talked to them, I liked them and we were friends. It's a lot in knowing the other fellow."

"You're th' Professor here, ain't you?" says Pa.

"Yes," says Professor Herbert, "and you are Dave's father."

3 "Yes," says Pa, pulling out his gun and laying it on the seat in Professor Herbert's office. Professor Herbert's eyes got big behind his black-rimmed glasses when he saw Pa's gun. Color came into his pale cheeks.

"Jist a few things about this school I want to know," says Pa. "I'm tryin' to make a scholar out'n Dave. He's the only one out'n eleven youngins I've sent to high school. Here he comes in late and leaves me all th' work to do! He said you's all out bug huntin' yesterday and broke a cherry tree down. He had to stay two hours atter school yesterday and work out money to pay on that cherry tree! Is that right?"

"Wwwwy," says Professor Herbert, "I guess it is."

He looked at Pa's gun.

"Well," says Pa, "this ain't no high school. It's a bug school, a lizard school, a snake school! It ain't no school nohow!"

"Why did you bring that gun?" says Professor Herbert to Pa.

"You see that little hole," says Pa as he picked up the long blue forty-four and put his finger on the end of the barrel, "a bullet can come out'n that hole that will kill a schoolteacher same as it will any other man. It will kill a rich man same as a poor man. It will kill a man. But atter I come in and saw you, I know'd I wouldn't need it. This maul[6] o' mine could do you up in a few minutes."

4 Pa stood there, big, hard, brown-skinned, and mighty, beside of Professor Herbert. I didn't know Pa was so much bigger and harder. I'd never seen Pa in a schoolhouse before. I'd seen Professor Herbert. He always looked big before to me. He didn't look big standing beside of Pa.

"I was only doing my duty, Mr. Sexton," says Professor Herbert, "and following the course of study the state provided us with."

"Course o'study," says Pa, "what study, bug study? Varmint study? Takin' youngins to th' woods. Boys and girls all out there together a-gallivantin' in the brush and kickin' up their heels and their poor old Ma's and Pa's at home a-slavin' to keep 'em in school and give 'em a education! You know that's dangerous, too, puttin' a lot o' boys and girls out together like that!"

Students were coming into the schoolhouse now.

Professor Herbert says, "Close the door, Dave, so others won't hear."

I walked over and closed the door. I was shaking like a leaf in the wind. I thought Pa was going to hit Professor Herbert every minute. He was doing all the talking. His face was getting red. The red color was coming through the brown, weather-beaten skin on Pa's face.

"I was right with these students," says Professor Herbert. "I know what they got into and

---

5. **gone to seed:** become worn out or shabby.

6. **maul** [môl]: heavy hammer; here, Pa's fist.

GUIDED READING

LITERAL QUESTIONS

1a. What does Pa put on the seat in Professor Herbert's office? (a gun)

2a. What does Professor Herbert say in defense of his teaching methods? (He says he was following the state's course of study.)

INFERENTIAL QUESTIONS

1b. What does this action indicate about Pa's ideas about resolving a difference? (He is a tough-minded person who seems to think that the threat of violence will resolve a dispute.)

2b. Why do you think Professor Herbert responds to Pa's threat in this way? (to calm Pa down in order to avoid a physical confrontation)

what they didn't. I didn't send one of the other teachers with them on this field trip. I went myself. Yes, I took the boys and girls together. Why not?"

"It jist don't look good to me," says Pa, "a-takin' all this swarm of youngins out to pillage th' whole deestrict. Breakin' down cherry trees. Keepin' boys in atter school."

"What else could I have done with Dave, Mr. Sexton?" says Professor Herbert. "The boys didn't have any business all climbing that cherry tree after one lizard. One boy could have gone up in the tree and got it. The farmer charged us six dollars. It was a little steep, I think, but we had to pay. Must I make five boys pay and let your boy off? He said he didn't have the dollar and couldn't get it. So I put it in for him. I'm letting him work it out. He's not working for me. He's working for the school!"

"I jist don't know what you could a-done with 'im," says Pa, "only a-larruped 'im with a withe! That's what he needed!"

"He's too big to whip," says Professor Herbert, pointing at me. "He's a man in size."

"He's not too big fer me to whip," says Pa. "They ain't too big until they're over twenty-one! It just didn't look fair to me! Work one and let th' rest out because they got th' money. I don't see what bugs has got to do with a high school! It don't look good to me nohow!"

Pa picked up his gun and put it back in its holster. The red color left Professor Herbert's face. He talked more to Pa. Pa softened a little. It looked funny to see Pa in the high school building. It was the first time he'd ever been there.

"We were not only hunting snakes, toads, flowers, butterflies, lizards," says Professor Herbert, "but, Mr. Sexton, I was hunting dry timothy grass to put in an incubator and raise some protozoa."

"I don't know what that is," says Pa. "Th' incubator is th' newfangled way o' cheatin' th' hens and raisin' chickens. I ain't so sure about th' breed o' chickens you mentioned."

2 "You've heard of germs, Mr. Sexton, haven't you?" says Professor Herbert.

"Jist call me Luster, if you don't mind," says Pa, very casual like.

"All right, Luster, you've heard of germs, haven't you?"

"Yes," says Pa, "but I don't believe in germs. I'm sixty-five years old and I ain't seen one yet!"

"You can't see them with your naked eye," says Professor Herbert. "Just keep that gun in the holster and stay with me in the high school today. I have a few things I want to show you. That scum on your teeth has germs in it."

"What," says Pa, "you mean to tell me I've got germs on my teeth!"

"Yes," says Professor Herbert. "The same kind as we might be able to find in a living black snake if we dissect it!"

"I don't mean to dispute your word," says Pa, "but I don't believe it. I don't believe I have germs on my teeth!"

"Stay with me today and I'll show you. I want to take you through the school anyway! School has changed a lot in the hills since you went to school. I don't guess we had high schools in this county when you went to school!"

3 "No," says Pa, "jist readin', writin', and cipherin'. We didn't have all this bug larnin', frog larnin', and findin' germs on your teeth and in the middle o' black snakes! Th' world's changin'."

"It is," says Professor Herbert, "and we hope all for the better. Boys like your own there are going to help change it. He's your boy. He knows all of what I've told you. You stay with me today."

"I'll shore stay with you," says Pa. "I want to see th' germs off'n my teeth. I jist want to see a germ. I've never seen one in my life. 'Seein' is believin',' Pap allus told me."

Pa walks out of the office with Professor Herbert. I just hoped Professor Herbert didn't have Pa arrested for pulling his gun. Pa's gun has

AT A GLANCE

- Professor Herbert explains the purpose of field trips.
- Pa puts his gun away.
- The professor tells Pa about germs; Pa agrees to stay at school for the day.

1 CHARACTERIZATION

Pa is a dynamic character, capable of change; he softens toward Professor Herbert and puts his gun away. Then, Dave can relax and think about the incongruity of his father in the school environment.

2 READING SKILLS: INFERENCE

When Pa tells the professor to call him Luster, the reader sees that the anger Pa felt before is diminishing.

3 THEME

Despite his bluster Pa may be willing to learn how the world has changed since he went to school.

GUIDED READING

LITERAL QUESTIONS

1a. What does Pa do with his gun after he picks it up from the chair? (He puts it in its holster.)

2a. What makes Pa want to stay in school for the day? (The professor offers to show him germs.)

INFERENTIAL QUESTIONS

1b. Why is this event important? (It shows that Pa is willing to relax and listen to what Professor Herbert has to say.)

2b. What does this willingness to stay tell you about Pa? (Although he initially thinks that "nature study" is a waste of time, he becomes interested.)

AT A GLANCE

- Pa spends the day with Professor Herbert at the school.
- Pa and Professor Herbert sit in on classes and have lunch together in the high school cafeteria.

1 SETTING

Pa's rugged clothes contrast with those of the clean and well-dressed students around him. In the schoolyard he stands alone under a tree, out of touch with the rhythms of school life.

2 STYLE: SIMILE

Pa's "big and gnarled" hands are compared to the roots of an elm tree to emphasize his strength and his connection to the land.

always been a friend to him when he goes to settle disputes.

The bell rang. School took up. I saw the students when they marched in the schoolhouse look at Pa. They would grin and punch each
1 other. Pa just stood and watched them pass in at the schoolhouse door. Two long lines marched in the house. The boys and girls were clean and well dressed. Pa stood over in the schoolyard under a leafless elm, in his sheepskin coat, his big boots laced in front with buckskin, and his heavy socks stuck above his boot tops. Pa's overalls legs were baggy and wrinkled between his coat and boot tops. His blue work shirt showed at the collar. His big black hat showed his gray-streaked black hair. His face was hard and weath-
2 er-tanned to the color of a ripe fodder blade. His hands were big and gnarled like the roots of the elm tree he stood beside.

When I went to my first class I saw Pa and Professor Herbert going around over the schoolhouse. I was in my geometry class when Pa and Professor Herbert came in the room. We were explaining our propositions[7] on the blackboard. Professor Herbert and Pa just quietly came in and sat down for a while. I heard Fred Wurts whisper to Glenn Armstrong, "Who is that old man? Lord, he's a rough-looking scamp." Glenn whispered back, "I think he's Dave's Pap." The students in geometry looked at Pa. They must have wondered what he was doing in school. Before the class was over, Pa and Professor Herbert got up and went out. I saw them together down on the playground. Professor Herbert was explaining to Pa. I could see the prints of Pa's gun under his coat when he'd walk around.

At noon in the high school cafeteria Pa and Professor Herbert sat together at the little table where Professor Herbert always ate by himself. They ate together. The students watched the way Pa ate. He ate with his knife instead of his fork. A lot of the students felt sorry for me after they found out he was my father. They didn't have to feel sorry for me. I wasn't ashamed of Pa after I found out he wasn't going to shoot Professor Herbert. I was glad they had made friends.

7. **propositions:** in mathematics, statements that must be proven.

GUIDED READING

LITERAL QUESTION

1a. What does Dave notice about Pa in the cafeteria? (He eats with his knife instead of his fork.)

INFERENTIAL QUESTION

1b. Why is Pa's handling of utensils significant? (He is not a cultured or educated person, a fact that makes his willingness to visit the school for the day remarkable.)

I wasn't ashamed of Pa. I wouldn't be as long as he behaved. He would find out about the high school as I had found out about the Lambert boys across the hill.

In the afternoon when we went to biology Pa was in the class. He was sitting on one of the high stools beside the microscope. We went ahead with our work just as if Pa wasn't in the class. I saw Pa take his knife and scrape tartar from one of his teeth. Professor Herbert put it on the lens and adjusted the microscope for Pa. He adjusted it and worked awhile. Then he says, "Now Luster, look! Put your eye right down to the light. Squint the other eye!"

Pa put his head down and did as Professor Herbert said. "I see 'im," says Pa. "Who'd a ever thought that? Right on a body's teeth! Right in a body's mouth. You're right certain they ain't no fake to this, Professor Herbert?"

"No, Luster," says Professor Herbert. "It's there. That's the germ. Germs live in a world we cannot see with the naked eye. We must use the microscope. There are millions of them in our bodies. Some are harmful. Others are helpful."

Pa holds his face down and looks through the microscope. We stop and watch Pa. He sits upon the tall stool. His knees are against the table. His legs are long. His coat slips up behind when he bends over. The handle of his gun shows. Professor Herbert pulls his coat down quickly.

"Oh, yes," says Pa. He gets up and pulls his coat down. Pa's face gets a little red. He knows about his gun and he knows he doesn't have any use for it in high school.

"We have a big black snake over here we caught yesterday," says Professor Herbert. "We'll chloroform him and dissect him and show you he has germs in his body, too."

"Don't do it," says Pa. "I believe you. I jist don't want to see you kill the black snake. I never kill one. They are good mousers[8] and a lot o' help to us on the farm. I like black snakes. I jist hate to see people kill 'em. I don't allow 'em killed on my place."

The students look at Pa. They seem to like him better after he said that. Pa with a gun in his pocket but a tender heart beneath his ribs for snakes, but not for man! Pa won't whip a mule at home. He won't whip his cattle.

"Man can defend hisself," says Pa, "but cattle and mules can't. We have the drop on 'em. Ain't nothin' to man that'll beat a good pullin' mule. He ain't got th' right kind o' a heart!"

2 Professor Herbert took Pa through the laboratory. He showed him the different kinds of work we were doing. He showed him our equipment. They stood and talked while we worked. Then they walked out together. They talked louder when they got out in the hall.

When our biology class was over I walked out of the room. It was our last class for the day. I would have to take my broom and sweep two hours to finish paying for the split cherry tree. I just wondered if Pa would want me to stay. He was standing in the hallway watching the stu-
3 dents march out. He looked lost among us. He looked like a leaf turned brown on the tree among the treetop filled with growing leaves.

I got my broom and started to sweep. Professor Herbert walked up and says, "I'm going to let you do that some other time. You can go home with your father. He is waiting out there."

I laid my broom down, got my books, and went down the steps.

Pa says, "Ain't you got two hours o' sweepin' yet to do?"

I says, "Professor Herbert said I could do it some other time. He said for me to go home with you."

"No," says Pa. "You are goin' to do as he
4 says. He's a good man. School has changed from my day and time. I'm a dead leaf, Dave. I'm behind. I don't belong here. If he'll let me I'll get a broom and we'll both sweep one hour. That pays your debt. I'll hep you pay it. I'll ast 'im and

8. **mousers:** any animals like cats and snakes that catch mice.

AT A GLANCE

- Dave realizes he is not ashamed of his father.
- Pa looks through a microscope at the germs from his teeth.
- Pa insists a black snake not be killed.
- After school Dave begins to sweep; Pa offers to help.

1 CHARACTERIZATION

Although he is presented as hard and tough, Pa has a tender spot in his heart for animals.

2 RESPONSE JOURNAL

Have students write about what it would be like to take an older person on a tour of their school.

3 SETTING

Even after spending a day in the school, Pa still looks out of place there: He is not in his natural element.

4 STYLE: METAPHOR

Pa, comparing himself to a dead leaf, realizes that times have changed and that he has not kept pace with them.

GUIDED READING

LITERAL QUESTION

1a. What does Pa say to Dave after school? ("I'm a dead leaf, Dave. I'm behind.")

INFERENTIAL QUESTION

1b. What does this statement indicate about Pa's self-awareness? (He is now aware of how little he knows about education.)

see if he won't let me hep you."

"I'm going to cancel the debt," says Professor Herbert. "I just wanted you to understand, Luster."

"I understand," says Pa, "and since I understand, he must pay his debt fer th' tree and I'm goin' to hep 'im."

"Don't do that," says Professor Herbert. "It's all on me."

"We don't do things like that," says Pa, "we're just and honest people. We don't want somethin' fer nothin'. Professor Herbert, you're wrong now and I'm right. You'll haf to listen to
1 me. I've larned a lot from you. My boy must go on. Th' world has left me. It changed while I've raised my family and plowed th' hills. I'm a just and honest man. I don't skip debts. I ain't larned 'em to do that. I ain't got much larnin' myself but I do know right from wrong atter I see through a thing."

Professor Herbert went home. Pa and I stayed and swept one hour. It looked funny to see Pa use a broom. He never used one at home. Mom used the broom. Pa used the plow. Pa did hard work. Pa says, "I can't sweep. Durned if I can. Look at th' streaks o'dirt I leave on th'
2 floor! Seems like no work a-tall fer me. Brooms is too light'r somethin'. I'll jist do th' best I can, Dave. I've been wrong about th' school."

I says, "Did you know Professor Herbert can get a warrant out for you for bringing your pistol to school and showing it in his office! They can railroad[9] you for that!"

"That's all made right," says Pa. "I've made that right. Professor Herbert ain't goin' to take it to court. He likes me. I like 'im. We jist had to get together. He had the remedies. He showed me. You must go on to school. I am as strong a man as ever come out'n th' hills fer my years and th' hard work I've done. But I'm behind, Dave. I'm a little man. Your hands will be softer than mine. Your clothes will be better. You'll allus look cleaner than your old Pap. Jist remember, Dave, to pay your debts and be honest. Jist be kind to animals and don't bother th' snakes. That's all I got agin th' school. Puttin' black snakes to sleep and cuttin' 'em open."

It was late when we got home. Stars were in the sky. The moon was up. The ground was frozen. Pa took his time going home. I couldn't run like I did the night before. It was ten o'clock before we got the work finished, our suppers eaten. Pa sat before the fire and told Mom he was going to take her and show her a germ some-
3 time. Mom hadn't seen one either. Pa told her about the high school and the fine man Professor Herbert was. He told Mom about the strange school across the hill and how different it was from the school in their day and time.

9. **railroad:** slang for "imprison without fair trial."

STUDY QUESTIONS

Recalling

1. Explain why Dave is late returning home from school.
2. What responsibilities does Dave have at home that make him concerned about being late?
3. Summarize Pa's reaction to Dave's reason for being late.
4. Give three statements or actions by Pa at the end of the school day that show he now approves of Dave's school.

Interpreting

5. Dave says that he learned to like the Lambert boys because "it's a lot in knowing the other fellow." What does Pa learn about Professor Herbert that causes him to like the teacher?

AT A GLANCE

- Pa helps Dave finish sweeping.
- He admits he was wrong about school.
- At home Pa tells his wife about the school.

1 PLOT: CLIMAX

Pa acknowledges that school has changed and that he is behind.

2 CHARACTERIZATION

Pa's character has developed during the story: He is no longer annoyed by the school's methods and has become more aware of his own limitations.

3 PLOT: RESOLUTION

Upon arriving home, Pa—now able to accept a changing world—tells his wife about the school and the new things he has encountered.

REFLECTING ON THE STORY

Who seems to learn the most in this story, Pa or Dave? (Although Pa learns many new things at school, a case could also be made for Dave, who learns to recognize his father's strengths *and* weaknesses.)

STUDY QUESTIONS

1. stays after school to pay his share of damage to tree
2. milks cows, cares for animals, cuts wood, draws water
3. He is furious and blames Herbert for unfair treatment.
4. - calls professor "a good man"
   - helps Dave work off debt
   - tells Dave, "You must go on to school."
   - tells wife about his day
5. They share mutual respect for discipline and responsibility.

6. Explain what we learn about Pa from his feelings toward the black snakes and toward cattle and mules.
7. What reasons does Dave have to be proud of his father?

VIEWPOINT

Although "Split Cherry Tree" is primarily about Pa, the role of Professor Herbert would be important to Jesse Stuart, who was himself a teacher in the hills of Kentucky. One biographer of Stuart says that his principles have their root in America's pioneer past. Stuart, she says, believes the following:

> Responsibility develops self-confidence. Discipline is a necessary corollary [accompaniment] to learning. Nature is a great teacher. Every student is an individual.
>
> —M. W. Clarke,
> *Jesse Stuart: Essays on His Work*

- Explain how Professor Herbert illustrates Stuart's philosophy of education.

LITERARY FOCUS

Dynamic and Static Characters

By definition, the word *dynamic* means "changing," and the word *static*, "unchanging." **Dynamic characters** change in the course of a story, just as people do, because of the influence of events or other people. **Static characters** remain primarily the same throughout a story.

For example, in Charles Dickens' *Christmas Carol* Ebenezer Scrooge is a dynamic character because he changes his miserly ways. His clerk, Bob Cratchit, is a static character because he is basically the same man at the end of the story as at the beginning.

Thinking About Characterization

Explain how Pa's attitude expressed in each of the following quotations has changed by the end of the story.

1. "...I'll keep you at home, Dave. I've got work here fer you to do."
2. "I don't see what bugs has got to do with a high school!"

Figurative Language

Figurative language is language used for descriptive effect; it is *not* **literal language**, which states facts or ideas directly. The most common forms of figurative language are metaphor and simile. A **metaphor** is a comparison of seemingly unlike things. For example, in "The Most Dangerous Game" (page 11) Rainsford describes the hunt with metaphors: "The Cossack was the cat; he [Rainsford] was the mouse." A **simile** is a comparison of seemingly unlike things using *like* or *as*. For example, Rainsford describes the damp, dark night by saying, "It's like moist black velvet."

Thinking About Figurative Language

- Find two metaphors and two similes in "Split Cherry Tree."

COMPOSITION

Writing About Character

- Compare and contrast Pa and Professor Herbert. You may want to consider the following: (a) their everyday lives, (b) their backgrounds, and (c) their relationships with other people. *For help with this assignment, see Lesson 4 in the Writing About Literature Handbook at the back of this book.*

Writing with Metaphors and Similes

- Metaphors and similes are techniques of descriptive writing. Using metaphors and similes, write a description of either Dave or Professor Herbert. First describe how the character looks. Then describe how the character acts, walks, and speaks.

COMPARING STORIES

- We remember vividly an action by a person when the action tells us a great deal about that person. Think about Mrs. Markham in "A Day's Pleasure," Squeaky in "Raymond's Run," Jerry in "A Mother in Mannville," and Pa in "Split Cherry Tree." Compare the characters in two or more stories. For each character describe one action that you consider the best example of that character's personality. Then explain what the action reveals about personality.

STUDY QUESTIONS

6. He is humane, respects useful life, and believes in fair play.
7. Pa gracefully admits his error, displays an interest in knowledge, is capable of change.

VIEWPOINT

- "Responsibility develops self-confidence": He makes the boys pay for the tree, defends his decision to Dave's father.
- "Discipline is a necessary corollary to learning": He makes Dave work as a way of paying his share of the damages.
- "Nature is a great teacher": He teaches biology and includes field trips in his course.
- "Every student is an individual": He alters Dave's punishment, asks Dave to close the door to protect him from embarrassment.

LITERARY FOCUS

Thinking About Characterization

1. Pa discovers that education will give Dave a chance for a better life. He says, "You must go on to school."
2. Pa's experience in biology class shows him that learning about nature is interesting and an important part of a complete education in the modern world.

Thinking About Figurative Language

- *Metaphor:* "I'm a dead leaf"; "his eyes danced fire"
- *Similes:* "I was shaking like a leaf in the wind"; "His hands were big and gnarled like the roots of the elm tree he stood beside"; "He looked like a leaf turned brown on the tree"

COMPARING STORIES

Answers will vary.

COMPOSITION: GUIDELINES FOR EVALUATION

WRITING ABOUT CHARACTER

Objective

To compare and contrast Pa and Professor Herbert

Guidelines for Evaluation

- suggested length: four to six paragraphs
- should contain a thesis statement in the first paragraph
- should develop each comparison and contrast
- should make references to the story

WRITING WITH METAPHORS AND SIMILES

Objective

To describe either Dave or Professor Herbert

Guidelines for Evaluation

- suggested length: two paragraphs
- should describe appearance, actions
- should use at least four metaphors and/or similes to enhance description

AT A GLANCE

- Arnold is awakened by a rooster outside the window of the Talbots' guest room.
- Arnold's annual visit excites Duncan and George, the Talbots' two sons.
- Arnold joins Mrs. Talbot and her younger son, George, for breakfast.

LITERARY OPTIONS

- setting
- theme
- characterization

THEMATIC OPTIONS

- the family
- responding to nature
- solitude

1 SETTING

The sound of a rooster's crowing from a tree outside the window places the action in a rural setting.

2 THEME

The natural cycle of the seasons is a central theme throughout the story.

3 CHARACTERIZATION

The friendly, relaxed exchange between Arnold and George shows their comfortable, natural relationship.

LITERARY FOCUS: Setting

William Maxwell (born 1908) was raised in a small town and was part of a large, affectionate family. The following story involves a man from the city observing family life in the country.

- What does the word *patterns* bring to mind?

William Maxwell

The Patterns of Love

1 Kate Talbot's bantam[1] rooster, awakened by the sudden appearance of the moon from behind a cloud on a white June night, began to crow. There were three bantams—a cock and two hens—and their roost[2] was in a tree just outside the guest-room windows. The guest room was on the first floor and the Talbots' guest that weekend was a young man by the name of Arnold, a rather light sleeper. He got up and closed the windows and went back to bed. In the sealed room he slept, but was awakened at frequent intervals until daylight Saturday morning.

Arnold had been coming to the Talbots' place in Wilton[3] sometime during the spring or early
2 summer for a number of years. His visits were, for the children, one of a thousand seasonal events that could be counted on, less exciting than the appearance of the first robin or the arrival of violets in the marsh at the foot of the Talbots' hill but akin to them. Sometimes Duncan, the Talbots' older boy, who for a long time was under the impression that Arnold came to see *him*, slept in the guest room when Arnold was there. Last year, George, Duncan's younger brother, had been given that privilege. This time, Mrs. Talbot, knowing how talkative the boys were when they awoke in the morning, had left Arnold to himself.

When he came out of his room, Mrs. Talbot and George, the apple of her eye, were still at breakfast. George was six, small and delicate and very blond, not really interested in food at any time, and certainly not now, when there was a guest in the house. He was in his pajamas and a
3 pink quilted bathrobe. He smiled at Arnold with his large and very gentle eyes and said, "Did you miss me?"

"Yes, of course," Arnold said. "I woke up and there was the other bed, flat and empty. Nobody to talk to while I looked at the ceiling. Nobody to watch me shave."

George was very pleased that his absence had been felt. "What is your favorite color?" he asked.

1. **bantam:** miniature breed of fowl.
2. **roost:** perch for birds to rest and sleep.
3. **Wilton:** rural, residential community in Connecticut.

GUIDED READING

LITERAL QUESTION

1a. What is the first sound Arnold hears in the story? (a rooster crowing)

INFERENTIAL QUESTION

1b. What does this indicate about the story's setting? (The rooster's crowing indicates that the story is set in a rural area where there are outdoor animals.)

"Red," Arnold said, without having to consider.

"Mine, too," George said, and his face became so illuminated with pleasure at this coincidence that for a moment he looked angelic.

"No matter how much we disagree about other things," Arnold said, "we'll always have that in common, won't we?"

"Yes," George said.

"You'd both better eat your cereal," Mrs. Talbot said.

Arnold looked at her while she was pouring his coffee and wondered if there wasn't something back of her remark—jealousy, perhaps. Mrs. Talbot was a very soft-hearted woman, but for some reason she seemed to be ashamed—or perhaps afraid—to let other people know it. She took refuge continually behind a dry humor. There was probably very little likelihood that George would be as fond of anyone else as he was of his mother, Arnold decided, for many years to come. There was no real reason for her to be jealous.

"Did the bantams keep you awake?" she asked.

Arnold shook his head.

"Something tells me you're lying," Mrs. Talbot said. "John didn't wake up, but he felt his responsibilities as a host even so. He cried 'Oh!' in his sleep every time a bantam crowed. You'll have to put up with them on Kate's account. She loves them more than her life."

Excluded from the conversation of the grownups, George finished his cereal and ate part of a soft-boiled egg. Then he asked to be excused and, with pillows and pads which had been brought in from the garden furniture the night before, he made a train right across the dining-room floor. The cook had to step over it when she brought a fresh pot of coffee, and Mrs. Talbot and Arnold had to do likewise when they went out through the dining-room door to look at the bantams. There were only two—the cock and one hen—walking around under the Japanese cherry tree on the terrace. Kate was leaning out of an upstairs window, watching them fondly.

"Have you made your bed?" Mrs. Talbot asked.

The head withdrew.

"Kate is going to a houseparty," Mrs. Talbot said, looking at the bantams. "A sort of houseparty. She's going to stay all night at Mary Sherman's house and there are going to be some boys and they're going to dance to the victrola."[4]

"How old is she, for heaven's sake?" Arnold asked.

"Thirteen," Mrs. Talbot said. "She had her hair cut yesterday and it's too short. It doesn't look right, so I have to do something about it."

4 "White of egg?" Arnold asked.

"How did you know that?" Mrs. Talbot asked in surprise.

"I remembered it from the last time," Arnold said. "I remembered it because it sounded so drastic."

"It only works with blonds," Mrs. Talbot said. "Will you be able to entertain yourself for a while?"

"Easily," Arnold said. "I saw *Anna Karenina*[5] in the library and I think I'll take that and go up to the little house."

"Maybe I'd better come with you," Mrs. Talbot said.

The little house was a one-room studio halfway up the hill, about a hundred feet from the big house, with casement windows[6] on two sides and a Franklin stove.[7] It had been built several years before, after Mrs. Talbot had read *A Room of One's Own,*[8] and by now it had a slightly musty odor which included lingering traces of wood smoke.

---

4. **victrola:** phonograph.
5. ***Anna Karenina:*** novel by Leo Tolstoy.
6. **casement windows:** windows that open on hinges along the side.
7. **Franklin stove:** cast-iron heating stove invented by Benjamin Franklin.
8. ***A Room of One's Own:*** essay by Virginia Woolf.

AT A GLANCE

- Mrs. Talbot tells Arnold that her daughter, Kate, loves the bantams.
- Kate must prepare for her first dancing party.
- Arnold decides to read in "the little house."

1 POINT OF VIEW

Maxwell uses the third-person limited point of view to share Arnold's thoughts and view of the scene.

2 THEME

Mrs. Talbot's mild annoyance of the bantams is overshadowed by her awareness of Kate's love for them. The Talbots respond to animals with affection and concern.

3 THEME

George is allowed to inconvenience the grown-ups: The family accepts him as a child and lets him play wherever he wants.

4 CHARACTERIZATION

Arnold seems to have an exceptional memory for minute details of the Talbots' life.

GUIDED READING

LITERAL QUESTION

1a. What does Mrs. Talbot say Kate feels about the bantams? ("She loves them more than her life.")

INFERENTIAL QUESTION

1b. What can you infer from Mrs. Talbot "putting up" with the crowing on Kate's account? (She is tolerant and easy-going.)

AT A GLANCE

- Arnold hears the song of a wood thrush, and is visited by Duncan, George, and the Talbots' Great Dane.
- Mr. Talbot fears a rat has been burrowing near the little house.
- The family takes Kate to her party.

1 CHARACTERIZATION

Arnold, the city dweller, is more aware of the bird sounds than Mrs. Talbot, who is surrounded by family activity and affection.

2 THEME

Arnold takes special note of the natural fluctuations of family life: The two children move from hostility to affection without difficulty or ado.

3 THEME

Mrs. Talbot perceives the likely consequences of training a tree to grow in an unnatural way.

1 "Hear the wood thrush?" Arnold asked, as Mrs. Talbot threw open the windows for him. They both listened.

"No," she said. "All birds sound alike to me."

"Listen," he said.

This time there was no mistaking it—the liquid notes up and then down the same scale.

"Oh, that," she said. "Yes, I love that," and went off to wash Kate's hair.

From time to time Arnold raised his head from the book he was reading and heard not only the wood thrush but also Duncan and George, quarreling in the meadow. George's voice was shrill and unhappy and sounded as if he were on the verge of tears. Both boys appeared at the window eventually and asked for permission to come in. The little house was out of bounds to them. Arnold nodded. Duncan, who was nine, crawled in without much difficulty, but George had to be hoisted. No sooner were they inside than they began to fight over a wooden gun which had been broken and mended and was rightly George's, it seemed, though Duncan had it and refused to give it up. He refused to give it up one moment, and the next moment, after a sudden change of heart, pressed it upon George—*forced* George to take it, actually, for by that time George was more concerned about the Talbots' dog, who also wanted to come in.

The dog was a Great Dane, very mild but also very enormous. He answered to the name of Satan. Once Satan was admitted to the little house, it became quite full and rather noisy, but John Talbot appeared and sent the dog out and made the children leave Arnold in peace. They left as they had come, by the window. Arnold
2 watched them and was touched by the way Duncan turned and helped George, who was too small to jump. Also by the way George accepted this help. It was as if their hostility had two faces and one of them was the face of love. Cain and Abel,[9] Arnold thought, and the wood thrush. All immortal.

John Talbot lingered outside the little house. Something had been burrowing in the lily-of-the-valley bed, he said, and had also uprooted several lady slippers. Arnold suggested that it might be moles.

"More likely a rat," John Talbot said, and his eyes wandered to a two-foot espaliered[10] pear tree. "That pear tree," he said, "we put in over a year ago."

Mrs. Talbot joined them. She had shampooed not only Kate's hair but her own as well.

"It's still alive," John Talbot said, staring at the pear tree, "but it doesn't put out any leaves."

3 "I should think it would be a shock to a pear tree to be espaliered," Mrs. Talbot said. "Kate's ready to go."

They all piled into the station wagon and took Kate to her party. Her too-short blond hair

9. **Cain and Abel:** In the Old Testament, the sons of Adam and Eve. Cain, the older brother, murdered Abel. Here, the storyteller refers to the childish fighting between the two brothers.
10. **espaliered** [is pal′yərd]: trained to grow flat along a trellis.

GUIDED READING

LITERAL QUESTION

1a. What does Arnold hear from the little house? (the sound of a wood thrush)

INFERENTIAL QUESTION

1b. What does his awareness of the sound tell you about him? (He is especially able to appreciate nature.)

looked quite satisfactory after the egg shampoo, and Mrs. Talbot had made a boutonniere out of a pink geranium and some little blue and white flowers for Kate to wear on her coat. She got out of the car with her suitcase and waved at them from the front steps of the house.

"I hope she has a good time," John Talbot said uneasily as he shifted gears. "It's her first dance with boys. It would be terrible if she didn't have any partners." In his eyes there was a vague threat toward the boys who, in their young callowness, might not appreciate his daughter.

"Kate always has a good time," Mrs. Talbot said. "By the way, have you seen both of the bantam hens today?"

"No," John Talbot said.

"One of them is missing," Mrs. Talbot said.

One of the things that impressed Arnold whenever he stayed with the Talbots was the number and variety of animals they had. Their place was not a farm, after all, but merely a big white brick house in the country, and yet they usually had a dog and a cat, kittens, rabbits, and chickens, all actively involved in the family life. This summer the Talbots weren't able to go in and out by the front door, because a phoebe[11] had built a nest in the porch light. They used the dining-room door instead, and were careful not to leave the porch light on more than a minute or two, lest the eggs be cooked. Arnold came upon some turtle food in his room, and when he asked about it, Mrs. Talbot informed him that there were turtles in the guest room, too. He never came upon the turtles.

The bantams were new this year, and so were the two very small ducklings that at night were put in a paper carton in the sewing room, with an electric light bulb to keep them warm. In the daytime they hopped in and out of a saucer of milk on the terrace. One of them was called Mr. Rochester[12] because of his distinguished air. The other had no name.

All the while that Mrs. Talbot was making conversation with Arnold, after lunch, she kept her eyes on the dog, who, she explained, was jealous of the ducklings. Once his great head swooped down and he pretended to take a nip at them. A nip would have been enough. Mrs. Talbot spoke to him sharply and he turned his head away in shame.

"They probably smell the way George did when he first came home from the hospital," she said.

"What did George smell like?" Arnold asked.

"Sweetish, actually. Actually awful."

"Was Satan jealous of George when he was a baby?"

"Frightfully," Mrs. Talbot said. "Call Satan!" she shouted to her husband, who was up by the little house. He had found a rat hole near the ravaged lady slippers and was setting a trap. He called the dog, and the dog went bounding off, devotion in every leap.

While Mrs. Talbot was telling Arnold how they found Satan at the baby's crib one night, Duncan, who was playing only a few yards away with George, suddenly, and for no apparent reason, made his younger brother cry. Mrs. Talbot got up and separated them.

3 "I wouldn't be surprised if it wasn't time for your nap, George," she said, but he was not willing to let go of even a small part of the day. He wiped his tears away with his fist and ran from her. She ran after him, laughing, and caught him at the foot of the terrace.

Duncan wandered off into a solitary world of his own, and Arnold, after yawning twice, got
4 up and went into the house. Stretched out on the bed in his room, with the Venetian blinds closed, he began to compare the life of the Talbots with his own well-ordered but childless and animal-

11. **phoebe** [fē′bē]: small gray bird.

12. **Mr. Rochester:** major character in Charlotte Brontë's novel *Jane Eyre.* He was an impressive, noble gentleman.

AT A GLANCE

- The family drops Kate off; Mr. Talbot worries that she will not have a good time at the party.
- Mrs. Talbot says that one of the hens is missing.
- Arnold begins to compare the life of the Talbots to his own.

1 PLOT: NARRATIVE HOOK

The announcement of the missing hen injects an element of uncertainty and the possibility of bad news into the happy Talbot home.

2 THEME

All the animals in the Talbot home are "actively involved in the family life." The family's pets symbolize their unity.

3 READING SKILLS: CAUSE AND EFFECT

George's desire to skip his nap and participate in the entire day causes him to shed cranky tears and run off.

4 THEME

Arnold reflects on the well-ordered but solitary life he lives in the city and the hectic but affectionate life he observes and enjoys at the Talbot home.

GUIDED READING

LITERAL QUESTION

1a. What does Arnold think about in his room? (He compares his life in the city with the life of the Talbots.)

INFERENTIAL QUESTION

1b. Do you think he would prefer not to live in the city? (Possible answer: He doesn't seem to crave the country, though he may not be entirely happy with his city routines.)

AT A GLANCE

- Arnold realizes that the Talbots' lives and concerns intersect with one another.
- The whole family respects Kate's sorrow over the loss of her hen.
- The family entertains other guests.
- The family takes Arnold to the train station.

1 STYLE: METAPHOR

The title of the story is a metaphor indirectly comparing the Talbots' lives and acts of affection with visual geometric patterns.

2 THEME

The Talbots' family love forms an intricate pattern in which each life intertwines with all others.

3 CONFLICT

Arnold will return to his own world, which lacks both the "patterns of love" formed by a loving family and the elements of nature he appreciates.

REFLECTING ON THE STORY

Are love's "patterns" simple or complex? Why? (Possible answers: complex, because a person can love many people at once in different ways; simple, because love *can* be clear and straightforward.)

less life in town. Everywhere they go, he thought, they leave tracks behind them, like people walking in the snow. Paths crisscrossing, lines that are perpetually meeting: the mother's loving pursuit of her youngest, the man's love for his daughter, the dog's love for the man, the
1 two boys' preoccupation with each other. Wheels and diagrams, Arnold said to himself. The patterns of love.

That night Arnold was much less bothered by the crowing, which came to him dimly, through dreams. When he awoke finally and was fully awake, he was conscious of the silence and the sun shining in his eyes. His watch had stopped and it was later than he thought. The Talbots had finished breakfast and the Sunday *Times* was waiting beside his place at the table. While he was eating, John Talbot came in and sat down for a minute, across the table. He had been out early that morning, he said, and had found a chipmunk in the rat trap and also a nest with three bantam eggs in it. The eggs were cold.

He was usually a very quiet, self-contained man. This was the first time Arnold had ever seen him disturbed about anything. "I don't know how we're going to tell Kate," he said. "She'll be very upset."

Kate came home sooner than they expected her, on the bus. She came up the driveway, lugging her suitcase.

"Did you have a good time?" Mrs. Talbot called to her from the terrace.

"Yes," she said, "I had a beautiful time."

Arnold looked at the two boys, expecting them to blurt out the tragedy as soon as Kate put down her suitcase, but they didn't. It was her father who told her, in such a roundabout way that she didn't seem to understand at all what he was saying. Mrs. Talbot interrupted him with the flat facts; the bantam hen was not on her nest and therefore, in all probability, had been killed, maybe by the rat.

Kate went into the house. The others remained on the terrace. The dog didn't snap at the ducklings, though his mind was on them still,
2 and the two boys didn't quarrel. In spite of the patterns on which they seem so intent, Arnold thought, what happens to one of them happens to all. They are helplessly involved in Kate's loss.

At noon other guests arrived, two families with children. There was a picnic, with hot dogs and bowls of salad, cake, and wine, out under the grape arbor. When the guests departed, toward the end of the afternoon, the family came together again on the terrace. Kate was lying on the ground, on her stomach, with her face resting on her arms, her head practically in the ducklings' saucer of milk. Mrs. Talbot, who had stretched out on the garden chaise longue,[13] discovered suddenly that Mr. Rochester was missing. She sat up in alarm and cried, "Where is he?"

"Down my neck," Kate said.

The duck emerged from her crossed arms. He crawled around them and climbed up on the back of her neck. Kate smiled. The sight of the duck's tiny downy head among her pale ash-blond curls made them all burst out laughing. The cloud that had been hanging over the household evaporated into bright sunshine, and Arnold seized that moment to glance surreptitiously at his watch.

They all went to the train with him, including the dog. At the last moment Mrs. Talbot, out of a sudden perception of his lonely life, tried to give him some radishes, but he refused them. When he stepped out of the car at the station, the boys were arguing and were with dif-
3 ficulty persuaded to say goodbye to him. He watched the station wagon drive away and then stood listening for the sound of the wood thrush. But, of course, in the center of South Norwalk[14] there was no such sound.

---

13. **chaise longue** [shāz′ lông′]: chair with a long seat that supports the legs.
14. **South Norwalk:** small industrial city in Connecticut.

GUIDED READING

LITERAL QUESTIONS

1a. When the Talbots tell Kate of the death of her hen, how do the two boys behave? (They neither blurt out the tragedy nor quarrel.)

2a. What does Arnold listen for at the end of the story? (the sound of the wood thrush)

INFERENTIAL QUESTIONS

1b. What does the family's reaction to the death of the hen tell you about them? (They respect Kate's sorrow; they are involved in each other's lives.)

2b. What does the fact that Arnold listens for the sound of the wood thrush suggest about him? (He wishes he could establish for himself a kind of communion with natural things.)

STUDY QUESTIONS

Recalling

1. Animals in the story are treated with affection and concern, almost as members of the family. Give three examples from the story of this attitude toward animals.
2. What happens to distract Arnold from his reading in "the little house"? Who finally restores peace?
3. What news is broken to Kate near the end of the story? According to Arnold, what do the reactions of the family to this news tell us about the family relationships?

Interpreting

4. Give evidence from the story to show why Arnold's yearly visits with the Talbots are important to him.
5. Why is "the little house" important to Mrs. Talbot? What does its importance tell us about her?
6. Considering what he says about his life in the city, why is Arnold more likely to notice the songs of birds and the sounds of the children than his hosts are?

Extending

7. In the story a single man from the city shares a weekend with a family in the country. What benefits can be achieved when people who have very different life styles share experiences with each other?

VIEWPOINT

Many of William Maxwell's stories have rural settings. Reviewing a collection of his stories, the *New York Times* said:

> Hope and joy, frequently represented by their traditional symbols of music, birds, and trees, appear as the good things of life; the bad things are often in the form of possessions made and paid for by men.

■ Explain how the good things in life are pictured in "The Patterns of Love." What hints does the story contain about the bad things in life?

LITERARY FOCUS

Details of Setting

The **setting** of a story is the place and time in which the story happens. The setting is described so that we can picture the scene and enter the world of the story. Since a story is usually short, the author must choose specific details of description that will inspire our imagination to fill in the rest. For example, in "A Mother in Manville" (page 48) the woman mentions "the flaming of maples in October." This one telling detail helps us to imagine much more about the North Carolina countryside.

The details that are used to sketch a setting need not be only visual, for the author may successfully appeal to any of our senses. For example, the sense of sound might be important in a story about a violent storm.

Whatever the details of setting are, they have an impact on the characters. For example, most people act differently in different settings—in school, at home, in a house of worship.

Thinking About Setting

1. List five details of the setting that tell a great deal about the Talbot family. Be sure that at least two examples are details that appeal to a sense other than sight.
2. What hints does the story give that Arnold acts differently while staying with the Talbots than he does at home?

COMPOSITION

Writing About Setting

■ Explain how the setting of "The Patterns of Love" reveals the characters in the story. You may want to consider the following: (a) the kinds of descriptive details used, (b) the effect of their surroundings on the Talbot children, and (c) the effect of the setting on Arnold. *For help with this assignment, see Lesson 5 in the Writing About Literature Handbook at the back of this book.*

Writing a Description

■ Close your eyes, and imagine or recall a place that can be recognized by its sounds. Emphasizing details of sound, write a description of a place, such as a jungle, a classroom, or a beach.

STUDY QUESTIONS

1. Kate watches hens fondly; dog rides to depot; turtles in the guest room; ducklings put in bulb-lit carton
2. the boys and dog; Mr. Talbot
3. hen is missing; they're closely connected
4. he's alone; he appreciates natural surroundings and family life
5. She needs privacy.
6. He is unaccustomed to them.
7. They may gain new perspectives and achieve greater understanding of other life styles.

VIEWPOINT

- *good*—the country, children, pets, song of wood thrush
- *bad*—city life; loneliness

LITERARY FOCUS

1. *Sight*—"little house," nest, pear tree, turtles; *sound*—rooster's crow, dog's bark, song of thrush; *smell*—wood smoke, smell of ducklings
2. He oversleeps, adapts to disorder.

COMPOSITION: GUIDELINES FOR EVALUATION

WRITING ABOUT SETTING

Objective

To show how setting reveals character

Guidelines for Evaluation

- suggested length: three to four paragraphs
- should state relationship between setting and characterization in thesis statement
- should use specific examples from story

WRITING A DESCRIPTION

Objective

To describe a place with auditory details

Guidelines for Evaluation

- suggested length: one paragraph
- should establish place
- should use images that appeal to the sense of hearing

AT A GLANCE

- Berl and Berlcha live in Lentshin, a tiny village in Poland.
- Their son, Samuel, went to America forty years ago and sends them money, which they do not spend.
- Although poor, they are content.

LITERARY OPTIONS

- setting
- conflict
- irony

THEMATIC OPTIONS

- spiritual vs. material wealth
- relationships between generations
- hopes and ideals

1 SETTING

The tiny village setting is central to the story: Only in such a place would the isolated self-sufficiency of the people seem plausible.

2 CONFLICT

The central conflict of the story is presented as one between two ways of life: Samuel's and that of the Lentshin villagers.

3 THEME

Although the old couple have little material wealth, they feel they have all that they need.

Photograph © 1982 by Jill Krementz

Isaac Bashevis Singer (born 1904) immigrated to the United States from Poland in 1935. Many of his stories and novels contrast the life style of a small European village with the metropolitan life style of the United States. In this story, translated by the author and Dorothea Strauss, Singer draws a vivid picture of the Old World.

■ A famous writer once said, "You can't go home again"—a remark that may apply to Samuel in this story. What does it mean?

Isaac Bashevis Singer

The Son from America

1 The village of Lentshin was tiny—a sandy marketplace where the peasants of the area met once a week. It was surrounded by little huts with thatched roofs or shingles green with moss. The chimneys looked like pots. Between the huts there were fields, where the owners planted vegetables or pastured their goats.

In the smallest of these huts lived old Berl, a man in his eighties, and his wife, who was called Berlcha (wife of Berl). Old Berl was one of the Jews who had been driven from their villages in Russia and had settled in Poland. In Lentshin, they mocked the mistakes he made while praying aloud. He spoke with a sharp "r." He was short, broad-shouldered, and had a small white beard, and summer and winter he wore a sheepskin hat, a padded cotton jacket, and stout boots. He walked slowly, shuffling his feet. He had a half acre of field, a cow, a goat, and chickens.

2 The couple had a son, Samuel, who had gone to America forty years ago. It was said in Lentshin that he became a millionaire there. Every month, the Lentshin letter carrier brought old Berl a money order and a letter that no one could read because many of the words were English. How much money Samuel sent his parents remained a secret. Three times a year, Berl and his wife went on foot to Zakroczym and cashed the
3 money orders there. But they never seemed to use the money. What for? The garden, the cow, and the goat provided most of their needs. Besides, Berlcha sold chickens and eggs, and from these there was enough to buy flour for bread.

No one cared to know where Berl kept the money that his son sent him. There were no thieves in Lentshin. The hut consisted of one room, which contained all their belongings: the table, the shelf for meat, the shelf for milk foods, the two beds, and the clay oven. Sometimes the chickens roosted in the woodshed and sometimes, when it was cold, in a coop near the oven. The goat, too, found shelter inside when the weather was bad. The more prosperous villagers had kerosene lamps, but Berl and his wife did not believe in newfangled gadgets. What was wrong with a wick in a dish of oil? Only for the Sabbath would Berlcha buy three tallow candles at the store. In summer, the couple got up at sunrise and retired with the chickens. In the long

GUIDED READING

LITERAL QUESTION

1a. Why doesn't anyone steal Berl's money? (There are no thieves in Lentshin.)

INFERENTIAL QUESTION

1b. What does this tell you about the village? (Everyone feels they have all they need, so there is no reason to steal.)

winter evenings, Berlcha spun flax[1] at her spinning wheel and Berl sat beside her in the silence of those who enjoy their rest.

Once in a while when Berl came home from the synagogue[2] after evening prayers, he brought news to his wife. In Warsaw there were strikers who demanded that the czar[3] abdicate. A heretic by the name of Dr. Herzl had come up with the idea that Jews should settle again in Palestine.[4] Berlcha listened and shook her bonneted head. Her face was yellowish and wrinkled like a cabbage leaf. There were bluish sacks under her eyes. She was half deaf. Berl had to repeat each word he said to her. She would say, "The things that happen in the big cities!"

Here in Lentshin nothing happened except usual events: a cow gave birth to a calf, a young couple had a bris,[5] or a girl was born and there was no party. Occasionally, someone died. Lentshin had no cemetery, and the corpse had to be taken to Zakroczym. Actually, Lentshin had become a village with few young people. The young men left for Zakroczym, for Nowy Dwor, for Warsaw, and sometimes for the United States. Like Samuel's, their letters were illegible, the Yiddish[6] mixed with the languages of the countries where they were now living. They sent photographs in which the men wore top hats and the women fancy dresses like squiresses.

Berl and Berlcha also received such photographs. But their eyes were failing and neither he nor she had glasses. They could barely make out the pictures. Samuel had sons and daughters with Gentile[7] names—and grandchildren who had married and had their own offspring. Their names were so strange that Berl and Berlcha could never remember them. But what difference do names make? America was far, far away on the other side of the ocean, at the edge of the world. A Talmud[8] teacher who came to Lentshin had said that Americans walked with their heads down and their feet up. Berl and Berlcha could not grasp this. How was it possi-
3 ble? But since the teacher said so it must be true. Berlcha pondered for some time and then she said, "One can get accustomed to everything."

And so it remained. From too much thinking—God forbid—one may lose one's wits.

One Friday morning, when Berlcha was kneading the dough for the Sabbath loaves, the
4 door opened and a nobleman entered. He was so tall that he had to bend down to get through the door. He wore a beaver hat and a cloak bordered with fur. He was followed by Chazkel, the coachman from Zakroczym, who carried two leather valises with brass locks. In astonishment Berlcha raised her eyes.

The nobleman looked around and said to the coachman in Yiddish, "Here it is." He took out a silver ruble[9] and paid him. The coachman tried to hand him change but he said, "You can go now."

5 When the coachman closed the door, the nobleman said, "Mother, it's me, your son Samuel—Sam."

Berlcha heard the words and her legs grew numb. Her hands, to which pieces of dough were sticking, lost their power. The nobleman

1. **flax:** fiber made from the stem of a plant.
2. **synagogue** [sin'ə gog']: building used by Jews for worship and religious instruction.
3. **czar** [zär]: title of the rulers of Russia until the revolution in 1917. Russia governed Poland at the time of the story.
4. **A heretic . . . Palestine:** Theodor Herzl (1860–1904) was the founder of Zionism, the movement to establish a Jewish state in Palestine, the biblical homeland of the Jews. Berlcha considers him a heretic, or one who believes doctrines that are not officially accepted, because his ideas had not yet been widely accepted.
5. **bris:** Jewish ritual and party accompanying the birth of a male child.
6. **Yiddish:** language that is a combination of German, Hebrew, and Slavic. It is spoken by eastern European Jews.
7. **Gentile** [jen'tīl]: person who is not a Jew, usually a Christian.
8. **Talmud** [täl'mo͞od]: collection of Jewish civil and religious laws. A Talmud teacher explains the complications of the law to the people.
9. **ruble** [ro͞o'bəl]: unit of money in Russia and, here, in Russian-occupied Poland.

AT A GLANCE

- Berl and Berlcha know little about the outside world.
- They have received photos from Samuel, but their eyes are weak.
- Samuel visits them.
- His mother mistakes him for a nobleman.

1 SETTING

The backwardness of the village is shown in the couple's limited awareness of events.

2 THEME

The villagers are content with their tiny, static, insular world where little changes.

3 TONE

Through the depiction of Berlcha's superstitiousness, the author gently mocks the villagers' simple ways.

4 STYLE: IMAGERY

That Berlcha believes it is a "tall nobleman" who enters her hut indicates that this person has "outgrown" the tiny village.

5 PLOT: NARRATIVE HOOK

Samuel's arrival sets the stage for the conflict between two different ways of life.

GUIDED READING

LITERAL QUESTIONS

1a. How do the villagers learn about the outside world? (They learn at the synagogue and from wandering Talmud teachers.)

2a. What does Samuel look like when he arrives at his parents' hut? (He is tall, well dressed, and has two leather valises.)

INFERENTIAL QUESTIONS

1b. Why is this significant? (It shows that the villagers are isolated and generally ignorant of the outside world.)

2b. What does the description of Samuel's appearance tell you about him? (He is vividly different from the villagers; he has come from another culture.)

AT A GLANCE

- Samuel greets his mother, then his awestruck father.
- Berlcha worries about finishing Sabbath preparations; Samuel helps her.

1 CONFLICT

Berl does not recognize his son; his first reaction is confusion and anger.

2 POINT OF VIEW

Singer's omniscient narrator relates both parents' amazement.

3 BACKGROUND

By Jewish tradition no work can be done from sundown on Friday to sundown on Saturday. Berlcha worries about having insufficient time to prepare because of the early sunset in winter.

hugged her, kissed her forehead, both her cheeks. Berlcha began to cackle like a hen, "My son!" At that moment Berl came in from the woodshed, his arms piled with logs. The goat
1 followed him. When he saw a nobleman kissing his wife, Berl dropped the wood and exclaimed, "What is this?"

The nobleman let go of Berlcha and embraced Berl. "Father!"

For a long time Berl was unable to utter a sound. He wanted to recite holy words that he had read in the Yiddish Bible, but he could remember nothing. Then he asked, "Are you Samuel?"

"Yes, Father, I am Samuel."

"Well, peace be with you." Berl grasped his son's hand. He was still not sure that he was not being fooled. Samuel wasn't as tall and heavy as this man, but then Berl reminded himself that Samuel was only fifteen years old when he had left home. He must have grown in that faraway country. Berl asked, "Why didn't you let us know that you were coming?"

"Didn't you receive my cable?" Samuel asked.

Berl did not know what a cable was.

Berlcha had scraped the dough from her hands and enfolded her son. He kissed her again and asked, "Mother, didn't you receive a cable?"

2 "What? If I lived to see this, I am happy to die," Berlcha said, amazed by her own words. Berl, too, was amazed. These were just the words he would have said earlier if he had been able to remember. After a while Berl came to himself and said, "Pescha, you will have to make a double Sabbath pudding in addition to the stew."

It was years since Berl had called Berlcha by her given name. When he wanted to address her, he would say, "Listen," or "Say." It is the young or those from the big cities who call a wife by her name. Only now did Berlcha begin to cry. Yellow tears ran from her eyes, and everything
3 became dim. Then she called out, "It's Friday—I have to prepare for the Sabbath." Yes, she had to knead the dough and braid the loaves. With such a guest, she had to make a larger Sabbath stew. The winter day is short and she must hurry.

Her son understood what was worrying her, because he said, "Mother, I will help you."

Berlcha wanted to laugh, but a choked sob came out. "What are you saying? God forbid."

The nobleman took off his cloak and jacket and remained in his vest, on which hung a solid-gold watch chain. He rolled up his sleeves and came to the trough. "Mother, I was a baker for

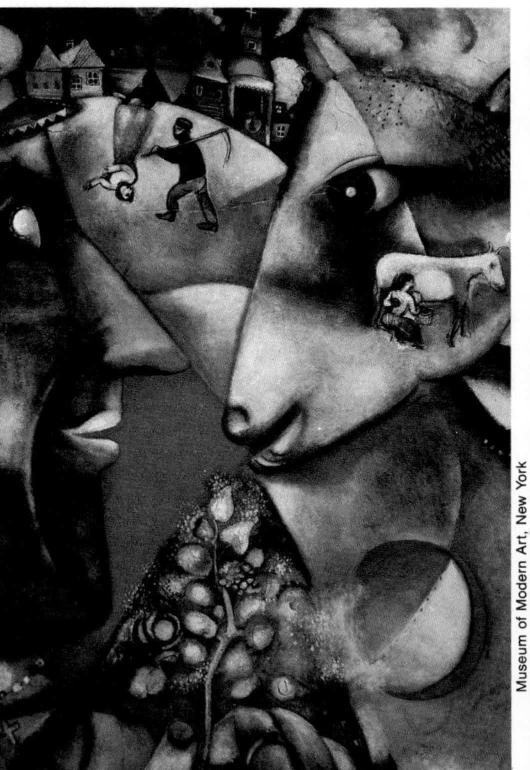

Museum of Modern Art, New York

Detail,
I and My Village,
Marc Chagall
(1887–1985).

GUIDED READING

LITERAL QUESTION

1a. Why doesn't Berl recognize his son? (He still thinks of Samuel as he was when he left home at fifteen.)

INFERENTIAL QUESTION

1b. What does this tell you about Berl's sense of time and change? (Time has stood still for Berl.)

many years in New York," he said, and he began to knead the dough.

"What! You are my darling son who will say Kaddish[10] for me." She wept raspingly. Her strength left her, and she slumped onto the bed.

Berl said, "Women will always be women." And he went to the shed to get more wood. The goat sat down near the oven; she gazed with surprise at this strange man—his height and his bizarre clothes.

1 The neighbors had heard the good news that Berl's son had arrived from America and they came to greet him. The women began to help Berlcha prepare for the Sabbath. Some laughed, some cried. The room was full of people, as at a wedding. They asked Berl's son, "What is new in America?" And Berl's son answered, "America is all right."

"Do Jews make a living?"

"One eats white bread there on weekdays."

"Do they remain Jews?"

"I am not a Gentile."

2 After Berlcha blessed the candles, father and son went to the little synagogue across the street. A new snow had fallen. The son took large steps, but Berl warned him, "Slow down."

In the synagogue the Jews recited "Let Us Exult" and "Come, My Groom." All the time, the snow outside kept falling. After prayers, when Berl and Samuel left the Holy Place, the village was unrecognizable. Everything was covered in snow. One could see only the contours of the roofs and the candles in the windows. Samuel said, "Nothing has changed here."

Berlcha had prepared gefilte fish,[11] chicken soup with rice, meat, carrot stew. Berl recited the benediction over a glass of ritual wine. The family ate and drank, and when it grew quiet for a while one could hear the chirping of the house cricket. The son talked a lot, but Berl and Berlcha understood little. His Yiddish was different and contained foreign words.

After the final blessing Samuel asked, "Father, what did you do with all the money I sent you?"

Berl raised his white brows. "It's here."

"Didn't you put it in a bank?"

"There is no bank in Lentshin."

"Where do you keep it?"

Berl hesitated. "One is not allowed to touch money on the Sabbath, but I will show you." He crouched beside the bed and began to shove something heavy. A boot appeared. Its top was stuffed with straw. Berl removed the straw and the son saw that the boot was full of gold coins. He lifted it.

"Father, this is a treasure!" he called out.

"Well."

3 "Why didn't you spend it?"

"On what? Thank God, we have everything."

"Why didn't you travel somewhere?"

"Where to? This is our home."

The son asked one question after the other, but Berl's answer was always the same: they wanted for nothing. The garden, the cow, the goat, the chickens provided them with all they needed. The son said, "If thieves knew about this, your lives wouldn't be safe."

"There are no thieves here."

"What will happen to the money?"

"You take it."

Slowly, Berl and Berlcha grew accustomed to their son and his American Yiddish. Berlcha could hear him better now. She even recognized

4 his voice. He was saying, "Perhaps we should build a larger synagogue."

"The synagogue is big enough," Berl replied.

"Perhaps a home for old people."

"No one sleeps in the street."

The next day after the Sabbath meal was eaten, a Gentile from Zakroczym brought a paper—it was the cable. Berl and Berlcha lay down for a nap. They soon began to snore. The goat, too, dozed off. The son put on his cloak

10. **Kaddish** [kä'dish]: Jewish hymn of mourning sung especially by a son for a deceased parent.

11. **gefilte** [gə fil'tə] **fish:** cakes made of fish chopped and mixed with other ingredients.

AT A GLANCE

- Neighbors help Berlcha and ask Samuel about America.
- Samuel discovers that his parents have never spent the money he sent them.
- Berl says that he and Berlcha have everything they want.

1 THEME

Neighbors treat Samuel's arrival as an occasion, and the women help Berlcha. The villagers' self-sufficiency contributes to their sense of satisfaction.

2 CHARACTERIZATION

Even Samuel's stride has "outgrown" the tiny village of his boyhood.

3 THEME

Although Samuel's parents live very simply and seem to have nothing, they believe they have "everything."

4 CONFLICT

Samuel cannot accept the view that the villagers lack nothing; from his perspective they lack many progressive things.

GUIDED READING

LITERAL QUESTIONS

1a. What do the neighbors do when they hear of Samuel's arrival? (They visit with him, and the women help Berlcha prepare dinner.)

2a. What does Samuel learn about the money he has sent his parents? (It was never spent.)

INFERENTIAL QUESTIONS

1b. What do their actions tell you about the villagers' involvement in each other's lives? (They feel a strong sense of community.)

2b. Why is Samuel amazed at this fact? (He has assumed that they need his help.)

AT A GLANCE

- A man in the synagogue tells Samuel that contentment is the greatest wealth.
- Samuel realizes that his plans for the village are pointless.

1 IRONY

The old man has never associated "living" with material wealth. The fact that he does "not understand" ironically underscores what Samuel has never understood: Good health and contentment are the keys to a good life.

REFLECTING ON THE STORY

What would make Berl and Berlcha proud of their son? (They would probably be proud if they saw in him a sense of true happiness and gratitude for the basic necessities of life.)

STUDY QUESTIONS

1. table, shelves, two beds, oven, chicken coop, oil bowl and wick, spinning wheel, goat
2. tall, fur hat and cloak, gold watch chain, valises
3. Their land and animals provide all they need; hidden it in a boot
4. He has outgrown the village.
5. They have all they need.
6.
   - old man: staying alive
   - Samuel: salary, wealth

and his hat and went for a walk. He strode with his long legs across the marketplace. He stretched out a hand and touched a roof. He wanted to smoke a cigar, but he remembered it was forbidden on the Sabbath. He had a desire to talk to someone, but it seemed that the whole of Lentshin was asleep. He entered the synagogue. An old man was sitting there, reciting psalms. Samuel asked, "Are you praying?"

"What else is there to do when one gets old?"

1 "Do you make a living?"

The old man did not understand the meaning of these words. He smiled, showing his empty gums, and then he said, "If God gives health, one keeps on living."

Samuel returned home. Dusk had fallen. Berl went to the synagogue for the evening prayers and the son remained with his mother. The room was filled with shadows.

Berlcha began to recite in a solemn singsong, "God of Abraham, Isaac, and Jacob,[12] defend the poor people of Israel and Thy name. The Holy Sabbath is departing; the welcome week is coming to us. Let it be one of health, wealth, and good deeds."

"Mother, you don't need to pray for wealth," Samuel said. "You are wealthy already."

Berlcha did not hear—or pretended not to. Her face had turned into a cluster of shadows.

In the twilight Samuel put his hand into his jacket pocket and touched his passport, his checkbook, his letters of credit. He had come here with big plans. He had a valise filled with presents for his parents. He wanted to bestow gifts on the village. He brought not only his own money but funds from the Lentshin Society in New York, which had organized a ball for the benefit of the village. But this village in the hinterland needed nothing. From the synagogue one could hear hoarse chanting. The cricket, silent all day, started again its chirping. Berlcha began to sway and utter holy rhymes inherited from mothers and grandmothers:

Thy holy sheep
In mercy keep,
In Torah[13] and good deeds;
Provide for all their needs,
Shoes, clothes, and bread
And the Messiah's tread.

12. **Abraham, Isaac, and Jacob:** figures from the Old Testament, the original fathers or ancestors of the Jewish people. Abraham was the father of Isaac, who was the father of Jacob.

13. **Torah** [tôr'ə]: body of Jewish religious thinking and law, collected from scripture and tradition. Berlcha is praying that God help His people follow the law.

STUDY QUESTIONS

Recalling

1. List the things that can be found inside the tiny one-room hut of the old couple.
2. Find four details of Samuel's appearance that lead Berlcha to think that her son is a nobleman.
3. Explain why the old couple seldom use money. What have they done with the money Samuel has sent them?

Interpreting

4. In what way does the detail about Samuel's height illustrate his relationship to his native village?
5. Lentshin contains no thieves, and no old people sleep in the streets. What do these facts teach us about the people who live in the village?
6. Find the conversation in which Samuel asks the old man if he makes a living. How would Samuel

and the old man each define the word *living* according to this conversation?

Extending

7. At the end of the story, Samuel realizes that his parents and the village do not need his money and his help. What lesson does Samuel learn about people and about life?

LITERARY FOCUS

Setting and Atmosphere

Setting is more important in some stories than in others because some stories could take place almost anywhere or at any time. For example, a simple story about people getting to know each other could take place in ancient Rome or in a modern American city. In some stories, however, the setting is more than a background for the action. Setting can help us to understand the people in the story; it can influence what happens in the story.

When the setting is important, the author usually describes it in detail at the beginning, and the setting then creates an **atmosphere**, or mood, that runs through the entire story. "The Son from America" has a slightly unrealistic, country atmosphere that reminds us of a folk tale about the lives of ordinary rural people. In other words, the atmosphere seems to produce certain kinds of characters who reflect that atmosphere.

To decide the importance of the setting to a story, ask this question: "Could this story take place anywhere else?"

Thinking About Setting

- Would you be able to believe this story if it took place in a larger village or a village that is closer to a big city? Why or why not?

VOCABULARY

Word Origins

The origin and history of a word is called its **etymology**. You can find a word's etymology in a dictionary by reading the information that is usually given in brackets [ ] just before or after the definitions. The information includes the spelling and meaning of the word in each language from which it develops. A dictionary would print the etymology for the word *sabbath* as follows:

> **Sab · bath** (sab'əth) *n.* [Latin *sabbatum* the Jewish Sabbath, from Greek *sabbaton,* from Hebrew *sabbāth* rest, the Jewish Sabbath.]
> —*Macmillan Dictionary*

This entry tells us that the word appeared in Latin, in Greek, and, earliest of all, in Hebrew.

Czar was the title of the Russian emperors who ruled until 1917. If you look up *czar,* you will see that *czar* comes from the Latin word *Caesar,* which was the title of the ancient Roman emperors.

Not all words have come to us from or through Latin. Look up *hinterland.* Where has this word come from? Write what you find out about its etymology.

Using a dictionary, answer the questions about the following words from "The Son from America":

abdicate	gentile	tallow
exult	synagogue	

1. Which word comes from Middle Low German?
2. Which word has a French background?
3. Which word comes from the Latin word meaning "to leap"?
4. Which word is related to the Latin word *dicare*?
5. Which word comes from a Greek word meaning "to bring together"?

COMPOSITION

Writing About Setting

- Explain how the setting of "The Son from America" helps to reveal the personalities of the characters. What do we learn about the old couple from their cabin and from their village? *For help with this assignment, see Lesson 5 in the Writing About Literature Handbook at the back of this book.*

Writing a Description

- Reread the first and fourth paragraphs of the story. Notice how carefully the author creates a picture of the town of Lentshin and the hut of Samuel's parents. Imagine that you are Samuel's father and have returned with Samuel to the United States for a short visit. Write a letter to your wife, Berlcha, describing in detail either the city that Samuel lives in or Samuel's house.

STUDY QUESTIONS

7. People can be content with less than he considered necessary.

LITERARY FOCUS

Larger villages would probably be less self-sufficient than Lentshin. People would be less superstitious and more aware of world events.

VOCABULARY

- hinterland: from German *Hinterland,* back country; from *hinter,* behind + *land,* land
- from Middle Low German: tallow
- from French: gentile
- from Latin "to leap": exult
- from Latin *dicare:* abdicate
- from Greek "to bring together": synagogue

COMPOSITION: GUIDELINES FOR EVALUATION

WRITING ABOUT SETTING

Objective

To show how setting reveals character

Guidelines for Evaluation

- suggested length: two to three paragraphs
- should contain a thesis statement
- should explain how hut reveals personalities of the old couple
- should make specific references to the story

WRITING A DESCRIPTION

Objective

To write a letter containing a description

Guidelines for Evaluation

- suggested length: 200–400 words
- should use personal letter form
- should assume the persona of Berl
- should describe several details of Samuel's city or home

AT A GLANCE

- On a winter night Ulrich von Gradwitz hunts his neighbor Georg Znaeym, who he suspects is poaching on his land.
- For three generations the two families have feuded over a narrow strip of land.

LITERARY OPTIONS

- setting
- conflict
- characterization

THEMATIC OPTIONS

- neighbors should live in peace
- friendship and love
- responding to nature

1 POINT OF VIEW

The omniscient narrator concisely states background details for the reader.

2 CONFLICT

The external conflict between Ulrich von Gradwitz and Georg Znaeym is the basis for the entire story. It continues a long conflict between two families.

3 SETTING

The story's setting—a dark forest in the Carpathian mountains on a cold, dark, "wind-scourged" winter night—underscores the sense of impending trouble.

Saki is the pen name of Hector Hugh Munro (1870–1916). Once a famous London journalist, Munro is now best known for stories that end with surprise twists. "The Interlopers" is one of his most famous stories.

■ When is it appropriate to help an enemy?

Saki

The Interlopers

In a forest of mixed growth somewhere on the eastern spurs of the Carpathians,[1] a man stood one winter night watching and listening, as though he waited for some beast of the woods to come within the range of his vision and, later, of his rifle. But the game for whose presence he kept so keen an outlook was none that figured in the sportsman's calendar as lawful and proper for the chase; Ulrich von Gradwitz[2] patrolled the dark forest in quest of a human enemy.

The forest lands of Gradwitz were of wide extent and well stocked with game; the narrow strip of precipitous woodland that lay on its outskirt was not remarkable for the game it harbored or the shooting it afforded, but it was the most jealously guarded of all its owner's ter-
1 ritorial possessions. A famous lawsuit, in the days of his grandfather, had wrested it from the illegal possession of a neighboring family of petty landowners; the dispossessed party had never acquiesced in the judgment of the Courts, and a long series of poaching[3] affrays and similar scandals had embittered the relationships between
2 the families for three generations. The neighbor feud had grown into a personal one since Ulrich had come to be head of his family; if there was a man in the world whom he detested and wished ill to it was Georg Znaeym,[4] the inheritor of the quarrel and the tireless game-snatcher and raider of the disputed border forest. The feud might, perhaps, have died down or been compromised if the personal ill-will of the two men had not stood in the way; as boys they had thirsted for one another's blood, as men each prayed that
3 misfortune might fall on the other; and this wind-scourged winter night Ulrich had banded together his foresters to watch the dark forest, not in quest of four-footed quarry, but to keep a lookout for the prowling thieves whom he suspected of being afoot from across the land boundary. The roebuck,[5] which usually kept in the sheltered hollows during a storm wind, were running like driven things tonight, and there was movement and unrest among the creatures that were wont to sleep through the dark hours. Assuredly there was a disturbing element in the

1. **Carpathians** [kär pā'thē ənz]: mountain range in central and eastern Europe.
2. **Ulrich von Gradwitz** [ool'rik fôn gräd'vitz]
3. **poaching** [pōch'ing]: hunting or fishing on another person's property. At one time in Europe, poaching was considered a severe crime.
4. **Georg Znaeym** [gā'ôrg znä'im]
5. **roebuck** [rō'buk']: male roe, small deer from Europe and northern Asia.

GUIDED READING

LITERAL QUESTION

1a. How do the forest animals behave? (Roebuck are "running like driven things" and other animals are awake and uneasy.)

INFERENTIAL QUESTION

1b. In what way does the animals' behavior contribute to the story's atmosphere? (Their unrest creates a sense of danger and suspense.)

forest, and Ulrich could guess the quarter from whence it came.

He strayed away by himself from the watchers whom he had placed in ambush on the crest of the hill and wandered far down the steep slopes amid the wild tangle of undergrowth, peering through the tree trunks and listening through the whistling and skirling of the wind and the restless beating of the branches for sight or sound of the marauders. If only on this wild night, in this dark, lone spot, he might come across Georg Znaeym, man to man, with none to witness—that was the wish that was uppermost in his thoughts. And as he stepped round the trunk of a huge beech he came face to face with the man he sought.

The two enemies stood glaring at one another for a long silent moment. Each had a rifle in his hand, each had hate in his heart and murder uppermost in his mind. The chance had come to give full play to the passions of a lifetime. But a man who has been brought up under the code of a restraining civilization cannot easily nerve himself to shoot down his neighbor in cold blood and without word spoken, except for an offense against his hearth and honor. And before the moment of hesitation had given way to action a deed of Nature's own violence overwhelmed them both. A fierce shriek of the storm had been answered by a splitting crash over their heads, and ere they could leap aside a mass of falling beech tree had thundered down on them. Ulrich von Gradwitz found himself stretched on the ground, one arm numb beneath him and the other held almost as helplessly in a tight tangle of forked branches, while both legs were pinned beneath the fallen mass. His heavy shooting boots had saved his feet from being crushed to pieces, but if his fractures were not as serious as they might have been, at least it was evident that he could not move from his present position till someone came to release him. The descending twigs had slashed the skin of his face, and he had to wink away some drops of blood from his eyelashes before he could take in a general view of
4 the disaster. At his side, so near that under ordinary circumstances he could almost have touched him, lay Georg Znaeym, alive and struggling, but obviously as helplessly pinioned down as himself. All round them lay a thick-strewn wreckage of splintered branches and broken twigs.

Relief at being alive and exasperation at his captive plight brought a strange medley of pious thank-offerings and sharp curses to Ulrich's lips. Georg, who was nearly blinded with the blood which trickled across his eyes, stopped his struggling for a moment to listen and then gave a short, snarling laugh.

"So you're not killed, as you ought to be, but you're caught, anyway," he cried; "caught fast.
5 Ho, what a jest, Ulrich von Gradwitz snared in his stolen forest. There's real justice for you!"

And he laughed again, mockingly and savagely.

"I'm caught in my own forest land," retorted Ulrich. "When my men come to release us you will wish, perhaps, that you were in a better plight than caught poaching on a neighbor's land, shame on you."

Georg was silent for a moment; then he answered quietly:

"Are you sure that your men will find much to release? I have men, too, in the forest tonight, close behind me, and *they* will be here first and do the releasing. When they drag me out from under these branches it won't need much clumsiness on their part to roll this mass of trunk right over on the top of you. Your men will find you dead under a fallen beech tree. For form's sake I shall send my condolences to your family."

"It is a useful hint," said Ulrich fiercely. "My men had orders to follow in ten minutes' time, seven of which must have gone by already, and when they get me out—I will remember the hint. Only as you will have met your death poaching on my lands I don't think I can decently send any message of condolence to your family."

AT A GLANCE

- Ulrich and Georg meet under a huge beech tree.
- The wind knocks the tree on top of them.
- Pinned by the tree, tney exchange insults and threats.
- Each man asserts that his foresters will rescue him first.

1 PLOT: NARRATIVE HOOK

When the two enemies meet face-to-face, the narrative's suspense is heightened.

2 IRONY

Ulrich and Georg do not shoot each other in cold blood because the "code of a restraining civilization" prevents them. Ironically, that code has also allowed them to hunt each other like animals.

3 SETTING

The code of civilization is meaningless before nature's power.

4 PLOT: RISING ACTION

Ulrich realizes that he and his enemy are pinned to the ground at an unnerving proximity.

5 CONFLICT

The two enemies exchange insults and threats, each asserting the justice of his claim to the land.

GUIDED READING

LITERAL QUESTION

1a. How do the two men speak to each other when they are pinned by the tree? What do they say? (They exchange insults and threats and each bluffs about the nearness of his foresters.)

INFERENTIAL QUESTION

1b. What does this tell you about them? (They hate each other; their boasting emphasizes the feud's bitterness; they attempt to intimidate each other.)

AT A GLANCE

- The men continue their threats.
- Ulrich drinks from his wine flask and offers some to Georg.

1 SYMBOL

Both men have been held down by their mutual hatred, much as they are now pinned down by the tree.

2 CHARACTERIZATION

Ulrich is a dynamic character: As he begins to realize his "enemy's" humanity, he feels pity for him.

Return from the Hunt, 1565, Pieter Brueghel. Kunsthistorisches Museum, Vienna.

"Good," snarled Georg, "good. We fight this quarrel out to the death, you and I and our foresters, with no cursed interlopers to come between us. Death and damnation to you, Ulrich von Gradwitz."

"The same to you, Georg Znaeym, forest-thief, game-snatcher."

Both men spoke with the bitterness of possible defeat before them, for each knew that it might be long before his men would seek him out or find him; it was a bare matter of chance which party would arrive first on the scene.

1 Both had now given up the useless struggle to free themselves from the mass of wood that held them down; Ulrich limited his endeavors to an effort to bring his one partially free arm near enough to his outer coat pocket to draw out his wine flask. Even when he had accomplished that operation, it was long before he could manage the unscrewing of the stopper or get any of the liquid down his throat. But what a heaven-sent draft it seemed! It was an open winter, and little snow had fallen as yet, hence the captives suffered less from the cold than might have been the case at that season of the year; nevertheless, the wine was warming and reviving to the
2 wounded man, and he looked across with something like a throb of pity to where his enemy lay, just keeping the groans of pain and weariness from crossing his lips.

"Could you reach this flask if I threw it over to you?" asked Ulrich suddenly; "there is good wine in it, and one may as well be as comfortable as one can. Let us drink, even if tonight one of us dies."

"No, I can scarcely see anything; there is so much blood caked round my eyes," said Georg, "and in any case I don't drink wine with an enemy."

Ulrich was silent for a few minutes, and lay

GUIDED READING

LITERAL QUESTION

1a. What does Ulrich offer Georg? (his wine flask)

INFERENTIAL QUESTION

1b. Why do you think he does this? (Because they are suffering together, Ulrich is probably beginning to see their common humanity.)

listening to the weary screeching of the wind. An idea was slowly forming and growing in his brain, an idea that gained strength every time that he looked across at the man who was fighting so grimly against pain and exhaustion. In the pain and languor that Ulrich himself was feeling the old fierce hatred seemed to be dying down.

"Neighbor," he said presently, "do as you please if your men come first. It was a fair compact. But as for me, I've changed my mind. If my men are the first to come you shall be the first to be helped, as though you were my guest. We have quarreled like devils all our lives over this stupid strip of forest, where the trees can't even stand upright in a breath of wind. Lying here tonight, thinking, I've come to think we've been rather fools; there are better things in life than getting the better of a boundary dispute. Neighbor, if you will help me to bury the old quarrel, I—I will ask you to be my friend."

Georg Znaeym was silent for so long that Ulrich thought, perhaps, he had fainted with the pain of his injuries. Then he spoke slowly and in jerks.

"How the whole region would stare and gabble if we rode into the market square together. No one living can remember seeing a Znaeym and a von Gradwitz talking to one another in friendship. And what peace there would be among the forester folk if we ended our feud tonight. And if we choose to make peace among our people there is none other to interfere, no interlopers from outside. . . . You would come and keep the Sylvester night[6] beneath my roof, and I would come and feast on some high day at your castle. . . . I would never fire a shot on your land, save when you invited me as a guest; and you should come and shoot with me down in the marshes where the wildfowl are. In all the countryside there are none that could hinder if we willed to make peace. I never thought to have wanted to do other than hate you all my life, but
3 I think I have changed my mind about things too, this last half hour. And you offered me your wine-flask. . . . Ulrich von Gradwitz, I will be your friend."

For a space both men were silent, turning over in their minds the wonderful changes that this dramatic reconciliation would bring about.
4 In the cold, gloomy forest, with the wind tearing in fitful gusts through the naked branches and whistling round the tree trunks, they lay and waited for the help that would now bring release and succor to both parties. And each prayed a private prayer that his men might be the first to arrive, so that he might be the first to show honorable attention to the enemy that had become a friend.

Presently, as the wind dropped for a moment, Ulrich broke silence.

"Let's shout for help," he said; "in this lull our voices may carry a little way."

"They won't carry far through the trees and undergrowth," said Georg, "but we can try. Together, then."

The two raised their voices in a prolonged hunting call.

"Together again," said Ulrich a few minutes later, after listening in vain for an answering halloo.

"I heard something that time, I think," said Ulrich.

"I heard nothing but the pestilential wind," said Georg hoarsely.

There was silence again for some minutes, and then Ulrich gave a joyful cry.

"I can see figures coming through the wood. They are following in the way I came down the hillside."

Both men raised their voices in as loud a shout as they could muster.

"They hear us! They've stopped. Now they see us. They're running down the hill toward us," cried Ulrich.

6. **Sylvester** [sil ves′tər] **night:** New Year's Eve.

AT A GLANCE

- Ulrich offers Georg his friendship, and Georg accepts.
- As they wait to be rescued, both men hope to be able to free the other man first; together they cry for help.
- Ulrich sees figures coming through the wood.

1 CHARACTERIZATION

Ulrich begins to change his mind about Georg when he sees how bravely Georg is bearing pain and exhaustion. He cannot maintain his hatred in the face of the respect and empathy he now feels.

2 CONFLICT

Ulrich's unexpected offer of peace indicates that he has resolved an internal conflict: He may have wanted to end the feud but until now has been too stubborn to do so.

3 CHARACTERIZATION

Georg follows Ulrich in repenting his earlier insults and threats.

4 SETTING

The "cold, gloomy forest" and the menacing wind remind the reader of potential dangers that surround the two men.

GUIDED READING

LITERAL QUESTION

1a. What does each man now pray for? (that his foresters will arrive first so that he can free the other)

INFERENTIAL QUESTION

1b. What does this tell you about them? (They are now filled with respect and compassion for each other. Each wants to do the honorable thing by freeing his new friend.)

AT A GLANCE

- Ulrich realizes the figures approaching them through the forest are wolves.

1 PLOT: RESOLUTION

The plot is resolved ironically: Nature presents its own interlopers who resolve the feud with finality.

REFLECTING ON THE STORY

Who are the "interlopers" of the title? (Possible answers: the wolves; at first both men see the other as interloper; both are interlopers in the natural world.)

STUDY QUESTIONS

1. strip of unremarkable land
2. three generations
3. social restraints—a "code of civilization"
4. to escape and kill the other; to free the other first
5. cries attract a pack of wolves
6. to intimidate each other
7. pities George's pain; realizes the feud is ridiculous
8. each man to the other; both men in forest; wolves to the men
9. irrational; results from lack of communication

VIEWPOINT

it is suspenseful, sudden ironic ending; petty quarreling, greed

COMPARING STORIES

1. "Patterns": pets part of warm atmosphere of home; "Son": animals give Berl and Berlcha sustenance; "Interlopers": animals ironically end feud
2. "Patterns": indoor and outdoor settings create sense of open space; "Son": village, hut, winter create closed-in feeling; "Interlopers": tree pinning men on strip of land creates closed, small atmosphere

"How many of them are there?" asked Georg.

"I can't see distinctly," said Ulrich; "nine or ten."

"Then they are yours," said Georg; "I had only seven out with me."

"They are making all the speed they can, brave lads," said Ulrich gladly.

"Are they your men?" asked Georg. "Are they your men?" he repeated impatiently as Ulrich did not answer.

"No," said Ulrich with a laugh, the idiotic chattering laugh of a man unstrung with hideous fear.

1 "Who are they?" asked Georg quickly, straining his eyes to see what the other would gladly not have seen.

"Wolves."

STUDY QUESTIONS

Recalling

1. Describe the land that is the cause of the dispute.
2. How long has the feud lasted?
3. Explain why Ulrich and Georg do not fight when they meet.
4. Give two reasons—one from early in the story and one from later on—that each man hopes to be found by his own foresters.
5. What response do the men finally receive to their calls for help?

Interpreting

6. Why do the two men bluff about the number and nearness of their own foresters?
7. Why does Ulrich begin to change his mind about his feud with Georg?
8. Who are the interlopers? Give two different interpretations of the meaning of the term in the story.

Extending

9. Explain how the story illustrates the nature of a long feud.

VIEWPOINT

Saki's best-known stories are either humorous or suspenseful, but all of his stories reflect his criticism of human weaknesses. One writer said:

> Saki was not merely intent upon entertaining his readers; rather...he desired to vex [annoy] them into an awareness of their follies.
>
> —G. Spears, *The Satire of Saki*

- In what sense do you think this story is entertaining? What human follies is Saki showing?

COMPOSITION

Writing About Setting

- The setting of "The Interlopers" plays an important role in what happens in the story. Explain the role of setting in the story. You may want to consider the following: (a) the role of the land in the feud and (b) the ways in which setting interferes with the intentions of the characters.

Writing a New Ending for a Story

- Write a new ending for the story so that Ulrich and Georg are saved. Whose foresters find them? Do they become friends as they say they will? Do they resolve their argument?

COMPARING STORIES

1. In "The Patterns of Love," "The Son from America," and "The Interlopers" animals play an important part in the setting. Compare the roles of animals in the settings of two or more stories.
2. "The Patterns of Love" has an atmosphere that includes a feeling of open space. In "The Son from America" the atmosphere often suggests feeling cramped or closed-in. "The Interlopers" happens in open space, yet the atmosphere suggests a closed-in feeling. For two or more of these stories, compare specific details of setting to show how the authors create the different atmospheres.

COMPOSITION: GUIDELINES FOR EVALUATION

WRITING ABOUT SETTING

Objective

To determine the effect of setting in the story

Guidelines for Evaluation

- suggested length: two to three paragraphs
- should contain a thesis statement explaining how setting affects story
- support thesis with references to story
- show how setting thwarts characters

WRITING A NEW ENDING

Objective

To write brief narrative changing story's ending

Guidelines for Evaluation

- suggested length: 300 words
- should logically extend story
- should include some dramatic action
- should provide a satisfying conclusion

LITERARY FOCUS: Point of View

Edgar Allan Poe (1809–1849) was one of America's earliest short story writers. Poe was actually the first to describe the short story: short enough to be read in one sitting and constructed to create a single effect. Often, as in the following story, the single effect of a Poe story is horror.

■ What effect does the emotion of guilt have on people, including the fictional character who tells this story?

Edgar Allan Poe

The Tell-Tale Heart

True!—nervous—very, very dreadfully nervous I had been and am; but why *will* you say that I am mad? The disease had sharpened my senses—not destroyed—not dulled them. Above all was the sense of hearing acute. I heard all things in the heaven and in the earth. I heard many things in hell. How, then, am I mad? Hearken! and observe how healthily—how calmly I can tell you the whole story.

It is impossible to say how first the idea entered my brain; but once conceived, it haunted me day and night. Object there was none. Passion there was none. I loved the old man. He had never wronged me. He had never given me insult. For his gold I had no desire. I think it was his eye! yes, it was this! He had the eye of a vulture[1]—a pale blue eye, with a film over it. Whenever it fell upon me, my blood ran cold; and so by degrees—very gradually—I made up my mind to take the life of the old man, and thus rid myself of the eye forever.

Now this is the point. You fancy me mad. Madmen know nothing. But you should have
3 seen *me*. You should have seen how wisely I proceeded—with what caution—with what foresight—with what dissimulation I went to work! I was never kinder to the old man than during the whole week before I killed him. And every night, about midnight, I turned the latch of his door and opened it—oh, so gently! And then, when I had made an opening sufficient for my head, I put in a dark lantern, all closed, closed, so that no light shone out, and then I thrust in my head. Oh, you would have laughed to see how cunningly I thrust it in! I moved it slowly—very, very slowly, so that I might not disturb the old man's sleep. It took me an hour to place my whole head within the opening so far that I could see him as he lay upon his bed. Ha!—would a madman have been so wise as this? And then, when my head was well in the room, I undid the lantern cautiously—oh, so cautiously—cautiously (for the hinges creaked)—I undid it just so much that a single thin ray fell upon the vulture eye. And this I did for seven long nights—every night just at midnight—but I found the eye always closed; and so it was impossible to do the work; for it was not the old

1. **vulture** [vul′chər]: large, hawklike bird.

AT A GLANCE

- The narrator insists he is not mad but that a disease has made his hearing acute.
- He plans to murder an old man because the old man's eye disturbs him.
- For seven nights he begins to enter the old man's room but does not kill him because the eye is always closed.

LITERARY OPTIONS

- point of view
- characterization
- setting

THEMATIC OPTIONS

- guilt vs. innocence
- identity and self-respect

1 POINT OF VIEW

In the first sentences we learn that the first-person narrator is a person whose sanity (thus, reliability) is questionable.

2 PLOT: NARRATIVE HOOK

When the narrator reveals that he has decided to kill the old man, the reader is drawn into a world of madness and suspense.

3 CHARACTERIZATION

The narrator is a man who vehemently attests to his sanity, yet calmly plots a murder with obsessive attention to detail.

GUIDED READING

LITERAL QUESTION

1a. Why does the narrator want to kill the old man? (He cannot stand the old man's eye.)

INFERENTIAL QUESTION

1b. What does this tell you about the narrator's sanity? (His obsession suggests that he is not sane.)

SELECTION FOR PRACTICE IN ACTIVE READING
(TCR 5, p. 53)

AT A GLANCE

- As the narrator enters the room on the eighth night, the old man wakes.
- The narrator stands still in the doorway for an hour.
- The narrator shines a beam of light into the room.

1 SETTING

The "thick darkness" of the room creates a sense of fear and suspense.

2 CHARACTERIZATION

The narrator identifies with the old man's "mortal terror" and says that he, too, has felt it; nonetheless, he delivers this information with a disturbing sense of excitement and impending doom.

3 STYLE: REPETITION

Poe's narrator repeats key words and phrases, especially when he becomes agitated. Here, repetition of *all in vain, shadow,* and *feel* is accompanied by five references to the old man (four pronouns plus *the victim*).

man who vexed me, but his Evil Eye. And every morning, when the day broke, I went boldly into the chamber, and spoke courageously to him, calling him by name in a hearty tone, and inquiring how he had passed the night. So you see he would have been a very profound old man, indeed, to suspect that every night, just at twelve, I looked in upon him while he slept.

Upon the eighth night I was more than usually cautious in opening the door. A watch's minute hand moves more quickly than did mine. Never before that night had I *felt* the extent of my own powers—of my sagacity. I could scarcely contain my feelings of triumph. To think that there I was, opening the door, little by little, and he not even to dream of my secret deeds or thoughts. I fairly chuckled at the idea; and perhaps he heard me; for he moved on the bed
1 suddenly, as if startled. Now you may think that I drew back—but no. His room was as black as pitch with the thick darkness (for the shutters were close fastened, through fear of robbers), and so I knew that he could not see the opening of the door, and I kept pushing it on steadily, steadily.

I had my head in, and was about to open the lantern, when my thumb slipped upon the tin fastening, and the old man sprang up in bed, crying out—"Who's there?"

I kept quite still and said nothing. For a whole hour I did not move a muscle, and in the meantime I did not hear him lie down. He was still sitting up in the bed listening—just as I have done, night after night, hearkening to the deathwatches in the wall.

Presently I heard a slight groan, and I knew it was the groan of mortal terror. It was not a groan of pain or of grief—oh, no!—it was the
2 low stifled sound that arises from the bottom of the soul when overcharged with awe. I knew the sound well. Many a night, just at midnight, when all the world slept, it has welled up from my own bosom, deepening, with its dreadful echo, the terrors that distracted me. I say I knew it well. I knew what the old man felt, and pitied

Man with Arm Raised, 1960, Francis Bacon.

him, although I chuckled at heart. I knew that he had been lying awake ever since the first slight noise, when he had turned in the bed. His fears had been ever since growing upon him. He had been trying to fancy them causeless, but could not. He had been saying to himself, "It is nothing but the wind in the chimney—it is only a mouse crossing the floor," or "It is merely a cricket which has made a single chirp." Yes, he
3 had been trying to comfort himself with these suppositions: but he had found all in vain. *All in vain;* because Death, in approaching him, had stalked with his black shadow before him, and enveloped the victim. And it was the mournful influence of the unperceived shadow that caused him to feel—although he neither saw nor heard—to *feel* the presence of my head within the room.

When I had waited a long time, very patiently, without hearing him lie down, I resolved to open a little—a very, very little crevice in the lantern. So I opened it—you cannot imagine how stealthily, stealthily—until, at length, a simple dim ray, like the thread of the spider, shot

GUIDED READING

LITERAL QUESTION

1a. What happens on the eighth night? (The old man wakes.)

INFERENTIAL QUESTION

1b. Why is his waking significant? (His waking implies that his eye will be open, and the narrator will be able to kill him.)

from out the crevice and fell full upon the vulture eye.

It was open—wide, wide open—and I grew furious as I gazed upon it. I saw it with perfect distinctness—all a dull blue, with a hideous veil over it that chilled the very marrow in my bones; but I could see nothing else of the old man's face or person: for I had directed the ray as if by instinct, precisely upon the spot.

And have I not told you that what you mistake for madness is but overacuteness of the senses?—now, I say, there came to my ears a low, dull, quick sound, such as a watch makes when enveloped in cotton. I knew *that* sound well, too. It was the beating of the old man's heart. It increased my fury, as the beating of a drum stimulates the soldier into courage.

But even yet I refrained and kept still. I scarcely breathed. I held the lantern motionless. I tried how steadily I could maintain the ray upon the eye. Meantime the hellish tattoo of the heart increased. It grew quicker and quicker, and louder and louder every instant. The old man's terror *must* have been extreme! It grew louder, I say, louder every moment!—do you mark me well? I have told you that I am nervous: so I am. And now at the dead hour of the night, amid the dreadful silence of that old house, so strange a noise as this excited me to uncontrollable terror. Yet, for some minutes longer I refrained and stood still. But the beating grew louder, louder! I thought the heart must burst. And now a new anxiety seized me—the sound would be heard by a neighbor! The old man's hour had come! With a loud yell, I threw open the lantern and leaped into the room. He shrieked once—once only. In an instant I dragged him to the floor, and pulled the heavy bed over him. I then smiled gaily, to find the deed so far done. But, for many minutes, the heart beat on with a muffled sound. This, however, did not vex me; it would not be heard through the wall. At length it ceased. The old man was dead. I removed the bed and examined the corpse. Yes, he was stone, stone dead. I placed my hand upon the heart and held it there many minutes. There was no pulsation. He was stone dead. His eye would trouble me no more.

If still you think me mad, you will think so no longer when I describe the wise precautions I took for the concealment of the body. The night waned, and I worked hastily, but in silence. First of all I dismembered the corpse. I cut off the head and the arms and the legs.

I then took up three planks from the flooring of the chamber, and deposited all between the scantlings.[2] I then replaced the boards so cleverly, so cunningly, that no human eye—not even *his*—could have detected anything wrong. There was nothing to wash out—no stain of any kind—no blood spot whatever. I had been too wary for that. A tub had caught all—ha! ha!

When I had made an end of these labors, it was four o'clock—still dark as midnight. As the bell sounded the hour, there came a knocking at the street door. I went down to open it with a light heart, for what had I *now* to fear? There entered three men, who introduced themselves, with perfect suavity, as officers of the police. A shriek had been heard by a neighbor during the night; suspicion of foul play had been aroused; information had been lodged at the police office, and they (the officers) had been deputed to search the premises.

I smiled, for *what* had I to fear? I bade the gentlemen welcome. The shriek, I said, was my own in a dream. The old man, I mentioned, was absent in the country. I took my visitors all over the house. I bade them search—search *well*. I led them, at length, to *his* chamber. I showed them his treasures, secure, undisturbed. In the enthusiasm of my confidence, I brought chairs into
3 the room, and desired them *here* to rest from their fatigues, while I myself, in the wild audacity of my perfect triumph, placed my own seat upon the very spot beneath which reposed the corpse of the victim.

The officers were satisfied. My *manner* had

2. **scantlings:** small beams.

AT A GLANCE

- The old man's eye is open.
- The narrator says he hears the beating of the old man's heart.
- He kills the man, dismembers the corpse, and hides the body parts.
- The narrator shows three policemen through the house.

1 POINT OF VIEW

Poe's use of the first-person point of view enhances the reader's awareness of the narrator's insanity: It is not possible that he hears the old man's heart.

2 PLOT: RISING ACTION

When the murder is committed the story begins to move with sudden swiftness of action and detail.

3 THEME

The narrator, feeling madly triumphant and powerful, tempts fate; inadvertently he creates a situation in which his guilt will surface and overwhelm him.

GUIDED READING

LITERAL QUESTION

1a. What does the narrator do with the old man's body? (He dismembers it and hides the parts under the floor boards.)

INFERENTIAL QUESTION

1b. Why do these actions strike the narrator as "wise precautions"? (They seem the most expedient way to avoid detection.)

AT A GLANCE

- The narrator grows alarmed, begins to argue wildly with the police, and confesses his crime.

1 THEME

The narrator's guilt and madness overwhelm him: He believes he can hear the dead man's heartbeat.

2 POINT OF VIEW

Poe's use of the mad first-person narrator makes the climactic scene intriguing and enigmatic: The reader cannot *know* how the policemen behave.

REFLECTING ON THE STORY

Whose heart is the "tell-tale" heart? (It is the narrator's own heartbeat that impels him to confess the crime, and it is his "heart" that lacks humanity and accepts the idea of murder.)

STUDY QUESTIONS

1. "the disease"
2. "He had the eye of a vulture—a pale blue eye with a film over it."
3. kindness to old man; slow entry into his room; limitation of one ray on man's eye
4. on the eighth night; smothers him with the bed
5. encourages their search, invites them to sit and chat, sits over burial place; thinks police hear beating heart
6. he's losing self-control
7. it spurs him on; his own heart; he is fearful and guilty
8. descriptions are sensual and easily imagined by reader

VIEWPOINT

Answers will vary.

convinced them. I was singularly at ease. They sat, and while I answered cheerily, they chatted of familiar things. But, ere long, I felt myself getting pale and wished them gone. My head ached, and I fancied a ringing in my ears; but still they sat and still chatted. The ringing became more distinct—it continued and became more distinct; I talked more freely to get rid of the feeling; but it continued and gained definiteness—until, at length, I found that the noise was *not* within my ears.

No doubt, I now grew *very* pale—but I talked more fluently, and with a heightened voice. Yet
1 the sound increased—and what could I do? It was *a low, dull, quick sound—much such a sound as a watch makes when enveloped in cotton*. I gasped for breath—and yet the officers heard it not. I talked more quickly—more vehemently; but the noise steadily increased. I arose and argued about trifles, in a high key and with violent gesticulations; but the noise steadily increased. Why *would* they not be gone? I paced the floor to and fro with heavy strides, as if excited to fury by the observations of the men—but the noise steadily increased. Oh what *could* I do? I foamed—I raved—I swore! I swung the chair upon which I had been sitting, and grated it upon the boards, but the noise arose over all and continually increased. It grew louder—louder—*louder!* And still the men chatted pleasantly, and smiled. Was it possible they heard not? No, no! They heard!—they suspected—they *knew!*—they were making a *mockery* of my horror—this I thought, and this I think. But anything was better than this agony! Anything was more tolerable than this derision! I could bear those hypocritical smiles no longer! I felt that I must scream or die!—and now—again!—hark! louder! louder! louder! *louder!*—

2 "Villains!" I shrieked, "dissemble no more! I admit the deed!—tear up the planks!—here, here!—it is the beating of his hideous heart!"

STUDY QUESTIONS

Recalling

1. At the beginning of the story, what reason does the narrator give for his nervous condition?
2. Describe in detail what disturbs the narrator about the old man.
3. What details of his caution does the narrator give as evidence of his sanity?
4. When and how does the narrator finally commit his crime?
5. Give two examples of the narrator's confidence with the police. Why does he finally confess?

Interpreting

6. In spite of his claims of calm and cautious behavior, the narrator acts in an increasingly frenzied manner. What do his movements tell us about his state of mind?
7. Explain how the narrator's supposedly sharpened sense of hearing contributes to the murder and to the narrator's confession. What might he actually be hearing in each instance? Why?

Extending

8. Explain how the repeated mention of the narrator's sensitivity to the eye, the scream, and the heartbeat increases the mood of horror in the story.

VIEWPOINT

We might be tempted to dismiss "The Tell-Tale Heart" as a fantastic, unbelievable horror story. However, one critic says that Poe has the

> ability to give the appearance of truth to the implausible or incredible.
>
> —A. Voss, *American Short Story*

- Do you consider "The Tell-Tale Heart" believable? What in the story caused you to believe it or not to believe it?

LITERARY FOCUS

First-Person Point of View

Point of view is the relationship of the storyteller to the story. A story told from the **first-person point of view** is told by one of the characters, who refers to himself or herself as "I." This character, who is the narrator, speaks directly to the reader to tell the story. We have the advantage of an immediate report by someone actually involved in the events of the story.

One possible disadvantage of the first-person narrator is that he or she provides only a partial view of the story. The narrator cannot tell what another character is thinking or what happens elsewhere. We read only what the narrator sees and hears—or what the narrator wants us to know. A first-person narrator can be unreliable. The narrator may be too involved in the story to be honest.

Thinking About Point of View

- The narrator of "The Tell-Tale Heart" insists on his own sanity, but much of the proof he offers is actually proof that he is mad. Give examples of his own arguments that prove him insane.

VOCABULARY

Context Clues

Context clues allow us to unlock the meaning of an unfamiliar word by studying the sentence or sentences surrounding the word. Consider the following segment from "The Tell-Tale Heart":

> He had been saying to himself, "It is nothing but the wind in the chimney—it is only a mouse crossing the floor," or "It is merely a cricket which has made a single chirp." Yes, he had been trying to comfort himself with these *suppositions*....

The old man guesses about the source of the sound that woke him. These guesses are given as examples of *suppositions*. *Suppositions* must mean "assumptions."

Choose the best meaning for each italicized word in the following sentences by studying its *context*. That is, examine the ideas found in the sentence in which the word appears or in adjoining sentences. Write the number of each item and the letter of your choice on a separate sheet.

1. The disease had sharpened my senses—not destroyed—not dulled them. Above all was the sense of hearing *acute*. I heard all things in the heaven and in the earth.
   (a) dull (c) weak
   (b) sharp (d) natural
2. Never before that night had I felt the extent of my own powers—of my *sagacity*.
   (a) confusion (c) cleverness
   (b) clumsiness (d) spite
3. I resolved to open a little—a very, very little *crevice* in the lantern.
   (a) door (c) candle
   (b) box (d) slit
4. It was not a groan of pain or of grief—oh, no!—it was the low *stifled* sound that arises from the bottom of the soul when overcharged with awe.
   (a) sharp (c) banging
   (b) muffled (d) shrill
5. It increased my fury, as the beating of a drum *stimulates* the soldier into courage.
   (a) excites (c) depresses
   (b) convinces (d) discourages

COMPOSITION

Writing About Point of View

- Because of the first-person point of view, we are given a partial view of the story. Explain what is revealed about the characters and events of "The Tell-Tale Heart" by the narrator. Then explain what is not revealed. *For help with this assignment, see Lesson 6 in the Writing About Literature Handbook at the back of this book.*

Writing a Fictional Account

- Imagine that you are one of the police officers who goes to the house after the murder, hoping to get credit for solving the case. Write a report to your sergeant describing the events that occurred after your arrival. You may want to consider the following: How did the narrator act when you first met him? What in his behavior first made you suspicious of him? How did you get him to confess to the crime?

LITERARY FOCUS

"Hearken! and observe how healthily—how calmly I can tell you the whole story"; "You should have seen how wisely I proceeded"; "If you still think me mad, you will think so no longer when I describe the wise precautions I took for the concealment of the body"; "A tub had caught all—ha! ha!"

VOCABULARY

1. (b) sharp
2. (c) cleverness
3. (d) slit
4. (b) muffled
5. (a) excites

COMPOSITION: GUIDELINES FOR EVALUATION

WRITING ABOUT POINT OF VIEW

Objective

To analyze characterization and plot development in terms of point of view

Guidelines for Evaluation

- suggested length: three or more paragraphs
- should explain what narrator reveals about himself
- should show how his point of view gives partial account of story, determines outcome

WRITING A FICTIONAL ACCOUNT

Objective

To write a chronological report

Guidelines for Evaluation

- suggested length: three paragraphs
- should answer three questions given
- should assume *persona* of a police officer
- should refer to story and list events chronologically

AT A GLANCE

- The author describes a pilot flying his plane.
- The pilot tells himself he will be home in half an hour; he has lost a leg.
- He tries to invent a humorous way to tell others about his leg.

LITERARY OPTIONS

- point of view
- characterization
- style

THEMATIC OPTIONS

- powers of observation
- adventure and suspense
- self-reliance and leadership

1 POINT OF VIEW

The author uses a limited third person point of view: The reader is told only what the pilot sees and thinks.

2 PLOT: EXPOSITION

Dahl describes the pilot, who has lost his leg in combat, flying his plane. It is unclear whether the description concerns the actual event or a recollection of it.

3 CHARACTERIZATION

The pilot remains calm in a crisis, trying to retain his sense of humor amid a grisly situation.

Roald Dahl (born 1916) served as a fighter pilot for the British Royal Air Force in World War II. He was shot down while flying over the Libyan desert and spent fifteen weeks in a German hospital. His experiences during the war have become the basis for some of his fiction.

■ What are the advantages of remaining calm in a crisis situation?

Roald Dahl

Beware of the Dog

Down below there was only a vast white undulating sea of cloud. Above there was the sun, and the sun was white like the clouds, because it is never yellow when one looks at it from high in the air.

He was still flying the Spitfire.[1] His right hand was on the stick, and he was working the rudder-bar with his left leg alone. It was quite
1 easy. The machine was flying well. He knew what he was doing.

Everything is fine, he thought. I'm doing all right. I'm doing nicely. I know my way home. I'll be there in half an hour. When I land, I shall taxi in and switch off my engine, and I shall say, "Help me to get out, will you?" I shall make my voice sound ordinary and natural, and none of them will take any notice. Then I shall say, "Someone help me to get out. I can't do it alone because I've lost one of my legs." They'll all laugh and think that I'm joking.

2 He glanced down again at his right leg. There was not much of it left. The cannon-shell had taken him on the thigh, just above the knee, and now there was nothing but a great mess and a lot of blood. But there was no pain. When he looked down, he felt as though he were seeing something that did not belong to him. It had nothing to do with him. It was just a mess which happened to be there in the cockpit, something strange and unusual and rather interesting. It was like finding a dead cat on the sofa.

He really felt fine, and because he still felt fine, he felt excited and unafraid.

I won't even bother to call up on the radio for the blood-wagon, he thought. It isn't necessary. And when I land, I'll sit there quite
3 normally and say, "Some of you fellows come and help me out, will you, because I've lost one of my legs." That will be funny. I'll laugh a little while I'm saying it; I'll say it calmly and slowly, and they'll think I'm joking. . . .

Then he saw the sun shining on the engine cowling[2] of his machine. He saw the sun shining on the rivets in the metal, and he remembered the airplane and he remembered where he was. He realized that he was no longer feeling good,

1. **Spitfire:** single-engine British fighter plane used in World War II.

2. **cowling:** detachable, streamlined metal covering for an airplane engine.

GUIDED READING

LITERAL QUESTION

1a. What is the first thing we learn about the pilot? (He has lost a leg.)

INFERENTIAL QUESTION

1b. What does the pilot's reaction to his lost leg tell us about his personality? (He is trying to remain calm in a crisis.)

that he was sick and giddy. His head kept falling forward onto his chest because his neck seemed no longer to have any strength. But he knew that he was flying the Spitfire. He could feel the handle of the stick between the fingers of his right hand.

I'm going to pass out, he thought. Any moment now I'm going to pass out.

He looked at his altimeter.[3] Twenty-one thousand. To test himself he tried to read the hundreds as well as the thousands. Twenty-one thousand and what? As he looked, the dial became blurred and he could not even see the needle. He knew then that he must bail out, that there was not a second to lose; otherwise he would become unconscious. Quickly, frantically, he tried to slide back the hood with his left hand, but he had not the strength. For a second he took his right hand off the stick and with both hands he managed to push the hood back. The rush of cold air on his face seemed to help. He had a moment of great clearness. His actions became orderly and precise. That is what happens with a good pilot. He took some quick deep breaths from his oxygen mask, and as he did so, he looked out over the side of the cockpit. Down below there was only a vast white sea of cloud, and he realized that he did not know where he was.

It'll be the Channel,[4] he thought. I'm sure to fall in the drink.

He throttled back, pulled off his helmet, undid his straps, and pushed the stick hard over to the left. The Spitfire dipped its port wing and turned smoothly over onto its back. The pilot fell out.

As he fell, he opened his eyes, because he knew that he must not pass out before he had pulled the cord. On one side he saw the sun; on the other he saw the whiteness of the clouds, and as he fell, as he somersaulted in the air, the white clouds chased the sun and the sun chased the clouds. They chased each other in a small circle; they ran faster and faster and there was the sun and the clouds and the clouds and the sun, and the clouds came nearer until suddenly there was no longer any sun but only a great whiteness. The whole world was white and there was
3 nothing in it. It was so white that sometimes it looked black, and after a time it was either white or black, but mostly it was white. He watched as it turned from white to black, then back to white again, and the white stayed for a long time, but the black lasted only for a few seconds. He got into the habit of going to sleep during the white periods, of waking up just in time to see the world when it was black. The black was very quick. Sometimes it was only a flash, a flash of black lightning. The white was slow, and in the slowness of it he always dozed off.

One day, when it was white, he put out a hand and he touched something. He took it between his fingers and crumpled it. For a time he lay there, idly letting the tips of his fingers play with the thing which they had touched. Then slowly he opened his eyes, looked down at his
4 hand, and saw that he was holding something which was white. It was the edge of a sheet. He knew it was a sheet because he could see the texture of the material and the stitchings on the hem. He screwed up his eyes and opened them again quickly. This time he saw the room. He saw the bed in which he was lying; he saw the gray walls and the door and the green curtains over the window. There were some roses on the table by his bed.

Then he saw the basin on the table near the roses. It was a white enamel basin and beside it
5 there was a small medicine glass.

This is a hospital, he thought. I am in a hospital. But he could remember nothing. He lay back on his pillow, looking at the ceiling and wondering what had happened. He was gazing at the smooth grayness of the ceiling which was so

3. **altimeter** [al tim′ə tər]: in an aircraft the instrument that measures altitude.
4. **Channel:** the English Channel between England and France. France was occupied by Germany during World War II, and British planes often crossed the Channel.

AT A GLANCE

- The pilot tries to read the altimeter.
- He bails out of the plane.
- He realizes he is in a hospital.

1 THEME

The pilot's realization that his senses are dulling may have saved his life; his judgment is crucial.

2 MOOD

The pilot's "moment of great clearness" is juxtaposed with one of disorientation; the combination of sensations heightens the mood of confusion and suspense.

3 STYLE: IMAGERY

Dahl moves the pilot from the whiteness of the sun to the unconscious state of the pilot to the whiteness of the hospital room. The imagery is abstract, and the pilot's responses to the two colors are both intense and dreamy.

4 POINT OF VIEW

The limited third-person point of view allows the reader to recognize the sheet only as the pilot does.

5 SETTING

The stark hospital room heightens the sense of the pilot's alienation.

GUIDED READING

LITERAL QUESTIONS

1a. How does the pilot test himself in the plane? (He tries to read the altimeter.)

2a. What is the "whiteness" he keeps seeing? (a sheet)

INFERENTIAL QUESTIONS

1b. Why does he want to read the altimeter? (to prove to himself that he is conscious and coherent)

2b. Why do you think the author uses such complicated language to describe what the pilot sees? (He wants the reader to experience the same difficulty and confusion that the pilot feels.)

AT A GLANCE

- The pilot sees a fly on the ceiling and remembers what happened.
- A nurse enters and tells him he is in Brighton, England.
- A doctor checks up on him and says he cannot have visitors yet.
- The pilot hears a German bomber.

1 STYLE: IMAGERY

The small black fly—a tiny but tangible thing amid an abstract "sea of gray"—reminds the pilot of his recent crisis.

2 THEME

Both the pilot's desire to observe his surroundings keenly and his exhaustion are illustrated by his basic, unemotional description of the nurse.

3 SETTING

The pilot's keen powers of observation are emphasized by his acute awareness of his surroundings. Dahl maintains the anxious mood by focusing that acute awareness on an insignificant element of the setting.

4 PLOT: NARRATIVE HOOK

The pilot, who can distinguish the sounds of different planes, hears the sound of a German bomber; he is jolted out of his vague apprehension of the room.

clean and gray, and then suddenly he saw a fly
1 walking upon it. The sight of this fly, the suddenness of seeing this small black speck on a sea of gray, brushed the surface of his brain, and quickly, in that second, he remembered everything. He remembered the Spitfire and he remembered the altimeter showing twenty-one thousand feet. He remembered the pushing back of the hood and both hands and he remembered the bailing out. He remembered his leg.

It seemed all right now. He looked down at the end of the bed, but he could not tell. He put one hand underneath the bedclothes and felt for his knees. He found one of them, but when he felt for the other, his hand touched something which was soft and covered in bandages.

Just then the door opened and a nurse came in. "Hello," she said. "So you've waked up at last."

2 She was not good-looking, but she was large and clean. She was between thirty and forty and she had fair hair. More than that he did not notice.

"Where am I?"

"You're a lucky fellow. You landed in a wood near the beach. You're in Brighton.[5] They brought you in two days ago, and now you're all fixed up. You look fine."

"I've lost a leg," he said.

"That's nothing. We'll get you another one. Now you must go to sleep. The doctor will be coming to see you in about an hour." She picked up the basin and the medicine glass and went out.

But he did not sleep. He wanted to keep his eyes open because he was frightened that if he shut them again everything would go away. He
3 lay looking at the ceiling. The fly was still there. It was very energetic. It would run forward very fast for a few inches, then it would stop. Then it would run forward again, stop, run forward, stop, and every now and then it would take off and buzz around viciously in small circles. It always landed back in the same place on the ceiling and started running and stopping all over again. He watched it for so long that after a while it was no longer a fly, but only a black speck upon a sea of gray, and he was still watching it when the nurse opened the door and stood aside while the doctor came in.

He was an Army doctor, a major, and he had some last-war ribbons on his chest. He was bald and small, but he had a cheerful face and kind eyes. "Well, well," he said. "So you've decided to wake up at last. How are you feeling?"

"I feel all right."

"That's the stuff. You'll be up and about in no time."

The doctor took his wrist to feel his pulse. "By the way," he said, "some of the lads from your squadron were ringing up and asking about you. They wanted to come along and see you, but I said that they'd better wait a day or two. Told them you were all right and that they could come and see you a little later on. Just lie quiet and take it easy for a bit. Got something to read?" He glanced at the table with the roses. "No. Well, Nurse will look after you. She'll get you anything you want." With that he waved his hand and went out, followed by the large, clean nurse.

When they had gone, he lay back and looked at the ceiling again. The fly was still there, and as he lay watching it, he heard the noise of an airplane in the distance. He lay listening to the sound of its engines. It was a long way away. I
4 wonder what it is, he thought. Let me see if I can place it. Suddenly he jerked his head sharply to one side. Anyone who has been bombed can tell the noise of a Junkers 88. They can tell most other German bombers for that matter, but especially a Junkers 88. The engines seem to sing a duet. There is a deep, vibrating bass voice, and with it there is a high-pitched tenor. It is the singing of the tenor which makes the sound of a JU-88 something which one cannot mistake.

5. **Brighton** [brī′tən]: city on the southern coast of England.

GUIDED READING

LITERAL QUESTION

1a. Where does the nurse tell the pilot he is? (Brighton, England)

INFERENTIAL QUESTION

1b. How do you think the pilot will feel about being in Brighton? (The pilot, realizing that he has landed back in England, will probably feel safe.)

He lay listening to the noise and he felt quite certain about what it was. But where were the sirens and where the guns? That German pilot certainly had a nerve coming near Brighton alone in daylight.

The aircraft was always far away and soon the noise faded away into the distance. Later on there was another. This one, too, was far away, but there was the same deep, undulating bass and the high, singing tenor and there was no mistaking it. He had heard that noise every day during the Battle.[6]

He was puzzled. There was a bell on the table by the bed. He reached out his hand and rang it. He heard the noise of footsteps down the corridor. The nurse came in.

"Nurse, what were those airplanes?"

"I'm sure I don't know. I didn't hear them. Probably fighters or bombers. I expect they were returning from France. Why, what's the matter?"

"They were JU-88's. I'm sure they were JU-88's. I know the sound of the engines. There were two of them. What were they doing over here?"

The nurse came up to the side of his bed and began to straighten out the sheets and tuck them in under the mattress. "Gracious me, what things you imagine. You mustn't worry about a thing like that. Would you like me to get you something to read?"

"No, thank you."

She patted his pillow and brushed back the hair from his forehead with her hand. "They never come over in daylight any longer. You know that. They were probably Lancasters[7] or Flying Fortresses."[8]

"Nurse."

"Yes."

"Could I have a cigarette?"

"Why, certainly you can."

She went out and came back almost at once with a packet of Players and some matches. She handed one to him, and when he had put it in his mouth, she struck a match and lit it. "If you want me again," she said, "just ring the bell," and she went out.

Once toward evening he heard the noise of another aircraft. It was far away, but even so he knew that it was a single-engined machine. It was going fast; he could tell that. He could not place it. It wasn't a Spit, and it wasn't a
3 Hurricane.[9] It did not sound like an American engine either. They make more noise. He did not know what it was, and it worried him greatly. Perhaps I am very ill, he thought. Perhaps I am imagining things. Perhaps I am a little delirious. I simply do not know what to think.

That evening the nurse came in with a basin of hot water and began to wash him. "Well," she said, "I hope you don't still think that we're being bombed."

She had taken off his pajama top and was soaping his right arm with a flannel. He did not answer.

She rinsed the flannel in the water, rubbed more soap on it, and began to wash his chest. "You're looking fine this evening," she said. "They operated on you as soon as you came in. They did a marvelous job. You'll be all right. I've got a brother in the R.A.F.,"[10] she added. "Flying
4 bombers."

He said, "I went to school in Brighton."

She looked up quickly. "Well, that's fine," she said. "I expect you'll know some people in the town."

"Yes," he said, "I know quite a few."

She had finished washing his chest and arms. Now she turned back the bedclothes so that his

---

6. **the Battle:** the Battle of Britain, between Britain's Royal Air Force and Germany's Luftwaffe for control of the skies over England. The battle was fought early in World War II, from August to October 1940, and ended with a British victory.
7. **Lancasters:** British heavy bombers.
8. **Flying Fortresses:** American heavy bombers.
9. **Hurricane:** British fighter plane.
10. **R.A.F.:** Britain's Royal Air Force.

AT A GLANCE

- The pilot is confused to hear no sirens or guns.
- He fears he is imagining things.
- He asks the nurse about the planes; she says she didn't hear them.
- While the nurse bathes him, the pilot says he went to school in Brighton.

1 STYLE: METAPHOR

The sound of the bombers is compared to two singing voices, one a deep bass and the other a high tenor, a strange comparison that seems apt for the ill pilot to make.

2 PLOT: CONFLICT

The basic external conflict between the pilot and the nurse begins when she says that she didn't hear the German bombers.

3 PLOT: CONFLICT

The pilot's internal conflict begins as he doubts his own judgment: He knows he is physically ill and cannot verify what he believes he has heard.

4 PLOT: RISING ACTION

The pilot tells the nurse he went to school in Brighton, and she realizes that he will be able to recognize the city.

GUIDED READING

LITERAL QUESTIONS

1a. What disturbs the pilot when he hears the German bombers? (He doesn't hear sirens or guns.)

2a. Why does the pilot worry when he hears another aircraft he cannot identify? (He is afraid that he is imagining things.)

INFERENTIAL QUESTIONS

1b. Why does he expect to hear sirens and guns? (The English would attempt to stop a German bomber flying over Brighton.)

2b. Why is he worried about imagining things? (He is used to relying on his reason; now he needs to rely on his mental faculties more than ever before.)

AT A GLANCE

- As the nurse bathes the pilot, she complains about the hard water.
- The pilot remembers that Brighton had soft water.
- He lies awake at night.

1 STYLE: IMAGERY

Water *(as hard as nails)* and soap that won't lather are images that emphasize the barrenness of the hospital room.

2 PLOT: RISING ACTION

The pilot's memory of bathing at school in Brighton with soft water contradicts the nurse's statement.

3 THEME

The pilot lies awake trying to reconcile what he has been told with what he actually knows from his own experience. Physically disabled, he must rely on his mind for resolution of his difficulties.

left leg was uncovered. She did it in such a way that his bandaged stump remained under the sheets. She began to wash his left leg and the rest of his body. This was the first time he had had a bedbath and he was embarrassed. She laid a towel under his leg and began washing his foot
1 with the flannel. She said, "This wretched soap won't lather at all. It's the water. It's as hard as nails."

He said, "None of the soap is very good now and, of course, with hard water it's hopeless." As he said it, he remembered something. He remembered the baths which he used to take at school in Brighton, in the long stone-floored bathroom which had four baths in a room. He
2 remembered how the water was so soft that you had to take a shower afterwards to get all the soap off your body, and he remembered how the foam used to float on the surface of the water, so that you could not see your legs underneath. He remembered that sometimes they were given calcium tablets because the school doctor used to say that soft water was bad for the teeth.

"In Brighton," he said, "the water isn't. . . ." He did not finish the sentence. Something had occurred to him, something so fantastic and absurd that for a moment he felt like telling the nurse about it and having a good laugh.

She looked up. "The water isn't what?" she said.

"Nothing," he answered. "I was dreaming."

She rinsed the flannel in the basin, wiped the soap off his leg, and dried him with a towel.

"It's nice to be washed," he said, "I feel better." He was feeling his face with his hand. "I need a shave."

"We'll do that tomorrow," she said. "Perhaps you can do it yourself then."

3 That night he could not sleep. He lay awake thinking of the Junkers 88's and of the hardness of the water. He could think of nothing else. They *were* JU-88's, he said to himself. I know they were. And yet it is not possible, because they would not be flying around so low over here in

GUIDED READING

LITERAL QUESTION

1a. What does the pilot remember about Brighton's water? (It was soft.)

INFERENTIAL QUESTION

1b. What is the significance of the pilot's memory? (It does not fit with the information the nurse has given him.)

broad daylight. I know that it is true and yet I know that it is impossible. Perhaps I am ill. Perhaps I am behaving like a fool and do not know what I am doing or saying. Perhaps I am delirious. For a long time he lay awake thinking these things, and once he sat up in bed and said aloud, "I will prove that I am not crazy. I will make a little speech about something complicated and intellectual. I will talk about what to do with Germany after the war." But before he had time to begin, he was asleep.

He woke just as the first light of day was showing through the slit in the curtains over the window. The room was still dark, but he could tell that it was already beginning to get light outside. He lay looking at the gray light which was showing through the slit in the curtain, and as he lay there, he remembered the day before. He remembered the Junkers 88's and the hardness of the water; he remembered the large, pleasant nurse and the kind doctor, and now a small grain of doubt took root in his mind and it began to grow.

He looked around the room. The nurse had taken the roses out the night before. There was nothing except the table with a packet of ciga-
1 rettes, a box of matches, and an ashtray. The room was bare. It was no longer warm or friendly. It was not even comfortable. It was cold and empty and very quiet.

Slowly the grain of doubt grew, and with it came fear, a light, dancing fear that warned but did not frighten—the kind of fear that one gets not because one is afraid, but because one feels that there is something wrong. Quickly the doubt and the fear grew so that he became restless and angry, and when he touched his forehead with his hand, he found that it was damp
2 with sweat. He knew then that he must do something, that he must find some way of proving to himself that he was either right or wrong, and he

AT A GLANCE

- The pilot worries about his ability to think rationally.
- A "grain of doubt" begins to grow in his mind.
- He decides to act to resolve his doubt.

1 SETTING

The cold, empty, and uncomfortable hospital room increases the mood of fear and apprehension.

2 PLOT: RISING ACTION

The pilot resolves to act: He must find out the truth.

GUIDED READING

LITERAL QUESTION

1a. What begins "to grow" in the pilot's mind? ("a small grain of doubt")

INFERENTIAL QUESTION

1b. Why does he decide to "find some way of proving to himself that he was either right or wrong"? (He must decisively test his suspicions.)

AT A GLANCE

- The pilot decides to reach the window and look out.
- He crawls to the window.
- He realizes he is in France.
- He returns to bed before the nurse enters.

1 THEME

The pilot has calmly analyzed the situation and chosen a course of action despite its difficulty.

2 CHARACTERIZATION

The pilot's slow, painful, and determined progress demonstrates his bravery and fortitude.

3 SETTING

The precise description of the scene outside the hospital window not only contrasts with the room's blandness but also indicates the pilot's healing mental faculties.

4 PLOT: CLIMAX

The pilot's suspicions are confirmed. Instantly, the bucolic domestic scene takes on a deeper meaning: The nurse lied.

looked up and saw again the window and the
1 green curtains. From where he lay, that window was right in front of him, but it was fully ten yards away. Somehow he must reach it and look out. The idea became an obsession with him and soon he could think of nothing except the window. But what about his leg? He put his hand underneath the bedclothes and felt the thick bandaged stump, which was all that was left on the right-hand side. It seemed all right. It didn't hurt. But it would not be easy.

He sat up. Then he pushed the bedclothes aside and put his left leg on the floor. Slowly, carefully, he swung his body over until he had both hands on the floor as well; then he was out of bed, kneeling on the carpet. He looked at the stump. It was very short and thick, covered with bandages. It was beginning to hurt and he could feel it throbbing. He wanted to collapse, lie down on the carpet and do nothing, but he knew that he must go on.

With two arms and one leg he crawled over
2 toward the window. He would reach forward as far as he could with his arms; then he would give a little jump and slide his left leg along after them. Each time he did it, it jarred his wound so that he gave a soft grunt of pain, but he continued to crawl across the floor on two hands and one knee. When he got to the window, he reached up, and one at a time he placed both hands on the sill. Slowly he raised himself up until he was standing on his left leg. Then quickly he pushed aside the curtains and looked out.

3 He saw a small house with a gray tiled roof standing alone beside a narrow lane, and immediately behind it there was a plowed field. In front of the house there was an untidy garden, and there was a green hedge separating the garden from the lane. He was looking at the hedge when he saw the sign. It was just a piece of board nailed to the top of a short pole, and because the hedge had not been trimmed for a long time, the branches had grown out around the sign so that it seemed almost as though it had been placed in the middle of the hedge. There was something written on the board with white paint. He pressed his head against the glass of the window, trying to read what it said. The first letter was a G, he could see that. The second was an A, and the third was an R. One after another he managed to see what the letters were. There were three words, and slowly he spelled the letters out aloud to himself as he managed to read them, "G-A-R-D-E A-U C-H-I-E-N." *Garde au chien.*[11] That is what it said.

He stood there, balancing on one leg and holding tightly to the edges of the window sill with his hands, staring at the sign and at the whitewashed lettering of the words. For a moment he could think of nothing at all. He stood there, looking at the sign, repeating the words
4 over and over to himself. Slowly he began to realize the full meaning of the thing. He looked up at the cottage and at the plowed field. He looked at the small orchard on the left of the cottage and he looked at the green countryside beyond. "So this is France," he said. "I am in France."

Now the throbbing in his right thigh was very great. It felt as though someone was pounding the end of his stump with a hammer, and suddenly the pain became so intense that it affected his head. For a moment he thought he was going to fall. Quickly he knelt down again, crawled back to the bed and hoisted himself in. He pulled the bedclothes over himself and lay back on the pillow, exhausted. He could still think of nothing at all except the small sign by the hedge and the plowed field and the orchard. It was the words on the sign that he could not forget.

It was some time before the nurse came in. She came carrying a basin of hot water and she said, "Good morning, how are you today?"

---

11. **"Garde au chien"** [gärd ō shyen]: French for "Beware of the dog."

GUIDED READING

LITERAL QUESTION

1a. What does the pilot decide he must do? (reach the window and look out)

INFERENTIAL QUESTION

1b. Why does he decide to look out the window? (He will be able to recognize the city and settle his doubts.)

He said, "Good morning, Nurse."

The pain was still great under the bandages, but he did not wish to tell this woman anything. He looked at her as she busied herself with getting the washing things ready. He looked at her more carefully now. Her hair was very fair. She was tall and big-boned and her face seemed pleasant. But there was something a little uneasy about her eyes. They were never still. They never looked at anything for more than a moment and they moved too quickly from one place to another in the room. There was something about her movements also. They were too sharp and nervous to go well with the casual manner in which she spoke.

She set down the basin, took off his pajama top, and began to wash him. "Did you sleep well?"

"Yes."

"Good," she said. She was washing his arms and chest. "I believe there's someone coming down to see you from the Air Ministry after breakfast," she went on. "They want a report or something. I expect you know all about it. How you got shot down and all that. I won't let him stay long, so don't worry."

He did not answer. She finished washing him and gave him a toothbrush and some toothpowder. He brushed his teeth, rinsed his mouth and spat the water out into the basin.

Later she brought him his breakfast on a tray, but he did not want to eat. He was still feeling weak and sick, and he wished only to lie still and think about what had happened. And there was a sentence running through his head. It was a sentence which Johnny, the Intelligence Officer of his squadron, always repeated to the pilots every day before they went out. He could see Johnny now, leaning against the wall of the dispersal hut with his pipe in his hand, saying, "And if they get you, don't forget: just your name, rank, and number. Nothing else. For God's sake, say nothing else."

"There you are," she said as she put the tray on his lap, "I've got you an egg. Can you manage all right?"

"Yes."

She stood beside the bed. "Are you feeling all right?"

"Yes."

"Good. If you want another egg, I might be able to get you one."

"This is all right."

"Well, just ring the bell if you want any more." And she went out.

He had just finished eating when the nurse came in again. She said, "Wing Commander Roberts is here. I've told him that he can only stay for a few minutes."

She beckoned with her hand and the Wing Commander came in. "Sorry to bother you like this," he said.

He was an ordinary R.A.F. officer, dressed in a uniform which was a little shabby. He wore wings and a D.F.C.[12] He was fairly tall and thin, with plenty of black hair. His teeth, which were irregular and widely spaced, stuck out a little, even when he closed his mouth. As he spoke, he took a printed form and a pencil from his pocket, and he pulled up a chair and sat down.

3 "How are you feeling?"

There was no answer.

"Tough luck about your leg. I know how you feel. I hear you put up a fine show before they got you."

The man in the bed was lying quite still, watching the man in the chair. The man in the chair said, "Well, let's get this stuff over. I'm afraid you'll have to answer a few questions so that I can fill in this combat report. Let me see now, first of all, what was your squadron?"

4 The man in the bed did not move. He looked straight at the Wing Commander and he said, "My name is Peter Williamson. My rank is Squadron Leader and my number is nine seven two four five seven."

12. **D.F.C.:** Distinguished Flying Cross, a medal.

AT A GLANCE

- The pilot knows the nurse is an enemy but does not confront her.
- He remembers his Intelligence Officer telling him not to reveal any information if he is captured.
- An R.A.F. Wing Commander enters; the pilot gives only his name, rank, and serial number.

1 POINT OF VIEW

The pilot now notices that the nurse's eyes are uneasy and that her actions betray a nervousness and discomfort.

2 THEME

The pilot's keen powers of observation have prevented an accidental betrayal of his country's military secrets.

3 PLOT: CONFLICT

Since the pilot is now aware of his circumstances, the external conflict between the pilot and the enemy will now begin in earnest.

4 PLOT: RESOLUTION

The pilot's stalwart words indicate that he will continue to defy the enemy and fulfill his patriotic duties.

REFLECTING ON THE STORY

In what way is the pilot a hero? (He demonstrates bravery both in battle and in the hospital: Faced with disorientation and pain, he heroically ascertains the truth of his situation and protects his country.)

GUIDED READING

LITERAL QUESTIONS

1a. What does the pilot remember being told by the Intelligence Officer? (to give only his name, rank, and serial number if he is captured)

2a. What does the Wing Commander ask the pilot? (He asks the pilot what his squadron is.)

INFERENTIAL QUESTIONS

1b. Why shouldn't the pilot provide any additional information? (He might undermine his country's military strategy and endanger other pilots.)

2b. What does this question reveal about the Wing Commander? (that he is not British and that he wants useful military information)

STUDY QUESTIONS

1. clouds below; sun above; remains of his right leg
2. hears engines of German planes but no sirens or guns; notes water in hospital is hard
3. a sign reading "Garde au chien"; he is in German–occupied France
4. In the plane he keeps his head despite his leg injury; he is keenly aware of his surroundings, for example, the fly.
5. If Peter were a British officer, he would know; he is a prisoner of war and has been instructed to give only basic information.
6. Answers will vary but may include that he will remain in the hospital, then will be moved to a camp for war prisoners.

VIEWPOINT

Dahl never explicitly relates Peter's fear that he has been captured. Readers sense that Peter fears something but are not sure what he fears. When they discover what the problem is, they still must wait to find out the man's response.

LITERARY FOCUS

1. strengthen; demonstrate he is rational
2. would destroy suspense; diminish our identification with Peter

STUDY QUESTIONS

Recalling

1. What details about himself and his surroundings does Peter Williamson notice before bailing out of his plane?
2. While Peter is in the hospital, what clues lead him to suspect that something is wrong?
3. What does Peter see when he looks out the window? Why is this object significant?

Interpreting

4. Peter Williamson is our only source of information in the story. What do we learn about him and his powers of observation that make us trust his perceptions and judgment?
5. The man identified as the British Wing Commander asks Peter, "What was your squadron?" Why is that question suspect? Why does Peter answer it in the way he does?

Extending

6. What do you think is going to happen to Peter Williamson?

VIEWPOINT

A reviewer for *Time* magazine wrote of Dahl and his ability to create suspense:

> The greatest danger facing a writer of this genre is that of tipping his hand too early in the story.

■ How does Dahl avoid the danger of "tipping his hand" too early? How does he keep the suspense alive for the rest of the story?

LITERARY FOCUS

Limited Third-Person Point of View

In a story told from the **limited third-person point of view**, the narrator reveals the thoughts and feelings of only one character, often the main character. The reader does not know the thoughts and feelings of the other characters. On the other hand, the reader may know more about the main character than that character does. Also, the reader has to remember that this character may not *entirely* understand what is going on.

The limited third-person point of view works well in stories like "Beware of the Dog," in which the central character is intelligent and trustworthy but lacks an important piece of information. As readers, we stumble along with the character, trying to figure out what is happening.

Thinking About Point of View

1. Occasionally, Peter doubts his own judgment, wondering if he could be delirious. Do these doubts weaken or strengthen our trust in Peter's judgment? Why?
2. In what ways would the story be different if the narrator revealed to us the thoughts and feelings of the nurse?

COMPOSITION

Writing About Point of View

■ Because Roald Dahl uses a limited third-person point of view, we see the other characters only as Peter sees them. Using specific examples, describe his first impressions of the nurse. Then contrast these impressions with his view of her at the end.

Writing a Description

■ Details often go unnoticed because we do not take the time to observe an object carefully. This point is illustrated in the story by Peter Williamson's keen awareness of the fly on the ceiling of his hospital room. Select a familiar object near you. Look at it, look away from it, and then write a brief description of it.

COMPOSITION: GUIDELINES FOR EVALUATION

WRITING ABOUT POINT OF VIEW

Objective

To write a paragraph contrasting two impressions of the nurse

Guidelines for Evaluation

- suggested length: one paragraph
- should make a clear contrast in the topic sentence
- should support the statement with references and contain a concluding statement

WRITING A DESCRIPTION

Objective

To write a brief description of something after having observed it carefully

Guidelines for Evaluation

- suggested length: 150 words
- should clearly identify object
- should include several details about object
- should use vivid, precise language

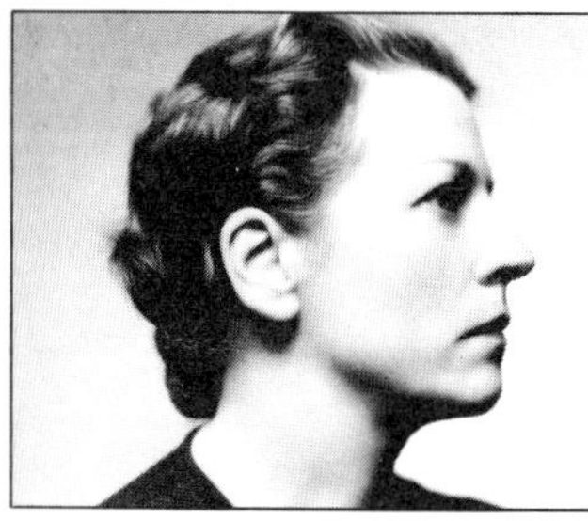

Born in West Virginia, Pearl Buck (1892–1973) lived most of her life in China. Many of her novels and short stories, such as the following one, show her appreciation of both eastern and western cultures.

■ The expression "One good deed deserves another" might apply to this story. What associations do you have with that expression?

Pearl Buck

The Good Deed

New York Chinatown 1953

Mr. Pan was worried about his mother. He had been worried about her when she was in China, and now he was worried about her in New York, although he had thought that once he got her out of his ancestral village in the province of Szechuen[1] and safely away from the local bullies, who took over when the distant government fell, his anxieties would be ended. To this end he had risked his own life and paid out large sums of sound American money, and he felt that day when he saw her on the wharf, a tiny, dazed little old woman, in a lavender silk coat and black skirt, that now they would live happily together, he and his wife, their four small children and his beloved mother, in the huge safety of the American city.

It soon became clear, however, that safety was not enough for old Mrs. Pan. She did not even appreciate the fact, which he repeated again and again, that had she remained in the village, she would now have been dead, because she was the widow of the large landowner who had been his father and therefore deserved death in the eyes of the rowdies in power.

Old Mrs. Pan listened to this without reply, but her eyes, looking very large in her small withered face, were haunted with homesickness.

2 "There are many things worse than death, especially at my age," she replied at last, when again her son reminded her of her good fortune in being where she was.

He became impassioned when she said this. He struck his breast with his clenched fists and he shouted, "Could I have forgiven myself if I had allowed you to die? Would the ghost of my father have given me rest?"

"I doubt his ghost would have traveled over such a wide sea," she replied. "That man was always afraid of the water."

3 Yet there was nothing that Mr. Pan and his wife did not try to do for his mother in order to make her happy. They prepared the food that she had once enjoyed, but she was now beyond the age of pleasure in food, and she had no appetite. She touched one dish and another with

1. **Szechuen** [se'chwän']: also Szechwan, a province of southwestern China.

AT A GLANCE

- Mr. Pan is worried about his mother, whom he has brought to New York from China.
- Old Mrs. Pan has moved in with her son, his wife and four grandchildren, but she is homesick and unhappy.

LITERARY OPTIONS

- point of view
- style
- characterization

THEMATIC OPTIONS

- compromise
- recognizing different lifestyles
- relationships between generations

1 PLOT: EXPOSITION

The narrator describes the reasons for old Mrs. Pan's move to New York City.

2 CONFLICT

The clash of two cultures is apparent in the different perspectives of old Mrs. Pan and her son.

3 CHARACTERIZATION

Mr. and Mrs. Pan try hard to make his mother comfortable.

GUIDED READING

LITERAL QUESTION

1a. How does old Mrs. Pan show her unhappiness? (Her eyes look haunted with homesickness.)

INFERENTIAL QUESTION

1b. What are her chances for adjusting to the new American culture? (Since she refuses to eat and continually yearns for her country, the chances seem small.)

AT A GLANCE

- Old Mrs. Pan dislikes New York water.
- She does not communicate with her grandchildren.

1 POINT OF VIEW

The omniscient point of view reveals the thoughts inside Mrs. Pan's mind.

2 THEME

The language difficulties create an unbridgeable gulf between Mrs. Pan and her grandchildren.

the ends of her ivory chopsticks, which she had brought with her from her home, and she thanked them prettily. "It is all good," she said, "but the water is not the same as our village water; it tastes of metal and not of earth, and so the flavor is not the same. Please allow the children to eat it."

1 She was afraid of the children. They went to an American school and they spoke English very well and Chinese very badly, and since she could speak no English, it distressed her to hear her own language maltreated by their careless
2 tongues. For a time she tried to coax them to a few lessons, or she told them stories, to which they were too busy to listen. Instead they pre-

GUIDED READING

LITERAL QUESTION

1a. What stops Mrs. Pan from communicating with her grandchildren? (They speak Chinese badly and are too busy to learn from her.)

INFERENTIAL QUESTION

1b. Why does her grandchildrens' inability to speak Chinese well distress Mrs. Pan? (She is distressed that they are abandoning their heritage by forgetting the Chinese language.)

ferred to look at the moving pictures in the box that stood on the table in the living room. She gave them up finally and merely watched them contemplatively when they were in the same room with her and was glad when they were gone. She liked her son's wife. She did not understand how there could be a Chinese woman who had never been in China, but such her son's wife was. When her son was away, she could not say to her daughter-in-law, "Do you remember how the willows grew over the gate?" For her son's wife had no such memories. She had grown up here in the city and she did not even hear its noise. At the same time, though she was so foreign, she was very kind to the old lady, and she spoke to her always in a gentle voice, however she might shout at the children, who were often disobedient.

The disobedience of the children was another grief to old Mrs. Pan. She did not understand how it was that four children could all be disobedient, for this meant that they had never been taught to obey their parents and revere their elders, which are the first lessons a child should learn.

"How is it," she once asked her son, "that the children do not know how to obey?"

Mr. Pan had laughed, though uncomfortably. "Here in America the children are not taught as we were in China," he explained.

"But my grandchildren are Chinese nevertheless," old Mrs. Pan said in some astonishment.

"They are always with Americans," Mr. Pan explained. "It is very difficult to teach them."

Old Mrs. Pan did not understand, for Chinese and Americans are different beings, one on the west side of the sea and one on the east, and the sea is always between. Therefore, why should they not continue to live apart even in the same city? She felt in her heart that the children should be kept at home and taught those things which must be learned, but she said nothing. She felt lonely and there was no one who understood the things she felt and she was quite useless. That was the most difficult thing: She was of no use here. She could not even remember which spout the hot water came from and which brought the cold. Sometimes she turned on one and then the other, until her son's wife came in briskly and said, "Let me, Mother."

4 So she gave up and sat uselessly all day, not by the window, because the machines and the many people frightened her. She sat where she could not see out; she looked at a few books, and day by day she grew thinner and thinner until Mr. Pan was concerned beyond endurance.

One day he said to his wife, "Sophia, we must do something for my mother. There is no use in saving her from death in our village if she dies here in the city. Do you see how thin her hands are?"

"I have seen," his good wife said. "But what can we do?"

"Is there no woman you know who can speak Chinese with her?" Mr. Pan asked. "She needs to have someone to whom she can talk about the village and all the things she knows. She cannot talk to you because you can only speak English, and I am too busy making our living to sit and listen to her."

5 Young Mrs. Pan considered. "I have a friend," she said at last, "a schoolmate whose family compelled her to speak Chinese. Now she is a social worker here in the city. She visits families in Chinatown and this is her work. I will call her up and ask her to spend some time here so that our old mother can be happy enough to eat again."

"Do so," Mr. Pan said.

That very morning, when Mr. Pan was gone, young Mrs. Pan made the call and found her friend, Lili Yang, and she explained everything to her.

"We are really in very much trouble," she said finally. "His mother is thinner every day, and she is so afraid she will die here. She has

AT A GLANCE

- Old Mrs. Pan is distressed by the disobedience of the children.
- Seeing his mother's suffering, Mr. Pan decides they must find someone she can talk Chinese with during the day.
- Mrs. Pan asks her friend Lili Yang to visit old Mrs. Pan.

1 CONFLICT

The conflict between two different life styles is shown in the lack of shared memories.

2 CHARACTERIZATION

Old Mrs. Pan is used to the ways of her country and cannot understand the less rigid American life style.

3 THEME

Old Mrs. Pan does not understand that although two cultures may be different, they can exist in the same city with some compromise from each.

4 SETTING

The noises of a crowded city frighten old Mrs. Pan.

5 PLOT: EXPOSITION

The family decides to bring in Lili Yang to speak to old Mrs. Pan in Chinese.

GUIDED READING

LITERAL QUESTIONS

1a. What does old Mrs. Pan do during the day? (She does nothing.)

2a. What do Mr. and Mrs. Pan decide to do? (They decide to ask Lili Yang to come and visit with old Mrs. Pan.)

INFERENTIAL QUESTIONS

1b. What does old Mrs. Pan's idleness all day tell you about her? (She feels useless and that her life is empty.)

2b. What do Mr. and Mrs. Pan hope will happen when Lili Yang visits? (They hope old Mrs. Pan's spirits will be lifted.)

AT A GLANCE

- Lili visits old Mrs. Pan.
- Mrs. Pan brightens up as she is able to reminisce in Chinese.

1 CONFLICT

Old Mrs. Pan feels so alienated in New York that she refuses even to be buried there.

2 POINT OF VIEW

The omniscient point of view shows us old Mrs. Pan's inner thoughts and helps us understand her depression and feelings of alienation.

3 THEME

Mrs. Pan's words remind us of the differences between the two cultures and of her unwillingness to accept American ways.

4 CHARACTERIZATION

Lili's interested attitude reveals her kindness and understanding of the older woman's needs.

1 made us promise that we will not bury her in foreign soil but will send her coffin back to the ancestral village. We have promised, but can we keep this promise, Lili? Yet I am so afraid, because I think she will die, and Billy will think he must keep his promise and he will try to take the coffin back and then he will be killed. Please help us, Lili."

Lili Yang promised and within a few days she came to the apartment and young Mrs. Pan led her into the inner room, which was old Mrs. Pan's room and where she always sat, wrapped in her satin coat and holding a magazine at whose pictures she did not care to look. She took up that magazine when her daughter-in-law came in, because she did not want to hurt her feelings, but the pictures frightened her. The women looked bold and evil, and sometimes they wore only a little silk stuff over their legs and this
2 shocked her. She wondered that her son's wife would put such a magazine into her hands, but she did not ask questions. There would have been no end to them had she once begun, and the ways of foreigners did not interest her. Most of the time she sat silent and still, her head sunk on her breast, dreaming of the village, the big house there where she and her husband had lived together with his parents and where their children were born. She knew that the village had fallen into the hands of their enemies and that strangers lived in the house, but she hoped even so that the land was tilled. All that she remembered was the way it had been when she was a young woman and before the evil had come to pass.

She heard now her daughter-in-law's voice, "Mother, this is a friend. She is Miss Lili Yang. She has come to see you."

Old Mrs. Pan remembered her manners. She tried to rise but Lili took her hands and begged her to keep seated.

"You must not rise to one so much younger," she exclaimed.

Old Mrs. Pan lifted her head. "You speak such good Chinese!"

"I was taught by my parents," Lili said. She sat down on a chair near the old lady.

Mrs. Pan leaned forward and put her hand on Lili's knee. "Have you been in our own country?" she asked eagerly.

Lili shook her head. "That is my sorrow. I have not and I want to know about it. I have come here to listen to you tell me."

"Excuse me," young Mrs. Pan said, "I must prepare the dinner for the family."

She slipped away so that the two could be alone and old Mrs. Pan looked after her sadly. "She never wishes to hear; she is always busy."

"You must remember in this country we have no servants," Lili reminded her gently.

"Yes," old Mrs Pan said, "and why not? I have told my son it is not fitting to have my daughter-in-law cooking and washing in the
3 kitchen. We should have at least three servants: one for me, one for the children and one to clean and cook. At home we had many more but here we have only a few rooms."

Lili did not try to explain. "Everything is different here and let us not talk about it," she said. "Let us talk about your home and the village. I want to know how it looks and what goes on there."

Old Mrs. Pan was delighted. She smoothed the gray satin of her coat as it lay on her knees and she began.

4 "You must know that our village lies in a wide valley from which the mountains rise as sharply as tiger's teeth."

"It is so?" Lili said, making a voice of wonder.

"It is, and the village is not a small one. On the contrary, the walls encircle more than one thousand souls, all of whom are relatives of our family."

"A large family," Lili said.

"It is," old Mrs. Pan said, "and my son's

GUIDED READING

LITERAL QUESTIONS

1a. Where does old Mrs. Pan want to be buried? (in China)

2a. What does Lili ask old Mrs. Pan about? (She asks her about her village in China.)

INFERENTIAL QUESTIONS

1b. Why does she want to be buried in China? (She wants be buried in her homeland.)

2b. What is old Mrs. Pan's response? (She is thrilled to talk about the things that matter to her.)

father was the head of it. We lived in a house with seventy rooms. It was in the midst of the village. We had gardens in the courtyards. My own garden contained also a pool wherein are aged goldfish, very fat. I fed them millet and they knew me."

"How amusing." Lili saw with pleasure that the old lady's cheeks were faintly pink and that her large beautiful eyes were beginning to shine and glow. "And how many years did you live there, Ancient One?"

"I went there as a bride. I was seventeen." She looked at Lili, questioning, "How old are you?"

Lili smiled, somewhat ashamed, "I am twenty-seven."

Mrs. Pan was shocked. "Twenty-seven? But my son's wife called you Miss."

"I am not married," Lili confessed.

Mrs. Pan was instantly concerned. "How is this?" she asked. "Are your parents dead?"

"They are dead," Lili said, "but it is not their fault that I am not married."

Old Mrs. Pan would not agree to this. She shook her head with decision. "It is the duty of the parents to arrange the marriage of the children. When death approached, they should have attended to this for you. Now who is left to perform the task? Have you brothers?"

"No," Lili said, "I am an only child. But please don't worry yourself, Madame Pan. I am earning my own living and there are many young women like me in this country."

Old Mrs. Pan was dignified about this. "I cannot be responsible for what other persons do, but I must be responsible for my own kind," she declared. "Allow me to know the names of the suitable persons who can arrange your marriage. I will stand in the place of your mother. We are all in a foreign country now and we must keep together and the old must help the young in these important matters."

Lili was kind and she knew that Mrs. Pan meant kindness. "Dear Madame Pan," she said. "Marriage in America is very different from marriage in China. Here the young people choose their own mates."

"Why do you not choose, then?" Mrs. Pan said with some spirit.

Lili Yang looked abashed. "Perhaps it would be better for me to say that only the young men choose. It is they who must ask the young women."

"What do the young women do?" Mrs. Pan inquired.

"They wait," Lili confessed.

"And if they are not asked?"

"They continue to wait," Lili said gently.

"How long?" Mrs. Pan demanded.

"As long as they live."

3 Old Mrs. Pan was profoundly shocked. "Do you tell me that there is no person who arranges such matters when it is necessary?"

"Such an arrangement is not thought of here," Lili told her.

"And they allow their women to remain unmarried?" Mrs. Pan exclaimed. "Are there also sons who do not marry?"

"Here men do not marry unless they wish to do so."

Mrs. Pan was even more shocked. "How can this be?" she asked. "Of course, men will not marry unless they are compelled to do so to provide grandchildren for the family. It is necessary to make laws and create customs so that a man who will not marry is denounced as an unfilial son and one who does not fulfill his duty to his ancestors."

"Here the ancestors are forgotten and parents are not important," Lili said unwillingly.

"What a country is this," Mrs. Pan exclaimed. "How can such a country endure?"

4 Lili did not reply. Old Mrs. Pan had unknowingly touched upon a wound in her heart. No man had ever asked her to marry him. Yet above all else she would like to be married and to have

AT A GLANCE

- Old Mrs. Pan learns that Lili is twenty-seven, unmarried, and has no living relatives.
- She offers to arrange Lili's marriage but is shocked to find this is not the American custom.

1 STYLE: DIALOGUE

The use of an expression like "Ancient One" conveys the sense of a different culture.

2 PLOT: NARRATIVE HOOK

Old Mrs. Pan learns that Lili is unmarried and has no living relatives who can "arrange" her marriage.

3 THEME

Old Mrs. Pan continues to be shocked by a culture so totally different from her own.

4 POINT OF VIEW

Here, the author offers a glimpse into Lili's secret thoughts that reveals a hidden vulnerability.

GUIDED READING

LITERAL QUESTION

1a. What title does Lili use for old Mrs. Pan? ("Ancient One")

INFERENTIAL QUESTION

1b. Why does Lili use this traditional form of address? (She wants to make Mrs. Pan comfortable by addressing her the way she was used to being addressed in China.)

AT A GLANCE

- Lili thinks about how difficult it is to find a husband and how much she wants to be a wife and mother.
- Old Mrs. Pan decides to find a husband for Lili.

1 POINT OF VIEW

Old Mrs. Pan perceives Lili as plain.

2 STYLE: SIMILE

Lili is compared to a flower that is withering away. The reader gets a sense of youth and vitality going to waste.

3 PLOT: RISING ACTION

Old Mrs. Pan decides to find a husband for Lili.

4 READING SKILLS: CAUSE AND EFFECT

Old Mrs. Pan's insights into Lili's predicament touch the younger woman and cause her to confess her sadness.

children. She was a good social worker, and the head of the Children's Bureau sometimes told her that he would not know what to do without her and she must never leave them, for then there would be no one to serve the people in Chinatown. She did not wish to leave except to be married, but how could she find a husband? She looked down at her hands, clasped in her lap, and thought that if she had been in her own country, if her father had not come here as a young man and married here, she would have been in China and by now the mother of many children. Instead what would become of her? She would grow older and older, and twenty-seven was already old, and at last hope must die. She knew several American girls quite well; they liked her, and she knew that they faced the same fate. They, too, were waiting. They tried very hard; they went in summer to hotels and in winter to ski lodges, where men gathered and were at leisure enough to think about them, and in confidence they told one another of their efforts. They compared their experiences and they asked anxious questions. "Do you think men like talkative women or quiet ones?" "Do you think men like lipstick or none?" Such questions they asked of one another and who could answer them? If a girl succeeded in winning a proposal from a man, then all the other girls envied her and asked her special questions and immediately she became someone above them all, a successful woman. The job which had once been so valuable then became worthless and it was given away easily and gladly. But how could she explain this to old Mrs. Pan?

Meanwhile Mrs. Pan had been studying Lili's face carefully and with thought. This was not a pretty girl. Her face was too flat, and her mouth was large. She looked like a girl from Canton and not from Hangchow or Soochow.[2] But she had nice
1 skin, and her eyes, though small, were kind. She was the sort of girl, Mrs. Pan could see, who would make an excellent wife and a good mother, but certainly she was one for whom a marriage must be arranged. She was a decent, plain, good girl and, left to herself, Mrs. Pan could predict, nothing at
2 all would happen. She would wither away like a dying flower.

Old Mrs. Pan forgot herself and for the first time since she had been hurried away from the village without even being allowed to stop and see that the salted cabbage, drying on ropes across the big courtyard, was brought in for the winter. She had been compelled to leave it there and she had often thought of it with regret. She could have brought some with her had she known it was not to be had here. But there it was, and it was only one thing among others that she had left undone. Many people depended upon her and she had left them, because her son compelled her, and she was not used to this idleness that was killing her day by day.

3 Now as she looked at Lili's kind, ugly face it occurred to her that here there was something she could do. She could find a husband for this good girl, and it would be counted for merit when she went to heaven. A good deed is a good deed, whether one is in China or in America, for the same heaven stretches above all.

She patted Lili's clasped hands. "Do not grieve anymore," she said tenderly. "I will arrange everything."

"I am not grieving, " Lili said.

"Of course, you are," Mrs. Pan retorted. "I see you are a true woman, and women grieve when they are not wed so that they can have children. You are grieving for your children."

4 Lili could not deny it. She would have been ashamed to confess to any other person except this old Chinese lady who might have been her grandmother. She bent her head and bit her lip; she let a tear or two fall upon her hands. Then she nodded. Yes, she grieved in the secret places of her heart, in the darkness of the lonely nights,

---

2. **Canton, Hangchow, Soochow** [can′ton′, hang′ chou′, sōō′chou′]: cities in China. Canton is in southeastern China; Hangchow is a port in eastern China; Soochow is in the east.

GUIDED READING

LITERAL QUESTION

1a. What does old Mrs. Pan think her reward will be for finding a husband for Lili? (She sees it as a good deed and hopes that it will be counted for merit when she goes to heaven.)

INFERENTIAL QUESTION

1b. What is the actual effect of this decision on old Mrs. Pan? (It gives her an immediate reward—a purpose in life.)

when she thought of the empty future of her life.

"Do not grieve," old Mrs. Pan was saying, "I will arrange it; I will do it."

It was so comforting a murmur that Lili could not bear it. She said, "I came to comfort you, but it is you who comfort me." Then she got up and went out of the room quickly because she did not want to sob aloud. She was unseen, for young Mrs. Pan had gone to market and the children were at school, and Lili went away telling herself that it was all absurd, that an old woman from the middle of China who could not speak a word of English would not be able to change this American world, even for her.

Old Mrs. Pan could scarcely wait for her son to come home at noon. She declined to join the family at the table, saying that she must speak to her son first.

1 When he came in, he saw at once that she was changed. She held up her head and she spoke to him sharply when he came into the room, as though it was her house and not his in which they now were.

"Let the children eat first," she commanded, "I shall need time to talk with you and I am not hungry."

He repressed his inclination to tell her that he was hungry and that he must get back to the office. Something in her look made it impossible for him to be disobedient to her. He went away and gave the children direction and then returned.

"Yes, my mother," he said, seating himself on a small and uncomfortable chair.

Then she related to him with much detail and repetition what had happened that morning; she declared with indignation that she had never before heard of a country where no marriages were arranged for the young, leaving to them the most important event of their lives and that at a time when their judgment was still unripe, and a mistake could bring disaster upon the whole family.

"Your own marriage," she reminded him, "was arranged by your father with great care, our two families knowing each other well. Even though you and my daughter-in-law were distant in this country, yet we met her parents through a suitable go-between, and her uncle here stood in her father's place, and your father's friend in place of your father, and so it was all done according to custom though so far away."

2 Mr. Pan did not have the heart to tell his mother that he and his wife Sophia had fallen in love first, and then, out of kindness to their elders, had allowed the marriage to be arranged for them as though they were not in love, and as though, indeed, they did not know each other. They were both young people of heart, and although it would have been much easier to be married in the American fashion, they considered their elders.

"What has all this to do with us now, my mother?" he asked.

"This is what is to do," she replied with spirit. "A nice, ugly girl of our own people came here today to see me. She is twenty-seven years old and she is not married. What will become of her?"

"Do you mean Lili Yang?" her son asked.

"I do," she replied. "When I heard that she has no way of being married because, according to the custom of this country, she must wait for a man to ask her—"

Old Mrs. Pan broke off and gazed at her son with horrified eyes.

"What now?" he asked.

"Suppose the only man who asks is one who is not at all suitable?"

"It is quite possible that it often happens thus," her son said, trying not to laugh.

3 "Then she has no choice," old Mrs. Pan said indignantly. "She can only remain unmarried or accept one who is unsuitable."

"Here she has no choice," Mr. Pan agreed, "unless she is very pretty, my mother, when several men may ask and then she has choice." It

AT A GLANCE

- Lili is skeptical of a successful outcome of Mrs. Pan's marriage plans for her.
- Old Mrs. Pan discusses arranged marriages and her plans for Lili with her son.

1 CHARACTERIZATION

Her strong manner of speaking and the new way she carries herself show that old Mrs. Pan has regained her authority and recovered a sense of purpose.

2 THEME

Young Mr. and Mrs. Pan showed a willingness to compromise to avoid a clash of cultures. Though they married for love, they, out of kindness to their elders, pretended to follow tradition and have their marriage "arranged."

3 STYLE: DIALOGUE

The dialogue conveys a flavor of the Chinese language that the characters are actually speaking.

GUIDED READING

LITERAL QUESTION

1a. What does Lili think about old Mrs. Pan's marriage plans? (She thinks they are absurd.)

INFERENTIAL QUESTION

1b. Why does Lili think the plans are absurd? (She is aware of the obstacles old Mrs. Pan would have to face in trying to follow Chinese custom in America.)

AT A GLANCE

- Mr. Pan explains American courtship customs to his mother.
- Old Mrs. Pan asks her son to help find a husband for Lili at his office.
- Young Mrs. Pan argues that an arranged marriage might be good for Lili.

1 THEME

Old Mrs. Pan regards American courtship methods as barbarous.

2 STYLE: DICTION

The stilted dialogue reminds the reader that the characters are speaking in Chinese.

3 PLOT: RISING ACTION

Old Mrs. Pan enlists her son's assistance in her plans to arrange a marriage for Lili.

4 CHARACTERIZATION

Old Mrs. Pan continues to demonstrate rigidity in attitudes as well as actions.

was on the tip of his tongue to tell how at least six young men had proposed to his Sophia, thereby distressing him continually until he was finally chosen, but he thought better of it. Would it not be very hard to explain so much to his old mother, and could she understand? He doubted it. Nevertheless, he felt it necessary at least to make one point.

"Something must be said for the man also, my mother. Sometimes he asks a girl who will not have him, because she chooses another, and then his sufferings are intense. Unless he wishes to remain unmarried he must ask a second girl, who is not the first one. Here also is some injustice."

Old Mrs. Pan listened to this attentively and
1 then declared, "It is all barbarous. Certainly it is very embarrassing to be compelled to speak of these matters, man and woman, face to face. They should be spared; others should speak for them."

She considered for a few seconds and then she said with fresh indignation, "And what woman can change the appearance her ancestors have given her? Because she is not pretty is she less a woman? Are not her feelings like any woman's; is it not her right to have husband and home and children? It is well-known that men have no wisdom in such matters; they believe that a woman's face is all she has, forgetting that everything else is the same. They gather about the pretty woman, who is surfeited with them, and leave alone the good woman. And I do not know why heaven has created ugly women always good but so it is, whether here or in our own country, but what man is wise enough to know that? Therefore his wife should be chosen for him, so that the family is not burdened with his follies."

2 Mr. Pan allowed all this to be said and then he inquired, "What is on your mind, my mother?"

Old Mrs. Pan leaned toward him and lifted her forefinger. "This is what I command you to do for me, my son. I myself will find a husband for this good girl of our people. She is helpless and alone. But I know no one; I am a stranger, and I
3 must depend upon you. In your business there must be young men. Inquire of them and see who stands for them, so that we can arrange a meeting between them and me; I will stand for the girl's mother. I promised it."

Now Mr. Pan laughed heartily. "Oh, my mother!" he cried. "You are too kind, but it cannot be done. They would laugh at me, and do you believe that Lili Yang herself would like such an arrangement? I think she would not. She has been in America too long."

4 Old Mrs. Pan would not yield, however, and in the end he was compelled to promise that he would see what he could do. Upon this promise she consented to eat her meal, and he led her out, her right hand resting upon his left wrist. The children were gone and they had a quiet meal together, and after it she said she felt that she would sleep. This was good news, for she had not slept well since she came, and young Mrs. Pan led her into the bedroom and helped her to lie down and placed a thin quilt over her.

When young Mrs. Pan went back to the small dining room where her husband waited to tell her what his mother had said, she listened thoughtfully.

"It is absurd," her husband said, "but what shall we do to satisfy my mother? She sees it as a good deed if she can find a husband for Lili Yang."

Here his wife surprised him. "I can see some good in it myself," she declared. "I have often felt for Lili. It is a problem, and our mother is right to see it as such. It is not only Lili—it is a problem here for all young women, especially if they are not pretty." She looked quizzically at her husband for a moment and then said, "I too used to worry when I was very young, lest I should not find a husband for myself. It is a great burden for a young woman. It would be nice to have someone else arrange the matter."

"Remember," he told her, "how often in the

GUIDED READING

LITERAL QUESTIONS

1a. What does Mr. Pan try to explain to his mother? (He tries to explain American courtship customs.)

2a. What does old Mrs. Pan try to explain to her son? (She explains the benefits of arranged marriages.)

INFERENTIAL QUESTIONS

1b. Why does he try to explain these customs to her? (He wants her to understand the vast differences between American and Chinese courtship customs.)

2b. Why does she explain the benefits of this custom to him? (to convince him to help her find a husband for Lili)

old country the wrong men are arranged for and how often the young men leave home because they do not like the wives their parents choose for them."

1 "Well, so do they here," she said pertly. "Divorce, divorce, divorce!"

"Come, come," he told her. "It is not so bad."

"It is very bad for women," she insisted. "When there is divorce here, then she is thrown out of the family. The ties are broken. But in the
2 old country, it is the man who leaves home and the woman stays on, for she is still the daughter-in-law and her children will belong to the family, and however far away the man wants to go, she has her place and she is safe."

Mr. Pan looked at his watch. "It is late and I must go to the office."

"Oh, your office," young Mrs. Pan said in an uppish voice, "what would you do without it?"

They did not know it but their voices roused old Mrs. Pan in the bedroom, and she opened her eyes. She could not understand what they said for they spoke in English, but she understood that there was an argument. She sat up on the bed to listen, then she heard the door slam and
3 she knew her son was gone. She was about to lie down again when it occurred to her that it would be interesting to look out of the window to the street and see what young men there were coming to and fro. One did not choose men from the street, of course, but still she could see what their looks were.

She got up and tidied her hair and tottered on her small feet over to the window and opening the curtains a little she gazed into the street really for the first time since she came. She was pleased to see many Chinese men, some of them

AT A GLANCE

- Mr. and Mrs. Pan argue about the advantages and disadvantages of arranged marriages.
- Old Mrs. Pan decides to look out at the world beyond her window for the first time.

1 STYLE: DICTION

The idiomatic style of the dialogue indicates that the characters are arguing in English.

2 THEME

Young Mrs. Pan shows spirit and independence in disagreeing with her husband's views, something old Mrs. Pan probably never would have done.

3 CHARACTERIZATION

Old Mrs. Pan's new project has given her a sense of purpose, encouraging her to expand her horizons beyond her tiny room.

GUIDED READING

LITERAL QUESTION

1a. What do Mr. and Mrs. Pan argue about? (They argue about the advantages and disadvantages of American and Chinese marriage customs.)

INFERENTIAL QUESTION

1b. Why does young Mrs. Pan defend the Chinese customs? (As a woman, she chooses the tradition that seems to protect the wives.)

AT A GLANCE

- One day, as old Mrs. Pan looks out of her window, a young man from a shop across the street smiles at her.
- She decides that he will be Lili's husband and plans to speak to him.

1 CHARACTERIZATION

Old Mrs. Pan has progressed from an awareness of the outside world to an active pleasure in observing it.

2 CONFLICT

The opposing viewpoints of mother and son clash again as they consider the same person differently.

3 CHARACTERIZATION

Mr. Pan's gesture reveals a patronizing attitude toward women, also shown earlier in the "concealed amusement" with which he listens to his mother.

4 PLOT: RISING ACTION

Old Mrs. Pan realizes she will have to go out and speak to the young man herself.

young. It was still not late, and they loitered in the sunshine before going back to work, talking
1 and laughing and looking happy. It was interesting to her to watch them, keeping in mind Lili Yang and thinking to herself that it might be this one or that one, although still one did not choose men from the street. She stood so long that at last she became tired and she pulled a small chair to the window and kept looking through the parted curtain.

Here her daughter-in-law saw her a little later, when she opened the door to see if her mother-in-law was awake, but she did not speak. She looked at the little satin-clad figure, and went away again, wondering why it was that the old lady found it pleasant today to look out of the window when every other day she had refused the same pleasure.

It became a pastime for old Mrs. Pan to look out of the window every day from then on. Gradually she came to know some of the young men, not by name but by their faces and by the way they walked by her window, never, of course looking up at her, until one day a certain young man did look up and smile. It was a warm day, and she had asked that the window be opened, which until now she had not allowed, for fear she might be assailed by the foreign winds and made ill. Today, however, was near to summer, she felt the room airless and she longed for freshness.

After this the young man habitually smiled when he passed or nodded his head. She was too old to have it mean anything but courtesy and so bit by bit she allowed herself to make a gesture of her hand in return. It was evident that he belonged in a china shop across the narrow street. She watched him go in and come out; she watched him stand at the door in his shirt sleeves on a fine day and talk and laugh, showing, as she observed, strong white teeth set off by two gold ones. Evidently he made money. She did not believe he was married, for she saw an old man who must be his father, who smoked a water pipe,[3] and now and then an elderly woman, perhaps his mother, and a younger brother, but there was no young woman.

She began after some weeks of watching to fix upon this young man as a husband for Lili. But who could be the go-between except her own son?

She confided her plans one night to him, and, as always, he listened to her with courtesy and
2 concealed amusement. "But the young man, my mother, is the son of Mr. Lim, who is the richest man on our street."

"That is nothing against him," she declared.

"No, but he will not submit to an arrangement, my mother. He is a college graduate. He is only spending the summer at home in the shop to help his father."

"Lili Yang has also been to school."

"I know, my mother, but, you see, the young man will want to choose his own wife, and it will not be someone who looks like Lili Yang. It will be someone who—"

3 He broke off and made a gesture which suggested curled hair, a fine figure and an air. Mrs. Pan watched him with disgust. "You are like all these other men, though you are my son," she said and dismissed him sternly.

Nevertheless, she thought over what he had said when she went back to the window. The young man was standing on the street picking his fine teeth and laughing at friends who passed, the sun shining on his glistening black hair. It was true he did not look at all obedient; it was perhaps true that he was no more wise than other men and so saw only what a girl's face
4 was. She wished that she could speak to him, but that, of course, was impossible. Unless—

She drew in a long breath. Unless she went downstairs and out into that street and crossed it

3. **water pipe:** smoking pipe in which the smoke is drawn through water.

GUIDED READING

LITERAL QUESTION

1a. What does old Mrs. Pan notice about young Mr. Lim? (She notices his smile, his gold teeth, and his glistening hair.)

INFERENTIAL QUESTION

1b. Why does she feel that these attitudes would make him a good husband? (He seems to be kind, wealthy, and handsome.)

and entered the shop, pretending that she came to buy something! If she did this, she could speak to him. But what would she say, and who would help her cross the street? She did not want to tell her son or her son's wife, for they would suspect her and laugh. They teased her often even now about her purpose, and Lili was so embarrassed by their laughter that she did not want to come anymore.

Old Mrs. Pan reflected on the difficulty of her position as a lady in a barbarous and strange country. Then she thought of her eldest grandson, Johnnie. On Saturday, when her son was at his office and her son's wife was at the market, she would coax Johnnie to lead her across the street to the china shop; she would pay him some money, and in the shop she would say she was looking for two bowls to match some that had been broken. It would be an expedition, but she might speak to the young man and tell him—what should she tell him? That must first be planned.

This was only Thursday and she had only two days to prepare. She was very restless during those two days, and she could not eat. Mr. Pan spoke of a doctor whom she indignantly refused to see, because he was a man and also because she was not ill. But Saturday came at last and everything came about as she planned. Her son went away, and then her son's wife, and she
1 crept downstairs with much effort to the sidewalk where her grandson was playing marbles and beckoned him to her. The child was terrified to see her there and came at once, and she pressed a coin into his palm and pointed across the street with her cane.

"Lead me there," she commanded and, shutting her eyes tightly, she put her hand on his shoulder and allowed him to lead her to the shop. Then to her dismay he left her and ran back to play and she stood wavering on the threshold, feeling dizzy, and the young man saw her and came hurrying toward her. To her joy he
2 spoke good Chinese, and the words fell sweetly upon her old ears.

"Ancient One, Ancient One," he chided her kindly. "Come in and sit down. It is too much for you."

He led her inside the cool, dark shop and she sat down on a bamboo chair.

"I came to look for two bowls," she said faintly.

"Tell me the pattern and I will get them for you," he said. "Are they blue willow pattern or the thousand flowers?"

"Thousand flowers," she said in the same faint voice, "but I do not wish to disturb you."

"I am here to be disturbed," he replied with the utmost courtesy.

He brought out some bowls and set them on a small table before her and she fell to talking with him. He was very pleasant; his rather large face was shining with kindness and he laughed
3 easily. Now that she saw him close, she was glad to notice that he was not too handsome; his nose and mouth were big, and he had big hands and feet.

"You look like a countryman," she said. "Where is your ancestral home?"

"It is in the province of Shantung,"[4] he replied, "and there are not many of us here."

"That explains why you are so tall," she said. "These people from Canton[5] are small. We of Szechuen are also big and our language is yours. I cannot understand the people of Canton."

4 From this they fell to talking of their own country, which he had never seen, and she told him about the village and how her son's father had left it many years ago to do business here in this foreign country and how he had sent for their son and then how she had been compelled to flee because the country was in fragments and torn between many leaders. When she had told

4. **Shantung** [shan'tung']: province of northeastern China.
5. **Canton** [can'ton']: province of southeastern China.

AT A GLANCE

- Old Mrs. Pan decides to go to the shop on Saturday.
- Her grandson helps her across the street to the shop.
- Young Mr. Lim leads her inside and shows her some bowls.

1 CHARACTERIZATION

To achieve her goal, old Mrs. Pan is prepared to overcome her fears about facing the outside world.

2 STYLE: DIALOGUE

The young man speaks to her in a way that reminds us of Lili's respectful dialogue with the older woman.

3 POINT OF VIEW

Old Mrs. Pan sees young Mr. Lim in a less flattering light than before.

4 THEME

Old Mrs. Pan feels comfortable with young Mr. Lim because he speaks good Chinese and observes old traditions.

GUIDED READING

LITERAL QUESTION

1a. How does old Mrs. Pan see young Mr. Lim up close? (She sees a large face, a big mouth and nose, and big hands and feet.)

INFERENTIAL QUESTION

1b. Why does the way she sees him make her glad? (She feels that a less handsome man will be more receptive to a plain woman.)

AT A GLANCE

- Old Mrs. Pan mentions Lili Yang to Mr. Lim and praises plain, virtuous women.
- Mr. Pan secretly invites Lili to drop by again.
- Old Mrs. Pan decides to introduce Lili to Mr. Lim.

1 VOCABULARY: CONNOTATION

Beauty is in the eye of the beholder. This concept also applies to the clash-of-cultures theme—the same culture can have predominantly positive or predominantly negative aspects to different observers.

2 PLOT: RISING ACTION

Mr. Pan helps his mother's purpose along by doing his own "good deed" in inviting Lili to visit again.

3 THEME

The main theme of the story is stated here.

this much, she found herself telling him how difficult it was to live here and how strange the city was to her and how she would never have looked out of the window had it not been for the sake of Lili Yang.

"Who is Lili Yang?" he asked.

Old Mrs. Pan did not answer him directly. That would not have been suitable. One does not speak of a reputable young woman to any man, not even one as good as this one. Instead she began a long speech about the virtues of young women who were not pretty, and how beauty in a woman made virtue unlikely, and how a woman not beautiful was always grateful to her husband and did not consider that she had done him a favor by the marriage, but rather that it was he who conferred the favor, so that she served him far better than she could have done were she beautiful.

To all this the young man listened, his small eyes twinkling with laughter.

"I take it that this Lili Yang is not beautiful," he said.

Old Mrs. Pan looked astonished. "I did not
1 say so," she replied with spirit. "I will not say she is beautiful and I will not say she is ugly. What is beautiful to one is not so to another. Suppose you see her sometime for yourself, and then we will discuss it."

"Discuss what?" he demanded.

"Whether she is beautiful."

Suddenly she felt that she had come to a point and that she had better go home. It was enough for the first visit. She chose two bowls and paid for them and while he wrapped them up she waited in silence, for to say too much is worse than to say too little.

When the bowls were wrapped, the young man said courteously, "Let me lead you across the street, Ancient One."

So, putting her right hand on his left wrist, she let him lead her across and this time she did not shut her eyes, and she came home again feeling that she had been a long way and had accomplished much. When her daughter-in-law came home she said quite easily, "I went across the street and bought these two bowls."

Young Mrs. Pan opened her eyes wide. "My mother, how could you go alone?"

"I did not go alone," old Mrs. Pan said tranquilly. "My grandson led me across and young Mr. Lim brought me back."

Each had spoken in her own language with helpful gestures.

Young Mrs. Pan was astonished and she said no more until her husband came home, when she told him. He laughed a great deal and said, "Do not interfere with our old one. She is enjoying herself. It is good for her."

But all the time he knew what his mother was doing and he joined in it without her
2 knowledge. That is to say, he telephoned the same afternoon from his office to Miss Lili Yang, and when she answered, he said, "Please come and see my old mother again. She asks after you every day. Your visit did her much good."

Lili Yang promised, not for today but for a week hence, and when Mr. Pan went home he told his mother carelessly, as though it were nothing, that Lili Yang had called him up to say she was coming again next week.

Old Mrs. Pan heard this with secret excitement. She had not gone out again, but every day young Mr. Lim nodded to her and smiled, and once he sent her a small gift of fresh ginger root. She made up her mind slowly but she made it up well. When Lili Yang came again, she would ask her to take her to the china shop, pretending that
3 she wanted to buy something, and she would introduce the two to each other; that much she would do. It was too much, but, after all, these were modern times, and this was a barbarous country, where it did not matter greatly whether the old customs were kept or not. The important thing was to find a husband for Lili, who was already twenty-seven years old.

So it all came about, and when Lili walked into her room the next week, while the fine weather

GUIDED READING

LITERAL QUESTIONS

1a. How does old Mrs. Pan respond to the question: "Who is Lili Yang?" (She answers indirectly by referring to the virtues of plain women.)

2a. What does Mr. Pan do? (He invites Lili to visit his mother again.)

INFERENTIAL QUESTIONS

1b. Why doesn't old Mrs. Pan answer the question? (She wants to make Mr. Lim curious about Lili and not reject her on the basis of looks alone.)

2b. Why does he invite Lili? (He wants to help his mother in her project because it is doing her good, even if nothing comes of it.)

still held, old Mrs. Pan greeted her with smiles. She seized Lili's small hand and noticed that the hand was very soft and pretty, as the hands of most plain-faced girls are, the gods being kind to such women and giving them pretty bodies when they see that ancestors have not bestowed pretty faces.

"Do not take off your foreign hat," she told Lili. "I wish to go across the street to that shop and buy some dishes as a gift for my son's wife. She is very kind to me."

Lili Yang was pleased to see the old lady so changed and cheerful and in all innocence she agreed and they went across the street and into the shop. Today there were customers, and old Mr. Lim was there too, as well as his son. He was a tall, withered man, and he wore a small beard under his chin. When he saw old Mrs. Pan he stopped what he was doing and brought her a chair to sit upon while she waited. As soon as his customer was gone, he introduced himself, saying that he knew her son.

1 "My son has told me of your honored visit last week," he said. "Please come inside and have some tea. I will have my son bring the dishes, and you can look at them in quiet. It is too noisy here."

She accepted his courtesy, and in a few minutes young Mr. Lim came back to the inner room with the dishes while a servant brought tea.

2 Old Mrs. Pan did not introduce Lili Yang, for it was not well to embarrass a woman, but young Mr. Lim boldly introduced himself, in English.

"Are you Miss Lili Yang?" he asked. "I am James Lim."

"How did you know my name?" Lili asked, astonished.

"I have met you before, not face to face, but through Mrs. Pan," he said, his small eyes twinkling. "She has told me more about you than she knows."

Lili blushed. "Mrs. Pan is so old-fashioned," she murmured. "You must not believe her."

AT A GLANCE

- Old Mrs. Pan asks Lili to take her to the shop to buy some dishes.
- Old Mr. Lim greets old Mrs. Pan and offers her a chair and tea.
- Young Mr. Lim introduces himself to Lili.

1 SETTING

The description and activities of old Mr. Lim emphasize the difference between a Chinese store and an American one.

2 THEME

Here two different life styles are back to back. While Mrs. Pan is acting formally, the two young people immediately converse easily.

GUIDED READING

LITERAL QUESTION

1a. What does James Lim do when he sees Lili? (He introduces himself to her.)

INFERENTIAL QUESTION

1b. What does this introduction tell you about his way of life? (He is not hampered by Chinese customs; he follows American ways.)

AT A GLANCE

- Old Mrs. Pan and old Mr. Lim talk about Lili and Jim.
- Lili accepts a date with Jim on Sunday.
- Mr. and Mrs. Pan agree to arrange the marriage on Sunday.

1 POINT OF VIEW

In James Lim's eyes Lili is an attractive woman.

2 PLOT: CLIMAX

Lili and James make a date.

3 PLOT: FALLING ACTION

Old Mrs. Pan is still determined to arrange a marriage for James and Lili.

4 THEME

Both Chinese tradition and American custom combine to bring James and Lili together.

REFLECTING ON THE STORY

Why did the author choose the omniscient point of view? (He shows the conflicting thoughts of the characters, underscoring the differences between American and Chinese cultures.)

"I shall only believe what I see for myself," he said gallantly. He looked at her frankly and
1 Lili kept blushing. Old Mrs. Pan had not done her justice, he thought. The young woman had a nice, round face, the sort of face he liked. She was shy, and he liked that also. It was something new.

Meanwhile old Mrs. Pan watched all this with amazement. So this was the way it was: The young man began speaking immediately, and the young woman blushed. She wished that she knew what they were saying but perhaps it was better that she did not know.

She turned to old Mr. Lim, who was sitting across the square table sipping tea. At least here she could do her duty. "I hear your son is not married," she said in a tentative way.

"Not yet," Mr. Lim said. "He wants first to finish learning how to be a Western doctor."

"How old is he?" Mrs. Pan inquired.

"He is twenty-eight. It is very old but he did not make up his mind for some years, and the learning is long."

"Miss Lili Yang is twenty-seven," Mrs. Pan said in the same tentative voice.

The young people were still talking in English and not listening to them. Lili was telling James Lim about her work and about old Mrs. Pan. She was not blushing anymore; she had forgotten, it seemed, that he was a young man and she a young woman. Suddenly she stopped and blushed again. A woman was supposed to let a man talk about himself, not about her.

"Tell me about your work," she said. "I wanted to be a doctor, too, but it cost too much."

"I can't tell you here," he said. "There are customers waiting in the shop and it will take a long time. Let me come to see you, may I? I could come on Sunday when the shop is closed. Or we could take a ride on one of the riverboats. Will you? The weather is so fine."

"I have never been on a riverboat," she said. "It would be delightful."

She forgot her work and remembered that he was a young man and that she was a young woman. She liked his big face and the way his black hair fell back from his forehead and she knew that a day on the river could be a day in
2 heaven.

The customers were getting impatient. They began to call out and he got up. "Next Sunday," he said in a low voice. "Let's start early. I'll be at the wharf at nine o'clock."

"We do not know each other," she said, reluctant and yet eager. Would he think she was too eager?

He laughed. "You see my respectable father, and I know old Mrs. Pan very well. Let them guarantee us."

He hurried away, and old Mrs. Pan said immediately to Lili, "I have chosen these four dishes. Please take them and have them wrapped. Then we will go home."

Lili obeyed, and when she was gone, old Mrs. Pan leaned toward old Mr. Lim.

3 "I wanted to get her out of the way," she said in a low and important voice. "Now, while she is gone, what do you say? Shall we arrange a match? We do not need a go-between. I stand as her mother, let us say, and you are his father. We must have their horoscopes read, of course, but just between us, it looks as though it is suitable, does it not?"

Mr. Lim wagged his head. "If you recommend her, Honorable Old Lady, why not?"

Why not, indeed? After all, things were not so different here, after all.

"What day is convenient for you?" she asked.

"Shall we say Sunday?" old Mr. Lim suggested.

"Why not?" she replied. "All days are good, when one performs a good deed, and what is better than to arrange a marriage?"

4 "Nothing is better," old Mr. Lim agreed. "Of all good deeds under heaven, it is the best."

They fell silent, both pleased with themselves, while they waited.

GUIDED READING

LITERAL QUESTIONS

1a. What do James and Lili decide to do on Sunday? (They plan a date on a riverboat.)

2a. What do Mrs. Pan and Mr. Lim do at the end of the story? (They fell silent and waited.)

INFERENTIAL QUESTIONS

1b. How will they get along on their first date? (They will probably get along well, since they seem to like each other.)

2b. What are they waiting for at the end? (They are waiting to achieve their goal, whether in the traditional Chinese way, or in the American way.)

STUDY QUESTIONS

Recalling

1. Give three examples of old Mrs. Pan's dissatisfaction with customs in the New World.
2. In what way was the arranging of Mr. Pan's marriage a compromise between old ways and new?
3. In what way does old Mrs. Pan come to forget her own unhappiness?
4. At the end of the story, what do Lili and Mrs. Pan each plan for Sunday?

Interpreting

5. On what other thresholds might Mrs. Pan be wavering when her grandson leaves her "wavering on the threshold" of Mr. Lim's door?
6. Speaking of Lili, old Mrs. Pan tells Mr. Lim, "What is beautiful to one is not so to another." How might this statement also be applied to culture as pictured in the story?
7. What good deeds by others help to bring about the final good deed by old Mrs. Pan?

Extending

8. What message does "The Good Deed" imply about the conflicts that often exist between old and new ways and between different cultures?

VIEWPOINT

In most of her stories, Pearl S. Buck presents characters who struggle to overcome personal or cultural barriers. One author states that Buck's work illustrates the following principle:

> Every knot can be untied or loosened if one acts with selfless intent and altruistic consideration.
>
> —P. Doyle, *Pearl S. Buck*

■ What evidence does "The Good Deed" provide of Buck's belief in selflessness and its power?

LITERARY FOCUS

Omniscient Point of View

The word *omniscient* means "all-knowing." A story told from the **omniscient point of view** is told by the author, acting as an omniscient narrator who stands outside the story. The omniscient narrator knows and can tell the reader everything, including the thoughts and feelings of every character. As a result, we usually know more than any one character does. The narrator's personality does not interfere with the storytelling, and we can trust the narrator completely.

Thinking About Point of View

1. What, according to the omniscient narrator, do Lili, Mr. Pan, and his wife feel about the plan to find Lili a husband?
2. In what ways would this story be different if old Mrs. Pan were the narrator?

COMPOSITION

Writing About Character

■ Select the character you like the most from the story, and, using specific references from the story, explain why this is your favorite character. After you have identified the character, first tell what you like about the character's opinions. Then tell what you like about the character's actions. (Make sure to base your decision on what you know about the character as revealed by the omniscient point of view.)

Writing a Dialogue

■ In the story we see many differences between traditional Chinese customs and customs of the New World. Mr. Pan has decided that it is important for his mother to gain a better understanding of the New World and its different customs. Choose one of the following areas of differing traditions, and write a dialogue in which Mr. Pan and his mother discuss their different attitudes: (a) older family members, (b) raising children, (c) courtship and marriage.

COMPARING STORIES

■ In "The Tell-Tale Heart" the murderer has a dark secret. In "Beware of the Dog" Peter Williamson is the victim of a secret conspiracy. In "The Good Deed" Mrs. Pan does not tell Lili what she is planning. For at least two of these stories, explain how the point of view determines how much you know about the secret as you read. Then discuss how your knowledge determines the overall impact of the story on you.

STUDY QUESTIONS

1. marriages not arranged; no servants; children disrespectful
2. They met, fell in love but let marriage be arranged according to tradition.
3. Arranging Lili's marriage gives her a purpose.
4. Lili: a date; Mrs. Pan: to meet James's father
5. of plan to find Lili a husband; of adapting to her new life
6. culture of New York attractive to young Chinese, unappealing to Mrs. Pan; culture of China unappealing to younger characters
7. Daughter-in-law invites Lili; Lili visits Mrs. Pan.
8. They can be settled by compromise.

VIEWPOINT

One act of altruism inspires another.

LITERARY FOCUS

1. ■ Lili: embarrassed but hopeful
   ■ Mr. Pan: skeptical but helpful
   ■ wife: thinks it's a good idea
2. wouldn't know other's conflicting thoughts; would get one-sided view of conflicting cultures

COMPARING STORIES

"Heart": First-person point of view reveals entire plan. "Beware": Limited third-person withholds truth until end. "Deed": Omniscient narrator reveals plan slowly as story unfolds.

COMPOSITION: GUIDELINES FOR EVALUATION

WRITING ABOUT CHARACTER

Objective

To express an opinion about a character and support it with examples and reasons

Guidelines for Evaluation

- suggested length: three paragraphs
- should include clear thesis statement
- should cite character's opinions and actions and writer's reasons for liking them

WRITING A DIALOGUE

Objective

To write a short dialogue

Guidelines for Evaluation

- suggested length: 200–300 words
- should use direct quotations or dramatic form
- should employ one of the suggested topics
- should give reasons for character's attitudes

AT A GLANCE

- Della and Jim live spartan lives on little money.
- She has only $1.87 to buy a Christmas present for him.

LITERARY OPTIONS

- theme
- characterization
- irony

THEMATIC OPTIONS

- selfless love
- identity and self-respect
- hopes and ideals

1 TONE

The author's thematic asides and elevated vocabulary show a tongue-in-cheek attitude toward his story and characters.

2 SETTING

The economic difficulties of the couple are symbolized by an empty mailbox and a broken doorbell.

3 PLOT: CONFLICT

Della's lack of funds for a Christmas present sets up the basic conflict of the story.

LITERARY FOCUS: Theme

O. Henry is the pen name for American short story writer William Sydney Porter. In the course of his life (1862–1910), O. Henry completed twelve volumes of stories. He is most famous for mastering the art of stories with twist, or surprise, endings.

■ What examples of *selflessness* can you suggest from other stories?

O. Henry

The Gift of the Magi[1]

One dollar and eighty-seven cents. That was all. And sixty cents of it was in pennies. Pennies saved one and two at a time by bulldozing the grocer and the vegetable man and the butcher until one's cheek burned with the silent imputation of parsimony[2] that such close dealing implied. Three times Della counted it. One dollar and eighty-seven cents. And the next day would be Christmas.

There was clearly nothing to do but flop down on the shabby little couch and howl. So
1 Della did it. Which instigates the moral reflection that life is made up of sobs, sniffles, and smiles, with sniffles predominating.

While the mistress of the home is gradually subsiding from the first stage to the second, take a look at the home. A furnished flat[3] at eight dollars per week. It did not exactly beggar description,[4] but it certainly had that word on the lookout for the mendicancy squad.[5]

2 In the vestibule[6] below was a letter box into which no letter would go, and an electric button from which no mortal finger could coax a ring. Also appertaining thereunto was a card bearing the name "Mr. James Dillingham Young."

The "Dillingham" had been flung to the breeze during a former period of prosperity when its possessor was being paid thirty dollars per week. Now, when the income was shrunk to twenty dollars, the letters of "Dillingham" looked blurred, as though they were thinking seriously of contracting to a modest and unassuming *D.* But whenever Mr. James Dillingham Young came home and reached his flat above he was called "Jim" and greatly hugged by Mrs. James Dillingham Young, already introduced to you as Della. Which is all very good.

Della finished her cry and attended to her cheeks with the powder rag. She stood by the window and looked out dully at a gray cat walk-
3 ing a gray fence in a gray backyard. Tomorrow would be Christmas Day, and she had only one dollar and eighty-seven cents with which to buy Jim a present. She had been saving every penny

1. **Magi** [mā′jī]
2. **imputation** [im′pyə tā′shən] **of parsimony** [pär′sə mō′nē]: silent accusation of stinginess.
3. **flat:** apartment.
4. **beggar description:** defy description.
5. **mendicancy** [men′di kən sē] **squad:** police squad that arrested beggars.
6. **vestibule** [ves′tə būl′]: small entrance hallway.

GUIDED READING

LITERAL QUESTION

1a. How does O. Henry first describe the Youngs' home? ("a furnished flat at eight dollars per week")

INFERENTIAL QUESTION

1b. What can you infer from the description of the flat? (It shows that they are living on very little money and may be having trouble making ends meet.)

she could for months, with this result. Twenty dollars a week doesn't go far. Expenses had been greater than she had calculated. They always are. Only one dollar and eighty-seven cents to buy a present for Jim. Her Jim. Many a happy hour she had spent planning for something nice for him. Something fine and rare and sterling—something just a little bit near to being worthy of the honor of being owned by Jim.

There was a pier glass[7] between the windows of the room. Perhaps you have seen a pier glass in an eight-dollar flat. A very thin and very agile person may, by observing his reflection in a rapid sequence of longitudinal strips, obtain a fairly accurate conception of his looks. Della, being slender, had mastered the art.

Suddenly she whirled from the window and stood before the glass. Her eyes were shining brilliantly, but her face had lost its color within twenty seconds. Rapidly she pulled down her hair and let it fall to its full length.

Now there were two possessions of the James Dillingham Youngs in which they both took a mighty pride. One was Jim's gold watch that had been his father's and his grandfather's. The other was Della's hair. Had the Queen of Sheba[8] lived in the flat across the air shaft, Della would have let her hair hang out the window someday to dry, just to depreciate Her Majesty's jewels and gifts. Had King Solomon[9] been the janitor, with all his treasures piled up in the basement, Jim would have pulled out his watch every time he passed, just to see him pluck at his beard from envy.

So now Della's beautiful hair fell about her, rippling and shining like a cascade of brown waters. It reached below her knee and made itself almost a garment for her. And then she did it up again nervously and quickly. Once she faltered for a minute and stood still while a tear or two splashed on the worn red carpet.

On went her old brown jacket; on went her old brown hat. With a whirl of skirts and with the brilliant sparkle still in her eyes, she fluttered out the door and down the stairs to the street.

Where she stopped the sign read: "Mme. Sofronie. Hair Goods of All Kinds." One flight up Della ran—and collected herself, panting. Madame, large, too white, chilly, hardly looked the "Sofronie."

"Will you buy my hair?" asked Della.

"I buy hair," said Madame. "Take yer hat off and let's have a sight at the looks of it."

Down rippled the brown cascade.

4 "Twenty dollars," said Madame, lifting the mass with a practiced hand.

"Give it to me quick," said Della.

Oh, and the next two hours tripped by on rosy wings. Forget the hashed metaphor. She was ransacking the stores for Jim's present.

She found it at last. It surely had been made for Jim and no one else. There was no other like it in any of the stores, and she had turned all of them inside out. It was a platinum fob chain,[10] simple and chaste in design, properly proclaiming its value by substance alone and not by meretricious ornamentation[11]—as all good things should do. It was even worthy of The Watch. As
5 soon as she saw it she knew that it must be Jim's. It was like him. Quietness and value—the description applied to both. Twenty-one dollars they took from her for it, and she hurried home with the eighty-seven cents. With that chain on his watch Jim might be properly anxious about the time in any company. Grand as the watch was, he sometimes looked at it on the sly on account of the old leather strap that he used in place of a chain.

When Della reached home her intoxication

7. **pier** [pēr] **glass:** narrow mirror between two windows.
8. **Queen of Sheba** [shē′bə]: biblical queen legendary for her beauty.
9. **King Solomon** [sol′ə mən]: biblical king of Israel noted for his wealth and wisdom.

10. **platinum fob chain:** silvery chain connecting a pocket watch to the pocket.
11. **meretricious** [mer′ə trish′əs] **ornamentation:** falsely attractive, flashy decoration.

AT A GLANCE

- Della looks at her long, beautiful hair in the mirror.
- She sells her hair for twenty dollars and buys a platinum chain for Jim's watch.

1 CHARACTERIZATION

Through Della's eyes we understand her devotion; Jim is so special that a gift must be worthy of his ownership.

2 TONE

The author gently exaggerates the beauty of Della's hair by comparing her with a legendary woman of beauty.

3 STYLE: IMAGERY

Comparing Della's hair first to a waterfall and then to "a garment" emphasizes its beauty and magnificence.

4 PLOT: NARRATIVE HOOK

Della sells her most prized possession for twenty dollars in order to buy Jim an expensive present; she performs the act quickly to avoid changing her mind.

5 READING SKILLS: COMPARISON

Jim's character is likened to the "quietness and value" of the platinum chain.

GUIDED READING

LITERAL QUESTIONS

1a. What is Della's most prized possession? (her hair)

2a. What does she do with her hair? (She sells it for twenty dollars.)

INFERENTIAL QUESTIONS

1b. What does this tell you about her circumstances? (Her only valuable possession is a natural one; she cannot buy anything of value.)

2b. What does this sale tell you about Della's relationship with Jim? (Della is devoted to him; she parts with her most prized possession for him.)

AT A GLANCE

- Della curls her short hair.
- Jim arrives and stares at her.
- He tosses a package on the table for her.
- He says that she will soon understand.

1 TONE

The author repeatedly intrudes on the narrative to comment in an amused but kindly way on the actions of his characters.

2 SETTING

The meager Christmas Eve dinner reminds the reader of the meanness of the Youngs' physical surroundings.

3 POINT OF VIEW

The limited third-person point of view enables us to look into Jim's eyes with as much confusion as Della.

gave way a little to prudence and reason. She got out her curling irons and lighted the gas and
1 went to work repairing the ravages made by generosity added to love. Which is always a tremendous task, dear friends—a mammoth task.

Within forty minutes her head was covered with tiny, close-lying curls that made her look wonderfully like a truant schoolboy. She looked at her reflection in the mirror long, carefully, and critically.

"If Jim doesn't kill me," she said to herself, "before he takes a second look at me, he'll say I look like a Coney Island[12] chorus girl. But what could I do—oh! what could I do with a dollar and eighty-seven cents?"

2 At seven o'clock the coffee was made and the frying pan was on the back of the stove hot and ready to cook the chops.

Jim was never late. Della doubled the fob chain in her hand and sat on the corner of the table near the door that he always entered. Then she heard his step on the stair away down on the first flight, and she turned white for just a moment. She had a habit of saying little silent prayers about the simplest everyday things, and now she whispered, "Please, God, make him think I am still pretty."

The door opened and Jim stepped in and closed it. He looked thin and very serious. Poor fellow, he was only twenty-two—and to be burdened with a family! He needed a new overcoat and he was without gloves.

Jim stopped inside the door, as immovable as
3 a setter at the scent of quail. His eyes were fixed upon Della; and there was an expression in them that she could not read, and it terrified her. It was not anger, nor surprise, nor disapproval, nor horror, nor any of the sentiments that she had been prepared for. He simply stared at her fixedly with that peculiar expression on his face.

Della wriggled off the table and went to him.

"Jim, darling," she cried, "don't look at me that way. I had my hair cut off and sold it because I couldn't have lived through Christmas without giving you a present. It'll grow out again—you won't mind, will you? I just had to do it. My hair grows awfully fast. Say 'Merry Christmas!' Jim, and let's be happy. You don't know what a nice—what a beautiful, nice gift I've got for you."

"You've cut off your hair?" asked Jim laboriously, as if he had not arrived at that patent fact yet even after the hardest mental labor.

"Cut it off and sold it," said Della. "Don't you like me just as well, anyhow? I'm me without my hair, ain't I?"

Jim looked about the room curiously.

"You say your hair is gone?" he said, with an air almost of idiocy.

"You needn't look for it," said Della. "It's sold, I tell you—sold and gone, too. It's Christmas Eve, boy. Be good to me, for it went for you. Maybe the hairs of my head were numbered," she went on with a sudden serious sweetness, "but nobody could ever count my love for you. Shall I put the chops on, Jim?"

Out of his trance Jim seemed quickly to wake. He enfolded his Della. For ten seconds let us regard with discreet scrutiny some inconsequential object in the other direction. Eight dollars a week or a million a year—what is the difference? A mathematician or a wit would give you the wrong answer. The Magi brought valuable gifts, but that was not among them. This dark assertion will be illuminated later on.

Jim drew a package from his overcoat pocket and threw it upon the table.

"Don't make any mistake, Dell," he said, "about me. I don't think there's anything in the way of a haircut or a shave or a shampoo that could make me like my girl any less. But if you'll unwrap that package you may see why you had me going awhile at first."

White fingers and nimble tore at the string and paper. And then an ecstatic scream of joy;

12. **Coney Island:** beach and amusement park in Brooklyn, New York.

GUIDED READING

LITERAL QUESTION

1a. What is Jim's reaction when he enters the room? (He stares at Della with a peculiar expression on his face.)

INFERENTIAL QUESTION

1b. Why is Jim's reaction so important to the story? (It creates a mood of suspense: How will he react to both of her "surprises"?)

and then, alas! a quick feminine change to hysterical tears and wails, necessitating the immediate employment of all the comforting powers of the lord of the flat.

For there lay The Combs—the set of combs, side and back, that Della had worshipped for long in a Broadway[13] window. Beautiful combs, pure tortoise shell, with jeweled rims—just the shade to wear in the beautiful vanished hair. They were expensive combs, she knew, and her heart had simply craved and yearned over them without the least hope of possession. And now they were hers, but the tresses that should have adorned the coveted adornments were gone.

But she hugged them to her bosom, and at length she was able to look up with dim eyes and a smile and say, "My hair grows so fast, Jim!"

And then Della leaped up like a little singed cat and cried, "Oh, oh!"

Jim had not yet seen his beautiful present. She held it out to him eagerly upon her open palm. The dull precious metal seemed to flash with a reflection of her bright and ardent spirit.

"Isn't it a dandy, Jim? I hunted all over town to find it. You'll have to look at the time a hundred times a day now. Give me your watch. I want to see how it looks on it."

Instead of obeying, Jim tumbled down on the couch and put his hands under the back of his head and smiled.

"Della," said he, "let's put our Christmas presents away and keep 'em awhile. They're too nice to use just at present. I sold the watch to get the money to buy your combs. And now suppose you put the chops on."

The Magi, as you know, were wise men—wonderfully wise men—who brought gifts to the Babe in the manger. They invented the art of giving Christmas presents. Being wise, their gifts were no doubt wise ones, possibly bearing the privilege of exchange in case of duplication. And here I have lamely related to you the uneventful

Detail, *Woman Brushing Her Hair,* Henri de Toulouse-Lautrec (1864–1901).

4 chronicle of two foolish children in a flat who most unwisely sacrificed for each other the greatest treasures of their house. But in a last word to the wise of these days let it be said that of all who give gifts these two were the wisest. Of all who give and receive gifts, such as they are wisest. Everywhere they are wisest. They are the Magi.

13. **Broadway:** major avenue in New York.

AT A GLANCE

- Jim gives Della her present—a set of combs.
- She gives him the chain and learns that he sold his watch.
- The narrator compares them to the Magi.

1 IRONY

Della no longer possesses the beautiful hair for which Jim acquired the wonderful combs. She sold it to get *his* present.

2 CHARACTERIZATION

After describing Della indirectly throughout the story, the author now directly says she was a "bright and ardent spirit."

3 IRONY

The irony is compounded when Jim reveals that he too has sold his most prized possession to buy Della a present.

4 THEME

The author directly states the theme of the story: Those who give gifts out of selfless love are the wisest.

REFLECTING ON THE STORY

What is the meaning of the title? (The Magi were the wise men who brought gifts to the Christ child. The truly "wise" are those who give gifts out of selfless love.)

GUIDED READING

LITERAL QUESTION

1a. What does O. Henry say he has "lamely related"? ("the uneventful chronicle of two foolish children")

INFERENTIAL QUESTION

1b. How would you describe O. Henry's tone here? (His tone is ironic: He feels that the two are in fact "the wisest" and comparable to the Magi.)

STUDY QUESTIONS

1. "letter box into which no letter would go"; "furnished flat at eight dollars a week"; "shabby little couch"
2. Della's hair yields watch chain; Jim's watch yields combs.
3. He stares fixedly with a peculiar expression.
4. He reacts calmly, comforts Della.
5. She is affectionate with Jim; sells hair; wants to please Jim.
6.
   - three wise men
   - They give gifts out of selfless love.
7. Statement is meant to be ironic; the sentences that follow disprove it.

VIEWPOINT

selfless giving, quick forgiveness, poverty

LITERARY FOCUS

1. Selfless giving is true giving.
2. It compares Della and Jim to the Magi, who gave first Christmas gifts.

VOCABULARY

1. (d) discourages
2. (c) increase in value
3. (c) important
4. (b) clumsy
5. (b) avoidance

STUDY QUESTIONS

Recalling

1. Mention three details that the author uses to illustrate the poverty of the couple's apartment.
2. What do Della and Jim give up for each other? What gifts do they buy for each other?
3. Describe Jim's reaction when he enters the flat and sees Della.

Interpreting

4. Della compares the watch chain to Jim: "Quietness and value—the description applied to both." What evidence do we see, once he enters, that the description fits Jim?
5. From what she says and does, give three examples of Della's "bright and ardent [devoted] spirit."
6. Who were the Magi? Why does the author compare Della and Jim to them?

Extending

7. Near the end of the story, the narrator claims to have related "the uneventful chronicle of two foolish children in a flat." Do you agree or disagree with the narrator's opinion? Why?

VIEWPOINT

About "The Gift of the Magi" one critic has noted:

> O. Henry builds up to his surprise twist very artfully, and with deft touches he elicits the reader's admiration and sympathy for the young couple.
>
> —A. Voss, *American Short Story*

■ What details about Della and Jim cause us to feel admiration and sympathy for them?

LITERARY FOCUS

Stated Theme

The **theme** of a story, or its main idea, can usually be expressed as a general statement about life. An author writes a story because of a desire to communicate that general statement. Some stories have a **stated theme,** a theme that is directly announced in the text, usually at the end of the story. A stated theme can be expressed by the author or by a character in the story. The moral lesson at the end of a **fable**, a very brief story told to teach the lesson, can sometimes be a good example of stated theme. Aesop's fable about the boy who cried "Wolf!" ends with a statement that liars are not believed even when they tell the truth.

Thinking About Stated Theme

1. What is the theme of "The Gift of the Magi"?
2. Explain how the title directs us to the theme.

VOCABULARY

Antonyms

Antonyms are words that have opposite or nearly opposite meanings. *Strength* and *weakness* are antonyms. The words in capitals are from "The Gift of the Magi." Choose the word that is *most nearly the opposite* of each word in capitals, *as the word is used in the story*. Write the number of each item and the letter of your choice on a separate sheet.

1. INSTIGATES: (a) treats (b) provokes (c) looks over (d) discourages
2. DEPRECIATE: (a) make over (b) approve of (c) increase in value (d) be grateful for
3. INCONSEQUENTIAL: (a) in order (b) known (c) important (d) resulting
4. AGILE: (a) strong (b) clumsy (c) quick (d) honest
5. SCRUTINY: (a) search (b) avoidance (c) inspection (d) observation

COMPOSITION

Writing About Theme

■ State the theme of "The Gift of the Magi." Then show how O. Henry illustrates the theme of the story through the characterization of Della and Jim as well as through the setting and the events of the story. *For help with this assignment, see Lesson 7 in the Writing About Literature Handbook at the back of this book.*

Writing a Speech

■ Imagine that you have been requested to give a short speech to an audience of ninth-graders. Write a short speech that presents one of the following opinions: "It is better to give than to receive" or "It is better to receive."

COMPOSITION: GUIDELINES FOR EVALUATION

WRITING ABOUT THEME

Objective

To show how characterization, setting, and plot illustrate theme

Guidelines for Evaluation

- suggested length: one to three paragraphs
- should state story's theme
- should use references from the story
- should maintain coherence within and between paragraphs

WRITING A SPEECH

Objective

To write a short speech presenting an opinion

Guidelines for Evaluation

- suggested length: three-minute presentation
- should state the opinion
- should support opinion with reasons and examples
- should be written for peer audience

Anton Chekhov (1860–1904) was a medical doctor as well as a writer of plays and short stories. He lived in Russia during the rule of the czars, or emperors. His work often shows a comic attitude toward the behavior expected from members of the strict social classes of that time.

■ How does the expression "You're your own worst enemy" apply to this story?

Anton Chekhov

A Slander

The penmanship teacher Sergei Kapitonich Ahineyev[1] was marrying his daughter Natalia to the history and geography teacher. The wedding gaiety was at its height. People sang, played, and danced in the ballroom. Hired waiters, dressed in black tails and dirty white ties, scurried back and forth like madmen. Noise filled the air. The mathematics teacher, the French teacher, and the tax assessor, sitting side by side on the sofa, talked hurriedly, interrupting each other to tell the guests about cases of people buried alive, and expressing their opinions of spiritualism.[2] None of the three believed in spiritualism, but all admitted that there are many things in this world which a human mind will never understand. In the next room the literature teacher was explaining the cases in which a sentry has the right to shoot at passers-by. As you can see, the conversations were terrifying but highly pleasant. From the yard, people whose social standing did not give them the right to enter looked through the windows.

Exactly at midnight, Ahineyev, the host, walked into the kitchen to see whether everything was ready for supper. The kitchen was full of fumes from the goose and duck, mixed with many other smells. Appetizers and drinks were spread in artistic disorder on two tables. Marfa, the cook, a red-faced woman whose figure was like a balloon with a belt around it, bustled near the tables.

"Show me the sturgeon,[3] Marfa," said Ahineyev, rubbing his hands and licking his lips. "What an aroma! I could eat up the whole kitchen. Now then, show me the sturgeon!"

Marfa went to a bench and carefully lifted a greasy newspaper. Under the paper, on an enormous platter, rested a big jellied sturgeon, dazzling with olives and carrots. Ahineyev looked at the sturgeon and gasped. His face beamed, his eyes rolled up. He bent over and made a sound like an ungreased wheel. After a while he snapped his fingers with pleasure and smacked his lips once more.

3 "Oh, the sound of a passionate kiss! . . . Who are you kissing in there, little Marfa?" asked a voice from the next room, and Vankin, an assistant teacher, stuck his cropped head through the door. "Who are you with? Ah, ah, ah . . .

1. **Sergei Kapitonich Ahineyev** [ser gā′ kä pē tō′nēch akh ē nā′yef]
2. **spiritualism:** belief that the dead can communicate with the living.
3. **sturgeon** [stur′jən]: large fish.

AT A GLANCE

- Ahineyev, a penmanship teacher, celebrates his daughter's wedding.
- At midnight he goes to the kitchen to check on the food and smacks his lips over the sturgeon.
- Vankin, an assistant teacher, teases him about kissing the cook.

LITERARY OPTIONS

- theme
- conflict
- characterization

THEMATIC OPTIONS

- vanity
- communication
- identity and self-respect

1 SETTING

The story is set amid a lighthearted, cheerful, chatty gathering—a social event typified by scurrying people and noise.

2 THEME

With their idle chatter and vain talk the wedding guests communicate one social message to each other and another message to the "lower classes," who are literally on the outside looking in.

3 PLOT: NARRATIVE HOOK

Vankin's teasing Ahineyev about kissing the cook ignites the main action of the story.

GUIDED READING

LITERAL QUESTION

1a. What does Vankin say to Ahineyev in the kitchen? (Vankin kids him about kissing the cook.)

INFERENTIAL QUESTION

1b. Do you think Vankin is serious? (He is probably being playful, as Marfa is described as unattractive and not a likely candidate for a tryst.)

AT A GLANCE

- Ahineyev corrects Vankin but later worries that Vankin is telling others about the kiss.
- Ahineyev decides to protect his reputation by telling what actually happened.

1 CONFLICT

Ahineyev's internal conflict begins when he starts to worry about what others think of him.

2 THEME

In his eagerness to save his reputation, Ahineyev decides to spread the story himself; he fails to consider the possible consequences.

3 CHARACTERIZATION

This one-dimensional, insecure man is so shallow that he does not even realize he is in the process of slandering himself.

4 POINT OF VIEW

The limited third-person point of view allows us to witness Ahineyev's frantic and comical thought process.

very nice! With Sergei Kapitonich! You're a fine grandfather, alone here with a woman!"

"Not at all, I am not kissing her," said Ahineyev with embarrassment. "Who told you that, you fool? I just . . . smacked my lips because of . . . my pleasure . . . at the sight of the fish."

"Tell me another one!" Vankin's head smiled broadly and disappeared behind the door. Ahineyev blushed.

1 "What now?" he thought. "The scoundrel will go now and gossip. He will put me to shame before the whole town, the beast . . ."

Ahineyev timidly entered the ballroom and looked around: where was Vankin? Vankin was standing at the piano and dashingly bent over to whisper something to the laughing sister-in-law of the inspector.

2 "It is about me," thought Ahineyev, "about me. He should be torn apart! And she believes . . . believes! She's laughing. I can't let this go on . . . no . . . I must arrange it so that no one will believe him . . . I will talk to everybody and show what a fool and gossip he is."

Ahineyev scratched himself and, still embarrassed, approached the French teacher.

"I was just in the kitchen, arranging the supper," he told the Frenchman. "I know you love fish and I have a sturgeon, old chap. Two yards long. Ha, ha, ha . . . oh, yes, I almost forgot . . . in the kitchen now, with the sturgeon . . . it was a real joke! I went to the kitchen and wanted to examine the food . . . I looked at the sturgeon
3 and from the pleasure, the aroma of it, I smacked my lips! But at this moment suddenly this fool Vankin came in and said . . . ha, ha, ha . . . and said . . . 'Ah, are you kissing in here?' Kissing Marfa, the cook! He made it all up, the fool. The woman looks like a beast, such a face, such skin . . . and he . . . kissing! Funny man!"

"Who is funny?" asked the mathematics teacher, coming over.

"That one there, Vankin! I came into the kitchen . . ." and he told the story of Vankin. "He made me laugh, he's so funny! I think I'd rather kiss a stray dog than Marfa," added Ahineyev, turning around and seeing the tax assessor behind him.

"We are talking about Vankin," said he. "Such a funny man! He came in the kitchen, saw me near Marfa . . . well, he started to invent all kinds of stories. 'Why,' he says, 'are you kissing?' He was drunk and made it up. And I said, 'I would rather kiss a turkey than Marfa. I have a wife,' I told him, 'you are such a fool.' He made me laugh."

"Who made you laugh?" asked the priest who taught Scripture in the school, coming to Ahineyev.

"Vankin. I was, you know, standing in the kitchen and looking at the sturgeon . . ."

And so forth. In half an hour all the guests knew the story of the sturgeon and Vankin.

4 "Let him tell the stories now!" thought Ahineyev, rubbing his hands. "Let him! He'll start telling stories, and everyone will say right away: 'Stop talking nonsense, you fool! We know all about it.' "

And Ahineyev was so reassured that he drank four glasses too much from joy. After supper he saw the newlyweds to their room, went home, and slept like an innocent child, and the next day he had already forgotten the story of the sturgeon. But, alas! Man supposes, but God disposes.[4] Wicked tongues will wag, and Ahineyev's cunning did not help him. Exactly a week later, after the third lesson on Wednesday, when Ahineyev was standing in the staff room discussing the evil ways of one of his students, the principal came to him and called him aside.

"Well, Sergei Kapitonich," said the principal, "excuse me . . . it's not my business, but still I must explain . . . my duty. You see, there is talk that you have kissed this . . . cook. It is not my

4. **Man . . . disposes:** a proverb. No matter how much man may plan, God can cause unexpected events.

GUIDED READING

LITERAL QUESTIONS

1a. What is Ahineyev worried about? (that Vankin will slander him about "the kiss")

2a. What does Ahineyev decide to do? (to explain to everyone what actually happened)

INFERENTIAL QUESTIONS

1b. Could Ahineyev have avoided his troubles? (He could have spoken directly to Vankin about his joke and laughed along with him.)

2b. What does this decision tell you about his character? (He is shallow, vain, and humorless; he cannot see the ramifications of his rash "remedy.")

business, but . . . kiss her . . . anything you want but, please, not so publicly. Please! Don't forget, you are a teacher."

Ahineyev got chilly and faint. He felt as if he had been stung by a swarm of bees and scalded in boiling water. As he walked home, it seemed to him that the whole town was looking at him as if he were smeared with tar. New trouble awaited him at home.

"Why don't you eat anything?" his wife asked him during dinner. "What are you thinking about? Your love life? Lonesome without little Marfa? I know all about it, Mohammedan![5] Good people opened my eyes! O-o-oh, barbarian!"

And she slapped him on the cheek. He left the table in a daze, without his hat and coat, and wandered to Vankin. Vankin was home.

2 "You scoundrel!" Ahineyev addressed Vankin. "Why did you smear me with mud before the entire world? Why did you slander me?"

"What slander? What are you inventing?"

"Who gossiped that I kissed Marfa? Not you? Not you, robber?"

Vankin blinked and winked with all his worn face, raised his eyes to the icon,[6] and said, "Let God punish me! Let my eyes burst, let me die, if I ever said one word about you! Bad luck to me! Cholera[7] is not enough!"

The sincerity of Vankin could not be doubted. Evidently he had not gossiped.

3 "But who? Who?" thought Ahineyev, turning over in his mind all his acquaintances and beating his breast. "Who else?"

"Who else?" we will also ask the reader . . .

---

5. **Mohammedan** [mō ham'id en]: Moslem. Ahineyev's wife implies that Moslem men have more than one wife.

6. **icon** [ī'kon]: painting of a holy person or saint.

7. **Cholera** [kol'ər ə]: infectious disease of the intestines.

AT A GLANCE

- Ahineyev's wife accuses him of infidelity and slaps his face.
- He accuses Vankin of slander, but Vankin swears his innocence.
- Ahineyev wonders who spread the rumor.
- The author asks the reader.

1 CHARACTERIZATION

Ahineyev is self-conscious and paranoid. His literal-minded vanity shields him from the truth.

2 CONFLICT

Ahineyev blusters into a wrongful accusation: He mistakes Vankin as his enemy. In fact he has offended himself.

3 PLOT: RESOLUTION

Ahineyev still does not realize that he himself has spread the slander, but the author refers the question back to the reader (who understands the humor of the situation).

REFLECTING ON THE STORY

What does the last line of the story mean? (Chekhov thinks the reader realizes Ahineyev spread the slander himself by trying to deny it. The author emphasizes Ahineyev's blind self-centeredness and lack of humor.)

GUIDED READING

LITERAL QUESTION

1a. What does Vankin tell Ahineyev? (He tells Ahineyev that he did not spread the slander.)

INFERENTIAL QUESTION

1b. What does Vankin's believable protestation reveal to Ahineyev? (It reveals that Ahineyev has wrongly thought Vankin a slanderer; it does *not* help Ahineyev realize that the guilty party is himself.)

STUDY QUESTIONS

1. ■ to check on supper, to look at sturgeon
   ■ Vankin accuses him of kissing the cook.
2. He is afraid Vankin will spread rumor.
3. Principal and wife chide him.
4. He swears his innocence.
5. He thinks all are talking about him.
6. He should have laughed it off.
7. Ahineyev spreads it; Chekhov lets reader come to this conclusion.
8. He would have responded the same way.
9. yes; idle chatter in first paragraph; Ahineyev's vanity; Vankin's humor; Ahineyev's wife's jealousy

VIEWPOINT

He could have avoided it by speaking to Vankin immediately.

LITERARY FOCUS

1. The answer is obvious.
2. Vanity makes people act foolishly.

STUDY QUESTIONS

Recalling

1. Why does Ahineyev go into the kitchen during the wedding party? What happens there?
2. For what reason does Ahineyev talk to many different people after he leaves the kitchen?
3. Give two examples to show that the rumor about Ahineyev and Marfa has spread.
4. What is Vankin's response when Ahineyev accuses him of spreading lies?

Interpreting

5. Explain how Ahineyev's trouble develops because he is vain.
6. In what way should Ahineyev have responded to Vankin about what happened in the kitchen?
7. Explain how the rumor actually spread. What does the last line of the story mean?

Extending

8. Imagine that Ahineyev really did kiss Marfa in the kitchen. Describe how you think he would have acted after Vankin's remarks.
9. Do you think this story is realistic in the way it portrays human behavior? Explain your opinion with specific examples from the story.

VIEWPOINT

Whether serious or humorous, most of Chekhov's short stories involve

> the inability of human beings to respond to or even to communicate with one another....
>
> —W. R. Benét, *The Reader's Encyclopedia*

■ In what sense does Ahineyev's trouble grow out of an inability to communicate?

LITERARY FOCUS

Implied Theme

A theme is a generalization about life that the author wants to communicate by writing a specific story. An **implied theme** is not directly stated but is gradually revealed to us by the other elements of the story. Theme can be implied in the following ways:

- A story's title may suggest the author's opinion of what happens in the story.
- A major character may learn a lesson about life from events of the plot and from the resolution of the conflict.
- Personality traits of a character may suggest the author's ideas about people.
- Details of setting may suggest the author's ideas about the world.
- The author's choice of point of view may tell us how the author wants us to react to the events in the story.

For example, if a character is threatened by a lion and gets away by outsmarting the beast, the character's personality, the conflict and its resolution show us that reason is superior to brute force.

A story with an implied theme is much more common than a story with a stated theme. When a reader finds a story's implied theme and wishes to express it, the theme always takes the form of a sentence.

Thinking About Implied Theme

1. Why does Chekhov ask the reader, "Who else?" instead of directly revealing who spread the rumor?
2. State the theme of "A Slander" in one or two sentences.

COMPOSITION

Writing About Theme

■ Explain how in the course of the story you gradually became aware of the implied theme of "A Slander." When did you first think that Ahineyev was acting foolishly? What did you think of (a) Ahineyev's behavior at the party, (b) his conviction that people are watching him and talking about him, and (c) his confrontation with Vankin? When did you realize Chekhov's theme?

Writing a Fable

■ Imagine that you are the teacher of a third-grade class. Your students have been telling tales about one another, and you want to teach them that gossip can hurt innocent people. To teach the lesson, you write a fable that you plan to read to your students. Write a short fable using animal characters. Create a plot in which a character learns that gossip is harmful. (If necessary, see page 114 for a definition of *fable*.)

COMPOSITION: GUIDELINES FOR EVALUATION

WRITING ABOUT THEME

Objective

To explain how character's behavior leads to discovery of implied theme

Guidelines for Evaluation

- suggested length: two to three paragraphs
- should state the theme
- should explain how incidents in the story reveal theme
- should explain first realization of theme

WRITING A FABLE

Objective

To write a fable with a moral

Guidelines for Evaluation

- suggested length: 150–300 words
- should have the form of a fable
- should illustrate the moral
- should have narrative action
- should state the moral at the end

Dorothy Canfield Fisher (1879–1958) spent much of her life on a farm near Arlington, Vermont, and many of her stories such as "The Heyday of the Blood" reflect the deep admiration she had for the strength and character of her New England neighbors.

■ What can very old people teach very young people about living?

Dorothy Canfield Fisher

The Heyday of the Blood

The older professor looked up at the assistant, fumbling fretfully with a pile of papers. "Farrar, what's the *matter* with you lately?" he said sharply.

The younger man started, "Why . . . why . . ." The brusqueness of the other's manner shocked him suddenly into confession. "I've lost my nerve, Professor Mallory, that's what's the matter with me. I'm frightened to death," he said melodramatically.

"What *of?*" asked Mallory, with a little challenge in his tone.

The floodgates were open. The younger man burst out in exclamations, waving his thin, nervous, knotted fingers, his face twitching as he spoke. "Of myself . . . no, not myself, but my body! I'm not well . . . I'm getting worse all the time. The doctors don't make out what is the matter . . . I don't sleep . . . I worry . . . I forget things, I take no interest in life . . .the doctors intimate a nervous breakdown ahead of me . . .and yet I rest . . .I rest . . .more than I can afford to! I never go out. Every evening I'm in bed by nine o'clock. I take no part in college life beyond my work, for fear of the nervous strain. I've refused to take charge of that summer school in New York, you know, that would be such an opportunity for me . . .if I could only sleep! But though I never do anything exciting in the evening . . .heavens! what nights I have. Black hours of seeing myself in a sanitarium,[1] dependent on my brother! I never . . .why, I'm in hell . . .that's what's the matter with me, a perfect hell of ignoble terror!"

He sat silent, his drawn face turned to the window. The older man looked at him speculatively. When he spoke it was with a cheerful, casual quality in his voice which made the other look up at him surprised.

2 "You don't suppose those great friends of yours, the nerve specialists, would object to my telling you a story, do you? It's very quiet and unexciting. You're not too busy?"

"Busy! I've forgotten the meaning of the word! I don't dare to be!"

3 "Very well, then; I mean to carry you back to the stony little farm in the Green Mountains, where I had the extreme good luck to be born and raised. You've heard me speak of Hillsboro; and the story is all about my great-grandfather,

1. **sanitarium:** institution for the care of invalids.

AT A GLANCE

- Professor Mallory's assistant complains about his health and extreme nervousness.
- The doctors are confused but warn of an impending nervous breakdown.
- The professor begins a story about his great-grandfather.

LITERARY OPTIONS

- frame story
- theme
- characterization

THEMATIC OPTIONS

- attitudes toward life
- relationship between generations
- learning a lesson

1 CONFLICT

This dynamic opening immediately presents the central conflict of the story: a professor confronted with his assistant's exaggerated nervousness.

2 FRAME STORY

In response to his assistant's complaints, Professor Mallory begins a story about his great-grandfather.

3 SETTING

The author shifts from the frame story world of papers and books to the inner story setting of a Vermont farm in the Green Mountains.

GUIDED READING

LITERAL QUESTION

1a. What does the young assistant complain about? (He complains about his health and nervousness.)

INFERENTIAL QUESTION

1b. What can you infer about the young assistant from his complaints? (He seems to be afraid of living; the doctors can find nothing wrong with him.)

AT A GLANCE

- Gran'ther was eighty-eight and still active when he came to live with the professor's family.
- One August a county fair was held fourteen miles away.
- The professor's father refused to take Gran'ther to the county fair.

1 RESPONSE JOURNAL

Have students respond to this statement by writing about their memories of an elderly relative.

2 CHARACTERIZATION

Gran'ther's zest for life is illustrated through his actions and words: The old man is vigorous spiritually if not physically.

3 THEME

Gran'ther, who enjoys life and does not dwell morbidly upon illnesses or let them "cramp his style," contrasts with the professor's nervous assistant.

4 CONFLICT

Gran'ther's hardy attitude toward living puts him in conflict with the grandson and doctor who worry about his well-being.

5 SYMBOL

The image of the knot tied in an empty sleeve represents Gran'ther's determination and stubbornness.

who came to live with us when I was a little boy."

1 "Your great-grandfather?" said the other incredulously. "People don't remember their great-grandfathers!"

"Oh, yes, they do, in Vermont. There was my father on one farm, and my grandfather on another, without a thought that he was no longer young, and there was 'Gran'ther' as we called him, eighty-eight years old and just persuaded to settle back, let his descendants take care of him, and consent to be an old man. He had been in the War of 1812[2]—think of that, you mushroom!—and had lost an arm and a good deal of his health there. He had lately begun to get a pension of twelve dollars a month, so that for an old man he was quite independent financially, as poor Vermont farmers look at things; and he was a most extraordinary character, so that his arrival in our family was quite an event.

"He took precedence at once of the oldest man in the township, who was only eighty-four and not very bright. I can remember bragging at school about Gran'ther Pendleton, who'd be eighty-nine come next Woodchuck Day, and
2 could see to read without glasses. He had been ailing all his life, ever since the fever he took in the war. He used to remark triumphantly that he had now outlived six doctors who had each given him but a year to live; 'and the seventh is going downhill fast, so I hear!' This last was his never-failing answer to the attempts of my conscientious mother and anxious, dutiful father to check the old man's reckless indifference to any of the rules of hygiene.

"They were good disciplinarians with their children, and this naughty old man, who would give his weak stomach frightful attacks of indigestion by stealing out to the pantry and devouring a whole mince pie because he had been refused two pieces at the table—this rebellious, unreasonable, whimsical old madcap[3] was an electric element in our quiet, orderly life. He insisted on going to every picnic and church sociable,
3 where he ate recklessly of all the indigestible dainties he could lay his hands on, stood in drafts, tired himself to the verge of fainting away by playing games with the children, and returned home, exhausted, animated, and quite ready to pay the price of a day in bed, groaning and screaming out with pain as heartily and unaffectedly as he had laughed with the pretty girls the evening before.

"The climax came, however, in the middle of August, when he announced his desire to go to the county fair, held some fourteen miles down the valley from our farm. Father never dared let Gran'ther go anywhere without him-
4 self accompanying the old man, but he was perfectly sincere in saying that it was not because he could not spare a day from the haying that he refused point-blank to consider it. The doctor who had been taking care of Gran'ther since he came to live with us said that it would be crazy to think of such a thing. He added that the wonder was that Gran'ther lived at all, for his heart was all wrong, his asthma was enough to kill a young man, and he had no digestion; in short, if Father wished to kill his old grandfather, there was no surer way than to drive fourteen miles in the heat of August to the noisy excitement of a county fair.

"So Father for once said 'No,' in the tone that we children had come to recognize as final.
5 Gran'ther grimly tied a knot in his empty sleeve—a curious, enigmatic mode of his to express strong emotion—put his one hand on his cane, and his chin on his hand, and withdrew himself into that incalculable distance from the life about him where very old people spend so many hours.

"He did not emerge from this until one morning toward the middle of fair-week, when all the

2. **War of 1812:** war between England and the United States.

3. **madcap:** impulsive, reckless person.

GUIDED READING

LITERAL QUESTIONS

1a. What impressed the professor about Gran'ther? (He was eighty-eight and weak but still enjoyed life fully.)

2a. How does the professor's father respond to Gran'ther's request to go to the fair? (He says no.)

INFERENTIAL QUESTIONS

1b. What does his attitude tell you about the professor's values? (It shows that he admires someone who can live life to the fullest.)

2b. Why won't he take Gran'ther to the fair? (He is worried that such a trip would harm his grandfather.)

rest of the family were away—Father and the bigger boys on the far-off upland meadows haying, and Mother and the girls off blackberrying. I was too little to be of any help, so I had been left to wait on Gran'ther, and to set out our lunch of bread and milk and huckleberries. We had not been alone half an hour when Gran'ther sent me to extract, from under the mattress of his bed, the wallet in which he kept his pension money. There was six dollars and forty-three cents—he counted it over carefully, sticking out his tongue like a schoolboy doing a sum, and when he had finished he began to laugh and snap his fingers and sing out in his high, cracked old voice:

" 'We're goin' to go a skylarkin'! Little Jo Mallory is going to the county fair with his Gran'ther Pendleton, an' he's goin' to have more fun than ever was in the world, and he—'

" 'But, Gran'ther, Father said we mustn't!' I protested, horrified.

" 'But I say we *shall!* I was your gre't-gran'ther long before he was your feyther, and anyway I'm here and he's not—so, *march!* Out to the barn!'

"He took me by the collar, and, executing a shuffling fandango[4] of triumph, he pushed me ahead of him to the stable, where old white Peggy, the only horse left at home, looked at us amazed.

" 'But it'll be twenty-eight miles, and Peg's never driven over eight!' I cried, my old-established world of rules and orders reeling before my eyes.

" 'Eight—and—twenty-eight!
But I—am—*eighty*-eight!'

"Gran'ther improvised a sort of whooping chant of scorn as he pulled the harness from the peg. 'It'll do her good to drink some pink lemonade—old Peggy! An' if she gits tired comin' home, I'll git out and carry her part way myself!'

"His adventurous spirit was irresistible. I made no further objection, and we hitched up together, I standing on a chair to fix the checkrein,[5] and Gran'ther doing wonders with his one

3 hand. Then, just as we were—Gran'ther in a hickory shirt, and with an old hat flapping over his wizened face, I barelegged, in ragged old clothes—so we drove out of the grassy yard, down the steep, stony hill that led to the main valley road, and along the hot, white turnpike, deep with the dust which had been stirred up by the teams on their way to the fair. Gran'ther sniffed the air jubilantly, and exchanged hilarious greetings with the people who constantly overtook old Peg's jogging trot. Between times he regaled me with spicy stories of the hundreds of thousands—they seemed no less numerous to me then—of county fairs he had attended in his youth. He was horrified to find that I had never been even to one.

4 " 'Why, Joey, how old be ye? 'Most eight, ain't it? When I was your age I had run away and been to two fairs an' a hangin'.'

" 'But didn't they lick you when you got home?' I asked shudderingly.

" 'You *bet* they did!' cried Gran'ther with gusto.

5 "I felt the world changing into an infinitely larger place with every word he said.

" 'Now, this is somethin' *like!*' he exclaimed, as we drew near to Granville and fell into a procession of wagons all filled with country people in their best clothes, who looked with friendly curiosity at the little, shriveled cripple, his face shining with perspiring animation, and at the little boy beside him, his bare feet dangling high above the floor of the battered buckboard, overcome with the responsibility of driving a horse for the first time in his life, and filled with such a flood of new emotions and ideas that he must have been quite pale."

Professor Mallory leaned back and laughed

4. **fandango** [fan dang'gō]: lively Spanish dance.

5. **checkrein** [chek'rān']: short strap attached to the bridle to keep a horse from lowering its head.

AT A GLANCE

- One day Gran'ther tells Joey they are going to the fair.
- They hitch up an old mare.
- As Joey drives a horse for the first time and listens to Gran'ther, he feels his world expanding.

1 POINT OF VIEW

The professor's story is told in a first-person narrative; everything is relayed through memories of his youth.

2 PLOT: NARRATIVE HOOK

Gran'ther, defying everyone's advice, suddenly announces that they are going to the fair.

3 READING SKILLS: DETAILS

The world of the Vermont farmer is vividly portrayed through these images of old clothing. It is a picturesque view of the old man and boy setting out on an adventure.

4 VOCABULARY: DIALECT

The use of "ye" for "you" and "ain't it" for "isn't it" adds realism and flavor to the story.

5 THEME

Joey's world begins to expand as he learns from his great-grandfather that there are other ways of looking at experiences and other ways of living.

GUIDED READING

LITERAL QUESTIONS

1a. What does Gran'ther suddenly announce? (He tells Joey that they are going to the fair.)

2a. What does Joey feel when Gran'ther tells him about his adventures? (He feels that his world is changing into a larger place.)

INFERENTIAL QUESTIONS

1b. What does this announcement reveal about Gran'ther's philosophy of living? (It shows that he likes to live life fully and will not be limited by "infirmity.")

2b. In what ways do you think Joey's world is expanding? (Joey is becoming aware of different ways of looking at life.)

AT A GLANCE

- Gran'ther and Joey arrive at the fair and see many exhibits.
- They order the most expensive lunch and ride the merry-go-round.

1 SYMBOLISM

Gran'ther had stubbornly vowed to keep his sleeve knotted until he got to the fair.

2 CHARACTERIZATION

For all his bluster Gran'ther is a compassionate and open-minded individual, interested in other people and willing to continue to learn about them and the world.

3 VOCABULARY: SLANG

The use of colorful expressions like "Sufferin' Hezekiah!" makes Gran'ther a more vivid personality for the reader.

4 THEME

Gran'ther's "King Solomon" pronouncement demonstrates his basic philosophy of life: Live life to the fullest while you can.

aloud at the vision he had been evoking—laughed with so joyous a relish in his reminiscences that the drawn, impatient face of his listener relaxed a little. He drew a long breath, he even smiled a little absently.

"Oh, that was a day!" went on the professor, still laughing and wiping his eyes. "Never will I have such another! At the entrance to the grounds
1 Gran'ther stopped me while he solemnly untied the knot in his empty sleeve. I don't know what kind of harebrained vow he had tied up in it, but with the little ceremony disappeared every trace of restraint, and we plunged head over ears into the saturnalia[6] of delights that was an old-time county fair.

"People had little cash in those days, and Gran'ther's six dollars and forty-three cents lasted like the widow's cruse of oil.[7] We went to see the fat lady, who, if she was really as big as she looked to me then, must have weighed at least a ton. My admiration for Gran'ther's daredevil qualities rose to infinity when he entered into free-and-easy talk with her, about how much she ate, and could she raise her arms enough to do up her own hair, and how many yards of velvet it took to make her gorgeous,
2 gold-trimmed robe. She laughed a great deal at us, but she was evidently touched by his human interest, for she confided to him that it was not velvet at all but furniture covering; and when we went away she pressed on us a bag of peanuts. She said she had more peanuts than she could eat—a state of unbridled opulence which fitted in for me with all the other superlatives of that day.

"We saw the dog-faced boy, whom we did not like at all; Gran'ther expressing, with a candidly outspoken cynicism, his belief that 'them whiskers was glued to him.' We wandered about the stock exhibit, gazing at the monstrous oxen and hanging over the railings where the prize pigs lived to scratch their backs. In order to miss nothing, we even conscientiously passed through the Woman's Building, where we were very much bored by the serried[8] ranks of preserve jars.

3 " 'Sufferin' Hezekiah!' cried Gran'ther irritably. 'Who cares how gooseberry jel *looks*. If they'd give a felly a taste, now—'

"This reminded him that we were hungry, and we went to a restaurant under a tent, where, after taking stock of the wealth that yet remained of Gran'ther's hoard, he ordered the most expensive things on the bill of fare."

Professor Mallory suddenly laughed out again. "Perhaps in heaven, but certainly not until then, shall I ever taste anything so ambrosial[9] as that fried chicken and coffee ice cream! I have not lived in vain that I have such a memory back of me!"

This time the younger man laughed with the narrator, settling back in his chair as the professor went on:

"After lunch we rode on the merry-go-round, both of us, Gran'ther clinging desperately with his one hand to his red camel's wooden hump, and crying out shrilly to me to be sure and not lose his cane. The merry-go-round had just come in at that time, and Gran'ther had never experi-
4 enced it before. After the first giddy flight we retired to a lemonade stand to exchange impressions, and finding that we both alike had fallen completely under the spell of the new sensation, Gran'ther said that we 'sh'd keep on a-ridin' till we'd had enough! King Solomon[10] couldn't tell when we'd ever git a chance again!' So we returned to the charge, and rode and rode and rode, through blinding clouds of happy excite-

6. **saturnalia** [sat′ər nā′lē ə]: festival characterized by unrestrained merrymaking.
7. **the widow's cruse** [krōōz] **of oil:** a cruse is an earthen jug. The phrase implies that a poor woman would use oil sparingly to make it last.
8. **serried** [ser′ēd]: tightly packed.
9. **ambrosial** [am brō′zhəl]: delicious, worthy of being tasted by the gods.
10. **King Solomon** [sol′ə mən]: Biblical king of Israel known for his wisdom.

GUIDED READING

LITERAL QUESTIONS

1a. What do they do at the fair? (They go to all the sideshows, the food tent, and the merry-go-round.)

2a. What do they do after their first ride on a merry-go-round? (They go back and ride it again and again.)

INFERENTIAL QUESTIONS

1b. Why does Gran'ther do all these things? (He does not want to miss out on any experiences that the fair can offer.)

2b. In what way does this decision demonstrate Gran'ther's childlike ability to enjoy experiences? (He is willing to repeat the thrill of the merry-go-round ride with the enthusiasm of a child.)

ment, so it seems to me now, such as I was never to know again. The sweat was pouring off from us, and we had tried all the different animals on the machine before we could tear ourselves away to follow the crowd to the race track.

"We took reserved seats, which cost a quarter apiece, instead of the unshaded ten-cent benches, and Gran'ther began at once to pour out to me a flood of horse talk and knowing race-track aphorisms,[11] which finally made a young fellow sitting next to us laugh superciliously. Gran'ther turned on him heatedly.

" 'I bet-che fifty cents I pick the winner in the next race!' he said sportily.

" 'Done!' said the other, still laughing.

"Gran'ther picked a big black mare, who came in almost last, but he did not flinch. As he paid over the half dollar he said: 'Everybody's likely to make mistakes about *some* things; King Solomon was a fool in the head about women-
2 folks! I bet-che a dollar I pick the winner in *this* race!' and 'Done!' said the disagreeable young man, still laughing. I gasped, for I knew we had only eighty-seven cents left, but Gran'ther shot

11. **aphorisms** [af'ə riz'əmz]: proverbs.

AT A GLANCE

- Gran'ther and Joey follow the crowd to the race track.
- Gran'ther bets on a race with a young man and loses fifty cents.
- He doubles his bet on the next race.

1 READING SKILLS: SEQUENCE OF EVENTS

The quick shift of location gives a sense of the rapid succession of experiences that Gran'ther and Joey enjoy.

2 CHARACTERIZATION

Gran'ther's actions show that he is impulsive and fun-loving, willing to gamble without a care about the future.

GUIDED READING

LITERAL QUESTION

1a. What does Gran'ther do when he loses the bet? (He doubles his bet for the next race.)

INFERENTIAL QUESTION

1b. Do you think this is a wise bet? (It seems impetuous, since he does not even have the money to cover it.)

AT A GLANCE

- Gran'ther wins the second bet.
- Gran'ther and Joey buy presents for the family with the last of their money and head for home.
- They arrive home after dark and Gran'ther collapses into unconsciousness.

1 VOCABULARY: DICTION

The use of standard English by the professor is another way that the author separates the frame structure from the slang and dialect used by Gran'ther in the narrative.

2 THEME

The theme of the story is announced by Gran'ther in his colorful image of going "the whole hog."

3 SETTING

The quiet beauty of the gathering darkness contrasts with the "carnival of joy" they have just left.

4 CONFLICT

Gran'ther's determination to enjoy life fully in spite of his poor health is a conflict he must repeatedly endure.

5 PLOT: RISING ACTION

Gran'ther has become ill as a result of his impulsive day of merriment at the county fair.

me a command to silence out of the corner of his eyes, and announced that he bet on the sorrel gelding.

1 "If I live to be a hundred and break the bank at Monte Carlo three times a week," said Mallory, shaking his head reminiscently, "I could not know a tenth part of the frantic excitement of that race or of the mad triumph when our horse won. Gran'ther cast his hat upon the ground, screaming like a steam calliope[12] with exultation as the sorrel swept past the judges' stand ahead of all the others, and I jumped up and down in an agony of delight which was almost more than my little body could hold.

"After that we went away, feeling that the world could hold nothing more glorious. It was five o'clock, and we decided to start back. We paid for Peggy's dinner out of the dollar we had won on the race—I say 'we,' for by that time we were welded into one organism—and we still
2 had a dollar and a quarter left. 'While ye're about it, always go the whole hog!' said Gran'ther, and we spent twenty minutes in laying out that money in trinkets for all the folks at home. Then, dusty, penniless, laden with bundles, we bestowed our exhausted bodies and our uplifted hearts in the old buckboard, and turned Peg's head toward the mountains. We did not talk much during that drive, and though I thought at the time only of the carnival of joy we had left, I can now recall every detail of the trip—how the sun sank behind Indian Mountain, a peak I had known before only through distant
3 views; then, as we journeyed on, how the stars came out above Hemlock Mountain—our own home mountain behind our house, and later, how the fireflies filled the darkening meadows along the river below us, so that we seemed to be floating between the steady stars of heaven and their dancing, twinkling reflection in the valley.

"Gran'ther's dauntless spirit still surrounded me. I put out of mind doubts of our reception at home, and lost myself in delightful ruminatings on the splendors of the day. At first, every once in a while, Gran'ther made a brief remark, such as, ''Twas the hindquarters of the sorrel I bet on. He was the only one in the hull kit and bilin' of 'em that his quarters didn't fall away'; or, 'You needn't tell *me* that them Siamese twins ain't unpinned every night as separate as you and me!' But later on, as the damp evening air began to bring on his asthma, he subsided into silence, only broken by great gasping coughs.

"These were heard by the anxious, heartsick watchers at home, and, as old Peg stumbled wearily up the hill, Father came running down to meet us. 'Where you be'n?' he demanded, his
4 face pale and stern in the light of his lantern. 'We be'n to the county fair!' croaked Gran'ther with a last flare of triumph, and fell over sideways against me. Old Peg stopped short, hanging her head as if she, too, were at the limit of her strength. I was frightfully tired myself, and frozen with terror of what Father would say. Gran'ther's collapse was the last straw. I began to cry loudly, but Father ignored my distress with an indifference which cut me to the heart. He lifted Gran'ther out of the buckboard, carrying the unconscious little old body into the house without a glance backward at me. But when I crawled down to the ground, sobbing and digging my fists into my eyes, I felt Mother's arms close around me.

" 'Oh, poor, naughty little Joey!' she said. 'Mother's bad, dear little boy!' "

Professor Mallory stopped short.

"Perhaps that's something else I'll know again in heaven," he said soberly, and waited a moment before he went on: "Well, that was the end of our day. I was so worn out that I fell asleep over my supper, in spite of the excitement
5 in the house about sending for a doctor for Gran'ther, who was, so one of my awe-struck sisters told me, having some kind of 'fits.'

12. **steam calliope** [kə lī'ə pē']: musical instrument consisting of keyboard and steam whistles that produces a sound identified with fairs and circuses.

GUIDED READING

LITERAL QUESTIONS

1a. What does Gran'ther do with the last of his money? (He buys presents for all the family.)

2a. What happens to Gran'ther when they arrive home? (He collapses into unconsciousness.)

INFERENTIAL QUESTIONS

1b. Why does he spend the last of his money? (He likes to "go the whole hog" whenever he does anything.)

2b. What does this collapse tell you about Gran'ther's condition? (It shows that he is truly a sick man; his desire to live life fully is a spirited rebellion against the physical limitations that challenge him.)

Mother must have put me to bed, for the next thing I remember, she was shaking me by the shoulder and saying, 'Wake up, Joey. Your great-grandfather wants to speak to you. He's been suffering terribly all night, and the doctor thinks he's dying.'

"I followed her into Gran'ther's room, where the family was assembled about the bed. Gran'ther lay drawn up in a ball, groaning so dreadfully that I felt a chill like cold water at the roots of my hair; but a moment or two after I came in, all at once he gave a great sigh and relaxed, stretching out his legs and laying his arms down on the coverlid. He looked at me and attempted a smile.

" 'Well, it was wuth it, warn't it, Joey?' he said gallantly, and closed his eyes peacefully to sleep."

"Did he die?" asked the younger professor, leaning forward eagerly.

"Die? Gran'ther Pendleton? Not much! He came tottering down to breakfast the next morning, as white as an old ghost, with no voice left, his legs trembling under him, but he kept the whole family an hour and a half at the table, telling them in a loud whisper all about the fair, until Father said really he would have to take us to the one next year. Afterward he sat out on the porch watching old Peg graze around the yard. I thought he was in one of his absent-minded fits, but when I came out, he called me to him, and setting his lips to my ear, he whispered:

" 'An' the seventh is a-goin' down-hill fast, so I hear!' He chuckled to himself over this for some time, wagging his head feebly, and then he said: 'I tell ye, Joey, I've lived a long time, and I've larned a lot about the way folks is made. The trouble with most of 'em is, they're 'fraid-cats! As Jeroboam Warner used to say—he was in the
2 same rigiment with me in 1812—the only way to manage this business of livin' is to give a whoop and let her rip! If ye just about half-live, ye just the same as half-die; and if ye spend yer time half-dyin', some day ye turn in and die all over, without rightly meanin' to at all—just a kind o' bad habit ye've got yerself inter.' Gran'ther fell into a meditative silence for a moment. 'Jeroboam, he said that the evenin' before the battle of Lundy's Lane, and he got killed the next day. Some live, and some die; but folks that live all over die happy, anyhow! Now I tell you what's my motto, an' what I've lived to be eighty-eight on—' "

Professor Mallory stood up and, towering over the younger man, struck one hand into the
3 other as he cried: "This was the motto he told me: 'Live while you live, and then die and be done with it!' "

STUDY QUESTIONS

Recalling

1. What reasons does the young assistant give for being frightened?
2. What experiences do Joey and his great-grandfather share during their day together at the county fair?
3. What happens to Gran'ther after he and Joey return from the fair? What does Gran'ther say when Joey visits his room?

Interpreting

4. Which recollections about Gran'ther's comments and habits show him to be truly unusual?
5. While listening to his great-grandfather's adventures, Joey felt "the world changing into an infinitely larger place with every word he said." Explain this statement.
6. At the end of the professor's story, why does the assistant ask, "Did he die?"

AT A GLANCE

- Gran'ther asks to see Joey and says that the fair was worth his present pain.
- The next morning he shows up at breakfast confident he will outlive yet another doctor.
- Professor Mallory tells his assistant to live life to the fullest.

1 PLOT: CLIMAX

To the pessimistic assistant's amazement Gran'ther does not die but appears the next morning at breakfast.

2 THEME

By quoting these words of Gran'ther, the professor hopes to snap the assistant out of his self-centered morbidity and depression.

3 INTERPRETING

In a final effort to impress his assistant, Professor Mallory proclaims the moral of his story: Cowards die many times, but it is better to enjoy life and not worry about death, which will take care of itself.

REFLECTING ON THE STORY

What do you think will happen to the young assistant? (If he takes the story to heart, his condition will probably disappear; however, since he thought that the fair had killed the old man, he may never learn to think positively.)

STUDY QUESTIONS

1. He is not well, can't sleep, and has no interest in life.
2. the shows, food, races
3.
   - has seizure
   - "It was wuth it."
4. trip to fair: strength and independence; chat with fat lady: compassion
5. His experience has been limited.
6. He is obsessed with death.

STUDY QUESTIONS

7. a broader outlook
8. His condition may improve if he learns to appreciate life.

VIEWPOINT

death; by straining himself physically

LITERARY FOCUS

- to enjoy life to the fullest
- Assistant is afraid to live and, as a result, is sickly.

VOCABULARY

1. dialect
2. standard
3. dialect
4. dialect
5. standard

COMPARING STORIES

- Della sacrifices pride to get money to buy suitable gift for Jim; she demonstrates that giving should express love.
- Ahineyev's actions demonstrate the theme that vanity can make people appear foolish.
- Gran'ther embodies theme of living life to fullest; he has done so, though he has supposedly been on borrowed time.

Extending

7. Explain what this story implies about the things young people can gain by spending time with older people.
8. In what way may the young assistant change after hearing the story of Gran'ther?

VIEWPOINT

One quality that Fisher's characters share is the strength to endure. One writer describes a typical Fisher character as

> a mere human being holding the tremendous at bay, a frail hero calling fate to come on.
>
> —M. L. Becker, *Golden Tales of New England*

- What is Gran'ther holding off? In what way does he dare fate?

LITERARY FOCUS

Frame Story to Highlight Theme

"The Heyday of the Blood" is actually two stories—one inside the other. The author tells us a story about the professor, who in turn tells a story to his frightened young assistant. The outer story about the assistant is the **frame** because it appears before and after the main story about the great-grandfather.

An author uses a frame as a reflection of the main story, and the frame usually echoes the theme of the main story. In effect, the reader receives a second example of the author's message about life to make the impression stronger.

Thinking About the Frame Story and Theme

- What is the theme of "The Heyday of the Blood," and in what way does the frame support that theme?

VOCABULARY

Recognizing Dialect

Standard American English is the most widely known and accepted kind of English spoken and written in the United States. **Dialect** is a variation of a language, sometimes spoken by a particular group but most often associated with a particular region. Regional dialects differ from standard English because they contain words with different sounds, forms, and meanings. The dialect of the American frontier, the dialect of the hill country of the South, and the dialect of Brooklyn, New York, are all regional dialects.

In this story which of the following sentences would you regard as standard English and which as regional dialect? On a separate sheet write the number of each item. Next to each number mark the item *standard* or *dialect*.

1. "Why, Joey, how old be ye?"
2. "His adventurous spirit was irresistible."
3. "While ye're about it, always go the whole hog!"
4. "Most eight, ain't it?"
5. "But I say we shall!"

For each sentence that you marked *dialect*, explain briefly why you made your decision. Then find three more examples of dialect in the story.

COMPOSITION

Writing About Character

- Describe Gran'ther, and then describe the assistant. In each description concentrate on the man's attitude toward life. Explain how his attitude affects each man's everyday life. Then in another paragraph contrast the two men.

Writing an Anecdote

- Gran'ther lived according to aphorisms, or sayings. Select one of the following sayings, and write a short anecdote, or brief story, that will reinforce the idea brought out in the saying.

a. "The grass is always greener on the other side of the fence."
b. "A rolling stone gathers no moss."
c. "Live and let live."

COMPARING STORIES

- The themes of "The Gift of the Magi," "A Slander," and "The Heyday of the Blood" are different, but each story has a character who embodies, or is an example of, its theme: Della, Ahineyev, and Gran'ther. Choose two or more stories. Explain how the character in each story embodies the theme of the story.

COMPOSITION: GUIDELINES FOR EVALUATION

WRITING ABOUT CHARACTER

Objective

To contrast two dissimilar characters

Guidelines for Evaluation

- suggested length: three paragraphs
- should show how character's attitudes affect their activities
- should contrast their attitudes and outlooks
- should make references to the story

WRITING AN ANECDOTE

Objective

To write an anecdote in support of one of three aphorisms

Guidelines for Evaluation

- suggested length: 150–300 words
- should state the aphorism
- should illustrate the idea of the aphorism
- should use informal style

LITERARY FOCUS: *The Total Effect*

To get the greatest pleasure from a well-written short story, you must participate actively in the experience of reading. As you read a story, you should not only follow the plot line, but you should also become aware of information or clues about the characters, the setting, the point of view, and the theme. Then you should think about how all the elements interact.

As you read, you can silently make observations about the words and the sentences in front of you. In that way you will be able to extract meaning from the printed page, see connections among parts of a story, and find pleasure in seeing it "all add up."

Of course, no two readers will make exactly the same observations when going through a story. Nevertheless, a truly active reader will always consider the following reminders about the elements of fiction:

Reminders for Active Reading of Short Stories

1. The **title** can help you to understand the author's theme.
2. The **plot** will generally consist of several stages: exposition, narrative hook, rising action, climax, falling action, and resolution. At the heart of the plot will be one or more conflicts and, often, suspense.
3. **Characters** can be directly or indirectly portrayed. They can be round or flat, static or dynamic.
4. The **setting** can tell you more about the characters and can also create an atmosphere for the story.
5. **Point of view** concerns the relationship of the storyteller to the story.
6. The **theme,** or generalization about life, may be stated directly, but usually it is implied. The theme grows out of the interaction of the preceding elements.

Model for Active Reading

On the following pages you will see how an alert reader kept the elements of fiction in mind while reading one particular story, "About Two Nice People" by Shirley Jackson. You will find marginal notations that represent the reader's observations. Each notation includes a page reference for further information on the element in question. Ideally, you should first read the story alone purely for pleasure. Then, on your second reading, consider the marginal notations. Afterward, you can use the process illustrated in this model as you read other short stories.

MODEL FOR ACTIVE READING

The annotations in the Pupil's Edition that accompany this story bring to students' attention each of the elements of the short story along with various techniques of fiction. Review the six steps under "Reminders for Active Reading of Short Stories" (page 127), and have students tell how each has been illustrated in one or two of the stories they have studied. Then have students apply each of the eight reminders to Jackson's story, by pointing to specific passages in the story and notations in the text.

AT A GLANCE

- The narrator says that anger can be an intense emotion, even in "nice" people.
- Ellen Webster is a "sweet" girl ready for marriage.

LITERARY OPTIONS

- plot
- characterization
- point of view

THEMATIC OPTIONS

- anger
- love
- communication

Shirley Jackson (1919–1965) published many short stories in magazines like the *New Yorker*; she also wrote novels. Most of her work seems to appeal to one of two very different emotions—fear or humor. At the heart of all, however, is a fascination with everyday human behavior that gets out of hand.

- Do relationships ever turn out totally different from what you would expect?

Shirley Jackson

About Two Nice People

Title (p. 118): The author may be serious or sarcastic in titling the story.

A problem of some importance, certainly, these days, is that of anger. When one half of the world is angry at the other half, or one half of a nation is angry at the rest, or one side of town feuds with the other side, it is hardly surprising, when you stop to think about it, that so many people lose their tempers with so many other people. Even if, as in this case, they are two people not usually angry, two people whose lives are obscure and whose emotions are gentle, whose smiles are amiable and whose voices are more apt to be cheerful than raised in fury. Two people, in other words, who would much rather be friends than not and who yet, for some reason, perhaps chemical or sociological or environmental, enter upon a mutual feeling of dislike so intense that only a very drastic means can bring them out of it.

Theme (p. 114): A general observation about life points to a possible theme and ties the *title* of the story to that theme.

Take two such people:

Ellen Webster was what is referred to among her friends as a "sweet" girl. She had pretty, soft hair and dark, soft eyes, and she dressed in soft colors and wore frequently a lovely old-fashioned brooch which had belonged to her grandmother. Ellen thought of herself as a very happy and very lucky person, because she had a good job, was able to buy herself a fair number of soft-colored dresses and skirts and sweaters and coats and hats; she had, by working hard at it evenings, transformed her one-room apartment from a bare, neat place into a charming little refuge with her sewing basket on the table and a canary at the window; she had a reasonable conviction that someday, perhaps soon, she would fall in love with a nice young man and they would be married and Ellen would devote herself whole-

Setting (p. 69): Ellen's apartment is a clue to her personality and contributes to *characterization*.

GUIDED READING

LITERAL QUESTION

1a. What kinds of anger does the narrator talk about in the first paragraph? (conflicts between nations, conflicts between parts of a nation, feuds within a town, individuals losing their tempers)

INFERENTIAL QUESTION

1b. What effect does she create by lumping these types of anger together? (The effect is ironic and amusing, since a quarrel between individuals is not of the same seriousness or danger as a conflict between nations.)

heartedly to children and baking cakes and mending socks. This not-very-unusual situation, with its perfectly ordinary state of mind, was a source of great happiness to Ellen. She was, in a word, not one of those who rail against their fate, who live in sullen hatred of the world. She was—her friends were right—a sweet girl.

Plot (p. 10): Ellen's goals are stated; the plot will probably involve reaching those goals. The hint early on is *foreshadowing* (p. 26).

On the other hand, even if you would not have called Walter Nesmith sweet, you would very readily have thought of him as a "nice" fellow, or an "agreeable" person, or even—if you happened to be a little old white-haired lady—a "dear boy." There was a subtle resemblance between Ellen Webster and Walter Nesmith. Both of them were the first resort of their friends in trouble, for instance. Walter's ambitions, which included the rest of his life, were refreshingly similar to Ellen's: Walter thought that someday he might meet some sweet girl, and would then devote himself wholeheartedly to coming home of an evening to read his paper and perhaps work in the garden on Sundays.

Direct characterization (p. 40): The author states that Walter is agreeable and describes both him and Ellen as helpful.

Walter thought that he would like to have two children, a boy and a girl. Ellen thought that she would like to have three children, a boy and two girls. Walter was very fond of cherry pie, Ellen preferred Boston cream. Ellen enjoyed romantic movies, Walter preferred Westerns. They read almost exactly the same books.

In the ordinary course of events, the friction between Ellen and Walter would have been very slight. But—and what could cause a thing like this?—the ordinary course of events was shattered by a trifle like a telephone call.

External conflict (p. 26): The conflict will be between two people, Ellen and Walter.

Ellen's telephone number was 3–4126. Walter's telephone number was 3–4216. Ellen lived in apartment 3–A and Walter lived in apartment 3–B; these apartments were across the hall from each other and very often Ellen, opening her door at precisely quarter of nine in the morning and going toward the elevator, met Walter, who opened *his* door at precisely quarter of nine in the morning and went toward the elevator. On these occasions Ellen customarily said "Good morning" and looked steadfastly the other way, Walter usually answered "Good morning," and avoided looking in her direction. Ellen thought that a girl who allowed herself to be informal with strangers created a bad impression, and Walter thought that a man who took advantage of living in the same building to strike up an acquaintance with a girl was a man of little principle. One particularly fine morning, he said to Ellen in the elevator, "Lovely day," and she replied, "Yes, isn't it?" and both of them felt scarcely that they had been bold. How this mutual respect for each other's dignity could have degenerated into fury is a mystery not easily understood.

Exposition (p. 10): The author has been providing background information.

It happened that one evening—and, to do her strict justice, Ellen had had a hard day, she was coming down with a cold, it had rained

AT A GLANCE

- Walter Nesmith, also a nice person, wants to get married and have children.
- Ellen and Walter have similar phone numbers; they live across the hall from each other.

GUIDED READING

LITERAL QUESTIONS

1a. What qualities do Ellen and Walter have in common? (Both are "nice," helpful, and want to get married and have children; both are domestic; they enjoy the same books.)

2a. What is Ellen's telephone number? (3-4126) What is Walter's (3-4216)

INFERENTIAL QUESTIONS

1b. What type of story might you expect to follow such a list of what a man and a woman have in common? (a romance)

2b. What conflict can you predict from these numbers? (Either Ellen or Walter is likely to get calls that are meant for the other.)

AT A GLANCE

- After Ellen has had a hard day, someone calls her number by mistake several times and asks for Walter.
- Ellen's anger grows.

steadily for a week, her stockings were unwashed, and she had broken a fingernail—the phone which had the number 3–4126 rang. Ellen had been opening a can of chicken soup in the kitchenette, and she had her hands full; she said, "Darn," and managed to drop and break a cup in her hurry to answer the phone.

"Hello?" she said, thinking, *This is going to be something cheerful.*

"Hello, is Walter there?"

"Walter?"

"Walter Nesmith. I want to speak to Walter, please."

"This is the wrong number," Ellen said thinking with the self-pity that comes with the first stages of a head cold that no one ever called *her*.

"Is this three—four two one six?"

"This is three—four one two six," Ellen said, and hung up.

Narrative hook (p. 10): A simple wrong number begins the *conflict* between Ellen and Walter.

At that time, although she knew that the person in the apartment across the hall was named Walter Nesmith, she could not have told the color of his hair or even of the outside of his apartment door. She went back to her soup and had a match in her hand to light the stove when the phone rang again.

"Hello?" Ellen said without enthusiasm; this *could* be someone cheerful, she was thinking.

"Hello, is Walter there?"

"This is the wrong number again," Ellen said; if she had not been such a very sweet girl she might have let more irritation show in her voice.

"I *want* to *speak* to Walter Nesmith, *please*."

"This is three—four one two six again," Ellen said patiently. "You want three—four two one six."

"What?" said the voice.

"This," said Ellen, "is number three—four one two six. The number you want is three—four two one six." Like anyone who has tried to say a series of numbers several times, she found her anger growing. Surely anyone of *normal* intelligence, she was thinking, surely anyone *ought* to be able to dial a phone, anyone who can't dial a phone shouldn't be allowed to have a nickel.

She had got all the way back into the kitchenette and was reaching out for the can of soup before the phone rang again. This time when she answered she said "Hello?" rather sharply for Ellen, and with no illusions about who it was going to be.

"Hello, may I please speak to Walter?"

At that point it started. Ellen had a headache and it was raining and she was tired and she was apparently not going to get any chicken soup until this annoyance was stopped.

"Just a minute," she said into the phone.

She put the phone down with an understandable bang on the

GUIDED READING

LITERAL QUESTION

1a. What details does the narrator give to suggest how Ellen is feeling the night of the wrong numbers? (She's had a hard day and is coming down with a cold; it has rained steadily for a week; her stockings are unwashed.)

INFERENTIAL QUESTION

1b. Why do you think the narrator gives so many details? (to emphasize that it takes a lot of stress and things going wrong to push a "nice" person like Ellen to anger)

table, and she marched, without taking time to think, out of her apartment and up to the door across the hall. "Walter Nesmith" said a small card at the doorbell. Ellen rang the doorbell with what was, for her, a vicious poke. When the door opened she said immediately, without looking at him:

"Are you Walter Nesmith?"

Now Walter had had a hard day, too, and *he* was coming down with a cold, and *he* had been trying ineffectually to make himself a cup of hot tea in which he intended to put a spoonful of honey to ease his throat, that being the remedy his aunt had always recommended for the first onslaught of a cold. If there had been one fraction less irritation in Ellen's voice, or if Walter had not taken off his shoes when he came home that night, it might very probably have turned out to be a pleasant introduction, with Walter and Ellen dining together on chicken soup and hot tea, and perhaps even sharing a bottle of cough medicine. But when Walter opened the door and heard Ellen's voice, he was unable to answer her cordially, and so he said briefly:

"I am. Why?"

"Will you please come and answer my phone?" said Ellen, too annoyed to realize that this request might perhaps bewilder Walter.

"Answer your phone?" said Walter stupidly.

"Answer my phone," said Ellen firmly. She turned and went back across the hall, and Walter, wondering briefly if they allowed harmless lunatics to live alone as though they were just like other people, hesitated for an instant and then followed her, on the theory that it would be wiser to do what she said when she seemed so cross, and reassuring himself that he could leave the door open and yell for help if necessary. Ellen stamped into her apartment and pointed at the phone where it lay on the table. "There. Answer it."

Point of view (p. 85): The author tells the thoughts of both Ellen and Walter. The story has an *omniscient third-person point of view* (p. 109).

Eyeing her sideways, Walter edged over to the phone and picked it up. "Hello," he said nervously. Then, "Hello? Hello?" Looking at her over the top of the phone, he said, "What do you want me to do now?"

"Do you mean to say," said Ellen ominously, "that that terrible terrible person has hung up?"

"I guess so," said Walter, and fled back to his apartment.

The door had only just closed behind him when the phone rang again, and Ellen, answering it, heard, "May I speak to Walter, please?"

Not a very serious mischance, surely. But the next morning Walter pointedly avoided going down in the elevator with Ellen, and sometime during that day the deliveryman left a package addressed to Ellen at Walter's door.

Setting (p. 69): The fact that Ellen and Walter live next door is very important to the plot.

When Walter found the package he took it manfully under his arm and went boldly across the hall and rang Ellen's doorbell. When Ellen

AT A GLANCE

- Ellen rings Walter's doorbell and demands that he answer her phone.
- When Walter picks up the phone, no one is on the line.
- A package for Ellen is delivered to Walter by mistake.

GUIDED READING

LITERAL QUESTIONS

1a. What does Ellen say to Walter when she goes to his door? ("Are you Walter Nesmith? . . . Will you please come and answer my phone?")

2a. What happens when Walter picks up the phone? (The person on the other end has hung up.)

INFERENTIAL QUESTIONS

1b. Why doesn't Ellen explain the situation to Walter when she goes to his door? (She is too angry and thinks that he'll find out soon enough.)

2b. Why doesn't Ellen explain the situation to Walter then? (She can't; Walter flees her apartment immediately.)

AT A GLANCE

- When Walter brings Ellen the package, she thinks he is apologizing with a gift.
- She is annoyed to discover the truth.
- Other misunderstandings occur, and the situation disintegrates into "white-hot fury."

opened her door she thought at first—and she may have been justified—that Walter had come to apologize for the phone call the evening before, and she even thought that the package under his arm might contain something delightfully unexpected, like a box of candy. They lost another chance then; if Walter had not held out the package and said "Here," Ellen would not have gone on thinking that he was trying to apologize in his own shy way, and she would certainly not have smiled warmly, and said, "You ***shouldn't*** have bothered."

Walter, who regarded transporting a misdelivered parcel across the hall as relatively little bother, said blankly, "No bother at all," and Ellen, still deceived, said, "But it really wasn't ***that*** important."

Walter went back into his own apartment convinced that this was a very odd girl indeed, and Ellen, finding that the package had been mailed to her and contained a wool scarf knitted by a cousin, was as much angry as embarrassed because, once having imagined that an apology is forthcoming, it is very annoying not to have one after all, and particularly to have a wool scarf instead of a box of candy.

How this situation disintegrated into the white-hot fury which rose between these two is a puzzle, except for the basic fact that when once a series of misadventures has begun between two people, everything tends to contribute further to a state of misunderstanding. Thus, Ellen opened a letter of Walter's by mistake, and Walter dropped a bottle of milk—he was still trying to cure his cold, and thought that perhaps milk toast was the thing—directly outside Ellen's door, so that even after his nervous attempts to clear it up, the floor was still littered with fragments of glass, and puddled with milk.

Rising action (p. 10): Each prank complicates the *conflict* and adds *suspense*.

Then Ellen—who believed by now that Walter had thrown the bottle of milk against her door—allowed herself to become so far confused by this succession of small annoyances that she actually wrote and mailed a letter to Walter, asking politely that he try to turn down his radio a little in the late evenings. Walter replied with a frigid letter to the effect that certainly if he had known that she was bothered by his radio, he should surely never have dreamed—

That evening, perhaps by accident, his radio was so loud that Ellen's canary woke up and chirped hysterically, and Ellen, pacing her floor in incoherent fury, might have been heard—if there had been anyone to hear her, and if Walter's radio had not been so loud—to say, "I'll get even with him!" A phrase, it must be said, which Ellen had never used before in her life.

Ellen made her preparation with a sort of loving care that might well have been lavished on some more worthy object. When the alarm went off she turned in her sleep and smiled before quite waking up, and, once awake and the alarm turned off, she almost laughed out loud. In her slippers and gown, the clock in her hand, she went across her small apartment to the phone; the number was one she was not

GUIDED READING

LITERAL QUESTION

1a. What does Ellen do when she wants Walter to turn down his radio? (She writes and mails him a letter.)

INFERENTIAL QUESTION

1b. Why doesn't she address him in person? (She wants to create a dramatic effect.)

soon apt to forget. The dial tone sounded amazingly loud, and for a minute she was almost frightened out of her resolution. Then, setting her teeth, she dialed the number, her hand steady. After a second's interminable wait, the ringing began. The phone at the other end rang three times, four times, with what seemed interminable waits between, as though even the mechanical phone system hesitated at this act. Then, at last, there was an irritable crash at the other end of the line, and a voice said, "Wah?"

"Good morning," said Ellen brightly. "I called to tell you that my clock has stopped—"

"Wah?"

"This is Ellen Webster," said Ellen still brightly. "I called to tell you that my clock has stopped—"

"Wah?"

"—and I wonder if you could tell me what time it is?"

There was a short pause at the other end of the line. Then after a minute, his voice came back: "Tenny minna fah."

" I beg your pardon?"

There was another short pause at the other end of the line, as of someone opening his eyes with a shock. "Twenty minutes after four," he said. *"Twenty minutes after four."*

"The reason I thought of asking you," Ellen said sweetly, "was that you were so *very* obliging before. About the radio, I mean."

"—calling a person at—"

"Thanks so much," said Ellen. "Good-by."

She felt fairly certain that he would not call her back, but she sat on her bed and giggled a little before she went back to sleep.

Walter's response to this was miserably weak: he contacted a neighboring delicatessen a day or so later, and had an assortment of evil-smelling cheese left in Ellen's apartment while she was out. This, which required persuading the superintendent to open Ellen's apartment so that the package might be left inside, was a poor revenge but a monstrous exercise of imagination upon Walter's part, so that, in one sense, Ellen was already bringing out in him qualities he never knew he had. The cheese, it turned out, more than evened the score: the apartment was small, the day was warm, and Ellen did not get home until late, and long after most of the other tenants on the floor had gone to the superintendent with their complaints about something dead in the woodwork.

Since breaking and entering had thus become one of the rules of their game, Ellen felt privileged to retaliate in kind upon Walter. It was with great joy, some evenings later, that Ellen, sitting in her odorous apartment, heard Walter's scream of pure terror when he put his feet into his slippers and found a raw egg in each.

Walter had another weapon, however, which he had been so far

Internal conflict (p. 33): Ellen struggles briefly with her decision to play this trick on Walter. Acting in ways to which they are not accustomed, both characters experience internal conflict.

Indirect characterization (p. 47): Their actions and words reveal that Ellen and Walter can be childish.

Round characters (p. 53): Walter and Ellen act in new ways, revealing more about their various personality traits.

AT A GLANCE

- Ellen phones Walter in the middle of the night to get revenge.
- Walter has evil-smelling cheese delivered to Ellen's apartment.
- Ellen sneaks raw eggs into Walter's slippers.

GUIDED READING

LITERAL QUESTIONS

1a. What does Ellen do after hanging up the phone? (sits on her bed and giggles a little before going to sleep)

2a. What does the narrator say that Ellen is bringing out in Walter? (qualities he never knew he had)

INFERENTIAL QUESTIONS

1b. Why does Ellen giggle? (She has gotten revenge on Walter for his loud radio; she is beginning to enjoy these childish games.)

2b. What qualities do you think the narrator means? (both a negative childishness and a playful, childlike imagination)

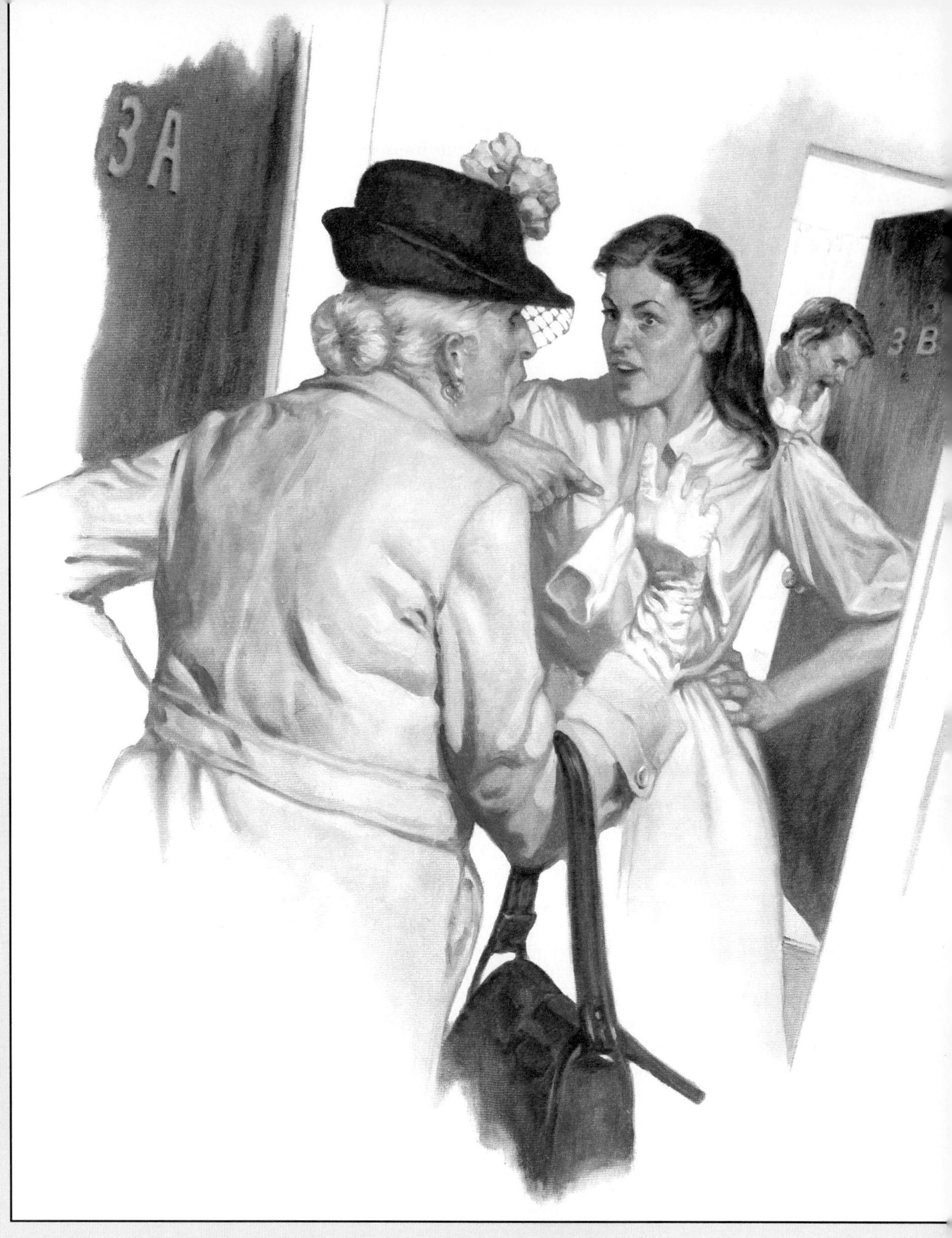

3A
3B

reluctant to use; it was a howitzer[1] of such proportions that Walter felt its use would end warfare utterly. After the raw eggs he felt no compunction whatever in bringing out his heavy artillery.

It seemed to Ellen, at first, as though peace had been declared. For almost a week things went along smoothly; Walter kept his radio tuned down almost to inaudibility, so that Ellen got plenty of sleep. She was over her cold, the sun had come out, and on Saturday morning she spent three hours shopping, and found exactly the dress she wanted at less than she expected to pay.

About Saturday noon she stepped out of the elevator, her packages under her arm, and walked briskly down the hall to her apartment, making, as usual, a wide half circle to avoid coming into contact with the area around Walter's door.

Her apartment door, to her surprise, was open, but before she had time to phrase a question in her own mind, she had stepped inside and come face to face with a lady who—not to make any more mysteries— was Walter Nesmith's aunt, and a wicked old lady in her own way, possessing none of Walter's timidity and none of his tact.

"Who?" said Ellen weakly, standing in the doorway.

"Come in and close the door," said the old lady darkly. "I don't think you'll want your neighbors to hear what I have to say. I," she continued as Ellen obeyed mechanically, "am Mrs. Harold Vongarten Nesmith. Walter Nesmith, young woman, is my nephew."

"Then you are in the wrong apartment," said Ellen, quite politely considering the reaction which Walter Nesmith's name was beginning by now to arouse in her. "You want Apartment Three–B, across the hall."

"I do *not*," said the old lady firmly. "I came here to see the designing young woman who has been shamelessly pursuing my nephew, and to warn her"—the old lady shook her gloves menacingly —"to warn her that *not one cent* shall she have from me if she marries Walter Nesmith."

"Marries?" said Ellen, thoughts too great for words in her heart.

"It has long been my opinion that some young woman would be after Walter Nesmith for his money," said Walter's aunt with satisfaction.

"Believe me," said Ellen wholeheartedly, "there is not that much money in the world."

"You deny it?" The old lady leaned back and smiled triumphantly. "I expected something of the sort. Walter," she called suddenly, and then, putting her head back and howling. "Wal-l-l-l-ter."

"Sh-h-h," said Ellen fearfully. "They'll hear you all over."

1. **howitzer** [hou′it sər]: short cannon; here, horrible weapon

Characterization (pp. 40, 47): The author uses *direct characterization* (by telling us Walter's aunt has no timidity or tact) and *indirect characterization* (by showing us her words and actions).

AT A GLANCE

- Walter plans to bring out his "heavy artillery."
- Things go smoothly for two weeks.
- One day Ellen returns home to find Walter's aunt in her apartment.
- The aunt accuses Ellen of wanting to marry Walter for his money.

GUIDED READING

LITERAL QUESTION

1a. How does the narrator describe Walter's next plan of action? (as a "howitzer," as "bringing out his heavy artillery")

INFERENTIAL QUESTION

1b. Why is what actually happens to Ellen ironic after this description? (One wouldn't ordinarily describe a visit from an old woman as bringing out "heavy artillery.")

AT A GLANCE

- Walter arrives on the scene, and total confusion reigns.
- Walter wanted his aunt to scare Ellen into leaving him alone.
- Ellen's phone rings, and it is for Walter.

"I expect them to," said the old lady. "Wal-l-l-l-l--- Oh, there you are."

Ellen turned and saw Walter Nesmith, with triumph in his eyes, peering around the edge of the door. "Did it work?" he asked.

"She denies everything," said his aunt.

"About the eggs?" Walter said, confused. "You mean, she denies about the eggs and the phone call and---"

"Look," Ellen said to Walter, stamping across the floor to look him straight in the eye, "of all the insufferable, conceited, rude, self-satisfied---"

"What?" said Walter.

"I wouldn't want to marry you," said Ellen, "if—if---" She stopped for a word, helpless.

"If he were the last man on earth," Walter's aunt supplied obligingly. "I think she's really after your *money*, Walter."

Walter stared at his aunt. "I didn't tell you to tell her---" he began. He gasped, and tried again. "I mean," he said, "I never thought---" He appealed to Ellen. "I don't want to marry you, either," he said, and then gasped again, and said, "I mean, I told my aunt to come and tell you---"

"If this is a proposal," Ellen said coldly, "I decline."

"All I wanted her to do was scare you," Walter said finally.

"It's a good way," his aunt said complacently. "Turned out to be the only way with your Uncle Charles and a Hungarian adventuress."

"I mean," Walter said desperately to Ellen, "she owns the building. I mean, I wanted her to tell you that if you didn't stop—I mean, I wanted her to scare you---"

"Apartments are too hard to get these days," his aunt said. "That would have been *too* unkind."

"That's how I got my apartment at all, you see," Walter said to Ellen, still under the impression he was explaining something Ellen wanted to understand.

"Since you have an apartment," Ellen said with restraint, "may I suggest that you take your aunt and the both of you---"

The phone rang.

"Excuse me," said Ellen mechanically, moving to answer it. "Hello?" she said.

"Hello, may I speak to Walter, please?"

Ellen smiled rather in the manner that Lady Macbeth[2] might have smiled if she found a run in her stocking.

"It's for you," she said, holding the phone out to Walter.

---

2. **Lady Macbeth:** coldblooded, murderous woman in Shakespeare's *Macbeth*. Ellen's smile shows her desire for revenge.

GUIDED READING

LITERAL QUESTION

1a. What does Walter's aunt say when he asks, "Did it work?" (Walter's aunt answers, "She denies everything.")

INFERENTIAL QUESTION

1b. What does Walter mean by his question? (He wants to know whether his aunt was able to scare Ellen out of playing tricks.) What does his aunt mean by her answer? (that Ellen denies wanting to marry Walter)

"For me?" he said, surprised. "Who is it?"

"I really could not say," said Ellen sweetly. "Since you have so many friends that one phone is not adequate to answer all their calls---"

Since Walter made no move to take the phone, she put it gently back on the hook.

"They'll call again," she assured him, still smiling in that terrible fashion.

"I ought to turn you both out," said Walter's aunt. She turned to Ellen. "Young woman," she said, "do you deny that all this nonsense with eggs and telephone calls is an attempt to entangle my nephew into matrimony?"

"Certainly not," Ellen said, "I mean, I *do* deny it."

"Walter Nesmith," said his aunt, "do you admit that all your finagling with cheeses and radios is an attempt to strike up an acquaintance with this young woman?"

"Certainly," said Walter. "I mean, I do *not* admit it."

"Good," said Walter's aunt. "You are precisely the pair of silly fools I would have picked out for each other." She rose with great dignity, motioned Walter away from her, and started for the door. "Remember," she said, shaking her gloves again at Ellen, "not one cent."

She opened the door and started down the hall, her handkerchief over her eyes, and—a sorry thing in such an old lady—laughing until she had to stop and lean against the wall near the elevator.

"I'm sorry," Walter was saying to Ellen, almost babbling, "I'm *really* sorry this time—please believe me, I had *no* idea—I wouldn't for the world—nothing but the most profound respect—a joke, you know—hope you didn't really think---"

"I understand perfectly," Ellen said icily. "It is all perfectly clear. It only goes to show what I have always believed about young men who think that all they have to do is---"

The phone rang.

Ellen waited a minute before she spoke. Then she said, "You might as well answer it."

"I'm *terribly* sorry," Walter said, not moving toward the phone. "I mean, I'm *terribly* sorry." He waved his hands in the air. "About what she said about what she thought about what you wanted me to do---" His voice trailed off miserably.

Suddenly Ellen began to giggle.

Anger is certainly a problem that will bear much analysis. It is hardly surprising that one person may be angry at another, particularly if these are two people who are gentle, usually, and rarely angry, whose emotions tend to be mild and who would rather be friends

Climax (p. 10): Walter apologizes, and Ellen fails to become angry at another wrong number; we know how the *conflict* is going to be resolved.

Theme (p. 114): The author again speaks about life in general, *stating the theme.*

AT A GLANCE

- Walter's aunt accuses Ellen and Walter of using childish tricks to get acquainted.
- They deny it.
- Walter's aunt leaves in a state of uncontrollable laughter.
- Walter apologizes, and Ellen begins to giggle when the phone rings.

GUIDED READING

LITERAL QUESTIONS

1a. What does Walter's aunt accuse Ellen and Walter of? (using their tricks and practical jokes as excuses to get to know each other)

2a. What does Walter's aunt do as soon as she leaves Ellen's apartment? (starts laughing)

INFERENTIAL QUESTIONS

1b. Do you think she is right? (In a way; although on a conscious level Ellen and Walter were motivated by revenge, they have also been having fun with each other.)

2b. Why do you think she starts laughing? (She sees that the two young people have been falling in love without knowing it; she is amused and pleased by their relationship.)

AT A GLANCE

- Walter and Ellen resolve their differences.
- Walter's aunt sends them a down payment for a house.
- They marry and have children.

REFLECTING ON THE STORY

Do you think that it is good to poke fun at angry emotions, as this author does? (Sometimes it helps to laugh at ourselves and see how silly our anger can be; at other times anger can be more serious, and it might be dangerous, unkind, and unwise to poke fun at it.)

STUDY QUESTIONS

1. Ellen's wardrobe; Walter's reputation
2. domestic ambitions; books they read
3. with four phone calls; series of misunderstandings
4. Ellen wants to marry for money; they marry and move to the country.
5. plot is exaggerated for comic effect
6. first quality: anger; second: love
7. She is optimistic that anger's problems can be resolved.

with everyone than be enemies with anyone. Such an anger argues a situation so acute that only the most drastic readjustment can remedy it.

Either Walter Nesmith or Ellen Webster could have moved, of course. But, as Walter's aunt had pointed out, apartments are not that easy to come by, and their motives and their telephone numbers were by now so inextricably mixed that on the whole it seemed more reasonable not to bother.

Moreover, Walter's aunt, who still snickers when her nephew's name is mentioned, did not keep them long in suspense, after all. She was not lavish, certainly, but she wrote them a letter which both of them found completely confusing and which enclosed a check adequate for a down payment on the extremely modest house in the country they decided upon without disagreement. They even compromised and had four children—two boys and two girls.

Falling Action and Resolution (p. 10): Ellen and Walter solve their differences. "And they lived happily ever after!"

STUDY QUESTIONS

Recalling

1. What details early in the story support the opinions that Ellen is sweet and Walter is agreeable?
2. In what ways are Ellen and Walter similar, according to the narrator?
3. How does the conflict between Ellen and Walter begin? What chain of events leads to the visit of Walter's aunt?
4. According to Walter's aunt, why do Ellen and Walter play tricks on each other? What finally happens to their feud?

Interpreting

5. Do Ellen's and Walter's actions seem justified by the circumstances? Why or why not?
6. Referring to Walter, the narrator notes that "Ellen was already bringing out in him qualities he never knew he had." In what ways does this comment prepare us for the ending of the story?

Extending

7. Why does Jackson make her point about anger with a romantic story rather than with a story about a bitter quarrel that is never resolved?

COMPOSITION

Writing About Plot

■ In spite of their conflict, Ellen and Walter solve their problems and are happily married at the end of the story. Find three or four details of foreshadowing that prepare the reader for this happy ending. Explain fully how each detail foreshadows the outcome of the story. Then explain whether you think foreshadowing helps or hurts the impact of the story. (If necessary, see page 26 for a definition of *foreshadowing*.)

Writing a Dramatic Scene

■ Imagine two people, one who is extremely neat and organized and one who is extremely sloppy and disorganized. They share a hall locker in school and, because of their different habits, are constantly irritated with each other. One day, they have an argument over these differences. Write a dramatic episode between the two people. You may choose either to end the incident with a solution to the problem or to leave the matter unresolved with the tension still in the air.

COMPOSITION: GUIDELINES FOR EVALUATION

WRITING ABOUT PLOT

Objective

To illustrate how author foreshadows ending

Guidelines for Evaluation

- suggested length: three to four paragraphs
- should cite details of foreshadowing
- should connect each detail with the outcome

WRITING A DRAMATIC SCENE

Objective

To dramatize a verbal confrontation

Guidelines for Evaluation

- suggested length: 300–400 words
- should be written in narrative or dramatic form
- should display dramatic tension by depicting character's opposing habits

While working as a government clerk in Paris, Guy de Maupassant (1850–1893) was encouraged and advised in his writing by some of the most important French authors of his day, including Gustave Flaubert. Although Maupassant also wrote novels, he now ranks among the masters of the short story.

- What do people—including the main character of this story—learn about appearance versus reality as they grow older?

Guy de Maupassant

The Necklace

She was one of those pretty and charming girls, born, as if by an accident of fate, into a family of clerks. With no dowry, no prospects, no way of any kind of being met, understood, loved, and married by a man both prosperous and famous, she was finally married to a minor clerk in the Ministry of Education.

She dressed plainly because she could not afford fine clothes, but was as unhappy as a woman who has come down in the world; for women have no family rank or social class. With them, beauty, grace, and charm take the place of birth and breeding. Their natural poise, their instinctive good taste, and their mental cleverness are the sole guiding principles which make daughters of the common people the equals of ladies in high society.

She grieved incessantly, feeling that she had been born for all the little niceties and luxuries of living. She grieved over the shabbiness of her apartment, the dinginess of the walls, the worn-out appearance of the chairs, the ugliness of the draperies. All these things, which another woman of her class would not even have noticed, gnawed at her and made her furious. The sight of the little Breton[1] girl who did her humble housework roused in her disconsolate regrets
2 and wild daydreams. She would dream of silent chambers, draped with Oriental tapestries and lighted by tall bronze floor lamps, and of two handsome butlers in knee breeches, who, drowsy from the heavy warmth cast by the central stove, dozed in large overstuffed armchairs.

She would dream of great reception halls hung with old silks, of fine furniture filled with priceless curios, and of small, stylish, scented sitting rooms just right for the four o'clock chat with intimate friends, with distinguished and sought-after men whose attention every woman envies and longs to attract.

3 When dining at the round table covered for the third day with the same cloth, opposite her husband, who would raise the cover of the soup tureen, declaring delightedly, "Ah! a good stew! There's nothing I like better . . ." she would dream of fashionable dinner parties, of gleaming silverware, of tapestries making the walls alive

1. **Breton** [bret′ən]: from Brittany, a province of northwestern France.

AT A GLANCE

- A pretty and charming woman with no money marries a minor clerk.
- She dreams of luxurious surroundings.
- Her husband is content with his lifestyle.

LITERARY OPTIONS

- plot
- irony
- character

THEMATIC OPTIONS

- appearance vs. reality
- hopes and ideals
- happiness vs. misery

1 SETTING

The author's description of the apartment emphasizes the woman's discontent with her surroundings.

2 CONFLICT

The setting of the story clashes with the woman's dreams of a finer life style; the contrast dramatizes her internal conflict about her position in society.

3 CHARACTERIZATION

Her husband's contentment with his way of life is dramatized by his love of simple food.

GUIDED READING

LITERAL QUESTION

1a. How does the author first describe the woman in the story? (He describes her as "pretty and charming" with no money.)

INFERENTIAL QUESTION

1b. How do you think her external appearance has influenced the way she thinks about herself? (She believes that because of her beauty and charm she deserves to live a life of luxury.)

AT A GLANCE

- One day Madame Loisel's husband comes home with an invitation to a ball.
- Madame Loisel weeps because she has nothing suitable to wear.
- Her husband says she may have 400 francs for a new dress.

1 THEME

Madame Loisel's desire for the clothing and jewelry creates a constant state of unhappiness in her.

2 PLOT: NARRATIVE HOOK

The Loisels receive a special invitation that has a serious impact on Madame Loisel.

3 STYLE: DIALOGUE

The author uses the clerk's words to convey the drama and importance of the reception of this invitation.

4 IRONY

Madame Loisel's reaction is not what her husband expects: She responds with tears instead of joy.

5 CHARACTERIZATION

Monsieur Loisel recovers from his disappointment at his wife's reaction and seeks to salvage the situation by gently placating her.

with characters out of history and strange birds in a fairyland forest; she would dream of delicious dishes served on wonderful china, of gallant compliments whispered and listened to with a sphinxlike[2] smile as one eats the rosy flesh of a trout or nibbles at the wings of a grouse.

1 She had no evening clothes, no jewels, nothing. But those were the things she wanted; she felt that was the kind of life for her. She so much longed to please, be envied, be fascinating and sought after.

She had a well-to-do friend, a classmate of convent-school days whom she would no longer go to see, simply because she would feel so distressed on returning home. And she would weep for days on end from vexation, regret, despair, and anguish.

Then one evening, her husband came home proudly holding out a large envelope.

"Look," he said, "I've got something for you."

She excitedly tore open the envelope and pulled out a printed card bearing these words:

2 "The Minister of Education and Mme. Georges Ramponneau[3] beg M. and Mme. Loisel[4] to do them the honor of attending an evening reception at the Ministerial Mansion on Friday, January 18."

Instead of being delighted, as her husband had hoped, she scornfully tossed the invitation on the table, murmuring, "What good is that to me?"

3 "But, my dear, I thought you'd be thrilled to death. You never get a chance to go out, and this is a real affair, a wonderful one! I had an awful time getting a card. Everybody wants one: it's much sought after, and not many clerks have a chance at one. You'll see all the most important people there."

She gave him an irritated glance and burst out impatiently, "What do you think I have to go in?"

He hadn't given that a thought. He stammered, "Why, the dress you wear when we go to the theater. That looks quite nice, I think."

4 He stopped talking, dazed and distracted to see his wife burst out weeping. Two large tears slowly rolled from the corners of her eyes to the corners of her mouth; he gasped, "Why, what's the matter? What's the trouble?"

By sheer will power she overcame her outburst and answered in a calm voice while wiping the tears from her wet cheeks:

"Oh, nothing. Only I don't have an evening dress and therefore I can't go to that affair. Give the card to some friend at the office whose wife can dress better than I can."

5 He was stunned. He resumed, "Let's see, Mathilde.[5] How much would a suitable outfit cost—one you could wear for other affairs too—something very simple?"

She thought it over for several seconds, going over her allowance and thinking also of the amount she could ask for without bringing an immediate refusal and an exclamation of dismay from the thrifty clerk.

Finally, she answered hestitatingly, "I'm not sure exactly, but I think with four hundred francs[6] I could manage it."

He turned a bit pale, for he had set aside just that amount to buy a rifle so that, the following summer, he could join some friends who were getting up a group to shoot larks on the plain near Nanterre.[7]

However, he said, "All right. I'll give you four hundred francs. But try to get a nice dress."

As the day of the party approached, Mme. Loisel seemed sad, moody, and ill at ease. Her

2. **sphinxlike** [sfingks'līk]: mysterious, like the Sphinx in Egypt.
3. **Mme. Georges Ramponneau** [ma dam' zhôrzh ram pə nō']
4. **M. Loisel** [mə syœ'lwa zel']
5. **Mathilde** [ma tēld']
6. **four hundred francs:** French currency, approximately eighty dollars at the time the story was written. The franc is the central monetary unit in France.
7. **Nanterre** [nan ter']: village near Paris.

GUIDED READING

LITERAL QUESTIONS

1a. What upsets Madame Loisel about the invitation? (She is upset because she has nothing appropriate to wear to the ball.)

2a. What does Monsieur Loisel offer to do when he learns what is upsetting his wife? (He offers to give her the money for a new dress.)

INFERENTIAL QUESTIONS

1b. What does her concern about her clothing indicate? (She is so preoccupied with appearances that she fails to appreciate a unique opportunity to spend an evening in luxurious surroundings.)

2b. What can you infer about his personality from this act? (In his willingness to deny himself a rifle, this "thrifty" clerk shows he is willing to make sacrifices to make his wife happy.)

Too Early, 1873, James Tissot. Guildhall Art Gallery, City of London.

outfit was ready, however. Her husband said to her one evening, "What's the matter? You've been all out of sorts for three days."

1 And she answered, "It's embarrassing not to have a jewel or a gem—nothing to wear on my dress. I'll look like a pauper: I'd almost rather not go to that party."

He answered, "Why not wear some flowers? They're very fashionable this season. For ten francs you can get two or three gorgeous roses."

2 She wasn't at all convinced. "No. . . . There's nothing more humiliating than to look poor among a lot of rich women."

But her husband exclaimed, "My, but you're silly! Go see your friend Mme. Forestier[8] and ask her to lend you some jewelry. You and she know each other well enough for you to do that."

She gave a cry of joy, "Why, that's so! I hadn't thought of it."

The next day she paid her friend a visit and told her of her predicament.

Mme. Forestier went toward a large closet with mirrored doors, took out a large jewel box, brought it over, opened it, and said to Mme. Loisel: "Pick something out, my dear."

At first her eyes noted some bracelets, then a pearl necklace, then a Venetian cross, gold and gems, of marvelous workmanship. She tried on these adornments in front of the mirror, but hesitated, unable to decide which to part with and put back. She kept on asking, "Haven't you something else?"

"Oh, yes, keep on looking. I don't know just what you'd like."

3 All at once she found, in a black satin box, a superb diamond necklace; and her pulse beat faster with longing. Her hands trembled as she took it up. Clasping it around her throat, outside her high-necked dress, she stood in ecstasy looking at her reflection.

Then she asked, hesitatingly, pleading, "Could I borrow that, just that and nothing else?"

8. **Forestier** [fô rə styā′]

GUIDED READING

LITERAL QUESTION

1a. What item of jewelry does Madame Loisel decide to borrow? (a diamond necklace)

INFERENTIAL QUESTION

1b. What does the author's description of the necklace imply? (He describes it as a "superb diamond necklace" in a "black satin box," which suggests that it has great value.)

AT A GLANCE

- Madame Loisel is still unhappy because she has no jewelry.
- At her husband's suggestion she borrows a diamond necklace from her friend, Madame Forestier.

1 CONFLICT

Madame Loisel, not content with her new dress, is still unhappy because she has no jewelry to go with it.

2 IRONY

Madame Loisel is unaware of the qualities she possesses that make her look naturally elegant: her beauty and charm.

3 PLOT: RISING ACTION

The "superb diamond necklace" of the story's title comes into the hands of Madame Loisel.

AT A GLANCE

- Madame Loisel, admired by all the men at the party, is elated and stays until four A.M.
- Monsieur Loisel has trouble finding a cab.
- At home they discover the necklace is missing.
- Monsieur Loisel tries unsuccessfully to find the necklace.

1 THEME

Madame Loisel does not realize that she is a sensation at the party because of her natural charm.

2 CONTRAST

The difference between Madame Loisel's modest wraps and her evening clothes emphasizes the Cinderella aspect of her adventure: She is about to reenter the world of pumpkins.

3 CHARACTERIZATION

Monsieur Loisel's plodding, down-to-earth simplicity is shown by his practical thoughts about going to work in the morning.

4 STYLE: DIALOGUE

The author employs dialogue to convey the drama of this critical moment when the Loisels realize that the necklace is missing.

"Why, of course."

She threw her arms around her friend, kissed her warmly, and fled with her treasure.

1 The day of the party arrived. Mme. Loisel was a sensation. She was the prettiest one there, fashionable, gracious, smiling, and wild with joy. All the men turned to look at her, asked who she was, begged to be introduced. All the Cabinet officials wanted to waltz with her. The minister took notice of her.

She danced madly, wildly, drunk with pleasure, giving no thought to anything in the triumph of her beauty, the pride of her success, in a kind of happy cloud composed of all the adulation, of all the admiring glances, of all the awakened longings, of a sense of complete victory that is so sweet to a woman's heart.

She left around four o'clock in the morning. Her husband, since midnight, had been dozing in a small empty sitting room with three other gentlemen whose wives were having too good a time.

2 He threw over her shoulders the wraps he had brought for going home, modest garments of everyday life whose shabbiness clashed with the stylishness of her evening clothes. She felt this and longed to escape, unseen by the other women who were draped in expensive furs.

Loisel held her back.

"Hold on! You'll catch cold outside. I'll call a cab."

But she wouldn't listen to him and went rapidly down the stairs. When they were on the street, they didn't find a carriage; and they set out to hunt for one, hailing drivers whom they saw going by at a distance.

They walked toward the Seine,[9] disconsolate and shivering. Finally on the docks they found one of those carriages that one sees in Paris only after nightfall, as if they were ashamed to show their drabness during daylight hours.

It dropped them at their door in the Rue des Martyrs,[10] and they climbed wearily up to their
3 apartment. For her, it was all over. For him, there was the thought that he would have to be at the Ministry at ten o'clock.

Before the mirror, she let the wraps fall from her shoulders to see herself once again in all her glory. Suddenly she gave a cry. The necklace was gone.

4 Her husband, already half undressed, said, "What's the trouble?"

She turned toward him despairingly, "I . . . I . . . I don't have Mme. Forestier's necklace."

"What! You can't mean it! It's impossible!"

They hunted everywhere, through the folds of the dress, through the folds of the coat, in the pockets. They found nothing.

He asked, "Are you sure you had it when leaving the dance?"

"Yes, I felt it when I was in the hall of the Ministry."

"But if you had lost it on the street we'd have heard it drop. It must be in the cab."

"Yes, quite likely. Did you get its number?"

"No. Didn't you notice it either?"

"No."

They looked at each other aghast. Finally Loisel got dressed again.

"I'll retrace our steps on foot," he said, "to see if I can find it."

And he went out. She remained in her evening clothes, without the strength to go to bed, slumped in a chair in the unheated room, her mind a blank.

Her husband came in about seven o'clock. He had had no luck.

He went to the police station, to the newspapers to post a reward, to the cab companies, everywhere the slightest hope drove him.

That evening Loisel returned, pale, his face lined; still he had learned nothing.

---

9. **Seine** [sān]: river that flows through the heart of the city of Paris.

10. **Rue des Martyrs** [ro͞o dā mär tĕr′]: French for "Street of the Martyrs."

GUIDED READING

LITERAL QUESTIONS

1a. What happens to Madame Loisel at the party? (She is the prettiest woman there; all the men admire her and dance with her.)

2a. What do the Loisels discover when they finally get home? (The necklace is missing.)

INFERENTIAL QUESTIONS

1b. Why is she so attractive at the party? (her natural beauty and charm)

2b. Why are they so upset by the loss of the necklace? (It is a diamond necklace, and they cannot afford to replace it.)

"We'll have to write your friend," he said, "to tell her you have broken the catch and are having it repaired. That will give us a little time to turn around."

She wrote to his dictation.

At the end of a week, they had given up all hope.

And Loisel, looking five years older, declared, "We must take steps to replace that piece of jewelry."

The next day they took the case to the jeweler whose name they found inside. He consulted his records. "I didn't sell that necklace, madame," he said. "I only supplied the case."

Then they went from one jeweler to another hunting for a similar necklace, going over their recollections, both sick with despair and anxiety.

They found, in a shop in Palais Royal,[11] a string of diamonds which seemed exactly like the one they were seeking. It was priced at forty thousand francs. They could get it for thirty-six.

They asked the jeweler to hold it for them for three days. And they reached an agreement that he would take it back for thirty-four thousand if the lost one was found before the end of February.

Loisel had eighteen thousand francs he had inherited from his father. He would borrow the rest.

He went about raising the money, asking a thousand francs from one, four hundred from another, a hundred here, sixty there. He signed notes, made ruinous deals, did business with loan sharks, ran the whole gamut of moneylenders. He compromised the rest of his life, risked his signature without knowing if he'd be able to honor it, and then, terrified by the outlook for the future, by the blackness of despair about to close around him, by the prospect of all the privations of the body and tortures of the spirit, he went to claim the new necklace with the thirty-six thousand francs which he placed on the counter of the shopkeeper.

When Mme. Loisel took the necklace back, Mme. Forestier said to her frostily, "You should have brought it back sooner; I might have needed it."

2 She didn't open the case, an action her friend was afraid of. If she had noticed the substitution, what would she have thought? What would she have said? Would she have thought her a thief?

Mme. Loisel experienced the horrible life the needy live. She played her part, however, with sudden heroism. That frightful debt had to be paid. She would pay it. She dismissed her maid; they rented a garret under the eaves.

3 She learned to do the heavy housework, to perform the hateful duties of cooking. She washed dishes, wearing down her shell-pink nails scouring the grease from pots and pans; she scrubbed dirty linen, shirts, and cleaning rags which she hung on a line to dry; she took the garbage down to the street each morning and brought up water, stopping on each landing to get her breath. And, clad like a peasant woman, basket on arm, guarding sou[12] by sou her scanty allowance, she bargained with the fruit dealers, the grocer, the butcher, and was insulted by them.

Each month notes had to be paid, and others renewed to give more time.

Her husband labored evenings to balance a tradesman's accounts, and at night, often, he copied documents at five sous a page.

And this went on for ten years.

Finally, all was paid back, everything including the exorbitant rates of the loan sharks and accumulated compound interest.

Mme. Loisel appeared an old woman, now. She became heavy, rough, harsh, like one of the

11. **Palais Royal** [pa lā′ rwa yal′]: upperclass neighborhood in Paris with expensive shops.

12. **sou** [so͞o]: French coin, then worth about one cent. Madame Loisel must watch every penny.

AT A GLANCE

- The Loisels are forced to replace the necklace.
- Monsieur Loisel uses up his inheritance and borrows heavily to buy one.
- They spend ten years in poverty and hard work to pay off the debt.

1 THEME

The Loisels find a necklace that looks just like the one they lost so that they can deceive Madame Forestier with it.

2 POINT OF VIEW

This limited third-person viewpoint enables us to tap Madame Loisel's fearful thoughts about being discovered. Ironically, discovery would mean salvation in this case.

3 IRONY

Because she had to have an evening of glamour, her simple life style has been transformed into a much worse existence.

GUIDED READING

LITERAL QUESTIONS

1a. What do the Loisels decide to do about the lost necklace? (They decide to replace it with an exact duplicate without telling Madame Forestier.)

2a. What happens to Madame Loisel as a result of buying the new necklace? (She is forced to live a life of poverty and hard work.)

INFERENTIAL QUESTIONS

1b. Do you think this is a wise decision on their part? (They cannot afford to replace the necklace. They should tell Madame Forestier the truth and hope she will understand.)

2b. How does her desire for material things destroy her natural gifts? (Hard work and poverty rob her of youth, beauty, and charm—priceless and irreplaceable assets.)

AT A GLANCE

- One day Madame Loisel meets Madame Forestier.
- Madame Loisel tells her the truth about the necklace and the struggle to pay off the debt.
- She learns that the necklace was made not of diamonds but of inexpensive glass.

1 THEME

The author suggests that the reader contemplate the "what ifs." Mathilde's happiness was not destroyed by the loss of the necklace but by her desire to have and wear jewelry. She may have been miserable in any case.

2 PLOT: CLIMAX, FALLING ACTION, RESOLUTION

Madame Forestier's revelation shows that the external appearance of the necklace was no indication of its true value; ironically, appearances ruin Mathilde's life in more ways than one.

REFLECTING ON THE STORY

Do you think Madame Loisel is a better person at the end of the story? (She may have learned not to let appearances deceive her.)

STUDY QUESTIONS

1. lavish home, servants, feasts
2. needs jewels; borrowing them
3. prettiest woman at party; men admired her greatly
4. It is lost; they search for it, borrow money, replace it.
5. Mme. Forestier does not recognize her, tells her necklace was fake.
6. moves to poorer quarters, works and bargains; surprising because she aspired to higher social position

poor. Her hair untended, her skirts askew, her hands red, her voice shrill, she even slopped water on her floors and scrubbed them herself. But, sometimes, while her husband was at work, she would sit near the window and think of that long-ago evening when, at the dance, she had been so beautiful and admired.

1 What would have happened if she had not lost that necklace? Who knows? Who can say? How strange and unpredictable life is! How little there is between happiness and misery!

Then one Sunday when she had gone for a walk on the Champs Élysées[13] to relax a bit from the week's labors, she suddenly noticed a woman strolling with a child. It was Mme. Forestier, still young-looking, still beautiful, still charming.

Mme. Loisel felt a rush of emotion. Should she speak to her? Of course. And now that everything was paid off, she would tell her the whole story. Why not?

She went toward her. "Hello, Jeanne."

The other, not recognizing her, showed astonishment at being spoken to so familiarly by this common person. She stammered, "But . . . madame . . . I don't recognize . . . You must be mistaken."

"No, I'm Mathilde Loisel."

Her friend gave a cry, "Oh, my poor Mathilde how you've changed!"

"Yes, I've had a hard time since last seeing you. And plenty of misfortunes—and all on account of you!"

"Of me . . . How do you mean?"

"Do you remember that diamond necklace you loaned me to wear to the dance at the Ministry?"

"Yes, but what about it?"

"Well, I lost it."

"You lost it! But you returned it."

"I brought you another just like it. And we've been paying for it for ten years now. You can imagine that wasn't easy for us who had nothing. Well, it's over now, and I am glad of it."

Mme. Forestier stopped short. "You mean to say you bought a diamond necklace to replace mine?"

"Yes. You never noticed, then? They were quite alike."

And she smiled with proud and simple joy.

2 Mme. Forestier, quite overcome, clasped her by the hands. "Oh, my poor Mathilde. But mine was only paste.[14] Why, at most it was worth only five hundred francs!"

---

13. **Champs Élysées** [shanz ā lē zā']: fashionable wide avenue, the main boulevard of Paris.

14. **paste:** bright but inexpensive glass used in costume jewelry.

STUDY QUESTIONS

Recalling

1. Summarize three specific things that Madame Loisel dreams about at the beginning of the story.
2. Why is Madame Loisel still unhappy after buying a dress? What does her husband suggest?
3. Describe Madame Loisel's success at the party.
4. What happens to the necklace? In what ways do the Loisels react?
5. Briefly describe Madame Loisel's encounter with Madame Forestier at the end of the story. What information does Madame Forestier give Madame Loisel?

Interpreting

6. When she found herself in debt, Madame Loisel "played the part...with sudden heroism." What did she do that could be called heroic? Why might those actions seem surprising?

WRITING A MAGAZINE ARTICLE

Objective

To describe changes wealth can bring

Guidelines for Evaluation

- suggested length: 300–400 words
- should identify object and tell of its discovery
- should describe lives before discovery and five years after

7. An old and worn Madame Loisel meets the still beautiful Madame Forestier and tells her about the lost necklace. Why does Madame Loisel decide to tell the truth?

Extending

8. When might dreams for a better life be beneficial to the dreamer, and when might they be harmful?

VIEWPOINT

Like "The Necklace," a number of Maupassant's other stories have titles that are the names of objects—for example "The Piece of String" and "The Mask." One writer described the center of these stories as

> a single object...dominating the lives of the people concerned.... It is the object which is to mold the lives of the people and can even decide their fate.
>
> —J. R. Dugan, *Illusion and Reality*

- To what extent is Madame Loisel's life molded by the necklace? To what extent is her fate the result of her own personality?

LITERARY FOCUS

The Elements of the Short Story

The five major elements of a short story are (1) plot, (2) character, (3) setting, (4) point of view, and (5) theme. Although in a particular story one of these elements may dominate, all of the elements will usually be present and important if the story is a good one. "The Necklace" is a good example of a story in which each of these elements is significant.

Thinking About the Elements of the Short Story

1. **Plot:** What is the climax of "The Necklace"?
2. **Character:** In what way has Madame Loisel's appearance influenced her personality?
3. **Setting:** Compare the scene at the Loisels' dinner table to Madame Loisel's dream dinner.
4. **Point of View:** In what way would the story be different if the storyteller were Madame Loisel herself?
5. **Theme:** Prove from the story that the author wants readers to disagree with Madame Loisel and her attitude toward appearances. What is the theme of the story?

Irony

Irony is a broad term used to talk about a contrast between reality and what seems to be real. **Situational irony** exists when what actually happens in a particular situation is the opposite of what we expect to happen. An author may use irony to give a story a surprise ending. For example, the ending of O. Henry's "Gift of the Magi" is ironic. We are surprised to learn that Jim has sold his watch to buy combs for Della, who sold her hair to buy Jim a watch chain.

Thinking About Irony

- In what way is the ending of "The Necklace" ironic?

COMPOSITION

Writing About the Total Effect

- What is the total effect of "The Necklace"? That is, what is its impact on the reader? Defend your answer by explaining how the author uses the following elements of fiction to achieve this effect: (a) plot, (b) character, (c) setting, (d) point of view, and (e) theme. Give examples from the story to support what you say. *For help with this assignment, see Lesson 11 in the Writing About Literature Handbook at the back of this book.*

Writing About Character

- By the end of the story, Madame Loisel has spent ten years in poverty in order to repay her debt. Explain (a) how Madame Loisel changed as a result of that experience and (b) what she learned about herself and about life. Use specific evidence from the story to support your answer.

Writing a Magazine Article

- In "The Necklace" Maupassant tells the story of a couple whose lives change drastically because they believe that a piece of jewelry is valuable when it actually is not. Write a brief magazine article about a poor couple who find out the reverse—that something they own and consider worthless is actually very valuable. First tell what the object is and where they got it. Then describe their lives before this discovery, immediately afterward, and five years later.

STUDY QUESTIONS

7. satisfied pride, obligation by paying debt
8. harmful when better life out of reach; beneficial when attainable

VIEWPOINT

- She must alter her existence to pay for it.
- dreams, vanity lead to need to borrow necklace; pride leads her to replace it secretly.

LITERARY FOCUS

Elements of the Short Story

1. Madame Loisel's meeting with Madame Forestier
2. She believes her beauty and charm entitle her to a better life.
3. Stew on a stained cloth contrasts unfavorably with the dinner of trout and grouse.
4. Her version would be less self-critical, would concentrate more on her sacrifices.
5.
   - She becomes a more heroic person as she loses her fine appearance.
   - True value is not always apparent.

Irony

Irony: The valueless necklace is paid for by ten priceless years of the Loisels' lives.

COMPOSITION: GUIDELINES FOR EVALUATION

WRITING ABOUT THE TOTAL EFFECT

Objective

To explain how author uses five elements of fiction to achieve the total impact

Guidelines for Evaluation

- suggested length: three to six paragraphs
- should support thesis with references to story
- should contain clear topic sentences
- should maintain coherence between paragraphs

WRITING ABOUT CHARACTER

Objective

To explain the change in Madame Loisel's looks and outlook as a result of her experience

Guidelines for Evaluation

- suggested length: two to three paragraphs
- should include an introduction stating cause of physical and spiritual change
- should use ample illustration from story
- should cite examples of what she learned

AT A GLANCE

- A semibarbarous king uses an amphitheater to try accused persons.
- An accused person must choose one of two doors in the arena.
- Behind one door is a tiger.

LITERARY OPTIONS

- interaction of plot and point of view
- characterization
- conflict

THEMATIC OPTIONS

- jealousy and love
- identity and self-respect
- mystery and adventure

1 SETTING

The opening sentence lends an aura of fairy tale to the story by setting the action "in the very olden time."

2 CHARACTERIZATION

The king is characterized directly as a person of great power who crushed all opposition.

3 PLOT: EXPOSITION

Early in the story the author explains the king's unusual method of administering "justice."

Frank R. Stockton (1834–1902) worked all his life as a wood engraver while writing short stories for periodicals. When "The Lady, or the Tiger?" appeared in 1882, it stirred up debates throughout the country. The story has remained popular reading since its first appearance.

- Based on your reading and your life experience, which choices in life are the most difficult?

Frank R. Stockton

The Lady, or the Tiger?

1 In the very olden time, there lived a semibarbaric[1] king who was a man of exuberant fancy and of an authority so irresistible that, at his will, he turned his varied fancies into facts. He was greatly given to self-communing; and when he and himself agreed upon anything, the thing was done. When everything moved smoothly, his nature was bland and genial; but whenever there was a little hitch, he was blander and more
2 genial still, for nothing pleased him so much as to make the crooked straight, and crush down uneven places.

Among his borrowed notions was that of the public arena, in which, by exhibitions of manly and beastly valor, the minds of his subjects were refined and cultured.

But even here the exuberant and barbaric fancy asserted itself. This vast amphitheater,[2] with its encircling galleries, its mysterious vault, and its unseen passages, was an agent of poetic justice, in which crime was punished, or virtue rewarded, by the decrees of an impartial and incorruptible chance.

When a subject was accused of a crime of sufficient importance to interest the king, public notice was given that on an appointed day the fate of the accused person would be decided in the king's arena.

When all the people had assembled in the galleries, and the king, surrounded by his court, sat high up on his throne of royal state on one side of the arena, he gave a signal, a door beneath him opened, and the accused subject stepped out into
3 the amphitheater. Directly opposite him, on the other side of the enclosed space, were two doors, exactly alike and side by side. It was the duty and the privilege of the person on trial to walk directly to these doors and open one of them. He could open either door he pleased. He was subject to no guidance or influence but that of the aforementioned impartial and incorruptible chance. If he opened the one, there came out of it a hungry tiger, the fiercest and most cruel that could be procured, which immediately sprang upon him and tore him to pieces, as a punishment for his guilt. The moment that the case of the criminal was thus decided, doleful iron bells were clanged, great wails went up from the hired mourners posted on the outer rim of the arena, and the vast audience, with bowed heads and downcast hearts, wended slowly their

1. **semibarbaric** [sem′ē bär bar′ik]: half savage.
2. **amphitheater** [am′fə thē′ə tər]: round open stadium surrounded by tiers of seats.

GUIDED READING

LITERAL QUESTION

1a. What word does the author use to describe the king in the first sentence of the story? *(semibarbaric)*

INFERENTIAL QUESTION

1b. What does the author wish to convey with this word? (The king is something of a savage; he puts little value on human life while demonstrating some limited sense of culture.)

SELECTION FOR PRACTICE IN ACTIVE READING
(TCR 5, p. 59)

omeward way, mourning greatly that one so oung and fair, or so old and respected, should ave merited so dire a fate.

But if the accused person opened the other oor, there came forth from it a lady, the most iitable to his years and station that His Majesty ould select among his fair subjects; and to this dy he was immediately married, as a reward of is innocence. It mattered not that he might aleady possess a wife and family, or that his affecons might be engaged upon an object of his wn selection. The king allowed no such arangements to interfere with his great scheme of unishment and reward. The exercises, as in the ther instance, took place immediately, and in he arena. Another door opened beneath the ing, and a priest, followed by a band of chorsters, and dancing maidens blowing joyous airs n golden horns, advanced to where the pair ood, side by side; and the wedding was promptly and cheerily solemnized. Then the gay brass ells rang forth their merry peals, and the people houted glad hurrahs, and the innocent man, receded by children strewing flowers on his ath, led his bride to his home.

This was the king's semibarbaric method of dministering justice. Its perfect fairness is obious. The criminal could not know out of which door would come the lady. He opened ither he pleased, without having the slightest dea whether, in the next instant, he was to be levoured or married. On some occasions the iger came out of one door, and on some, out of the other. The decisions were not only fair, hey were positively decisive. The accused peron was instantly punished if he found himself guilty; and, if innocent, he was rewarded on the pot, whether he liked it or not. There was no scape from the judgments of the king's arena.

The institution was a very popular one. When he people gathered together on one of the great rial days, they never knew whether they were o witness a bloody slaughter or a hilarious wedling. This element of uncertainty lent an interest to the occasion which it could not otherwise have attained. Thus, the masses were entertained and pleased, and the thinking part of the community could bring no charge of unfairness against this plan; for did not the accused person have the whole matter in his own hands?

4 This semibarbaric king had a daughter as blooming as his most florid fancies, and with a soul as fervent and imperious as his own. As is usual in such cases, she was the apple of his eye, and was loved by him above all humanity. Among his courtiers was a young man of that fineness of blood and lowness of station common to the heroes of romance who love royal maidens. This royal maiden was well satisfied with her lover, for he was handsome and brave to a degree unsurpassed in all this kingdom; and she loved him with an ardor that had enough of barbarism in it to make it exceedingly warm and strong. This love affair moved on happily for many months,
5 until one day the king happened to discover its existence. He did not hesitate nor waver in regard to his duty. The youth was immediately cast into prison, and a day was appointed for his trial in the king's arena. This, of course, was an especially important occasion; and His Majesty, as well as all the people, was greatly interested in the workings and development of this trial. Never before had such a case occurred—never before had a subject dared to love the daughter of a king. In after years such things became commonplace enough; but then they were, in no slight degree, novel and startling.

The tiger cages of the kingdom were searched for the most savage and relentless beasts, from which the fiercest monster might be selected for the arena; and the ranks of maiden youth and beauty throughout the land were carefully surveyed by competent judges, in order that the young man might have a fitting bride in case fate did not determine for him a different destiny. Of course, everybody knew that the deed with which the accused was charged had been done. He had loved the princess, and neither he, she,

AT A GLANCE

- Behind the other door is a beautiful lady.
- The king has a daughter who loves a lowly courtier.
- The king discovers their love; he sets a date for a trial.

1 THEME

A correct choice is rewarded by marriage to a young lady regardless of the affections of either party.

2 TONE

The omniscient narrator dismisses the method of "justice" with a thinly veiled attitude of sarcasm.

3 RESPONSE JOURNAL

Have students comment on the king's concept of justice.

4 CHARACTERIZATION

The king's daughter is characterized as the king's equal in every aspect of "semibarbarism."

5 PLOT: NARRATIVE HOOK

Discovering his daughter's love affair with a commoner impels the king to take extreme action.

GUIDED READING

LITERAL QUESTIONS

1a. What determines the guilt or innocence of the accused? (the appearance of tiger or lady)

2a. How does the author describe the king's daughter's soul? ("as fervent and imperious" as his)

INFERENTIAL QUESTIONS

1b. Why is this an unfair method of obtaining justice? (The choice of a "correct" door is no basis for determining guilt or innocence.)

2b. What can you infer about her character from her similarity to her father? (She also has a peculiar mixture of savagery and civilization.)

AT A GLANCE

- The king and princess join the masses in the arena.
- The courtier enters the arena.
- The princess has learned the secret of the doors.

1 SETTING

The description of the gathering masses reinforces the "semibarbaric" nature of the king's subjects—people who come to witness and thrill at possible death.

2 CHARACTERIZATION

The princess also possesses a nature that allows her to go where a more "refined" lady would never venture.

3 CONFLICT

The princess's knowledge of the doors seems to grant her a terrible power.

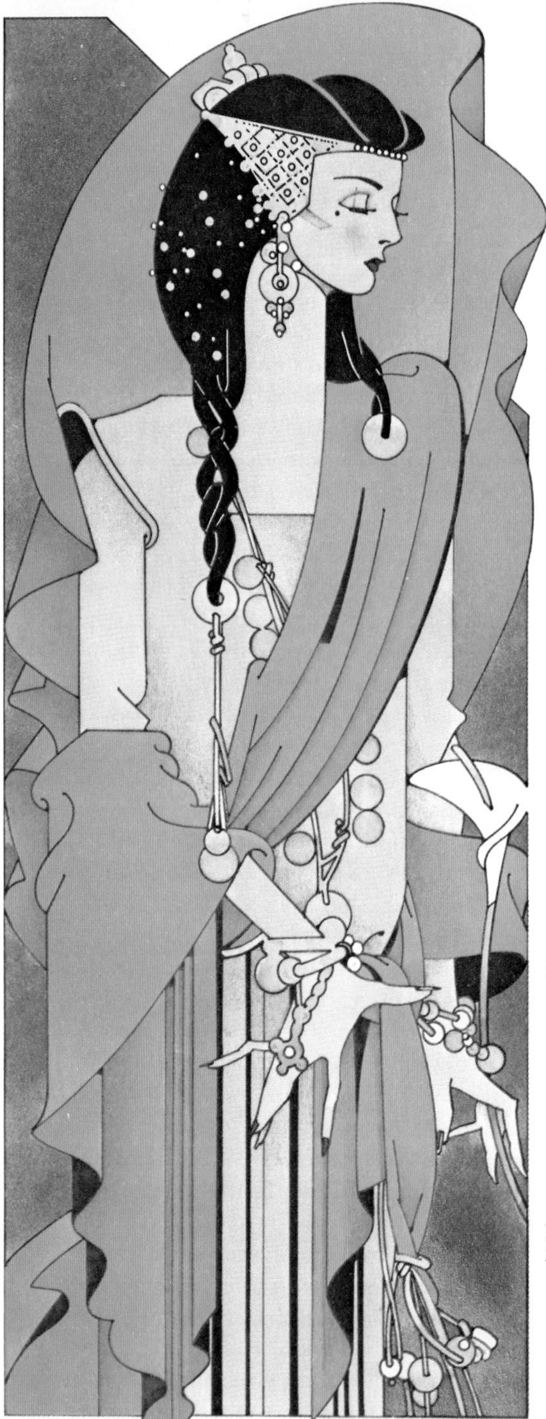

nor anyone else thought of denying the fact. But the king would not think of allowing any fact of this kind to interfere with the workings of the court of judgment, in which he took such great delight and satisfaction. No matter how the affair turned out, the youth would be disposed of; and the king would take pleasure in watching the course of events, which would determine whether or not the young man had done wrong in allowing himself to love the princess.

1 The appointed day arrived. From far and near the people gathered, and thronged the great galleries of the arena; and crowds, unable to gain admittance, massed themselves against its outside walls. The king and his court were in their places, opposite the twin doors—those fateful portals, so terrible in their similarity.

All was ready. The signal was given. A door beneath the royal party opened, and the lover of the princess walked into the arena. Tall, beautiful, fair, his appearance was greeted with a low hum of admiration and anxiety. Half the audience had not known so grand a youth had lived among them. No wonder the princess loved him! What a terrible thing for him to be there!

As the youth advanced into the arena, he turned, as the custom was, to bow to the king. But he did not think at all of that royal personage; his eyes were fixed upon the princess,
2 who sat to the right of her father. Had it not been
for the barbarism in her nature, it is probable
that lady would not have been there. But her intense and fervid soul would not allow her to be absent on an occasion in which she was so terribly interested. From the moment that the decree had gone forth that her lover should decide his fate in the king's arena, she had thought of nothing, night or day, but this great event and
3 the various subjects connected with it. Possessed
of more power, influence, and force of character than anyone who had ever before been interested in such a case, she had done what no other person had done—she had possessed herself of the secret of the doors. She knew in which of the

GUIDED READING

LITERAL QUESTION

1a. When the courtier enters the arena, what does he do? (He looks at the princess.)

INFERENTIAL QUESTION

1b. Why do you think he does this? (He may hope that she knows where the tiger is and will signal him with the information.)

two rooms that lay behind those doors stood the cage of the tiger, with its open front, and in which waited the lady. Through these thick doors, heavily curtained with skins on the inside, it was impossible that any noise or suggestion should come from within to the person who should approach to raise the latch of one of them. But gold, and the power of a woman's will, had brought the secret to the princess.

And not only did she know in which room stood the lady, ready to emerge, all blushing and radiant, should her door be opened, but she knew who the lady was. It was one of the fairest and loveliest of the damsels of the court who had been selected as the reward of the accused youth, should he be proved innocent of the crime of aspiring to one so far above him; and the princess hated her. Often had she seen, or imagined that she had seen, this fair creature throwing glances of admiration upon the person of her lover, and sometimes she thought these glances were perceived and even returned. Now and then she had seen them talking together. It was but for a moment or two, but much can be said in a brief space. It may have been on most unimportant topics, but how could she know that? The girl was lovely, but she had dared to raise her eyes to the loved one of the princess; and, with all the intensity of the savage blood transmitted to her through long lines of wholly barbaric ancestors, she hated the woman who blushed and trembled behind that silent door.

When her lover turned and looked at her, and his eye met hers as she sat there paler and whiter than anyone in the vast ocean of anxious faces about her, he saw, by that power of quick perception which is given to those whose souls are one, that she knew behind which door crouched the tiger, and behind which stood the lady. He had expected her to know it. He understood her nature, and his soul was assured that she would never rest until she had made plain to herself this thing, hidden to all other lookers-on, even to the king. The only hope for the youth in

AT A GLANCE

- The princess knows the lady behind the other door.
- She hates this woman, who is a rival for her lover's affections.
- The courtier sees that the princess knows which door hides the tiger.

1 CHARACTERIZATION

Since the courtier must marry the lady if he chooses the correct door, the princess has made sure she knows who that lady is.

2 THEME

The jealousy of the princess toward the lady behind the door is a strong and powerful emotion; the implication that the princess would knowingly allow her lover to die indicates that this jealousy seems out of control.

3 CONFLICT

The love that exists between the princess and the courtier makes their two souls "one." The princess's internal conflict concerns true love versus jealousy.

GUIDED READING

LITERAL QUESTION

1a. Who is the lady behind the door? (A damsel of the court whom the princess hates.)

INFERENTIAL QUESTION

1b. Why does the author introduce the notion of jealousy? (He wants to show that the princess may have a reason to direct her lover to the door with the tiger behind it.)

AT A GLANCE

- The princess points to the right door, and the courtier opens it.
- The narrator asks the reader to consider what was behind the door.

1 PLOT: CLIMAX

The courtier follows the princess's advice; the narrative halts at this point.

2 THEME

The narrator wishes the reader to decide whether jealousy or love ruled the princess.

3 CONFLICT

The princess's internal (and her lover's external) conflict is never resolved; the narrator insists that the reader think about two opposite motivations.

4 INTERACTION OF PLOT AND POINT OF VIEW

The story works because the omniscient narrator chooses not to reveal the decision of the princess; thus, the suspense of the plot remains unresolved.

REFLECTING ON THE STORY

Which door did the princess point to? (Either answer should be supported with references to the princess's love or jealousy.)

which there was any element of certainty was based upon the success of the princess in discovering this mystery; and the moment he looked upon her, he saw she had succeeded.

Then it was that his quick and anxious glance asked the question: "Which?" It was as plain to her as if he shouted it from where he stood. There was not an instant to be lost. The question was asked in a flash; it must be answered in another.

Her right arm lay on the cushioned parapet before her. She raised her hand, and made a slight, quick movement toward the right. No one but her lover saw her. Every eye but his was fixed on the man in the arena.

He turned, and with a firm and rapid step he walked across the empty space. Every heart stopped beating, every breath was held, every
1 eye was fixed immovably upon that man. Without the slightest hesitation, he went to the door on the right, and opened it.

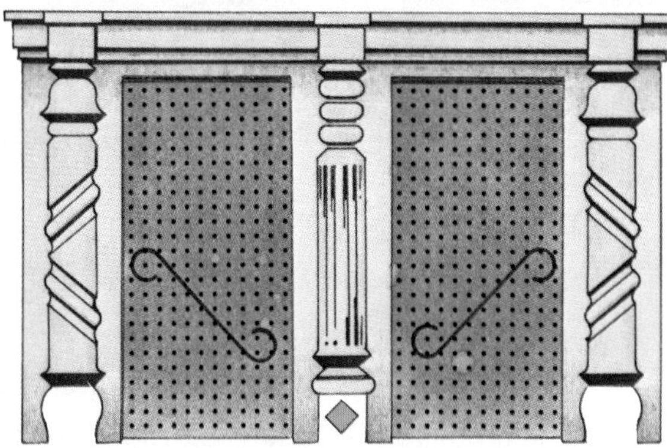

Now, the point of the story is this: Did the tiger come out of that door, or did the lady?

2 The more we reflect upon this question, the harder it is to answer. It involved a study of the human heart which leads us through roundabout pathways of passion, out of which it is difficult to find our way. Think of it, fair reader, not as if the decision of the question depended upon yourself, but upon that hotblooded, semibarbar-
3 ic princess, her soul at a white heat beneath the combined fires of despair and jealousy. She had lost him, but who should have him?

How often, in her waking hours and in her dreams, had she started in wild horror and covered her face with her hands as she thought of her lover opening the door on the other side of which waited the cruel fangs of the tiger!

But how much oftener had she seen him at the other door! How in her grievous reveries had she gnashed her teeth and torn her hair, when she saw his start of rapturous delight as he opened the door of the lady! How her soul had burned in agony when she had seen him rush to meet that woman, with her flushing cheek and sparkling eye of triumph; when she had seen him lead her forth, his whole frame kindled with the joy of recovered life; when she had heard the glad shouts from the multitude, and the wild ringing of the happy bells; when she had seen the priest, with his joyous followers, advance to the couple, and make them man and wife before her very eyes; and when she had seen them walk away together upon their path of flowers, followed by the tremendous shouts of the hilarious multitude in which her one despairing shriek was lost and drowned!

Would it not be better for him to die at once and go to wait for her in the blessed regions of semibarbaric futurity?

And yet, that awful tiger, those shrieks, that blood!

Her decision had been indicated in an instant, but it had been made after days and nights of anguished deliberation. She had known she would be asked, she had decided what she would answer, and, without the slightest hesitation, she had moved her hand to the right.

4 The question of her decision is one not to be lightly considered, and it is not for me to presume to set up myself as the one person able to answer it. And so I leave it with all of you: Which came out of the opened door—the lady, or the tiger?

GUIDED READING

LITERAL QUESTION

1a. How does the young man open the door? (without the slightest hesitation)

INFERENTIAL QUESTION

1b. What does this indicate about the man's feelings? (He trusts completely in the goodness of his princess.)

STUDY QUESTIONS

Recalling

1. How does the king determine the guilt or innocence of persons accused of crimes in his country? Why do his subjects regard this system of justice as a perfectly fair one?
2. For what crime is the young man imprisoned?
3. Once he is in the arena, why does the young man stare at the princess? What does she do?
4. According to the narrator, for what reasons might the princess save the hero's life? For what reasons might she send him to his doom?

Interpreting

5. Why is the princess described as "semibarbaric" rather than civilized or completely barbaric? In what ways does her *semi*barbaric nature make her decision more difficult?

Extending

6. Which door do you think the princess pointed toward—the lady's or the tiger's? Why?

VIEWPOINT

Some people might dismiss "The Lady, or the Tiger?" as a mere trick because of its ending. One writer has defended the story against such a charge by speaking of the story's last eight paragraphs:

> It is this epilogue which raises the story above the level of the "trick," and invests it with the dignity of an exposition of human strength and human frailty.
>
> —M. Griffin, *Frank R. Stockton: A Critical Biography*

■ What do the last eight paragraphs of the story tell us about human strength and weakness?

LITERARY FOCUS

Interaction of Plot and Point of View

In any good story all of the various elements of the short story should **interact**, or work together. The interaction is often so complete that it is difficult to discuss, for example, plot or theme without also mentioning character, setting, or point of view. As an example, notice how plot and point of view are intertwined in "The Lady, or the Tiger?"

Thinking About Plot and Point of View

■ Why would Stockton's ending to the story not have been possible if the story were told from the first-person point of view of the princess?

VOCABULARY

Word Origins

The word *arena* is actually the Latin word for "sand." The Romans used sand to cover the floors of the amphitheaters in which their gladiators fought. Later on, the term *arena* was applied to any area in which athletic or other contests were held.

In the word *amphitheater*, the prefix *amphi-* means "around." While a regular theater has seats that face the stage, an amphitheater has tiers of seats on all sides around the stage or playing area.

Barbaric is an "echoic" word—that is, it imitates some familiar sound. The Greeks called foreigners *barbarous*, because all unknown languages sounded like *bar-bar-bar* to them. Can you think of other *echoic* words?

Look up the origins of three of the following words in a good dictionary. Most dictionaries place this information in brackets [ ] just before or just after the definitions.

1. imperious
2. florid
3. incorruptible
4. parapet
5. wended
6. damsels

COMPOSITION

Writing About Plot and Point of View

■ The narrator plays an important role in the plot of this story. He is careful not to lead the reader to expect either ending. Explain what details he might have emphasized, added, or eliminated if he had wanted to prepare for the "lady" ending. Then explain how he might have prepared for the "tiger" ending.

Writing a Description of a New Story

■ Imagine a new version of the story that takes place in modern times. Do not write the complete story, but describe, with a paragraph devoted to each, the modern versions of the following: (a) the setting, (b) the king, (c) the princess, (d) the hero, and (e) the choice to be made.

STUDY QUESTIONS

1. allows them to choose between two doors; accused holds fate "in his own hands"
2. loving the princess
3. expects a sign; motions to right
4. her love; her jealousy
5. A totally barbaric princess would probably allow her lover to die; a civilized one would probably allow him to live. Being "semibarbaric," she appears capable of either.
6. Answers will vary.

VIEWPOINT

True love should be unselfish, but possessive love leads to jealousy.

LITERARY FOCUS

The story's suspense would be lost, for she would probably reveal the courtier's fate.

VOCABULARY

1. *imperious* from Latin *imperiosus,* "powerful, tyrannical" from *imperium,* "rule, empire"
2. *florid* from Latin *floridus,* "full of flowers" from *flos,* "a flower"
3. *incorruptible* from Middle English *incorruptyble* from Late Latin *incorruptibilis,* from *in,* "not" + *corruptibilis,* "breakable"
4. *parapet,* French, from Italian *parapetto,* "breast-high wall," from *para,* "ward off" + *petto* "breast"
5. *wended* from Middle English *wenden,* from Old English *wendan,* "to turn, go"
6. *damsels* from Middle English *dameseles,* from Old French *dameiseles,* from Vulgar Latin *dominicellas,* from Latin *domina,* "lady, mistress"

COMPOSITION: GUIDELINES FOR EVALUATION

WRITING ABOUT PLOT AND POINT OF VIEW

Objective

To suggest changes to make ending predictable

Guidelines for Evaluation

- suggested length: two paragraphs
- should have a clear topic sentence for each alternate ending
- should make logical suggestions based on evidence in the story

WRITING A DESCRIPTION OF A NEW STORY

Objective

To suggest changes to set story in modern times

Guidelines for Evaluation

- suggested length: five paragraphs
- should have a one-sentence thesis stating general change to be made
- should devote a paragraph to each element

AT A GLANCE

- A commander directs a hydroplane through a hurricane.
- Walter Mitty's wife wakes him from his daydream.
- As they drive to Waterbury, she orders him to do errands.

LITERARY OPTIONS

- interaction of character and theme
- plot
- tone

THEMATIC OPTIONS

- dreams vs. reality
- leadership
- identity and self-respect

1 THEME

Mitty and the reader are jolted from his dream world by reality throughout the story.

2 SETTING

The story's occasional setting is Walter Mitty's imagination. The exterior suburban locales prompt his daydreams.

3 CHARACTERIZATION

In real life Mitty is a suggestible person without the power to command—the opposite of his persona in his daydreams.

One of this country's most widely read humorists, James Thurber (1894–1961) specialized in the presentation of slightly unusual human behavior. "The Secret Life of Walter Mitty" is probably his most popular story.

- What intrigues you about daydreams—such as the ones in this story?

James Thurber

The Secret Life of Walter Mitty

"We're going through!" The Commander's voice was like thin ice breaking. He wore his full-dress uniform, with the heavily braided white cap pulled down rakishly over one cold gray eye. "We can't make it, sir. It's spoiling for a hurricane, if you ask me." "I'm not asking you, Lieutenant Berg," said the Commander. "Throw on the power lights! Rev her up to 8,500! We're going through!" The pounding of the cylinders increased: ta-pocketa-pocketa-pocketa-*pocketa-pocketa*. The Commander stared at the ice forming on the pilot window. He walked over and twisted a row of complicated dials. "Switch on No. 8 auxiliary!" he shouted. "Switch on No. 8 auxiliary!" repeated Lieutenant Berg. "Full strength in No. 3 turret!" shouted the Commander. "Full strength in No. 3 turret!" The crew, bending to their various tasks in the huge, hurtling eight-engined Navy hydroplane,[1] look-
1 ed at each other and grinned. "The Old Man'll get us through," they said to one another. "The Old Man ain't afraid of Hell!" . . .

"Not so fast! You're driving too fast!" said Mrs. Mitty. "What are you driving so fast for?"

"Hmm?" said Walter Mitty. He looked at his wife, in the seat beside him, with shocked astonishment. She seemed grossly unfamiliar, like a strange woman who had yelled at him in a crowd. "You were up to fifty-five," she said. "You know I don't like to go more than forty. You
2 were up to fifty-five." Walter Mitty drove on toward Waterbury[2] in silence, the roaring of the SN202 through the worst storm in twenty years of Navy flying fading in the remote, intimate airways of his mind. "You're tensed up again," said Mrs. Mitty. "It's one of your days. I wish you'd let Dr. Renshaw look you over."

Walter Mitty stopped the car in front of the building where his wife went to have her hair
3 done. "Remember to get those overshoes while I'm having my hair done," she said. "I don't need overshoes," said Mitty. She put her mirror back into her bag. "We've been all through that," she said, getting out of the car. "You're not a young man any longer." He raced the engine a little. "Why don't you wear your gloves? Have you lost your gloves?" Walter Mitty reached in a pocket and brought out the gloves. He put them on, but after she had turned and gone into the building and he had driven on

1. **hydroplane** [hī′drə plān′]: seaplane.

2. **Waterbury:** city in Connecticut.

GUIDED READING

LITERAL QUESTION

1a. What is the daydream that opens the story? (A commander directs a hydroplane through a hurricane.)

INFERENTIAL QUESTION

1b. How does this dream contrast with reality? (In reality Mitty drives a car; he meekly slows down when his wife complains of the car's speed.)

to a red light, he took them off again. "Pick it up, brother!" snapped a cop as the light changed, and Mitty hastily pulled on his gloves and lurched ahead. He drove around the streets aimlessly for a time, and then he drove past the hospital on his way to the parking lot.

. . . "It's the millionaire banker, Wellington McMillan," said the pretty nurse. "Yes?" said Walter Mitty, removing his gloves slowly. "Who has the case?" "Dr. Renshaw and Dr. Benbow, but there are two specialists here, Dr. Remington from New York and Dr. Pritchard-Mitford from London. He flew over!" A door opened down a long cool corridor and Dr. Renshaw came out. He looked distraught and haggard. "Hello, Mitty," he said. "We're having the devil's own time with McMillan, the millionaire banker and close personal friend of Roosevelt.[3] Obstreosis of the ductal tract. Tertiary.[4] Wish you'd take a look at him." "Glad to," said Mitty.

In the operating room there were whispered introductions: "Dr. Remington, Dr. Mitty. Dr. Pritchard-Mitford, Dr. Mitty." "I've read your book on streptothricosis," said Pritchard-Mitford, shaking hands. "A brilliant performance, sir." "Thank you," said Walter Mitty. "Didn't know you were in the States, Mitty," grumbled Remington. "Coals to Newcastle,[5] bringing Mitford and me up here for a tertiary." "You are very kind," said Mitty. A huge, complicated machine, connected to the operating table, with many tubes and wires, began at this moment to go pocketa-pocketa-pocketa. "The new anesthetizer is giving way!" shouted an intern. "There is no one in the East who knows how to fix it!" "Quiet, man!" said Mitty, in a low, cool voice. He sprang to the machine, which was now going pocketa-pocketa-queep-pocketa-queep. He began fingering delicately a row of glistening dials. "Give me a fountain pen!" he snapped. Someone handed
3 him a fountain pen. He pulled a faulty piston out of the machine and inserted the pen in its place. "That will hold for ten minutes," he said. "Get on with the operation." A nurse hurried over and whispered to Renshaw, and Mitty saw the man turn pale. "Coreopsis has set in," said Renshaw nervously. "If you would take over, Mitty?" Mitty looked at him and at the craven figure of Benbow, who drank, and at the grave, uncertain faces of the two great specialists. "If you wish," he said. They slipped a white gown on him; he adjusted a mask and drew on thin gloves; nurses handed him shining . . .

4 "Back it up, Mac! Look out for that Buick!" Walter Mitty jammed on the brakes. "Wrong lane, Mac," said the parking-lot attendant, looking at Mitty closely. "Gee. Yeh," muttered Mitty. He began cautiously to back out of the lane marked "Exit Only." "Leave her sit there," said the attendant. "I'll put her away." Mitty got out of the car. "Hey, better leave the key." "Oh," said Mitty, handing the man the ignition key. The attendant vaulted into the car, backed it up with insolent skill, and put it where it belonged.

They're so cocky, thought Walter Mitty, walking along Main Street; they think they know
5 everything. Once he had tried to take his chains off, outside New Milford, and he had got them wound around the axles. A man had had to come out in a wrecking car and unwind them, a young, grinning garageman. Since then Mrs. Mitty always made him drive to a garage to have the chains taken off. The next time, he thought, I'll wear my right arm in a sling; they won't grin at me then. I'll have my right arm in a sling and they'll see I couldn't possibly take the chains off myself. He kicked at the slush on the sidewalk. "Overshoes," he said to himself, and he began looking for a shoe store.

When he came out into the street again, with the overshoes in a box under his arm, Walter

3. **Roosevelt:** President Franklin D. Roosevelt (1882–1945).
4. **obstreosis . . . . Tertiary:** nonsensical diagnosis indicating that some details of Mitty's dreams are imaginary.
5. **coals to Newcastle:** proverb about unnecessary effort. Newcastle is a city in England known for its production of coal. The doctor implies that, with Mitty on the case, it is unnecessary to call for further help.

AT A GLANCE

- As Mitty drives past a hospital, he dreams he is a famous surgeon.
- He drives into an exit lane of a parking lot.
- He remembers that he cannot take the chains off his tires without help.

1 THEME

The gloves Mitty puts on in the car transform him into a famous surgeon taking off his gloves in the hospital.

2 TONE

The sound of the malfunctioning anesthetizer is the same sound the cylinders of the hydroplane made. The author's bemused attitude toward his protagonist is relayed via this amusing, recurring sound effect.

3 THEME

In his dreams Mitty is self-assured and calm with unusual manual dexterity—the opposite of Mitty's comportment in the world.

4 CHARACTERIZATION

In reality Mitty absent-mindedly drives his car into the exit lane of a parking lot and lets the attendant order him about.

5 CONFLICT

Mitty's inability to cope with the ordinary problems of daily life reveals the internal conflict that impels him to daydream of being brave and famous.

GUIDED READING

LITERAL QUESTIONS

1a. What is Mitty's second fantasy? (He dreams he is a famous surgeon saving the life of a rich banker.)

2a. What suddenly rouses Mitty from this fantasy? (The parking attendant yells at him.)

INFERENTIAL QUESTIONS

1b. Why does Mitty dream of being a famous surgeon? (The gloves he puts on in the car remind him of his lack of manual dexterity, and a surgeon is a master at using his hands.)

2b. Why is the attendant's yelling at Mitty ironic? (Mitty is the opposite of a capable, dexterous person.)

AT A GLANCE

- Mitty cannot remember what his wife told him to buy.
- He dreams he is a star witness in a murder trial.
- He remembers to buy puppy biscuit.

1 READING SKILLS: CAUSE AND EFFECT

The newsboy's shouts about a controversial trial cause Mitty to fantasize about being a star witness.

2 PLOT: TRANSITION

Thurber's deft juxtaposition of real and imaginary events creates a comic momentum that moves the plot forward. In this case the word *cur* is used to leap to the term *puppy biscuit.*

3 TONE

The author makes the story humorous by contrasting the silliness of this slogan with Mitty's fantasy of being the "greatest pistol shot in the world."

Mitty began to wonder what the other thing was his wife had told him to get. She had told him twice before they set out from their house for Waterbury. In a way he hated these weekly trips to town—he was always getting something wrong. Kleenex, he thought, Squibb's, razor blades? No. Toothpaste, toothbrush, bicarbonate, carborundum, initiative and referendum? He gave it up. But she would remember it. "Where's the what's-its-name?" she would ask. "Don't tell me you
1 forgot the what's-its-name." A newsboy went by shouting something about the Waterbury trial.

. . . "Perhaps this will refresh your memory." The District Attorney suddenly thrust a heavy automatic at the quiet figure on the witness stand. "Have you ever seen this before?" Walter Mitty took the gun and examined it expertly. "This is my Webley-Vickers 50.80," he said calmly. An excited buzz ran around the courtroom. The Judge rapped for order. "You are a crack shot with any sort of firearms, I believe?" said the District Attorney, insinuatingly. "Objection!" shouted Mitty's attorney. "We have shown that the defendant could not have fired the shot. We have shown that he wore his right arm in a sling on the night of the fourteenth of July." Walter Mitty raised his hand briefly and the bickering attorneys were stilled. "With any known make of gun," he said evenly, "I could have killed Gregory Fitzhurst at three hundred feet *with my left hand.*" Pandemonium broke loose in the courtroom. A woman's scream rose above the bedlam and suddenly a lovely, dark-haired girl was in Walter Mitty's arms. The District Attorney struck at her savagely. Without rising from his chair, Mitty let the man have it on the point of the chin. "You miserable cur!" . . .

2 "Puppy biscuit," said Walter Mitty. He stopped walking and the buildings of Waterbury rose up out of the misty courtroom and surrounded him again. A woman who was passing laughed. "He said 'Puppy biscuit,' " she said to her companion. "That man said 'Puppy biscuit' to himself." Walter Mitty hurried on. He went into an A&P, not the first one he came to but a smaller one farther up the street. "I want some biscuit for small, young dogs," he said to the clerk. "Any
3 special brand, sir?" The greatest pistol shot in the world thought a moment. "It says 'Puppies Bark for It' on the box," said Walter Mitty.

His wife would be through at the hairdresser's in fifteen minutes, Mitty saw in looking at his watch, unless they had trouble drying it; sometimes they had trouble drying it. She didn't like to get to the hotel first; she would want him to be there waiting for her as usual. He found a big leather chair in the lobby, facing a window, and he put the overshoes and the puppy biscuit on the floor beside it. He picked up an old copy of *Liberty*[6] and sank down into the chair. "Can Germany Conquer the World Through the Air?" Walter Mitty looked at the pictures of bombing planes and of ruined streets.

6. **Liberty:** weekly magazine that is no longer published.

GUIDED READING

LITERAL QUESTION

1a. What can't Mitty remember to buy? (puppy biscuit)

INFERENTIAL QUESTION

1b. Why does the author choose this item for Mitty to forget? (It sounds humorous and is a relatively unimportant item that can be comically compared to a heroic man.)

US NAVY

AT A GLANCE

- Mitty dreams he is an intrepid World War I bomber pilot.
- His wife interrupts the dream.
- As he leans against a store wall, Mitty fantasizes that he is facing a firing squad.

1 THEME

Each fantasy emphasizes that even people who lead humdrum lives can become heroes in their dreams.

2 POINT OF VIEW

The author employs a limited third-person point of view to underscore the humor of Mitty's fantasy life.

3 INTERACTION OF CHARACTER AND THEME

There is a sharp contrast between Mitty's dreams of daring exploits and the reality of his being ordered about by everyone he encounters.

REFLECTING ON THE STORY

Do you think Walter Mitty should spend so much of his time daydreaming? (Although some students may think it is better to live life in the real world, others may feel that Mitty's dreams relieve him of a mediocre life in which he seems to have neither influence nor skill.)

STUDY QUESTIONS

1. commander; surgeon; criminal; pilot; man facing firing squad
2. driving; headline; article; lighting cigarette
3. wife yells at him; lot attendant yells at him; remembers to buy dog biscuits; wife strikes his shoulder

. . . "The cannonading has got the wind up in young Raleigh, sir," said the sergeant. Captain Mitty looked up at him through tousled hair. "Get him to bed," he said wearily, "with the others. I'll fly alone." "But you can't, sir," said the sergeant anxiously. "It takes two men to handle that bomber and the Archies[7] are pounding hell out of the air. Von Richtman's circus[8] is between here and Saulier." "Somebody's got to get that ammunition dump," said Mitty. "I'm going over. Spot of brandy?" He poured a drink for the sergeant and one for himself. War thundered and whined around the dugout and battered at the door. There was a rending of wood and splinters flew through the room. "A bit of a near thing," said Captain Mitty carelessly. "The box barrage is closing in," said the sergeant. "We only live once, Sergeant," said Mitty, with his faint, fleeting smile. "Or do we?" He poured another brandy and tossed it off. "I never see a man could hold his brandy like you, sir," said the sergeant. "Begging your pardon, sir." Captain Mitty stood up and strapped on his huge Webley-Vickers auto-
1 matic. "It's forty kilometers through hell, sir," said the sergeant. Mitty finished one last brandy. "After all," he said softly, "what isn't?" The pounding of the cannon increased; there was the rat-tat-tatting of machine guns, and from somewhere came the menacing pocketa-pocketa-pocketa of the new flame-throwers. Walter Mitty walked to the door of the dugout humming "Auprès de Ma Blonde."[9] He turned and waved to the sergeant. "Cheerio!" he said. . . .

Something struck his shoulder. "I've been looking all over this hotel for you," said Mrs. Mitty. "Why do you have to hide in this old chair? How did you expect me to find you?" "Things close in," said Walter Mitty vaguely. "What?" Mrs. Mitty said. "Did you get the what's-its-name? The puppy biscuit? What's in that box?" "Overshoes," said Mitty. "Couldn't you have put them on in the store?" "I was thinking," said Walter Mitty. "Does it ever occur to you that I am sometimes thinking?" She looked at him. "I'm going to take your temperature when I get you home," she said.

They went out through the revolving doors that made a faintly derisive whistling sound when you pushed them. It was two blocks to the parking lot. At the drugstore on the corner she said, "Wait here for me. I forgot something. I won't be a minute."
2 She was more than a minute. Walter Mitty lighted a cigarette. It began to rain, rain with sleet in it. He stood up against the wall of the drugstore, smoking. . . . He put his shoulders back and his heels together. "To hell with the handkerchief," said Walter Mitty scornfully. He took one last
3 drag on his cigarette and snapped it away. Then, with that faint, fleeting smile playing about his lips, he faced the firing squad; erect and motionless, proud and disdainful, Walter Mitty the Undefeated, inscrutable to the last.

---

7. **Archies:** slang for antiaircraft guns during World War I.
8. **circus:** squadron of fighter planes flying in formation.
9. **Auprès de Ma Blonde** [ō prā′ də mä blond]: French song, "Near My Blonde."

STUDY QUESTIONS

Recalling

1. Name the characters Mitty imagines himself to be. Describe the situation he creates for each of those characters.
2. Mitty drives past a hospital and imagines that he is a surgeon. What other situations lead Mitty into other dreams?
3. Give two examples of how Mitty is suddenly roused from his dreams.

Interpreting

4. What personality traits does Mitty possess in his dreams?
5. Compare the way Mitty is treated by people in his dreams with the way he is actually treated in his real life.

Extending

6. Explain two methods by which Thurber makes the story humorous.

VIEWPOINT

People all over the world have come to know Walter Mitty and his dream life. For example, the journalist Lewis Gannet once saw a reference to "Walter Mitty types" in an editorial in a newspaper in Pakistan. The editorial writer clearly expected readers to understand the reference without any further explanation.

- How would you describe a "Walter Mitty type"? In what ways is the character of Walter Mitty a recognizable and well-known human type?

LITERARY FOCUS

Interaction of Character and Theme

A character often reveals a story's theme, or central idea. A writer developing theme through character usually gives the reader a very clear picture of the thoughts, words, and actions of the main character. Because the focus on the character is so strong, the reader understands that this character's life is meant to illustrate an idea or message about life in general. Any change that a character undergoes or lesson that a character learns in a story usually points to the story's theme.

Thinking About Character and Theme

1. What is the theme of "The Secret Life of Walter Mitty"?
2. Explain how the theme is revealed through the character of Mitty.

VOCABULARY

Antonyms

Antonyms are words that have opposite or nearly opposite meanings. *Entertaining* and *boring* are antonyms. The words in capitals are from "The Secret Life of Walter Mitty." Choose the word that is *most nearly the opposite* of the word in capitals, *as the word is used in the story.* Write the number of each item and the letter of your choice on a separate sheet.

1. REV: (a) soar up (b) dive (c) slow down (d) turn aside
2. HURTLING: (a) sluggish (b) speeding (c) unsteady (d) powerful
3. DISTRAUGHT: (a) concerned (b) confused (c) cheerful (d) disappointed
4. INSOLENT: (a) modest (b) insulting (c) wary (d) carefree
5. INSCRUTABLE: (a) understandable (b) unafraid (c) invisible (d) unthinkable

COMPOSITION

Writing About Character and Theme

- Explain how the character of Walter Mitty illustrates the theme of the story. First state the theme of the story in a sentence or two. Then explain how Mitty's personality demonstrates that theme. Cite evidence from the story to support your answer.

Writing a Sequel to the Story

- "The Secret Life of Walter Mitty" is really a series of episodes. In each episode Mitty escapes into a new fantasy situation. Write one more episode for the story. First describe Mitty in a real world situation that inspires his imagination. Then describe his fantasy. Finally, describe his return to the real world.

COMPARING STORIES

1. Both "The Necklace" and "The Secret Life of Walter Mitty" involve characters who dream because they are unhappy with their present lives. In what different ways do Mitty's and Madame Loisel's dreams affect their lives?
2. Both "The Lady, or the Tiger?" and "About Two Nice People" are love stories that contain conflicts. What is the conflict in each of the stories? Explain how love leads to conflict in one story and how conflict leads to love in the other.

STUDY QUESTIONS

4. calm leadership, manual dexterity, self-assurance, daring, scornfulness, pride, fearlessness, disdain
5. dreams: with respect and admiration; real life: is scoffed at and ignored
6. comic words and expressions; incongruity of real and fantasy life; the way events in real life inspire Mitty's dreams; the hyperbole and melodrama of Mitty's dreams

VIEWPOINT

- He is self-effacing, timid, and largely ignored.
- There are far more followers than leaders in the world; there is a Walter Mitty in nearly all of us.

LITERARY FOCUS

1. People can become heroes in daydreams.
2. the sharp contrast between his personality and his dreams

VOCABULARY

1. (c) slow down
2. (a) sluggish
3. (c) cheerful
4. (a) modest
5. (a) understandable

COMPARING STORIES

1. Mme. Loisel: Dreams cause chronic misery. Mitty: dreams bring relief
2. "Lady/Tiger": Love of courtier leads to conflicts with king and within princess. "About Two": Worsening conflict between Ellen and Walter is resolved when they uncover their real feelings.

COMPOSITION: GUIDELINES FOR EVALUATION

WRITING ABOUT CHARACTER AND THEME

Objective

To demonstrate that Mitty's personality illustrates Thurber's theme

Guidelines for Evaluation

- suggested length: three paragraphs
- should state the theme in first paragraph and end with summary conclusion
- should analyze Mitty's real and fantasized personalities

WRITING A SEQUEL TO THE STORY

Objective

To write another episode to the story

Guidelines for Evaluation

- suggested length: 300–400 words
- should begin with real situation that inspires daydreams
- should make dream appropriate to character
- should interrupt daydream with real situation

ACTIVE READING

To have students appreciate the care that authors use to supply the words and details necessary to understand their meaning, have students read this essay about significant detail. Then discuss the following points:

- Too often students ask, "Do you think that the author really *meant* to put that in?" The answer is, of course, yes and no. Sometimes in the multiple revisions of a story, the authors see that they have quite accidentally inserted something remarkably germane to the structure. Just as often, probably more often, authors see that something they intended is not clear or else obstructs their intentions. Students should realize, however, that multiple revision is an important part of the creation of a short story. By the time the process is complete, every word and detail in a good story contributes to its impact.
- To show the importance of every incident and action to a whole story, read the sections that apply to "The Monkey's Paw" and "Raymond's Run" after the class has studied each of those stories. Later, as a review of the unit, take a class period to examine carefully a selection which the class has already read and discussed. You might begin by having the first paragraphs of a story read aloud. Interrupt that reading frequently to point out such significant details as bits of characterization or foreshadowing. Then let everyone search through the remainder of the story for small details that provide clues to the author's intentions.

You will find among the materials for this unit in your *Teacher's Classroom Resources* the related blackline master Significant Details in Short Stories.

ACTIVE READING

Significant Details in Short Stories

Almost any story, even a long one, can be summed up in a paragraph or two. The plot of a story, the "what happens," can be sketched in a few words. The bare outline of a story, however, is not very interesting or convincing without the rich details that give a story color, life, complication, and meaning.

For example, a brief summary of "The Monkey's Paw" (page 2) would not contain the many details that create suspense, atmosphere, character, and psychological drama. Let us look at one detail that adds meaning to "The Monkey's Paw." When the father makes a poor move in a game of chess, the author remarks that the father has "seen a fatal mistake after it was too late." Later we can see how the remark connects to the larger meaning of the story. In innocently wishing for the money, the Whites make a "fatal mistake" that they see only after it is too late. To appreciate such details in the story is to increase our pleasure, for we come to recognize the depth of the theme and W.W. Jacobs' skill as a writer.

Toni Cade Bambara's "Raymond's Run" (page 41) is largely a character study of a girl called Squeaky. By paying attention to significant details, we may know Squeaky better than she knows herself. She presents herself to us as a tough, aggressive, competitive character with "the baddest rep around." The details tell us otherwise, but we are likely to miss their meaning if we are not reading carefully.

Listen to Squeaky while she waits for the race to begin: "I'm on my back looking at the sky, trying to pretend I'm in the country." Then she remembers that she is in the "concrete jungle." A few minutes later, however, her dream returns: "I dream I'm flying over a sandy beach in the early morning sun, kissing the leaves of the trees as I fly by." These images and this kind of language conflict with the picture that Squeaky has of herself and with the tougher language she uses most of the time. Squeaky has another side to her character. She has a dream that she is not telling us as she struggles for an identity in her concrete jungle. Understanding the meaning of these details opens up the meaning of the story itself.

A good writer makes every word count. If we pay close attention to the details in a story, we will be amply rewarded in the pleasure we gain from our careful reading.

THE SHORT STORY

Guide for Studying the Short Story

As you read short stories, review the following guide in order to appreciate how an author creates a fictional world.

Plot

1. What type of **conflict** does the main character face?
2. What is the **exposition**? The **narrative hook**?
3. What complications in the **rising action** increase the conflict?
4. What is the **climax**, the point of highest reader interest?
5. Does the **resolution** logically follow the conflict and climax?

Character

1. What does the author **directly tell** about the character?
2. What does the author **indirectly show** about the character through the actions and words of the character?
3. Is the character **round** or **flat**?
4. Do the character's attitudes and opinions change in the course of the story? Is the character **dynamic** or **static**?

Setting

1. What details does the author use to describe the time and place of the story?
2. What insight does the **setting** provide into the personalities of the characters?
3. What **atmosphere** is created by the setting?

Point of View

1. Does the author use **first-person point of view,** with a character as storyteller?
2. Does the author reveal the thoughts of only one character through **limited third-person point of view**?
3. Does the author reveal the thoughts of all the characters through **omniscient third-person point of view**?

Theme

1. Is the theme directly **stated**?
2. If the theme is not stated directly, what theme, or central idea, is **implied** by the other elements of the story?

REVIEW

The Guide for Studying the Elements of the Short Story is a series of questions that can serve as an inventory for each story in turn or as a review for the unit as a whole. You may want students to keep the questions in mind as they read each story. This approach may demonstrate to them that such informed reading enhances understanding and enjoyment even of independent reading. You may prefer to use the guide as a review of the unit as a whole. Apply the questions to one or two stories in class, and suggest that students adopt the approach in studying the remainder of the unit at home.

The questions in the Guide for Studying the Elements of the Short Story appear with write-on lines, in blackline master form, among the materials for this unit in your *Teacher's Classroom Resources*.

PREVIEW: POETRY

We are all poets when we read a poem well.

—Thomas Carlyle

Poetry makes the senses sizzle. It is a special kind of writing in which language, pictures, and sounds combine, creating a special emotional effect.

Poetry is different from prose, the kind of writing that you find in short stories, novels, and newspapers. Poetry packs meaning into a small number of words, while prose is looser and more lengthy. A line of poetry ends in a particular place because the poet has made an artistic decision based on sense or sound. A line of prose ends when the typewriter rings or the pen hits the right-hand margin of the paper. Poetry is usually written in units called stanzas, while prose is organized into paragraphs. Poetry also tends to be more visual and musical than prose. In short, prose speaks, and poetry sings.

The subject matter of poetry is wide in range. Not all poems are about "truth and beauty." Any subject—from baseball to battles, from fingerprints to funerals—can be shaped into a poem.

The following pages place poems into two major classes—poems as stories (narratives) and poems as expressions of feelings (lyrics). In addition, these pages explore some of the basic elements of poetry: speaker, word choice, sound, and imagery. A final selection of poems shows how all of these elements work together to create a unique effect. An understanding of these elements and their interaction will enable any reader to feel poetry's high-voltage effect—an intellectual and emotional response—and to be a poet by reading poetry well.

PREVIEW

After students have read the Preview, ask them to discuss poems they have liked and disliked. As they give reasons for their feelings, list them on the board. You may find some of these reactions valuable because discussing feelings about poetry helps to overcome prejudices students sometimes form about the genre.

Ask students to interpret the quotation by Thomas Carlyle—"We are all poets when we read a poem well." Point out that poetry generally allows for a variety of meanings and that interpretations depend in part on the personal experiences and emotions of the reader. Remind them, however, that personal interpretations must always be based on evidence that can clearly be found in the poem.

LITERARY FOCUS: Narrative Poetry

A **narrative poem** tells a story. Narrative poetry has plot and characters but differs from the short story in important ways besides its arrangement into lines and stanzas. While a short story has a beginning, a middle, and an end, a narrative poem generally focuses on just one part of a story, spotlighting only a few key events. The selection and arrangement of these events makes a narrative poem unique.

Narrative poems can vary in length and sophistication from a short, simple ballad to an inspiring epic (see page 433) comprised of thousands of lines. Poems that tell stories have been popular for centuries; for example, early English ballads were composed before most people could write and were passed to us orally. Modern poets continue to write narrative poems on a wide range of subjects and in a variety of styles.

The narrative poems on the following pages take us from a baseball diamond to a medieval castle. Like all good storytellers, the creators of these poems keep us interested in what is happening and what will happen next.

Ernest Lawrence Thayer (1863–1940) worked as a reporter in California and New York. He often published his poems—some based on actual news items—in the newspapers for which he worked. "Casey at the Bat" is his famous "baseball epic."

- What qualities do you think make an athlete, such as the Mighty Casey, a champion?

Alfred, Lord Tennyson (1809–1892) was poet laureate, or official poet, of England and wrote poems about important national events. Though his secluded country home was far away from such events, his poems capture them with passion. "The Charge of the Light Brigade" was inspired by a battle of the Crimean War, in which England, France, and Turkey fought against Russia.

- How can a terrible defeat, like the battle described in this poem, be turned into a victory?

The **anonymous** author of "Lord Randal" lived in the fifteenth century and is unknown because, like other tales of its day, the poem was passed on by word of mouth before being written down. It tells only part of a tragic tale, leaving the reader to imagine details and draw conclusions.

- Do you think "love is blind"? What happens to Lord Randal because of his love?

Robert Frost (1874–1963) was born in California but spent most of his life in New Hampshire and Vermont. This "New England Poet," as Frost is often called, worked as a newspaper editor, cobbler, and chicken farmer. Frost's poems describe ordinary people and simple settings, but the thoughts and emotions behind the poems are more complex.

- The runaway horse in this poem learns a bitter lesson. What valuable lessons about living must be learned "the hard way"?

William Butler Yeats (1865–1939) was an Irish poet who worked for Irish independence and for an Irish literature separate from British literature. He admired and collected old Irish folk tales and legends. Inspired by the heroes, the romance, and the magic of these legends, he often scattered parts of many legends into a single poem as he does in "The Song of Wandering Aengus."

- What makes adventurous people, like Aengus, try to make their dreams come true—love, fear, courage, curiosity?

Ernest Lawrence Thayer

Casey at the Bat

It looked extremely rocky for the Mudville nine that day;
The score stood two to four, with but one inning left to play.
So, when Cooney died at second, and Burrows did the same,
A pallor wreathed the features of the patrons[1] of the game.

A straggling few got up to go, leaving there the rest,
With that hope which springs eternal within the human breast.
For they thought: "If only Casey could get a whack at that,"
They'd put even money now, with Casey at the bat.

But Flynn preceded Casey, and likewise so did Blake,
And the former was a pudd'n, and the latter was a fake.
So on that stricken multitude a deathlike silence sat;
For there seemed but little chance of Casey's getting to the bat.

But Flynn let drive a "single," to the wonderment of all.
And the much-despised Blakey "tore the cover off the ball."
And when the dust had lifted, and they saw what had occurred,
There was Blakey safe at second, and Flynn a-huggin' third.

Then from the gladdened multitude went up a joyous yell—
It rumbled in the mountaintops, it rattled in the dell;[2]
It struck upon the hillside and rebounded on the flat;
For Casey, mighty Casey, was advancing to the bat.

1. **A pallor . . . patrons:** Paleness overcame the faces of the spectators.
2. **dell:** small valley.

AT A GLANCE

- The Mudville baseball team is losing by two runs in the last inning.
- The crowd longs for the mighty Casey to save the day.
- After two weak hitters surprise everyone by getting on base, Casey comes to the plate.

LITERARY OPTIONS

- narrative poetry
- exaggeration
- parallelism

THEMATIC OPTIONS

- pride
- idealized heroes

NARRATIVE POETRY

The first lines quickly set the scene (the last inning of the Mudville baseball game) and establish the conflict (the home team is losing) (ll. 1–4).

EXAGGERATION

Exaggerated language *(struck, rumbled, rattled)* describes the crowd's cheering and its impact on the surrounding countryside, creating suspense and adding to the wondrous tone of the poem (ll. 17–19).

PARALLELISM

The poet uses four similar phrases to describe the sound and resonance of the crowd's wild cheering and to build suspense as Casey approaches the plate (ll. 18–19).

GUIDED READING

LITERAL QUESTIONS

1a. What events take place in the fourth stanza of the poem? (Flynn hits a single; Blakey hits a double; Blakey gets to second base and Flynn to third.)

2a. What caused the crowd to cheer in the fifth stanza? (Casey was stepping up to bat.)

INFERENTIAL QUESTIONS

1b. How do the descriptions of these and other events effect the suspense of the poem? (They change the complexion of the game by creating the possibility of a Mudville victory.)

2b. What do the fans expect from Casey? (They expect him to get a hit to win the game.)

AT A GLANCE

- The fans cheer and admire their hero, Casey, as he prepares to bat.
- Casey grandly lets two pitches pass, and the fans shout at the umpire.
- Casey strikes out.

MAIN IDEA

Thayer shows Casey's pride with visual images (*defiance gleamed, sneer curled*) and the tone of his actual words (*That ain't my style*).

SIMILE

Thayer compares the sound of the crowd's angry protest to the roar of a stormy sea, adding further to the humorous, exaggerated description of the scene (ll. 33–34).

IRONY

Casey is described as if he were a saint soothing angry hordes, an image that contrasts powerfully with previous descriptions of the larger-than-life, prideful hero (ll. 37–38).

SPEAKER

The speaker heightens the drama and humor of the ending by using elevated, philosophical language (ll. 49–52). The speaker increases the immediacy of the poem's climax by using the present tense (ll. 45–52).

REFLECTING ON THE POEM

Why are the characters and their emotions described in such extreme terms? (Answers should suggest that the descriptions heighten the dramatic effect of the poem and depict the intensity of emotion felt by sportsman and spectator.)

There was ease in Casey's manner as he stepped into his place,
There was pride in Casey's bearing and a smile on Casey's face;
And when responding to the cheers he lightly doffed[3] his hat,
No stranger in the crowd could doubt 'twas Casey at the bat.

Ten thousand eyes were on him as he rubbed his hands with dirt.
Five thousand tongues applauded when he wiped them on his shirt;
Then when the writhing pitcher ground the ball into his hip,
Defiance gleamed in Casey's eye, a sneer curled Casey's lip.

And now the leather-covered sphere came hurtling through the air,
And Casey stood a-watching it in haughty grandeur there.
Close by the sturdy batsman the ball unheeded sped;
"That ain't my style," said Casey. "Strike one," the umpire said.

From the benches, black with people, there went up a muffled roar,
Like the beating of the storm waves on the stern and distant shore.
"Kill him! kill the umpire!" shouted someone on the stand;
And it's likely they'd have killed him had not Casey raised his hand.

With a smile of Christian charity great Casey's visage[4] shone;
He stilled the rising tumult, he made the game go on;
He signaled to the pitcher, and once more the spheroid[5] flew;
But Casey still ignored it, and the umpire said, "Strike two."

"Fraud!" cried the maddened thousands, and the echo answered "Fraud!"
But one scornful look from Casey and the audience was awed;
They saw his face grow stern and cold, they saw his muscles strain,
And they knew that Casey wouldn't let the ball go by again.

The sneer is gone from Casey's lips, his teeth are clenched in hate,
He pounds with cruel vengeance his bat upon the plate;
And now the pitcher holds the ball, and now he lets it go,
And now the air is shattered by the force of Casey's blow.

Oh, somewhere in this favored land the sun is shining bright,
The band is playing somewhere, and somewhere hearts are light;
And somewhere men are laughing, and somewhere children shout,
But there is no joy in Mudville—Mighty Casey has struck out.

---

3. **doffed** [dofd]: removed.
4. **visage** [viz′ij]: face.
5. **spheroid** [sfēr′oid]: round three-dimensional figure; here, the ball.

GUIDED READING

LITERAL QUESTIONS

1a. How does Casey's manner change during his time at bat? (He starts out proud and confident, becomes haughty and defiant, turns charitable, and finally becomes scornful, stern, and cold.)

2a. How does the crowd react when the umpire calls the first strike against Casey? (They threaten to "kill the umpire.")

INFERENTIAL QUESTIONS

1b. In what ways is Casey a heroic character? In what ways is he not? (Casey is larger than life. His responses *seem* to indicate power and heroism, but in the end he fails because he is too proud.)

2b. How do you think the poet feels about fans like these? (Thayer seems amused by the fans' strong and exaggerated responses.)

STUDY QUESTIONS

Recalling

1. At the beginning of the poem, why is the outlook for Casey's team "extremely rocky"?
2. Give two examples of the crowd's enthusiasm for Casey.
3. What is the result of each of the three pitches to Casey?
4. What is the reaction of the people of Mudville after the game?

Interpreting

5. What effect does the name Mudville have on your attitude toward the story of Casey?
6. Explain how self-confidence is the cause of both Casey's popularity and his failure.
7. Why do you think the author saves the information that Casey struck out for the last line?

Extending

8. In what ways is the poem like a short story? In what ways is it different?

COMPOSITION

Writing About Narrative Poetry

- Explain how "Casey at the Bat" tells its story through the use of plot and character. Consider, in turn, each of the following: (a) the personality of Casey and whether it is realistic, (b) the information given at the beginning of the poem, (c) the use of suspense, and (d) the climax. Give specific examples from the poem to support your opinions.

Writing a Poem of Contrasts

- Write a four-line poem that uses a pattern of contrasts like the pattern in the last stanza of "Casey at the Bat." Begin lines 1 and 3 with the word *Somewhere*, and complete those lines with a positive thought. Begin lines 2 and 4 with the words *But in Mudville*, and complete those lines with a negative thought. Use specific, colorful details. You may write with or without rhyme.

STUDY QUESTIONS

1. There are two outs in ninth inning; score is 4–2 against Mudville.
2. stanza 5: the shout that "rattled the dell"; stanza 7: enthusiasm as Casey stands at plate
3. He ignores first two strikes; strikes out on third pitch.
4. "There is no joy in Mudville."
5. It suggests a very small town; Casey's name is mud after losing.
6. - *popularity:* The crowd admires his heroic pose as he calmly lets two pitches go.
   - *failure:* He might have scored if he had taken a chance on an earlier pitch.
7. It sustains the suspense for a climactic effect.
8. *similar:* has conflict, resolution; *different:* set in stanzas, has little characterization, rhymes, focuses on one incident

COMPOSITION: GUIDELINES FOR EVALUATION

WRITING ABOUT NARRATIVE POETRY

Objective

To analyze poet's use of narrative elements

Guidelines for Evaluation

- suggested length: three to five paragraphs
- should describe situation and examine character
- should discuss the suspense in stanzas 8–13

WRITING A POEM OF CONTRASTS

Objective

To write a four-line stanza containing a twist

Guidelines for Evaluation

- suggested length: four lines
- should give a positive thought in the first and third lines
- should develop a twist in the second and fourth lines
- should be in the form of a poem

AT A GLANCE

- Armed only with sabers, the British Light Brigade is ordered to charge Russian guns.
- Fighting valiantly and unquestioningly, the brigade loses the battle; the author asks the world to honor their memory.

LITERARY OPTIONS

- repetition
- metaphor

THEMATIC OPTIONS

- courage and honor
- leaders and followers

REPETITION

The rhythm of repeated phrases in the first stanza suggests soldiers on the march (ll. 1–8).

METAPHOR

Tennyson uses fiercely dramatic metaphors *(jaws of Death, mouth of hell)* to describe the challenge the British soldiers face in battle with the Russians (ll. 22–26).

MAIN IDEA

The poet portrays the brigade's courage against overwhelming odds through the graphic image of men surrounded by cannons. *Cannon behind them* especially suggests their courage, as all escape has been cut off (ll. 18–20, 39–41).

REFLECTING ON THE POEM

Do you agree that the Light Brigade should be honored? Why or why not? (Some may admire their courage; others may feel that following orders blindly is not a virtue.)

SELECTION FOR PRACTICE IN ACTIVE READING

(TCR 5, p. 61)

Alfred, Lord Tennyson

The Charge of the Light Brigade[1]

Half a league,[2] half a league,
Half a league, onward,
All in the valley of Death
  Rode the six hundred.
"Forward, the Light Brigade!
Charge for the guns!" he said.
Into the valley of Death
  Rode the six hundred.

"Forward, the Light Brigade!"
Was there a man dismayed?
Not though the soldier knew
  Someone had blundered.
Theirs not to make reply,
Theirs not to reason why,
Theirs but to do and die.
Into the valley of Death
  Rode the six hundred.

Cannon to right of them,
Cannon to left of them,
Cannon in front of them
  Volleyed[3] and thundered;
Stormed at with shot and shell,
Boldly they rode and well,
Into the jaws of Death,
Into the mouth of hell
  Rode the six hundred.

Flashed all their sabers[4] bare,
Flashed as they turned in air
Sabering the gunners there,
Charging an army, while
  All the world wondered.
Plunged in the battery smoke
Right through the line they broke;
Cossack[5] and Russian
Reeled from the saber stroke
  Shattered and sundered.
Then they rode back, but not,
  Not the six hundred.

Cannon to right of them,
Cannon to left of them,
Cannon behind them
  Volleyed and thundered;
Stormed at with shot and shell,
While horse and hero fell,
They that had fought so well
Came through the jaws of Death,
Back from the mouth of hell,
All that was left of them,
  Left of six hundred.

When can their glory fade?
O the wild charge they made!
  All the world wondered.
Honor the charge they made!
Honor the Light Brigade,
  Noble six hundred!

---

1. **the Light Brigade:** British Light Cavalry Brigade armed with light, or small, weapons. They fought in the Crimean War, which was waged by England, France, and Turkey against Russia. On October 25, 1854, they made a heroic but fruitless charge against Russian artillery positions near Sebastopol, Russia.
2. **league:** measure of distance, approximately three miles.
3. **Volleyed** [vol′ēd]: fired.
4. **sabers** [sā′bərz]: single-edged swords.
5. **Cossack** [kos′ak]: cavalry soldiers from southeastern Russia.

Charge of the Light Brigade, H. Barraud, nineteenth century. Mary Evans Picture Library.

STUDY QUESTIONS

Recalling

1. According to stanza 2, why do the men of the Light Brigade charge when they know the order is a mistake?
2. What weapons are used by the Light Brigade? By the enemy?
3. According to stanza 5, what is the outcome of the battle?
4. In the last stanza how does the poet urge us to regard the Light Brigade?

Interpreting

5. What effect does the repetition of words and lines have on the story of the battle?
6. List some of the verbs used in stanzas 1, 3, and 5. What effect do these verbs have on the plot of the poem?
7. What specific details suggest that very few members of the Light Brigade survived the famous charge?

Extending

8. While most people never heard of the Battle of Balaklava, which inspired this poem, many people remember lines from the poem. Explain how this fact demonstrates the proverb that the pen is mightier than the sword.

VIEWPOINT

After reading a newspaper account of the battle, Tennyson composed "The Charge of the Light Brigade" in just a few minutes. The poem was an instant and lasting success; thousands of soldiers asked for copies. One British critic called the poem

> a fine rolling war-chant, with thunderous echo . . . which gained hearty applause from the British soldiers of the Crimea. . . .
>
> —A. Lyall, *English Men of Letters*

■ In what ways do you think the poem is a "war chant"? What do you think made the poem popular with soldiers?

STUDY QUESTIONS

1. They're trained to follow orders.
2. sabers; cannons and guns
3. Few survived.
4. to honor them as heroes
5. emphasizes action, loss of men, bravery of men
6. In stanza 1 *rode, charge* depict action. In stanza 3 *volleyed, thundered, rode* depict strength of enemy. In stanza 5 *volleyed, thundered* depict failure of charge.
7. last two lines of stanzas 4, 5: "not the six hundred"; "all that was left of them"
8. Poetic technique illustrates universal themes.

VIEWPOINT

drumlike beat; its patriotism

AT A GLANCE

- Lord Randal returns home weary from hunting.
- His mother learns that he has been poisoned and will die.

LITERARY OPTIONS

- ballad
- repetition

THEMATIC OPTIONS

- trust and betrayal
- communication

REPETITION

Each stanza opens with the mother asking a question; this repetition creates the impression that the son is answering reluctantly (ll. 1, 5, 9, 13, 17).

MAIN IDEA

The mother's question suggests that Lord Randal did not realize he had been poisoned until he saw his dogs die; he put blind faith in this true-love (ll. 13–15).

BALLAD

In typical ballad form, the love story has reached its tragic end through dialogue, repetition, simplicity of detail, and a limited number of characters (ll. 19–20).

REFLECTING ON THE POEM

Why do you think Lord Randal is so unwilling to tell his mother what happened? (Possible answers: It is often humiliating to admit a betrayal; he wants to deny what happened; or he is too weary.)

SELECTION FOR PRACTICE IN ACTIVE READING
(TCR 5, p. 65)

Anonymous

Lord Randal

"O where hae[1] ye been, Lord Randal my son?
O where hae ye been, my handsome young man?"
"I hae been to the wild wood; mother, make my bed soon,
For I'm weary wi'[2] hunting, and fain wald[3] lie down."

"Where got ye your dinner, Lord Randal my son?
Where got ye your dinner, my handsome young man?"
"I dined wi' my true-love; mother, make my bed soon,
For I'm weary wi' hunting, and fain wald lie down."

"What got ye to your dinner, Lord Randal my son?
What got ye to your dinner, my handsome young man?"
"I got eels boiled in broo;[4] mother, make my bed soon,
For I'm weary wi' hunting, and fain wald lie down."

"What became of your bloodhounds, Lord Randal my son?
What became of your bloodhounds, my handsome young man?"
"O they swelled[5] and they died; mother, make my bed soon,
For I'm weary wi' hunting, and fain wald lie down."

"O I fear ye are poisoned, Lord Randal my son!
O I fear ye are poisoned, my handsome young man!"
"O yes, I am poisoned; mother, make my bed soon,
For I'm sick at the heart, and I fain wald lie down."

1. **hae** [hā]: have.
2. **wi':** with.
3. **fain** [fān] **wald:** gladly would.
4. **broo:** broth.
5. **swelled:** expanded, bulged.

STUDY QUESTIONS

Recalling

1. Who are the two speakers in the poem?
2. What activity does Lord Randal claim has made him weary?
3. With whom has Lord Randal had dinner? What has he eaten?
4. What has happened to Lord Randal's bloodhounds?
5. What does his mother fear has happened to Lord Randal? Is she correct?

Interpreting

6. Who is suspected of murder in the poem? What evidence incriminates the suspect? Who are the victims?
7. Why do you think Lord Randal is reluctant to tell his mother the complete story of what happened to him?
8. Give two different meanings of Lord Randal's statement at the end of the poem that he is "sick at the heart."

Extending

9. Give an example from history or literature of a person's being betrayed by a close friend or loved one. What was the outcome of the betrayal for each person?

LITERARY FOCUS

The Ballad

The word *ballad* is often used to refer to a song. In poetry a **ballad** is a short, musical, narrative poem. Ballads are the most common form of narrative poetry. "Lord Randal" is a folk ballad. **Folk ballads** or **popular ballads** are anonymous. They were passed on by word of mouth for generations before they were written down. **Literary ballads** are imitations of folk ballads. They are often longer, and their authors are known.

A ballad focuses on a single situation that is a very dramatic, often tragic episode about love, death, or physical courage. A ballad has few characters, and the action usually develops through dialogue. The plot is simple, and the poem starts in the middle of the story.

The stanzas of a ballad are made up of either two or four lines each. A ballad also has a refrain or chorus. A **refrain** is a word, phrase, line, or group of lines that is repeated throughout a poem, usually at the ends of stanzas.

Thinking About the Ballad

1. Why is the plot of "Lord Randal" a typical plot for a ballad?
2. Give examples from the poem of other characteristics of the ballad.

STUDY QUESTIONS

1. Lord Randal; his mother
2. hunting
3. his "true-love"; eels in broth
4. they have swollen and died
5. he's been poisoned; yes
6. suspect: the "true-love" evidence: Lord Randal both poisoned and "sick at heart" victims: Lord Randal; hounds
7. to protect his sweetheart (out of love or shame)
8. close to death; betrayed by his love
9. Answers will vary. Suggestions: history—Brutus/Julius Ceasar, Benedict Arnold, Judas/Christ; literature—Mordred/King Arthur, pigs in *Animal Farm*

LITERARY FOCUS

1. it is simple; starts in middle of story; dramatizes tragic love
2. few characters; development by dialogue; simplicity; little attention to details

AT A GLANCE

- In falling snow, the speaker and his companion stop to watch a colt alone in a pasture.
- The speaker thinks the skittish colt is afraid of the snow.
- He criticizes his owner for leaving it outside.

LITERARY OPTIONS

- imagery
- main idea

THEMATIC OPTION

- youth and age
- innocence and experience

IMAGERY

Surprising images *(miniature thunder, shadow against the curtain)* create the sound of the colt's hooves and the animal's appearance; both suggest his vulnerability (ll. 6–8).

MAIN IDEA

That the colt would think his mother "didn't know" implies that experience is sometimes necessary in addition to guidance from elders (ll. 12–14).

DETAILS

Specific details (*clatter of stone, whited eyes,* and tail *up straight*) create a portrait of a lively, fearful colt (ll. 15–18).

REFLECTING ON THE POEM

Why does the speaker tell his feelings about the colt? (Possible answers: He has compassion for the young, understanding of fear, interest in animals and nature.)

Robert Frost

The Runaway

Once when the snow of the year was beginning to fall,
We stopped by a mountain pasture to say, "Whose colt?"
A little Morgan[1] had one forefoot on the wall,
The other curled at his breast. He dipped his head
And snorted at us. And then he had to bolt.[2]
We heard the miniature thunder where he fled,
And we saw him, or thought we saw him, dim and grey
Like a shadow against the curtain of falling flakes.
"I think the little fellow's afraid of the snow.
He isn't winter-broken. It isn't play
With the little fellow at all. He's running away.
I doubt if even his mother could tell him, 'Sakes,
It's only weather.' He'd think she didn't know!
Where is his mother? He can't be out alone."
And now he comes again with clatter of stone,
And mounts the wall again with whited eyes
And all his tail that isn't hair up straight.
He shudders his coat as if to throw off flies.
"Whoever it is that leaves him out so late,
When other creatures have gone to stall and bin,
Ought to be told to come and take him in."

---

1. **Morgan:** horse of a breed of light horses noted for their strength and gentle disposition.
2. **bolt:** run off suddenly.

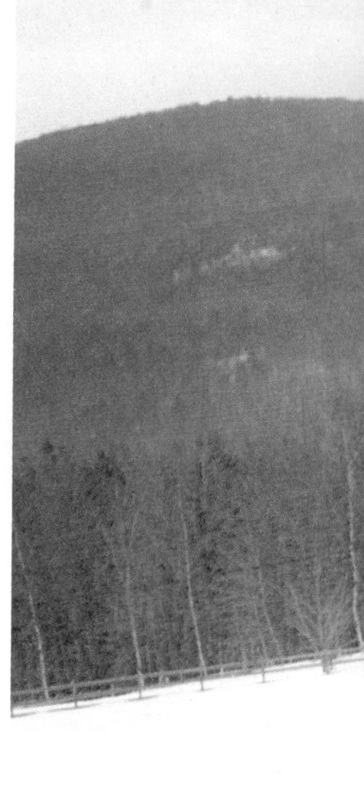

STUDY QUESTIONS

Recalling

1. What is the weather in the scene that the poem presents?
2. Describe in detail the colt's actions.
3. Give two reasons that the colt should not be outside.

Interpreting

4. What is the meaning of the term *winter-broken* in line 10?
5. Explain what the speaker says about the colt's mother in lines 12 and 13.
6. What does the poem imply about having to learn from experience? Quote the lines that present this topic.
7. What is the attitude of the speaker toward the colt? Toward its owner? Support your opinions with lines from the poem.
8. Why do you think Frost titled his poem "The Runaway"?

Extending

9. Why do you think that people sometimes assume that animals share human emotions?

COMPOSITION

Writing About Narrative Poetry

- Narrative poetry often uses dialogue to present a character's emotions. Reread "The Runaway" leaving out all the lines in quotation marks. Then write a paragraph or two that answers the following questions: How does the loss of the dialogue affect the emotional force of the poem? Do you care as much about the colt in the shorter version? Why or why not?

Writing from Another Point of View

- In Frost's poem people stare at a colt and imagine what he is feeling. Write a nonrhyming narrative poem of at least four lines in which you describe the reverse—a colt's impression of the behavior and feelings of two people.

STUDY QUESTIONS

1. first snow falling
2. has forefoot on wall; snorts; runs away; returns; remounts wall; shows fright
3. afraid of weather; should not be out alone; "other creatures have gone . . . "
4. used to winter weather
5. she couldn't explain the weather; colt must learn for himself
6. experience is best teacher; "It isn't play . . . "; "He'd think she didn't know."
7. colt: sympathetic; calls him "little fellow"
   owner: critical; "ought to be told to take him in"
8. colt runs away from speaker; from what he can't yet understand
9. Suggested answers: they have physical needs, react to pain and fear; humans project own feelings onto animals.

COMPOSITION: GUIDELINES FOR EVALUATION

WRITING ABOUT NARRATIVE POETRY

Objective

To explain effect of dialogue in a narrative poem

Guidelines for Evaluation

- suggested length: one to two paragraphs
- should state an opinion about the change in emotional force, and support with quotes
- note loss of sympathy and identification with colt's experience

WRITING FROM ANOTHER POINT OF VIEW

Objective

To write nonrhyming narrative poem

Guidelines for Evaluation

- suggested length: at least four lines
- should use colt as speaker
- convey impression of the people
- follow poetic form

LITERARY OPTIONS

- sensory language
- narrative poetry

THEMATIC OPTIONS

- ideals
- love

SENSORY LANGUAGE

Yeats uses surprising, vivid, sensory images throughout the poem to intensify the reader's experience. Examples are *moth-like stars, rustled, apple blossom, pluck* (ll. 5–6, 11, 14, 22).

NARRATIVE POETRY

Yeats's use of a first-person narrator to tell about himself and his dreams makes this poem intimate and immediate (ll. 9–12).

REFLECTING ON THE POEM

Do you think Aengus has led a good life? Why or why not? (Answers may suggest that he has not succeeded, or that the search has expanded his horizons.)

STUDY QUESTIONS

1. a hazel branch, thread, berry
2. a silver trout; changes into a "glimmering girl"
3. has wandered searching for girl
4. find girl; kiss her; take her hands and walk with her
5. sense of restlessness
6. Girl is magical; he must recapture vision.
7. Answers may suggest: youth, ideal beauty.
8. "silver apples"; "golden apples"; suggest night / day imagery; magic
9.
   - suggestions: They symbolize man's quest for achievement.
   - gain: growth, progress; loss: achievement of lesser goals

William Butler Yeats

The Song of Wandering Aengus[1]

I went out to the hazel wood,
Because a fire was in my head,
And cut and peeled a hazel wand,
And hooked a berry to a thread;
And when white moths were on the wing,
And moth-like stars were flickering out,
I dropped the berry in a stream
And caught a little silver trout.

When I had laid it on the floor
I went to blow the fire aflame,
But something rustled on the floor,
And some one called me by my name:
It had become a glimmering girl[2]
With apple blossom in her hair
Who called me by my name and ran
And faded through the brightening air.

Though I am old with wandering
Through hollow lands and hilly lands,
I will find out where she has gone,
And kiss her lips and take her hands;
And walk among long dappled grass,
And pluck till time and times are done
The silver apples of the moon,
The golden apples of the sun.

---

1. **Aengus** [ang′gəs]: in ancient Irish lore, the god of youth, beauty, poetry, and love.
2. **It had . . . girl:** In Irish lore mythical women disguised themselves as fish and cast spells over the men who caught them.

STUDY QUESTIONS

Recalling

1. Out of what does Aengus make his fishing gear?
2. What does he catch? What happens to it?
3. Describe the life that Aengus has led since the fishing incident.
4. Name three things that Aengus hopes to do some day as he wanders.

Interpreting

5. Based on what he does to relieve it, what do you think Aengus means by a "fire" in his head?
6. Why do you think Aengus has been unsuccessful in his search? Why does he continue wandering?
7. What do you think Aengus is actually looking for in his search for the "glimmering girl"?
8. What words does Yeats use to describe the moon and the sun? In what way are these descriptions appropriate for the poem?

Extending

9. Why do you think people sometimes reach for unrealistic goals? What might be gained or lost by doing this reaching?

COMPARING POEMS

1. Choose two or more of the poems in this section: "Casey at the Bat," "The Charge of the Light Brigade," "Lord Randal," "The Runaway," and "The Song of Wandering Aengus." Compare their use of dialogue, or written speech. How much of each poem is actual dialogue? In what ways does the dialogue advance the plot? In what ways does the dialogue add emotion to each narrative poem?
2. Compare characters from two or more of the poems in this section. Use one character from each poem. How much detail is used to describe each character? In what ways are the characters similar and different?

COMPARING POEMS

1.
   - "Casey": 24 words; portrays action; sense of participation
   - "Brigade": 3 lines; conveys order to charge; turns reader against the one who gives order
   - "Randal": all dialogue; reveals entire plot; lessens sympathy by withholding motive for betrayal
   - "Runaway": 10 lines; learn colt's feelings; sympathize with colt
   - "Aengus": poetic soliloquy; reveals plot; allows reader to form own opinion
2. Narrative poetry uses few details of description.
   - "Casey": superiority; pride
   - "Brigade": no individual characters
   - "Randal": handsome
   - "Runaway": colt: young, confused; speaker not described
   - "Aengus": character implied, not described

   Students may notice character's individualism and heroic stature.

LITERARY FOCUS: *Speaker and Word Choice*

When we read a poem, the poet is speaking to us. Sometimes the poet speaks directly to us as if we were chatting at the kitchen table. Sometimes the poet wears the "mask" of a **speaker** by pretending to be someone or something else—a child, a tiger, a chair. In still other poems two speakers may talk only with each other, forcing us to "eavesdrop."

The poet is concerned not only with the speaker in a poem but also with the speech. A poem might require the language of a child, of a midwesterner, or of a nurse. Any poem needs just the right word to capture exactly the poet's meaning or emotion. The overall effect of this **word choice** can be a poem as chatty and informal as a talk on the telephone or as serious and formal as a graduation address.

The poems on the following pages demonstrate a "feel" for words—for their different textures, colors, and flavors. In addition, the author of each of these poems chooses to play a role that is the speaker of the poem.

Nikki Giovanni (born 1943) is a native of Knoxville, Tennessee. She has been a professor of black studies and of English at several universities. In her poem "Knoxville, Tennessee" she illustrates that she can still identify closely with the southern child who is the speaker of her poem.

- What do you predict you will remember twenty years from now about summer in your community?

Theodore Roethke [ret′kē] (1908–1963) spent much of his early life in his father and uncle's greenhouse. "Child on Top of a Greenhouse" seems to re-create a moment from his past.

- Do you think that sometimes everyone—like the speaker of this poem—needs to be the center of attention?

Philip Booth (born 1925) has been a professor of English at many colleges and universities. He spends his nonteaching time on the coast of Maine. Booth draws on his World War II Air Force experience in "Ego," a poem filled with the language of planes and flight.

- What do our jobs and career experiences contribute to making us the people we really are?

Robert Francis (born 1901) began a formal writing career after graduating from Harvard. His work is known for its lively language and sometimes unusual word choice.

- In baseball a base stealer is a good decision maker. What qualities does a good decision maker possess?

Nikki Giovanni

Knoxville, Tennessee

I always like summer
best
you can eat fresh corn
from daddy's garden
and okra[1]
and greens
and cabbage
and lots of
barbecue
and buttermilk
and homemade ice-cream
at the church picnic
and listen to
gospel music
outside
at the church
homecoming
and go to the mountains with
your grandmother
and go barefooted
and be warm
all the time
not only when you go to bed
and sleep

1. **okra** [ō′krə]: green vegetable.

STUDY QUESTIONS

Recalling

1. Name five foods that the speaker associates with summer.
2. Name three of her favorite summer activities.
3. What can the speaker be "all the time" in summer that she cannot be the rest of the year?

Interpreting

4. Explain how the speaker's youth is revealed by sentence structure, line length, and punctuation.
5. At what point in the poem does the mood change? What does the change imply about the speaker's feelings toward seasons other than summer?
6. In what ways is the poem more than just a list of details?

Extending

7. List favorite foods and pastimes of young people in your community during the summer. In what ways is your local summer similar or dissimilar to summer in Knoxville?

LITERARY FOCUS

The Speaker

The **speaker** is the voice of a poem, or the role that the poet plays in a poem. The speaker of a poem can seem to be the poet, or the speaker can be a person, animal, or object that the poet pretends to be. Playing a role in a poem enables the poet to state a message or to explain a feeling more clearly than speaking as himself or herself. For example, one poet may speak as an eagle to describe the wonders of flight. Another poet may pretend to be a mother in order to express an ideal of unselfish love.

When reading a poem, we need to identify the speaker and to understand the speaker's attitude toward the subject of the poem. Is the speaker being honest or "tongue-in-cheek"? Is the speaker sharing emotions? Is the speaker trying to prove a point? Recognizing the speaker and the speaker's attitude is an important step toward "reading between the lines."

Thinking About the Speaker

■ Explain how the poem might be different if the poet had chosen an adult speaker.

LITERARY OPTIONS

- speaker
- parallelism

THEMATIC OPTIONS

- the seasons
- childhood

SPEAKER

The reference to *daddy* establishes the speaker as a child; the informal construction *you can* and lack of punctuation help establish her personal tone (ll. 3–4).

PARALLELISM

The word *and* ties images together and encourages the reader to add them to reach a "total" effect (ll. 1–24).

REFLECTING ON THE POEM

How might the poem differ if the speaker were adult? (An adult might cite negative aspects, use formal language, show less joy.)

STUDY QUESTIONS

1. corn, okra, cabbage, barbecue, greens, buttermilk, ice cream
2. eating; going to church picnics; going barefooted
3. warm
4. are only two sentences—one short, one consisting of twenty-two lines held together by *and*; no punctuation; short lines reveal straightforwardness
5. final two lines; dislikes other seasons
6. It reveals child's character by her likes and dislikes.
7. Answers will vary.

LITERARY FOCUS

Adult speaker might have broader range of interests; might use less simplistic language; might have used shorter, more formal lines.

LITERARY OPTIONS

- speaker
- word choice

THEMATIC OPTIONS

- individualism
- youth and age

SPEAKER

The use of the pronoun *my*, long lines, and sophisticated words establishes the speaker as an adult looking back on an exhilirating childhood scene (ll. 1–3).

WORD CHOICE

The poet uses vivid participles (*flashing, rushing, plunging, tossing*) to denote the child's sensual delight in the crowd's reaction (ll. 4–6).

REFLECTING ON THE POEM

How do you think the child on the roof feels? (Answers might include frightened, proud, excited, joyful, surprised, exhilarated, smug, wondering.)

STUDY QUESTIONS

1. child stands atop greenhouse on a windy day
2. watching and accusing him
3. They are pointing and shouting.
4. wind *billowing* britches; clouds *rushing;* elms *tossing* and *plunging*
5. imagines chrysanthemums accuse him; sees elms move like horses
6. use of *my*; effectively reveals speaker's elation and guilt
7. *billowing, crackling, rushing, plunging, flashing;* suggest dangerous excitement
8. unaware of danger; realizes his audacity; enjoys attention
9. Answers will vary.

Theodore Roethke

Child on Top of a Greenhouse

The wind billowing[1] out the seat of my britches,[2]
My feet crackling splinters of glass and dried putty,[3]
The half-grown chrysanthemums staring up like accusers,
Up through the streaked glass, flashing with sunlight,
A few white clouds all rushing eastward,
A line of elms plunging and tossing like horses,
And everyone, everyone pointing up and shouting!

1. **billowing:** causing to fill with air.
2. **britches:** breeches, pants.
3. **putty:** soft rubbery compound used to seal panes of glass in place.

STUDY QUESTIONS

Recalling

1. Describe the scene that Roethke presents in the poem.
2. What do the half-grown chrysanthemums seem to be doing?
3. According to the last line, in what way does "everyone" behave?

Interpreting

4. Give three examples from the poem to show that the wind is strong.
5. Give two specific examples from the poem that demonstrate that the speaker of the poem has an active imagination.
6. How do we know that the poem has a first-person point of view? Explain whether or not you think this point of view is effective for the poem.
7. Find three or four words that show motion. What effect do the words have on your impression of the child's position?
8. What emotions do you think the child feels? Support your answer with specific examples from the poem.

Extending

9. The child in the poem assumes he is the center o attention. In what ways do you think this attitud is typical of children? Explain how you thin children view themselves in relation to the rest o the world.

COMPOSITION

Writing About the Speaker

■ One reason Roethke's poem is powerful i that the speaker's senses are fully used ir the description of the scene. Explain how th poem appeals to the senses of sight, touch, an hearing. Give examples from the poem. Then te how this affects the impact of the poem.

Writing Through a Speaker

■ Write a paragraph in which the speaker is ar animal or an object. Select a speaker of you choice, or select one of the following: a tiger's tooth, a tarantula, a bicycle wheel, or a stere needle. Have your speaker describe a typical da in its life. Include its favorite and least favorit parts of the day.

COMPOSITION: GUIDELINES FOR EVALUATION

WRITING ABOUT THE SPEAKER

Objective

To analyze the sensory language of a poem

Guidelines for Evaluation

- suggested length: two to three paragraphs
- should mention specific sensory images from poem
- should explain how each contributes to overall emotional impact

WRITING THROUGH A SPEAKER

Objective

To assume a convincing persona in a description

Guidelines for Evaluation

- suggested length: 150–200 words
- should encompass a full day in life of the speaker
- should include likes and dislikes of the day
- should use vocabulary appropriate to speaker

Philip Booth

Ego

When I was on Night Line,
flying my hands to park
a big-bird B-29,[1]
I used to command the dark:
four engines were mine

to jazz; I was ground crew,
an unfledged pfc,[2]
but when I waved planes through
that flight line[3] in Tennessee,
my yonder was wild blue.

Warming up, I was hot
on the throttle,[4] logging an hour
of combat, I was the pilot
who rogered the tower.
I used to take off a lot.

With a flat-hat[5] for furlough[6]
and tin wings to sleep on,
I fueled my high-octane[7] ego:
I buzzed, I landed my jeep on
the ramp, I flew low.

When a cross-country hop
let down, I was the big deal
who signaled big wheels to stop.
That's how I used to feel.
I used to get all revved up.

1. **B-29:** World War II bomber.
2. **pfc:** private first class.
3. **flight line:** area where planes are parked and serviced.
4. **throttle:** valve that regulates the amount of fuel that flows into an engine and, therefore, controls speed.
5. **flat-hat:** flat-topped cloth military hat with brim.
6. **furlough** [fur′lō]: official leave from military duty.
7. **high-octane:** referring to a highly combustible liquid fuel; here, powerful.

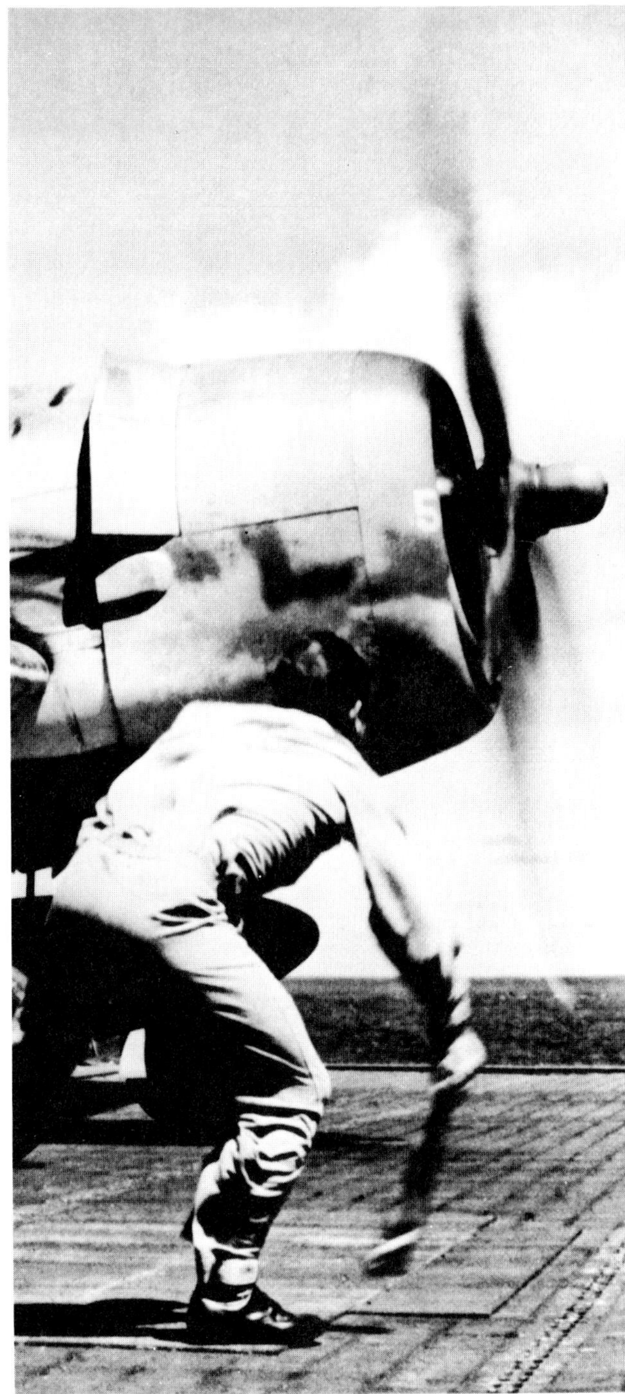

AT A GLANCE

- The speaker recalls helping military planes to land in Tennessee.
- He felt powerful and imagined flying the planes.

LITERARY OPTIONS

- word choice
- speaker

THEMATIC OPTIONS

- pride in work
- imagination's power

HYPERBOLE

The speaker describes how powerful he felt on his night job in this stunning overstatement: "I used to command the dark" (l. 4).

WORD CHOICE

The speaker uses airplane jargon, describing himself as an engine "warming up"; a pilot "hot on the throttle," "logging an hour of combat," and getting an okay from the control tower; as a plane taking off (ll. 11–15).

MAIN IDEA

The young man's ability to see his jeep as a plane expresses his overwhelming pride in his work, as well as the transforming power of his imagination (ll. 19–20).

SPEAKER

The poet sums up his feelings in aircraft jargon ("I used to get all revved up") and implies that both pride and imagination have lessened with age (ll. 24–25).

REFLECTING ON THE POEM

Why did the speaker feel so powerful when he worked on the ground crew? (Answers may suggest that his imagination transformed him into a pilot, that being part of the war effort made him feel important, and that the planes were exciting.)

AT A GLANCE

A baseball player moves lightly and teasingly and finally makes his move to steal a base.

LITERARY OPTIONS

- speaker
- word choice
- simile

THEMATIC OPTION

- taking risks

SPEAKER

The poem begins with a series of close descriptions that leave the speaker unidentified. The speaker's relationship to the subject is finally established as an observer when the third-person pronoun *he* is used (l. 7).

WORD CHOICE

The poet interjects into his descriptions of the base stealer the informal, "under-the-breath" urgings of an excited fan: "come on, come on," "crowd him, crowd him," and "Delicate, delicate, delicate, delicate—now!" (ll. 5, 9, 10).

SIMILE

Francis compares the base stealer to a tightrope-walker, a bouncing ball, a child skipping rope, and an ecstatic bird (ll. 2, 4, 5, 8).

MAIN IDEA

The poet suggests the exhilaration of taking risks by his use of the word *ecstatic* and by the exclamatory "now!" at the climax of the poem. The base stealer's urgency suggests the necessity of taking risks (ll. 8, 10).

REFLECTING ON THE POEM

How does Robert Francis make you feel about this "small" event? (Possible answers include nervous, excited, involved, hopeful.)

Robert Francis

The Base Stealer

Poised between going on and back, pulled
Both ways taut like a tightrope-walker,
Fingertips pointing the opposites,
Now bouncing tiptoe like a dropped ball
Or a kid skipping rope, come on, come on,
Running a scattering of steps sidewise,
How he teeters, skitters, tingles, teases,
Taunts them, hovers like an ecstatic bird,
He's only flirting, crowd him, crowd him,
Delicate, delicate, delicate, delicate—now!

Ego

STUDY QUESTIONS

Recalling

1. Name the speaker's duties on the landing strip.
2. What is his military rank?
3. How does his job make the speaker feel?

Interpreting

4. Explain the relationship of the title and the repetition of the word *I* to the speaker's job on the landing strip.
5. In what ways does the speaker's imagination come into play during his work?
6. Did the speaker take himself seriously in his military days? Does he take himself seriously now? Give examples from the poem.

Extending

7. Name two or three jobs that you think might expand a person's ego and explain why.

LITERARY FOCUS

Word Choice

A poet is especially careful about the selection of words because poetry tries to say a great deal in a few words. A scientist who is writing a lab report wants just one exact meaning for each word used. A poet, however, may choose a word for its many meanings. A particular word may add a double meaning or a tricky twist to a poem.

A poet may select formal words or informal words. A poet may create new words and rearrange word order. Some poems use slang or **jargon**, which is slang that is associated with a specific career.

A poet usually chooses concrete, specific words instead of abstract, general words. Though poems both show and tell, a poet emphasizes showing by using colorful language. A poet is more likely to say "My stomach is doing flips to the drumming of my head" than to say "I do not feel well."

Thinking About Word Choice

1. Find at least four examples of military or airplane jargon in the poem.
2. What do we learn about the speaker from his use of jargon to describe his own on-land behavior?

The Base Stealer

STUDY QUESTIONS

Recalling

1. Find three people or things to which the base stealer is compared.
2. Give examples to show that he is tense from his fingertips to his toes.
3. Name three movements that the base stealer makes.

Interpreting

4. Which words does the poet choose to illustrate the starting, stopping, and "go-for-it" actions of the base stealer?
5. What does the word *delicate* describe in the last line? Why does the poet repeat the word four times?
6. For what action does the final word, *now*, stand? Do you think this action will be successful? Why or why not?
7. Which words or arrangements of words build suspense?

Extending

8. "The Base Stealer" takes an emotional approach to a baseball game. Why do you think spectators become emotionally involved in sporting events?

COMPARING POEMS

1. Choose two or more of the poems in this section: "Knoxville, Tennessee," "Child on Top of a Greenhouse," "Ego," and "The Base Stealer." Compare the speakers of the poems. In what ways is the speaker's age and sex important to the poem? How well does the word choice of the poem match its speaker? What attitudes and emotions do the speakers of the different poems have in common?
2. Compare the word choice of two or more of the poems in this section. Explain how the word choice adds to the emotion and power of each poem. In what ways does the word choice affect your reaction to the poem?

STUDY QUESTIONS

Ego

1. helps to land and park aircraft
2. private first class
3. important, "revved up"
4. Ego, Latin for *I*, connotes pride; helping planes makes him feel important
5. imagines he flies planes
6. had a playful attitude; *used to* indicates change of feeling
7. Possible answers: doctors save lives; actors elicit emotion, applause

The Base Stealer

1. tightrope walker, dropped ball, kid skipping rope
2. *both ways taut* (l. 2); fingertips . . . *opposites* (l. 3); *tingles* (l. 7); *hovers* (l. 8)
3. bounces, teeters, skitters, runs, hovers
4.
   - starting: *taut, teeters, teases*
   - stopping: *hovers*
   - go-for-it: *now*
5. skill in judging conditions; repetition reveals tension
6. starting his run; expect success
7. *come on, come on; crowd him, crowd him; delicate . . . now*
8. Answers may suggest that they identify with player's skill or see team as a symbol of region or city.

LITERARY FOCUS

1. *big-bird B-29; pfc; flat-hat* for *furlough; revved up,* etc.
2. has good imagination; would like to be a pilot instead of ground worker

COMPARING POEMS

1. *"Knoxville":* age determines the uncomplicated loves of the child; word choice is appropriate to child
   "Child": age determines child's audacity; word choice relates vividness of memory
   "Ego": age/sex determine pride of speaker; word choice adds wit; meaning
   "Stealer": age/sex unimportant; speaker not directly involved; word choice builds suspense; speakers all relate pleasant experiences
2. *"Knoxville":* evokes specific images; creates sympathy
   "Child": suggests nostalgia; captures emotion vividly
   "Ego": adds wit; nostalgia
   "Stealer": builds suspense

LITERARY FOCUS: The Sound of Poetry

Anyone who enjoys music knows that it has the power to transmit ideas and emotions. Because words have sound, they can be combined to create patterns of sound—or music. The poet chooses words not only to communicate ideas but also to create a distinct sound. The sound of poetry is not mere decoration. The music of a poem contributes to its meaning and emotional effect.

Try reading the poems on the following pages aloud because the poets represented here all use sound to achieve their effects.

John Masefield (1878–1967) was an orphan who ran away to sea when he was only fourteen. He read the great English poets while working at a series of jobs in New York and decided to write poetry after he returned to his native England. In "Sea Fever" Masefield uses rhythm to capture the magic and movement of the sea.

- If you were to go on a long sea voyage—as the speaker in this poem desires to do—what would you expect to learn from the experience?

William Wordsworth (1770–1850) was one of the poets whom Masefield studied. The first of the great English Romantic poets, Wordsworth rebelled against the traditional, artificial language of poetry in favor of more natural sound and language. "She Dwelt Among the Untrodden Ways" employs rhythm and rhyme to communicate emotion through poetry.

- Does this poem demonstrate that basic human emotions can be communicated in words?

Eve Merriam (born 1916) has written poetry, fiction, and nonfiction, much of it for young people. Some of her poems are about poetry. "Onomatopoeia," for example, actually uses onomatopoeia, one of poetry's special musical devices.

- What popular songs can you name that do what this poem does—use words to imitate sounds?

Lewis Carroll (1832–1898), whose real name was Charles Lutwidge Dodgson, was a professor of mathematics at Oxford University in England. Shy with adults, he felt comfortable with children and composed the books *Alice in Wonderland* and *Through the Looking Glass* solely for the entertainment of a friend's daughter.

- What is the most extraordinary sound you have ever heard a movie monster make? How would you describe the sound made by the Jabberwock in the poem on page 189?

Edgar Allan Poe (1809–1849) is as famous for his highly musical poems, though he wrote only fifty of them, as for his suspenseful stories. His poems often share the eerie mood of his stories. "The Bells" clearly illustrates Poe's belief that the musical quality of poetry is essential to what he called the "Rhythmical Creation of Beauty."

- Which qualities of the bells described in the poem also apply to *school* bells?

AT A GLANCE

- The speaker longs to be aboard a sailing ship—to enjoy the wind and tide and spray, the "vagrant gypsy life," and the companionship of other wanderers.
- He asks for simple pleasures and a "quiet sleep and a sweet dream" when his tour is over.

LITERARY OPTIONS

- rhythm
- alliteration
- imagery

THEMATIC OPTIONS

- the power of nature
- self-fulfillment

RHYTHM

Note the regular rhythm and the undulating sound of the phrases in each line. Words that are naturally emphasized (*wheel's, wind's, white*) are like the crests in a series of waves (l. 3).

ALLITERATION

The poem's repeated *s* sounds suggest the hissing of sea spray and the hush of breaking waves: *must, seas, sky,* etc. (ll. 1–4, 8, 12).

MAIN IDEA

The repeated first line of each stanza, "I must go down to the seas again," stresses the magnetism of the sea for the speaker. The rhythmic invocation suggests the sea's hypnotic power and movement (ll. 1, 5, 9).

IMAGERY

Masefield evokes the sense of touch with images such as *wheel's kick* and *flung spray,* sight with *white sail's shaking,* and hearing with *wind's song* and *sea-gulls crying* (ll. 3, 8).

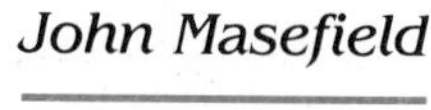

John Masefield

Sea Fever

I must go down to the seas again, to the lonely sea and the sky,
And all I ask is a tall ship and a star to steer her by,
And the wheel's[1] kick and the wind's song and the white sail's shaking
And a gray mist on the sea's face and a gray dawn breaking.

I must go down to the seas again, for the call of the running tide
Is a wild call and a clear call that may not be denied;
And all I ask is a windy day with the white clouds flying,
And the flung spray and the blown spume,[2] and the sea-gulls crying.

I must go down to the seas again, to the vagrant gypsy life,
To the gull's way and the whale's way where the wind's like a whetted[3]
knife;
And all I ask is a merry yarn[4] from a laughing fellow rover,
And quiet sleep and a sweet dream when the long trick's[5] over.

1. **wheel:** referring to the wheel used to control the rudder and to steer a ship.
2. **spume** [spūm]: foam.
3. **whetted** [hwet′id]: sharpened.
4. **yarn:** story or tall tale.
5. **trick:** turn, or period, of duty.

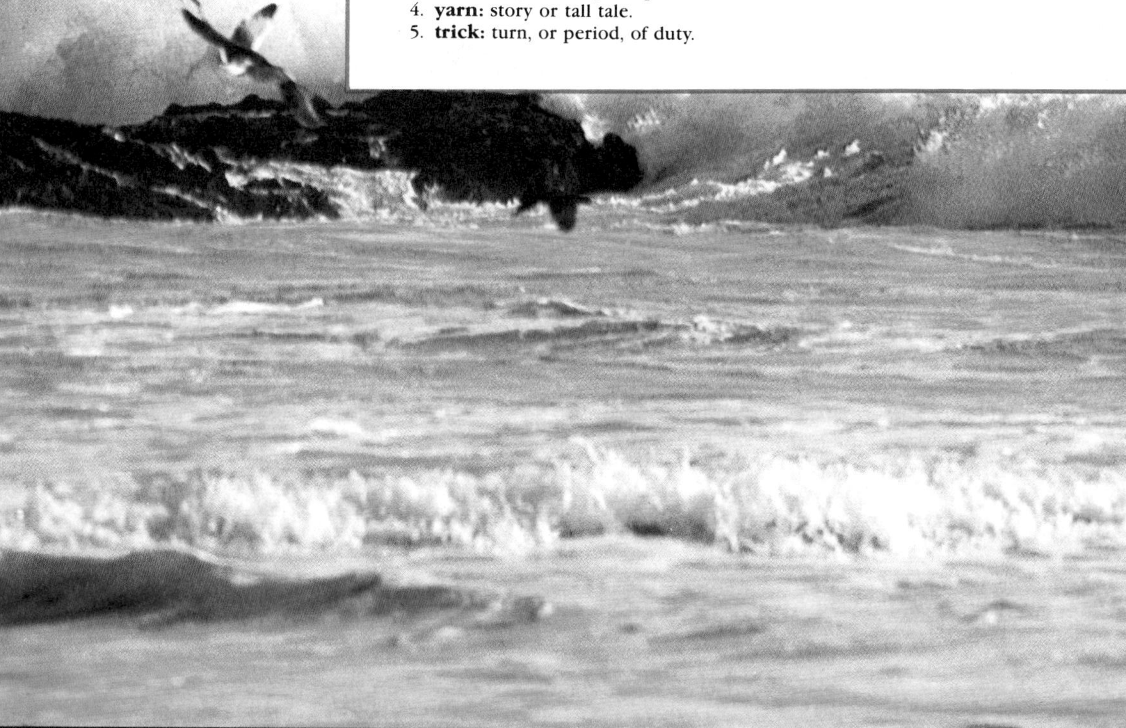

REFLECTING ON THE POEM

How would you describe the speaker's character? (Answers may suggest that he loves freedom; he is not particularly attached to or dependent upon a community; he is sensitive to natural beauty; he is sociable and enjoys humor.)

TUDY QUESTIONS

ecalling

What does the speaker feel he must do?
What are the characteristics of the call of the sea?
In each stanza the speaker asks for several sea-related items. Name one such item from each stanza.
What two adjectives are used in the last stanza to describe the life that the speaker wants to live at sea?
Who is the only human being besides the speaker mentioned in the poem? What role does the speaker plan for him?
What does the speaker look forward to after returning from the sea?

terpreting

Explain how the title is appropriate to the meaning of the poem.
From what he looks for at sea, what can we assume about the speaker's present life?

xtending

What specific properties of an ocean, including some not mentioned in the poem, cause many people to be fascinated by the sea?

ITERARY FOCUS

hythm

When we speak, we naturally stress, or accent, ome syllables and not others. In poetry **rhythm** is ne pattern created by arranging stressed and nstressed syllables. Rhythm causes a poem to ound musical whether the sound is a heavy ngsong or a gentle lilt.

The proper matching of rhythm with meaning is nportant in a poem. A soft rhythm may suit a poem bout sleep. A jumpy rhythm may be appropriate in a oem about a basketball game.

Rhythm can be regular, following a predictable attern, or irregular. When the rhythm of a poem has regular, measurable pattern, the poem has **meter**. *Meter* comes from the Greek word *metron* meaning "measure.") The basic unit in the measurement of rhythm is the **foot.** A foot contains one accented syllable. For example, the word *lonely* has one foot made up of one accented and one unaccented syllable. The line "I must go down to the seas again, to the lonely sea and the sky" is made up of seven feet.

The rhythm of a poem can be shown with accent marks over accented syllables and rounded marks over unaccented syllables:

Ĭ múst / gŏ dówn / tŏ thĕ séas / ăgáin, / tŏ thĕ
lóne /lў̆ séa /ănd thĕ ský,

Finding the rhythm of a poem is called **scanning.** Scanning enables us to determine whether the rhythm is regular and, if it is, to identify the specific pattern used.

Thinking About Rhythm

1. Copy the first stanza of "Sea Fever" on a separate sheet, and try to scan it. Is the rhythm regular or irregular?
2. Explain why the rhythm of "Sea Fever" is appropriate to a poem about the sea.

VOCABULARY

Sensory Language

Sensory language appeals to the senses and represents concrete objects, people, or events. Poets use sensory language to enable the reader to picture what happens in the poem and, therefore, to understand the abstract ideas or emotions behind the poem. For example, "Sea Fever" helps us to understand the lure of the sea by representing that abstract idea with concrete examples of the sea's attraction.

For each example of the sea's lure, decide to which of the senses Masefield is appealing:

1. "the wheel's kick"
2. "a gray dawn breaking"
3. "the flung spray"
4. "the sea-gulls crying"
5. "the wind's like a whetted knife"

STUDY QUESTIONS

1. return to the sea
2. it is wild, clear; must be obeyed
3. ▪ *Stanza 1:* wheel's kick, star
   ▪ *Stanza 2:* spray, spume
   ▪ *Stanza 3:* gull's way; whale's way
4. *vagrant, gypsy* life
5. "a laughing fellow rover"; storyteller
6. "quiet sleep and a sweet dream"
7. speaker burns with desire to return to the sea
8. lives in city; finds life there tame, stifling, serious
9. its vastness, depth, abundant and varied sea life, power, mystery

LITERARY FOCUS

1. Types of metric feet vary within lines, but the pattern of seven stressed syllables per line is regular.
2. has a soft insistent rhythm like the sea; regular with small variations

VOCABULARY

1. touch
2. sight
3. touch, sight, taste, smell
4. sound
5. touch

AT A GLANCE

- Lucy lived in such isolation that no one could appreciate her beauty, and few could love her.
- Few people knew she died, but the speaker grieves deeply.

LITERARY OPTIONS

- rhyme
- metaphor

THEMATIC OPTIONS

- human relationships
- beauty

RHYME

The regularly repeated end rhymes help to unify each stanza and give the poem resonance. Note that lines 5 and 7 end in approximate rhymes.

METAPHOR

The speaker says that Lucy is as beautiful as a half-hidden violet and as fair as a single star, delicate images of obscurity and distance (ll. 5–8).

SPEAKER

The speaker does not reveal his deep feelings for Lucy until the last lines of the poem in order to give them the greatest impact (ll. 11–12).

MAIN IDEA

The sudden, wistful intimacy of the last exclamation and the sudden shift into personal confession from a more objective tone underscore Lucy's great impact on the speaker's life (ll. 11–12).

REFLECTING ON THE POEM

What kind of relationship do you think the speaker had with Lucy? (Answers might suggest that he did not know her well because she was so reclusive but that he was deeply impressed by what he saw of her beauty, bearing, and style.)

William Wordsworth

She Dwelt Among the Untrodden Ways

She dwelt among the untrodden[1] ways
  Beside the springs of Dove,[2]
A maid whom there were none to praise
  And very few to love:

A violet by a mossy stone
  Half hidden from the eye!
—Fair as a star, when only one
  Is shining in the sky.

She lived unknown, and few could know
  When Lucy ceased to be;
But she is in her grave, and, oh,
  The difference to me!

1. **untrodden:** not walked upon.
2. **Dove:** small rural river in England.

SELECTION FOR PRACTICE IN ACTIVE READING

(TCR 5, p. 66)

STUDY QUESTIONS

Recalling

1. Where did Lucy live? Where is she now?
2. Name two natural objects to which the speaker compares Lucy.
3. What fact makes a difference to the speaker?

Interpreting

4. Define *dwelt* and *untrodden.* What does the poem's title mean?
5. Describe Lucy's relationships with people other than the speaker.
6. In the second stanza what is the poet telling us about Lucy?
7. Describe the speaker's emotions. Explain how the poem's punctuation supports these emotions.

Extending

8. Without realizing it, anyone—even the least likely person—can have an important influence on another person's life. Use the poem as an example, and explain this idea.

LITERARY FOCUS

Rhyme and Rhyme Scheme

Rhyme occurs when accented vowel sounds and all succeeding consonant sounds are the same. For example, *scribble* and *dribble* rhyme, but *mother* and *father,* despite identical endings, do not rhyme. In **approximate rhyme** the final sounds are similar but not exactly alike. *Pain* and *frame* are approximate rhymes. Most rhymes are **end rhymes**, meaning that the words that rhyme occur at the ends of lines. Rhymes that happen within a line are **internal rhymes.**

End rhymes often fall into a repeating pattern called a **rhyme scheme**. To determine the rhyme scheme of a poem, assign a new letter of the alphabet to each new end rhyme. Lines that rhyme have the same letter. For example, the rhyme scheme of the following poem by Emily Dickinson is *aabcdb.*

A word is dead (*a*)
When it is said, (*a*)
Some say. (*b*)
I say it just (*c*)
Begins to live (*d*)
That day. (*b*)

A rhyme scheme unifies a poem by creating sound echoes and by giving the poem a pattern.

Thinking About Rhyme and Rhyme Scheme

- What is the rhyme scheme of Wordsworth's poem? Which lines end in an approximate rhyme?

STUDY QUESTIONS

1. apart from people "Beside the springs of Dove"; in her grave
2. violet, star
3. her death
4. dwelt: *lived,* untrodden: *not walked upon;* she lived in remote place away from people
5. No one loved or appreciated her.
6. He praises her beauty, rarity, and remoteness.
7. ■ admired and loved Lucy
   ■ exclamation highlights feelings about Lucy's beauty and death
8. Speaker does not mention relationship with Lucy; he only sees her, yet grieves deeply. Without knowing it, a person can influence others through attitude, life style, accomplishment, appearance.

LITERARY FOCUS

- rhyme scheme: *abab cdcd efef*
- lines 5 and 7

LITERARY OPTIONS

- onomatopoeia
- rhythm

THEMATIC OPTIONS

- language and communication
- imagination

RHYTHM

The irregular rhythm of the poem echoes the irregular flow of water as it builds from a few drops to a rushing stream (ll. 1–14).

ONOMATOPOEIA

The shift from percussive to sibilant consonant sounds echoes the water's sudden gush. *Plash,* the sound that marks the transition, combines both kinds of consonant sounds (l. 12).

REFLECTING ON THE POEM

How do you think the poet felt writing this poem? (amused, challenged, alert)

STUDY QUESTIONS

1. turning on faucet
2. *rusty* (old)
3. *spatters, splatters, scatters, spurts, gushes*
4. faucet coughs, trickles; gathers force, gushes clear water
5. to convey sound and motion
6. Commas create pauses that imitate sound; exclamation point marks sudden rush of water.
7. to draw attention to things often taken for granted (both questions)

LITERARY FOCUS

1. She intended poem to illustrate onomatopoeia.
2. opening sounds: *sputters, splutters;* gaining force: *gashes, slash, spatters;* full force: *gushes, rushes*

Eve Merriam

Onomatopoeia[1]

The rusty spigot[2]
sputters,
utters
a splutter,
spatters a smattering[3] of drops,
gashes wider;
slash,
splatters,
scatters,
spurts,
finally stops sputtering
and plash!
gushes rushes splashes
clear water dashes.

1. **Onomatopoeia** [on'ə mat'ə pē'ə]
2. **spigot** [spig'ət]: faucet.
3. **smattering:** small number.

STUDY QUESTIONS

Recalling

1. What simple action is taking place in the poem?
2. What adjective tells us whether the spigot is old or new?
3. Give five verbs the poet uses to portray the motion of the water.

Interpreting

4. Describe the changes in the water's activity from the beginning of the poem to the end.
5. Why do you think the poet uses so many verbs?
6. Reread the poem and notice its punctuation. Explain how the use and absence of punctuation adds to the poem's meaning.

Extending

7. Why do you think poets sometimes write about very simple objects or events? What effect do you think such poems are intended to have on readers?

LITERARY FOCUS

Onomatopoeia

Onomatopoeia [on'ə mat'ə pē'ə] is the use of a word or phrase that actually imitates or suggests the sound of what it describes. Onomatopoeia is a musical device often used in poetry, whether in a single word like *buzz* or in an entire line that imitates a sound. For example, in the following lines from "The Raven," Edgar Allan Poe imitates the sound of a whisper by using the letters *s* and *w.*

> But the silence was unbroken, and the stillness gave no token,
> And the only word there spoken was the whispered word, "Lenore?"

Such sound imitation can add to a poem's meaning. Soft, whispering words may be used in a poem about fresh snow. Loud, crashing words may be used in a poem about a traffic jam.

Thinking About Onomatopoeia

1. Why do you think Merriam chose the title for her poem?
2. Find the particular words or letters within words that suggest water coming from the spigot in different degrees of force.

Lewis Carroll

Jabberwocky[1]

'Twas brillig, and the slithy toves
  Did gyre and gimble in the wabe:
All mimsy were the borogoves,
  And the mome raths outgrabe.

"Beware the Jabberwock, my son!
  The jaws that bite, the claws that catch!
Beware the Jubjub bird, and shun
  The frumious Bandersnatch!"

He took his vorpal sword in hand;
  Long time the manxome foe he sought—
So rested he by the Tumtum tree,
  And stood awhile in thought.

And, as in uffish thought he stood,
  The Jabberwock, with eyes of flame,
Came whiffling through the tulgey wood,
  And burbled as it came!

One, two! One, two! And through and through
  The vorpal blade went snicker-snack!
He left it dead, and with its head
  He went galumphing back.

"And hast thou slain the Jabberwock?
  Come to my arms, my beamish boy!
O frabjous day! Callooh, Callay!"
  He chortled in his joy.

'Twas brillig, and the slithy toves
  Did gyre and gimble in the wabe:
All mimsy were the borogoves,
  And the mome raths outgrabe.

Jabberwocky, 1871, Sir John Tenniel. Rare Book Division, New York Public Library, Astor, Lenox and Tilden Division.

1. **Jabberwocky** [jab′ər wok′ē]

AT A GLANCE

- An adult warns a boy about the Jabberwock.
- The boy waits under a tree with a sword.
- When the Jabberwock appears, the boy slays and beheads it.
- His return home is celebrated by the adult.

LITERARY OPTIONS

- narrative poem
- onomatopoeia

THEMATIC OPTION

- conquering the unknown

NARRATIVE POEM

Though many of the words are unfamiliar, the poem clearly tells the story of a heroic child and a monster. The mysterious setting, introduced in the first stanza, is almost familiar when it reappears at the end of the poem.

ONOMATOPOEIA

The reader is encouraged to speculate on the meaning of the nonsense words, based on their sounds: *frumious, uffish, whiffling, burbled, etc.* (ll. 8, 13, 15, 16).

MAIN IDEA

The adult's delight in the child's accomplishment—he asks the child to come to his arms; he feels joy—dramatizes the child's return to a familiar home after conquering the unknown (ll. 21–24).

REFLECTING ON THE POEM

Why do people play with words? (Answers may suggest that through word play people can shape, control, and personalize language; that it is an entertaining, harmless way of breaking rules.)

STUDY QUESTIONS

1. It has jaws that bite, claws that catch.
2. They meet; he slashes it; decapitates it; returns.
3. He is overjoyed; praises boy.
4. an adult; could be parent, mentor, friend
5. Plot told with familiar words; only first and last stanzas are nonsensical.
6. ■ *adj.:* slithy, mimsy, frumious
   ■ *nouns:* toves, wabe, borogoves
   ■ *verbs:* gyre, gimble, outgrabe
   ■ *interj.:* Callooh, Callay
7. It adds nothing to the plot; contains nonsensical language; frames poem.
8. David/Goliath, Jack/Beanstalk's giant, Hansel, Gretel/witch, Peter/Wolf; they symbolize children's desire to overcome things that frighten them.

VIEWPOINT

Answers will vary. Some may dislike lack of definitions for words. Others may enjoy using imagination.

VOCABULARY

Answers will vary. Glossary is not necessary but adds humor.

STUDY QUESTIONS

Recalling

1. Give two reasons that the boy is warned to "beware the Jabberwock."
2. Describe in your own words the encounter between the boy and the Jabberwock.
3. The person who had warned the boy returns at the end of the poem. What is that person's reaction to what has happened?

Interpreting

4. Who do you think is the person who speaks in the two stanzas that are in quotation marks? Give reasons for your opinion.
5. Explain how you were able to understand what happens in the poem even though many of the words are not recognizable. Which parts of the poem clearly state the plot?
6. We can often determine the part of speech of a word from its suffix, or ending, or from its position in a sentence. Find at least four unrecognizable words and give the part of speech for each.
7. The first stanza of "Jabberwocky" was probably written seventeen years before the rest of the poem as part of a parlor game. Explain how this division can be seen in the poem.

Extending

8. Throughout history the story of a child slaying a beast has been repeated often. Give examples. What makes this plot so popular?

VIEWPOINT

Alice reads "Jabberwocky" in the first chapter of *Through the Looking Glass.* One critic describes the result:

> Alice hates to be defeated. She doesn't like to confess even to herself that she fails to understand "Jabberwocky," that she can't break its system. She insists that she gets the main point, which is that "somebody kills something."
>
> —K. Blake, *Play, Games and Sport: The Literary Works of Lewis Carroll*

■ In what ways were your reactions to reading the poem similar to or different from Alice's?

VOCABULARY

Word Invention

Poets often invent words to achieve startling effects, but must provide clues to the meanings of these new words. In *Through the Looking Glass* Alice receives help in understanding "Jabberwocky" from Humpty Dumpty, who says:

> "*Brillig* means four o'clock in the afternoon—the time when you begin broiling things for dinner."
>
> "Well, *slithy* means *lithe* and *slimy. Lithe* is the same as *active.* You see, it's like a portmanteau [suitcase]—there are two meanings packed up into one word."
>
> "Well, *toves* are something like badgers—they're something like lizards—and they're something like corkscrews. . . . also they make their nests under sun-dials—also they live on cheese."
>
> "To *gyre* is to go round and round like a gyroscope. To *gimble* is to make holes like a gimlet [a small tool]."
>
> "And the *wabe* is the grass plot around a sun-dial, I suppose?" said Alice, surprised at her own ingenuity.
>
> "Of course it is. It's called *wabe*, you know, because it goes a long way before it, and a long way behind it—"
> "And a long way beyond it on each side," Alice added.
>
> "Well then, *mimsy* is *flimsy* and *miserable* (there's another portmanteau for you), and a *borogove* is a thin, shabby-looking bird with its feathers sticking out all around—something like a live mop."
>
> "Well, a *rath* is a sort of green pig; but *mome* I'm not certain about. I think it's short for *from home* — meaning that they'd lost their way, you know."
>
> "Well, *outgribing* is something between bellowing and whistling with a kind of sneeze in the middle . . ."

■ Explain whether you think the glossary is necessary to enjoy "Jabberwocky."

Edgar Allan Poe

The Bells

I

Hear the sledges[1] with the bells—
Silver bells!
What a world of merriment their melody foretells!
How they tinkle, tinkle, tinkle,
In the icy air of night!
While the stars that oversprinkle
All the heavens, seem to twinkle
With a crystalline delight;
Keeping time, time, time,
In a sort of Runic[2] rhyme,
To the tintinnabulation[3] that so musically wells
From the bells, bells, bells, bells,
Bells, bells, bells—
From the jingling and the tinkling of the bells.

1. **sledges:** sleds or sleighs.
2. **Runic** [rōōn′ik]: referring to the letters in an ancient Germanic system of writing or to a magical Norse chant.
3. **tintinnabulation** [tin′tə nab′yə lā′shən]: ringing of bells.

AT A GLANCE

The first stanza evokes the sound of sleigh bells on a winter night.

LITERARY OPTIONS

- repetition
- parallelism
- imagery

THEMATIC OPTIONS

- emotional effects of sound
- joy and horror

SPEAKER

The speaker of the poem begins each stanza by urging the reader to "listen" to a different kind of bell; these lines link speaker to reader. For the rest of the poem, the speaker is a detached observer.

IMAGERY

The poet's use of phrases like *icy air of night, stars that oversprinkle,* and *crystalline delight* help to suggest the wonder and excitement of a clear winter night (ll. 5, 6, and 8).

REPETITION

Poe exploits almost every kind of repetition in this poem. In the first stanza, for instance, he repeats words like *bells, tinkle,* and *time* to give the poem a simple musicality and the rhythm of a trotting horse (ll. 1, 2, 4, 9, 12, 13, 14).

ALLITERATION/ASSONANCE

The repetition of the consonant sounds *t, k,* and *l* give the stanza a light, metallic jingling sound, while long vowels create a clear, high-pitched one (ll. 1–14).

GUIDED READING

LITERAL QUESTION

1a. What two words does Poe use in the last line of the stanza to describe the sound of the bells? *(jingling, tinkling)*

INFERENTIAL QUESTION

1b. What feeling or emotion do these words convey to the reader? (happiness, lightness, playfulness)

AT A GLANCE

- Wedding bells sound.
- Alarm bells signal a fire.

MAIN IDEA

The poet relates sound to emotion by making harmony a metaphor for happiness through such words as *mellow, harmony, delight, in tune, euphony, and rapture* (ll. 15, 17, 19, 21, 26, 30).

ASSONANCE

The rounded wedding-bell tones are echoed in the *o* of *molten-golden notes, floats, gloats;* in the *u* of *through, tune, moon, euphony, voluminously,* and *future* (ll. 20, 22, 23; 18, 21, 24, 26, 29).

PARALLELISM

The first lines of the second and third stanzas are almost identical in rhythm and word pattern, except that gold has become brass and happiness has become terror (ll. 15–19, 36–40).

PERSONIFICATION

Poe personifies night and fire, then links these metaphors. The alarm bells ring in "the startled ear of night," then plead for mercy from "the deaf and frantic fire" (ll. 39, 44–45).

ALLITERATION

The use of alliteration and harsh *t, c,* and *z* sounds seems to underscore the alarm of the bells—*brazen bells, tale of terror . . . their turbulency tells, frantic fire, desperate desire* (ll. 37, 38, 45, 47).

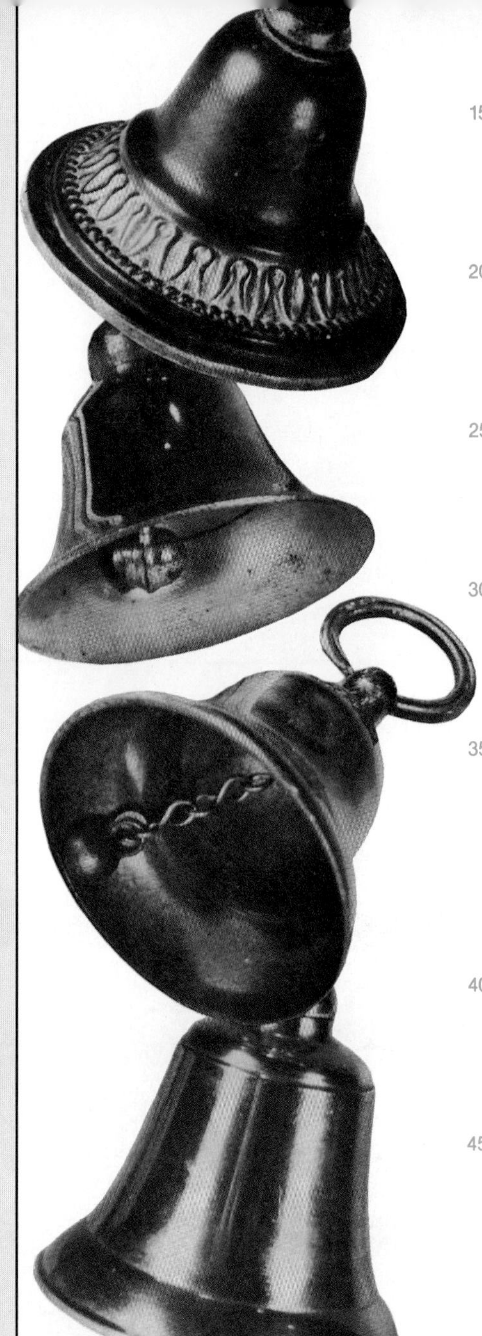

II

Hear the mellow wedding bells—
Golden bells!
What a world of happiness their harmony foretells!
Through the balmy air of night
How they ring out their delight!—
From the molten-golden notes,
And all in tune,
What a liquid ditty floats
To the turtle-dove[4] that listens, while she gloats[5]
On the moon!
Oh, from out the sounding cells,
What a gush of euphony[6] voluminously wells!
How it swells![7]
How it dwells
On the Future!—how it tells
Of the rapture that impels
To the swinging and the ringing
Of the bells, bells, bells—
Of the bells, bells, bells, bells,
Bells, bells, bells—
To the rhyming and the chiming of the bells!

III

Hear the loud alarum bells[8]—
Brazen[9] bells!
What a tale of terror, now, their turbulency tells!
In the startled ear of night
How they scream out their affright!
Too much horrified to speak,
They can only shriek, shriek,
Out of tune,
In a clamorous appealing to the mercy of the fire,
In a mad expostulation[10] with the deaf and frantic fire,
Leaping higher, higher, higher,
With a desperate desire,

---

4. **turtle dove:** small, wild bird noted for its soft cooing.
5. **gloats** [glōtz]: gazes.
6. **euphony** [ū′fə nē]: pleasant sound.
7. **swells:** grows louder.
8. **alarum bells:** alarm bells. Loud bells were used to alert the public that some danger threatened a given area.
9. **Brazen** [brā′zən]: made of brass; also, loud and rude.
10. **expostulation** [iks pos′chə lā′shən]: protest.

GUIDED READING

LITERAL QUESTION

1a. What two words does Poe use (one in l. 16, one in l. 37) to describe the bells? (*Golden, Brazen*)

INFERENTIAL QUESTION

1b. In what way does the sound of each word match the type of bell it describes? (*Golden* has a round, warm sound that aptly describes the wedding scene; *Brazen*'s harsh, jagged quality evokes alarm and fear.)

And a resolute endeavor
Now—now to sit, or never,
By the side of the pale-faced moon.
Oh, the bells, bells, bells!
What a tale their terror tells
Of Despair!
How they clang, and clash, and roar!
What a horror they outpour
On the bosom of the palpitating air!
Yet the ear, it fully knows,
By the twanging
And the clanging,
How the danger ebbs and flows;[11]
Yet the ear distinctly tells,
In the jangling
And the wrangling,
How the danger sinks and swells,
By the sinking or the swelling in the anger of the bells—
Of the bells,—
Of the bells, bells, bells, bells,
Bells, bells, bells—
In the clamour and the clangor of the bells!

IV

Hear the tolling[12] of the bells—
Iron bells!
What a world of solemn thought their monody[13] compels!
In the silence of the night,
How we shiver with affright
At the melancholy menace of their tone!
For every sound that floats
From the rust within their throats
Is a groan.
And the people—ah, the people—
They that dwell up in the steeple,
All alone,
And who tolling, tolling, tolling,
In that muffled monotone,
Feel a glory in so rolling
On the human heart a stone—

11. **ebbs and flows:** recedes and advances like the tide.
12. **tolling** [tōl′ing]: ringing with slow, regular strokes.
13. **monody** [mon′ə dē]: lament sung by one voice.

AT A GLANCE

- The third stanza (of alarm bells) concludes.
- The fourth stanza begins to describe the sound of funeral bells.

ONOMATOPOEIA

Poe uses loud, ringing, urgent onomatopoeic words like *clang, clash, roar, twanging, clanging, jangling, wrangling, clamour,* and *clangor* to describe the sound of alarm bells (ll. 54–69).

PERSONIFICATION

In each stanza Poe has the bells speak: They predict happiness in the first two stanzas, send an alarm in the third, and groan "within their throats" in the fourth (ll. 77–78).

PARALLELISM

The first three lines of each part of the poem are very similar. The poet urges the reader to listen to the bells, describes the metal of the bells, and follows the word "what" with an exclamation.

STRUCTURE

Although each stanza begins and ends similarly, each stanza's middle section is progressively larger and more fully developed. This allows Poe to show how horror gradually grows out of joy.

GUIDED READING

LITERAL QUESTION

1a. What words does Poe use to describe the bells in stanza IV? *(Iron, solemn, monody, melancholy menace, groan)*

INFERENTIAL QUESTION

1b. Given these descriptive words, why do you think these bells are tolling? (A funeral is taking place.)

AT A GLANCE

- The fourth stanza (of funeral bells) concludes.

IMAGERY

With strange and jarring imagery Poe describes people (whom he later calls "ghouls") who live in the church steeple and celebrate each time they ring funeral bells (ll. 86–89).

REPETITION

Poe repeats lines 9 and 10 from the first stanza to stress the frightening similarity between terror and joy (ll. 96–97, 100–101, 105, 107).

RHYTHM

The rhythm pattern of the poem is based on alternating stressed and unstressed syllables. Many lines, especially those that repeat the word *bells,* contain extra syllables that imitate a monotonous ringing and convey emotion through sound.

REFLECTING ON THE POEM

In what ways are the four types of bells different? In what ways the same? (Respectively they evoke happiness, hope and love, terror, and dread; each type of bell sounds like its meaning, and each is vivid and purposeful.)

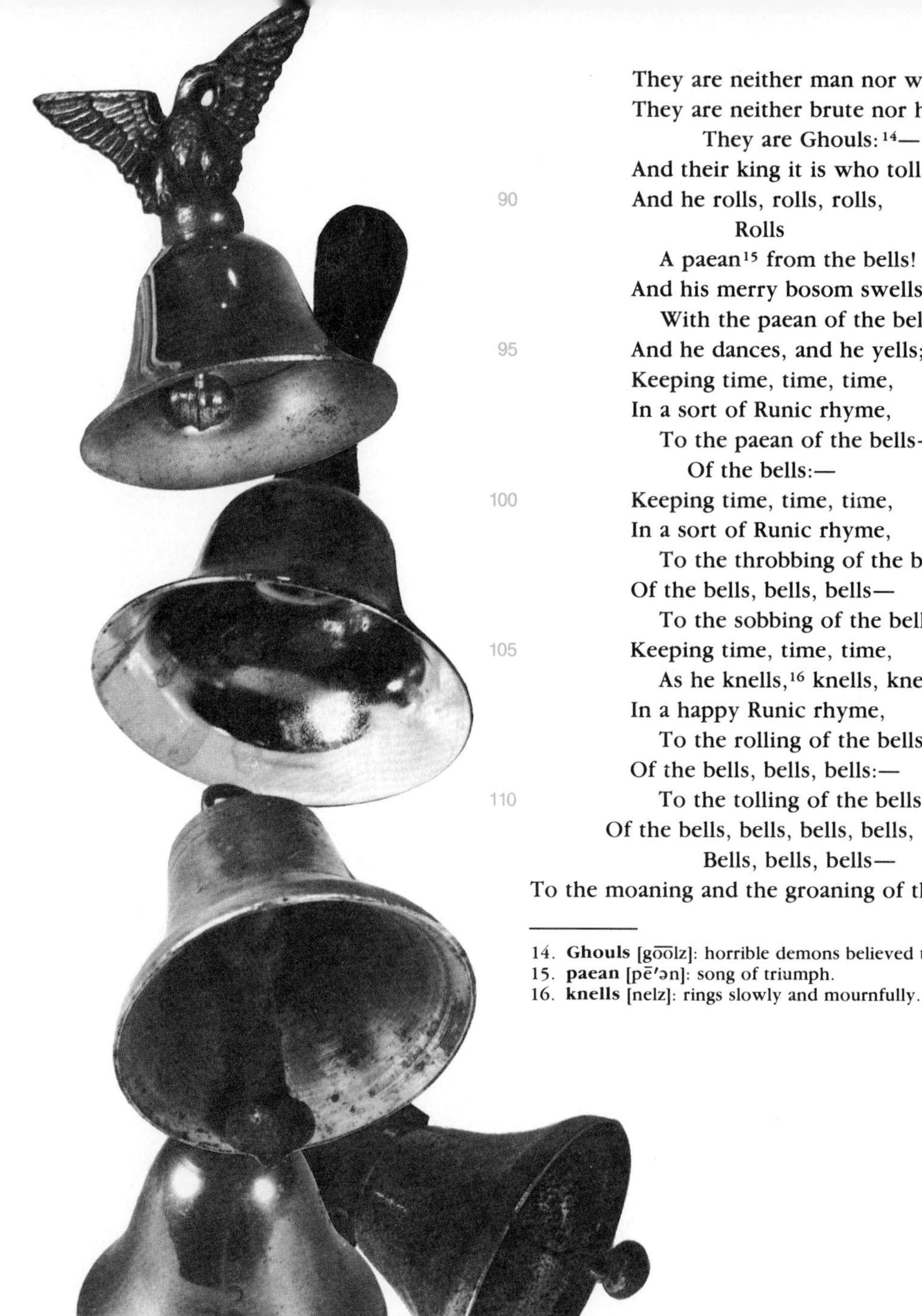

They are neither man nor woman—
They are neither brute nor human—
They are Ghouls:[14]—
And their king it is who tolls:—
And he rolls, rolls, rolls,
Rolls
A paean[15] from the bells!
And his merry bosom swells
With the paean of the bells!
And he dances, and he yells;
Keeping time, time, time,
In a sort of Runic rhyme,
To the paean of the bells—
Of the bells:—
Keeping time, time, time,
In a sort of Runic rhyme,
To the throbbing of the bells—
Of the bells, bells, bells—
To the sobbing of the bells;
Keeping time, time, time,
As he knells,[16] knells, knells,
In a happy Runic rhyme,
To the rolling of the bells—
Of the bells, bells, bells:—
To the tolling of the bells—
Of the bells, bells, bells, bells,
Bells, bells, bells—
To the moaning and the groaning of the bells.

14. **Ghouls** [go͞olz]: horrible demons believed to rob graves.
15. **paean** [pē′ən]: song of triumph.
16. **knells** [nelz]: rings slowly and mournfully.

GUIDED READING

LITERAL QUESTION

1a. What word is repeated nine times in lines 96, 100, 105? *(time)*

INFERENTIAL QUESTION

1b. In the first stanza "keeping time" referred to a kind of musical beat. What sort of time is suggested here? (a lifetime)

STUDY QUESTIONS

Recalling

1. Find the line in each stanza that tells us at what part of the day the bells ring.
2. Name three metals from which the different bells are made.
3. What type of bell is ringing in the first stanza?
4. Why are the bells ringing in the second stanza?
5. What is happening in the third stanza? Too horrified to speak, what do the bells do instead?
6. Describe the beings that live in the steeple in the fourth stanza. Who rings the bells?

Interpreting

7. What letters, words, and lines imitate the sounds of the different kinds of bells?
8. What mood is created in each of the four stanzas? What is the total effect of combining these four moods into one poem?
9. What is the effect of using lines of different lengths?
10. Do you think the main focus of the poem is on meaning or sound? Explain your answer.

Extending

11. Can the same sound have different effects on a listener, depending on the person's mood? Explain your answer with specific examples like the sound of an alarm clock, laughter, or the surf.

LITERARY FOCUS

Repetition: Alliteration, Assonance, Parallelism

The **repetition** of sounds, letters, words, or lines helps give poetry its meaning, form, and sound. Rhyme and rhythm repeat sounds; a refrain repeats important lines. Other common forms of repetition in poetry are alliteration, assonance, and parallelism.

Alliteration is the repeating of consonant sounds, most often at the beginnings of words. The following line from Poe's "Raven" is an example of alliteration:

*D*oubting, *d*reaming *d*reams no mortal ever
*d*ared to *d*ream before. . .

Assonance is the repeating of vowel sounds. For example, Poe used assonance in these lines from "To Helen":

The weary way-w*o*rn wanderer b*o*re
To his *o*wn native sh*o*re.

Parallelism is the repeating of phrases or sentences so that the repeated parts are alike in structure or in meaning. Parallelism can take many forms, but it always creates a pattern that is recognizable. For example, the poet may begin each sentence or each stanza with the prepositional phrase "In the muggy morning. . ." or with a simple word like *I*. In another poem half of each stanza may be made of happy thoughts, the second half of sad thoughts.

Thinking About Repetition

1. Find at least one example of alliteration and one example of assonance in each stanza of "The Bells."
2. In what ways do alliteration and assonance help to create the mood of each stanza?
3. In what ways are the four stanzas parallel? Give examples to support your answer.

COMPARING POEMS

1. Compare the meaning of two or more of the poems in this section: "Sea Fever," "She Dwelt Among the Untrodden Ways," "Onomatopoeia," "Jabberwocky," and "The Bells." How important is the sound of each poem to its meaning? How well does the sound of each poem match its meaning? Do you think that the sound helps you to understand the poem or distracts you? Give reasons for your opinion.
2. Compare the sounds of two or more of the poems in this section. Imagine that you do not read English but hear the poems read aloud. What impression would you have of each poem based solely on its sound?
3. Do you enjoy poetry with distinctive sound? Why or why not? Use two or more poems in this section to explain your opinion.

STUDY QUESTIONS

1. stanza 1, l. 5; stanza 2, l. 18; stanza 3, l. 39; stanza 4, l. 73
2. silver, gold, brass
3. sleigh bell
4. for a wedding
5. fire alarm sounding; shriek out of tune
6. ghouls; their king
7. sleigh: letters *t, kl;* words *tinkle, jingle;* ll. 4, 14
   wedding: letters *l, r, m, n;* words *ring, chime;* ll. 31, 35
   alarm: letters *cl;* words *shriek, clang;* ll. 42, 54, 58–59, 62–63, 69
   funeral: letters *o, e;* words *groan, throb;* ll. 78, 82, 102, 104, 106, 113
8. 1st: merry; 2nd: happy; 3rd: turbulent; 4th: menacing; total effect: portrays span of life
9. varies emotional effect
10. sound; poem illogical, repetitions detract from meaning but add sound
11. Answers will vary. Mood can determine a reaction to sound; sound can also affect mood.

LITERARY FOCUS

1.
   - *1:* alliteration: lines 3, 10; assonance: lines 3, 14
   - *2:* alliteration: lines 17, 25; assonance: lines 17, 20, 22, 26
   - *3:* alliteration: lines 37, 38; assonance: lines 47–49
   - *4:* alliteration: lines 75, 83; assonance: 72, 73–74
2.
   - *1:* suggest merry sleigh bells
   - *2:* suggest harmony
   - *3:* create frightening effect
   - *4:* imitate groans
3. Each stanza begins with same words, becomes longer but maintains repetition, ends with two lines in same rhythm.

COMPARING POEMS

1.
   - "Sea": imitates sound of waves; rhythm matches meaning; sound not important
   - "Ways": sound least important; rhythm matches meaning
   - "Onomatopoeia": Sound is meaning.
   - "Jabberwocky": Nonsense words may distract or add to meaning.
   - "Bells": Sound is meaning.
2.
   - "Sea": noticeable rhythm, rhyme
   - "Ways": musical rhythm, rhyme
   - "Onomatopoeia": imitative sounds
   - "Jabberwocky": rhyme, rhythm, onomatopoeia
   - "Bells": Sound suggests meaning.
3. Answers will vary.

LITERARY FOCUS: Imagery, Figurative Language

Poetry wakens our senses with **imagery.** Poetry startles us by replacing **literal language** (the ordinary language of everyday) with figurative language. **Figurative language** and its devices—**figures of speech**—surprise us with unique comparisons.

Bashō (1644-1694) was a poet and a samurai, a member of Japan's feudal warrior class. His poems "paint" detailed, vivid pictures.

■ Which picture presented in these haiku is most vivid to you?

Richard Wright (1908–1960) was born in Mississippi to a poor black family and decided to be a writer while still a teen-ager. In "Hokku Poems" he experiments with Bashō's style, but the pictures he creates are his own.

■ Which of the hokku is most like the poems of Bashō?

Emily Dickinson (1830–1886) spent most of her adult life in seclusion in Amherst, Massachusetts, and scribbled her poems secretly on scraps of paper. Poems like "A Narrow Fellow in the Grass" are celebrated today for their surprising figures of speech.

■ What animal that you have seen has given you a feeling as powerful as the feeling described in the poem on page 200?

Walter de la Mare (1873–1956) often scratched down poems during lunch breaks while working as a bookkeeper for an oil company in London. "Silver" demonstrates his lively language and fresh descriptions.

■ Do you think people living in the space age can be as romantic about a moonlit night as the speaker is in the poem on page 201?

Elinor Wylie (1885–1928) began writing poems while still a teenager. Although she also wrote prose, Wylie is best known as a poet and was married to another poet, William Rose Benét. The vivid use of imagery that characterizes her work is evident in "Velvet Shoes."

- What strong memories or vivid images of snow do you have that are like or unlike the ones in the poem on page 202?

Langston Hughes (1902–1967) spent his early years as a cook, busboy, and seaman. His poetry was first recognized during the 1920s black cultural movement called The Harlem Renaissance. In "Dreams" Hughes employs figurative language to offer encouragement to the people about whom he wrote.

- Do you agree with Hughes about what happens "if dreams die"?

May Swenson (born 1919) has defined poetry as "a craving to get through the curtains of things as they appear. . . ." In "Water Picture," as in much of her work, she writes about appearances and illustrates that the senses can both delight and deceive.

- Why do you think people—like the speaker in this poem—often take delight in being deceived by appearances?

William Shakespeare (1564–1616) wrote his plays in verse, and he also wrote narrative poems and sonnets. "The Seven Ages of Man" is taken from the play *As You Like It,* and it demonstrates his mastery of lively figurative speech.

- Which of the seven ages of human life do you believe is the most interesting one?

LITERARY OPTIONS

- haiku
- imagery

THEMATIC OPTIONS

- nature
- permanence and change

"HAIKU": IMAGERY

Bashō uses images to evoke sight *(plum orchard, flowering blooms, moon glows)* and hearing *(in silence, roar of waterfall).*

MAIN IDEA

Each poem teaches a lesson the poet learned by observing nature: The mighty ignore the young; reality persists despite "clouds" of illusion; little things can accumulate into a "roar."

"HOKKU POEMS": SPEAKER

In the third, fifth, and seventh poems the speaker is a detached observer; in the second, fourth, and sixth he directly addresses the reader; in the first he speaks of himself.

MAIN IDEA

By close observation and direct address to nature, the poet reveals the deep impact nature has on him; the first poem stresses nature's power to overwhelm his identity.

REFLECTING ON THE POEMS

Why do the poets focus on such minute, specific details of nature? (In details the poets find many of nature's truths revealed; specific images can be more vivid than abstract ones.)

Bashō

Haiku

Within plum orchard,
sturdy oak takes no notice
of flowering blooms.

The moon glows the same:
it is the drifting cloud forms
make it seem to change.

Yellow rose petals
drop one-by-one in silence:
roar of waterfall.

Richard Wright

Hokku Poems

I am nobody
A red sinking autumn sun
Took my name away

Make up your mind snail!
You are half inside your house
And halfway out!

In the falling snow
A laughing boy holds out his palms
Until they are white

Keep straight down this block
Then turn right where you will find
A peach tree blooming

The spring lingers on
In the scent of a damp log
Rotting in the sun

Whose town did you leave
O wild and drowning spring rain
And where do you go?

The crow flew so fast
That he left his lonely caw
Behind in the fields

STUDY QUESTIONS

Recalling

1. Where does the first poem take place? What does the oak fail to notice?
2. In the second poem what stays the same? What makes it seem to change?
3. What two natural objects appear in the third poem?

Interpreting

4. Describe in detail the relationship that exists in each poem. In what ways are the three relationships similar?
5. Explain what human traits might be suggested by the first and second poems.
6. Compare and contrast the two separate pictures in the third poem. What effect is created by putting them together?

Extending

7. Haiku is effective because it is brief. Poet Robert Browning once said, "Less is more." Name other situations in which this attitude is true.

LITERARY FOCUS

Haiku

A **haiku** is a three-line poem, usually about nature. The haiku, developed in seventeenth-century Japan, presents one or two simple natural scenes without direct comment but often with the suggestion of a deeper meaning. A traditional haiku follows a strict form. Each poem contains seventeen syllables, five in the first and third lines, seven in the second.

Thinking About Haiku

1. Explain why Bashō's poems are typical of traditional haiku.
2. Reread the poems filling in missing words like *that, the*, and *an*. What effect does the addition have on the poems' forcefulness?

STUDY QUESTIONS

Recalling

1. What took the speaker's name away in the first poem?
2. In your own words describe the central pictures of the second and third poems.
3. In the fourth poem what will be found by following the speaker's directions?
4. Give three details about the log pictured in the fifth poem.
5. Name three traits of the rain in poem six.
6. In the last poem what did the crow leave behind?

Interpreting

7. What order or reason can you find in the arrangement of the poems?
8. A haiku sometimes contains a surprising twist. Which of these poems demonstrates this trait?
9. In what ways are Wright's poems like traditional haiku? How are they different?

Extending

10. Poets often use the seasons to suggest moods. What moods do you associate with each season?

LITERARY FOCUS

Imagery

Image means "picture" or "likeness." In poetry an **image** is a picture made with words. Poetic images are usually visual, and they help us to form a mental portrait of what a poem is describing. A poet, however, may also use images that help us to imagine a sound, a smell, a taste, or a texture. The collection of these images within a poem is called its **imagery,** the language in the poem that appeals to the senses. A poet uses imagery to re-create a scene, a person, or an object in the reader's mind through the use of colors, sounds, and other sensations. In this way we share the poet's experience.

Thinking About Imagery

- From *Hokku Poems* give one example each for images that appeal to the senses of sight, sound, smell, and touch.

STUDY QUESTIONS

"Haiku"

1. in plum orchard; plum blossoms
2. moon; drifting clouds
3. yellow rose petals, waterfall
4. - 1st: contrast between sturdy oak/fragile blossoms; 2nd: moon/drifting clouds; 3rd: rose petals dropping/waterfall
   - poems contrast strength/delicacy, stillness/motion, silence/roar
5. Answers may suggest the strong ignore the weak; nature can deceive.
6. silent, delicate petals and noisy, powerful waterfall; suggests variety of nature
7. Possible answers: Proverbs use few words; jewels are often small.

STUDY QUESTIONS

"Hokku"

1. red sinking autumn sun
2. - *2nd:* snail halfway out of shell
   - *3rd:* boy, palms up in snow storm
3. peach tree in bloom
4. damp, rotting, spring smell
5. wild, downpour, travels
6. its caw
7. arranged according to season
8. each in its last line
9. like: traditional pattern, syllables; unlike: joining words complete sentences; deal with human world
10. Answers will vary.

LITERARY FOCUS

"Haiku"

1. deal with natural phenomena; follow classical form
2. dilutes forcefulness

"Hokku"

- sight: "red sinking . . . sun"
- sound: "laughing boy"
- smell: "scent of a damp log"
- touch: "palms held out . . . snow"

LITERARY OPTIONS

- imagery
- rhythm

THEMATIC OPTION

- responses to nature

SPEAKER

Dickinson chose a male speaker for this poem, which recalls boyhood encounters with snakes (l. 11).

RHYTHM

Dickinson alters word order to accommodate her rhythm; this device interrupts the natural flow of language and gives the poem a startled, breathless quality (ll. 4, 17–18).

IMAGERY

The poet uses concrete, sensory images (*tighter breathing* and *Zero at the Bone*) to convey the fear the speaker feels of the snake (ll. 21–24).

REFLECTING ON THE POEM

Why might the poet fear the snake? (Snakes can kill, hide, be deceptive; there is something "otherworldly" about them.)

STUDY QUESTIONS

1. snake parting grass, comb parting hair
2. cool, wet places; also in sun
3. line 11: male
4. whip lash "unbraiding" in sun
5. cordiality; startled, frightened
6. snake; "narrow fellow," grass parting, habits described; lets reader discover identity through sudden images
7. Cold is often associated with fear.
8. *words:* unbraiding, wrinkling, etc., provide visual images; *order:* lines 4, 11, 15–16, emphasize abruptness of meeting snake and fit rhythm better
9. *serious:* description of fear; *playful:* whimsical descriptions
10. Unpleasant associations: Some are harmful.

VIEWPOINT

"Comb" is common item; author uses terms familiar to farming populace.

Emily Dickinson

A Narrow Fellow in the Grass

A narrow Fellow in the Grass
Occasionally rides—
You may have met Him—did you not
His notice sudden is—

The Grass divides as with a Comb—
A spotted shaft is seen—
And then it closes at your feet
And opens further on—

He likes a Boggy[1] Acre
A Floor too cool for Corn—
Yet when a Boy, and Barefoot—
I more than once at Noon

Have passed, I thought, a Whip lash[2]
Unbraiding in the Sun
When stooping to secure it
It wrinkled, and was gone—

Several of Nature's People
I know, and they know me—
I feel for them a transport[3]
Of cordiality—

But never met this Fellow
Attended, or alone
Without a tighter breathing
And Zero at the Bone—

---

1. **Boggy** [bog′gē]: swamp-like.
2. **Whip lash:** flexible, braided part of a whip.
3. **transport:** strong emotion.

STUDY QUESTIONS

Recalling

1. What comparison is made in the second stanza?
2. In what temperatures can the "fellow" be found?
3. What line tells us the sex of the speaker?
4. For what item has the speaker mistaken the "fellow" according to the fourth stanza?
5. What does the speaker normally feel for "nature's people"? Explain how the speaker feels upon encountering the "fellow."

Interpreting

6. What is the "fellow" being described? What images lead you to this conclusion? Why do you think the poet chose not to name it directly?
7. Explain the meaning of the phrase "zero at the bone."
8. Find two examples each of Dickinson's use of unusual words and her odd word order. What effect do you think they have on the poem?
9. In what ways is the poem both serious and playful?

Extending

10. For what reasons do you think people sometimes have unreasonable fear of harmless animals and insects?

VIEWPOINT

Because Emily Dickinson's images are unique, many readers can easily recognize a poem as hers. One group of critics said:

> The concrete images for much of her poetry . . .[are] provided by matter-of-fact domestic life: household activities and the sights and smells of the yards and fields about the house.
>
> —Brooks, Purser, and Warren, *An Approach to Literature*

■ In what sense is the imagery of "A Narrow Fellow in the Grass" domestic and ordinary?

Walter de la Mare

Silver

Slowly, silently, now the moon
Walks the night in her silver shoon.[1]
This way, and that, she peers, and sees
Silver fruit upon silver trees:
One by one the casements[2] catch
Her beams beneath the silvery thatch;[3]
Couched[4] in his kennel, like a log,
With paws of silver sleeps the dog;
From their shadowy cote[5] the white breasts peep
Of doves in a silver-feathered sleep;
A harvest mouse goes scampering by,
With silver claws and a silver eye;
And moveless fish in the water gleam,
By silver reeds in a silver stream.

---

1. **shoon:** shoes.
2. **casements:** windows that open on hinges on the sides.
3. **thatch:** roof covered with straw.
4. **couched:** lying in a place of rest.
5. **cote** [kōt]: small shelter for animals or birds.

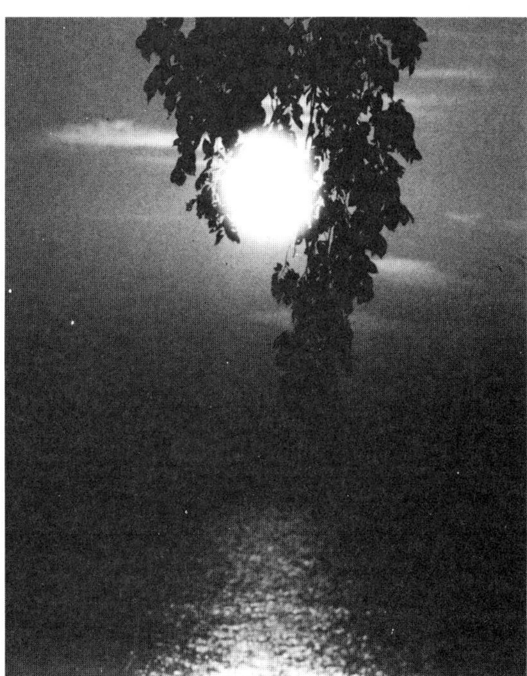

STUDY QUESTIONS

Recalling

1. What "walks the night" in the first two lines?
2. Name four animals mentioned in the poem.
3. How many times is the word *silver* repeated? Give five specific items that are described as being silver.

Interpreting

4. What effect does the repetition of the word *silver* have on the meaning and sound of the poem?
5. In what ways are de la Mare's images unusual or mysterious?
6. Explain how the poem is like a painting.

Extending

7. Reread the poem leaving out all references to color. Does the new version have more or less emotional power? Explain your opinion.

LITERARY FOCUS

Personification

Personification is a figure of speech in which an animal, object, or idea is described as having human form or characteristics. Personification implies that a nonhuman thing has personality, intelligence, and emotion. For example, when a poem states that window shades "let down their eyelids" or that a willow tree "shakes wet streamers from her hair," the poem contains personification.

Thinking About Personification

1. Find three words or phrases that personify the moon in "Silver."
2. Using just a few adjectives, describe the personality of de la Mare's moon.

LITERARY OPTIONS

- personification
- alliteration

THEMATIC OPTIONS

- responses to nature
- human perception

PERSONIFICATION

The moon is described in human terms: It "walks the night" and "sees" (ll. 1–3).

ALLITERATION

The poet uses alliteration in almost every line; because *s* sounds predominate, the poem becomes (like the silent scene it describes) a hushed whisper. The harsh *k* sounds (ll. 5, 7) provide contrast.

IMAGERY

The poet creates images of stillness with repeated descriptions of sleep. Although a mouse "goes scampering by," the stillness is reestablished by the image of the "moveless fish" (ll. 11–14).

REFLECTING ON THE POEM

Why do you think poets sometimes describe nature as human? (It can make nature more understandable and connect it to human life.)

STUDY QUESTIONS

1. the moon
2. dog, doves, mouse, fish
3. nine times; moon's shoes, fruits, trees, dog's paws, mouse's eye, thatch, feathers, reeds, stream
4. slows reading and emphasizes image's power
5. describes still night scene; no people; uses unusual terms for common objects
6. describes a detailed scene that seems old
7. less; scene becomes common

LITERARY FOCUS

1. walks, peers, sees, she, her
2. Answers will vary, and may suggest: curious, kind, gentle, relaxed.

LITERARY OPTION

- simile

THEMATIC OPTION

- nature

SIMILE

Wylie doubles elements in her similes to underscore their purity: Walkers' shoes will be "*white* as a *white* cow's milk" (l. 8).

PARALLELISM

Six lines of the poem start with "Let us walk " or a slight variation of this phrase. These lines establish a calm and soothing rhythmic pattern and suggest a tranquil mood (ll. 1, 6, 11, 13, 16, 20).

REFLECTING ON THE POEM

Is this poem about velvet shoes? (yes, in the sense that velvet shoes embody softness, silence, and delight)

STUDY QUESTIONS

1. will walk in white snow; will walk quietly, slowly
2. silk, wool
3. through town upon white down, silver fleece
4.
- stanza 1: *soundless, quiet*
- stanza 3: *still town*
- stanza 4: *white silence*

5. Shoes connote quiet softness.
6. Lines act as frame, add reassuring tone.
7.
- *veils of . . . lace, white down, silver fleece, white silence*
- She stresses color, beauty, softness, silence.

8.
- coldness, wetness
- to focus on sensual beauty

LITERARY FOCUS

- similes: *white . . . milk; more . . . gull; silence . . . dews*
- She compares whiteness of silk shoes to that of milk and breast of gull; compares silence to dew.
- White and soft similes are apt; *silence/dew* simile unusual—one is abstract, one concrete—but dew does appear silently and mysteriously.

Elinor Wylie

Velvet Shoes

Let us walk in the white snow
  In a soundless space;
With footsteps quiet and slow,
  At a tranquil pace,
  Under veils of white lace.

I shall go shod in silk
  And you in wool,
White as a white cow's milk,
  More beautiful
  Than the breast of a gull.

We shall walk through the still town
  In a windless peace;
We shall step upon white down,
  Upon silver fleece,
  Upon softer than these.

We shall walk in velvet shoes;
  Wherever we go
Silence will fall like dews
  On white silence below.
  We shall walk in the snow.

STUDY QUESTIONS

Recalling

1. From the first stanza give at least two details of the walk that the speaker plans.
2. Of what materials are the shoes in the second stanza made?
3. Where and upon what does the speaker say they will walk?
4. Find at least four references to silence in the poem.

Interpreting

5. Explain the title and the mention of shoes within the poem.
6. Why do you think the poet states clearly her topic in the poem's first and last lines?
7. Name at least four things to which snow is compared in the poem. What qualities of snow is the author stressing?

Extending

8. What qualities of snow has the poet chosen not to mention? Why do you think these qualities have been omitted?

LITERARY FOCUS

Simile

A **simile** is a figure of speech that directly compares two seemingly unlike things using a comparing word such as *like* or *as*. For example, the following are similes from the poetry of William Wordsworth: "I wheeled about, / Proud and exulting *like* an untired horse" ("The Prelude") and "impatient *as* the wind / I turned" ("Surprised by Joy").

The items that are being compared in a simile are basically not alike, but they do share some characteristics. Statements comparing items that are alike are not similes. For example, "My dog looks like a guard dog" is not a simile; "My dog looks like a bank guard on duty" is a simile.

Thinking About Simile

- Point out the similes in "Velvet Shoes." What comparisons is Wylie making? Compare and contrast the items she compares.

Langston Hughes

Dreams

Hold fast to dreams
For if dreams die
Life is a broken-winged bird
That cannot fly.

Hold fast to dreams
For when dreams go
Life is a barren field
Frozen with snow.

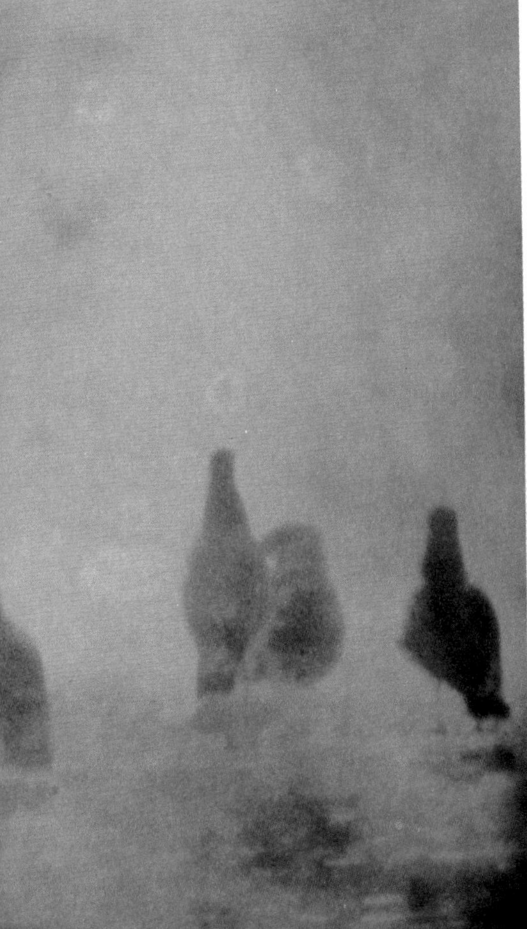

STUDY QUESTIONS

Recalling

1. According to the poem, what should we do with our dreams?
2. Give two traits of the bird mentioned in the first stanza.
3. Describe the field that is mentioned in the second stanza.
4. Under what conditions will the reader's life be like the bird or the field?

Interpreting

5. Define the word *dreams* as it is used in the poem.
6. What is the poet's attitude about a life without dreams?
7. Explain how the two stanzas are parallel.

Extending

8. Explain how dreams, as Hughes defines them, can make harsh situations more bearable.

LITERARY FOCUS

Metaphor

A **metaphor** is a figure of speech that makes an implied comparison between two seemingly unlike things. Unlike a simile, a metaphor does not use a comparing word such as *like* or *as.* For example, "My hand is like a starfish" is a simile, but "My hand is a starfish" is a metaphor. Metaphors excite our imaginations by finding surprising similarities in objects that we would not normally consider alike.

Thinking About Metaphor

1. Point out the metaphors in "Dreams." What comparisons is Hughes making? What similarities can you find in the things being compared?
2. Explain how these particular metaphors make Hughes's warning more powerful.

LITERARY OPTION

- metaphor

THEMATIC OPTION

- the necessity of dreams

METAPHOR

The poet links two poignant metaphors: a broken-winged bird and a barren, snow-covered field. The simplicity of both images reinforces their essences—frustration and emptiness.

WORD CHOICE

The first stanza's *if* suggests that dreams might die, while the second stanza's *when* insists they *will.* The poet's warning has gained considerable urgency (ll. 2, 6).

REFLECTING ON THE POEM

Do you think the poet has experienced life without dreams? (Answers may suggest that the moving images indicate that the poet experienced periods without dreams or knew people who did.)

STUDY QUESTIONS

1. hold fast to them
2. has broken wing; cannot fly
3. barren; frozen with snow
4. if or when dreams die
5. "hopes for the future"
6. futile, empty, sterile
7. first lines use same words, second lines change one word, third lines contain "Life is" and metaphor that concludes in fourth lines
8. Dreams of better future make present more tolerable, create goals to strive toward.

LITERARY FOCUS

1.
   - lines 2–3; 7–8
   - compares life without dreams to barren field, to injured bird
   - similarities: inability to fulfill purpose
2. They offer concrete examples.

AT A GLANCE

- The speaker describes a park scene as displayed in a pool's reflection.
- A swan swims into the scene, destroying the images.

LITERARY OPTIONS

- metaphor
- imagery

THEMATIC OPTIONS

- responding to nature
- originality

SPEAKER

The speaker of this poem—probably the poet—is keenly observant and willing to enjoy the surprises she sees in the water's surface.

METAPHOR

Swenson uses metaphors to show how things are not what they seem. These metaphors emphasize distortion: chimneys as bent legs, the bridge as an eye, cherry blossoms as roots, and the hill as a bowl (ll. 4–6, 9–11, 18–21).

IMAGERY

The poem is an extended image, a vivid word picture of the magical world of a pond's surface. The scene's quiet, peaceful subjects—a baby feeding ducks, birds coasting on air, children eating peanuts—are made slightly less quiet and peaceful by being reversed.

REFLECTING ON THE POEM

How do you think seeing this "water picture" made the writer feel? (She may have felt surprised, amused, fascinated.)

May Swenson

Water Picture

In the pond in the park
all things are doubled:
Long buildings hang and
wriggle gently. Chimneys
are bent legs bouncing
on clouds below. A flag
wags like a fishhook
down there in the sky.

The arched stone bridge
is an eye, with underlid
in the water. In its lens
dip crinkled heads with hats
that don't fall off. Dogs go by,
barking on their backs.
A baby, taken to feed the
ducks, dangles upside-down,
a pink balloon for a buoy.

Treetops deploy[1] a haze of
cherry bloom for roots,
where birds coast belly-up
in the glass bowl of a hill;
from its bottom a bunch
of peanut-munching children
is suspended by their
sneakers, waveringly.

A swan, with twin necks
forming the figure three,
steers between two dimpled
towers doubled. Fondly
hissing, she kisses herself,
and all the scene is troubled:
water-windows splinter,
tree-limbs tangle, the bridge
folds like a fan.

1. **deploy** [di ploi′]: spread out.

STUDY QUESTIONS

Recalling

1 What is the setting of the poem?
2. Name at least six objects that are part of the scene.
3. Describe the swan that appears in the fourth stanza.
4. What causes the scene to become "troubled"?

Interpreting

5. Explain the phrase "all things are doubled."
6. Describe three of the distorted images in the poem. What words tell you that each object is not real?
7. When "the scene is troubled," in what ways does the poet's view change?

Extending

8. From literature, mythology, and life, give examples of the fascination that people seem to have with mirror images.

COMPOSITION

Writing About Poetry

- Explain what techniques reveal the meaning of "Water Picture." First, explain the meaning of the poem. Then, tell what techniques the author uses to reveal this meaning. Techniques include speaker, sound, imagery, and figures of speech. *For help with this assignment, see Lesson 10 in the Writing About Literature Handbook at the back of this book.*

Writing a Description

- Write a poem or a paragraph in which you describe an object, scene, or event that is recognizable but distorted. Choose one of the following ideas: (a) seeing through a red glass window, (b) hearing with earmuffs on, (c) touching with thick mittens, (d) tasting with your nose pinched shut.

STUDY QUESTIONS

1. urban park with pond, bridge
2. buildings, bridge, people, dogs, baby, swan
3. seems to have two necks and to pass between two towers
4. swan's movement
5. includes objects and reflections
6. baby "dangles upside-down"; children "suspended by . . . sneakers"; bridge folds "like a fan"
7. movement of swan shatters reflection
8. ▪ *literature:* Snow White's stepmother, Alice/Looking Glass
   ▪ *mythology:* Narcissus/pool
   ▪ *life:* concern with appearance; fun house mirrors

COMPOSITION: GUIDELINES FOR EVALUATION

WRITING ABOUT POETRY

Objective

To explicate a poem by discussing its figures of speech and other poetic devices

Guidelines for Evaluation

- suggested length: three to five paragraphs
- should summarize meaning of poem
- should name poetic techniques that contribute to meaning: rhythm, rhyme, repetition, simile, metaphor, personification

WRITING A DESCRIPTION

Objective

To describe a scene in which senses are fooled

Guidelines for Evaluation

- suggested length: short poem or one prose paragraph
- should identify cause of distortion
- should present three results of distortion
- should use figurative language

AT A GLANCE

- The speaker suggests that "All the world's a stage" and that each person plays many parts.
- The speaker catalogs the ages of man: infant, schoolboy, lover, soldier, judge, old man trying to look young, old man with physical and mental losses.

LITERARY OPTIONS

- extended metaphor
- imagery

THEMATIC OPTIONS

- the human life cycle
- life and art

SPEAKER

Jaques (a character in *As You Like It*) is the speaker. His cynical eye notes that people are "merely players," "mewling and puking," "whining," "creeping," etc. Clearly, he believes that people are laughable, predictable creatures.

EXTENDED METAPHOR

The poem begins with a reference to a stage and players with exits and entrances; it goes on to describe roles, costumes, actions, and the ways of playing parts. The extended metaphor links life and theater.

IMAGERY

Images appeal to sight and hearing: The schoolboy creeps "like snail"; the lover sighs "like furnace"; the soldier seeks reputation "in the cannon's mouth"; the old man's sound has "pipes / And whistles" (ll. 8, 10, 15, 25).

MAIN IDEA

The poet states directly that life has "seven ages" or stages, then proceeds to prove his case by detailing each stage. Because he includes such recognizable detail, the reader is apt to agree with his analysis of human experience (ll. 4–5).

William Shakespeare

The Seven Ages of Man

All the world's a stage,
And all the men and women merely players;
They have their exits and their entrances;
And one man in his time plays many parts,
His acts being seven ages. At first the infant,
Mewling[1] and puking in the nurse's arms;
Then the whining school-boy, with his satchel[2]
And shining morning face, creeping like snail
Unwillingly to school. And then the lover,
Sighing like furnace, with a woeful ballad
Made to his mistress' eyebrow. Then a soldier,
Full of strange oaths, and bearded like the pard,[3]
Jealous in honor,[4] sudden and quick in quarrel,
Seeking the bubble reputation
Even in the cannon's mouth. And then the justice,
In fair round belly with good capon[5] lin'd,
With eyes severe and beard of formal cut,
Full of wise saws and modern instances;[6]
And so he plays his part. The sixth age shifts
Into the lean and slipper'd pantaloon,[7]
With spectacles on nose and pouch on side;
His youthful hose,[8] well sav'd, a world too wide
For his shrunk shank;[9] and his big manly voice,
Turning again toward childish treble,[10] pipes
And whistles in his sound. Last scene of all,
That ends this strange eventful history,
Is second childishness and mere oblivion;[11]
Sans[12] teeth, sans eyes, sans taste, sans everything.

---

1. **Mewling** [mūl'ing]: crying weakly, whimpering.
2. **satchel** [sach'əl]: bag for carrying books or other articles.
3. **pard:** leopard.
4. **Jealous in honor:** careful to defend his reputation.
5. **capon** [kā'pon]: chicken.
6. **saws and modern instances:** familiar old sayings and trite examples.
7. **pantaloon** [pant'əl o͞on']: stock character in Italian comedy, a foolish old man wearing pantaloons, or tight-fitting trousers.
8. **hose** [hōz]: close-fitting trousers like tights.
9. **shrunk shank:** shrunken leg.
10. **treble** [treb'əl]: high-pitched voice.
11. **oblivion:** forgetfulness, senility.
12. **Sans:** without.

REFLECTING ON THE POEM

What aspects of Shakespeare's seven ages can still be seen today? (Answers will probably suggest that all seven exist today. Shakespeare's accurate, universal images allow the reader to see the "timeless" nature of the seven ages.)

The Seven Ages of Man, William Mulready (1786-1863). Victoria and Albert Museum, London.

STUDY QUESTIONS

Recalling

1. This poem is actually a speech from Shakespeare's comedy *As You Like It,* spoken by a character named Jaques [jā'kwēz]. To what does Jaques compare the world and all its men and women?
2. Name the seven stages of human life according to Jaques.
3. At the end of the poem, Jaques describes man as being "sans," or without, what things?

Interpreting

4. What is the implied meaning of "exits" and "entrances"?
5. Give an image that represents each stage. What metaphors and similes are used to describe the different stages?
6. Find places in the poem where Jaques seems to be making fun of his subject. Show that his attitude is maintained throughout the poem.
7. What is the effect of presenting an entire life in just twenty-eight lines?

Extending

8. In *As You Like It* Jaques is a cynic, a man who doubts the goodness and kindness of human beings. Explain how your reaction to the poem changes once you know Jaques' personality.

COMPARING POEMS

1. Choose two or more of the poems in this section: Haiku, "Hokku Poems," "A Narrow Fellow in the Grass," "Silver," "Velvet Shoes," "Dreams," "Water Picture," and "The Seven Ages of Man." Imagine that the scenes or events in the poems have been captured by a photographer. Compare the photographs. Which picture is more colorful, more detailed, more memorable, more meaningful? Give reasons for your opinions.
2. Compare the imagery and figurative language of two or more of the poems in this section. Which images and figures of speech are you more likely to remember? Why? What emotions do you associate with these memorable images and figures of speech?

STUDY QUESTIONS

1. a stage and actors
2. infancy, childhood, youth of a lover, later youth of a soldier, maturity and middle age of a judge, old age, senility
3. teeth, eyesight, taste, everything
4. death and birth
5.
   - infant: *mewling and puking*
   - child: *whining school boy*
   - lover: *sighing like furnace* (simile)
   - soldier: *bearded like the pard* (simile)
   - justice: *in fair round belly* (metaphor)
   - old age: *spectacles on nose*
   - senility: *second childishness*
6. He depicts unflattering images of each age.
7. makes generalization seem like universal truth
8. generalizations, negative views easier to understand when reader understands Jaques is a cynic

COMPARING POEMS

1.
   - "Haiku": simple, little detail, contrasts memorable
   - "Hokku": simple, little detail, could not capture sound, smell
   - "Fellow": startling images, would reveal snake's identity
   - "Silver": detailed, black/white
   - "Shoes": few details, black/white could not capture sound, texture
   - "Dreams": could capture images
   - "Picture": detailed, colorful, literal, would lose humor and mystery
   - "Man": would capture theme, not attitude
2.
   - "Haiku"/"Hokku": contain little figurative language; imagery, precise words are memorable
   - "Fellow": images for snake, fear
   - "Silver": sharp images
   - "Shoes": similes, imagery, quiet
   - "Dreams": metaphors and a warning
   - "Picture": sharp imagery, humor
   - "Man": vivid images, similes, cynicism

LITERARY FOCUS: Lyric Poetry

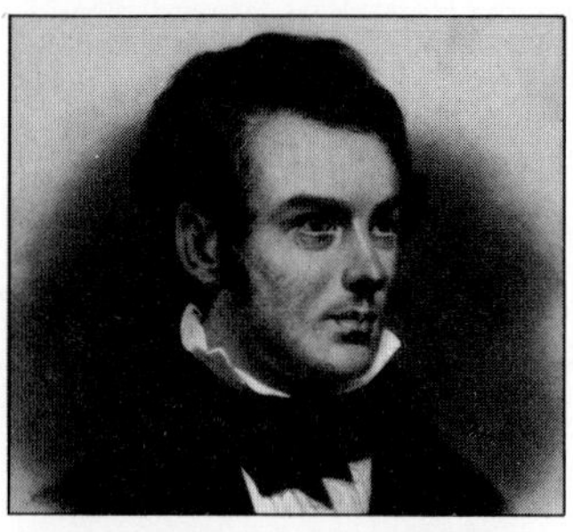

Lyric poetry is poetry in which the speaker reveals personal thoughts and feelings. *Lyric* comes from the Greek *lyrikos*, a short poem sung to the music of a lyre, a small harplike instrument.

Robert Burns (1759–1796), sometimes called the national poet of Scotland, was influenced by Scottish songs and folklore.

- What feelings of the speaker are typical of love songs?

William Wordsworth (1770–1850) called upon his early life in England's Lake District to write poems like "I Wandered Lonely as a Cloud." This lyric illustrates Wordsworth's conviction that poetry is the "spontaneous overflow of powerful feelings."

- Wordsworth uses a single cloud to suggest his loneliness. What natural object would you use to convey the same feeling?

Edna St. Vincent Millay (1892–1950) wrote political and social poetry later in her career, but her early work is lyrical and romantic. In "The Courage That My Mother Had," one of Millay's lyric poems, she expresses deeply personal feelings.

- Millay says she wishes she had her mother's courage. Do you think it takes courage to say what she says in this poem?

Photograph © 1982 by Jill Krementz

Gordon Parks (born 1912) is best known as a photographer and a poet. He was also the first black film director in Hollywood. "The Funeral" movingly compares a present-day setting with childhood memories.

- How believable do you find the poet's memory of this scene from his past? Can a person's powerful feelings be more "true" than any facts?

Claude McKay (1890–1948) was born in Jamaica, British West Indies, and came to the United States in 1912. McKay's musical lyric "The Tropics in New York" relies on images from both locations to create a vivid emotional impression.

- Has a certain place—a room, a street, a city—ever reminded you of another place? What details triggered your memory as they trigger McKay's memory in this poem?

N. Scott Momaday (born 1934) is a Kiowa Indian born in Lawton, Oklahoma. He grew up on various southwestern reservations and attended the University of New Mexico. Among his books are *House Made of Dawn*, awarded the Pulitzer Prize for fiction in 1969, *Angle of Geese and Other Poems* (1974), and *The Way to Rainy Mountain* (1969).

- How is the behavior of the child in the poem on page 216 typical of small children?

Evangelina Vigil-Piñón (born 1949) is a San Antonio native who currently resides in Houston, Texas, where she is an editor of *The Americas Review*. She is a fellow of the National Endowment of the Arts.

- Whether you live in a small community or a large metropolis, there is one thing that is completely your own. According to the poem on page 217, what is it?

Photograph © 1982 by Jill Krementz

Alice Walker (born 1944) has taught English and black studies. She frequently writes about women's concerns and experiences, and in "Women" she applauds her mother's generation.

- What details about the women in the poem on page 218 remind you of any people you have known?

LITERARY OPTIONS

- repetition
- exaggeration

THEMATIC OPTIONS

- love
- nature

EXAGGERATION

The smitten speaker uses exaggeration to insist that his love will endure extreme changes—seas going dry and rocks melting (ll. 8–10).

REPETITION

Burns uses repetition *(red red; my dear; seas gang dry)* to emphasize the speaker's enduring love (ll. 1, 7–11).

REFLECTING ON THE POEM

Is the poem an effective expression of love? (Some students may feel that exaggerations make a powerful statement, others that they make an empty one.)

STUDY QUESTIONS

1. compares love to rose, melody
2. the world ends; he dies
3. *fare thee weel; will come again*
4. "ten thousand mile"
5. lines 8, 9, 10, 16; to illustrate intensity of feelings
6. Soft, gentle sounds are suitable for love song.
7. has rhythm, rhyme; popular topic
8. Answers will vary.

VOCABULARY

1.
- *art thou:* "are you"
- *bonnie lass:* Scottish dialect for "pretty girl"

2.
- *a' the seas:* "all the seas"
- *gang:* Scottish dialect for "go"

3. *fare thee weel:* "farewell"

Robert Burns

My Love Is Like a Red Red Rose

My love is like a red red rose
    That's newly sprung in June:
My love is like the melodie
    That's sweetly played in tune.

So fair art thou, my bonnie lass,
    So deep in love am I:
And I will love thee still, my dear,
    Till a' the seas gang dry.

Till a' the seas gang dry, my dear,
    And the rocks melt wi' the sun:
And I will love thee still, my dear,
    While the sands o' life shall run.

And fare thee weel, my only love,
    And fare thee weel awhile!
And I will come again, my love,
    Tho' it were ten thousand mile.

STUDY QUESTIONS

Recalling

1. What two comparisons does the speaker make in the first stanza?
2. The speaker declares that he will love his "lass" until what two things happen?
3. What words in the last stanza show that the speaker is about to leave his love?
4. How far is he willing to travel to see her again?

Interpreting

5. Where in the poem does the speaker exaggerate? For what purpose does he overstate his feelings?
6. The poem contains only a few harsh consonant sounds. Explain how the resulting sound is suitable to the meaning of the poem.
7. Burns set some of his poems to traditional Scottish tunes. In what ways is this poem like a song?

Extending

8. Do you consider the very musical sound of this poem an important part of its effect or a distraction? Explain your opinion.

VOCABULARY

Recognizing Dialect

A **dialect** is a variation of a language spoken by a particular group. **Regional dialects** are particular to an area. Regional dialects differ from standard English because they contain words with different sounds, forms, and meanings. Robert Burns uses a type of Scottish dialect in this poem.

In the following lines from the poem, identify variations on standard English. Look up unfamiliar words in a dictionary; they may be listed as Scottish dialect. For each example of dialect, give the standard English word or form.

1. "So fair art thou, my bonnie lass,"
2. "Till a' the seas gang dry."
3. "And fare thee weel, my only love,"

Private collection

Detail, *The Daydream*, Ferdinand Hodler.

William Wordsworth

I Wandered Lonely as a Cloud

I wandered lonely as a cloud
That floats on high o'er vales[1] and hills,
When all at once I saw a crowd,
A host,[2] of golden daffodils;
Beside the lake, beneath the trees,
Fluttering and dancing in the breeze.

Continuous as the stars that shine
And twinkle on the Milky Way,[3]
They stretched in never-ending line
Along the margin of a bay:
Ten thousand saw I at a glance,
Tossing their heads in sprightly dance.

The waves beside them danced; but they
Outdid the sparkling waves in glee:
A poet could not but be gay,
In such a jocund[4] company:
I gazed—and gazed—but little thought
What wealth the show to me had brought:

For oft,[5] when on my couch I lie
In vacant or in pensive mood,[6]
They flash upon that inward eye
Which is the bliss of solitude;
And then my heart with pleasure fills,
And dances with the daffodils.

---

1. **o'er vales** [ôr vālz]: over valleys.
2. **host:** large number.
3. **Milky Way:** galaxy made up of more than a hundred billion stars and planets including Earth and its solar system.
4. **jocund** [jok'ənd]: cheerful.
5. **oft:** often.
6. **In vacant . . . mood:** in an idle or in a thoughtful mood.

STUDY QUESTIONS

Recalling

1. When did the speaker see the daffodils?
2. In what lines does the speaker tell us that the daffodils were numerous?
3. Describe the scene that surrounds the flowers.
4. According to the speaker, in what activity do the flowers take part?
5. At what times does the speaker remember the flowery scene? What effect does the memory have on his mood?

Interpreting

6. What was the speaker's mood before he saw the daffodils? How do you know?
7. Find three examples of personification in the poem. What human characteristics are given to nonhuman things?
8. What is the speaker's "inward eye"? Why is it the "bliss of solitude"?
9. Where does Wordsworth change word order for the sake of rhythm? Do you think the new word order adds to or takes away from the poem's sound?

Extending

10. Wordsworth once described poetry as "powerful feelings recollected in tranquility." Explain how this famous phrase relates to "I Wandered Lonely as a Cloud."

VIEWPOINT

Wordsworth's lyric poem is known for its vivid images and music. Not all critics, however, have found it flawless. One writer said that the final stanza

> is tacked on; more than that, it is prose commentary. . . [and] ought to have been worked into the poem, never permitted to stand in isolation, sticking out like a sore thumb from the rest.
>
> —E. Daniels, *The Art of Reading Poetry*

- Do you agree with the critic, or do you think the last stanza is connected smoothly with the rest of the poem? Why might the last stanza be called prose?

LITERARY OPTIONS

- personification
- main idea

THEMATIC OPTIONS

- memory
- nature

PERSONIFICATION

The poet turns daffodils and waves into companions with whom his heart can "dance" (ll. 12–13, 24–25).

MAIN IDEA

The poet describes his memory's ability to change his "vacant" or "pensive" mood to pleasure (ll. 20–24). He feels the seemingly trivial moment brought him great and unexpected "wealth" (l. 18).

REFLECTING ON THE POEM

What other memories can reawaken feelings? (Recalling something funny can make one laugh again; recalling an insult might bring back anger.)

STUDY QUESTIONS

1. while wandering by himself
2. lines 3, 4, 7–11
3. They bloom beneath trees along a bay; a breeze blows.
4. toss their heads in dance
5. at rest, in deep thought; changes his mood to joy
6. Line 1 says he was lonely.
7. poet's heart, daffodils, waves; to dance they need legs, ability to feel joy
8. memory; memories are the only company for a solitary person
9. lines 11, 18, 23; adds to sound and meaning
10. First three stanzas describe experience; last stanza recalls event in tranquility.

VIEWPOINT

Answers will vary.

- Last stanza develops thematically from rest of poem, changes mood, becomes more abstract.
- It is more abstract and literal; it has less imagery and figurative language.

LITERARY OPTIONS

- rhyme
- main idea

THEMATIC OPTIONS

- courage in the face of loss
- families

RHYME

The poem's *abab* rhyme scheme includes approximate rhymes (*had/quarried, grave/have)* and fits the poem's simple, direct language. Rhymes give each stanza an air of finality that mirrors final loss (ll. 1–12).

MAIN IDEA

Loss leads the speaker to turn to her inheritance as a consolation, yet she yearns for a less tangible inheritance.

REFLECTING ON THE POEM

What do people inherit, other than material things? (Possible answers include physical characteristics, certain health conditions, temperament, and the truths and values parents teach.)

STUDY QUESTIONS

1. It is buried with her.
2. a rock
3. gold brooch; treasures it; would exchange it for courage
4. *literal:* New England rock has returned to hills; *figurative:* rocklike courage has been buried with mother in hills
5. Granite is less decorative but more useful, durable, and secure; courage is more valuable trait.
6. regret; discordant note of the approximate rhyme
7. reminder of meaningful event or special person

Edna St. Vincent Millay

The Courage That My Mother Had

The courage that my mother had
Went with her, and is with her still:
Rock from New England quarried;
Now granite in a granite hill.

The golden brooch[1] my mother wore
She left behind for me to wear;
I have no thing I treasure more:
Yet, it is something I could spare.

Oh, if instead she'd left to me
The thing she took into the grave!—
That courage like a rock, which she
Has no more need of, and I have.

1. **brooch** [brōch]: ornamental pin.

STUDY QUESTIONS

Recalling

1. What has happened to the courage of the speaker's mother?
2. To what does the speaker compare her mother's courage?
3. What possession did her mother leave behind? What different feelings does the speaker have toward this possession? What inheritance would she have preferred?

Interpreting

4. Explain in your own words the literal meaning of lines 3 and 4. Then explain the figurative meaning of the lines.
5. What message is implied in the contrast between granite and gold?
6. Describe the mood of the speaker. Explain how the poet shows the strength of the emotion in the last stanza.

Extending

7. Explain why a person might value a possession as a "treasure" though it has no monetary value.

COMPOSITION

Writing About Poetry

■ Explain what poetic techniques influence your reaction to Millay's poem. First describe your reaction to the poem. Then tell what words, figures of speech, and sounds prompted your feeling. *For help with this assignment, see Lesson 10 in the Writing About Literature Handbook at the back of this book.*

Writing with Rhyme

■ Write a four-line poem with the rhyme scheme of Millay's poem—*abab*. Use any topic you wish or one of the following: the first day of a long vacation, helpful hints on learning to swim, or travel directions to a new neighbor.

COMPOSITION: GUIDELINES FOR EVALUATION

WRITING ABOUT POETRY

Objective

To support personal opinion with reasons and examples

Guidelines for Evaluation

- suggested length: two to three paragraphs
- should state reaction to poem
- should give reasons for reaction
- should support reasons with examples of poet's use of word choice, figurative language, sound

WRITING WITH RHYME

Objective

To write a four-line poem

Guidelines for Evaluation

- suggested length: four lines
- should demonstrate an *abab* rhyme
- should more closely resemble poetry than rhymed prose

Gordon Parks

The Funeral

After many snows I was home again.
Time had whittled[1] down to mere hills
The great mountains of my childhood.
Raging rivers I once swam trickled now
like gentle streams.
And the wide road curving on to China or
Kansas City or perhaps Calcutta,[2]
Had withered to a crooked path of dust
Ending abruptly at the county burying ground.
Only the giant who was my father
remained the same.
A hundred strong men strained beneath his coffin
When they bore him to his grave.

---

1. **whittled** [hwit′əld]: gradually reduced in size as if by whittling, or shaving away piece by piece with a knife.
2. **Calcutta** [kal kut′ə]: city in northeastern India.

STUDY QUESTIONS

Recalling

1. Where in the poem does the speaker tell us when he was last home? How much time has passed since then?
2. What have the "great mountains," "raging rivers," and "wide road" of the speaker's childhood now become?
3. Where does the road now end?
4. What one item has remained the same for the speaker?
5. How many men bore the father to his grave? What words show the great weight they carried?

Interpreting

6. Why have the speaker's impressions of the local mountains, rivers, and road changed?
7. What do you think the speaker means when he calls his father a "giant"? Why do you think this impression of his father has remained the same?
8. Why does Parks exaggerate in the last two lines?

Extending

9. What qualities do you think make a person a "giant" in the sense that Parks uses the word?

VOCABULARY

Connotations

Connotations are the unspoken or unwritten meanings associated with a word beyond its dictionary definition, or **denotation.** A word has many different connotations depending on the context in which it is used. The following words are from "The Funeral." For each word list at least two words that the poet could have used instead. Then explain what connotations the actual word has that make it the right word for the poem.

1. snows
2. trickled
3. curving
4. crooked
5. giant

LITERARY OPTIONS

- word choice
- main idea

THEMATIC OPTIONS

- love and respect
- the passage of time

WORD CHOICE

Parks contrasts his childhood impression of the world's grandeur and mystery with his present diminished view—"raging rivers . . . trickled" and "the wide road curving on . . . Had withered to a crooked path of dust" (ll. 4, 6–8).

MAIN IDEA

Parks focuses on the gap between a child's and an adult's view of the world and stresses the passage of time in order to affirm what has not changed: his admiration for his father.

REFLECTING ON THE POEM

What other "death" might this poem be said to describe? (The speaker mourns also the death of his youthful vision of the world.)

STUDY QUESTIONS

1. line 1; "many snows"
2. hills; streams; a path
3. at burying ground
4. his father
5. one hundred; *strained, bore*
6. He has grown older.
7. He remembers him as great man; has retained childhood admiration.
8. to emphasize intensity of emotion
9. Answers should discuss such traits as compassion, tolerance, kindness.

VOCABULARY

1. *years, winters;* suggests years have been difficult
2. *flowed, ran;* suggests narrowness
3. *leading, running;* connotes road with limited vistas
4. *winding, narrow;* describes path
5. *man, corpse;* reveals admiration

AT A GLANCE

- The speaker describes a New York fruit stand that reminds him of his tropical home.
- He longs for home and weeps.

LITERARY OPTIONS

- imagery
- rhyme

THEMATIC OPTIONS

- nostalgia
- aspects of loss

SPEAKER

The poet introduces the speaker—a person from the tropics living in New York—after richly describing the present scene and past memories. The speaker's reaction in the last stanza is thus given added emphasis (ll. 9–12).

IMAGERY

McKay evokes devotion and reverence for his childhood home by using religious language: *parish, mystical, benediction, nunlike,* and *bowed my head* (ll. 4, 7, 8, 12).

WORD CHOICE

The phrase *hungry for the old familiar ways* links the vision of tropical fruit (and physical hunger) with the speaker's spiritual hunger for his homeland (l. 11).

RHYME

McKay's rhymes and rhythm give the poem the measured tones of an invocation.

REFLECTING ON THE POEM

Do you think the speaker will ever return to his homeland? Why or why not? (Possible answers: Yes, he feels strongly enough to find a way to return; no, one can feel strongly about home and still not go back.)

Claude McKay

The Tropics in New York

Bananas ripe and green, the gingerroot,[1]
Cocoa in pods and alligator pears,[2]
And tangerines and mangoes[3] and grapefruit,
Fit for the highest prize at parish fairs,[4]

Set in the window, bringing memories
Of fruit trees laden by low-singing rills,[5]
And dewy dawns, and mystical blue skies
In benediction over nunlike hills.

My eyes grew dim, and I could no more gaze;
A wave of longing through my body swept,
And, hungry for the old familiar ways,
I turned aside and bowed my head and wept.

1. **gingerroot** [jin′jə ro͞ot]: aromatic, edible root of ginger plants.
2. **alligator pears:** avocados, pear-shaped fruit with a buttery texture and a nutty taste.
3. **mangoes:** yellowish-red, oval-shaped fruit with a sweet, spicy taste.
4. **parish fairs:** district festivals at which farmers enter their produce into competition.
5. **rills:** small streams.

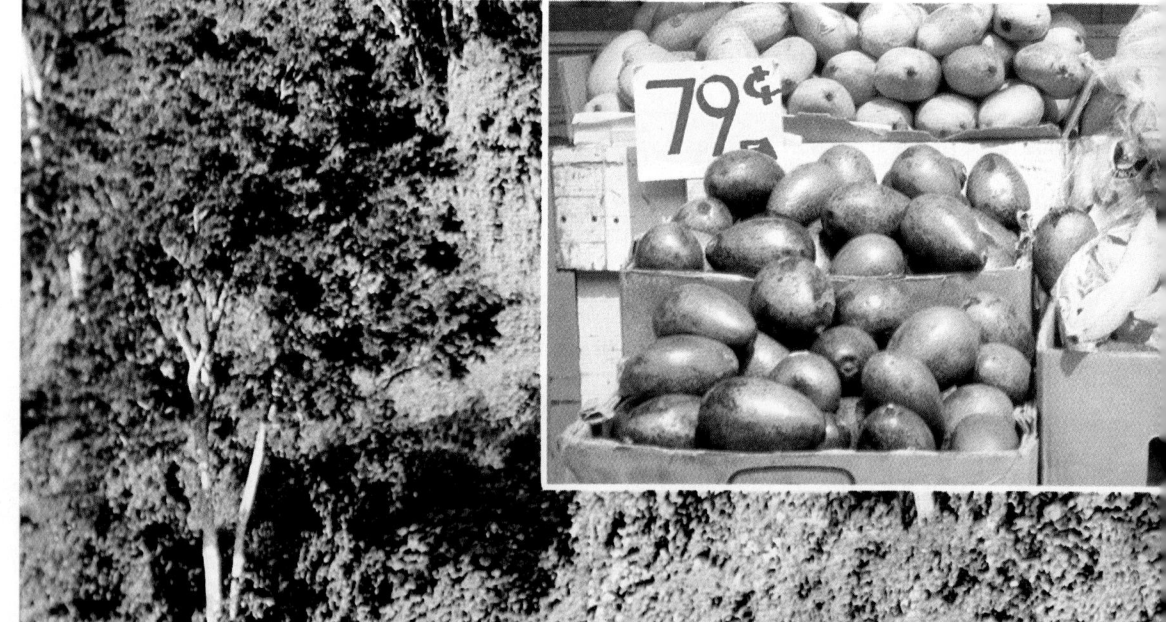

STUDY QUESTIONS

Recalling

1. Name five kinds of fruit mentioned in the first stanza.
2. Where is the fruit that the speaker sees?
3. What memories are caused by the sight of the fruit?
4. According to the last stanza, what sweeps through the speaker's body?
5. For what is the speaker "hungry"? What actions does this hunger cause?

Interpreting

6. Where in the poem do you find changes in mood? What are the moods?
7. In what ways is the title appropriate to the content of the poem?
8. In lines 7 and 8 what do the words *mystical, benediction,* and *nunlike* tell us about the speaker's attitude toward home?
9. What parts of the poem contain colorful images, and what part does not? What does this arrangement of images mean?

COMPOSITION

Writing About Poetry

■ An important part of lyric poetry is its sound. Explain how the sound of "The Tropics in New York" contributes to the meaning of the poem. First explain the meaning of the poem. Then discuss in general the rhyme, rhythm, and alliteration in the poem. Then tell in what ways the sound is different in each stanza. Finally, explain how the sound is appropriate to the message of the poem. *For help with this assignment, see Lesson 10 in the Writing About Literature Handbook at the back of this book.*

Writing a Poem

■ Write a poem of three stanzas. Each stanza should have at least two lines. In the first stanza describe specific objects that might remind someone of a particular place. In the second stanza describe the place that is recalled by the objects. In the third stanza record the feelings that are awakened by these memories. The poem need not rhyme.

STUDY QUESTIONS

1. bananas, avocados, tangerines, mangoes, grapefruit
2. in a store window
3. fruit trees, tropical streams, "dewy dawns," blue skies
4. a wave of longing
5. home; weeping
6. line 5: admiring fruit leads to reminiscing; line 9: nostalgia, sadness
7. memories bring tropics to New York; locates store window
8. suggest his spiritual feelings
9. ■ colorful: stanzas 1, 2; colorless: last stanza
   ■ contrasts former and present life

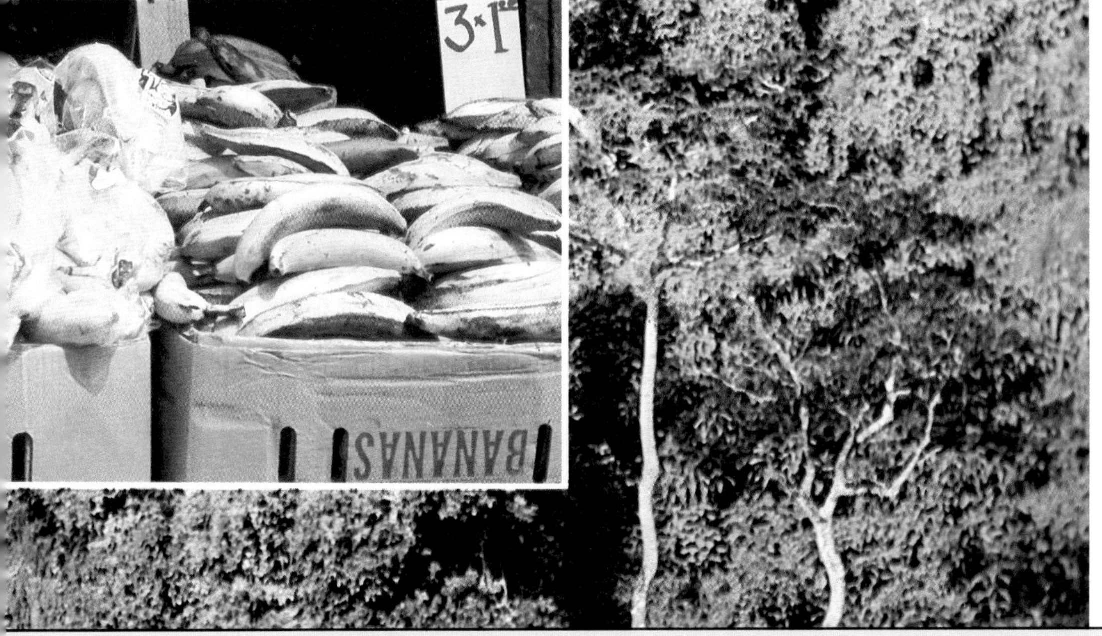

COMPOSITION: GUIDELINES FOR EVALUATION

WRITING ABOUT POETRY

Objective

To explain how sound contributes to poem

Guidelines for Evaluation

- suggested length: three to four paragraphs
- should discuss at least three sound devices
- should show how sound in each stanza changes to reflect mood change
- should cite examples of each sound device

WRITING A POEM

Objective

To write a poem about memories

Guidelines for Evaluation

- suggested length: six or more lines
- should follow prescribed sequence of stanzas: (1) description of objects; (2) description of place; (3) description of feelings
- should use appropriate imagery

LITERARY OPTIONS

- word choice
- imagery

THEMATIC OPTIONS

- youth vs. age
- aspects of nature

WORD CHOICE

Note the adjectives *small, intense,* and *whole,* which present the child as a compact, passionate bit of life in a vast landscape (ll. 1–2).

IMAGERY

With the image of sand drifts breaking like waves through the canyon, the poet suggests the similarity of child and sand as each moves through "cleavages of light / And shadow" (ll. 6–7).

REFLECTING ON THE POEM

How does the child seem to "embrace the spirit" of the canyon? (The child's arms seem ready to hug it; the child's response to nature is true and mighty.)

STUDY QUESTIONS

1. outstretched arms; in Canyon de Chelly
2. *small, intense, whole*
3. "The spirit of this place"
4. Lines 1 and 4 contrast the child's smallness with the canyon's vastness.
5. delight; *Running with Outstretched Arms; Embodied in delight; embrace / The spirit of this place*
6. shadows and light make sand drifts appear like waves
7. more open to experience, better able to forget worries and enjoy the immediate

N. Scott Momaday

To a Child Running with Outstretched Arms in Canyon de Chelly[1]

You are small and intense
In your excitement, whole,
Embodied in delight.
The backdrop is immense;

The sand drifts break and roll
Through cleavages of light
And shadow. You embrace
The spirit of this place.

1. **Canyon de Chelly** [kan′ yən də shā′]: national monument in northeastern Arizona, containing records of an ancient Native American civilization.

STUDY QUESTIONS

Recalling

1. According to the title, with what is the child running? Where does this action take place?
2. What three adjectives does the poet use to describe the child in the first stanza?
3. In stanza 2 what does the child embrace?

Interpreting

4. How does the poet contrast the child with the place where the poem is set? Quote specific lines to support your answer.
5. What is the child's attitude toward the setting? Which images in particular suggest the child's emotional response to the place?
6. Summarize the meaning of lines 5 and 6.

Extending

7. Why do you think children are sometimes better able to enjoy nature than adults?

COMPOSITION

Writing About Imagery

■ Momaday uses images of light and dark, land and water, and largeness and smallness. In a paragraph explain how these contrasting images create a vivid picture. Give specific examples from the poem. Then relate the images to the meaning of the poem.

Writing a Description

■ In a short poem or paragraph describe a landscape that is undergoing a sudden physical change. A scene might shift from dark to light, dry to wet, or hot to cold. You might, for example, describe moving shadows, a tornado, a snow squall, or a surprise downpour. Rely on your senses to create a vivid and shifting picture.

COMPOSITION: GUIDELINES FOR EVALUATION

WRITING ABOUT IMAGERY

Objective

To explain how images create a picture and relate to meaning

Guidelines for Evaluation

- suggested length: two to three paragraphs
- should refer to images: light and dark, land and water, large and small
- should explain how images make a vivid picture

WRITING A DESCRIPTION

Objective

To write a description of sudden physical change in the landscape

Guidelines for Evaluation

- suggested length: three four-line stanzas or two to three paragraphs
- should describe initial landscape, how it changes, and its final appearance
- should rely on sensory imagery

Evangelina Vigil-Piñón

space

privacy that no one owns
a silent moment
outdoors, in the city
the shade of a tree at a park
a vacant table at a library
your own office window with your own view
beaches and sea
body-free
your own breath of air
an expansive horizon
viewed by many
but singularly

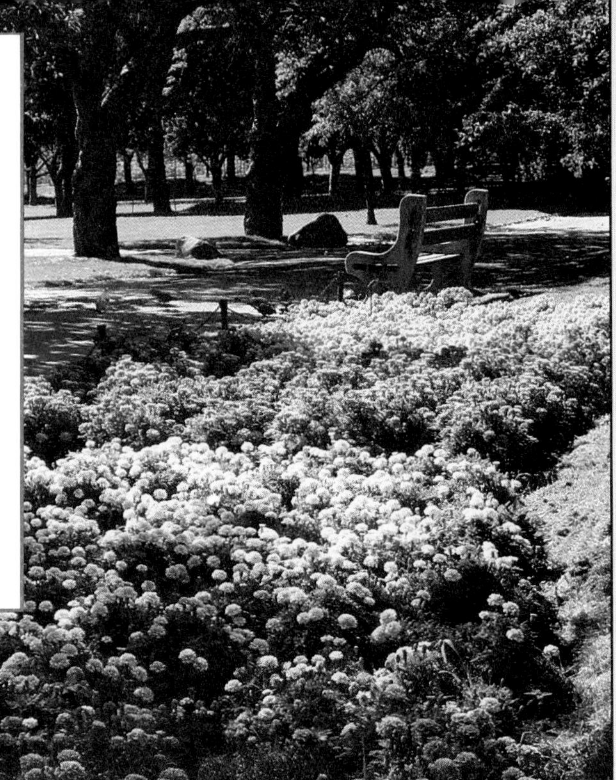

STUDY QUESTIONS

Recalling

1. According to the speaker, what does no one own?
2. Name each of the spaces mentioned in the poem.
3. What is "viewed by many"?

Interpreting

4. Which of the spaces described in the poem are not actual physical spaces? What are they?
5. Why might Vigil-Piñón have omitted capital letters and standard punctuation in her poem? What effect do these omissions have on the poem's meaning?
6. According to the poem, do you have to be alone to achieve a sense of space? Refer to specific lines.
7. In what ways can an experience be "viewed by many/but singularly"?

Extending

8. What are some of the ways people react when they do not get enough physical space? Psychological space?

COMPOSITION

Writing About Structure

■ Structure refers to how something is built, organized, or put together. In "space" Vigil-Piñón abandons traditional sentence structure. In a paragraph describe how she "builds" or structures her lines without using traditional sentences. End by stating how the poet's technique enhances the poem's meaning.

Writing a Poem

■ Write a poem of at least six lines that describes a favorite private space. In the title name the space, following that name with a comma and the words "a Private Space." In each of the lines of your poem, include one vivid description of an aspect of your special space. You may wish to omit standard sentence structure, capitalization, and punctuation.

LITERARY OPTIONS

- repetition
- rhyme
- lyric poetry

THEMATIC OPTIONS

- individuality
- privacy

REPETITION

Repetition of *own* and *owns* underscore the poet's interest in a certain kind of possession—moments of privacy that give people a sense of themselves (ll. 1, 6, 9).

RHYME

Nine words end with the long *e* sound: *privacy, city, tree, library, sea, body-free, many, singularly*. These rhymes give the poem a high, bright sound.

REFLECTING ON THE POEM

What do you think the title "space" means? (Space allows people to experience themselves as alive and separate.)

STUDY QUESTIONS

1. privacy
2. silent moment, shade of tree at park, vacant table, office window view, beaches and sea, breath of air, horizon
3. an expansive horizon
4. privacy, silent moment, breath of air; psychological spaces
5. to minimize barriers between images and thoughts in order to create sense of open space; underscores theme of individual perceptions and taste
6. No; several "private" spaces suggest proximity to others: *city, park, library, office.*
7. Each interprets individually.
8. argue, hoard, or hide belongings, become ill; sever contact with surroundings, become enmeshed in others' problems, suffer stress

COMPOSITION: GUIDELINES FOR EVALUATION

WRITING ABOUT STRUCTURE

Objective

To write about the structure of a poem

Guidelines for Evaluation

- suggested length: two paragraphs
- should describe particulars of structure
- should state how non–traditional structures help to express sense of openness

WRITING A POEM

Objective

To write a poem that describes a private space

Guidelines for Evaluation

- suggested length: at least six lines
- should describe a favorite private space
- each line should have one vivid description of some aspect of the space

AT A GLANCE

- The speaker praises the women of her mother's generation for their strength and hard work.
- Their work helped provide their children with an education and "a place."

LITERARY OPTIONS

- imagery
- parallelism

THEMATIC OPTIONS

- relations between generations
- social change

IMAGERY

Women's strength and persistence are conveyed through the juxtaposition of images of battle with those of domestic chores: *fists as well as / Hands; battered down / Doors / And ironed / Starched white / Shirts; led / Armies / . . . Across mined / Fields* (ll. 5–16).

MAIN IDEA

Although the author uses powerful images of warfare, they lead—perhaps surprisingly—to a peaceful end: the women's discovery of books, desks, and necessary knowledge for their children.

PARALLELISM

Two similar phrases describe the mother's generation: *Husky of voice* and *Stout of / Step*. Much of the rest of the poem takes the form of three exclamations, each beginning with the words *How they* (ll. 3–4, 7, 12, 22).

REFLECTING ON THE POEM

What kinds of social change have been won by leaders fighting for rights or conditions that they do not have? (Answers may include abolition of slavery, women's suffrage, civil rights, etc.)

Alice Walker

Women

They were women then
My mama's generation
Husky of voice—Stout of
Step
With fists as well as
Hands
How they battered down
Doors
And ironed
Starched white
Shirts
How they led
Armies
Headragged[1] Generals
Across mined[2]
Fields
Booby-trapped[3]
Ditches
To discover books
Desks
A place for us
How they knew what we
Must know
Without knowing a page
Of it
Themselves.

1. **Headragged** [hed′ragd]: with heads covered by kerchiefs.
2. **mined:** containing secret, buried weapons.
3. **Booby-trapped:** containing a dangerous trick or device that is disguised to seem harmless.

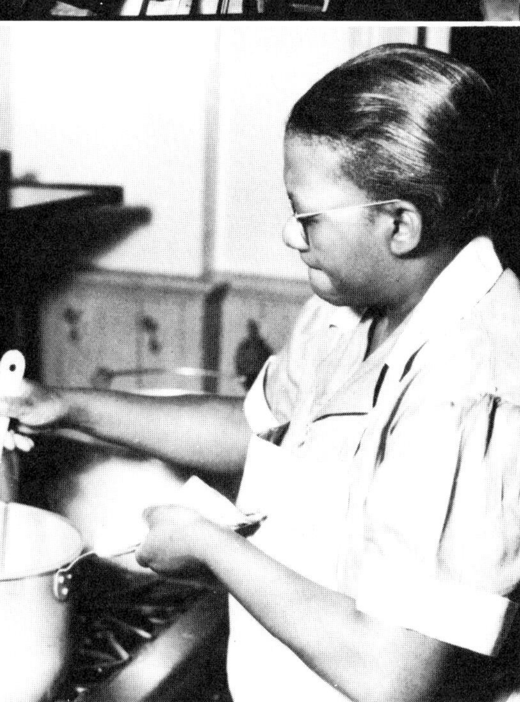

STUDY QUESTIONS

Recalling

1. From what generation do the women of the poem come?
2. What physical characteristics are given the women in the first six lines?
3. Find three activities of these women.
4. What three things did they discover?

Interpreting

5. What words and images in the poem show the strength of the women?
6. Explain the last five lines of the poem. Why do you think the poet italicized the word *must*?
7. What improvements does the poem imply have taken place from one generation to the next? What has been lost?

Extending

8. Explain how sacrifice and hardship can be positive experiences.

COMPARING POEMS

1. Compare two or more of the poems in this section (pages 210–218). What are the different emotions in each poem? In what ways does each poet inspire the reader to share these feelings?
2. Since the lyric poem conveys emotion, it often indirectly gives information about the speaker. Compare two or more of the poems in this section. What do you learn about the speakers of each poem? Explain how the poems convey this information.
3. Lyric poetry is musical. Compare two or more of the poems in this section. To what extent does each poem's sound help to capture the emotion of the poem? Be sure to point out specific techniques of sound that each poem uses.

STUDY QUESTIONS

1. generation of speaker's mother
2. husky voices, firm steps, hands that can be used as fists
3. battered down doors, led armies, ironed shirts
4. books, desks, place for children
5. All suggest strength.
6. Women realized importance of education; it emphasizes this message.
7. *improvements:* better education, greater opportunities; *lost:* strength and determination
8. Answers will vary.

COMPARING POEMS

1.
   - "Rose": love; rhythms, exaggerations
   - "Cloud": pleasure; imagery
   - "Courage": loss; contrasts
   - "Funeral": admiration and respect; contrast between past and present
   - "Tropics": nostalgia; images
   - "Women": admiration; rhythm, imagery
2.
   - "Rose": Exaggerations suggest speaker's ardor.
   - "Cloud": Speaker is solitary person; first, last stanzas convey loneliness.
   - "Courage": Speaker is female, mother is from New England.
   - "Funeral": Speaker's long absence due to his/her seeking destiny in faraway city.
   - "Tropics": Speaker is a stranger from warmer climate.
   - "Women": Speaker probably a woman, better educated than mother.
3.
   - "Rose": Soft *l, r* sounds hook reader; repetition, meter are fitting for love song.
   - "Cloud": rhyme and rhythm
   - "Courage": Hard consonants, rhyme, rhythm emphasize regret.
   - "Funeral": Assonance, word choice, metric variations underscore important images.
   - "Tropics": Exotic sounds help reader share nostalgia.
   - "Women": Consonants and various line lengths emphasize strength.

LITERARY FOCUS: The Total Effect

A poem, even more than a short story or an essay, is meant to be an experience for the reader. The experience of poetry treats our senses, challenges our imaginations, and tugs at our emotions. This unique response to poetry is its total effect, the sum of message and technique.

Each of the poets represented on the following pages creates for us a unique total effect.

E. (Edward) E. (Estlin) Cummings (1894–1962) experimented with the look of his poems, bending the rules of spelling, capitalization, punctuation, and word arrangement. In "maggie and milly and molly and may" he plays with several poetic devices to create a unique total effect.

- Which of the four characters in this poem does what you would probably do?

David Wagoner (born 1926) has studied with poet Theodore Roethke (pages 175, 178), and he himself teaches at the University of Washington in Seattle. "Lament for the Non-Swimmers" concerns people with whom Wagoner sympathizes, people who are "out of their element."

- What does it mean to feel "like a fish out of water"? Do the people in this poem share that feeling?

Carl Sandburg (1878–1967) became known as a typically American voice through poetry that carries on the themes and style of Walt Whitman. In "Lost" he fills a simple scene with deep emotion.

- Have you ever been lost? Why do you think the image of a lost child—like the one in this poem—has such a powerful appeal?

Robert Herrick (1591–1674) apprenticed as a goldsmith, studied law, and eventually became a clergyman. He served in the English countryside, where he studied colorful rural customs. Herrick's poetry, including "To Daffodils," is often about love and the passage of time.

- What element in nature makes you most aware of the passing of time? Do you think Herrick would agree with you?

Walt Whitman (1819–1892) began working as a carpenter before his twelfth birthday. He also worked as a printer, teacher, and editor and was a volunteer nurse during the Civil War. Whitman's poetry is known for its free rhythms and lack of rhyme. "I Hear America Singing" presents an example of Whitman's enthusiasm for American democracy and individualism.

- Do you think Whitman's belief in American individuals is as justified today as it was when he wrote the poem?

MODEL FOR ACTIVE READING

The annotations in the Pupil's Edition that accompany this poem bring to students' attention each of the elements of poetry along with various techniques of poetry. Review the five steps under "Reminders for Active Reading of Poetry" (page 222), and have students tell how each has been illustrated in one or two of the poems they have studied. Then have students apply each of the five reminders to Cummings' poem, by pointing to specific verses / lines in the poem and notations in the text.

The Total Effect

When you first read a poem, you should try to experience and enjoy it as a whole. This introduction to a poem should include two readings, one aloud and one silent. Appreciate the sound; allow specific images to seize your imagination. Only then should you zoom in on details, study techniques, and interpret the message. Once you are comfortable with the poem, a final reading will allow you to feel its total effect.

Analyzing a poem is easier when you know what to look for. Of course, no two people respond in exactly the same way to a poem. An active reader, however, will always consider the following points as an important step to understanding any poem.

Reminders for Active Reading of Poetry

1. The **title** will direct you to the poet's major concern.
2. The **speaker** is the person or thing that is the voice in a poem. The **choice of words** should fit the speaker.
3. The **sound** of the poem—its use of rhyme, rhythm, onomatopoeia, repetition, alliteration, assonance, and parallelism—should suit its subject and mood.
4. **Imagery** and **figures of speech**, such as personification, simile, and metaphor, should allow the poem to appeal directly to your senses and, therefore, to your own experience.
5. A **narrative poem** tells a story; a **lyric poem** expresses emotions.

Model for Active Reading

With the following poem, "maggie and milly and molly and may" by E. E. Cummings, you can see how an alert reader approaches poetry. First read the poem aloud, and then read it silently. Then consider the marginal notations as an aid in understanding the poem. Finally read the poem again to appreciate its total effect. Afterward you can use this process as you read other poetry.

E. E. Cummings

maggie and milly and molly and may

maggie and milly and molly and may
went down to the beach (to play one day)

and maggie discovered a shell that sang
so sweetly she couldn't remember her troubles, and

milly befriended a stranded star
whose rays five languid fingers were;

and molly was chased by a horrible thing
which raced sideways while blowing bubbles and

may came home with a smooth round stone
as small as a world and as large as alone.

For whatever we lose (like a you or a me)
it's always ourselves we find in the sea

Alliteration (p. 195): The repetition of the *m* sound gives the first line a musical sound. **Assonance** (p. 195) repeats vowel sounds in line 9.

Personification (p. 201): The singing shell is a nonhuman thing with human qualities.

Metaphor (p. 203): This is an implied comparison between the rays of a star and fingers.

Simile (p. 202): The stone is directly compared, using the word *as*, to a world and to being alone.

Rhyme (p. 187) **and Rhythm** (p. 185): The last two lines are *end rhyme.* Some lines have *approximate rhyme* (sang/thing, star/were). The *rhyme scheme* is *aa/bc/dd/bc/ee/ff.* The *meter* is somewhat irregular.

STUDY QUESTIONS

Recalling

1. Where did Maggie, Milly, Molly, and May go? Why?
2. What did Maggie find? What effect did it have on her?
3. Describe the item that Milly "befriended."
4. Give two details to describe the thing that chased Molly.
5. What item did May bring home?

Interpreting

6. Explain the only capital letter in the poem.
7. Why do you think the speaker chooses not to name the "horrible thing" that chased Molly?
8. Explain the last two lines of the poem.
9. What can we infer about the personality of each girl from what she found in the sea?

Extending

10. Do you agree with Cummings' statement about the sea in the last stanza? Explain your opinion.

STUDY QUESTIONS

1. to the seashore; to play
2. a shell; helped her forget her troubles
3. a starfish
4. it raced sideways; blew bubbles
5. a stone
6. emphasizes theme
7. Description playfully identifies it as a crab.
8. Each girl's discovery reveals strong personal characteristics.
9.
   - Maggie: troubled; sea comforts her
   - Milly: friendly, poetic
   - Molly: timid, not inquisitive
   - May: alone in own small world
10. Answers will vary.

AT A GLANCE

Maggie, Milly, Molly, and May go to the beach. Each discovers a special part of herself in what she sees on the shore.

LITERARY OPTIONS

- alliteration
- assonance
- figurative language

THEMATIC OPTIONS

- effects of nature
- self-awareness

REFLECTING ON THE POEM

How do the four girls' reactions to finding themselves compare and contrast? (Maggie and Millie seem pleased, Molly seems to fear her discovery, and May's reaction is ambiguous.)

LITERARY OPTIONS

- personification
- simile

THEMATIC OPTIONS

- insecurity
- response to nature

PERSONIFICATION

Wagoner shows the non-swimmers' confusion and disjointedness by describing body parts as if they were alive and independent of each other: "their cupped hands hesitate" "Their bones believe in heaviness" (ll. 3, 6).

SIMILE

Non-swimmers are compared to herons. But unlike the birds the frightened people "hope for nothing / Under the surface," fearing "eels and sharks." Their imaginary fears force them to leave the water (ll. 13–15).

MAIN IDEA

The poet uses strong images (*fluttering, scissoring legs, knees touching*) to convey the non-swimmer's intense insecurity and discomfort in water (ll. 5, 11).

REFLECTING ON THE POEM

What might the non-swimmers "want" in line 4? (Answers might suggest that they want something they *know,* something solid to hold onto, or something that will grant them comfort and grace.)

David Wagoner

Lament for the Non-Swimmers

They never feel they can be well in the water,
Can come to rest, that their bodies are light.
When they reach out, their cupped hands hesitate:
What they wanted runs between their fingers.
Their fluttering, scissoring legs sink under.

Their bones believe in heaviness, their ears
Shake out the cold invasion of privacy,
Their eyes squeeze shut. Each breath,
Only half air, is too breath-taking.
The dead man's float seems strictly for dead men.

They stand in the shallows, their knees touching,
Their feet where they belong in the sand.
They wade as carefully as herons,[1] but hope for nothing
Under the surface, that wilderness
Where eels and sharks slip out of their element.

Those who tread water and call see their blurred eyes
Turn distant,[2] not away from a sky's reflection
As easy to cross as the dependable earth
But from a sight as blue as drowned men's faces.
They splash ashore, pretending to feel buoyant.

---

1. **herons** [her'ənz]: birds that wade along the shore hunting for fish.
2. **see . . . distant:** see the eyes of the nonswimmers look toward land.

STUDY QUESTIONS

Recalling

1. From the first two lines, give three ways that nonswimmers feel in the water.
2. Name four or five actions of the nonswimmers that show their fear of the water.
3. From the end of the poem, describe how the nonswimmers cover up their fear.

Interpreting

4. A lament is a poem that expresses serious grief. Do you think this poem is a lament? Why or why not?
5. Find the speaker's references to death. What do these references add to the poem's impact?
6. Find two images that describe the nonswimmers' being out of place in the water.

Extending

7. Explain how fear can be a sensible or a dangerous response to a situation.

COMPOSITION

Writing a Paraphrase

■ Sometimes the meaning of a poem is clear and direct, but sometimes some interpretation is necessary to arrive at the meaning. Write a paraphrase, a summary in your own words, of the meaning of the last stanza of "Lament for the Non-Swimmers."

Writing a Story for Children

■ Write a story in poetry or prose intended for children. Describe an adventure in which you are immersed in an unusual substance such as the following: (a) a pool full of gelatin, (b) a vat of popcorn, (c) a valley of neck-high snow, or (d) a field of giant feathers. Be sure to describe your movements and your emotional responses to the situation.

STUDY QUESTIONS

1. heavy-bodied, unwell, incapable of rest
2. scoop water; legs sink; avoid floating; gaze at land; close eyes; stand in shallows
3. splash to shore and pretend to feel buoyant
4. No; it expresses little pity or sympathy for nonswimmers, but rather amusement.
5. Lines 10, 19; give strong reasons for fear, but reasons are expressed humorously.
6. lines 6–7: "cold invasion of privacy"; line 15: "out of their element"
7. *sensible:* to avoid a threatening situation; *dangerous:* when it becomes panic or prevents growth

COMPOSITION: GUIDELINES FOR EVALUATION

WRITING A PARAPHRASE

Objective

To paraphrase the meaning of poem

Guidelines for Evaluation

- suggested length: 25–75 words
- should include main ideas and images of poem
- should be in writer's own words
- should attempt to explain difficult lines

WRITING A STORY FOR CHILDREN

Objective

To write a fantastic story for children

Guidelines for Evaluation

- suggested length: 100 prose words or six lines of poetry
- should contain at least one incident
- should present conflict and resolve it
- should be suitable for intended audience

LITERARY OPTIONS

- sound devices
- main idea

THEMATIC OPTIONS

- dependence vs. independence
- loneliness

ASSONANCE

Long vowel sounds (ll. 1–6) suggest both boat whistles and human moaning.

ALLITERATION

The repeated l sounds (ll. 1–2, 6) help to unify and give the poem a soothing, lulling sound, appropriate to the "childlike" sadness of the ship.

MAIN IDEA

The poem's strong visual images allow Sandburg to compare a fogbound ship to a lost child (ll. 1–9).

REFLECTING ON THE POEM

What does this poem show about Sandburg's character? (Possible answers: He is sensitive to sounds and moved by fog whistles.)

STUDY QUESTIONS

1. night beside a lake
2. boat's whistle; fog on lake
3. a lost child
4. the harbor
5. somber, lonely; *desolate, lone, lost, tears, fog, mist, cries*
6. a mother; represents security, home
7. alliteration, assonance; fits slow pace
8. socially at party, mentally in problems, academically in difficult tasks; feel insecure, need help

Carl Sandburg

Lost

Desolate and lone
All night long on the lake
Where fog trails and mist creeps,
The whistle of a boat
Calls and cries unendingly,
Like some lost child
In tears and trouble
Hunting the harbor's breast
And the harbor's eyes.

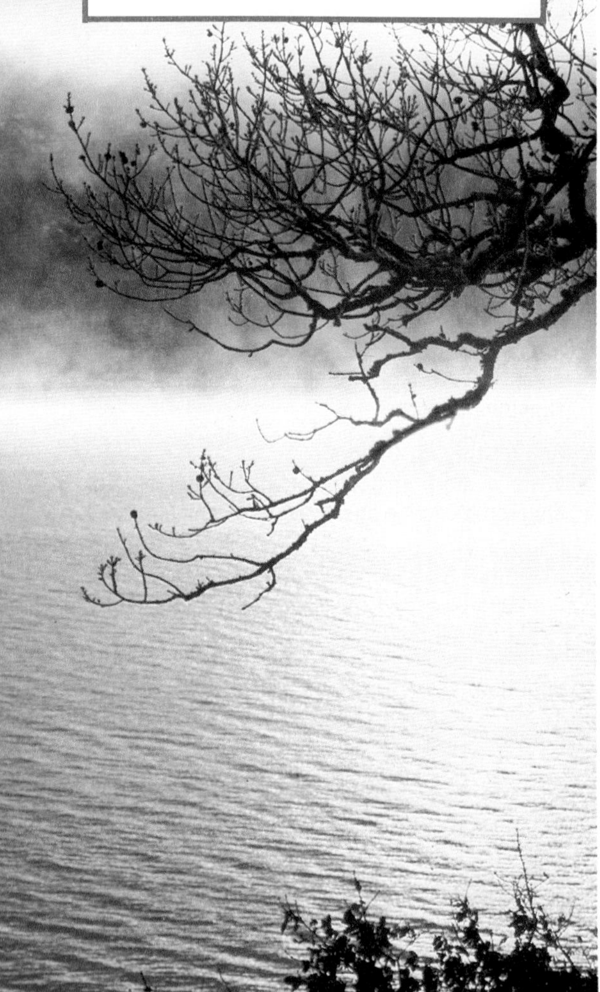

STUDY QUESTIONS

Recalling

1. What is the time and place of the poem?
2. What "calls and cries"? Why?
3. To what is the "crier" compared?
4. What is the "crier" seeking?

Interpreting

5. What mood is created by the poem? What words help to create this mood?
6. To what is the harbor compared? Why is this a fitting comparison?
7. What techniques of sound does the poet use? In what ways does the sound match the mood of the poem?

Extending

8. In what ways can people get lost other than physically? Explain how people who are lost in any manner are like children.

COMPOSITION

Writing About Form and Meaning in Poetry

Explain the relationship between the form of Sandburg's poem and its meaning. In discussing the form of the poem, you may want to consider the following: (a) its length, (b) its one-sentence structure, (c) its sound, and (d) its imagery.

Writing a Poem

Sometimes a mechanical noise can suggest a human sound. Write a poem of at least four lines. In the first two lines describe a mechanical sound, making sure that you indicate what is producing the sound. In the following lines compare that noise to a human sound. Explain the emotions that are associated with the sound.

COMPOSITION: GUIDELINES FOR EVALUATION

WRITING ABOUT FORM AND MEANING IN POETRY

Objective

To relate a poem's form to its meaning

Guidelines for Evaluation

- suggested length: one to two paragraphs
- should state what poem meant to writer
- should mention length, sound, structure, and imagery
- should relate these devices to meaning

WRITING A POEM

Objective

To compare a mechanical sound to a human one

Guidelines for Evaluation

- suggested length: four lines or more
- indicate source of mechanical sound
- use simile or metaphor to compare to human sound
- should suggest emotions connected to sound

Robert Herrick

To Daffodils

Fair daffodils, we weep to see
You haste away so soon;
As yet the early rising sun
Has not attained his noon.
Stay, stay,
Until the hasting day
Has run
But to the evensong;[1]
And, having prayed together, we
Will go with you along.

We have short time to stay, as you
We have as short a spring;
As quick a growth to meet decay
As you, or anything.
We die,
As your hours do, and dry
Away,
Like to the summer's rain;
Or as the pearls of morning's dew,
Ne'er[2] to be found again.

1. **evensong:** evening prayer service.
2. **Ne'er** [nār]: never.

STUDY QUESTIONS

Recalling

1. To whom does the speaker address the poem?
2. What time of day does the speaker say it is?
3. What does the speaker want the daffodils to do?
4. Name three things that, according to the speaker, "dry away."

Interpreting

5. What do you think the speaker means by the phrase "haste away"?
6. Who are "we"? What do "we" and the daffodils have in common?
7. What is the speaker's unstated reason for not wanting the daffodils to "haste away"?
8. What does Herrick's poem imply about the passage of time?

Extending

9. Why do you think people tend to compare plants and animals to human beings? For example, we consider an owl wise or think that a willow tree weeps.

LITERARY FOCUS

The Total Effect

The total effect of a poem is the complete experience communicated to the reader by that poem. This includes the meaning of a poem, but the total effect is greater than a list of the ideas that a poem contains. The complete impact of a poem is made up of meaning, sound, emotion, and imagination. The result is a unique experience because the poem should inspire the reader to supply personal experiences and imagination to bring the poet's words to life. The result is the total effect, a personal response to the poem that is unlike that of anyone else.

Thinking About the Total Effect

1. This poem has been read for more than three hundred years. What do you think has made it meaningful to people for so long?
2. What specific techniques of sound or imagery help to create the total effect that the poem has on you?

LITERARY OPTIONS

- total effect
- personification

THEMATIC OPTIONS

- life's brevity
- ephemeral beauty

TOTAL EFFECT

The poem's iambic rhythm and regular rhyme are appropriate for a poem that deals traditionally with nature.

PERSONIFICATION

Daffodils rush and pray with the speaker, and the day hurries to evening prayers. These comparisons emphasize the kinship of all things that the poem describes (ll. 2, 7–9).

REFLECTING ON THE POEM

Why do you think poets write about life's brevity? (Possible answer: It is arguably the most important universal truth of humanity.)

STUDY QUESTIONS

1. daffodils in bloom
2. not yet noon
3. stay through evensong and prayer
4. "We," summer rain, morning dew
5. refers to flowers quickly dying
6. speaker and all people; short span of life, death
7. Their fading and dying is symbol of speaker's own eventual death.
8. passage of time inevitable; life of people is short
9. Possible answer: comparison suggests shared traits.

LITERARY FOCUS

1. Possible answer: deals with universal theme.
2. regular rhythm, rhyme; images of people/flowers praying contrasted with death

LITERARY OPTIONS

- parallelism
- repetition

THEMATIC OPTIONS

- the nature of work
- individuality

SPEAKER

The first word identifies the first-person speaker and gives the poem immediacy and directness.

PARALLELISM

Whitman identifies one or two workers in each line and uses the word *singing* or *song* for each. The parallel structures insist on the beauty and strength of the workers' songs (ll. 2–11).

REPETITION

By repeating words and phrases (*each one singing; The boatman singing; Each singing what belongs to him or her),* the poet insists on individuality as he links the individuals through repetition (ll. 2–11).

MAIN IDEA

By opening with the image *America singing* and then cataloging the components of this song as each worker's special melody, Whitman shows that America's workers create her music and greatness.

REFLECTING ON THE POEM

Do you think the poem's message is still valid today? (Students may point out that many jobs today do not involve craft or manual labor; still, today's workers are integral to the nation and their work is part of its greatness.)

Walt Whitman

I Hear America Singing

I hear America singing, the varied carols I hear,
Those of mechanics, each one singing his as it should be blithe and strong,
The carpenter singing his as he measures his plank or beam,
The mason[1] singing his as he makes ready for work, or leaves off work,
The boatman singing what belongs to him in his boat, the deckhand singing on the steamboat deck,
The shoemaker singing as he sits on his bench, the hatter singing as he stands,
The wood-cutter's song, the ploughboy's on his way in the morning, or at noon intermission or at sundown,
The delicious singing of the mother, or of the young wife at work, or of the girl sewing or washing,
Each singing what belongs to him or her and to none else,
The day what belongs to the day—at night the party of young fellows, robust, friendly.
Singing with open mouths their strong melodious songs.

1. **mason:** one who builds with brick, concrete, or stone.

STUDY QUESTIONS

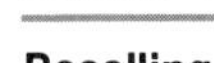

Recalling

1. List at least five occupations of the singers in the poem.
2. To whom does each song belong?
3. What adjectives are used to describe the songs in the first and last lines?

Interpreting

4. What does the poem imply about the American worker?
5. Whitman is known for his love of democracy. Explain how the poem is democratic.
6. In what ways is the form of the poem parallel? Explain how this parallelism is fitting to the topic.

Extending

7. If Whitman were writing this poem today, how might the roles of women in the poem be different?
8. Explain how a person's attitude toward his or her work affects the efficiency and enjoyment of that work.

COMPARING POEMS

1. Choose two or more poems in this section: "maggie and milly and molly and may," "Lament for the Non-Swimmers," "Lost," "To Daffodils," and "I Hear America Singing." Compare their total effects. What elements and techniques contribute most to the overall impact of each poem?
2. Of the poems in this section, which had the greatest impact on you? Which had the least impact? Explain why each poem had the effect it did.

Changing West, 1930, Thomas Hart Benton. Maurice Segoura Gallery, New York.

STUDY QUESTIONS

1. mechanics, carpenters, masons, deckhands, mothers, young wives
2. to the singer only
3. *varied, strong, melodious*
4. He is happy at his labor, an individual working for the common good.
5. extols variety of common workers; treats all workers equally
6. - lists occupations at opening of each image; repeats verbs; places laborers in situation or time
   - demonstrates how varied songs can make melodious whole
7. women's roles more varied, important
8. People who enjoy work perform more efficiently; positive attitudes create harmony, pride.

COMPARING POEMS

1. "Maggie": rhyme, rhythm, word choice, surprise
   "Non-Swimmers": imagery, humor
   "Lost": Pace, sound, simile create lonely mood.
   "Daffodils": contrast of beauty/brevity illustrates theme; regular rhythm, rhyme
   "America Singing": Parallelism, lists celebrate theme.
2. Possible answers:
   "Maggie": pleasing melody; idea "childish"
   "Non-Swimmers": pleasing imagery, irony; some difficult images
   "Lost": Simile, sound, brevity may create enjoyment/dislike.
   "Daffodils": message, lyricism; some may dislike subject of death, figurative language
   "America Singing": patriotic spirit enjoyable; some may feel poem is dated, women depicted stereotypically

ACTIVE READING

Throughout this unit encourage students to read poetry aloud in the manner outlined in this essay. Have each poem that your students study read aloud in class. You may wish to read some of the poems yourself to illustrate the proper method, but give a number of students the opportunity to read as well. You may wish to ask students to practice their reading before class.

After the class has read this essay, ask if they prefer poems with or without rhythm and rhyme, and discuss their reasons. Then discuss with the class the idea that poetry predates writing. To explain this primitive fascination with poetry, point out that young children often enjoy hearing, remembering, and reciting simple poems such as jingles and nursery rhymes. The musical sound of poetry facilitates memorization and makes reciting and hearing poetry enjoyable. To illustrate this idea, ask whether students still remember nursery rhymes and poems from childhood and elementary school.

You will find among the materials for this unit in your *Teacher's Classroom Resources* the related blackline master The Sound of Poetry.

ACTIVE READING

The Sound of Poetry

Long before people knew how to write, there was poetry. The art of poetry began with words chanted to music; often the singers danced as they sang. Poetry was performance. After writing was invented, people began to write down the words of poems. Then, over the centuries, more and more of the music was gone, and poetry became increasingly a matter of words on a page.

When modern poets write, however, they are still working with rhythms and sounds. As readers, we will not enjoy poetry if we just *see* it, no matter how many images, metaphors and meanings we find. We have to *hear* it, too, but hearing it takes practice. In reading a poem—aloud or silently—we want to avoid two things: (1) turning a poem into prose with a flat, monotonous voice and (2) turning a poem into a pulsing singsong without variety.

The pleasure of reading a poem lies in making it sound as natural as possible and yet allowing the words to have their way. There should be phrasing and rhythm. The rhymes should be stated, but not shouted. Pauses should gently announce the ends of lines. The sound of poetry is a mixture of speech and song.

Think of each poem as a unique work, not as something belonging to a larger substance called "poetry." Not all poems sound alike. For example, Poe's "Bells" is filled with sound effects of the most exaggerated sort:

> How they clang, and clash, and roar!
> What a horror they outpour
> On the bosom of the palpitating air!

"The Charge of the Light Brigade" has rolling rhythms and obvious repetitions in which we take pleasure:

> Half a league, half a league,
> Half a league, onward,
> All in the valley of Death
> Rode the six hundred.

"The Funeral" has a quieter voice, quieter music:

> Time had whittled down to mere hills
> The great mountains of my childhood.

The best approach for finding the sound of a poem is to know what the rhythm is, to know where the rhymes are (or are not), and then to try to make the whole poem sound as natural as possible.

POETRY

Guide for Studying Poetry

As you read poetry, review the following guide in order to recognize the types of poetry and to appreciate the techniques that enable the poet to speak to our senses and to our emotions.

Types of Poetry

1. What events happen in the poem to form a **narrative**?
2. What thoughts and feelings is the poet sharing in a **lyric**?

Speaker and Word Choice

1. Who is the poem's **speaker**?
2. What interesting word choices does the poet make? In what ways do these word choices fit the personality of the speaker?

Sound

1. What pattern can you find in the **rhythm** of the poem? Does it have **meter**?
2. What is the poem's **rhyme scheme**?
3. What words in the poem imitate sounds through **onomatopoeia**?
4. What examples can you find of **alliteration**?
5. What lines contain examples of **assonance**?
6. What words, lines, or stanzas are repeated to give the poem **parallelism**?

Imagery, Figurative Language

1. What particularly vivid **images** stand out in the poem? To what senses do they appeal?
2. What examples can you find of **personification**?
3. What examples can you find of **simile**?
4. What implied comparisons are made with **metaphors?**

REVIEW

When you have completed the poems in this unit, refer to the Review, the Guide for Studying Poetry. Advise students to use the guide to review the unit and to help them to interpret other poetry as well. Point out that, although many students are intimidated by poetry, they can interpret most poems by following the step-by-step analysis that is outlined in the Review.

The questions in the Guide for Studying Poetry appear with write-on lines, in blackline master form, among the materials for this unit in your *Teacher's Classroom Resources*.

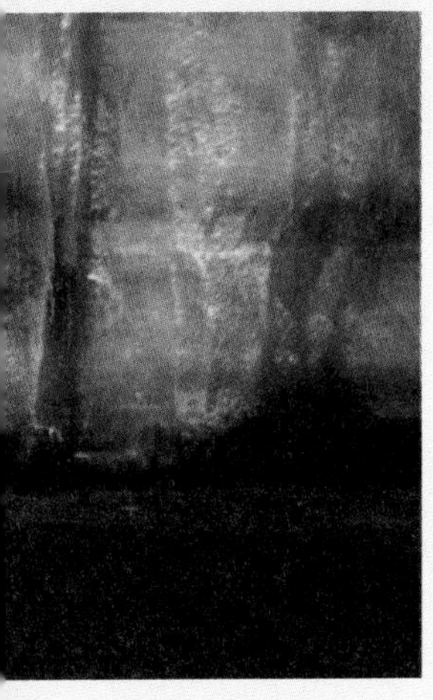

PREVIEW: NONFICTION

What is needed in nonfiction is. . . facts—mind-boggling, verifiable facts that settle arguments and arouse to action.

—William C. Knott

Nonfiction is factual prose writing. While **fiction** is the work of the imagination, nonfiction concerns real people and true experiences. The nonfiction on the following pages is divided into two sections to represent the two main types of nonfiction: (1) biography and autobiography and (2) essays.

An author writes nonfiction for a definite purpose and a specific audience. In nonfiction **purpose** is the central idea, or general statement about life, that the author wants to make. The author often states a purpose directly but can also imply a purpose in the following ways:

- The author may use a title that suggests an attitude toward the subject.
- The author may relate an experience that suggests an opinion about life.
- The author may provide details about people and their behavior that suggest an opinion about people in general.
- The author may provide details of place that suggest ideas about the world in general.
- The author's **style,** or choice and arrangement of words, may reveal an attitude toward the subject.

The **audience** of a work of nonfiction is the type of reader for which the work is intended. A work of nonfiction may be intended for experts or for casual readers.

PREVIEW

After students have read the Preview, you might discuss it with the class in terms of nonfiction's similarities to the short story, because at its best nonfiction is a demanding art that requires as much control of language as a short story does. In fact, except for expository and persuasive essays, nonfiction employs most of the elements of the short story. Make sure, however, that the class understands the major difference: Nonfiction deals with "verifiable facts" and fiction is a work of the imagination. To check, ask students to name examples of nonfiction that they have read. Use a newspaper to introduce the types of nonfiction: Human-interest stories can be descriptive or narrative; reviews are persuasive; how-to articles are expository; interviews often contain biographical sketches.

LITERARY FOCUS: *Biography, Autobiography*

A **biography** is the account of a person's life written by someone other than the subject. The key ingredient in a good biography is integrity—completeness and honesty. A biography with integrity is not simply hero worship or criticism but rather an effort to tell the truth about a life.

More than a collection of facts, a biography explains the motives behind actions, the methods behind achievements, the lessons learned from setbacks. A biographer researches and uses personal letters, diaries, public documents, and interviews as sources of information.

Many characteristics of good fiction appear also in biography: lively recounting of events; crisp, authentic dialogue; richness of detail; many-sided characterization. Though rooted in fact, the biography does not just report a life but makes that life rewarding, entertaining reading.

To present fully the life of an individual, most biographies are book length. Biographical sketches, however, present only a few events that illustrate important characteristics of the subject's personality. In this way the author of a biographical sketch can capture the essence of a person's life in a few carefully selected episodes or even in a single crucial event.

An **autobiography** is the story of a person's life written by that person. The author of an autobiography re-creates personal events as objectively as possible and tries to see the pattern they form and the meaning they hold.

One form of autobiography is the **diary,** a day-by-day account of events in a person's own life. The author of a diary usually writes for personal satisfaction and greater self-awareness and not for immediate publication. Some diaries, however, are intended to be read by a wider audience.

The next few selections are short biographical and autobiographical portraits of five men and women, famous and unknown, young and old. Though these people also represent different places and periods of time, we can read about each life with equal interest because each offers us another approach to living.

Yoshiko Uchida (born 1921) has written many books for children and adolescents. Uchida writes about the Japanese American experience, and her strong pride in that heritage is evident throughout her work.

As a child of immigrants, Uchida understands that America has always been a land of dreams for those who come from foreign lands. The following selection demonstrates the changing course of one man's dream.

■ What does the expression *self-made man* mean to you?

Yoshiko Uchida[1]

Of Dry Goods[2] and Black Bow Ties

Long after reaching the age of sixty, when my father was persuaded at last to wear a conservative four-in-hand tie,[3] it was not because of his family's urging, but because Mr. Shimada[4] (I shall call him that) had died. Until then, for some forty years, my father had always worn a plain black bow tie, a formality which was required on his first job in America and which he had continued to observe as faithfully as his father before him had worn his samurai[5] sword.

My father came to America in 1906 when he was not yet twenty-one. Sailing from Japan on a small six-thousand-ton ship which was buffeted all the way by rough seas, he landed in Seattle on a bleak January day. He revived himself with the first solid meal he had enjoyed in many days, and then allowed himself one day of rest to restore his sagging spirits. Early on the second morning, wearing a stiff new bowler,[6] he went to see Mr. Shozo Shimada to whom he carried a letter of introduction.

At that time, Shozo Shimada was Seattle's most successful Japanese business man. He owned a chain of dry goods stores which extended not only from Vancouver to Portland, but to cities in Japan as well. He had come to America in 1880, penniless but enterprising, and sought work as a laborer. It wasn't long, however, before he saw the futility of trying to compete with American laborers whose bodies were twice his in muscle and bulk. He knew he would never go far as a laborer, but he did possess another skill that could give him a start
3 toward better things. He knew how to sew. It was a matter of expediency over masculine pride. He set aside his shovel, bought a second-hand sewing machine, and hung a dressmaker's sign in his window. He was in business.

In those days, there were some Japanese women in Seattle who had neither homes nor

1. **Yoshiko Uchida** [yōsh'kō o͞o chē'dä]
2. **Dry Goods:** cloth, cloth products, and related items.
3. **four-in-hand tie:** necktie.
4. **Shimada** [shē mä'dä]
5. **samurai** [sam'oo rī']: Japan's feudal warrior class. A samurai wore two swords as signs of his position.
6. **bowler** [bō'lər]: derby hat.

AT A GLANCE

- Uchida's father, at sixty, was finally persuaded to wear a regular necktie.
- In 1906, at twenty, he arrives in America and goes to see Mr. Shimada.
- Mr. Shimada has become a successful Japanese businessman.

LITERARY OPTIONS

- description
- characterization
- plot

THEMATIC OPTIONS

- self-identity
- success
- different life styles

1 DESCRIPTION

Uchida describes her father's bow tie, which represents respect, self-esteem, and tradition.

2 PLOT: CHRONOLOGY

The author moves the action to the more distant past, having established the importance of Mr. Shimada and the bow tie.

3 CHARACTERIZATION

Uchida identifies Mr. Shimada as a man who is practical, intelligent, and willing to make sacrifices in order to succeed.

GUIDED READING

LITERAL QUESTION

1a. To what does the author compare her father's wearing the black bow tie? (to her grandfather's wearing a samurai sword)

INFERENTIAL QUESTION

1b. What do these two articles of dress represent to their wearers? (They represent a certain position in society and a mark of respect.)

AT A GLANCE

- Mr. Shimada's dressmaking business is successful.
- Japanese customers bring Mr. Shimada their money for safekeeping.
- Mr. Shimada decides he must invest their money.

1 MAIN IDEA

Mr. Shimada is respected by the women for whom he sews; recognizing his honesty, they give him their money to guard.

2 BACKGROUND

In the early years of the century, a dry-goods store was the equivalent of today's department store. Usually it featured all kinds of goods except food.

Japanese Americans in California during the 1930s with decorations for a Japanese festival.

families nor sewing machines, and were delighted to find a friendly Japanese person to do some sewing for them. They flocked to Mr. Shimada with bolts of cloth, elated to discover a dressmaker who could speak their native tongue and, although a male, sew western-styled dresses for them.

Mr. Shimada acquainted himself with the fine points of turning a seam, fitting sleeves, and coping with the slippery folds of silk, and soon the women told their friends and gave him enough business to keep him thriving and able to
1 establish a healthy bank account. He became a trusted friend and confidant to many of them and soon they began to bring him what money they earned for safekeeping.

"Keep our money for us, Shimada-san,"[7] they urged, refusing to go to American banks whose tellers spoke in a language they could not understand.

At first the money accumulated slowly and Mr. Shimada used a pair of old socks as a repository, stuffing them into a far corner of his drawer beneath his union suits. But after a time, Mr. Shimada's private bank began to overflow and he soon found it necessary to replenish his supply of socks.

2 He went to a small dry goods store downtown, and as he glanced about at the buttons, threads, needles and laces, it occurred to him that he owed it to the women to invest their savings in a business venture with more future than the dark recesses of his bureau drawer. That night he called a group of them together.

"Think, ladies." he began. "What are the two basic needs of the Japanese living in Seattle? Clothes to wear and food to eat," he answered himself. "Is that not right? Every man must buy a

7. **san:** in Japanese a polite form of address.

GUIDED READING

LITERAL QUESTION

1a. What does Mr. Shimada do for the women who are his customers? (He sews for them and keeps their money safe.)

INFERENTIAL QUESTION

1b. Why do the women give Mr. Shimada their money? (They trust him; he speaks their language and is a part of their culture.)

shirt to put on his back and pickles and rice for his stomach."

The women marveled at Mr. Shimada's cleverness as he spread before them his fine plans for a Japanese dry goods store that would not only carry everything available in an American dry goods store, but Japanese foodstuff as well. That was the beginning of the first Shimada Dry Goods Store on State Street.

By the time my father appeared, Mr. Shimada had long since abandoned his sewing machine and was well on his way to becoming a business tycoon. Although he had opened cautiously with such stock items as ginghams, flannel, handkerchiefs, socks, shirts, overalls, umbrellas and ladies' silk and cotton stockings, he now carried tins of salt rice crackers, bottles of soy sauce, vinegar, ginger root, fish-paste cakes, bean paste, Japanese pickles, dried mushrooms, salt fish, red beans, and just about every item of canned food that could be shipped from Japan. In addition, his was the first Japanese store to install a U.S. Post Office Station, and he thereby attained the right to fly an American flag in front of the large sign that bore the name of his shop.

When my father first saw the big American flag fluttering in front of Mr. Shimada's shop, he was overcome with admiration and awe. He expected that Mr. Shozo Shimada would be the finest of Americanized Japanese gentlemen, and when he met him, he was not disappointed.

Although Mr. Shimada was not very tall, he gave the illusion of height because of his erect carriage. He wore a spotless black alpaca suit, an immaculate white shirt and a white collar so stiff it might have overcome a lesser man. He also wore a black bow tie, black shoes that buttoned up the side and a gold watch whose thick chain looped grandly on his vest. He was probably in his fifties then, a ruddy-faced man whose hair, already turning white, was parted carefully in the center. He was an imposing figure to confront a young man fresh from Japan with scarcely a future to look forward to. My father bowed, summoned as much dignity as he could muster, and presented the letter of introduction he carried to him.

Mr. Shimada was quick to sense his need. "Do you know anything about bookkeeping?" he inquired.

"I intend to go to night school to learn this very skill," my father answered.

Mr. Shimada could assess a man's qualities in a very few minutes. He looked my father straight in the eye and said, "Consider yourself hired."
3 Then he added, "I have a few basic rules. My employees must at all times wear a clean white shirt and a black bow tie. They must answer the telephone promptly with the words, 'Good morning or good afternoon, Shimada's Dry Goods,' and they must always treat each customer with respect. It never hurts to be polite," he said thoughtfully. "One never knows when one might be indebted to even the lowliest of beggars."

My father was impressed with these modest words from a man of such success. He accepted them with a sense of mission and from that day was committed to white shirts and black bow ties, and treated every customer, no matter how
4 humble, with respect and courtesy. When, in later years, he had his own home, he never failed to answer the phone before it could ring twice if at all possible.

My father worked with Mr. Shimada for ten years, becoming first the buyer for his Seattle store and later, manager of the Portland branch. During this time Mr. Shimada continued on a course of exhilarated expansion. He established two Japanese banks in Seattle, bought a fifteen-room house outside the dreary confines of the Japanese community and dressed his wife and daughter in velvets and ostrich feathers. When his daughter became eighteen, he sent her to study in Paris, and the party he gave on the eve of her departure, hiring musicians, as well as caterers to serve roast turkey, venison, baked

AT A GLANCE

- Mr. Shimada's store succeeds.
- Mr. Shimada hires Mr. Uchida and explains his basic rules.
- Mr. Shimada expands his business; he establishes two banks and buys a house.

1 DETAILS

The details of inventory explain Mr. Shimada's success: He competes with ordinary dry-goods stores by offering flannel, umbrellas, etc., yet he also sells unique products for Japanese customers.

2 DESCRIPTION

Mr. Shimada's clothes *(spotless, immaculate, grand)*, reflect his dignity and self-respect.

3 CHARACTERIZATION

Shimada's basic rules reflect not only his self-esteem but also his attention to the dignity of others.

4 PURPOSE

The author shows how Mr. Shimada influenced her father: Simple courtesies that Shimada taught him, such as answering the phone promptly, became part of his own way of living.

GUIDED READING

LITERAL QUESTIONS

1a. What does Mr. Shimada hang outside his shop? (an American flag)

2a. What are Mr. Shimada's rules for his employees? (They must wear a white shirt and black bow tie, answer the phone promptly, and treat customers with respect.)

INFERENTIAL QUESTIONS

1b. Why does Mr. Shimada want to fly an American flag outside his shop? (He is proud to be an American and grateful to the country for his success.)

2b. What do these rules show about Mr. Shimada's attitude toward his customers? (He respects them and wants them to think well of him and his store.)

AT A GLANCE

- Mr. Shimada lends money to friends without collateral.
- Mr. Uchida leaves Mr. Shimada's employ for a new position.
- Mr. Shimada's banks fail.

1 CHARACTERIZATION

Mr. Shimada's desire to help friends illustrates his generosity; he gives not only of his money but also of himself.

2 IRONY

Mr. Shimada's offer of help to Mr. Uchida is poignant in its irony: It is Mr. Shimada who will need help.

A popular drug store in the Japanese American community in Sacramento, California, in 1903.

ham and champagne, seemed to verify rumors that he had become one of the first Japanese millionaires of America.

In spite of his phenomenal success, however, Mr. Shimada never forgot his early friends nor lost any of his generosity, and this, ironically enough, was his undoing. Many of the women for whom he had once sewn dresses were now well established, and they came to him requesting loans with which they and their husbands might open grocery stores and laundries and
1 shoe repair shops. Mr. Shimada helped them all and never demanded any collateral. He operated his banks on faith and trust and gave no thought to such common prudence as maintaining a reserve.

When my father was called to a new position with a large Japanese firm in San Francisco, Mr. Shimada came down to Portland to extend personally his good wishes. He took Father to a Chinese dinner and told him over the peanut duck and chow mein that he would like always to be considered a friend.

2 "If I can ever be of assistance to you," he said, "don't ever hesitate to call." And with a firm shake of the hand, he wished my father well.

That was in 1916. My father wrote regularly to Mr. Shimada telling him of his new job, of his bride, and later, of his two children. Mr. Shimada did not write often, but each Christmas he sent a box of Oregon apples and pears, and at New Year's a slab of heavy white rice paste from his Seattle shop.

In 1929 the letters and gifts stopped coming, and Father learned from friends in Seattle that both of Mr. Shimada's banks had failed.[8] He immediately dispatched a letter to Mr. Shimada, but it was returned unopened. The next news he had

8. **In 1929 . . . failed:** After the stock market crash of 1929, many banks and businesses became bankrupt, and the Great Depression began.

GUIDED READING

LITERAL QUESTION

1a. After Mr. Uchida goes to San Francisco, how does his relationship with Mr. Shimada continue? (Mr. Uchida writes letters, and Mr. Shimada sends boxes of fruit and rice paste.)

INFERENTIAL QUESTION

1b. How do you think the two men feel about each other? (They respect and enjoy each other.)

was that Mr. Shimada had had to sell all of his shops. My father was now manager of the San Francisco branch of his firm. He wrote once more asking Mr. Shimada if there was anything he could do to help. The letter did not come back, but there was no reply, and my father did not write again. After all, how do you offer help to the head of a fallen empire? It seemed almost irreverent.

It was many years later that Mr. Shimada appeared one night at our home in Berkeley.[9] In the dim light of the front porch my mother was startled to see an elderly gentleman wearing striped pants, a morning coat[10] and a shabby black hat. In his hand he carried a small black satchel. When she invited him inside, she saw that the morning coat was faded, and his shoes badly in need of a shine.

"I am Shimada," he announced with a courtly bow, and it was my mother who felt inadequate to the occasion. She hurriedly pulled off her apron and went to call my father. When he heard who was in the living room, he put on his coat and tie before going out to greet his old friend.

Mr. Shimada spoke to them about Father's friends in Seattle and about his daughter who was now married and living in Denver. He spoke of a typhoon that had recently swept over Japan, and he drank the tea my mother served and ate a piece of her chocolate cake. Only then did he open his black satchel.

"I thought your girls might enjoy these books," he said, as he drew out a brochure describing *The Book of Knowledge*.

"Fourteen volumes that will tell them of the wonders of this world." He spread his arms in a magnificent gesture that recalled his eloquence of the past. "I wish I could give them to your children as a personal gift," he added softly.

Without asking the price of the set, my father wrote a check for one hundred dollars and gave it to Mr. Shimada.

3 Mr. Shimada glanced at the check and said, "You have given me fifty dollars too much." He seemed troubled for only a moment, however, and quickly added, "Ah, the balance is for a deposit, is it? Very well, yours will be the first deposit in my next bank."

"Is your home still in Seattle then?" Father asked cautiously.

"I am living there, yes," Mr. Shimada answered.

And then, suddenly overcome with memories of the past, he spoke in a voice so low he could scarcely be heard.

4 "I paid back every cent," he murmured. "It took ten years, but I paid it back. All of it. I owe nothing."

"You are a true gentleman, Shimada-san," Father said. "You always will be." Then he pointed to the black tie he wore, saying, "You see, I am still one of the Shimada men."

A young Japanese American in San Francisco in 1872.

9. **Berkeley** [burk′lē]: city in California on San Francisco Bay.
10. **morning coat:** jacket with tails in back, worn for daytime formal events.

AT A GLANCE

- Years later Mr. Shimada visits the Uchidas, selling encyclopedias.
- Mr. Uchida buys an encyclopedia and gives Mr. Shimada extra money.
- Mr. Shimada says the extra money will be a deposit for his next bank.

1 DESCRIPTION

Though Mr. Shimada's clothes are now "shabby" and "faded," and his shoes are "badly in need of a shine," he is still elegantly dressed in a morning coat and hat. He still clings to his self-respect.

2 PURPOSE

Uchida shows that her father's respect for his old employer (illustrated by his dressing in coat and tie before meeting with him) does not depend on Mr. Shimada's wealth or success.

3 MAIN IDEA

Although he has no money, Mr. Shimada will not accept a handout; he takes the money from Mr. Uchida only because he can justify it as a "deposit" in his "next bank."

4 CHARACTERIZATION

Mr. Shimada shows his honor when he states that he has paid back all the money he owed.

GUIDED READING

LITERAL QUESTION

1a. What does Mr. Uchida give to Mr. Shimada? (a check for one hundred dollars)

INFERENTIAL QUESTION

1b. Why does Mr. Uchida write the check without asking the price of the books? (He feels bad for Mr. Shimada and wants to help him financially.)

AT A GLANCE

- Mr. Shimada dies penniless.
- Mr. Uchida puts away black ties.

1 MAIN IDEA

Mr. Uchida learns that the tie is no longer necessary; he can carry his respect in his heart.

REFLECTING ON THE SELECTION

When Mr. Uchida takes off his bow tie, how is he still respectful of Shimada? (He still lives by the important values of honor and self-respect that Shimada taught him.)

STUDY QUESTIONS

1. not strong enough to work as laborer; knows how to sew
2. Japanese women become customers, invest their money.
3. wears white shirts, black ties; respects customers; keeps in touch with Mr. Shimada
4. doesn't maintain reserves at banks; freely extends credit
5. hopes to sell them a book
6. represents opportunities America has provided
7. clothes proper, neat; will use extra money as deposit; has repaid debts
8. Mr. Shimada has died.
9. Mr. Shimada retains respect, courtesy, responsibility, enterprising spirit.

VIEWPOINT

hires Mr. Uchida after brief interview; freely gives loans; respects customers; gives without expecting anything in return

LITERARY FOCUS

- *Before:* Spotless alpaca suits, immaculate shirts, stiff collars suggest confidence, success.
- *After:* Striped pants, faded coat, shabby hat, dull shoes suggest dignity and pride in defeat.

That was the last time my father saw Shozo Shimada. Some time later he heard that he had returned to Japan as penniless as the day he set out for America.

It wasn't until the Christmas after we heard of Mr. Shimada's death that I ventured to give my father a silk four-in-hand tie. It was charcoal gray and flecked with threads of silver. My father looked at it for a long time before he tried it
1 on, and then fingering it gently, he said, "Well, perhaps it is time now that I put away my black bow ties."

STUDY QUESTIONS

Recalling

1. Why does Mr. Shimada become a dressmaker?
2. What are the steps that lead to Mr. Shimada's owning banks and a chain of stores?
3. Find three examples of the respect that Uchida's father has for Mr. Shimada.
4. In what way is Mr. Shimada's "undoing" the result of his generosity?
5. For what reason does Mr. Shimada visit Uchida's family at the end of the selection?

Interpreting

6. Why is the American flag outside his first store a source of pride to Mr. Shimada?
7. From his last meeting with the author's father, give three examples of Mr. Shimada's pride.
8. Why do you think Uchida's father decides that the time has come to put away his black bow ties?

Extending

9. Using Mr. Shimada as an example, explain how success in life can be measured by what a person is rather than by what a person has.

VIEWPOINT

A review in the *New York Times* stated that Uchida's writings

> possess dramatic quality, humor and a gently insinuated [suggested] doctrine of human kindness and generosity.

- Explain how Uchida's sketch of Mr. Shimada demonstrates the value of kindness and generosity.

LITERARY FOCUS

Description in Biography

A biographer can suggest much about the inner life of an individual through **descriptive details** such as clothing and mannerisms. These details are often expressions of personality, and physical characteristics can influence a person's life. The biographer chooses from the subject's appearance details that provide clues to personality.

Thinking About Biography

- Compare the description of Mr. Shimada's clothing before and after his business failure. What clues to his personality does the comparison provide?

COMPOSITION

Writing About a Biography

- Some biographies are purely factual; others are biased for or against their subject. Is "Of Dry Goods and Black Bow Ties" purely factual or biased? First describe your opinion of Mr. Shimada after you read Uchida's portrait of him. Then show how Uchida led you to that conclusion. Cite character traits she chooses to mention and the descriptive details she uses.

Writing a Character Sketch

- Uchida provides a vivid character sketch of Mr. Shimada by describing his appearance and his actions. Write a character sketch about a person whom you admire. Begin by explaining what you admire about the person. Then provide physical details that give clues to the personality of your subject. Conclude with one or two actions that reveal personality.

COMPOSITION: GUIDELINES FOR EVALUATION

WRITING ABOUT A BIOGRAPHY

Objective

To show how Uchida's description of Mr. Shimada influences reader's opinion of that character

Guidelines for Evaluation

- suggested length: three to five paragraphs
- should state reader's opinion of Mr. Shimada
- should include thesis statement
- should cite example of character traits and descriptive details that reinforce opinion

WRITING A CHARACTER SKETCH

Objective

To write a character sketch of an admirable person

Guidelines for Evaluation

- suggested length: 150–300 words
- should state person's most admirable qualities
- should relate physical details that enhance qualities
- should describe actions that reveal qualities

Carl Sandburg (1878–1967) gained a knowledge and love of America and its people through much travel, as well as through a variety of odd jobs such as milk deliverer, firefighter, truck driver, house painter, and reporter. Sandburg won two Pulitzer Prizes, one for *Collected Poems* and one for his biography of Abraham Lincoln.

Sandburg added new dimensions to the world's understanding of Lincoln, showing him to be a man of strength as well as compassion, of tears as well as laughter. The following is an excerpt from the preface to *Abraham Lincoln: The Prairie Years,* the beginning of a six-volume work about Lincoln.

■ What do details of personality and of family life add to your picture of a public figure?

AT A GLANCE

- Abraham Lincoln is shot in 1865, and America mourns.
- The author begins his examination of Lincoln.
- Lincoln takes steps necessary to win the Civil War.
- Lincoln meets with Harriet Beecher Stowe.

LITERARY OPTIONS

- anecdotes in biography
- figurative language
- characterization

THEMATIC OPTIONS

- distinguishing myth from reality
- qualities of leadership
- conflict

1 BACKGROUND

On April 14, 1865, Lincoln was shot and killed by John Wilkes Booth during a performance of *Our American Cousin.* It was the fifth year of his presidency.

2 VOCABULARY

The word *chattel* (which means "a piece of personal property") emphasizes both the dehumanizing horror of slavery and the courage it took Lincoln to outlaw the institution.

3 ANECDOTE IN BIOGRAPHY

This anecdote illustrates Lincoln's gift for comic exaggeration ("the little woman . . . that made this great war") and his bleak, realistic idea of his own future ("I shan't last long . . . ").

Carl Sandburg

from A Lincoln Preface

In the time of the April lilacs in the year 1865, a man in the city of Washington, D.C., trusted a guard to watch at a door, and the guard was careless, left the door, and the man was shot, lingered a night, passed away, was laid in a box, and carried north and west a thousand miles; bells sobbed; cities wore crepe;[1] people stood with hats off as the railroad burial car came past at midnight, dawn, or noon.

During the four years of time before he gave up the ghost, this man was clothed with despotic power, commanding the most powerful armies till then assembled in modern warfare, enforcing draft of soldiers, abolishing the right of habeas corpus,[2] directing politically and spiritually the wild, massive forces loosed in civil war.

Four billion dollars' worth of property was taken from those who had been legal owners of
2 it, confiscated, wiped out as by fire, at his instigation and executive direction; a class of chattel property recognized as lawful for two hundred years went to the scrap pile.

When the woman who wrote *Uncle Tom's Cabin*[3] came to see him in the White House, he
3 greeted her, "So you're the little woman who wrote the book that made this great war," and as they seated themselves at a fireplace, "I do love an open fire; I always had one to home." As they were finishing their talk of the days of blood, he said, "I shan't last long after it's over."

An Illinois Congressman looked in on him as he had his face lathered for a shave in the White House, and remarked, "If anybody had told me

1. **crepe** [krāp]: type of cloth which, when black, is used for mourning.
2. **habeas corpus** [hā'bē əs kôr'pəs]: right of a citizen who is in prison to have a hearing. During the Civil War Lincoln abolished this right for military prisoners.
3. **woman . . . *Cabin:*** Harriet Beecher Stowe, whose book aroused public sentiment against slavery. As a result some people consider her book one cause of the Civil War.

GUIDED READING

LITERAL QUESTION

1a. How does Lincoln spend the four years before his death? (like a despot: commanding armies, abolishing *habeas corpus,* enforcing a military draft)

INFERENTIAL QUESTION

1b. Why do you think Sandburg highlights such negative examples of Lincoln's activities? (He wants to show Lincoln in other than rosy hues; in fact, Lincoln is not above criticism.)

AT A GLANCE

- Lincoln discusses the Constitution.
- He gives his opinion of various public figures.
- He works to win the Civil War and to prepare the country for the war's aftermath.
- He faces danger and conflict.

1 MAIN IDEA

Sandburg quotes Lincoln to show readers that he worked, as everyone does, from day to day.

2 RESPONSE JOURNAL

Ask students to discuss Lincoln's attitude toward the Constitution in their journals: Was he justified in violating the Constitution? Why or why not?

3 STYLE: METAPHOR

By quoting Lincoln's comparison of Horace Greeley to a rotten shoe, Sandburg illustrates the president's flair for inventive, comic language as well as his strong feelings about dishonesty.

4 CHARACTERIZATION

Sandburg portrays Lincoln as a man who knew when to speak and when to remain silent—a vitally important ability for one who was forced to be responsible for a country rent by civil war.

5 CONFLICT

Sandburg points out Lincoln's courage and loyalty in the face of adversity, qualities that both humanize him and make him seem larger than life.

that in a great crisis like this the people were going out to a little one-horse town and pick out a one-horse lawyer for President, I wouldn't have believed it.'' The answer was, ''Neither would I. But it was a time when a man with a policy
1 would have been fatal to the country. I never had a policy. I have simply tried to do what seemed best each day, as each day came.''

''I don't intend precisely to throw the Constitution overboard, but I will stick it in a hole if I can,'' he told a Cabinet officer. The enemy was violating the Constitution to destroy the Union,
2 he argued, and therefore, ''I will violate the Constitution, if necessary, to save the Union.'' He instructed a messenger to the Secretary of the Treasury, ''Tell him not to bother himself about the Constitution, say that I have that sacred instrument here at the White House, and I am guarding it with great care.''

His life, mind, and heart ran in contrasts. When his white kid gloves broke into tatters while shaking hands at a White House reception, he remarked, ''This looks like a general bustification.'' When he talked with an Ohio friend one day during the 1864 campaign, he mentioned one public man, and murmured, ''He's a thistle! I don't see why God lets him live.'' Of a devious Senator, he said, ''He's too crooked to lie still!'' And of a New York editor, ''In early life in the
3 West, we used to make our shoes last a great while with much mending, and sometimes, when far gone, we found the leather so rotten the stitches would not hold. Greeley is so rotten that nothing can be done with him. He is not truthful; the stitches all tear out.''

While the luck of war wavered and broke and came again, as generals failed and campaigns were lost, he held enough forces of the Union together to raise new armies and supply them, until generals were found who made war as victorious war has always been made, with terror, frightfulness, destruction, and valor and sacrifice past words of man to tell.

His own speeches, letters, telegrams, and of-

ficial messages during that war form the most significant and enduring document from any one man on why the war began, why it went on, and the dangers beyond its end. As the platoons filed before him at a review of an army corps, he asked, ''What is to become of these boys when the war is over?''

4 He was a chosen spokesman; yet there were times he was silent; nothing but silence could at those times have fitted a chosen spokesman; in the mixed shame and blame of the immense wrongs of two crashing civilizations, with nothing to say, he said nothing, slept not at all, and wept at those times in a way that made weeping appropriate, decent, majestic.

5 His hat was shot off as he rode alone one night in Washington; a son he loved died as he watched at the bed; his wife was accused of betraying information to the enemy, until denials from him were necessary; his best companion was a fine-hearted and brilliant son with a deformed palate and an impediment of speech; when a Pennsylvania Congressman told him the enemy had declared they would break into the city and hang him to a lamppost, he said he had considered ''the violent preliminaries'' to such a scene; on his left thumb was a scar where an ax

GUIDED READING

LITERAL QUESTIONS

1a. What words does Sandburg use to describe how war is made? (*terror, frightfulness, destruction, valor, sacrifice*)

2a. How did Lincoln occasionally react as spokesman of the nation? (He was silent, didn't sleep, and wept.)

INFERENTIAL QUESTIONS

1b. Why do you think Sandburg uses these particular contrasting words? (He wants to show that war can contain both good and bad elements.)

2b. What do Lincoln's reactions show about his character? (He felt deeply the injustices of the war and didn't try to glorify what was wrong about it.)

1 had nearly chopped the thumb off when he was a boy; over one eye was a scar where he had been hit with a club in the hands of a man trying to steal the cargo off a Mississippi River flatboat; he threw a cashiered[4] officer out of his room in the White House, crying, "I can bear censure, but not insult, I never wish to see your face again."

2 He rebuked with anger a woman who got to her knees to thank him for a pardon that saved her son from being shot at sunrise; and when an Iowa woman said she had journeyed out of her way to Washington just for a look at him, he grinned, "Well, in the matter of looking at one another, I have altogether the advantage."

He sent hundreds of telegrams, "Suspend death sentence" or "Suspend execution" of so-and-so, who was to be shot at sunrise. The telegrams varied oddly at times, as in one, "If Thomas Samplogh, of the First Delaware Regiment, has been sentenced to death, and is not yet executed, suspend and report the case to me." And

4. **cashiered** [ka shērd′]: dismissed dishonorably.

Abraham Lincoln. *Opposite page,* photographed in Springfield, Illinois, about 1860, the year he was first elected President; *this page top,* with son Tad in April 1865, shortly before his assassination; *this page bottom,* the train, *Nashville,* which carried Lincoln's body back to Springfield.

AT A GLANCE

- Lincoln reacts with anger to both insult and adulation.
- Lincoln pardons soldiers sentenced to death.

1 MAIN IDEA

Lincoln's physical clumsiness and injuries—an accident with an ax, a scar over his eye—stress that Lincoln was an ordinary man as well as a legend.

2 ANECDOTE IN BIOGRAPHY

Anecdotes that illustrate Lincoln's anger and his appreciation of an attractive woman make him seem more human.

GUIDED READING

LITERAL QUESTION

1a. How does Lincoln react to the woman who thanks him on her knees? (He is angry and rebukes her.)

INFERENTIAL QUESTION

1b. Why do you think Lincoln reacts this way? (He does not want to be treated like a king or a god.)

AT A GLANCE

- Enemies and friends praise him.
- Sandburg illustrates why Lincoln will be remembered and mythologized.

1 MAIN IDEA

Lincoln is called a "matchless man," compared to Christ, and described as a baby crawling on a dirt floor. Again Sandburg points up the contrast between the myth and the man.

2 PURPOSE

As Sandburg calls Lincoln a "Strange Friend and a Friendly Stranger," he juxtaposes human being with myth. The combination of these qualities comprises the Lincoln who lives in our memories.

REFLECTING ON THE SELECTION

Which aspect of Lincoln's personality—the ordinary man or the extraordinary leader—do you find most interesting? Why? (Answers will likely focus on his humanity, courage, ethics, and honesty.)

STUDY QUESTIONS

1. bells sobbed; cities wore crepe
2. commanded armies; enforced draft; abolished habeas corpus; emancipated slaves
3. had scar over one eye; watched as son died; wife accused of being traitor; son had deformed palate
4. good, appealing, humorous
5. ■ gracious toward soldiers; empathized with them
   ■ harsh toward men who were making profits from war; many were suffering
6. raised armies/hated bloodshed; could be silent/make speeches; could laugh/weep; would endure censure/intolerant of insult

another, "Is it Lieutenant Samuel B. Davis whose death sentence is commuted? If not done, let it be done."

While the war drums beat, he liked best, of all the stories told of him, one about two Quakeresses[5] heard talking in a railway car. "I think that Jefferson[6] will succeed." "Why does thee think so?" "Because Jefferson is a praying man." "And so is Abraham a praying man." "Yes, but the Lord will think Abraham is joking."

An Indiana man at the White House heard him say, "Voorhees, don't it seem strange to you that I, who could never so much as cut off the head of a chicken, should be elected, or selected, into the midst of all this blood?"

Of men taking too fat profits out of the war, he said, "Where the carcass is there will the eagles be gathered together."

1 An enemy general, Longstreet, after the war, declared him to have been "the one matchless man in forty millions of people," while one of his private secretaries, Hay, declared his life to have been the most perfect in its relationships and adjustments since that of Christ.

Between the days in which he crawled as a baby on the dirt floor of a Kentucky cabin, and the time when he gave his final breath in Washington, he packed a rich life with work, thought, laughter, tears, hate, love.

With vast reservoirs of the comic and the droll, and notwithstanding a mastery of mirth and nonsense, he delivered a volume of addresses and letters of terrible and serious appeal, with import beyond his own day, shot through here and there with far, thin ironies, with paragraphs having raillery of the quality of the Book of Job,[7] and echoes as subtle as the whispers of wind in prairie grass.

Perhaps no human clay pot has held more laughter and tears.

The facts and myths of his life are to be an American possession, shared widely over the world, for thousands of years, as the traditions of Knute or Alfred, Lao-tse or Diogenes, Pericles
2 or Caesar,[8] are kept. This because he was not only a genius in the science of neighborly human relationships and an artist in the personal handling of life from day to day, but a Strange Friend and a Friendly Stranger to all forms of life that he met.

He lived fifty-six years, of which fifty-two were lived in the West—the prairie years.

5. **Quakeresses** [kwā′kər es əz]: women of the Society of Friends, a Christian sect, commonly known as Quakers.
6. **Jefferson:** Jefferson Davis (1808-1889), president of the Confederate States of America during the Civil War.
7. **Book of Job** [jōb]: book of the Old Testament. Job patiently accepted the trials sent him by God.
8. **Knute** [no͞ot], **Alfred, Lao-tse** [lou′dzu′], **Diogenes** [dī oj′ə nēz], **Pericles** [per′ə klēz′], **Caesar** [sē′zər]: famous leaders and thinkers from different periods of history.

STUDY QUESTIONS

Recalling

1. Give two details of the mourning that occurred after Lincoln's death.
2. Name four examples of the power held by Lincoln as President.
3. Give four details that Sandburg mentions about Lincoln's personal life.
4. How does Sandburg, a prominent poet and biographer, rate Lincoln as a writer?

Interpreting

5. Lincoln was gracious to some people and harsh to others. Give one example of each type of behavior, and explain why it was justified.
6. Give four examples to prove that Sandburg shows many sides of Lincoln's personality.

Extending

7. Lincoln had devoted admirers and fanatical enemies. Why do you think this situation is common for a major leader?

VIEWPOINT

Sandburg's love of the common people is reflected in his work, including his biography of Lincoln. One critic said:

> His intent was to separate Lincoln the man from Lincoln the myth, to avoid hero worship, to relate with graphic detail and humanness the man...he...admired.
>
> —*Contemporary Authors*

- Which events as related by Sandburg make Lincoln more human and less like a myth?

LITERARY FOCUS

Anecdotes in Biography

An **anecdote** is a brief account of a true event, usually intended to entertain and to reveal personality through a person's actions. Using a series of anecdotes, an author can create a biography that is more than a list of dates, places, and major events. The author shows us the subject in a number of different settings and creates an impression that is based on a broad range of the subject's experiences. The choice of anecdotes makes clear the author's attitude toward the subject and the impression that the biography is intended to convey.

Thinking About Anecdotes in Biography

- Find two of Sandburg's anecdotes that surprised you. What new insights into Lincoln's personality did these anecdotes give you?

VOCABULARY

Synonyms

A **synonym** is a word that has the same or nearly the same meaning as another word. *Autumn* and *fall* are synonyms. The words in capitals are from *A Lincoln Preface*. Choose the word that is *nearest* the meaning of each word in capitals, *as the word is used in the selection.* Write the number of each item and the letter of your choice on a separate sheet.

1. CONFISCATED: (a) ruined (b) sold (c) seized (d) isolated
2. DEVIOUS: (a) dishonest (b) opposing (c) undependable (d) direct
3. VALOR: (a) discipline (b) obedience (c) savagery (d) bravery
4. CENSURE: (a) ridicule (b) blame (c) approval (d) slander
5. REBUKED: (a) resented (b) received (c) scolded (d) scorned

COMPOSITION

Writing About a Biography

- Sandburg's biography of Lincoln not only presents a vivid picture of Lincoln but also makes clear how Sandburg wants the reader to view Lincoln. In a brief essay first explain how Sandburg's selection of details illustrates Lincoln's outlook on life. Then show how these details support Sandburg's purpose in writing the biography. *For help with this assignment, see Lesson 8 in the Writing About Literature Handbook at the back of this book.*

Writing an Editorial

- Imagine that you are living in the year 1865 and have just heard of President Lincoln's assassination. As editor of the local newspaper, you are responsible for writing an editorial about Lincoln. Begin with a statement of your general impression of Lincoln. Then support your opinion with facts from the selection. You may discuss two or three of the following: (a) Lincoln's wit, (b) his honesty, (c) his concern for others, (d) one major event of his life, (e) his effect as a political leader.

COMPARING BIOGRAPHIES

- Carl Sandburg, writing about a great President, had a wealth of information about Lincoln to use in his biography. Yoshiko Uchida, writing about an unknown businessman, had little more than her father's recollections as the source for her biographical sketch. What problems does the wealth of information cause for Sandburg? How does Uchida compensate for the lack of information on Mr. Shimada?

7. It is impossible to please all people.

VIEWPOINT

meeting with Harriet Beecher Stowe; shaving while talking with Congressman; rebuke of woman who got on her knees

LITERARY FOCUS

Possible answers:

- his rebuking woman who got on her knees to thank him for saving son's life; demonstrates humility, impatience
- his enjoyment in listening to stories told about himself; demonstrates ability to laugh at himself

VOCABULARY

1. (c) seized
2. (a) dishonest
3. (d) bravery
4. (b) blame
5. (c) scolded

COMPARING BIOGRAPHIES

Sandburg: wealth of information poses task of sorting, arranging; *Uchida:* compensates for lack of information by focusing on a few of Mr. Shimada's personality traits

COMPOSITION: GUIDELINES FOR EVALUATION

WRITING ABOUT A BIOGRAPHY

Objective

To determine Sandburg's purpose in writing the biography by analyzing details

Guidelines for Evaluation

- suggested length: three to five paragraphs
- should state Sandburg's purpose
- should choose details that illustrate Lincoln's outlook and behavior
- should show how details support stated purpose

WRITING AN EDITORIAL

Objective

To write an editorial giving an impression of Lincoln and supporting opinion with facts

Guidelines for Evaluation

- suggested length: three to five paragraphs
- should state general impression that editor wishes to convey
- should use facts from selection
- should discuss at least two suggested topics

AT A GLANCE

- Marguerite mopes for nearly a year.
- Mrs. Flowers, a well-off neighbor greatly admired by Marguerite, is described.

LITERARY OPTIONS

- autobiography
- characterization
- plot

THEMATIC OPTIONS

- identity
- relationships between generations
- communication

1 AUTOBIOGRAPHY

Angelou writes about herself in the first person, focusing on a difficult period in her childhood.

2 CHARACTERIZATION

The narrator describes Mrs. Flowers as appearing warm in cold weather and cool in hot, creating an impression of a calm, unflappable person.

3 STYLE: SIMILE

Angelou compares Mrs. Flowers' skin to a rich, ripe plum, a comparison that may have occurred to her as a child and helped her to remember details of Mrs. Flowers' appearance.

Photograph © 1982 by Jill Krementz

Maya Angelou (born 1928) has had a great variety of experiences: She toured twenty-two nations as a dancer, worked on a newspaper in Egypt, lectured at the University of Ghana in western Africa, and directed a film in Hollywood. She has written poetry, fiction, and plays.

Born Marguerite Johnson, Angelou and her brother, Bailey, were raised by their grandmother Annie Henderson (whom they called Momma), the owner of a general store in the black area of Stamps, Arkansas. The following excerpt from her autobiography covers the time when Marguerite is about ten years old. Unusually bright but painfully self-conscious, she has become withdrawn and refuses to speak to anyone.

■ What is the connection between being liked by others and liking yourself?

Maya Angelou

from I Know Why the Caged Bird Sings

1 For nearly a year, I sopped around the house, the Store, the school and the church, like an old biscuit, dirty and inedible. Then I met, or rather got to know, the lady who threw me my first life line.

Mrs. Bertha Flowers was the aristocrat of
2 Black Stamps. She had the grace of control to appear warm in the coldest weather, and on the Arkansas summer days it seemed she had a private breeze which swirled around, cooling her. She was thin without the taut look of wiry people, and her printed voile[1] dresses and flowered hats were as right for her as denim overalls for a farmer. She was our side's answer to the riches white woman in town.

3 Her skin was a rich black that would hav peeled like a plum if snagged, but then no on would have thought of getting close enough t Mrs. Flowers to ruffle her dress, let alone snag her skin. She didn't encourage familiarity. Sh wore gloves too.

I don't think I ever saw Mrs. Flowers laugh but she smiled often. A slow widening of he thin black lips to show even, small white teeth then the slow effortless closing. When she chos to smile on me, I always wanted to thank her The action was so graceful and inclusively benign.

1. **voile** [voil]: lightweight, sheer fabric.

GUIDED READING

LITERAL QUESTION

1a. How does the author describe Mrs. Flowers' attitude toward familiarity? (She says that Mrs. Flowers didn't encourage familiarity.)

INFERENTIAL QUESTION

1b. Does this attitude make her a snob? (Not necessarily; she is just different from the other people in Black Stamps. Mrs. Flowers does smile often, and Marguerite regards her smile as "inclusively benign.")

She was one of the few gentlewomen I have ever known, and has remained throughout my life the measure of what a human being can be.

Momma had a strange relationship with her. Most often when she passed on the road in front of the Store, she spoke to Momma in that soft yet carrying voice, "Good day, Mrs. Henderson." Momma responded with "How you, Sister Flowers?"

Mrs. Flowers didn't belong to our church, nor was she Momma's familiar. Why on earth did she insist on calling her Sister Flowers? Shame made me want to hide my face. Mrs. Flowers deserved better than to be called Sister. Then, Momma left out the verb. Why not ask, "How *are* you, *Mrs.* Flowers?" With the unbalanced passion of the young, I hated her for showing her ignorance to Mrs. Flowers. It didn't occur to me for many years that they were as alike as sisters, separated only by formal education.

Although I was upset, neither of the women was in the least shaken by what I thought an unceremonious greeting. Mrs. Flowers would continue her easy gait up the hill to her little bungalow, and Momma kept on shelling peas or doing whatever had brought her to the front porch.

Occasionally, though, Mrs. Flowers would drift off the road and down to the Store and Momma would say to me, "Sister, you go on and play." As I left I would hear the beginning of an intimate conversation. Momma persistently using the wrong verb, or none at all.

"Brother and Sister Wilcox is sho'ly the meanest"—"Is," Momma? "Is"? Oh, please, not "is," Momma, for two or more. But they talked, and from the side of the building where I waited for the ground to open up and swallow me, I heard the soft-voiced Mrs. Flowers and the textured voice of my grandmother merging and melting. They were interrupted from time to time by giggles that must have come from Mrs. Flowers (Momma never giggled in her life). Then she was gone.

She appealed to me because she was like people I had never met personally. Like women in English novels who walked the moors[2] (whatever they were) with their loyal dogs racing at a respectful distance. Like the women who sat in front of roaring fireplaces, drinking tea incessantly from silver trays full of scones and crumpets. Women who walked over the "heath" and read morocco-bound books and had two last
2 names divided by a hyphen. It would be safe to say that she made me proud to be Negro, just by being herself. . . .

One summer afternoon, sweet-milk fresh in my memory, she stopped at the Store to buy provisions. Another Negro woman of her health and age would have been expected to carry the paper sacks home in one hand, but Momma said, "Sister Flowers, I'll send Bailey up to your house with these things."

3 She smiled that slow dragging smile, "Thank you, Mrs. Henderson. I'd prefer Marguerite, though." My name was beautiful when she said it. "I've been meaning to talk to her, anyway." They gave each other age-group looks.

Momma said, "Well, that's all right then. Sister, go and change your dress. You going to Sister Flowers'."

The chifforobe[3] was a maze. What on earth
4 did one put on to go to Mrs. Flowers' house? I knew I shouldn't put on a Sunday dress. It might be sacrilegious. Certainly not a house dress, since I was already wearing a fresh one. I chose a school dress, naturally. It was formal without suggesting that going to Mrs. Flowers' house was equivalent to attending church.

I trusted myself back into the Store.

"Now, don't you look nice." I had chosen the right thing, for once.

---

2. **moors:** also called "heath"; open, wild land.
3. **chifforobe** [shif'ə rōb]: cabinet for storing clothing.

AT A GLANCE

- Mrs. Flowers and Momma converse from time to time; Marguerite is ashamed of her grandmother.
- Mrs. Flowers stops to buy groceries.
- She asks that Marguerite carry the supplies to her house.
- Marguerite dresses up to accompany Mrs. Flowers home.

1 RELATIONSHIPS BETWEEN GENERATIONS

Angelou describes her embarrassment and anger over her grandmother's ignorance and notes her blindness to her grandmother's worth.

2 MAIN IDEA

Angelou, as an adult, sums up the influence Mrs. Flowers had on her: "She made me proud to be Negro"; because of Mrs. Flowers' pride and self-respect, Angelou grew to see that she, too, had self-worth.

3 PLOT: RISING ACTION

The action of the plot accelerates when Mrs. Flowers requests Marguerite's help in carrying her groceries, a rare honor for the girl.

4 DETAILS

By describing the various dresses Marguerite considers, the narrator makes clear the importance of Mrs. Flowers for the girl: She is too important for a mere house dress.

GUIDED READING

LITERAL QUESTIONS

1a. How does the narrator describe her grandmother's relationship with Mrs. Flowers? (She says it was "strange.")

2a. Why does Mrs. Flowers appeal to the narrator? (She is like people whom the narrator has never met personally.)

INFERENTIAL QUESTIONS

1b. In what way does Marguerite think the relationship strange? (Though educationally and economically unequal, the two women were good friends.)

2b. Why is Mrs. Flowers' unfamiliarity so fascinating? (She is so different that she seems more important than the familiar people in Marguerite's life.)

AT A GLANCE

- Momma shows Mrs. Flowers the stitching on Marguerite's dress, much to Marguerite's embarrassment.
- Mrs. Flowers and Marguerite walk toward Mrs. Flower's house.
- Mrs. Flowers talks about Marguerite's schoolwork.

1 CHARACTERIZATION

When Mrs. Flowers compliments Momma's sewing, two facts are disclosed about her: She does not sew herself, and she is gracious in her recognition of others' talents.

2 STYLE: DIALOGUE

The conversation reveals that Mrs. Flowers, though gracious and friendly, is very different from Momma: She does not take the Bible as seriously as Momma does.

3 VOCABULARY: WORD CHOICE

Marguerite knows she ought not act "womanish" because Momma would interpret it as an inappropriate display of pride.

4 THEME

The "unasked and unanswerable questions" that hang between Marguerite and Mrs. Flowers concern Marguerite's work and behavior in school, but Mrs. Flowers knows that to ask them would close the lines of communication.

Celestine Birge, a photograph by P. H. Polk, official photographer of Tuskegee Institute in Alabama. Polk photographed this young girl in 1933, the approximate time in which this excerpt from Angelou's autobiography is set.

"Mrs. Henderson, you make most of the children's clothes, don't you?"

"Yes, ma'am. Sure do. Store-bought clothes ain't hardly worth the thread it take to stitch them."

"I'll say you do a lovely job, though, so neat. That dress looks professional."

Momma was enjoying the seldom-received
1 compliments. Since everyone we knew (except Mrs. Flowers, of course) could sew competently, praise was rarely handed out for the commonly practiced craft.

"I try, with the help of the Lord, Sister Flowers, to finish the inside just like I does the outside. Come here, Sister."

I had buttoned up the collar and tied the belt, apronlike, in back. Momma told me to turn around. With one hand she pulled the strings and the belt fell free at both sides of my waist. Then her large hands were at my neck, opening the button loops. I was terrified. What was happening?

"Take it off, Sister." She had her hands on the hem of the dress.

"I don't need to see the inside, Mrs. Henderson, I can tell. . ." But the dress was over my head and my arms were stuck in the sleeves. Momma said, "That'll do. See here, Sister Flowers, I French-seams around the armholes." Through the cloth film, I saw the shadow approach. "That makes it last longer. Children these days would bust out of sheet-metal clothes. They so rough."

2 "That is a very good job, Mrs. Henderson. You should be proud. You can put your dress back on, Marguerite."

"No ma'am. Pride is a sin. And 'cording to the Good Book, it goeth before a fall."

"That's right. So the Bible says. It's a good thing to keep in mind."

I wouldn't look at either of them. Momma hadn't thought that taking off my dress in front
3 of Mrs. Flowers would kill me stone dead. If I had refused, she would have thought I was trying to be "womanish". . . . Mrs. Flowers had known that I would be embarrassed and that was even worse. I picked up the groceries and went out to wait in the hot sunshine. It would be fitting if I got a sunstroke and died before they came outside. Just dropped dead on the slanting porch.

There was a little path beside the rocky road, and Mrs. Flowers walked in front swinging her arms and picking her way over the stones.

She said, without turning her head, to me, "I hear you're doing very good school work, Marguerite, but that it's all written. The teachers report that they have trouble getting you to talk in
4 class." We passed the triangular farm on our left and the path widened to allow us to walk together. I hung back in the separate unasked and unanswerable questions.

"Come and walk along with me, Marguerite." I couldn't have refused even if I wanted to. She

GUIDED READING

LITERAL QUESTION

1a. What does Momma do that embarrasses Marguerite? (She takes off Marguerite's dress to show the stitching.)

INFERENTIAL QUESTION

1b. Why does she do this? (to show Mrs. Flowers that the inside of the dress is as well made as the outside)

pronounced my name so nicely. Or more correctly, she spoke each word with such clarity that I was certain a foreigner who didn't understand English could have understood her.

"Now no one is going to make you talk—possibly no one can. But bear in mind, language is man's way of communicating with his fellow man and it is language alone which separates him from the lower animals." That was a totally new idea to me, and I would need time to think about it.

"Your grandmother says you read a lot. Every chance you get. That's good, but not good enough. Words mean more than what is set down on paper. It takes the human voice to infuse them with the shades of deeper meaning."

I memorized the part about the human voice infusing words. It seemed so valid and poetic.

She said she was going to give me some books and that I not only must read them, I must read them aloud. She suggested that I try to make a sentence sound in as many different ways as possible.

"I'll accept no excuse if you return a book to me that has been badly handled." My imagination boggled at the punishment I would deserve if in fact I did abuse a book of Mrs. Flowers. Death would be too kind and brief.

The odors in the house surprised me. Somehow I had never connected Mrs. Flowers with food or eating or any other common experience of common people. There must have been an outhouse, too, but my mind never recorded it.

The sweet scent of vanilla had met us as she opened the door.

"I made tea cookies this morning. You see, I had planned to invite you for cookies and lemonade so we could have this little chat. The lemonade is in the icebox."[4]

It followed that Mrs. Flowers would have ice on an ordinary day, when most families in our town bought ice late on Saturdays only a few times during the summer to be used in the wooden ice-cream freezers.[5]

She took the bags from me and disappeared
3 through the kitchen door. I looked around the room that I had never in my wildest fantasies imagined I would see. Browned photographs leered or threatened from the walls and the white, freshly done curtains pushed against themselves and against the wind. I wanted to gobble up the room entire and take it to Bailey, who would help me analyze and enjoy it.

"Have a seat, Marguerite. Over there by the table." She carried a platter covered with a tea towel. Although she warned that she hadn't tried her hand at baking sweets for some time, I was certain that like everything else about her the cookies would be perfect.

4 They were flat round wafers, slightly browned on the edges and butter-yellow in the center. With the cold lemonade they were sufficient for childhood's lifelong diet. Remembering my manners, I took nice little lady-like bites off the edges. She said she had made them expressly for me and that she had a few in the kitchen that I could take home to my brother. So I jammed one whole cake in my mouth and the rough crumbs scratched the insides of my jaws, and if I hadn't had to swallow, it would have been a dream come true.

As I ate she began the first of what we later called "my lessons in living." She said that I must always be intolerant of ignorance but understanding of illiteracy. That some people, unable to go to school, were more educated and even more intelligent than college professors.
5 She encouraged me to listen carefully to what country people called mother wit. That in those homely sayings was couched the collective wisdom of generations.

When I finished the cookies she brushed off

---

4. **icebox:** chest for storing food that was cooled with blocks of ice, used before electric refrigeration.

5. **wooden ice-cream freezers:** wooden buckets equipped with crank-operated mechanisms for making ice cream.

AT A GLANCE

- Mrs. Flowers discusses oral communication and books.
- Marguerite eats cookies and drinks lemonade that Mrs. Flowers made. Mrs. Flowers begins Marguerite's "lessons in living."

1 THEME

Marguerite learns that language separates humanity from "the lower animals" and begins to understand that communication is vital for understanding among people.

2 AUTOBIOGRAPHY

The narrator of this reminiscence recalls the scent of food in the house, but her memory is selective: Unable to remember an outhouse, she speculates that she never noticed it.

3 SETTING

The contrast of leering photographs and fresh white curtains in the room echoes Marguerite's own contrasting fear and exhilaration at being in Mrs. Flowers' home.

4 DETAILS

The narrator recalls details about the meal that had such great importance for her.

5 THEME

Marguerite learns that the "country" speech that has embarrassed her in the past contains "the collective wisdom of generations," and she learns that listening as well as speaking is important.

GUIDED READING

LITERAL QUESTIONS

1a. What does Mrs. Flowers tell Marguerite to do with the books she loans her? (She should read them aloud.)

2a. What is Mrs. Flowers' first "lesson in living"? (Some people who are not educated are more intelligent than those who are highly educated.)

INFERENTIAL QUESTIONS

1b. Why does Mrs. Flowers want Marguerite to read aloud? (so Marguerite can hear all of the words' possible meanings; to gain confidence in speaking)

2b. How does the lesson apply to Marguerite's own life? (She might see that her grandmother, though uneducated, is smart and worthy of respect.)

AT A GLANCE

- Mrs. Flowers reads aloud to Marguerite.
- Mrs. Flowers asks her to recite a poem.
- She realizes Mrs. Flowers likes her and begins to like herself more.

1 PLOT: CLIMAX

When Mrs. Flowers reads aloud from Dickens, Marguerite hears "poetry" for the first time; it is a momentous experience that changes her life.

2 AUTOBIOGRAPHY

The narrator cannot recapture the true feeling of her encounters with Mrs. Flowers, but she can recall the meaning, the "aura," of the discussions.

3 PURPOSE

The author has illustrated that Mrs. Flowers' approval made a difference in her life. Being liked by a person she respects, she is able to like herself.

REFLECTING ON THE SELECTION

Do you think that Marguerite is less of a "caged bird" by the end of the story? Why or why not? (possible answer: yes, because she has learned to speak and listen and thus has greater freedom)

STUDY QUESTIONS

1. had grace; appeared warm in cold weather; didn't encourage familiarity; wore gloves
2. improper grammar; makes her take off dress
3. carries sacks; to have a chat
4. book, cookies; recite a poem
5. Being liked for herself made a great difference to her.

the table and brought a thick, small book from
1 the bookcase. I had read *A Tale of Two Cities*[6] and found it up to my standards as a romantic novel. She opened the first page and I heard poetry for the first time in my life.

"It was the best of times and the worst of times . . ." Her voice slid in and curved down through and over the words. She was nearly singing. I wanted to look at the pages. Were they the same that I had read? Or were there notes, music, lined on the pages, as in a hymn book? Her sounds began cascading gently. I knew from listening to a thousand preachers that she was nearing the end of her reading, and I hadn't really heard, heard to understand, a single word.

"How do you like that?"

It occurred to me that she expected a response. The sweet vanilla flavor was still on my tongue and her reading was a wonder in my ears. I had to speak.

I said, "Yes, ma'am." It was the least I could do, but it was the most also.

"There's one more thing. Take this book of poems and memorize one for me. Next time you pay me a visit, I want you to recite."

2 I have tried often to search behind the sophistication of years for the enchantment I so easily found in those gifts. The essence escapes but its aura remains. To be allowed, no, invited, into the private lives of strangers, and to share their joys and fears, was a chance to exchang the Southern bitter wormwood[7] for a cup c mead[8] with Beowulf[9] or a hot cup of tea an milk with Oliver Twist.[10] When I said aloud, "I is a far, far better thing that I do, than I have eve done . . ."[11] tears of love filled my eyes at m selflessness.

On that first day, I ran down the hill and int the road (few cars ever came along it) and ha the good sense to stop running before I reache the Store.

3 I was liked, and what a difference it made. was respected not as Mrs. Henderson's grand child or Bailey's sister but for just bein Marguerite Johnson.

Childhood's logic never asks to be prove (all conclusions are absolute). I didn't questio why Mrs. Flowers had singled me out for atten tion, nor did it occur to me that Momma migh have asked her to give me a little talking to. All cared about was that she had made tea cookie for *me* and read to *me* from her favorite book It was enough to prove that she liked me.

6. ***A Tale of Two Cities:*** novel by Charles Dickens.

7. **wormwood:** anything bitter or unpleasant.
8. **mead:** drink made from fermented honey and herbs, usually associated with literary characters from the Middle Ages.
9. **Beowulf** [bā'ə woolf']: title character and hero of an Old English epic poem.
10. **Oliver Twist:** title character and hero of a novel by Charles Dickens.
11. **"It is . . . done":** from Dickens' novel *A Tale of Two Cities*. The line expresses the feelings of a man who is about to die so that another may live.

STUDY QUESTIONS

Recalling

1. Give four details about Mrs. Flowers that support Marguerite's impression of her as "the aristocrat of Black Stamps."
2. Name two ways in which Momma embarrasses Marguerite.
3. For what reasons does Marguerite go to Mrs Flowers' home?
4. What two things does Mrs. Flowers give to Marguerite to take home? What does she ask Marguerite to do on her next visit?
5. In what way does Marguerite describe her feelings after the visit with Mrs. Flowers?

Interpreting

6. Explain how Mrs. Flowers uses Marguerite's love of reading to break her silence. What does this show about the woman's understanding of people?
7. What is Marguerite's first "lesson in living"? Why does Mrs. Flowers consider this lesson necessary for Marguerite?
8. In what way does Mrs. Flowers serve as a "life line" for Marguerite?

Extending

9. At the end of the selection, Marguerite is amazed at being liked for herself. Explain why being liked helps people to like themselves.

VIEWPOINT

Readers of Maya Angelou's autobiography marvel that, while telling her own story, she captures experiences that are common childhood and adolescent concerns such as

> worries of not being normal...of being incompetent...and, finally, of wondering what will happen in the future.
>
> —C. Amato, *Survey of Contemporary Authors*

■ Give at least four examples of Marguerite's experiences and concerns that are typical for a ten-year-old.

LITERARY FOCUS

Autobiography

An **autobiography** describes the events of the author's life and also records the insights that time gives. Especially when writing about childhood, autobiographers approach the events of their lives both as participants and as spectators. They can narrate events through a child's eyes, but they can also speak at times from an adult's viewpoint. Maya Angelou records a child's impression when she says, "Her skin was a rich black that would have peeled like a plum if snagged...." However, she is speaking as an adult when she says, "She was one of the few gentlewomen I have ever known, and has remained throughout my life the measure of what a human being can be."

Thinking About Autobiography

■ Find three statements by Angelou that could not have been made by a child but are interpretations by an adult.

VOCABULARY

Vivid Word Choice

Vivid words startle the reader into thinking about the author's meaning. Speaking of a special day in her life, Maya Angelou recalls "a summer afternoon, sweet-milk fresh in my memory." This colorful phrase tells us several things in a few words: The author's memories of that day are as fresh as new milk; the events of that day have left a sweet, wholesome flavor in her mind; it was a summer afternoon, a time we associate with light, warmth, and leisure. From one vivid phrase we know that the author will recount a good and important time.

Sometimes a single word can give a colorful effect. "She smiled that slow *dragging* smile...." "They gave each other *age-group* looks."

■ Find three other examples of vivid language in the selection. On a separate sheet write the examples, and explain what each adds to your understanding of a person or a situation.

COMPOSITION

Writing About an Autobiography

■ A good autobiography is honest. The author describes success and admits failure, accepts blame and claims credit. In what ways do you think Maya Angelou is honest in writing about her own childhood? Use specific references from the autobiography as examples.

Writing an Autobiographical Sketch

■ Our lives are constantly being shaped and molded by the influence of people around us. Marguerite becomes a better person because of the positive influence of Mrs. Flowers. Write a short sketch describing an important encounter with a teacher or some other adult who had a positive influence on you or someone else of Marguerite's age. Tell what change the adult may have brought about.

6. explains that human voice gives written words deeper meaning; understands she must make Marguerite want to speak; is good judge of character

7.
- Lesson: Ignorance is intolerable, but illiteracy should be understood.
- Necessary: senses she is embarrassed by grandmother

8. rescues her from difficult period of her life; teaches her to value herself

9. People often judge their worth by other's opinions of them.

VIEWPOINT

embarrassed by Momma's grammar; mortified when Momma takes off her dress; thrilled to be treated as individual by an adult; considers punishment for abusing Mrs. Flower's book

LITERARY FOCUS

- "Mrs. Bertha Flowers was the aristocrat of Black Stamps."
- "The action (a smile) was so graceful. . . ."
- "Momma had a strange relationship with her."

VOCABULARY

Possible answers:
- "I *sopped* around the house"; conveys low self-esteem
- "The chiffrobe was a *maze*"; suggests both she and closet were in state of confusion
- "Her sounds began *cascading*"; suggests soothing effect, inspires Marguerite to speak

COMPOSITION: GUIDELINES FOR EVALUATION

WRITING ABOUT AN AUTOBIOGRAPHY

Objective

To show how Angelou is honest in writing about her childhood

Guidelines for Evaluation

- suggested length: one paragraph
- should state ways Angelou is honest in writing
- should use examples from text as support

WRITING AN AUTOBIOGRAPHICAL SKETCH

Objective

To describe an encounter with an influential person and explain resulting changes

Guidelines for Evaluation

- suggested length: 150–300 words
- should clearly report encounter
- should tell what positive influence was gained
- should explain changes that occurred as a result of the positive influence

AT A GLANCE

- The narrator goes to the train yard.
- The narrator's mother explains some differences between Mexico and the United States.
- The narrator and his mother will go to Tucson.

LITERARY OPTIONS

- purpose
- setting
- atmosphere

THEMATIC OPTIONS

- cultural differences and similarities
- communication
- the immigrant experience

1 MAIN IDEA

The first thing the narrator notices as he enters the United States from the Mexican border is how close the two countries are; the only things that look different are the American and Mexican flags.

2 POINT OF VIEW

Until now the narrative has been told through the point of view of the child-narrator; here, the narrator as adult is commenting: "It was the closest thing we did to saying good-bye. . . ."

Ernesto Galarza (1905–1984) was uprooted from his home in western Mexico by the revolution of 1910 and moved to the United States while a young child.

This excerpt from Galarza's autobiography tells the story of his journey in 1910 from the Mexican border into the United States. The boy and his mother (Doña Henriqueta) are left alone as his uncles Gustavo and José travel ahead. The uncles, unable to find work in war-torn Mexico, now work for the railroad and are earning passage for the small family. Although unable to speak English and unfamiliar with the people and customs in the United States, the six-year-old Galarza and his mother bravely make their way to a new life in the *barrio*, or Mexican neighborhood, of Sacramento, California. More than a trip across a border and through a few states, this is a journey into another world for the young Ernesto.

- What is frightening and what is amusing about moving to a new community?

Ernesto Galarza

from Barrio Boy

In the sunny morning of the next day we walked back to the station. Our train was still there, the flats and boxcars and coaches deserted, Mexican and American soldiers walking
1 back and forth. "Look, the American flag," my mother said. It was flying over a building near us. Down the street, beyond the depot, there was a Mexican flag on a staff. "We are in the United States. Mexico is over there."

It took further explaining to clear up certain points to my satisfaction. The North was the same place as the United States, and we had finally arrived. The Americans never drew an eagle on their flag. The red and the white were the same as on ours but why they liked blue better than green was just one of those peculiar things about Americans. Where did Mexico begin? Just beyond the railway station. How far did it go? "A long way," said Doña Henriqueta,[1] "far
2 down the track, farther than Jalcocotán."[2] It was the closest thing we did to saying good-bye to our country.

That evening at the *mesón*,[3] José and my mother and I reread Gustavo's letter, the last we had received in Mazatlán.[4] José was to work his way on the railroad to a place called Sacramento.[5] My mother and I were to go to another city called

1. **Doña Henriqueta** [dōn'yə hān rē kā'tə]
2. **Jalcocotán** [yäl kō kō tän']: a mountain village in western Mexico.
3. ***mesón*** [mā sōn']: Spanish for "inn."
4. **Mazatlán** [mä zät län']: a city on the west coast of central Mexico.
5. **Sacramento:** city in central California, the capital of the state.

GUIDED READING

LITERAL QUESTION

1a. With what words does the narrator compare the American and Mexican flags? (He says the Americans don't put an eagle on theirs, and though the red and white are the same, the Americans like blue better than green.)

INFERENTIAL QUESTION

1b. What does this comparison reflect? (It reflects both the similarities and differences between the two countries.)

Tucson[6] and wait there until another pass and money could be obtained.

José then explained a remarkable thing about our money. Mexican centavos and tostones and pesos[7] were good for nothing in the United States. He had already exchanged some of our Mexican currency for dollars. "Listen carefully," he told us. "You have to give two pesos for one dollar. For one tostón you get one quarter. For ten centavos you get one nickel." On the table he laid out the coins, in rows two for one.

He turned to me.

"Now, Ernesto, you are the man of the family. You will take care of your mother until we are together in Sacramento. How do you say *por favor*?"

"Plees."

"Right, how do you say *cuánto es*?"

"Hau-mochee"

"How do you say *qué hora es, por favor*?"

"Hua-tinees, plees."

"Correct."

"Now say the numbers."

"Huan, too, tree."

"Correct. If you don't know the numbers, hold up your fingers and count in Spanish."

In Nogales[8] we sold the extra blankets. José bought us two cardboard suitcases and one for himself, and an alarm clock like the one we used to try to win in the lottery tent in Mazatlán. With our new luggage and the tin trunk, we set off for Tucson, saying good-bye to José. In one of the suitcases there was a brown folder tied with a blue tape. In it were the pass, the letters from Gustavo with certain names and addresses, and the instructions for our arrival in Sacramento. The suitcase with its precious papers was never out of our sight, and the American paper money
3 that José had exchanged. Gustavo's forwarding address was puzzling. The best we could make out it was a General Delibri. It sounded as if generals were in charge of the mail in the United States, nothing like our *lista del correo*[9] in Acaponeta.

In Tucson we found our way to the address Gustavo had sent. It was a small hotel where the clerk spoke Spanish. He took us down a long, dark hall to a room, where I immediately began to explore the remarkable inventions of the Americans.

Hanging from a cord attached to the middle of the ceiling there was an electric bulb, low enough for an adult to reach and turn the black
4 switch. I realized that this was our own electric light for us to turn on and off as we pleased. I pushed a chair under it and after some instruction from my mother proceeded to create lightening in the room by turning the switch as fast as I could.

Next I discovered the bedsprings. When I sat on the bed it sank deliciously. Jumping on it in my stocking feet, I held my balance dangerously as I made the bed creak and the mattress bounce. The head and foot of the bed were made of iron scrollwork in loops and rosettes painted white. On each of the four posts there was a large brass knob that unscrewed. I took one off, deciding to take it with us since it matched the three cartridges in the cedar box. My plan didn't work. Doña Henriqueta ordered me to screw it back....

We stayed only one day at the hotel, long enough for me to become acquainted with the bathtub, located in a closet next to the toilet. A rope of water twisted and whirled from a brass faucet, filling the tub. I sat in the cold water up to my neck and discovered that I could slide down the back of the tub and hit the bottom

---

6. **Tucson** [to͞o′son]: a city in southeastern Arizona.
7. **centavo** [sen tä′vō], **tostón** [tōs tōn′], **peso** [pā′sō]: Mexican money. The peso is the monetary unit and contains one hundred centavos. A tostón is a fifty centavo piece.
8. **Nogales** [nō gä′lās]: a Mexican city on the border with Arizona.

9. ***lista del correo*** [lēs′tä dāl kōr rā′ō]: Spanish for "general delivery." General delivery is a postal service that delivers mail to a post office where the addressee calls for it.

AT A GLANCE

- Ernesto practices English.
- Ernesto and his mother spend one day at a hotel in Tucson.
- Ernesto discovers American "inventions."

1 THEME

José teaches Ernesto that being able to speak to others is vitally important to survival in a new country; the words Ernesto learns will help him take care of his mother.

2 THEME

Ernesto and his family begin to acquire the things they will need in America and discard items that are no longer useful: They sell blankets to buy suitcases and a clock.

3 VOCABULARY

Ernesto's Mexican accent has changed the words "general delivery" to "General Deliberi," showing how easy it is for foreigners to confuse English words that have more than one meaning.

4 POINT OF VIEW

The author describes the hotel room through a child's eyes; what might seem unpleasant or mundane to an adult—bare bulbs, soft mattress—are sources of fascination to a child.

GUIDED READING

LITERAL QUESTIONS

1a. What words and phrases does José teach Ernesto? (*please, How much? What time is it?* and *one, two, three.*)

2a. What does Ernesto do with the electric light switch? (He plays with it, turning the switch on and off rapidly to "create lightening.")

INFERENTIAL QUESTIONS

1b. Why does José choose to teach Ernesto these specific words and phrases? (They are the language's most basic and most practical words.)

2b. Why is he so excited about the electric light switch? (It seems he has never been able to switch one on and off before; perhaps his family has never had electricity at home.)

AT A GLANCE

- Ernesto and his mother board with a couple.
- Ernesto examines his new surroundings.
- After many weeks Gustavo sends for Ernesto and his mother in Sacramento.

1 SETTING

The author describes the setting as bleak, summing it up in shades of muddy brown and dirty gray—a contrast to the excitement Ernesto feels in his temporary home.

2 RESPONSE JOURNAL

Have the students write in their journals about how they might feels if they had to move to a country where language and customs were unfamiliar.

3 ATMOSPHERE

The rose-patterned tablecloth, the "amber kerosene," and the "yellow crown of flames" convey the warmth Ernesto and his mother found in the old couple's home.

4 BACKGROUND

The narrator calls his feeling of respect for the old couple "genuinely Mexican." In Mexico children are taught that the old are wise and should be treated with great respect.

5 THEME

Ernesto is chased by unfriendly American boys and is exposed to a situation many immigrants have faced: a cruel reception by the natives of an area.

with a great splash. When my water party was interrupted, both the bathroom and I got a scrubbing.

With the help of the hotel clerk we located the family with whom we were to stay, an elderly couple who took in boarders and rented a spare room. They lived in a muddy alley with narrow board sidewalks and rickety planks connecting the walks with the droopy unpainted
1 porches. The whole scene was in two colors—the mud-brown of the alley, the empty lots between the houses, the plank fences propped from behind to keep them from falling; and the dirty gray of everything else—like the fronts of the houses and the winter sky.

Our temporary home was halfway down the alley between two streets. Our landlady was plump, quiet, slow-moving, and wore her greying hair in two thick braids. The husband, a fat man with sad eyes who talked even less than his wife, did odd jobs around town.

Our front room had two small beds. Mine swayed and squeaked when I got into it. There was a dresser between the two windows with a washbowl and a white pitcher on the marble top. The blinds were ragged at the bottom and were kept down all the time because there were no curtains. I discovered the blinds could snap and roll up with a whir and a clap if I jerked them, but Doña Henriqueta immediately stopped my game.

2 Because there was nothing to do outside but get wet and muddy we spent the first days helping with the housework and looking at the people who sloshed by. All of them were Mexicans, *barrio*[10] people. The empty lot next door was a sump of drainage from the alley, littered with tin cans and empty bottles that had become stuck in the gumbo. We had to walk alongside this swamp of garbage to get to the toilet, an outhouse connected to the back porch by planks raised on bricks.

Since the kitchen was the only heated room, we spent our evenings there, feeding the fire one stick at a time, the adults talking as I listened.
3 The oil cloth on the kitchen table was covered with a design of huge red roses. In the center, the oil lamp, its glass belly full of amber kerosene, burned in a yellow crown of flames. The old couple told us about Tucson and my mother told them of Jalco, of the siege of Mazatlán, the revolution,[11] and our mishaps on the way to
4 Nogales. Privately we called the old couple *los abuelitos*,[12] and our visit with them gave me some idea of what it was like to have a grandfather and grandmother in the house. They were not our kinfolk but the *respeto*[13] I felt for them, after Doña Henriqueta's lectures, was genuinely Mexican.

Except for the quiet company of the *abuelitos*, we were locked in the alley, my mother with no work and I with no friends. The Mexican boys who lived in the other row houses had no place
5 to play where we could become acquainted. The one time I ventured out of the alley and down the street I was chased back by three American boys who yelled something I could not understand but which didn't sound friendly. . . .

Regularly we went to the hotel to ask for mail from Gustavo. Almost always there was a letter with money, but it was many weeks before we received the most important one of all, the one that had the pass and the instructions for the trip. We were to take the train to Sacramento, go to the Hotel Español and stay there until Gustavo and José came for us.

The *abuelitos* walked us to the railroad station, helping us with our tin trunk and suitcases. As if we had lived together all our lives every-

10. ***barrio*** [bär′rē ō]: Spanish for "neighborhood."

11. **the revolution:** The Mexico Revolution of 1910 was led by Francisco Madero against President Diaz, who had been a dictator for thirty-four years. Madero won but was murdered in 1911. A renewed revolutionary struggle began in 1914.

12. ***los abuelitos*** [lōs ä bwä lē′tōs]: Spanish for "grandparents."

13. ***respeto*** [rās pā′to]: Spanish for "respect."

GUIDED READING

LITERAL QUESTIONS

1a. How does the narrator describe the surroundings in the Tucson neighborhood? (It is muddy, near "a sump of drainage," littered with cans and bottles.)

2a. What happens when Ernesto tries to play outside? (He is chased and yelled at by three American boys.)

INFERENTIAL QUESTIONS

1b. What do these details tell you about the neighborhood? (It is very poor and not well tended.)

2b. Why do you think the boys chase him? (They may see him as some sort of threat; they may be trying to show that they are protective of their neighborhood.)

body embraced everybody and the old couple waited to wave good-bye as our train pulled out of the station.

As soon as we were in the coach I knew we were riding first-class. The seat was a green felt cushion, plump and comfortable. The packages and suitcases were placed on the racks and under the seats, not in the aisles, so I could walk up and down when I felt stiff or when I wanted a drink of ice water which came out of a silver faucet. . . .

When the conductor came by to check tickets, he punched two colored tabs and slipped them through a metal frame on the seat in front of us. I discovered to my delight that the brass letters on his cap were exactly like those of the conductor in Mazatlán. I spelled them out silently as I watched him—c-o-n, con, d-u-c, duc, t-o-r, tor, conductor. In a whispered conversation with my mother over the subject, we agreed that a gringo con-

The Sacramento, California, railroad station in 1910, approximately the time when Galarza arrived there.

ductor would not be wearing Mexican letters on his cap, and that *conductor* in Spanish was the
2 same as conductor in English. This started a guessing game that kept us amused the rest of the trip. Some words worked out neatly in both languages, like *conductor*, others failed to match by a syllable or a letter, in which case we thought English spelling idiotic.

I had never moved as fast as on this train which sped along faster even than the *diligencia.*[14] The telephone poles whizzed by, making me dizzy if I watched them, and around the curves the coach leaned a little.

3 We began to notice the eating habits of the gringos. The man with the large tray strapped to his shoulders did not have tortillas or tacos[15] or meat snacks with pepper sauce. He sold slices of white bread cut in triangles with mushy stuff between the slices. After one bite I wrapped mine in a napkin and didn't touch it again until I realized that it was either sandwiches or starvation. Once a day we bought peanuts and fruit, which we selected by pointing to the tray. To pay the vendor I held out on the palm of my hand an assortment of nickles and dimes and quarters. It was not even necessary for me to ask "hua-mochee." At the station stops, hawkers did not rush up to the coach windows to sell us food. In the middle of the train there was a car where you could eat a meal sitting at a table, but we never went there.

I asked the conductor several times while we were on the long journey, "hua-tinees, plees."
4 One conductor pulled the watch out of his vest pocket, flipped open the gold lid and read the time to us, which meant nothing at all since we didn't know the numbers in English. Another, after looking us over and guessing our difficulty, snapped his watch open and held the face up for us to read.

---

14. ***diligencia*** [dē lē hän′sē ä]: Spanish for "stagecoach."
15. **tortillas** [tôr tē′yəz], **tacos** [ta′kōz]: Mexican food. A tortilla is a round, flat cake of cornmeal. A taco is a fried tortilla wrapped around a filling of meat.

AT A GLANCE

- Ernesto and his mother board the train to Sacramento; he considers the details of the coach.
- They discover differences and similarities between Mexican and American words.
- They eat American food on board the train.
- Ernesto asks conductors for the time.

1 ATMOSPHERE

Simple details (the plumpness of cushions, the suitcase racks, the unblocked aisles, the "silver" faucet) create a sense of luxury on what was probably a fairly ordinary train car.

2 MAIN IDEA

Ernesto and his mother find similarities as well as differences between Spanish and English; they become more comfortable with the differences by making fun of English spelling.

3 DETAILS

Ernesto compares the food sold on the train (white bread sandwiches) with the food he ate in Mexico (tacos and tamales). He eats the sandwiches only when he sees there is no alternative.

4 THEME

Ernesto tries to speak to two conductors; he finds that one is aware of his language difficulty and is helpful, and one is impatient.

GUIDED READING

LITERAL QUESTIONS

1a. How does the narrator describe the railroad car? (He says it is first-class, with green felt cushions, roomy racks, and ice water from silver faucets.)

2a. What does the second conductor do when Ernesto asks the time? (He shows the boy his watch.)

INFERENTIAL QUESTIONS

1b. Do you think the car actually was first-class? (Ernesto's family had little money; the car probably only seemed first-class to a boy who had never ridden a train.)

2b. Why does the conductor do this? (He realizes Ernesto cannot understand spoken English and instead lets him read the time himself.)

AT A GLANCE

- Enresto observes American manners.
- Ernesto and his mother disembark into the bustling station.

1 POINT OF VIEW

From the child-narrator's point of view it seems incredible that a country can be at peace, since the one he has just fled is at war.

2 THEME

The narrator finds American behavior and manners boorish compared with those of Mexicans: The Americans put their feet on seats, laugh loudly, wear their hats inside the coach, and blow their noses with their fingers.

3 BACKGROUND

In the early 1900's when railroads began to extend through the West, many railroad companies used foreign labor to build tracks because they could pay foreigners less and force them to work harder than American labor.

4 SETTING

The narrator's first view of Sacramento is strange and "frightening," as much of his journey through an unfamiliar land must have been.

1 Not seeing any soldiers with rifles and bayonets I asked my mother if the Americans were not having a revolution. "No," and when I asked why, she only said, "People are different."

And from what I saw in the coach on that long ride, the Americans were indeed different. They ate the repulsive sandwiches with relish. They put their feet, shoes and all, on the seats in front of them. When the men laughed it seemed more like a roar, and if they were close by it scared me. Doña Henriqueta frowned and admonished me. "Be careful I never hear you bray-
2 ing like that." Many of them kept their hats on as if they didn't know that the inside of a coach was like the inside of a house, and wearing your hat in either a sure sign of being *mal educado.*[16] On the station platforms gentlemen in bowler hats, suits, and shiny boots blew their noses first with their fingers and then with their handkerchiefs. "What a thing," my mother said. "Asquerosos."[17]

It was late in the afternoon after countless hours from Tucson that the conductor stopped by our seat, picked up our stubs and pointing to us, said, "Sacramento." With the greatest of ease I said "Tanks yoo" and felt again the excitement of arriving somewhere. We looked out at the countryside to be sure we didn't miss the first sights of the city with the Mexican name where we were going to live. As far as I could see there were rows on rows of bushes, some standing by themselves, some leaning on wires and posts, all of them without leaves. "Vineyards," my mother said. I always wanted to know the number or quantity of things. "How many?" I asked. "A heap," she answered, not just *un montón,* but *un montonal,*[18] which meant more than you could count, nobody really knows, sky-high, infinity, millions.

We left the vineyards behind, passing by orchards and pastures with cattle. At the crossroads, our locomotive hooted a salute to droves of cattle, automobiles and horse-drawn buggies with school children waiting to cross.

Our train began to make a great circle, slowing down. The roadbed carried the train higher than the roof tops, giving us a panorama of the
3 city. Track crews standing by with the familiar brown faces of Mexicans waved to us. I looked hard for Gustavo and José, for the last we had heard they were working on the Southern Pacific, making tracks or locomotives. Through the window we could see long buildings with stacks belching smoke like a dozen Casas Redondas,[19] boxcars, flatcars, coaches, gondolas, cabooses, and locomotives dismantled or waiting for repairs.

A brakeman opened the door at the front of the coach and called, "Sack-men-ah," by which we knew he meant Sa-cra-men-to, for we had passed a large sign with the name in black and white at the entrance to the corporation yard.

Unlike the Mexicans, the Americans were not in a great hurry to leave the coach. We were the last, carrying our luggage.

4 We stepped down into a frightening scene, a huge barn filled with smoke and noise and the smell of burnt oil. This was the station, nearly as long as the train and with a sooty roof twice as high as the *mercado*[20] in Mazatlán. Our locomotive was still belching black clouds from the stack. Men were hurrying along pulling four-wheeled carts loaded with baggage, jerking hoses close to the train and thrusting the nozzles into holes here and there, washing windows with brushes on long sticks, opening the axle boxes with hammers and banging them shut.

We dashed through the confusion over the tracks and into the waiting room, myself drag-

16. ***mal educado*** [mäl ā do͞o kä′dō]: Spanish for "ill-mannered."
17. **asquerosos** [äs ke rō′sōs]: Spanish for "disgusting."
18. ***un montón*** [o͞on mōn tōn′] . . . ***un montonal*** [mōn tō näl′]
19. **Casas Redondas** [kä′säs rā dōn′däs]: Spanish for "roundhouses," buildings used for the storage and repair of railroad locomotives.
20. ***mercado*** [mär kä′dō]: Spanish for "market"; here, a vast space.

GUIDED READING

LITERAL QUESTIONS

1a. What do Ernesto and his mother think of the Americans on the train? (that they have bad manners and are disgusting)

2a. How many vineyards does Doña Henriqueta say she sees? (*un montonal*—millions, infinity)

INFERENTIAL QUESTIONS

1b. According to Ernesto, how do the Americans' manners differ from Mexicans' manners? (Mexicans would not put their feet up on seats, laugh so roughly, keep their hats on indoors, or blow their noses with their fingers.)

2b. Why do you think she uses this word to describe the number of vineyards? (In Mexico she probably had not seen vines or plants in such great quantity.)

ging one of the shopping bags. The depot was a gloomy, dangerous place. We sat watching the crowd thin out. Our train departed, headed in the same direction, and I felt that we were being left behind.

Out of the bag my mother pulled the small envelope with the address of the Hotel Español. She handed me the paper. Holding it I watched the men in uniforms and green visors who passed by us and the clerks behind the ticket counters. Taking a chance I stopped one and thrust the paper at him. I said, "Plees" and waited, pinching one corner of the envelope while he read it. Like the conductor, the man guessed our prob-
2 lem. He smiled, and held up a forefinger, crooking and straightening it while he looked at us. I had no idea what he meant, for in Mexico you signaled people to follow you by holding up your hand and closing all the fingers over the palm with a snap a few times. But Doña Henriqueta knew instantly and he guided us under an arch and out of the station. Handing back the envelope he pointed down the street and smiled us on.

One more stop to ask our way with another "plees" and we were at the Hotel Español.

STUDY QUESTIONS

Recalling

1. Summarize the plan by which Ernesto and his mother will eventually arrive in Sacramento.
2. Describe three items in the Tucson hotel that are new to Ernesto, and explain his reaction to each of them.
3. Name four observations Ernesto and his mother make about Americans during the ride from Tucson to Sacramento.

Interpreting

4. The border separating Mexico and the United States is an invisible line. According to Ernesto's experiences, what other "borders" that are more difficult to cross separate the two nations?
5. Considering Ernesto's reactions to things he sees in America, what can we assume about his life in Mexico?
6. What traits of young Ernesto's personality will make it easy for him to adapt to a new country?

Extending

7. Which Mexican custom as demonstrated by Ernesto and his family do you admire? Why?

VIEWPOINT

The *New York Review of Books* called *Barrio Boy* an important work because it records the Mexican American experience and also because it speaks about the lives of all immigrants:

> The passage on the flight north from Mexico...belongs among the choicest accounts of debarkation [arrival] into America.

- What parts of Ernesto's story are probably shared by all people coming to a new place?

COMPOSITION

Writing About an Autobiography

- We see everything in the selection from Galarza's viewpoint as a child. Explain how this viewpoint as well as the choice of other details illustrates (a) Galarza's outlook on life and (b) his purpose in writing this section of his autobiography. *For help with this assignment, see Lesson 8 in the Writing About Literature Handbook at the back of this book.*

Writing an Explanation

- Imagine that you are speaking to someone your age who, like Ernesto, has not seen many modern conveniences. Explain to that person one of the following items: (a) a computer, (b) a telephone, (c) a television, (d) a stereo, (e) an automobile. Include an explanation of the device's purpose, its good and bad features, and instructions for its use.

COMPOSITION: GUIDELINES FOR EVALUATION

WRITING ABOUT AN AUTOBIOGRAPHY

Objective

To determine Galarza's outlook and purpose by analyzing his viewpoint as a child

Guidelines for Evaluation

- suggested length: three to five paragraphs
- should state in introduction Galarza's outlook and purpose
- should cite details that indicate Galarza's viewpoint as a child

WRITING AN EXPLANATION

Objective

To explain an item's purpose, features, means of use

Guidelines for Evaluation

- suggested length: three paragraphs
- should identify device and its purpose
- should thoroughly describe its features
- should provide logical instructions for the use of the device

AT A GLANCE

- A clerk guides Ernesto and his mother from the station and directs them toward the hotel.
- Ernesto and his mother arrive at their hotel.

1 THEME

That Ernesto felt he was "being left behind" is an indication of how an immigrant's fear and loneliness in the face of change can be temporarily calmed by something as unlikely as a train.

2 PURPOSE

The author shows that patience on the part of natives can narrow the immigrant–American gap. Here, the clerk's assistance eases the adjustment of Ernesto and his mother to their new life.

REFLECTING ON THE SELECTION

Do you think Ernesto is like or unlike the Americans he meets? Why? (Both: In many matters of lifestyle and customs, Ernesto is unlike the Americans. At bottom, however, he shares important human characteristics with them.)

STUDY QUESTIONS

1. They will wait in Tucson until uncles send money for trip.
2.
   - *electric bulb:* flicks it on/off
   - *bedsprings:* jumps up/down
   - *bathtub:* slides down tub into water
3. have strange eating habits; put feet on seats; laugh too loudly; men don't remove hats in coach
4. language, wealth, culture, fear
5. He was poor.
6. friendliness, inquisitiveness
7. possible answers: courtesy, propriety, family loyalty

VIEWPOINT

fear of unknown; different language, customs, eating habits

AT A GLANCE

- Anne muses about her reasons for keeping a diary.
- She reveals that she has no "real" friends.
- She describes her family and acquaintances.

LITERARY OPTIONS

- audience
- characterization
- conflict

THEMATIC OPTIONS

- upholding ideals
- adolescence
- friends and family

1 AUDIENCE

Anne doesn't intend that others should read her diary; nevertheless, she is aware of a potential audience, which she reveals by saying she doesn't think anyone else "would be interested" in reading it.

2 THEME

Anne reveals that she loves her family, but she is also lonely and longs for a "real friend" who would truly understand her.

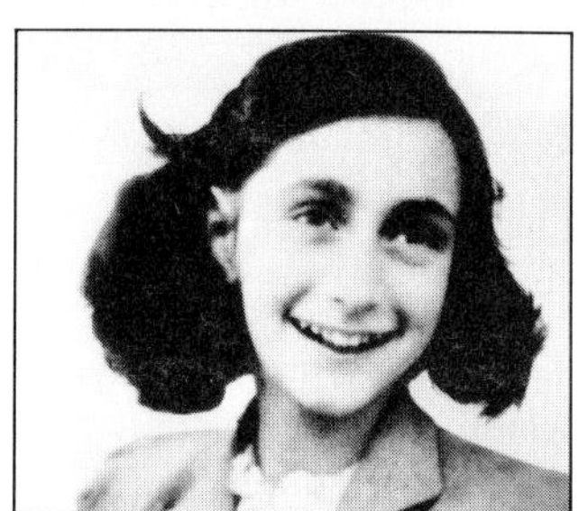

Anne Frank (1929–1945), a German Jewish girl, moved with her family to the Netherlands in 1933 after Adolf Hitler's Nazi party came to power. In 1942 the Nazis occupied the Netherlands. Anne and her family—and others who later joined them—went into hiding in a small attic above a warehouse in Amsterdam to escape persecution. The family was captured in August 1944; they were sent to different concentration camps. Anne died in 1945 of typhus at the Bergen-Belsen camp in Germany.

During the two years of confinement in the attic, Anne Frank kept a diary. Anne's father, the lone survivor of the family, discovered the diary after the war. The book has since been translated into more than twenty languages and has been adapted for the stage and film.

The first of the excerpts that follow was written shortly before the family went into hiding; the second, shortly before their capture. Anne died before her sixteenth birthday.

■ How does keeping a diary help an individual? A society?

Anne Frank

from Diary of a Young Girl

Saturday, 20 June, 1942

I haven't written for a few days, because I wanted first of all to think about my diary. It's an odd idea for someone like me to keep a diary; not only because I have never done so before,
1 but because it seems to me that neither I—nor for that matter anyone else—will be interested in the unbosomings of a thirteen-year-old schoolgirl. Still, what does that matter? I want to write, but more than that, I want to bring out all kinds of things that lie buried deep in my heart.

There is a saying that "paper is more patient than man"; it came back to me on one of my slightly melancholy days, while I sat chin in hand, feeling too bored and limp even to make up my mind whether to go out or stay at home. Yes, there is no doubt that paper is patient and as I don't intend to show this cardboard-covered notebook, bearing the proud name of "diary," to anyone, unless I find a real friend, boy or
2 girl, probably nobody cares. And now I come to the root of the matter, the reason for my starting a diary: it is that I have no such real friend.

Let me put it more clearly, since no one will believe that a girl of thirteen feels herself quite alone in the world, nor is it so. I have darling parents and a sister of sixteen. I know about thirty people whom one might call friends—I have strings of boy friends, anxious to catch a glimpse of me and who, failing that, peep at me through mirrors in class. I have relations, aunts and

GUIDED READING

LITERAL QUESTION

1a. What saying does Anne quote when she gives her reasons for keeping a journal? ("Paper is more patient than man.")

INFERENTIAL QUESTION

1b. Why do you think Anne feels her diary must be "patient"? (because she tells it things she feels would interest no one else)

uncles, who are darlings too, a good home, no—I don't seem to lack anything. But it's the same with all my friends, just fun and joking, nothing more. I can never bring myself to talk of anything outside the common round. We don't seem to be able to get any closer, that is the root of the trouble. Perhaps I lack confidence, but anyway, there it is, a stubborn fact and I don't seem to be able to do anything about it.

Hence, this diary. In order to enhance in my mind's eye the picture of the friend for whom I have waited so long, I don't want to set down a series of bald facts in a diary like most people do, but I want this diary itself to be my friend, and I shall call my friend Kitty. No one will grasp what I'm talking about if I begin my letters to Kitty just out of the blue, so albeit unwillingly, I will start by sketching in brief the story of my life.

My father was thirty-six when he married my mother, who was then twenty-five. My sister Margot was born in 1926 in Frankfort-on-Main,[1] I followed on June 12, 1929, and, as we are Jewish, we emigrated to Holland in 1933, where my father was appointed Managing Director of Travies N.V. This firm is in close relationship with the firm of Kolen & Co. in the same building, of which my father is a partner.

The rest of our family, however, felt the full impact of Hitler's anti-Jewish laws, so life was filled with anxiety. In 1938 after the pogroms,[2] my two uncles (my mother's brothers) escaped to the U.S.A. My old grandmother came to us, she was then seventy-three. After May 1940 good times rapidly fled: first the war, then the capitulation,[3] followed by the arrival of the Germans, which is when the sufferings of us Jews really began. Anti-Jewish decrees followed each other in quick succession. Jews must wear a yellow star,[4] Jews must hand in their bicycles, Jews are banned from trains and are forbidden to drive. Jews are only allowed to do their shopping between three and five o'clock and then only in shops which bear the placard "Jewish shop." Jews must be indoors by eight o'clock and cannot even sit in their own gardens after that hour. Jews are forbidden to visit theaters, cinemas, and other places of entertainment. Jews may not take part in public sports. Swimming baths, tennis courts, hockey fields, and other sports grounds are all prohibited to them. Jews may not visit Christians. Jews must go to Jewish schools, and many more restrictions of a similar kind.

So we could not do this and were forbidden to do that. But life went on in spite of it all. Jopie[5] used to say to me, "You're scared to do anything, because it may be forbidden." Our freedom was strictly limited. Yet things were still bearable.

Granny died in January 1942; no one will ever know how much she is present in my thoughts and how much I love her still.

In 1934 I went to school at the Montessori
4 Kindergarten and continued there. It was at the end of the school year, I was in form[6] 6B, when I had to say good-by to Mrs. K. We both wept, it was very sad. In 1941 I went, with my sister Margot, to the Jewish Secondary School, she into the fourth form and I into the first.

So far everything is all right with the four of us and here I come to the present day.

Saturday, 15 July, 1944

Dear Kitty,

We have had a book from the library with the challenging title of: ***What Do You Think of the***

---

1. **Frankfort-on-Main:** also known as Frankfurt, a city in what is now central West Germany.
2. **pogroms** [pō′grəmz]: organized persecution of a minority group; here, a wave of persecution of Jews throughout Germany in November, 1938.
3. **capitulation** [kə pich′ə lā′shən]: surrender; here, the surrender of the Dutch army to Germany in May, 1940.
4. **yellow star:** During World War II the Jews in German-occupied countries were forced to wear a yellow star of David to make them more recognizable.
5. **Jopie:** Anne's classmate and friend at the Jewish Secondary School.
6. **form:** grade or class.

AT A GLANCE

- She decides her diary will be her friend; she names it "Kitty."
- Anne describes the growing anti-Jewish sentiment in Europe.
- Anne describes her departure from the Montessori school.
- A second diary entry from two years later begins.

1 CONFLICT

Anne's description of her friends' activities reveals her inner conflict: She joins them in "fun and joking," though she wants to share her more serious feelings about life with them.

2 AUDIENCE

Anne names her diary "Kitty" and treats it like a friend, stressing that she is writing for herself and her "friend"; again she shows her awareness of a wider audience by saying, "No one will grasp what I'm talking about . . . ."

3 BACKGROUND

From 1933 until 1945 Adolf Hitler was chancellor of Germany. He brought the Nazi party to power. Hitler was responsible for the slaughter of millions of Jews and others.

4 THEME

This passage shows not only the sadness inherent in the situation but also Anne's desperation for close ties in a world where everything familiar is crumbling.

GUIDED READING

LITERAL QUESTION

1a. What does Anne do when she is with her friends? (She jokes and has fun.)

INFERENTIAL QUESTION

1b. Why do you think such normal behavior upsets her? (She wishes to be closer to them and to talk of deeper, more meaningful matters.)

AT A GLANCE

- Anne discusses a book that criticizes young people.
- She tells of her self–awareness and courage.
- She feels young people have more difficulty in life than adults have.

1 CHARACTERIZATION

Anne believes that she knows herself and can judge herself honestly; that she watches herself "just like an outsider" reveals she may not be entirely comfortable with herself.

2 CONFLICT

Anne states that "there are so many things about myself that I condemn . . . ," showing that she feels conflict between what she believes and how she acts.

Modern Young Girl? I want to talk about this subject today.

The author of this book criticizes "the youth of today" from top to toe, without, however, condemning the whole of the young brigade as "incapable of anything good." On the contrary, she is rather of the opinion that if young people wished, they have it in their hands to make a bigger, more beautiful and better world, but that they occupy themselves with superficial things, without giving a thought to real beauty.

The Amsterdam warehouse where Anne Frank, her family, and others hid in a secret attic for two years. The building was photographed in 1952, the year *Diary of a Young Girl* was published in the United States; since then it has been refurbished as a museum called Anne Frank House.

In some passages, the writer gave me very much the feeling she was directing her criticism at me, and that's why I want to lay myself completely bare to you for once and defend myself against this attack.

1 I have one outstanding trait in my character, which must strike anyone who knows me for any length of time, and that is my knowledge of myself. I can watch myself and my actions, just like an outsider. The Anne of every day I can face entirely without prejudice, without making excuses for her, and watch what's good and what's bad about her. This "self-consciousness" haunts me, and every time I open my mouth I know as soon as I've spoken whether "that ought to have been different" or "that was right
2 as it was." There are so many things about myself that I condemn; I couldn't begin to name them all. I understand more and more how true Daddy's words were when he said: "All children must look after their own upbringing." Parents can only give good advice or put them on the right paths, but the final forming of a person's character lies in their own hands.

In addition to this, I have lots of courage, I always feel so strong and as if I can bear a great deal, I feel so free and so young! I was glad when I first realized it, because I don't think I shall easily bow down before the blows that inevitably come to everyone. . . .

"For in its innermost depths youth is lonelier than old age."

I read this saying in some book and I've always remembered it, and found it to be true. Is it true then that grownups have a more difficult time here than we do? No. I know it isn't. Older people have formed their opinions about everything, and don't waver before they act. It's twice as hard

GUIDED READING

LITERAL QUESTIONS

1a. What criticism is directed toward young people by the author of the book Anne reads? (Young people occupy themselves with superficial concerns without giving thought to real beauty.)

2a. How does Anne describe her own attitude toward danger? (She says that she has "lots of courage.")

INFERENTIAL QUESTIONS

1b. Anne feels that this criticism applies to her. Do you agree? (No; she thinks and feels deeply and wants to make a better world.)

2b. Do you think she is correct in her assessment? Why or why not? (Yes; the entry was written while she was hiding bravely from the Nazis in an attic.)

for us young ones to hold our ground, and maintain our opinions, in a time when all ideals are being shattered and destroyed, when people are showing their worst side, and do not know whether to believe in truth and right and God.

Anyone who claims that the older ones have a more difficult time here certainly doesn't realize to what extent our problems weigh down on us, problems for which we are probably much too young, but which thrust themselves upon us continually, until, after a long time, we think we've found a solution, but the solution doesn't seem able to resist the facts which reduce it to nothing again. That's the difficulty in these times: ideals, dreams, and cherished hopes rise within us, only to meet the horrible truth and be shattered.

1 It's really a wonder that I haven't dropped all my ideals, because they seem so absurd and impossible to carry out. Yet I keep them, because in spite of everything I still believe that people are really good at heart. I simply can't build up my hopes on a foundation consisting of confusion, misery, and death. I see the world gradually being
2 turned into a wilderness, I hear the ever approaching thunder, which will destroy us too, I can feel the sufferings of millions and yet, if I look up into the heavens, I think that it will all come right, that this cruelty too will end, and that peace and tranquillity will return again.

In the meantime, I must uphold my ideals, for perhaps the time will come when I shall be able to carry them out.

Yours, Anne

STUDY QUESTIONS

Recalling

1. According to the first entry, what is Anne's purpose in keeping a diary? Who is "Kitty"?
2. In the second entry what does Anne call her two outstanding character traits?
3. From the second entry find the reason Anne gives for holding on to her ideals.

Interpreting

4. What does Anne mean when, at the beginning, she says, "Paper is more patient than man"?
5. What do we learn about Anne's personality from what she says about friends and family?
6. In what ways does Anne change between the two entries? In what ways is she the same?

Extending

7. The book that Anne had from the library, *What Do You Think of the Modern Young Girl?*, says that young people "occupy themselves with superficial things, without giving a thought to real beauty." Can this statement be applied to today's youth? Why or why not?

VIEWPOINT

Anne Frank touches a responsive chord in many young people who read her diary. One girl from Boston wrote:

> Anne's struggles for maturity have reminded me of mine, and yet she was so much more mature than I who am now sixteen.
>
> —*The Works of Anne Frank*

■ Give two examples of Anne's maturity. Explain why Anne may have been more mature than most people her age.

LITERARY FOCUS

The Diarist's Audience

The **audience** of a piece of literature is the type of reader for whom the work is intended. Most diarists write their diaries just for themselves. Since no one else will read the diaries, the writers can be honest about themselves and others without fear of hurting anyone or appearing foolish or boastful. Still, many diarists seem aware that their work may

AT A GLANCE

- Anne writes about the difficulties youths have in finding solutions for their problems.
- She maintains her ideals and hopes to act on them one day.

1 MAIN IDEA

Anne declares that—although her world is falling to pieces—she still believes that "people are really good at heart." She upholds her belief in basic goodness.

2 PURPOSE

Anne declares that people must uphold their ideals because ultimately cruelty will give way to peace.

REFLECTING ON THE SELECTION

Is Anne's belief that "people are really good at heart" naive, given her situation? (Possible answers: *Yes*—she did not fully understand the Nazi horror; *no*—she would have said that the Nazis didn't realize the results of their own actions.)

STUDY QUESTIONS

1. she has no true friend; her diary
2. self-knowledge, courage
3. believes people are good at heart; thinks cruelty will end
4. one can write without fear of being rejected or criticized
5. she is mature; has insight into human nature
6. becomes more introspective; maintains understanding of self
7. Students might try to define real beauty/superficial things and give examples.

VIEWPOINT

- has good insight into own character; understands there are things she cannot change
- has experienced worst side of human nature; has not been sheltered

LITERARY FOCUS

that she has no real friend; names two outstanding character traits: courage, self-knowledge; questions why she maintains her ideals in the face of the world situation

VOCABULARY

1. (a) reward: punish
2. (b) honored: respected
3. (c) action: act
4. (c) damage: harm
5. (c) armed: defenseless

COMPARING AUTOBIOGRAPHIES

1. Students may compare by ranking autobiographies from most aware to least aware.
   - Anne Frank: most aware; not written for publication
   - Angelou: takes middle ground; childhood experiences are revealed by the adult
   - Galarza: seemed less aware as child; reveals few feelings
2. The immediacy of Anne Frank's account creates an intimacy; the other works are more objective because they are told by an adult recalling the past.

eventually have a wider use. They may use their diaries now to record impressions and events that they will later incorporate into other writing. Some diaries of famous people actually seem designed to be published, perhaps after the author's death.

Thinking About the Diarist's Audience

■ Find at least three statements about herself or others that Anne probably would not have made if she had thought that other people might read her diary.

VOCABULARY

Analogies

Analogies are comparisons stated as double relationships: "*A* is to *B* as *C* is to *D*." On tests analogies are printed as "*A* : *B* : : *C* : *D*." You may be given the first pair and asked to find a second pair that has the same kind of relationship as the first pair. See the following example:

FAUCET : WATER : : switch : light

Here the first word in each pair *sets off* the second.

Many different kinds of relationships can be stated in analogies. *A* may be greater than *B* or an extreme of *B*, as in FEAST : SNACK. *A* may mean approximately the same as *B* or the opposite. *A* may cause *B*, as in HARD WORK : SUCCESS. *A* and *B* may be different forms of the same word, as in DETERMINE : DETERMINATION.

Each numbered item below begins with two related words in capital letters, one of which is from *Diary of a Young Girl*. First decide how these two capitalized words relate to each other. Then choose the pair with the relationship most like the relationship between the pair in capital letters. Write the number of each item and the letter of your choice on a separate sheet.

1. ENHANCE : DIMINISH : :
   (a) reward : punish (c) disappear : vanish
   (b) emerge : enter (d) relate : confide
2. MELANCHOLY : SAD : :
   (a) general : specific (c) noisy : nosy
   (b) honored : respected (d) angry : sorrowful
3. CAPITULATION : CAPITULATE : :
   (a) emigrate : emigration (c) action : act
   (b) succeed : succession (d) surrender : give up
4. IMPACT : FORCE : :
   (a) suffering : complaint (c) damage : harm
   (b) pack : journey (d) joke : giggle
5. SUPERFICIAL : PROFOUND : :
   (a) superior : preferred (c) armed : defenseless
   (b) artificial : fake (d) created : produced

COMPOSITION

Writing About a Diary

■ The writers of diaries reveal their own states of mind as well as report current events. First give two examples of outside events and two examples of personal feelings that Anne reports. Then explain whether you think Anne reveals more about herself or about the events occurring around her.

Writing a Diary Entry

■ Anne Frank wrote about both the frightening events of her time and her personal hopes and fears. Imagine that you are a teen-ager living at the time of some great event in history. Write one entry in your diary in which you describe your reactions to the events of the day.

COMPARING AUTOBIOGRAPHIES

1. Compare two or more of the following autobiographies: *I Know Why the Caged Bird Sings, Barrio Boy,* and *Diary of a Young Girl.* How self-aware and honest do you think each author has been in the personal statements contained in the works you choose? Use examples from the works to support your opinions.
2. Maya Angelou and Ernesto Galarza wrote their accounts as adults looking back on their childhood, but Anne Frank wrote her diary when she was a teen-ager. Choose two or more of these autobiographies and explain how the impact of each work is affected by the time relationship between the actual events and the writing of the book.

COMPOSITION: GUIDELINES FOR EVALUATION

WRITING ABOUT A DIARY

Objective

To compare the extent to which Anne reveals herself and the events occurring around her

Guidelines for Evaluation

- suggested length: three to five paragraphs
- should state two examples of outside events and two of personal feelings that Anne reports
- should state opinion as to whether Anne reveals more about herself or outside events

WRITING A DIARY ENTRY

Objective

To describe a reaction to an event

Guidelines for Evaluation

- suggested length: 150–300 words
- should describe event
- should describe writer's reaction to event
- should use informal, first-person narration

LITERARY FOCUS: Essay

The **essay** is a short piece of nonfiction writing on any topic. The form of the essay was developed by the sixteenth-century French writer Michel de Montaigne [mē shel′ də mon tān′]. Montaigne used the term *J'essai,* which means "I try," for short nonfiction that attempts to inform and explain. Today, popular essays have been written by scientists, explorers, sports figures, and politicians.

Essays are classified as formal and informal. The **formal essay** is serious and impersonal. The **informal essay** entertains while it informs and usually displays a light approach and a conversational style. The author of an informal essay often indirectly creates a self-portrait. Most popular essays—including the essays on the following pages—are informal essays.

An author always has a definite purpose in writing an essay, a general idea or opinion to communicate. As indicated on page 233, there are several ways an author can alert us to the purpose of an essay. Apart from communicating one general idea, the essay may affect its audience in one way or another: It may entertain the audience, inform the audience, rouse the audience to action. Regardless of its specific effect, however, the successful essay must communicate its general idea—its purpose—to its audience.

Different writers often specialize in different kinds of essays. A **narrative essay** recounts true events. Examples of narrative essays include "human interest" stories in newspapers or magazines. A **descriptive essay** describes actual people, places, or things. Magazine columns devoted to travel or architecture are examples of descriptive essays. A **persuasive essay** aims to convince the reader of the author's opinion and perhaps to rouse the reader to action. Persuasive essays include newspaper editorials and some reviews of books, plays, and movies. An **expository essay** presents information and explains an idea. Articles about cooking, gardening, and fishing are usually expository.

Effective essays, like the four essays that follow, often combine the different types of writing. "Kilimanjaro!" is basically a narrative about a mountain climb, yet it also contains detailed description. "Sayonara" is a descriptive essay that also explains a serious truth about language. "The Spreading 'You Know' " is persuasive with the help of both explanation and narration. Finally, narration and description help the expository essay, an excerpt from *Shakespeare of London,* to provide information about actors in Shakespeare's day.

AT A GLANCE

- The narrator describes the surroundings and Mount Kilimanjaro.
- The climbing party approaches the mountain.

LITERARY OPTIONS

- narrative essay
- setting
- style

THEMATIC OPTIONS

- accomplishment
- adventure
- responses to nature

1 VOCABULARY: CONNOTATION

The author uses the word *apex*, which can mean "highest point" or "culmination," to show that Kilimanjaro is not only the highest mountain in Africa but represents the greatest challenge in Africa.

2 THEME

The narrator communicates his enthusiasm for the adventure by noting that everything seems "new and fresh and different."

3 STYLE: METAPHOR

The author calls Kilimanjaro "the white ghost in the sky," a metaphor that stresses both the frightening and elusive aspects of the mountain.

By writing about his mountain-climbing expeditions, James Ramsey Ullman (1907–1971) combines his two favorite activities. He was a member of the first American expedition to Mount Everest in Asia's Himalayas in 1963 and wrote of the climb in his book *Americans on Everest*.

This narrative essay relates a grueling climb up Mount Kilimanjaro in Africa. Ullman shows that mountain climbers purposely seek out mountains that will test their skills, endurance, and courage.

■ Answer the famous question "Why do people climb mountains?"

James Ramsey Ullman

Kilimanjaro!

I

It has been called the House of God. It has been called the High One. The Cold One. The White One. On close acquaintance, by climbers, it has been called a variety of names rather less
1 printable. But to the world at large it is Kilimanjaro, the apex of Africa and one of the great mountains of the earth.

For two weeks we had been on safari in southern Kenya and northern Tanganyika,[1] and it was a realm of glorious variety. We moved from the red lands of Tsavo to the white lands of Amboseli; from prairie to parkland to forest to swamp to desert. We rode out from the towns of
2 the settlers, through the villages of the Masai,[2] into the domain of the lion, the rhino, and the elephant, and everywhere was something new and fresh and different from what we had seen before. Only one thing remained constant. Raise our eyes, wherever we were, and there *it* was. Above the giraffes' ears, above the baobab trees,
3 above the bright white cloud puffs in the African sunlight. Changeless above change unending, the white ghost in the sky.

Slowly we circled it, and the circle grew tighter. "They say it's one of the easiest big mountains in the world," I said to son Jim; and Jim nodded, but awkwardly, because his neck was craned back so far. "And it's only a mile higher than the Matterhorn,"[3] I added cheerfully.

Our white hunter, to whom mountaineers were a stranger breed than albino zebras, kept pointing off in sundry directions across what he affectionately called MMBA. Translation: Miles and Miles of Bloody[4] Africa. But by now we were incapable of focusing on anything except the center of our magic circle, the Miles and Miles of Bloody Kilimanjaro.

---

1. **Kenya** [ken′yə], **Tanganyika** [tang′gən yē′kə]: countries in eastern Africa. Tanganyika united with Zanzibar in 1964 to form the new nation of Tanzania [tan′zə nē′ə].
2. **Masai** [mä sī′]: the people of Kenya and Tanzania.
3. **Matterhorn:** mountain peak in the Alps on the border between Switzerland and Italy.
4. **Bloody:** British slang expression for "amazing" or "terrible."

GUIDED READING

LITERAL QUESTION

1a. What does MMBA stand for? (miles and miles of bloody Africa)

INFERENTIAL QUESTION

1b. Why do you think the hunter calls the plains MMBA? (He is both enthralled and frustrated by them, and he is awed by their huge expanse.)

It is a thing of contradictions; a long-dead volcano built up from the plains in vast gentle slopes and known to expert cragsmen[5] as a "nothing" mountain, an antagonist that calls for neither rope nor ax nor crampon nor any special climbing skills. It is, at the same time, an awful lot of nothing. The surrounding plains are at a mere 3000-foot elevation, its summit at 19,340—and Everest itself boasts no such three-mile leap from base to tip. A German scientist, Dr. Hans Meyer, first conquered Kilimanjaro in 1889, and since then it has been challenged by more climbers than any peak of its size on earth. Few have ever fallen from it, but well over half its challengers, through the years, have run out of gas on its upper flanks and had to turn back defeated.

Until a little more than a century ago the very existence of Kilimanjaro was unsuspected by the outside world. It was during the great European land grabs in Africa, when Kenya fell to the British and Tanganyika to the Germans, that it was discovered that the highest point of the continent stood flush on their borders. In a moment of generosity, Queen Victoria[6] (who had plenty of mountains in her realm) presented a gift to her nephew the Kaiser[7] (who had none) by authorizing a bulge in the boundary whereby the peak became all German. But the British got it back, with compound interest, in the first World War, and it has been theirs ever since.[8]

II

Road's end was the village of Marangu, sprawled on the mountain's southern flank at about the 5000-foot level. There Jim and I bade temporary farewell to jeep and white hunter (no neck-craner he), picked up our provisions and equipment, and joined forces with our porters. These added up to nine: a headman-guide, a cook, and seven rank-and-file load bearers. All were men of the Wachagga tribe (called Chaggas for short), and they ranged in age from a sixteen-year-old boy, who was having his first go at the mountain, to Thomas, the headman, who, at fifty-four, would be making his uncounted-
2 hundredth ascent. Of the lot of them only Thomas had the job of going all the way to the top—*if* his employers were able to follow him. We also joined forces with a third *bwana:*[9] Fred Hughes, an official in the Tanganyika Forestry Service and secretary of the local mountaineering club.

If we followed the usual schedule we would be gone five days: three and a half up, one and a half down. "Got your dark glasses for the snowfields?" Fred asked. And it was a startling thought in that tropical world of black Africa. We were in shorts and T shirts. We sweated. We plodded. We hiked ten miles to climb the three thousand feet of our first day's ascent.

3 During the first two hours we were in inhabited country—primitive but not squalid or poverty-stricken. On the contrary, it had a bright multihued Land of Oz[10] quality, a mixture of sunshine and greenery and gay clothing and chatter and laughter.

Then we entered the forest. This was pure jungleland: a maze of black boles, dense shrubbery, ferns, fronds and lianas.[11] Orchids and begonias winked on and off like lights in the
4 surrounding shadow. Birds cawed. Monkeys jabbered. Jabbering right back at them, our long file wound its way between the great green-bearded trees.

By now we were strung out loosely, each going at his own pace, meaning that Fred and Jim

5. **cragsmen:** mountain climbers.
6. **Queen Victoria:** (1819-1901) queen of England from 1837 to her death.
7. **the Kaiser** [kī'zər]: German for "emperor"; here, Kaiser Wilhelm I (1797-1888), king of Germany.
8. **it has . . . since:** This essay was written in 1957. Kilimanjaro is now in Tanzania.
9. ***bwana:*** "boss" in Swahili, a language of eastern and central Africa.
10. **Land of Oz:** magic fictional land in *The Wonderful Wizard of Oz* and other books by L. Frank Baum (1856-1919).
11. **boles . . . lianas** [lē ä'nəz]: types of tropical vegetation.

AT A GLANCE

- The author presents facts about Kilimanjaro and its history.
- The climbing party is described; they begin their ascent.
- They walk through jungle, observing plant and animal life.

1 NARRATIVE ESSAY

Ullman firms his narrative by giving facts about the mountain—its elevation, the number who have challenged it—that allow the reader a better understanding of his adventure.

2 THEME

Ullman makes it clear that the ascent of Kilimanjaro will not be easy by mentioning the possibility that he and the others might not complete the climb.

3 SETTING

The unreal atmosphere surrounding the expedition is established when the author compares the landscape to the Land of Oz.

4 STYLE: PERSONIFICATION

The moss-hung trees, past which the party walks, seem spooky and threatening when described as "green-bearded," as if they were human.

GUIDED READING

LITERAL QUESTIONS

1a. How do experts describe Kilimanjaro? (as a "nothing" mountain)

2a. What does Fred ask the narrator? (if he has dark glasses for the snowfield)

INFERENTIAL QUESTIONS

1b. Why do you think expert mountain climbers would still want to climb Kilimanjaro? (Although it can be climbed without special skills, over half its challengers have failed to reach the top.)

2b. Why is blinding snow a startling thought? (It is hard to imagine blinding snow and ice when one is surrounded by steamy hot jungle.)

AT A GLANCE

- The narrator talks with Thomas, the tribal headman and guide.
- The company camps at the first hut on Kilimanjaro.
- The second day's trek begins.
- The author comments on one of the mountain's summits.

1 STYLE: SIMILE

The author describes a bank of clouds as "white and frozen as a polar snowfield," anticipating the cold and snow he will encounter later in the climb.

2 SETTING

The description of Kilimanjaro conveys its seeming omnipresence and inaccessibility.

A climbing expedition on Kilimanjaro sets up camp at an altitude of approximately 16,500 feet.

were up ahead, well out of my ken, and I dead last in the procession. Well, next to dead last. Headman Thomas considered it his duty to stay with the feeblest of his *bwanas* and crept loyally behind me.

Unfortunately there was not much communication between us. Thomas' English was pretty well limited to his own name, presumably acquired in a mission house. And my mastery of the African tongues was somewhat less than that. Our major attempt at conversation came during a brief stop, when Thomas pointed at me and inquired, "Nairobi?"

"No, America," I told him.

"Ah," he said, "missionary."

And we let it go at that.

The lowest of Kilimanjaro's three huts, at about 9000 feet, is called the Bismarck. The head of our column took four hours to reach it. I needed about five.

The second day's trek, to Pieter's Hut, was another ten-odd miles, another 3000-plus feet higher. At first we were still in dense forest, but then the vegetation began to thin, we came out onto great moorlike slopes, and the surrounding
1 world swung slowly into view. To the east, and the Indian Ocean, a cloud bank spread away beneath us into blue miles, gleaming white and frozen as a polar snowfield. To south and west, there was not white but brown, no cloud but only distance—an incredible sweep of MMBA stretching to horizons so distant that the eye faltered trying to reach them.

Then the eye turned. It looked north. It looked
2 up. And there, again, was Kilimanjaro. It is not a single tapering peak but a huge and sprawling massif, almost a range in itself. To our right—the east—was the lesser of its two ultimate summits, called Mawenzi, an ancient volcanic core of red crumbling rock, raising its jagged towers to a

GUIDED READING

LITERAL QUESTION

1a. What does Thomas think the narrator does in Africa? (He thinks he is a missionary.)

INFERENTIAL QUESTION

1b. Why do you think Thomas believes this? (Perhaps many Americans with whom he has come in contact have been missionaries.)

height of some 17,000 feet. Then to the west, and directly above us, its walls leveled out into a long skyline saddle which swept on for some seven miles before beginning to rise again—this time into the slopes of Kibo. Kibo is *the* top of the mountain, and utterly unlike Mawenzi: a symmetrical truncated cone, perpetually snow-capped, and so vast it dwarfs its rival. This is the Kilimanjaro of the stories, the legends, the photographs: the fabulous white-topped pudding athwart the equatorial sky.

I have, in my day, described the great silences on certain mountains, but there were no silences that day on Kilimanjaro. The porters jabbered; they laughed; they told each other stories at a distance of a quarter of a mile. And though almost all were barefoot, they moved like chamois[12] over rocks and gravel that were trying hard to tear my stout boots to ribbons. On their heads, nonchalantly, swayed their forty-pound loads of foodstuffs, utensils, and blankets. Two men, I noted, carried fine new capacious knapsacks—presumably the gifts of previous employers—but even these went balanced atop their craniums.

And so up we went, now through long slanting meadows, with Alpine flowers bright around us, and by the time my private rear guard reached Pieter's Hut it was midafternoon. Here at 12,300 feet, it was cold even in the sunshine, and when night came we sat huddled in blankets long before turning into our bunks. Far below us, on the plains, we could see the pinprick lights of towns and villages, and in the emptiness beyond them the orange glow of bush fires. From the Chaggas' lean-to, bursting with smoke, came a low, slow sing-song that was half mission-house hymn and half ancient tribal chant.

In the morning the fires below were invisible. But there was fire above: the ice-white summit of Kibo ablaze in the rising sun. In the stainless clarity of air, it seemed close enough to reach out and touch, but there was still another full day's climb ahead of us before we would be even at the base of the final cone. Toward noon we reached our first major goal: the great 14,000-foot saddle between Kibo and Mawenzi. Seven miles long and almost as broad, it is utterly barren and flat as a ball field, and I had been told by previous climbers how terribly the wind could blow across its unprotected wastes. Our luck held, however. We had no wind. Only sun.

The trail came out close to the base of Mawenzi, and its tattered spires rose sheer above us. Then we turned our backs and slogged across the saddle. At this altitude, I knew all too well, a whole encyclopedia of ailments can afflict the climber, among them headache, nausea, sore throat, thumping heart. But so far I was all right; and even after we crossed the seven flat miles and began the ascent of Kibo's skirts, my anatomy continued to hold together. Right foot, left foot. Right, left. Perhaps a hundred steps— ten seconds' rest—a hundred more. Ahead, a slowly emerging speck on the scree[13] slopes, was Kibo Hut—about 16,500 feet up, higher than the highest peak of the Alps.

4 Kibo Hut was tiny. It was dirty. It was freezing. Here there was neither water nor firewood, and all we had brought up was the minimal amount needed for drinking and cooking. Such problems, however, did not prevent our cook, Samuel, from dispensing a de luxe tea and supper, complete with serving cloth and napkins. And for the eighth time in eight meals he hopefully set out the prize item in his larder—a jar of ferocious-looking mustard pickles that, to his great distress, no one had yet deigned to touch.

"Jim, don't you think we owe it to Samuel—"

That was as far as I got. Suddenly I was conscious of something even yellower than the hor-

12. **chamois** [sham′ē]: antelope native to the mountains of Europe and Asia.

13. **scree** [skrē]: loose stones on the slope or at the base of a mountain.

AT A GLANCE

- The author describes the porters' method of carrying heavy loads.
- The climbers camp for a second night.
- The third day's climb ends at the undersupplied and freezing Kibo Hut.
- The cook prepares another "de luxe" meal, despite the conditions.

1 STYLE: METAPHOR

The author compares Kilimanjaro to a "fabulous white-topped pudding," an amusing description that makes the mountain less threatening.

2 THEME

The native porters walk barefoot carrying huge packs on their heads; they are easy and natural in meeting the demands of the mountain, whereas the climbers walk in boots and are burdened by their backpacks.

3 SETTING

The "pinprick lights of towns and villages" far below emphasize the isolation that the narrator feels as he climbs the mountain.

4 THEME

In the author's description of Kibo Hut—*tiny . . . dirty . . . freezing,* the reader can sense that he sees the inconveniences as an integral part of the challenge and adventure of climbing Kilimanjaro.

GUIDED READING

LITERAL QUESTION

1a. When the narrator begins to ascend, how does he describe the way he climbs? (He moves step by step for one hundred steps, then rests for several seconds.)

INFERENTIAL QUESTION

1b. What does this tell you about the climb? (It is very difficult and tiring.)

AT A GLANCE

- The narrator's son suffers altitude sickness and must descend.
- The narrator and Thomas continue the climb in the early morning.
- The steep climb becomes maddeningly slow and difficult.
- They approach Leopard Point.

1 NARRATIVE ESSAY

As Jim, ill with altitude sickness, must give up, and Ullman goes on alone, the narrative continues to build toward its climactic moment.

2 STYLE: SIMILE

The narrator compares the summit to a "great beacon lighted from within," showing his strong compulsion to complete the ascent.

3 MAIN IDEA

The narrator is beginning to push himself to physical exhaustion: In order to accomplish his goal he must rest frequently and fight headaches.

4 SETTING

The sunrise, described as "savage," underscores the awesome quality of natural wilderness.

5 THEME

A light "too brilliant for mere human eyes" reveals the narrator's sense of being a sort of intruder on the slopes of Kilimanjaro.

rid pickles, and that something was Jim's face.

"Ex-cuse me," he mumbled weakly, and lurched from the hut.

It was the demon Altitude, striking without warning; and from then on Jim had no respite from nausea and racking headaches. We gave him aspirin. No effect. Sundry other pills. No effect. "A night's sleep will fix you up," we told him. But there was no sleep for poor Jim. When I awoke at 3:30—the grim hour of up-and-at-it—it was to find him miserably climbing back into his bunk after still another bout of sickness outside.

It was obvious that he could go no higher.

"Don't feel too bad about it," Fred comforted him. "Even George Mallory—the *Everest* Mallory—got sick up here at Kibo and had to go back."

This information didn't seem to cheer Jim greatly, but he was realist enough to know the score, and it was decided that at daylight he would go down to Pieter's. Fred, too, would be going no higher, but this was according to plan. He had already been up the mountain three
1 times. So now it was I alone who bestirred myself, sloshing down the tea that Samuel brought me and pulling on my heavy clothing in the cold candlelit hut.

Then the door opened and Thomas stomped in, dressed now in heavy boots, woolen helmet, and a too-small British-army overcoat that must have dated from the Zulu Wars.[14] And a moment later there were just we two—and Kilimanjaro.

2 It was still full night, but the stars and a late-waning moon gave light enough to see by, and above us Kibo's snow dome loomed like a great beacon lighted from within. There remained some 3500 vertical feet to go to the top—no more, to be sure, than we had climbed on each of the previous days, but now the angle of ascent steeped sharply. There was no solid rock, but only loose scree and crumbled lava in which one floundered and backslid maddeningly. And with each foot gained the lungs struggled harder and more futilely for breathable air.

Step—slip. Step—slip. Multiplied a hundred times, and then a thousand.

We followed a long shallow gully up to our
3 left; then another to the right. My rests were no longer at hundred-step intervals but at fifty, and then thirty and then twenty. Yet, basically, there was no sign of *real* trouble. Heart, lungs, and legs, to be sure, were working overtime—but still working. My stomach behaved, and aspirin dissolved a gathering headache. Best of all, the mountain was keeping its sharpest claws sheathed, for there was neither wind nor bitter cold.

As we climbed on, the night thinned and the
4 stars faded. For perhaps half an hour we crept on in gray twilight, and then the grayness was shattered by the wildest, most savage sunrise I have ever seen. The whole eastern horizon was banded with crimson. Mawenzi, its summit already beneath us, flamed red as fire. And Kibo's snowcap, above us, was suddenly no longer a mountaintop but a vast spectrum, itself a sun in the
5 gleaming sky. I put on dark goggles, and so did Thomas. But even through their green film the light seemed too brilliant for mere human eyes.

We were at 17,000 feet—seventeen-five—eighteen. Kibo's walls now rose up smoothly. No gullies, no humps or ridges; only an endless hateful grind of scree and lava.

At the end of the endlessness, clamped into the sky above, were the rocks of Gillman's Point, lowest notch in the crater's rim, and through the minutes, and then the hours, it seemed to remain exactly the same distance above us.

Step—slip. Step—slip. I was half convinced we were not moving at all. But apparently we were, for around us there were changes. Red Mawenzi was remote below. To the left and right were snow slopes and glaciers. And to the right, too, and only a little below the rim, we could see the bulge in the mountainside known as Leopard Point. Kibo's famous leopard is no

14. **Zulu** [zo͞o′lo͞o] **Wars:** England conquered the Zulus of South Africa in 1879.

GUIDED READING

LITERAL QUESTION

1a. When Jim gets sick, what are his symptoms? (He is nauseous and has terrible headaches.)

INFERENTIAL QUESTION

1b. Why does he get sick? (The air is thinner, and he may not be getting enough oxygen.)

legend. He was not invented by Ernest Hemingway for "The Snows of Kilimanjaro,"[15] but was right there for years, a carcass frozen amid the ice and rock—with no one knowing how, or why, he had climbed to it. And the reason he is there no longer is that he was gradually hacked to bits by climbers and carried away as souvenirs.

Leopard Point is at 18,500 feet, and now it was below us. Gillman's is at 18,635, and at last it seemed closer. It was very close. We had almost reached it. We *had* reached it. We were standing, not on scree but on solid rock, and before us the mountain no longer climbed skyward but fell sharply away into its summit crater.

"Is O.K., *bwana,*" said Thomas.

"Yes, O.K."

O.K.? It was marvelous. It was heaven. To be there, to stand there. To *sit down.*

Kilimanjaro's crater, like the rest of the mountain, is on the grand scale. More than a mile across and some three and a half in circumference, it is a double crater whose deepest point is about 900 feet lower than the highest summit. Gillman's Point, where we now were, is on the crater scarp.[16] Six hundred feet down steep walls is the crater floor, a piebald sweep of black and white, lava and snow, almost perfectly level, except for a number of huge and fantastic ice masses that have been given such names as the Dome, the Battleship, and the Cathedral. At the center of this circle, like a bull's-eye in a target, is the inner crater, another 300 feet deep, complete with a second scarp, steep walls and, at the very bottom, the volcano's cold core, called the Ash Pit.

I would have liked to go down and see the Ash Pit, but there was something I wanted more—and that something was not down but up. In the rulebook of Kilimanjaro, Gillman's Point "counts"; if you reach it you have climbed
3 the mountain. But it is not the top. *The* top is some 700 feet higher and a mile and a quarter distant to the south and west, along the ups and downs of the crater rim. It is still known by its old German name, the Kaiser Wilhelm Spitze, and it is only there that all of Africa is beneath you.

Par for the climb from Kibo Hut to Gillman's is five hours. It had taken me seven, and I was thoroughly conscious that I had not spent the morning in bed. In all honesty, I had not expected to get this far. I was surprised and delighted that I had, and decided the only sane
4 course was to leave well enough alone. "Gillman's counts," I told myself. "It's enough, and we'll go down." Then Thomas looked at me inquiringly, and my hand, quite on its own, pointed up.

The hateful scree was below us. We were on blessed solid rock. For all of ten steps, that is. Then we came off the rock onto snow, the snow was soft and crustless in the midday sunshine, and we sank in to the knee, the thigh, the waist. I lurched. I floundered. In no time my mouth was open like a boated fish's, gasping for air, and my heart was pounding fit to crack my ribs.

Even Thomas was not quite superhuman. He sank in too. But sinking or not, he was able to keep going steadily, whereas my ratio of movement to rest was about one to three. On the downslopes of the ragged rim my gait was a stumbling crawl. On the upgrades, which of course predominated, the crawl seemed in comparison to have been a light-footed sprint.

We searched for snowless rock. But now there was snow everywhere. Ahead, on the endless hummocks[17] of the rim; to the right, choking the crater; to the left, falling away

15. **Ernest . . . Kilimanjaro:** Hemingway's story contains the following lines: "Close to the western summit there is the dried and frozen carcass of a leopard. No one has explained what the leopard was seeking at that altitude."
16. **scarp:** line of cliffs.

17. **hummocks** [hum'əks]: hills or ridges of ice in an ice field.

AT A GLANCE

- The narrator and his guide reach Gillman's Point.
- They scale the crater wall.
- They continue upward toward Kaiser Wilhelm Spitze.

1 STYLE: ALLUSION

In Hemingway's story the protagonist lies dying of gangrene on the side of the mountain. He realizes that one must live life fully and face danger squarely as the leopard does—a lesson that the narrator is also learning.

2 SETTING

The author describes the interior of the crater, giving the reader an idea of the immensity of Kilimanjaro: It is a double crater, a mile wide and nine hundred feet deep.

3 THEME

To get the proper perspective on his adventure, the narrator believes he must scale the Kaiser Wilhelm Spitze. Until he can see all of Africa, he feels his climb will not be complete.

4 MAIN IDEA

Although the narrator is exhausted, he chooses to continue his climb, pushing his endurance to the limit.

GUIDED READING

LITERAL QUESTIONS

1a. What does the narrator decide when he reaches Gillman's Point? (to continue to the Kaiser Wilhelm Spitze)

2a. What happens after the climbers reach "blessed solid rock"? (They come to the snow line and sink in to the waist.)

INFERENTIAL QUESTIONS

1b. Why does he want to go on? (He wants to feel he has truly conquered the mountain.)

2b. Given the difficulty of continuing in the snow, do you think the narrator will be able to reach the Spitze? (Yes; he is determined to finish the climb.)

AT A GLANCE

- The narrator reaches the snow line and is stricken with snow blindness.
- He fights the overwhelming exhaustion caused by the high altitude and begins to feel disoriented.

1 THEME

The narrator finds that the physical challenges he has faced—the cold, the altitude—now seem minor in contrast to the sun's glare. Again he faces unexpected difficulties.

2 MAIN IDEA

The narrator fights an overwhelming exhaustion caused by the high altitude, but he pushes himself to finish the climb.

One climber rests amid snow and glacier near Gillman's Point on Kilimanjaro.

endlessly in billowing waves of glacier. The snow gleamed. The snow glared. The billows were no longer static but undulating, and from their crests darted long white lances of light that struck blindingly into my eyes. I fumbled in a pocket for my goggles but didn't find them. I had them on. The whiteness beat against their green lenses as if it would crack them with its force.

1 In that frozen world it was not cold. It was warm, even hot. Sweat was trickling on my back and down my forehead, under the goggles, into my eyes. My eyes were bothering me even more now than legs, lungs, or heart. Sweat and snow seemed to mingle, forming patterns and images that wove before me. Soon the whole mountaintop was weaving. Crater and rim revolved slowly in space, like an enormous wheel.

I was terribly tired, and the snow was soft. It was a great pillow, a featherbed, all around me, and in the deep drifts, leaning against it, I closed my eyes. I had read, sometimes even written, of climbers overwhelmed by sleep at high altitudes, and now for the first time it was actually happening to me. With eyes closed, the awful glare
2 was gone. Resting motionless in my featherbed, I felt breathing and heartbeat ease, and I sank gently, deliciously, into a shadowed doze. Luckily the shadows never closed in entirely. My head jerked back. My eyes opened. I crept on again, willing myself to move, my eyes to stay open.

I had estimated an hour from Gillman's Point to the summit, but now, after twice that, we seemed to be nowhere at all. All recognizable features of rim and crater were gone. There were the endless humps, the snow, the sky; and now something was happening to the sky, too, for it was no longer blue but white. Like the mountain, it was covered with snow—or was it cloud? Yes, it was cloud, I decided. And then

GUIDED READING

LITERAL QUESTION

1a. What happens to the narrator as he climbs through the snow? (He has trouble seeing properly; he fights exhaustion caused by the high altitude.)

INFERENTIAL QUESTION

1b. In what way does the snow blindness and altitude exhaustion add to the difficulty of his climb? (He is growing confused and is no longer as clear about his goal.)

suddenly, through a rent in the cloud, I saw a sight that I thought was hallucination: a soaring plane. It was not silver, as a plane should be, but gleaming amber, and it moved high and still, like a specter, and then vanished in the gulfs of space.

It had not been illusion, I learned later; Thomas had seen the plane too. But then I didn't know. I couldn't even find Thomas. Like the spectral thing in the sky, he had disappeared, too, into the whiteness. And then a second hallucination: a black disk. The disk was not in the sky but on the rim before me. It grew larger as I approached. It was Thomas's face, and he had turned and was waiting.

Down—up. Up—down. Then up and more up. The cloud seemed to be gone, and there was only the rim and the crater spinning around me. Then they, too, dissolved, as I tripped and fell headlong into the snow. When I arose it was to see still another hallucination. In the whiteness ahead, there was something that was not white. On a hump of snow there was what seemed to be a pile of stones—a pile fashioned not by nature but by man—and rising from the stones two bamboo poles. I climbed another few steps and the pile didn't vanish. I reached out to touch it, and it was there. *We* were there. On the Kaiser Wilhelm Spitze, 19,340 feet high. I shook hands with Thomas and sat down. Or maybe I sat down first.

After a few minutes my head was clear, my breathing normal. I smoked a cigarette, and it was good. From beneath the stones I pulled a black metal box, took out the summit register and signed it; and that was good, too, except that I wished Jim were there to sign with me.

Then I looked slowly around. MMBK lay all below us. MMBA lay all around us. If I say I could see the Indian Ocean, Johannesburg, the Nile, the Congo, I am obviously lying. But I would not have thought so then, for it seemed to me I could see *everything*—the whole of Africa—lying clear and bright in crystal space. There are few men in
3 the world as happy as the mountaineer atop his mountain, and for half an hour, on that magical summit, I savored my reward to the full.

Then—*"Bwana—"*

"Yes, Thomas."

He pointed at my wristwatch. There was still a full installment of the price to be paid: those Miles and Miles of Bloody Kilimanjaro in reverse.

III

I shall make it brief, which it wasn't. First there was the crater rim again: the humps, the whiteness, the ups, the downs; but now, at least, the downs predominated. There was our self-made trail to follow; and in half the time of our upward crawl we were back on the rocks of Gillman's Point. Here I was greeted by another hallucination. A figure was moving. A voice was speaking. Presently they turned into Fred Hughes, and Fred said, "Have some chocolate." Then he added, "I thought I'd amble up and see how you were doing."

"So the worst is over," I thought—and failed to hear the sound of off-stage laughter. But I heard it clearly enough during the hours that followed, as I crept and lurched and stumbled down the endless slopes of scree and lava. The proper way to descend a mountain like Kilimanjaro is on the double-quick—sliding, almost running, as gravity pulls you along. But for me gravity was no ally, for I had not the strength to brace against it. Every time I tried to advance at more than a crawl, my knees buckled, and I swayed and fell.

So a crawl it was. Down the miles. Through the hours. Sometimes Fred and Thomas were with me; sometimes they were no more than
4 specks far below. But always there were knees, calves, feet, toes. There were stones, stones, stones. There was an ache spreading upward that would have been almost unendurable if I had not been at least half asleep from fatigue.

Day was ending; Kibo Hut appeared. But this

AT A GLANCE

- The narrator and Thomas reach the top of Kilimanjaro.
- They admire the view, and the narrator savors his accomplishment.
- They begin the descent.

1 STYLE: METAPHOR

The author uses metaphor—comparing Thomas' face to a featureless disk—to show how he is treading a fine line between reality and hallucination.

2 NARRATIVE ESSAY: CLIMAX

The narrator finally achieves his goal: the top of the highest peak of Kilimanjaro.

3 MAIN IDEA

The pain of the ascent is forgotten as the narrator rests and looks at the view; despite his exhaustion he feels a supreme happiness.

4 MAIN IDEA

The narrator perseveres as exhaustion dulls the pain and his drive to finish the journey remains a constant, automatic thing.

GUIDED READING

LITERAL QUESTIONS

1a. What does the narrator see in the sky? (a soaring plane)

2a. What does the narrator do atop the Kaiser Wilhelm Spitze? (He smokes a cigarette, signs the register, looks at the view, and savors his achievement.)

INFERENTIAL QUESTIONS

1b. Why do you think the plane seems unreal to him? (because it is amber; because it moves freely when he can barely struggle along)

2b. What is his "reward"? (to see "the whole of Africa" and to know that he has succeeded)

AT A GLANCE

- The narrator rests.
- He completes his descent.
- He decides that the experience was worth the effort.

1 STYLE: SIMILE

The author compares his face to "a red balloon" and his movements to "a puppet's"; these images of children's toys contrast vividly with the suffering he is enduring.

2 PURPOSE

The author clearly believes that the experience (which tested his skills and endurance to the limit) was worth the pain he suffered.

REFLECTING ON THE SELECTION

Do you think the author will go on to climb other mountains? Why or why not? (Possible answer: Yes; although he swears he won't, he enjoys challenge and will want again to overcome obstacles.)

STUDY QUESTIONS

1. Ullman, Jim, Fred Hughes, nine porters; Ullman and headman
2. effects of the altitude
3. counts as completing climb; not the highest point
4. swollen face, blistered toes, weak knees, exhausted
5. - *orchids and begonias winked*
   - *Birds cawed.*
   - *Kilimanjaro is a huge and sprawling massif.*
   - *Mawenzi flamed red as fire.*
   - *The snow is a great pillow, a featherbed.*
6. on first day; on climb down
7. feels thrill of accomplishment
8. marathon running; performing before an audience

VIEWPOINT

risks danger; prepares carefully; is aware of his shortcomings as a climber but determined to succeed

---

was not journey's end. Not only Jim but all the porters had gone on down to Pieter's, taking our food and blankets along.

"Can you keep going?" Fred asked me.

"I most certainly cannot," I assured him. But after an hour's rest, somehow, I did; and on through the night I went, hobbling into Pieter's Hut a little before midnight.

This time it was Jim who was the nurse and I the patient.

Then came the last day—the walk down to Marangu. "There's nothing to it," Fred and Jim reminded me cheerfully. But by now there was
1 nothing much to me either. My face was round and swollen as a red balloon; my knees jerked and twitched like a puppet's; and my toes wore monstrous blisters.

Hobble, hobble, hobble. Sway, stumble, trip. I tried walking pigeon-toed; I tried walking duck-footed. No good. Nothing was any good. At every step the rocks in the path seemed to rise gleefully and kick me, and I kicked them savagely back, and groaned.

"Snows!" I thought. Mr. Hemingway could have his snows. What I would remember would be the *toes* of Kilimanjaro.

Still, all things have an end—even MMBK. And at five that afternoon our 1957 Kilimanjaro Expedition had passed into history. We were on the terrace of the hotel at Marangu. I was barefoot. I was pouring the third beer into my swollen face. I was swearing silently that in the rest of my life I would climb nothing higher than New York's Murray Hill.[18]

Then our white hunter joined us.

"Well, how was it?" he asked.

2 "It was wonderful," I heard myself saying, and the darndest thing is that I was telling the truth.

18. **New York's Murray Hill:** gently sloping hill and a neighborhood in New York City.

STUDY QUESTIONS

Recalling

1. List the members of the climbing party. Which of them actually reach the top?
2. What danger keeps most climbers from reaching the top of Kilimanjaro?
3. What is the significance of reaching Gillman's Point? Why is that not enough for the author?
4. Describe Ullman's physical condition at the end of the selection.

Interpreting

5. Ullman creates a vivid picture of the mountain by using descriptive details that appeal to the various senses. Find five examples of descriptive detail. Include at least one detail of sight, one of sound, and one of touch.
6. At what two points in this essay can you find humor as the author mocks his own skills and endurance?
7. After describing the physical agony that results from the climb, why does Ullman say that the experience was wonderful?

Extending

8. Give other examples of people working very hard for a brief, exhilarating moment.

VIEWPOINT

One critic has said:

> Mr. Ullman achieves success through his convincing awareness of the spell of mountains and the urge to climb, his depiction of a kind of heroism that is intelligence and nobility of spirit more than mere courage....
>
> —*Horn Book* magazine

- Explain how Ullman possesses courage, intelligence, and nobility of spirit.

LITERARY FOCUS

The Narrative Essay

The **narrative essay** tells a true story. To maintain our interest, the author of a narrative essay often uses techniques and elements of the short story. To begin with, an author of a narrative essay usually presents events in chronological order. The **plot** of a narrative essay provides the same basic structure as the plot in a story. The **exposition** introduces people and setting. The **rising action** presents a **conflict**, a struggle between two forces, and its complications. The **climax** is the point of our highest interest and emotional involvement in the narrative. The **falling action** shows the result of the climax. The **resolution** ends the falling action of the plot.

This form is particularly noticeable in "Kilimanjaro!" because of the way that Ullman has divided his essay. Part I of the essay provides the exposition. Part II relates the rising action. Part III contains the falling action.

Dialogue is the conversation between characters in a story. The author of a narrative essay also uses dialogue to help us feel like eyewitnesses to the events being related.

Just as a short story has a theme that expresses the author's idea, a narrative essay is built around a central idea, or generalization about life, that the author wants to communicate. This is the **purpose**.

Thinking About the Narrative Essay

1. What details about Kilimanjaro that are important to the climb are given in the exposition (Part I)?
2. From the rising action (Part II) identify the major conflict, one minor conflict, and the climax of the essay.
3. What information is given in the falling action (Part III) to complete the story of Ullman's adventure?
4. What do you think is this essay's purpose, the generalization about life that Ullman communicates through the incidents he narrates? Be sure that the purpose is a statement about life in general and *not* about mountain climbing.

VOCABULARY

Sentence Completions

Each of the following sentences contains a blank with four possible words for completing the sentence. The words are from "Kilimanjaro!" Choose the word that completes each sentence correctly and that uses the word *as the word is used in the selection.* Write the number of each item and the letter of your choice on a separate sheet.

1. The tree fell _____ the path.
   (a) atop (c) athwart
   (b) sloshing (d) slanting
2. None of the others _____ to reply to the whining child.
   (a) deigned (c) followed
   (b) resigned (d) challenged
3. The _____ across the valley was long and difficult.
   (a) sprint (c) ascent
   (b) trek (d) altitude
4. Grandma reached into her _____ suitcase for the children's gifts.
   (a) dense (c) steep
   (b) monstrous (d) capacious
5. When she was elected president, she reached the _____ of her career.
   (a) ascent (c) upgrade
   (b) apex (d) climb

COMPOSITION

Writing About a Narrative Essay

- Explain how Ullman uses short story techniques to make his true story more exciting. You may want to consider (a) dialogue, (b) descriptive details, (c) suspense, and (d) characterization.

Writing a Narrative Essay

- Write a brief account of a true event in which an obstacle is overcome or a challenge is met. Divide your essay into three parts. In Part I write an exposition providing background to the event. In Part II relate the rising action with its conflict and climax. In Part III cover the falling action and resolution.

LITERARY FOCUS

1. is mile higher than the Matterhorn; slopes gently upward; climbers do not need special equipment or skills
2. *major conflict:* conquering summit; *minor conflict:* Jim's problems with altitude; *climax:* signing summit register
3. trip down is harder than Ullman expects; describes his physical condition; evaluates experience
4. the greater the challenge, the more rewarding the experience

VOCABULARY

1. (c) athwart
2. (a) deigned
3. (b) trek
4. (d) capacious
5. (b) apex

COMPOSITION: GUIDELINES FOR EVALUATION

WRITING ABOUT A NARRATIVE ESSAY

Objective

To explain how short story techniques contribute to the effect of the narrative

Guidelines for Evaluation

- suggested length: three to five paragraphs
- should discuss at least two techniques
- should show how techniques enhance narrative essay
- should cite examples from essay

WRITING A NARRATIVE ESSAY

Objective

To narrate a true event in the manner of "Kilimanjaro!"

Guidelines for Evaluation

- suggested length: four paragraphs
- should give background information
- should relate rising action with conflict and climax
- should relate falling action and resolution

AT A GLANCE

- The author describes a scene at a Chinese harbor.
- She travels across Japan by train and describes the bustling scene at a railroad station.

LITERARY OPTIONS

- descriptive essay
- style

THEMATIC OPTIONS

- comparing customs and languages
- acceptance and denial

1 STYLE: SIMILE

The author compares the voices of the departing Japanese to "a flock of frightened birds," stressing both the musical quality of the language and the nervous excitement of saying good-by.

2 DESCRIPTIVE ESSAY

Lindbergh concentrates on the trip's most foreign aspects to show that the sights and sounds of Japan are as different as the language.

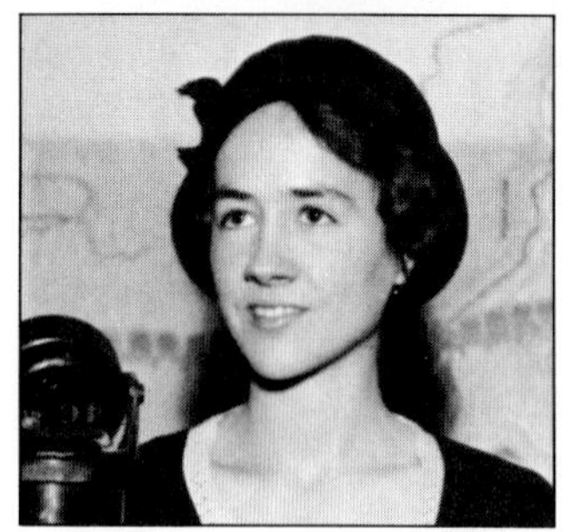

A licensed pilot and radio operator herself, Anne Morrow Lindbergh (born 1906) is the widow of Charles Lindbergh, the first person to fly alone across the Atlantic. The Lindberghs traveled to the farthest reaches of the globe, and Mrs. Lindbergh has written about those trips. She has also written other nonfiction and poetry.

This descriptive essay is taken from *North to the Orient,* an account of the Lindberghs' 1931 trip to the Far East in their own plane. When the plane was damaged in China, the Lindberghs traveled by boat to Japan and by train across Japan to the ship that would carry them home.

■ Is one way of saying "good-by" better than another?

Anne Morrow Lindbergh

Sayonara[1]

"Sayonara, Sayonara!" I was in my stateroom[2] but I could hear them, outside on the deck of the Japanese boat, calling to friends and relatives on the dock at Shanghai.[3] "Sayonara"—up and down the gangplank and over the rails. A boatload of Japanese were leaving China for home, as we were. "Sayonara," the chains clanked
1 and the warning whistle shook the boat. The voices outside rose in a flurry of noise, like a flock of frightened birds. But above the conglomerate sound there was always one voice, clean and sharp and individual and yet representative of the mass like that one face in the front line that holds the meaning of the whole crowd—one cry, "Sayonara." The impression was intensified perhaps because it was the one word of Japanese I understood—"Sayonara" ("Good-by").

I was to hear it again, all along our trip home. For we crossed Japan by train from the southern tip to Yokohama,[4] where we boarded the boat for America.

2 "Sayonara": the clatter of wooden clogs[5] along the station platform; the flutter of kimonos;[6] babies jogging on their mothers' backs; men carrying four or five small bundles tied up in different-colored furoshiki (squares of parti-colored silk or cotton); old women knocking along with their sticks, their brown faces hidden under enormous rooflike hats of straw; a man shouting his wares. We leaned out of the window at one of these stations and motioned to a vender for some tea. He poured out of his big tin into a little brown clay teapot like a child's toy, with a saucer for a lid and an inverted cup on top. "Two! Two!" we shouted and signaled

1. **Sayonara** [sä'yə nä'rə]: Japanese for "good-by."
2. **stateroom:** private room aboard a ship.
3. **Shanghai** [shang'hī]: seaport in China.
4. **Yokohama** [yō kə häm'ə]: seaport in eastern central Japan
5. **clogs:** wooden shoes.
6. **kimonos** [ki mō'nəz]: loose gowns tied with a sash; part of the traditional costume worn by Japanese men and women.

GUIDED READING

LITERAL QUESTION

1a. What does the voice that rises above the noise of the crowd represent? (It represents the whole mass of people.)

INFERENTIAL QUESTION

1b. In what way does it represent them all? (It is saying *Sayonara,* which is what all of the departing people are saying or feeling.)

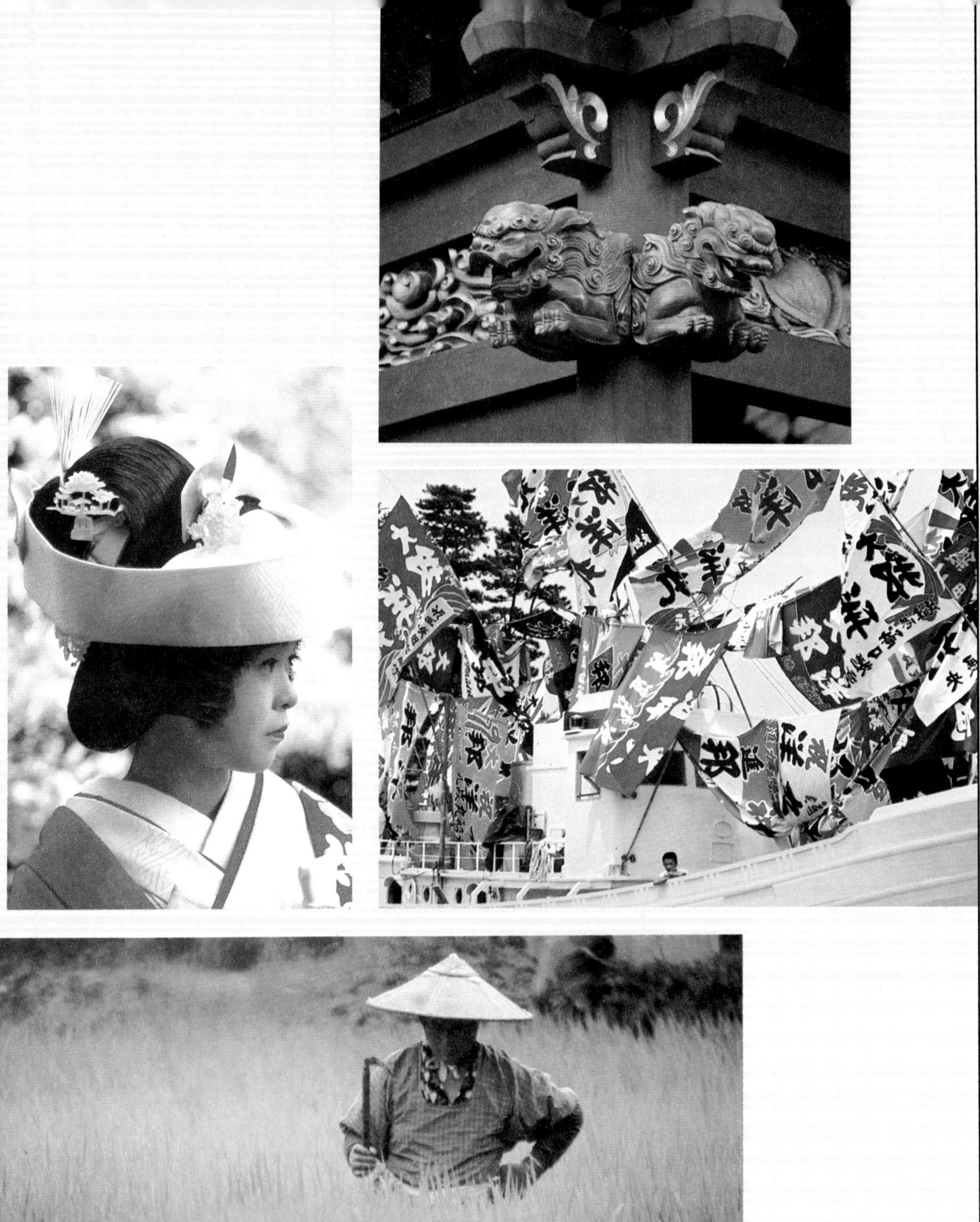

AT A GLANCE

- A Japanese family says good-by from the train.
- The train travels through Japan to the harbor.
- In Yokohama the passengers board the boat; the boat departs.
- The author discusses various languages' words for "good-by."

1 STYLE: PARALLELISM

The author begins some of her paragraphs with the word *Sayonara* to underscore its deep meaning for the Japanese who use it: It is a word that links them to what they are leaving.

2 DESCRIPTIVE ESSAY

As the author describes the things she is leaving behind as she moves through the countryside, she reveals her love for details of Japanese culture.

3 STYLE: METAPHOR

Lindbergh compares the paper ribbons to a web that is at once strong and fragile: Departing passengers are bound to the land by their feeling for it as they leave it.

4 MAIN IDEA

In contrast to other languages' words for "good-by," the Japanese *Sayonara* implies the sorrow of leave-taking, which makes it the most honest and beautiful.

5 THEME

The author states that *Sayonara*, unlike other words of parting, contains an understanding of life because it signifies an acceptance of fate.

REFLECTING ON THE SELECTION

In what ways do you think the word *Sayonara* reflects attitudes toward life that are different from Americans'? (Possible answer: The Japanese hold on until the last moment and then let go; they acknowledge the true meaning of an ending.)

as the train jerked forward, starting to pull out. The vender ran after us with another teapot swinging from its wire handle and pushed it in our window.

1 "Sayonara—Sayonara!" cried the passengers who had just stepped on board. A Japanese family across the aisle from us leaned out of the window to say a few last words. They occupied two long seats raised on a slight platform, separated from the next family by a partition. The mother and nurse (or older sister) were dressed in Japanese kimonos, the father in Western business suit, the two little girls in green challis[7] suits with Irish-lace collars, and the baby in woolens. They had already kicked off their shoes, in Japanese fashion, and were squatting on their feet on the blue plush seats. They held the baby up to the window for the last good-by—"Sayonara"; and then the monotonous doggerel rhythm of the train, quickening to a roar, drowned all noise. We were off.

It was good-by for us too, as we rushed
2 through Japan on our way to the boat. Good-by to the rice fields terraced up a narrow gully in the hills; to thatched roofs and paper walls; to heavy-headed grain bent to a curve; to a field of awkward lotus leaves, like big elephant ears, flapping on their tall stalks; to a white road leading up a hill to a pine grove and the flicker of red of a shrine gate. Good-by to the little towns we rattled through, with their narrow cobbled streets lined with shops, open to the passer-by except for fluttering blue-toweling curtains or bright paper and cloth flag-signs. Good-by to blue paper umbrellas in the rain and little boys chasing dragon flies.

Our real good-by was not until the boat pulled out of the dock at Yokohama, when the crowd of Japanese leaning over the rails of the decks shot twirling strands of serpentine[8] across to those they had left behind on shore—a rain of
3 bright fireworks. One end of these colored paper ribbons was held in the hands of those on deck, the other, by those on shore, until a brilliant multicolored web was spun between ship and shore. This and the shouts of conversation, unintelligible to me, interlacing back and forth across the gap, made up a finely woven band—a tissue, intricately patterned and rich in texture which held together for a few more seconds those remaining and those departing. Then the gap of water slowly widening between dock and ship, the ribbons tautened and snapped, the broken and raveled ends twirling off idly into the water, floating away with the unfinished ends of sentences. And nothing could bridge the gap but "Sayonara!"

4 For *Sayonara*, literally translated, "Since it must be so," of all the good-bys I have heard is the most beautiful. Unlike the *Auf Wiedersehens* and *Au revoirs*, it does not try to cheat itself by any bravado "Till we meet again," any sedative to postpone the pain of separation. It does not evade the issue like the sturdy blinking *Farewell. Farewell* is a father's *good-by.* It is—"Go out in the world and do well, my son." It is encouragement and admonition. It is hope and faith. But it passes over the significance of the moment; of parting it says nothing. It hides its emotion. It says too little. While *Good-by* ("God be with you") and *Adios* say too much. They try to bridge the distance, almost to deny it. *Good-by* is a prayer, a ringing cry. "You must not go—I cannot bear to have you go! But you shall not go alone, unwatched. God will be with you. God's hand will be over you" and even—underneath, hidden, but it is there, incorrigible—"I will be with you; I will watch you—always." It is a
5 mother's *good-by.* But *Sayonara* says neither too much nor too little. It is a simple acceptance of fact. All understanding of life lies in its limits. All emotion, smoldering, is banked up behind it. But it says nothing. It is really the unspoken good-by, the pressure of a hand, "Sayonara."

---

7. **challis** [shal′ē]: lightweight cloth made of cotton or wool.
8. **serpentine:** streamers of rolled colored paper that unwind when thrown.

GUIDED READING

LITERAL QUESTIONS

1a. What does the family across the train aisle from the author wear? (The adult women are in kimonos; the man and children wear Western clothing.)

2a. What words of parting does the author think say too much? (*Adios* and *Good-by*)

INFERENTIAL QUESTIONS

1b. Does the family seem more Western or Japanese? Why? (Japanese; they say *Sayonara* as they leave.)

2b. In what way do they say too much? (Rather than accepting parting, they lament it and try to make promises for the future.)

STUDY QUESTIONS

Recalling

1. Briefly describe one picture that the author sees from the train and one from the dock in Yokohama.
2. What is the literal translation of *sayonara*?
3. Why does the author say that *farewell* says too little?

Interpreting

4. Based on the people and things she chooses to describe, what do you think the author's feelings are about Japan?
5. What does the meaning of *sayonara* suggest about a Japanese attitude toward life?
6. Why does the author feel that expressions like "till we meet again" are "sedative"?

Extending

7. Why do you think there are so many ways to convey the idea of parting? What does the existence of so many alternate expressions say about people's attitudes toward parting?

VIEWPOINT

By describing the sights encountered in her travels, Anne Morrow Lindbergh also reveals herself. One review of *North to the Orient* said:

> She gives proof of a personality which finds expression in a love for simplicity and naturalness in all things.
>
> —*Catholic World*

■ Find three examples of simplicity and naturalness among the people, places, and objects that Lindbergh describes.

LITERARY FOCUS

The Descriptive Essay

The **descriptive essay** creates a picture of an actual person, object, place, or scene. Like the poet or short story writer, the essayist uses rich descriptive details and concrete language to give us a vivid picture of the subject. **Concrete language** is another name for sensory language, or words that appeal to the senses. The use of color and visual details appeals to the sense of sight. The description of sounds and the use of words that imitate sounds appeal to the sense of hearing. An author can even describe specific odors, flavors, and textures to appeal to the senses of smell, taste, and touch.

The scenes and details that an author chooses to describe can add up to create a generalization about life. This generalization is the **purpose** of the essay. The author also uses a particular style, which may reveal the purpose of the essay. **Style** is the author's choice and arrangement of words.

Thinking About the Descriptive Essay

■ Lindbergh lists only a few details in her description of the train platform. Classify the various details as details of sight or details of sound. Then explain the overall impression of the scene she creates by these few details.

COMPOSITION

Writing About an Essay

■ Explain Lindbergh's purpose in writing "Sayonara." Then tell what techniques she uses to accomplish this purpose. You may wish to include the following: (a) sensory details, (b) examples, and (c) opinions. Cite evidence from the selection to support your answer. *For help with this assignment, see Lesson 9 in the Writing About Literature Handbook at the back of this book.*

Writing a Description of a Place

■ Lindbergh's descriptions are short and colorful like vivid post card messages. Remember a place you once visited. Pretend that you are writing three post cards from a vacation there. On each card describe vividly one scene, person, or object that you associate with the place. You may describe a view, a local costume, a landmark, the native wildlife, or a local inhabitant.

STUDY QUESTIONS

1. *train:* station platform, little towns with cobbled streets
   dock: people holding colored ribbons
2. "Since it must be so"
3. masks true emotions
4. fascination, admiration
5. acceptance of the inevitable
6. deny parting, suggest reunion that may not occur
7. ■ There are many types of parting.
   ■ Attitudes about separation vary because of cultural differences.

VIEWPOINT

- *. . . babies jogging on their mothers' backs . . .*
- *. . . rice fields terraced up a narrow gully in the hills . . .*
- *. . . awkward lotus leaves . . . flapping on their tall stalks*

LITERARY FOCUS

- *sight:* babies on mothers' backs, men carrying bundles, women wearing enormous hats
- *sound:* clatter of clogs, flutter of kimonos, men shouting wares
- *overall impression:* colorful, gentle confusion

COMPOSITION: GUIDELINES FOR EVALUATION

WRITING ABOUT AN ESSAY

Objective

To explain Lindbergh's purpose in writing "Sayonara"

Guidelines for Evaluation

- suggested length: three to five paragraphs
- should state Lindbergh's purpose
- should discuss two techniques used to accomplish purpose
- should cite details and examples

WRITING A DESCRIPTION OF A PLACE

Objective

To describe a scene, person, and object

Guidelines for Evaluation

- suggested length: should contain three paragraphs, one for each description
- should use vivid details for each description
- should use informal style

AT A GLANCE

- Thurber discusses the use of the phrase *you know.*
- He counts "you know"s in conversation.
- The phrase creates irritation and confusion.
- He guesses at its origins.

LITERARY OPTIONS

- persuasive essay
- style

THEMATIC OPTIONS

- language
- trends

1 MAIN IDEA

Thurber explains how the phrase *you know* interferes with correct usage: It garbles meaning, ruins rhythm, and sounds awkward.

2 STYLE: HUMOR

Thurber tells a humorous story about a repetitive whippoorwill, which parallels his annoyance at the repetitive use of "you know."

3 PERSUASIVE ESSAY

Thurber gives an example of a "you know"–ridden speech to convince readers that the phrase sounds awkward and muddles meaning.

James Thurber (1894–1961) worked as a reporter in his native Columbus, Ohio, and then in New York and Paris. In New York he played an important role on the staff of the *New Yorker* magazine. As an essayist, short story writer, and cartoonist, Thurber set the witty tone for which the *New Yorker* has become famous. Thurber is a humorist whose work often reveals his exasperation with life's smaller problems.

- Is Thurber's concern about *you know* outdated?

James Thurber

The Spreading "You Know"

1 The latest blight to afflict the spoken word in the United States is the rapidly spreading reiteration of the phrase "*you* know." I don't know just when it began moving like a rainstorm through the language, but I tremble at its increasing garbling of meaning, ruining of rhythm, and drumming upon my hapless ears. One man, in a phone conversation with me last summer, used the phrase thirty-four times in about five minutes, by my own count; a young matron in Chicago got seven "*you* know"s into one wavy sentence, and I have also heard it as far west as Denver, where an otherwise charming woman at a garden party in August said it almost as often as a whippoorwill[1] says "Whippoorwill." Once, speaking of whippoorwills, I was waked after midnight by one of those feathered hellions,[2] and lay there counting his chants. He got up to a hundred and fifty-eight and then suddenly said
2 "Whip—"and stopped dead. I like to believe that his mate, at the end of her patience, finally let him have it.

My unfortunate tendency to count "*you* know"s is practically making a female whippoorwill out of me. Listening to a radio commentator not long ago discussing the recent General Assembly meeting of the United Nations, I thought I was going mad when I heard him using "*you* know" as a noun, until I realized that he had shortened "United Nations Organization" to "UNO" and was pronouncing it, you know, as if it were "*you* know."

3 A typical example of speech *you*-knowed to death goes like this: "The other day I saw, *you* know, Harry Johnson, the, *you* know, former publicity man for, *you* know, the Charteris Publishing Company, and, *you* know, what he wanted to talk about, strangely enough, was, *you* know, something you'd never guess. . . ."

This curse may have originated simultaneously on Broadway and in Hollywood, where such curses often originate. About twenty-five years ago, or perhaps longer, theater

1. **whippoorwill** [hwip′ər wil′]: a North American bird whose call sounds like its name.
2. **hellions** [hel′yənz]: mischievous or troublesome people; rascals.

GUIDED READING

LITERAL QUESTION

1a. What was the radio commentator actually saying in his discussion of the U.N. meeting? (UNO, an abbreviation for United Nations Organization)

INFERENTIAL QUESTION

1b. How does this anecdote fit in with Thurber's main idea? (It helps prove that the use of "you know" is confusing and makes language harder to understand.)

nd movie people jammed their sentences with 'you know what I mean?,'' which was soon hortened to "you *know*?" That had followed he overuse, in the nineteen-twenties, of "you ee?" or just plain "see?" These blights often isappear finally, but a few have stayed and will ontinue to stay, such as "well" and "I mean to ay" and "I mean" and "the fact is." Others eem to have mercifully passed out of lingo into imbo, such as, to go back a long way, "Twenty-hree, skiddoo" and "So's your old man" and "I lon't know nothin' from nothin'" and "Believe ou me." About five years ago, both men and vomen were saying things like "He has a new Cadillac job with a built-in bar deal in the back eat," and in 1958 almost everything anybody nentioned, or even wrote about, was "trig-gered." Arguments were triggered, and allergies, and divorces, and even love affairs. This gun-and-bomb verb seemed to make the jumpiest of the jumpy even jumpier, but it has almost died out now, and I trust that I have not triggered its revival.

It was in Paris, from late 1918 until early 1920, that there was a glut—an American glut, to be sure—of "You said it" and "You can say that again," and an American Marine I knew, from Montana, could not speak any sentence of agreement or concurrence without saying, "It *is*, you *know*." Fortunately, that perhaps original use of "*you* know" did not seem to be imported into America.

I am reluctantly making notes for a possible future volume to be called "A Farewell to Speech" or "The Decline and Fall of the King's English." I hope and pray that I shall not have to write the book. Maybe everything, or at least the language, will clear up before it is too late. Let's face it, it better had, that's for sure, and I don't mean maybe.

STUDY QUESTIONS

Recalling

1. According to Thurber, in what ways does the phrase *you know* hurt the language?
2. Where does Thurber believe the spread of *you know* began? Why does he think so?
3. Find five other overused phrases that Thurber mentions.

Interpreting

4. Thurber's protest against careless language is strengthened by his own vivid language. Find three examples of Thurber's lively, original use of language.
5. Beyond the spread of one overused phrase, what is the real topic of this essay?
6. What effect does the last sentence have on Thurber's message?

Extending

7. What overworked expressions are common today? Why do you think people use such phrases?

VIEWPOINT

"The Spreading 'You Know'" was collected in *Lanterns and Lances*, a book of Thurber's essays. Explaining the book's title, Thurber said that his intention was

> to throw a few lantern beams here and there. But I also cast a few lances [spears] at the people and the ideas that have disturbed me.

■ What light [information or explanation] is shed by Thurber in "The Spreading 'You Know'"? What or who are the targets of Thurber's lances [criticism or sarcasm] ?

AT A GLANCE

- Thurber discusses the history of overused words and phrases.
- He hopes the use of English will improve.

1 MAIN IDEA

Thurber notes how language evolves by tracing the development of such useless phrases as *you see, I mean to say,* and *the fact is.*

2 STYLE: HUMOR

Citing a ridiculous, slangy statement (*He has a new Cadillac job with a built-in bar deal in the back seat*), Thurber shows how unnecessary words and phrases clutter language.

REFLECTING ON THE SELECTION

Do you think Thurber believes the phrase *you know* is here to stay? (Possible answer: No; he talks about other phrases that have faded out of use.)

STUDY QUESTIONS

1. garbles meanings; ruins rhythms
2. on Broadway, in Hollywood; such phrases often originate there
3. *you see, well, I mean, the fact is, believe you me*
4. *feathered hellions; passed out of lingo into limbo; gun-and-bomb verb*
5. People are careless with language.
6. demonstrates effect of resorting to clichés
7. possible answers: well, I mean, you know; easier than selecting distinct words and phrases

VIEWPOINT

- *light:* abuses of language cloud meaning
- *target:* people who abuse and debase English language

LITERARY FOCUS

1. Thurber expresses personal feelings.
2. *exaggeration* emphasizes theme; *humor* gives light tone; *examples and statistics* reinforce opinion.

VOCABULARY

1. *blight:* disease that kills plants; implies comparison
2. *garbling:* mixing up so as to mislead; echoes *tremble*
3. *limbo:* place of oblivion; adds clever twist
4. *glut:* oversupply; more forceful

LITERARY FOCUS

The Persuasive Essay

The **persuasive essay** tries to convince the reader (1) to accept the author's opinion or (2) to take some kind of action. Writing which uses reason to affect people's opinions and actions is also known as **argument.** The **purpose**, or central idea, is usually clear and can be determined by examining (1) the author's opinion or (2) the specific action that the author wants readers to take. Common persuasive techniques include exaggeration, humor, and the use of examples and statistics. Such techniques hold our interest and encourage us to accept the author's opinion as logical and well researched.

Thinking About the Persuasive Essay

1. In what way is the selection an essay of opinion rather than one of fact?
2. In what ways does Thurber's use of exaggeration, humor, examples, and statistics help to convince you of his opinion?

VOCABULARY

Exact Words

Thurber was careful to say exactly what he meant. For example, take the sentence from the selection, "I was waked up after midnight by one of those feathered hellions and lay there counting his chants." The words *tunes, songs, melodies, chirps,* or *trills* do not have the repetitive, monotonous quality of *chants.*

The following sentences from "The Spreading 'You Know'" have been altered to include a word whose meaning is *not* exact. For each numbered item do the following: (1) Find the exact word that Thurber used in the selection, (2) check the word in the dictionary, and explain why it fits Thurber's purpose so precisely (consider the sound of the word as part of its meaning), and (3) write your own sentence using that exact word.

1. The latest blemish to afflict the spoken word in the United States is the rapidly spreading reiteration of the phrase "you know."
2. ...I tremble at its increasing confusion of meaning.
3. Others seem to have mercifully passed out of lingo into neglect....
4. ...there was a supply—an American supply to be sure—of "You said it" and "You can say that again,"....

COMPOSITION

Writing About a Persuasive Essay

■ To convince the reader, the author of a persuasive essay uses different types of support such as examples, statistics, exaggeration, and humor. Explain Thurber's purpose in the essay. Then identify two or three methods used by Thurber to accomplish his purpose, and explain whether each method is successful as a persuasive technique. *For help with this assignment, see Lesson 9 in the Writing About Literature Handbook at the back of this book.*

Writing a Persuasive Essay

■ Select a word or phrase that you feel is overused. Write a persuasive essay of three paragraphs in which you relate the problem of its overuse and a possible solution. Include specific actions that you wish your readers to take in order to solve the problem.

COMPOSITION: GUIDELINES FOR EVALUATION

WRITING ABOUT A PERSUASIVE ESSAY

Objective

To evaluate Thurber's technique in light of his purpose

Guidelines for Evaluation

- suggested length: three to five paragraphs
- should state Thurber's purpose
- should identify two or three methods used to achieve purpose
- should cite examples and discuss their effectiveness

WRITING A PERSUASIVE ESSAY

Objective

To persuade readers to take action to solve a problem

Guidelines for Evaluation

- suggested length: three paragraphs
- should develop reader's understanding of problem and offer solution
- should include at least two specific actions as possible solutions

Marchette Chute (born 1909) is one of three famous writing sisters from Minnesota who gained an interest in English history and literature from their English mother. Chute's best-known work is *Shakespeare of London*, which brings Shakespeare's life, times, and theater to vivid life.

■ Was acting more or less demanding as a profession five hundred years ago?

Marchette Chute

from Shakespeare of London

Acting was not an easy profession on the Elizabethan[1] stage or one to be taken up lightly. An actor went through a strenuous period of training before he could be entrusted with an important part by one of the great city companies. He worked on a raised stage in the glare of the afternoon sun, with none of the softening illusions that can be achieved in the modern theater, and in plays that made strenuous demands upon his skill as a fencer, a dancer, and an acrobat.

Many of the men in the London companies had been "trained up from their childhood" in the art, and an actor like Shakespeare, who entered the profession in his twenties, had an initial handicap that could only be overcome by intelligence and rigorous discipline. Since he was a well-known actor by 1592, and Chettle[2] says he was an excellent one, he must have had the initial advantages of a strong body and a good voice and have taught himself in the hard school of the Elizabethan theater how to use them to advantage.

One of the most famous of the London companies, that of Lord Strange, began its career as a company of tumblers, and a standard production like "The Forces of Hercules" was at least half
3 acrobatics. Training of this kind was extremely useful to the actors, for the normal London stage consisted of several different levels. Battles and sieges were very popular with the audiences, with the upper levels of the stage used as the town walls and turrets, and an actor had to know how to take violent falls without damaging either himself or his expensive costume.

Nearly all plays involved some kind of fighting, and in staging hand-to-hand combats the actor's training had to be excellent. The average Londoner was an expert on the subject of fencing, and he did not pay his penny to see two professional actors make ineffectual jabs at each other with rapiers[3] when the script claimed

1. **Elizabethan** [i liz′ə bē′thən]: relating to the reign of Queen Elizabeth I of England, 1558 to 1603.
2. **Chettle:** Henry Chettle (died 1607?), an English publisher and playwright.

3. **rapiers** [rā′pē ərz]: slender, two-edged swords.

AT A GLANCE

- Elizabethan actors trained from early youth in acrobatics, dancing, and fencing.
- Shakespeare became an actor in his twenties.
- Chute tells of Lord Strange's company, which featured acrobatics.

LITERARY OPTIONS

- expository essay
- anecdote
- historical details

THEMATIC OPTIONS

- professions
- comparing past and present
- communication

1 EXPOSITORY ESSAY

Chute reveals her purpose in a thesis statement: She will show that acting in Elizabethan times was a difficult profession.

2 MAIN IDEA

By explaining that most actors trained for the stage from childhood, Chute stresses both the difficulty of acting and Shakespeare's skill (since he began acting at a much later age than was usual).

3 STYLE: DETAILS

The stage's several levels illustrates some of the physical difficulties an actor faced.

GUIDED READING

LITERAL QUESTION

1a. What three skills did an Elizabethan actor need? (to dance, fence, and do acrobatics)

INFERENTIAL QUESTION

1b. Which do you think would be the most difficult to learn? Why? (Possibilities: fencing, because of dangerous swords; acrobatics, because it requires precision and grace, etc.)

AT A GLANCE

- Chute discusses the use of fencing in theater.
- She tells how dancing was employed in Elizabethan theater.

1 ANECDOTE

An anecdote about a fencing accident stresses the dangers inherent in acting and the skill needed.

2 STYLE: DETAILS

The favored dance styles of the time are given detailed description to illustrate specific difficulties actors faced.

they were fighting to the death. A young actor like Shakespeare must have gone through long grueling hours of practice to learn the ruthless technique of Elizabethan fencing. He had to learn how to handle a long, heavy rapier in one hand, with a dagger for parrying[4] in the other, and to make a series of savage, calculated thrusts at close quarters from the wrist and forearm, aiming at either his opponent's eyes or below the ribs. The actor had to achieve the brutal reality of an actual Elizabethan duel without injuring himself or his opponent, a problem that required a high degree of training and of physical coor-
1 dination. The theaters and inn-yards were frequently rented by the fencing societies to put on exhibition matches, and on one such occasion at the Swan[5] a fencer was run through the eye and died, an indication of the risks this sort of work involved even with trained, experienced fencers. The actors had to be extremely skilled, since they faced precisely the same audience. Richard Talleton, a comic actor of the 80's who was the first great popular star of the Elizabethan theater, was made Master of Fence the year before he died and this was the highest degree the fencing schools could award. . . .

Another test of an actor's physical control was in dancing. Apart from the dances that were written into the actual texts of the plays, it was usual to end the performance with a dance performed by some of the members of the company. A traveler from abroad who saw Shakespeare's company act *Julius Caesar* said that "when the play was over they danced very marvelously and gracefully together," and when the English actors traveled abroad, special mention was
2 always made of their ability as dancers. The fashion of the time was for violent, spectacular dances and the schools in London taught intricate steps like those of the galliard, the exaggerated leap called the "capriole" and the violent lifting of one's partner high into the air that was the "volte." A visitor to one of these dancing schools of London watched a performer do a galliard and noted how "wonderfully he leaped, flung, and took on"; and if amateurs were talented at this kind of work, professionals on the stage were expected to be very much better.

---

4. **parrying:** in fencing, moving to stop the opponent's attack.
5. **the Swan:** a theater in London during Shakespeare's time.

GUIDED READING

LITERAL QUESTION

1a. What weapons were used in Elizabethan fencing? (a rapier and dagger)

INFERENTIAL QUESTION

1b. In what ways might Elizabethan actors have avoided injury during duels? (undoubtedly directed intense concentration on each movement; probably memorized every "move" of opponents and themselves)

In addition to all this, subordinate or beginning actors were expected to handle several roles in an afternoon instead of only one. A major company seldom had more than twelve actors in it and could not afford to hire an indefinite number of extra ones for a single production. This meant that the men who had short speaking parts or none were constantly racing about and leaping into different costumes to get onstage with a different characterization as soon as they heard their cues. In one of Alleyn's[6] productions a single actor played a Tartar[7] nobleman, a spirit, an attendant, a hostage, a ghost, a child, a captain, and a Persian;[8] and while none of the parts made any special demands on his acting ability, he must have had very little time to catch his breath. The London theater was no place for physical weaklings; and, in the same way it is safe to assume that John Shakespeare must have had a strong, well-made body or he would not have been appointed a constable in Stratford; it is safe to assume that he must have passed the inheritance on to his eldest son.

2 There was one more physical qualification an Elizabethan actor had to possess, and this was perhaps more important than any of the others. He had to have a good voice. An Elizabethan play was full of action, but in the final analysis it was not the physical activity that caught and held the emotions of the audience; it was the words. An audience was an assembly of listeners and it was through the ear, not the eye, that the audience learned the location of each of the scenes, the emotions of each of the characters, and the poetry and excitement of the play as a whole.
3 More especially, since the actors were men and boys and close physical contact could not carry the illusion of love-making, words had to be depended upon in the parts that were written for women.

An Elizabethan audience had become highly susceptible to the use of words, trained and alert to catch their exact meaning and full of joy if
4 they were used well. But this meant, as the basis of any successful stage production, that all the words had to be heard clearly. The actors used a fairly rapid delivery of their lines and this meant that breath control, emphasis, and enunciation had to be perfect if the link that was being forged

6. **Alleyn:** Edward Alleyn (1566–1626), an actor, theater owner, and patron of actors.
7. **Tartar** [tär′tər]: Mongol or Turk.
8. **Persian:** native of Persia, an ancient middle eastern empire.

AT A GLANCE

- Actors played many parts in a production.
- Chute discusses the importance of a good voice and the audience's response to language.

1 ANECDOTE

As Chute lists the eight roles a single man played in a production, she stresses the exhausting physical and intellectual demands on an actor.

2 MAIN IDEA

Chute emphasizes the need for a good voice—the skill she places foremost among physical qualifications for good acting.

3 THEME

Chute points out a major difference between acting in the past and today: In Shakespeare's time all actors were men, a fact that put unique demands on Elizabethan actors.

4 THEME

Chute notes the importance of strong, clear speech as a link between actor and audience.

GUIDED READING

LITERAL QUESTION

1a. What does the author think was the most important part of the play for Elizabethan audiences? (the words)

INFERENTIAL QUESTION

1b. Do you think language is apt to have such significance for an audience today? (In some cases, yes; primarily, though, visual images dominate, especially in television and film performances.)

AT A GLANCE

- Chute discusses the evolution of blank verse, the repertory system, and the complexity of stage arrangements.
- She details the insecure position of actors and discusses companies outside London.

1 STYLE: DETAILS

Dramatic verse changed in Shakespeare's day, from a style that allowed frequent stops for breath to Shakespeare's own more elegant and difficult blank verse.

2 EXPOSITORY ESSAY

Chute's topic sentences support her thesis statement and state the main idea of each paragraph. Here she emphasizes the difficulty of acting by specifying the difficulty of remembering lines.

3 THEME

In Shakespeare's time acting was a very competitive profession with more actors than parts—a situation that is equally true today.

4 EXPOSITORY ESSAY

Chute restates her thesis in a slightly indirect way: Since Shakespeare managed to remain on the stage for two decades, he must have been an extraordinary actor.

REFLECTING ON THE SELECTION

Do you think it was harder to be an actor in Shakespeare's time or today? Why? (Possible answers: in Shakespeare's time, for reasons Chute explains; today, because actors still use special skills, and the body of work they must know is bigger and more varied)

between the emotions of the audience and the
1 action on the stage was not to be broken. When Shakespeare first came to London, the problem of effective stage delivery was made somewhat easier by the use of a heavily end-stopped line,[9] where the actor could draw his breath at regular intervals and proceed at a kind of jog-trot. But during the following decade this kind of writing became increasingly old-fashioned, giving way to an intricate and supple blank verse that was much more difficult to handle intelligently; and no one was more instrumental in bringing the new way of writing into general use than Shakespeare himself.

2 Even with all the assistance given him by the old way of writing, with mechanical accenting and heavy use of rhyme, an Elizabethan actor had no easy time remembering his part. A repertory system[10] was used and no play was given two days in succession. The actor played a different part every night, and he had no opportunity to settle into a comfortable routine while the lines of the part became second nature to him. He could expect very little help from the prompter, for that overworked individual was chiefly occupied in seeing that the actors came on in proper order, that they had their properties available, and that the intricate stage arrangements that controlled the pulleys from the "heavens"[11] and the springs to the trapdoors were worked with quick, accurate timing. These stage effects, which naturally had to be changed each afternoon for each new play, were extremely complicated. A single play in which Greene and Lodge collaborated required the descent of a prophet and an angel let down on a throne, a woman blackened by a thunderstroke, sailors coming in wet from the sea, a serpent devouring a vine, a hand with a burning sword emerging from a cloud, and "Jonah the prophet cast out of the whale's belly upon the stage." Any production that had to wrestle with as many complications as this had no room for an actor who could not remember his lines.

3 Moreover, an actor who forgot his lines would not have lasted long in what was a highly competitive profession. There were more actors than there were parts for them, judging by the number of people who were listed as players in the parish registers.[12] Even the actor who had achieved the position of a sharer in one of the large London companies was not secure. Richard Jones, for instance, was the owner of costumes and properties and playbooks worth nearly forty pounds, which was an enormous sum in those days, and yet three years later he was working in the theater at whatever stray acting jobs he could get. "Sometimes I have a shilling a day and sometimes nothing," he told Edward Alleyn, asking for help in getting his suit and cloak out of pawn.

The usual solution for an actor who could not keep his place in the competitive London theater was to join one of the country companies, where the standards were less exacting, or to go abroad. English actors were extravagantly admired abroad and even a second-string company with poor equipment became the hit of the Frankfort[13] Fair, so that "both men and
4 women flocked wonderfully" to see them. An actor like Shakespeare who maintained his position on the London stage for two decades could legitimately be praised, as Chettle praised him, for being "excellent in the quality he professes." If it had been otherwise, he would not have remained for long on the London stage.

9. **end-stopped line:** line of verse that has a natural pause at the end such as a period or comma.

10. **repertory system:** theatrical system in which a permanent company of actors alternates performances of several different plays.

11. **the "heavens":** a canopy over the stage in some Elizabethan theaters. Theatrical effects could be achieved by lowering people or objects from it.

12. **parish registers:** records of births, marriages, and deaths in a district.

13. **Frankfort:** Frankfurt, a city in what is now central West Germany.

GUIDED READING

LITERAL QUESTION

1a. Who was most instrumental in bringing blank verse into popular use? (Shakespeare)

INFERENTIAL QUESTION

1b. Since he knew how hard it would be to recite blank verse, why do you think he wrote it? (He may have believed its grace more than outweighed its difficulty for the actor.)

STUDY QUESTIONS

Recalling

1. Why was Shakespeare at a disadvantage as an actor? What advantages did he probably have?
2. Name two reasons that an actor needed physical strength.
3. Why were actors often required to play several roles in one day?
4. In an Elizabethan play what important information was conveyed by the lines?
5. Why did actors sometimes have difficulty remembering lines?
6. Why does Chute conclude that Shakespeare must have been a skilled actor?

Interpreting

7. Describe the type of entertainment that was popular with Elizabethan audiences.
8. In what sense was the skill of a good Elizabethan actor both intellectual and physical?

Extending

9. What aspects of Elizabethan theater do you think are similar to popular entertainment today?

LITERARY FOCUS

The Expository Essay

Exposition means "explanation of facts." At the beginning of a short story, novel, or play, exposition provides information that is necessary to follow the action. The **expository essay** presents facts or explains an idea. The essayist seeks to inform the reader. Most expository essays follow a pattern. The author states the central idea, or the **purpose** for writing the essay. Then the author presents support in the form of examples, reasons, statistics, and anecdotes. The clear statement of the central idea of the essay is the **thesis statement.** The thesis statement is often the first sentence of an expository essay or falls within the first paragraph. It is often repeated in other words in or near the last sentence.

In addition, each paragraph of an expository essay generally contains a **topic sentence** which states the central point of that paragraph. This pattern of thesis statement and topic sentences presents the explanation in a logical, straightforward manner.

Thinking About the Expository Essay

- List the thesis statement for this excerpt from *Shakespeare of London* and the topic sentence for each paragraph. Explain the relationship of each paragraph's topic sentence to the thesis statement of the essay.

COMPOSITION

Writing About an Expository Essay

- Explain whether you think this selection is successful in conveying information in a straightforward manner. First explain the purpose of the essay. Then name some techniques that the author uses, and explain how each helps her to convey her purpose. You may consider the following techniques: (a) thesis statement, (b) use of examples, (c) statistics, and (d) anecdotes. *For help with this assignment, see Lesson 9 in the Writing About Literature Handbook at the back of this book.*

Writing an Expository Essay

- Use a play or film that you have seen as the basis for writing an expository essay of three paragraphs on one of the following topics: (a) "The Difficult Life of a Modern Actor" or (b) "The Easy Life of a Modern Actor." Be sure to use a thesis statement and to use examples from the play or film to support that statement.

COMPARING ESSAYS

1. The author's purpose in writing an essay often determines the type of essay that results. "Kilimanjaro!" is a narrative essay; "Sayonara" is descriptive. "The Spreading 'You Know'" is persuasive, and the excerpt from *Shakespeare of London* is expository. Choose two or more of these essays, and compare them. What is the purpose of each essay? In what way is the type of each essay determined by that purpose?
2. Essays can inform the reader, but an effective essay may also entertain. Compare two or more of the following essays: "Kilimanjaro!" "Sayonara," "The Spreading 'You Know,'" and the excerpt from *Shakespeare of London.* Explain how they entertain while presenting serious information.

COMPOSITION: GUIDELINES FOR EVALUATION

WRITING ABOUT AN EXPOSITORY ESSAY

Objective

To evaluate essay in light of author's purpose and techniques

Guidelines for Evaluation

- suggested length: three to five paragraphs
- should include statement of writer's opinion regarding success of essay
- should state purpose of essay
- should name two techniques used

WRITING AN EXPOSITORY ESSAY

Objective

To use examples to support a statement

Guidelines for Evaluation

- suggested length: three paragraphs
- should include suggested thesis statement
- should use examples from play or film

STUDY QUESTIONS

1. *disadvantages:* started acting in his twenties
   advantages: had strong body, good voice, disciplined mind
2. to perform acrobatics; to fence; to dance
3. Companies had no more than twelve actors.
4. location, emotions, excitement
5. Each played several parts.
6. Competition was keen; he was on London stage for two decades.
7. acrobatics, battles, fencing, dancing, special effects
8. had to remember many lines, had to have good voice; had to be able to fight, dance
9. People still enjoy good acting, staging, dancing, drama.

LITERARY FOCUS

Thesis—acting on the Elizabethan stage was not an easy profession; *topic sentence*—first sentence in each paragraph; *relationship*—each topic sentence further defines thesis statement.

COMPARING ESSAYS

1. "Kilimanjaro!": narrative; illustrates challenge of climbing
   "Sayonara": descriptive, about language and culture; best conveyed with symbolism
   "You Know": persuasive, wishes to convince readers of his views; uses examples to illustrate
   Shakespeare: exposition, illustrates actor's life; explains points with examples
2. "Kilimanjaro!": humor, suspense, conflict, characterization
   "Sayonara": poetic language, depicts exotic lands; serious universal theme
   "You Know": familiar foibles, humor
   Shakespeare: behind-the-scenes look; insight into Elizabethan theater

MODEL FOR ACTIVE READING

The annotations in the Pupil's Edition that accompany this autobiography bring to students' attention various elements and techniques of fiction which likewise apply to nonfiction. Review the five steps under "Reminders for Active Reading of Nonfiction" (page 286), and have students tell how each has been illustrated in one or two of the pieces of nonfiction they have studied. Then have students apply each of the five reminders to Garland's story, by pointing to specific passages in the autobiography and notations in the text.

LITERARY FOCUS: *The Total Effect*

Whether you are reading fiction or nonfiction, active reading enhances enjoyment. Active reading is especially important in nonfiction so that you will be able to separate fact from impression and to distinguish truth from the author's interpretation of truth. A real appreciation of nonfiction involves observing details, recognizing writing techniques, accepting facts, and evaluating impressions. A successful reader will always consider the following reminders about varieties and ingredients of nonfiction.

Reminders for Active Reading of Nonfiction

1. The **title** can point to the author's purpose and audience.
2. The author of a **biography** uses **concrete language** to emphasize **descriptive details** that bring an individual to life.
3. The author of an **autobiography** combines memories with the insights that time allows.
4. Authors of nonfiction—**biography, autobiography,** or **essays**—use various elements and techniques that are appropriate to the interests and knowledge of the **audience.** These include the following:
   - plot (A narrative essay, in particular, will contain exposition, rising action with a conflict, climax, falling action, resolution.)
   - sensory language and other supporting details such as examples and statistics
   - thesis statement or clearly implied central idea
   - anecdotes to reveal character traits and to portray key events
   - dialogue between people
5. The author of any piece of nonfiction has a **purpose** in mind. The reader should uncover that purpose.

Model for Active Reading

On the following pages you will see how an alert reader considered the preceding reminders about nonfiction while reading one particular selection, an excerpt from *A Son of the Middle Border* by Hamlin Garland. You will find marginal notations that represent the reader's observations. Each notation includes a page reference for further information on the item in question. Ideally, you should first read the selection alone purely for pleasure. Then, on your second reading, consider the marginal notations. Afterward, you can use the process illustrated in this model as you read any nonfiction.

Hamlin Garland (1860–1940) was born on a farm in Wisconsin and grew up on farms in Iowa and South Dakota. Garland resisted his family's frequent moves toward the West and traveled to Boston to begin his writing career. Although he gave up the life of a prairie farmer, Garland's work—fiction and nonfiction—reflects his background and his concern for the hard, lonely lives of pioneer men and women. *A Son of the Middle Border* is Garland's autobiography, but it combines elements of the autobiography, the biography, the narrative essay, the descriptive essay, and the expository essay. The following excerpt documents one of the westward moves that were made by the Garland family.

- How does this nonfiction piece compare to fiction you have read or movies you have seen about pioneers?

AT A GLANCE

- Garland remembers his family's move westward to the plains in the late 1800s.

LITERARY OPTIONS

- purpose
- audience
- figurative language

THEMATIC OPTIONS

- hopes and ideals
- relationships between generations
- nature

Hamlin Garland

from A Son of the Middle Border

Late in August my father again loaded our household goods into wagons, and with our small herd of cattle following, set out toward the west, bound once again to overtake the actual line of the middle border.

Exposition (p. 273): Background information prepares us for the *narrative* aspect of the selection.

This journey has an unforgettable epic charm as I look back upon it. Each mile took us farther and farther into the unsettled prairie until in the afternoon of the second day, we came to a meadow so wide that its western rim touched the sky without revealing a sign of man's habitation other than the road in which we traveled.

Thesis statement (p. 285): The author states his central idea.

The plain was covered with grass as tall as ripe wheat and when my father stopped his team and came back to us and said, "Well, children, here we are on The Big Prairie," we looked about us with awe, so endless seemed this spread of wild oats and waving bluejoint.

Dialogue (p. 273): The father's words increase our understanding of him.

Far away dim clumps of trees showed, but no chimney was in sight, and no living thing moved save our own cattle and the hawks lazily wheeling in the air. My heart filled with awe as well as wonder. The majesty of this primeval world exalted me. I felt for the first time the poetry of the unplowed spaces. It seemed that the "herds of deer and buffalo" of our song might, at any moment, present themselves—

Supporting details (p. 285): The author's awe at the vast plain and his sensory language help to illustrate the "epic charm" of the journey.

GUIDED READING

LITERAL QUESTION

1a. What emotions does the author remember feeling when he saw the plains for the first time? ("awe" and "wonder")

INFERENTIAL QUESTION

1b. What qualities of the plains inspired these feelings? (its size, its lack of living things, the lack of evidence of civilization, the sense of something ancient and untouched)

AT A GLANCE

- Garland's father cheerfully pushes ever westward until nightfall; Garland's mother is unhappy.
- The family arrives at their new house.
- Garland and his brother camp there; the rest of the family stays with an uncle.

but they did not, and my father took no account even of the marsh fowl.

"Forward march!" he shouted, and on we went.

Hour after hour he pushed into the west, the heads of his tired horses hanging ever lower, and on my mother's face the shadow deepened, but her chieftain's voice cheerily urging his team lost nothing of its clarion resolution. He was in his element. He loved this shelterless sweep of prairie. This westward march entranced him, I think he would have gladly kept on until the snowy wall of the Rocky Mountains met his eyes, for he was a natural explorer.

Conflict (p. 273): The author's mother is unhappy about the father's westward march.

Sunset came at last, but still he drove steadily on through the sparse settlements. Just at nightfall we came to a beautiful little stream, and stopped to let the horses drink. I heard its rippling, reassuring song on the pebbles. Thereafter all is dim and vague to me until my mother called out sharply, "Wake up, children! Here we are!"

Struggling to my feet I looked about me. Nothing could be seen but the dim form of a small house. On every side the land melted into blackness, silent and without boundary.

Driving into the yard, father hastily unloaded one of the wagons and taking mother and Harriet and Jessie drove away to spend the night with Uncle David who had preceded us, as I now learned, and was living on a farm not far away. My brother and I were left to camp as best we could with the hired man.

Spreading a rude bed on the floor, he told us to "hop in" and in ten minutes we were all fast asleep.

The sound of a clattering poker awakened me next morning and when I opened my sleepy eyes and looked out a new world displayed itself before me.

The cabin faced a level plain with no tree in sight. A mile away to the west stood a low stone house and immediately in front of us opened a half-section of unfenced sod. To the north, as far as I could see, the land billowed like a russet ocean with scarcely a roof to fleck its lonely spread. I cannot say that I liked or disliked it. I merely marveled at it, and while I wandered about the yard, the hired man scorched some cornmeal mush in a skillet and this with some butter and gingerbread made up my first breakfast in Mitchell County.

Concrete language (p. 277): Details appeal to the senses of sound, sight, and smell.

An hour or two later father and mother and the girls returned and the work of setting up the stove and getting the furniture in place began. In a very short time the experienced clock was voicing its contentment on a new shelf, and the kettle was singing busily on its familiar stove. Once more and for the sixth time since her marriage, Belle Garland adjusted herself to a pioneer environment, comforted no doubt by the knowledge that David and Deborah were near and

Climax (p. 273): We know how the mother's conflict about moving will be resolved as we see her set up a new home.

GUIDED READING

LITERAL QUESTIONS

1a. How does Garland's mother look as the family proceeds westward? (The "shadow deepened" on her face.) What words does Garland use to describe his mother's relationship to his father? ("her chieftain")

2a. What details does Garland remember about setting up furniture and other belongings in the new house? (the clock "voicing its contentment" and the kettle "singing busily")

INFERENTIAL QUESTIONS

1b. What can you infer about the parents' relationship from these descriptions? (The father is in charge, and the mother must go along with his decisions.)

2b. What do these details suggest about the family's relationship with their new house? (that they have quickly made it their home by filling it with familiar items of warmth and contentment)

that her father was coming soon. No doubt she also congratulated herself on the fact that she had not been carried beyond the Missouri River. . . .

A few hours later, while my brother and I were on the roof of the house with intent to peer "over the edge of the prairie" something grandly significant happened. Upon a low hill to the west a herd of horses suddenly appeared running swiftly, led by a beautiful sorrel pony with shining white mane. On they came like a platoon of cavalry rushing down across the open sod which lay before our door. The leader moved with lofty and graceful action, easily outstretching all his fellows. Forward they swept, their long tails floating in the wind like banners—on in a great curve as if scenting danger in the smoke of our fire. The thunder of their feet filled me with delight. Surely, next to a herd of buffalo this squadron of wild horses was the most satisfactory evidence of the wilderness into which we had been thrust.

Riding as if to intercept the leader, a solitary herder now appeared, mounted upon a horse which very evidently was the mate of the leader. He rode magnificently, and under him the lithe mare strove resolutely to overtake and head off the leader. All to no purpose! The halterless steeds of the prairie snorted derisively at their former companion, bridled and saddled, and carrying the weight of a master. Swiftly they thundered across the sod, dropped into a ravine, and disappeared in a cloud of dust.

Silently we watched the rider turn and ride slowly homeward. The plain had become our new domain, the horseman our ideal.

Autobiographer's insight (p. 251): The author combines his childhood memory with an adult interpretation of it as "grandly significant."

Anecdote (p. 245): This brief story illustrates the author's attraction to the wilderness.

Restatement of thesis statement (p. 285): The last sentence returns to the "epic charm" mentioned in the *thesis statement*.

STUDY QUESTIONS

Recalling

1. Give two details that Garland uses to describe "The Big Prairie" at the beginning of the selection.
2. How does each of Garland's parents feel about moving west?
3. Describe briefly the scene that Garland and his brother view from the roof of their cabin.

Interpreting

4. Why is the author's mother pleased at not going farther west than the Missouri River?
5. Why does the lone horseman become the author's hero?

COMPOSITION

Writing About Your Reaction to Nonfiction

■ Explain how Garland shows understanding for each parent in their disagreement about moving. First explain how he creates sympathy for his father and then for his mother. Finally, tell which parent you eventually understand better, and explain why.

Writing a Description of a Place

■ The vast prairie fills Garland with awe because the land is empty and untouched. Write a description of a vast empty place that you know, or base your description on a place about which you have read.

AT A GLANCE

- Garland and his brother stand on the roof of their house and see a herd of wild horses approach.
- A solitary herder tries to overtake the leader of the horses but fails.
- The lone horseman becomes the boys' ideal.

REFLECTING ON THE SELECTION

What positive emotions does Garland remember feeling about his family's move westward? (awe, wonder, delight) What negative emotions do you think he might have experienced? (fear, loneliness, boredom, worry about the conflict between his parents, sadness for his mother)

STUDY QUESTIONS

1. The meadow was *so wide that its western rim touched the sky; the plain was covered with grass as tall as ripe wheat.*
2. *father:* in his element; *mother:* adjusted to pioneer life
3. see herd of wild horses being chased by herder
4. prefers to stay near family and civilization
5. He symbolizes freedom.

COMPOSITION: GUIDELINES FOR EVALUATION

WRITING ABOUT REACTION TO NONFICTION

Objective

To explain how Garland uses technique

Guidelines for Evaluation

- suggested length: four to six paragraphs
- should state which parent the writer understands better and explain why
- should explain how Garland creates sympathy for each parent

WRITING A DESCRIPTION OF A PLACE

Objective

To describe a vast empty place

Guidelines for Evaluation

- suggested length: 150–300 words
- should identify specific place
- should provide concrete details
- should create mood or feeling about place

ACTIVE READING

Students must learn to make inferences, to draw conclusions from the given information, when they read. For instance, in order to understand and appreciate Uchida's "Of Dry Goods and Black Bow Ties," students must do a great deal of inferring: (1) Uchida's grandfather was a samurai warrior; therefore, Uchida's family has a noble background. (2) Uchida's father wears black bow ties until after Mr. Shimada's death; therefore, Uchida's father retains and continues to show his respect for Mr. Shimada as if he were the lord that a samurai serves.

You might assign this section and discuss it with the class after they have read Uchida's piece. Then throughout the unit remind them to read actively and to be alert to details from which they can make inferences. For example, inferring is also an important aspect of understanding Lincoln in the excerpt from Sandburg's *Lincoln Preface*. Sandburg relates various anecdotes and expects the reader to draw conclusions about Lincoln based on these anecdotes. You might have students review the selection, relate some of the episodes, and discuss what they can infer about Lincoln based on the information Sandburg presents.

You will find among the materials for this unit in your *Teacher's Classroom Resources* the related blackline master Making Inferences in Nonfiction.

ACTIVE READING

Making Inferences

Writers expect readers to participate actively in their work; active participation includes making inferences. An **inference** is a conclusion we draw from available information.

In reading Yoshiko Uchida's "Of Dry Goods and Black Bow Ties" (page 235), we must do a good deal of inferring. In the first paragraph, for example, we hear that Uchida's father wore a black bow tie, a formality "he had continued to observe as faithfully as his father before him had worn his samurai sword." If we know that the samurai were the proud, aristocratic warrior class of Japan, we can infer (1) that Uchida's family had a noble background and (2) that her father had not only migrated but had somehow "come down" in the world. Later she tells us about the party the prosperous Mr. Shimada gave to send his daughter off to Paris. The caterers served "roast turkey, venison, baked ham and champagne." All the food served is of the European or American type. We can infer that Mr. Shimada adopted American culture and ways of life; in some ways he left his Japanese culture behind. The author expects us to infer a good deal about what happened to some Japanese American families as they attempted to adapt to their new surroundings.

More important is the fact that Uchida could not persuade her father to give up his black bow tie until he was almost sixty years old and had learned that Mr. Shimada was dead. We can infer a great deal from this. Even though the father no longer worked for Mr. Shimada and had become prosperous himself, and even though Mr. Shimada had lost his power and his fortune, Uchida's father never abandoned his respect for his former employer. We learn about traditional Japanese respect for authority. We see that the relation between employer and employee in traditional Japanese culture is more of a "family" relationship than is usually the case in America.

If Uchida's tale shows us many ways in which Japanese families became "Americanized," it also shows us that in some ways they kept one of the admirable values of their native culture—a respect and mutual assistance that goes beyond the values that can be measured by money.

REVIEW: NONFICTION

Guide for Studying Nonfiction

As you read nonfiction, review the following guide in order to recognize the methods a nonfiction author uses to communicate facts and impressions to the reader.

Biography

1. What seems to be the prime **purpose** of the biography? That is, what generalization about the subject—or about people in general—does the author make?
2. On what part of the subject's life does the author concentrate? Why?
3. What flattering information about the subject does the author convey? What unflattering information does the author use?
4. What **details of appearance** and which mannerisms does the author include? Why?
5. What **anecdotes** convey the human qualities of the subject? How well do you get to know the subject as a person?

Autobiography

1. For what **purpose** is the author writing the autobiography? That is, what generalization about himself or herself—or about people in general—is the author making?
2. What virtues and successes does the author claim? What faults and defeats does the author admit?

Essay

1. What seems to be the prime **purpose** of the essay? That is, what opinion or generalization is the author trying to communicate?
2. If the essay is **narrative**, what is the main conflict? What is the climax?
3. If the essay is **descriptive**, what concrete language is used?
4. If the essay is **persuasive**, what methods does the author use to persuade you?
5. If the essay is **expository**, what is the thesis statement? In what ways does the rest of the essay support the thesis statement?

REVIEW

Refer to the review in the text, Guide for Studying Nonfiction. It offers a variety of questions that can be used in reviewing the selections in turn or the unit as a whole. You might also request that students keep these questions in mind to aid their comprehension as they read the selections and all nonfiction.

The questions in the Guide for Studying Nonfiction appear with write-on lines, in blackline master form, among the materials for this unit in your *Teacher's Classroom Resources.*

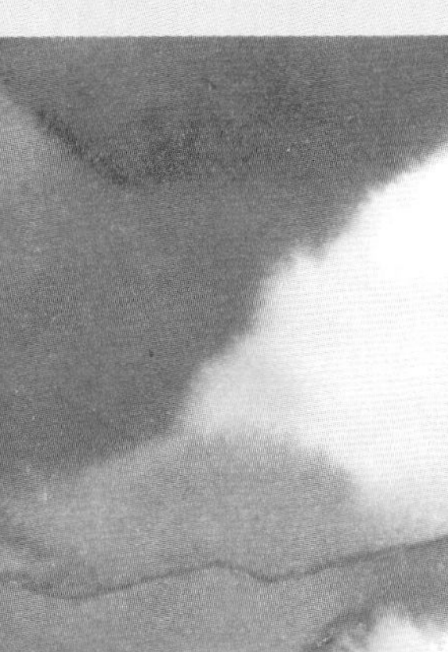

PREVIEW: DRAMA

On the stage it is always now; *the personages are standing on that razor-edge, between the past and the future. . . .*
—Thornton Wilder

A **drama** is a play, a story meant to be performed for an audience. The drama on the following pages is divided into two sections: (1) one-act plays and (2) Shakespearean drama.

Drama traces its ancestry to ancient times. The first plays that we know of were performed as part of religious festivals in Greece, and, by 400 B.C., playgoing was already a popular pastime. The classic plays of the Greek playwrights Aeschylus, Aristophanes, Sophocles, and Euripides are still performed today—on stage and film—throughout the world.

Greek theater presented two basic types of drama: tragedy and comedy. A **tragedy** is a play in which a hero suffers a major downfall. A **comedy** is a humorous play with a happy ending. Today we still have both types; most plays, however, fall somewhere between the two extremes.

Since drama is meant to be performed, the reader of a play should understand the two basic parts of any drama: (1) the script and (2) the staging. The script of a play is made up of (1) **dialogue**, which is the speech of the characters, and (2) **stage directions**, which include instructions for performing the play and descriptions of settings, characters, and actions. To enjoy reading drama, we should read stage directions and visualize the play. The staging—scenery, costumes, lighting, and the actors' gestures, facial expressions, and tone of voice—can help us to understand a play's setting, mood, characters, plot, and even theme.

PREVIEW

Have students read the Preview. Help them to understand that a play usually contains no narrative voice to describe characters directly and that all characterization is indirect. We learn about characters in a play as we learn about people in everyday life—from their appearance, from what they do and say, and from what others say about them. You may need to remind students that, although stage directions sometimes contain direct statements about characters' personalities, an audience never sees stage directions, which are intended as instructions for the director, designers, and actors.

Have students bring in programs from plays that they have seen. First have them turn to one of the plays in their text, and point out the list of characters, the setting, stage directions, dialogue, and speakers' names. Use the term *script* in speaking of this text. Then have them examine programs from actual performances. Point out the various interpretive artists responsible for turning *script* into *performance:* director, actors, designers of scenery, costumes, and lighting, and, perhaps, composers, musicians, and choreographers. Show them that the audience at a performance is usually provided with a list of characters (usually in order of appearance) and with a setting for each scene.

LITERARY FOCUS: *The One-Act Play*

A **full-length play** usually has several major characters and a complicated plot. The play is usually divided into acts, and the acts are divided into scenes. A **one-act play** usually has few characters, a simple plot, and only a few or even one scene.

One-act plays have existed for as long as drama itself; Greek dramatists wrote short as well as full-length plays. Modern authors often use this short form to try out experimental ideas. They can also present situations that may be tragic or funny or enlightening but that cannot be stretched to fill a longer work. As the following plays demonstrate, the one-act format has been used for light comedy as well as for more realistic dramas.

Because one-act plays usually have one setting and few characters, they are easy to read and to perform. Short plays, however, can sometimes have greater impact than longer drama. Although a one-act play presents a single incident or situation, it can nevertheless suggest much more. For example, a brief glimpse into a character's day can suggest an entire life; a single conversation between two characters can suggest a relationship.

In spite of their brevity, the one-act plays that follow present a wealth of observation about human nature and a wealth of entertainment. *A Sunny Morning* is a Spanish play, a simple scene of a chance encounter by long-lost friends. *The Dancers* is a "coming-of-age" play, in which a young man makes a decision that adds a new maturity to his character.

Serafín (1871–1938) and Joaquín (1873–1944) Alvarez Quintero were brothers who collaborated on many plays, both comedies and tragedies. They worked together so closely that, to many people, their plays seem to be the product of a single mind. Like all their light comedies, *A Sunny Morning,* which is translated from its original Spanish, is a brief, humorous sketch about life in Madrid.

- One of the characters in this play quotes a line from a poem: "All love is sad, but sad as it is, it is the best thing that we know." Do you agree? Do you think the characters in the play have earned the right to feel this way?

Serafín and Joaquín Alvarez Quintero

A Sunny Morning

CHARACTERS

DON GONZALO [gan za'lō]
JUANITO [hwän ē'tō]: his servant
DOÑA LAURA
PETRA [pā'tra]: her maid

AT A GLANCE

- Elderly Doña Laura comes to the park with her maid, Petra.
- Petra is young and in love.
- Doña Laura encourages Petra to chat with her lover while she feeds the birds.

LITERARY OPTIONS

- characterization
- aside
- theme

THEMATIC OPTIONS

- friendship and love
- youth and age
- hopes and ideals

1 THEME

Doña Laura is appreciative of life's small pleasures. Her enthusiastic response to the available bench and to the weather is contrasted with the youthful Petra's impatience with the heat.

2 CHARACTERIZATION

Doña Laura is seen initially to be both pragmatic and sympathetic about love.

3 STAGING

The actress through gestures and eye movements will help us "see" the invisible pigeons.

CIVIC REPERTORY THEATRE, INC.

APRIL 1929

EVA LE GALLIENNE, Director

A SUNNY MORNING

SERAFIN and JOAQUIN ALVAREZ QUINTERO

CAST (in order of appearance)

Doña Laura . . . . *Eva Le Gallienne*
Petra, (her maid) . . . . *Josephine Hutchinson*
Don Gonzalo . . . . *Egon Brecher*
Juanito, (his servant) . . . . *Robert Ross*

SCENE—A retired corner in a park in Madrid
TIME—The Present

***Scene:* *A park in Madrid*[1]**
Time:* *The present

[***A sunny morning in a retired corner of a park in Madrid. Autumn. A bench at right.*** DOÑA[2] LAURA, ***a handsome, white-haired old lady of about seventy, refined in appearance, her bright eyes and entire manner giving evidence that despite her age her mental faculties are unimpaired, enters leaning upon the arm of her maid,*** PETRA[3]. ***In her free hand she carries a parasol,[4] which serves also as a cane.***]

1 DOÑA LAURA. I am so glad to be here. I feared my seat would be occupied. What a beautiful morning!

PETRA. The sun is hot.

DOÑA LAURA. Yes, you are only twenty. [***She sits down on the bench.***] Oh, I feel more tired today than usual. [***Noticing*** PETRA, ***who seems impatient.***] Go, if you wish to chat with your guard.

2 PETRA. He is not mine, señora[5]; he belongs to the park.

DOÑA LAURA. He belongs more to you than he does to the park. Go find him, but remain within calling distance.

PETRA. I see him over there waiting for me.

DOÑA LAURA. Do not remain more than ten minutes.

PETRA. Very well, señora. [***Walks toward right.***]

DOÑA LAURA. Wait a moment.

PETRA. What does the señora wish?

DOÑA LAURA. Give me the bread crumbs.

PETRA. I don't know what is the matter with me.

DOÑA LAURA. [***Smiling.***] I do. Your head is where your heart is—with the guard.

PETRA. Here, señora. [***She hands*** DOÑA LAURA ***a small bag. Exit*** PETRA ***by right.***]

3 DOÑA LAURA. Adiós. [***Glances toward trees at right.***] Here they come! They know just when to expect me. [***She rises, walks toward right, and throws three handfuls of bread crumbs.***] These are for the spryest, these for the gluttons, and these for the little ones which are the most persistent. [***Laughs. She returns to her seat and watches, with a pleased expression, the pigeons feeding.***] There, that big one is always first! I

---

1. **Madrid** [mə drid′]: capital city of Spain, located in the central part of the country.
2. **Doña** [dōn′yə]: Spanish for "Lady" or "Madam," title of respect for married women. Men are addressed as "Don."
3. **Petra** [pā′tra]
4. **parasol** [par′ə sol′]: small, decorative umbrella used for protection from the sun.
5. **señora** [sen yôr′ə]: madame; term of address for married women. Men are addressed as "señor," mister or sir.

GUIDED READING

LITERAL QUESTION

1a. What does Petra forget? (to leave the bread crumbs)

INFERENTIAL QUESTION

1b. What attitude does Doña Laura take toward Petra's forgetfulness? (She smiles because she understands the girl's preoccupation.)

know him by his big head. Now one, now another, now two, now three—That little fellow is the least timid. I believe he would eat from my hand. That one takes his piece and flies up to that branch alone. He is a philosopher. But where do they all come from? It seems as if the news had spread. Ha, ha! Don't quarrel. There is enough for all. I'll bring more tomorrow.

[*Enter* DON GONZALO[6] *and* JUANITO[7] *from left center.* DON GONZALO *is an old gentleman of seventy, gouty*[8] *and impatient. He leans upon* JUANITO*'s arm and drags his feet somewhat as he walks.*]

DON GONZALO. Idling their time away! They should be saying mass.

JUANITO. You can sit here, señor. There is only a lady. [DOÑA LAURA *turns her head and listens.*]

DON GONZALO. I won't, Juanito. I want a bench to myself.

JUANITO. But there is none.

DON GONZALO. That one over there is mine.

JUANITO. There are three priests sitting there.

DON GONZALO. Rout them out. Have they gone?

JUANITO. No, indeed. They are talking.

DON GONZALO. Just as if they were glued to the seat. No hope of their leaving. Come this way, Juanito. [*They walk toward the birds, right.*]

2 DOÑA LAURA. [*Indignantly.*] Look out!

DON GONZALO. Are you speaking to me, señora?

DOÑA LAURA. Yes, to you.

DON GONZALO. What do you wish?

DOÑA LAURA. You have scared away the birds who were feeding on my crumbs.

DON GONZALO. What do I care about the birds?

DOÑA LAURA. But I do.

DON GONZALO. This is a public park.

DOÑA LAURA. Then why do you complain that the priests have taken your bench?

DON GONZALO. Señora, we have not met. I cannot imagine why you take the liberty of addressing me. Come, Juanito. [BOTH *go out right.*]

DOÑA LAURA. What an ill-natured old man! Why must people get so fussy and cross when they reach a certain age? [*Looking toward right.*] I am glad. He lost that bench, too. Serves him right for scaring the birds. He is furious. Yes, yes; find a seat if you can. Poor man! He is wiping the perspiration from his face. Here he comes. A carriage would not raise more dust than his feet. [*Enter* DON GONZALO *and* JUANITO *by right and walk toward left.*]

DON GONZALO. Have the priests gone yet, Juanito?

JUANITO. No, indeed, señor. They are still there.

DON GONZALO. The authorities should place more benches here for these sunny mornings.
3 Well, I suppose I must resign myself and sit on the bench with the old lady. [*Muttering to himself, he sits at the extreme end of* DOÑA LAURA*'s bench and looks at her indignantly. Touches his hat as he greets her.*] Good morning.

DOÑA LAURA. What, you here again?

DON GONZALO. I repeat that we have not met.

DOÑA LAURA. I was responding to your salute.

DON GONZALO. "Good morning" should be answered by "good morning," and that is all you should have said.

DOÑA LAURA. You should have asked permission to sit on this bench, which is mine.

DON GONZALO. The benches here are public property.

---

6. **Gonzalo** [gan za′lō]
7. **Juanito** [hwän ē′tō]
8. **gouty** [gout′ē]: suffering from gout, a disease that causes swelling and pain, especially in the big toe.

AT A GLANCE

- Don Gonzalo, aged and irritable, enters with his servant.
- Doña Laura rebukes him for scaring away the birds.
- Chafing and scolding, they sit on the same bench.

1 CHARACTERIZATION

Don Gonzalo is first seen as a short-tempered, opinionated, somewhat selfish man. His belief that a certain bench is *his* parallels Doña Laura's.

2 PLOT: CONFLICT

The first interaction between them is laden with anger, impatience, and scorn.

3 STAGING

Don Gonzalo joins Doña Laura on the bench, where their similarities and differences will be vividly shown to the audience.

GUIDED READING

LITERAL QUESTION

1a. How does Doña Laura first get Don Gonzalo's attention? (She says "Look out!")

INFERENTIAL QUESTION

1b. When he answers her rudely, why does she continue to speak to him? (She treats their conversation as a battle of wits.)

AT A GLANCE

- Doña Laura continues to tease and criticize Don Gonzalo.
- He tries to ignore her by reading.
- She provokes a volley of challenges and boasts.
- They share a pinch of snuff together.

1 TONE

Her witty turn of phrase lightens her criticism with humor.

2 DIALOGUE

She will not let him ignore her. We see that her barbed remarks are a way of keeping his attention.

3 CHARACTERIZATION

His vanity and her challenges lead him to boast.

4 DIALOGUE

"What a coincidence!" underplays the newly revealed likeness of the pair.

DOÑA LAURA. Why, you said the one the priests have was yours.

DON GONZALO. Very well, very well. I have nothing more to say. [*Between his teeth.*] Senile old lady! She ought to be at home knitting and counting her beads.

DOÑA LAURA. Don't grumble any more. I'm not going to leave just to please you.

DON GONZALO. [*Brushing the dust from his shoes with his handkerchief.*] If the ground were sprinkled a little it would be an improvement.

1 DOÑA LAURA. Do you use your handkerchief as a shoe brush?

DON GONZALO. Why not?

DOÑA LAURA. Do you use a shoe brush as a handkerchief?

DON GONZALO. What right have you to criticize my actions?

DOÑA LAURA. A neighbor's right.

DON GONZALO. Juanito, my book. I do not care to listen to nonsense.

DOÑA LAURA. You are very polite.

DON GONZALO. Pardon me, señora, but never interfere with what does not concern you.

DOÑA LAURA. I generally say what I think.

DON GONZALO. And more to the same effect. Give me the book, Juanito.

JUANITO. Here, señor. [JUANITO *takes a book from his pocket, hands it to* DON GONZALO, *then exits by right.* DON GONZALO, *casting indignant glances at* DOÑA LAURA, *puts on an enormous pair of glasses, takes from his pocket a reading-glass, adjusts both to suit him, and opens his book.*]

DOÑA LAURA. I thought you were taking out a telescope.

DON GONZALO. Was that you?

2 DOÑA LAURA. Your sight must be keen.

DON GONZALO. Keener than yours is.

DOÑA LAURA. Yes, evidently.

DON GONZALO. Ask the hares and partridges.

DOÑA LAURA. Ah! Do you hunt?

DON GONZALO. I did, and even now—

DOÑA LAURA. Oh, yes, of course!

DON GONZALO. Yes, señora. Every Sunday I take my gun and dog, you understand, and go to one of my estates near Aravaca[9] and kill time.

3 DOÑA LAURA. Yes, kill time. That is all you kill.

DON GONZALO. Do you think so? I could show you a wild boar's head in my study—

DOÑA LAURA. Yes, and I could show you a tiger's skin in my boudoir.[10] What does that prove?

DON GONZALO. Very well, señora, please allow me to read. Enough conversation.

DOÑA LAURA. Well, you subside, then.

DON GONZALO. But first I shall take a pinch of snuff. [*Takes out snuff box.*] Will you have some? [*Offers box to* DOÑA LAURA.]

DOÑA LAURA. If it is good.

DON GONZALO. It is of the finest. You will like it.

4 DOÑA LAURA. [*Taking pinch of snuff.*] It clears my head.

DON GONZALO. And mine.

DOÑA LAURA. Do you sneeze?

DON GONZALO. Yes, señora, three times.

DOÑA LAURA. And so do I. What a coincidence!

---

9. **Aravaca** [a rə va'kə]: village near Madrid.
10. **boudoir** [bo͞od'wär]: woman's bedroom.

GUIDED READING

LITERAL QUESTION

1a. How many times does Don Gonzalo attempt to break off the conversation? (Three: *Very well, very well; Give me the book . . . ; Enough conversation. . . .*)

INFERENTIAL QUESTION

1b. Why would he want to resume the conversation each time he has stopped it? (Her comments are provocative; he feels compelled to defend himself.)

After taking the snuff, they await the sneezes, both anxiously, and sneeze alternately three times each.]

DON GONZALO. There, I feel better.

DOÑA LAURA. So do I. [*Aside.*] The snuff has made peace between us.

DON GONZALO. You will excuse me if I read aloud?

DOÑA LAURA. Read as loud as you please; you will not disturb me.

DON GONZALO. [*Reading.*] "All love is sad, but sad as it is, it is the best thing that we know." That is from Campoamor.[11]

DOÑA LAURA. Ah!

DON GONZALO. [*Reading.*] "The daughters of the mothers I once loved kiss me now as they would a graven image." Those lines, I take it, are in a humorous vein.

DOÑA LAURA. [*Laughing.*] I take them so, too.

DON GONZALO. There are some beautiful poems in this book. Here. "Twenty years pass. He returns."

DOÑA LAURA. You cannot imagine how it affects me to see you reading with all those glasses.

DON GONZALO. Can you read without any?

DOÑA LAURA. Certainly.

DON GONZALO. At your age? You're jesting.

DOÑA LAURA. Pass me the book, then. [*Takes book; reads aloud.*]

"Twenty years pass. He returns.
And each, beholding the other, exclaims—
Can it be that this is he?
Heavens, is it she?"

11. **Campoamor** [kam′pwa mōr′]: Ramón de Campoamor (1817–1901), Spanish poet.

[DOÑA LAURA *returns the book to* DON GONZALO.]

4 DON GONZALO. Indeed, I envy you your wonderful eyesight.

DOÑA LAURA. [*Aside.*] I know every word by heart.

DON GONZALO. I am very fond of good verses, very fond. I even composed some in my youth.

DOÑA LAURA. Good ones?

DON GONZALO. Of all kinds. I was a great friend of Espronceda, Zorrilla, Bécquer,[12] and others. I first met Zorrilla in America.

DOÑA LAURA. Why, have you been in America?

DON GONZALO. Several times. The first time I went I was only six years old.

DOÑA LAURA. You must have gone with Columbus in one of his caravels![13]

DON GONZALO. [*Laughing.*] Not quite as bad as that. I am old, I admit, but I did not know Ferdinand and Isabella.[14] [*They both laugh.*] I was also a great friend of Campoamor. I met him in Valencia.[15] I am a native of that city.

DOÑA LAURA. You are?

DON GONZALO. I was brought up there and there I spent my early youth. Have you ever visited that city?

DOÑA LAURA. Yes, señor. Not far from Valencia there was a villa that, if still there, should retain

12. **Espronceda** [äs prōn sā′da], **Zorrilla** [zô rē′ya], **Bécquer** [bā′ker]: José de Espronceda (1808–1842), José Zorrilla (1817–1893), and Gustavo Adolfo Bécquer (1836–1870), Spanish poets.
13. **caravels** [kar′ə velz′]: ships built in Spain and Portugal in the fifteenth century. Two of Columbus' ships were caravels.
14. **Ferdinand and Isabella:** King Ferdinand V (1452–1516) and Queen Isabella I (1451–1504), the first rulers of a united Spain and the monarchs who financed Columbus' discovery of America.
15. **Valencia** [və len′sē ə]: coastal city in eastern Spain.

AT A GLANCE

- Doña Laura takes his book from him and reads it perfectly.
- She confides to the audience that she has memorized the poem.

1 ASIDE

Doña Laura's comment helps confirm for the audience the growing attraction between the pair.

2 THEME

The authors draw attention to the play's theme by showing the woman giving her permission, the man reading the statement aloud, and her reacting emotionally to it.

3 PLOT: RISING ACTION

The poem foreshadows each character's realization of the other's identity.

4 CHARACTERIZATION

On a literal level the woman has craftily fooled the man about her "wonderful eyesight." Doña Laura's having memorized the poem reveals a romantic side of her nature and further allies her sensibilities with Don Gonzalo's.

GUIDED READING

LITERAL QUESTION

1a. What is Don Gonzalo's relationship to the poet Campoamor? (He admires his work; he had met Campoamor in his youth.)

INFERENTIAL QUESTION

1b. Why does the poem seem appropriate to his current situation? (It speaks of an older man seen no longer as an object of love but as a "graven image.")

AT A GLANCE

- The poem sets off a chain of memories leading to the revelation that Doña Laura and Don Gonzalo were once in love.
- Doña Laura realizes that Don Gonzalo no longer recognizes her.
- They recall details of their love affair.

1 CHARACTERIZATION

She recognizes her own name and is shaken; she decides to pretend it is the name of a friend.

2 CHARACTERIZATION

The depth of Don Gonzalo's feelings are evident as he idealizes the love of his youth.

3 THEME

Doña Laura regrets that time has faded his lovely dream.

4 ASIDE

She recognizes him as her lost love, but tells only the audience.

5 IMAGE PATTERN

In recalling their love affair the two characters focus on the romantic image of a *bouquet of flowers.*

memories of me. I spent several seasons there. It was many, many years ago. It was near the sea, hidden away among lemon and orange trees. They called it—let me see, what did they call it—Maricela.[16]

DON GONZALO. [*Startled.*] Maricela?

DOÑA LAURA. Maricela. Is the name familiar to you?

DON GONZALO. Yes, very familiar. If my memory serves me right, for we forget as we grow old, there lived in that villa the most beautiful woman I have ever seen, and I assure you I have seen many. Let me see—what was her name? Laura—Laura—Laura Llorente.

1 DOÑA LAURA. [*Startled.*] Laura Llorente?

DON GONZALO. Yes. [*They look at each other intently.*]

DOÑA LAURA. [*Recovering herself.*] Nothing. You reminded me of my best friend.

DON GONZALO. How strange!

DOÑA LAURA. It is strange. She was called "The Silver Maiden."

DON GONZALO. Precisely, "The Silver Maiden." By that name she was known in that locality. I seem to see her as if she were before me now, at that window with the red roses. Do you remember that window?

DOÑA LAURA. Yes, I remember. It was the window of her room.

DON GONZALO. She spent many hours there. I mean in my day.

DOÑA LAURA. [*Sighing.*] And in mine, too.

2 DON GONZALO. She was ideal. Fair as a lily, jet black hair and black eyes, with an uncommonly sweet expression. She seemed to cast a radiance wherever she was. Her figure was beautiful perfect. "What forms of sovereign beauty God models in human clay!" She was a dream.

3 DOÑA LAURA. [*Aside.*] If you but knew that dream was now by your side, you would realize what dreams come to. [*Aloud.*] She was very unfortunate and had a sad love affair.

DON GONZALO. Very sad. [*They look at each other.*]

DOÑA LAURA. Did you hear of it?

DON GONZALO. Yes.

4 DOÑA LAURA. The ways of Providence are strange. [*Aside.*] Gonzalo!

DON GONZALO. The gallant lover, in the same affair—

DOÑA LAURA. Ah, the duel!

DON GONZALO. Precisely, the duel. The gallant lover was—my cousin, of whom I was very fond.

DOÑA LAURA. Oh, yes, a cousin? My friend told me in one of her letters the story of that affair, which was truly romantic. He, your cousin, passed by on horseback every morning down
5 the rose path under her window, and tossed up to her balcony a bouquet of flowers which she caught.

DON GONZALO. And later in the afternoon the gallant horseman would return by the same path, and catch the bouquet of flowers she would toss him. Am I right?

DOÑA LAURA. Yes. They wanted to marry her to a merchant whom she would not have.

DON GONZALO. And one night, when my cousin waited under her window to hear her sing, this other person presented himself unexpectedly.

DOÑA LAURA. And insulted your cousin.

DON GONZALO. There was a quarrel.

16. **Maricela** [mar ē sä′la]

GUIDED READING

LITERAL QUESTION

1a. What does the "letter" reveal about the lovers in Maricela? (Doña Laura waited on a balcony to catch his bouquet. He caught her flowers when he returned in the afternoon.)

INFERENTIAL QUESTION

1b. In what spirit do they recall these details? (They remember with fondness and excitement.)

DOÑA LAURA. And later a duel.

DON GONZALO. Yes, at sunrise, on the beach, and the merchant was badly wounded. My cousin had to conceal himself for a few days and later to fly.

DOÑA LAURA. You seem to know the story well.

DON GONZALO. And so do you.

DOÑA LAURA. I have explained that a friend repeated it to me.

DON GONZALO. As my cousin did to me. [*Aside.*] This is Laura!

1 DOÑA LAURA. [*Aside.*] Why tell him? He does not suspect.

DON GONZALO. [*Aside.*] She is entirely innocent.

DOÑA LAURA. And was it you, by any chance, who advised your cousin to forget Laura?

DON GONZALO. Why, my cousin never forgot her!

DOÑA LAURA. How do you account, then, for his conduct?

DON GONZALO. I will tell you. The young man took refuge in my house, fearful of the consequences of a duel with a person highly regarded in that locality. From my home he went to

AT A GLANCE

- In the past forbidden affection led to a duel.
- Don Gonzalo recognizes Doña Laura but does not tell her.
- Both continue to speak of the affair as having happened to her cousin and his friend.

1 ASIDE

Both characters reveal to the audience that they will not declare their identities. Both claim to have the other's welfare in mind.

GUIDED READING

LITERAL QUESTION

1a. Following the duel what happened to the young Don Gonzalo? (He ran away.)

INFERENTIAL QUESTION

1b. From the young Doña Laura's point of view, what happened after the duel? (She was abandoned.)

AT A GLANCE

- The two exchange made-up stories of the deaths of their younger selves.
- To the audience they confide that their lives went on normally.
- They agree to meet the next day.

1 ASIDE

Successive asides sustain the dramatic tension and provide humor.

2 TONE

Doña Laura outdoes him in her fictional account of her demise; her story provides both comedy and pathos.

3 PLOT

We learn the truth: both led happy lives with other mates. The much-anticipated disclosure to each other does not occur.

4 THEME

In Petra and Juanito we see the cycle of hopeful new love starting again.

Seville,[17] then came to Madrid. He wrote Laura many letters, some of them in verse. But undoubtedly they were intercepted by her parents, for she never answered at all. Gonzalo then, in despair, believing his love lost to him forever, joined the army, went to Africa, and there, in a trench, met a glorious death, grasping the flag of Spain and whispering the name of his beloved Laura—

1 DOÑA LAURA. [*Aside.*] What an atrocious lie!

DON GONZALO. [*Aside.*] I could not have killed myself more gloriously.

DOÑA LAURA. You must have been prostrated by the calamity.

DON GONZALO. Yes, indeed, señora. As if he were my brother. I presume, though, on the contrary, that Laura in a short time was chasing butterflies in her garden, indifferent to regret.

DOÑA LAURA. No señor, no!

DON GONZALO. It is woman's way.

DOÑA LAURA. Even if it were woman's way, "The Silver Maiden" was not of that disposition. My friend awaited news for days, months, a year, and no letter came. One afternoon, just at sunset, as the first stars were appearing, she was seen to leave the house, and with quickening steps wend her way toward the beach, the beach
2 where her beloved had risked his life. She wrote his name on the sand, then sat down upon a rock, her gaze fixed upon the horizon. The waves murmured their eternal threnody[18] and slowly crept up to the rock where the maiden sat. The tide rose with a boom and swept her out to sea.

DON GONZALO. Good heavens!

DOÑA LAURA. The fishermen of that shore who often tell the story affirm that it was a long time before the waves washed away that name written on the sand. [*Aside.*] You will not get ahead of me in decorating my own funeral.

DON GONZALO. [*Aside.*] She lies worse than I do.

DOÑA LAURA. Poor Laura!

DON GONZALO. Poor Gonzalo!

3 DOÑA LAURA. [*Aside.*] I will not tell him that I married two years later.

DON GONZALO. [*Aside.*] In three months I ran off to Paris with a ballet dancer.

DOÑA LAURA. Fate is curious. Here are you and I, complete strangers, met by chance, discussing the romance of old friends of long ago! We have been conversing as if we were old friends.

DON GONZALO. Yes, it is curious, considering the ill-natured prelude to our conversation.

DOÑA LAURA. You scared away the birds.

DON GONZALO. I was unreasonable, perhaps.

DOÑA LAURA. Yes, that was evident. [*Sweetly.*] Are you coming again tomorrow?

DON GONZALO. Most certainly, if it is a sunny morning. And not only will I not scare away the birds, but I will bring a few crumbs.

DOÑA LAURA. Thank you very much. Birds are grateful and repay attention. I wonder where my maid is? Petra! [*Signals for her maid.*]

DON GONZALO. [*Aside, looking at* LAURA, *whose back is turned.*] No, no, I will not reveal myself. I am grotesque now. Better that she recall the gallant horseman who passed daily beneath her window tossing flowers.

4 DOÑA LAURA. Here she comes.

DON GONZALO. That Juanito! He plays havoc with the nursemaids. [*Looks right and signals with his hand.*]

DOÑA LAURA. [*Aside, looking at* GONZALO, *whose back is turned.*] No, I am too sadly changed. It is

---

17. **Seville** [sə vil′]: city in southern Spain.
18. **threnody** [thren′ə dē]: song of mourning.

GUIDED READING

LITERAL QUESTION

1a. Where does Doña Laura set the story of the Silver Maiden's death? (on a beach)

INFERENTIAL QUESTION

1b. What details about her story seem artificial and far-fetched? (that the water would not wash away the name written in the sand, among others)

etter he should remember me as the black-eyed irl tossing flowers as he passed among the roses ı the garden. [JUANITO *enters by right,* PETRA *by ·ft. She has a bunch of violets in her hand.*]

OÑA LAURA. Well, Petra! At last!

ON GONZALO. Juanito, you are late.

ETRA. [*To* DOÑA LAURA.] The gard gave me ıese violets for you, señora.

OÑA LAURA. How very nice! Thank him for me. 'hey are fragrant. [*As she takes the violets from er maid a few loose ones fall to the ground.*]

ON GONZALO. My dear lady, this has been a reat honor and a great pleasure.

OÑA LAURA. It has also been a pleasure to me.

ON GONZALO. Goodbye until tomorrow.

OÑA LAURA. Until tomorrow.

ON GONZALO. If it is sunny.

OÑA LAURA. A sunny morning. Will you go to our bench?

ON GONZALO. No, I will come to this—if you do ıot object?

DOÑA LAURA. This bench is at your disposal.

DON GONZALO. And I will surely bring the crumbs.

DOÑA LAURA. Tomorrow, then?

DON GONZALO. Tomorrow!

1 [LAURA *walks away toward right, supported by her* MAID. GONZALO, *before leaving with* JUANITO, *trembling and with a great effort, stoops to pick up the violets* LAURA *dropped. Just then* LAURA *turns her head and surprises him picking up the flowers.*]

JUANITO. What are you doing, señor?

DON GONZALO. Juanito, wait—

DOÑA LAURA. [*Aside.*] Yes, it is he!

DON GONZALO. [*Aside.*] It is she, and no mistake. [DOÑA LAURA *and* DON GONZALO *wave farewell.*]

2 DOÑA LAURA. "Can it be that this is he?"

DON GONZALO. "Heavens, is it she?" [*They smile once more, as if she were again at the window and he below in the rose garden, and then disappear upon the arms of their servants.*]

STUDY QUESTIONS

Recalling

1. From stage directions, describe what Doña Laura and Don Gonzalo look like.
2. Give two reasons that the two main characters argue at the beginning of the play.
3. Name the other characters in the play. How are they related to the main characters? What do they do while the main characters are speaking?
4. Briefly tell the story of the old romance between the main characters.
5. What story does each main character create to cover up the truth?
6. What reasons do the main characters give for not revealing their true identities?
7. What plans do they make for the next day?

Interpreting

8. Explain how the poem that Don Gonzalo reads gives a summary of the play and states its theme.
9. Why might both characters exaggerate and glorify the ending of their romance?
10. Explain how the minor characters are similar to the main characters and how they are different.
11. Why do you think this play could take place anywhere and at any time?

AT A GLANCE

- Doña Laura drops some violets from her bouquet.
- As Don Gonzalo picks them up, the Don and Doña exchange lines from the poem.

1 IMAGE PATTERN

Their prior courtship is echoed by this reenactment of their exchange of flowers.

2 PLOT: RESOLUTION

The characters indirectly reveal their identities to each other by reciting lines from the poem that has meant so much to them.

REFLECTING ON THE PLAY

How do you think their relationship will proceed? (Probably they will maintain a fond, friendly relationship.)

STUDY QUESTIONS

1.
   - *Laura:* seventy, handsome, white-haired, refined, bright-eyed
   - *Gonzalo:* same age, gouty, impatient, drags feet as he walks
2. his scaring birds, possession of benches, eyesight
3. Petra, maid to Doña Laura, chats with guard; Juanito, servant to Gonzalo, talks with maids
4. they courted; she was to be married to merchant; Gonzalo wounded him in duel, fled
5.
   - *Gonzalo:* died in African war
   - *Laura:* carried away by the tide
6. Both wish to be remembered as they were in youth.
7. to meet on same bench
8. First line states theme, second refers to aging, third brings play to present, foreshadows remainder of play
9. Both are embarrassed to reveal how quickly they recovered from their romance.
10. both in love; servants cannot court as masters do
11. theme is universal; setting is a simple park bench

STUDY QUESTIONS

12. suggests they will be more honest

LITERARY FOCUS

Thinking About the Aside

1.
- true identities
- Tales are lies.
- Laura's eyesight is not good.
- true endings of affair

2. conveys their regrets and desire to preserve memories

3.
- Laura: "I know every word by heart."
- Gonzalo: "I could not have killed myself more gloriously."

Thinking About Staging and Setting

1. Students' responses should be consistent with stage directions.

2. requires bright light of autumn morning; changes slowly to suggest time passing, cloudiness

3. Mood is light and playful. Sunny morning in park suggests happiness; autumn symbolizes aging.

Extending

12. Do you think that Doña Laura and Don Gonzalo will continue to conceal their identities? Why or why not?

LITERARY FOCUS

The Aside

In a play an **aside** is a comment by a character that is heard by the audience but not by the other characters. Sometimes two or more characters exchange asides that are not heard by other characters on the stage. Asides reveal directly to the audience what a character is thinking and feeling. Therefore, we know more about the character than the other characters do. At times, asides are humorous because they show us the difference between a character's words and thoughts.

Thinking About the Aside

1. What information do Doña Laura and Don Gonzalo keep from each other but reveal to us through asides?
2. Explain how our knowing more than the characters gives the end of the play a more emotional impact.
3. Give two examples of asides that give the play humor.

Staging and Setting

Like a short story, a play has **setting,** which is its time and place, and **atmosphere,** which can also be called mood. When we read a play, we should try to visualize the scene based on the **stage directions,** or the instructions for staging. When a play is performed, a director and designers interpret the stage directions to create the elements of staging that form setting: scenery, costumes, and lighting. Scenery tells us where and when a play takes place. Costumes also sometimes place a play in a specific country and time period. The brightness and color of light on the stage can create mood. For example, lighting can create the bright, golden feel of morning or the deep blue, quiet mood of evening.

Thinking About Staging and Setting

1. From the stage directions at the beginning of the play, describe how you picture the play's scenery.
2. Explain how the play would probably use lighting to suggest time.
3. What do the time and place of the play add to its mood?

COMPOSITION

Writing About Dialogue

■ In a play we learn about a character's personality through what the character says, but our first impressions based on the character's appearance are also important. Explain how your first impressions of Doña Laura and Don Gonzalo are confirmed by what they say. First, give the personality traits that can be implied from the stage directions about their physical appearance. Then, find examples of those personality traits in what the characters say.

Writing Stage Directions for Setting

■ Imagine a place where two old friends might meet by chance after a long separation. Write the stage directions describing this place. Be sure to include (a) the exact location, (b) the year, season, and time of day, (c) furnishings and their placement on the stage, and (d) any details that make the place more recognizable. You may create your own setting, or you may want to use one of the following: (a) an airport waiting room, (b) a reunion in a school gym, (c) a restaurant in an exotic land, or (d) the box office of a theater or sports arena.

COMPOSITION: GUIDELINES FOR EVALUATION

WRITING ABOUT DIALOGUE

Objective

To demonstrate that characters' personality traits are consistent with their appearance

Guidelines for Evaluation

- suggested length: one to two paragraphs
- should state at least one trait that may be inferred from each character's appearance
- should cite two specific illustrations for each trait

WRITING STAGE DIRECTIONS FOR SETTING

Objective

To write stage directions for a meeting of friends long separated

Guidelines for Evaluation

- suggested length: 50–100 words
- should specify place, year, season, time
- should describe setting and props

Horton Foote (born 1916) began his career as an actor and became a playwright. He is also a novelist, a television writer, and an Oscar-winning screen writer (*To Kill a Mockingbird,* 1964, and *Tender Mercies,* 1983). Three of his plays—*The Chase, The Traveling Lady,* and *The Trip to Bountiful*—were produced on Broadway before being made into films.

The Dancers is from a collection of television plays entitled *Harrison, Texas* (1956). The play takes place in 1952 in the imaginary Gulf Coast town of Harrison, a place resembling Foote's hometown of Wharton, Texas. In fact, the setting for many of Foote's plays is the fertile, river-bottom farmland near the Gulf of Mexico. His family came to that area in the 1830s to grow cotton, and many members of his family are still involved in cotton farming.

Despite his fondness for his hometown, Foote left immediately after high school in order to go to acting school. He studied first at the Pasadena Playhouse in California and then later in New York City, where he formed an off-Broadway theater company with fellow acting students. In New York he met playwrights and developed an interest in writing. Since then his life has been devoted to "writing or struggling with the problems of a writer."

Through his writing Foote has retained a strong connection to his home and to the local people. While he admits that his portrayal of small-town residents may be an unlikely subject in today's theater, he says, "I did not choose this task, this place, or these people to write about, so much as they chose me. . . ."

Foote is known for his understated realism in dialogue and behavior and for his perceptive and compassionate characterization. In *The Dancers,* as in many of Foote's plays, a character becomes aware of a situation that has long existed but now must be faced and understood.

■ How believable do you find the portrayal of the teen-agers and the adults in this play?

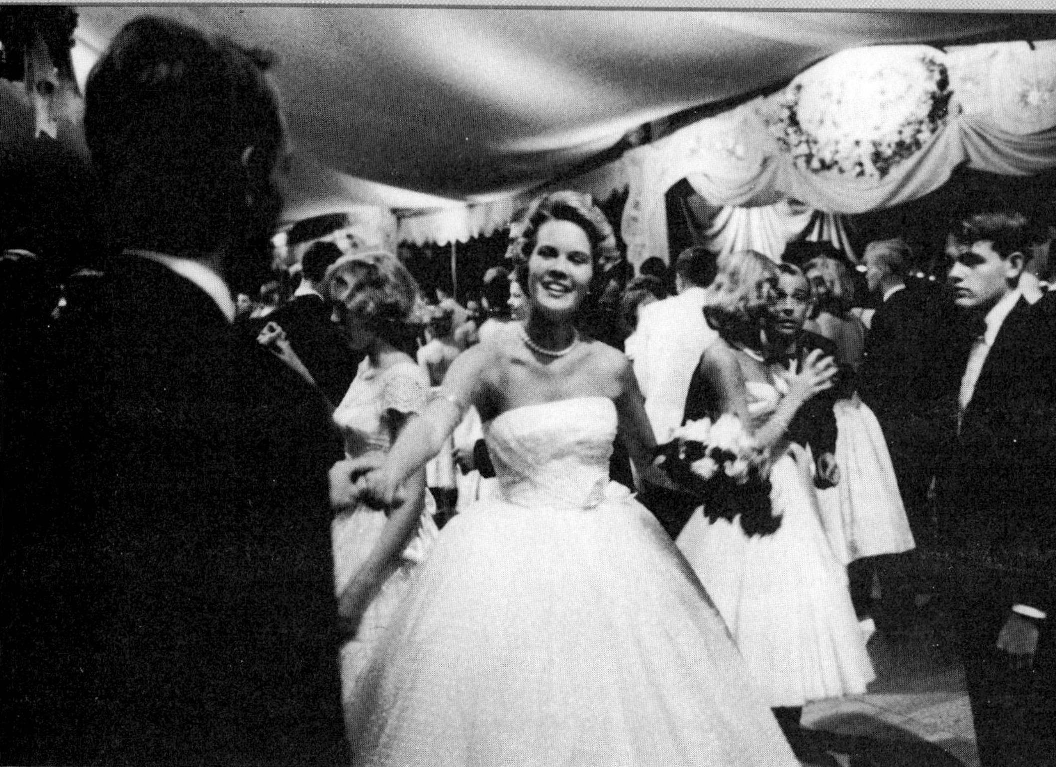

Horton Foote

The Dancers

CHARACTERS

WAITRESS in the local drugstore
EMILY CREWS, a popular seventeen year old
ELIZABETH CREWS, Emily's mother
HORACE, a sensitive eighteen year old
INEZ STANLEY Horace's older sister
HERMAN STANLEY, Inez's husband
MARY CATHERINE DAVIS, a plainer girl of Emily's age
VELMA MORRISON, another young girl
TOM DAVIS, Mary Catherine's father
MRS. DAVIS, Mary Catherine's mother

arrison, Texas

cene: The stage is divided into four acting areas: *ownstage left is the living room of* INEZ *and* :RMAN STANLEY. *Downstage right is part of a nall-town drugstore. Upstage right is the living oom of* ELIZABETH CREWS. *Upstage left, the yard nd living room of* MARY CATHERINE DAVIS. *Since the :tion should flow continuously from one area to* 1 *the other, only the barest amount of furnishings should be used to suggest what each area represents. The lights are brought up on the drugstore, downstage right. A* WAITRESS *is there.* INEZ STANLEY *comes into the drugstore. She stands for a moment thinking. The* WAITRESS *goes over to her.*]

'AITRESS. Can I help you?

NEZ. Yes, you can if I can think of what I came in ere for. Just gone completely out of my mind. I've een running around all day. You see, I'm expecting company tonight. My brother Horace. He's oming on a visit.

[ELIZABETH CREWS *and her daughter* EMILY *come into the drugstore.* EMILY *is about seventeen and very pretty. This afternoon, however, it is evident that she is unhappy.*]

Iey. . .

LIZABETH. We've just been by your house.

NEZ. You have? Hello, Emily.

MILY. Hello.

:LIZABETH. We made some divinity[1] and took it over for Horace.

NEZ. Well, that's so sweet of you.

:LIZABETH. What time is he coming in?

NEZ. Six thirty.

:LIZABETH. Are you meeting him?

INEZ. No—Herman. I've got to cook supper. Can I buy you all a drink?

ELIZABETH. No, we have to get Emily over to the beauty parlor.

INEZ. What are you wearing tonight, Emily?

ELIZABETH. She's wearing that sweet little net I got her the end of last summer. She's never worn it to a dance here.

INEZ. I don't think I've ever seen it. I'll bet it looks beautiful on her. I'm gonna make Horace bring you by the house so I can see you before the dance.

WAITRESS. Excuse me. . . .

INEZ. Yes?

WAITRESS. Have you thought of what you wanted yet? I thought I could be getting it for you.

INEZ. That's sweet, honey. . . but I haven't thought of what I wanted yet. [*To* ELIZABETH *and* EMILY.] I feel so foolish, I came in here for something, and I can't remember what.

WAITRESS. Cosmetics?

INEZ. No. . .you go on. I'll think and call you.

WAITRESS. All right. [*She goes.*]

INEZ. Emily, I think it's so sweet of you to go to the

1. **divinity:** soft, creamy candy made of sugar, egg whites, :orn syrup, flavoring, and nuts.

AT A GLANCE

- In a drugstore Inez Stanley meets her friend, Elizabeth Crews, and her daughter Emily Crews.
- The two women have persuaded Emily to go to a dance with Inez's younger brother, Horace.

LITERARY OPTIONS

- staging and audience
- characterization
- parallelism

THEMATIC OPTIONS

- identity and self-respect
- helping others
- love and friendship

1 STAGING AND AUDIENCE

By limiting directions for the set, Foote frees the audience to imagine the environment for themselves.

2 DIALOGUE

The first lines of dialogue in the play establish a key element in the plot: Horace's visit. The lines indicate that Inez is excited and distracted by this prospect.

GUIDED READING

LITERAL QUESTION

1a. What does Inez tell Elizabeth and Emily after she dismisses the waitress? ("I feel so foolish. I came in here for something, and I can't remember what.")

INFERENTIAL QUESTION

1b. How do you know that Horace's date is the real source of Inez's excitement? (She spends a lot of time reviewing details of the preparation—especially what Emily will be wearing.)

AT A GLANCE

- Elizabeth has arranged the date between Emily and Horace.
- Inez remembers she has to order flowers that coordinate with Emily's dress.
- Horace arrives at Inez's house, and they chat casually.

1 THEME

After compelling her daughter to deny her real feelings about the arranged date, Elizabeth tells Inez that Emily will be thankful for her help one day.

2 CHARACTERIZATION

Inez repeatedly uses the word "sweet" to tell people they are thoughtful, kind, or considerate. These repetitions indicate that she responds automatically or, perhaps, that she lacks imagination.

3 STAGING AND AUDIENCE

Audience attention is moved from one part of the stage to the next by changes in lighting. The play's events follow chronological order as locations change.

4 CHARACTERIZATION

Inez reveals that her powerful determination to change her younger brother extends to changing his physical appearance.

dance with Horace. I know he's going to be thrilled when I tell him.

1 **ELIZABETH.** Well, you're thrilled too, aren't you, Emily?

EMILY. Yes, ma'am.

ELIZABETH. I told Emily she'd thank me some day for not permitting her to sit home and miss all the fun.

EMILY. Mama, it's five to four. My appointment is at four o'clock.

ELIZABETH. Well, you go on in the car.

EMILY. How are you gonna get home?

ELIZABETH. I'll get home. Don't worry about me.

EMILY. OK. [*She starts out.*]

INEZ. 'Bye, Emily.

EMILY. 'Bye. [*She goes on out.*]

ELIZABETH. Does Horace have a car for tonight?

INEZ. Oh, yes. He's taking Herman's.

ELIZABETH. I just wondered. I wanted to offer ours if he didn't have one.

2 **INEZ.** That's very sweet—but we're giving him our car every night for the two weeks of his visit. Oh—I know what I'm after. Flowers. I have to order Emily's corsage for Horace. I came in here to use the telephone to call you to find out what color Emily's dress was going to be.

ELIZABETH. Blue.

INEZ. My favorite color. Walk me over to the florist.

3 **ELIZABETH.** All right.

[*They go out as the lights fade. The lights are brought up downstage left on the living room of* INEZ STANLEY. HERMAN STANLEY *and his brother-in-law,* HORACE, *come in.* HERMAN *is carrying* HORACE*'s suitcase.* HERMAN *is in his middle thirties.* HORACE *is eighteen, thin, sensitive, but a likable boy.*]

HERMAN. Inez. Inez. We're here.

[*He puts the bag down in the living room.* INE*Z comes running in from stage right.*]

INEZ. You're early.

HERMAN. The bus was five minutes ahead of tim[e].

INEZ. Is that so? Why, I never heard of that. [*Sh[e] kisses her brother.*] Hello, honey.

HORACE. Hello, sis.

INEZ. You look fine.

HORACE. Thank you.

INEZ. You haven't put on a bit of weight though

HORACE. Haven't I?

4 **INEZ.** Not a bit. I'm just going to stuff food dow[n] you and put some weight on you while you're her[e]. How's your appetite?

HORACE. Oh, it's real good. I eat all the time.

INEZ. Then why don't you put on some weight?

HORACE. I don't know. I guess I'm just the skinn[y] type.

INEZ. How are the folks?

HORACE. Fine.

INEZ. Mother over her cold?

HORACE. Yes, she is.

INEZ. Dad's fine?

HORACE. Just fine.

INEZ. Oh, Herman, did you ask him?

HERMAN. Ask him what?

GUIDED READING

LITERAL QUESTIONS

1a. What does Elizabeth ask Emily about the prospects of going to the dance? ("Well, you're thrilled too, aren't you, Emily?")

2a. What does Inez tell Horace will happen during his visit? ("I'm just going to stuff food down you and put some weight on you.")

INFERENTIAL QUESTIONS

1b. Why can we legitimately suspect that Emily *isn't* thrilled? (Elizabeth admits that she has arranged the date.)

2b. What does this remark tell you about Inez? (She is somewhat controlling and manipulative.)

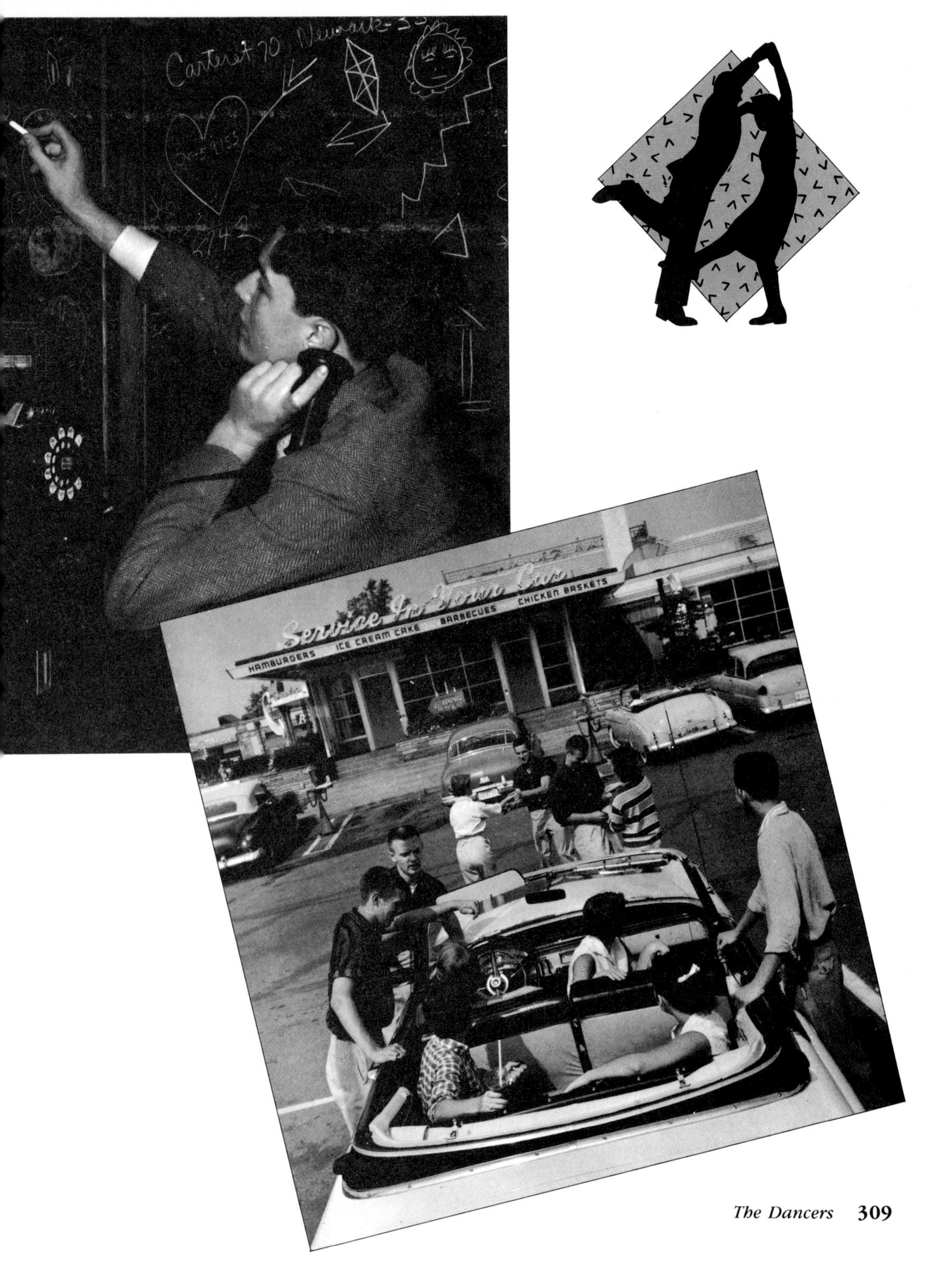
Service In Your Car
HAMBURGERS
ICE CREAM CAKE
BARBECUES
CHICKEN BASKETS

AT A GLANCE

- Inez tells Horace about the arranged date.
- Horace worries about his dancing ability.
- Inez assures her brother that he lacks only confidence.

1 STAGING AND AUDIENCE

Foote's stage directions help to reveal Horace's shyness and the fact that he finds it difficult to perform in front of others.

2 CHARACTERIZATION

Horace is not distracted from his real concerns by his sister's complicated explanation. He reveals himself to be a person who cares about others' feelings.

3 PLOT: RISING ACTION

Both Emily and Horace have conflicts that keep them from wanting to go to the dance: Emily already has a boyfriend, and Horace fears he cannot dance well enough.

4 THEME

Horace again indicates that he hopes to change. He is a character who sees possibilities for improvement.

5 PARALLELISM

Inez uses virtually the same words about Horace as Elizabeth used about Emily. Both women feel responsible for younger family members' not missing "all the fun in life."

INEZ. Ask him what? About his tux.

HERMAN. No, I didn't. . . .

INEZ. Honestly, Herman. Here we have him a date with the prettiest and most popular girl in Harrison and Herman says ask him what. You did bring it, didn't you, Bubber?

HORACE. Bring what?

INEZ. Your tux.

HORACE. Oh, sure.

INEZ. Well, guess who I've got you a date with. Aren't you curious?

HORACE. Uh. Huh.

INEZ. Well, guess. . .

[*A pause. He thinks.*]

HORACE. I don't know.

INEZ. Well, just try guessing. . . .

1 **HORACE.** Well. . .uh. . . [*He is a little embarrassed. He stands trying to think. No names come to him.*] I don't know.

INEZ. Emily Crews. Now isn't she a pretty girl?

HORACE. Yes. She is.

INEZ. And the most popular girl in this town. You know her mother is a very close friend of mine and she called me day before yesterday and she said I hear Horace is coming to town and I said yes you were and she said that the boy Emily is going with
2 is in summer school and couldn't get away this week-end and Emily said she wouldn't go to the dance at all but her mother said that she had insisted and wondered if you'd take her. . . .

HORACE. Her mother said. Does Emily want me to take her?

INEZ. That isn't the point, Bubber. The point is that her mother doesn't approve of the boy Emily is in love with and she likes you. . . .

HORACE. Who likes me?

INEZ. Emily's mother. And she thinks you would make a very nice couple.

HORACE. Oh. [*A pause*] But what does Emily think

3 **INEZ.** Emily doesn't know what to think, honey. I'm trying to explain that to you. She's in love.

HORACE. Where am I supposed to take her to?

INEZ. The dance.

HORACE. But, Inez, I don't dance well enough. . . . I don't like to go to dances. . .yet. . . .

INEZ. Oh, Horace, Mother wrote me you were learning.

4 **HORACE.** Well. . . I am learning. But I don't dance well enough yet.

INEZ. Horace, you just make me sick. The trouble with you is that you have no confidence in yourself. I bet you can dance.

HORACE. No, I can't. . . .

INEZ. Now let's see. [INEZ *goes to the radio and turns it on. She comes back to him.*] Now, come on. Show me what you've learned. . . .

HORACE. Aw, sis. . . .

HERMAN. Inez. Why don't you let the boy alone?

5 **INEZ.** Now you keep out of this, Herman Stanley. He's my brother and he's a stick. He's missing all the fun in life and I'm not going to have him a stick. I've sat up nights thinking of social engagements to keep him busy every minute of these next two weeks—I've got three dances scheduled for him. So he can*not* dance. Now come on, dance with me. . . . [*He takes her by the arm awkwardly. He begins to lead her around the room.*] Now, that's fine. That's just fine. Isn't that fine, Herman?

HERMAN. Uh. Huh.

INEZ. You see all you need is confidence. And I want you to promise me you'll talk plenty when

GUIDED READING

LITERAL QUESTION

1a. What does Horace say when Inez announces that he is a stand-in date for Emily? ("Her mother said. Does Emily want me to take her?")

INFERENTIAL QUESTION

1b. What does this statement reveal about Horace? (He cares about the feelings of others.)

·ou're with the girl, not just sit there in silence and ›nly answer when you're asked a question. . . . ·Jow promise me.

·IORACE. I promise.

·NEZ. Fine. Why, I think he dances real well. Don't ·ou, Herman?

·IERMAN. Yes, I do. Just fine, Inez.

·NEZ. Just a lovely dancer, all he needs is confi- ·lence. He is very light on his feet. And he has a fine ·ense of rhythm—why, brother, you're a born ·lancer—

[HORACE *is smiling over the compliments, half wanting to believe what they say, but then not so sure. He is dancing with her around the room as the lights fade. They are brought up on the area upstage right.* EMILY CREWS *is in her living room. She has on her dressing gown. She is crying.* ELIZABETH, *her mother, comes in from upstage right.*]

·LIZABETH. Emily.

·MILY. Yes, ma'am

·LIZABETH. Do you know what time it is?

·MILY. Yes, ma'am.

·LIZABETH. Then why in the world aren't you ·lressed?

·EMILY. Because I don't feel good.

ELIZABETH. Emily. . . .

EMILY. I don't feel good. . . . [*She begins to cry.*] Oh, Mother. I don't want to go to the dance tonight. Please, ma'am, don't make me. I'll do anything in this world for you if you promise me. . . .

ELIZABETH. Emily. This is all settled. You are going to that dance. Do you understand me. You are going to that dance. That sweet, nice brother of Inez Stanley's will be here any minute. . . .

EMILY. Sweet, nice brother. He's a goon. That's what
3 he is. A regular goon. A bore and a goon. . . .

ELIZABETH. Emily. . . .

EMILY. That's all he is. Just sits and doesn't talk. Can't dance. I'm not going to any dance or any place else with him and that's final.

[*She runs out stage right.*]

ELIZABETH. Emily. . . Emily. . .You get ready this minute. . . . [*The doorbell rings. Yelling.*] Emily. . . Emily. . . Horace is here. I want you down those stairs in five minutes. . .dressed.

[*She goes out stage left and comes back in followed by* HORACE, *all dressed up. He has a corsage box in his hand.*]

Hello, Horace.

HORACE. Good evening.

ELIZABETH. Sit down, won't you, Horace? Emily is a little late getting dressed. You know how girls are.

HORACE. Yes, ma'am.

[*He sits down. He seems a little awkward and shy.*]

ELIZABETH. Can I get you something to drink, Horace?

HORACE. No, ma'am.

[*A pause.* ELIZABETH *is obviously very nervous about whether* EMILY *will behave or not.*]

ELIZABETH. Are you sure I can't get you a Coca-Cola or something?

4 **HORACE.** No. Thank you.

ELIZABETH. How's your family?

HORACE. Just fine, thank you.

ELIZABETH. I bet your sister was glad to see you.

HORACE. Yes, she was.

ELIZABETH. How's your family? Oh, I guess I asked you that, didn't I?

AT A GLANCE

- Emily does not want to go to the dance with Horace; she thinks he is a bore.
- Her mother sends her upstairs to dress as Horace arrives.

1 MAIN IDEA

Though she criticizes nearly everything about her brother, Inez also tries to bolster his confidence. Telling him he is "a born dancer," she suggests that he has innate talent for whatever he wants to achieve.

2 CONFLICT

The conflict between Elizabeth and her daughter is fully revealed as Emily tries to bargain with her mother to get out of her date with Horace.

3 CHARACTERIZATION

Emily's and her mother's perceptions of Horace's character are completely different. These contradictory perceptions inform the heart of a second important conflict within the play: the older vs. the younger generation.

4 DIALOGUE

In this stiff and formal conversation between Horace and Elizabeth, Foote captures not only the awkwardness that often occurs when a young man meets his date's parents but also Inez's discomfort over her pending announcement.

GUIDED READING

LITERAL QUESTION

1a. What does Emily say about Horace? (She thinks he's a bore.)

INFERENTIAL QUESTION

1b. Based on the discussion between Elizabeth and Emily, who do you think will have her way and why? (Emily, if her parents respect her feelings; Elizabeth, if parental authority overrides Emily's objections)

AT A GLANCE

- Mother and daughter argue; Elizabeth tells Horace that Emily is ill.
- After Horace leaves, Elizabeth announces that she has summoned her husband home.

1 STAGING AND AUDIENCE

In a single moment the playwright presents the play's two most important conflicts: The audience sees Horace trying to overcome his sense of social inadequacy and hears the disagreement between Emily and her mother.

2 CHARACTERIZATION

Elizabeth seems blind to the notion that she has disregarded Horace's and Emily's feelings.

HORACE. Yes, you did.

[ELIZABETH *keeps glancing off stage right, praying that* EMILY *will put in an appearance.*]

ELIZABETH. I understand you've become quite an accomplished dancer. . . .

HORACE. Oh. . .well. . .I. . . .

ELIZABETH. Inez tells me you do all the new steps.

HORACE. Well—I. . . .

ELIZABETH. Excuse me. Let me see what is keeping that girl.

[*She goes running off stage right.* HORACE *gets up. He seems very nervous. He begins to practice his dancing. He seems more unsure of himself and awkward. . . . We can hear* ELIZABETH *offstage knocking on* EMILY*'s door. At first* HORACE *isn't conscious of the knocking or the ensuing conversation and goes on practicing*
1 *his dancing. When he first becomes conscious of what's to follow he tries to pay no attention. Then gradually he moves over to the far stage-left side of the stage. The first thing we hear is* ELIZABETH*'s genteel tapping at* EMILY*'s door. Then she begins to call, softly at first, then louder and louder.*]

Emily. Emily. Emily Crews. Emily Carter Crews . . . [*The pounding offstage is getting louder and louder.*] Emily. I can hear you in there. Now open that door.

EMILY. [*Screaming back.*] I won't. I told you I won't.

ELIZABETH. Emily Carter Crews. You open that door immediately.

EMILY. I won't.

ELIZABETH. I'm calling your father from downtown if you don't open that door right this very minute.

EMILY. I don't care. I won't come out.

ELIZABETH. Then I'll call him. [*She comes runnin in from right stage.* HORACE *quickly gets back to hi chair and sits.*] Excuse me, Horace.

[*She crosses through the room and goes ou upstage right.* HORACE *seems very ill at ease. H looks at the box of flowers. He is very warm. H begins to fan himself.* ELIZABETH *comes back i the room from upstage right. She is very ner vous. But she tries to hide her nervousness in a overly social manner.* ELIZABETH *has decided t tell a fib.*]

Horace, I am so sorry to have to ruin your evening but my little girl isn't feeling well. She has a head ache and a slight temperature and I've just called th doctor and he says he thinks it's very advisable tha she stay in this evening. She's upstairs insisting sh go, but I do feel under the circumstances I had jus better keep her in. I hope you understand.

HORACE. Oh, yes ma'am. I do understand.

ELIZABETH. How long do you plan to visit us Horace?

HORACE. Two weeks.

ELIZABETH. That's nice. [*They start walking off-stage left.*] Please call Emily tomorrow and ask her out again. She'll just be heartbroken if you don't.

HORACE. Yes, ma'am. Good night.

ELIZABETH. Good night, Horace. [HORACE *goes out.* ELIZABETH *calls out after him.*] Can you see, Horace? [*In the distance we hear* HORACE *answer.*]

HORACE. Yes, ma'am.

ELIZABETH. Now you be sure and call us tomorrow. You hear? [*She stands waiting for a moment. Then she walks back across stage to upstage right, screaming at the top of her voice.*] Emily Carter
2 Crews. You have mortified me. You have mortified me to death. I have, for your information, called your father and he is interrupting his work and is coming home this very minute and he says to tell

GUIDED READING

LITERAL QUESTION

1a. What does Horace do as Elizabeth returns to the living room? (He begins to fan himself.)

INFERENTIAL QUESTION

1b. What might Horace really mean when he says, "Oh, yes ma'am. I do understand"? (He knows that Elizabeth is really trying to shield him from the truth.)

AT A GLANCE

- Horace goes to the drugstore.
- Emily's friend Mary Catherine and the waitress discuss Emily's date.

1 IRONY

Having learned how long Horace will be in town and urged him to ask Emily out again, Elizabeth punishes her daughter by grounding her, ironically, for Horace's entire visit.

2 CHARACTERIZATION

Even in his brief encounter with a lazy waitress, Horace shows his consideration by asking what she would like to make.

3 CHARACTERIZATION

From her first appearance on stage, Mary Catherine seems in sharp contrast to Emily: Her undisguised plainness reflects her honesty and directness.

4 STAGING AND AUDIENCE

For a second time the playwright allows the audience to watch Horace overhear other characters talking about him. By witnessing Horace's discomfort as he finds out how others perceive him, the audience develops empathy for him.

1 you that you are not to be allowed to leave this house again for two solid weeks. Is that perfectly clear?

[*She is screaming as she goes out upstage right. The lights are brought down. They are brought up immediately downstage right on the drugstore. It is half an hour later.* HORACE *comes in. He seats himself at the counter. He still has the box of flowers. The drugstore is deserted. A* WAITRESS *is up near the front with her arms on the counter. She keeps glancing at a clock.* HORACE *is examining a menu.*]

HORACE. Can I have a chicken salad sandwich?

WAITRESS. We're all out of that.

HORACE. Oh.

[*He goes back to reading the menu.*]

2 **WAITRESS.** If it's all the same to you, I'd rather not make a sandwich. I'm closing my doors in ten minutes.

HORACE. Oh. Well, what would you like to make?

WAITRESS. Any kind of ice cream or soft drinks. [*She looks up at the ice cream menu.*] Coffee is all gone.

HORACE. How about a chocolate ice cream soda?

WAITRESS. OK. Coming up. [*She starts to mix the soda. She talks as she works.*] Going to the dance?

HORACE. No.

WAITRESS. The way you're all dressed up I thought for sure you were going.

3 **HORACE.** No. I was, but I changed my mind.

[MARY CATHERINE DAVIS *comes in the drugstore from downstage right. Somehow in her young head she has gotten the idea that she is a plain girl and in defiance for the pain of that fact she does everything she can to make herself look plainer.*]

WAITRESS. Hello, Mary Catherine. Been to the movies?

MARY CATHERINE. Yes, I have.

[*The* WAITRESS *puts the drink down in front of* HORACE. *He begins to drink.*]

WAITRESS. What'll you have, Mary Catherine?

MARY CATHERINE. Vanilla ice cream.

WAITRESS. OK. [*She gets the ice cream. She talks as she does so.*] There weren't many at the picture show tonight, I bet. I can always tell by whether we have a crowd in here or not after the first show. I guess everybody is at the dance.

4 **MARY CATHERINE.** I could have gone, but I didn't want to. I didn't want to miss the picture show. Emily Crews didn't go. Leo couldn't get home from summer school and she said she was refusing to go. Her mother made a date for her with some bore from out of town without consulting her and she was furious about it. I talked to her this afternoon. She said she didn't know yet how she would get out of it, but she would. She said she had some rights. Her mother doesn't approve of Leo and that's a shame because they are practically engaged.

WAITRESS. I think Emily is a very cute girl, don't you?

MARY CATHERINE. Oh, yes. I think she's darling.

[HORACE *has finished his drink and is embarrassed by their talk. He is trying to get the* WAITRESS'*s attention but doesn't quite know how. He finally calls to the* WAITRESS.]

HORACE. Miss. . . .

WAITRESS. Yes?

HORACE. How much do I owe you?

WAITRESS. Twenty cents.[2]

---

2. **Twenty cents:** price of an ice cream soda at the time the play is set.

GUIDED READING

LITERAL QUESTION

1a. What reason does Mary Catherine give for Emily's not going to the dance? (Her boyfriend Leo couldn't take her.)

INFERENTIAL QUESTION

1b. What is the real reason Emily refused to go to the dance? (She doesn't like Horace.)

HORACE. Thank you.

[*He reaches in his pocket for the money.*]

WAITRESS. Emily has beautiful clothes, doesn't she?

MARY CATHERINE. Oh, yes. She does.

WAITRESS. Her folks are rich?

MARY CATHERINE. She has the prettiest things. But she's not a bit stuck up. . . .

[*He holds the money out to the* WAITRESS.]

HORACE. Here you are.

WAITRESS. Thank you. [*She takes the money and rings it up in the cash register.* HORACE *goes on out.* WAITRESS *shakes her head as he goes.*] There's a goofy nut if I ever saw one. He's got flowers under his arm. He's wearing a tux and yet he's not going to the dance. Who is he?

MARY CATHERINE. I don't know. I never saw him before.

[*The* WAITRESS *walks to the edge of the area and looks out. She comes back shaking her head. She sits on the stool beside* MARY CATHERINE.]

WAITRESS. [*While laughing and shaking her head.*] I ought to call the Sheriff and have him locked up. Do you know what he's doing?

MARY CATHERINE. No. What?

WAITRESS. Standing on the corner. Dancing back and forth. He's holding his arm up like he's got a girl and everything. Wouldn't it kill you? [*Goes to the front and looks out.*] See him?

MARY CATHERINE. No. He's stopped.

WAITRESS. What's he doing?

MARY CATHERINE. Just standing there. Looking kind of lost.

[MARY CATHERINE *comes back to the counter. She starts eating her ice cream again.*]

WAITRESS. Well—it takes all kinds.

MARY CATHERINE. I guess so.

[*She goes back to eating her ice cream. The lights are brought down. The lights are brought up on the area downstage left. The living room of the* STANLEYS. INEZ *is there reading a book.* HERMAN *comes in.*]

HERMAN. Hi, hon.

INEZ. Hello. . . .

HERMAN. What's the matter with you? You look down in the dumps.

INEZ. No. I'm just disgusted.

HERMAN. What are you disgusted about?

INEZ. Horace. I had everything planned so beautifully for him and then that silly Emily has to go and hurt his feelings.

HERMAN. Well, honey, that was pretty raw, the trick she pulled.

2 **INEZ.** I know. But he's a fool to let that get him down. He should have just gone to the dance by himself and proved her wrong. . . . Why like I told him. Show her up. Rush a different girl every night. Be charming. Make yourself popular. But it's like trying to talk to a stone wall. He refused to go out any more. He says he's going home tomorrow.

HERMAN. Where is he now?

INEZ. Gone to the movies.

3 **HERMAN.** Well, honey. I hate to say it, but in a way it serves you right. I've told you a thousand times if I've told you once. Leave the boy alone. He'll be all right. Only don't push him. You and your mother have pushed the boy and pushed him and pushed him.

INEZ. And I'm going to keep on pushing him. I let him off tonight because his feelings were hurt, but tomorrow I'm going to have a long talk with him.

AT A GLANCE

- The two women discuss Horace's dancing on the street corner.
- Inez and her husband, Herman, discuss Horace.
- Horace, his feelings hurt, has gone to the movies.
- Herman advises Inez to leave her brother alone.

1 CHARACTER

Although each of the four other women in the play has described Horace differently, Mary Catherine is the first to perceive him as he sees himself; a person who is "kind of lost."

2 THEME

Inez does not realize that she is not being helpful when she advises her younger brother to act in a way that is totally alien to him. She resents his refusal to be "helped."

3 THEME

Herman opposes Inez's interventions with her brother. He sees those actions that she believes are helpful as intrusive.

GUIDED READING

LITERAL QUESTION

1a. How does Mary Catherine answer the waitress' question about what Horace is doing? ("Just standing there. Looking kind of lost.")

INFERENTIAL QUESTION

1b. Why do you think the playwright created this exchange between the waitress and Mary Catherine? (to show Mary Catherine's perception and sensitivity)

AT A GLANCE

- Mary Catherine tells the waitress that Horace was to have been Emily's date.
- Horace and then Emily enter the drugstore.
- Emily introduces Horace to Mary Catherine and apologizes to him.

1 CHARACTERIZATION

Mary Catherine realizes how much her remarks must have hurt Horace. Like him, she cares about other people's feelings.

2 STYLE: HUMOR

The waitress' repeated inability to serve customers what they want is an amusing touch that suggests ongoing limitations of life in the little town.

3 PLOT: RISING ACTION

Emily's honest explanation invites Horace's trust and forgiveness. With the resolution of a minor conflict, Foote can focus on the main one—Horace's lack of confidence.

HERMAN. Inez. Leave the boy alone.

INEZ. I won't leave him alone. He is my brother and I'm going to see he that learns to have a good time.

HERMAN. Inez. . . .

INEZ. Now you just let me handle this, Herman. He's starting to college next year and it's a most important time in his life. He had no fun in high school. . . .

HERMAN. Now. He must have had some fun. . . .

INEZ. Not like other people. And he's not going through four years of college like a hermit with his nose stuck in some old book. . . . [*She jumps up.*] I'll never forgive Elizabeth for letting Emily behave this way. And I told her so. I said Elizabeth Crews, I am very upset. . . .

[*She is angrily walking up and down as the lights fade. They are brought up downstage right on the drugstore area. The* WAITRESS *is there alone.* MARY CATHERINE *comes in from downstage right.*]

WAITRESS. Did you go to the movies again tonight?

MARY CATHERINE. Uh-huh. Lila, do you remember when I was telling you about Emily's date and how she wouldn't go out with him because he was such a bore?

WAITRESS. Uh. . . .

1 **MARY CATHERINE.** Oh. I just feel awful. That was the boy sitting in here. . . .

WAITRESS. Last night . . .?

MARY CATHERINE. Yes. I went riding with Emily and some of the girls this afternoon and we passed by his sister's house and there sat the boy.

WAITRESS. Sh. . . sh. . . . [*She has seen* HORACE *come into the area from downstage right. He comes to the counter. He seems very silent. He picks up a menu.*] Back again tonight?

HORACE. Uh-huh.

2 **WAITRESS.** What'll you have?

HORACE. A cup of coffee. . . .

WAITRESS. All out. We don't serve coffee after eight unless we happen to have some left over from suppertime. . . .

HORACE. Thanks. [*He gets up.*]

WAITRESS. Nothing else?

HORACE. No, thanks.

[*He goes over to the magazine rack. He picks up a magazine and starts looking through it.* EMILY CREWS *comes in from downstage right. She doensn't see* HORACE. *She goes right over to* MARY CATHERINE.]

EMILY. Leora and I were riding around the square and we saw you sitting here. . . .

[MARY CATHERINE *points to* HORACE. *She turns around and sees him.* EMILY *looks a little embarrassed. He happens to glance up and sees her.*]

HORACE. Hello, Emily.

EMILY. Hello, Horace. . . . Do you know Mary Catherine Davis?

HORACE. No. How do you do.

MARY CATHERINE. How do you do.

3 **EMILY.** I feel awfully bad about last night, Horace. My mother says you know I wasn't really sick. I just wanted to tell you that it had nothing to do with you, Horace. It was a battle between me and my mother. Mary Catherine can tell you. I promised the boy I go with not to go with any other boys. . . .

HORACE. Oh, that's all right, I understand.

EMILY. You see, we've gone steady for two years. All the other boys in town understand it and their feelings are not a bit hurt if I turn them down. Are they, Mary Catherine?

GUIDED READING

LITERAL QUESTION

1a. What does Emily do after introducing Horace and Mary Catherine? (apologizes to Horace)

INFERENTIAL QUESTION

1b. How do you know that Emily is unaware of the real source of Horace's hurt feelings? (She tells him that Mary Catherine will back up the story about the battle with her mother.)

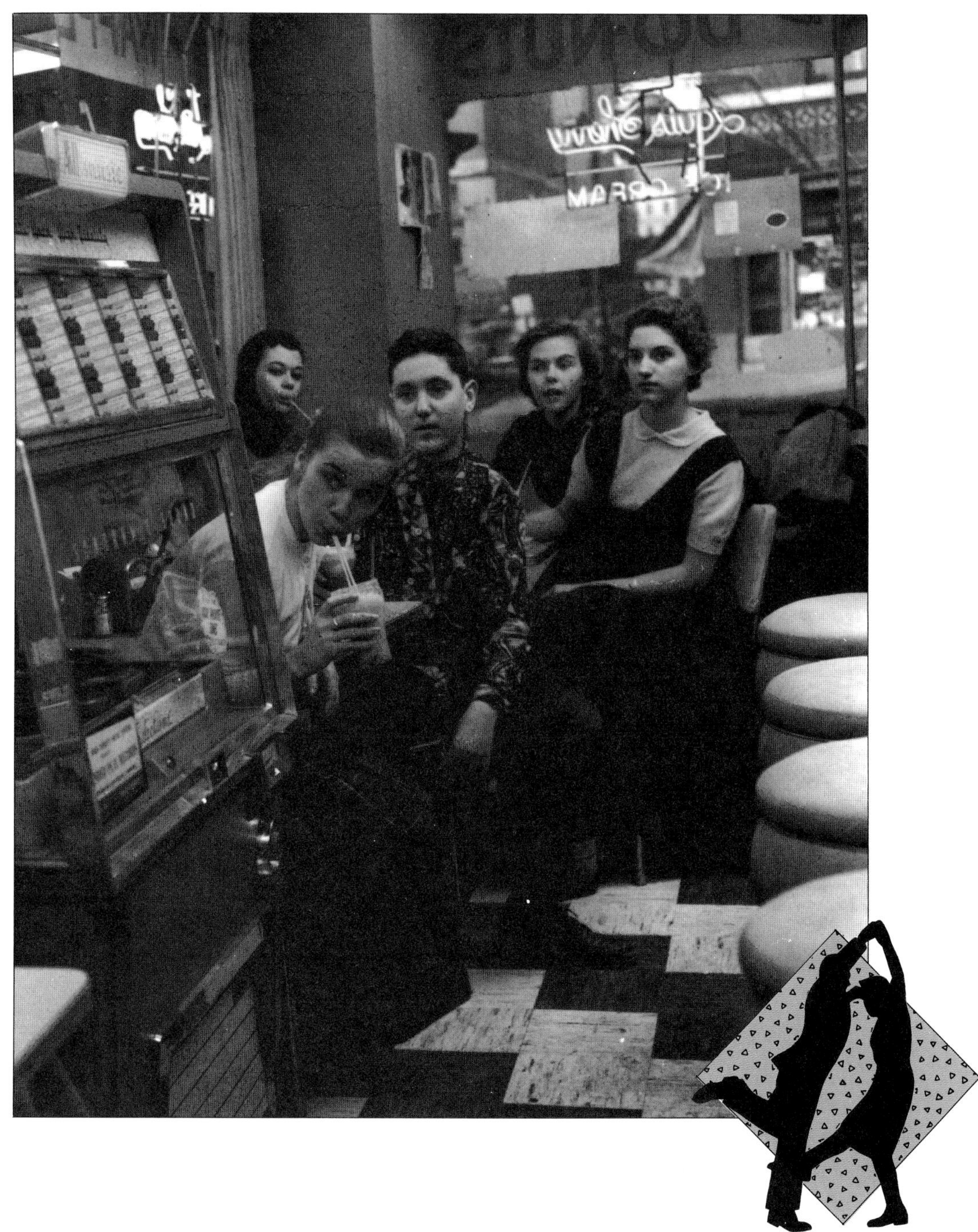

AT A GLANCE

- Mary Catherine's friendship with Emily has weakened.
- Horace and Mary Catherine discuss college.
- Velma, Mary Catherine's friend, announces she has a date.

1 THEME

In a difficult situation Emily calls on a friend to support her. Mary Catherine communicates her understanding and total allegiance.

2 CONFLICT

Mary Catherine considers Velma's sensitivity and is willing to sacrifice her own pleasure rather than hurt her friend.

3 CHARACTERIZATION

This speech reveals another aspect of Mary Catherine's character: She understands and accepts changes in friendships and is able to talk openly about them.

MARY CATHERINE. No.

EMILY. Mary Catherine is my best friend and she can tell you I'm not stuck up. And I would have gone, anyway, except I was so mad at my mother. . . .

1 **MARY CATHERINE.** Emily is not stuck up a bit. Emily used to date all the boys before she began going with Leo steadily. Didn't you, Emily?

EMILY. Uh-huh. How long are you going to be here, Horace?

HORACE. Well, I haven't decided, Emily.

EMILY. Well, I hope you're not still hurt with me.

HORACE. No, I'm not, Emily.

EMILY. Well, I'm glad for that. Mary Catherine, can you come with us?

MARY CATHERINE. No, I can't, Emily. Velma came in after the first show started and I promised to wait here for her and we'd walk home together.

EMILY. Come on. We can ride around and watch for her.

2 **MARY CATHERINE.** No, I don't dare. You know how sensitive Velma is. If she looked in here and saw I wasn't sitting at this counter she'd go right home and not speak to me again for two or three months.

EMILY. Velma's too sensitive. You shouldn't indulge her in it.

MARY CATHERINE. I'm willing to grant you that. But you all are going off to college next year and Velma and I are the only ones that are going to be left here and I can't afford to get her mad at me.

EMILY. OK. I'll watch out for you and if we're still riding around when Velma gets out, we'll pick you up.

MARY CATHERINE. Fine. . . .

EMILY. 'Bye. . . .

MARY CATHERINE. 'Bye. . . .

EMILY. 'Bye, Horace.

HORACE. Good-bye, Emily.

[*She goes out downstage right.*]

MARY CATHERINE. She's a lovely girl. She was my closest friend until this year. Now we're still good friends, but we're not as close as we were. We had
3 a long talk about it last week. I told her I understood. She and Eloise Dayton just naturally have a little more in common now. They're both going steady and they're going to the same college. [*A pause.*] They're going to Sophie Newcomb.[3] Are you going to college?

HORACE. Uh-huh.

MARY CATHERINE. You are? What college?

HORACE. The university. . . .

MARY CATHERINE. Oh. I know lots of people there. [*A pause.*] I had a long talk with Emily about my not getting to go. She said she thought it was wonderful that I wasn't showing any bitterness about it. [*A pause*] I'm getting a job next week so I can save up enough money to go into Houston to business school. I'll probably work in Houston some day. If I don't get too lonely. Velma Morrison's oldest sister went into Houston and got herself a job but she almost died from loneliness. She's back here now working at the courthouse. Oh, well . . . I don't think I'll get lonely. I think a change of scenery would be good for me.

[VELMA MORRISON *comes in downstage right. She is about the same age as* MARY CATHERINE. *She is filled with excitement.*]

VELMA. Mary Catherine, you're going to be furious with me. But Stanley Sewell came in right after you left and he said he'd never forgive me if I didn't go riding with him. . . . I said I had to ask you first. As

---

3. **Sophie Newcomb:** H. Sophie Newcomb College for Women in New Orleans, Louisiana.

GUIDED READING

LITERAL QUESTION

1a. What do Horace and Mary Catherine discuss? (going to college)

INFERENTIAL QUESTION

1b. What qualities of Mary Catherine's are revealed through her conversation with Horace? (She seems honest, focused, and capable; she knows a lot about herself.)

I had asked you to wait particularly for me and that I knew you were very sensitive.

MARY CATHERINE. I'm very sensitive. You're very sensitive. . . . I have never in my life stopped speaking to you over anything.

[*A car horn is heard off stage.*]

VELMA. Will you forgive me if I go?

MARY CATHERINE. Oh, sure.

[VELMA *goes running out.*]

VELMA. Thank you.

[*She disappears out the door.*]

MARY CATHERINE. I'm not nearly as close to Velma as I am to Emily. I think Emily's beautiful, don't you?

HORACE. Yes. She's very pretty.

MARY CATHERINE. Well, Lila's going to kill us if we don't stop holding her up. Which way do you go?

HORACE. Home.

MARY CATHERINE. I go that way, too. We can walk together.

HORACE. OK. [*They go out of the area.*]

MARY CATHERINE. Good night, Lila.

WAITRESS. Good night.

[*They continue walking out downstage left as the lights fade. The lights are brought up on the living room of the* CREWS*'s house.* ELIZABETH CREWS is there, crying. EMILY *comes in.*]

EMILY. Mother, what is it? Has something happened to Daddy?

ELIZABETH. No. He's in bed asleep.

EMILY. Then what is it?

ELIZABETH. Inez blessed me out and stopped speaking to me over last night. She says we've ruined the boy's whole vacation. You've broken his heart, given him all kinds of complexes and he's going home tomorrow. . . .

EMILY. But I saw him at the drugstore tonight and I had a long talk with him and he said he understood. . . .

ELIZABETH. But Inez doesn't understand. She says she'll never forgive either of us again.

[*She starts to cry.*]

EMILY. Oh, Mother. I'm sorry. . . .

2 **ELIZABETH**. Emily, if you'll do me one favor. I promise you I'll never ask another thing of you again as long as I live. And I will never nag you about going out with Leo again as long as I live. . . .

EMILY. What is the favor, Mother?

ELIZABETH. Let that boy take you to the dance day after tomorrow. . . .

EMILY. Now, Mother. . . .

ELIZABETH. Emily. I get down on my knees to you. Do me this one favor. . . . [*A pause.*] Emily. . . . Emily. . . . [*She is crying again.*]

3 **EMILY**. Now, Mother, please. Don't cry. I'll think about it. I'll call Leo and see what he says. But please don't cry like this. . . . Mother. . . Mother.

[*She is trying to console her as the lights fade. The lights are brought up on upstage left. It is* MARY CATHERINE*'s yard and living room. Music can be heard in the distance.* HORACE *and* MARY CATHERINE *come walking in downstage left, go up the center of the stage until they reach the upstage area.*]

MARY CATHERINE. Well, this is where I live.

HORACE. In that house there?

MARY CATHERINE. Uh-huh. [*A pause.*]

HORACE. Where is that music coming from?

AT A GLANCE

- That night Emily arrives home to find her mother crying.
- Elizabeth tells Emily that Horace's heart is broken.
- She begs Emily to accompany him to the next dance.

1 PLOT: NARRATIVE HOOK

Foote has reduced the tension of Horace's conflicts, creating circumstances that lead him to walk home with Mary Catherine.

2 PARALLELISM

Elizabeth, like her daughter, cries and uses extravagant promises to bargain for what she wants. Foote seems to be commenting wryly on how children imitate their parents.

3 THEME

Emily's love and compassion for her mother lead her to consider reversing her decision not to go with Horace. Foote provides another example of loving sacrifice.

GUIDED READING

LITERAL QUESTION

1a. Why does Elizabeth cry? (because her friend Inez is angry with her)

INFERENTIAL QUESTION

1b. What new crisis does this create? (Emily is forced to choose between pleasing her mother and being loyal to Leo.)

AT A GLANCE

- Horace and Mary Catherine hear music.
- She tells him that dancing is nothing but confidence.
- She invites him in to talk; Horace asks her about gaining confidence.

1 CONFLICT

Inspired by the music from nearby restaurants, Mary Catherine innocently asks Horace if he likes to dance. Once again Horace must confront both fear and feelings of inadequacy.

2 STAGING AND AUDIENCE

With only two details in the stage directions, Foote provides important clues to Mary Catherine's father's character: He is an unpretentious, hard-working man worthy of respect.

3 THEME

Tom Davis' respect for his daughter's social interests and his quiet confidence in her sharply contrast with Elizabeth Crews's and Inez Stanley's distrust of young people.

4 THEME

Here the playwright offers another example of loving sacrifice: A daughter sacrifices her ambitions to avoid causing pain to her hard-working father.

MARY CATHERINE. The Flats. . . .

HORACE. What's the Flats?

MARY CATHERINE. I don't know what it is. That's just what they call it. It's nothing but a bunch of barbecue restaurants and beer joints down there and they call it the Flats. There used to be a creek running down there that they called Willow Creek but it's all dry now. My father says when he was a boy, every time the river flooded, Willow Creek would fill up. The river doesn't overflow any more since they took the raft[4] out of it. I like to come out here
1 at night and listen to the music. Do you like to dance. . . ?

HORACE. Well. . . I. . . .

MARY CATHERINE. I love to dance.

HORACE. Well . . . I don't dance too well.

MARY CATHERINE. There's nothing to it but confidence.

HORACE. That's what my sister says. . . .

MARY CATHERINE. I didn't learn for the longest kind of time for lack of confidence and then Emily gave me a long lecture about it and I got confidence and went ahead and learned. Would you like to come in for a while?

HORACE. Well. . . if it's all right with you. . . .

MARY CATHERINE. I'd be glad to have you.

2 **HORACE**. Thank you.

[*They go into the area.* MARY CATHERINE'S *father,* TOM DAVIS, *is seated there in his undershirt. He works in a garage.*]

MARY CATHERINE. Hello, Daddy.

TOM. Hello, baby.

MARY CATHERINE. Daddy, this is Horace.

TOM. Hello, son.

HORACE. Howdy do, sir.

[*They shake hands.*]

MARY CATHERINE. Horace is Mrs. Inez Stanley's brother. He's here on a visit.

TOM. That's nice. Where's your home, son?

HORACE. Flatonia.

3 **TOM**. Oh, I see. Well, are you young people going to visit for a while?

MARY CATHERINE. Yes, sir.

TOM. Well, I'll leave you then. Good night.

MARY CATHERINE. Good night, Daddy.

HORACE. Good night, sir. [*He goes out upstage left.*] What does your father do?

MARY CATHERINE. He works in a garage. He's a mechanic. What does your father do?

HORACE. He's a judge.

MARY CATHERINE. My father worries so because he can't afford to send me to college. My mother told him that was all foolishness. That I'd rather go to business school anyway.

HORACE. Had you rather go to business school?

MARY CATHERINE. I don't know. [*A pause.*] Not really. But I'd never tell him that. When I was in the
4 seventh grade I thought I would die if I couldn't get there, but then when I was in the ninth, Mother talked to me one day and told me Daddy wasn't sleeping at nights for fear I'd be disappointed if he couldn't send me, so I told him the next night I decided I'd rather go to business school. He seemed relieved. [*A pause.*]

HORACE. Mary Catherine. I. . . uh. . . heard you say a while ago that you didn't dance because you lacked confidence and uh. . . then I heard you say you talked it over with Emily and she told you what

4. **raft:** natural dam formed by debris, leaves, and trees.

GUIDED READING

LITERAL QUESTION

1a. What does Mary Catherine say about her preference for school? (She would not prefer going to business school.)

INFERENTIAL QUESTION

1b. How does her remark affect Horace? (Her honesty inspires him to ask about gaining confidence.)

AT A GLANCE

- Horace asks how a person gets confidence; Mary Catherine offers a method.
- Horace admits he's comfortable being with her and asks her to the dance.
- She accepts.

1 CHARACTERIZATION

Horace's tentative exploration of how to obtain confidence is rewarded, and he declares his appreciation of Mary Catherine's relatively mature perspective.

2 MAIN IDEA

Horace believes that if he can go to the next dance with Mary Catherine, he will gain confidence. She is important to him both as a new friend and as a means of improving and changing himself.

3 CHARACTERIZATION

In a rush of enthusiasm and pleasure, Horace assures Mary Catherine that he will practice dancing nonstop.

was wrong and you got the confidence and you went ahead . . .

MARY CATHERINE. That's right. . . .

HORACE. Well . . . It may sound silly and all to you . . . seeing I'm about to start my first year of college . . . but I'd like to ask you a question. . . .

MARY CATHERINE. What is it, Horace?

HORACE. How do you get confidence?

MARY CATHERINE. Well, you just get it. Someone points it out to you that you lack it and then you get it. . . .

HORACE. Oh, is that how it's done?

MARY CATHERINE. That's how I did it.

HORACE. You see I lack confidence. And I . . . sure would like to get it. . . .

MARY CATHERINE. In what way do you lack confidence, Horace . . . ?

HORACE. Oh, in all kinds of ways. [*A pause.*] I'm not much of a mixer. . . .

1 **MARY CATHERINE.** I think you're just mixing fine tonight.

HORACE. I know. That's what's giving me a little encouragement. You're the first girl I've ever really been able to talk to. I mean this way. . . .

MARY CATHERINE. Am I, Horace . . . ?

HORACE. Yes.

MARY CATHERINE. Well, I feel in some ways that's quite a compliment.

HORACE. Well, you should feel that way. [*A pause.*] Mary Catherine. . . .

MARY CATHERINE. Yes, Horace?

HORACE. I had about decided to go back home tomorrow or the next day, but I understand there's another dance at the end of the week. . . .

MARY CATHERINE. Uh-huh. Day after tomorrow.

2 **HORACE.** Well . . . I . . . don't know if you have a date or not . . . but if you don't have . . . I feel if I could take you . . . I would gain the confidence to go. . . . I mean. . . .

MARY CATHERINE. Well, Horace. . . . You see. . . .

HORACE. I know I'd gain the confidence. My sister is a swell dancer and she'll let me practice with her every living minute until it's time for the dance. Of course I don't know if I could learn to jitterbug by then or rumba or do anything fancy, you understand, but I know I could learn the fox trot and I can waltz a little now. . . .

MARY CATHERINE. I'm sure you could.

HORACE. Well, will you go with me?

MARY CATHERINE. Yes, Horace. I'd love to. . . .

3 **HORACE.** Oh, thank you, Mary Catherine. I'll just practice night and day. I can't tell you how grateful Inez is going to be to you. . . . Mary Catherine, if we played the radio softly could we dance now?

MARY CATHERINE. Why certainly, Horace.

HORACE. You understand I'll make mistakes. . . .

MARY CATHERINE. I understand. . . .

[*She turns the radio on very softly.*]

HORACE. All right.

MARY CATHERINE. Yes. . . .

[*He approaches her very cautiously and takes her in his arms. He begins awkwardly to dance.* MARY CATHERINE *is very pleased and happy.*]

Why, you're doing fine, Horace. Just fine.

HORACE. Thank you, Mary Catherine. Thank you.

[*They continue dancing.* HORACE *is very pleased with himself although he is still dancing quite awkwardly. The lights fade. The lights are brought up on the area downstage left. It is early*

GUIDED READING

LITERAL QUESTION

1a. In what ways does Horace lack confidence? (He says, "in all kinds of ways," and specifically, "I'm not much of a mixer.")

INFERENTIAL QUESTION

1b. How has Horace already gained confidence? (He wanted to go home but changed his mind; he invites Mary Catherine to the dance.)

next morning. INEZ *is there reading.* HORACE *comes in whistling. He seems brimming over with happiness.*]

INEZ. What are you so happy about?

HORACE. I'm just happy.

INEZ. Wait until you hear my news and you'll be happier.

HORACE. Is that so?

INEZ. Miss Emily has seen the light.

HORACE. What?

INEZ. She has succumbed.

HORACE. What do you mean?

INEZ. She has crawled on her knees.

HORACE. She's crawled on her knees? I don't get it. . . .

INEZ. She has eaten dirt.

HORACE. Sister, what's this all about?

INEZ. Last night around ten o'clock she called in the meekest kind of voice possible and said, Inez, I've called up to apologize to you. I have apologized to Horace in the drugstore. Did she?

HORACE. Uh. Huh.

INEZ. And now I want to apologize to you and to tell you how sorry I am I behaved so badly. . . .

HORACE. Well. Isn't that nice of her, Inez?

1 **INEZ**. Wait a minute. You haven't heard the whole thing. And then her highness added, tell Horace if he would like to invite me to the dance to call me and I'd be glad to accept. And furthermore, Elizabeth called this morning and said they were leaving for Houston to buy her the most expensive evening dress in sight. Just to impress you with.

HORACE. Oh. . . . [*He sits down on a chair.*]

INEZ. Brother. What is the matter with you? Now are you gonna start worrying about this dancin' business all over again? You are the biggest fool sometimes. We've got today and tomorrow to practice.

HORACE. Inez. . . .

INEZ. Yes?

HORACE. I already have a date with someone tomorrow. . . .

INEZ. You do?

HORACE. Yes. I met a girl last night at the drugstore and I asked her.

INEZ. What girl did you ask?

HORACE. Mary Catherine Davis. . . .

INEZ. Well, you've got to get right out of it. You've got to call her up and explain what just happened.

HORACE. But, Inez. . . .

INEZ. You've got to do it, Horace. They told me they are spending all kinds of money for that dress. I practically had to threaten Elizabeth with never
2 speaking to her again to bring this all about. Why, she will never forgive me now if I turn around and tell her you can't go. . . . Horace. Don't look that way. I can't help it. For my sake, for your sister's sake you've got to get out of this date with Mary Catherine Davis. . . . Tell her. . .tell her. . .anything. . . .

HORACE. OK. [*A pause. He starts out.*] What can I say?

INEZ. I don't know, Horace. [*A pause.*] Say. . .well just tell her the truth. That's the best thing. Tell her that Emily's mother is your sister's best friend and that Emily's mother has taken her into Houston to buy her a very expensive dress. . . .

HORACE. What if Mary Catherine has bought a dress. . .?

AT A GLANCE

- Early next morning at his sister's home, Horace is happy.
- Emily has agreed to go to tomorrow's dance with him.
- He tells Inez that he has a date with Mary Catherine.
- She insists that he break it.

1 CHARACTERIZATION

Inez sees Emily's agreement to go to the dance as the surrender of a proud and mighty queen. She seems to believe relationships are like contests.

2 STYLE: EXAGGERATION

The playwright uses exaggeration to heighten dramatic conflict. Inez's emotional recounting of Emily's apology and the detailed description of the pending trip create an uncomfortable situation for Horace.

GUIDED READING

LITERAL QUESTION

1a. How does Horace reply when Inez tells him what to say to Mary Catherine? ("What if Mary Catherine has bought a dress?")

INFERENTIAL QUESTION

1b. What choice do you think Horace will make and why? (Answers include Mary Catherine, who helps him to build confidence and independence; or Inez, who can elicit his guilt about straining family ties.)

AT A GLANCE

- Horace declares that he will take Mary Catherine.
- Her parents prepare for Horace's arrival.
- Horace arrives in a tuxedo.

1 CHARACTERIZATION

In her appeal to Horace, Inez reveals her values. She believes her brother will gain status and popularity if he goes with the wealthy girl.

2 PLOT: CLIMAX

Applying his newly developing wisdom, Horace is adamant in his refusal to Inez.

3 READING SKILLS: COMPARISON AND CONTRAST

In contrast to Inez, Mr. and Mrs. Davis use every valid technique for affirming Mary Catherine's confidence.

INEZ. Well, she can't have bought an expensive dress. . . .

HORACE. Why not?

1 **INEZ**. Because her people can't afford it. Honey, you'll be the envy of every young man in Harrison, bringing Emily Crews to the dance. . . . Why, everybody will wonder just what it is you have. . . .

HORACE. I'm not going to do it.

INEZ. Horace. . . .

HORACE. I don't want to take Emily, I want to take Mary Catherine and that's just what I'm going to do.

INEZ. Horace. . . .

HORACE. My mind is made up. Once and for all. . . .

INEZ. Then what am I gonna do? [*She starts to cry.*] Who's gonna speak to Elizabeth? She'll bless me out putting her to all this trouble. Making her spend all
2 this money and time. . . . [*She is crying loudly now.*] Horace. You just can't do this to me. You just simply can't. . . .

HORACE. I can't help it. I'm not taking Emily Crews—

INEZ. Horace. . . .

HORACE. I am not taking Emily Crews.

[*He is firm. She is crying as the lights fade. The lights are brought up on the upstage left area.* MARY CATHERINE'S FATHER *is seated there. He is in his undershirt. In the distance dance music can be heard.* MRS. DAVIS *comes in from stage left.*]

MRS. DAVIS. Don't you think you'd better put your shirt on, Tom? Mary Catherine's date will be here any minute.

TOM. What time is it?

MRS. DAVIS. Nine o'clock.

TOM. The dance has already started. I can hear the music from here.

MRS. DAVIS. I know. But you know young people, they'd die before they'd be the first to a dance. Put your shirt on, Tom.

TOM. OK.

MRS. DAVIS. As soon as her date arrives we'll go.

TOM. OK.

[MARY CATHERINE *comes in from stage left. She has on an evening dress and she looks very pretty.*]

3 **MRS. DAVIS**. Why, Mary Catherine. You look lovely. Doesn't she look lovely, Tom?

TOM. Yes, she does.

MRS. DAVIS. Turn around, honey, and let me see you from the back. [*She does so.*] Just as pretty as you can be, Mary Catherine.

MARY CATHERINE. Thank you.

[HORACE *comes in from downstage left in his tux with a corsage box. He walks up the center of the stage to the upstage left area.*]

That's Horace. [*She goes to the corner of the area.*] Hello, Horace.

HORACE. Hello, Mary Catherine.

MARY CATHERINE. You've met my mother and father.

HORACE. Yes. I have. I met your father the other night and your mother yesterday afternoon.

MRS. DAVIS. Hello, Horace.

TOM. Hello, son.

MRS. DAVIS. Well, we were just going. You all have a good time tonight.

HORACE. Thank you.

GUIDED READING

LITERAL QUESTION

1a. Why would bringing Emily to the dance make Horace the envy of Harrison, according to Inez? ("Everybody will wonder just what it is you have.")

INFERENTIAL QUESTION

1b. In fact, what *does* Horace have? (a growing sense of independence and self-confidence; a true appreciation of values, such as loyalty and reliability)

MRS. DAVIS. Come on, Tom.

TOM. All right. Good night and have a nice time.

MARY CATHERINE. Thank you, Daddy. [*They go out stage left.* HORACE *hands her the corsage box. She takes it and opens it.*] Oh, thank you, Horace. Thank you so much. [*She takes the flowers out.*] They're just lovely. Will you pin them on for me?

HORACE. I'll try. [*He takes the corsage and the pin. He begins to pin it on.*] Will about here be all right?

MARY CATHERINE. Just fine. [*He pins the corsage on.*] Emily told me about the mix-up between your sister and her mother. I appreciate your going ahead and taking me anyway. If you had wanted to get out of it I would have understood. Emily and I are very good friends. . . and. . . .

HORACE. I didn't want to get out of it, Mary Catherine. I wanted to take you.

MARY CATHERINE. I'm glad you didn't want to get out of it. Emily offered to let me wear her new dress. But I had already bought one of my own.

HORACE. It's very pretty, Mary Catherine.

MARY CATHERINE. Thank you. [*A pause.*] Well, the dance has started. I can hear the music. Can't you?

HORACE Yes.

MARY CATHERINE. Well, we'd better get going. . . .

HORACE. All right. [*They start out.*] Mary Catherine. I hope you don't think this is silly, but could we practice just once more. . . .

MARY CATHERINE. Certainly we could. . . .

[*They start to dance.* HORACE *has improved although he is no Fred Astaire. They are dancing around and suddenly* HORACE *breaks away.*]

HORACE. Mary Catherine. I'm not good enough yet. I can't go. I'm sorry. Please let's just stay here.

MARY CATHERINE. No, Horace. We have to go.

HORACE. Please, Mary Catherine. . . .

2 **MARY CATHERINE**. I know just how you feel, Horace, but we have to go. [*A pause.*] I haven't told you the whole truth, Horace. This is my first dance, too. . . .

HORACE. It is?

MARY CATHERINE. Yes. I've been afraid to go. Afraid I wouldn't be popular. The last two dances I was asked to go and I said no.

HORACE. Then why did you accept when I asked you?

MARY CATHERINE. I don't know. I asked myself that afterwards. I guess because you gave me a kind of confidence. [*A pause. They dance again.*] You gave me confidence and I gave you confidence. What's the sense of getting confidence, Horace, if you're not going to use it?

[*A pause. They continue dancing.*]

HORACE. That's a pretty piece.

MARY CATHERINE. Yes, it is.

[*A pause. They dance again.* HORACE *stops.*]

HORACE. I'm ready to go if you are, Mary Catherine.

3 **MARY CATHERINE**. I'm ready. [*They start out.*] Scared?

HORACE. A little.

MARY CATHERINE. So am I. But let's go.

HORACE. OK.

[*They continue out the area down the center of the stage and off downstage right as the music from the dance is heard.*]

AT A GLANCE

- Mary Catherine tells Horace she knows about the mix-up involving Emily.
- Horace prefers Mary Catherine, who admits that this is also her first dance.
- They practice and then leave for the dance.

1 PLOT: FALLING ACTION

Mary Catherine reveals her own insecurity as well as her loyalty to a long friendship when she assures Horace that she would have understood if he had wanted to go to the dance with Emily.

2 MAIN IDEA

When Mary Catherine says she understands exactly how Horace feels, the audience cannot appreciate the full truth of it; seconds later we see that they have similar fears. Honesty and open communication will help them to outgrow those fears.

3 PLOT: RESOLUTION

Mary Catherine's and Horace's candid admissions provide an honest and realistic resolution to the plot.

REFLECTING ON THE PLAY

In what sense do Horace and Mary Catherine "have to go" to the dance? (They have to "use" their newfound confidence; they have to grow, even though it may seem momentarily uncomfortable.)

STUDY QUESTIONS

1. to go to a dance
2. ■ does not dance well enough
   ■ He is a "bore and a goon."
3. Horace; awful
4. "Someone points it out to you . . . and then you get it."
5. "I'm not going to do it."
6. gave her confidence
7. to a great extent: cannot stand up to Inez or Emily; afraid to go to dance
8. wants to go with Mary Catherine more than to please Inez; before timid, now firm
9. liked him as he was
10. Answers will vary. Students might say change of character should carry into other areas.

VIEWPOINT

Limited audience: subtle, simple, not much action; *mass audience:* universal human emotions and theme

LITERARY FOCUS

Dramatic Plot

(1) situation, characters introduced; (2) Horace's lack of confidence (inner conflict); (3) Emily stands him up, Horace meets Mary; (4) asks Mary to dance; (5) refuses to cancel date, exchanges fears with Mary; (6) Horace and Mary go to dance.

STUDY QUESTIONS

Recalling

1. What plans have Inez and Elizabeth made for Horace and Emily at the beginning of the play?
2. What reason does Horace give for not wanting to go to the dance? What reason does Emily give her mother for not wanting to go to the dance with Horace?
3. Who overhears Mary Catherine tell the waitress about Emily's date for the dance? How does Mary Catherine feel after she finds out who overheard her conversation?
4. What is Mary Catherine's reply when Horace asks her how a person gets confidence?
5. What does Horace tell Inez when she insists that he cancel his date with Mary Catherine?
6. After Mary Catherine admits that she has been afraid to go to dances, what reason does she give Horace for accepting his invitation?

Interpreting

7. To what extent is Inez correct when she says that the trouble with Horace is that he has no confidence in himself? Provide examples from the play to support your answer.
8. Why does Horace refuse to cancel his date with Mary Catherine when his sister pressures him to do so? In what way does Horace's refusal show a change in his character?
9. Mary Catherine tells Horace, "You gave me confidence and I gave you confidence." Explain how Mary Catherine gave Horace confidence.

Extending

10. Do you think that Horace will be able to transfer his newly gained social confidence to other areas of his life? Why or why not?

VIEWPOINT

Of Horton Foote's television plays, one critic wrote that they are

> more suggestive of short stories written for a limited "quality" audience than of mass-medium entertainment.
>
> —Anthony Boucher

■ What aspects of the play would appeal to the majority of television viewers? In what respects do you think that *The Dancers* would appeal to only a limited television audience?

LITERARY FOCUS

Dramatic Plot

The **plot structure** of a play—even a one-act play—is very similar to the plot structure of a story. As a matter of fact, since drama is an older form of literature than fiction, we derived many of our concepts about plot from ancient writers' observations of drama. However, since an audience in a theater does not have the opportunity to reread what they have just seen, the plot structure of a play is usually more sharply defined than the plot structure of a story or novel. Every speech and event in a play must clearly advance the action and develop the characters.

In a traditional play the **exposition** establishes the setting, introduces the main characters, and presents the situation when the curtain goes up. The **conflict**, or struggle the main character undergoes, appears early in a play. The **rising action** adds complications to the conflict until the climax is reached. The **climax** is the part of the play that points toward the final outcome. The **falling action** grows logically from the climax, and the **resolution** provides a satisfying conclusion to the play.

Thinking About Dramatic Plot

■ Identify the parts of *The Dancers* that represent the (1) exposition, (2) conflict, (3) rising action, (4) climax, (5) falling action, and (6) resolution.

Staging and Character

We learn about the characters in a play from what they say, or the **dialogue**, but we can also learn about characters from staging. Stage directions describe the appearance and actions of characters. When reading a play, we should try to visualize the characters as the author describes them. The elements of staging that reveal character include costumes and scenery; we can learn about people from their appearance and from their surroundings. The elements of staging used by the actors to interpret the characters include gesture, facial expression, and tone of voice.

Thinking About Staging and Character

1. Explain how the differences between Emily and Mary Catherine are reflected by their appearances.
2. Find two stage directions for tone of voice and two for gestures. What does each stage direction reveal about the character?

Staging and Audience

The audience at the performance of any play must use its imagination to believe that what is happening on the stage is real. Some plays, however, require more imagination than others. Many plays have scenery, costumes, and other elements of staging that are as realistic as possible. These plays leave little to the imagination. Other plays, like *The Dancers*, call upon the audience to become more involved in the production by imagining elements of staging like scenery, props, and details of costuming. In such plays the dialogue and the actions of the characters provide clues to help the audience picture the play as the author wants it to look.

Thinking About Staging and Audience

- Find three points in the play where words, actions, or objects help the audience to imagine what is not actually on the stage.

Staging and Theme

The staging of a play can inform the audience about setting and characters, but elements of staging can also hint at the plot of a play and its theme. For example, consider a play whose theme is the diversity of America's young, their many talents, and the many opportunities open to them. The scenery of the play represents a classroom. Students enter dressed in many different styles; they carry an assortment of props that includes sports equipment, books, musical instruments, and art supplies. The theme of the play is thus reflected in the appearance of the stage and the actors even before a single word is spoken.

Thinking About Staging and Theme

- Explain how the scarcity of scenery and props and the division of the stage into four acting areas contribute to a sense of thematic unity in *The Dancers*.

COMPOSITION

Writing About Dialogue

- Explain how we learn about the characters in *The Dancers* from what they say. First choose two characters from the play. Then find at least three revealing statements made by each character. Finally tell what we learn about each character from the statements.

Writing Stage Directions for Characters

- Write stage directions that describe two characters who are strangers but who are about to become friends. Describe their physical characteristics, their clothing, and their gestures. Your descriptions should show a similarity between the two characters that foreshadows their friendship.

COMPARING PLAYS

1. Compare *A Sunny Morning* and *The Dancers*. Which do you think would benefit more from being seen on stage? Which would benefit less? What qualities of each play cause you to make your choice? Give examples from the plays to support your opinions.
2. Plays are said to hold a mirror to life, to show us ourselves. Compare *A Sunny Morning* and *The Dancers*. In what ways does each show us typical human behavior? Give examples from the plays to support your opinions.

Staging and Character

1. *Emily:* pretty—confident, popular; *Mary:* plain—lacks confidence, shy
2. *Tone of voice:* Elizabeth (begins to call, softly . . . then louder)—well-mannered, but determined; Emily (screaming back)—stubborn, thoughtless; *Gestures:* Elizabeth (keeps glancing off R.)—nervous, embarrassed; Horace: (begins to fan himself)—anxious, embarrassed

Staging and Audience

(doorbell rings . . . She goes off L. and comes back in followed by Horace)—appears that Horace has come in from outside; (hear Elizabeth offstage knocking on Emily's door)—impression of Emily's room, though not part of the set; (walks to the edge of the area and looks out)—appearance of looking through window.

Staging and Theme

- Staging simple, like theme
- domestic aspect shown by living rooms and yard, small town aspect by drugstore
- Limited set underscores inner conflicts.

COMPARING PLAYS

1. *A Sunny Morning:* readable as humor derived from words, but expressions, gestures help; *The Dancers:* reads easily—depends less on action than language, but expressions, gestures help
2. *A Sunny Morning:* grumpiness—Gonzalo's petulance; vanity—characters' lies; *The Dancers:* Insecurity—Horace's and Mary's lack of confidence; thoughtlessness—Emily's treatment of Horace

COMPOSITION: GUIDELINES FOR EVALUATION

WRITING ABOUT DIALOGUE

Objective

To show how dialogue reveals character

Guidelines for Evaluation

- suggested length: three to four paragraphs
- should cite three revealing statements about each of two characters
- should make clear what these speeches reveal about the characters

WRITING STAGE DIRECTIONS FOR CHARACTERS

Objective

To reveal character through stage directions

Guidelines for Evaluation

- suggested length: 75–150 words
- should include details about physical characterization, clothing, and mannerisms
- should reveal similarities that foreshadow a future friendship

LITERARY FOCUS: *Romeo and Juliet*

William Shakespeare

William Shakespeare lived in England four hundred years ago. Because biographical information was compiled only for royalty at that time, we know little about Shakespeare beyond what a few public documents tell us. He was born in Stratford-on-Avon, a market town about ninety miles northwest of London. Church records show that he was christened on April 26, 1564. His birth is traditionally celebrated on April 23 because baptisms were usually performed three days after birth and possibly because April 23 is also the date of his death. From this point few records exist until his marriage to Anne Hathaway in 1582 and the eventual births of their three children.

We do not know when or why Shakespeare left Stratford, but by 1592 he was established as a London playwright and actor. In 1594 he joined a theater company, the Lord Chamberlain's Men. After James I became king in 1603, the group became known as the King's Men.

Shakespeare wrote thirty-seven plays—histories such as ***Richard III,*** comedies such as *A Midsummer Night's Dream,* and tragedies such as *Julius Caesar.* Most of the plays were performed by his theater company, and he acted in several.

Shakespeare retired to Stratford in 1610. He died in 1616 and was buried in the parish church.

Elizabethan England

Shakespeare lived in Elizabethan England—that is, during the reign of Queen Elizabeth I. During this time England defeated the Spanish Armada to become the world's greatest naval power. As a result, explorers like Sir Walter Raleigh and Sir Francis Drake led the English to new trade routes and faraway colonies. Their travels led to the founding, four years after Elizabeth's death, of Jamestown, Virginia, England's first permanent colony in America.

England experienced a golden age of peace and prosperity, an atmosphere in which the arts flourished. The literature of the day, produced by authors such as Ben Jonson, Edmund Spenser, Francis Bacon, and William Shakespeare, reflected the self-confidence and energy of the times. Queen Elizabeth had a splendid court where court masques, plays with fancy costumes and elaborate decorations, were often performed.

The love of theater filtered down from the court through the entire society. Crowds composed of all segments of society filled the public theaters every afternoon, making drama one of the most popular forms of entertainment in Elizabethan England.

Shakespeare's Theater

During Shakespeare's life a number of public theaters were built just outside the city of London. Before these permanent theaters were built, most theater companies performed on wooden platforms set up in the courtyards of inns. The physical arrangement of inn theaters influenced the design of the permanent theaters.

The Globe Theater, where most of Shakespeare's plays were performed, was an eight-sided structure with a large open area in the middle. A straw-thatched roof covered the three-tiered galleries surrounding the open courtyard. At one end of the courtyard was a large wooden stage that jutted out into the open space. At the back of the

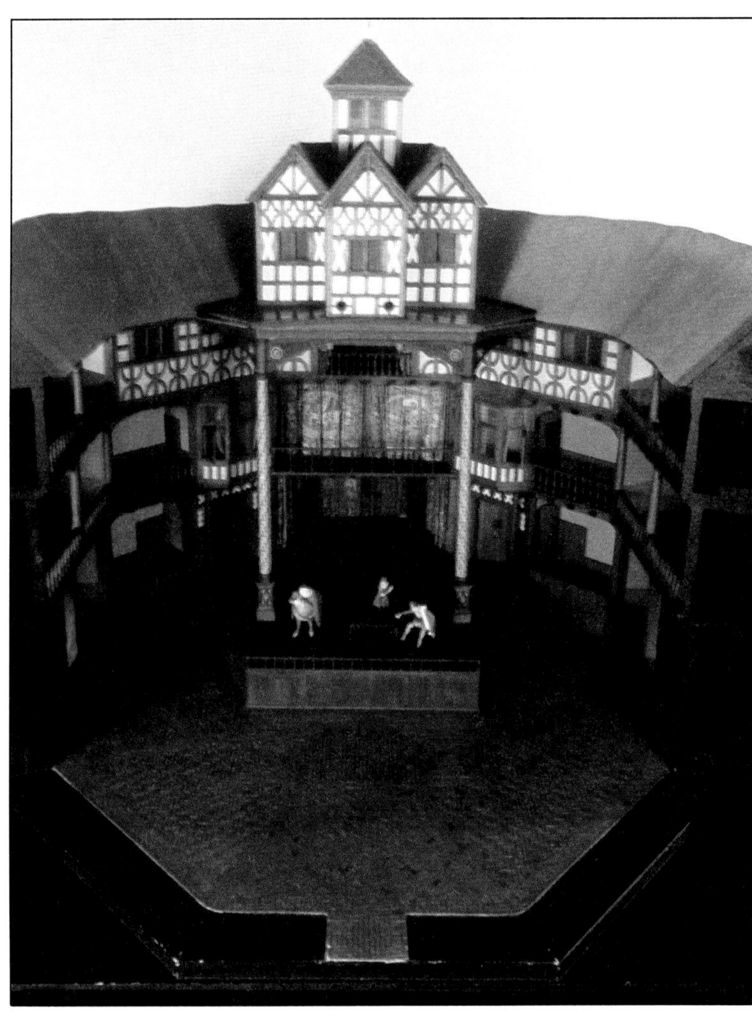

Model of the Globe Theater by John Cranford Adams. By Courtesy of the Folger Shakespeare Library, Washington, D.C.

main stage was a curtained inner stage that was used for scenes set in small, dark areas like a tomb or a private chamber. Above the inner stage was a balcony that could become a watchtower for soldiers or a balcony for lovers.

Because the stage was thrust into the courtyard, the audience surrounded the actors on three sides. Most of the audience paid a penny admission and stood on the ground surrounding the stage. These groundlings, as they were called, were a noisy and demanding audience. Wealthier playgoers paid an extra penny to sit in the galleries that surrounded the courtyard.

Groundlings and gallery patrons alike wanted entertainment that contained poetic language, action, word play, dancing, and sword fighting. They often knew the plot of a play in advance and were interested in the style of presentation.

The pace of a performance was rapid; Shakespeare's plays were put on in two hours. There was no scenery, no artificial lighting, few props, and no curtain on the main stage. As a result, the action moved quickly from one scene to the next.

Since there was no scenery or lighting, playwrights used language to set scenes and to create atmosphere. A play's dialogue had to inspire audiences to imagine setting and mood. Shakespeare's rich language and skillfully constructed verse also created vivid characters, exciting plots, and strong messages. The result, then and now, is an unusual theatrical experience.

Scene from the 1961 film version of *West Side Story*, a modern musical adaptation of *Romeo and Juliet.*

Romeo and Juliet

Romeo and Juliet is a **tragedy,** a play in which a main character suffers a major downfall. Shakespeare wrote the play early in his career, probably between 1594 and 1596. Like many of Shakespeare's plays, it is based on a story that was well known to Elizabethans. Shakespeare borrowed the plot from Arthur Brooke's poem *The Tragicall Historye of Romeus and Juliet.* Earlier versions of the story also exist including an Italian novella, or short novel, by Matteo Bandello. Shakespeare turned the stiff characters of his model into realistic people. He also told the story in language that is uniquely his own and beautifully poetic.

Romeo and Juliet was immediately popular, and its popularity has grown through nearly four hundred years. Today the romantic tragedy is performed in many languages and in many countries as well as on television and on film. In addition, Shakespeare's young lovers have inspired composers, choreographers, and artists.

The play takes place during the 1300s in Italy, a country that Shakespeare favored as a setting for his plays. In the northern Italian city of Verona, a feud between two wealthy, powerful families— the Capulets and the Montagues—has raged for many years. This feud provides a background and a contrast to the tragic love of Romeo and Juliet.

Romeo and Juliet in an illustration from a 1535 Italian novel about them that predates Shakespeare's play.

Elizabethan Language

Language changes constantly, and the four hundred years since Shakespeare's time have made English a different language in many ways. In addition, Shakespeare occasionally needed to alter a word in order for the word to fit into the rhythm of a line of verse. Listed below are some common Elizabethan expressions that you will find in *Romeo and Juliet.*

against: for
alack: alas
an, and: if
art thou: are you
aught: anything
aye: yes, alas
but: except for, only
dost: you do
doth: do
e'en: even
e'er: ever
ere: before
fie: for shame!
forsooth: indeed
go to: stop this!
haply: perhaps
happy: convenient
hence: from here
hie: hurry
hither: here
marry: indeed
morrow: morning
naught: nothing
nay: no
ne'er: never
o'er: over
thither: there
thrice: three times
'tis: it is
unto: to
wench: young woman
whence: where
wherefore: why
whither: where
wilt: will
would: wish
yonder, yon: over there

Key Ideas in *Romeo and Juliet*

■ As you read *Romeo and Juliet,* look for references to each of the following topics. If you keep track of what the play says about each topic, you will begin to grasp the most important themes of *Romeo and Juliet.*

- the lessons taught by love
- the effect of love on hostility
- the influence of fate
- the importance of moderation—acting with thought and caution
- the importance of order, the smooth running of government and society

Key Quotations in *Romeo and Juliet*

As you read *Romeo and Juliet,* you will probably recognize a few lines because the play contains some of the most famous lines in English drama. Here are a few familiar quotations from the play.

A pair of star-crossed lovers
—Prologue to Act I, line 6

True, I talk of dreams;
Which are the children of an idle brain,
Begot of nothing but vain fantasy.
—MERCUTIO, Act I, Scene iv, 68–70

But soft! What light through yonder window breaks?
It is the East, and Juliet is the sun!
—ROMEO, Act II, Scene ii, 2–3

O Romeo, Romeo! Wherefore art thou Romeo?
—JULIET, Act II, Scene ii, 33

What's in a name? That which we call a rose
By any other word would smell as sweet.
—JULIET, Act II, Scene ii, 43–44

Good night, good night! Parting is such sweet sorrow
That I shall say good night till it be morrow.
—JULIET, Act II, Scene ii, 184–185

A plague a both your houses!
—MERCUTIO, Act III, Scene i, 97–98

O, I am fortune's fool!
—ROMEO, Act III, Scene i, 134

Then I defy you, stars!
—ROMEO, Act V, Scene i, 24

A gentlewoman of Verona as depicted in a sixteenth-century Italian book of costumes.

William Shakespeare

The Tragedy of Romeo and Juliet
(abridged)

CHARACTERS

The Montagues

LORD MONTAGUE: wealthy nobleman of Verona and enemy to Capulet
LADY MONTAGUE: his wife
ROMEO: their son
BENVOLIO: Lord Montague's nephew and Romeo's friend
BALTHASAR: Romeo's servant
ABRAM: a servant

The Capulets

LORD CAPULET: wealthy nobleman of Verona and enemy to Montague
LADY CAPULET: his wife
JULIET: their daughter, who is thirteen years old
TYBALT: Lady Capulet's nephew
OLD MAN OF THE FAMILY
NURSE: servant who has cared for Juliet since her infancy
PETER: the Nurse's servant
SAMPSON: servant
GREGORY: servant

Others

CHORUS: actor who speaks directly to the audience to introduce the play
PRINCE ESCALUS: ruler of Verona
COUNT PARIS: relative of the Prince and suitor to Juliet
MERCUTIO: relative of the Prince and Romeo's friend
FRIAR LAWRENCE: Catholic priest of the order of Franciscans and a pharmacist
APOTHECARY: pharmacist in Mantua
FRIAR JOHN: Franciscan priest
PAGE: servant to Paris

Officers and Citizens of Verona, Relatives of both families, Maskers, Officers, Guards, Watchmen, Servants, and Attendants

Scene: *Italy—the cities of Verona and Mantua. The fourteenth century.*

AT A GLANCE

- *Prologue:* The Chorus states that a feud between two Veronese families leads to the tragic death of two "star-crossed lovers."
- *Scene i:* Two Capulet servants enter in a mood to fight.

LITERARY OPTIONS

- characterization
- style
- plot

THEMATIC OPTIONS

- friendship and love
- methods of communication
- individual responsibility

1 BACKGROUND

A Chorus that directly addresses the audience is a dramatic device as old as Greek tragedy. The role of the Chorus is to clarify or amplify themes and actions in the play. Here it directly states the story's outcome.

2 STYLE: RHYME

The rhyming prologue contrasts with the blank verse and prose that Shakespeare will use elsewhere in the play. The *abab* rhyme lends formality and finality to the words.

3 PLOT: FORESHADOWING

The "star-crossed lovers" will take their lives, a tragic act that will end their parents' feud.

4 CHARACTERIZATION

Of the two servants, Sampson seems the more belligerent. Shakespeare is known for giving distinct characteristics to even the most minor characters.

SELECTION FOR PRACTICE IN ACTIVE READING
(TCR 5, p. 67)

ACT I

Prologue

1 *[Elizabethan dramatists sometimes imitated classical Greek theater by using a chorus, an actor or group of actors who comment on the action of the play and explain the theme. An actor, serving as the* CHORUS, *enters and directly addresses the audience. The* CHORUS *speaks first about a long-standing feud between two of Verona's most important families, the Capulets and the Montagues.]*

2 CHORUS. Two households, both alike in dignity,[1]
In fair Verona, where we lay our scene,
From ancient grudge break to new mutiny,
Where civil blood makes civil hands unclean.[2]
From forth the fatal loins of these two foes
3 A pair of star-crossed[3] lovers take their life;
Whose misadventured piteous overthrows[4]
Doth with their death bury their parents' strife.
The fearful passage of their death-marked love,
And the continuance of their parents' rage,
Which, but[5] their children's end, naught could remove,
Is now the two hours' traffic of our stage;[6]
The which if you with patient ears attend,
What here shall miss, our toil shall strive to mend.[7]

[The CHORUS *exits.]*

1 **dignity:** high position in society.
2 **mutiny . . . unclean:** rioting in which citizens soil their hands with each other's blood.
3 **star-crossed:** doomed because of the positions of the stars when they were born. People in Shakespeare's time followed astrology very seriously.
4 **overthrows:** ruin.
5 **but:** except for.
6 **traffic of our stage:** action or topic of our play.
7 **mend:** clarify.

Scene i. *Early morning. A public square in Verona.*

*[*SAMPSON *and* GREGORY, *servants of the Capulets, enter. Because of the feud between the powerful Capulet and Montague families, they are armed with swords and bucklers, or small shields. They are always ready to fight for the Capulets. While they discuss the possibility of a fight,* SAMPSON *and* GREGORY *joke with each other and play with words.]*

SAMPSON. Gregory, on my word, we'll not carry coals.[1]

GREGORY. No, for then we should be colliers.[2]

SAMPSON. I mean, and we be in choler, we'll draw.[3]

GREGORY. Ay, while you live, draw your neck out of collar.[4]

4 SAMPSON. I strike quickly, being moved.

1 **carry coals:** put up with insults. Men who carried coals, a dirty job, were targets for insults.
2 **colliers:** coal dealers.
3 **and . . . draw:** if we are made angry, we will draw out our swords. The servants are making a pun, or play on words, with collier and choler (anger).
4 **collar:** hangman's noose. The characters add *collar* to the pun with *collier* and *choler.*

GUIDED READING

LITERAL QUESTION

1a. How do the "two households" get along? (They have had a long-standing feud that will break out again.)

INFERENTIAL QUESTION

1b. As the first scene begins, why might we suspect that the households don't get along? (The two Capulet servants are ready for a fight.)

GREGORY. But thou art not quickly moved to strike.

SAMPSON. A dog of the house of Montague moves me.

GREGORY. To move is to stir, and to be valiant is to stand. Therefore, if thou art moved, thou run'st away.

SAMPSON. A dog of that house shall move me to stand.

GREGORY. The quarrel is between our masters and us their men.

SAMPSON. 'Tis all one. I will show myself a tyrant.

GREGORY. Here comes two of the house of Montagues.

1 [ABRAM *and* BALTHASAR, *servants of the Montagues, enter. They, too, are armed and ready to fight for their masters.*]

SAMPSON. My naked weapon is out. Quarrel! I will back thee.

GREGORY. How? Turn thy back and run?

SAMPSON. Fear me not.

GREGORY. No, marry.[5] I fear thee!

2 **SAMPSON.** Let us take the law of our sides; let them begin.[6]

GREGORY. I will frown as I pass by, and let them take it as they list.[7]

SAMPSON. Nay, as they dare. I will bite my thumb[8] at them, which is disgrace to them if they bear it.

3 **ABRAM.** Do you bite your thumb at us, sir?

SAMPSON. I do bite my thumb, sir.

ABRAM. Do you bite your thumb at us, sir?

SAMPSON. [*Aside to* GREGORY.] Is the law of our side if I say ay?

GREGORY. [*Aside to* SAMPSON.] No.

SAMPSON. No, sir, I do not bite my thumb at you, sir; but I bite my thumb, sir.

GREGORY. Do you quarrel, sir?

ABRAM. Quarrel, sir? No, sir.

SAMPSON. But if you do, sir, I am for you. I serve as good a man as you.

ABRAM. No better.

SAMPSON. Well, sir.

[*Enter* BENVOLIO, LORD MONTAGUE'*s nephew.*]

5 **marry:** indeed.

6 **Let . . . begin:** Let them begin the fight; then we can fight back legally in self-defense.

7 **list:** please.

8 **bite my thumb:** an insulting gesture.

AT A GLANCE

- *Scene i (continued):* Montague servants enter and meet the Capulet servants.
- Sampson tries to provoke a fight.

1 PLOT: CONFLICT

The two feuding families—represented by their servants—face off on stage and Sampson immediately tries to engage the Montague servants in a fight.

2 CHARACTERIZATION

Though belligerent, Sampson knows that the law forbids fighting: He cleverly tries to start a fight in a way that will cause the other side to be blamed.

3 THEME

Sampson chooses a method of communication—a gesture—that he knows will be more insulting than words.

GUIDED READING

LITERAL QUESTION

1a. What does Sampson do to insult Abram and Balthasar? (He bites his thumb.)

INFERENTIAL QUESTION

1b. Why does Sampson hesitate to say he bit his thumb *at* them? (He doesn't want to be blamed for starting the fight.)

AT A GLANCE

- *Scene i (continued):* The servants fight.
- As Benvolio, a Montague, tries to stop them, Tybalt, a Capulet, challenges him.
- A brawl breaks out between the two families.
- The heads of both families arrive.

1 THEME

The fight has escalated from servants to family members, and we see how lack of individual responsibility leads to public disorder.

2 STYLE: BLANK VERSE

In contrast to the servants, the more "noble" family members speak in blank verse, marking a contrast between "lower" and "more elevated" characters.

3 PLOT: RISING ACTION

The terrible consequences of the feud are made plainly visible: The stage is filled with excited, angry people who fight noisily.

4 CHARACTERIZATION

In the midst of the tumult, Lady Capulet tries to restrain her husband. She comically insults him by calling attention to his age.

5 PLOT: SYMMETRY

Lady Montague likewise tries to restrain her husband, furthering Shakespeare's symmetrical presentation of the two households.

GREGORY. Say "better." Here comes one of my master's kinsmen.

SAMPSON. Yes, better, sir.

ABRAM. You lie.

SAMPSON. Draw, if you be men. Gregory, remember thy swashing blow.[9]

[*They fight.*]

1 BENVOLIO. Part, fools!
Put up your swords. You know not what you do.

[TYBALT, LADY CAPULET'S *nephew, enters with his sword drawn. He speaks first to* BENVOLIO.]

TYBALT. What, art thou drawn among these heartless hinds?[10]
Turn thee, Benvolio; look upon thy death.

BENVOLIO. I do but keep the peace. Put up thy sword,
Or manage it to part these men with me.

2 TYBALT. What, drawn, and talk of peace? I hate the word
As I hate hell, all Montagues, and thee.
Have at thee, coward!

3 [BENVOLIO *and* TYBALT *fight as men of both families enter and join the brawl. Then an* OFFICER *of the town and several* CITIZENS *enter. They carry clubs, battle-axes (bills), and spears (partisans).*]

OFFICER. Clubs, bills and partisans! Strike! Beat them down!
Down with the Capulets! Down with the Montagues!

[LORD CAPULET, *in his dressing gown, and* LADY CAPULET *enter.*]

4 CAPULET. What noise is this? Give me my long sword, ho!

LADY CAPULET. A crutch, a crutch! Why call you for a sword?

CAPULET. My sword, I say! Old Montague is come
And flourishes his blade in spite of me.[11]

5 [LORD MONTAGUE *and* LADY MONTAGUE *enter.* LADY MONTAGUE *tries to hold back her husband.*]

MONTAGUE. Thou villain Capulet!—Hold me not; let me go.

LADY MONTAGUE. Thou shalt not stir one foot to seek a foe.

[PRINCE ESCALUS *enters with his* ATTENDANTS.]

9 **swashing blow:** heavy downward stroke.

10 **heartless hinds:** cowardly servants.

11. **in spite of me:** to defy me.

GUIDED READING

LITERAL QUESTIONS

1a. Which Montagues have been introduced? (Abram, Balthasar, Benvolio, Lord and Lady Montague)

2a. What does the Officer tell the Citizens to do? ("Strike" and "Beat . . . down" the feuding Capulets and Montagues)

INFERENTIAL QUESTIONS

1b. How have the Montagues tried to keep the peace? (Abram tried to ignore the insult; Benvolio tried to stop the fight; Lady Montague tried to restrain her husband.)

2b. What does this tell us about how the townspeople feel about the feud? (They seem tired of it and ready to blame both houses.)

1 **PRINCE.** Rebellious subjects, enemies to peace,
Profaners[12] of this neighbor-stainèd steel[13]—
Will they not hear? What, ho! You men, you beasts,
That quench the fire of your pernicious[14] rage
With purple fountains issuing from your veins!
On pain of torture, from those bloody hands
Throw your mistempered[15] weapons to the ground
And hear the sentence of your movèd prince.
Three civil brawls, bred of an airy word
By thee, old Capulet, and Montague,
Have thrice disturbed the quiet of our streets
And made Verona's ancient citizens
Cast by their grave beseeming ornaments[16]
To wield old partisans, in hands as old,
Cank'red with peace, to part your cank'red[17] hate.
2 If ever you disturb our streets again,
Your lives shall pay the forfeit of the peace.[18]
For this time all the rest depart away.
You, Capulet, shall go along with me;
And, Montague, come you this afternoon,
To know our farther pleasure in this case,
To old Freetown, our common judgment place.
Once more, on pain of death, all men depart.

[*Everyone leaves except* MONTAGUE, LADY MONTAGUE, *and their nephew* BENVOLIO.]

MONTAGUE. Who set this ancient quarrel new abroach?[19]
Speak, nephew, were you by when it began?

3 **BENVOLIO.** Here were the servants of your adversary
And yours, close fighting ere I did approach.
I drew to part them. In the instant came
The fiery Tybalt, with his sword prepared;
Which, as he breathed defiance to my ears,
He swung about his head and cut the winds,
Who, nothing hurt withal,[20] hissed him in scorn.
While we were interchanging thrusts and blows,
Came more and more, and fought on part and part,[21]
Till the Prince came, who parted either part.

4 **LADY MONTAGUE.** O, where is Romeo? Saw you him today?
Right glad I am he was not at this fray.

BENVOLIO. Madam, an hour before the worshiped sun
Peered forth the golden window of the East,

12 **Profaners:** those who show disrespect.
13 **neighbor-stained steel:** swords stained with the blood of neighbors.
14 **pernicious:** fatal, deadly.
15 **mistempered:** poorly made, and used in bad will.
16 **Cast . . . ornaments:** discard the dignified clothing of the aged.
17 **cank'red:** Swords cank'red (rusted) with disuse are being used in the cank'red (dangerous) feud.
18 **Your lives . . . peace:** The Prince threatens death for anyone who again disturbs the peace with brawling.
19 **Who . . . abroach?:** Who reopened this old feud?
20 **nothing hurt withal:** not hurt by this.
21 **Came more . . . part:** While the fight progressed, more members of each house arrived, took sides, and joined the fight.

AT A GLANCE

- *Scene i (continued):* The Prince orders the fighting to stop and threatens the feuders with death if another brawl starts.
- All exit except Lord and Lady Montague and Benvolio.
- Montague asks Benvolio how the fight started.

1 READING SKILLS: INFERENCE

The Prince's "Will they not hear?" suggests that he must shout to make himself heard above the noise of the fight. It also conveys his impatience with the feuders.

2 PLOT: CONFLICT

The Prince's threat heightens the tense mood by making the stakes in every potential conflict very high—life and death.

3 STYLE: BLANK VERSE

Iambic rhythm allows for "natural" pauses in characters' speech. Pauses are underscored by the period after *them* and the comma after *Tybalt.*

4 CHARACTERIZATION

Lady Montague's concern for Romeo builds interest in him. Her relief at his safety is a kind of ironic foreshadowing.

GUIDED READING

LITERAL QUESTIONS

1a. What does the Prince say will happen to anyone caught fighting again? (He will be put to death.)

2a. What does Lady Montague say about Romeo? (She is glad that he was "not at this fray.")

INFERENTIAL QUESTIONS

1b. Why does the Prince impose such a strict penalty? (He seems to think that only an extreme penalty will end the fighting.)

2b. What does this tell us about Lady Montague's feelings for Romeo? (She is fond of him and worried about him.)

AT A GLANCE

- *Scene i (continued):* Montague and Benvolio discuss the strange behavior of Romeo.
- Romeo enters without seeing them.
- Benvolio offers to question him, and the Montagues leave.

1 MAIN IDEA

Benvolio measures his friend's mood by his own, demonstrating the sort of empathy that forms their friendship.

2 STYLE: IMAGERY

Shakespeare portrays the sun as a person drawing curtains from a personified dawn's bed. Note the contrast between the "all-cheering" sunlight and the "shady," sinister curtains.

3 STYLE: RHYME

Shakespearean speeches often end in rhyming couplets. The rhyme gives a kind of twist to the end of the speech.

4 STYLE: SIMILE

Montague compares Romeo's secretive, dark mood to a worm that spoils a bud—a comparison that suggests that Romeo will be destroyed.

5 CHARACTERIZATION

The audience's first impression of Romeo is informed by his extreme distraction and self-involvement.

A troubled mind drave me to walk abroad;
Where, underneath the grove of sycamore
That westward rooteth from this city side,
So early walking did I see your son.
Towards him I made, but he was ware[22] of me
And stole into the covert[23] of the wood.
1 I, measuring his affections,[24] by my own,
Which then most sought where most might not be found,[25]
Being one too many by my weary self,
Pursued my humor not pursuing his,[26]
And gladly shunned who gladly fled from me.

MONTAGUE. Many a morning hath he there been seen,
With tears augmenting the fresh morning's dew,
Adding to clouds more clouds with his deep sighs;
2 But all so soon as the all-cheering sun
Should in the farthest East begin to draw
The shady curtains from Aurora's[27] bed,
Away from light steals home my heavy[28] son
And private in his chamber pens himself,
Shuts up his windows, locks fair daylight out,
And makes himself an artificial night.
3 Black and portentous[29] must this humor prove
Unless good counsel may the cause remove.

BENVOLIO. My noble uncle, do you know the cause?

MONTAGUE. I neither know it nor can learn of him.

BENVOLIO. Have you importuned[30] him by any means?

MONTAGUE. Both by myself and many other friends;
But he, his own affections' counselor,
Is to himself—I will not say how true—
4 But to himself so secret and so close,
So far from sounding and discovery,
As is the bud bit with an envious worm
Ere he can spread his sweet leaves to the air[31]
Or dedicate his beauty to the sun.
Could we but learn from whence his sorrows grow,
We would as willingly give cure as know.

5 [ROMEO *enters. He appears distracted and does not notice the others on stage.*]

BENVOLIO. See where he comes. So please you step aside;
I'll know his grievance, or be much denied.

MONTAGUE. I would thou wert so happy by thy stay[32]
To hear true shrift.[33] Come, madam, let's away.

22 **ware:** aware.
23 **covert:** shelter.
24 **affections:** mood.
25 **most . . . found:** wanted to be alone.
26 **Pursued . . . his:** followed my own mood (humor) by not following him.
27 **Aurora:** goddess of the dawn. References to light and to dark occur throughout the play.
28 **heavy:** sad.
29 **portentous:** leading to trouble.
30 **importuned:** questioned.
31 **so far . . . air:** Montague compares Romeo, whom he cannot understand, to a bud that is bitten by a harmful worm and remains tightly closed.
32 **happy . . . stay:** successful for your patience.
33 **shrift:** confession.

GUIDED READING

LITERAL QUESTIONS

1a. At what time of day has Benvolio seen Romeo? (an hour before dawn)

2a. What does Montague say that Romeo does at dawn? (He comes home and locks himself in a darkened room.)

INFERENTIAL QUESTIONS

1b. How do night walks seem appropriate to Romeo's mood? (He is gloomy, literally and emotionally.)

2b. What kind of father does Montague seem to be? (He seems loving, caring, and concerned.)

[MONTAGUE *and* LADY MONTAGUE *leave.*]

BENVOLIO. Good morrow,[34] cousin.

ROMEO. Is the day so young?

BENVOLIO. But new struck nine.

ROMEO. Ay me! Sad hours seem long.
Was that my father that went hence so fast?

BENVOLIO. It was. What sadness lengthens Romeo's hours?

ROMEO. Not having that which having makes them short.

2 BENVOLIO. In love?

ROMEO. Out—

BENVOLIO. Of love?

ROMEO. Out of her favor where I am in love.

BENVOLIO. Alas that love, so gentle in his view,[35]
Should be so tyrannous and rough in proof!

ROMEO. Alas that love, whose view is muffled still,[36]
Should without eyes see pathways to his will!
3 Where shall we dine? O me! What fray was here?
Yet tell me not, for I have heard it all.

34 **Good morrow:** Good morning.

35 **love . . . view:** Cupid, the god of love, was pictured as a child—therefore, gentle in appearance.

36 **view . . . still:** Cupid is pictured as being blindfolded; thus the source of the expression, "Love is blind."

AT A GLANCE

Scene i (continued): Romeo confides to Benvolio that he is in love.

1 STYLE: BLANK VERSE

Benvolio's and Romeo's lines taken together make up the five feet of the line: The iambic pentameter interlocks the two friends.

2 PLOT: EXPOSITION

We learn that Romeo is in love and that his love is not returned. Benvolio's ability to finish Romeo's sentences reiterates their close friendship.

3 READING SKILLS: INFERENCE

We can infer Romeo's distractedness as he moves rapidly between subjects: the nature of love, dining, the brawl.

GUIDED READING

LITERAL QUESTION

1a. What question does Benvolio ask Romeo? (He asks what is making Romeo sad.)

INFERENTIAL QUESTION

1b. What kind of relationship do Benvolio and Romeo seem to have? (close friendship)

AT A GLANCE

- *Scene i (continued):* Romeo rails at love, which brings only pain.
- Benvolio asks for the name of Romeo's lady, but Romeo refuses to disclose it.

1 MAIN IDEA

In a series of paradoxical remarks, Romeo claims that love and hate can be bound together, thus love can become a travesty of itself.

2 CHARACTERIZATION

As Romeo tells Benvolio that the latter's loving concern only adds to his own sorrows, Romeo displays the sort of moroseness that has elicited his parents' concern.

3 STYLE: METAPHOR

Romeo defines love in a series of metaphors that has led some Shakespearean scholars to remark that he is "in love with love."

4 CHARACTERIZATION

Romeo feels lost, which he stresses by speaking of himself in the third person.

5 PLOT: SUSPENSE

Romeo's intense unhappiness and his secrecy about the object of his love increases our interest in his predicament.

1 Here's much to do with hate, but more with love.[37]
Why then, O brawling love, O loving hate,
O anything, of nothing first created!
O heavy lightness, serious vanity,
Misshapen chaos of well-seeming forms,
Feather of lead, bright smoke, cold fire, sick health,
Still-waking sleep, that is not what it is!
This love feel I, that feel no love in this.[38]
Dost thou not laugh?

BENVOLIO. No, coz,[39] I rather weep.

ROMEO. Good heart, at what?

BENVOLIO. At thy good heart's oppression.

2 ROMEO. Why, such is love's transgression.
Griefs of mine own lie heavy in my breast,
Which thou wilt propagate, to have it prest
With more of thine.[40] This love that thou hast shown
Doth add more grief to too much of mine own.
Love is a smoke made with the fume of sighs;
Being purged, a fire sparkling in lovers' eyes;
Being vexed, a sea nourished with loving tears.
3 What is it else? A madness most discreet,
A choking gall,[41] and a preserving sweet.
Farewell, my coz.

BENVOLIO. Soft![42] I will go along.
And if you leave me so, you do me wrong.

4 ROMEO. Tut! I have lost myself; I am not here;
This is not Romeo, he's some other where.

BENVOLIO. Tell me in sadness,[43] who is that you love?

ROMEO. What, shall I groan and tell thee?

5 BENVOLIO. Groan? Why, no;
But sadly tell me who.

ROMEO. Bid a sick man in sadness make his will.
Ah, word ill urged to one that is so ill!
In sadness, cousin, I do love a woman.

BENVOLIO. I aimed so near when I supposed you loved.

ROMEO. A right good markman. And she's fair I love.

BENVOLIO. A right fair mark,[44] fair coz, is soonest hit.

37 **Here's much . . . love:** The feu[d] started with hatred but continues because of loyalty to family and the love of fighting. Romeo goes on to show his belief that all love is a contradiction.

38 **This love . . . this:** I feel no happiness in this love.

39 **coz:** cousin.

40 **Which thou . . . thine:** Burdenin[g] you with my grief will increase my sorrow.

41 **gall:** bitter liquid.

42 **Soft!:** Wait a minute!

43 **in sadness:** seriously.

44 **right fair mark:** target that is easily seen.

GUIDED READING

LITERAL QUESTIONS

1a. How does Romeo claim to feel about his new love? (He feels no happiness in it.)

2a. What is Romeo's answer when Benvolio asks him whom he loves? (*a woman*)

INFERENTIAL QUESTIONS

1b. Why is he so unhappy? (The love is not returned; he has discovered that love has a darker side.)

2b. Why does Romeo give this answer? (He is teasing Benvolio to avoid having to tell his love's name.)

ROMEO. Well, in that hit you miss. She'll not be hit
With Cupid's arrow. She hath Dian's wit,[45]
And, in strong proof[46] of chastity well armed,
From Love's weak childish bow she lives uncharmed.
She will not stay[47] the siege of loving terms,
Nor bide th' encounter of assailing eyes,
Nor ope her lap to saint-seducing gold.
O, she is rich in beauty; only poor
That, when she dies, with beauty dies her store.[48]
She hath forsworn to[49] love, and in that vow
Do I live dead that live to tell it now.

BENVOLIO. Be ruled by me; forget to think of her.

ROMEO. O, teach me how I should forget to think!

BENVOLIO. By giving liberty unto thine eyes.
Examine other beauties.

ROMEO. 'Tis the way
To call hers, exquisite, in question more.[50]
These happy masks[51] that kiss fair ladies' brows,
Being black puts us in mind they hide the fair.
He that is strucken blind cannot forget
The precious treasure of his eyesight lost.
Show me a mistress that is passing fair:
What doth her beauty serve but as a note
Where I may read who passed that passing fair?[52]
Farewell. Thou canst not teach me to forget.

BENVOLIO. I'll pay that doctrine, or else die in debt.[53]

[They exit.]

45 **Dian's wit:** the wisdom of Diana, Roman goddess of chastity.
46 **proof:** armor.
47 **stay:** put up with.
48 **with . . . store:** She will die without children, and, therefore, her beauty will die with her.
49 **forsworn to:** sworn not to.
50 **'Tis . . . more:** Seeing other women only convinces me that she is most beautiful.
51 **masks:** Fashionable Elizabethan women sometimes wore black masks to protect fair complexions from the sun.
52 **passed . . . fair:** is even more fair.
53 **I'll . . . debt:** I will teach you to forget or die owing you a lesson.

Scene ii. *Later that afternoon. A street near* CAPULET'S *house in Verona.*

[CAPULET *enters with* COUNT PARIS, *a young relative of the* PRINCE, *and with a* SERVANT. *They speak of the feud and of the* PRINCE'S *warning against further public fighting, but the topic soon changes to the request that* PARIS *has made for permission to marry* JULIET, CAPULET'S *daughter.*]

CAPULET. But Montague is bound as well as I,
In penalty alike; and 'tis not hard, I think,
For men so old as we to keep the peace.

AT A GLANCE

- *Scene i (continued):* Romeo tells Benvolio that the woman he loves has sworn a vow of chastity.
- *Scene ii:* Later that day, Capulet speaks with Count Paris, a suitor for Juliet's hand.

1 CHARACTERIZATION

Romeo's comparing his love to chaste Diana, the Roman goddess, suggests his tendency to glorify and exaggerate.

2 PLOT: FORESHADOWING

Benvolio suggests that Romeo look for someone else. Although Romeo dismisses the suggestion, he will soon find Juliet.

3 CHARACTERIZATION

The youthful Romeo imagines that he will always remember the unattainable lover as the only true beauty.

4 THEME

Capulet seems committed to keeping the peace and patching the feud. He seems ignorant of the fact that the "old" men who started the feud have planted their hateful passions in younger family members.

GUIDED READING

LITERAL QUESTION

1a. How does Romeo describe his beloved? (chaste, virtuous, and impervious to passion; *Love's weak childish bow.*)

INFERENTIAL QUESTION

1b. How does he feel about his beloved's supposed commitment to remain chaste? (He seems almost proud of his own hopeless devotion.)

AT A GLANCE

- *Scene ii (continued):* Capulet contemplates the betrothal of his daughter Juliet to Paris.
- He invites Paris to a ball that evening.
- He gives a written invitation list for his servant to deliver.

1 PLOT: EXPOSITION

Juliet is thirteen years old and may not be ready for marriage for two more years.

2 CHARACTERIZATION

Capulet shows his sensitivity and caring for Juliet by stating that she must consent to the marriage; he points out that she is his only child and especially dear to him.

3 STYLE: IMAGERY

Lovely women, described here as stars, bring light to darkness, much as love brings joy to life.

PARIS. Of honorable reckoning[1] are you both,
And pity 'tis you lived at odds so long.
But now, my lord, what say you to my suit?

CAPULET. But saying o'er what I have said before:
1 My child is yet a stranger in the world,
She hath not seen the change of fourteen years;
Let two more summers wither in their pride
Ere we may think her ripe to be a bride.

PARIS. Younger than she are happy mothers made.

CAPULET. And too soon marred are those so early made.
2 Earth hath swallowèd all my hopes but she;[2]
She is the hopeful lady of my earth.[3]
But woo her, gentle Paris, get her heart;
My will to her consent is but a part.
And she agreed[4] within her scope of choice[5]
Lies my consent and fair according[6] voice.
This night I hold an old accustomed feast,
Whereto I have invited many a guest,
Such as I love; and you among the store,
One more, most welcome, makes my number more.
3 At my poor house look to behold this night
Earth-treading stars[7] that make dark heaven light.
Such comfort as do lusty young men feel
When well-appareled April on the heel
Of limping Winter treads, even such delight
Among fresh fennel buds shall you this night
Inherit at my house.[8] Hear all, all see,
And like her most whose merit most shall be;
Which, on more view of many, mine, being one,
May stand in number, though in reck'ning none.[9]
Come, go with me.

[CAPULET *speaks to his* SERVANT *and hands him a piece of paper that contains the names of the people he is inviting to his party.*]

Go, sirrah,[10] trudge about
Through fair Verona; find those persons out
Whose names are written there, and to them say
My house and welcome on their pleasure stay.

[CAPULET *and* PARIS *leave. The* SERVANT, *who cannot read, looks at the paper.*]

1 **reckoning:** reputation.

2 **Earth hath . . . she:** She is my only surviving child.

3 **my earth:** my flesh and blood.

4 **And she agreed:** if she agrees. At the time parents arranged marriages. Capulet is unusual in looking for Juliet's approval.

5 **within . . . choice:** with her decision.

6 **according:** agreeing

7 **Earth-treading stars:** young women.

8 **Such comfort . . . house:** Tonight the pleasure you will take at my home is like the joy that young men feel when spring replaces winter.

9 **in reck'ning none:** not worth considering. Capulet suggests that Paris may change his mind about Juliet when he has compared her to other women.

10 **sirrah:** a term of address used when speaking to someone who is younger or inferior in rank.

GUIDED READING

LITERAL QUESTION

1a. How many daughters does Capulet have? (one)

INFERENTIAL QUESTION

1b. Why is Capulet being so cautious about his daughter's marriage? (He seems concerned for her lasting happiness.)

SERVANT. Find them out whose names are written here? It is written that the shoemaker should meddle with his yard and the tailor with his last, the fisher with his pencil and the painter with his nets;[11] but I am sent to find those persons whose names are here writ, and can never find what names the writing person hath here writ. I must to the learned. In good time![12]

[ROMEO *and* BENVOLIO *enter, still talking about* ROMEO'S *unhappiness in love.*]

BENVOLIO. Tut, man, one fire burns out another's burning;
One pain is less'ned by another's anguish;
Turn giddy, and be holp[13] by backward turning;
One desperate grief cures with another's languish.
Take thou some new infection to thy eye,
And the rank poison of the old will die.

ROMEO. Your plantain leaf[14] is excellent for that.

BENVOLIO. For what, I pray thee?

ROMEO. For your broken shin.

BENVOLIO. Why, Romeo, art thou mad?

ROMEO. Not mad, but bound more than a madman is;
Shut up in prison, kept without my food,
Whipped and tormented and—God-den,[15] good fellow.

SERVANT. God gi'[16] god-den. I pray, sir, can you read?

ROMEO. Ay, mine own fortune in my misery.

SERVANT. Perhaps you have learned it without book.
But, I pray, can you read anything you see?

ROMEO. Ay, if I know the letters and the language.

SERVANT. Ye say honestly. Rest you merry.[17]

ROMEO. Stay, fellow; I can read. [*He reads.*]
"Signior Martino and his wife and daughters;
County[18] Anselm and his beauteous sisters;
The lady widow of Vitruvio;
Signior Placentio and his lovely nieces;
Mercutio and his brother Valentine;
Mine uncle Capulet, his wife and daughters;
My fair niece Rosaline; Livia;
Signior Valentio and his cousin Tybalt;

11 **the shoemaker . . . nets:** The servant shows his ignorance by mixing up types of workers and their tools. He means that people should stick to what they do best.

12 **In good time!:** Just in time! He sees learned men arrive just when he needs them.

13 **holp:** helped.

14 **plantain leaf:** leaf used as a bandage to stop bleeding.

15 **God-den:** "Good afternoon" or "Good evening."

16 **God gi':** God give you.

17 **Rest you merry:** May you be happy. The servant missed Romeo's joke and starts to leave.

18 **County:** count.

AT A GLANCE

- *Scene ii (continued):* The illiterate servant shows the list to Romeo and Benvolio.
- Romeo reads the guest list to him.

1 STYLE: PROSE

Unlike the more "noble" characters, the servant does not speak in blank or rhymed verse, but in prose. This shows his lower station and identifies his concerns as comic or trivial rather than tragic.

2 STYLE: METAPHOR

Through a series of comparisons, Benvolio tries to show Romeo how to get over his unrequited love: Let a new grief erase the memory of an old one.

3 CHARACTERIZATION

Romeo's sense of humor (especially his facility at wordplay) emerges in this banter with the servant.

GUIDED READING

LITERAL QUESTION

1a. Which women are invited to the party? (Martino's daughters; Count Anselm's sisters; the widow of Vitruvio; Placentio's nieces; Capulet's nieces, including Rosaline and Livia)

INFERENTIAL QUESTION

1b. What does the guest list tell us about the type of party Capulet is planning? (It will be a large, important gathering, well attended by many Capulet relatives.)

AT A GLANCE

- *Scene ii (continued):* The servant invites Romeo and Benvolio to the party.
- Benvolio urges Romeo to attend in order to compare his love, Rosaline, to other women; Romeo agrees to go.
- *Scene iii:* Lady Capulet and the Nurse enter a Capulet room.

1 PLOT: CONFLICT

The servant's invitation explicitly repeats the terms of the dramatic conflict: Montagues and Capulets will not welcome one another.

2 STYLE: RHYME

Most of this dialogue between Romeo and Benvolio is written in rhyming couplets. The contrast between light banter and more serious conversations, which are written in blank verse, is further emphasized.

3 STAGING

A room in Capulet's house might actually be shown in a different portion of the stage; or stagehands or actors might carry on props such as tables and candlesticks to show that the scene has changed to an interior room.

Lucio and the lively Helena.''
A fair assembly. Whither[19] should they come?

SERVANT. Up.

ROMEO. Whither? To supper?

SERVANT. To our house.

ROMEO. Whose house?

SERVANT. My master's.

ROMEO. Indeed I should have asked you that before.

1 **SERVANT.** Now I'll tell you without asking. My master is the great rich Capulet; and if you be not of the house of Montagues, I pray come and crush a cup[20] of wine. Rest you merry.

[*The* SERVANT *leaves.*]

BENVOLIO. At this same ancient[21] feast of Capulet's
Sups the fair Rosaline whom thou so loves;
With all the admired beauties of Verona.
Go thither, and with unattainted eye[22]
Compare her face with some that I shall show,
And I will make thee think thy swan a crow.

ROMEO. One fairer than my love? The all-seeing sun
Ne'er saw her match since first the world begun.

2 **BENVOLIO.** Tut! you saw her fair, none else being by,
Herself poised[23] with herself in either eye;
But in that crystal scales[24] let there be weighed
Your lady's love against some other maid
That I will show you shining at this feast,
And she shall scant[25] show well that now seems best.

ROMEO. I'll go along, no such sight to be shown,
But to rejoice in splendor of mine own.[26]

[*They exit.*]

19 **Whither:** where

20 **crush a cup:** have a drink.

21 **ancient:** customary, traditional.

22 **Go . . . eye:** Go there, and with impartial eye.

23 **poised:** balanced.

24 **crystal scales:** Romeo's eyes.

25 **scant:** scarcely.

26 **in splendor of mine own:** in the beauty of my own fair lady (Rosaline).

3 ***Scene iii. Later that evening, before the party. A room in*** CAPULET'S ***house.***

[LADY CAPULET *and the Capulets'* NURSE *enter.*]

LADY CAPULET. Nurse, where's my daughter? Call her forth to me.

GUIDED READING

LITERAL QUESTION

1a. What does Benvolio want Romeo to do? (come to the party to meet women other than Rosaline)

INFERENTIAL QUESTION

1b. Why does Benvolio want Romeo to meet other women? (He wants to relieve Romeo's morbid obsession with Rosaline.)

NURSE. I bade her come. What, lamb! What, ladybird!
Where's this girl? What, Juliet!

[JULIET *enters.*]

JULIET. How now? Who calls?

NURSE. Your mother.

JULIET. Madam, I am here.
What is your will?

1 LADY CAPULET. This is the matter—Nurse, give leave[1] awhile;
We must talk in secret. Nurse, come back again.
I have rememb'red me; thou's hear our counsel.[2]
Thou knowest my daughter's of a pretty age.

NURSE. Faith, I can tell her age unto an hour.

LADY CAPULET. She's not fourteen.

2 NURSE. I'll lay fourteen of my teeth—
And yet, to my teen[3] be it spoken, I have but four—
She's not fourteen. How long is it now
To Lammastide?[4]

LADY CAPULET. A fortnight and odd days.[5]

1 **give leave:** leave us alone.

2 **thou's hear our counsel:** you should hear our conversation.

3 **teen:** sorrow.

4 **Lammastide:** August 1, a religious feast day.

5 **A fortnight . . . days:** two weeks plus a few days.

AT A GLANCE

- *Scene iii (continued):* Lady Capulet asks the Nurse how old her daughter Juliet is as Juliet listens.

1 CHARACTERIZATION

Lady Capulet's first impulse is to dismiss the Nurse, but (because the Nurse is so close to Juliet) she changes her mind and asks her to stay.

2 CHARACTERIZATION

Comic associations such as this immediately establish the Nurse as an attractive character who can provide comic relief.

GUIDED READING

LITERAL QUESTION

1a. What nicknames does the nurse use to call Juliet? (*lamb, ladybird, this girl*)

INFERENTIAL QUESTION

1b. What relationship do these names suggest? (familiarity, love, a difference in ages)

AT A GLANCE

- *Scene iii (continued):* Lady Capulet asks Juliet if she has ever thought of marriage.
- Lady Capulet urges Juliet to look carefully at Paris this evening and to consider his proposal of marriage.

1 SETTING

The month is July, based on the reference to Lammastide. Summer seems an appropriate month for this love story, much of which is set outdoors in warm summer nights.

2 STYLE: WORD CHOICE

Some form of the word "marry" appears several times on this page—as an exclamation, as a reference to marriage itself, and as a metaphor for harmony.

3 STYLE: METAPHOR

Paris is compared to a book lacking only a cover, or wife. The word *unbound* contrasts Paris and Romeo, who in the previous scene described himself as "bound" by love.

1 NURSE. Even or odd, of all days in the year,
Come Lammas Eve at night shall she be fourteen.
Susan and she (God rest all Christian souls!)
Were of an age.[6] Well, Susan is with God;
She was too good for me. But, as I said,
On Lammas Eve at night shall she be fourteen;
That shall she, marry; I remember it well.
'Tis since the earthquake now eleven years;
Thou wast the prettiest babe that e'er I nursed.
And I might live to see thee married once,
I have my wish.

LADY CAPULET. Marry, that "marry" is the very theme
I came to talk of. Tell me, daughter Juliet,
How stands your dispositions to be married?

JULIET. It is an honor that I dream not of.

LADY CAPULET. Well, think of marriage now. Younger than you,
Here in Verona, ladies of esteem,
Are made already mothers. By my count,
I was your mother much upon these years[7]
That you are now a maid. Thus then in brief:
The valiant Paris seeks you for his love.

NURSE. A man, young lady! Lady, such a man
As all the world— Why, he's a man of wax.[8]

LADY CAPULET. Verona's summer hath not such a flower.

NURSE. Nay, he's a flower, in faith—a very flower.

LADY CAPULET. What say you? Can you love the gentleman?
This night you shall behold him at our feast.
Read o'er the volume[9] of young Paris' face,
And find delight writ there with beauty's pen;
2 Examine every married lineament,[10]
And see how one another lends content;
And what obscured in this fair volume lies
Find written in the margent[11] of his eyes.
3 This precious book of love, this unbound lover,
To beautify him only lacks a cover.[12]
The fish lives in the sea, and 'tis much pride
For fair without the fair within to hide.
That book in many's eyes doth share the glory,
That in gold clasps locks in the golden story;
So shall you share all that he doth possess,
By having him making yourself no less.

6 **of an age:** The nurse had a daughter, now dead, who was the same age as Juliet.

7 **much . . . years:** at about your age.

8 **man of wax:** a model man, perfect like a wax statue.

9 **volume:** book; in the following lines Paris' face is compared to a book that Juliet can read in order to get to know him.

10 **every married lineament:** all the harmonious features of his face.

11 **margent:** margin; his eyes, like marginal notes in a book, will reveal whatever is not clear in the rest of his face.

12 **cover:** Paris lacks only a wife, compared to a book's binding.

GUIDED READING

LITERAL QUESTION

1a. How does the nurse praise Paris? (She calls him a model man, a "flower.")

INFERENTIAL QUESTION

1b. What does the nurse seem to want Juliet to do? (marry Paris)

Speak briefly, can you like of Paris' love?

JULIET. I'll look to like, if looking liking move;[13]
But no more deep will I endart mine eye
Than your consent gives strength to make it fly.[14]

[*A* SERVANT *enters.*]

SERVINGMAN. Madam, the guests are come, supper served up, you called, my young lady asked for, the nurse cursed[15] in the pantry, and everything in extremity. I must hence to wait. I beseech you follow straight.

[*The* SERVANT *leaves.*]

LADY CAPULET. We follow thee. Juliet, the County stays.[16]

[*They exit.*]

13 **I'll . . . move:** I'll try to like him if his appearance is pleasing.

14 **But . . . fly:** I will be no more serious about Paris than you advise.

15 **the nurse cursed:** The other servants are angry with the nurse because she is not helping them to prepare for the party.

16 **the County stays:** The Count (Paris) is waiting.

Scene iv. Later that night. A street in Verona.

[ROMEO *enters with his friends* MERCUTIO *and* BENVOLIO. *They are on their way to* CAPULET'S *party; they wear masks to conceal their identities because* ROMEO *and* BENVOLIO *are Montagues. As they walk along, they joke and play with words. Several other* MASKERS *and* TORCHBEARERS *accompany them. Maskers, usually young men, could arrive at a party even without being invited and expect hospitality.*]

ROMEO. Give me a torch. I am not for this ambling.
Being but heavy,[1] I will bear the light.

MERCUTIO. Nay, gentle Romeo, we must have you dance.

ROMEO. Not I, believe me. You have dancing shoes
With nimble soles; I have a soul of lead
So stakes me to the ground I cannot move.

MERCUTIO. You are a lover. Borrow Cupid's wings
And soar with them above a common bound.[2]

ROMEO. I am too sore enpiercèd with his shaft[3]
To soar with his light feathers; and so bound
I cannot bound a pitch[4] above dull woe.
Under love's heavy burden do I sink.

MERCUTIO. And, to sink in it, should you burden love—
Too great oppression for a tender thing.

ROMEO. Is love a tender thing? It is too rough,
Too rude, too boist'rous.

1 **heavy:** sad; weighted down with sorrow.

2 **bound:** leap; part of a dance.

3 **empiercèd . . . shaft:** wounded with Cupid's arrow.

4 **a pitch:** any height.

AT A GLANCE

- *Scene iii (continued):* Juliet says she will be ruled by her mother's wishes.
- A servant announces that the party is beginning.
- *Scene iv:* Romeo, Mercutio, and others proceed to Capulet's party.

1 CHARACTERIZATION

Juliet seems more interested in pleasing her mother than in pursuing any love affair.

2 CHARACTERIZATION

Romeo's melancholy mood persists; Shakespeare uses strong imagery (*soul of lead*) to suggest Romeo's emotional burden.

3 STYLE: WORD CHOICE

Romeo and Mercutio indulge in yet more punning and wordplay with the word *bound.*

GUIDED READING

LITERAL QUESTION

1a. How often has Juliet spoken in Scene iii? Does she speak at length or briefly? (She speaks only four times, and briefly.)

INFERENTIAL QUESTION

1b. What impression do we have of Juliet? (She is childlike, obedient, innocent, shy.)

AT A GLANCE

- *Scene iv (continued):* To raise Romeo's spirits, Mercutio relates a story about Queen Mab.

1 CHARACTERIZATION

Mercutio refuses to wear a mask, saying he doesn't care how he is seen. In contrast to Romeo, he seems both confident and *not* self-involved.

2 STYLE: RHYME

The use of rhyme here (*I*/*lie*) ties the banter of Romeo and Mercutio together. Note, also, the pun on the word *lie*.

3 VOCABULARY: CONNOTATION

Queen Mab is a "midwife" to humans in the sense that she helps give birth to dreams.

4 STYLE: IMAGERY

Mab's chariot and company is pictured as being made of common and natural objects of the day. The interplay of day and night, light and dark, is echoed throughout the play.

MERCUTIO. If love be rough with you, be rough with love.
Give me a case to put my visage[5] in.
1 A visor for a visor![6] What care I
What curious eye doth quote[7] deformities?
Here are the beetle brows[8] shall blush for me.

BENVOLIO. Come, knock and enter; and no sooner in
But every man betake him to his legs.[9]

ROMEO. A torch for me! Let wantons light of heart
Tickle the senseless rushes with their heels;[10]
For I am proverbed with a grandsire phrase,[11]
I'll be a candleholder[12] and look on;
The game was ne'er so fair, and I am done.[13]
I dreamt a dream tonight.[14]

2 MERCUTIO. And so did I.

ROMEO. Well, what was yours?

MERCUTIO. That dreamers often lie.

ROMEO. In bed asleep, while they do dream things true.

[*As* ROMEO *speaks with his friends, the* MASKERS *and* TORCHBEARERS *march about the stage.* MERCUTIO *continues trying to cheer* ROMEO. *He uses* ROMEO'S *mention of his dream to make a long speech about Queen Mab. Queen Mab is a queen of fairies who causes sleepers to dream. Mercutio describes her and the kinds of dreams she sends to different people.*]

MERCUTIO. O, then I see Queen Mab[15] hath been with you.
3 She is the fairies' midwife, and she comes
In shape no bigger than an agate stone[16]
On the forefinger of an alderman,
Drawn with a team of little atomies[17]
Over men's noses as they lie asleep;
4 Her wagon spokes made of long spinners'[18] legs,
The cover, of the wings of grasshoppers;
Her traces,[19] of the smallest spider web;
Her collars, of the moonshine's wat'ry beams;
Her whip, of cricket's bone; the lash, of film;[20]
Her wagoner, a small gray-coated gnat,
Not half so big as a round little worm
Pricked from the lazy finger of a maid;[21]
Her chariot is an empty hazelnut,
Made by the joiner[22] squirrel or old grub,

5 **visage:** mask.
6 **visor . . . visor:** mask for my mask. Because his face is a mask, Mercutio will not wear one. (He was invited to the party.)
7 **quote:** make note of.
8 **beetle brows:** overhanging eyebrows.
9 **betake . . . legs:** begin to dance.
10 **Let . . . heels:** Let the happy ones dance on straw mats.
11 **proverbed . . . phrase:** guided by an old saying.
12 **candleholder:** spectator.
13 **The game . . . done:** I give up dancing no matter how pleasant it may be.
14 **tonight:** last night.
15 **Queen Mab:** the fairy queen.
16 **agate stone:** gem set in a ring.
17 **little atomies:** tiny creatures.
18 **spinners:** spiders.
19 **traces:** harness.
20 **film:** spider's thread.
21 **worm . . . maid:** Worms were said to grow in the fingers of lazy maids.
22 **joiner:** carpenter.

GUIDED READING

LITERAL QUESTIONS

1a. What does Romeo intend to be at the party? (a candleholder)

2a. How does Mab travel? (in a tiny chariot pulled by creatures as small as motes of dust, steered by a gnat)

INFERENTIAL QUESTIONS

1b. Why will Romeo not take part in the pleasure of the evening? (He is lovelorn.)

2b. What reasons do we have for liking Mercutio? (He is quick-witted, imaginative, expressive, and compassionate.)

Time out o'mind the fairies' coachmakers.
And in this state[23] she gallops night by night
Through lovers' brains, and then they dream of love;
On courtiers' knees, that dream on curtsies straight;
O'er lawyers' fingers, who straight dream on fees;
O'er ladies' lips, who straight on kisses dream,
Which oft the angry Mab with blisters plagues,
Because their breath with sweetmeats[24] tainted are.
Sometime she gallops o'er a courtier's nose,
And then dreams he of smelling out a suit;[25]
1 And sometime comes she with a tithe pig's[26] tail
Tickling a parson's nose as 'a lies asleep,
Then he dreams of another benefice.[27]
Sometime she driveth o'er a soldier's neck,
And then dreams he of cutting foreign throats,

23 **state:** majestic style.

24 **sweetmeats:** sweets.

25 **smelling . . . suit:** having someone pay him for his influence with the king.
26 **tithe pig:** a pig given to a parson as a contribution. Parishioners were expected to contribute a tenth (tithe) of their earnings to the church.
27 **benefice:** church appointment with an assured income.

AT A GLANCE

Scene iv (continued): Mercutio describes the dreams Mab brings.

1 CHARACTERIZATION

Mercutio shows himself to be a sharp-witted cynic when he portrays the parson as more concerned with benefices than with spiritual matters.

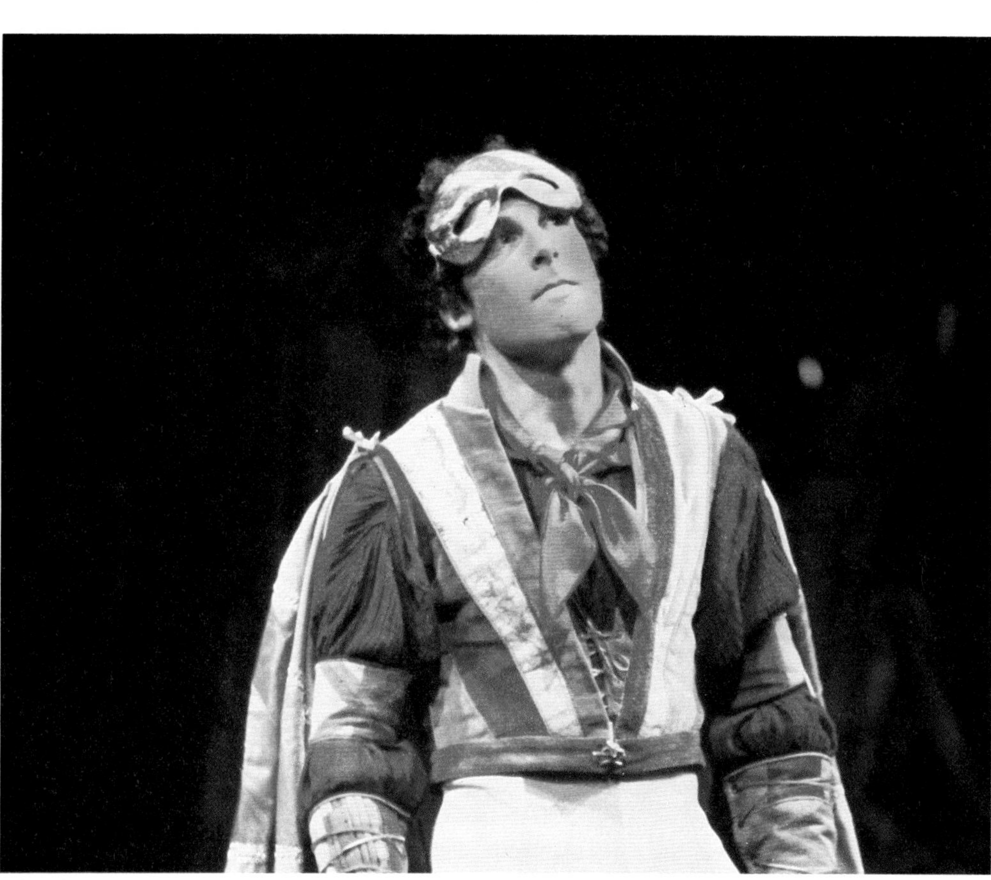

GUIDED READING

LITERAL QUESTION

1a. How does Mab influence the dreams of her victims? (She gallops over the part of their body that they are to dream about.)

INFERENTIAL QUESTION

1b. What mood is conveyed by this story? (The Mab story is fanciful and playful.)

AT A GLANCE

- *Scene iv (continued):* Romeo and Benvolio urge Mercutio to be quiet so as not to make them late.
- *Scene v:* At Capulet's house, the party is in progress.

1 MOOD

Mercutio's speech, having begun with the playful image of Mab and progressing through cynical portraits of dreamers, ends with a more sober image: The renewed sleep suggests death.

2 STYLE: METAPHOR

The image of the wind's wooing of the North suggests Romeo's wooing of the frozen Rosaline.

3 PLOT: FORESHADOWING

Romeo's premonition echoes the Chorus's Prologue: The audience is reminded of the lovers' fate once again.

Of breaches, ambuscadoes,[28] Spanish blades,
Of healths[29] five fathom deep; and then anon[30]
Drums in his ear, at which he starts and wakes,
1 And being thus frighted, swears a prayer or two
And sleeps again.

ROMEO. Peace, peace Mercutio, peace!
Thou talk'st of nothing.

MERCUTIO. True, I talk of dreams;
Which are the children of an idle brain,
Begot of nothing but vain fantasy;
Which is as thin of substance as the air,
2 And more inconstant[31] than the wind, who woos
Even now the frozen bosom of the North
And, being angered, puffs away from thence,
Turning his side to the dew-dropping South.

BENVOLIO. This wind you talk of blows us from ourselves.
Supper is done, and we shall come too late.

3 ROMEO. I fear, too early; for my mind misgives
Some consequence yet hanging in the stars[32]
Shall bitterly begin his fearful date[33]
With this night's revels and expire the term
Of a despisèd life, closed in my breast,
By some vile forfeit of untimely death.[34]
But he that hath the steerage of my course
Direct my sail! On, lusty gentlemen!

BENVOLIO. Strike, drum.

[*They march about the stage and exit.*]

28 **ambuscadoes:** ambushes.
29 **healths:** drinking toasts.
30 **anon:** at once.
31 **inconstant:** fickle, changing.
32 **misgives . . . stars:** fears a chain of events still being arranged by the stars.
33 **date:** time, duration.
34 **expire . . . death:** Romeo is afraid that something that happens tonight will lead to his death. He compares a short life to a loan that comes due too soon.

Scene v. *Immediately following the previous scene. A hall in* CAPULET'S *house.*

[SERVANTS *enter carrying napkins. They are clearing away the tables from dinner and making the hall ready for dancing. This is the party at which* JULIET *plans to notice* PARIS. ROMEO *is looking for Rosaline, while* BENVOLIO *hopes to show him a beautiful woman who will cause him to forget Rosaline.*]

FIRST SERVINGMAN. Where's Potpan, that he helps not to take away?[1] He shift a trencher![2] He scrape a trencher!

1 **take away:** clean up after dinner.
2 **trencher:** wooden platter.

GUIDED READING

LITERAL QUESTIONS

1a. In Mercutio's opinion, what produces dreams? (*an idle brain, vain fantasy*)

2a. What does Romeo fear? (something that will lead to his untimely death)

INFERENTIAL QUESTIONS

1b. How would you describe Mercutio's opinion of dreams? (He seems gently scornful of both dreams and dreamers.)

2b. What is Romeo's attitude toward his fears? (He seems to accept his fate, saying ". . . he that hath the steerage of my course/Direct my sail!"; *i.e.*, let fate take its course.)

SECOND SERVINGMAN. When good manners shall lie all in one or two men's hands, and they unwashed too, 'tis a foul thing.

FIRST SERVINGMAN. Away with the join-stools,[3] remove the court cupboard,[4] look to the plate.[5] Good thou, save me a piece of marchpane,[6] and, as thou loves me, let the porter let in Susan Grindstone and Nell. Anthony, and Potpan!

SECOND SERVINGMAN. Ay, boy, ready.

FIRST SERVINGMAN. You are looked for and called for, asked for and sought for, in the great chamber.

THIRD SERVINGMAN. We cannot be here and there too. Cheerly, boys! Be brisk awhile, and the longer liver take all.[7]

[The SERVANTS *retire to the back.* CAPULET *enters with* LADY CAPULET, JULIET, TYBALT, *and other* CAPULETS, *the* NURSE, *and all the* GUESTS. *The* MASKERS *join the group.]*

CAPULET. Welcome, gentlemen! Ladies that have their toes
Unplagued with corns will walk a bout[8] with you.
Ah, my mistresses, which of you all
1 Will now deny to dance? She that makes dainty,[9]
She I'll swear hath corns. Am I come near ye now?[10]

*[*CAPULET *notices the* MASKERS *and speaks to them.]*

Welcome, gentlemen! I have seen the day
That I have worn a visor and could tell
A whispering tale in a fair lady's ear,
Such as would please. 'Tis gone, 'tis gone, 'tis gone.
2 You are welcome, gentlemen! Come, musicians, play.

[Music plays, and the GUESTS *dance.]*

A hall, a hall! Give room![11] And foot it, girls.
More light, you knaves, and turn the tables up,
And quench the fire; the room is grown too hot.
Ah, sirrah, this unlooked-for sport[12] comes well.
Nay, sit; nay, sit, good cousin Capulet;
For you and I are past our dancing days.
How long is't now since last yourself and I
Were in a mask?

SECOND CAPULET. By'r Lady, thirty years.

CAPULET. What, man? 'Tis not so much, 'tis not so much;
'Tis since the nuptial[13] of Lucentio,
Come Pentecost[14] as quickly as it will,
Some five-and-twenty years, and then we masked.

3 **join-stools:** sturdy stools made by a joiner, or carpenter.
4 **court cupboard:** cabinet that holds linen, silver, and china.
5 **plate:** silver-plated utensils.
6 **marchpane:** marzipan, a sweet made of sugar and almonds.

7 **longer . . . all:** The last survivor takes all.

8 **walk a bout:** dance.

9 **makes dainty:** pretends to be shy.

10 **Am I . . . now:** Have I eliminated your excuses for not dancing?

11 **A hall . . . room:** Clear the hall! Make room for dancing!

12 **unlooked-for sport:** The maskers were unexpected.

13 **nuptial:** wedding.

14 **Pentecost:** seventh Sunday after Easter.

AT A GLANCE

- *Scene v (continued):* Dinner being over, the hall is prepared for dancing.
- Capulet welcomes the masked young men to his party.

1 CHARACTERIZATION

Capulet teases his guests in a good-humored way that helps to set a mood of fellowship and cheer and contrasts strongly with the previous one of foreboding.

2 BACKGROUND

Elizabethan musicians played string and wind instruments whose sounds were muted, not brassy.

GUIDED READING

LITERAL QUESTION

1a. When the servants have made the hall ready, who enters besides the Capulet family? (invited guests and the masked young men)

INFERENTIAL QUESTION

1b. Among the invited guests, what man and woman would we see onstage, even though neither is specifically named? (Count Paris and Rosaline)

AT A GLANCE

- *Scene v (continued):* Romeo falls in love with Juliet.
- Tybalt recognizes Romeo and becomes enraged.
- Capulet forbids Tybalt to fight.

1 STAGING

Romeo first glances at Juliet as she dances with someone else (possibly Count Paris).

2 PLOT: RISING ACTION

Romeo's love for Juliet takes the place of his now forgotten love for Rosaline.

3 THEME

In the privacy of his house, Capulet is temperate and wise once again—a responsible individual who maintains both the festive mood of his party and the public order.

SECOND CAPULET. 'Tis more, 'tis more. His son is elder, sir;
His son is thirty.

CAPULET. Will you tell me that?
His son was but a ward[15] two years ago.

[ROMEO *has been watching* JULIET *and stops a* SERVANT *to ask about her.*]

1 ROMEO. What lady's that which doth enrich the hand
Of yonder knight?

SERVINGMAN. I know not, sir.

ROMEO. O, she doth teach the torches to burn bright!
It seems she hangs upon the cheek of night
As a rich jewel in an Ethiop's ear—
Beauty too rich for use, for earth too dear!
So shows a snowy dove trooping with crows
As yonder lady o'er her fellows shows.
The measure done, I'll watch her place of stand[16]
And, touching hers, make blessèd my rude[17] hand.
2 Did my heart love till now? Forswear[18] it, sight!
For I ne'er saw true beauty till this night.

TYBALT. This, by his voice, should be a Montague.
Fetch me my rapier,[19] boy. What! Dares the slave
Come hither, covered with an antic face,[20]
To fleer and scorn at our solemnity?[21]
Now, by the stock and honor of my kin,
To strike him dead I hold it not a sin.

CAPULET. Why, how now, kinsman? Wherefore[22] storm you so?

TYBALT. Uncle, this is a Montague, our foe,
A villain, that is hither come in spite
To scorn at our solemnity this night.

CAPULET. Young Romeo is it?

TYBALT. 'Tis he, that villain Romeo.

CAPULET. Content thee, gentle coz,[23] let him alone.
'A bears him like a portly gentleman,[24]
3 And, to say truth, Verona brags of him
To be a virtuous and well-governed youth.
I would not for the wealth of all this town
Here in my house do him disparagement.[25]
Therefore be patient; take no note of him.
It is my will, the which if thou respect,

15 **but a ward:** only a boy.

16 **The measure . . . stand:** After this dance I will approach her.

17 **rude:** rough.

18 **Forswear:** deny.

19 **rapier:** sword.

20 **antic face:** grotesque mask.

21 **fleer . . . solemnity:** to mock our celebration.

22 **Wherefore:** why.

23 **Content . . . coz:** Be calm, cousin. *Coz* was often used for any relative.

24 **'A bears . . . gentleman:** He is behaving like a dignified gentleman.

25 **do him disparagement:** insult him.

GUIDED READING

LITERAL QUESTIONS

1a. What two comparisons does Romeo make concerning Juliet? (He compares her to a "rich jewel" and to a dove among crows.)

2a. What does Tybalt ask for when he recognizes Romeo? (a rapier)

INFERENTIAL QUESTIONS

1b. Why might Shakespeare have Romeo utter these compliments in rhymed couplets? (to emphasize his love)

2b. What sort of first impression does Tybalt make on the audience? (He seems extreme and obsessed with his hatred for the Montagues.)

Show a fair presence and put off these frowns,
And ill-beseeming semblance[26] for a feast.

TYBALT. It fits when such a villain is a guest.
I'll not endure him.

CAPULET. He shall be endured.
What, goodman boy![27] I say he shall. Go to![28]
Am I the master here, or you? Go to!
You'll not endure him, God shall mend my soul![29]
You'll make a mutiny[30] among my guests!

TYBALT. Why, uncle, 'tis a shame.

CAPULET. Go to, go to!
You are a saucy boy. Is't so, indeed?
This trick[31] may chance to scathe[32] you. I know what.
You must contrary me! Marry, 'tis time—
Well said, my hearts[33]—You are a princox[34]—go!
Be quiet, or— More light, more light!—For shame!
I'll make you quiet. What!—Cheerly, my hearts!

TYBALT. Patience perforce[35] with willful choler meeting
Makes my flesh tremble in their different greeting.
I will withdraw; but this intrusion shall,
Now seeming sweet, convert to bitt'rest gall.

[*Trembling with anger,* TYBALT *leaves. At the same time,* ROMEO *walks over to* JULIET *and speaks to her.*]

ROMEO. If I profane[36] with my unworthiest hand
This holy shrine,[37] the gentle sin is this:
My lips, two blushing pilgrims, ready stand
To smooth that rough touch with a tender kiss.

JULIET. Good pilgrim, you do wrong your hand too much,
Which mannerly devotion shows in this;
For saints have hands that pilgrims' hands do touch,
And palm to palm is holy palmers' kiss.[38]

ROMEO. Have not saints lips, and holy palmers too?

JULIET. Ay, pilgrim, lips that they must use in prayer.

ROMEO. O, then, dear saint, let lips do what hands do!
They pray; grant thou, lest faith turn to despair.

JULIET. Saints do not move, though grant for prayers' sake.[39]

ROMEO. Then move not while my prayer's effect I take.
Thus from my lips, by thine my sin is purged.

26 **ill-beseeming semblance:** inappropriate appearance.

27 **goodman boy:** an insulting term that refers to a person below the rank of gentleman.
28 **Go to:** Stop this!
29 **God . . . soul:** God save me!
30 **mutiny:** disturbance.

31 **trick:** habit.
32 **scathe:** harm.

33 **Well . . . hearts:** Capulet goes back and forth between scolding Tybalt and greeting his guests.
34 **princox:** conceited youngster.

35 **Patience perforce:** enforced self-control.

36 **profane:** treat with irreverence.

37 **shrine:** place of worship; here, Juliet's hand which Romeo now takes. In the following exchange Romeo compares Juliet to a saint and himself to a pilgrim.

38 **For saints . . . kiss:** Juliet suggests that pilgrims usually kiss by touching the palms of their hands. Pilgrims were called *palmers* because they carried palms from the Holy Land.

39 **Saints . . . sake:** Saints take part in human affairs only if they are moved by prayer.

AT A GLANCE

- *Scene v (continued):* Capulet barely keeps Tybalt under control; Tybalt vows to attack Romeo when he has the chance.
- Romeo and Juliet speak.

1 CHARACTERIZATION

Tybalt's obsession with the feud is so great that he is willing even to disobey his uncle.

2 STYLE: RHYME

The last instance of rhyme we heard was Romeo's rhymed couplets of love for Juliet. Now Tybalt uses rhymed couplets to swear revenge on Romeo, an ironic linking of love and hate.

3 CHARACTERIZATION

Juliet welcomes Romeo's advances, then teasingly deflects him by offering to touch palms rather than kiss.

GUIDED READING

LITERAL QUESTIONS

1a. How many times does Capulet seem to break off what he is saying in lines 79–85? (four, at least)

2a. What do Juliet and Romeo call each other? (Romeo is a "pilgrim"; Juliet is a "saint.")

INFERENTIAL QUESTIONS

1b. Why do you think the speech is written this way? (Apparently, Tybalt's actions, posture, and facial expressions are defiant, and Capulet cannot turn his attention to his guests.)

2b. How does the metaphor of saints and pilgrims affect the tone of their meeting? (It elevates and idealizes it.)

AT A GLANCE

- *Scene v (continued):* Romeo kisses Juliet twice.
- He learns she is a Capulet.
- Capulet urges Romeo and his party to remain, but they leave.
- Juliet, interested in Romeo, asks the Nurse about him.

1 CHARACTERIZATION

The talkative Nurse is a bit crude: To a stranger she speaks of nursing Juliet and of how much money Juliet's future husband may look forward to.

2 THEME

Juliet, suddenly cunning, disguises her interest in Romeo by asking about other men.

[He kisses her.]

JULIET. Then have my lips the sin that they have took.

ROMEO. Sin from my lips? O trespass sweetly urged!
Give me my sin again.

[He kisses her again.]

JULIET. You kiss by th' book.[40]

[The NURSE *joins* JULIET.*]*

NURSE. Madam, your mother craves a word with you.

*[*JULIET *goes to speak with her mother.]*

ROMEO. What is her mother?

NURSE. Marry, bachelor,
Her mother is the lady of the house,
And a good lady, and a wise and virtuous.
1 I nursed her daughter that you talked withal.[41]
I tell you, he that can lay hold of her
Shall have the chinks.[42]

ROMEO. Is she a Capulet?
O dear account! My life is my foe's debt.[43]

BENVOLIO. Away, be gone; the sport is at the best.[44]

ROMEO. Ay, so I fear; the more is my unrest.

CAPULET. Nay, gentlemen, prepare not to be gone;
We have a trifling foolish banquet towards.[45]
Is it e'en so?[46] Why then, I thank you all.
I thank you, honest gentlemen. Good night.
More torches here! Come on then; let's to bed.
Ah, sirrah, by my fay,[47] it waxes[48] late;
I'll to my rest.

*[*JULIET *returns to the* NURSE *as everyone else starts to leave.* JULIET *disguises her interest in* ROMEO *by asking about other men first.]*

2 JULIET. Come hither, nurse. What is yond gentleman?

NURSE. The son and heir of old Tiberio.

JULIET. What's he that now is going out of door?

NURSE. Marry, that, I think, be young Petruchio.

JULIET. What's he that follows here, that would not dance?

40 **You kiss . . . book:** You take my words too seriously in order to have an excuse to kiss me again.

41 **withal:** with.

42 **chinks:** money.

43 **My life . . . debt:** My life belongs to an enemy. Romeo would die without Juliet.

44 **the sport . . . best:** the best part of our fun is over.

45 **towards:** in preparation.

46 **Is it e'en so:** Do you insist (on leaving)?

47 **fay:** faith.

48 **waxes:** grows.

GUIDED READING

LITERAL QUESTION

1a. Whose idea is it to leave? (Benvolio's)

INFERENTIAL QUESTION

1b. Why might Benvolio have chosen this time to take Romeo away? (He realizes the conflict that has been introduced, and so wants to protect Romeo.)

NURSE. I know not.

JULIET. Go ask his name.

[*The* NURSE *goes to ask* ROMEO*'s name.*]

—If he is married,
My grave is like to be my wedding bed.

[*The* NURSE *returns.*]

NURSE. His name is Romeo, and a Montague,
The only son of your great enemy.

JULIET. My only love, sprung from my only hate!
Too early seen unknown, and known too late!
Prodigious[49] birth of love it is to me
That I must love a loathèd enemy.

NURSE. What's this? What's this?

JULIET. A rhyme I learnt even now
Of one I danced withal.

[*Someone calls from another room,* "Juliet."]

NURSE. Anon, anon!
Come, let's away; the strangers all are gone.

[*They exit.*]

49 **Prodigious:** unnatural and, therefore, promising bad luck.

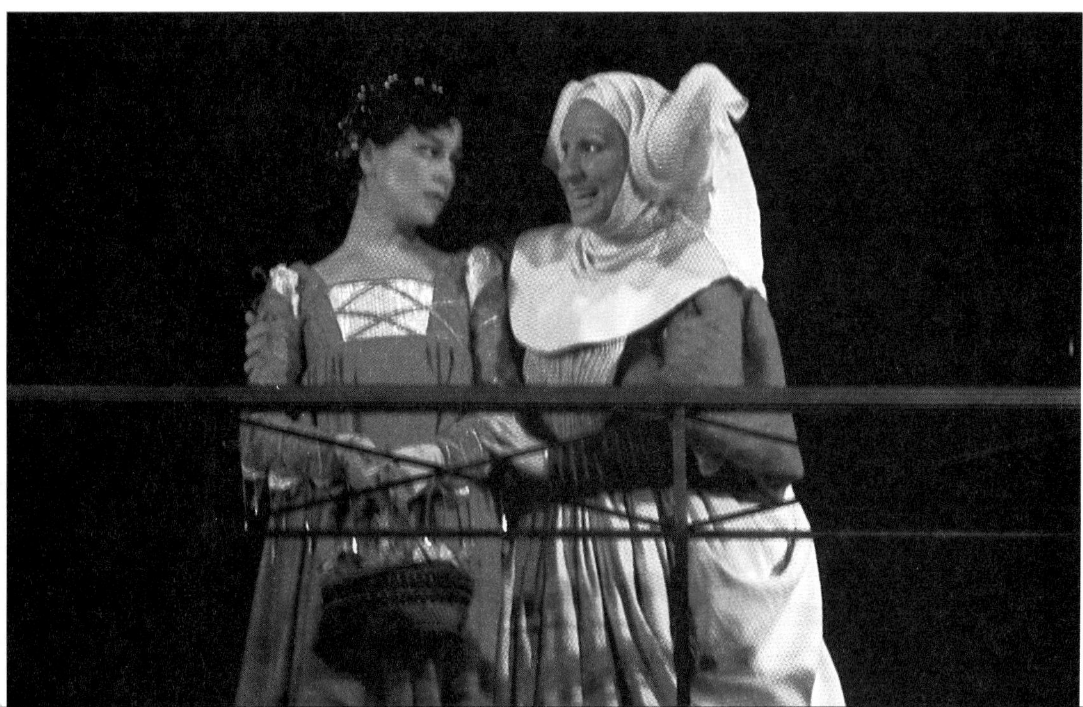

AT A GLANCE

Scene v (continued): Juliet learns that she has fallen in love with a Montague.

1 PLOT: FORESHADOWING

Ironically, Juliet accurately predicts her future. Note the symmetry between her prediction and Romeo's premonition of "untimely death" in Scene iv.

2 STYLE: RHYME

Rhymed couplets frame the drama of Juliet's discovery. Shakespeare juxtaposes words (*love/hate, unknown/known, early/late*) to underscore the light and the dark sides of love.

REFLECTING ON THE ACT

In what ways has love been portrayed so far? (as the silly obsession of an infatuated young man; as a lunatic's prison for a "bound" lover; as an emotion with a dark and painful side; as an ennobling emotion fit for saints and pilgrims)

GUIDED READING

LITERAL QUESTION

1a. What does Juliet say will happen to her if the young man is married? (Her grave will be her wedding bed.)

INFERENTIAL QUESTION

1b. Why does she say this? (She has already fallen deeply in love with him, and cannot bear to marry anyone else.)

STUDY QUESTIONS

1. It has caused three public brawls; death will be punishment for next disturbance.
2. ▪ He is sad, cries often, and shuns company.
   ▪ He loves someone who does not love him.
3. to see Rosaline; to show him there are women more desirable
4. Paris will woo her; Juliet must approve of him.
5. dance, be happy
6. wants to fight; has a good reputation and can stay
7. Romeo falls in love with Juliet as she dances, compliments her; he begs a kiss; Nurse reveals their identities.
8. "Star-crossed" lovers cannot escape death; it states he will die.
9. Benvolio: sensible, good-humored, watches over Romeo, avoids trouble; Tybalt: proud, arrogant, eager to fight
10. has poetic, witty mind; is good friend to Romeo
11. ▪ Montague: concerned, loving father
    ▪ Capulet: reasonable: wants to avoid fight; loving father: wants Juliet to marry someone she loves; hospitable: allows Romeo to stay at party
12. torch, jewel, dove; values her as something brilliant, precious, and rare
13. Answers will vary.

LITERARY FOCUS

1. ▪ verse: expresses range of emotions; has richness, color; suggests matters of importance
   ▪ prose: suggests trivial concerns of everyday life; suggests speech of lower classes
2. ▪ ROMEO: Farewell. Thou canst not teach me to forget.
   BENVOLIO: I'll pay that doctrine, or else die in debt.
   ▪ ROMEO: I'll go along, no such sight to be shown, / But to rejoice in splendor of mine own.

STUDY QUESTIONS

Recalling

1. According to the Prince in Scene i, in what ways has the feud between Capulets and Montagues affected the city of Verona? What warning does the Prince give the two families?
2. In Scene i explain how Benvolio and Lord Montague describe Romeo's mood at the beginning of the play. What reason does Romeo give for this mood?
3. In Scene ii why does Romeo want to go to Capulet's party? Why does Benvolio want him to go?
4. What decisions are made in Scenes ii and iii about a marriage for Juliet?
5. In Scene iv, lines 3–17, what does Mercutio suggest Romeo do to improve his mood?
6. How does Tybalt react to Romeo's presence at the party during Scene v? What does Lord Capulet say about Romeo?
7. Explain the circumstances of Romeo and Juliet's meeting in Scene v. In what way does each find out the identity of the other?

Interpreting

8. What does the Prologue say about fate? What does Romeo say about fate in Scene iv, lines 78–85? In what way does the Prologue show us that Romeo's misgivings are correct?
9. From their fight and from their relationships with other characters, contrast Benvolio and Tybalt.
10. What does Mercutio's speech about Queen Mab reveal about his personality? What do you think of Mercutio as a friend?
11. Explain what we learn about Lord Montague's personality from his conversation with Benvolio in Scene i. Describe Lord Capulet's personality by giving three different personality traits with examples from this act.
12. In Scene v, lines 42–51, find three things to which Romeo compares Juliet. What does his language when speaking of her tell us about his feelings for her?

Extending

13. Describe a plan that Romeo and Juliet could use to try to solve the problem they find themselves facing at the end of Act I. Explain why your plan might or might not work.

LITERARY FOCUS

Blank Verse

Shakespeare followed a custom of the Elizabethan theater and wrote his plays in blank verse. **Blank verse** is poetry written in unrhymed iambic pentameter. Lines of iambic pentameter contain ten syllables with an accent on every other syllable:

For I / ne'er saw / true beau / ty till / this night.

The result is a gentle rhythm throughout the play even though Shakespeare introduced enough irregularities to provide variety. Shakespeare preserved the pattern even when two characters must share a line:

ROMEO. I dreamed / a dream / tonight.
MERCUTIO. And so / did I.

Shakespeare reserved prose in his plays for dialogue by servants and common people and for comic passages.

Although some passages in *Romeo and Juliet* rhyme, the majority of lines do not. Shakespeare, however, used **rhymed couplets,** two consecutive lines that rhyme, at the end of most scenes. In a theater that contained no scenery and no curtains, the couplet was a signal to the audience that a change of scene was about to take place.

Thinking About Verse

1. Explain how the mood of the play changes when Shakespeare switches from verse to prose. For a prose speech see Scene ii, lines 38–44.
2. Find two examples of rhymed couplets that end scenes in Act I.

ACT II

Prologue

[The CHORUS *enters and addresses the audience, commenting on what has happened in Act I and introducing the action of Act II.]*

CHORUS. Now old desire[1] doth in his deathbed lie,
And young affection gapes[2] to be his heir;
That fair[3] for which love groaned for and would die,
With tender Juliet matched, is now not fair.
Now Romeo is beloved and loves again,
Alike bewitchèd by the charm of looks;
But to his foe supposed he must complain,[4]
And she steal love's sweet bait from fearful hooks.
Being held a foe, he may not have access
To breathe such vows as lovers use to[5] swear,
And she as much in love, her means much less
To meet her new belovèd anywhere;
But passion lends them power, time means, to meet,
Temp'ring extremities with extreme sweet.[6]

[The CHORUS *exits.]*

1 **old desire:** Romeo's love for Rosaline.
2 **young affection gapes:** new love is eager.
3 **fair:** beautiful woman (Rosaline).
4 **complain:** express his love.
5 **use to:** usually.
6 **Temp'ring . . . sweet:** mixing difficulties with delights.

Scene i. Later the same night. Outside the wall that surrounds CAPULET'S *orchard.*

[ROMEO *enters. He is walking alone after the party.]*

ROMEO. Can I go forward when my heart is here?
Turn back, dull earth,[1] and find thy center[2] out.

[BENVOLIO *and* MERCUTIO *enter; they are looking for* ROMEO. *Because he wishes to remain near* JULIET *and because he prefers to be alone,* ROMEO *avoids his friends and climbs the wall into* CAPULET'S *orchard.]*

BENVOLIO. Romeo! My cousin Romeo! Romeo!

MERCUTIO. He is wise
And, on my life, hath stol'n him home to bed.

BENVOLIO. He ran this way and leapt this orchard wall.
Call, good Mercutio.

MERCUTIO. Nay, I'll conjure[3] too.
Romeo! Humors! Madman! Passion! Lover!

1 **earth:** body.
2 **center:** heart.
3 **conjure:** make him appear by magic.

AT A GLANCE

- *Act II, Prologue:* The Chorus reminds us that Romeo has forgotten Rosaline and that the feud will make Romeo's new love difficult.
- *Scene i:* Romeo, sought by his friends, leaps into Capulet's orchard.

LITERARY OPTIONS

- conflict
- style
- staging

THEMATIC OPTIONS

- loyalty and devotion
- hopes and ideals
- relations between generations

1 THEME

The theme of relations between generations is introduced immediately in the Chorus's image of old desire dying so that young affection may inherit.

2 CHARACTERIZATION

As a young lady of good family, Juliet's movement is even more restricted than that of Romeo.

3 CHARACTERIZATION

Unlike the strait-laced Benvolio, Mercutio seizes any opportunity to inject wit and energy into conversations. Here he equates *Romeo* with four alternate names.

GUIDED READING

LITERAL QUESTION

1a. How does Romeo avoid his friends? (He climbs the wall into Capulet's orchard.)

INFERENTIAL QUESTION

1b. Why do you think he wants to avoid them? (Possible answers: Having fallen in love, he craves solitude; he is going to see Juliet; he doesn't want to be interrogated or mocked by Mercutio.)

AT A GLANCE

- *Scene i (continued):* Benvolio and Mercutio search in vain for Romeo.
- *Scene ii:* Romeo sees Juliet at her bedroom window.

1 DRAMATIC IRONY

Mercutio assumes Romeo is still in love with Rosaline, but the audience knows that Juliet is his new love.

2 STAGING

Elizabethan theaters did not have elaborate sets or lighting; thus, a character's description of trees and dark sets the stage for the audience.

3 STYLE: METAPHOR

Romeo idealizes Juliet by comparing her to the sun. He continues the metaphor by describing the personified moon's envy of Juliet's greater beauty and radiance.

Appear thou in the likeness of a sigh;
Speak but one rhyme, and I am satisfied!
Cry but "Ay me!" pronounce but "love" and "dove."
He heareth not, he stirreth not, he moveth not;
The ape is dead,[4] and I must conjure him.
1 I conjure thee by Rosaline's bright eyes,
By her high forehead and her scarlet lip,
That in thy likeness thou appear to us!

BENVOLIO. And if he hear thee, thou wilt anger him.

MERCUTIO. This cannot anger him.
My invocation[5]
Is fair and honest: in his mistress' name,
I conjure only but to raise up him.

2 BENVOLIO. Come, he hath hid himself among these trees
To be consorted[6] with the humorous[7] night.
Blind is his love and best befits the dark.

MERCUTIO. If love be blind, love cannot hit the mark.
Romeo, good night. I'll to my truckle bed;[8]
This field bed is too cold for me to sleep.
Come, shall we go?

BENVOLIO. Go then, for 'tis in vain
To seek him here that means not to be found.

[*They exit.*]

4 **The ape is dead:** He (Romeo) is playing dead like a trained monkey. Throughout this speech, Mercutio makes fun of Romeo's lovesickness in a friendly manner.

5 **invocation:** prayer; here, the words of a magic spell to raise a spirit.

6 **consorted:** blended.
7 **humorous:** damp.

8 **truckle bed:** trundle bed, a child's small bed that rolls under a big bed when not in use.

Scene ii. Immediately following the previous scene.
CAPULET'*s orchard.*

[ROMEO, *alone, comments on* MERCUTIO'*s joking.*]

ROMEO. He jests at scars that never felt a wound.

[JULIET *enters at a window above and stands on a balcony. She does not know that* ROMEO *is nearby.*]

3 But soft! What light through yonder window breaks?
It is the East, and Juliet is the sun!
Arise, fair sun, and kill the envious moon,
Who is already sick and pale with grief
That thou her maid art far more fair than she.
Be not her maid, since she is envious.
Her vestal livery[1] is but sick and green,
And none but fools do wear it. Cast it off.

1 **Her vestal livery:** the moon's white dress. The moon becomes pale beside Juliet, the sun.

GUIDED READING

LITERAL QUESTION

1a. What does Romeo do when he first sees Juliet? (He speaks softly to himself about her beauty.)

INFERENTIAL QUESTION

1b. Why do you think he speaks to himself rather than to her? (Possible answers: He wants to regard her beauty first; he is fearful of speaking to her, or of being in the Capulet orchard; he is unsure of what to do.)

It is my lady! O, it is my love!
O, that she knew she were!
She speaks, yet she says nothing. What of that?
Her eye discourses;[2] I will answer it.
I am too bold; 'tis not to me she speaks.
1 Two of the fairest stars in all the heaven,
Having some business, do entreat her eyes
To twinkle in their spheres[3] till they return.
What if her eyes were there, they in her head?
The brightness of her cheek would shame those stars
As daylight doth a lamp; her eyes in heaven
Would through the airy region stream so bright
That birds would sing and think it were not night.
See how she leans her cheek upon her hand!
O, that I were a glove upon that hand,
That I might touch that cheek!

JULIET. Ay me!

2 ROMEO. [*Aside.*] She speaks.
O, speak again, bright angel, for thou art
As glorious to this night, being o'er my head,
As is a winged messenger of heaven
Unto the white-upturned wond'ring eyes

2 **discourses:** speaks.

3 **spheres:** orbits.

AT A GLANCE

- *Scene ii (continued):* Romeo exclaims upon Juliet's beauty.
- She does not know he sees her.

1 STYLE: METAPHOR

Romeo idealizes Juliet by comparing her eyes to stars. Further, he suggests that the stars are beholden to her; they must "entreat her eyes."

2 ASIDE

Though Romeo seems to be addressing Juliet, he voices his hopes to himself and to the audience. An aside allows the audience and one character to interact without the knowledge of other characters on stage.

GUIDED READING

LITERAL QUESTION

1a. What are Juliet's first words in this scene? ("Ay me!")

INFERENTIAL QUESTION

1b. What might she be feeling? (She may be thinking about Romeo and feeling concerned about loving a man whom her family will not permit her to marry.)

AT A GLANCE

- *Scene ii (continued):* Juliet wishes Romeo were not a Montague.
- His identity is no barrier to her love.
- Romeo speaks lovingly to her.

1 STYLE: BLANK VERSE

Juliet elevates her love (as Romeo did) by speaking of it in blank verse.

2 STYLE: METAPHOR

Juliet compares Romeo's sweetness to that of a rose: Neither's good qualities depend on a name. Juliet will go beyond the family feud to devote herself to Romeo.

3 CONFLICT

Juliet warns Romeo that he is in danger. Our awareness of the constant risk to his life adds tension to the love scene.

Of mortals that fall back to gaze on him
When he bestrides the lazy puffing clouds
And sails upon the bosom of the air.

JULIET. O Romeo, Romeo! Wherefore art thou Romeo?[4]
1 Deny thy father and refuse thy name;
Or, if thou wilt not, be but sworn my love,
And I'll no longer be a Capulet.

ROMEO. [*Aside.*] Shall I hear more, or shall I speak at this?

JULIET. 'Tis but thy name that is my enemy.
Thou art thyself, though not[5] a Montague.
What's Montague? It is nor[6] hand, nor foot,
Nor arm, nor face. O, be some other name
Belonging to a man.
2 What's in a name? That which we call a rose
By any other word would smell as sweet.
So Romeo would, were he not Romeo called,
Retain that dear perfection which he owes[7]
Without that title. Romeo, doff[8] thy name;
And for thy name, which is no part of thee,
Take all myself.

[ROMEO *speaks aloud so that* JULIET *can hear him for the first time.*]

ROMEO. I take thee at thy word.
Call me but love, and I'll be new baptized;
Henceforth I never will be Romeo.

JULIET. What man art thou, that, thus bescreened[9] in night,
So stumblest on my counsel?[10]

ROMEO. By a name
I know not how to tell thee who I am.
My name, dear saint, is hateful to myself
Because it is an enemy to thee.
Had I it written, I would tear the word.

JULIET. My ears have yet not drunk a hundred words
Of thy tongue's uttering, yet I know the sound.
Art thou not Romeo, and a Montague?

ROMEO. Neither, fair maid, if either thee dislike.

JULIET. How camest thou hither, tell me, and wherefore?
3 The orchard walls are high and hard to climb,
And the place death, considering who thou art,
If any of my kinsmen find thee here.

4 **Wherefore . . . Romeo:** Why are you called *Romeo* (a Montague)?

5 **though not:** even if you were not.

6 **nor:** neither.

7 **owes:** owns.

8 **doff:** remove.

9 **bescreened:** hidden.

10 **counsel:** secret thoughts.

GUIDED READING

LITERAL QUESTION

1a. In her opening speech what solution does Juliet propose to their dilemma? (that they "refuse their names")

INFERENTIAL QUESTION

1b. Why does Juliet speak so openly? (She believes she is alone and unheard.)

1 ROMEO. With love's light wings did I o'erperch[11] these walls;
For stony limits cannot hold love out,
And what love can do, that dares love attempt.
Therefore thy kinsmen are no stop to me.

JULIET. If they do see thee, they will murder thee.

ROMEO. Alack, there lies more peril in thine eye
Than twenty of their swords! Look thou but sweet,
And I am proof[12] against their enmity.

JULIET. I would not for the world they saw thee here.

ROMEO. I have night's cloak to hide me from their eyes;
And but[13] thou love me, let them find me here.
My life were better ended by their hate
Than death proroguèd,[14] wanting of[15] thy love.

JULIET. By whose direction found'st thou out this place?

2 ROMEO. By love, that first did prompt me to inquire.
He lent me counsel, and I lent him eyes.
I am no pilot; yet, wert thou as far
As that vast shore washed with the farthest sea,
I should adventure[16] for such merchandise.

JULIET. Thou knowest the mask of night is on my face;
Else would a maiden blush bepaint my cheek
For that which thou hast heard me speak tonight.
3 Fain would I dwell on form[17]—fain, fain deny
What I have spoke; but farewell compliment![18]
Dost thou love me? I know thou wilt say "Ay";
And I will take thy word. Yet, if thou swear'st,
Thou mayst prove false. At lovers' perjuries,
They say Jove[19] laughs. O gentle Romeo,
If thou dost love, pronounce it faithfully.
Or if thou thinkest I am too quickly won,
I'll frown and be perverse and say thee nay,[20]
So thou wilt woo; but else, not for the world.
In truth, fair Montague, I am too fond,
And therefore thou mayst think my havior light;[21]
But trust me, gentleman, I'll prove more true
Than those that have more cunning to be strange.[22]
4 I should have been more strange, I must confess,
But that thou overheard'st, ere I was ware,[23]
My truelove passion. Therefore pardon me,
And not impute this yielding[24] to light love,

11 **o'erperch:** fly over.

12 **proof:** protected.

13 **And but:** unless.

14 **prorogued:** postponed.

15 **wanting of:** lacking.

16 **adventure:** risk a dangerous journey.

17 **Fain . . . form:** Gladly would I behave in the usual, more shy manner.

18 **compliment:** formal manners.

19 **Jove:** For ancient Romans, Jove was ruler of all the gods.

20 **be . . . nay:** act against my own wishes and discourage you.

21 **my havior light:** my behavior not serious enough.

22 **cunning to be strange:** cleverness to pretend to be aloof, or distant.

23 **ere I was ware:** before I knew you were there.

24 **impute this yielding:** trace my giving in so easily.

AT A GLANCE

- *Scene ii (continued):* Juliet warns Romeo that he is in extreme danger.
- She pledges her love but worries that Romeo may not truly love her.

1 STYLE: METAPHOR

Cupid has lent Romeo his wings. Romeo's loyalty to Juliet is already great: Inspired by love, he is willing to risk death for her.

2 STYLE: PERSONIFICATION

"Love" (with whom Romeo can speak) is so powerful that his "counsel" allows Romeo to find Juliet without using his eyes. Romeo implicitly admits to a certain "blindness."

3 CHARACTERIZATION

Juliet regrets that she has broken the rules of polite conduct, yet she impulsively continues to express her true feelings and to wonder about Romeo's.

4 CHARACTERIZATION

Juliet worries that Romeo may think her fickle for "yielding" so quickly. Whereas Romeo tends to speak of the beauties of feeling itself, Juliet tends to speak of how love's problems might be solved.

GUIDED READING

LITERAL QUESTION

1a. What does Juliet say will happen if her kinsmen find Romeo? (They will murder him.)

INFERENTIAL QUESTION

1b. How does Romeo seem to feel about this possibility? (He seems to ignore the idea of danger.)

AT A GLANCE

- *Scene ii (continued):* Juliet worries that their exchange of vows is too sudden.
- Called by her nurse, she goes into the house but asks Romeo to wait for her.

1 CHARACTERIZATION

Juliet worries that their declarations of love have been premature, although she readily admits her feelings at the same time *(I joy in thee).*

2 STYLE: METAPHOR

Juliet compares their love to a bud that will flower in the summer weather.

3 MAIN IDEA

The idea of gaining love as one gives love suggests a higher level of love and devotion.

Which the dark night hath so discoverèd.[25]

ROMEO. Lady, by yonder blessèd moon I vow,
That tips with silver all these fruit-tree tops—

JULIET. O, swear not by the moon, th' inconstant moon,
That monthly changes in her circle orb,
Lest that thy love prove likewise variable.

ROMEO. What shall I swear by?

JULIET. Do not swear at all;
Or if thou wilt, swear by thy gracious self,
Which is the god of my idolatry,[26]
And I'll believe thee.

ROMEO. If my heart's dear love—

1 JULIET. Well, do not swear. Although I joy in thee,
I have no joy of this contract[27] tonight.
It is too rash, too unadvised, too sudden;
Too like the lightning, which doth cease to be
Ere one can say it lightens. Sweet, good night!
2 This bud of love, by summer's ripening breath,
May prove a beauteous flow'r when next we meet.
Good night, good night! As sweet repose and rest
Come to thy heart as that within my breast!

ROMEO. O, wilt thou leave me so unsatisfied?

JULIET. What satisfaction canst thou have tonight?

ROMEO. Th' exchange of thy love's faithful vow for mine.

JULIET. I gave thee mine before thou didst request it;
And yet I would it were[28] to give again.

ROMEO. Wouldst thou withdraw it? For what purpose, love?

JULIET. But to be frank[29] and give it thee again.
And yet I wish but for the thing I have.
My bounty[30] is as boundless as the sea,
3 My love as deep; the more I give to thee,
The more I have, for both are infinite.
I hear some noise within. Dear love, adieu!

[*The* NURSE *calls from within the house.*]

Anon, good nurse! Sweet Montague, be true.
Stay but a little, I will come again.

[JULIET *goes into the house.*]

25 **discovered:** revealed.

26 **idolatry:** devotion.

27 **contract:** betrothal, engagement.

28 **I would it were:** I wish I had my vow back.

29 **frank:** generous.

30 **bounty:** generosity.

GUIDED READING

LITERAL QUESTIONS

1a. How does Juliet answer Romeo's offer to swear on the moon? ("O, swear not by the moon . . .")

2a. What does Juliet ask Romeo to do as she leaves? (wait until she comes out)

INFERENTIAL QUESTIONS

1b. How do the lovers look at the moon differently? (Romeo sees it as an object of beauty and a symbol of love; Juliet portrays it as changeable, not to be trusted.)

2b. What does Juliet's request reveal about her feelings? (Despite her wish to act without rashness, she does not wish to cut the evening short.)

ROMEO. O blessèd, blessèd night! I am afeard,
Being in night, all this is but a dream,
Too flattering-sweet to be substantial.[31]

[JULIET *reappears on the balcony.*]

JULIET. Three words, dear Romeo, and good night indeed.
1 If that thy bent[32] of love be honorable,
Thy purpose marriage, send me word tomorrow,
By one that I'll procure[33] to come to thee,
Where and what time thou wilt perform the rite;[34]
And all my fortunes at thy foot I'll lay
And follow thee my lord throughout the world.

NURSE. [*She calls from within the house.*] Madam!

2 **JULIET.** [*To the* NURSE.] I come anon. [*To* ROMEO.]—But if thou
meanest not well,
I do beseech[35] thee—

NURSE. [*From within again.*] Madam!

JULIET [*To the* NURSE.] By and by[36] I come.—
[*To* ROMEO.] To cease thy strife[37] and leave me to my grief.
Tomorrow will I send.

ROMEO. So thrive my soul—

JULIET. A thousand times good night!

[JULIET *goes into the house.*]

ROMEO. A thousand times the worse, to want thy light!
Love goes toward love as schoolboys from their books;
But love from love, toward school with heavy looks.

[JULIET *returns to the balcony.*]

JULIET. Hist! Romeo, hist! O for a falc'ner's voice[38]
To lure this tassel gentle[39] back again!
3 Bondage is hoarse and may not speak aloud,[40]
Else would I tear the cave where Echo[41] lies
And make her airy tongue more hoarse than mine
With repetition of "My Romeo!"

ROMEO. It is my soul that calls upon my name.
How silver-sweet sound lovers' tongues by night,
Like softest music to attending[42] ears!

JULIET. Romeo!

ROMEO. My sweet?

31 **substantial:** real.
32 **bent:** intention.
33 **procure:** obtain.
34 **rite:** ceremony; here, marriage.
35 **beseech:** beg.
36 **By and by:** at once.
37 **strife:** efforts.
38 **O for . . . voice:** If only I had the loud voice of a hawk trainer.
39 **tassel gentle:** male hawk.
40 **Bondage . . . aloud:** Bound by my family, I must not be overheard.
41 **Echo:** In classical mythology Echo was a wood nymph. When rejected in love, she retired to a cave where she wasted away until only her voice was left.
42 **attending:** attentive.

AT A GLANCE

- *Scene ii (continued):* Juliet tells Romeo that she will marry him immediately if he is sincere; he must leave her alone if he is not true.
- The Nurse calls Juliet, who goes inside and then returns.

1 PLOT: RISING ACTION

Juliet propels the action by offering to marry Romeo immediately. Their marriage could have much more serious ramifications for the family feud than a love affair.

2 CHARACTERIZATION

Juliet wants Romeo to break off his attentions if he is not as sincere as she is: In dealing openly and honorably with him, she hopes he will do the same.

3 CONFLICT

The lovers' meeting is marked by reminders of the dangers they face and the terrible conflicts they may provoke.

GUIDED READING

LITERAL QUESTIONS

1a. Which third character interrupts this scene? (the Nurse)

2a. What does Juliet do as soon as she returns? (She calls for Romeo.)

INFERENTIAL QUESTIONS

1b. What effect might the interruptions have on the audience? (fear and excitement that the lovers may be found out)

2b. Why is Juliet afraid to speak aloud? (She fears punishment for herself and death for Romeo.)

AT A GLANCE

- *Scene ii (continued):* The lovers part.
- Romeo goes to find Friar Lawrence, his spiritual advisor.
- *Scene iii:* The Friar enters his cell.

1 PLOT: FORESHADOWING

In declaring her deep love for Romeo, Juliet unwittingly foretells their sad future as lovers: Romeo is pictured as a "poor prisoner" in chains and as one whose death is caused by love.

2 BACKGROUND

Romeo's rhymed couplet sets the stage for the next scene. In Shakespeare's day such verbal reminders were necessary to remind actors and audience of a change of scene.

3 SETTING

Friar Lawrence's opening lines establish the setting: The magical night is over and the lovers must face the cold reality of the "gray-eyed morn."

JULIET. What o'clock tomorrow
Shall I send to thee?

ROMEO. By the hour of nine.

JULIET. I will not fail. 'Tis twenty year till then.
I have forgot why I did call thee back.

ROMEO. Let me stand here till thou remember it.

JULIET. I shall forget, to have thee still stand there,
Rememb'ring how I love thy company.

ROMEO. And I'll still stay, to have thee still forget,
Forgetting any other home but this.

JULIET. 'Tis almost morning. I would have thee gone—
And yet no farther than a wanton's bird,[43]
That lets it hop a little from his hand,
1 Like a poor prisoner in his twisted gyves,[44]
And with a silken thread plucks it back again,
So loving-jealous of his liberty.

ROMEO. I would I were thy bird.

JULIET. Sweet, so would I.
Yet I should kill thee with much cherishing.
Good night, good night! Parting is such sweet sorrow
That I shall say good night till it be morrow.

[JULIET *goes into the house.*]

ROMEO. Sleep dwell upon thine eyes, peace in thy breast!
Would I were sleep and peace, so sweet to rest!
2 Hence will I to my ghostly friar's[45] close cell,[46]
His help to crave[47] and my dear hap[48] to tell.

[ROMEO *leaves to find the* FRIAR.]

43 **wanton's bird:** bird belonging to a selfish child.

44 **gyves:** chains.

45 **ghostly friar's:** spiritual father's.
46 **close cell:** small, bare room.
47 **crave:** beg.
48 **hap:** luck.

Scene iii. Early the next morning. FRIAR LAWRENCE'*s cell.*

[FRIAR LAWRENCE, ROMEO'*s spritual advisor, enters alone carrying a basket full of herbs. He speaks about the harmful and helpful effects of the various plants.*]

3 FRIAR. The gray-eyed morn smiles on the frowning night,
Check'ring the eastern clouds with streaks of light;
And fleckèd[1] darkness like a drunkard reels
From forth day's path and Titan's burning wheels.[2]
Now, ere the sun advance his burning eye

1 **fleckèd:** spotted.
2 **From . . . wheels:** out of the path of the sun god, who was thought to drive a fiery chariot (the sun) across the sky.

GUIDED READING

LITERAL QUESTION

1a. Why does Juliet call Romeo back? (She has forgotten the reason.)

INFERENTIAL QUESTION

1b. Why do you think she is suddenly forgetful? (She is flustered and reluctant to let Romeo go.)

The day to cheer and night's dank dew to dry,
I must upfill this osier cage[3] of ours
With baleful[4] weeds and precious-juicèd flowers.
O, mickle is the powerful grace[5] that lies
In plants, herbs, stones, and their true qualities;
1 For naught so vile that on the earth doth live
But to the earth some special good doth give;
Nor aught so good but, strained from that fair use,[6]
Revolts from true birth,[7] stumbling on abuse.
Virtue itself turns vice, being misapplied,
And vice sometime by action dignified.[8]

[ROMEO *enters. The* FRIAR *does not see him and continues speaking until* ROMEO *interrupts him.*]

Within the infant rind[9] of this weak flower
Poison hath residence and medicine[10] power;
2 For this, being smelt, with that part cheers each part;
Being tasted, stays all senses with the heart.[11]
Two such opposèd kings encamp them still[12]
In man as well as herbs—grace and rude will;[13]
And where the worser is predominant,
Full soon the canker[14] death eats up that plant.

ROMEO. Good morrow, father.

FRIAR. *Benedicite!*[15]
What early tongue so sweet saluteth me?
Young son, it argues a distemperèd head[16]
So soon to bid good morrow to thy bed.
3 Care keeps his watch in every old man's eye,
And where care lodges, sleep will never lie;
But where unbruisèd youth with unstuffed brain[17]
Doth couch his limbs, there golden sleep doth reign.
Therefore thy earliness doth me assure
Thou art uproused with some distemp'rature;[18]
Or if not so, then here I hit it right—
Our Romeo hath not been in bed tonight.

ROMEO. That last is true. The sweeter rest was mine.

FRIAR. God pardon sin! Wast thou with Rosaline?

ROMEO. With Rosaline, my ghostly father? No.
I have forgot that name and that name's woe.

FRIAR. That's my good son! But where hast thou been then?

ROMEO. I'll tell thee ere thou ask it me again.

3 **upfill . . . cage:** fill up this willow basket.
4 **baleful:** poisonous.
5 **mickle . . . grace:** great is the goodness.
6 **strained . . . use:** used improperly or for the wrong purpose.
7 **Revolts . . . birth:** turns away from its real purpose.
8 **Virtue . . . dignified:** Whether a thing is helpful or harmful depends on the way it is used.
9 **infant rind:** tender skin.
10 **medicine:** medicinal.
11 **For this . . . heart:** When smelled, the juice of this plant stimulates the entire body. When tasted, it can cause death.
12 **still:** always.
13 **In man . . . will:** Men, like herbs, have both good and evil properties.
14 **canker:** cankerworm, a worm that feeds on plants.
15 **Benedicite** [bā nā dē ′chē tā]: Latin for "Bless you."
16 **argues . . . head:** is a sign of a troubled mind.
17 **unstuffed brain:** clear, untroubled mind.
18 **uproused . . . distemp'rature:** not still asleep because of some illness.

AT A GLANCE

- *Scene iii (continued):* Romeo finds the friar.
- The friar, who knows about Rosaline, worries that Romeo has been with her all night and is relieved to hear Romeo deny that.

1 THEME

Friar Lawrence observes that good and evil are inextricably bound even in the world of plants.

2 PLOT: FORESHADOWING

As Friar Lawrence sorts through his herbs, he comes upon one that both smells sweet and causes death, as love will be shown to do.

3 THEME

As the friar contrasts a youth's "unstuffed" mind with an old man's restive spirit, he implies that it is unnatural for Romeo to resist sleep. Yet Romeo seems the opposite of the friar's picture of "unbruisèd youth."

GUIDED READING

LITERAL QUESTION

1a. What does Friar Lawrence ask Romeo about Rosaline? (if Romeo has seen her that night)

INFERENTIAL QUESTION

1b. What relationship do Romeo and the friar seem to have? (They seem to be on rather intimate terms with each other.)

AT A GLANCE

- *Scene iii (continued):* Romeo asks that Friar Lawrence marry him to Juliet.
- Friar Lawrence accuses Romeo of being fickle.

1 STYLE: METAPHOR

Romeo uses the common metaphor of Cupid and his arrows to refer to Juliet's and his mutual "wounds."

2 PLOT: RISING ACTION

As Romeo asks the friar to perform the marriage ceremony, his impatience ("When and where and how . . . I'll tell thee as we pass") heightens the sense of conflict and impending trouble.

3 CHARACTERIZATION

Romeo defends himself by explaining that Juliet (unlike Rosaline) returns his love.

I have been feasting with mine enemy,
1 Where on a sudden one hath wounded me
That's by me wounded. Both our remedies
Within thy help and holy physic[19] lies.
I bear no hatred, blessed man, for, lo,
My intercession likewise steads my foe.[20]

FRIAR. Be plain, good son, and homely in thy drift.[21]
Riddling confession finds but riddling shrift.[22]

ROMEO. Then plainly know my heart's dear love is set
On the fair daughter of rich Capulet;
As mine on hers, so hers is set on mine,
2 And all combined, save[23] what thou must combine
By holy marriage. When and where and how
We met, we wooed, and made exchange of vow,
I'll tell thee as we pass; but this I pray,
That thou consent to marry us today.

FRIAR. Holy Saint Francis! What a change is here!
Is Rosaline, that thou didst love so dear,
So soon forsaken? Young men's love then lies
Not truly in their hearts, but in their eyes.
Jesu Maria! What a deal of brine[24]
Hath washed thy sallow cheeks for Rosaline!
How much salt water thrown away in waste
To season love, that of it doth not taste!
The sun not yet thy sighs from heaven clears,
Thy old groans ring yet in mine ancient ears.
Lo, here upon thy cheek the stain doth sit
Of an old tear that is not washed off yet.
If e'er thou wast thyself, and these woes thine,
Thou and these woes were all for Rosaline.
And art thou changed? Pronounce this sentence then:
Women may fall when there's no strength in men.[25]

ROMEO. Thou chidst[26] me oft for loving Rosaline.

FRIAR. For doting,[27] not for loving, pupil mine.

ROMEO. And badst me[28] bury love.

FRIAR. Not in a grave
To lay one in, another out to have.

3 **ROMEO.** I pray thee chide me not. Her I love now
Doth grace[29] for grace and love for love allow.[30]
The other did not so.

19 **physic:** cure.
20 **My intercession . . . foe:** My plea is also on behalf of my enemy (Juliet).
21 **homely . . . drift:** speak simply.
22 **Riddling . . . shrift:** A confusing confession will receive a confusing forgiveness.
23 **all combined, save:** everything is arranged, except for.
24 **brine:** salt water, tears.
25 **Women . . . men:** Women can be expected to be unfaithful when men are so fickle.
26 **chidst:** scolded.
27 **doting:** being foolishly fond.
28 **badst me:** urged me to.
29 **grace:** favor.
30 **allow:** give.

GUIDED READING

LITERAL QUESTION

1a. What does Romeo request of the friar? (that he marry Romeo and Juliet)

INFERENTIAL QUESTION

1b. How does the friar react to this request? (He is amazed but does not refuse; he seems more alarmed by Romeo's fickleness than by the news that the object of his love is a Capulet.)

FRIAR. O, she knew well
Thy love did read by rote, that could not spell.[31]
But come, young waverer, come go with me.
In one respect I'll thy assistant be;
For this alliance may so happy prove
To turn your households' rancor[32] to pure love.

ROMEO. O, let us hence! I stand on sudden haste.[33]

FRIAR. Wisely and slow. They stumble that run fast.

[They exit.]

31 **did read . . . spell:** read by memorization without understanding the meaning.

32 **rancor:** hatred.

33 **stand . . . haste:** insist on hurrying.

***Scene iv.** Approximately nine o'clock in the morning, the time at which* JULIET *was to send a messenger to* ROMEO. *A street in Verona.*

[BENVOLIO *and* MERCUTIO *enter; they are still concerned about* ROMEO*'s disappearance the night before.*]

MERCUTIO. Where the devil should this Romeo be?
Came he not home tonight?

BENVOLIO. Not to his father's. I spoke with his man.[1]

MERCUTIO. Why, that same pale hardhearted wench, that Rosaline,
Torments him so that he will sure run mad.

BENVOLIO. Tybalt, the kinsman to old Capulet,
Hath sent a letter to his father's house.

MERCUTIO. A challenge,[2] on my life.

BENVOLIO. Romeo will answer it.

MERCUTIO. Any man that can write may answer a letter.

BENVOLIO. Nay, he will answer the letter's master, how he dares, being dared.

MERCUTIO. Alas, poor Romeo, he is already dead: stabbed with a white wench's black eye; run through the ear with a love song; the very pin of his heart cleft with the blind bow-boy's butt-shaft;[3] and is he a man to encounter Tybalt?

BENVOLIO. Why, what is Tybalt?

MERCUTIO. More than Prince of Cats.[4] O, he's the courageous captain of compliments.[5] The very butcher of a silk

1 **man:** servant.

2 **challenge:** challenge to a duel.

3 **pin . . . butt-shaft:** the center of Romeo's heart is pierced by Cupid's unpointed practice arrow. Mercutio means that Romeo was wounded by Cupid's least powerful weapon.
4 **Prince of Cats:** a pun on Tybalt's name. In stories of the time, Tybert is the Prince of Cats.
5 **captain of compliments:** expert in formalities. Tybalt duels according to all the rules.

AT A GLANCE

- *Scene iii (continued):* Friar Lawrence agrees to help the young lovers.
- *Scene iv:* Benvolio and Mercutio discuss Tybalt's challenge to Romeo.

1 THEME

Friar Lawrence agrees to perform the marriage in the hope that the two warring houses may be reconciled.

2 CONFLICT

Romeo has received a challenge to duel with Tybalt—news that strikes an ominous note, since Romeo and Juliet are in love.

3 STYLE: PROSE

Mercutio uses prose to mock Romeo, rather than the more elevated blank verse style in which he conversed with Benvolio a few lines earlier.

GUIDED READING

LITERAL QUESTIONS

1a. What does Friar Lawrence say about Romeo's love for Rosaline? (that he read "by rote"—he did not really understand the meaning of the love he professed)

2a. With whom does Mercutio believe Romeo is in love? (Rosaline)

INFERENTIAL QUESTIONS

1b. Do you think the friar has the same assessment of Romeo's love for Juliet? (He does not seem to take it seriously, calling Romeo "young waverer.")

2b. How does this mistake affect our assessment of Romeo's love for Juliet? (It may make us suspicious of Romeo's ability to know his own mind.)

AT A GLANCE

- *Scene iv (continued):* Romeo joins Benvolio and Mercutio.
- The Nurse, Juliet's messenger, enters, seeking Romeo.

1 FORESHADOWING

The playful Mercutio makes teasing references to dueling; his words are a kind of ironic foreshadowing of his future involvement in the duel.

2 CHARACTERIZATION

Mercutio is both coarse and witty: He takes pleasure in mocking the Nurse, and his insults are delivered in clever wordplay.

3 CHARACTERIZATION

Romeo's own teasing wordplay with the Nurse recalls the similar jesting he undertook with the Capulet servant who invited him to the party; Romeo has a playful and, perhaps, arrogant side.

button,[6] a duelist, a duelist! A gentleman of the very first 1 house,[7] of the first and second cause.[8] Ah, the immortal *passado!* The *punto reverso!* The hay![9]

[ROMEO *enters. He seems much happier than he was at the beginning of the play.*]

BENVOLIO. Here comes Romeo! Here comes Romeo!

MERCUTIO. You gave us the counterfeit[10] fairly last night.

ROMEO. Good morrow to you both. What counterfeit did I give you?

MERCUTIO. The slip, sir, the slip. Can you not conceive?

ROMEO. Pardon, good Mercutio. My business was great, and in such a case as mine a man may strain courtesy. Here's goodly gear![11]

[*The* NURSE *enters with* PETER, *a servant.*]

A sail, a sail!

MERCUTIO. Two, two! A shirt and a smock.[12]

NURSE. Peter!

PETER. Anon.

NURSE. My fan, Peter.

2 MERCUTIO. Good Peter, to hide her face; for her fan's the fairer face.

NURSE. God ye good morrow, gentlemen. Can any of you tell me where I may find the young Romeo?

3 ROMEO. I can tell you; but young Romeo will be older when you have found him than he was when you sought him. I am the youngest of that name, for fault[13] of a worse.

NURSE. You say well.

MERCUTIO. Yea, is the worst well? Very well took, i' faith! Wisely, wisely.

NURSE. If you be he, sir, I desire some confidence[14] with you.

MERCUTIO. Romeo, will you come to your father's? We'll to dinner thither.

ROMEO. I will follow you.

MERCUTIO. Farewell, ancient lady. Farewell.

6 **button:** that is, the button on an opponent's shirt.
7 **first house:** highest rank.
8 **first and second cause:** the reasons that one gentleman would challenge another to a duel.
9 **passado . . . hay:** Italian dueling terms *Passado* is a lunge; *punto reverso* is a backhand stroke; hay [hai] is the cry as a fencer thrusts at his opponent.

10 **counterfeit:** A counterfeit coin was called a *slip,* a word that also means "escape."

11 **goodly gear:** fine stuff. Romeo refers to the Nurse and her servant.

12 **a shirt . . . smock:** a man and a woman.

13 **fault:** lack.

14 **confidence:** conference. The Nurse often confuses words that sound alike.

GUIDED READING

LITERAL QUESTION

1a. How do both Romeo and Mercutio treat the Nurse? (They tease her.)

INFERENTIAL QUESTION

1b. Why is it ironic that Romeo treats her this way? (He doesn't realize she bears a message from Juliet.)

[BENVOLIO *and* MERCUTIO *leave.*]

NURSE. I pray you, sir, what saucy merchant[15] was this that was so full of his ropery?[16]

ROMEO. A gentleman, nurse, that loves to hear himself talk and will speak more in a minute than he will stand to in a month.

NURSE. Scurvy Knave![17] Pray you, sir, a word; and, as I told you, my young lady bid me inquire you out. What she bid me say, I
1 will keep to myself; but first let me tell ye, if ye should lead her in a fool's paradise, as they say, it were a very gross kind of behavior, as they say; for the gentlewoman is young; and therefore, if you should deal double with her, truly it were an ill thing to be off'red to any gentlewoman, and very weak[18] dealing.

ROMEO. Nurse, commend me[19] to thy lady and mistress. I protest[20] unto thee—

2 **NURSE.** Good heart, and i' faith I will tell her as much. Lord, Lord, she will be a joyful woman.

15 **saucy merchant:** rude fellow.

16 **ropery:** The Nurse means "roguery," jokes.

17 **Scurvy knave:** contemptible rascal.

18 **weak:** unmanly.

19 **commend me:** give my regards.

20 **protest:** declare.

AT A GLANCE

Scene iv (continued): The Nurse wants to know for herself if Romeo is sincere.

1 CHARACTERIZATION

The Nurse questions Romeo's motives and reminds him of Juliet's youth and inexperience, using the now-famous phrase *fool's paradise.*

2 STYLE: HUMOR

The Nurse is so eager to believe Romeo's sincerity that she does not wait for him to prove it.

GUIDED READING

LITERAL QUESTION

1a. What does the Nurse do before she relays Juliet's message? (She questions Romeo about Mercutio.)

INFERENTIAL QUESTION

1b. Why does the Nurse postpone relaying her message? (She wants to test Romeo's sincerity and to warn him to be good to Juliet.)

AT A GLANCE

- *Scene iv (continued):* Romeo tells the Nurse that the marriage has been arranged for that afternoon; Juliet is to come to Friar Lawrence's cell.
- Romeo plans to visit Juliet secretly that night.
- The Nurse reveals that Juliet prefers Romeo to Paris.

1 BACKGROUND

The marriage is scheduled for a time when Juliet might go to see Friar Lawrence for confession.

2 PLOT: RISING ACTION

Romeo plans to carry out the marriage without the family's knowledge or consent, which will provoke conflict between the feuding families.

3 CONFLICT

The Nurse reveals that she thinks Paris is a better man than Romeo, but that Juliet disagrees. With this comic touch Shakespeare reminds us of a source of conflict—Paris's competing claim.

ROMEO. What wilt thou tell her, nurse? Thou dost not mark me.[21]

NURSE. I will tell her, sir, that you do protest, which, as I take it, is a gentlemanlike offer.

ROMEO. Bid her devise
1 Some means to come to shrift[22] this afternoon;
And there she shall at Friar Lawrence' cell
Be shrived[23] and married. Here is for thy pains.

[*He puts money into her hand.*]

NURSE. No, truly, sir; not a penny.

ROMEO. Go to! I say you shall.

NURSE. This afternoon, sir? Well, she shall be there.

ROMEO. And stay, good nurse, behind the abbey wall.
2 Within this hour my man shall be with thee
And bring thee cords made like a tackled stair,[24]
Which to the high topgallant[25] of my joy
Must be my convoy[26] in the secret night.
Farewell. Be trusty, and I'll quit thy pains.[27]
Farewell. Commend me to thy mistress.

NURSE. Now God in heaven bless thee! Hark you,[28] sir.

ROMEO. What say'st, thou, my dear nurse?

NURSE. Is your man secret? Did you ne'er hear say,
Two may keep counsel, putting one away?[29]

ROMEO. Warrant thee my man's as true as steel.

NURSE. Well, sir, my mistress is the sweetest lady. Lord, Lord! When 'twas a little prating[30] thing—O, there is a nobleman
3 in town, one Paris, that would fain lay knife aboard;[31] but she, good soul, had as lieve[32] see a toad, a very toad, as see him. I anger her sometimes, and tell her that Paris is the properer man; but I'll warrant you, when I say so, she looks as pale as any clout in the versal world.[33] Doth not rosemary and Romeo begin both with a letter?

ROMEO. Ay, nurse; what of that? Both with an *R*.

NURSE. Ah, mocker! That's the dog's name.[34] *R* is for the—No; I know it begins with some other letter; and she hath the prettiest sententious[35] of it, of you and rosemary, that it would do you good to hear it.

ROMEO. Commend me to thy lady.

21 **mark me:** pay attention to me.

22 **shrift:** the sacrament of confession in which sins are confessed for forgiveness.

23 **shrived:** forgiven for her sins.

24 **tackled stair:** rope ladder.

25 **topgallant:** topmast, highest part.

26 **convoy:** vehicle. He is speaking of the ladder.

27 **quit thy pains:** reward your trouble.

28 **Hark you:** Listen.

29 **Two . . . away:** Two people can keep a secret if one is dead.

30 **prating:** chattering

31 **fain . . . aboard:** take her for himself.

32 **had as lieve:** would rather.

33 **as any . . . world:** as any cloth in the universe.

34 **That's . . . name:** The letter *R* sounds like a dog's growl.

35 **sententious:** The Nurse means *sentences.*

GUIDED READING

LITERAL QUESTION

1a. What part do the Nurse and Friar Lawrence play in devising this scheme? (Friar Lawrence helped plan it; the Nurse consents to it.)

INFERENTIAL QUESTION

1b. Both Friar Lawrence and the Nurse are sympathetic, likeable figures—how does their support fit the tragic theme of the play? (example of how good motives can lead to tragic results)

NURSE. Ay, a thousand times. [ROMEO *leaves.*] Peter!

PETER. Anon.

NURSE. Before, and apace.[36]

[PETER *exits, followed by the* NURSE.]

Scene v. Later that day. CAPULET'S *orchard.*

[JULIET, *waiting for the* NURSE *to return from the meeting with* ROMEO, *paces impatiently.*]

1 JULIET. The clock struck nine when I did send the nurse;
In half an hour she promised to return.
Perchance she cannot meet him. That's not so.
2 O, she is lame! Love's heralds should be thoughts,
Which ten times faster glides than the sun's beams
Driving back shadows over low'ring[1] hills.
Therefore do nimble-pinioned doves draw Love,[2]
And therefore hath the wind-swift Cupid wings.
Now is the sun upon the highmost hill
3 Of this day's journey, and from nine till twelve
Is three long hours; yet she is not come.
Had she affections and warm youthful blood,
She would be as swift in motion as a ball;
My words would bandy her[3] to my sweet love,
And his to me.
But old folks, many feign as[4] they were dead—
Unwieldy, slow, heavy and pale as lead.

[*The* NURSE *enters, with* PETER.]

O God, she comes! O honey nurse, what news?
Hast thou met with him? Send thy man away.

NURSE. Peter, stay at the gate. [PETER *leaves.*]

JULIET. Now, good sweet nurse—O Lord, why lookest thou sad?
Though news be sad, yet tell them merrily;
If good, thou shamest the music of sweet news
By playing it to me with so sour a face.

4 NURSE. I am aweary, give me leave awhile.[5]
Fie, how my bones ache! What a jaunce[6] have I!

JULIET. I would thou hadst my bones, and I thy news.
Nay, come, I pray thee speak. Good, good nurse, speak.

36 **Before, and apace:** Go before me, and hurry.

1 **low'ring:** darkening.

2 **nimble-pinioned . . . Love:** Light-winged, very fast doves were believed to pull the chariot of Venus, goddess of love.

3 **bandy her:** toss her quickly back and forth.

4 **feign as:** act as if.

5 **give . . . awhile:** excuse me for a minute.

6 **jaunce:** rough trip.

AT A GLANCE

- *Scene iv (continued):* The Nurse and Peter exit.
- *Scene v:* Juliet impatiently awaits the Nurse.
- The Nurse returns; she teasingly withholds her news.

1 BLANK VERSE

Juliet's blank verse elevates her discourse on love.

2 STYLE: METAPHOR

Juliet amuses herself with insights into why love is associated with winged creatures. Again light and shadow are pictured as opposites; here, love's light drives away dangerous shadows.

3 CHARACTERIZATION

Juliet's lines announce the passage of time from nine A.M. to noon and convey her impatience as they remind us of her youthful love and difficult situation.

4 STYLE: HUMOR

The Nurse teases Juliet as she herself was teased, and Juliet's reply shows wit as well as impatience.

GUIDED READING

LITERAL QUESTION

1a. To whom does Juliet refer in line 16? ("old folks," perhaps the Nurse)

INFERENTIAL QUESTION

1b. What comparison does Juliet draw between the young and the old? (The young are quick and lively; the old, slow and lifeless.)

AT A GLANCE

Scene v (continued): The Nurse plays with Juliet's impatience by not answering her questions.

1 CHARACTERIZATION

Juliet softens her chastisement of the Nurse by playing with words.

2 STYLE: PROSE

Juliet's more sublime thoughts on love contrast with the Nurse's earthier reflections, rendered in prose.

3 CHARACTERIZATION

The Nurse changes the subject, content to take her time telling Juliet the news; Juliet's pleading helps create a comic tension that grows from the grave matter being discussed.

NURSE. Jesu, what haste! Can you not stay awhile?
Do you not see that I am out of breath?

1 JULIET. How art thou out of breath when thou hast breath
To say to me that thou art out of breath?
The excuse that thou dost make in this delay
Is longer than the tale thou dost excuse.
Is thy news good or bad? Answer to that.
Say either, and I'll stay the circumstance.[7]
Let me be satisfied, is't good or bad?

2 NURSE. Well, you have made a simple[8] choice; you know not how to choose a man. Romeo? No, not he. Though his face be better than any man's, yet his leg excels all men's; and for a hand and a foot, and a body, though they be not to be talked on, yet they are past compare. He is not the flower of
3 courtesy, but, I'll warrant him, as gentle as a lamb. Go thy ways, wench; serve God. What, have you dined at home?

JULIET. No, no. But all this did I know before.
What says he of our marriage? What of that?

NURSE. Lord, how my head aches! What a head have I!
It beats as it would fall in twenty pieces.
My back a t'other side—ah, my back, my back!
Beshrew[9] your heart for sending me about
To catch my death with jauncing up and down!

JULIET. I'faith, I am sorry that thou art not well.
Sweet, sweet, sweet nurse, tell me, what says my love?

NURSE. Your love says, like an honest gentleman, and a courteous, and a kind, and a handsome, and, I warrant, a virtuous— Where is your mother?

JULIET. Where is my mother? Why, she is within.
Where should she be? How oddly thou repliest!
"Your love says, like an honest gentleman,
'Where is your mother?' "

NURSE. O God's Lady dear!
Are you so hot?[10] Marry come up, I trow.[11]
Is this the poultice[12] for my aching bones?
Henceforward do your messages yourself.

JULIET. Here's such a coil![13] Come, what says Romeo?

NURSE. Have you got leave to go to shrift today?

JULIET. I have.

7 **stay the circumstance:** wait for the details.

8 **simple:** foolish.

9 **Beshrew:** shame on.

10 **hot:** impatient.

11 **Marry . . . trow:** Come, contain yourself; I declare.

12 **poultice:** remedy.

13 **coil:** fuss.

GUIDED READING

LITERAL QUESTIONS

1a. What does the Nurse complain about? (She says that she is tired.)

2a. How does Juliet respond to the Nurse's complaint? (She expresses sorrow and impatience.)

INFERENTIAL QUESTIONS

1b. What might be the Nurse's motive for this complaint? (to tease Juliet; to remind her to be grateful)

2b. What does her response tell you about Juliet's relationship to the Nurse? (She cares for the Nurse and probably often must listen to her complaints.)

NURSE. Then hie[14] you hence to Friar Lawrence' cell;
There stays a husband to make you a wife.
Now comes the wanton[15] blood up in your cheeks:
They'll be in scarlet straight at any news.
Hie you to church; I must another way,
To fetch a ladder, by the which your love
Must climb a bird's nest soon when it is dark.
Go; I'll to dinner; hie you to the cell.

JULIET. Hie to high fortune! Honest nurse, farewell.

[*They exit in separate directions.*]

14 **hie:** hurry.

15 **wanton:** playful.

Scene vi. Later that afternoon. FRIAR LAWRENCE'S *cell.*

[ROMEO *and* FRIAR LAWRENCE *are waiting for* JULIET *so that the wedding can take place.*]

FRIAR. So smile the heavens upon this holy act
That afterhours with sorrow chide us not![1]

ROMEO. Amen, amen! But come what sorrow can,
It cannot countervail[2] the exchange of joy
That one short minute gives me in her sight.
Do thou but close our hands with holy words,
Then love-devouring death do what he dare—
It is enough I may but call her mine.

FRIAR. These violent delights have violent ends
And, in their triumph die, like fire and powder,
Which, as they kiss, consume.[3] The sweetest honey
Is loathsome in his own deliciousness
And in the taste confounds the appetite.[4]
Therefore love moderately: long love doth so;
Too swift arrives as tardy as too slow.

[JULIET *enters.*]

Here comes the lady. O, so light a foot
Will ne'er wear out the everlasting flint.[5]
A lover may bestride the gossamers[6]
That idles in the wanton summer air,
And yet not fall; so light is vanity.[7]

JULIET. Good even to my ghostly confessor.

FRIAR. Romeo shall thank thee, daughter, for us both.

JULIET. As much to him,[8] else is his thanks too much.

1 **That . . . not:** and not punish us for it later.

2 **countervail:** outweigh.

3 **These violent . . . consume:** Extreme happiness burns itself out like gunpowder.

4 **The sweetest . . . appetite:** The sweeter the honey, the sooner we tire of it.

5 **flint:** hard stone. The Friar refers to a proverb that says small drops of water can wear away stones.

6 **bestride the gossamers:** walk on spiders' webs.

7 **vanity:** the unreality of lovers.

8 **As much to him:** the same to him.

AT A GLANCE

- *Scene v (continued):* Juliet learns that Romeo plans to marry her at Friar Lawrence's cell.
- *Scene vi:* In Friar Lawrence's cell the friar and Romeo await Juliet, who finally arrives.

1 MOOD

Shakespeare develops tension in the scene by having the Nurse withhold news; as soon as she reveals the information, the scene ends.

2 FORESHADOWING

Even at this happy moment of marriage, Friar Lawrence invokes the unhappy fate *(the heavens)* that may yet bring "sorrow."

3 FORESHADOWING

Friar Lawrence's metaphors of violent matings and "loathsome" sweetness underscore the tragic potential of Romeo's hasty, all-consuming love.

4 PLOT: RISING ACTION

As Friar Lawrence paints a word picture of Juliet's arrival, Shakespeare tantalizes us with the foreboding of doom; Juliet's entrance propels the tragedy.

GUIDED READING

LITERAL QUESTIONS

1a. What is the friar's concluding advice to Romeo before Juliet's entrance? (to "love moderately" and not "too swift")

2a. How lightly does Juliet run, according to Friar Lawrence? (so lightly that she could run upon spider webs)

INFERENTIAL QUESTIONS

1b. Why, in your opinion, is the friar so troubled? (He may be having second thoughts. He is aware that he has risked a great deal of their happiness and feels responsible.)

2b. How does the sight of Juliet seem to change Friar Lawrence's mood? (He seems to lighten at seeing her beauty.)

AT A GLANCE

- *Scene vi (continued):* The lovers reaffirm their desire to be wed.
- Friar Lawrence invites them into the chapel, where he will perform the ceremony.

1 THEME

Friar Lawrence assures the lovers that a proper ceremony will be performed, legitimizing their union and ending the act with a reminder of the conflict.

REFLECTING ON ACT II

In what way are Friar Lawrence and the Nurse similar? (Each consents to the lovers' wishes and helps the couple: The Nurse acts as a messenger and counsel, and Friar Lawrence agrees to marry them.)

ROMEO. Ah, Juliet, if the measure of thy joy
Be heaped like mine, and that thy skill be more
To blazon it,[9] then sweeten with thy breath
This neighbor air, and let rich music's tongue
Unfold the imagined happiness that both
Receive in either by this dear encounter.

JULIET. Conceit, more rich in matter than in words,
Brags of his substance, not of ornament.[10]
They are but beggars that can count their worth;
But my true love is grown to such excess
I cannot sum up sum of half my wealth.

FRIAR. Come, come with me, and we will make short work;
1 For, by your leaves, you shall not stay alone
Till Holy Church incorporate two in one.

[*They exit to perform the wedding ceremony.*]

9 **that thy . . . it:** if you are better able than I to announce it.

10 **Conceit . . . ornament:** True understanding does not need words.

GUIDED READING

LITERAL QUESTION

1a. With what word does Shakespeare have Romeo describe the lovers' happiness? *(imagined)*

INFERENTIAL QUESTION

1b. Why might this description help to foreshadow the tragedy? (Their happiness will be fleeting.)

STUDY QUESTIONS

Recalling

1. To what three heavenly bodies does Romeo compare Juliet at the beginning of Act II, Scene ii?
2. In Scene ii, lines 33–49, what does Romeo overhear Juliet saying about him and about her feelings for him?
3. What does Juliet ask of Romeo in Scene ii, lines 143–148? What offer does she make to him in return?
4. What is Friar Lawrence doing when we first meet him in Scene iii?
5. In Scene iii with what trait in Romeo does Friar Lawrence find fault? At the end of the scene, what reason does Friar Lawrence give for helping Romeo and Juliet?
6. In Scene iv why is Tybalt looking for Romeo?
7. During Scene iv what directions does Romeo have for Juliet and for the Nurse? What is about to happen at the end of Act II?

Interpreting

8. What do we learn about Juliet from her speech in Scene ii, lines 85–106?
9. Contrast Romeo's love for Juliet with his love for Rosaline. Consider his reaction to being in love with each woman and the resulting actions.
10. According to Scene vi, lines 1–15, what fears does Friar Lawrence have about the marriage? Explain his advice to Romeo.

Extending

11. Do you agree with the Nurse's and Friar Lawrence's decisions to help Romeo and Juliet? Why or why not? What else might they have done?

LITERARY FOCUS

Dramatic Conventions

One meaning of *convention* is "custom." A **dramatic convention** is a device that a playwright uses to present a story on stage and that the audience accepts as realistic. For example, today's moviegoers accept as realistic the music that accompanies the action in films even though music does not actually accompany life's dramatic moments. In addition to using the convention of blank verse (page 356), Shakespeare followed a number of other Elizabethan dramatic conventions. For example, because Elizabethans considered acting unrespectable for women, boys who were apprentice actors played the parts of women.

Acting companies did not use scenery and they performed during daylight without special lighting. As a result, the action moved quickly because no time was needed to change scenes. Because of the lack of scenery and special lighting, dialogue was the key to establishing action. For example, at the beginning of Act I, Scene iv, Romeo calls for a torch. Therefore, the audience knows that it is night. Capulet's greeting at the start of the next scene tells us that we are at his home at the time of his party.

Thinking About Dramatic Conventions

1. Reread Act II, Scene i, lines 1–6, and Scene ii, lines 1–6. What does the beginning of each scene tell us about time and place?
2. Reread Act II, Scene ii, lines 186–189, and Scene iii, lines 1–8. What do we learn about the setting of Scene iii? Based on these lines, explain how dialogue creates setting.
3. What clues about the time and place are contained in Act II, Scene v, lines 1–17?

STUDY QUESTIONS

1. sun, moon, stars
2. wonders why he is a Montague; declares love in spite of name
3. if his purpose is marriage; her fortunes, to follow him
4. returning from gathering herbs
5. fickleness; hopes that marriage will end feud
6. to challenge him to a duel
7.
   - Juliet is to come to Friar's cell to be married; Nurse is to hang rope ladder out window.
   - They are about to be married.
8. Her love is genuine; she is aware of her boldness in declaring love, speaking so soon.
9. Rosaline, an infatuation: He mopes and mourns. Juliet, sincere: He rushes into danger in hopes of seeing her, and accepts fate.
10. its haste; that immoderation will bring trouble
11. Answers will vary.

LITERARY FOCUS

1. *Scene i:* late night, outside Capulet orchard; *Scene ii:* before daybreak, under Juliet's balcony
2.
   - It is dawn at the friar's cell.
   - Scenes end as characters leave and announce destinations, begin with some hint of location and time, and rhymed couplets signal end of scenes.
3. Juliet's words *from nine to twelve* and her description of sun make us assume she is at home, as she is waiting for Nurse to return.

AT A GLANCE

Act III, Scene i: Mercutio and Benvolio pass the time on a Verona street.

LITERARY OPTIONS

- monologue and soliloquy
- imagery
- dramatic conventions

THEMATIC OPTIONS

- moderation
- revenge
- good and evil

1 THEME

Benvolio speaks of excessive heat, which drives intemperate men to seek relief in fighting. Though playful, the following dialogue reminds us that excessive passions can lead to conflict.

2 CHARACTERIZATION

Mercutio again entertains himself and his friend with a long, inventive speech about the trivial and improbable causes of argument.

3 PARAPHRASING

Mercutio's fanciful description compares Benvolio's brains to a scrambled egg.

4 CHARACTERIZATION

The good-humored Benvolio brushes aside Mercutio's taunts. Ironically, Mercutio's and Tybalt's imminent quarrel will lead to the loss of life that Benvolio jokes about.

ACT III

Scene i. The same afternoon. A street in Verona.

[BENVOLIO *and* MERCUTIO *enter with some of their* SERVANTS. BENVOLIO *worries about meeting Capulets (Capels) on such a hot summer day when tempers are short.* MERCUTIO*, however, mocks* BENVOLIO*'s concern and calls him quarrelsome.*]

1 **BENVOLIO.** I pray thee, good Mercutio, let's retire.
The day is hot, the Capels are abroad,
And, if we meet, we shall not 'scape a brawl,
For now, these hot days, is the mad blood stirring.

MERCUTIO. Thou art like one of these fellows that, when he enters the confines of a tavern, claps me his sword upon the table and says, "God send me no need of thee!" and by the operation of the second cup draws him on the drawer,[1] when indeed there is no need.

BENVOLIO. Am I like such a fellow?

MERCUTIO. Come, come, thou art as hot a Jack in thy mood as any in Italy; and as soon moved to be moody, and as soon moody to be moved.[2]

BENVOLIO. And what to?

MERCUTIO. Nay, and there were two such, we should have none
2 shortly, for one would kill the other. Thou! Why, thou wilt
quarrel with a man that hath a hair more or a hair less in his
beard than thou hast. Thou wilt quarrel with a man for
cracking nuts, having no other reason but because thou hast
hazel eyes. What eye but such an eye would spy out such a
3 quarrel? Thy head is as full of quarrels as an egg is full of
meat; and yet thy head hath been beaten as addle[3] as an egg
for quarreling. Thou hast quarreled with a man for coughing in the street, because he hath wakened thy dog that hath
lain asleep in the sun. Didst thou not fall out with a tailor
for wearing his new doublet[4] before Easter? With another
for tying his new shoes with old riband?[5] And yet thou wilt
tutor me from quarreling![6]

4 **BENVOLIO.** And I were so apt to quarrel as thou art, any man should buy the fee simple[7] of my life for an hour and a quarter[8]

MERCUTIO. The fee simple? O simple![9]

1 **by . . . drawer:** by the time he has his second drink, he draws his sword on the waiter.

2 **as soon moved . . . to be moved:** as angry as you are quick-tempered.

3 **addle:** scrambled.

4 **doublet:** short, close-fitting jacket.

5 **riband:** ribbon.

6 **tutor me from quarreling:** teach me not to quarrel.

7 **fee simple:** complete ownership.

8 **an hour and a quarter:** with payment no more than the brief time someone as quarrelsome as Mercutio could be expected to live.

9 **O simple!:** O stupid!

GUIDED READING

LITERAL QUESTIONS

1a. What does Benvolio ask Mercutio to do at the opening of the act? (to retire from the street)

2a. What is the subject of Mercutio's speech? (Benvolio's supposedly quarrelsome personality)

INFERENTIAL QUESTIONS

1b. What does this action reveal about Benvolio's character? (He is a peacemaker who wants to avoid trouble.)

2b. How do we know Mercutio is joking? (In Act I Benvolio broke up the street fight in the interests of peace.)

[TYBALT, JULIET*'s cousin, enters with other* CAPULETS. *He is still angry about* ROMEO*'s intruding at the party the night before.* TYBALT *has not been able to find* ROMEO *since sending him a challenge earlier that day.*]

BENVOLIO. By my head, here comes the Capulets.

MERCUTIO. By my heel, I care not.

TYBALT. [*To his companions.*] Follow me close, for I will speak to them. [*To* BENVOLIO *and* MERCUTIO.] Gentlemen, good-den. A word with one of you.

MERCUTIO. And but one word with one of us? Couple it with something; make it a word and a blow.

TYBALT. You shall find me apt enough to that, sir, and you will give me occasion![10]

MERCUTIO. Could you not take some occasion without giving?

TYBALT. Mercutio, thou consortest[11] with Romeo.

MERCUTIO. Consort? What, dost thou make us minstrels? And thou make minstrels of us, look to hear nothing but discords.[12] [*He places his hand on the hilt of his sword.*] Here's my fiddlestick;[13] here's that shall make you dance. Zounds,[14] consort!

BENVOLIO. We talk here in the public haunt of men.
Either withdraw unto some private place,
Or reason coldly of your grievances,
Or else depart. Here all eyes gaze on us.

MERCUTIO. Men's eyes were made to look, and let them gaze.
I will not budge for no man's pleasure, I.

[ROMEO *enters. He is calm and happy after his secret marriage to* JULIET.]

TYBALT. Well, peace be with you, sir. Here comes my man.[15]

MERCUTIO. But I'll be hanged, sir, if he wear your livery.[16]
Marry, go before to field,[17] he'll be your follower!
Your worship in that sense may call him man.

TYBALT. Romeo, the love I bear thee can afford
No better term than this: thou art a villain.[18]

ROMEO. Tybalt, the reason that I have to love thee
Doth much excuse the appertaining rage[19]
To such a greeting. Villain am I none.

10 **occasion:** reason.

11 **consortest:** keep company. A consort is also a group of musicians (minstrels). Mercutio will use this second meaning for a joke.

12 **discords:** inharmonious sounds.

13 **fiddlestick:** bow for a fiddle; here, sword.

14 **Zounds:** an exclamation of surprise or anger. It derives from "by God's wounds."

15 **man:** the man I am looking for. Mercutio takes another meaning of the word, "servant."

16 **livery:** servant's uniform.

17 **field:** dueling field.

18 **villain:** person of low class.

19 **appertaining rage:** the appropriate angry response.

AT A GLANCE

- *Scene i (continued):* Tybalt enters and quarrels with Mercutio.
- Romeo, newly married to Tybalt's cousin, greets Tybalt civilly.

1 CONFLICT

Tybalt, whose immoderate temper is never entirely under control, enters the quarrel simply because Mercutio is Romeo's friend.

2 THEME

Benvolio's wise words, delivered in blank verse, attempt to persuade the men to moderate their passions ("reason coldly").

3 THEME

Fate has decreed that good and evil will struggle together; it delivers the bridegroom, Romeo, just as the fight begins.

4 DRAMATIC IRONY

Whereas Tybalt uses the word *love* sarcastically, Romeo uses it sincerely—but no one present knows why.

GUIDED READING

LITERAL QUESTION

1a. How many of Romeo's friends know that he has fallen in love with Juliet? (none)

INFERENTIAL QUESTION

1b. Had Romeo confided in his friends, how might the action have been different? (Benvolio and Mercutio would have understood his meaning in lines 61–63 and discouraged the fight.)

AT A GLANCE

- *Scene i (continued):* Mercutio provokes Tybalt; they fight.
- Romeo steps between them, blocking Mercutio.
- Tybalt stabs Mercutio and flees.

1 THEME

Romeo tries to diffuse the situation, but the inflamed tempers of Tybalt and Mercutio overpower his reason.

2 PLOT: RISING ACTION

Mercutio has called Tybalt "Prince of Cats" once before—it is a literary reference that amuses him. The insult further inflames Tybalt.

3 THEME

Romeo's good intentions—to make peace—lead to tragic evil: the death of Mercutio.

4 IRONY

Mercutio, who has partly precipitated the tragedy, does not belong to either feuding family.

Therefore farewell. I see thou knowest me not.[20]

TYBALT. Boy, this shall not excuse the injuries
That thou hast done me; therefore turn and draw.

ROMEO. I do protest I never injured thee,
But love thee better than thou canst devise[21]
Till thou shalt know the reason of my love;
1 And so, good Capulet, which name I tender[22]
As dearly as mine own, be satisfied.

MERCUTIO. O calm, dishonorable, vile submission!
Alla stoccata[23] carries it away.

[MERCUTIO, *upset at* TYBALT'S *insults and at* ROMEO'S *refusal to fight, draws his sword.*]

Tybalt, you ratcatcher, will you walk?

TYBALT. What wouldst thou have with me?

2 MERCUTIO. Good King of Cats, nothing but one of your nine lives. That I mean to make bold withal,[24] and, as you shall use me hereafter, dry-beat[25] the rest of the eight. Will you pluck your sword out of his pilcher[26] by the ears? Make haste, lest mine be about your ears ere it be out.

TYBALT. I am for you. [TYBALT *draws his sword.*]

ROMEO. Gentle Mercutio, put thy rapier up.

MERCUTIO. Come sir, your *passado!*

[MERCUTIO *and* TYBALT *fight.* ROMEO, *trying to stop the fight, turns to* BENVOLIO *for help.*]

ROMEO. Draw, Benvolio; beat down their weapons.
Gentlemen, for shame! Forbear this outrage!
Tybalt, Mercutio, the Prince expressly hath
Forbid this bandying in Verona streets.
Hold, Tybalt! Good Mercutio!

3 [ROMEO, *trying to separate the two men, steps between them and blocks* MERCUTIO'S *sword arm. At that moment* TYBALT *thrusts his sword under* ROMEO'S *arm and stabs* MERCUTIO. TYBALT *flees with his followers.*]

MERCUTIO. I am hurt.
4 A plague a[27] both houses! I am sped.[28]
Is he gone and hath nothing?

BENVOLIO. What, art thou hurt?

20 **knowest me not:** Tybalt does not know that Romeo and he are now related because of the marriage.

21 **devise:** imagine.

22 **tender:** value.

23 **Alla stoccata:** Italian fencing term meaning "at the thrust." Mercutio gives Tybalt this nickname because Tybalt's insults are like thrusts.

24 **make bold withal:** take.

25 **dry-beat:** thrash.

26 **pilcher:** scabbard, case.

27 **a:** on.

28 **sped:** done for.

GUIDED READING

LITERAL QUESTION

1a. What reason does Romeo give to Tybalt and Mercutio for stopping their fight? ("The Prince expressly hath forbid" such fighting.)

INFERENTIAL QUESTION

1b. Of what does this reason remind the audience? (Anyone caught fighting will face the death penalty; the fight is dangerous even for its survivors.)

MERCUTIO. Ay, ay, a scratch, a scratch. Marry, 'tis enough.
Where is my page? Go, villain, fetch a surgeon.

[*The* PAGE, *a servant, leaves to find a doctor.*]

ROMEO. Courage, man. The hurt cannot be much.

1 **MERCUTIO.** No, 'tis not so deep as a well, nor so wide as a church door; but 'tis enough, 'twill serve. Ask for me tomorrow, and you shall find me a grave[29] man. I am peppered,[30] I warrant, for this world. A plague a both your houses! Zounds, a dog, a rat, a mouse, a cat, to scratch a man to death! A braggart, a rogue, a villain, that fights by the book of arithmetic![31] Why the devil came you between us? I was hurt under your arm.

ROMEO. I thought all for the best.

MERCUTIO. Help me into some house, Benvolio,
2 Or I shall faint. A plague o' both your houses!
They have made worms' meat of me. I have it,
And soundly too. Your houses!

[MERCUTIO *leaves, supported by* BENVOLIO *and his men.*]

3 **ROMEO.** This gentleman, the Prince's near ally,[32]
My very friend, hath got his mortal hurt
In my behalf—my reputation stained
With Tybalt's slander—Tybalt, that an hour
Hath been my cousin. O sweet Juliet,
Thy beauty hath made me effeminate[33]
And in my temper soft'ned valor's steel!

[BENVOLIO *returns.*]

BENVOLIO. O Romeo, Romeo, brave Mercutio is dead!
That gallant spirit hath aspired[34] the clouds,
Which too untimely here did scorn the earth.

4 **ROMEO.** This day's black fate on moe days doth depend;[35]
This but begins the woe others must end.

[TYBALT *returns.*]

BENVOLIO. Here comes the furious Tybalt back again.

ROMEO. Alive in triumph, and Mercutio slain?
Away to heaven respective lenity,[36]
And fire-eyed fury be my conduct[37] now!
Now, Tybalt, take the "villain" back again
That late thou gavest me; for Mercutio's soul

29 **grave:** serious, dead. Mercutio puns even while dying.
30 **peppered:** finished.
31 **by . . . arithmetic:** by the rules.
32 **ally:** relative. Mercutio is related to the Prince and is neither a Capulet nor a Montague.
33 **effeminate:** like a woman.
34 **aspired:** risen to.
35 **This . . . depend:** Today's fatal happening will lead to more dark days.
36 **respective lenity:** reasonable mercy.
37 **conduct:** guide.

AT A GLANCE

- *Scene i (continued):* Mercutio dies.
- Romeo challenges Tybalt.

1 STYLE: IMAGERY

Mercutio, knowing he has been fatally wounded, creates a riddle about his wound and about his grave.

2 CHARACTERIZATION

Mercutio bitterly curses the feud that he believes has taken his life.

3 PLOT: RISING ACTION

Mercutio has died defending Romeo's name, and honor now demands that Romeo take his friend's place.

4 THEME

Romeo begins to see the tragic chain of events but cannot extricate himself from a fateful encounter.

GUIDED READING

LITERAL QUESTION

1a. What are Mercutio's last words? ("Your houses!")

INFERENTIAL QUESTION

1b. Why does he curse *both* houses? (Both houses are equally responsible for the feud.)

AT A GLANCE

- *Scene i (continued):* Tybalt is slain by Romeo.
- A crowd gathers.
- The Prince demands to know what happened.

1 STYLE: IMAGERY

Mercutio's ghost is depicted as hovering over their heads, waiting for Tybalt's spirit to join him.

2 THEME

As soon as he hears Benvolio speak of the Prince's edict, Romeo recognizes that in killing a Capulet he has been goaded into a tragic act of revenge.

3 STYLE: RHYTHM

Lady Capulet's broken lines indicate strong emotion. In her anguish she calls out for revenge.

1 Is but a little way above our heads,
Staying for thine to keep him company.
Either thou or I, or both, must go with him.

TYBALT. Thou, wretched boy, that didst consort him here,
Shalt with him hence.

ROMEO. This shall determine that.

[ROMEO *draws his sword;* TYBALT *draws his in response. They fight until* ROMEO *stabs* TYBALT, *who falls.*]

BENVOLIO. Romeo, away, be gone!
The citizens are up, and Tybalt slain.
2 Stand not amazed. The Prince will doom thee death
If thou art taken. Hence, be gone, away!

ROMEO. O, I am fortune's fool![38]

BENVOLIO. Why dost thou stay?

[ROMEO *flees just before a group of angry* CITIZENS *enters.*]

CITIZEN. Which way ran he that killed Mercutio?
Tybalt, that murderer, which way ran he?

BENVOLIO. There lies that Tybalt.

CITIZEN. Up, sir, go with me.
I charge thee in the Prince's name obey.

[PRINCE ESCALUS, LORD MONTAGUE, LADY MONTAGUE, LORD CAPULET, *and* LADY CAPULET *enter with various followers.*]

PRINCE. Where are the vile beginners of this fray?

BENVOLIO. O noble Prince, I can discover[39] all
The unlucky manage[40] of this fatal brawl.
There lies the man, slain by young Romeo,
That slew thy kinsman, brave Mercutio.

3 LADY CAPULET. Tybalt, my cousin! O my brother's child!
O Prince! O cousin! Husband! O, the blood is spilled
Of my dear kinsman! Prince, as thou art true,
For blood of ours shed blood of Montague.
O cousin, cousin!

PRINCE. Benvolio, who began this bloody fray?

BENVOLIO. Tybalt, here slain, whom Romeo's hand did slay.
Romeo, that spoke him fair, bid him bethink
How nice[41] the quarrel was, and urged withal
Your high displeasure. All this—utterèd

38 **fortune's fool:** fate's plaything.

39 **discover:** reveal.

40 **manage:** circumstances.

41 **nice:** trivial.

GUIDED READING

LITERAL QUESTIONS

1a. Which member of the Capulet family expresses grief for Tybalt's death? (Lady Capulet)

2a. What question does the Prince ask repeatedly? (Who started the fight?)

INFERENTIAL QUESTIONS

1b. What reasons could be found for her outburst? (Tybalt was a relative; she feels familial grief.)

2b. Why does he ask this? (He needs to know how to assign responsibility for the fight so that he can mete out punishment.)

1 With gentle breath, calm look, knees humbly bowed—
Could not take truce with the unruly spleen[42]
Of Tybalt deaf to peace, but that he tilts[43]
With piercing steel at bold Mercutio's breast;
Who, all as hot, turns deadly point to point,
And, with a martial scorn,[44] with one hand beats
Cold death aside and with the other sends
It back to Tybalt, whose dexterity
Retorts it.[45] Romeo he cries aloud,
"Hold, friends! Friends, part!" and swifter than his tongue,
His agile arm beats down their fatal points,
And 'twixt them rushes; underneath whose arm
An envious[46] thrust from Tybalt hit the life
Of stout[47] Mercutio, and then Tybalt fled;
But by and by comes back to Romeo,
Who had but newly entertained[48] revenge,
2 And to't they go like lightning; for, ere I
Could draw to part them, was stout Tybalt slain;
And, as he fell, did Romeo turn and fly.
This is the truth, or let Benvolio die.

LADY CAPULET. He is a kinsman to the Montague;
Affection makes him false, he speaks not true.
Some twenty of them fought in this black strife,

42 **spleen:** anger.

43 **tilts:** thrusts.

44 **martial scorn:** warlike hatred.

45 **dexterity retorts it:** skill returns it.

46 **envious:** hateful.

47 **stout:** courageous.

48 **entertained:** thought of.

AT A GLANCE

- *Scene i (continued):* Benvolio reports the events to the Prince.
- Lady Capulet accuses him of lying.

1 MONOLOGUE

Comparing Benvolio's account of Romeo's departure to the actual scene, we see that Benvolio is trying to give an honest account.

2 IRONY

We learn that Benvolio contemplated the same action Romeo undertook with such unfortunate consequence.

GUIDED READING

LITERAL QUESTION

1a. How does Benvolio report Romeo's part in the quarrel? (He presents Romeo as calm and as urging peace on bended knee (l. 154); he tells how Romeo tried to break up the fight (l. 163).

INFERENTIAL QUESTION

1b. Why might Benvolio think the motive of revenge could be a point in Romeo's favor? (The Prince might have wanted someone to avenge the murder of his relative Mercutio.)

AT A GLANCE

- *Scene i (continued):* The Prince banishes Romeo.
- *Scene ii:* Juliet awaits Romeo in her bedroom.
- The Nurse enters with a rope ladder.

1 CONFLICT

Lady Capulet urges that Romeo be put to death for the murder of her kinsman.

2 PLOT: RISING ACTION

The angry Prince sentences Romeo to banishment rather than death.

3 DRAMATIC CONVENTION

The scene ends with a rhymed couplet that expresses the idea that to pardon killers is to murder justice itself.

4 STYLE: IMAGERY

Juliet addresses the sun—urging it to travel faster across the sky—as though it were pulled by wonderfully swift horses.

1 And all those twenty could but kill one life.
I beg for justice, which thou, Prince, must give.
Romeo slew Tybalt; Romeo must not live.

PRINCE. Romeo slew him; he slew Mercutio.
Who now the price of his dear blood doth owe?

MONTAGUE. Not Romeo, Prince; he was Mercutio's friend;
His fault concludes but what the law should end,
The life of Tybalt.[49]

2 **PRINCE.** And for that offense
Immediately we do exile him hence.
I have an interest in your hate's proceeding,
My blood[50] for your rude brawls doth lie a-bleeding;
But I'll amerce[51] you with so strong a fine
That you shall all repent the loss of mine.
I will be deaf to pleading and excuses;
Nor tears nor prayers shall purchase out abuses.
Therefore use none. Let Romeo hence in haste,
Else, when he is found, that hour is his last.
3 Bear hence this body and attend our will.[52]
Mercy but murders, pardoning those that kill.

[*They all exit.*]

49 **His fault . . . Tybalt:** Romeo only carried out what the law would have required, the death of Tybalt.

50 **blood:** relative.

51 **amerce:** punish.

52 **attend our will:** wait to hear my complete judgment.

Scene ii. Later that day. CAPULET'*s orchard.*

[JULIET, *unaware of what has happened, waits impatiently for the night so that she can see* ROMEO *again.*]

4 **JULIET.** Gallop apace, you fiery-footed steeds,
Towards Phoebus' lodging![1] Such a wagoner
As Phaëton[2] would whip you to the west
And bring in cloudy night immediately.
Come, gentle night; come, loving, black-browed night;
Give me my Romeo; and, when I shall die,
Take him and cut him out in little stars,
And he will make the face of heaven so fine
That all the world will be in love with night
And pay no worship to the garish sun.
O, here comes my nurse,

[*The* NURSE *enters carrying a rope ladder.*]

And she brings news; and every tongue that speaks
But Romeo's name speaks heavenly eloquence.

1 **Gallop . . . lodging:** Phoebus Apollo, the Greek god of light, is often confused with Helios, the sun god. Here, Juliet refers to Phoebus as the sun god driving his chariot home at the end of the day.

2 **Phaëton:** According to Greek myth, young Phaëton tried to drive the sun god's chariot but was unable to control the horses.

GUIDED READING

LITERAL QUESTION

1a. How does the opening of Scene 2 contrast with the end of Scene 1? (Juliet is alone—happy, ignorant, awaiting the night. The previous scene involved an angry crowd, violence, and death.)

INFERENTIAL QUESTION

1b. In what ways is Juliet a tragic victim of the events of the previous scene? (Her only fault has been to fall in love, yet she will have to suffer the consequences as if guilty of some greater crime.)

Now, nurse, what news? What hast thou there, the cords
That Romeo bid thee fetch?

NURSE. Ay, ay, the cords.

[*She throws down the ladder.*]

JULIET. Ay me! What news? Why dost thou wring thy hands?

NURSE. Ah, weraday![3] He's dead, he's dead, he's dead!
We are undone, lady, we are undone!
Alack the day! He's gone, he's killed, he's dead!

JULIET. Can heaven be so envious?[4]

NURSE. Romeo can,
Though heaven cannot. O Romeo, Romeo!
Who ever would have thought it? Romeo!

JULIET. What devil art thou that dost torment me thus?
This torture should be roared in dismal hell.
Hath Romeo slain himself?

1 NURSE. I saw the wound, I saw it with mine eyes,
(God save the mark![5]) here on his manly breast.
A piteous corse,[6] a bloody piteous corse;
Pale, pale as ashes, all bedaubed in blood,
All in gore-blood. I sounded[7] at the sight.

JULIET. O, break, my heart! Poor bankrout,[8] break at once!
To prison, eyes; ne'er look on liberty!
2 Vile earth, to earth resign;[9] end motion here,
And thou and Romeo press one heavy bier![10]

NURSE. O Tybalt, Tybalt, the best friend I had!
O courteous Tybalt! Honest gentleman!
That ever I should live to see thee dead!

JULIET. What storm is this that blows so contrary?[11]
Is Romeo slaught'red, and is Tybalt dead?
My dearest cousin, and my dearer lord?
Then, dreadful trumpet, sound the general doom![12]
For who is living, if those two are gone?

NURSE. Tybalt is gone, and Romeo banishèd;
Romeo that killed him, he is banishèd.

JULIET. O God! Did Romeo's hand shed Tybalt's blood?

NURSE. It did, it did! Alas the day, it did!

JULIET. O serpent heart, hid with a flow'ring face!

3 **weraday:** wellaway, alas.

4 **envious:** cruel.

5 **God . . . mark:** God keep this from being a sign of more evil to come.

6 **corse:** corpse.

7 **sounded:** swooned, fainted.

8 **bankrout:** bankrupt.

9 **Vile . . . resign:** Juliet wishes her own worthless body to return into the earth, to die.

10 **bier:** platform on which a corpse is displayed before burial.

11 **contrary:** in opposite directions.

12 **dreadful . . . doom:** frightening trumpet, announce the end of the world.

AT A GLANCE

- *Scene ii (continued):* The grief-stricken Nurse brings a garbled account of a death.
- Juliet imagines that Romeo has been killed.
- The Nurse explains, and Juliet condemns Romeo.

1 BLANK VERSE

At this moment of high tension, when the Nurse depicts the corpse that caused her to faint, she speaks in iambic pentameter.

2 FORESHADOWING

An overwhelmed Juliet, imagining that Romeo is dead, speaks of their sharing a common grave.

GUIDED READING

LITERAL QUESTION

1a. What does Juliet learn from the Nurse? (Her husband slew her cousin.)

INFERENTIAL QUESTION

1b. How does this news fit the idea that good and evil are intertwined? (The wedding night is disturbed by sorrow, anger, and confusion.)

AT A GLANCE

- *Scene ii (continued):* Juliet is torn between conflicting loyalties.

1 STYLE: IMAGERY

By comparing Romeo to a dragon, a book, and a palace, Juliet tries to capture her shock at his deceitfulness.

2 CHARACTERIZATION

Her second thought is that Romeo is an honorable man, one to whom she owes wifely loyalty.

3 MONOLOGUE

In this long speech Juliet tries to sort out her thoughts and to determine which has hurt her most—Tybalt's death or Romeo's banishment.

1
Did ever dragon keep so fair a cave?
Was ever book containing such vile matter
So fairly bound? O, that deceit should dwell
In such a gorgeous palace!

NURSE. There's no trust,
No faith, no honesty in men; all perjured,
All forsworn, all naught, all dissemblers.[13]
Ah, where's my man? Give me some *aqua vitae.*[14]
These griefs, these woes, these sorrows make me old.
Shame come to Romeo!

2
JULIET. Blistered be thy tongue
For such a wish! He was not born to shame.
Upon his brow shame is ashamed to sit;
For 'tis a throne where honor may be crowned
Sole monarch of the universal earth.
O, what a beast was I to chide at him!

NURSE. Will you speak well of him that killed your cousin?

3
JULIET. Shall I speak ill of him that is my husband?
Ah, poor my lord, what tongue shall smooth thy name
When I, thy three-hours wife, have mangled it?
But wherefore, villain, didst thou kill my cousin?
That villain cousin would have killed my husband.
Back, foolish tears, back to your native spring!
Your tributary[15] drops belong to woe,
Which you, mistaking, offer up to joy.
My husband lives, that Tybalt would have slain;
And Tybalt's dead, that would have slain my husband.
All this is comfort; wherefore weep I then?
Some word there was, worser than Tybalt's death,
That murd'red me. I would forget it fain;
But O, it presses to my memory
Like damnèd guilty deeds to sinners' minds!
"Tybalt is dead, and Romeo—banishèd."
That "banishèd," that one word "banishèd,"
Hath slain ten thousand Tybalts. Tybalt's death
Was woe enough, if it had ended there;
Or, if sour woe delights in fellowship
And needly will be ranked with[16] other griefs,
Why followed not, when she said "Tybalt's dead,"
Thy father, or thy mother, nay, or both,
Which modern lamentation[17] might have moved?
But with a rearward[18] following Tybalt's death,
"Romeo is banishèd"—to speak that word

13 **dissemblers:** liars.

14 **aqua vitae:** brandy.

15 **tributary drops:** tears in tribute.

16 **needly . . . with:** necessarily must be accompanied by.

17 **modern lamentation:** ordinary grief.

18 **rearward:** rear guard, follow up.

GUIDED READING

LITERAL QUESTION

1a. What word is "worser than Tybalt's death"? (*banishèd*)

INFERENTIAL QUESTION

1b. How does Juliet express her fear of Romeo's banishment? (She says the word has "murdered" her happiness, and believes it to be so powerful it has killed even the memory of her love for Tybalt.)

Is father, mother, Tybalt, Romeo, Juliet,
All slain, all dead. "Romeo is banishèd"—
There is no end, no limit, measure, bound,
In that word's death; no words can that woe sound.
Where is my father and my mother, nurse?

NURSE. Weeping and wailing over Tybalt's corse.
Will you go to them? I will bring you thither.

JULIET. Wash they his wounds with tears? Mine shall be spent,
When theirs are dry, for Romeo's banishment.

NURSE. Hie to your chamber. I'll find Romeo
To comfort you. I wot[19] well where he is.
Hark ye, your Romeo will be here at night.
I'll to him; he is hid at Lawrence' cell.

JULIET. O, find him! Give this ring to my true knight
And bid him come to take his last farewell.

[*They exit.*]

19 **wot:** know.

Scene iii. Later. FRIAR LAWRENCE'*s cell.*

[FRIAR LAWRENCE *enters and notices that* ROMEO *is hiding in the room.*]

FRIAR. Romeo, come forth; come forth, thou fearful man.
Affliction is enamored of thy parts,[1]
And thou art wedded to calamity.[2]

[ROMEO *steps forward.*]

ROMEO. Father, what news? What is the Prince's doom?[3]
What sorrow craves acquaintance at my hand
That I yet know not?

FRIAR. Too familiar
Is my dear son with such sour company.
I bring thee tidings of the Prince's doom.

ROMEO. What less than doomsday[4] is the Prince's doom?

FRIAR. A gentler judgment vanished[5] from his lips—
Not body's death, but body's banishment.

ROMEO. Ha, banishment? Be merciful, say "death";
For exile hath more terror in his look,
Much more than death. Do not say "banishment."

FRIAR. Here from Verona art thou banishèd.
Be patient, for the world is broad and wide.

1 **Affliction . . . parts:** Misfortune has fallen in love with your good qualities.
2 **calamity:** disaster.
3 **doom:** final sentence or decision.
4 **doomsday:** my death.
5 **vanished:** escaped.

AT A GLANCE

- *Scene ii (continued):* Juliet sends the Nurse to invite Romeo to visit her.
- *Scene iii:* Friar Lawrence finds Romeo hiding in his cell.
- He tells Romeo that he is banished, not sentenced to die.

1 STYLE: RHYME

The scene ends with a variation on rhymed couplets: *abab.* The rhymes join the Nurse and Juliet in mutual understanding and succinctly end the scene.

2 THEME

Friar Lawrence expresses the ironic consequence of the marriage: Misfortune, rather than Juliet, is the bride.

GUIDED READING

LITERAL QUESTIONS

1a. What is both lovers' response to the sentence of exile? (Both consider it worse than death.)

2a. How does Friar Lawrence describe the Prince's sentence? (He calls it "gentle.")

INFERENTIAL QUESTIONS

1b. Why don't they see the blessing in staying alive? (To lovers, being apart is torture more painful than death.)

2b. What does Friar Lawrence's view of exile show about his character? (It may be taken to show that he is experienced and realistic.)

AT A GLANCE

- *Scene iii (continued):* Romeo considers the agony of banishment.

1 STYLE: IMAGERY

Like Juliet, Romeo sees exile as a sort of murder. He sees himself decapitated by a golden ax—a weapon whose beauty betrays its deadly nature.

2 CHARACTERIZATION

Friar Lawrence offers comfort, gently calling Romeo "mad": He recognizes that Romeo is temporarily beyond reason.

ROMEO. There is no world without[6] Verona walls,
But purgatory, torture, hell itself.
Hence banishèd is banished from the world,
And world's exile is death. Then "banishèd"
1 Is death mistermed. Calling death "banishèd,"
Thou cut'st my head off with a golden ax
And smilest upon the stroke that murders me.

FRIAR. O deadly sin! O rude unthankfulness!
Thy fault our law calls death;[7] but the kind Prince,
Taking thy part, hath rushed[8] aside the law,
And turned that black word "death" to "banishment."
This is dear[9] mercy, and thou seest it not.

ROMEO. 'Tis torture, and not mercy. Heaven is here,
Where Juliet lives; and every cat and dog
And little mouse, every unworthy thing,
Live here in heaven and may look on her;
But Romeo may not. More validity,[10]
More honorable state, more courtship lives
In carrion flies than Romeo. They may seize
On the white wonder of dear Juliet's hand
And steal immortal blessing from her lips.
But Romeo may not, he is banishèd.
Flies may do this but I from this must fly;
They are freemen, but I am banishèd.
And sayest thou yet that exile is not death?
Hadst thou no poison mixed, no sharp-ground knife,
No sudden mean[11] of death, though ne'er so mean,[12]
But "banishèd" to kill me—"banishèd"?
O friar, the damned use that word in hell;
Howling attends it! How hast thou the heart,
Being a divine, a ghostly confessor,
A sin-absolver, and my friend professed,
To mangle me with that word "banishèd"?

2 FRIAR. Thou fond[13] mad man, hear me a little speak.

ROMEO. O, thou wilt speak again of banishment.

FRIAR. I'll give thee armor to keep off that word;
Adversity's sweet milk, philosophy,[14]
To comfort thee, though thou art banishèd.

ROMEO. Yet "banishèd"? Hang up philosophy!
Unless philosophy can make a Juliet,
Displant a town, reverse a prince's doom,
It helps not, it prevails not. Talk no more.

6 **without:** outside.

7 **Thy fault . . . death:** Your crime is usually punishable by death.

8 **rushed:** pushed.

9 **dear:** uncommon.

10 **validity:** value.

11 **mean:** method.

12 **mean:** lowly.

13 **fond:** foolish.

14 **Adversity's sweet milk, philosophy:** Misfortune can be soothed by calm, reasonable thinking, according to the Friar.

GUIDED READING

LITERAL QUESTIONS

1a. To what animals does Romeo compare himself? (cats, dogs, mice, flies)

2a. How does Romeo accuse Friar Lawrence in lines 42–49? (He attacks Friar Lawrence for uttering the word *banishment.*)

INFERENTIAL QUESTIONS

1b. What is the effect of these unworthy comparisons? (They strike a note of self-pity and express Romeo's extreme despair.)

2b. How do these attacks on Friar Lawrence's character reflect on Romeo's character? (When hurt, Romeo strikes out blindly and without caution.)

FRIAR. O, then I see that madmen have no ears.

ROMEO. How should they, when that wise men have no eyes?

FRIAR. Let me dispute with thee of thy estate.[15]

1 **ROMEO.** Thou canst not speak of that thou dost not feel.
Wert thou as young as I, Juliet thy love,
An hour but married, Tybalt murderèd,
Doting like me, and like me banishèd,
Then mightst thou speak, then mightst thou tear thy hair,
2 And fall upon the ground, as I do now,

[ROMEO *throws himself on the floor.*]

Taking the measure of an unmade grave.

[*There is a knock at the door to the cell.*]

FRIAR. Arise, one knocks. Good Romeo, hide thyself.

ROMEO. Not I; unless the breath of heartsick groans
Mistlike infold me[16] from the search of eyes.

[*Another knock.*]

FRIAR. Hark, how they knock! Who's there? Romeo, arise;
Thou wilt be taken.—Stay awhile!—Stand up;

[*The knocking continues more loudly than before.*]

Run to my study.—By and by![17]—God's will,
What simpleness[18] is this.—I come, I come!

[*There is a very loud knock. The* FRIAR *goes to the door.*]

Who knocks so hard? Whence come you? What's your will?

NURSE. Let me come in, and you shall know my errand.
I come from Lady Juliet.

FRIAR. Welcome then.

[*The* NURSE *enters.*]

NURSE. O holy friar, O, tell me, holy friar,
Where is my lady's lord, where's Romeo?

FRIAR. There on the ground, with his own tears made drunk.

NURSE. O, he is even in my mistress' case,
Just in her case! O woeful sympathy!
Piteous predicament! Even so lies she,
Blubb'ring and weeping, weeping and blubb'ring.
Stand up, stand up! Stand, and you be a man.

15 **dispute . . . estate:** discuss with you your situation.

16 **unless . . . me:** unless my sighs form a mist to hide me.

17 **By and by:** Wait a minute.

18 **simpleness:** silly behavior (Romeo refuses to rise).

AT A GLANCE

- *Scene iii (continued):* The Nurse arrives with Juliet's message.
- She finds Romeo prostrate with grief.

1 CHARACTERIZATION

Romeo believes that he can receive no comfort from people who have not felt what he has felt; he assumes that the friar has never experienced loss.

2 FORESHADOWING

In his grief Romeo unwittingly suggests the conclusion of the play, and the audience is reminded of fate's inevitability.

GUIDED READING

LITERAL QUESTION

1a. According to Romeo, why can't he take the friar's advice? (He says that the friar cannot understand him because the friar has not felt what he has.)

INFERENTIAL QUESTION

1b. How does this point of view reveal his immaturity? (He assumes that Friar Lawrence has not felt what he does.)

AT A GLANCE

- *Scene iii (continued):* Romeo, in his grief and sorrow, threatens to kill himself.
- Friar Lawrence bids him be patient.

1 STYLE: METAPHOR

Romeo threatens to cut his name out of his anatomy with a knife; his despair rules his actions at the dire moment when he considers Juliet's pain. The reference recalls Juliet's "What's in a name?"

2 MONOLOGUE

The aroused friar sermonizes Romeo, using oratorical repetition of the statement "There art thou happy" to rekindle Romeo's interest in life.

For Juliet's sake, for her sake, rise and stand!
Why should you fall into so deep an O?[19]

ROMEO. [*He rises.*] Nurse—

NURSE. Ah sir, ah sir! Death's the end of all.

ROMEO. Spakest thou of Juliet? How is it with her?
Doth not she think me an old murderer,
Now I have stained the childhood of our joy
With blood removed but little from her own?
Where is she? And how doth she! And what says
My concealed lady[20] to our canceled love?

NURSE. O, she says nothing, sir, but weeps and weeps;
And now falls on her bed, and then starts up,
And Tybalt calls; and then on Romeo cries,
And then down falls again.

ROMEO. As if that name,
Shot from the deadly level[21] of a gun,
Did murder her; as that name's cursèd hand
Murdered her kinsman. O, tell me, friar, tell me,
1 In what vile part of this anatomy[22]
Doth my name lodge? Tell me, that I may sack[23]
The hateful mansion.

[ROMEO *takes out his dagger and offers to stab himself. The* NURSE *snatches the dagger away.*]

FRIAR. Hold thy desperate hand.
Art thou a man? Thy form cries out thou art;
Thy tears are womanish, thy wild acts denote
The unreasonable fury of a beast.
Thou hast amazed me. By my holy order,
I thought thy disposition better tempered.
Hast thou slain Tybalt? Wilt thou slay thyself?
And slay thy lady that in thy life lives,
By doing damnèd hate upon thyself?
What, rouse thee, man! Thy Juliet is alive,
For whose dear sake thou wast but lately dead.[24]
2 There art thou happy.[25] Tybalt would kill thee,
But thou slewest Tybalt. There art thou happy.
The law, that threat'ned death, becomes thy friend
And turns it to exile. There art thou happy.
A pack of blessings light upon thy back;
Happiness courts thee in her best array;[26]
But, like a misbehaved and sullen wench,[27]

19 **so deep an O:** so heavy a cry of grief.
20 **concealed lady:** secret bride.
21 **level:** aim.
22 **anatomy:** body.
23 **sack:** plunder.
24 **lately dead:** declaring yourself dead.
25 **happy:** fortunate.
26 **array:** costume.
27 **wench:** girl.

GUIDED READING

LITERAL QUESTION

1a. What finally rouses Romeo to action? (the sound of Juliet's name)

INFERENTIAL QUESTION

1b. Why does Romeo try to kill himself? (He imagines that Juliet blames him for Tybalt's death.)

Thou pout'st thy fortune and thy love.
Take heed, take heed, for such die miserable.
Go get thee to thy love, as was decreed,
Ascend her chamber, hence and comfort her.
But look thou stay not till the watch be set,[28]
1 For then thou canst not pass to Mantua,
Where thou shalt live till we can find a time
To blaze[29] your marriage, reconcile your friends,
Beg pardon of the Prince, and call thee back
With twenty hundred thousand times more joy
Than thou went'st forth in lamentation.
Go before, nurse. Commend me to thy lady,
And bid her hasten all the house to bed,
Which heavy sorrow makes them apt to unto.[30]
Romeo is coming.

NURSE. O Lord, I could have stayed here all the night
2 To hear good counsel. O, what learning is!
My lord, I'll tell my lady you will come.

ROMEO. Do so, and bid my sweet prepare to chide.[31]

[*The* NURSE *begins to leave but turns again to* ROMEO *handing him a ring.*]

NURSE. Here, sir, a ring she bid me give you, sir.
Hie you, make haste, for it grows very late.

[*She leaves.*]

28 **watch be set:** the watchmen go on duty at the gates of the city.

29 **blaze:** publicly announce.

30 **apt unto:** likely to do.

31 **prepare to chide:** be ready to scold. Romeo expects Juliet to be angry with him because of Tybalt's death.

AT A GLANCE

- *Scene iii (continued):* Friar Lawrence tells his plan to hide Romeo.
- Romeo agrees to see Juliet.

1 BACKGROUND

Mantua is about ten miles from Verona; Romeo would be able to return to Verona easily after hiding until the families can be reconciled.

2 CHARACTERIZATION

The naive Nurse believes that what Friar Lawrence has said will come true. The audience, warned by the Chorus and foreshadowing, knows better.

GUIDED READING

LITERAL QUESTION

1a. What is the friar's plan for Romeo's safety? (to hide him in Mantua until the families can be reconciled)

INFERENTIAL QUESTION

1b. What does this plan show about the friar's character? (He is calm and sensible in a crisis; he has the lovers' interests at heart.)

AT A GLANCE

- *Scene iii (continued):* Friar Lawrence reminds Romeo to leave Juliet before dawn.
- *Scene iv:* The Capulets, meeting with Paris, plan a sudden wedding for their daughter.

1 SETTING

Friar Lawrence reminds us that it is late the same night: Less than forty-eight hours have passed since the play began. The rapid movement of events suggests the swift inevitability of tragedy.

2 READING SKILLS: SEQUENCE OF EVENTS

Lord Capulet is planning the wedding ceremony for Thursday; it is now late Monday night.

ROMEO. How well my comfort is revived by this!

FRIAR. Go hence; good night; and here stands all your state:[32]
1 Either be gone before the watch be set,
Or by the break of day disguised from hence.
Sojourn[33] in Mantua. I'll find out your man,
And he shall signify from time to time
Every good hap to you that chances here.[34]
Give me thy hand. 'Tis late. Farewell; good night.

ROMEO. But that a joy past joy calls out on me,
It were a grief so brief to part with thee.
Farewell.

[ROMEO *and* FRIAR LAWRENCE *clasp hands and then leave in opposite directions.*]

32 **here . . . state:** everything depends on what I am about to tell you.

33 **Sojourn:** stay for a while.

34 **signify . . . here:** bring you news occasionally of every good event that happens here.

Scene iv. Late that night. A room in* CAPULET'*s house.

[PARIS, LORD CAPULET, *and* LADY CAPULET *enter. At this time of sorrow, they are discussing* PARIS' *offer to marry* JULIET.]

CAPULET. Things have fall'n out, sir, so unluckily
That we have had no time to move[1] our daughter.
Look you, she loved her kinsman Tybalt dearly,
And so did I. Well, we were born to die.
'Tis very late; she'll not come down tonight.
I promise you, but for your company,
I would have been abed an hour ago.

PARIS. These times of woe afford no times to woo.
Madam, good night. Commend me to your daughter.

LADY. I will, and know her mind early tomorrow;
Tonight she's mewed up to her heaviness.[2]

CAPULET. Sir Paris, I will make a desperate tender[3]
Of my child's love. I think she will be ruled
In all respects by me; nay more, I doubt it not.
Wife, go you to her ere you go to bed;
Acquaint her here of my son[4] Paris' love
And bid her (mark you me?) on Wednesday next—
2 But soft! What day is this?

PARIS. Monday, my lord.

CAPULET. Monday! Ha, ha! Well, Wednesday is too soon.
A[5] Thursday let it be—a Thursday, tell her,

1 **move:** offer your proposal to.

2 **mewed . . . heaviness:** shut up with her grief. Hawks were kept in cages called mews.

3 **desperate tender:** risky offer.

4 **son:** future son-in-law.

5 **A:** On.

GUIDED READING

LITERAL QUESTION

1a. What order does Lord Capulet give Lady Capulet? ("Wife, go you to her ere you go to bed.")

INFERENTIAL QUESTION

1b. Why might Lord Capulet be especially eager to get the wedding over with? (He may be looking to blot out the present sorrow; he may worry that the killings will discourage Paris' suit.)

She shall be married to this noble earl.
Will you be ready? Do you like this haste?
We'll keep no great ado[6]—a friend or two;
For hark you, Tybalt being slain so late,[7]
1 It may be thought we held him carelessly,[8]
Being our kinsman, if we revel[9] much.
Therefore we'll have some half a dozen friends,
And there an end. But what say you to Thursday?

PARIS. My lord, I would that Thursday were tomorrow.

CAPULET. Well, get you gone. A Thursday be it then.
2 [*To his wife.*] Go you to Juliet ere you go to bed;
Prepare her, wife, against[10] this wedding day.
Farewell, my lord.—Light to my chamber, ho!
Afore me,[11] it is so very late
That we may call it early by and by.
Good night.

[*They exit.*]

6 **keep no great ado:** make no big fuss.
7 **late:** recently.
8 **held him carelessly:** had little regard for him.
9 **revel:** celebrate.
10 **against:** for.
11 **Afore me:** for goodness' sake.

Scene v. Later that night, just before daybreak. CAPULET'S ***orchard and, above,*** JULIET'S ***room and balcony.***

[ROMEO *and* JULIET *are on the balcony. The rope ladder hangs down from the balcony into the garden.* ROMEO *must leave before the day is light, or he will be killed. In Shakespeare's theater this scene utilized the balcony* (JULIET'S *balcony), the inner stage behind the balcony* (JULIET'S *bedroom), and the main stage (the garden).*]

JULIET. Wilt thou be gone? It is not yet near day.
It was the nightingale, and not the lark,[1]
That pierced the fearful hollow of thine ear.
3 Nightly she sings on yond pomegranate tree.
Believe me, love, it was the nightingale.

ROMEO. It was the lark, the herald of the morn;
No nightingale. Look, love, what envious streaks
Do lace[2] the severing[3] clouds in yonder East.
4 Night's candles[4] are burnt out, and jocund[5] day
Stands tiptoe on the misty mountaintops.
I must be gone and live, or stay and die.

JULIET. Yond light is not daylight; I know it, I.
It is some meteor that the sun exhales[6]

1 **nightingale . . . lark:** The nightingale sings at night, and the lark sings at dawn.
2 **lace:** speckle.
3 **severing:** scattering.
4 **Night's candles:** the stars.
5 **jocund:** cheerful.
6 **exhales:** breathes out. Some people believed that meteors were made of gases from the sun.

AT A GLANCE

- *Scene iv (continued):* The wedding will take place in three days.
- *Scene v:* Romeo prepares to leave Verona.

1 PARAPHRASING

Capulet offers a reason to keep the wedding small: the possibility that others will say the Capulets did not mourn Tybalt properly.

2 CHARACTERIZATION

Capulet, as though unsure of his wife's response, repeats his order to her to prepare Juliet for her wedding.

3 STYLE: IMAGERY

The lovers depict the sights and sounds of dawn in images that reflect the beauty of the morning and of their love.

4 THEME

Fate's part in the tragedy is suggested with imagery: The loveliness of night is over and the day about to begin.

GUIDED READING

LITERAL QUESTION

1a. What do Capulet and Paris decide? (to schedule a wedding between Juliet and Paris)

INFERENTIAL QUESTION

1b. How does our knowledge of the wedding add to the play's tension? (The happiness of the lovers can be preserved only if Romeo goes away—but how can he prevent the marriage from Mantua?)

AT A GLANCE

- *Scene v (continued):* Romeo leaves the balcony.
- The Nurse warns Juliet that her mother is coming to her room.

1 STYLE: METAPHOR

Juliet sees the heavens as protecting Romeo and lighting his way to Mantua with a special torch.

2 CHARACTERIZATION

Romeo imagines death a pleasant end and echoes his dramatically threatened suicide. He seems to believe in the relief death can offer.

3 CHARACTERIZATION

Juliet, aware of the tangible realities of their situation, will not let him indulge his fanciful allusion to death: She urges him to go.

4 PLOT: RISING ACTION

The Nurse warns Juliet that her mother is coming. Lady Capulet (who does not know Romeo and Juliet are married) will bring news that increases the conflict.

1 To be to thee this night a torchbearer
And light thee on thy way to Mantua.
Therefore stay yet; thou need'st not to be gone.

ROMEO. Let me be ta'en, let me be put to death.
I am content, so thou wilt have it so.
I'll say yon gray is not the morning's eye,[7]
'Tis but the pale reflex of Cynthia's brow;[8]
Nor that is not the lark whose notes do beat
The vaulty heaven so high above our heads.
2 I have more care to stay than will to go.
Come, death, and welcome! Juliet wills it so.
How is't, my soul! Let's talk; it is not day.

3 JULIET. It is, it is! Hie hence, be gone, away!
It is the lark that sings so out of tune,
Straining harsh discords and unpleasing sharps.[9]
Some say the lark makes sweet division;[10]
This doth not so, for she divideth us.
Some say the lark and loathèd toad change eyes;[11]
O, now I would they had changed voices too,
Since arm from arm that voice doth us affray,[12]
Hunting thee hence with hunt's-up[13] to the day.
O, now be gone! More light and light it grows.

ROMEO. More light and light—more dark and dark our woes.

[*The* NURSE *enters* JULIET*'s room.*]

NURSE. Madam!

JULIET. Nurse?

4 NURSE. Your lady mother is coming to your chamber.
The day is broke; be wary, look about.

[*She leaves.*]

JULIET. Then, window, let day in, and let life out.

ROMEO. Farewell, farewell! One kiss, and I'll descend.

[*They kiss. Then* ROMEO *climbs down the rope ladder to the garden below.*]

JULIET. Art thou gone so, love-lord, ay husband-friend?
I must hear from thee every day in the hour,
For in a minute there are many days.
O, by this count I shall be much in years[14]
Ere I again behold my Romeo!

7 **morning's eye:** sunrise.

8 **reflex . . . brow:** reflection of the moon's forehead. Cynthia was an Elizabethan name for the moon goddess, Diana, often depicted with a crescent moon on her forehead.

9 **sharps:** type of musical note.

10 **division:** melody.

11 **lark . . . eyes:** Some people believed that the lark and toad exchanged eyes. The lark has a beautiful body with ugly eyes and the toad has an ugly body with beautiful eyes.

12 **affray:** frighten.

13 **hunt's up:** an early morning song to wake the hunters.

14 **much in years:** much older.

GUIDED READING

LITERAL QUESTION

1a. Whose arrival does the Nurse announce? (Lady Capulet's)

INFERENTIAL QUESTION

1b. Lady Capulet intended to speak to Juliet the previous night. Why didn't she? (Juliet may have gone to bed; Lady Capulet may have been too tired and grief-stricken.)

ROMEO. Farewell!
I will omit no opportunity
That may convey my greetings, love, to thee.

JULIET. O, think'st thou we shall ever meet again?

ROMEO. I doubt it not; and all these woes shall serve
For sweet discourses[15] in our times to come.

1 JULIET. O God, I have an ill-divining soul![16]
Methinks I see thee, now thou art so low,
As one dead in the bottom of a tomb.
Either my eyesight fails, or thou lookest pale.

ROMEO. And trust me, love, in my eye so do you.
Dry sorrow drinks our blood.[17] Adieu, adieu!

[ROMEO *leaves.*]

JULIET. O Fortune, Fortune! All men call thee fickle.
If thou art fickle, what dost thou with him
That is renowned for faith?[18] Be fickle, Fortune,
For then I hope thou wilt not keep him long
But send him back.

[LADY CAPULET *enters* JULIET'*s room.*]

LADY CAPULET. Ho, daughter! Are you up?

JULIET. Who is't that calls? It is my lady mother.
Is she not down so late,[19] or up so early?
What unaccustomed cause procures her hither?[20]

[JULIET *returns to her room from the balcony.*]

LADY CAPULET. Why, how now, Juliet?

2 JULIET. Madam, I am not well.

LADY CAPULET. Evermore weeping for your cousin's death?
What, wilt thou wash him from his grave with tears?
And if thou couldst, thou couldst not make him live.
3 Therefore have done. Some grief shows much of love;
But much of grief shows still some want of wit.[21]

JULIET. Yet let me weep for such a feeling[22] loss.

LADY CAPULET. So shall you feel the loss, but not the friend
Which you weep for.

JULIET. Feeling so the loss,
I cannot choose but ever weep the friend.

15 **discourses:** conversations.

16 **ill-divining soul:** soul that foresees evil.

17 **Dry . . . blood:** They are pale because sorrow was believed to dry up the blood.

18 **If thou . . . faith:** What does unfaithful fate have to do with faithful Romeo?

19 **down:** gone to bed.

20 **unaccustomed . . . hither:** unusual reason causes her to come this way.

21 **wit:** common sense.

22 **feeling:** deeply felt.

AT A GLANCE

- *Scene v (continued):* Romeo leaves.
- Lady Capulet mistakes Juliet's grieving as being for Tybalt.
- Juliet deceives her mother.

1 FORESHADOWING

Juliet's premonition of Romeo in a tomb intensifies the sense of tragic doom.

2 CHARACTERIZATION

Juliet has been changed by recent events: Her childish manner has given way to cunning, and she protects herself and Romeo by deceiving her mother.

3 CHARACTERIZATION

Lady Capulet's advice seems cold: Tybalt was killed less than twenty-four hours before, yet she says Juliet's grief is prolonged and makes her look silly.

GUIDED READING

LITERAL QUESTION

1a. What advice does Lady Capulet give Juliet? (She advises her to stop crying.)

INFERENTIAL QUESTION

1b. Why is her advice ironic? (She doesn't realize that Juliet weeps not for Tybalt, but for Romeo.)

AT A GLANCE

- *Scene v (continued):* Lady Capulet threatens to have Romeo poisoned.
- She announces that Juliet will be married to Paris.
- Juliet pretends to agree.

1 ASIDE

Juliet tells the audience that she does not subscribe to her mother's idea that Romeo is a villain. The aside furthers the sense of Juliet's cunning.

2 CHARACTERIZATION

Juliet deceives her mother by speaking with double meanings. Her mother hears these words as hate for Romeo; we know she is speaking of love.

LADY CAPULET. Well, girl, thou weep'st not so much for his death
As that the villain lives which slaughtered him.

JULIET. What villain, madam?

LADY CAPULET. That same villain Romeo.

1 JULIET. [*Aside.*] Villain and he be many miles asunder.[23]—
[*To* LADY CAPULET.] God pardon him! I do, with all my heart;
And yet no man like[24] he doth grieve my heart.

LADY CAPULET. That is because the traitor murderer lives.

JULIET. Ay, madam, from the reach of these my hands.
Would none but I might venge my cousin's death!

LADY CAPULET. We will have vengeance for it, fear thou not.
Then weep no more. I'll send to one in Mantua,
Where that same banished runagate[25] doth live,
Shall give him such an unaccustomed dram[26]
That he shall soon keep Tybalt company;
And then I hope thou wilt be satisfied.

2 JULIET. Indeed I never shall be satisfied
With Romeo till I behold him—dead[27]—
Is my poor heart so for a kinsman vexed.
Madam, if you could find out but a man
To bear a poison, I would temper[28] it;
That Romeo should, upon receipt thereof,
Soon sleep in quiet. O, how my heart abhors
To hear him named and cannot come to him,
To wreak[29] the love I bore my cousin
Upon his body that hath slaughtered him!

LADY CAPULET. Find thou the means, and I'll find such a man.
But now I'll tell thee joyful tidings, girl.

JULIET. And joy comes well in such a needy time.
What are they, beseech your ladyship?

LADY CAPULET. Well, well, thou hast a careful[30] father, child;
One who, to put thee from thy heaviness,
Hath sorted out[31] a sudden day of joy
That thou expects not nor I looked not for.

JULIET. Madam, in happy time![32] What day is that?

LADY CAPULET. Marry, my child, early next Thursday morn
The gallant, young, and noble gentleman,
The County Paris, at Saint Peter's Church,
Shall happily make thee there a joyful bride.

23 **asunder:** apart.

24 **like:** as much as.

25 **runagate:** runaway.

26 **unaccustomed dram:** unexpected dose (of poison).

27 **dead:** Juliet used the word *dead* as part of the next line (*dead is my poor heart*). Lady Capulet associates the word with the previous line (*till I behold him dead*).

28 **temper:** mix.

29 **wreak:** Juliet deceives her mother by using a word with two meanings. The first meaning, for her mother, is "revenge." The second meaning, the one Juliet feels, is "express."

30 **careful:** considerate.

31 **sorted out:** chosen.

32 **in happy time:** just in time!

GUIDED READING

LITERAL QUESTION

1a. Why does Lady Capulet say that Juliet's father has decided on this sudden marriage? (He was thinking of Juliet's happiness.)

INFERENTIAL QUESTION

1b. Why does the Capulets' haste seem unfair? (Juliet hasn't been consulted about the marriage plans.)

JULIET. Now by Saint Peter's Church, and Peter too,
He shall not make me there a joyful bride!
I wonder at this haste, that I must wed
Ere he that should be husband comes to woo.
I pray you tell my lord and father, madam,
I will not marry yet; and when I do, I swear
It shall be Romeo, whom you know I hate,
Rather than Paris. These are news indeed!

LADY CAPULET. Here comes your father. Tell him so yourself,
And see how he will take it at your hands.

[CAPULET *and the* NURSE *enter.*]

CAPULET. When the sun sets the earth doth drizzle dew,
But for the sunset of my brother's son
It rains downright.
How now? A conduit,[33] girl? What, still in tears?
Evermore show'ring? In one little body
Thou counterfeits[34] a bark,[35] a sea, a wind:
For still thy eyes, which I may call the sea,
Do ebb and flow with tears; the bark thy body is,
Sailing in this salt flood; the winds, thy sighs,
Who, raging with thy tears and they with them,
Without a sudden calm will overset
Thy tempest-tossèd body. How now, wife?
Have you delivered to her our decree?

LADY CAPULET. Ay, sir; but she will none, she gives you thanks.
I would the fool were married to her grave!

CAPULET. Soft! Take me with you,[36] take me with you, wife.
How? Will she none? Doth she not give us thanks?
Is she not proud?[37] Doth she not count her blest,
Unworthy as she is, that we have wrought[38]
So worthy a gentleman to be her bride?

JULIET. Not proud you have, but thankful that you have.
Proud can I never be of what I hate,
But thankful even for hate that is meant love.

CAPULET. How, how, how, how, chopped-logic?[39]
What is this?
"Proud"—and "I thank you"—and "I thank you not"—
And yet "not proud"? Mistress minion[40] you,
Thank me no thankings, nor proud me no prouds,
But fettle[41] your fine joints 'gainst Thursday next
To go with Paris to Saint Peter's Church,

33 **conduit:** fountain.

34 **counterfeits:** imitates.

35 **bark:** boat.

36 **Soft . . . you:** Wait! Help me to understand you.

37 **proud:** pleased.

38 **wrought:** arranged.

39 **chopped-logic:** quibbling.

40 **Mistress minion:** spoiled miss.

41 **fettle:** prepare.

AT A GLANCE

- *Scene v (continued):* Juliet refuses to marry Paris.
- Her surprised parents grow angry.
- They argue and her father orders her to obey.

1 CHARACTERIZATION

Juliet finally speaks plainly: She loves Romeo, whom Lady Capulet had thought she hated.

2 CHARACTERIZATION

Lady Capulet's cold anger finds expression in this strikingly hateful speech. Excessive feelings again spur the tragedy.

3 CHARACTERIZATION

Juliet speaks to her father with great courtesy, thanking him for the opportunity to marry while turning it down.

GUIDED READING

LITERAL QUESTION

1a. How does Lord Capulet characterize Juliet's worth? (He calls her "unworthy.")

INFERENTIAL QUESTION

1b. How could Lord Capulet be so sweet to Juliet at first and then call her unworthy of the marriage he has arranged? (He may think of Juliet as a child who needs care by a father or husband; her subsequent disobedience angers him.)

AT A GLANCE

- *Scene v (continued):* Lord Capulet orders Juliet to be married.

1 CHARACTERIZATION

Capulet, overwhelmed with emotion, threatens to drag her to the church. His grotesque name-calling underscores the depth and breadth of the tragedy's consequences.

1 Or I will drag thee on a hurdle[42] thither.
Out, you greensickness carrion![43] Out, you baggage![44]
You tallow-face![45]

LADY CAPULET. [*To* CAPULET.] Fie, fie! What, are you mad?

JULIET. [*She kneels before her father.*] Good father, I beseech you on my knees,
Hear me with patience but to speak a word.

CAPULET. Hang thee, young baggage! Disobedient wretch!
I tell thee what—get thee to church a Thursday
Or never after look me in the face.
Speak not, reply not, do not answer me!
My fingers itch. Wife, we scarce thought us blest
That God had lent us but this only child;
But now I see this one is one too much,
And that we have a curse in having her.
Out on her, hilding![46]

NURSE. God in heaven bless her!
You are to blame, my lord, to rate[47] her so.

CAPULET. And why, my Lady Wisdom? Hold your tongue,
Good Prudence. Smatter with your gossips, go![48]

42 **hurdle:** sled used to carry prisoners to their executions.
43 **greensickness carrion:** anemic flesh.
44 **baggage:** shameless girl.
45 **tallow-face:** pale face.
46 **hilding:** worthless person.
47 **rate:** scold.
48 **Smatter . . . go:** Go chatter with the other old women.

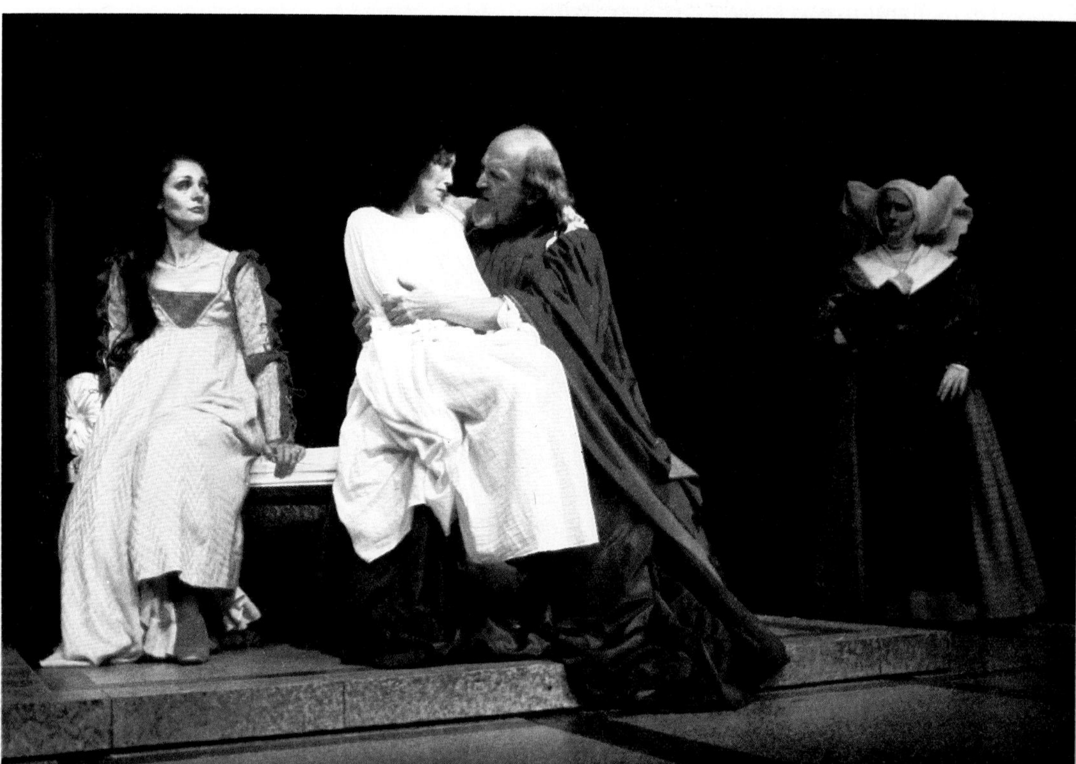

GUIDED READING

LITERAL QUESTION

1a. What names does Capulet call his daughter? (*carrion, baggage, tallow-face, disobedient wretch, hilding*)

INFERENTIAL QUESTION

1b. What insight does this scene give us into Lord Capulet? (His temper is extreme, as are his feelings about Juliet and the events of the past forty-eight hours.)

NURSE. I speak no treason.

CAPULET. O, God-i-god-en!

NURSE. May not one speak?

CAPULET. Peace, you mumbling fool!
Utter your gravity[49] o'er a gossip's bowl,
For here we need it not.

LADY CAPULET. You are too hot.

CAPULET. God's bread![50] It makes me mad.
Day, night; hour, tide, time; work, play;
Alone, in company; still my care hath been
To have her matched; and having now provided
A gentleman of noble parentage,
Of fair demesnes,[51] youthful, and nobly trained,
Stuffed, as they say, with honorable parts,[52]
Proportioned as one's thought would wish a man—
And then to have a wretched puling[53] fool,
A whining mammet,[54] in her fortune's tender,[55]
To answer "I'll not wed, I cannot love;
I am too young, I pray you pardon me"!
1 But, and you will not wed, I'll pardon you!
Graze where you will, you shall not house with me.
Look to't, think on't; I do not use to jest.
Thursday is near; lay hand on heart, advise:[56]
And you be mine, I'll give you to my friend;
And you be not, hang, beg, starve, die in the streets,
For, by my soul, I'll ne'er acknowledge thee,
Nor what is mine shall never do thee good.
Trust to't. Bethink you. I'll not be forsworn.[57]

[CAPULET *leaves.* JULIET *rises and speaks to her mother.*]

JULIET. Is there no pity sitting in the clouds
That sees into the bottom of my grief?
O sweet my mother, cast me not away!
Delay this marriage for a month, a week;
Or if you do not, make the bridal bed
In that dim monument where Tybalt lies.

2 LADY CAPULET. Talk not to me, for I'll not speak a word.
Do as thou wilt, for I have done with thee.

[LADY CAPULET *leaves.*]

JULIET. O God!—O nurse, how shall this be prevented?
My husband is on earth, my faith in heaven.[58]

49 **gravity:** wisdom.

50 **God's bread!:** By the sacred host!

51 **demesnes [di mānz′]:** wealth and property.

52 **parts:** qualities.

53 **puling:** whimpering.

54 **mammet:** doll.

55 **in her fortune's tender:** when good fortune is offered her.

56 **advise:** think carefully.

57 **be forsworn:** break my vow.

58 **my faith in heaven:** My marriage vow is recorded in heaven.

AT A GLANCE

- *Scene v (continued):* Capulet orders Juliet to marry Paris or leave the family.
- Juliet's mother refuses to help her.
- She is left alone with the Nurse.

1 THEME

Lord Capulet delivers an ultimatum: Marry Paris or get out of the house. With excessive rage he swears that no one in his household will help Juliet if she is expelled.

2 CHARACTERIZATION

Lady Capulet turns her back on her daughter's request and on Juliet herself. Since we know she is capable of opposing her husband, this response indicates lack of sympathetic feeling toward her daughter.

GUIDED READING

LITERAL QUESTIONS

1a. What consequences will Juliet face if she refuses marriage? (According to Lord Capulet, she "shall not house with me"; she can "hang, beg, starve, die in the streets.")

2a. How does Lady Capulet answer Juliet's request for assistance? (She refuses.)

INFERENTIAL QUESTIONS

1b. What resources is Juliet left with at this point? (Her own judgment, the Nurse, and Friar Lawrence.)

2b. How does the picture of the Capulet household help us to understand Lady Capulet's behavior? (Lord Capulet uses his temper to demand obedience from both Lady Capulet and Juliet.)

AT A GLANCE

- *Scene v (continued):* Juliet turns to the Nurse for advice.
- The Nurse suggests that she go ahead with the marriage to Paris.
- Juliet repudiates the Nurse and turns to Friar Lawrence.

1 PERSONIFICATION

Juliet turns to the Nurse for comfort and counsel, feeling that even heaven has abandoned her.

2 CHARACTERIZATION

The Nurse advises Juliet to marry Paris (l. 219) because Romeo is banished and she thinks Paris the better man; she seems to have Juliet's interests at heart.

3 CHARACTERIZATION

Juliet responds to the Nurse's advice as she earlier answered her mother: Her words conceal two opposite meanings.

REFLECTING ON ACT III

How does lack of moderation make itself felt in this act? (Tybalt, Mercutio, and Romeo are too eager to fight; the Prince's edict is too hasty; Capulet's marriage plans are made too quickly; the Capulets are too angry to heed Juliet's feelings.)

1 How shall that faith return again to earth
Unless that husband send it me from heaven
By leaving earth?[59] Comfort me, counsel me.
Alack, alack, that heaven should practice stratagems[60]
Upon so soft a subject as myself!
What say'st thou? Hast thou not a word of joy?
Some comfort, nurse.

NURSE. Faith, here it is.
Romeo is banished; and all the world to nothing[61]
That he dares ne'er come back to challenge[62] you;
Or if he do, it needs must be by stealth.
2 Then, since the case so stands as now it doth,
I think it best you married with the County.
O, he's a lovely gentleman!
Romeo's a dishclout to him.[63] An eagle, madam,
Hath not so green, so quick, so fair an eye
As Paris hath. Beshrew my very heart,
I think you are happy in this second match,
For it excels your first; or if it did not,
Your first is dead—or 'twere as good he were
As living here and you no use of him.

JULIET. Speak'st thou from thy heart?

NURSE. And from my soul too; else beshrew them both.

JULIET. Amen!

NURSE. What?

3 JULIET. Well, thou hast comforted me marvelous much.
Go in; and tell my lady I am gone,
Having displeased my father, to Lawrence' cell,
To make confession and to be absolved.[64]

NURSE. Marry, I will; and this is wisely done.

[*The* NURSE *leaves to find* LADY CAPULET.]

JULIET. Ancient damnation![65] O most wicked fiend!
Is it more sin to wish me thus forsworn,[66]
Or to dispraise my lord with that same tongue
Which she hath praised him with above compare
So many thousand times? Go, counselor!
Thou and my bosom henceforth shall be twain.[67]
I'll to the friar to know his remedy.
If all else fail, myself have power to die.

[JULIET *exits.*]

59 **leaving earth:** dying.
60 **stratagems:** tricks.
61 **all . . . nothing:** the odds are everything to nothing.
62 **challenge:** claim.
63 **dishclout to him:** a dish cloth compared to him.
64 **absolved:** forgiven.
65 **Ancient damnation:** Old devil!
66 **forsworn:** guilty of breaking my marriage vow.
67 **Thou . . . twain:** You and my confidences from here on will be separated.

GUIDED READING

LITERAL QUESTION

1a. Does the Nurse think Juliet should marry Paris? (yes)

INFERENTIAL QUESTION

1b. Why does the Nurse suggest that Juliet marry Paris? (She doubts that Romeo will ever be pardoned and thinks Paris is the better man.)

STUDY QUESTIONS

Recalling

1. In Act III, Scene i, what part does Romeo play in the deaths of Mercutio and Tybalt? What punishment does the Prince set for Romeo?
2. In Scene iii why does the Nurse look for Romeo after the fight? Where does she find him?
3. In Scene iii, lines 126–134, what plan for the future does the Friar propose to Romeo?
4. In Scene iv what plan does Capulet make for Juliet? Why does Capulet threaten Juliet in Scene v? What is the threat?
5. What reason does Juliet give for visiting the friar? Why does she really want to see him?

Interpreting

6. Explain the internal conflict that Romeo faces in Act III, Scene i. At the end of the scene, why does he call himself "fortune's fool"?
7. In what ways are Mercutio and Tybalt true to their personalities up to their deaths?
8. What are the mixed emotions that Juliet feels when she learns of Tybalt's death?
9. Explain how Juliet's relationship with the Nurse changes during this act.
10. What does this act reveal about the depth of Romeo and Juliet's love? Give examples to support your answer.

Extending

11. The Prologue to the play tells us how it will end. What effect do you imagine this information has on readers and theater audiences during Acts I–III?

VIEWPOINT

Because of Mercutio's death Act III changes the mood of *Romeo and Juliet*. One critic said:

> The whole play is challenged and re-directed by this scene. . . . The shock of the scene is used to precipitate [cause] a change of key in the play.
>
> — N. Brooke, *Shakespeare's English Tragedies*

- In what sense is Mercutio's death a shock? In what ways does the mood of the play change in Act III?

LITERARY FOCUS

Imagery

An **image** is a picture made with words. A collection of images within a piece of literature is called its **imagery,** the language in the work that appeals to the senses. Images are most often visual, but they can also help the audience to hear, see, smell, or feel what the author is describing. Shakespeare used many colorful images; audiences of his day enjoyed hearing rich, poetic language. In addition, the colorful language was often necessary to compensate for the lack of scenery.

Shakespeare often repeated important images many times within a play. As a result, the imagery of a play often acts as a clue to the play's meaning. Images of light and darkness are repeated throughout *Romeo and Juliet*. For example, during the famous balcony scene (Act II, Scene ii) the light from Juliet's window pierces the black night, and Romeo identifies Juliet with the sun and compares her to the moon and stars.

Thinking About Imagery

1. Describe Juliet's comparison of Romeo to the stars in the beginning of Act III, Scene ii.
2. Give two examples of images for the night and the dawn in Act III, Scene v.

Monologue and Soliloquy

A **monologue** is a long speech by a character in a play. For example, Mercutio's long speech about Queen Mab in Act I, Scene iv, is a monologue. In that speech Mercutio is speaking to Romeo and Benvolio. A long speech spoken by a character who is alone on stage is a **soliloquy**. Since the character is alone, the soliloquy usually reveals personal thoughts and emotions and can be accepted as sincere. Romeo's long speech under Juliet's balcony at the beginning of Act II, Scene ii, is a soliloquy because, although Juliet is on stage, she does not see or hear him yet.

Thinking About Monologue and Soliloquy

1. What do we learn about Mercutio from his monologue in Act III, Scene i, lines 15–28?
2. Reread Juliet's soliloquy at the beginning of Scene ii (lines 1–15). What personal thoughts does she express in this speech?

STUDY QUESTIONS

1. steps between them, allowing Mercutio to be stabbed, and avenges Mercutio's death by slaying Tybalt; banishment
2. to give him ring as sign of Juliet's forgiveness; in Friar's cell
3. Romeo will stay in Mantua until Friar announces marriage; Romeo to be pardoned by Prince
4. She will marry Paris in three days; she refuses; he will disown her.
5. She wants to confess her disobedience; wants him to help prevent marriage.
6. related to Tybalt by marriage; must not fight; must avenge the death of Mercutio; felt powerless to prevent violence
7. Mercutio remains witty; Tybalt remains proud, humorless
8. torn between love for cousin, husband; confused by irony
9. loses trust in her
10. Juliet is loyal; Romeo grieves for separation from Juliet.
11. casts pall; tragedy becomes inevitable

VIEWPOINT

- He is neither Capulet nor Montague.
- removes humor, makes tragedy seem inevitable

LITERARY FOCUS

Imagery

1. She wishes that upon her death Romeo will be "cut out in little stars" so brilliant that people will prefer night to day.
2. Stars are "night's candles"; Juliet pretends dawn is meteor to guide Romeo.

Monologue and Soliloquy

1. He demonstrates wit, wordiness; describes his own temper.
2. She thinks Romeo is brilliant enough to light the world at night.

ACT IV

Scene i. Later that morning. FRIAR LAWRENCE'S *cell.*

[FRIAR LAWRENCE ***and*** PARIS ***enter.*** PARIS ***has just explained to the confused*** FRIAR ***that he will marry*** JULIET.]

FRIAR. On Thursday, sir? The time is very short.

1 PARIS. My father[1] Capulet will have it so,
And I am nothing slow to slack his haste.[2]

FRIAR. You say you do not know the lady's mind.
Uneven is the course;[3] I like it not.

2 PARIS. Immoderately she weeps for Tybalt's death,
And therefore have I little talked of love;
For Venus smiles not in a house of tears.
Now, sir, her father counts it dangerous
That she do give her sorrow so much sway,
And in his wisdom hastes our marriage
To stop the inundation[4] of her tears,
Which, too much minded[5] by herself alone,
May be put from her by society.
Now do you know the reason of this haste.

3 FRIAR. [*Aside.*] I would I knew not why it should be slowed.—
Look, sir, here comes the lady toward my cell.

[JULIET *enters. Surprised to see* PARIS *there, she pretends to be in good spirits.*]

PARIS. Happily met, my lady and my wife!

JULIET. That may be, sir, when I may be a wife.

PARIS. That "may be" must be, love, on Thursday next.

JULIET. What must be shall be.

FRIAR. That's a certain text.[6]

PARIS. Come you to make confession to this father?

JULIET. To answer that, I should confess to you.

4 PARIS. Do not deny to him that you love me.

JULIET. I will confess to you that I love him.

PARIS. So will ye, I am sure, that you love me.

1 **father:** future father-in-law.

2 **nothing . . . haste:** not willing to slow him down.

3 **Uneven . . . course:** Unusual is the plan.

4 **inundation:** flood.

5 **minded:** brooded over.

6 **That's . . . text:** That comment is certainly true.

AT A GLANCE

- *Scene i:* Juliet meets Paris, who has arranged the wedding with the friar.
- Paris asks her to tell Friar Lawrence of her love for him.
- She evades answering directly.

LITERARY OPTIONS

- monologue and soliloquy
- inner conflict
- imagery

THEMATIC OPTIONS

- love
- human will vs. destiny
- deception and secrecy

1 THEME

Capulet's first thought regarding Paris' proposal was that Juliet was too young. In his desire to bring her the happiness he wants for her, he will play a part in bringing on her ruin.

2 CHARACTERIZATION

Paris speaks here with affection and respect for both Juliet and her father; he presents his case reasonably. Though he lacks Romeo's flair and passion, we see that, ironically, he might have made a good husband for Juliet.

3 ASIDE

Friar Lawrence tells us privately that he regrets knowing the reason why the wedding must not take place. This complication is one he did not foresee.

4 CONFLICT

As Paris tries to get a declaration of Juliet's love, she tries to avoid showing her feelings. She uses wit and wordplay to conceal the truth.

GUIDED READING

LITERAL QUESTION

1a. Has Paris asked Juliet whether she wants to marry him? (no)

INFERENTIAL QUESTION

1b. Why do Paris and Lord Capulet feel justified in arranging Juliet's marriage? (They may believe they are doing what's best for her.)

JULIET. If I do so, it will be of more price,[7]
Being spoke behind your back, than to your face.

PARIS. Poor soul, thy face is much abused with tears.

JULIET. The tears have got small victory by that,
For it was bad enough before their spite.[8]

PARIS. Thou wrong'st it more than tears with that report.

1 **JULIET.** That is no slander,[9] sir, which is a truth;
And what I spake, I spake it to my face.

PARIS. Thy face is mine, and thou hast sland'red it.

JULIET. It may be so, for it is not mine own.
[*To* FRIAR LAWRENCE.] Are you at leisure, holy father, now,
Or shall I come to you at evening mass?

FRIAR. My leisure serves me, pensive[10] daughter, now.
[*To* PARIS.] My lord, we must entreat the time alone.[11]

PARIS. God shield[12] I should disturb devotion!
Juliet, on Thursday early will I rouse ye.
Till then, adieu, and keep this holy kiss.

[PARIS *leaves.*]

JULIET. O, shut the door, and when thou hast done so,
Come weep with me—past hope, past care, past help!

FRIAR. O Juliet, I already know thy grief;
It strains me past the compass of my wits.[13]
I hear thou must, and nothing may prorogue[14] it,
On Thursday next be married to this County.

2 **JULIET.** Tell me not, friar, that thou hearest of this,
Unless thou tell me how I may prevent it.
If in thy wisdom thou canst give no help,
Do thou but call my resolution wise
And with this knife I'll help it presently.[15]
God joined my heart and Romeo's, thou our hands;
And ere this hand, by thee to Romeo's sealed,
Shall be the label to another deed,[16]
Or my true heart with treacherous revolt
Turn to another, this shall slay them both.
Therefore, out of thy long-experienced time,
Give me some present counsel; or, behold,
'Twixt my extremes and me[17] this bloody knife
Shall play the umpire, arbitrating[18] that

7 **price:** value.

8 **For . . . spite:** because my face was bad enough before the tears marred it.

9 **slander:** a lie told deliberately to injure another's reputation.

10 **pensive:** thoughtful.

11 **entreat . . . alone:** ask to be left alone.

12 **shield:** forbid.

13 **past . . . wits:** beyond the limits of my understanding.

14 **prorogue:** postpone.

15 **help it presently:** solve the problem immediately.

16 **be . . . deed:** agree to another contract (marriage).

17 **'Twixt . . . me:** between my misfortunes and me.

18 **umpire, arbitrating:** judge, solving.

AT A GLANCE

- *Scene i (continued):* Paris leaves.
- Juliet threatens to kill herself rather than agree to the marriage.

1 VOCABULARY: CONNOTATION

Juliet and Paris play with the word "face," which can also mean "dignity" and "self-respect." Juliet's statement that her face is not her own is an underhanded way of indicating that she does not speak the truth to Paris.

2 CHARACTERIZATION

Juliet now considers death as an answer to her plight: She will die before permitting her heart or hand to rebel against her true love, Romeo.

GUIDED READING

LITERAL QUESTION

1a. How does Paris leave Juliet? (He kisses her and says he will see her early Thursday.)

INFERENTIAL QUESTION

1b. What does Paris seem to feel for Juliet? (He seems to love her.)

AT A GLANCE

- *Scene i (continued):* Friar Lawrence offers Juliet a solution that is not death but something "like death."

1 PLOT: RISING ACTION

Friar Lawrence, ever hopeful, suggests to Juliet that if she is willing to die rather than marry Paris, she might undertake something equally daring and brave, though not fatal.

2 STYLE: IMAGERY

Juliet imagines more preferable fates than marriage to Paris. Her feverish imagination conjures up a string of explicit images of death and decay.

Which the commission of thy years and art
Could to no issue of true honor bring.[19]
Be not so long to speak. I long to die
If what thou speak'st speak not of remedy.

FRIAR. Hold, daughter. I do spy a kind of hope,
Which craves[20] as desperate an execution
As that is desperate which we would prevent.
1 If, rather than to marry County Paris,
Thou hast the strength of will to slay thyself,
Then is it likely thou wilt undertake
A thing like death to chide away this shame,
That cop'st with death himself to scape from it;[21]
And, if thou darest, I'll give thee remedy.

JULIET. O, bid me leap, rather than marry Paris,
From off the battlements of any tower,
Or walk in thievish ways,[22] or bid me lurk
Where serpents are; chain me with roaring bears,
2 Or hide me nightly in a charnel house,[23]
O'ercovered quite with dead men's rattling bones,
With reeky[24] shanks and yellow chapless[25] skulls;
Or bid me go into a new-made grave
And hide me with a dead man in his shroud—
Things that, to hear them told, have made me tremble—

19 **Which . . . bring:** which the authority of your age and skills could not solve honorably.

20 **craves:** requires.

21 **That cop'st . . . from it:** that bargains with death itself in order to escape from death.

22 **in thievish ways:** on roads where thieves lurk.
23 **charnel house:** vault where old bones were stored. As a common practice, bones were removed from old graves that could then be reused.
24 **reeky:** foul-smelling.
25 **chapless:** jawless.

GUIDED READING

LITERAL QUESTION

1a. How does Friar Lawrence describe his solution to Juliet's dilemma? (It is a thing like death that bargains with death itself to escape from being actual death.)

INFERENTIAL QUESTION

1b. In what way does this trigger Juliet's imagination? (She seems to be willing to endure extraordinary discomforts if he will help her; she imagines grisly tombs and bones.)

And I will do it without fear or doubt,
To live an unstained wife to my sweet love.

FRIAR. Hold, then. Go home, be merry, give consent
To marry Paris. Wednesday is tomorrow.
Tomorrow night look that thou lie alone;
Let not the nurse lie with thee in thy chamber.
Take thou this vial, being then in bed,
And this distilling liquor drink thou off;
When presently through all thy veins shall run
A cold and drowsy humor;[26] for no pulse
Shall keep his native[27] progress, but surcease;[28]
No warmth, no breath, shall testify thou livest;
The roses in thy lips and cheeks shall fade
To wanny ashes,[29] thy eyes' windows[30] fall
Like death when he shuts up the day of life;
Each part, deprived of supple government,[31]
Shall, stiff and stark and cold, appear like death;
And in this borrowed likeness of shrunk death
Thou shalt continue two-and-forty hours,
And then awake as from a pleasant sleep.
Now, when the bridegroom in the morning comes
To rouse thee from thy bed, there art thou dead.
Then, as the manner of our country is,
In thy best robes uncovered on the bier[32]
Thou shalt be borne to that same ancient vault
Where all the kindred of the Capulets lie.
In the meantime, against[33] thou shalt awake,
Shall Romeo by my letters know our drift;[34]
And hither shall he come; and he and I
Will watch thy waking, and that very night
Shall Romeo bear thee hence to Mantua.
And this shall free thee from this present shame,
If no inconstant toy[35] nor womanish fear
Abate thy valor[36] in the acting it.

[JULIET *takes the vial.*]

JULIET. Give me, give me! O, tell not me of fear!

FRIAR. Hold! Get you gone, be strong and prosperous
In this resolve. I'll send a friar with speed
2 To Mantua, with my letters to thy lord.

JULIET. Love give me strength, and strength shall help afford.
Farewell, dear father.

[*They exit.*]

26 **humor:** liquid.

27 **native:** natural.
28 **surcease:** stop.

29 **to wanny ashes:** to the color of pale ashes.
30 **eyes' windows:** lids.

31 **supple government:** ability to move easily.

32 **uncovered on the bier:** displayed for mourners. Friar Lawrence's plan could work because the Capulets do not bury their dead but lay them in a family tomb.
33 **against:** before.

34 **drift:** plan.

35 **inconstant toy:** foolish whim.

36 **Abate thy valor:** lessen your courage.

AT A GLANCE

- *Scene i (continued):* Friar Lawrence offers her a potion that will make her seem dead for forty-two hours; he will send for Romeo; Romeo will take her away to Mantua.
- Juliet agrees to the plan.

1 PLOT: RISING ACTION

Friar Lawrence's potion will cause her to *seem* dead. She will be taken to the family tomb, where Romeo will rescue her and take her to Mantua.

2 STYLE: RHYME

The friar and Juliet reach an agreement on this dangerous plan, and the rhymes help us understand their agreement as the scene ends.

GUIDED READING

LITERAL QUESTIONS

1a. What is Juliet's response to Friar Lawrence's offer of the sleeping potion? ("Give me [the vial]!")

2a. How will Romeo know that Juliet is not dead? (Friar Lawrence will write a letter to him.)

INFERENTIAL QUESTIONS

1b. Why is she so quick to agree to the plan? (She is emotionally upset and deeply in love; love has blinded her to the need for caution.)

2b. Why does this plan seem dangerous? (Only Romeo and Friar Lawrence will know that Juliet is still alive, and Romeo is far away.)

AT A GLANCE

- *Scene ii:* Juliet promises to obey her father.
- Capulet moves the wedding ahead one day.

1 STYLE: HUMOR

Shakespeare uses humor to contrast the tragic scenes that precede and follow this one. Here, a servant furnishes wit.

2 CHARACTERIZATION

The Nurse tells us that Juliet wears a "merry look"; the girl, of course, has conspired with the Friar to deceive the family.

3 THEME

To throw her parents off track, Juliet professes absolute devotion to her father's wishes. She so completely succeeds that her father moves the wedding ahead one day. An ominous and ironic consequence suggests itself: Friar Lawrence may not be able to tell Romeo in time.

Scene ii. *The afternoon of the same day. A ball in* CAPULET'S *house.*

[LORD CAPULET, LADY CAPULET, *and the* NURSE *enter with several* SERVANTS. *They are making arrangements for the wedding that will be held in just two days.*]

CAPULET. So many guests invite as here are writ.

[CAPULET *hands a* SERVANT *a guest list, and the* SERVANT *leaves to invite the wedding guests.*]

1 Sirrah, go hire me twenty cunning[1] cooks.

SERVINGMAN. You shall have none ill, sir; for I'll try[2] if they can lick their fingers.

CAPULET. How canst thou try them so?

SERVINGMAN. Marry, sir, 'tis an ill cook that cannot lick his own fingers.[3] Therefore he that cannot lick his fingers goes not with me.

[*The second* SERVANT *leaves to hire more cooks.*]

CAPULET. Go begone.
We shall be much unfurnished[4] for this time.
What, is my daughter gone to Friar Lawrence?

NURSE. Ay, forsooth.[5]

CAPULET. Well, he may chance to do some good on her.
A peevish self-willed harlotry it is.[6]

2 [JULIET *enters, returning from* FRIAR LAWRENCE'S *cell.*]

NURSE. See where she comes from shrift with merry look.

CAPULET. How now, my headstrong? Where have you been gadding?

JULIET. Where I have learnt me to repent the sin
Of disobedient opposition
To you and your behests,[7] and am enjoined
By holy Lawrence to fall prostrate[8] here
To beg your pardon.

[*She kneels before her father.*]

3 Pardon, I beseech you!
Henceforward I am ever ruled by you.

CAPULET. Send for the County. Go tell him of this.
I'll have this knot knit up tomorrow morning.[9]

1 **cunning:** talented.

2 **try:** test.

3 **'tis . . . fingers:** It is a poor cook who will not eat his own cooking.

4 **unfurnished:** unprepared.

5 **forsooth:** in truth.

6 **A peevish . . . it is:** She is an ill-tempered, selfish hussy.

7 **behests:** requests.

8 **fall prostrate:** lie face down in humility and obedience.

9 **tomorrow morning:** that is, Wednesday. Capulet is so happy about Juliet's agreeing that he decides to have the wedding a day earlier.

GUIDED READING

LITERAL QUESTIONS

1a. What decision does Capulet make about the wedding? (He moves it from Thursday to Wednesday.)

2a. What lies does Juliet tell her father? (She plans to obey him from now on.)

INFERENTIAL QUESTIONS

1b. How does this decision intensify the tension of the play? (The pace of events, which was already fast, seems to be accelerating and may go out of control.)

2b. How do the events of the past few days seem to have changed Juliet's character? (She has turned from an open, innocent girl to a desperate, alienated person.)

JULIET. I met the youthful lord at Lawrence' cell
And gave him what becomed[10] love I might,
Not stepping o'er the bounds of modesty.

CAPULET. Why, I am glad on't. This is well. Stand up.

[JULIET *rises.*]

This is as't should be. Let me see the County.
Ay, marry, go, I say, and fetch him hither.
Now, afore God, this reverend holy friar,
All our whole city is much bound[11] to him.

JULIET. Nurse, will you go with me into my closet[12]
To help me sort such needful ornaments[13]
As you think fit to furnish me tomorrow?

LADY CAPULET. No, not till Thursday. There is time enough.

CAPULET. Go, nurse, go with her. We'll to church tomorrow.

[JULIET *and the* NURSE *leave.*]

LADY CAPULET. We shall be short in our provision.[14]
'Tis now near night.

CAPULET. Tush, I will stir about,
And all things shall be well, I warrant thee, wife.
2 Go thou to Juliet, help to deck up her.[15]
I'll not to bed tonight; let me alone.
I'll play the housewife for this once. What, ho!
They are all forth;[16] well, I will walk myself
To County Paris, to prepare up him
Against tomorrow. My heart is wondrous light,
Since this same wayward girl is so reclaimed.

[CAPULET *and* LADY CAPULET *exit.*]

Scene iii. The evening of the same day, the night before the wedding. JULIET'*s room.*

[JULIET *and the* NURSE *have been preparing* JULIET'*s clothing for the wedding.*]

3 JULIET. Ay, those attires are best; but, gentle nurse,
I pray thee leave me to myself tonight;
For I have need of many orisons[1]
To move the heavens to smile upon my state,
Which, well thou knowest, is cross[2] and full of sin.

10 **becomed:** proper.

11 **bound:** indebted.

12 **closet:** bedroom.

13 **sort . . . ornaments:** choose necessary clothing.

14 **be . . . provision:** not have enough time for preparation.

15 **deck up her:** get her ready.

16 **What ho! . . . forth:** Capulet calls for a servant but realizes that he has already sent them all on errands.

1 **orisons:** prayers.

2 **cross:** wrong.

AT A GLANCE

- *Scene ii (continued):* Capulet praises Friar Lawrence.
- Juliet prepares for her wedding.
- *Scene iii:* Juliet asks the Nurse to let her be alone.

1 IRONY

Capulet praises the friar for his daughter's transformation; although Friar Lawrence's plan was to bring the feud to an end, so far it has succeeded only in causing deception.

2 PLOT: SUSPENSE

Capulet's command leaves open the possibility that his wife will enter Juliet's room at the wrong time and spoil Juliet's plan to avoid the marriage to Paris.

3 CHARACTERIZATION

Juliet and the Nurse are in the middle of looking through her gowns and apparently have chosen the ones they like. Juliet asks the Nurse to leave her alone, giving a false reason—her need to pray for her sins.

GUIDED READING

LITERAL QUESTION

1a. How does Capulet plan to get ready for the wedding so quickly? (by staying up all night)

INFERENTIAL QUESTION

1b. Does the father's behavior seem to fit his character? (Quick-tempered people are often spontaneous people; we know Capulet loves a party. These two factors seem to make his character consistent.)

AT A GLANCE

- *Scene iii (continued):* Alone, Juliet tries to take the potion, but fear overwhelms her.

1 SOLILOQUY

Juliet's moral and emotional isolation is underscored by her being alone on the stage: She has often been presented alone to think out some new development in her life.

2 STYLE: BLANK VERSE

The break in the rhythm caused by the three-syllable line shows us that a significant pause follows before Juliet speaks again.

3 THEME

Although she is terrified, Juliet is determined to take the potion or use the dagger beside her bed. Love has blinded her to all thought of caution.

[LADY CAPULET *enters.*]

LADY CAPULET. What, are you busy, ho? Need you my help?

JULIET. No, madam; we have culled[3] such necessaries
As are behoveful[4] for our state tomorrow.
So please you, let me now be left alone,
And let the nurse this night sit up with you;
For I am sure you have your hands full all
In this so sudden business.

LADY CAPULET. Good night.
Get thee to bed, and rest; for thou hast need.

[LADY CAPULET *and the* NURSE *leave.*]

1 JULIET. Farewell! God knows when we shall meet again.
I have a faint cold fear thrills through my veins
That almost freezes up the heat of life.
I'll call them back again to comfort me.
Nurse!—What should she do here?
2 My dismal scene I needs must act alone.
Come, vial.
What if this mixture do not work at all?
Shall I be married then tomorrow morning?
No, no! This shall forbid it. Lie thou there.

[*She places a dagger beside the bed.*]

What if it be a poison which the friar
Subtly hath minist'red[5] to have me dead,
Lest in this marriage he should be dishonored
Because he married me before to Romeo?
I fear it is; and yet methinks it should not,
For he hath still been tried[6] a holy man.
3 How if, when I am laid into the tomb,
I wake before the time that Romeo
Come to redeem[7] me? There's a fearful point!
Shall I not then be stifled in the vault,
To whose foul mouth no healthsome air breathes in,
And there die strangled ere my Romeo comes?
Or, if I live, is it not very like
The horrible conceit[8] of death and night,
Together with the terror of the place—
As in a vault, an ancient receptacle
Where for this many hundred years the bones
Of all my buried ancestors are packed;
Where bloody Tybalt, yet but green in earth,[9]

3 **culled:** selected.

4 **behoveful:** appropriate.

5 **minist'red:** given to me.

6 **For he . . . tried:** because he has always proven to be.

7 **redeem:** rescue.

8 **conceit:** idea.

9 **green in earth:** newly buried.

GUIDED READING

LITERAL QUESTION

1a. What suspicion does Juliet develop about Friar Lawrence? (that he might have given her poison to protect his own reputation)

INFERENTIAL QUESTION

1b. Does this suspicion seem justified? (We have never seen Friar Lawrence act other than with kind concern toward both Romeo and Juliet.)

Lies fest'ring in his shroud; where, as they say,
At some hours in the night spirits resort—
Alack, alack, is it not like[10] that I,
So early waking—what with loathsome smells,
And shrieks like mandrakes[11] torn out of the earth,
That living mortals, hearing them, run mad—
1 O, if I wake, shall I not be distraught,[12]
Environèd[13] with all these hideous fears,
And madly play with my forefathers' joints,
And pluck the mangled Tybalt from his shroud,
And, in this rage, with some great kinsman's bone
As with a club dash out my desp'rate brains?
O, look! Methinks I see my cousin's ghost
Seeking out Romeo, that did spit his body
Upon a rapier's point. Stay, Tybalt, stay!
Romeo, Romeo, Romeo, I drink to thee.

[JULIET *drinks the contents of the vial and falls onto her bed, which is surrounded with curtains.*]

10 **like:** likely.

11 **mandrakes:** plants with forked roots that are shaped like a hand. According to superstition, the plant screamed when torn up, and whoever heard the sound became insane.

12 **distraught:** crazed.

13 **Environed:** surrounded.

AT A GLANCE

- *Scene iii (continued):* Juliet imagines the horrors of the Capulet tomb.
- She drinks the poison.

1 INNER CONFLICT

Juliet imagines waking in the hideous vault and being driven to madness and suicide by its horrors. Nevertheless, love spurs her on to her incautious act.

GUIDED READING

LITERAL QUESTION

1a. Which corpse does Juliet imagine encountering in the vault? (Tybalt's)

INFERENTIAL QUESTION

1b. Why is this image especially upsetting to Juliet? (Romeo is Tybalt's murderer.)

AT A GLANCE

- *Scene iv:* In continuing with the marriage preparations, members of the household work into the night.

1 **CHARACTERIZATION**

Lady Capulet seems never to miss an opportunity to remind her husband of his advanced age. He deflects her barb by taking it for jealousy.

2 **DRAMATIC IRONY**

While the servant and Capulet play with words, the audience knows these festive preparations are all for naught.

Scene iv. During the night. A hall in* CAPULET'S *house.

[Preparations for the wedding continue. LADY CAPULET *and the* NURSE *enter.]*

LADY CAPULET. Hold, take these keys and fetch more spices, nurse.

NURSE. They call for dates and quinces[1] in the pastry.[2]

[LORD CAPULET *enters.*]

CAPULET. Come, stir, stir, stir! The second cock hath crowed,
The curfew bell hath rung, 'tis three o'clock.
Look to the baked meats, good Angelica;[3]
Spare not for cost.

NURSE. Go, you cotquean,[4] go,
Get you to bed! Faith, you'll be sick tomorrow
For this night's watching.[5]

CAPULET. No, not a whit. What, I have watched ere now
All night for lesser cause, and ne'er been sick.

1 LADY CAPULET. Ay, you have been a mouse hunt[6] in your time;
But I will watch you from such watching now.

[LADY CAPULET *and the* NURSE *leave.*]

CAPULET. A jealous hood,[7] a jealous hood!

[Several SERVANTS *enter with spits, logs, and baskets for preparing the wedding feast.]*

Now, fellow,
What is there?

FIRST FELLOW. Things for the cook, sir; but I know not what.

CAPULET. Make haste, make haste.

[One SERVANT *leaves for the kitchen.]*

Sirrah, fetch drier logs.
Call Peter; he will show thee where they are.

2 SECOND FELLOW. I have a head, sir, that will find out logs
And never trouble Peter for the matter.

CAPULET. Mass,[8] and well said; ha!
Thou shalt be loggerhead.[9]

[The SERVANTS *leave.]*

1 **quinces:** golden, apple-shaped fruit.
2 **pastry:** room where baking is done.
3 **Angelica:** probably the Nurse's name.
4 **cotquean:** a man who does housework.
5 **night's watching:** staying awake all night.
6 **mouse hunt:** woman hunter.
7 **jealous hood:** jealousy.
8 **Mass:** by the Mass.
9 **loggerhead:** blockhead.

GUIDED READING

LITERAL QUESTION

1a. Where does this scene take place? (a hall in Capulet's house)

INFERENTIAL QUESTION

1b. What does the audience know that no one on stage knows? (Juliet is married to Romeo; she has taken the potion and will soon be discovered and taken for dead.)

Good faith, 'tis day.
The County will be here with music straight,
For so he said he would.

[*Music plays from offstage.* PARIS *is outside the house with musicians.*]

I hear him near.
Nurse! Wife! What, ho! What, nurse, I say!

[*The* NURSE *enters.*]

Go waken Juliet; go and trim her up.
I'll go and chat with Paris. Hie, make haste,
Make haste! The bridegroom he is come already:
Make haste, I say.

[*They exit.*]

Scene v. Immediately after the previous scene.* JULIET'S *room.

[JULIET *is behind the curtain that surrounds her bed. The* NURSE *enters in order to awaken* JULIET *and to prepare her for the wedding. The* NURSE *cannot see* JULIET *and assumes that she is asleep because of the stillness of the room.*]

NURSE. Mistress! What, mistress! Juliet! Fast,[1] I warrant her, she.
Why, lamb! Why, lady! Fie, you slugabed.[2]
Why, love, I say! Madam; Sweetheart! Why, bride!
What, not a word? How sound is she asleep!
I needs must wake her. Madam, madam, madam!

[*The* NURSE *pulls open the bed curtain. At first she thinks that* JULIET *has dressed and then fallen asleep again, but she becomes alarmed when* JULIET *fails to answer her calls.*]

What, dressed, and in your clothes, and down again?[3]
I must needs wake you. Lady! Lady! Lady!
Alas, alas! Help, Help! My lady's dead!
O weraday that ever I was born!
Some *aqua vitae*, ho! My lord! My lady!

[LADY CAPULET *enters.*]

LADY CAPULET. What noise is here?

NURSE. O lamentable day!

LADY CAPULET. What is the matter?

NURSE. Look, look! O heavy day!

1 **Fast:** fast asleep.

2 **slugabed:** sleepy head.

3 **down again:** gone back to bed.

AT A GLANCE

- *Scene iv (continued):* Capulet, hearing Paris, sends the Nurse to awaken Juliet.
- *Scene v:* The Nurse finds the "dead" Juliet.

1 BACKGROUND

To Shakespeare's audience, music was important; none of his plays is without it. In his tragedies music is carefully placed so that dramatic tension is not dissipated.

2 MOOD

The moment of discovery and suspense is prolonged because the Nurse must wake Juliet gently. She uses pet names that remind us that Juliet is not far from childhood.

3 STAGING

The Nurse's actions will reveal her conclusion that Juliet is dead: Because we can see her touch Juliet's body, recoil, listen to her heart, we will not find the repetition in her lines comical.

4 BLANK VERSE

The sharing of the iambic pentameter lines draw the Nurse and the mother together in the dawning of grief. In these lines *o* sounds predominate and reinforce the idea of mourning.

GUIDED READING

LITERAL QUESTION

1a. Who is sent to fetch Juliet? (the Nurse)

INFERENTIAL QUESTION

1b. How does the discovery by the Nurse add to the audience's sense of gloom? (The Nurse is an innocent victim of the deception; she might have been told the truth and spared the sight of Juliet "dead.")

AT A GLANCE

- *Scene v (continued):* The Capulets see the body and mourn.
- Paris and Friar Lawrence enter.

1 STAGING

Shakespeare gives the mother and the Nurse opportunity to express their grief through short phrases that can be mixed with sobs or other sounds of pain.

2 STYLE: IMAGERY

Lord Capulet notes the signs of death in Juliet's body, then compares her to a field-flower that has been stricken by a premature frost.

3 PERSONIFICATION

In revealing to Paris the news of Juliet's death, Capulet personifies death as Juliet's bridegroom.

1 LADY CAPULET. O me, O me! My child, my only life!
Revive, look up, or I will die with thee!
Help, help! Call help.

[LORD CAPULET *enters.*]

CAPULET. For shame, bring Juliet forth; her lord is come.

NURSE. She's dead, deceased; she's dead, alack the day!

LADY CAPULET. Alack the day, she's dead, she's dead, she's dead!

CAPULET. Ha! Let me see her. Out alas! She's cold,
2 Her blood is settled, and her joints are stiff;
Life and these lips have long been separated.
Death lies on her like an untimely frost
Upon the sweetest flower of all the field.

NURSE. O lamentable day!

LADY CAPULET. O woeful time!

CAPULET. Death, that hath ta'en her hence to make me wail,
Ties up my tongue and will not let me speak.

[FRIAR LAWRENCE *and* PARIS *enter.*]

FRIAR. Come, is the bride ready to go to church?

CAPULET. Ready to go, but never to return.
3 O son, the night before thy wedding day
Hath Death lain with thy wife. There she lies,
Death is my son-in-law, Death is my heir;
My daughter he hath wedded. I will die
And leave him all. Life, living, all is Death's.

PARIS. Have I thought, love, to see this morning's face,
And doth it give me such a sight as this?

LADY CAPULET. Accursed, unhappy, wretched, hateful day!
Most miserable hour that e'er time saw
In lasting labor of his pilgrimage!
But one, poor one, one poor and loving child,
But one thing to rejoice and solace[4] in,
And cruel Death hath catched it from my sight.

NURSE. O woe! O woeful, woeful, woeful day!
Most lamentable day, most woeful day
That ever ever I did yet behold!
O day, O day, O day! O hateful day!
Never was seen so black a day as this.
O woeful day! O woeful day!

4 **solace:** take comfort.

GUIDED READING

LITERAL QUESTION

1a. Who enters with Friar Lawrence? (Paris)

INFERENTIAL QUESTION

1b. How might the audience respond to Paris at this moment? (We feel sorry for him; quietly eloquent in his love for Juliet, he speaks of having looked forward to seeing her.)

1 **PARIS.** Beguiled,[5] divorcèd, wrongèd, spited, slain!
Most detestable Death, by thee beguiled,
By cruel, cruel thee quite overthrown.
O love! O life!—not life, but love in death!

2 **CAPULET.** Despised, distressèd, hated, martyred, killed!
Uncomfortable[6] time, why cam'st thou now
To murder, murder our solemnity?[7]
O child, O child! My soul, and not my child!
Dead art thou—alack, my child is dead,
And with my child my joys are burièd!

FRIAR. Peace, ho, for shame! Confusion's cure lives not
3 In these confusions.[8] Heaven and yourself
Had part in this fair maid—now heaven hath all,
And all the better is it for the maid.
Your part in her you could not keep from death,
But heaven keeps his part in eternal life.
The most you sought was her promotion,
For 'twas your heaven she should be advanced;
And weep ye now, seeing she is advanced

5 **Beguiled:** cheated.

6 **Uncomfortable:** distressing.

7 **solemnity:** celebration.

8 **Confusion's . . . confusions:** The confusion of your cries will not solve the confusion of this event.

AT A GLANCE

- *Scene v (continued):* Friar Lawrence tries to console the grieving family.

1 BLANK VERSE

The accents in *divorcèd* and *wrongèd* help us find the meter in this line. The line builds to the stressed word *slain.*

2 STYLE: BLANK VERSE

Capulet's line mirrors Paris' and reminds us that these two men shared the dream that Juliet would marry Paris. In their grief they each address her as Death's victim.

3 STYLE: MONOLOGUE

Friar Lawrence reminds the family that Juliet has gone to eternal life. In a play where fate guides the heroes to death, the idea of a fair heaven seems ironic.

GUIDED READING

LITERAL QUESTION

1a. According to Friar Lawrence, what two forces went into the making of Juliet? (heaven and her earthly parents)

INFERENTIAL QUESTION

1b. What double meanings might we find in his speech? (His references to heaven may be references to himself as its representative.)

AT A GLANCE

- *Scene v (continued):* Lawrence says Juliet is in a better place.
- He suggests that heaven may be punishing the Capulets for feuding.

1 CHARACTERIZATION

The measured cadence of these lines captures the dignity and weightiness of Lord Capulet.

REFLECTING ON ACT IV

In tragedy, ill-fated characters are often ruined by their own decisions. What choices have brought Juliet to this crisis? (She chose to be married secretly and to take the potion without confiding in any of her family.)

STUDY QUESTIONS

1. Juliet needs companionship to overcome grief.
2. He will give Juliet potion to induce deathlike sleep; she will be buried in vault; Romeo will be summoned there; they will flee to Mantua.
3. moves wedding to next day
4. fears it will not work, it is really poison, she will go mad with terror to awaken among dead
5. - *warm, loving:* talks to Juliet at friar's cell
   - *has self-control:* waits for Capulet to set wedding date and accepts grief of Juliet's death
6. Love has made her fearless.
7. loved her deeply
8. Juliet does not intend to marry Paris; Juliet is not dead.
9. He fears their anger; Romeo is Tybalt's murderer; too little time has passed.

Above the clouds, as high as heaven itself?
O, in this love, you love your child so ill
That you run mad, seeing that she is well.[9]
She's not well married that lives married long,
But she's best married that dies married young.
Dry up your tears and stick your rosemary[10]
On this fair corse, and, as the custom is,
And in her best array bear her to church;
For though fond nature bids us all lament,
Yet nature's tears are reason's merriment.[11]

CAPULET. All things that we ordainèd festival[12]
Turn from their office to black funeral—
1 Our instruments to melancholy bells,
Our wedding cheer to a sad burial feast;
Our solemn hymns to sullen dirges[13] change;
Our bridal flowers serve for a buried corse;
And all things change them to the contrary.

FRIAR. Sir, go you in; and, madam, go with him;
And go, Sir Paris. Everyone prepare
To follow this fair corse unto her grave.
The heavens do low'r[14] upon you for some ill;
Move them no more by crossing their high will.

[Each person casts rosemary leaves on JULIET *and then exits.]*

9 **well:** in heaven.

10 **rosemary:** an evergreen that was used at weddings and funerals because it signified everlasting love.

11 **Yet . . . merriment:** Although human nature tells us to cry, reason tells us to be happy (because she is in heaven).

12 **ordained festival:** intended as celebration.

13 **sullen dirges:** gloomy funeral music.

14 **low'r:** frown.

STUDY QUESTIONS

Recalling

1. In Act IV, Scene i, lines 2–15, what reason does Paris give Friar Lawrence for the hasty wedding plans?
2. Describe the friar's plan, explained in Scene i, lines 89–120, eventually to reunite Romeo and Juliet.
3. In Scene ii, after Juliet pretends to agree to marry Paris, what change does Capulet make in the wedding plans?
4. Explain three doubts that worry Juliet before she drinks Friar Lawrence's potion in Scene iii, lines 21–58.

Interpreting

5. Based on this act, describe Paris' personality, and cite examples.
6. What do we learn about Juliet in Act IV, Scene i, based on her reaction to Friar Lawrence's plan?
7. According to their reaction to her "death" in Act IV, Scene v, describe the Capulets' feelings for their daughter.
8. During Act IV what information does the audience have that various characters do not have?

Extending

9. Why do you think Friar Lawrence does not tell the Capulets that Juliet is already married to Romeo?

ACT V

***Scene i.** The next day. A street in Mantua, the city where* ROMEO *lives in exile.*

[ROMEO *enters; he is waiting for his servant,* BALTHASAR, *to return from Verona with news of* JULIET.]

ROMEO. If I may trust the flattering truth of sleep,[1]
My dreams presage,[2] some joyful news at hand.
My bosom's lord[3] sits lightly in his throne,
And all this day an unaccustomed spirit
Lifts me above the ground with cheerful thoughts.
1 I dreamt my lady came and found me dead
(Strange dream that gives a dead man leave to think!)
And breathed such life with kisses in my lips
That I revived and was an emperor.
Ah me! How sweet is love itself possessed,
When but love's shadows[4] are so rich in joy!

[ROMEO*'s servant,* BALTHASAR, *enters. He is still wearing the riding boots from his trip from Verona.*]

2 News from Verona! How now, Balthasar?
Dost thou not bring me letters from the friar?
How doth my lady? Is my father well?
How fares my Juliet? That I ask again,
For nothing can be ill if she be well.

MAN. Then she is well, and nothing can be ill.
Her body sleeps in Capel's monument,[5]
And her immortal part with angels lives.
3 I saw her laid low in her kindred's vault
And presently took post[6] to tell it you.
O, pardon me for bringing these ill news,
Since you did leave it for my office,[7] sir.

4 **ROMEO.** Is it e'en so? Then I defy you, stars!
Thou knowest my lodging. Get me ink and paper
And hire post horses. I will hence tonight.

MAN. I do beseech you, sir, have patience.
Your looks are pale and wild and do import[8]
Some misadventure.

ROMEO. Tush, thou art deceived.
Leave me and do the thing I bid thee do.
Hast thou no letters to me from the friar?

1 **flattering . . . sleep:** pleasant illusion of dreams.
2 **presage:** predict.
3 **bosom's lord:** heart.
4 **but love's shadows:** only love's dreams.
5 **Capel's monument:** Capulet's tomb.
6 **presently took post:** quickly set out on a post horse. Post horses were relay horses that could be changed at stations along the way to keep a messenger from being slowed down by tired horses.
7 **office:** duty.
8 **import some misadventure:** suggest some misfortune.

AT A GLANCE

- *Scene i:* Romeo waits anxiously in Mantua.
- His servant brings news that Juliet was placed in the Capulet tomb.

LITERARY OPTIONS

- dramatic irony
- setting
- characterization

THEMATIC OPTIONS

- love
- fate
- loss

1 THEME

Romeo's dream foreshadows the play's end and emphasizes the power of love.

2 SETTING

This scene is the first that has taken place outside of Verona. Love and exile seem to have changed Romeo: He thinks of his family and asks about Juliet.

3 DRAMATIC IRONY

While Balthasar gives his eyewitness account of Juliet's funeral, the audience watches—powerless to tell Romeo that there is a misunderstanding.

4 CHARACTERIZATION

Romeo responds to the news with action: Rather than sink into his feelings, he forms a plan to defy fate.

GUIDED READING

LITERAL QUESTIONS

1a. From whom does Romeo expect a letter? (the friar)

2a. Why does Romeo's servant think that Juliet is dead? (He saw her carried to her family's burial vault.)

INFERENTIAL QUESTIONS

1b. Why does the audience want Balthasar to be carrying a letter from the friar? (This is the only way Romeo will know that Juliet will awaken.)

2b. Does the servant's news destroy the suspense or quicken it? (The suspense is intensified, for we see a hope that Romeo might be brought to Juliet even if the friar's letter doesn't reach him.)

AT A GLANCE

- *Scene i (continued):* Romeo orders the servant to find horses to take him to Verona.
- He plans to join Juliet in death.

1 SOLILOQUY

Romeo intends to be faithful to his love by joining her forever in death. He describes his suicide as an act of marriage.

2 IMAGERY

Romeo's vivid description of the local apothecary portrays a man so poverty-stricken that he might be induced to sell anything.

MAN. No, my good lord.

ROMEO. No matter. Get thee gone.
And hire those horses. I'll be with thee straight.

1 [BALTHASAR *leaves.* ROMEO, *grief stricken, begins to walk aimlessly.*]

Well, Juliet, I will lie with thee tonight.
Let's see for means. O mischief, thou art swift
To enter in the thoughts of desperate men!
2 I do remember an apothecary,[9]
And hereabouts 'a dwells, which late I noted
In tatt'red weeds, with overwhelming brows,[10]
Culling of simples.[11] Meager[12] were his looks,
Sharp misery had worn him to the bones;
And in his needy shop a tortoise hung,
An alligator stuffed, and other skins
Of ill-shaped fishes; and about his shelves
A beggarly account[13] of empty boxes,
Green earthen pots, bladders, and musty seeds,
Remnants of packthread,[14] and old cakes of roses[15]
Were thinly scatterèd, to make up a show.
Noting this penury,[16] to myself I said,
"And if a man did need a poison now
Whose sale is present death in Mantua,[17]
Here lives a caitiff[18] wretch would sell it him."
O, this same thought did but forerun my need,
And this same needy man must sell it me.
As I remember, this should be the house.
Being holiday, the beggar's shop is shut.
What, ho! Apothecary!

APOTHECARY. Who calls so loud?

ROMEO. Come hither, man. I see that thou art poor.
Hold, there is forty ducats.[19] Let me have
A dram of poison, such soon-speeding gear[20]
As will disperse itself through all the veins
That the life-weary taker may fall dead.

APOTHECARY. Such mortal[21] drugs I have; but Mantua's law
Is death to any he that utters[22] them.

ROMEO. Art thou so bare and full of wretchedness
And fearest to die? Famine is in thy cheeks,
Need and oppression starveth in thy eyes,
Contempt and beggary hangs upon thy back:

9 **apothecary:** druggist.
10 **In tatt'red . . . brows:** in torn clothing and frowning eyebrows.
11 **Culling of simples:** sorting herbs.
12 **Meager:** thin.
13 **beggarly account:** small number.
14 **packthread:** twine for tying packages.
15 **old cakes of roses:** dried, pressed rose petals, used for perfume.
16 **penury:** poverty.
17 **Whose sale . . . Mantua:** the sale of which is punishable by death in Mantua.
18 **caitiff:** miserable.
19 **ducats:** gold coins.
20 **soon-speeding gear:** fast-working stuff.
21 **mortal:** deadly.
22 **utters:** sells.

GUIDED READING

LITERAL QUESTION

1a. What reason does the apothecary give for hesitating to sell the poison? (It is a capital crime in Mantua.)

INFERENTIAL QUESTION

1b. What irony does Romeo find in the apothecary's obedience to the law? (He wonders how death can be worse than the "waking death" of the man's miserable life.)

The world is not thy friend, nor the world's law;
The world affords no law to make thee rich;
Then be not poor, but break it and take this.

APOTHECARY. My poverty but not my will consents.

ROMEO. I pay thy poverty and not thy will.

APOTHECARY. Put this in any liquid thing you will
And drink it off, and if you had the strength
Of twenty men, it would dispatch you straight.

ROMEO. There is thy gold—worse poison to men's souls,
Doing more murder in this loathsome world,
Than these poor compounds[23] that thou mayst not sell.
I sell thee poison; thou hast sold me none.
Farewell. Buy food and get thyself in flesh.
Come, cordial[24] and not poison, go with me
To Juliet's grave; for there must I use thee.

[*They exit.*]

23 **compounds:** mixtures; here, poisons.

24 **cordial:** restoring liquid.

Scene ii. The same afternoon. FRIAR LAWRENCE'*s cell in Verona.*

[FRIAR JOHN *enters. Sent by* FRIAR LAWRENCE *to Mantua with a letter for* ROMEO, *he has just returned.*]

JOHN. Holy Franciscan friar, brother, ho!

[FRIAR LAWRENCE *enters.*]

LAWRENCE. This same should be the voice of Friar John.
Welcome from Mantua. What says Romeo?
Or, if his mind be writ,[1] give me his letter.

JOHN. Going to find a barefoot brother out,
One of our order, to associate[2] me
Here in this city visiting the sick,
And finding him, the searchers[3] of the town,
Suspecting that we both were in a house
Where the infectious pestilence[4] did reign,
Sealed up the doors, and would not let us forth,
So that my speed to Mantua there was stayed.

LAWRENCE. Who bare my letter, then, to Romeo?

JOHN. I could not send it—here it is again—
Nor get a messenger to bring it thee,
So fearful were they of infection.

1 **if his . . . writ:** if his message is written.

2 **associate:** accompany

3 **searchers:** health officials who searched houses for victims of the plague and quarantined them.

4 **infectious pestilence:** contagious disease.

AT A GLANCE

- *Scene i (continued):* Romeo buys poison.
- *Scene ii:* Friar John could not deliver Friar Lawrence's letter to Romeo.

1 THEME

The poison, according to Romeo, is not evil. Its real good lies in its power to restore him to Juliet's company in death.

2 PLOT: RISING ACTION

The letter could not be delivered because fear of the plague caused citizens to quarantine John and refuse to touch the letter to deliver it for him.

GUIDED READING

LITERAL QUESTION

1a. Why couldn't Friar John get to Mantua? (He stopped to pick up a friend who was visiting the sick; officials feared they carried disease and instituted a quarantine.)

INFERENTIAL QUESTION

1b. How do John's action and its consequences illustrate the theme that good and evil are intertwined? (It is good to visit the sick and to show friendship, yet Romeo's and Juliet's deaths will follow from this "good.")

AT A GLANCE

- *Scene ii (continued):* Friar Lawrence realizes he must be with Juliet when she wakes.
- *Scene iii:* Paris mourns at Juliet's tomb.

1 DRAMATIC IRONY

Friar Lawrence imagines that the worst result of these mishaps is that Juliet will scold him for not telling Romeo the plan.

2 STYLE: RHYME

Paris addresses Juliet as a flower. The rhyme scheme of his first four lines suggests that he alternates speaking to her and to himself about the sadness of their condition.

LAWRENCE. Unhappy fortune! By my brotherhood,
The letter was not nice, but full of charge,
Of dear import;[5] and the neglecting it
May do much danger. Friar John, go hence,
Get me an iron crow[6] and bring it straight
Unto my cell.

JOHN. Brother, I'll go and bring it thee.

[FRIAR JOHN *leaves.*]

LAWRENCE. Now must I to the monument alone.
1 Within this three hours will fair Juliet wake.
She will beshrew[7] me much that Romeo
Hath had no notice of these accidents,[8]
But I will write again to Mantua,
And keep her at my cell till Romeo come—
Poor living corse, closed in a dead man's tomb!

[*He exits.*]

5 **not nice . . . import:** not trivial but urgent and of great importance.

6 **crow:** crowbar.

7 **beshrew:** blame.

8 **accidents:** events.

***Scene iii.** Late that night. The churchyard that contains the Capulets' tomb.*

[PARIS *enters with his* PAGE *who carries a torch and flowers.*]

PARIS. Give me thy torch, boy. Hence, and stand aloof.[1]
Yet put it out, for I would not be seen.
Under yond yew trees lay thee all along,[2]
Holding thy ear close to the hollow ground.
So shall no foot upon the churchyard tread
(Being loose, unfirm, with digging up of graves)
But thou shalt hear it. Whistle then to me,
As signal that thou hearest something approach.
Give me those flowers. Do as I bid thee, go.

PAGE. [*Aside.*] I am almost afraid to stand alone
Here in the churchyard; yet I will adventure.[3]

[*The* PAGE *retires to a watching place while* PARIS *sprinkles the tomb with flowers.*]

2 PARIS. Sweet flower, with flowers thy bridal bed I strew
(O woe! thy canopy is dust and stones)
Which with sweet[4] water nightly I will dew;
Or, wanting that, with tears distilled by moans.
The obsequies[5] that I for thee will keep
Nightly shall be to strew thy grave and weep.

1 **aloof:** away from me.

2 **lay . . . along:** lie flat on the ground.

3 **adventure:** risk it.

4 **sweet:** perfumed.

5 **obsequies:** funeral ceremonies.

GUIDED READING

LITERAL QUESTION

1a. How does Friar Lawrence plan to cover the situation if Romeo does not come? (He will keep Juliet in secret at his cell.)

INFERENTIAL QUESTION

1b. How is Friar Lawrence also "fortune's fool"? (He cannot imagine his plan going seriously wrong.)

[*The* PAGE *whistles, his signal that someone is coming.*]

The boy gives warning something doth approach.
1 What cursèd foot wanders this way tonight
To cross[6] my obsequies and true love's rite?
What, with a torch? Muffle[7] me, night, awhile.

[PARIS *hides as* ROMEO *and* BALTHASAR *enter. They are carrying a torch, a pickaxe (mattock), and a crowbar (wrenching iron).*]

ROMEO. Give me that mattock and the wrenching iron.
Hold, take this letter. Early in the morning
See thou deliver it to my lord and father.
Give me the light. Upon thy life I charge thee,
Whate'er thou hearest or seest, stand all aloof
And do not interrupt me in my course.
Why I descend into this bed of death
Is partly to behold my lady's face,
2 But chiefly to take thence from her dead finger
A precious ring—a ring that I must use
In dear employment.[8] Therefore hence, be gone.
But if thou, jealous,[9] dost return to pry
In what I farther shall intend to do,
3 By heaven, I will tear thee joint by joint
And strew this hungry churchyard with thy limbs.
The time and my intents are savage-wild,
More fierce and more inexorable[10] far
Than empty[11] tigers or the roaring sea.

BALTHASAR. I will be gone, sir, and not trouble ye.

ROMEO. So shalt thou show me friendship. Take thou that.

[*He hands* BALTHASAR *money.*]

Live, and be prosperous; and farewell, good fellow.

BALTHASAR. [*Aside.*] For all this same, I'll hide me hereabout.
His looks I fear, and his intents I doubt.

[BALTHASAR *hides.*]

ROMEO. Thou detestable maw,[12] thou womb of death,
Gorged[13] with the dearest morsel of the earth,
Thus I enforce thy rotten jaws to open,
And in despite[14] I'll cram thee with more food.

[*As* ROMEO *forces open the tomb,* PARIS *watches from his hiding place.*]

6 **cross:** interrupt.

7 **Muffle:** hide.

8 **In dear employment:** for an important purpose.

9 **jealous:** curious.

10 **inexorable:** unable to be changed or influenced.

11 **empty:** hungry.

12 **maw:** stomach.

13 **Gorged:** stuffed.

14 **despite:** scorn.

AT A GLANCE

- *Scene iii (continued):* Paris hides.
- Romeo forces open the tomb.

1 IRONY

Paris, feeling himself Juliet's true love and rightful mourner, feels intruded upon by the presence of another.

2 THEME

Unaware of Juliet's deception, Romeo deceives Balthasar with a story; in actuality he plans to die beside Juliet.

3 CHARACTERIZATION

Romeo acknowledges to his servant that his motives are excessive and his behavior immoderate.

GUIDED READING

LITERAL QUESTION

1a. What does Paris do when interrupted? (He hides and keeps watch.)

INFERENTIAL QUESTION

1b. What seems to be Paris' mood in this scene? (He is sad and possessive of Juliet.)

AT A GLANCE

- *Scene iii (continued):* Paris interrupts Romeo.
- Romeo slays him.
- Romeo recognizes and feels compassion for him.

1 PLOT: RISING ACTION

Since Juliet was thought to be grieving for Tybalt, her death has been attributed indirectly to Romeo, who was Tybalt's killer. Paris thinks the villain has come to further harm the Capulets.

2 DRAMATIC IRONY

Paris' death seems as unnecessary as Mercutio's.

1 PARIS. This is that banished haughty Montague
That murd'red my love's cousin—with which grief
It is supposed the fair creature died—
And here is come to do some villainous shame
To the dead bodies. I will apprehend[15] him.

[PARIS *comes forward and speaks to* ROMEO.]

Stop thy unhallowed toil, vile Montague!
Can vengeance be pursued further than death?
Condemnèd villain, I do apprehend thee.
Obey, and go with me; for thou must die.

ROMEO. I must indeed; and therefore came I hither.
Good gentle youth, tempt not a desp'rate man.
Fly hence and leave me. Think upon these gone;
Let them affright thee. I beseech thee, youth,
Put not another sin upon my head
By urging me to fury. O, be gone!
By heaven, I love thee better than myself,
For I come hither armed against myself.
Stay not, be gone. Live, and hereafter say
A madman's mercy bid thee run away.

PARIS. I do defy thy conjurations.[16]
And apprehend thee for a felon[17] here.

ROMEO. Wilt thou provoke me? Then have at thee, boy!

[*They draw swords and fight.*]

PAGE. O Lord, they fight! I will go call the watch.

[*The* PAGE *runs off to call the* WATCHMEN. PARIS *is wounded and falls.*]

2 PARIS. O, I am slain! If thou be merciful,
Open the tomb, lay me with Juliet.

[PARIS *dies.*]

ROMEO. In faith, I will. Let me peruse[18] this face.
Mercutio's kinsman, noble County Paris!
What said my man when my betossèd[19] soul
Did not attend him[20] as we rode? I think
He told me Paris should have married Juliet.
Said he not so, or did I dream it so?
Or am I mad, hearing him talk of Juliet,
To think it was so? O, give me thy hand,
One writ with me in sour misfortune's book!
I'll bury thee in a triumphant grave.

15 **apprehend:** arrest.

16 **conjurations:** appeals.

17 **felon:** criminal.

18 **peruse:** examine.

19 **betossèd:** upset.

20 **attend him:** pay attention to him.

GUIDED READING

LITERAL QUESTIONS

1a. Why does Paris attack Romeo? (He believes Romeo has come to harm Tybalt's and Juliet's corpses.)

2a. How does Paris die? (Romeo kills him after urging him to retreat.)

INFERENTIAL QUESTIONS

1b. In what way does Paris continue the tradition of the feud? (He addresses Romeo as "vile Montague"; he sees himself defending the Capulets against their enemy.)

2b. In what way is Paris' death ironic and tragic? (It is unnecessary, the result of a series of untruths and misunderstandings.)

A grave? O, no, a lanthorn,[21] slaught'red youth,
For here lies Juliet, and her beauty makes
This vault a feasting presence,[22] full of light.
Death, lie thou there, by a dead man interred.[23]

[ROMEO *carries* PARIS *into the tomb and lays him there. Then he walks to* JULIET'S *body. In Shakespeare's day the inner stage represented the interior of the tomb.*]

How oft when men are at the point of death
Have they been merry! Which their keepers[24] call
A lightning before death.[25] O, how may I
Call this a lightning? O my love, my wife!
2 Death, that hath sucked the honey of thy breath,
Hath had no power yet upon thy beauty.
Thou art not conquered. Beauty's ensign[26] yet
Is crimson in thy lips and in thy cheeks,
And death's pale flag is not advancèd there.
Tybalt, liest thou there in thy bloody sheet?
O, what more favor can I do to thee
Than with that hand that cut thy youth in twain
To sunder[27] his that was thine enemy?
Forgive me, cousin! Ah, dear Juliet,
Why art thou yet so fair? Shall I believe
That unsubstantial[28] Death is amorous,[29]
3 And that the lean abhorrèd monster keeps
Thee here in dark to be his paramour?
For fear of that I still will stay with thee
And never from his pallet[30] of dim night
Depart again. Here, here will I remain
With worms that are thy chambermaids. O, here
Will I set up my everlasting rest
And shake the yoke of inauspicious stars[31]
From this world-wearied flesh. Eyes, look your last!
Arms, take your last embrace! And, lips, O you
The doors of breath, seal with a righteous kiss
A dateless[32] bargain to engrossing[33] death!
4 Come, bitter conduct;[34] come, unsavory guide!
Thou desperate pilot,[35] now at once run on
The dashing rocks thy seasick weary bark!
Here's to my love!

[*He takes out the poison and drinks it.*]

O true apothecary!
Thy drugs are quick. Thus with a kiss I die.

21 **lanthorn:** a dome with windows that made a room bright.

22 **feasting presence:** hall lit for a celebration, usually for royalty.

23 **interred:** buried.

24 **keepers:** jailers.

25 **lightning before death:** a proverbial phrase based on the idea that people revive their spirits just before dying.

26 **ensign:** flag.

27 **sunder:** cut off.

28 **unsubstantial:** spiritual.

29 **amorous:** in love.

30 **pallet:** bed.

31 **inauspicious:** unlucky.

32 **dateless:** eternal.

33 **engrossing:** all-encompassing.

34 **conduct:** guide (the poison).

35 **desperate pilot:** Romeo.

AT A GLANCE

- Romeo finds Juliet in the tomb.
- He drinks his poison.

1 STYLE: IMAGERY

Romeo has always found Juliet's beauty a source of light. At the ball she "taught the torches to burn bright"; in the balcony scene she was like the sun. Here she is "a lanthorn" that lights up the tomb.

2 STYLE: METAPHOR

By comparing Juliet's life to honey sucked away by death, Romeo indirectly calls her a flower.

3 PERSONIFICATION

Romeo imagines death as a "monster" who would keep Juliet as his own lover. In order to protect her from this and other fancied evils, Romeo will stay with her forever.

4 PLOT: FALLING ACTION

As Romeo addresses the poison itself and prepares to drink, we see the tragedy of his condition: Love has robbed him of the desire to live.

GUIDED READING

LITERAL QUESTION

1a. What does Romeo ask of Tybalt? (to be forgiven)

INFERENTIAL QUESTION

1b. How might Romeo's appeal to Tybalt affect the audience? (The audience might see that were Romeo to live, he would be a better man and the feud might be ended.)

AT A GLANCE

- Lawrence prepares to enter the tomb.
- He finds Romeo's servant.

1 IRONY

Friar Lawrence does not think himself late because he is trying only to arrive before Juliet wakes. He is unaware of the harm that has resulted from Romeo's arrival before him.

[ROMEO *kisses* JULIET *and falls. Outside the tomb,* FRIAR LAWRENCE *enters the churchyard carrying a lantern, crowbar, and spade.*]

1 FRIAR. Saint Francis be my speed![36] How oft tonight
Have my old feet stumbled[37] at graves! Who's there?

[BALTHASAR *steps out from his hiding place.*]

BALTHASAR. Here's one, a friend, and one that knows you well.

FRIAR. Bliss be upon you! Tell me, good my friend,
What torch is yond that vainly lends his light
To grubs[38] and eyeless skulls? As I discern,[39]
It burneth in the Capels' monument.

BALTHASAR. It doth so, holy sir; and there's my master,
One that you love.

36 **speed:** help.

37 **stumbled:** Stumbling was considered a bad omen.

38 **grubs:** worms.

39 **discern:** make out.

GUIDED READING

LITERAL QUESTION

1a. What two characters meet outside the tomb? (Balthasar and Friar Lawrence)

INFERENTIAL QUESTION

1b. Who will be the first person to see Romeo dead? (Friar Lawrence, because the servant Balthasar has been disobeying Romeo and does not want to be seen.)

FRIAR. Who is it?

BALTHASAR. Romeo.

FRIAR. How long hath he been there?

BALTHASAR. Full half an hour.

FRIAR. Go with me to the vault.

BALTHASAR. I dare not, sir.
My master knows not but I am gone hence,
And fearfully did menace me with death
If I did stay to look on his intents.

FRIAR. Stay then; I'll go alone. Fear comes upon me.
O, much I fear some ill unthrifty[40] thing.

1 **BALTHASAR.** As I did sleep under this yew tree here,
I dreamt my master and another fought,
And that my master slew him.

FRIAR. Romeo!
Alack, alack, what blood is this which stains
The stony entrance of this sepulcher?[41]
What mean these masterless[42] and gory swords
To lie discolored by this place of peace?

[*He enters the tomb.*]

Romeo! O, pale! Who else? What, Paris too?
And steeped in blood? Ah, what an unkind[43] hour
Is guilty of this lamentable chance!
The lady stirs.

[JULIET *wakes.*]

2 **JULIET.** O comfortable[44] friar! Where is my lord?
I do remember well where I should be,
And there I am. Where is my Romeo?

FRIAR. I hear some noise. Lady, come from that nest
Of death, contagion,[45] and unnatural sleep.
3 A greater power than we can contradict
Hath thwarted our intents.[46] Come, come away.
Thy husband in thy bosom there lies dead;
And Paris too. Come, I'll dispose of thee
Among a sisterhood of holy nuns.
Stay not to question, for the watch is coming.
4 Come, go, good Juliet. I dare no longer stay.

JULIET. Go, get thee hence, for I will not away.

40 **unthrifty:** unlucky.

41 **sepulcher:** tomb.

42 **masterless:** abandoned.

43 **unkind:** unnatural.

44 **comfortable:** comforting.

45 **contagion:** disease.

46 **thwarted our intents:** ruined our plans.

AT A GLANCE

- Lawrence discovers the swords of Romeo and Paris.
- He finds Romeo dead.
- Juliet awakens.
- Lawrence wants to help her escape to a convent.

1 MAIN IDEA

Fate has outsmarted the servant. Although he stayed to protect his master (and dreamed the truth), his sleep prevented his helping Romeo.

2 IRONY

Juliet wakens without the fearful vapors her imagination suggested before she took the potion, yet the harsher reality is unknown to her.

3 CHARACTERIZATION

Lawrence realizes that his plan has miscarried and blames a "greater power." He wants to hide Juliet, possibly because he will have to answer many questions if she is found there alive.

4 STYLE: RHYME

The rhymed lines emphasize the conflict between Juliet and Friar Lawrence: She directly refuses to follow him and orders him away.

GUIDED READING

LITERAL QUESTIONS

1a. Where does Lawrence suggest Juliet should go? (a nunnery)

2a. Why does Lawrence say they must both escape immediately? (He hears the watch coming.)

INFERENTIAL QUESTIONS

1b. Why doesn't Juliet run away? (She wants to stay with Romeo.)

2b. What would happen if the watchmen were to discover them? (The Capulets would want to know how they had been tricked into thinking Juliet was dead; Lawrence might also face questions about Paris and Romeo.)

AT A GLANCE

- Juliet discovers Romeo's poison.
- She stabs herself with his dagger.
- Watchmen enter and discover the bodies.

1 SUSPENSE

The audience's hopes are raised by the news of watchmen approaching: Juliet might be saved. Unfortunately, she resolutely defies their rescue.

2 PLOT: FALLING ACTION

As Juliet takes her own life she completes the prophecy that the lovers' deaths must precede the end of the feuding.

3 TOTAL EFFECT

We are reminded that the lovers' death has a wider meaning through the presence of the watchmen and the order to tell the Prince. Each time there has been a death, the entire town was assembled; this will be the third and last time.

[*Hearing the approaching* WATCHMAN, FRIAR LAWRENCE *hurries off.*]

What's here? A cup, closed in my truelove's hand?
Poison, I see, hath been his timeless[47] end.
O churl![48] Drunk all, and left no friendly drop
To help me after? I will kiss thy lips.
Haply[49] some poison yet doth hang on them
To make me die with a restorative.[50]

[*She kisses* ROMEO*'s lips.*]

Thy lips are warm!

1 CHIEF WATCHMAN. [*He calls from off stage.*]
Lead, boy. Which way?

JULIET. Yea, noise? Then I'll be brief. O happy[51] dagger!

[*She snatches* ROMEO*'s dagger.*]

2 This is thy sheath; there rust, and let me die.

[*She stabs herself, falls, and dies.* PARIS' PAGE *enters the churchyard with a troop of* WATCHMEN.]

BOY. This is the place. There, where the torch doth burn.

CHIEF WATCHMAN. The ground is bloody. Search about the churchyard.
Go, some of you; whoe'er you find attach.[52]

[*Some of the* WATCHMEN *leave to search the churchyard. The remainder of the* WATCHMEN, *with the* PAGE, *enter the tomb.*]

Pitiful sight! Here lies the County slain;
And Juliet bleeding, warm, and newly dead,
Who here hath lain this two days burièd.
3 Go, tell the Prince; run to the Capulets;
Raise up the Montagues; some others search.

[*Other* WATCHMEN *leave.*]

We see the ground whereon these woes do lie,
But the true ground[53] of all these piteous woes
We cannot without circumstance descry.[54]

[*Some* WATCHMEN *return with* BALTHASAR.]

SECOND WATCHMAN. Here's Romeo's man. We found him in the churchyard.

CHIEF WATCHMAN. Hold him in safety till the Prince come hither.

[*Another* WATCHMAN *returns with* FRIAR LAWRENCE.]

47 **timeless:** too early.
48 **churl:** selfish person.
49 **Haply:** perhaps.
50 **restorative:** medicine.
51 **happy:** convenient.
52 **attach:** arrest.
53 **ground:** cause.
54 **cannot . . . descry:** cannot understand without the facts.

GUIDED READING

LITERAL QUESTIONS

1a. What does the chief watchman send the others to do? (fetch the Prince and the feuding families)

2a. When Juliet kisses Romeo, what does she say? ("Thy lips are warm!" l. 167)

INFERENTIAL QUESTIONS

1b. What is the effect of the watchman's speech? (The lines mark the turning point from the lovers' tale to the larger story of the Capulet-Montague feud and its effect on the community.)

2b. What effect might her words have on the audience? (They allow us to feel how painful it must be to wake only a few minutes too late. This recognition may help us to accept her death.)

THIRD WATCHMAN. Here is a friar that trembles, sighs, and weeps.
1 We took this mattock and this spade from him
As he was coming from this churchyard's side.

CHIEF WATCHMAN. A great suspicion! Stay the friar too.

[PRINCE ESCALUS *enters with his* ATTENDANTS.]

PRINCE. What misadventure is so early up,
That calls our person from our morning rest?

[LORD CAPULET *and* LADY CAPULET *enter with others.*]

CAPULET. What should it be, that is so shrieked abroad?

LADY CAPULET. O, the people in the street cry "Romeo,"
Some "Juliet," and some "Paris"; and all run
With open outcry toward our monument.

PRINCE. What fear is this which startles in your ears?

CHIEF WATCHMAN. Sovereign,

[*He calls them to the entrance of the tomb.*]

here lies the County Paris slain;
And Romeo dead; and Juliet, dead before,
Warm and new killed.

PRINCE. Search, seek, and know how this foul murder comes.

CHIEF WATCHMAN. Here is a friar, and slaughtered Romeo's man,
With instruments upon them fit to open
These dead men's tombs.

CAPULET. O heavens! O wife, look how our daughter bleeds!
2 This dagger hath mista'en, for, lo, his house[55]
Is empty on the back of Montague,
And it missheathèd in my daughter's bosom!

LADY CAPULET. O me, this sight of death is as a bell
That warns my old age to a sepulcher.

[LORD MONTAGUE *enters with others. The* PRINCE *calls them to the entrance of the tomb.*]

PRINCE. Come, Montague; for thou art early up
To see thy son and heir more early down.

3 **MONTAGUE.** Alas, my liege,[56] my wife is dead tonight!
Grief of my son's exile hath stopped her breath.
What further woe conspires against mine age?

55 **house:** sheath.

56 **liege:** lord.

AT A GLANCE

- The watchmen find Friar Lawrence and take him to the tomb for questioning.
- The Prince, the Montagues, and the Capulets assemble; they see the three dead bodies.

1 MAIN IDEA

Good and evil are so disguised that we cannot easily tell them apart. Thus a crowbar and spade may be enough evidence to convict the friar of murder if no other explanation is found.

2 THEME

Capulet's mind is still taken up with the feud. Here he says the dagger which ought to have been found in Romeo's back has found his daughter by mistake.

3 IRONY

Lord Montague, who has shown less belligerence than anyone, has suffered a double loss—his son and his wife.

GUIDED READING

LITERAL QUESTION

1a. How do Lord and Lady Capulet react to the sight of the bodies? (Lord Capulet is in a rage at Romeo; Lady Capulet feels warned by the sight.)

INFERENTIAL QUESTION

1b. How might the audience react to Capulet's unrelenting hatred of the Montagues? (His hatred seems excessive after recent events.)

AT A GLANCE

- The Prince questions Lawrence, who tells what he knows to the gathered company.

1 CHARACTERIZATION

Even the Prince seems altered by the grave events of this night. He says that he, too, has reason to grieve and will do so after he has found out the facts.

2 STYLE: BLANK VERSE

The lack of rhymes, metaphors, and imagery makes this a plain speech, though more elevated than prose. The language reflects the friar's message: He does not dwell on his motivation but, rather, confines himself to the facts.

PRINCE. Look, and thou shalt see.

MONTAGUE. O thou untaught! What manners is in this,
To press before thy father to a grave?

PRINCE. Seal up the mouth of outrage[57] for a while,
Till we can clear these ambiguities[58]
And know their spring, their head, their true descent;
1 And then will I be general of your woes[59]
And lead you even to death. Meantime forbear,
And let mischance be slave to patience.[60]
Bring forth the parties of suspicion.

FRIAR. I am the greatest, able to do least,
Yet most suspected, as the time and place
Doth make against me, of this direful[61] murder;
And here I stand, both to impeach and purge[62]
Myself condemnèd and myself excusèd.

PRINCE. Then say at once what thou dost know in this.

FRIAR. I will be brief, for my short date of breath[63]
Is not so long as is a tedious tale.
Romeo, there dead, was husband to that Juliet;
And she, there dead, that's Romeo's faithful wife.
2 I married them; and their stol'n marriage day
Was Tybalt's doomsday, whose untimely death
Banished the new-made bridegroom from this city;
For whom, and not for Tybalt, Juliet pined.
You, to remove that siege of grief from her,
Betrothed and would have married her perforce
To County Paris. Then comes she to me
And with wild looks bid me devise some mean
To rid her from this second marriage,
Or in my cell there would she kill herself.
Then gave I her (so tutored by my art)
A sleeping potion; which so took effect
As I intended, for it wrought on her
The form of death. Meantime I writ to Romeo
That he should hither come as[64] this dire night
To help to take her from her borrowed[65] grave,
Being the time the potion's force should cease.
But he which bore my letter, Friar John,
Was stayed by accident, and yesternight
Returned my letter back. Then all alone
At the prefixèd hour of her waking
Came I to take her from her kindred's vault;

57 **Seal . . . outrage:** stop the cries of grief.
58 **ambiguities:** mysteries.
59 **general . . . woes:** leader of the grieving.
60 **let . . . patience:** let patience control your reactions to this misfortune.
61 **direful:** terrible.
62 **impeach and purge:** blame and free from blame.
63 **date of breath:** span of life.
64 **as:** on.
65 **borrowed:** temporary.

GUIDED READING

LITERAL QUESTION

1a. What four things does Lawrence take responsibility for? (He married the lovers—l. 233; he gave Juliet a sleeping potion—l. 244; he wrote to Romeo—l. 246; he came to take Juliet from the vault—l. 254.)

INFERENTIAL QUESTION

1b. Is Lawrence giving a fair and accurate report of his part in the tragedy? (He explains all the actions in detail except to discuss why he married the couple in secret.)

Meaning to keep her closely[66] at my cell
Till I conveniently could send to Romeo.
But when I came, some minute ere the time
Of her awakening, here untimely lay
The noble Paris and true Romeo dead.
1 She wakes; and I entreated her come forth
And bear this work of heaven with patience;
But then a noise did scare me from the tomb,
And she, too desperate, would not go with me,
But, as it seems, did violence on herself.
All this I know, and to the marriage
Her nurse is privy;[67] and if aught in this
Miscarried by my fault, let my old life
Be sacrificed some hour before his time
Unto the rigor[68] of severest law.

2 PRINCE. We still have known thee for a holy man.
Where's Romeo's man? What can he say to this?

BALTHASAR. I brought my master news of Juliet's death;
And then in post he came from Mantua
To this same place, to this same monument.

66 **closely:** secretly.

67 **is privy:** shares the secret.

68 **rigor:** strictness.

AT A GLANCE

- Lawrence offers to be sacrificed if any of his story be shown untrue.

1 MAIN IDEA

Lawrence believes that heaven has ordained these events to put an end to the feud. He thought himself an instrument of heaven, but in the tomb determined that heaven had found another means to the same end.

2 PLOT: FALLING ACTION

The Prince accepts Lawrence's account without questioning him. The Prince is the voice of moral authority in the play—the one who established a penalty for the feud. The resolution will be his final pronouncement on these events.

GUIDED READING

LITERAL QUESTION

1a. What does Lawrence say about the nurse? (that she shares the secret of the marriage)

INFERENTIAL QUESTION

1b. What might be his motive for mentioning the nurse? (He is telling *all* he knows; perhaps his story will need corroboration.)

AT A GLANCE

- The Prince questions the two servants and reads a letter explaining Romeo's intention to die with Juliet.
- The Prince lays the blame at the feet of Capulet, Montague, and himself.

1 MAIN IDEA

The Prince calls upon Montague and Capulet to see that heaven has punished them by taking away the causes of their joy, just as their feud takes away heaven's joy.

2 PLOT: RESOLUTION

The enemies show that they intend to change their ways by joining hands and promising to raise statues of each other's children in pure gold.

3 STYLE: RHYME

The formality, slow cadence, long vowels, and final couplet of this verse help us to sense the play's end.

REFLECTING ON ACT V

In Act V, what ironic consequences resulted from human attempts to outwit fate? (In trying to bring the lovers together again, Friar Lawrence brought them to the tomb. In pretending to be dead, Juliet deceived Romeo. In failing to stay in Mantua, Romeo came to the wrong place at the wrong time.)

This letter he early bid me give his father,
And threat'ned me with death, going in the vault,
If I departed not and left him there.

PRINCE. Give me the letter. I will look on it.

[BALTHASAR *hands the letter to the* PRINCE.]

Where is the County's page that raised the watch?
Sirrah, what made your master[69] in this place?

BOY. He came with flowers to strew his lady's grave;
And bid me stand aloof, and so I did.
Anon comes one with light to ope the tomb;
And by and by my master drew on him;
And then I ran away to call the watch.

PRINCE. [*He is reading* ROMEO'*s letter.*] This letter doth make good
the friar's words,
Their course of love, the tidings of her death;
And here he writes that he did buy a poison
Of a poor pothecary and therewithal
Came to this vault to die and lie with Juliet.
Where be these enemies? Capulet, Montague,
1 See what a scourge[70] is laid upon your hate,
That heaven finds means to kill your joys with love.
And I, for winking at[71] your discords too,
Have lost a brace of kinsmen.[72] All are punished.

2 CAPULET. O brother Montague, give me thy hand.
This is my daughter's jointure,[73] for no more
Can I demand.

MONTAGUE. But I can give thee more;
For I will raise her statue in pure gold,
That whiles Verona by that name is known,
There shall no figure at such rate[74] be set
As that of true and faithful Juliet.

CAPULET. As rich shall Romeo's by his lady's lie—
Poor sacrifices of our enmity![75]

3 PRINCE. A glooming[76] peace this morning with it brings.
The sun for sorrow will not show his head.
Go hence, to have more talk of these sad things;
Some shall be pardoned, and some punishèd;
For never was a story of more woe
Than this of Juliet and her Romeo.

[*Everyone exits.*]

69 **what . . . master:** What was your master doing?

70 **scourge:** punishment.

71 **winking at:** closing my eyes to.

72 **brace of kinsmen:** pair of relatives (Mercutio and Paris).

73 **jointure:** wedding gift.

74 **rate:** value.

75 **enmity:** hostility.

76 **glooming:** cloudy, gloomy.

GUIDED READING

LITERAL QUESTION

1a. How many relatives of the Prince have been killed in the feud? (two: Mercutio and Paris)

INFERENTIAL QUESTION

1b. How has Shakespeare created a symmetry in the losses of the three families? (Each has lost two members: Lady Montague and Romeo; Tybalt and Juliet; Paris and Mercutio.)

STUDY QUESTIONS

Recalling

1. In Act V, Scene i, what news does Balthasar bring to Romeo in Mantua? What does Romeo plan to do as a result?
2. According to Scene ii, why is Friar John unable to deliver Friar Lawrence's letter to Romeo?
3. In Scene iii why does Paris visit Juliet's tomb? Why does he challenge Romeo? What is his last request before dying?
4. Describe Romeo's last actions before dying in Scene iii, lines 74–120.
5. Describe Juliet's actions after the friar leaves the tomb in Scene iii (lines 160–170).
6. According to the Prince in Scene iii, in what ways are he, Capulet, and Montague punished (lines 291–295)? For what reasons are they punished?
7. According to the end of Scene iii, what memorials are planned for the lovers?

Interpreting

8. Explain the role that chance plays in the outcome of the play.
9. Before dying, Romeo speaks to the bodies of Paris and Tybalt (lines 81–101). What do his words show about his personality at this point?
10. Describe the manner in which Romeo and Juliet face their deaths.
11. What hints at the end of the play and in the Prologue to Act I tell us that peace will be restored in Verona?

Extending

12. The Prince says that some people will be punished and some pardoned. Whom do you think should be punished? Why?

VIEWPOINT

Different scholars of Shakespeare's work have different opinions on the idea of the lovers being "star-crossed":

> Romeo and Juliet—Romeo especially—are in several ways morally culpable [blameworthy] and are partly responsible for their own tragedy.
>
> —V. Whitaker, *Mirror up to Nature*

> The fates are perverse [contrary] and these lovers are the victims of some ill conjunction [closeness] of the stars from which there is no escape.
>
> —L. Wright and V. LaMar, introduction to *Romeo and Juliet*, Folger Edition

■ Do you think that Romeo and Juliet are in some way responsible for their own actions, or are they victims of fate or of chance? Explain your opinion.

LITERARY FOCUS

The Total Effect

Seeing a production of *Romeo and Juliet* will reinforce the idea that all of the elements of a Shakespearean play contribute to its total effect, or overall impact.

Thinking About Plot

Like a short story or novel, a play has a **plot** that is a sequence of events built around a **conflict**, or struggle. The conflict can be **internal,** within a character, or external. An **external conflict** pits a character against another person, or against nature, environment, society, or fate.

The plots of most plays follow a basic structure. The **exposition,** usually contained in the first act, prepares us for the action of the play. The exposition introduces us to the setting and tells us about important events that happened before the play began. We also receive a first impression of characters, an impression that is usually dependable.

The **rising action** presents the main conflict of the play and builds tension to hold our interest. The **climax** is the moment of our highest interest and greatest emotional involvement in the play. In a tragedy the climax usually comes in the middle of the play rather than at the end. At this point of a tragedy, the main character takes some action that will lead directly to a downfall. The **falling action** shows the results of the climax and ends with the **resolution.**

1. Identify an internal conflict from Act IV. Identify a person-against-person conflict from Act V.
2. What information that is important to the rest of the play do we learn in the exposition in Act I? What event in Act I begins the rising action?

STUDY QUESTIONS

1. Juliet is dead and buried in family's vault; he will go there and poison himself.
2. Health officials prevent his leaving Verona; they fear he has plague.
3. brings flowers, wants to mourn; thinks Romeo is there to shame the dead; to be lain next to Juliet in vault
4. puts Paris' body next to Juliet; asks Tybalt's forgiveness; embraces, kisses Juliet; swallows poison
5. tries to drink a drop of poison from Romeo's lips; kisses him; stabs herself
6. All lose relatives as a result of the feud.
7. Montague plans to raise statue of Juliet; Capulet will do same for Romeo
8. Romeo does not get Friar's letter; kills Paris and himself just before Juliet awakes.
9. He is conciliatory.
10. insist on being together, fearless about dying
11. Capulet offers hand to Montague, they plan monument to lovers; Prologue states strife will be buried with lovers' deaths
12. Possible answers: Friar Lawrence, Nurse for keeping marriage secret; parents for continuing feud; Balthasar, Count's page, for not reporting activities in graveyard

VIEWPOINT

- Responsible: They are responsible for their immoderation and secret marriage.
- Fate: They meet by chance; Friar John is detained; Romeo and friar cannot meet at tomb as planned.

LITERARY FOCUS

1.
   - Internal: Juliet questions her determination to take potion.
   - Person vs. person: Paris battles with Romeo to prevent his entering tomb.
2. explains feud, Romeo and Juliet's attitudes about love; meeting of Romeo and Juliet

LITERARY FOCUS

3. Romeo and Juliet meet alone, pledge love; Nurse acts as go-between; friar marries them; Romeo shows good will to Tybalt, sees Mercutio killed.

4. Romeo kills Tybalt.

5. Capulet's decision to marry Juliet to Paris; plan for her death; revival; confusion over message to Romeo; deaths of Paris, Romeo, Juliet

6. Prince passes judgment; families are reconciled.

7.
- strengths: brave, determined, loyal, loving
- weaknesses: impulsive, excitable, moody

8.
- Romeo: fickle to heroic loyalty
- Juliet: compliant girl to independent woman

9.
- Lady Capulet: vindictiveness
- Montague: parental concern
- Friar Lawrence: well-intentioned meddling
- Prince: judiciousness

10.
- daylight: brawl, Nurse's meeting with Romeo, duels; social interaction
- night: Romeo and Juliet's meeting, courtship, events in tomb; private emotion

11.
- Romeo, Juliet, Paris, Tybalt, parents, friar, Prince
- Tomb represents death of characters and feud.

12. *Act V: lanthorn* filling dark; *vault* of death; *Act II: sun* outshining moon; Juliet, a source of light for Romeo

13. Romeo does not want to fight because Tybalt is Juliet's relative; if Mercutio knew this, he would not have challenged him; both deaths could have been avoided.

14. Audience knows Romeo is Juliet's husband when Paris challenges him; Juliet is about to awake when Romeo kills himself.

3. Give examples of rising action in Acts II and III.
4. What event in Act III is the climax, the event that dooms the love of Romeo and Juliet?
5. What falling action happens in Act IV and Act V as a result of the climax?
6. What is the resolution of the play?

Thinking About Character

We learn about characters in a play from their actions and appearance, from what they say, and from what others say about them. The main characters usually develop and change in the course of a play. Minor characters are often flat characters (page 53) about whom we learn little.

7. What are the strengths and weaknesses of Romeo's personality? Give examples from the play to support your opinions.
8. Explain how Romeo and Juliet change during the course of the play. Give examples.
9. What is the main personality trait of each of the following minor characters: Lady Capulet, Lord Montague, Friar Lawrence, the Prince.

Thinking About Setting

Although Shakespeare's company did not use scenery, Shakespeare used language to conjure up the settings of his plays.

10. Choose two scenes that take place in daylight and two that take place at night. What kind of action happens in each?
11. The final setting of the play is the tomb. What characters come together here? Why is the tomb an appropriate setting for the end of the play?

Thinking About Imagery

The Elizabethan audience listened for an exciting use of language. Shakespeare's imagery made his plays popular in his own day and guaranteed his lasting appeal.

12. What image of light and dark does Romeo use to describe Juliet before he dies in Act V, Scene iii, lines 83–87? Explain the similarity between this image and his description of her in Act II, Scene ii, lines 2–25.

Thinking About Dramatic Irony

Irony is a broad term used to talk about a difference between appearance and reality. **Verbal irony** exists when a person says one thing and means another. For example, speaking with her mother about revenge on Romeo for Tybalt's death, Juliet says, "Would none but I might venge my cousin's death." These words have one meaning for Juliet and another meaning for her mother.

Dramatic irony occurs when the audience or reader of a play has important information that characters in the play do not have. For example, in the balcony scene in Act II, we know, but Juliet does not know, that Romeo is listening while she thinks aloud about her feelings for him. As another example, we know that Juliet is already married to Romeo when her parents are planning her marriage to Paris. Dramatic irony adds suspense and causes us to become more involved in the action of the play.

13. In what way does dramatic irony increase the shock of Mercutio's death in Act III, Scene i?
14. In what way does the ending of the play depend on dramatic irony?

Thinking About Theme

All the preceding elements work together to point to the play's **themes**, or general statements about life.

15. What theme is revealed in Friar Lawrence's speech at the beginning of Act II, Scene iii? Explain how the theme relates to the story of Romeo and Juliet.
16. What effect does the feud have on love? What effect does love have on the feud? What theme is implied?
17. Find three quotations from the play that show the characters' belief in the power of fate.

VOCABULARY

Puns

Puns are jokes based on words with several meanings, or on words that sound alike but have different meanings. For example, in Act III, Scene i, Mercutio puns with two meanings of *consort*, "friend" and "musical group." The play begins with puns based on three words that sound alike, *collier, choler,* and *collar.* Shakespeare's plays contain so many puns that we can be sure that Shakespeare and his audiences took great pleasure in playing with words. Even his most serious tragedies contain

WRITING A NEW ENDING

Objective

To write a logical ending for the play

Guidelines for Evaluation

- suggested length: one to two paragraphs
- should build upon events that occur in play up to Act V, Scene iii
- should contain a plausible solution

puns for comic relief from dramatic events. Puns remain popular today as comedians continue to play with our language for comic effect.

For each of the following quotations from *Romeo and Juliet*, explain the pun. You may need to consult the marginal notes in the play for definitions.

1. Marry, that "marry" is the very theme
   I came to talk of.
   —Act I, Scene iii, 26–27

2. Give me a torch. I am not for this ambling.
   Being but heavy, I will bear the light.
   —Act I, Scene iv, 1–2

3. You have dancing shoes
   With nimble soles. I have a soul of lead
   So stakes me to the ground I cannot move.
   —Act I, Scene iv, 4–6

4. MERCUTIO. That dreamers often lie.
   ROMEO. In bed asleep, while they do dream things true.
   —Act I, Scene iv, 30–31

5. Ask for me tomorrow and you shall find me a grave man.
   —Act III, Scene i, 95–96

6. We see the ground whereon these woes do lie,
   But the true ground of all these piteous woes
   We cannot without circumstance descry.
   —Act V, Scene iii, 179–181

COMPOSITION

Writing About the Total Effect

■ Once Romeo and Juliet meet at the end of the first act, the play carries us quickly to its end. Describe the total effect, the impact that *Romeo and Juliet* had on you. Explain how Shakespeare used the following elements to achieve this effect: (a) plot, (b) character, (c) setting, (d) imagery, and (e) theme. *For help with this assignment, see Lesson 11 in the Writing About Literature Handbook at the back of this book.*

Writing About Character

■ Describe the personality of one of the following characters from *Romeo and Juliet:* (a) the Nurse, (b) Tybalt, or (c) Paris. Consider each of the following in your description: (a) the character's actions, (b) the character's words and manner of speaking, (c) what other characters say about the character. Use examples from the play to support your opinion. *For help with this assignment, see Lesson 3 in the Writing About Literature Handbook at the back of this book.*

Writing a New Ending

■ For two hundred years after Shakespeare's death, *Romeo and Juliet* was performed with a happy ending. Write a happy ending to the play to replace Act V, Scene iii, the final scene. Write your ending in paragraph form and not as dialogue.

LITERARY FOCUS

15. Immoderation can lead to tragedy; their impulsive actions lead to their tragic ends.
16. Feud ends love; love ends feud; power of love overcomes hostility.
17. Act I, Scene iv, 78–83; Act III, Scene i, 134; Act V, Scene i, 24

VOCABULARY

1. First use means "indeed"; second, "to marry."
2. Romeo is heavy in spirit but will carry the torch.
3. Mercutio's shoes have dancing soles; Romeo's soul is heavy.
4. First use means "to tell a falsehood"; second, "to recline."
5. meaning "sober" and "burial place"
6. First use means "earth"; second, "cause."

COMPOSITION: GUIDELINES FOR EVALUATION

WRITING ABOUT THE TOTAL EFFECT

Objective

To explain the total effect of plot, characterization, setting, imagery, and theme

Guidelines for Evaluation

- suggested length: six to seven paragraphs
- should relate impact in first paragraph
- should show how each element adds or detracts
- should cite evidence from play

WRITING ABOUT CHARACTER

Objective

To show how a character's personality is revealed through actions, words, and what others say about him or her.

Guidelines for Evaluation

- suggested length: three to four paragraphs
- should describe character's personality in thesis statement
- should support each opinion with evidence

ACTIVE READING

As students read drama, encourage them to visualize the plays and imagine voices for the characters. In class discuss stage directions that describe characters, and ask what popular actors might fit the roles. Point out stage directions that describe gestures and tone of voice, and ask for interpretations. Assign the Reading for Appreciation essay either before or after students read the plays in this unit. Read before the plays, the essay will help students to imagine the plays in performance. After students have read the plays, the essay will reiterate the technique of reading drama for further, independent reading.

You will find among the materials for this unit in your *Teacher's Classroom Resources* the related blackline master Dramatic Voices.

ACTIVE READING

Dramatic Voices

Reading a play can supply some of the same satisfaction as seeing a performance or even acting in one. To read a play well, to bring it to life, we have to imagine the settings, the costumes, the ways in which the characters interact. Most of all, we have to imagine *voices* for the characters. If we do not almost hear their voices speaking to one another, then we are not fully enjoying the experience. We should become so absorbed that we are hardly aware of reading at all but seem to be *seeing* and *hearing*. Ideally, we become all the actors and the audience as well.

For example, Horton Foote's *The Dancers* asks us to place ourselves in a small Gulf Coast town in Texas in 1952. We imagine the counter in the local drugstore where the young people meet and socialize and the interiors of the homes of the parents of different incomes and social status. Most important we imagine the voices of the characters—the distinctive sound and pacing of south Texas speech and the traditional courtesy and respect with which characters address each other.

To decide how any speech should sound, we should think mostly about the character's *motivation* for speaking. Is the character trying to get something? To hide something? To impress someone? We should be concerned not just with the character's words but also with the thoughts beneath the words. For example, in Act III, Scene v, of *Romeo and Juliet*, Juliet speaks to her mother about Romeo's responsibility for Tybalt's death. Juliet says, "Would none but I might venge my cousin's death." Lady Capulet should hear this line as a wish for revenge, but the audience should detect the real meaning under Juliet's words. Juliet is actually praying for Romeo's safety and wishing that she could protect him from harm, especially harm from her own family. This line needs a voice that will convey the real sentiments along with the surface meaning. The situation demands that the words "none but I" be spoken slowly and with emphasis to suggest what Juliet is really saying under her words.

Whether reading drama quietly or aloud, our major tools—besides imagination—in turning print into dramatic voices are (1) pauses, short or long; (2) pitch, or the rising and falling of the voice; and (3) loudness and stress, or emphasis. With some practice it becomes easy to see action and hear voices as we read. When reading drama becomes more like seeing and hearing a play, we take more pleasure in it.

REVIEW: DRAMA

Guide for Studying Drama

Drama is unique because staging creates illusions that bring characters, words, and ideas to life, whether on stage or in a reader's imagination. Review the following questions when you read a play. The questions will add to your appreciation and enjoyment of drama, whether you are reading a play or watching a performance.

1. What is the **conflict** at the center of the **plot**? What is the **climax**?
2. What is the **setting** of the play? According to **stage directions,** in what ways do scenery, lights, and costumes create this time and place?
3. What do we learn about major **characters** from the scenery and costumes and from gestures, facial expressions, and tone of voice?
4. What do we learn about major **characters** from what they say and from what others say about them?
5. What major events do we learn about through **dialogue**?
6. What is the **theme** of the play? In what ways do dialogue and staging contribute to the theme?
7. What information, withheld from some characters, do we learn from **asides** and **dramatic irony**?
8. Is the play a **tragedy** or a **comedy**? In what sense is the play a combination of the two types?

REVIEW

Refer to the Review in the text, Guide for Studying Drama. Students can use the eight questions in the guide to study each play in turn or to review the unit as a whole. Encourage students to use the questions to aid their comprehension as they read all drama and to keep the questions in mind whenever they see a play in performance.

The questions in the Guide for Studying Drama appear with write-on lines, in blackline master form, among the materials for this unit in your *Teacher's Classroom Resources*.

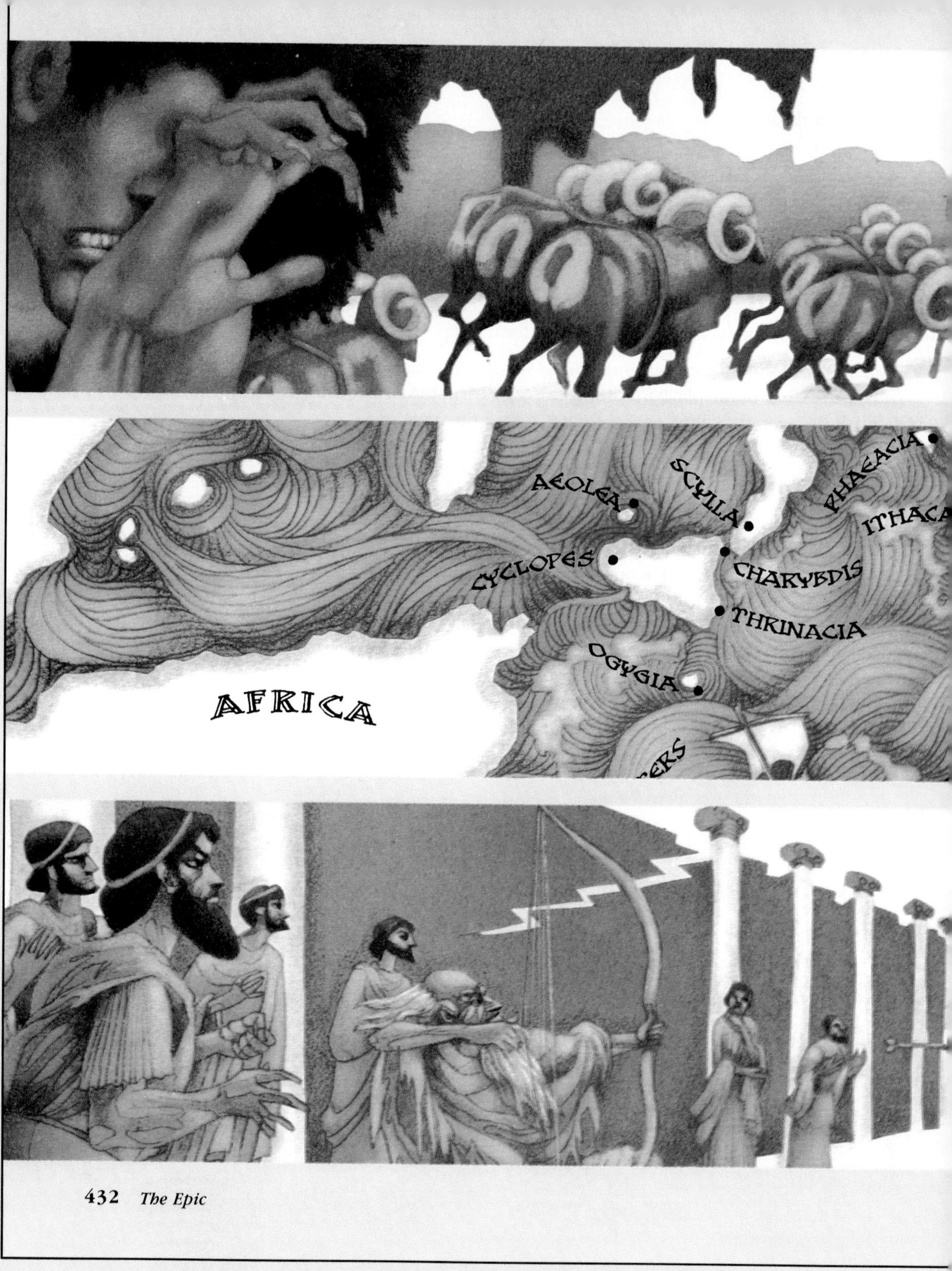
AEOLEA
SCYLLA
PHAEACIA
ITHACA
CYCLOPES
CHARYBDIS
THRINACIA
OGYGIA
AFRICA

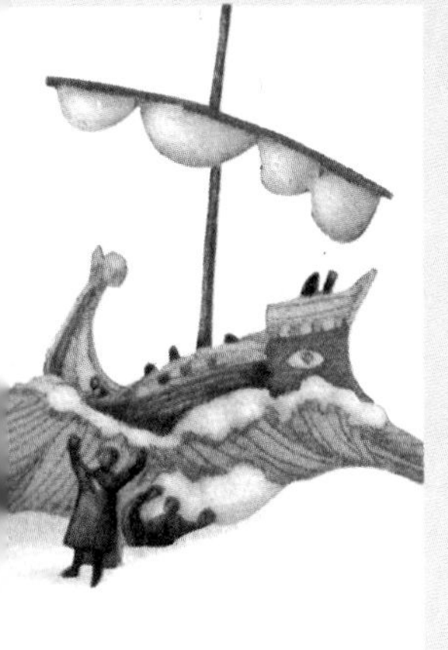

PREVIEW: THE EPIC

Heroic poetry . . . is the poetry of action, for such alone can arouse the whole nature of man. It touches all the strings—those of wonder and pity, of fear and joy.

—William Butler Yeats

The Epic and the Epic Hero

An **epic** is a long narrative poem that traces the adventures of a hero. The **epic hero** is a legendary figure who usually embodies the goals and virtues of an entire nation or culture. In an epic, gods and goddesses often interfere in the hero's affairs, sometimes to help and protect, sometimes to hurt and punish.

The epic usually opens with the poet making an invocation, or prayer, for inspiration to the muse, the goddess of poetry. The adventures of the hero take the form of a series of separate episodes, each a brief story on its own, as the hero moves from one challenge to another. The mood of the epic is serious; its language, elevated. The story, however, is clear and easy to follow. After all, originally, the epic was recited before an audience, not written on paper.

The Oral Tradition

Probably the best-known epics are the ancient Greek poems the *Iliad* [il′ē əd] and its sequel the *Odyssey* [od′ə sē]. Originally, these poems were not written down but were memorized and recited for an audience. Thus, through oral tradition they were passed from place to place and from one generation to the next.

Centuries ago, Greek minstrels, or traveling poets and singers, wandered from one town to another entertaining crowds with their tales of warriors and sea-faring adventurers. These minstrels would

PREVIEW

The introduction to this unit describes origins and characteristics of epic poetry. Before having students read the introduction to the *Odyssey*, discuss the following points in class:

- Tell students that the epic is always built around the adventures of a great hero. Ask for examples from popular entertainment of men and women whose exploits make them worthy of the name *superhero*, and then ask for qualities of these heroes. Students are likely to name characters such as Superman and James Bond. Look for qualities such as strength, integrity, courage, and cunning. Point out that some famous heroes, such as Superman, have supernatural resources at their disposal.
- Explain that epics and epic heroes usually represent the concerns and ideals of countries or geographical areas. To illustrate this idea, ask what local ideals and concerns would be used to characterize the hero of an epic about the area in which your students live. Have students suggest a name and adventures for such a hero.
- Explain that the first epics were passed on for centuries by word of mouth before they were written down. Ask students to consider the difference between writing a story and reciting it from memory. Ask them to write a joke down on paper and read it. Then ask them to tell another joke aloud. Note the greater interaction with audience in the oral narrative, and point out how the joke is likely to change as it is passed on to suit the nature of each audience. Ask students what stories and nursery rhymes they still remember from childhood and why. Much of what they remember will contain rhyme and rhythm. Explain that these musical techniques make a narrative easier to memorize and retain.

From left to right: (1) *Homer,* Greek marble statue. (2) Ithaca, the home of Odysseus, hero of the *Odyssey.* (3) *Head of Odysseus,* fragment of marble statue, first century B.C. (4) *Odysseus Disguised as Beggar with Penelope* [wife of Odysseus].

sometimes modify the stories to suit a particular audience. They might suggest that the hero was an ancestor of the people in the audience and describe the hero as having the concerns and ideals of the people listening to the tale.

The oral tradition influenced the style of the epics. The storytellers built frequent repetition and a highly musical sound into their long poems to make memorization easier. The same techniques survive today, for example, in the childhood nursery rhymes that many people remember throughout their lives.

Homer

Eventually, the Greek minstrels' stories were collected, organized, and set down in writing to become the *Iliad* and the *Odyssey.* Credit for this work has generally gone to a minstrel named Homer. We know little about Homer, but we do know that he lived about 800 B.C. and that he may have been blind.

The *Iliad* and the *Odyssey* represent a monumental artistic achievement in forming a full and complete whole from the bits and pieces of oral storytelling. They contain rounded characters (see page 53) and a language that is consistent yet fresh from one episode to the next, from beginning to end.

The Homeric poems became the basis for Greek education and culture. Every Greek who learned to read would read Homer. The epics had already achieved classic status in 400 B.C. The Greek philosophers Plato and Aristotle referred to them, and the Greek

playwrights Sophocles and Euripides based their dramas on the characters and events set down by Homer. Homer's influence spread throughout the world, too. Much of the literary heritage of the Western world has its roots in the two great Greek epics of Homer. Many great authors have imitated these epics and have referred to the heroes, settings, images, and themes of the *Iliad* and the *Odyssey* in their own works.

The Plot of the *Iliad*

Both epics are based on events that happened about 1200 B.C. The name of the *Iliad* comes from Ilion, another name for Troy, an ancient city located in what is now Turkey. The *Iliad* tells the story of the Trojan War, and it sets the stage for the *Odyssey.* Paris, a prince of Troy, kidnaps lovely Helen, the queen of the Greek city of Sparta. Helen has become known as "the face that launched a thousand ships" because the Greeks sail to Troy to avenge the insult and to bring her back to Sparta. The Greeks wage war against Troy for ten long years. Though each side loses many men, a stalemate results as the Greeks cannot penetrate the walled city of Troy, and the Trojans cannot destroy the Greek ships and fortifications.

During this conflict a second war is raging on Mount Olympus, the traditional home of the gods. Here, the gods who favor the Greeks struggle against those who favor the Trojans. Acting with surprisingly human emotions, the gods push the tide of war back and forth with their interfering.

From left to right. (1) *Trojan Horse,* relief on wine jar from Mykonos, Greece, seventh century B.C. (2) *Odysseus' Ship,* terra cotta relief, second century A.D. (3) The Parthenon in Athens, Greece, a temple dedicated to the goddess Athena and begun in 447 B.C. (4) Greek vase depicting Ajax and Achilles, Greek heroes of the Trojan War.

Odysseus at Troy

The link between the *Iliad* and the *Odyssey* is Odysseus [ō dis′ē əs], also known as Ulysses [ū lis′ēz], the crafty Greek chief who devises the masterful strategy that finally ends the Trojan War. The Greeks build a huge, hollow wooden horse, leave it on the Trojan shore, and sail away. Thinking it is a symbol of surrender, the Trojans drag the horse into the city and begin to celebrate their victory. In the dead of night, however, a band of Greek soldiers who have been concealed inside the horse slip out and open the gates of the city. Their comrades, who have been hiding just down the coast, return, enter Troy, and defeat the startled Trojans.

Although this trick leads to the end of the war, it angers the gods who favor Troy. They decree that Odysseus will not return to his home on the island of Ithaca, where he is king, but will wander the seas for ten more years, suffering great hardships.

The Plot of the *Odyssey*

When the *Odyssey* begins, ten years have passed since the fall of Troy. Odysseus has been wandering in search of home and has been kept from reaching his goal by the gods' decree. While Odysseus is striving for home, his wife and son are faced with troubles of their own. These troubles represent a second plot in the *Odyssey*. Dozens of suitors try to convince Odysseus' wife, Penelope, that Odysseus is dead. They take over Odysseus' house and refuse to leave until Penelope chooses one of them as her husband. The two plots meet to form a third when Odysseus returns home and must seek revenge against the suitors.

The setting of the *Iliad* is confined to the area around Troy, and the story concerns itself with the cruelty of war. In contrast, the mood of the *Odyssey* is more peaceful, and the settings change as Odysseus wanders slowly homeward. The virtues that are prized in

he *Odyssey* are love of home, loyalty to family, and hospitality—as well as the courage and cunning that motivate the heroes of the *Iliad.*

The *Odyssey* is one of the world's greatest adventure stories. Each episode of this epic pits the strength and cleverness of its hero against some natural, human, or superhuman foe.

Reading the *Odyssey* as an exciting, suspenseful adventure can provide great satisfaction. Yet, the *Odyssey* is also the story of all people who look for peace and a place to belong but who must overcome a series of external and internal obstacles to reach that contentment.

The Text of the *Odyssey*

The story of the *Odyssey* is long and involved. Homer needed 11,300 lines to relate Odysseus' adventures. Only excerpts of the story appear here, and naturally these are in translation from Homer's original Greek.

In spite of these changes, all of the flavor and excitement are here, starting with the invocation to the muse, which reviews Odysseus' role in the Trojan War and the god Poseidon's curse on him. Then the tale of the long journey begins, with Odysseus himself telling part of his unusual adventures.

Key Ideas in the *Odyssey*

As you read the *Odyssey,* look for references to each of the following topics. If you keep track of what the poem says about each topic, you will begin to grasp its most important themes.

- Wandering
- The sea
- Interference by the gods
- Home and family
- Characteristics of the epic hero

Odysseus Poseidon Polyphemus

CHARACTERS FROM THE *ODYSSEY*

Humans

Four groups of people figure prominently in these excerpts:

Achaeans [ə kē′ənz]: Greeks (The name comes from a section of northeastern Greece.)
Cicones [si kō′nēz]: people whom Odysseus' men attack soon after the Greeks leave Troy
Laestrygonians [les′tri gō′nē ənz]: cannibal tribe encountered by Odysseus
Lotus [lō′təs] **Eaters**: islanders who tempt Odysseus' crew with their lotus flowers

The following individuals have important roles in these excerpts:

Agamemnon [ag′ə mem′non]: commander of the Greek forces at Troy
Alcinous [al sin′ō əs]: king of the Phaeacians, in whose court Odysseus tells his story
Antinous [an tin′ō əs]: leader among Penelope's suitors during Odysseus' absence
Eumaeus [ū mē′əs]: swineherd and an old and loyal servant to Odysseus
Eurycleia [ū ri klē′yə]: Odysseus' old nurse
Eurylochus [ū ril′ə kəs]: member of Odysseus' crew
Eurymachus [ū ri′mə kəs]: one of the suitors for Penelope
Laertes [lā ər′tēz]: Odysseus' father
Odysseus [ō dis′ē əs]: king of Ithaca
Penelope [pə nel′ə pē]: Odysseus' wife
Perimedes [per ə mē′dēz]: member of Odysseus' crew
Telemachus [tə lem′ə kəs]: son of Odysseus and Penelope
Tiresias [tī rē′sē əs]: blind prophet whom Odysseus consults in the underworld

Sirens Scylla Penelope

Gods

Aeolus [ē′ə ləs]: Greek god of winds
Apollo [ə pol′ō]: Greek god of music, poetry, and prophecy
Athena [ə thē′nə]: Greek goddess of wisdom, skill, and warfare
Cronus [krō′nəs]: father of Zeus and leader of the Titans, an earlier generation of gods
Helios [hē′lē ōs′]: Greek sun god who keeps a herd of cattle on his own island
Muse [mūz]: any of the nine goddesses who preside over art, literature, and science (The muse addressed in the *Odyssey* is the goddess of poetry.)
Poseidon [pə sīd′ən]: Greek god of the sea and of earthquakes
Titans: an earlier generation of gods who were overthrown by Zeus and his followers
Zeus [zo͞os]: ruler of all the gods and goddesses

Supernatural Beings

Calypso [kə lip′sō]: sea nymph who keeps Odysseus on her island for seven years
Charybdis [kə rib′dis]: deadly whirlpool, across a narrow strait from Scylla
Circe [sur′sē]: witch who turns Odysseus' men into swine
Cyclopes [sī klō′pēz]: race of one-eyed giants
Polyphemus [pol′i fē′məs]: son of Poseidon; a Cyclops who briefly imprisons Odysseus and his men
Scylla [sil′ə]: six-headed monster who devours sailors when they sail too close trying to avoid Charybdis
Sirens: sea nymphs who lure sailors to their deaths by singing sweetly

PLACES IN THE *ODYSSEY*

Many of the following places that are mentioned in the *Odyssey* may actually exist and are identified here with possible modern locations. This identification of settings from the *Odyssey* with modern sites does not suggest that the adventures of Odysseus actually happened. Some scholars have suggested, however, that Homer may have had a knowledge of the geography of the Mediterranean Sea.

Aeaea [ē ē'ə]: island home of Circe (Cape Circeo is a peninsula on the Italian coast above Naples.)
Aeolea [ē ō'lē ə]: island home of Aeolus, god of winds (Aeolea may be Ustica, a small island north of Sicily.)
Charybdis: the deadly whirlpool (The location of Charybdis is widely believed to be the Straits of Messina, Sicily.)
Ismarus [iz'mar us]: a stronghold on the coast of the Cicones (The home of the Cicones is believed to be the coast of Thrace in Greece.)
Ithaca [ith'ə kə]: island homeland of Odysseus (Ithaca is off the southwestern coast of Greece.)

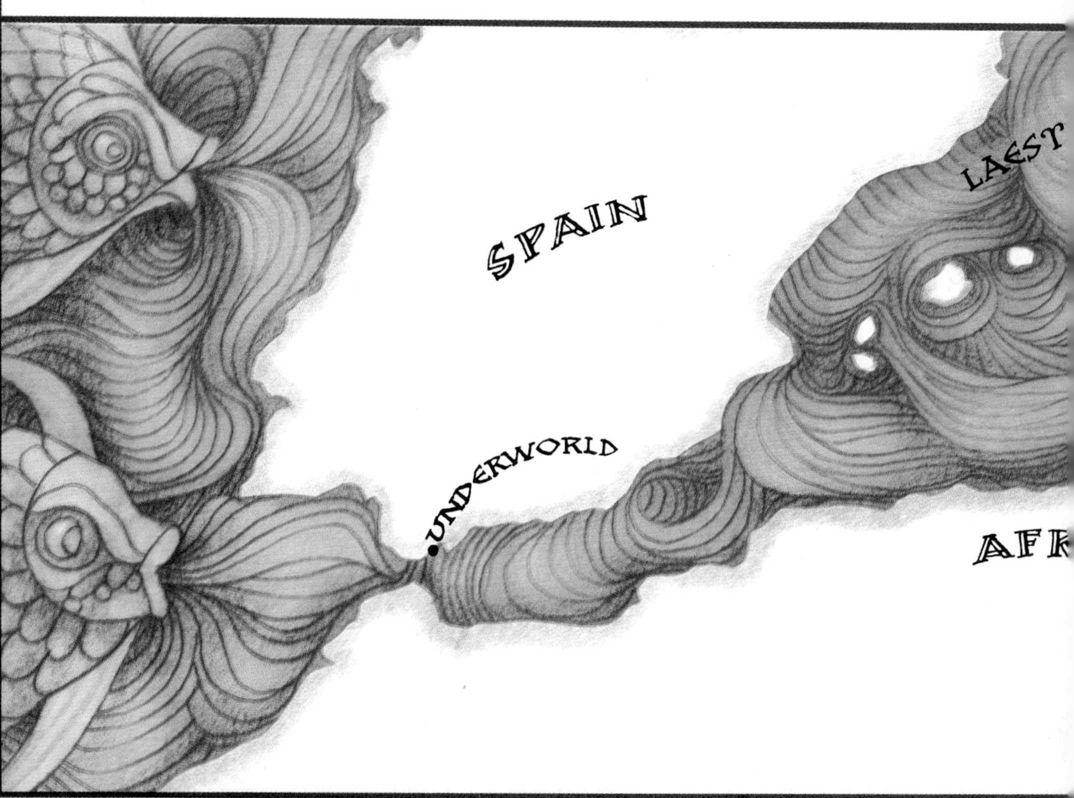

Ogygia [ō jij′ē ə]: island home of Calypso (Ogygia has been identified as the island of Malta near Sicily.)
Olympus [ō lim′pəs]: according to tradition, mountain home in northeastern Greece of the gods
Phaeacia [fē ā′shə]: island of shipbuilders and traders; ruled by Alcinous (Because of its short distance from Ithaca, the island of Corfu has been identified as the home of Alcinous.)
Scylla: the six-headed monster (The location of Scylla is widely believed to be the Straits of Messina, Sicily.)
Thrinacia [thrin ā′shə]: island of Helios, the sun god (The eastern coast of Sicily is identified as Thrinacia.)
Troy: also called Ilion, site of the Trojan War (Troy was uncovered in what is now Turkey.)
Underworld: land of the dead (Many people believe that Gibraltar, the edge of the known world in classical times, was considered the entrance to the underworld.)

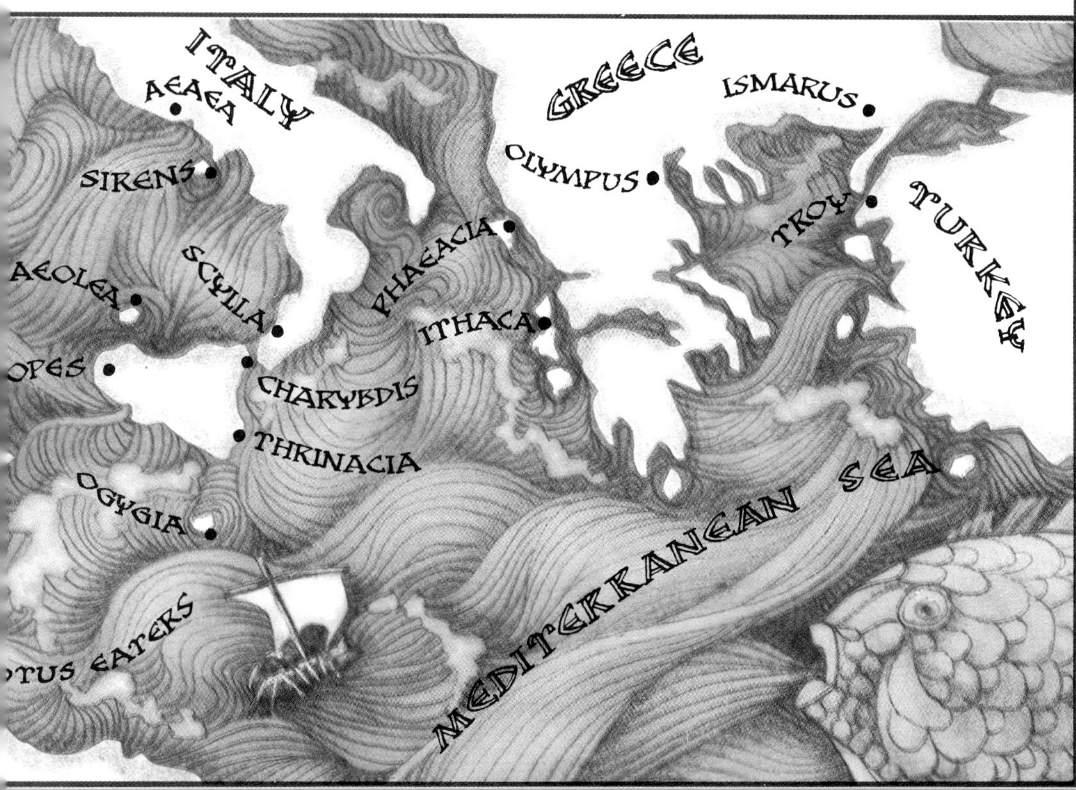

Homer

The Odyssey

translated by Robert Fitzgerald

PART ONE: TEN YEARS AT SEA

Invocation to the Muse

Homer prays for inspiration in his invocation to the muse, but he also gives his readers a hint of events that lie ahead in his long narrative.

Sing in me, Muse,[1] and through me tell the story
of that man skilled in all ways of contending,
the wanderer, harried for years on end,
after he plundered the stronghold
on the proud height of Troy[2] . . . .
And when the long years and seasons
wheeling brought around that point of time
ordained for him to make his passage homeward,
trials and dangers, even so, attended him
even in Ithaca,[3] near those he loved.
Yet all the gods had pitied Lord Odysseus,
all but Poseidon,[4] raging cold and rough
against the brave king till he came ashore
at last on his own land.

1 **Muse** [mūz]: one of nine goddesses who presided over art, literature, and science; here, the goddess of epic poetry.

2 **Troy:** also known as Ilion [il ′ē on], ancient city in what is now Turkey, site of the Trojan War.

3 **Ithaca** [ith ′ə kə]: home of Odysseus [ō dis ′ē əs], a rocky island off the southwestern coast of Greece.

4 **Poseidon** [pə sīd ′ən]: Greek god of the sea and of earthquakes.

AT A GLANCE

- Homer asks the muse to inspire him and to tell the story of Odysseus through him.
- The story will be about the challenges and dangers Odysseus faced after he conquered Troy.

LITERARY OPTIONS

- conflict
- imagery
- theme

THEMATIC OPTIONS

- longing for home
- fate
- leadership

SPEAKER

Homer, who prays to the muse for inspiration and help in telling the story, is the speaker of the first part of the poem; immediately he says that this is the story of a harried wanderer who longs for home (l. 1).

IMAGERY

Homer imagines the years and seasons as a great wheel turning to the point when Odysseus is fated to return home (ll. 6–8).

WORD CHOICE

The adjectives Homer uses to describe the sea god's temper *(raging cold and rough)* reflect the sea's characteristics (l. 11).

GUIDED READING

LITERAL QUESTION

1a. When and where did Odysseus have difficulty? (He was "harried for years on end" after conquering Troy and at home in Ithaca.)

INFERENTIAL QUESTION

1b. Why do you think nearly all of the gods pitied Odysseus? (Answers may suggest they pitied Odysseus' problems at home, where one should be safe.)

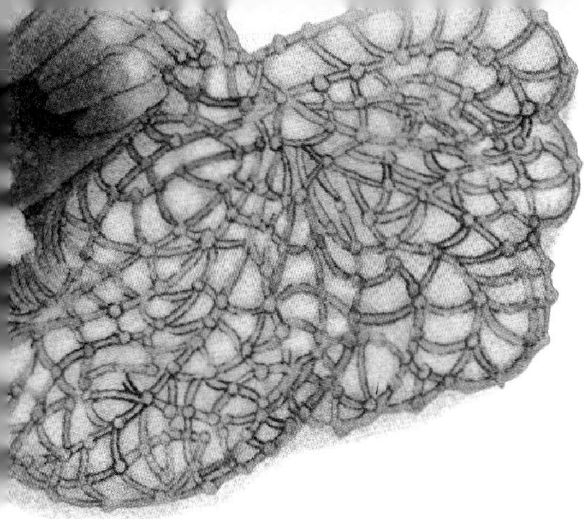

Odysseus Tells His Story

Ten years have passed since the fall of Troy. Odysseus [ō dis'ē əs] *is in the court of King Alcinous* [al sin'ō əs] *of Phaeacia* [fē ā'shə]. *His fleet has been destroyed; his comrades are all dead. At a banquet Odysseus weeps when a bard sings of the Trojan War. Because of this show of emotion, Alcinous asks the hero to reveal his identity, and Odysseus tells his story:*

"I am Laertes'[5] son, Odysseus.
Men hold me
formidable for guile in peace and war:
this fame has gone abroad to the sky's rim.
My home is on the peaked sea-mark of Ithaca
under Mount Neion's wind-blown robe of leaves,
in sight of other islands—Dulichium,
Same, wooded Zacynthus—Ithaca
being most lofty in that coastal sea,
and northwest, while the rest lie east and south.
A rocky isle, but good for a boy's training;
I shall not see on earth a place more dear,
though I have been detained long by Calypso,[6]
loveliest among goddesses, who held me
in her smooth caves, to be her heart's delight,
as Circe of Aeaea,[7] the enchantress,
desired me, and detained me in her hall.
But in my heart I never gave consent.
Where shall a man find sweetness to surpass
his own home and his parents? In far lands
he shall not, though he find a house of gold.
What of my sailing, then, from Troy?

5 **Laertes** [lā ər'tēz]

6 **Calypso** [kə lip'sō]

7 **Circe of Aeaea** [sur'sē, ē ē'ə]

AT A GLANCE

- Odysseus, Laertes' son, is famous for cunning in war and peace.
- He describes Ithaca, his home. He has traveled widely and been loved by goddesses.
- He admits that nothing has been sweeter than home.

SPEAKER

Odysseus tells his own story in the court of King Alcinous.

IMAGERY

The image of "the sky's rim" suggests that the heavens are a finite container like a bowl. The universe is a manageable size, over which rule the gods and an all-powerful fate (l. 16).

MAIN IDEA

Odysseus lovingly describes his rocky island home—a good vantage point from which to view the world and the scene of his excellent training (ll. 19–23).

GUIDED READING

LITERAL QUESTION

1a. Who detained Odysseus? (Calypso and Circe of Aeaea)

INFERENTIAL QUESTION

1b. How does Odysseus think home compares with the pleasures of traveling? (He feels home is sweeter than anywhere else, better than "a house of gold.")

AT A GLANCE

- Odysseus describes his voyage from Troy.
- After plundering the Cicones, Odysseus' soldiers refuse to set sail; consequently many are killed.
- Once underway, his ships are forced by a storm to lie offshore.

WORD CHOICE

Odysseus' dramatic description of a storm is preceded by references to years he "weathered" under Zeus and how he "stormed" the Cicones' fort (ll. 35, 39).

IMAGERY

The Cicones' soldiers looked deceptively innocent, "like the leaves and blades of spring"; Homer's use of natural imagery fills his epic poem (ll. 50–51).

IMAGERY

By showing us the empty benches in every ship and "each poor ghost/unfleshed by the Cicones," and by letting us "taste" the soldiers' grief, Homer makes loss and death poignantly concrete (ll. 59, 64–65, 74).

CONFLICT

As Homer shows Zeus's power and its impact upon Odysseus and his men, he reinforces the idea of human helplessness before the gods (ll. 66–71).

What of those years
of rough adventure, weathered under Zeus?[8]
The wind that carried west from Ilion
brought me to Ismarus,[9] on the far shore,
a strongpoint on the coast of the Cicones.[10]
I stormed that place and killed the men who fought.
Plunder we took, and we enslaved the women,
to make division, equal shares to all—
but on the spot I told them: 'Back, and quickly!
Out to sea again!' My men were mutinous,
fools, on stores of wine. Sheep after sheep
they butchered by the surf, and shambling cattle,[11]
feasting—while fugitives went inland, running
to call to arms the main force of Cicones.
This was an army, trained to fight on horseback
or, where the ground required, on foot. They came
with dawn over that terrain like the leaves
and blades of spring. So doom appeared to us,
dark word of Zeus for us, our evil days.
My men stood up and made a fight of it—
backed on the ships, with lances kept in play,
from bright morning through the blaze of noon
holding our beach, although so far outnumbered;
but when the sun passed toward unyoking time,[12]
then the Achaeans,[13] one by one, gave way.
Six benches were left empty in every ship
that evening when we pulled away from death.
And this new grief we bore with us to sea:
our precious lives we had, but not our friends.
No ship made sail next day until some shipmate
had raised a cry, three times, for each poor ghost
unfleshed by the Cicones on that field.

Now Zeus the lord of cloud roused in the north
a storm against the ships, and driving veils
of squall[14] moved down like night on land and sea.
The bows went plunging at the gust; sails
cracked and lashed out strips in the big wind.
We saw death in that fury, dropped the yards,
unshipped the oars, and pulled for the nearest lee:[15]
then two long days and nights we lay offshore
worn out and sick at heart, tasting our grief,
until a third Dawn came with ringlets shining.
Then we put up our masts, hauled sail,[16] and rested,
letting the steersmen and the breeze take over.

8 **Zeus** [zo͞os]: leader of all the Greek gods.

9 **Ismarus** [iz ′mar us]

10 **Cicones** [si kō ′nēz]

11 **shambling cattle:** cattle walking awkwardly.

12 **unyoking time:** late afternoon, the time when working animals are freed from their harnesses.

13 **Achaeans** [ə kē ′ənz]: another name for the Greeks.

14 **squall:** sudden violent storm.

15 **dropped . . . lee:** lowered the sails, put out the oars, and rowed toward a coast protected from the wind.

16 **put up . . . sail:** erected the mast and raised the sail.

GUIDED READING

LITERAL QUESTIONS

1a. What gave the Cicones an opportunity to attack Odysseus and his men after their victory? (The soldiers disobeyed Odysseus' orders to leave.)

2a. What does Zeus do to Odysseus and his men? (He rouses a storm that drives them ashore.)

INFERENTIAL QUESTIONS

1b. What does this detail reveal about Odysseus? (His leadership is failing; his instincts as a military strategist are excellent.)

2b. What does this action reveal about Zeus? (He is capable of cruel action that may seem arbitrary and unfair; he is strong and powerful.)

The Lotus Eaters

I might have made it safely home, that time,
but as I came round Malea[17] the current
took me out to sea, and from the north
a fresh gale drove me on, past Cythera.[18]
Nine days I drifted on the teeming sea
before dangerous high winds. Upon the tenth
we came to the coastline of the Lotus Eaters,
who live upon that flower. We landed there
to take on water. All ships' companies
mustered[19] alongside for the midday meal.
Then I sent out two picked men and a runner
to learn what race of men that land sustained.
They fell in, soon enough, with Lotus Eaters,
who showed no will to do us harm, only
offering the sweet Lotus to our friends—
but those who ate this honeyed plant, the Lotus,
never cared to report, nor to return:
they longed to stay forever, browsing on
that native bloom, forgetful of their homeland.
I drove them, all three wailing, to the ships,
tied them down under their rowing benches,
and called the rest: 'All hands aboard;
come, clear the beach and no one taste
the Lotus, or you lose your hope of home.'
Filing in to their places by the rowlocks[20]
my oarsmen dipped their long oars in the surf,
and we moved out again on our seafaring.

17 **Malea** [mə lē′ə]: point of land on the extreme southern coast of Greece.
18 **Cythera** [sith′ə rə]: island off the coast of Malea.
19 **mustered:** assembled.
20 **rowlocks:** devices that hold oars in place for rowing.

AT A GLANCE

- Odysseus tells how his ships attained the land of the Lotus Eaters.
- Three men sent ashore eat the sweet-tasting Lotus, which makes them forgetful.
- Odysseus regains them and sets sail.

SPEAKER

Odysseus continues his story in a conversational tone, which contrasts sharply with his evident frustration at the "fresh gale" that once again kept him from home (ll. 78–83).

CHARACTERIZATION

Homer deliberately has Odysseus encounter exotic characters. The drugged world of the Lotus Eaters is completely alien to him, and such characters intensify the hero's longing to return home (ll. 90–96).

GUIDED READING

LITERAL QUESTION

1a. What things do the men who eat the Lotus forget? (their mission, ship, and homeland)

INFERENTIAL QUESTION

1b. Why is Odysseus so angry about their forgetfulness? (It is a threat to his own desire to return home.)

AT A GLANCE

- Odysseus and his men land near the Cyclopes' mainland.
- The soldiers hunt and feast on the plentiful wild goats.
- At dawn Odysseus announces that he and a small company of soldiers will go ashore.

SETTING

The island is fertile and full of game; nature is gentle, generous, and beautiful. This idyllic setting (ll. 119–135) is in sharp contrast to the one they will encounter next.

PERSONIFICATION

Homer's personification of the dawn as a young woman with rosy fingertips became a literary tradition. The image suggests the "friendliness" of dawn after a dark night (ll. 117, 135).

CHARACTERIZATION

Odysseus and his men feast and drink whenever the opportunity arises: The men are flat characters with simple motives, and Odysseus' behavior is also stereotypical (ll. 126–130).

The Cyclops

In the next land we found were Cyclopes,[21]
giants, louts, without a law to bless them.
In ignorance leaving the fruitage of the earth in mystery
to the immortal gods, they neither plow
nor sow by hand, nor till the ground, though grain—
wild wheat and barley—grows untended, and
wine grapes, in clusters, ripen in heaven's rain.
Cyclopes have no muster and no meeting,
no consultation or old tribal ways,
but each one dwells in his own mountain cave
dealing out rough justice to wife and child,
indifferent to what the others do. . . .

Odysseus and his men go ashore on a small desert island near the mainland of the Cyclopes. They sleep on the beach until morning.

When Dawn spread out her fingertips of rose
we turned out marveling, to tour the isle,
while Zeus's shy nymph[22] daughters flushed wild goats
down from the heights—a breakfast for my men.
We ran to fetch our hunting bows and long-shanked
lances from the ships, and in three companies
we took our shots. Heaven gave us game a-plenty:
for every one of twelve ships in my squadron
nine goats fell to be shared; my lot was ten.
So there all day, until the sun went down, we made our
feast on meat galore, and wine—
wine from the ship, for our supply held out,
so many jars were filled at Ismarus,
from stores of the Cicones that we plundered.
We gazed, too, at Cyclopes Land, so near,
we saw their smoke, heard bleating from their flocks.
But after sundown, in the gathering dusk,
we slept again above the wash of ripples.

When the young Dawn with fingertips of rose
came in the east, I called my men together
and made a speech to them:
'Old shipmates, friends,
the rest of you stand by; I'll make the crossing
in my own ship, with my own company,
and find out what the mainland natives are—
for they may be wild savages, and lawless,
or hospitable and god fearing[23] men.'

21 **Cyclopes** [sī klō ′pēz]: plural of Cyclops [sī ′klops]; a band of one-eyed giants.

22 **nymph** [nimf]: beautiful goddess.

23 **hospitable and god fearing:** The Greeks believed that a person who respected the gods was kind to strangers because a stranger could be a god in disguise.

GUIDED READING

LITERAL QUESTIONS

1a. How does Odysseus describe the Cyclopes? (He says they are ignorant "louts" without ambition, laws, government, army, or age-old traditions. They are antisocial and not concerned with conformity.)

2a. Where does Odysseus say the wild goats come from? (He says that Zeus's beautiful daughters sent them to him and his soldiers.)

INFERENTIAL QUESTIONS

1b. What does Odysseus' opinion of the Cyclopes suggest about his own values? (Odysseus values all the things that the Cyclopes do not—hard work, the military, laws, and social conventions.)

2b. What does this suggest about Zeus? (The god and his relatives supply human needs, or are believed to do so.)

At this I went aboard, and gave the word
to cast off by the stern.[24] My oarsmen followed,
filing in to their benches by the rowlocks,
and all in line dipped oars in the grey sea.

As we rowed on, and nearer to the mainland,
at one end of the bay, we saw a cavern
yawning above the water, screened with laurel,[25]
and many rams and goats about the place
inside a sheepfold—made from slabs of stone
earthfast between tall trunks of pine and rugged
towering oak trees.
A prodigious man
slept in this cave alone, and took his flocks
to graze afield—remote from all companions,
knowing none but savage ways, a brute
so huge, he seemed no man at all of those
who eat good wheaten bread; but he seemed rather
a shaggy mountain reared in solitude.
We beached there, and I told the crew
to stand by and keep watch over the ship;
as for myself I took my twelve best fighters
and went ahead. I had a goatskin full
of that sweet liquor that Euanthes'[26] son,
Maron, had given me. He kept Apollo's[27]
holy grove at Ismarus; for kindness
we showed him there, and showed his wife and child,
he gave me seven shining golden talents[28]
perfectly formed, a solid silver winebowl,
and then this liquor—twelve two-handled jars
of brandy, pure and fiery. Not a slave
in Maron's household knew this drink; only
he, his wife and the storeroom mistress knew;
and they would put one cupful—ruby-colored,
honey-smooth—in twenty more of water,
but still the sweet scent hovered like a fume
over the winebowl. No man turned away
when cups of this came round.
A wineskin full
I brought along, and victuals[29] in a bag,
for in my bones I knew some towering brute
would be upon us soon—all outward power,
a wild man, ignorant of civility.

24 **stern:** rear of a ship.

25 **laurel:** evergreen tree.

26 **Euanthes** [ū an′thēz]

27 **Apollo** [ə pol′ō]: Greek god of music, poetry, and prophecy. A small grove, or forest, at Ismarus was dedicated to him.

28 **talents:** Greek coins.

29 **victuals:** food.

AT A GLANCE

- Odysseus and a small group of his best fighters row to the mainland, where they see a giant's cave.
- Odysseus brings food and liquor to appease the giant.

IMAGERY

Homer describes a series of actions that create an animated picture of the sailors preparing to row ashore (ll. 143–146).

SETTING

The setting is as fierce and monumental as the giants who live there. The "yawning" cavern and stone sheepfold "earthfast between tall trunks of pine and rugged/towering oak trees" are threatening and ominous (ll. 148–153).

MAIN IDEA

Odysseus strongly disapproves of the Cyclopes' solitary lives. He is a sociable character in his role as group leader and has strong feelings about home and family (ll. 154–155).

FIGURATIVE LANGUAGE

Odysseus painstakingly describes the beautiful color, tempting fragrance, and extraordinary potency of the liquor he carries, to prepare us for the important role it will play in his story (ll. 174–178).

FORESHADOWING

Homer gives his hero a premonition that the encounter with the giant will be terrible—a hint that helps to build suspense (180–183).

GUIDED READING

LITERAL QUESTION

1a. What words does Odysseus use to describe the giant? *(a prodigious man* who knows *none but savage ways; a brute so huge, he seemed . . . a shaggy mountain; a towering brute . . . all outward power; a wild man, ignorant of civility)*

INFERENTIAL QUESTION

1b. What emotions might these descriptions evoke in the reader? (fear and awe)

AT A GLANCE

- The men enter the giant's cave.
- Though his men urge him to take food and leave, Odysseus refuses.
- The giant returns and closes the cave with a slab of rock.

CHARACTERIZATION

In contrast to Odysseus' opinion that one-eyed giants are lazy and ignorant, this one is clearly a hard-working, well-organized farmer (ll. 186–191).

PLOT: FORESHADOWING

By hinting at the horror to come, the poet builds suspense. Odysseus' foreboding is part of a world view based in the idea that fate rules people's lives, often with unhappy endings (ll. 197–199).

IMAGERY

Odysseus shows how impossible it is to escape by providing an imaginative picture of twenty-four wagon teams unable to move the slab of rock the giant used to seal the cave (ll. 211–214).

We climbed, then, briskly to the cave. But Cyclops
had gone afield, to pasture his fat sheep,
so we looked round at everything inside:
a drying rack that sagged with cheese, pens
crowded with lambs and kids, each in its class:
firstlings apart from middlings, and the 'dewdrops,'
or newborn lambkins, penned apart from both.
And vessels full of whey[30] were brimming there—
bowls of earthenware and pails for milking.
My men came pressing round me, pleading:
'Why not
take these cheeses, get them stowed, come back,
throw open all the pens, and make a run for it?
We'll drive the kids and lambs aboard. We say
put out again on good salt water!'
Ah,
how sound that was! Yet I refused. I wished
to see the cave man, what he had to offer—
no pretty sight, it turned out, for my friends.

We lit a fire, burnt an offering,
and took some cheese to eat; then sat in silence
around the embers, waiting. When he came
he had a load of dry boughs on his shoulder
to stoke his fire at suppertime. He dumped it
with a great crash into that hollow cave,
and we all scattered fast to the far wall.
Then over the broad cavern floor he ushered
the ewes he meant to milk. He left his rams
and he-goats in the yard outside, and swung
high overhead a slab of solid rock
to close the cave. Two dozen four-wheeled wagons,
with heaving wagon teams, could not have stirred
the tonnage of that rock from where he wedged it
over the doorsill. Next he took his seat
and milked his bleating ewes. A practiced job
he made of it, giving each ewe her suckling;

30 **whey** [hwā]: watery part of milk when it thickens.

GUIDED READING

LITERAL QUESTION

1a. Why does Odysseus want to stay in the cave? (He wants to see the giant.)

INFERENTIAL QUESTION

1b. What does this suggest about Odysseus as a character and a leader? (He is daring and more curious than security-minded.)

thickened his milk, then, into curds[31] and whey,
sieved out the curds to drip in withy[32] baskets,
and poured the whey to stand in bowls
cooling until he drank it for his supper.
When all these chores were done, he poked the fire,
heaping on brushwood. In the glare he saw us.

'Strangers,' he said, 'who are you? And where from?
What brings you here by seaways—a fair traffic?
Or are you wandering rogues,[33] who cast your lives
like dice, and ravage other folk by sea?'

We felt pressure on our hearts, in dread
of that deep rumble and that mighty man.
But all the same I spoke up in reply:
'We are from Troy, Achaeans, blown off course
by shifting gales on the Great South Sea;
homeward bound, but taking routes and ways
uncommon; so the will of Zeus would have it.
We served under Agamemnon, son of Atreus[34]—
the whole world knows what city
he laid waste, what armies he destroyed.

31 **curds:** solid part of milk when it thickens.
32 **withy** [with'ē] **baskets:** baskets woven from flexible twigs.

33 **rogues** [rōgz]: dishonest, deceitful persons.

34 **Agamemnon** [ag'ə mem'non], **son of Atreus** [ā'trē əs]: king who led the Greek forces in the Trojan War.

AT A GLANCE

- The giant completes his dairying chores and stokes the fire.
- He sees Odysseus and his men and asks who they are.
- Odysseus tells of their history and journey.

SIMILE

The giant asks the men if they are legitimate traders or daring pirates who play out their lives like gambling games (ll. 223–226).

IMAGERY

Homer appeals to the senses of touch and hearing in his vivid description of the men's fear and the sound of the giant's voice (ll. 227–228).

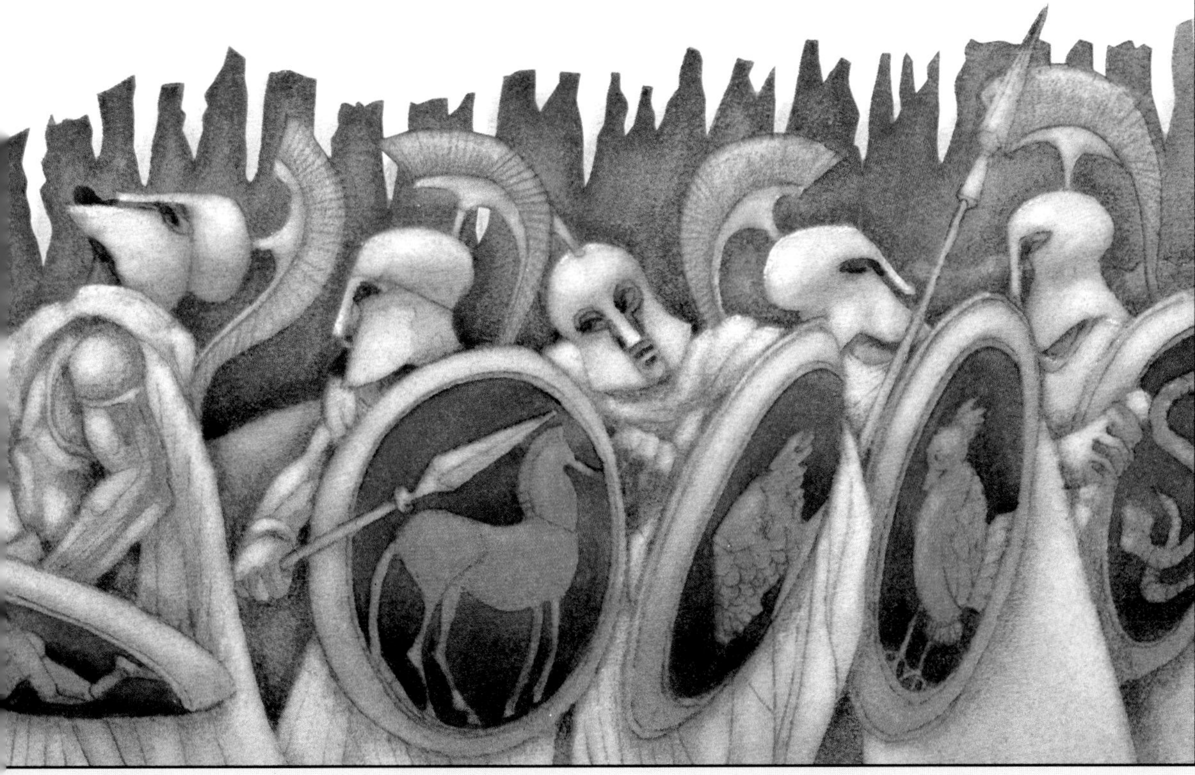

GUIDED READING

LITERAL QUESTION

1a. What do the giant and Odysseus say to each other? (The giant asks who the men are, where they are from, and if they are traders or pirates; Odysseus explains that they were on their way home when Zeus blew them off course, and that they are the famous soldiers of Agamemnon.)

INFERENTIAL QUESTION

1b. In what way is their dialogue surprising? (Their conversation is surprisingly reasonable, straightforward, and polite.)

AT A GLANCE

- Odysseus urges the giant to avoid offending the gods.
- The giant kills and eats two men.
- As the giant rests, Odysseus decides not to kill him.

MAIN IDEA

Odysseus reminds the giant of tradition and respectfully urges him not to offend the gods. Here Odysseus appears to be a conventional, humble man who expects others (even one-eyed giants) to be the same (ll. 240–242).

FIGURATIVE LANGUAGE

Contrasting sound words in the line *We Cyclopes care not a whistle for your thundering Zeus* effectively shows the giant's disrespect (ll. 245–246).

THEME

Odysseus says he and his men have been brought here by weather created by the gods—that is, by fate (ll. 254–256).

IMAGERY

Present participles like "squirming," "gaping," and "lifting" and onomatopoeias like "spattering" and "crunching" give this description excruciating immediacy (ll. 258–264).

It was our luck to come here; here we stand,
beholden for your help, or any gifts
you give—as custom is to honor strangers.
We would entreat you, great Sir, have a care
for the gods' courtesy; Zeus will avenge
the unoffending guest.'
He answered this
from his brute chest, unmoved:
'You are a ninny,
or else you come from the other end of nowhere,
telling me, mind the gods! We Cyclopes
care not a whistle for your thundering Zeus
or all the gods in bliss; we have more force by far.
I would not let you go for fear of Zeus—
you or your friends—unless I had a whim to.
Tell me, where was it, now, you left your ship—
around the point, or down the shore, I wonder?'

He thought he'd find out, but I saw through this,
and answered with a ready lie:
'My ship?
Poseidon Lord, who sets the earth a-tremble,[35]
broke it up on the rocks at your land's end.
A wind from seaward served him, drove us there.
We are survivors, these good men and I.'

Neither reply nor pity came from him,
but in one stride he clutched at my companions
and caught two in his hands like squirming puppies
to beat their brains out, spattering the floor.
Then he dismembered them and made his meal,
gaping and crunching like a mountain lion—
everything: innards, flesh, and marrowbones.
We cried aloud, lifting our hands to Zeus,
powerless, looking on at this, appalled;
but Cyclops went on filling up his belly
with manflesh and great gulps of whey,
then lay down like a mast among his sheep.
My heart beat high now at the chance of action,
and drawing the sharp sword from my hip I went
along his flank to stab him where the midriff
holds the liver. I had touched the spot
when sudden fear stayed me: if I killed him
we perished there as well, for we could never

35 **sets . . . a-tremble:** Poseidon was god of earthquakes.

GUIDED READING

LITERAL QUESTIONS

1a. What does the giant call Odysseus? (A "ninny" or someone "from the other end of nowhere.")

2a. What does Odysseus say happened to his ship? (He says it crashed and broke against rocks.)

INFERENTIAL QUESTIONS

1b. What seems to have made the giant angry? (Odysseus' urging him to honor them and not to offend the gods; Cyclops says he and other giants are more powerful than gods.)

2b. Why does he say this? (He thinks the giant might take the ship and leave them stranded or harm the men on board.)

move his ponderous doorway slab aside.
So we were left to groan and wait for morning.

When the young Dawn with fingertips of rose
lit up the world, the Cyclops built a fire
and milked his handsome ewes, all in due order,
putting the sucklings to the mothers. Then,
his chores being all dispatched, he caught
another brace[36] of men to make his breakfast,
and whisked away his great door slab
to let his sheep go through—but he, behind,
reset the stone as one would cap a quiver.[37]
There was a din of whistling as the Cyclops
rounded his flock to higher ground, then stillness.
And now I pondered how to hurt him worst,
if but Athena[38] granted what I prayed for.
Here are the means I thought would serve my turn:

A club, or staff, lay there along the fold—
an olive tree, felled green and left to season
for Cyclops' hand. And it was like a mast
a lugger of twenty oars, broad in the beam—
a deep-sea-going craft—might carry:
so long, so big around, it seemed. Now I
chopped out a six-foot section of this pole
and set it down before my men, who scraped it;
and when they had it smooth, I hewed again
to make a stake with pointed end. I held this
in the fire's heart and turned it, toughening it,
then hid it, well back in the cavern, under
one of the dung piles in profusion there.
Now came the time to toss for it: who ventured
along with me? whose hand could bear to thrust
and grind that spike in Cyclops' eye, when mild
sleep had mastered him? As luck would have it,
the men I would have chosen won the toss—
four strong men, and I made five as captain.

At evening came the shepherd with his flock,
his woolly flock. The rams as well, this time,
entered the cave: by some sheepherding whim—
or god's bidding—none were left outside.
He hefted his great boulder into place
and sat him down to milk the bleating ewes

36 **brace:** pair.

37 **quiver:** case for holding arrows.

38 **Athena** [ə thē′nə]: Greek goddess of wisdom.

AT A GLANCE

- Cyclops eats two more men and leaves the cave, sealing it with a stone.
- Odysseus plans to blind the giant and prepares a huge stake.
- That night the giant brings his flock inside the cave.

REPETITION

Homer repeats the image of Dawn as a young woman to mark the beginning of each day in his narrative (l. 278).

PLOT: RISING ACTION

Tension builds as the giant carefully caps the mouth of the cave, preventing the escape of Odysseus and his men (ll. 285–286).

CONFLICT

Odysseus displays cunning as he plans his attack. He admits that he cannot do it without divine help (ll. 289–290).

MAIN IDEA

Odysseus believes that the giant's decision to bring both rams and ewes is controlled by the gods. Thus what follows is also intended by the gods (ll. 312–314).

RESPONSE JOURNAL

Ask students to write about a time when they felt something that happened "was meant to be."

GUIDED READING

LITERAL QUESTIONS

1a. Which god or goddess does Odysseus hope will help him with his plan to kill the giant? (Athena)

2a. What words are used to describe the size of the stake? *(like a mast a lugger of twenty oars . . . might carry, six-foot section, pointed end)*

INFERENTIAL QUESTIONS

1b. Why is this choice apt? (Athena is goddess of wisdom; Odysseus must plan wisely if he and his men are to escape with their lives.)

2b. Why do you think Homer describes the size of the stake in such detail? (Answers should suggest that the description emphasizes the size of Odysseus' adversary and the drama of the confrontation.)

AT A GLANCE

- Cyclops eats two more men; Odysseus offers him wine.
- The drunk giant asks Odysseus' name.
- As the giant sleeps Odysseus' men heat the spike.

ALLITERATION

Certain key phrases are emphasized through alliteration. Note especially the musical sound of *dark drink* and *fuddle and flush* (ll. 321, 337).

CHARACTERIZATION

Odysseus and Cyclops are almost playful in their teasing: Cyclops offers Odysseus a "noble gift" (time to watch his friends be eaten), and Odysseus claims that he is "Nohbdy" (ll. 338–344).

IMAGERY

Homer creates a terrible picture of the fallen Cyclops: drunk and dribbling "streams of liquor and bits of men." This vision helps to rouse Odysseus' men to action (ll. 345–348).

in proper order, put the lambs to suck,
and swiftly ran through all his evening chores.
Then he caught two more men and feasted on them.
My moment was at hand, and I went forward
holding an ivy bowl of my dark drink,
looking up, saying:
'Cyclops, try some wine.
Here's liquor to wash down your scraps of men.
Taste it, and see the king of drink we carried
under our planks. I meant it for an offering
if you would help us home. But you are mad,
unbearable, a bloody monster! After this,
will any other traveler come to see you?'

He seized and drained the bowl, and it went down
so fiery and smooth he called for more:
'Give me another, thank you kindly. Tell me,
how are you called? I'll make a gift will please you.
Even Cyclopes know the wine grapes grow
out of grassland and loam in heaven's rain,
but here's a bit of nectar and ambrosia!'[39]

Three bowls I brought him, and he poured them down.
I saw the fuddle and flush come over him,
then I sang out in cordial tones:
'Cyclops,
you ask my honorable name? Remember
the gift you promised me, and I shall tell you.
My name is Nohbdy: mother, father, and friends,
everyone calls me Nohbdy.'
And he said:
'Nohbdy's my meat, then, after I eat his friends.
Others come first. There's a noble gift, now.'
Even as he spoke, he reeled and tumbled backward,
his great head lolling to one side; and sleep
took him like any creature. Drunk, hiccuping,
he dribbled streams of liquor and bits of men.
Now, by the gods, I drove my big hand spike
deep in the embers, charring it again,
and cheered my men along with battle talk
to keep their courage up: no quitting now.
The pike of olive, green though it had been,
reddened and glowed as if about to catch.
I drew it from the coals and my four fellows

39 **nectar and ambrosia** [am brō 'zhə]: drink and food of the gods.

GUIDED READING

LITERAL QUESTIONS

1a. What does Cyclops do before eating two more men? (his dairying chores)

2a. What does Odysseus do while heating up the spike? (He urges his men to action.)

INFERENTIAL QUESTIONS

1b. What do the giant's routines indicate about him? (In some ways he is "normal": He eats at regular times and does chores to provide for his own food.)

2b. What does this show about him? (Odysseus recognizes his men's fear and the importance of acting decisively.)

gave me a hand, lugging it near the Cyclops
as more than natural force nerved them; straight
forward they sprinted, lifted it, and rammed it
deep in his crater eye, and I leaned on it
turning it as a shipwright turns a drill
in planking, having men below to swing
the two-handled strap that spins it in the groove.
So with our brand we bored that great eye socket
while blood ran out around the red-hot bar.
Eyelid and lash were seared; the pierced ball
hissed broiling, and the roots popped.
In a smithy[40]
one sees a white-hot axhead or an adz[41]
plunged and wrung in a cold tub, screeching steam—
the way they make soft iron hale and hard:
just so that eyeball hissed around the spike.
The Cyclops bellowed and the rock roared round him,
and we fell back in fear. Clawing his face
he tugged the bloody spike out of his eye,
threw it away, and his wild hands went groping;
then he set up a howl for Cyclopes
who lived in caves on windy peaks nearby.
Some heard him; and they came by divers[42] ways
to clump around outside and call:
'What ails you,
Polyphemus?[43] Why do you cry so sore
in the starry night? You will not let us sleep.
Sure no man's driving off your flock? No man
has tricked you, ruined you?'
Out of the cave
the mammoth Polyphemus roared in answer:

'Nohbdy, Nohbdy's tricked me, Nohbdy's ruined me!'

To this rough shout they made a sage reply:

'Ah well, if nobody has played you foul
there in your lonely bed, we are no use in pain
given by great Zeus. Let it be your father,
Poseidon Lord, to whom you pray.'
So saying
they trailed away. And I was filled with laughter
to see how like a charm the name deceived them.
Now Cyclops, wheezing as the pain came on him,

40 **smithy:** blacksmith's workshop.

41 **adz:** axlike tool for trimming wood.

42 **divers** [dī′vərz]: various.

43 **Polyphemus** [pol′i fē′məs]

AT A GLANCE

- Odysseus and four men drill the spike into Cyclops' eye.
- Cyclops bellows and giants nearby ask who is harming him; he tells them "Nobody's ruined me!"
- The other giants say that he should pray for his father, Poseidon, to heal him.

MAIN IDEA

Odysseus claims his men are energized with "more than natural force." The gods are helping them to attack the giant (l. 357).

IMAGERY

Homer delights in describing energetic actions and their gory consequences. These descriptions heighten our sense of the men's heroism (ll. 358–371).

ALLITERATION

Cyclops' screams echo in the cave in the musical, alliterative phrase *the rock roared round him* (l. 371).

ONOMATOPOEIA

Word sounds *(hissed, popped, screeching, roared, clump)* lend vividness to the narrative (ll. 366, 368, 370, 371, 378).

MAIN IDEA

Cyclops' neighbors believe that if no one caused his pain then Zeus must be its source, because all things are governed by the gods (ll. 386–389).

GUIDED READING

LITERAL QUESTIONS

1a. What do the neighbors reveal about the blinded Cyclops? (They reveal that he is Polyphemus, son of Poseidon.)

2a. What name does Cyclops reply when asked who blinded him? ("Nohbdy")

INFERENTIAL QUESTIONS

1b. How does this relate to what was said about Poseidon and Odysseus at the beginning of the story? (Poseidon rages "cold and rough" against Odysseus; he now has more reason to hate Odysseus, who has blinded his son.)

2b. What effect does this have? (The Cyclops is unable to get help, because the other giants believe that no mortal being has hurt him.)

AT A GLANCE

- The giant moves the stone and reaches blindly for Odysseus' men.
- Odysseus decides to try to escape along with the rams; he ties the animals together in threes and slings a man under each center ram.

PERSONIFICATION

To stress the terror of the situation, Homer makes the giant the personification of death (l. 398).

MAIN IDEA

Again, Odysseus demonstrates his skill as a strategist: He sees the whole situation as a desperate game and reasons "as a man will for dear life" (l. 400).

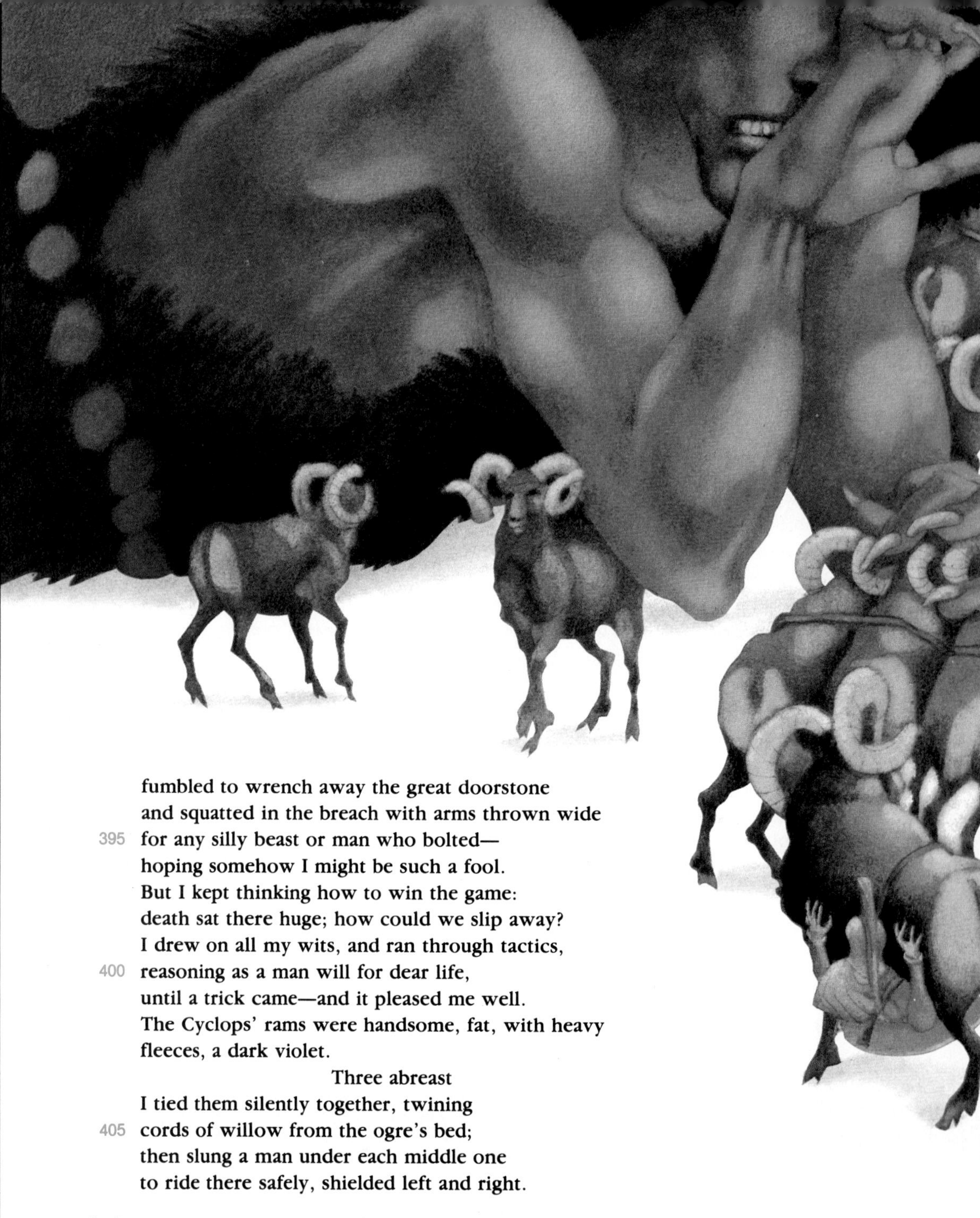

fumbled to wrench away the great doorstone
and squatted in the breach with arms thrown wide
for any silly beast or man who bolted—
hoping somehow I might be such a fool.
But I kept thinking how to win the game:
death sat there huge; how could we slip away?
I drew on all my wits, and ran through tactics,
reasoning as a man will for dear life,
until a trick came—and it pleased me well.
The Cyclops' rams were handsome, fat, with heavy
fleeces, a dark violet.
Three abreast
I tied them silently together, twining
cords of willow from the ogre's bed;
then slung a man under each middle one
to ride there safely, shielded left and right.

GUIDED READING

LITERAL QUESTION

1a. What does Odysseus do to escape? (He ties rams together in threes and puts one of his men beneath each of the center animals.)

INFERENTIAL QUESTION

1b. Why has he chosen this strategy for escape? (Blind Polyphemus could hear and feel the men if they tried to pass by on foot. However, the rams are strong enough to carry them and woolly enough to conceal them.)

So three sheep could convey each man. I took
the woolliest ram, the choicest of the flock,
and hung myself under his kinky belly,
pulled up tight, with fingers twisted deep
in sheepskin ringlets for an iron grip.
So, breathing hard, we waited until morning.

When Dawn spread out her fingertips of rose
the rams began to stir, moving for pasture,
and peals of bleating echoed round the pens
where dams with udders full called for a milking.
Blinded, and sick with pain from his head wound,
the master stroked each ram, then let it pass,
but my men riding on the pectoral[44] fleece
the giant's blind hands blundering never found.
Last of them all my ram, the leader, came,
weighted by wool and me with my meditations.
The Cyclops patted him, and then he said:

'Sweet cousin ram, why lag behind the rest
in the night cave? You never linger so,
but graze before them all, and go afar
to crop sweet grass, and take your stately way
leading along the streams, until at evening
you run to be the first one in the fold.
Why, now, so far behind? Can you be grieving
over your Master's eye? That carrion rogue[45]
and his accurst companions burnt it out
when he had conquered all my wits with wine.
Nohbdy will not get out alive, I swear.
Oh, had you brain and voice to tell
where he may be now, dodging all my fury!

44 **pectoral** [pek ′tər əl]: in the area of the chest.

45 **carrion rogue:** rotten scoundrel.

AT A GLANCE

- Odysseus hides in the wool of the largest ram; the men wait until morning.
- At dawn Polyphemus lets the rams out of the cave.
- The giant wishes the largest ram could tell him where the men are hiding.

IMAGERY

Homer appeals to three senses in this suspenseful scene: "the woolliest ram, the choicest of the flock" (sight), "peals of bleating echoed round the pens" (sound), "fingers twisted deep/In sheepskin ringlets" (touch)

IRONY

The giant asks the lead ram where Odysseus is, never guessing that Odysseus is there under his hands (ll. 436–437).

ALLITERATION

Alliteration lends music to the powerful lines *the giant's blind hands blundering* and *my ram . . . weighted by wool and me with my meditations* (ll. 421, 423).

GUIDED READING

LITERAL QUESTIONS

1a. What does Odysseus say weighs down the biggest ram? (himself and his thoughts)

2a. What does the giant ask the largest ram? (why he is lagging behind the others, whether he grieves over his master's wounded eye)

INFERENTIAL QUESTIONS

1b. Why is the image of a man with heavy thoughts apt? (Odysseus is worried that his plan may not work; his thoughts are weighty.)

2b. How does the giant's monologue make you feel about him? (Answers might suggest students feel pity or compassion for one baffled and in pain, or that they understand his wishing an animal could help him.)

Bashed by this hand and bashed on this rock wall
his brains would strew the floor, and I should have
rest from the outrage Nohbdy worked upon me.'

He sent us into the open, then. Close by,
I dropped and rolled clear of the ram's belly,
going this way and that to untie the men.
With many glances back, we rounded up
his fat, stiff-legged sheep to take aboard,
and drove them down to where the good ship lay.
We saw, as we came near, our fellows' faces
shining; then we saw them turn to grief
tallying those who had not fled from death.
I hushed them, jerking head and eyebrows up,
and in a low voice told them: 'Load this herd;
move fast, and put the ship's head toward the breakers.'
They all pitched in at loading, then embarked
and struck their oars into the sea. Far out,
as far offshore as shouted words would carry,
I sent a few back to the adversary: . . .

'Cyclops,
if ever mortal man inquire
how you were put to shame and blinded, tell him
Odysseus, raider of cities, took your eye:
Laertes' son, whose home's on Ithaca!'

At this he gave a mighty sob and rumbled:

'Now comes the weird[46] upon me, spoken of old.
A wizard, grand and wondrous, lived here—Telemus,
a son of Eurymus; great length of days
he had in wizardry among the Cyclopes,
and these things he foretold for time to come:
my great eye lost, and at Odysseus' hands.
Always I had in mind some giant, armed
in giant force, would come against me here.
But this, but you—small, pitiful and twiggy—
you put me down with wine, you blinded me.
Come back, Odysseus, and I'll treat you well,
praying the god of earthquake to befriend you—
his son I am, for he by his avowal
fathered me, and, if he will, he may
heal me of this black wound—he and no other

46 **weird:** predicted fate.

AT A GLANCE

- Odysseus and his men escape.
- Once at sea, Odysseus shouts to the giant and identifies himself.
- Polyphemus admits that this was predicted but that he had expected a giant.
- He asks Odysseus to return, promising to entreat Poseidon.

IMAGERY

Odysseus' men's moods change as they realize their losses. Their "shining" faces "turn to grief" (ll. 447–448).

CHARACTERIZATION

Odysseus' pride drives him to tell Polyphemus his real name and make a grave error: He wins Poseidon's undying enmity, which will cost him dearly in his efforts to sail home (ll. 456–460).

MAIN IDEA

Once again, we see that fate rules people's lives: These events were predicted years ago. Yet people's (or giants') limited vision keeps them from fully understanding prophecies (ll. 466–469).

IMAGERY

The giant stresses his vision of Odysseus as small and fragile in a series of adjectives. The last, *twiggy,* is a visual and poignant image (l. 470).

GUIDED READING

LITERAL QUESTIONS

1a. When does Odysseus tell Polyphemus who he really is? (When he is "as far offshore as words would carry.")

2a. What does the giant say happened long ago? (A wizard told him that Odysseus would blind him.)

INFERENTIAL QUESTIONS

1b. Why does Odysseus wait until then? (He is afraid of the awesome power of the giant.)

2b. What does this suggest about fate? (Even the lives of terrible flesh-eating giants are preordained and can be foretold.)

of all the happy gods or mortal men.'

Few words I shouted in reply to him:

'If I could take your life I would and take
your time away, and hurl you down to hell!
The god of earthquake could not heal you there!'

At this he stretched his hands out in his darkness
toward the sky of stars, and prayed Poseidon:

'O hear me, lord, blue girdler of the islands,
if I am thine indeed, and thou art father:
grant that Odysseus, raider of cities, never
sees his home: Laertes' son, I mean,
who kept his hall on Ithaca. Should destiny
intend that he shall see his roof again
among his family in his fatherland,
far be that day, and dark the years between.
Let him lose all companions, and return
under strange sail to bitter days at home.'

In these words he prayed, and the god heard him.
Now he laid hands upon a bigger stone
and wheeled around, titanic for the cast,
to let it fly in the black-prowed vessel's track.
But it fell short, just aft[47] the steering oar,
and whelming seas rose giant above the stone
to bear us onward toward the island.
There
as we ran in we saw the squadron waiting,
the trim ships drawn up side by side, and all
our troubled friends who waited, looking seaward.
We beached her, grinding keel[48] in the soft sand,
and waded in, ourselves, on the sandy beach.
Then we unloaded all the Cyclops' flock
to make division, share and share alike,
only my fighters voted that my ram,
the prize of all, should go to me. I slew him
by the seaside and burnt his long thighbones
to Zeus beyond the stormcloud, Cronus'[49] son,
who rules the world. But Zeus disdained my offering:
destruction for my ships he had in store
and death for those who sailed them, my companions.

47 **aft:** toward the rear of a ship.

48 **keel:** main central timber extending the length of the bottom of a ship.

49 **Cronus** [krō′nəs]: father of Zeus and leader of the Titans, an earlier generation of gods.

AT A GLANCE

- Odysseus would gladly kill Polyphemus if he could.
- The giant prays to his father, Poseidon, to punish Odysseus.
- The giant hurls a stone that pushes Odysseus' ship to the island.
- Odysseus sacrifices his biggest ram to Zeus, but the god disdains it.

CONFLICT

As a leader, Odysseus is so upset over the loss of his men that he wishes for still further revenge on Polyphemus (ll. 479–481).

WORD CHOICE

Homer uses brief descriptive phrases to stress his characters' most powerful traits. He calls Poseidon "blue girdler of the islands" and the "god of earthquake," and Odysseus the "raider of cities" (ll. 484, 486).

THEME

The worst curse that Polyphemus can imagine placing on Odysseus is that he shall never see his home. The giant acknowledges that destiny may have other plans and so chooses a "secondary" curse that will render home bitter (ll. 484–493).

MAIN IDEA

Odysseus seems to be a fair, almost democratic leader, for he does not simply seize the prize ram; his men vote it to him (ll. 508–509).

MAIN IDEA

Zeus, in addition to Polyphemus, is set against Odysseus and "disdains" his offering, a view that will have terrible consequences for Odysseus and his men (ll. 512–514).

GUIDED READING

LITERAL QUESTIONS

1a. What does Polyphemus pray will happen to Odysseus? (He prays Odysseus will never see his home, or that many years later he will sail there without companions.)

2a. What does Odysseus do with the sheep he and his men take from the giant? (He divides them "share and share alike.")

INFERENTIAL QUESTIONS

1b. Is Polyphemus' curse effective? How do you know? (Yes; Odysseus says that his ships will be destroyed and his companions will die.)

2b. What does this show about Odysseus? (Though he may be crafty and deceptive with others, he is scrupulously fair with his own men.)

AT A GLANCE

- Odysseus and his men relax.
- At dawn they set sail.

REPETITION

The end of the segment repeats motifs established earlier. The men feast until sunset, then sleep on the beach; when dawn comes they cast off as they have done before, grieving for their friends.

REFLECTING ON THE FIRST SEGMENT

What might inspire a person to do battle with the gods? (Arrogant, strong, or clever people might wish to prove they can control their lives.)

STUDY QUESTIONS

1. was skillful adversary; wandered for years; Poseidon disliked him; faced dangers on trip home; did return home
2. insist on feasting, which gives enemy chance to counterattack
3. eating the lotus makes one forget home and responsibilities; forces three who ate it back to ship, forbids men to taste it
4. imprisons them; eats six men
5. blinds him; ties men to bellies of rams sent out to pasture
6. fondly recalls boyhood; says no sweetness can surpass home and family
7. fears to kill him because only he can move rock from cave
8. *strength:* overcomes fear, outwits the Cyclops; *weakness:* explores cave, gives real name
9. pride
10. *same:* faces danger, inspires courage; *different:* would not endanger others out of pride

LITERARY FOCUS

1. tries to frustrate his return in revenge for blinding the Cyclops
2. delighted with his own cleverness; seems indifferent to fate

Now all day long until the sun went down
we made our feast on mutton and sweet wine,
till after sunset in the gathering dark
we went to sleep above the wash of ripples.

When the young Dawn with fingertips of rose
touched the world, I roused the men, gave orders
to man the ships, cast off the mooring lines;[50]
and filing in to sit beside the rowlocks
oarsmen in line dipped oars in the gray sea.
So we moved out, sad in the vast offing,
having our precious lives, but not our friends.

50 **mooring lines:** ropes that secure a ship in place in port.

STUDY QUESTIONS

Recalling

1. Find five facts about Odysseus in the invocation to the muse.
2. Explain how the disobedience of Odysseus' men creates problems in the land of the Cicones.
3. Describe the danger of the Lotus Eaters. Explain how Odysseus kept from losing his men there.
4. What offense does the Cyclops commit against Odysseus and his men?
5. Explain how Odysseus saves himself and his men from the Cyclops.

Interpreting

6. What attitudes about home can be found in Odysseus' introduction of himself to Alcinous and in the episode of the Lotus Eaters?
7. In what ways does fear help Odysseus to form his plan against the Cyclops?
8. Explain how the episode of the Cyclops shows both Odysseus' strength and weakness as a leader.
9. Why do you think Odysseus finally revealed his true identity to the Cyclops?

Extending

10. In what ways do you think the qualities of a good leader are the same today as in Odysseus' time? In what ways are they different?

LITERARY FOCUS

Conflict: Person Against Fate

In a narrative, **conflict** is a struggle between opposing forces. Many different types of conflict exist in the *Odyssey.* Odysseus must battle against other men like the Cicones and against nature, especially in the form of the sea. The greatest struggle that Odysseus must face, however, is against fate. In a conflict of **person against fate,** characters struggle against circumstances that cannot be changed. They try to change conditions that are beyond their control. Characters are responsible for their own fate. Once fate is determined, however, trying to change it is a futile struggle.

In the *Odyssey* fate takes the form of the gods who decree that Odysseus will return home only after a long period of wandering and hardship. In spite of the gods' decree, which cannot be changed, Odysseus continues to strive for home.

Thinking About the Person-Against-Fate Conflict

1. The god Poseidon is mentioned in the invocation to the muse and at the end of the Cyclops episode. What is Poseidon's role in Odysseus' future?
2. Why does Odysseus continue to insult the Cyclops after learning that the Cyclops is Poseidon's son? What does Odysseus' attitude toward fate seem to be?

The Sirens

Odysseus continues his story. He next tells Alcinous about his adventure on Aeolia, island of Aeolus [ē'ə ləs], *god of winds. To help Odysseus reach home, Aeolus gives him a bag in which unfavorable winds are trapped. Odysseus and his crew sail with a gentle breeze. Within sight of Ithaca, their homeland, curious crew members untie the bag and release the unfavorable winds. The ships are blown back to Aeolia. Realizing that it is Odysseus' fate to wander, Aeolus scorns him.*

The ships sail next to the land of the Laestrygonians [les'tri gō' nē ənz], *a tribe of cannibals. All but one of Odysseus' ships are destroyed, and their crews killed. In the last ship Odysseus escapes to Aeaea* [ē ē'ə], *home of the goddess Circe* [sur'sē]. *Circe turns the crew to swine, but Odysseus persuades her to return his men to human form.*

After a year with Circe, Odysseus journeys to the land of the dead at Circe's suggestion. There the blind prophet Tiresias [tī rē'sē əs] *tells Odysseus what to do to reach home. Then Odysseus meets the shade of his mother, who assures him of his wife's fidelity. Odysseus returns briefly to Aeaea, where Circe warns him of dangers ahead. Odysseus shares this knowledge with his men and then sets off with them.*

'Dear friends,
more than one man, or two, should know those things
Circe foresaw for us and shared with me,
so let me tell her forecast: then we die
with out eyes open, if we are going to die,
or know what death we baffle if we can. Sirens[1]
weaving a haunting song over the sea
we are to shun, she said, and their green shore
all sweet with clover; yet she urged that I
alone should listen to their song. Therefore
you are to tie me up, tight as a splint,
erect along the mast, lashed to the mast,
and if I shout and beg to be untied,
take more turns of the rope to muffle me.'

I rather dwelt on this part of the forecast
while our good ship made time, bound outward down
the wind for the strange island of Sirens.
Then all at once the wind fell, and a calm
came over all the sea, as though some power
lulled the swell.

1 **Sirens:** sea nymphs who lured sailors to their deaths by singing sweetly.

AT A GLANCE

- Odysseus starts for home again.
- Warned by the goddess Circe about the Sirens, Odysseus asks his men to tie him to the mast.
- On their way to the Sirens' island, Odysseus' ship is becalmed.

LITERARY OPTIONS

- epic hero
- imagery
- characterization

THEMATIC OPTIONS

- challenges and obstacles
- fate
- weather as fate's agent

SPEAKER

Odysseus, still speaking to Alcinous, continues the story of his adventures. The first-person point of view adds poignancy to his longing for home.

MAIN IDEA

Odysseus shares Circe's predictions about the dangerous obstacles he and his men will have to overcome before they can arrive home (ll. 526–531).

METAPHOR

The Sirens weave their song over the sea. Homer's metaphor suggests their alluring calls are a net in which sailors might be trapped (ll. 531–532).

EPIC HERO

As an epic hero Odysseus is fated to suffer in a special way. His torment will be unlike any other's (ll. 534–535).

GUIDED READING

LITERAL QUESTIONS

1a. Why does Odysseus tell his men Circe's predictions? (He wants them to die—or survive—with their "eyes open.")

2a. Which part of Circe's forecast does Odysseus stress? (The warning to stay away from the Sirens and to tie Odysseus to the mast of the ship.)

INFERENTIAL QUESTIONS

1b. What does this suggest Odysseus believes about his fate? (He feels clever enough to change his destiny.)

2b. How do Odysseus' orders show confidence in his men? (Answers may suggest that subordinates tying up a leader could easily rebel or revenge their powerlessness; Odysseus does not fear this.)

AT A GLANCE

- Odysseus covers his men's ears with wax; he is tied to the mast.
- Two Sirens sing to the men, promising companionship and joy.

IMAGERY

Homer lovingly describes the seafarers' work; his images appeal to the senses of sight and touch (ll. 545–548).

MAIN IDEA

The sun's heat helps Odysseus protect his men from the allure of the Sirens (ll. 551–552).

RHYME SCHEME

Shorter line lengths, four-line stanzas, and an *abab* rhyme scheme distinguish the Sirens' song from the rest of the narrative. In the first two and fourth stanzas the *b* rhymes are approximate.

IMAGERY

Homer uses images of "honey twining" from two throats, and of two sailors, "graybeard and rower-boy," in the Sirens' song. These images of pairs underscore the Sirens' offer of companionship (ll. 569, 575).

The crew were on their feet
briskly, to furl the sail, and stow it; then,
each in place, they poised the smooth oar blades
and sent the white foam scudding[2] by. I carved
a massive cake of beeswax into bits
and rolled them in my hands until they softened—
no long task, for a burning heat came down
from Helios,[3] lord of high noon. Going forward
I carried wax along the line, and laid it
thick on their ears. They tied me up, then, plumb
amidships, back to the mast, lashed to the mast,
and took themselves again to rowing. Soon,
as we came smartly within hailing distance,
the two Sirens, noting our fast ship
off their point, made ready, and they sang:

'This way, oh turn your bows,
Achaea's glory,
As all the world allows—
Moor and be merry.

Sweet coupled airs we sing.
No lonely seafarer
Holds clear of entering
Our green mirror.

Pleased by each purling note
Like honey twining
From her throat and my throat,
Who lies a-pining?

Sea rovers here take joy
Voyaging onward,
As from our song of Troy
Graybeard and rower-boy
Goeth more learned.

All feats on that great field
In the long warfare,
Dark days the bright gods willed,
Wounds you bore there,

2 **scudding:** flying swiftly in the wind.

3 **Helios** [hē′lē ōs′]: Greek god of the sun.

GUIDED READING

LITERAL QUESTION

1a. What do the Sirens urge the men to do? (to turn their boats toward the island, join them, and be merry.)

INFERENTIAL QUESTION

1b. Why would the Sirens' offer be appealing to the men? (They have been traveling a long time without the companionship of women; the Sirens are flattering and offer the men pleasure and understanding.)

Argos' old soldiery[4]
  On Troy beach teeming,
Charmed out of time we see.
No life on earth can be
  Hid from our dreaming.'

The lovely voices in ardor appealing over the water
made me crave to listen, and I tried to say
'Untie me!' to the crew, jerking my brows;
but they bent steady to the oars. Then Perimedes[5]
got to his feet, he and Eurylochus,[6]
and passed more line about, to hold me still.
So all rowed on, until the Sirens
dropped under the sea rim, and their singing
dwindled away.
                My faithful company
rested on their oars now, peeling off
the wax that I had laid thick on their ears;
then set me free.

4 **Argos' old soldiery:** warriors who fought in the Trojan War from the Greek city of Argos.

5 **Perimedes** [per ə mē′dēz]

6 **Eurylochus** [ū ril′ə kəs]

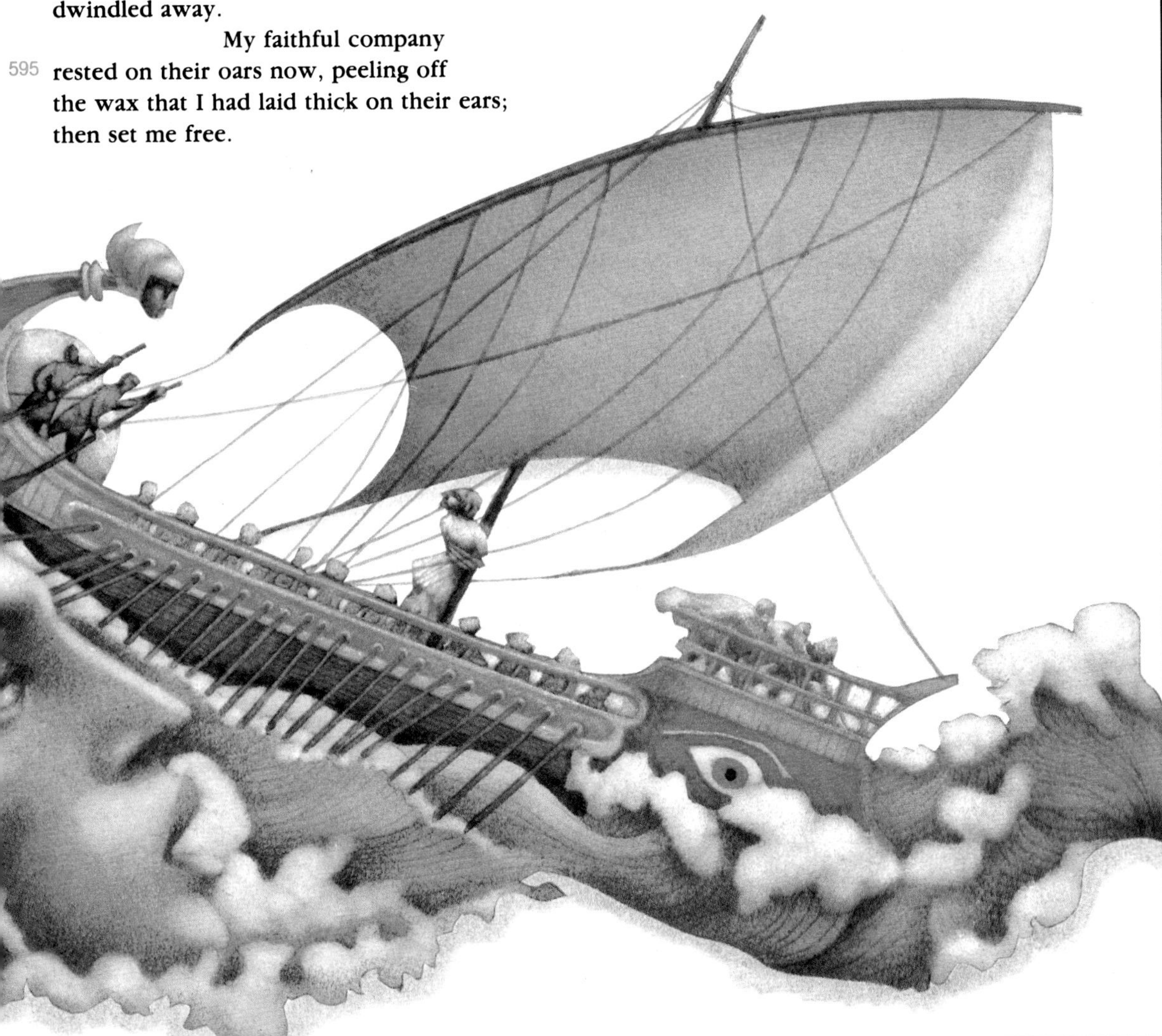

AT A GLANCE

- Odysseus urges his men to untie him; two men lash him tighter to the mast.
- Out of range of the Sirens' song, the men remove the wax and free Odysseus.

ASSONANCE

The welcoming open sounds of the Sirens' voices are echoed in repeated vowel sounds in Homer's description (l. 586).

IMAGERY

Homer embodies the dramatic conflict between Odysseus' confinement and his passionate longing to go to the Sirens in the small movements of his jerking brows (l. 588).

GUIDED READING

LITERAL QUESTION

1a. How does Odysseus describe his men after they have passed the Sirens? (He calls them "my faithful company.")

INFERENTIAL QUESTION

1b. How does Odysseus seem to feel about his men? (He is proud of them and pleased with their obedience during this trial.)

AT A GLANCE

- Odysseus discovers signs of danger nearby.
- The terrified men drop their oars.
- Odysseus urges them to be brave.

IMAGERY

Again Homer uses a small but significant detail to show human distress: The men dropped their oars and "the blades went knocking / wild alongside" (ll. 601–602).

EPIC HERO

Odysseus calms his frightened men by reminding them of all they have been through together and reminding them of his successes as a leader (ll. 604–611).

Scylla and Charybdis

Circe also warned Odysseus of the pass between Scylla [sil′ə] *and Charybdis* [kə rib′dis]. *According to Circe, Scylla is a six-headed monster who scoops men from ships that sail too close to her rocky shore. At the other side of the narrow pass is Charybdis, a violent whirlpool capable of swallowing the entire ship. Circe suggested that Odysseus avoid Charybdis and risk the smaller loss of six men to Scylla.*

But scarcely had that island
faded in blue air than I saw smoke
and white water, with sound of waves in tumult—
a sound the men heard, and it terrified them.
Oars flew from their hands; the blades went knocking
wild alongside till the ship lost way,
with no oarblades to drive her through the water.

Well, I walked up and down from bow to stern,
trying to put heart into them, standing over
every oarsman, saying gently,
'Friends,
have we never been in danger before this?
More fearsome is it now, than when the Cyclops
penned us in his cave? What power he had!
Did I not keep my nerve, and use my wits
to find a way out for us?

GUIDED READING

LITERAL QUESTION

1a. How do Odysseus' men react when they hear the waves? (They are terrified.)

INFERENTIAL QUESTION

1b. How do you think Odysseus feels? (He seems confident that he can lead his men through this danger, perhaps because Circe told him what would happen.)

Now I say
by hook or crook this peril too shall be
something that we remember.
Heads up, lads!
We must obey the orders as I give them,
Get the oarshafts in your hands, and lay back
hard on your benches; hit these breaking seas.
Zeus help us pull away before we founder.
You at the tiller,[7] listen, and take in
all that I say—the rudders are your duty;
keep her out of the combers[8] and the smoke;
steer for that headland; watch the drift, or we
fetch up in the smother,[9] and you drown us.'

That was all, and it brought them round to action.
But as I sent them on toward Scylla, I
told them nothing, as they could do nothing.
They would have dropped their oars again, in panic,
to roll for cover under the decking. Circe's
bidding against arms had slipped my mind,
so I tied on my cuirass[10] and took up
two heavy spears, then made my way along
to the foredeck[11]—thinking to see her first from there,

7 **tiller:** lever used to turn the rudder, or steering mechanism, of a ship.

8 **combers** [kō′mərz]: long, rolling waves.

9 **fetch . . . smother:** swerve into a cloud of spray.

10 **cuirass** [kwi ras′]: armor that covers the body from neck to waist.

11 **foredeck:** main deck in the front of a ship.

AT A GLANCE

- Odysseus tells his men that they must obey him.
- Odysseus arms himself and goes to the foredeck to watch for the monster and the whirlpool.

CHARACTERIZATION

Odysseus divides the tasks, orders his men to work, and warns them that making mistakes may kill them. He is stern and forceful because he feels the men's actions will have an impact on their fate (ll. 613–622).

MAIN IDEA

Even while ordering his men to do their best, Odysseus calls on Zeus to help them escape without capsizing (ll. 615–617).

CHARACTERIZATION

Odysseus does not share Circe's prediction that six of his men will die. He is concerned about the men's fears and tries to prevent panic (ll. 624–625).

GUIDED READING

LITERAL QUESTION

1a. What does Odysseus do and say as leader? (He assures the men that this peril will just be something to remember, gives specific orders to the oarsmen and others, and protects the men by not telling them what he knows Scylla will do.)

INFERENTIAL QUESTION

1b. How does Odysseus' belief about fate change the way he treats his men? (Odysseus is strict when he feels the men's actions are important; he is gentle and protective when he feels there is nothing his men can do about what will happen next.)

AT A GLANCE

- Scylla is a "monster of gray rock"; Charybdis is a terrible tidal whirlpool.
- Scylla devours six men.
- Odysseus suffers "deathly pity" as the men row on.

CHARACTERIZATION

Odysseus is sensitive to the focus of his crew's attention and their fear (ll. 648–650).

IMAGERY

Homer's image of the whirlpool presents the power of the water both visually and aurally. The description fairly hisses when the "mixture suddenly heaves and rises" and "shot spume" soars to the "landside heights" (ll. 640–644).

CONFLICT

The rocks are a living monster that grabs and eats Odysseus' men. Homer once again exploits the primordial human fear of being eaten alive (ll. 651–654, 663).

EPIC HERO

Seeing the dying men reach for him overwhelms Odysseus with pity. Such massive responses are typical of an epic hero (ll. 664–665).

the monster of the gray rock, harboring
torment for my friends. I strained my eyes
upon that cliffside veiled in cloud, but nowhere
could I catch sight of her.
And all this time,
in travail, sobbing, gaining on the current,
we rowed into the strait—Scylla to port[12]
and on our starboard[13] beam Charybdis, dire
gorge[14] of the salt-sea tide. By heaven! when she
vomited, all the sea was like a caldron
seething over intense fire, when the mixture
suddenly heaves and rises.
The shot spume
soared to the landside heights, and fell like rain.

But when she swallowed the sea water down
we saw the funnel of the maelstrom,[15] heard
the rock bellowing all around, and dark
sand raged on the bottom far below.
My men all blanched against the gloom, our eyes
were fixed upon that yawning mouth in fear
of being devoured.
Then Scylla made her strike,
whisking six of my best men from the ship.
I happened to glance aft at ship and oarsmen
and caught sight of their arms and legs, dangling
high overhead. Voices came down to me
in anguish, calling my name for the last time.

A man surf-casting on a point of rock
for bass or mackerel, whipping his long rod
to drop the sinker and the bait far out,
will hook a fish and rip it from the surface
to dangle wriggling through the air:
so these
were borne aloft in spasms toward the cliff.

She ate them as they shrieked there, in her den,
in the dire grapple, reaching still for me—
and deathly pity ran me through
at that sight—far the worst I ever suffered,
questing the passes of the strange sea.
We rowed on.
The Rocks were now behind; Charybdis, too,
and Scylla dropped astern. . . .

12 **port:** left side of a ship as one faces front.

13 **starboard:** right side of a ship.

14 **gorge:** throat.

15 **maelstrom** [māl′strəm]: whirlpool.

GUIDED READING

LITERAL QUESTION

1a. To what does Homer compare the rock monster, Scylla? (a man pulling a fish from the surf)

INFERENTIAL QUESTION

1b. Why is this an apt comparison? (Both the fisherman and the rocks disregard the pain and anguish of their catch.)

Odysseus Loses Everything

The crew insists on stopping for rest on Thrinacia [thrin ā'shə], *island of Helios, the sun god. Odysseus had been warned by Circe and Tiresias of the danger of harming the sun god's prized cattle. He forbids his men from disturbing the herd. However, the crew is short of supplies, and, when Odysseus goes inland to pray, they slaughter the cattle. In anger Zeus, the leader of the gods, promises Helios that the men will be punished when they are at sea.*

Now six full days my gallant crew could feast
upon the prime beef they had marked for slaughter
from Helios' herd; and Zeus, the son of Cronus,
added one fine morning.
                                        All the gales
had ceased, blown out, and with an offshore breeze
we launched again, stepping the mast[16] and sail,
to make for the open sea. Astern of us
the island coastline faded, and no land
showed anywhere, but only sea and heaven,
when Zeus Cronion piled a thunderhead
above the ship, while gloom spread on the ocean.
We held our course, but briefly. Then the squall
struck whining from the west, with gale force, breaking
both forestays,[17] and the mast came toppling aft
along the ship's length, so the running rigging[18]
showered into the bilge.[19]
                                        On the afterdeck
the mast had hit the steersman a slant blow
bashing the skull in, knocking him overside,
as the brave soul fled the body, like a diver.
With crack on crack of thunder, Zeus let fly
a bolt against the ship, a direct hit,
so that she bucked, in reeking fumes of sulfur,[20]
and all the men were flung into the sea.
They came up round the wreck, bobbing awhile
like petrels[21] on the waves.

16 **stepping the mast:** raising the mast.

17 **forestays:** lines that support the mast from the front of a ship.

18 **rigging:** rope used to support the mast and to work the sails.

19 **bilge:** lowest interior part of a ship.

20 **sulfur:** chemical element. Sulfur is odorless; the chemical odor produced by lightning is ozone. The smell here may be the burning of an object that contains a sulfur compound.

21 **petrels:** long-winged sea birds.

AT A GLANCE

- Odysseus' men feast on the sun god's prized cattle.
- Enraged, Zeus sends a thunderstorm to wreck Odysseus' ship and drown his men.

THEME

Weather conditions are excellent for the homeward voyage until Odysseus and his men are out in the open sea. Zeus lures the men away from land, then sends a storm to punish them for slaughtering Helios' cattle (ll. 675–679).

ALLITERATION

Homer describes the storm's coming in powerful language. The repetition of initial *th, s,* and *w* sounds propel the description: "Then the squall / struck whining from the west, with gale force . . ." (ll. 680–681).

SIMILE

Homer compares the steersman's departing soul to a diver, an apt and graceful image (l. 687).

WORD CHOICE

As usual, the verbs Homer uses are active and dramatic; most create visual images. In this passage one action is piled on another (ll. 680–693).

GUIDED READING

LITERAL QUESTION

1a. Why has Zeus sent the storm? (to punish the crew for taking Helios' cattle)

INFERENTIAL QUESTION

1b. What picture of the gods' involvement in human life has Homer presented so far? (Sometimes they punish men fairly, for real transgressions; other times they act out of petty jealousy or spite. Often they disagree among themselves.)

AT A GLANCE

- Odysseus rides out the storm.
- A southeasterly wind drives him toward Scylla and Charybdis.
- He holds onto a tree until his rig resurfaces.
- Odysseus uses his hands as oars, then drifts to Calypso's island.

THEME

Odysseus grieves over his drowned companions, mourning the fact that they will never reach home. Again Homer uses a simple human gesture to show fate abandoning them (l. 695).

EPIC HERO

Drifting alone on the wreckage, Odysseus is clearly a tragic hero who must face his next trials alone. He shows his bravery, physical strength, and endurance by clinging to a tree all night.

THEME

Odysseus feels his second encounter with Charybdis is "one more / twist of the knife," another opportunity for the gods to try his determination to go home (ll. 704–705).

REFLECTING ON THE SECOND SEGMENT

Which trial or danger seems most terrible to you? Why is Odysseus' reaction to it heroic? (Answers should suggest that Odysseus' responses are tempered by his acceptance of his fate and by an almost superhuman toughness.)

No more seafaring
homeward for these, no sweet day of return;
the god had turned his face from them.
I clambered
fore and aft my hulk until a comber
split her, keel from ribs, and the big timber
floated free; the mast, too, broke away.
A backstay[22] floated dangling from it, stout
rawhide rope, and I used this for lashing
mast and keel together. These I straddled,
riding the frightful storm.
Nor had I yet
seen the worst of it: for now the west wind
dropped, and a southeast gale came on—one more
twist of the knife—taking me north again,
straight for Charybdis. All that night I drifted,
and in the sunrise, sure enough, I lay
off Scylla mountain and Charybdis deep.
There, as the whirlpool drank the tide, a billow
tossed me, and I sprang for the great fig tree,
catching on like a bat under a bough.
Nowhere had I to stand, no way of climbing,
the root and bole[23] being far below, and far
above my head the branches and their leaves,
massed, overshadowing Charybdis pool.
But I clung grimly, thinking my mast and keel
would come back to the surface when she spouted.
And ah! how long, with what desire, I waited!
till, at the twilight hour, when one who hears
and judges pleas in the marketplace all day
between contentious men, goes home to supper,
the long poles at last reared from the sea.

Now I let go with hands and feet, plunging
straight into the foam beside the timbers,
pulled astride, and rowed hard with my hands
to pass by Scylla. Never could I have passed her
had not the Father of gods and men,[24] this time,
kept me from her eyes. Once through the strait,
nine days I drifted in the open sea
before I made shore, buoyed up by the gods,
upon Ogygia[25] Isle. The dangerous nymph
Calypso lives and sings there, in her beauty,
and she received me, loved me."

22 **backstay:** line that supports the mast from the back of a ship.

23 **bole:** tree trunk.

24 **the Father . . . men:** Zeus.

25 **Ogygia** [ō jij ′ē ə]: island home of Calypso.

GUIDED READING

LITERAL QUESTION

1a. What happens to Odysseus when Charybdis swallows the mast and keel? (A wave throws him ashore, where he clings to a fig tree.)

INFERENTIAL QUESTION

1b. Why has Odysseus no other choice except to hold on? (There is no place to stand, he cannot climb the trunk, the branches are out of reach, and if he lets go he will fall into the whirlpool.)

STUDY QUESTIONS

Recalling

1. What is the danger of the Sirens? Explain how Odysseus and his crew escape their alluring song.
2. Describe Scylla and Charybdis. What damage is suffered in the first passage through the strait between them?
3. Where is Odysseus when his men slaughter the cattle of the sun god? Explain how Zeus punishes them.
4. Alone, Odysseus faces Scylla and Charybdis a second time. Describe his method of escape. What happens to him afterwards?

Interpreting

5. In what ways is Odysseus more careful when approaching the Sirens than he was with the Cyclops?
6. What qualities of a good leader does Odysseus show in the first encounter with Scylla and Charybdis?
7. Does the slaughter of Helios' herd by Odysseus' men show a weakness in Odysseus as a leader? Explain your answer.
8. In what sense is the sea both a place of danger and a place of safety for Odysseus?

Extending

9. Many of the problems that Odysseus faces represent typical human problems. What messages about life are implied in the following situations in the *Odyssey*?
   a. The real danger of the Sirens is hidden beneath their beautiful song.
   b. Odysseus must choose between two frightening and destructive alternatives, Scylla and Charybdis.

VIEWPOINT

After centuries and in spite of its lofty reputation, the *Odyssey* can be approached as a great adventure story. In his introduction to one edition of the *Odyssey*, W. H. D. Rouse said:

> Those who like thrillers and detective novels will find excitement enough here. . . . Those who like fairy tales will find nothing better than the Goggleeye [Cyclops].

■ In what ways does the *Odyssey* provide excitement like that in a thriller or detective novel? Explain how the *Odyssey* might remind readers of a fairy tale.

LITERARY FOCUS

The Epic Hero

A person of almost superhuman qualities, the **epic hero** is stronger, smarter, more courageous, and more virtuous than most other people. An epic hero is not modest but is honest about achievements and proud of talents. In addition, the epic hero is "bigger than life" and embodies the ideals of a nation or a group of people. As a result, the heroes of the world's great epics have become part of the national pride of the nations that produced them. For example, El Cid is a national hero in Spain, and the hero of *The Song of Roland* is a legendary hero of France.

Thinking About the Epic Hero

1. The actions of an epic hero are often beyond what real people would be able to do. What actions of Odysseus seem superhuman?
2. From his adventures so far, which do you consider a greater help to Odysseus, his cleverness or his physical strength? Explain your answer.

STUDY QUESTIONS

1. Their singing enchants listeners, causing ships to be wrecked on their shore; Odysseus puts wax in men's ears, is tied to mast.
2. ■ Scylla: six-headed monster that grabs men from passing ships; Charybdis: whirlpool that swallows ships
   ■ Six men are lost to Scylla.
3. inland, praying; destroys ship and men with a sea storm
4. clings to fig tree until raft is flung up from whirlpool and paddles past Scylla into open sea; reaches Calypso after nine days
5. avoids risks by having men deafened and himself bound
6. warns and reassures men; conceals some of the danger to prevent panic
7. Possible answers: He cannot totally control men—their independence suggests resourcefulness; he fails to impress upon men the power of Zeus.
8. ■ danger: home of Poseidon, monsters; source of terrible winds, weather
   ■ safety: road home; refuge from dangers on land
9. a. Harmful things often appear attractive. b. One is often forced to choose the lesser of two evils.

VIEWPOINT

thriller: keeps reader in suspense about outcome; contains mysterious foes; *fairy tale:* magical, supernatural beings, monsters; gods' interference with humans; has happy ending

LITERARY FOCUS

1. ability to avoid whirlpool by clinging to branch; surviving shipwreck; blinding Cyclops
2. Answers will vary; Homer emphasizes both.

AT A GLANCE

- Alcinous helps Odysseus go home.
- Suitors have taken over Odysseus' house, pursuing his wife, Penelope, and plotting against his son, Telemachus.
- Telemachus thinks Odysseus is a god.
- Odysseus reassures his son.

LITERARY OPTIONS

- flashback
- epithet
- speaker

THEMATIC OPTIONS

- achieving justice at home
- the gods' power
- revealing the truth

SPEAKER

Odysseus no longer tells his story; instead, Homer chooses an omniscient narrator to describe events as Odysseus lives them. This type of narration heightens the sense of an uncertain outcome (ll. 734–735).

FLASHBACK

Part One of the story is a flashback: Odysseus tells the story of the adventures that brought him to Alcinous' court. In this instance the flashback (being a first-person narrative) presents a narrow view, as it reflects the perceptions and attitudes of the storyteller.

DIALOGUE

Telemachus' short sentences, many of them exclamations, show his excitement (ll. 737–742).

PART TWO: RETURN TO ITHACA

Father and Son

Odysseus completes his story for Alcinous. From here on, we follow Odysseus' adventures as he lives them. Moved by Odysseus' tale, Alcinous gives him a ship and crew. After twenty years, ten years at war with Troy and ten years trying to return home to Ithaca, Odysseus reaches his homeland, but he cannot yet go home.

The goddess Athena appears to warn Odysseus of suitors who have taken over his house. The suitors have been insisting that Odysseus is dead and have been pressuring his wife, Penelope, to choose one of them as her husband. Still believing that Odysseus is alive, Penelope refuses to remarry, but she cannot persuade the suitors to leave. In addition to living at her expense, the suitors are plotting to kill Odysseus' son, Telemachus [tə lem′ə kəs]. *Telemachus has gone to the Greek city of Sparta for news of his father.*

Athena disguises Odysseus as an old beggar and sends him to Eumaeus [ū mē′əs], *a loyal old swineherd. As Telemachus returns home, the disguised Odysseus meets him. Before Telemachus' eyes the disguise melts away.*

Then Lord Odysseus
reappeared—and his son was thunderstruck.
Fear in his eyes, he looked down and away
as though it were a god, and whispered:
"Stranger,
you are no longer what you were just now!
Your cloak is new; even your skin! You are
one of the gods who rule the sweep of heaven!
Be kind to us, we'll make you fair oblation[1]
and gifts of hammered gold. Have mercy on us!"

The noble and enduring man replied:

"No god. Why take me for a god? No, no.
I am that father whom your boyhood lacked
and suffered pain for lack of. I am he."

Held back too long, the tears ran down his cheeks
as he embraced his son.
Only Telemachus,
uncomprehending, wild
with incredulity,[2] cried out:

1 **oblation:** offering at an altar to god.

2 **incredulity:** disbelief.

GUIDED READING

LITERAL QUESTION

1a. What makes Telemachus think Odysseus is a god? (Odysseus changes form; his old-man disguise melts away.)

INFERENTIAL QUESTION

1b. Why do you think Telemachus is afraid to be in the presence of a god? (Answers should suggest that he is afraid of the gods' power.)

"You cannot
be my father Odysseus! Meddling spirits
conceived this trick to twist the knife in me!
No man of woman born could work these wonders
by his own craft, unless a god came into it
with ease to turn him young or old at will.
I swear you were in rags and old,
and here you stand like one of the immortals!"

Odysseus brought his ranging mind to bear
and said:
"This is not princely, to be swept
away by wonder at your father's presence.
No other Odysseus will ever come,
for he and I are one, the same; his bitter
fortune and his wanderings are mine.
Twenty years gone, and I am back again
on my own island.
As for my change of skin,
that is a charm Athena, Hope of Soldiers,
uses as she will; she has the knack
to make me seem a beggar man sometimes
and sometimes young, with finer clothes about me.
It is no hard thing for the gods of heaven
to glorify a man or bring him low."

AT A GLANCE

- Telemachus insists that the man before him is not his father.
- Odysseus scolds his son and explains that Athena helped to disguise him.

EPITHET

Homer stresses Athena's importance to soldiers in the epithet *Hope of Soldiers*. The goddess of wisdom's guidance is essential to their survival (l. 767).

THEME

Odysseus explains more than his disguise in this concise statement of one of the epic's major themes (ll. 770–771).

GUIDED READING

LITERAL QUESTION

1a. What does Telemachus insist? (He says the man before him could not be his father; no mortal could change from old to young at will.)

INFERENTIAL QUESTION

1b. How do you think Odysseus feels about his son's refusal to believe him? (Answers may suggest that he is impatient; he chides Telemachus and tells him that his reactions are not fitting for a prince.)

AT A GLANCE

- Telemachus weeps and asks his father how he came to Ithaca.
- Odysseus explains that he sailed with the Phaeacians.
- He asks Telemachus to help him by counting the men who are against them.

IMAGERY

The two men are overwhelmed with feelings. Their tears rise from "wells of longing," an image that suggests great emotional depth (l. 775).

SIMILE

Homer compares the men's cries to the sounds hawks make when farmers take their young. The simile is doubly apt because of the hawk's noble associations and because the separation of generations causes the cries (ll. 776–778).

MAIN IDEA

Odysseus lays out his plans to defeat the suitors. His first step is to convince Telemachus that in the dangerous conflict they are about to enter, they have the support and guidance of the gods (ll. 791–795).

When he had spoken, down he sat.
Then, throwing
his arms around this marvel of a father
Telemachus began to weep. Salt tears
rose from the wells of longing in both men,
and cries burst from both as keen and fluttering
as those of the great taloned hawk,
whose nestlings farmers take before they fly.
So helplessly they cried, pouring out tears,
and might have gone on weeping so till sundown,
had not Telemachus said:
"Dear father! Tell me
what kind of vessel put you here ashore
on Ithaca? Your sailors, who were they?
I doubt you made it, walking on the sea!"

Then said Odysseus, who had borne the barren sea:

"Only plain truth shall I tell you, child.
Great seafarers, the Phaeacians, gave me passage
as they give other wanderers. By night
over the open ocean, while I slept,
they brought me in their cutter,[3] set me down
on Ithaca, with gifts of bronze and gold
and stores of woven things. By the gods' will
these lie all hidden in a cave. I came
to this wild place, directed by Athena,
so that we might lay plans to kill our enemies.
Count up the suitors for me, let me know
what men at arms are there, how many men.
I must put all my mind to it, to see
if we two by ourselves can take them on
or if we should look round for help." . . .

3 **cutter:** ship with a single mast.

GUIDED READING

LITERAL QUESTION

1a. What does Odysseus promise to tell his son? (only the plain truth)

INFERENTIAL QUESTION

1b. Why might this promise be important at this point in the story? (Telemachus did not believe the man before him was truly his father; Odysseus had to overcome his son's distrust.)

Telemachus warns his father that the suitors are too numerous for only two men to fight. Odysseus replies that he and Telemachus will succeed with the help of Zeus and Athena. To set the plan in motion, Odysseus will arrive at his home in the disguise of the beggar. Although the suitors may abuse Odysseus, Telemachus is not to reveal his father's true identity. Odysseus continues to detail his plan for Telemachus:

"Athena,
counseling me, will give me word, and I
shall signal to you, nodding: at that point
round up all armor, lances, gear of war
left in our hall, and stow the lot away
back in the vaulted storeroom. When the suitors
miss those arms and question you, be soft
in what you say—answer:
'I thought I'd move them
out of the smoke. They seemed no longer those
bright arms Odysseus left us years ago
when he went off to Troy. Here where the fire's
hot breath came, they had grown black and drear.
One better reason, too, I had from Zeus:
Suppose a brawl starts up when you are drunk,
you might be crazed and bloody one another,
and that would stain your feast, your courtship. Tempered
iron can magnetize a man.'
Say that.
But put aside two broadswords and two spears
for our own use, two oxhide shields nearby
when we go into action. Pallas Athena
and Zeus All-Provident will see you through,
bemusing our young friends.
Now one thing more.
If son of mine you are and blood of mine,
let no one hear Odysseus is about.
Neither Laertes, nor the swineherd here,
nor any slave, nor even Penelope.
But you and I alone must learn how far
the women are corrupted; we should know
how to locate good men among our hands,
the loyal and respectful, and the shirkers[4]
who take you lightly, as alone and young."

4 **shirkers:** those who avoid doing what should be done.

AT A GLANCE

- Odysseus reassures his son that Athena and Zeus will help them fight the suitors.
- Odysseus plans to arrive home disguised as a beggar.
- He tells Telemachus to hide all but two weapons and to keep Odysseus' presence a secret.

CHARACTERIZATION

Zeus understands human motivation: Knowing that the most satisfying explanation for removing the weapons from the hall would appeal to the suitors' own self-interest, he tells Odysseus how to deceive them (ll. 812–816).

EPITHET

Odysseus uses a simple epithet to assure his son that he has on his side a god who provides everything (l. 820).

CHARACTERIZATION

Odysseus appeals to his son's desire to be important by telling him to keep the plan a secret (ll. 822–826).

GUIDED READING

LITERAL QUESTIONS

1a. What two reasons must Telemachus give the suitors for removing the arms from the hall? (The weapons were blackened by the fire; if a drunken fight occurred, someone might get hurt.)

2a. Why does Odysseus want Telemachus to keep his presence a secret? (Together they must find out which men and women are loyal to them.)

INFERENTIAL QUESTIONS

1b. What is the real reason Odysseus wants his son to remove the weapons? (The suitors will not have arms available when he begins the fight.)

2b. Why is this information important? (They need to know their allies for the coming fight.)

AT A GLANCE

- Odysseus returns home disguised as a beggar.
- A leading suitor insults him.
- Odysseus confronts the suitor, who throws a stool.
- Odysseus addresses the crowd.

CONFLICT

Homer has Odysseus deliberately insult Antinous in response to his taunting in order to narrow the conflict to two men (l. 840).

SPEAKER

The omniscient narrator reports not only the characters' words, actions, and facial expressions, but also visceral feelings and private thoughts (ll. 853–854).

IMAGERY

Odysseus uses graphic language to insult Antinous and to make clear the extent of his inhospitality to the reader and the other suitors (ll. 841–845).

Odysseus in Disguise

On the following day Odysseus returns to his home. He is disguised as an old beggar again and asks the suitors for food. Antinous [an tin'ō əs], *a leader of the suitors, complains bitterly about the presence of the old beggar.*

But here Antinous broke in, shouting:
"God!
What evil wind blew in this pest?
Get over,
stand in the passage! Nudge my table, will you?
Egyptian whips are sweet
to what you'll come to here, you nosing rat,
making your pitch to everyone!
These men have bread to throw away on you
because it is not theirs. Who cares? Who spares
another's food, when he has more than plenty?"

With guile Odysseus drew away, then said:

"A pity that you have more looks than heart.
You'd grudge a pinch of salt from your own larder[5]
to your own handyman. You sit here, fat
on others' meat, and cannot bring yourself
to rummage out a crust of bread for me!"

Then anger made Antinous' heart beat hard,
and, glowering under his brows, he answered:
"Now!
You think you'll shuffle off and get away
after that impudence? Oh, no you don't!"

The stool he let fly hit the man's right shoulder
on the packed muscle under the shoulder blade—
like solid rock, for all the effect one saw.
Odysseus only shook his head, containing
thoughts of bloody work, as he walked on,
then sat, and dropped his loaded bag again
upon the doorsill. Facing the whole crowd
he said, and eyed them all:
"One word only,
my lords, and suitors of the famous queen.
One thing I have to say.
There is no pain, no burden for the heart

5 **larder:** storage area for food.

GUIDED READING

LITERAL QUESTION

1a. How does Odysseus treat Antinous? (He insults him and deliberately provokes him, drawing away "with guile.")

INFERENTIAL QUESTION

1b. Why do you think Odysseus does this? (He sees that Antinous is the most imposing suitor and his major opponent; he wants to have reason to attack him.)

when blows come to a man, and he defending
his own cattle—his own cows and lambs.
Here it was otherwise. Antinous
hit me for being driven on by hunger—
how many bitter seas men cross for hunger!
If beggars interest the gods, if there are Furies[6]
pent in the dark to avenge a poor man's wrong, then may
Antinous meet his death before his wedding day!"

Then said Eupeithes' son, Antinous:
"Enough.
Eat and be quiet where you are, or shamble elsewhere,
unless you want these lads to stop your mouth
pulling you by the heels, or hands and feet,
over the whole floor, till your back is peeled!"

But now the rest were mortified, and someone
spoke from the crowd of young bucks to rebuke him:

"A poor show, that—hitting this famished tramp—
bad business, if he happened to be a god.
You know they go in foreign guise, the gods do,
looking like strangers, turning up
in towns and settlements to keep an eye
on manners, good or bad."
But at this notion
Antinous only shrugged.
Telemachus,
after the blow his father bore, sat still
without a tear, though his heart felt the blow.
Slowly he shook his head from side to side,
containing murderous thoughts.
Penelope
on the higher level of her room had heard
the blow, and knew who gave it. Now she murmured:

"Would god you could be hit yourself, Antinous—
hit by Apollo's bowshot!"
And Eurynome,[7]
her housekeeper, put in:
"He and no other?
If all we pray for came to pass, not one
would live till dawn!"

6 **Furies:** three spirits who punished wrongdoers.

7 **Eurynome** [ū rin ′ə mē]

AT A GLANCE

- Odysseus calls on the gods to avenge Antinous' insult.
- Antinous is scornful.
- Another suitor reminds Antinous that the gods may come in disguise.
- Telemachus, Penelope, and her housekeeper are enraged at Antinous and wish him dead.

DRAMATIC IRONY

Odysseus expresses a truth that he has just experienced: A man defending his own home does not feel the blows. His words are ironic because readers know who he is, while the suitors do not (ll. 860–862).

MAIN IDEA

Odysseus calls on the gods and spirits to avenge him, asking that Antinous die before his wedding (ll. 866–868).

DIALOGUE

The phrasing of the man's objection is lively and informal. The explanations that interrupt the flow of his ideas dramatically show his distraction (ll. 876–881).

FORESHADOWING

Homer makes even the loyal housekeeper's wish meaningful; it will come true in the next segment.

GUIDED READING

LITERAL QUESTION

1a. Which characters wish Antinous and the other suitors were dead? (Odysseus, Telemachus, Penelope, and Eurynome)

INFERENTIAL QUESTION

1b. Why are their similar feelings important to the story? (They are united; Homer has revealed the loyalty of Telemachus, Penelope, and the housekeeper, and Odysseus has said he needed this.)

AT A GLANCE

- Penelope decries the way the beggar was treated.
- She criticizes Antinous.
- Penelope asks a loyal servant to bring the beggar to her.

DIALOGUE

Penelope despairs over the maliciousness and stinginess of her suitors in this lively speech. She uses a dramatic metaphor to describe Antinous (l. 896).

DRAMATIC IRONY

Homer shows the audience the faithful husband and wife, each yearning for, but not available to, the other (l. 902).

Her gentle mistress said:

"Oh, Nan, they are a bad lot; they intend
ruin for all of us; but Antinous
appears a blacker-hearted hound than any.
Here is a poor man come, a wanderer,
driven by want to beg his bread, and everyone
in hall gave bits, to cram his bag—only
Antinous threw a stool, and banged his shoulder!"

So she described it, sitting in her chamber
among her maids—while her true lord was eating.
Then she called in the forester and said:

"Go to that man on my behalf, Eumaeus,
and send him here, so I can greet and question him.
Abroad in the great world, he may have heard
rumors about Odysseus—may have known him!"

GUIDED READING

LITERAL QUESTION

1a. How does Penelope feel about the old stranger? (She feels sorry that he must beg for food and that he was abused by Antinous.)

INFERENTIAL QUESTION

1b. What do her feelings reveal about her? (She is sympathetic to the poor, traditional, and—like other Greeks—kind to strangers because they may be gods in disguise.)

Penelope interviews the old man in the hope of learning news of her husband.

"Friend, let me ask you first of all:
who are you, where do you come from, of what nation
and parents were you born?"
And he replied:

"My lady, never a man in the wide world
should have a fault to find with you. Your name
has gone out under heaven like the sweet
honor of some god-fearing king, who rules
in equity[8] over the strong: his back lands bear
both wheat and barley, fruit trees laden bright,
new lambs at lambing time—and the deep sea
gives great hauls of fish by his good strategy,
so that his folk fare well.
O my dear lady,
this being so, let it suffice to ask me
of other matters—not my blood, my homeland.
Do not enforce me to recall my pain.
My heart is sore; but I must not be found
sitting in tears here, in another's house:
it is not well forever to be grieving.
One of the maids might say—or you might think—
I had got maudlin over cups of wine."

And Penelope replied:
"Stranger, my looks,
my face, my carriage,[9] were soon lost or faded

8 **equity:** fairness.

9 **carriage:** manner of holding and moving the head and body.

AT A GLANCE

- Penelope asks the old man where he is from.
- He tells her that she is loved everywhere and that he cannot answer her question without weeping.
- Penelope replies that her beauty faded when her husband left.

SIMILE

Odysseus does not want Penelope to think he is finding fault with her, so he begins his speech by comparing her fame to the reputation of the ruler of a peaceful, productive land. Such extended comparisons are called Homeric similes.

DIALOGUE

Much of this page and of other pages in this segment are dominated by characters' speech. Dialogue allows readers to feel the scenes' immediacy.

GUIDED READING

LITERAL QUESTION

1a. What does Penelope ask the old man? (She asks who is he, where is he from, and who his parents are.)

INFERENTIAL QUESTION

1b. What is the real reason the old man does not want to answer these questions? (He does not yet want to reveal who he is.)

AT A GLANCE

- For three years Penelope promised to marry after she had weaved a shroud; each night she unraveled her work.
- Her suitors discovered this and forced her to finish.
- Her parents are urging her to marry.

MAIN IDEA

Penelope denies that she is a famous beauty and attributes her faded looks to the years of grief the gods sent her (l. 934).

CHARACTERIZATION

Even in her deception of the suitors, Penelope shows that she is a traditional wife, sensitive to customs and eager to maintain a good reputation (ll. 951–952).

PARALLELISM

Homer uses parallel phrases to emphasize Penelope's sense of the time she spent deceiving the suitors—"long months," "long days"—as well as her dwindling choices—"I had no choice," "I have no strength" (ll. 958, 961, 963).

when the Achaeans crossed the sea to Troy,
Odysseus my lord among the rest.
If he returned, if he were here to care for me,
I might be happily renowned!
But grief instead heaven sent me—years of pain.
Sons of the noblest families on the islands,
Dulichium, Same, wooded Zacynthus,
with native Ithacans, are here to court me,
against my wish; and they consume this house.
Can I give proper heed to guest or suppliant
or herald on the realm's affairs?
How could I?
wasted with longing for Odysseus, while here
they press for marriage.
Ruses served my turn
to draw the time out—first a close-grained web
I had the happy thought to set up weaving
on my big loom in hall. I said, that day:

'Young men—my suitors, now my lord is dead,
let me finish my weaving before I marry,
or else my thread will have been spun in vain.
It is a shroud I weave for Lord Laertes
when cold Death comes to lay him on his bier.[10]
The country wives would hold me in dishonor
if he, with all his fortune, lay unshrouded.'
I reached their hearts that way, and they agreed.
So every day I wove on the great loom,
but every night by torchlight I unwove it;
and so for three years I deceived the Achaeans.
But when the seasons brought a fourth year on,
as long months waned, and the long days were spent,
through imprudent folly in the slinking maids
they caught me—clamored up to me at night;
I had no choice then but to finish it.
And now, as matters stand at last,
I have no strength left to evade a marriage,
cannot find any further way; my parents
urge it upon me, and my son
will not stand by while they eat up his property.
He comprehends it, being a man full-grown,
able to oversee the kind of house
Zeus would endow with honor."

10 **bier** [bēr]: stand on which a corpse is displayed.

GUIDED READING

LITERAL QUESTIONS

1a. Which people are pressing Penelope to marry? (the suitors and her parents)

2a. What does Penelope do in response to these pressures? (She resists; she deceives her suitors and delays the decision for three years.)

INFERENTIAL QUESTIONS

1b. Why do you think Penelope's parents want her to marry? (Answers may suggest that they might feel she would be happier married; they might feel marriage is appropriate for a woman of her age and status.)

2b. What does this show about her character? (She is strong-willed, loyal, and clever.)

The Test of the Bow

The old man tells Penelope that he has met Odysseus and describes his years of hardship and wandering. Penelope tells the old man of her dream in which Odysseus returns to slay the suitors. He assures her that her dream is true. Penelope tells the beggar about her idea for a contest to decide whom she will marry. He assures her that Odysseus will be home before the contest is over. Penelope then searches for Odysseus' long unused bow, which she will need for the competition.

Now the queen reached the storeroom door and halted.
Here was an oaken sill, cut long ago
and sanded clean and bedded true. Foursquare[11]
the doorjambs[12] and the shining doors were set
by the careful builder. Penelope untied the strap
around the curving handle, pushed her hook
into the slit, aimed at the bolts inside
and shot them back. Then came a rasping sound
as those bright doors the key had sprung gave way—
a bellow like a bull's vaunt in a meadow—
followed by her light footfall entering
over the plank floor. Herb-scented robes
lay there in chests, but the lady's milkwhite arms
went up to lift the bow down from a peg
in its own polished bowcase.
                                        Now Penelope
sank down, holding the weapon on her knees,
and drew her husband's great bow out, and sobbed
and bit her lip and let the salt tears flow.
Then back she went to face the crowded hall
tremendous bow in hand, and on her shoulder hung
the quiver spiked with coughing death. Behind her
maids bore a basket full of axeheads, bronze
and iron implements for the master's game.
Thus in her beauty she approached the suitors,
and near a pillar of the solid roof
she paused, her shining veil across her cheeks,
her maids on either hand and still,
then spoke to the banqueters:
                                        "My lords, hear me:
suitors indeed, you commandeered this house
to feast and drink in, day and night, my husband
being long gone, long out of mind. You found
no justification for yourselves—none

11 **Foursquare:** firmly.

12 **doorjambs:** vertical boards that form the sides of a doorway.

AT A GLANCE

- Penelope tells the old man about her idea for a contest to decide whom she will marry.
- She goes to the storeroom for Odysseus' longbow.
- She returns with the bow to address the feasting suitors.

NARRATION

Homer shifts from dialogue to narration to allow the reader to watch the beautiful, grieving queen enter the storeroom and find her husband's bow for the contest she dreads (ll. 970–987).

SETTING

This detailed description of the shining doors and the storeroom behind them creates an atmosphere of wealth and order. Note Homer's rich use of sensuous imagery, his descriptions of textures, shapes, colors, and sounds (ll. 970–984).

IMAGERY

Homer's image for the sharp tips of the arrows is especially vivid; they are "spiked with coughing death" (l. 990).

CHARACTERIZATION

Penelope has regained her composure; attended by her maids, she is calm and beautiful (ll. 990, 993–996).

GUIDED READING

LITERAL QUESTIONS

1a. What object does Penelope need for the contest? (her husband's bow)

2a. How does she react to holding it? (Penelope weeps.)

INFERENTIAL QUESTIONS

1b. Why do you think Homer described Penelope's entrance to the storeroom in such detail? (possible answers: to build suspense, to make the event more important, to emphasize the solidity of Odysseus' home and the value of his goods)

2b. Why do you think she reacts this way? (This object, so closely associated with her husband, may intensify her feelings of grief and loss.)

AT A GLANCE

- Penelope offers to marry the man who sends an arrow through twelve iron axes.
- When the suitors fail to bend the bow, the old beggar asks to try.
- Odysseus easily strings the bow.
- The suitors are amazed; Zeus thunders overhead.

DIALOGUE

The suitors' asides reflect their social backgrounds; the men scorn what they assume is the stranger's poverty and ignorance (ll. 1016–1020).

SIMILE

Homer compares the great warrior's handling of his powerful bow to a harpist's delicate handling of his instrument. The comparison is extended when Odysseus plucks the bowstring to make it sing (ll. 1021–1030).

except your lust to marry me. Stand up, then:
we now declare a contest for that prize.
Here is my lord Odysseus' hunting bow.
Bend and string it if you can. Who sends an arrow
through iron axe-helve sockets,[13] twelve in line?
I join my life with his, and leave this place, my home,
my rich and beautiful bridal house, forever
to be remembered, though I dream it only."

None of the suitors is able to bend the bow. When the old beggar asks to try, the suitors protest. Telemachus and Penelope, however, insist that he be given a chance.

And Odysseus took his time,
turning the bow, tapping it, every inch,
for borings that termites might have made
while the master of the weapon was abroad.
The suitors were now watching him, and some
jested among themselves:
"A bow lover!"
"Dealer in old bows!"
"Maybe he has one like it
at home!"
"Or has an itch to make one for himself."

"See how he handles it, the sly old buzzard!"

And one disdainful suitor added this:

"May his fortune grow an inch for every inch he bends it!"

But the man skilled in all ways of contending,
satisfied by the great bow's look and heft,
like a musician, like a harper, when
with quiet hand upon his instrument
he draws between his thumb and forefinger
a sweet new string upon a peg: so effortlessly
Odysseus in one motion strung the bow.
Then slid his right hand down the cord and plucked it,
so the taut gut vibrating hummed and sang
a swallow's note.
In the hushed hall it smote the suitors
and all their faces changed. Then Zeus thundered
overhead, one loud crack for a sign.

13 **axe-helve sockets:** The axe heads were fashioned with holes in their centers through which an arrow could pass.

GUIDED READING

LITERAL QUESTION

1a. What are the terms of the contest, and what is the prize that Penelope offers? (Whoever can shoot an arrow through the center of twelve iron axe heads can marry Penelope.)

INFERENTIAL QUESTION

1b. In what ways is this like a contest in a fairy tale? (Answers should suggest that brides are often prizes, contestants are often challenged to perform seemingly impossible tasks, and the winner is often the rightful owner of an object involved in the contest.)

And Odysseus laughed within him that the son
of crooked-minded Cronus had flung that omen down.
He picked one ready arrow from his table
where it lay bare: the rest were waiting still
in the quiver for the young men's turn to come.
He nocked[14] it, let it rest across the handgrip,
and drew the string and grooved butt of the arrow,
aiming from where he sat upon the stool.
Now flashed
arrow from twanging bow clean as a whistle
through every socket ring, and grazed not one,
to thud with heavy brazen head beyond.
Then quietly
Odysseus said:
"Telemachus, the stranger
you welcomed in your hall has not disgraced you.
I did not miss, neither did I take all day
stringing the bow. My hand and eye are sound,
not so contemptible as the young men say.
The hour has come to cook their lordships' mutton—
supper by daylight. Other amusements later,
with song and harping that adorn a feast."

He dropped his eyes and nodded, and the prince
Telemachus, true son of King Odysseus,
belted his sword on, clapped hand to his spear,
and with a clink and glitter of keen bronze
stood by his chair, in the forefront near his father.

14 **nocked:** fit the notch at the end of the arrow onto the string of the bow.

AT A GLANCE

- Odysseus fires an arrow clean through the axe heads.
- He tells Telemachus that the time has come "to cook their lordships' mutton."
- Telemachus dons his sword and stands by his father.

ALLITERATION/ONOMATOPOEIA

This vivid description of the arrow flashing through the axe heads zings with *s* and *z* sounds and resounds with onomatopoetic words like *twanging* and *thud* (ll. 1040–1043).

MAIN IDEA

Odysseus announces that the suitors will get what they deserve. His metaphor is aptly ironic because the men have been feasting on goods from his larder (ll. 1049–1051).

IMAGERY

The segment ends with the narrator's description of the hero and his son reunited and prepared to fight. Readers see the men's gestures, hear the "clink" and see the "glitter" of their ominous weapons (ll. 1052–1056).

REFLECTING ON THE FIRST SEGMENT

What are Odysseus' and Penelope's greatest strengths? (Answers may suggest that Odysseus and Penelope are both clever strategists; they are brave, persistent, and loyal; they conduct themselves honorably and nobly.)

GUIDED READING

LITERAL QUESTIONS

1a. What is Odysseus' secret reaction to the thunderclap? (He is pleased; he laughs "within him.")

2a. What happens after Odysseus finishes speaking and nods? (Telemachus belts on his sword, takes spear in hand, and stands near his father.)

INFERENTIAL QUESTIONS

1b. Why do you think Odysseus is pleased to hear Zeus's thunder? (He feels Zeus is now on his side and is glad to have his support.)

2b. What do you think will happen next? (Answers should suggest that Odysseus and his son will fight the suitors.)

STUDY QUESTIONS

1. warns him of suitors; disguises him as beggar; melts disguise for Telemachus
2. count suitors; hide weapons; identify loyal and disloyal servants
3. ▪ look at his act as impious
   ▪ Telemachus wishes Apollo would strike Antinous.
   ▪ Penelope says he is the worst of the suitors.
4. weaves shroud for Laertes, unweaves it at night; promises to choose when shroud is finished
5. Disloyal servants reveal trick; suitors become insistent; parents urge it.
6. ▪ She will marry one who can string bow and put arrow through twelve axe socket-rings.
   ▪ He strings bow so that it hums, performs feat.
7. He is cautious, a loving son.
8. He respects the gods.
9. She is resourceful, courageous, loyal.
10. He must remain in disguise until he defeats suitors.
11. ▪ realistic: Telemachus' wonder and joy
    ▪ fantasy: Odysseus' ability to change appearance; Athena's help

LITERARY FOCUS

Flashback

1. Part One
2. Different points of view give variety and drama to narrative.

Epithet

- *Athena, Hope of Soldiers:* protects warriors
- *Zeus, All-Provident:* supreme god
- *god-fearing king:* piety
- *man skilled in all ways of contending:* Odysseus' resourcefulness

STUDY QUESTIONS

Recalling

1. Find three ways in which the goddess Athena helps Odysseus in this section.
2. What three steps must Telemachus take as part of Odysseus' plan for revenge against the suitors?
3. When Antinous strikes the disguised Odysseus, what is the reaction of the other suitors? Of Telemachus? Of Penelope?
4. Explain how Penelope put off making a decision about choosing a suitor.
5. Why does Penelope finally agree to choose a husband?
6. What is Penelope's challenge to the suitors? Describe Odysseus' use of his old bow.

Interpreting

7. What do we learn of Telemachus' personality from his first meeting with Odysseus?
8. Odysseus says to Telemachus, "It is no hard thing for the gods of heaven / to glorify a man or bring him low." What does this statement reveal about Odysseus?
9. Explain how Penelope's actions show that she is well suited to be the wife of the crafty Odysseus.
10. In what sense is Odysseus still wandering even though he has arrived at Ithaca?

Extending

11. Explain how the reunion of Odysseus and Telemachus contains elements of fantasy as well as realistic human behavior.

LITERARY FOCUS

Flashback

A **flashback** is a scene in a narrative that breaks the normal time sequence of the plot to narrate events that happened earlier in time. For example, a movie uses a flashback when a character whom we meet as an adult relives a childhood experience. Epic poems usually begin **in medias res** [in mā′dē əs rās′], after much of the action has already happened. *In medias res* is a Latin term meaning "in the middle of things." Therefore, in an epic a flashback is usually necessary to provide the reader with background information.

Thinking About Flashback

1. What part of the *Odyssey* is a flashback?
2. Explain why the story switches from first-person point of view (see page 85) to third-person point of view (see page 109) when the flashback ends.

The Epithet

An **epithet** is a descriptive word or phrase attached to the name of a person or thing. An epithet usually stresses a particular characteristic of the subject: "Dawn *with fingertips of rose*," "*crafty* Odysseus," "Calypso, *loveliest of the goddesses*." Epithets were used often in early epic poems to lengthen lines or to make them more musical.

Thinking About the Epithet

■ Locate four epithets in this section (lines 734–1056) of the *Odyssey.* What characteristic of the person or thing is being stressed in each? (For example, "Helios, *lord of high noon*" tells us that Helios is god of the sun.)

Odysseus Against the Suitors

Suddenly Odysseus sheds his disguise and warns the suitors that their game is over. His first arrow kills Antinous, the suitor who had abused him earlier. The other suitors are outraged and look in vain for the weapons that Telemachus has hidden. Still not recognizing Odysseus, they condemn and threaten the stranger in their midst. Then Odysseus identifies himself:

"You yellow dogs, you thought I'd never make it
home from the land of Troy. You took my house
to plunder. . . .
You dared
bid for my wife while I was still alive.
Contempt was all you had for the gods who rule wide heaven,
contempt for what men say of you hereafter.
Your last hour has come. You die in blood."

As they all took this in, sickly green fear
pulled at their entrails, and their eyes flickered
looking for some hatch or hideaway from death.
Eurymachus[1] alone could speak. He said:

"If you are Odysseus of Ithaca come back,
all that you say these men have done is true.
Rash actions, many here, more in the countryside.
But here he lies, the man who caused them all.
Antinous was the ringleader, he whipped us on
to do these things. He cared less for a marriage
than for the power Cronion has denied him
as king of Ithaca. For that
he tried to trap your son and would have killed him.
He is dead now and has his portion. Spare
your own people. As for ourselves, we'll make
restitution of wine and meat consumed,
and add, each one, a tithe of twenty oxen
with gifts of bronze and gold to warm your heart.
Meanwhile we cannot blame you for your anger."

Odysseus glowered under his black brows
and said:
"Not for the whole treasure of your fathers,
all you enjoy, lands, flocks, or any gold
put up by others, would I hold my hand.

1 **Eurymachus** [ū ri'mə kəs]

AT A GLANCE

- Odysseus sheds his disguise and kills Antinous.
- He tells the other suitors they have treated him dishonorably.
- One suitor urges Odysseus' forgiveness; Odysseus refuses.

LITERARY OPTIONS

- Homeric simile
- imagery
- characterization

THEMATIC OPTIONS

- achieving justice at home
- the gods' power
- revealing the truth

SPEAKER

The story of Odysseus' struggle to achieve peace at home continues in the third person. An omniscient narrator provides details about the inner thoughts and feelings of the characters, while extensive dialogue provides immediacy and drama (l. 1064).

PARALLELISM

Homer uses parallelism to emphasize the suitors' most unforgivable crimes: their contempt for the gods and for their own reputations (ll. 1061–1062).

IMAGERY

Homer describes the suitors' reactions in visual and visceral terms: "sickly green fear pulled at their entrails" (ll. 1064–1065).

MAIN IDEA

Odysseus' concept of justice is absolute; he must destroy all of the contemptuous suitors. Nothing will stay his hand (ll. 1084–1086).

GUIDED READING

LITERAL QUESTION

1a. What does Eurymachus say the suitors will do for Odysseus? (He says they will restore the food and wine they consumed and give Odysseus additional gifts of oxen, bronze, and gold.)

INFERENTIAL QUESTION

1b. Why do you think the suitors' offer has no effect on Odysseus' desire for revenge? (He is not concerned with the restitution of his goods; the suitors have offended Odysseus' honor and the honor of the gods.)

AT A GLANCE

- With his son, servants, and Athena's aid, Odysseus slays the suitors.
- He contemplates the slaughter.

CHARACTERIZATION

Homer uses a small physical detail, Odysseus' searching eyes, to suggest the hero's fierce determination to be sure all the suitors are dead (ll. 1091–1093).

IMAGERY

In the image of "death's black fury," Homer gives color to an emotional state (l. 1093).

HOMERIC SIMILE

Homer reduces the suitors' final agonies to the twitching of dying fish to assure that Odysseus maintains the reader's sympathy (ll. 1095–1099).

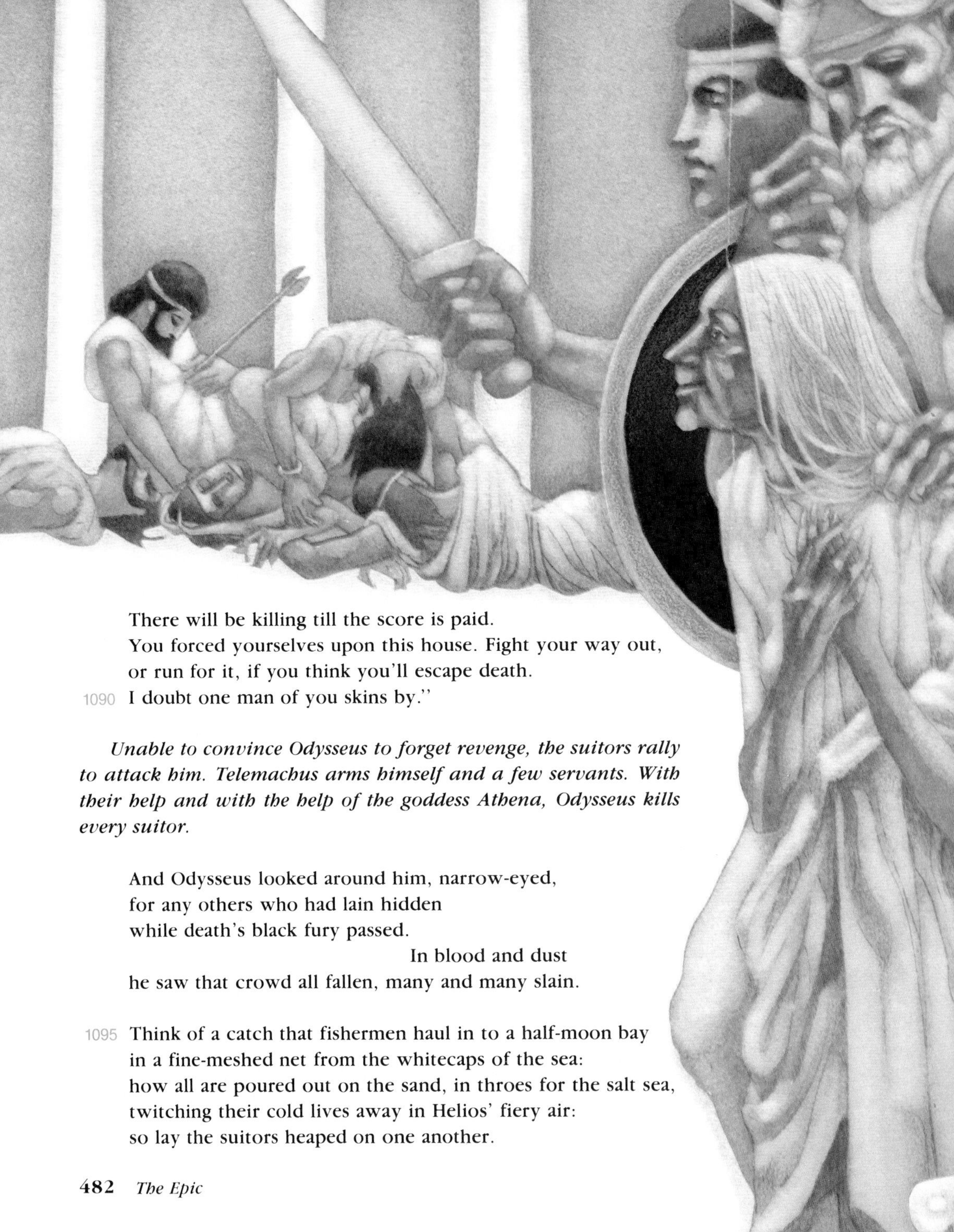

There will be killing till the score is paid.
You forced yourselves upon this house. Fight your way out,
or run for it, if you think you'll escape death.
I doubt one man of you skins by."

Unable to convince Odysseus to forget revenge, the suitors rally to attack him. Telemachus arms himself and a few servants. With their help and with the help of the goddess Athena, Odysseus kills every suitor.

And Odysseus looked around him, narrow-eyed,
for any others who had lain hidden
while death's black fury passed.
                                        In blood and dust
he saw that crowd all fallen, many and many slain.

Think of a catch that fishermen haul in to a half-moon bay
in a fine-meshed net from the whitecaps of the sea:
how all are poured out on the sand, in throes for the salt sea,
twitching their cold lives away in Helios' fiery air:
so lay the suitors heaped on one another.

GUIDED READING

LITERAL QUESTION

1a. What does Odysseus see when his murderous fury passes? (the crowd of dying suitors)

INFERENTIAL QUESTION

1b. Why do you think Homer compares the dying suitors to fish? (to emphasize the number of men killed and their powerlessness)

Odysseus at length said to his son:

"Go tell old Nurse I'll have a word with her." . . .

Telemachus knocked at the women's door and called:

"Eurycleia,[2] come out here! Move, old woman . . . .
Jump, my father is here and wants to see you."

2 **Eurycleia** [ū ri klē′yə]

His call brought no reply, only the doors
were opened, and she came. Telemachus
led her forward . . . .
As she gazed
from all the corpses to the bloody man
she raised her head to cry over his triumph,
but felt his grip upon her, checking her.
Said the great soldier then:
"Rejoice
inwardly. No crowing aloud, old woman.
To glory over slain men is no piety.
Destiny and the gods' will vanquished these,
and their own hardness. They respected no one,
good or bad, who came their way.
For this, and folly, a bad end befell them."

AT A GLANCE

- Odysseus sends Telemachus to find the family nurse.
- Odysseus warns her not to celebrate.

CHARACTERIZATION

Homer reveals Telemachus' imperious attitudes through his speech to the nurse. Though his manner may offend some readers, it might also be considered an indication of his growth and readiness to assume leadership (ll. 1103–1104).

EPITHET

Homer uses two very different epithets to describe Odysseus: He is both "the bloody man" and "the great soldier." Readers are urged to see him as a noble figure in the midst of carnage (ll. 1108, 1111).

THEME

Odysseus wants no credit and says that the men's own hardness, lack of respect, and folly made them destined to die. It was the gods' will (ll. 1114–1117).

GUIDED READING

LITERAL QUESTION

1a. With whom does Odysseus want to talk after the slaughter? (the old family nurse, Eurycleia)

INFERENTIAL QUESTION

1b. How are differences in Telemachus' and Odysseus' characters revealed in their treatment of the nurse? (The son is arrogant and wields his status over her; Odysseus is humble and gives the gods all credit.)

AT A GLANCE

- Penelope tests Odysseus to see if he is truly her husband.
- She tells the nurse to make up his bed outside the bedchamber.
- He proves his identity by revealing he knows how the bed was built.

EPITHET

Odysseus and Penelope call each other "strange man" and "strange woman." These epithets indicate they are uneasy with each other (ll. 1118, 1126).

THEME

Odysseus marvels that Penelope has held herself back from him and attributes her hardness and "iron heart" to the gods (l. 1119–1125).

CHARACTERIZATION

Penelope's speech reveals that she is a traditional wife: She assures the heroic stranger that neither her own pride nor scorn for him keeps her aloof (ll. 1126–1128).

CHARACTERIZATION

Odysseus rages when his wife suggests the bed be moved out of their bedroom, as if she has given up on their marriage (ll. 1135–1138).

A Final Test

Because it has been twenty years since she has seen Odysseus, Penelope does not believe that this man is actually her husband. She plans to test him. Odysseus understands her reluctance to believe but finally says to her:

"Strange woman,
the immortals of Olympus[3] made you hard,
harder than any. Who else in the world
would keep aloof as you do from her husband
if he returned to her from years of trouble,
cast on his own land in the twentieth year?

Nurse, make up a bed for me to sleep on.
Her heart is iron in her breast."
Penelope
spoke to Odysseus now. She said:
"Strange man,
if man you are . . . This is no pride on my part
nor scorn for you—not even wonder, merely.
I know so well how you—how he—appeared
boarding the ship for Troy. But all the same . . .

Make up his bed for him, Eurycleia.
Place it outside the bedchamber my lord
built with his own hands. Pile the big bed
with fleeces, rugs, and sheets of purest linen."

With this she tried him to the breaking point,
and he turned on her in a flash raging:

"Woman, by heaven you've stung me now!
Who dared to move my bed?
No builder had the skill for that—unless
a god came down to turn the trick. No mortal
in his best days could budge it with a crowbar.
There is our pact and pledge, our secret sign,
built into that bed—my handiwork
and no one else's!
An old trunk of olive
grew like a pillar on the building plot,
and I laid out our bedroom round that tree,
lined up the stone walls, built the walls and roof,
gave it a doorway and smooth-fitting doors.

3 **Olympus** [ō lim′pəs]: in northeastern Greece a mountain that was believed to be the home of the gods.

GUIDED READING

LITERAL QUESTION

1a. What epithets do Odysseus and Penelope use to describe each other? ("strange woman" and "strange man")

INFERENTIAL QUESTION

1b. What different meaning does the word *strange* have for each character? (Odysseus means Penelope's behavior is extraordinary; Penelope is not sure who he really is.)

Then I lopped off the silvery leaves and branches,
hewed and shaped that stump from the roots up
into a bedpost, drilled it, let it serve
as model for the rest. I planed them all,
inlaid them all with silver, gold and ivory,
and stretched a bed between—a pliant web
of oxhide thongs dyed crimson.
There's our sign!
I know no more. Could someone else's hand
have sawn that trunk and dragged the frame away?"

Their secret! as she heard it told, her knees
grew tremulous and weak, her heart failed her.
With eyes brimming tears she ran to him,
throwing her arms around his neck, and kissed him,
murmuring:
"Do not rage at me, Odysseus!
No one ever matched your caution! Think
what difficulty the gods gave: they denied us
life together in our prime and flowering years,
kept us from crossing into age together.
Forgive me, don't be angry. I could not
welcome you with love on sight! I armed myself
long ago against the frauds of men,
imposters who might come—and all those many
whose underhanded ways bring evil on!. . .

AT A GLANCE

- Odysseus tells how he built the bed.
- Penelope sees that the man is her husband; she explains her caution.

MAIN IDEA

Odysseus' knowledge of the way the marriage bed was built and rooted in the earth, and of the symbolic meaning it had for him and Penelope, proves his identity (ll. 1144–1157).

CHARACTERIZATION

Penelope tells Odysseus not to be angry with her, that he is even more cautious than she has been. Then she movingly enumerates the reasons they have had to protect themselves (ll. 1162–1171).

IMAGERY

Two simple images suggest all that the couple has missed: "life together in our prime and flowering years," enjoyment of each other's youthful beauty, and "crossing into age together" (ll. 1165–1166).

GUIDED READING

LITERAL QUESTION

1a. What reason does Penelope give for her caution? (She says she hardened herself to survive the difficulties the gods presented and the frauds of men.)

INFERENTIAL QUESTION

1b. How are Penelope and Odysseus alike? (Possible answers include that both are cautious, shrewd, strong-minded, loyal, respectful of the gods; both test people and meet great personal challenges.)

HOMERIC SIMILE

Homer compares Odysseus' longing for Penelope to the intense desire for land that a survivor of a sunken ship feels. This extended simile is particularly apt in its recollection of some of Odysseus' earlier trials (ll. 1178–1186).

REFLECTING ON THE SECOND SEGMENT

In what ways do Odysseus and Penelope seem larger than life in this segment? (Both are smart, powerful, demanding, and totally unambivalent; their actions are absolute and show great physical strength and moral fortitude.)

STUDY QUESTIONS

1. promises to pay for meat and wine suitors consumed; offers twenty oxen; apologizes for bad behavior
2. tells nurse to move bed; only he could know it is rooted to floor; Odysseus describes bed's construction; Penelope is convinced
3. There have been many impostors.
4. - *courage:* must defeat numerous foes
   - *cleverness:* hiding weapons reduces odds, outsmarts suitors
5. respects life
6. She is resourceful, independent.
7. He would approve.
8. loses men; is brought home in ship by strangers; must fight to regain home, family
9. Answers will vary.

But here and now, what sign could be so clear
as this of our own bed?
No other man has ever laid eyes on it—
only my own slave, Actoris, that my father
sent with me as a gift—she kept our door.
You make my stiff heart know that I am yours."

Now from his breast into his eyes the ache
of longing mounted, and he wept at last,
his dear wife, clear and faithful, in his arms,
longed for as the sunwarmed earth is longed for by a swimmer
spent in rough water where his ship went down
under Poseidon's blows, gale winds and tons of sea.
Few men can keep alive through a big surf
to crawl, clotted with brine, on kindly beaches
in joy, in joy, knowing the abyss behind:
and so she too rejoiced, her gaze upon her husband,
her white arms round him pressed as though forever.

On the next day with Telemachus at his side, Odysseus visits his father, Laertes. When the relatives of the slain suitors arrive and demand revenge, the goddess Athena appears to command that peace be restored. Odysseus finally rejoins his family in peace.

STUDY QUESTIONS

Recalling

1. Give two ways in which Eurymachus tries to make peace with Odysseus.
2. Explain how Penelope tests Odysseus. What is the result of the test?
3. What reasons does Penelope give for her reluctance to believe that Odysseus has returned?

Interpreting

4. Explain how Odysseus' revenge against the suitors shows both his courage and his cleverness.
5. What do we learn about Odysseus' personality when he tells the nurse not to rejoice at the deaths of the suitors?
6. Explain what is revealed about Penelope's personality by her test of Odysseus.
7. What do you think would be Odysseus' opinion of Penelope's test of him?
8. Praying to Poseidon for revenge, the Cyclops cried, "Let him lose all companions, and return / under strange sail to bitter days at home." In what ways has the Cyclops' prayer been answered?

Extending

9. After descriptions of Odysseus' many adventures, is the story of his return home satisfying or disappointing? Explain your answer.

VIEWPOINT

One reason for the classic status of the *Odyssey* is that its basic themes apply to people of any time or place. One writer attempted to identify those themes:

Love and justice are the themes of the poem, they are embodied in Odysseus as father and king. . . .

—H. Clark, *The Art of the Odyssey*

■ Explain how justice and love of family, home, and country are portrayed in the *Odyssey.*

LITERARY FOCUS

Homeric Simile

A **simile** is an expression that uses *like* or *as* to compare two seemingly unlike things. A **Homeric simile,** also called **epic simile,** is longer than a conventional simile because it extends the comparison with a more lengthy description. For example, in the following lines a Homeric simile describes Odysseus as he prepares to shoot his bow:

like a musician, like a harper, when
with quiet hand upon his instrument
he draws between his thumb and forefinger
a sweet new string upon a peg: so effortlessly
Odysseus in one motion strung the bow.
Then slid his right hand down the cord and plucked it,
so the taut gut vibrating hummed and sang
a swallow's note.

A conventional simile might have said, "Odysseus prepared the bow like a musician at his harp." The added details of the Homeric simile emphasize the skill and care with which Odysseus used his bow.

Thinking About the Homeric Simile

■ Find two Homeric similes in this last segment of the *Odyssey*. For each simile do the following: (a) Explain what things are being compared, and (b) explain what details expand the comparison into a Homeric simile.

VOCABULARY

Word Origins

The epic poetry of Homer is so much a part of Western culture that the names of characters and settings are somehow familiar. Allusions to the *Odyssey* are common in our literature. An **allusion** is a reference in a work of literature to a character, place, or situation from another work of literature, music, or art. For example, *Ithaca* often represents the ideal of home; *Penelope* is a name that is forever linked with the virtue of fidelity. Some proper names from Homer have even entered our vocabulary. For example, the name of Hector, a ferocious fighter in the *Iliad,* has become a verb, *to hector,* "to bully" or "to browbeat." In a segment of the *Odyssey* that is not reproduced here, the tutor of the young Telemachus is *Mentor,* a name that has come to mean "teacher" or "coach."

1. What are the current meanings of the words *siren* and *odyssey?* Explain how these definitions might have developed from the proper names in the *Odyssey.*
2. Many cities and towns in America are named for places that are settings in the *Odyssey.* Look up the following names in the index of an atlas or in a geographical dictionary. For each name list the American states that contain a city or town with that name.

   Athens Ithaca Troy

COMPOSITION

Writing About the Epic Hero

■ Each episode of the *Odyssey* pits the strength and cleverness of its hero against some foe. The opponent is (a) a human foe, (b) a natural foe, or (c) a superhuman foe. For each type of opponent, do the following: (1) Select an episode from the *Odyssey* in which Odysseus battles that type of opponent, and (2) discuss the ways in which Odysseus shows the characteristics of the epic hero in fighting that opponent. Characteristics you may consider are strength, courage, cleverness, and honesty.

Writing a Biographical Sketch

■ Imagine that twenty years have passed since Odysseus has returned to his family. Write a biographical sketch of Odysseus telling what has happened to him and to his family during the past twenty years. You may wish to consider the following: (a) Has Odysseus traveled to any new adventures? (b) Has Telemachus become as famous as his father? (c) Has Odysseus found peace?

VIEWPOINT

Odysseus' desire to return home; faith of Penelope, Telemachus; defeat of suitors; reunion of family

LITERARY FOCUS

- Lines 1095–99: (a) dying suitors, dying fish; (b) details of bay, descriptions of dying fish
- Lines 1178–88: (a) Odysseus' longing for Penelope, swimmer's longing for dry land; (b) details of rough seas, swimmer's exhaustion

VOCABULARY

1. - siren: woman who uses charm to entice men, device that produces warning signal; Sirens enticed sailors; song contains danger
   - odyssey: extended journey; reflects Odysseus' wanderings
2. *Athens:* Alabama, Georgia, Texas, Illinois, Louisiana, Maine, Ohio, New York, Pennsylvania, West Virginia, Wisconsin, Tennessee; *Ithaca:* Michigan, New York; *Troy:* Alabama, Idaho, Indiana, Kansas, Michigan, Missouri, Montana, North Carolina, New Hampshire, New York, Ohio, Oregon, Pennsylvania, South Carolina, Tennessee, Texas, Vermont

COMPOSITION: GUIDELINES FOR EVALUATION

WRITING ABOUT THE EPIC HERO

Objective

To analyze qualities of the epic hero revealed in contests against various types of foes

Guidelines for Evaluation

- suggested length: five paragraphs
- should define qualities of the epic hero
- should contain examples of each type of foe
- should show how each foe brings out qualities of the epic hero

WRITING A BIOGRAPHICAL SKETCH

Objective

To write a biographical sketch based on the characters of Odysseus and Telemachus

Guidelines for Evaluation

- suggested length: three paragraphs
- should contain details of character's later lives in Ithaca
- should be a logical extension of characters and conditions at end of poem

ACTIVE READING

Discovering Patterns

Throughout the *Odyssey* Homer harkens back to central images and themes that unify the narrative. You may wish to assign the reading of "Discovering Patterns" either *before* or *after* students have read the epic.

Before reading the *Odyssey*, have the invocation to the muse (page 442) read aloud in class, and then assign this section. All of the recurring images that are traced in "Discovering Patterns" first appear in the invocation. Once students have read both and understand the importance of such patterns, ask them to notice all further examples as they read the remainder of the epic. You may wish to have them list in their notebooks the examples that they find.

After reading the *Odyssey*, have students make their own lists of recurring images from the poem. Then assign this section, and ask students to compare their patterns and examples with those in the text.

ACTIVE READING

Discovering Patterns

One of the best clues to the meaning of a work of literature is the *pattern of repetition* we discover as we read. We notice that certain words, images, and themes keep recurring time after time. Such repetitions are not accidental. The patterns they form are often beautiful and are always significant.

Some of the words, images, and themes that recur frequently throughout the *Odyssey* are *Troy, wandering, the sea, the gods,* and *home* or *return*. Together, they form a unified pattern, the shape and feeling of this great story. Long after we have forgotten many of the details of the *Odyssey,* we remember the overall impression formed by these repetitions.

Troy. The sound of *Troy* rings throughout the poem. The *Odyssey* is part of a much larger story about how the Trojan War began, about the war itself, about all the heroes who fought, and about the problems they faced when the war was over. The Trojan War is over, yet it still remains an active force within the *Odyssey*. The violence and separation of the war form a contrast to the peace and homecoming that Odysseus seeks.

Wandering. Homer reminds us often that Odysseus is a wanderer. A sense of restlessness pervades the story. The adventures of Odysseus, fantastic and exciting as they are, are part of a larger pattern. They are all obstacles to Odysseus, all challenges to his famous cleverness and skill, all designed to keep him circling and wandering against his will.

The Sea. Water is everywhere in this story. Sometimes the sea is a place of danger, sometimes a place of hope and safety (as when Odysseus escapes from the Cyclops and other dangers he encounters when he touches land).

The Gods. They appear and disappear suddenly. They come in disguises to the world of men and women. They are actors in this story and take sides in human struggles. We remember especially Poseidon, god of the sea, who does everything he can to hinder the hero's safe journey home; and Athena, who is especially fond of the clever Odysseus, interceding with Zeus to aid him on his way.

Home. Through all his wanderings, his ten years of sailing and adventuring, Odysseus longs to return home. Yet even when he returns to Ithaca, he still must fight for his kingship and for recognition as son and husband. The final section of the *Odyssey* is called the *nostos,* which means "return home." (It is related to our word *nostalgia*.)

We have, then, a major pattern here, for these words thread themselves through the story in hundreds of repetitions. It is a pattern of *going forth* into the world of action and of *coming home* to safety and rest. In a sense it is a pattern very deep in all our lives. The *Odyssey* is the story of a hero who leaves his home to fight in the Trojan War, wanders on a long sea-journey, is helped and hindered by the gods, and finally returns home. Look again at the first thirteen lines of the poem. You will find all of these often-repeated topics mentioned for the first time within these thirteen opening lines.

REVIEW: THE EPIC

Guide for Studying the Epic

Epic poetry is not a very common form of writing, but many works from different periods of time and many media adopt themes, characters, and techniques from the epic. Review the following questions when you read an epic or epic-related work. The questions will help you to see the similarities among the few genuine epics and to recognize themes and techniques in other works.

1. What, if anything, does the poet ask for in the **invocation to the muse?** What hints does the invocation provide about the following epic?
2. What part of the story, if any, is told in **flashback?**
3. What superhuman qualities does the **epic hero** possess?
4. Which goals or virtues of an entire nation or large body of people does the hero represent?
5. What is the hero's fate? Does the hero try to resist fate in a **person-against-fate conflict**? What forces determine this fate?
6. Do supernatural forces work for or against the hero?
7. What **epithets,** descriptive words or phrases, are attached to the names of people or things?
8. What **Homeric** or **epic similes** are used to describe people or things?
9. In what ways is the language of the piece elevated?

REVIEW

Refer to the review in the text, Guide for Studying the Epic. The questions can be used by students to review their reading of the *Odyssey*. They might also use the questions to aid their comprehension as they read other examples of the epic form. The epic, however, is not a common genre, and students might use the guide more to evaluate and understand other reading and entertainment that use epic forms and themes. Introduce the guide by asking students to name a popular film that has epic qualities. Students might mention panoramic adventures such as westerns or historical or science fiction films. Choose a film that most of the class has seen, and subject the film to the list of questions. Students are most likely to see a parallel between the epic hero and the hero of the film. In addition, however, epic films often contain flashbacks, person-against-fate conflicts, hints about supernatural forces, and elevated language, and the names of characters are often descriptive in the manner of epithets.

PREVIEW: THE NOVEL

To me a novel is something that's built around the character of time, the nature of time, and the effects that time has on events and characters.

—Frank O'Connor

A **novel** is a long work of narrative prose fiction. Because of its length, a novel can picture life with all of its richness, complexity, and contradiction. The result is a lifelike world in which we become more involved than we would in a shorter work.

A novel uses the same elements as a short story: plot, character, setting, point of view, and theme. The greater length of the novel, however, allows novelists to deal with more complex aspects of these elements, to present characters of many dimensions in a variety of situations and settings.

Since its beginnings in eighteenth-century England, the novel has changed with the times and with new attitudes toward literature and life. Though fiction, the novel has become a record of changing ideas and behavior in a changing world. Therefore, when we read a novel, we can enjoy the adventures of the characters, but we can also learn about life at a given time and place. In addition, no matter how exotic its setting, a novel can help us to understand our own world, our own times. For example, the two novels that follow present very different settings, characters, and situations. *The Call of the Wild* by Jack London re-creates the hazardous adventure of the Klondike Gold Rush in 1897, and *Great Expectations* by Charles Dickens reflects the world of nineteenth-century England. Both novels, however, capture the challenge of a character's adapting to a new way of life, and both novels say something about how we all face change and grow.

PREVIEW

Before having students read the Preview, list a few short stories that the class particularly enjoyed. Ask what additional information they may have wanted about the characters and events in those stories. For example, they may be curious about whether Squeaky of "Raymond's Run" actually trains Raymond as a runner, about what Samuel's ("A Son from America") life in America is like, about how Loisel in "The Necklace" feels about the sacrifices he is forced to endure. Point out that the class has begun to detail the differences between a short story and a novel. Because it is longer than a short story, a novel can present more characters with deeper insight into their personalities, and it can provide multiple plots, settings, themes, and even points of view. A novel can record the changes caused by the passing of time. After they have read the Preview, ask the class to name some favorite novels, their characters, settings, and themes.

LITERARY FOCUS: *The Call of the Wild*

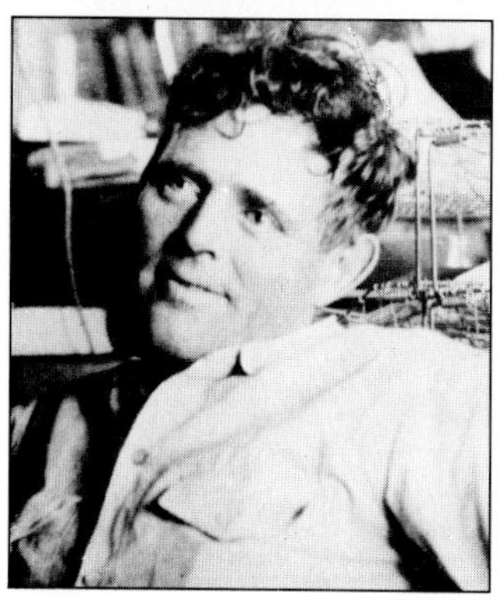

In 1896 gold was discovered near the Klondike River in the Yukon Territory of northwestern Canada. For the next two years the Klondike Gold Rush brought thousands of prospectors north. Once they arrived in the Yukon, these hopeful adventurers often became less concerned with gold than with the struggle against the savage climate. Average winter temperatures in the Yukon range from fifteen to thirty degrees below freezing; annual snowfall varies from forty to eighty inches.

Jack London (1876-1916) traveled to the Yukon in search of the precious yellow metal in 1897. He did not find gold, but he found the inspiration for his most famous novel, *The Call of the Wild.* London was well equipped to write this novel. He was a newspaper reporter and had a reporter's sharp eye and ear. He had also traveled, in a series of jobs, to Asia, across the United States, and, of course, to the dark and icy north. He wrote with realism about what he saw. For ten years after *The Call of the Wild* was written in 1903, London became the most popular and highest paid author in the United States. Other works by London that benefit from his experience as a prospector include his novel *White Fang* and the classic short story "To Build a Fire."

The Call of the Wild is the story of a sled dog in the Yukon where lives and fortunes depend on dog teams pulling pack sleds along frozen trails. London decided to tell his story through the eyes of Buck, the sled dog, the main character of the novel. This decision may reflect a desire to tell a tale of survival in its simplest terms. Uncomplicated by human thought and emotion, Buck makes simple, clear, life-and-death decisions. His impressions of human characters are based on their relationship with nature and, in turn, on their ability to survive.

Different readers can approach *The Call of the Wild* in different ways. It is an animal story, perhaps the greatest ever written. It is a realistic picture, an eyewitness account of the Klondike Gold Rush. It is an exciting adventure about animals and humans struggling against the cruelty of the Arctic. It is a **parable,** a simple story from which a lesson may be drawn, about civilization and wilderness.

Key Ideas in *The Call of the Wild*

■ As you read *The Call of the Wild*, look for references to each of the following topics. If you keep track of what the novel says about each topic, you will understand the major themes of *The Call of the Wild*.

- The relationship between humans and nature
- Nature versus civilization
- The search for wealth
- The power of love

Jack London

The Call of the Wild
(abridged)

1 Into the Primitive

Buck did not read the newspapers, or he would have known that trouble was brewing, not alone for himself, but for every tidewater[1] dog, strong of muscle and with warm, long hair, from Puget Sound[2] to San Diego.[3] Because men, groping in the Arctic[4] darkness, had found a yellow metal, and because steamship and transportation companies were booming the find, thousands of men were rushing into the Northland. These men wanted dogs, and the dogs they wanted were heavy dogs, with strong muscles by which to toil, and furry coats to protect them from the frost.

Buck lived at a big house in the sun-kissed Santa Clara Valley.[5] Judge Miller's place, it was called. It stood back from the road, half hidden among the trees, through which glimpses could be caught of the wide, cool veranda that ran around its four sides.

And over this great demesne[6] Buck ruled. Here he was born, and here he had lived the four years of his life. It was true, there were other
3 dogs. There could not but be other dogs on so vast a place, but they did not count. They came and went, resided in the populous kennels, or lived obscurely in the recesses of the house after the fashion of Toots, the Japanese pug, or Ysabel, the Mexican hairless—strange creatures that rarely put nose out of doors or set foot to ground. On the other hand, there were the fox

1. **tidewater:** seacoast.
2. **Puget** [pū′jit] **Sound:** inlet of the Pacific Ocean in northwestern Washington State.
3. **San Diego** [san′ dē ā′gō]: city on the western coast of southern California.
4. **Arctic** [är′tik]: region surrounding the North Pole.
5. **Santa Clara Valley:** valley in western California between San Francisco and Los Angeles.
6. **demesne** [di mān′]: estate.

AT A GLANCE

- It is 1897: Gold has been discovered in the Yukon.
- Buck, a ranch dog, is unaware of the need for strong dogs in the Arctic.

LITERARY OPTIONS

- point of view
- setting
- characterization

THEMATIC OPTIONS

- greed
- the power of nature
- survival

1 THEME

Because of the discovery of gold, dogs will be taken from civilization to a darkly brutal environment.

2 SETTING

Buck inhabits a world of sunshine, protected by trees and sheltered by a comfortable house; in contrast, the world of the Arctic is cold, dark, and starkly barren.

3 CHARACTERIZATION

The dogs that "did not count" include the pug and the hairless. These dogs live remote from nature, and Buck considers them "strange creatures" rather than fellow canines.

GUIDED READING

LITERAL QUESTION

1a. Where do the dogs live on the ranch? (some in the kennels, some in the house)

INFERENTIAL QUESTION

1b. According to Buck, which dogs seem superior? (Kennel dogs are superior to house dogs, who are too refined for their own good.)

AT A GLANCE

- During his four years on the Judge's ranch, Buck has not grown soft.
- Buck is kidnapped, taken to the train station, and sold.

1 CHARACTERIZATION

Buck is a singular example of the excellent individual: He roams freely, hunts, swims, and guards the children.

2 CHARACTERIZATION

Instinctively, Buck has known how to keep himself fit by challenging nature, seeking hardy entertainment, and swimming in cold water.

3 THEME

The gardener's greed has allowed him to be corrupted by the lottery, one of the forces of civilization. He is a failure for relying on human systems, rather than on instinct.

4 PLOT: CONFLICT

Manuel kidnaps Buck on an evening when the Judge is away. Buck's naive trust, born of his civilized life on the ranch, allows the gardener to take advantage of him.

terriers, a score of them at least, who yelped fearful promises at Toots and Ysabel looking out of the windows at them and protected by a legion of housemaids armed with brooms and mops.

1 But Buck was neither house dog nor kennel dog. The whole realm was his. He plunged into the swimming tank or went hunting with the Judge's sons; he escorted Mollie and Alice, the Judge's daughters, on long twilight or early-morning rambles; on wintry nights he lay at the Judge's feet before the roaring library fire; he carried the Judge's grandsons on his back, or rolled them in the grass, and guarded their footsteps through wild adventures down to the fountain in the stable yard, and even beyond, where the paddocks[7] were, and the berry patches. Among the terriers he stalked imperiously, and Toots and Ysabel he utterly ignored, for he was king—king over all creeping, crawling, flying things of Judge Miller's place, humans included.

His father, Elmo, a huge St. Bernard, had been the Judge's inseparable companion, and Buck bid fair to follow in the way of his father. He was not so large—he weighed only one hundred and forty pounds—for his mother, Shep, had been a Scotch shepherd dog. Nevertheless, one hundred and forty pounds, to which was added the dignity that comes of good living and universal respect, enabled him to carry himself in right royal fashion. During the four years since his puppyhood he had lived the life of a sated aristocrat; he had a fine pride in himself, was even a trifle egotistical, as country gentlemen sometimes become because of their in-
2 sular situation. But he had saved himself by not becoming a mere pampered house dog. Hunting and kindred outdoor delights had kept down the fat and hardened his muscles; and to him, as to the cold-tubbing races, the love of water had been a tonic and a health preserver.

And this was the manner of dog Buck was in the fall of 1897, when the Klondike strike[8] dragged men from all the world into the frozen North. But Buck did not read the newspapers, and he did not know that Manuel, one of the gardener's helpers, was an undesirable acquaintance. Manuel had one besetting sin. He loved to
3 play Chinese lottery. Also, in his gambling, he had one besetting weakness—faith in a system; and this made his damnation certain. For to play a system requires money, while the wages of a gardener's helper do not lap over the needs of a wife and numerous progeny.[9]

The Judge was at a meeting of the Raisin Growers' Association, and the boys were busy organizing an athletic club, on the memorable
4 night of Manuel's treachery. No one saw him and Buck go off through the orchard on what Buck imagined was merely a stroll. And with the exception of a solitary man, no one saw them arrive at the little flag station known as College Park. This man talked with Manuel, and money chinked between them.

"You might wrap up the goods before you deliver 'm," the stranger said gruffly, and Manuel doubled a piece of stout rope around Buck's neck under the collar.

"Twist it, an' you'll choke 'm plentee," said Manuel, and the stranger grunted a ready affirmative.

Buck had accepted the rope with quiet dignity. To be sure, it was an unwonted performance: but he had learned to trust in men he knew, and to give them credit for a wisdom that outreached his own. But when the ends of the rope were placed in the stranger's hands, he growled menacingly. He had merely intimated his displeasure, in his pride believing that to intimate was to command. But to his surprise the rope tightened around his neck, shutting off his

7. **paddocks:** fields for exercising horses.

8. **Klondike** [klän′dīk] **strike:** discovery of gold in 1896 near the Klondike River in the Yukon Territory of northwestern Canada.

9. **progeny** [proj′ə nē]: children.

GUIDED READING

LITERAL QUESTION

1a. What is Buck's lineage? (He is the offspring of a St. Bernard "father" and a Scotch shepherd "mother.")

INFERENTIAL QUESTION

1b. How does the author make Buck sound more like a human than a dog? (He uses human terms, rather than *dam* and *sire;* he gives Buck the qualities of pride and egotism; he calls him "king.")

breath. In quick rage he sprang at the man, who met him halfway, grappled him close by the throat, and with a deft twist threw him over on his back. Then the rope tightened mercilessly, while Buck struggled in a fury, his tongue lolling out of his mouth and his great chest panting futilely. Never in all his life had be been so vilely treated, and never in all his life had he been so angry. But his strength ebbed, his eyes glazed, and he knew nothing when the train was flagged and the two men threw him into the baggage car.

The next he knew, he was dimly aware that his tongue was hurting and that he was being jolted along in some kind of a conveyance. The hoarse shriek of a locomotive whistling a crossing told him where he was. He had traveled too often with the Judge not to know the sensation of riding in a baggage car.

Concerning that night's ride, the man spoke most eloquently for himself, in a little shed back of a saloon on the San Francisco waterfront.

"All I get is fifty for it," he grumbled; "an' I wouldn't do it over for a thousand, cold cash."

"How much did the other mug get?" the saloonkeeper demanded.

"A hundred," was the reply. "Wouldn't take a sou[10] less, so help me."

"That makes a hundred and fifty," the saloonkeeper calculated; "and he's worth it, or I'm a squarehead."

Dazed, suffering intolerable pain from throat and tongue, with the life half throttled out of him, Buck attempted to face his tormentors. But he was thrown down till they succeeded in filing the heavy brass collar from off his neck. Then the rope was removed, and he was flung into a cagelike crate.

There he lay for the remainder of the weary night, nursing his wrath and wounded pride. He could not understand what it all meant. What did they want with him, these strange men? Why were they keeping him pent up in this narrow crate? He did not know why, but he felt oppressed by the vague sense of impending calamity. Several times during the night he sprang to his feet when the shed door rattled open, expecting to see the Judge, or the boys at least. But each time it was the bulging face of the saloonkeeper that peered in at him by the sickly
3 light of a tallow candle. And each time the joyful bark that trembled in Buck's throat was twisted into a savage growl.

But the saloonkeeper let him alone, and in the morning four men entered and picked up the crate. More tormentors, Buck decided, for they were evil-looking creatures, ragged and unkempt; and he stormed and raged at them through the bars. They only laughed and poked sticks at him, which he promptly assailed with his teeth till he realized that that was what they wanted. Whereupon he lay down sullenly and allowed the crate to be lifted into a wagon. Then he, and the crate in which he was imprisoned, began a passage through many hands. Clerks in the express office took charge of him; he was carted about in another wagon; a truck carried him, with an assortment of boxes and parcels, upon a ferry steamer; he was trucked off the steamer into a great railway depot, and finally he was deposited in an express car.

For two days and nights this express car was dragged along at the tail of shrieking locomotives; and for two days and nights Buck
4 neither ate nor drank. In his anger he had met the first advances of the express messengers with growls, and they had retaliated by teasing him. When he flung himself against the bars, quivering and frothing, they laughed at him and taunted him. They growled and barked like detestable dogs, mewed, and flapped their arms and crowed. It was all very silly, he knew; but therefore the more outrage to his dignity, and his anger waxed and waxed. He did not mind the hunger so much, but the lack of water caused him severe suffering and fanned his wrath to fever pitch. For that matter, high-strung and

10. **sou** [so͞o]: French coin then worth about one cent.

AT A GLANCE

- Buck is taken away in the baggage car of a train.
- He is taken by wagon and truck to a ferry steamer.
- He rides for two days in an express train without food or water.

1 CHARACTERIZATION

Buck's first taste of brutality arouses fury and anger—emotions he has not felt amid the soft ranch life.

2 SETTING

London emphasizes Buck's dislocation with sudden shifts of scene. The setting moves rapidly from the baggage car to the inside of a shed in San Francisco.

3 CHARACTERIZATION

The "savage growl" that replaces the joyful bark is one of the first symptoms of Buck's reversion to a more primitive being.

4 PLOT: CONFLICT

Buck endures his new surroundings, where dignity and temperance are luxuries that must give way in the face of physical suffering. Ironically, the men who torment Buck "barked like detestable dogs."

GUIDED READING

LITERAL QUESTIONS

1a. What was the destination of the train that picked up Buck at the College Park Station? (San Francisco)

2a. What feeling does Buck's imprisonment arouse? (anger)

INFERENTIAL QUESTIONS

1b. What might be Buck's ultimate destination? (He is going up the coast of North America to the Klondike in the Yukon Territory of Canada.)

2b. How does Buck waste his strength during the long journey? (He hurls himself at antagonists whom he cannot reach; he rises to the bait of their teasing.)

AT A GLANCE

- Buck arrives in Seattle.
- He is met by a "dog-breaker," a man who strikes him with a club.
- Buck learns not to ignore superior strength.

1 CHARACTERIZATION

In the first stage of his atavism, Buck becomes a "raging fiend," ready to spring without judgment at any enemy.

2 READING SKILLS: DETAILS

The man and Buck are natural antagonists, and the color red is used to pair them: Buck's eyes are bloodshot, and the man's sweater is red.

3 PLOT: CONFLICT

Buck lunges at the man in the red sweater and is met with the blow of a club; this brutal action is his initiation into a more savage world.

4 THEME

The man in the red sweater is like Buck—a singular individual whose superior ability is admired by all who meet him. The man's experience is far greater: Buck is a novice, who must learn from him.

5 CHARACTERIZATION

Buck's ability to adapt is shown by his acceptance of the dog-breaker's offer of water; his unbroken spirit is shown by the involuntary bristling of his hair.

finely sensitive, the ill treatment had flung him into a fever, which was fed by the inflammation of his parched and swollen throat and tongue.

He was glad for one thing: the rope was off his neck. That had given them an unfair advantage; but now that it was off, he would show them. They would never get another rope around his neck. Upon that he was resolved. For two days and nights he neither ate nor drank, and during those two days and nights of tor-
1 ment, he accumulated a fund of wrath that boded ill for whoever first fell foul of him. His eyes turned bloodshot, and he was metamorphosed[11] into a raging fiend. So changed was he that the Judge himself would not have recognized him; and the express messengers breathed with relief when they bundled him off the train at Seattle.

Four men gingerly carried the crate from the wagon into a small, high-walled back yard. A stout man, with a red sweater that sagged generously at the neck, came out and signed the book for the driver. That was the man, Buck divined, the next tormentor, and he hurled himself savagely against the bars. The man smiled grimly, and brought a hatchet and a club.

"You ain't going to take him out now?" the driver asked.

"Sure," the man replied, driving the hatchet into the crate for a pry.

There was an instantaneous scattering of the four men who had carried it in, and from safe perches on top of the wall they prepared to watch the performance.

Buck rushed at the splintering wood, sinking his teeth into it, surging and wrestling with it. Wherever the hatchet fell on the outside, he was there on the inside, snarling and growling, as
2 furiously anxious to get out as the man in the red sweater was calmly intent on getting him out.

"Now, you red-eyed devil," he said, when he had made an opening sufficient for the passage of Buck's body. At the same time he dropped the hatchet and shifted the club to his right hand.

And Buck was truly a red-eyed devil, as he drew himself together for the spring, hair bristling, mouth foaming, a mad glitter in his bloodshot eyes. Straight at the man he launched his one hundred and forty pounds of fury, surcharged with the pent passion of two days and
3 nights. In midair, just as his jaws were about to close on the man, he received a shock that checked his body and brought his teeth together with an agonizing clip. He whirled over, fetching the ground on his back and side. He had never been struck by a club in his life, and did not understand.

4 "He's no slouch at dog-breakin', that's wot I say," one of the men on the wall cried enthusiastically.

"Druther break cayuses[12] any day, and twice on Sundays," was the reply of the driver, as he climbed on the wagon and started the horses.

Buck's senses came back to him, but not his strength. He lay where he had fallen, and from there he watched the man in the red sweater.

"'Answers to the name of Buck,'" the man soliloquized,[13] quoting from the saloonkeeper's letter, which had announced the consignment of the crate and contents. "Well, Buck, my boy," he went on in a genial voice, "we've had our little ruction, and the best thing we can do is to let it go at that. You've learned your place, and I know mine. Be a good dog and all'll go well and the goose hang high. Be a bad dog, and I'll whale the stuffin' outa you. Understand?"

5 As he spoke he fearlessly patted the head he had so mercilessly pounded, and though Buck's hair involuntarily bristled at touch of the hand, he endured it without protest. When the man brought him water he drank eagerly, and later

11. **metamorphosed** [met'ə môr'fōzd]: transformed.

12. **cayuses** [kī o͞os'iz]: small western horses used by cowboys.

13. **soliloquized** [sə lil'ə kwīzd]: said to himself.

GUIDED READING

LITERAL QUESTIONS

1a. What does the man hit Buck with? (a club)

2a. What does the man do with the hatchet? (He uses it to open the crate.)

INFERENTIAL QUESTIONS

1b. What defeats Buck in his tangle with the dog-breaker? (He does not recognize the club and has no idea what it can do.)

2b. Does Buck fear the hatchet? (Apparently not; he is so confident that he will be able to kill the man that he shows no caution around it.)

bolted a generous meal of raw meat, chunk by chunk, from the man's hand.

He was beaten (he knew that); but he was not broken. He saw, once for all, that he stood no chance against a man with a club. He had learned the lesson, and in all his after life he never forgot it. That club was a revelation. It was his introduction to the reign of primitive law, and he met the introduction halfway. The facts of life took on a fiercer aspect; and while he faced that aspect uncowed, he faced it with all the latent cunning of his nature aroused. As the days went by, other dogs came, in crates and at the ends of ropes, some docilely, and some raging and roaring as he had come; and, one and all, he watched them pass under the dominion of the man in the red sweater. Again and again, as he looked at each brutal performance, the lesson was driven home to Buck: a man with a club was a lawgiver, a master to be obeyed, though not necessarily conciliated.[14] Of this last Buck was never guilty, though he did see beaten dogs that fawned upon the man, and wagged their tails, and licked his
2 hand. Also he saw one dog, that would neither conciliate nor obey, finally killed in the struggle for mastery.

Now and again men came, strangers, who talked excitedly, wheedlingly and in all kinds of fashions to the man in the red sweater. And at such times that money passed between them the strangers took one or more of the dogs away with them. Buck wondered where they went, for they never came back; but the fear of the future was strong upon him, and he was glad each time when he was not selected.

3 Yet his time came, in the end, in the form of a little weazened man who spat broken English and many strange and uncouth exclamations which Buck could not understand.

His eyes lit upon Buck. "Eh? How moch?"

"Three hundred and a present at that," was the prompt reply of the man in the red sweater. "And seein' it's government money, you ain't got no kick coming, eh, Perrault?"[15]

Perrault grinned. Considering that the price of dogs had been boomed skyward by the unwonted demand, it was not an unfair sum for so

14. **conciliated** [kən sil′ē āt′id]: made friends with.

15. **Perrault** [pər ō′]

AT A GLANCE

- Buck sees many other dogs broken in Seattle.
- A dog who would not obey is killed.
- Buck is sold to Perrault, a French Canadian who works for the government.

1 THEME

Buck takes the facts of his new life as a challenge to his strength and cunning.

2 THEME

The dog who dies because he would not learn is a lesson to Buck: One must realistically assess obstacles before acting.

3 PLOT: EXPOSITION

Perrault, a dispatch carrier for the Canadian government who will figure prominently in the narrative, speaks "broken English," as in the opening question "Eh? How moch?"

GUIDED READING

LITERAL QUESTION

1a. What lesson does Buck learn from the man in the red sweater? ("A man with a club was a lawgiver, a master to be obeyed, though not necessarily conciliated.")

INFERENTIAL QUESTION

1b. How does Buck retain his pride even though he has been beaten? (He does not behave as though he likes the man or thinks him special in any way.)

AT A GLANCE

- Buck is sold to Perrault and François.
- The dogs leave Seattle with their new owners on the *Narwhal.*
- Buck discovers snow.
- They land on a Dyea beach.

1 SETTING

Buck passes from his initiation into the second phase of his transformation as he leaves the "warm Southland" and heads toward a colder climate.

2 CHARACTERIZATION

The white dog from Spitzbergen is more experienced than Buck: Adventures on the high seas have taught him to be crafty, and his dominance is a challenge to Buck.

3 BACKGROUND

Queen Charlotte Sound, at the head of the Inland Passage, is located along the coast of British Columbia.

4 POINT OF VIEW

The snowfall is described in terms that might occur to a dog as he experiences an unfamiliar phenomenon.

5 THEME

The new land's danger, confusion, and activity contrast Buck's past experience of a civilized land's safety, order, and boredom.

fine an animal. The Canadian Government would be no loser, nor would its dispatches travel the slower. Perrault knew dogs, and when he looked at Buck he knew that he was one in a thousand. "One in ten t'ousand," he commented mentally.

Buck saw money pass between them, and was not surprised when Curly, a good-natured Newfoundland, and he were led away by the little weazened man. That was the last he saw of
1 the man in the red sweater, and as Curly and he looked at receding Seattle from the deck of the *Narwhal,* it was the last he saw of the warm Southland. Curly and he were taken below by Perrault and turned over to a giant called François.[16] They were a new kind of men to Buck (of which he was destined to see many more), and while he developed no affection for them, he none the less grew honestly to respect them. He speedily learned that Perrault and François were fair men, calm and impartial in administering justice, and too wise in the way of dogs to be fooled by dogs.

In the 'tween decks of the *Narwhal,* Buck and Curly joined two other dogs. One of them was a big, snow-white fellow from Spitzbergen[17] who had been brought away by a whaling captain, and who had later accompanied a
2 Geological Survey into the Barrens. He was friendly, in a treacherous sort of way, smiling into one's face the while he meditated some underhand trick, as, for instance, when he stole from Buck's food at the first meal. As Buck sprang to punish him, the lash of François's whip sang through the air, reaching the culprit first; and nothing remained to Buck but to recover the bone. That was fair of François, he decided.

The other dog made no advances, nor received any; also, he did not attempt to steal from the newcomers. He was a gloomy, morose fellow, and he showed Curly plainly that all he desired was to be left alone, and further, that there would be trouble if he were not left alone. Dave he was called, and he ate and slept, or yawned between times, and took interest in nothing, not even when the *Narwhal* crossed
3 Queen Charlotte Sound and rolled and pitched and bucked like a thing possessed. When Buck and Curly grew excited, half wild with fear, he raised his head as though annoyed, favored them with an incurious glance, yawned, and went to sleep again.

Day and night the ship throbbed to the tireless pulse of the propeller, and though one day was very like another, it was apparent to Buck that the weather was steadily growing colder. At last, one morning, the propeller was quiet, and the *Narwhal* was pervaded with an atmosphere of excitement. He felt it, as did the other dogs, and knew that a change was at hand. François leashed them and brought them on
4 deck. At the first step upon the cold surface, Buck's feet sank into a white mushy something very like mud. He sprang back with a snort. More of this white stuff was falling through the air. He shook himself, but more of it fell upon him. He sniffed it curiously, then licked some up on his tongue. It bit like fire, and the next instant was gone. This puzzled him. He tried it again, with the same result. The onlookers laughed uproariously, and he felt ashamed, he knew not why, for it was his first snow.

2 The Law of Club and Fang

Buck's first day on the Dyea beach was like a nightmare. Every hour was filled with shock and surprise. He had been suddenly jerked from the heart of civilization and flung into the heart of
5 things primordial.[1] No lazy, sun-kissed life was this, with nothing to do but loaf and be bored. Here was neither peace, nor rest, nor a moment's safety. All was confusion and action,

---

16. **François** [fran'swa]
17. **Spitzbergen** [spits'bur'gən]: Norwegian islands in the Arctic Ocean.

1. **primordial** [prī mor'dē əl]: primitive.

GUIDED READING

LITERAL QUESTIONS

1a. What dogs accompany Buck on the *Narwhal*? (Curly, Dave, and Spitz)

2a. What is the title of Chapter 2? ("The Law of Club and Fang")

INFERENTIAL QUESTIONS

1b. What human types do Dave and Spitz resemble? (Dave is the old hand, whom nothing bothers; Spitz is the seasoned chief, who takes advantage of new recruits.)

2b. What would the words *club* and *fang* seem to represent? (human authority and animals' competition for survival)

and every moment life and limb were in peril. There was imperative need to be constantly alert; for these dogs and men were not town dogs and men. They were savages, all of them, who knew no law but the law of club and fang.

François fastened upon him an arrangement of straps and buckles. It was a harness, such as he had seen the grooms put on the horses at home. And as he had seen horses work, so he was set to work, hauling François on a sled to the forest that fringed the valley, and returning with a load of firewood. Though his dignity was sorely hurt by thus being made a draft animal,[2] he was too wise to rebel. He buckled down with a will and did his best, though it was all new and strange. François was stern, demanding instant obedience, and by virtue of his whip receiving instant obedience; while Dave, who was an experienced wheeler, nipped Buck's hind quarters whenever he was in error. Spitz was the leader, likewise experienced, and while he could not always get at Buck, he growled sharp reproof now and again, or cunningly threw his weight in the traces to jerk Buck into the way he should go. Buck learned easily, and under the combined tuition of his two mates and François made remarkable progress. Ere[3] they returned to camp he knew enough to stop at "ho," to go ahead at "mush," to swing wide on the bends, and to keep clear of the wheeler when the loaded sled shot downhill at their heels.

"T'ree vair' good dogs," François told Perrault. "Dat Buck, I tich heem queek as anyt'ing."

By afternoon, Perrault, who was in a hurry to be on the trail with his dispatches, returned with two more dogs. Billee and Joe he called them, two brothers, and true huskies both. Sons of the one mother though they were, they were as different as day and night. Billee's one fault was his excessive good nature, while Joe was the very opposite, sour and introspective, with a perpetual snarl and a malignant eye. Buck received them in comradely fashion, Dave ignored them, while Spitz proceeded to thrash first one and then the other. Billee wagged his tail appeasingly, turned to run when he saw that appeasement was of no avail, and cried (still appeasingly) when Spitz's sharp teeth scored his flank. But no
4 matter how Spitz circled, Joe whirled around on his heels to face him, mane bristling, ears laid back, lips writhing and snarling, jaws clipping together as fast as he could snap, and eyes diabolically gleaming—the incarnation of belligerent fear. So terrible was his appearance that Spitz was forced to forgo disciplining him; but to cover his own discomfiture he turned upon the inoffensive and wailing Billee and drove him to the confines of the camp.

By evening Perrault secured another dog, an old husky, long and lean and gaunt, with a battle-scarred face and a single eye which flashed a warning of prowess that commanded respect. He was called Sol-leks, which means The Angry One. Like Dave, he asked nothing, gave nothing, expected nothing; and when he marched slowly and deliberately into their midst, even Spitz left him alone. He had one peculiarity which Buck was unlucky enough to discover. He did not like to be approached on his blind side. Of this offense Buck was unwittingly guilty, and the first knowledge he had of his indiscretion was when Sol-leks whirled upon him and slashed his shoulder. Forever after Buck avoided his blind side, and to the last of their comradeship had no more trouble. His only apparent ambition, like Dave's, was to be left
5 alone; though, as Buck was afterward to learn, each of them possessed one other and even more vital ambition.

That night Buck faced the great problem of sleeping. The tent, illumined by a candle, glowed warmly in the midst of the white plain; and when he, as a matter of course, entered it, both Perrault and François bombarded him with

2. **draft animal:** animal used for pulling loads.
3. **Ere** [ãr]: before.

AT A GLANCE

- Buck is in a new world, governed by "the law of club and fang."
- He learns to pull a sled.
- Buck, Dave, and Spitz are joined by Billee, Joe, and Sol-leks.

1 THEME

In this new world the distinction between dogs and men breaks down: Both are a part of nature, "savages" who obey the law of club and fang.

2 CHARACTERIZATION

Buck must now relinquish his illusion of privileged status: He begins an education in work, instructed by the humans and tutored by his fellow dogs.

3 THEME

Buck will learn what happens to dogs who maintain soft, warm-weather manners in the Yukon. Billee, whose fault is his "good nature," is punished again and again by Spitz.

4 PLOT: EXPOSITION

Spitz establishes his authority with the new dogs, teaching them to obey the law of the fang: To belong to the pack, they must accept his discipline. Buck observes the defiance of Joe, who stands up to Spitz and gets some peace.

5 FORESHADOWING

The "one other and even more vital ambition" is part of the concealed motivation of the two veteran dogs. What this might be will form part of the novel's climax.

GUIDED READING

LITERAL QUESTIONS

1a. What must Buck learn to do to be part of the sled team? (pull the sled while in traces)

2a. What must Buck learn about getting along with Sol-leks? (to stay away from his blind side)

INFERENTIAL QUESTIONS

1b. What is Buck's attitude about learning this skill? (He feels humbled, but does not shirk.)

2b. What general lessons must Buck learn to survive in the company of the dogs? (He has to learn not only to hold back but also to defend himself if challenged.)

AT A GLANCE

- Buck learns to sleep outdoors by burrowing into the snow.
- He rediscovers his fear of the trap.
- He discovers that he likes the work of the sled team.

1 POINT OF VIEW

The reader experiences the problem of sleeping in the cold through the dog's mind. The process of his investigation is followed step by step.

2 CHARACTERIZATION

Buck instinctively knows to ignore Billee's friendly overtures: He must learn to dig his own sleeping pit. The offer of friendship is a false promise in this land where all take care of themselves.

3 THEME

We learn that Buck has been "unduly civilized" to the degree that he has lost his protective mechanism. Fortunately, his ancestral memory warns him to fear the enclosure he awakens in.

4 CHARACTERIZATION

Buck has mistaken the attitude of Dave and Sol-leks. Now that the work of the team is ready for them, they spring to life. Their apparent listlessness was mature conservation of energy.

curses and cooking utensils, till he recovered from his consternation and fled ignominiously into the outer cold. A chill wind was blowing that nipped him sharply and bit with especial venom into his wounded shoulder. He lay down on the snow and attempted to sleep, but the frost soon drove him shivering to his feet. Miserable and disconsolate, he wandered about among the many tents, only to find that one place was as cold as another. Here and there savage dogs rushed upon him, but he bristled his neck hair and snarled (for he was learning fast), and they let him go his way unmolested.

1 Finally an idea came to him. He would return and see how his own teammates were making out. To his astonishment, they had disappeared. Again he wandered about through the great camp, looking for them, and again he returned. Were they in the tent? No, that could not be, else he would not have been driven out. Then where could they possibly be? With drooping tail and shivering body, very forlorn indeed, he aimlessly circled the tent. Suddenly the snow gave way beneath his forelegs and he sank down. Something wriggled under his feet. He sprang back, bristling and snarling, fearful of the unseen and unknown. But a friendly little yelp reassured him, and he went back to investigate. A whiff of warm air ascended to his nostrils, and there, curled up under the snow in a snug ball, lay
2 Billee. He whined placatingly, squirmed and wriggled to show his good will and intentions, and even ventured, as a bribe for peace, to lick Buck's face with his warm, wet tongue.

Another lesson. So that was the way they did it, eh? Buck confidently selected a spot, and with much fuss and wasted effort proceeded to dig a hole for himself. In a trice the heat from his body filled the confined space and he was asleep. The day had been long and arduous, and he slept soundly and comfortably, though he growled and barked and wrestled with bad dreams.

Nor did he open his eyes till roused by the noises of the waking camp. At first he did not know where he was. It had snowed during the night and he was completely buried. The snow walls pressed him on every side, and a great surge of fear swept through him—the fear of the wild thing for the trap. It was a token that he was harking back through his own life to the
3 lives of his forebears; for he was a civilized dog, an unduly civilized dog, and of his own experience knew no trap and so could not of himself fear it. The muscles of his whole body contracted spasmodically and instinctively, the hair on his neck and shoulders stood on end, and with a ferocious snarl he bounded straight up into the blinding day, the snow flying about him in a flashing cloud. Ere he landed on his feet, he saw the white camp spread out before him and knew where he was and remembered all that had passed from the time he went for a stroll with Manuel to the hole he had dug for himself the night before.

A shout from François hailed his appearance. "Wot I say?" the dog driver cried to Perrault. "Dat Buck for sure learn queek as anyt'ing."

Perrault nodded gravely. As courier[4] for the Canadian Government, bearing important dispatches, he was anxious to secure the best dogs, and he was particularly gladdened by the possession of Buck.

Three more huskies were added to the team inside an hour, making a total of nine, and before another quarter of an hour had passed they were in harness and swinging up the trail toward the Dyea Canyon. Buck was glad to be gone, and though the work was hard he found he did not particularly despise it. He was surprised at the eagerness which animated the whole team and
4 which was communicated to him; but still more surprising was the change wrought in Dave and Sol-leks. They were new dogs, utterly transformed by the harness. All passiveness and unconcern had dropped from them. They were alert and active, anxious that the work should go

4. **courier** [kur'ē ər]: messenger.

GUIDED READING

LITERAL QUESTIONS

1a. How does Buck learn to keep warm at night? (He digs a hole in the snow and burrows into it.)

2a. What do Perrault and François think of Buck's solution? (They call him smart and a quick learner.)

INFERENTIAL QUESTIONS

1b. How does Buck know how to get out of the hole he has gotten buried in? (He *senses* it with his instinct.)

2b. Why didn't the French Canadian show Buck where to sleep and train him to dig himself in? (They have no use for a dog that must be shown how to take care of himself.)

well, and fiercely irritable with whatever, by delay or confusion, retarded that work. The toil of the traces seemed the supreme expression of their being, and all that they lived for and the only thing in which they took delight.

Dave was the wheeler or sled dog, pulling in front of him was Buck, then came Sol-leks; the rest of the team was strung out ahead, single file, to the leader, which position was filled by Spitz.

Buck had been purposely placed between Dave and Sol-leks so that he might receive instruction. Apt scholar that he was, they were equally apt teachers, never allowing him to linger long in error, and enforcing their teaching with their sharp teeth. Dave was fair and very wise. He never nipped Buck without cause, and he never failed to nip him when he stood in need of it. As François's whip backed him up, Buck found it to be cheaper to mend his ways than to retaliate. Once, during a brief halt, when he got tangled in the traces and delayed the start, both Dave and Sol-leks flew at him and administered a sound trouncing. The resulting tangle was even worse, but Buck took good care to keep the traces clear thereafter; and ere the day was done, so well had he mastered his work, his mates about ceased nagging him. François's whip snapped less frequently, and Perrault even honored Buck by lifting up his feet and carefully examining them.

They made good time down the chain of lakes which fills the craters of extinct volcanoes, and late that night pulled into the huge camp at the head of Lake Bennett, where thousands of gold seekers were building boats against the break-up of the ice in the spring. Buck made his hole in the snow and slept the sleep of the exhausted just, but all too early was routed out in the cold darkness and harnessed with his mates to the sled.

Day after day, for days unending, Buck toiled in the traces. Always, they broke camp in the dark, and the first gray of dawn found them hitting the trail with fresh miles reeled off behind them. And always they pitched camp after dark, eating their bit of fish, and crawling to sleep into
3 the snow. Buck was ravenous. The pound and a half of sun-dried salmon which was his ration for each day seemed to go nowhere. He never had enough, and suffered from perpetual hunger pangs. Yet the other dogs, because they weighed less and were born to the life, received a pound only of the fish and managed to keep in good condition.

He swiftly lost the fastidiousness which had characterized his old life. A dainty eater, he found that his mates, finishing first, robbed him of his unfinished ration. There was no defending it. While he was fighting off two or three, it was disappearing down the throats of the others. To remedy this, he ate as fast as they; and, so greatly did hunger compel him, he was not above taking what did not belong to him. He watched and learned. When he saw Pike, one of the new dogs, a clever malingerer and thief, slyly steal a slice of bacon when Perrault's back was turned, he duplicated the performance the following day, getting away with the whole chunk. A great uproar was raised, but he was unsuspected; while Dub, an awkward blunderer who was always getting caught, was punished for Buck's misdeed.

4 This first theft marked Buck as fit to survive in the hostile Northland environment. It marked his adaptability, his capacity to adjust himself to changing conditions, the lack of which would have meant swift and terrible death. It marked, further, the decay or going to pieces of his moral nature, a vain thing and a handicap in the ruthless struggle for existence.

Not that Buck reasoned it out. He was fit, that was all, and unconsciously he accommodated himself to the new mode of life. All his days, no matter what the odds, he had never run from a fight. But the club of the man in the red sweater had beaten into him a more fundamental and primitive code. Civilized, he could have died for a moral consideration, say the defense

AT A GLANCE

- Buck becomes the pupil of the two veterans, Dave and Sol-leks.
- Buck learns to live on a pound and a half of dried salmon a day.
- He learns to steal food.

1 CHARACTERIZATION

Dave and Sol-leks are described as teachers with extraordinary powers: They are fair, wise, and vigilant, and their punishment is swift.

2 POINT OF VIEW

The narrative contains passages that could not possibly have originated in Buck's mind. This passage shows the omniscience of the narrator.

3 READING SKILLS: DETAILS

We learn that Buck receives a pound and a half of fish each day, while other dogs receive one-third less. Buck's larger ration is partly because of his "civilized" past.

4 THEME

By stealing the bacon, Buck shows that he has rejected the "civilized" code of the South. He is able to adapt to the new environment and will survive its hostility.

GUIDED READING

LITERAL QUESTION

1a. Who gets the blame for the theft of the bacon? (Dub, a dog who always blunders)

INFERENTIAL QUESTION

1b. How does letting punishment fall to the other dog reflect well on Buck? (He senses that it's not enough to steal; a dog must succeed, even if it means that the innocent must suffer.)

AT A GLANCE

- Buck abandons the morality of the South and becomes a survivor.
- Hatred develops between Buck and Spitz.

1 STYLE: REPETITION

The author underscores his meaning by similar phrasing of similar points. "He did not steal for joy of it . . . ," "He did not rob openly . . . ," etc.

2 THEME

Once headed in the right direction, Buck's regression to his wild past proceeds rapidly and brings with it even greater ability to meet the challenge of the environment.

3 READING SKILLS: DETAILS

From these references to the behavior of a dog in an extreme climate, we see London's own observations of dogs in the Yukon.

4 STYLE: IMAGERY

As his instincts revive, Buck adopts the behavior of his most primitive relative, the wolf. The narrator's admiration is revealed in the comparison of the wolf howl to "the ancient song."

5 CHARACTERIZATION

Buck's manner conceals a growing hatred of the lead dog of the pack; Buck maintains an outward attitude of respect and avoids minor fights with Spitz.

of Judge Miller's riding whip; but the completeness of his decivilization was now evidenced by his ability to flee from the defense of a
1 moral consideration and so save his hide. He did not steal for joy of it, but because of the clamor of his stomach. He did not rob openly, but stole secretly and cunningly, out of respect for club and fang. In short, the things he did were done because it was easier to do them than not to do them.

2 His development (or retrogression[5]) was rapid. His muscles became hard as iron, and he grew callous to all ordinary pain. He achieved an internal as well as external economy. He could eat anything, no matter how loathsome or indigestible; and, once eaten, the juices of his stomach extracted the last least particle of nutriment; and his blood carried it to the farthest reaches of his body, building it into the toughest and stoutest of tissues. Sight and scent became remarkably keen, while his hearing developed such acuteness that in his sleep he heard the faintest sound and knew whether it heralded
3 peace or peril. He learned to bite the ice out with his teeth when it collected between his toes; and when he was thirsty and there was a thick scum of ice over the water hole, he would break it by rearing and striking it with stiff forelegs. His most conspicuous trait was an ability to scent the wind and forecast it a night in advance. No matter how breathless the air when he dug his nest by tree or bank, the wind that later blew inevitably found him to leeward, sheltered and snug.

And not only did he learn by experience, but instincts long dead became alive again. The domesticated generations fell from him. In vague ways he remembered back to the youth of the breed, to the time the wild dogs ranged in packs through the primeval forest and killed their meat as they ran it down. It was no task for him to learn to fight with cut and slash and the quick wolf snap. In this manner had fought forgotten ancestors. They quickened the old life within him, and the old tricks which they had stamped into the heredity of the breed were his tricks. They came to him without effort or discovery, as though they had been his always. And when, on the still, cold nights, he pointed his
4 nose at a star and howled long and wolflike, it was his ancestors, dead and dust, pointing nose at star and howling down through the centuries and through him. And his cadences[6] were their cadences, the cadences which voiced their woe and what to them was the meaning of the stillness, and the cold, and dark.

Thus, as token of what a puppet thing life is, the ancient song surged through him and he came into his own again; and he came because men had found a yellow metal in the North, and because Manuel was a gardener's helper whose wages did not lap over the needs of his wife and divers small copies of himself.

3 The Dominant Primordial Beast

The dominant primordial beast was strong in Buck, and under the fierce conditions of trail life it grew and grew. Yet it was a secret growth. His newborn cunning gave him poise and control. He was too busy adjusting himself to the new life to feel at ease, and not only did he not pick fights, but he avoided them whenever possible. A certain deliberateness characterized his attitude. He was not prone to rashness and precipi-
5 tate action; and in the bitter hatred between him and Spitz he betrayed no impatience, shunned all offensive acts.

On the other hand, possibly because he divined in Buck a dangerous rival, Spitz never lost an opportunity of showing his teeth. He even

5. **retrogression** [ret'rə gresh'ən]: process of changing to a worse condition.

6. **cadences** [kād'əns iz]: rhythms.

GUIDED READING

LITERAL QUESTION

1a. What physical changes come over Buck as he adapts to his environment? (He gets more out of food; his senses of sight, hearing, and smell improve.)

INFERENTIAL QUESTION

1b. How do these changes make Buck more fully alive? (With every sense alert and his attention engaged even in his sleep, Buck is completely in touch with his environment and its challenges.)

went out of his way to bully Buck, striving constantly to start the fight which could end only in the death of one or the other. Early in the trip this might have taken place had it not been for an unwonted accident. At the end of this day they made a bleak and miserable camp on the shore of Lake Laberge. Driving snow, a wind that cut like a white-hot knife, and darkness had forced them to grope for a camping place. They could hardly have fared worse. At their backs rose a perpendicular wall of rock, and Perrault and François were compelled to make their fire and spread their sleeping robes on the ice of the lake itself. The tent they had discarded at Dyea in order to travel light. A few sticks of driftwood furnished them with a fire that thawed down through the ice and left them to eat supper in the dark.

Close in under the sheltering rock Buck made his nest. So snug and warm was it, that he was loath to leave it when François distributed the fish which he had first thawed over the fire. But when Buck finished his ration and returned, he found his nest occupied. A warning snarl told him that the trespasser was Spitz. Till now Buck had avoided trouble with his enemy, but this was too much. The beast in him roared. He sprang upon Spitz with a fury which surprised them both, and Spitz particularly, for his whole experience with Buck had gone to teach him that his rival was an unusually timid dog, who managed to hold his own only because of his great weight and size.

François was surprised, too, when they shot out in a tangle from the disrupted nest and he divined the cause of the trouble. "A-a-ah!" he cried to Buck. "Gif it to heem, by Gar! Gif it to heem, the dirty t'eef!"

Spitz was equally willing. He was crying with sheer rage and eagerness as he circled back and forth for a chance to spring in. Buck was no less eager, and no less cautious, as he likewise circled back and forth for the advantage. But it was then that the unexpected happened, the thing which projected their struggle for supremacy far into the future, past many a weary mile of trail and toil.

An oath from Perrault, the resounding impact of a club upon a bony frame, and a shrill yelp of pain heralded the breaking forth of pan-
4 demonium. The camp was suddenly discovered to be alive with skulking furry forms—starving huskies, four or five score of them, who had scented the camp from some Indian village. They had crept in while Buck and Spitz were fighting, and when the two men sprang among them with stout clubs they showed their teeth and fought back. They were crazed by the smell of the food.

In the meantime the astonished team dogs had burst out of their nests only to be set upon by the fierce invaders. Never had Buck seen such dogs. It seemed as though their bones would burst through their skins. They were mere skeletons, draped loosely in draggled hides, with
5 blazing eyes and slavered fangs. But the hunger madness made them terrifying, irresistible. There was no opposing them. The team dogs were swept back against the cliff at the first onset. Buck was beset by three huskies, and in a trice his head and shoulders were ripped and slashed. The din was frightful.

Perrault and François, having cleaned out their part of the camp, hurried to save their sled dogs. The wild wave of famished beasts rolled back before them, and Buck shook himself free. But it was only for a moment. The two men were compelled to run back to save the grub, upon which the huskies returned to the attack on the team. Billee, terrified into bravery, sprang through the savage circle and fled away over the ice. Pike and Dub followed on his heels, with the rest of the team behind. As Buck drew himself together to spring after them, out of the tail of his eye he saw Spitz rush upon him with the evident intention of overthrowing him. Once off his feet and under that mass of huskies, there

AT A GLANCE

- A fight between Buck and Spitz breaks out; it is interrupted by an invasion of huskies.
- The sled dogs flee.

1 THEME

Spitz, sensing Buck's metamorphosis from a regal ranch dog to a dominant primordial beast, seeks the fight that will prove one superior to the other.

2 PLOT: RISING ACTION

Though Buck has avoided conflict with Spitz, he is faced with a predicament when Spitz steals his sleeping place: He must defend himself.

3 STYLE: DIALOGUE

Francois, understanding that Spitz started the fight, spurs Buck to "gif it to heem" by calling Spitz a "dirty t'eef."

4 PLOT: CONFLICT

In the midst of Buck and Spitz's fight, a challenge comes to the whole camp from nearly a hundred wild and starving dogs drawn by the smell of food.

5 THEME

The famished pack, ready to fight to the death, shows the fierceness and exhilaration of life in the wilderness. The team dogs find them terrifying and "irresistible."

GUIDED READING

LITERAL QUESTIONS

1a. How many dogs are in the wild pack that attack the camp? ("four or five score"—about eighty to one hundred)

2a. What does Spitz do after the attack is over? (He rushes Buck.)

INFERENTIAL QUESTIONS

1b. Why is there "no opposing" these wild dogs? (These dogs, closer to nature than the sled dogs, possess more of nature's primeval force.)

2b. Why does London show Spitz attacking Buck at this time? (The rivalry between the two dogs is far from over; Spitz will not rest until it is settled.)

AT A GLANCE

- The team returns the next morning to a pillaged camp.
- They undertake the last miles of the journey to Dawson.

1 BACKGROUND

The attack of the wild dogs takes place at Lake Laberge, which is only about two hundred statute miles (not four hundred) from Dawson. London's adherence to geographical facts makes it unlikely that he invented this mileage. It may be that the trail was very winding.

2 CHARACTERIZATION

Perrault is the human equivalent of the more competent and seasoned dogs. While not a dominant master, he exemplifies the man tested and proven by a strenuous life outdoors.

3 THEME

Although Buck is finding the instincts that generations of wild dogs have passed down to him, he cannot escape the physical effects of generations of breeding and living the easy life.

was no hope for him. But he braced himself to the shock of Spitz's charge, then joined the flight out on to the lake.

Later, the nine team dogs gathered together and sought shelter in the forest. Though unpursued, they were in sorry plight. There was not one who was not wounded in four or five places, while some were wounded grievously. At daybreak they limped warily back to camp, to find the marauders gone and the two men in bad tempers. Fully half their grub supply was gone. The huskies had chewed through the sled lashings and canvas coverings. In fact, nothing, no matter how remotely eatable, had escaped them. They had eaten a pair of Perrault's moose-hide moccasins, chunks out of the leather traces, and even two feet of lash from the end of François's whip. He broke from a mournful contemplation of it to look over his wounded dogs.

"Ah, my frien's," he said softly, "mebbe it mek you mad dog, dose many bites. Mebbe all mad dog. Wot you t'ink, eh, Perrault?"

1 The courier shook his head dubiously. With four hundred miles of trail still between him and Dawson,[1] he could ill afford to have madness break out among his dogs. Two hours of cursing and exertion got the harnesses into shape, and the wound-stiffened team was under way, struggling painfully over the hardest part of the trail they had yet encountered, and for that matter, the hardest between them and Dawson.

The Thirty Mile River was wide open. Its wild water defied the frost, and it was in the eddies only and in the quiet places that the ice held at all. Six days of exhausting toil were required to cover those thirty terrible miles. And terrible they were, for every foot of them was accomplished at the risk of life to dog and man. A dozen times Perrault, nosing the way, broke through the ice bridges, being saved by the long pole he carried, which he so held that it fell each time across the hole made by his body. But a cold snap was on, the thermometer registering fifty below zero, and each time he broke through he was compelled for very life to build a fire and dry his garments.

2 Nothing daunted him. It was because nothing daunted him that he had been chosen for government courier. He took all manner of risks, resolutely thrusting his little weazened face into the frost and struggling on from dim dawn to dark. He skirted the frowning shores on rim ice that bent and crackled under foot and upon which they dared not halt. Once, the sled broke through, with Dave and Buck, and they were half-frozen and all but drowned by the time they were dragged out. The usual fire was necessary to save them. They were coated solidly with ice, and the two men kept them on the run around the fire, sweating and thawing, so close that they were singed by the flames.

At another time Spitz went through, dragging the whole team after him up to Buck, who strained backward with all his strength, his forepaws on the slippery edge and the ice quivering and snapping all around. But behind him was Dave, likewise straining backward, and behind the sled was François, pulling until his tendons cracked.

By the time they made the Hootalinqua and good ice, Buck was played out. The rest of the dogs were in like condition; but Perrault, to make up lost time, pushed them late and early. The first day they covered thirty-five miles to the Big Salmon; the next day thirty-five more to the Little Salmon; the third day forty miles, which brought them well up toward the Five Fingers.

3 Buck's feet were not so compact and hard as the feet of the huskies. His had softened during the many generations since the day his last wild ancestor was tamed. All day long he limped in agony, and camp once made, lay down like a dead dog. Hungry as he was, he would not move to receive his ration of fish, which François had

1. **Dawson:** city in western central Yukon Territory, an important center during the Gold Rush.

GUIDED READING

LITERAL QUESTION

1a. How does Buck save the team when Spitz breaks through the ice? (He braces his legs against the ice, holding up the floundering dogs with tremendous strength.)

INFERENTIAL QUESTION

1b. What type of conflict is illustrated in this scene? (extreme conflict between characters and their environment)

o bring to him. Also, the dog driver rubbed uck's feet for half an hour each night after super, and sacrificed the tops of his own moccasins o make four moccasins for Buck. This was a reat relief, and Buck caused even the weazened ace of Perrault to twist itself into a grin one norning, when François forgot the moccasins nd Buck lay on his back, his four feet waving ppealingly in the air, and refused to budge vithout them. Later his feet grew hard to the rail, and the worn-out foot-gear was thrown way.

Spitz, as lead dog and acknowledged master of the team, felt his supremacy threatened by his strange Southland dog. And strange Buck vas to him, for of the many Southland dogs he ad known, not one had shown up worthily in amp and on trail. They were all too soft, dying inder the toil, the frost, and starvation. Buck vas the exception. He alone endured and prospered, matching the husky in strength, savagery, nd cunning. Then he was a masterful dog, and what made him dangerous was the fact that the lub of the man in the red sweater had knocked ll blind pluck and rashness out of his desire for nastery. He was pre-eminently cunning, and ould bide his time with a patience that was iothing less than primitive.

It was inevitable that the clash for leadership should come. Buck wanted it. He wanted it because it was his nature, because he had been gripped tight by that nameless, incomprehensible pride of the trail and trace—that pride which holds dogs in the toil to the last gasp, which lures them to die joyfully in the harness, and breaks their hearts if they are cut out of the harness. This was the pride of Dave as wheel dog, of Sol-leks as he pulled with all his strength; the pride that laid hold of them at break of camp, transforming them from sour and sullen brutes into straining, eager, ambitious creatures; the pride that spurred them on all day and dropped them at pitch of camp at night, letting them fall back into gloomy unrest and uncontent. This was the pride that bore up Spitz and made him thrash the sled dogs who blundered and shirked in the traces or hid away at harness-up time in the morning. Likewise it was this pride that made him fear Buck as a possible lead dog. And this was Buck's pride, too.

He openly threatened the other's leadership. He came between him and the shirks he should have punished. And he did it deliberately. One night there was a heavy snowfall, and in the morning Pike, the malingerer, did not appear. He was securely hidden in his nest under a foot of snow. François called him and sought him in vain. Spitz was wild with wrath. He raged through the camp, smelling and digging in every likely place, snarling so frightfully that Pike heard and shivered in his hiding place.

But when he was at last unearthed, and Spitz flew at him to punish him, Buck flew, with equal rage, in between. So unexpected was it, and so shrewdly managed, that Spitz was hurled backward and off his feet. Pike, who had been trembling abjectly, took heart at this open mutiny, and sprang upon his overthrown leader. Buck, to whom fair play was a forgotten code, likewise sprang upon Spitz. But François chuckling at the incident while unswerving in the administration of justice, brought his lash down upon Buck with all his might. This failed to drive Buck from his prostrate rival, and the butt of the whip was brought into play. Half-stunned by the blow, Buck was knocked backward and the lash laid upon him again and again, while Spitz soundly punished the many-times-offending Pike.

In the days that followed, as Dawson drew closer and closer, Buck still continued to interfere between Spitz and the culprits; but he did it
2 craftily, when François was not around. With the covert mutiny of Buck, a general insubordination sprang up and increased. Dave and Solleks were unaffected, but the rest of the team went from bad to worse. Things no longer went right. There was continual bickering and jang-

AT A GLANCE

- Spitz recognizes Buck's supremacy.
- Buck defends Pike against Spitz's attack; he is driven back by François.

1 CHARACTERIZATION

Buck has become the dominant primordial beast. His physical powers are matched by his inner character, in which savagery and cunning are held in check by patience.

2 PLOT: RISING ACTION

Buck begins to sow the seeds of Spitz's downfall by undermining the former lead dog's influence and encouraging the other dogs to mutiny.

GUIDED READING

LITERAL QUESTIONS

1a. Whom does Buck defend against Spitz? (Pike)

2a. What happens to Buck in this skirmish? (He is beaten back by François, who stuns him with the butt of his whip.)

INFERENTIAL QUESTIONS

1b. Why does Buck defend Pike against Spitz? (It is his nature to want to supplant Spitz.)

2b. What measures does Buck take to avoid another beating? (He becomes crafty and does not act in the presence of Francois.)

AT A GLANCE

- François knows that one day Buck and Spitz will fight to the finish.
- The team arrives in Dawson.
- After a week's rest, they begin their return trip, but discipline breaks down.

1 THEME

François does not intervene, though he knows he will end up losing one of his best dogs. He cannot interfere in this quarrel of nature.

2 SETTING

Everything is frozen—even the lights of heaven emanate a frosty glow. The sorrow and misery of life are sung by dogs whose ancestors endured similar fates.

3 PLOT: CONFLICT

The emerging conflict between the two great dogs grows as the intensity in the conflict with the environment wanes.

ling. Trouble was always afoot, and at the bottom of it was Buck. He kept François busy, for
1 the dog driver was in constant apprehension of the life-and-death struggle between the two which he knew must take place sooner or later; and on more than one night the sound of quarreling and strife among the other dogs turned him out of his sleeping robe, fearful that Buck and Spitz were at it.

But the opportunity did not present itself, and they pulled into Dawson one dreary afternoon with the great fight still to come. Here were many men, and countless dogs, and Buck found them all at work. It seemed the ordained order of things that dogs should work. All day they swung up and down the main street in long teams, and in the night their jingling bells still went by. They hauled cabin logs and firewood, freighted up to the mines, and did all manner of work that horses did in the Santa Clara Valley. Here and there Buck met Southland dogs, but in the main they were the wild wolf husky breed. Every night, regularly, at nine, at twelve, at three, they lifted a nocturnal song, a weird and eerie chant, in which it was Buck's delight to join.

2 With the aurora borealis[2] flaming coldly overhead, or the stars leaping in the frost dance, and the land numb and frozen under its pall of snow, this song of the huskies might have been the defiance of life, only it was pitched in minor key, with long-drawn wailings and half-sobs, and was more the pleading of life, the articulate travail[3] of existence. It was an old song, old as the breed itself—one of the first songs of the younger world in a day when songs were sad. It was invested with the woe of unnumbered generations, this plaint by which Buck was so strangely stirred. When he moaned and sobbed, it was with the pain of living that was of old the pain of his wild fathers, and the fear and mystery of the cold and dark that was to them fear and mystery.

Seven days from the time they pulled into Dawson, they dropped down the steep bank by the Barracks to the Yukon Trail,[4] and pulled for Dyea and Salt Water. Perrault was carrying dispatches if anything more urgent than those he had brought in; also, the travel pride had gripped him, and he purposed to make the record trip of the year. Several things favored him in this. The week's rest had recuperated the dogs and put them in thorough trim. The trail they had broken into the country was packed hard by later journeyers. And further, the police had arranged in two or three places deposits of grub for dog and man, and he was traveling light.

They made Sixty Mile, which is a fifty-mile run, on the first day; and the second day saw them booming up the Yukon well on their way to Pelly. But such splendid running was achieved not without great trouble and vexation on the
3 part of François. The insidious revolt led by Buck had destroyed the solidarity of the team. It no longer was as one dog leaping in the traces. The encouragement Buck gave the rebels led them into all kinds of petty misdemeanors. No more was Spitz a leader greatly to be feared. The old awe departed, and they grew equal to challenging his authority. Pike robbed him of half a fish one night, and gulped it down under the protection of Buck. Another night Dub and Joe fought Spitz and made him forego the punishment they deserved. And even Billee, the good-natured, was less good-natured, and whined not half so placatingly as in former days. Buck never came near Spitz without snarling and bristling menacingly. In fact, his conduct approached that of a bully, and he was given to swaggering up and down before Spitz's very nose.

The breaking down of discipline likewise af-

---

2. **aurora borealis** [ə rôr′ə bôr′ē al′is]: northern lights, bright bands of light visible in the night sky of northern regions.
3. **articulate** [är tik′yə lit]: **travail** [trə vāl′]: clearly expressed suffering.

4. **Yukon Trail:** trail between Dawson and the coast of southern Alaska. The team is heading south again.

GUIDED READING

LITERAL QUESTION

1a. Which dogs seem to predominate in Dawson? (the wild husky breed)

INFERENTIAL QUESTION

1b. What is Buck's response to these wild dogs? (He feels kinship with them and joins them at night in their "song.")

fected the dogs in their relations with one another. They quarreled and bickered more than ever among themselves, till at times the camp was a howling bedlam. Dave and Sol-leks alone were unaltered, though they were made irritable by the unending squabbling. François swore strange, barbarous oaths, and stamped the snow in futile rage, and tore his hair. His lash was always singing among the dogs, but it was of small avail. Directly his back was turned they were at it again. He backed up Spitz with his whip, while Buck backed up the remainder of the team. François knew he was behind all the trouble, and Buck knew he knew; but Buck was too clever ever again to be caught red-handed. He worked faithfully in the harness, for the toil had become a delight to him; yet it was a greater delight slyly to precipitate a fight amongst his mates and tangle the traces.

At the mouth of the Talkeetna, one night after supper, Dub turned up a snowshoe rabbit, blundered it and missed. In a second the whole team was in full cry. A hundred yards away was a camp of the Northwest Police, with fifty dogs, huskies all, who joined the chase. The rabbit sped down the river, turned off into a small creek, up the frozen bed of which it held steadily. It ran lightly on the surface of the snow, while the dogs ploughed through by main strength. Buck led the pack, sixty strong, around bend after bend, but he could not gain. He lay down low to the race, whining eagerly, his splendid body flashing forward, leap by leap, in the wan, white moonlight. And leap by leap, like some pale frost wraith[5] the snowshoe rabbit flashed on ahead.

2 There is an ecstasy that marks the summit of life, and beyond which life cannot rise. And such is the paradox of living, this ecstasy comes when one is most alive, and it comes as a complete forgetfulness that one is alive. This ecstasy, this forgetfulness of living, comes to the artist, caught up and out of himself in a sheet of flame; it

comes to the soldier, war-mad on a stricken field and refusing quarter; and it came to Buck, leading the pack, sounding the old wolf cry, straining after the food that was alive and that fled swiftly before him through the moonlight. He was sounding the deeps of his nature, and of the parts of his nature that were deeper than he. He was mastered by the sheer surging of life, the tidal wave of being, the perfect joy of each separate muscle, joint, and sinew in that it was everything that was not death, that it was aglow and rampant, expressing itself in movement, flying exultantly under the stars and over the face of dead matter that did not move.

3 But Spitz, cold and calculating even in his supreme moods, left the pack and cut across a narrow neck of land where the creek made a long bend around. Buck did not know of this, and as he rounded the bend, the frost wraith of a rabbit still flitting before him, he saw another and larger frost wraith leap from the overhanging bank into the immediate path of the rabbit. It was Spitz. The rabbit could not turn, and it shrieked as loudly as a stricken man may shriek.

Buck did not cry out. He did not check

5. **wraith** [rāth]: apparition, ghost.

AT A GLANCE

- Under Buck's influence the team loses its respect for Spitz.
- A rabbit chase becomes a moment of ecstasy for Buck and the other dogs.

1 CHARACTERIZATION

As ever, Buck learns from past mistakes. He is an absolute troublemaker but cleverly avoids punishment.

2 THEME

London's belief in the supreme happiness that comes to the wild being in nature is emphasized in this passage, which—along with the description of the howling of the dogs in Dawson—expresses a principal theme of the novel.

3 CHARACTERIZATION

London believed that only by the severest of conflicts with the most truthful and worthy foe can a creature's highest nature be developed. Thus it is important for Buck's victory that Spitz be a considerable opponent.

GUIDED READING

LITERAL QUESTION

1a. What creature do the dogs chase? (a snowshoe rabbit)

INFERENTIAL QUESTION

1b. How is life and death represented in the chase? (The rabbit is vainly trying to protect its life, and the dogs experience life at its fullest.)

AT A GLANCE

- Buck attacks Spitz.
- Sixty dogs from two camps form a ring around the fighting pair.
- They devour the loser, Spitz.

1 CHARACTERIZATION

Buck's instincts bring back to him the "memory" of the ritual of fighting for leadership, something he cannot have experienced directly before.

2 CHARACTERIZATION

Buck exhibits the trait that gives one creature the advantage over another and enables living things to improve over generations: imagination.

3 POINT OF VIEW

London closes the battle by drawing away from the scene: The savagery of the dogs' behavior is "a dot" and then nothing except the fitting end to a natural act.

REFLECTING ON CHAPTERS 1–3

What qualities make Buck the champion? (He has learned to steal and to hide his intentions, developed tremendous strength and stamina, and acquired ambition, the pride of the trail, and the desire for leadership.)

himself, but drove in upon Spitz, shoulder to shoulder, so hard that he missed the throat. They rolled over and over in the powdery snow. Spitz gained his feet almost as though he had not been overthrown, slashing Buck down the shoulder and leaping clear. Twice his teeth clipped together, like the steel jaws of a trap, as he backed away for better footing, with lean and lifting lips that writhed and snarled.

In a flash Buck knew it. The time had come. It was to the death. As they circled about, snarling, ears laid back, keenly watchful for the advantage,
1 the scene came to Buck with a sense of familiarity. He seemed to remember it all—the white woods, and earth, and moonlight, and the thrill of battle. Over the whiteness and silence brooded a ghostly calm. There was not the faintest whisper of air—nothing moved, not a leaf quivered, the visible breaths of the dogs rising slowly and lingering in the frosty air. They had made short work of the snowshoe rabbit, these dogs that were ill-tamed wolves; and they were now drawn up in an expectant circle. They, too, were silent, their eyes only gleaming and their breaths drifting slowly upward. To Buck it was nothing new or strange, this scene of old time. It was as though it had always been, the wonted way of things.

Spitz was a practiced fighter. From Spitzbergen through the Artic, and across Canada and the Barrens, he had held his own with all manner of dogs and achieved to mastery over them. Bitter rage was his, but never blind rage. In passion to rend and destroy, he never forgot that his enemy was in like passion to rend and destroy. He never rushed till he was prepared to receive a rush; never attacked till he had first defended that attack.

In vain Buck strove to sink his teeth in the neck of the big white dog. Then Buck took to rushing, as though for the throat, when, suddenly drawing back his head and curving in from the side, he would drive his shoulder at the shoulder of Spitz, as a ram by which to overthrow him. But instead, Buck's shoulder was slashed down each time as Spitz leaped lightly away.

The fight was growing desperate. And all the while the silent and wolfish circle waited to finish off whichever dog went down. As Buck grew winded, Spitz took to rushing, and he kept him staggering for footing. Once Buck went over, and the whole circle of sixty dogs started up; but he recovered himself, almost in midair, and the circle sank down again and waited.

2 But Buck possessed a quality that made for greatness—imagination. He fought by instinct, but he could fight by head as well. He rushed, as though attempting the old shoulder trick, but at the last instant swept low to the snow and in. His teeth closed on Spitz's left foreleg. Thrice he tried to knock him over, then repeated the trick and broke the right foreleg. Despite the pain and helplessness, Spitz struggled madly to keep up. He saw the silent circle, with gleaming eyes, lolling tongues, and silvery breaths drifting upward, closing in upon him as he had seen similar circles close in upon beaten antagonists in the past. Only this time he was the one who was beaten.

There was no hope for him. Buck was inexorable.[6] Mercy was a thing reserved for gentler climes. He maneuvered for the final rush. The circle had tightened till he could feel the breaths of the huskies on his flanks. He could see them, beyond Spitz and to either side, half-crouching for the spring, their eyes fixed upon him. A pause seemed to fall. Every animal was motionless as though turned to stone. Only Spitz quivered and bristled as he staggered back and forth, snarling with horrible menace, as though to frighten off impending death. Then Buck sprang in and out; but while he was in, shoulder had at
3 last squarely met shoulder. The dark circle became a dot on the moon-flooded snow as Spitz disappeared from view. Buck stood and looked on, the successful champion, the dominant primordial beast.

---

6. **inexorable** [i nek′sər ə bəl]: unyielding, relentless.

GUIDED READING

LITERAL QUESTION

1a. What is the difference between this fight and other, similar ones that Spitz has been in before? (This time Spitz is the loser.)

INFERENTIAL QUESTION

1b. What point does London make by reminding us that Spitz has won such fights before? (He reinforces the idea of survival of the fittest: A new champion takes the old one's place.)

STUDY QUESTIONS

Recalling

1. Based on Chapter 1, describe Buck and Judge Miller's place, giving three examples of Buck's relationships with the judge's family.
2. Briefly outline the steps in Chapter 1 that take Buck from Judge Miller's place to the man in the red sweater and then to the Yukon. Describe Buck's encounter with the man in the red sweater, and tell what lesson he learned.
3. According to Chapter 1, who are Buck's first owners in the north? What work do they do? What is Buck's opinion of them?
4. Describe the work Buck is made to do in Chapter 2 and his feelings about the work. What new skills does Buck learn in Chapter 2 in order to sleep and eat well?
5. According to Chapter 3, why does Buck want to become leader? Describe two things he does to gradually remove Spitz from the lead position.

Interpreting

6. In what ways does Buck change his attitudes about humans in the course of the first three chapters of the novel?
7. Explain how his experiences in the Klondike change Buck's relationship with nature.
8. What qualities enable Buck to remove Spitz from the lead position?
9. What actions of Buck show that he is losing the civilizing influence of the judge?

Extending

10. By the end of Chapter 3, do you think Buck misses his home with the judge? Explain your opinion.

LITERARY FOCUS

Point of View

In a novel as in a short story, **point of view** is the relationship of the storyteller to the story. A novel told from the **limited third-person point of view** is told by the author but from the limited point of view of only one character. The reader does not know the thoughts and feelings of any other character. *The Call of the Wild* is an unusual novel because London tells the story through the point of view of a dog, Buck. We know what Buck thinks and feels, and we learn about events through his eyes. We do not know the thoughts and feelings of other characters, animal or human.

Thinking About Point of View

■ Explain why Buck's point of view causes us to have more sympathy for him than the point of view of a human character would. You may consider incidents in which Buck is caged or is beaten, or in which he is made to sleep outdoors or is fed little.

Setting

The **setting** of a novel is the place and time in which the novel happens. Since a novel is longer than a short story, a novel can take place in a variety of settings and can describe a setting in more detail. Just as a new home or a trip may cause people to change, a change of setting in a novel is often a signal to the reader that a major character is undergoing some important change.

A change of setting can also provide clues to theme, or the novel's main idea. An author's use of settings may reveal an attitude about the world in general. For example, if a character in a novel moves from a humble shack to a luxurious home, the author may be revealing an optimism about life and a belief that situations improve with time.

Thinking About Setting

1. Contrast the two main settings of the first three chapters of *The Call of the Wild:* (1) the Judge's place and (2) the Yukon. Explain how the change of setting leads to a change in Buck.
2. What lesson about life does Buck learn from the change of settings?

STUDY QUESTIONS

1. big house on huge estate in California; hunts with sons, walks with daughters, lies at judge's feet before fire
2. ■ Buck stolen; sold to stranger; taken on train to San Francisco; crated, placed on trucks, wagons; after two days on another train without food and water, arrives in Seattle; meets man in red sweater
   ■ sold to Perrault; taken to Yukon on ship; clubbed; learns not to resist force
3. Francois and Perrault; couriers for Canadian government; respects them
4. ■ pulls sled hauling firewood, joins sled team; his dignity is offended
   ■ learns to make snow nest, to eat quickly, to steal food
5. his pride; interferes when Spitz disciplines other dogs, swaggers and growls at him
6. becomes wary of humans
7. begins to rely on instincts; experiences joy in wilderness
8. pride, imagination, cunning, strength, persistence
9. He bolts his food, steals food, fights to keep other dogs from challenging him.
10. Probably not—he has adapted to his new wilderness life.

LITERARY FOCUS

Point of View

He reveals his own sufferings, feelings.

Setting

1. ■ judge's place: warm, sunny, filled with luxuries; Yukon: cold, dangerous wilderness
   ■ Change awakens Buck's instincts to survive and makes him stronger.
2. He must fight to survive, rely on his own strength and intelligence.

AT A GLANCE

- François attempts to make Sol-leks the lead dog.
- Buck refuses to return to his old position.

LITERARY OPTIONS

- characterization
- plot
- point of view

THEMATIC OPTIONS

- civilization vs. nature
- in survival
- love of labor

1 PLOT: CONFLICT

Having survived conflict with the environment and with the most cunning and worthy of canine opponents, Buck encounters his third source of conflict: the men who are the masters.

2 CHARACTERIZATION

Buck has learned that the club is his enemy and stays out of its range. As his cunning tells him that the pack train cannot leave without him, his resistance takes passive form: He will wait out the men.

4 Who Has Won to Mastership

"Eh? Wot I say? I spik true w'en I say dat Buck two devils."

This was François's speech next morning when he discovered Spitz missing and Buck covered with wounds. He drew him to the fire and by its light pointed them out.

"An' now we make good time. No more Spitz, no more trouble, sure."

While Perrault packed the camp outfit and loaded the sled, the dog driver proceeded to
1 harness the dogs. Buck trotted up to the place Spitz would have occupied as leader; but François, not noticing him, brought Sol-leks to the coveted position. In his judgment, Sol-leks was the best lead dog left. Buck sprang upon Sol-leks in a fury, driving him back and standing in his place.

"Eh? eh?" François cried, slapping his thighs gleefully. "Look at dat Buck. Heem keel dat Spitz, heem t'ink to take de job."

"Go 'way, Chook." he cried, but Buck refused to budge.

He took Buck by the scruff of the neck, and though the dog growled threateningly, dragged him to one side and replaced Sol-leks. The old dog did not like it, and showed plainly that he was afraid of Buck. François was obdurate, but when he turned his back Buck again displaced Sol-leks, who was not at all unwilling to go.

François was angry. "Now, I feex you!" he cried, coming back with a heavy club in his hand.

Buck remembered the man in the red sweater, and retreated slowly; nor did he attempt to charge in when Sol-leks was once more brought
2 forward. But he circled just beyond the range of the club, snarling with bitterness and rage; and while he circled he watched the club so as to dodge it if thrown by François, for he was become wise in the way of clubs.

The driver went about his work, and he called to Buck when he was ready to put him in his old place in front of Dave. Buck retreated two or three steps. François followed him up, where-

GUIDED READING

LITERAL QUESTION

1a. Why doesn't Buck become lead dog after Spitz's death? (Francois thinks Sol-leks is the best potential lead dog.)

INFERENTIAL QUESTION

1b. Why do we sense that this fight with François will end happily for Buck? (Buck has the allegiance of the dogs: Sol-leks retreats whenever Buck approaches: the men need to proceed.)

upon he again retreated. After some time of this, François threw down the club, thinking that Buck feared a thrashing. But Buck was in open revolt. He wanted, not to escape a clubbing, but to have the leadership. It was his by right. He had earned it, and he would not be content with less.

Perrault took a hand. Between them they ran him about for the better part of an hour. They threw clubs at him. He dodged. He did not try to run away, but retreated around and around the camp, advertising plainly that when his desire was met, he would come in and be good.

François sat down and scratched his head. Perrault looked at his watch and swore. Time was flying, and they should have been on the trail an hour gone. François scratched his head again. He shook it and grinned sheepishly at the courier, who shrugged his shoulders in sign that they were beaten. Then François went up to where Sol-leks stood and called to Buck. Buck laughed, as dogs laugh, yet kept his distance. François unfastened Sol-leks's traces and put him back in his old place. The team stood harnessed to the sled in an unbroken line, ready for the trail. There was no place for Buck save at the front. Once more François called, and once more Buck laughed and kept away.

"T'row down de club," Perrault commanded.

François complied, whereupon Buck trotted in, laughing triumphantly, and swung around into position at the head of the team. His traces[1] were fastened, the sled broken out, and with both men running they dashed out on to the river trail.

Highly as the dog driver had forevalued Buck, with his two devils, he found, while the day was yet young, that he had undervalued. At a bound Buck took up the duties of leadership; and where judgment was required, and quick thinking and quick acting, he showed himself the superior even of Spitz, of whom François had never seen an equal.

But it was in giving the law and making his mates live up to it that Buck excelled. Dave and Sol-leks did not mind the change in leadership. It was none of their business. Their business was to toil, and toil mightily, in the traces. So long as that were not interfered with, they did not care what happened. Billee, the good-natured, could lead for all they cared, so long as he kept order. The rest of the team, however, had grown unruly during the last days of Spitz, and their surprise was great now that Buck proceeded to lick them into shape.

Pike, who pulled at Buck's heels, and who never put an ounce more of his weight against the breastband than he was compelled to do, was swiftly and repeatedly shaken for loafing; and ere the first day was done he was pulling more than ever before in his life. The first night in camp, Joe, the sour one, was punished roundly—a thing that Spitz had never succeeded in doing. Buck simply smothered him by virtue of superior weight, and cut him up till he ceased snapping and began to whine for mercy.

The general tone of the team picked up immediately. It recovered its old-time solidarity, and once more the dogs leaped as one dog in the
2 traces. At the Rink Rapids two native huskies, Teek and Koona, were added; and the celerity with which Buck broke them in took away François's breath.

"Nevaire such a dog as dat Buck!" he cried. "No, nevaire! Heem worth one t'ousan' dollair, by Gar! Eh? Wot you say, Perrault?"

And Perrault nodded. He was ahead of the
3 record then, and gaining day by day. The trail was in excellent condition, well packed and hard, and there was no new-fallen snow with which to contend. It was not too cold. The temperature dropped to fifty below zero and remained there the whole trip. The men rode and ran by turn, and the dogs were kept on the jump, with but infrequent stoppages.

1. **traces:** straps that connect the harness of a draft animal to the load it pulls.

AT A GLANCE

- Buck holds out for lead position.
- François and Perrault give in.
- Under Buck's leadership the team begins to regain its unity.

1 CHARACTERIZATION

Buck's victory over the men causes him to "laugh." This is Buck's greatest victory: He takes pleasure in knowing that the path to leadership is now clear.

2 THEME

As Buck becomes more adjusted to his new life, his company begins to change: The new dogs bear native names that carry no suggestion of a European, or "civilized," past.

3 SETTING

London uses ironically understated language (*It was not too cold . . . fifty below zero*) to suggest the genuine hardship of the environment; he also notes details (the hard-packed trail and lack of new-fallen snow) on which the team depends.

GUIDED READING

LITERAL QUESTIONS

1a. What, according to Dave and Sol-leks, is the purpose of the leader? (to keep order)

2a. How much does François think Buck is worth? (one thousand dollars)

INFERENTIAL QUESTIONS

1b. What wise qualities of leadership does Buck show? (He identifies the two troublemakers and metes out fair and effective punishments.)

2b. What do you predict will be the end of Buck's relationship with the men? (They will probably sell him.)

AT A GLANCE

- The team returns to Skagway.
- Buck and the team are sold to "a Scotsman."
- They travel with a dozen other teams delivering mail.

1 PLOT: RISING ACTION

Buck is sold to "a Scotsman." The parting from the French Canadian is abrupt and without sorrow on Buck's part.

2 CHARACTERIZATION

Buck's work ethic inspires him to apply himself wholeheartedly even to tasks he dislikes as he also keeps the others in line.

3 POINT OF VIEW

Under the influence of the new, routinely monotonous and uneventful life, Buck's thoughts drift back to his former life.

The Thirty Mile River was comparatively coated with ice, and they covered in one day going out what had taken them ten days coming in. In one run they made a sixty-mile dash from the foot of Lake Laberge to the Whitehorse Rapids. Across Marsh, Tagish, and Bennett (seventy miles of lakes), they flew so fast that the man whose turn it was to run towed behind the sled at the end of a rope. And on the last night of the second week they topped White Pass and dropped down the sea slope with the lights of Skagway[2] and of the shipping at their feet.

It was a record run. Each day for fourteen days they had averaged forty miles. For three days Perrault and François threw chests up and down the main street of Skagway while the team was the constant center of a worshipful crowd of dog busters and mushers.[3] Then three or four Western bad men aspired to clean out the town, and public interest turned to other idols. Next
1 came official orders. François called Buck to him, threw his arms around him, wept over him. And that was the last of François and Perrault. Like other men, they passed out of Buck's life for good.

A Scotsman took charge of him and his mates, and in company with a dozen other dog teams he started back over the weary trail to Dawson. It was no light running now, nor record time, but heavy toil each day, with a heavy load behind; for this was the mail train, carrying word from the world to the men who sought gold under the shadow of the Pole.

2 Buck did not like it, but he bore up well to the work, taking pride in it after the manner of Dave and Sol-leks, and seeing that his mates, whether they prided in it or not, did their fair share. It was a monotonous life, operating with machinelike regularity. One day was very like another. At a certain time each morning the cooks turned out, fires were built, and breakfast was eaten. Then, while some broke camp, others harnessed the dogs, and they were under way an hour or so before the darkness fell which gave warning of dawn. At night, camp was made. Some pitched the flies,[4] others cut firewood and pine boughs for the beds, and still others carried water or ice for the cooks. Also, the dogs were fed. To them, this was the one feature of the day, though it was good to loaf around, after the fish was eaten, for an hour or so with the other dogs, of which there were five score and odd. There were fierce fighters among them, but three battles with the fiercest brought Buck to mastery, so that when he bristled and showed his teeth they got out of his way.

3 Best of all, perhaps, he loved to lie near the fire, hind legs crouched under him, forelegs stretched out in front, head raised, and eyes blinking dreamily at the flames. Sometimes he thought of Judge Miller's big house in the sun-kissed Santa Clara Valley, and of the cement swimming tank, and Ysabel, the Mexican hairless, and Toots, the Japanese pug; but oftener he remembered the man in the red sweater, the great fight with Spitz, and the good things he had eaten or would like to eat. He was not homesick. The Sunland was very dim and distant, and such memories had no power over him. Far more potent were the memories of his heredity that gave things he had never seen before a seeming familiarity; the instincts (which were but the memories of his ancestors become habits) which had lapsed in later days, and still later, in him, quickened and became alive again.

It was a hard trip, with the mail behind them, and the heavy work wore them down. They were short of weight and in poor condition when they made Dawson, and should have had a ten days' or a week's rest at least. But in two days' time they dropped down the Yukon bank

2. **Skagway:** coastal city in southern Alaska, the southern end of the Yukon Trail. Most of the traveling in the novel is between Dawson and Skagway.
3. **busters and mushers:** those who train and drive sled dogs.
4. **pitched the flies:** erected the tents.

GUIDED READING

LITERAL QUESTION

1a. How fast does the team travel on its final trip to Skagway? (It covers forty miles on each of fourteen days—560 miles in two weeks.)

INFERENTIAL QUESTION

1b. How does the record-breaking run affect the theme of the novel? (It seems to be the stamp of approval to Buck's transformation: He has achieved excellence.)

from the Barracks, loaded with letters for the outside. The dogs were tired, the drivers grumbling, and to make matters worse, it snowed every day. This meant a soft trail, greater friction on the runners, and heavier pulling for the dogs; yet the drivers were fair through it all, and did their best for the animals.

Each night the dogs were attended to first. They ate before the drivers ate, and no man sought his sleeping robe till he had seen to the feet of the dogs he drove. Still, their strength went down. Since the beginning of the winter they had traveled eighteen hundred miles, dragging sleds the whole weary distance; and eighteen hundred miles will tell upon life of the toughest. Buck stood it, keeping his mates up to their work and maintaining discipline, though he, too, was very tired. Billee cried and whimpered regularly in his sleep each night. Joe was sourer than ever, and Sol-leks was unapproachable, blind side or other side.

But it was Dave who suffered most of all. Something had gone wrong with him. He became more morose and irritable, and when camp was pitched at once made his nest, where his driver fed him. Once out of the harness and down, he did not get on his feet again till harness-up time in the morning. Sometimes, in the traces, when jerked by a sudden stoppage of the sled, or by straining to start it, he would cry out with pain. The driver examined him, but could find nothing. All the drivers became interested in his case. They talked it over at mealtime, and over their last pipes before going to bed, and one night they held a consultation. He was brought up from his nest to the fire and was pressed and prodded till he cried out many times. Something was wrong inside, but they could locate no broken bones, could not make it out.

By the time Cassiar Bar was reached, he was so weak that he was falling repeatedly in the traces. The Scotsman called a halt and took him out of the team, making the next dog, Sol-leks, fast to the sled. His intention was to rest Dave, letting him run free behind the sled. Sick as he was, Dave resented being taken out, grunting and growling while the traces were unfastened, and whimpering brokenheartedly when he saw Sol-leks in the position he had held and served so long. For the pride of trace and trail was his, and, sick unto death, he could not bear that another dog should do his work.

When the sled started, he floundered in the soft snow alongside the beaten trail, attacking Sol-leks with his teeth, rushing against him and
1 trying to thrust him off into the soft snow on the other side, striving to leap inside his traces and get between him and the sled, and all the while whining and yelping and crying with grief and pain. Dave refused to run quietly on the trail behind the sled, where the going was easy, but continued to flounder alongside in the soft snow, where the going was most difficult, till exhausted. Then he fell, and lay where he fell, howling lugubriously[5] as the long train of sleds churned by.

With the last remnant of his strength he managed to stagger along behind till the train made another stop, when he floundered past the sleds to his own, where he stood alongside Sol-leks. His driver lingered a moment to get a light for his pipe from the man behind. Then he returned and started his dogs. They swung out on the trail with remarkable lack of exertion, turned their heads uneasily, and stopped in surprise. The driver was surprised, too; the sled had not moved. He called his comrades to witness the sight. Dave had bitten through both of Sol-leks's traces, and was standing directly in front of the sled in his proper place.

He pleaded with his eyes to remain there.
2 The driver was perplexed. His comrades talked of how a dog could break its heart through being denied the work that killed it, and recalled instances they had known, where dogs, too old for the toil, or injured, had died because they were

5. **lugubriously** [lo͞o go͞o′brē əs lē]: mournfully.

AT A GLANCE

- Dave becomes ill.
- He will not let his place be taken by another dog.

1 WORD CHOICE

The sounds of the weakened dog's protest at being cut out of the pack (*whining, yelping,* and *crying*) convey the pain of Dave's suffering.

2 FORESHADOWING

Talk among "comrades" suggests that Dave is going to die of a broken heart.

GUIDED READING

LITERAL QUESTIONS

1a. What happens to Dave by the time he reaches Cassiar Bar? (He becomes so weak that he falls repeatedly out of the traces.)

2a. Which sled dogs traveled with Buck on the *Narwhal* from Seattle to Skagway many weeks ago? (Dave and Spitz)

INFERENTIAL QUESTIONS

1b. What fate seems to be worse than death for Dave? (to be useless)

2b. How is Dave's illness part of a pattern of recent events? (Buck's ties are being severed one by one. Spitz is dead; Perrault and François are gone.)

AT A GLANCE

- Dave is unable to walk to the harness.
- The Scotsman shoots him.
- The exhausted team returns to Skagway and is purchased by two tenderfeet.

1 CHARACTERIZATION

The pain of Dave's condition indicates he should stop; the imperative of pride impels him to go on.

2 POINT OF VIEW

Dave's death is presented from the dogs' point of view: The language is dispassionate, except for the ironic use of the word *merrily*.

3 READING SKILLS: INFERENCE

The watery eyes, the fiercely twisted mustache, and the concealed, drooping lip suggest that Charles is a born loser.

1 cut out of the traces. Also, they held it a mercy, since Dave was to die anyway, that he should die in the traces, heart-easy and content. So he was harnessed in again, and proudly he pulled as of old, though more than once he cried out involuntarily from the bite of his inward hurt. Several times he fell down and was dragged in the traces, and once the sled ran upon him so that he limped thereafter in one of his hind legs.

But he held out till camp was reached, when his driver made a place for him by the fire. Morning found him to weak to travel. At harness-up time he tried to crawl to his driver. By convulsive efforts he got on his feet, staggered, and fell. Then he wormed his way forward slowly toward where the harnesses were being put on his mates. He would advance his forelegs and drag up his body with a sort of hitching movement, when he would advance his forelegs and hitch ahead again for a few more inches. His strength left him, and the last his mates saw of him he lay gasping in the snow and yearning toward them. But they could hear him mournfully howling till they passed out of sight behind a belt of river timber.

Here the train was halted. The Scotsman
2 slowly retraced his steps to the camp they had left. The men ceased talking. A revolver shot rang out. The man came back hurriedly. The whips snapped, the bells tinkled merrily, the sleds churned along the trail; but Buck knew, and every dog knew, what had taken place behind the belt of river trees.

5 The Toil of Trace and Trail

Thirty days from the time it left Dawson, the Salt Water Mail, with Buck and his mates at the fore, arrived at Skagway. They were in a wretched state, worn out and worn down. Buck's one hundred and forty pounds had dwindled to one hundred and fifteen. The rest of his mates, though lighter dogs, had relatively lost more weight than he. Pike, the malingerer, who, in his lifetime of deceit, had often successfully feigned a hurt leg, was now limping in earnest. Sol-leks was limping, and Dub was suffering from a wrenched shoulder blade.

"Mush on, poor sore feets," the driver encouraged them as they tottered down the main street of Skagway. "Dis is de las'. Den we get one long res'. Eh? For sure. One bully long res'."

The drivers confidently expected a long stopover. Themselves, they had covered twelve hundred miles with two days' rest, and in the nature of reason and common justice they deserved an interval of loafing. But so many were the men who had rushed into the Klondike, and so many were the sweethearts, wives, and kin that had not rushed in, that the congested mail was taking on Alpine proportions; also, there were official orders. Fresh batches of Hudson Bay[1] dogs were to take the places of those worthless for the trail. The worthless ones were to be got rid of, and, since dogs count for little against dollars, they were to be sold.

Three days passed, by which time Buck and his mates found how really tired and weak they were. Then, on the morning of the fourth day, two men from the States came along and bought them, harness and all, for a song. The men ad-
3 dressed each other as Hal and Charles. Charles was a middle-aged man, with weak and watery eyes and a mustache that twisted fiercely and vigorously up, giving the lie to the limply drooping lip it concealed. Hal was a youngster of nineteen or twenty, with a big Colt's revolver and a hunting knife strapped about him on a belt that fairly bristled with cartridges. This belt was the most salient thing about him. It advertised his callowness—a callowness sheer and unutterable. Both men were manifestly out of place, and why such as they should adventure the North is part of the mystery of things that passes understanding.

1. **Hudson Bay:** large inland sea in northeastern Canada. The Yukon Territory is the extreme northwest.

GUIDED READING

LITERAL QUESTIONS

1a. Who purchases the dog train from the Scotsman? (Hal and Charles)

2a. In what condition do the dogs return to Skagway? (emaciated and exhausted)

INFERENTIAL QUESTIONS

1b. Why does Hal's cartridge belt mark him as "callow"? (In his immaturity he has mistaken the kind of strength needed for life in the Yukon.)

2b. How is it possible such fine dogs could be sold to such ridiculous characters? (The dogs have been run to death and are no longer prime property; Hal and Charles may have offered a high price.)

Buck heard the chaffering,[2] saw the money pass between the man and the Government agent, and knew that the Scotsman and the mail-train drivers were passing out of his life on the heels of Perrault and François and the others who had gone before. When driven with his mates to the new owners' camp, Buck saw a slipshod and slovenly affair, tent half-stretched, dishes unwashed, everything in disorder; also, he saw a woman. Mercedes[3] the men called her. She was Charles's wife and Hal's sister—a nice family party.

Buck watched them apprehensively as they proceeded to take down the tent and load the sled. There was a great deal of effort about their
2 manner, but no businesslike method. The tent was rolled into an awkward bundle three times as large as it should have been. The tin dishes were packed away unwashed. Mercedes continually fluttered in the way of her men and kept up an unbroken chattering of remonstrance and advice. When they put a clothes sack on the front of the sled, she suggested it should go on the back; and when they had put it on the back, and covered it over with a couple of other bundles, she discovered overlooked articles which could abide nowhere else but in that very sack, and they unloaded again.

Three men from a neighboring tent came out

2. **chaffering:** bargaining.
3. **Mercedes** [mer sā'dēz]

AT A GLANCE

- Buck and the others are taken to the new camp.
- They discover that one of the residents is a woman.
- The camp is badly maintained.

1 POINT OF VIEW

The disarray, seen from the dog's point of view, seems to foretell disaster. However, there is also a light humor that enters at this point, perhaps because the animals know more than their new masters.

2 THEME

The devils of soft civilization—possessions, ineptitude, lack of real strength and authority—plague the party.

GUIDED READING

LITERAL QUESTION

1a. Who is Mercedes? (Charles's wife and Hal's sister)

INFERENTIAL QUESTION

1b. What is London's tone in the phrase *a nice family party*? (ironic)

AT A GLANCE

- Neighbors offer help to the threesome.
- Their advice is ignored.
- Hal tries to get the exhausted dogs to break out the sled.

1 STYLE: DIALOGUE

Mercedes' speech is full of outbursts that are inappropriate for the rugged arctic life.

2 CHARACTERIZATION

Hal arrogantly ignores good advice, and his sister winces at his language but not, ironically, at his foolishness.

and looked on, grinning and winking at one another.

"You've got a right smart load as it is," said one of them; "and it's not me should tell you your business, but I wouldn't tote that tent along if I was you."

1 "Undreamed of!" cried Mercedes, throwing up her hands in dainty dismay. "However in the world could I manage without a tent?"

"It's springtime, and you won't get any more cold weather," the man replied.

She shook her head decidedly, and Charles and Hal put the last odds and ends on top the mountainous load.

"Think it'll ride?" one of the men asked.

"Why shouldn't it?" Charles demanded rather shortly.

"Oh, that's all right, that's all right," the man hastened meekly to say. "I was just a-wonderin', that is all. It seemed a might top heavy."

Charles turned his back and drew the lashings down as well as he could, which was not in the least well.

"An' of course the dogs can hike along all day with that contraption behind them," affirmed a second of the men.

"Certainly," said Hal, with freezing politeness, taking hold of the gee pole[4] with one hand and swinging his whip from the other. "Mush!" he shouted. "Mush on there!"

The dogs sprang against the breastbands, strained hard for a few moments, then relaxed. They were unable to move the sled.

"The lazy brutes, I'll show them," he cried, preparing to lash out at them with the whip.

But Mercedes interfered, crying, "Oh, Hal, you mustn't," as she caught hold of the whip and wrenched it from him. "The poor dears! Now you must promise you won't be harsh with them for the rest of the trip, or I won't go a step."

"Precious lot you know about dogs," her brother sneered; "and I wish you'd leave me alone. They're lazy, I tell you, and you've got to whip them to get anything out of them. That's their way. You ask anyone. Ask one of those men."

Mercedes looked at them imploringly, untold repugnance at sight of pain written in her pretty face.

"They're weak as water, if you want to know," came the reply from one of the men. "Plumb tuckered out, that's what's the matter. They need a rest."

2 "Rest be blanked," said Hal, with his beardless lips; and Mercedes said, 'Oh!" in pain and sorrow at the oath.

But she was a clannish creature, and rushed at once to the defense of her brother. "Never mind that man," she said pointedly. "You're driving our dogs, and you do what you think best with them."

Again Hal's whip fell upon the dogs. They threw themselves against the breastbands, dug their feet into the packed snow, got down low to it, and put forth all their strength. The sled held as though it were an anchor. After two efforts, they stood still, panting. The whip was whistling savagely, when once more Mercedes interfered. She dropped on her knees before Buck, with tears in her eyes, and put her arms around his neck.

"You poor, poor dears," she cried sympathetically, "why don't you pull hard?—then you wouldn't be whipped." Buck did not like her, but he was feeling too miserable to resist her, taking it as part of the day's miserable work.

One of the onlookers, who had been clenching his teeth to suppress hot speech, now spoke up:

"It's not that I care a whoop what becomes of you, but for the dogs' sakes I just want to tell you, you can help them a mightly lot by breaking out that sled. The runners are froze fast. Throw your weight against the gee pole, right and left, and break it out."

A third time the attempt was made, but this

4. **gee pole:** pole at the rear of a sled by which the driver steers.

GUIDED READING

LITERAL QUESTION

1a. What advice do the old-timers offer the newcomers? (to fold the tent, to remember that the dogs are worn out, and to break out the runners)

INFERENTIAL QUESTION

1b. What phrases do the old-timers use that are typical of their characters? (*right smart load, tote that tent, I was just a-wonderin', contraption, not that I care a whoop*)

time, following the advice, Hal broke out the runners which had been frozen to the snow. The overloaded and unwieldy sled forged ahead, Buck and his mates struggling frantically under the rain of blows. A hundred yards ahead the path turned and sloped steeply into the main street. It would have required an experienced man to keep the top-heavy sled upright, and Hal was not such a man. As they swung on the turn the sled went over, spilling half its load through the loose lashings. The dogs never stopped. The lightened sled bounded on its side behind them. They were angry because of the ill treatment they had received and the unjust load. Buck was raging. He broke into a run, the team following his lead. Hal cried "Whoa! whoa!" but they gave no heed. He tripped and was pulled off his feet. The capsized sled ground over him, and the dogs dashed up the street, adding to the gaiety of Skagway as they scattered the remainder of the outfit along its chief thoroughfare.

Kindhearted citizens caught the dogs and gathered up the scattered belongings. Also, they gave advice. Half the load and twice the dogs, if they ever expected to reach Dawson, was what was said. Hal and his sister and brother-in-law listened unwillingly, pitched tent, and overhauled the outfit. Canned goods were turned out that made men laugh, for canned goods on the Long Trail are a thing to dream about. "Blankets for a hotel," quoth one of the men who laughed and helped. "Half as many is too much; get rid of them. Throw away that tent, and all those dishes—who's going to wash them, anyway? Good Lord, do you think you're traveling on a Pullman?"[5]

And so it went, the inexorable elimination of the superfluous. Mercedes cried when her clothes bags were dumped on the ground and article after article was thrown out. She cried in general, and she cried in particular over each discarded thing. She clasped hands about knees, rocking back and forth brokenheartedly. She averred[6] she would not go an inch, not for a dozen Charleses. She appealed to everybody and to everything, finally wiping her eyes and proceeding to cast out even articles of apparel that were imperative necessaries. And in her zeal, when she had finished with her own, she attacked the belongings of her men and went through them like a tornado.

This accomplished, the outfit, though cut in half, was still a formidable bulk. Charles and Hal went out in the evening and bought six Outside dogs. These, added to the six of the original team, and Teek and Koona, the huskies obtained at the Rink Rapids on the record trip, brought the team up to fourteen. But the Outside dogs, though practically broken in since their landing, did not amount to much. Three were short-haired pointers, one was a Newfoundland, and the other two were mongrels of indeterminate
2 breed. They did not seem to know anything, these newcomers. Buck and his comrades looked upon them with disgust, and though he speedily taught them their places and what not to do, he could not teach them what to do. They did not take kindly to trace and trail. With the exception of the two mongrels, they were bewildered and spirit-broken by the strange, savage environment in which they found themselves and by the ill treatment they had received. The two mongrels were without spirit at all; bones were the only things breakable about them.

With the newcomers hopeless and forlorn, and the old team worn out by twenty-five hundred miles of continuous trail, the outlook was
3 anything but bright. The two men, however, were quite cheerful. And they were proud, too. They were doing the thing in style, with fourteen dogs. They had seen other sleds depart over the Pass for Dawson, or come in from Dawson, but never had they seen a sled with so many as fourteen dogs. In the nature of Arctic travel there was a reason why fourteen dogs should

5. **Pullman:** railroad car with sleeping accommodations.

6. **averred:** insisted.

AT A GLANCE

- Hal lets the sled tip over.
- The dogs run away with the sled.
- The townspeople persuade the party to fortify the team.

1 CHARACTERIZATION

Indirectly (through the comments of the citizens) we learn how soft and naive the threesome are. They deserve to be ridiculed because they stubbornly refuse to recognize that they are misplaced.

2 CHARACTERIZATION

Buck seems to forget his own inexperience of the past: He assesses the newcomers (in a haughty and superior manner) as unequal to the tasks before them.

3 CHARACTERIZATION

Again, the inappropriate response of Hal and Charles to their predicament makes them seem like clowns. Their fourteen dogs are a ragtag, worn-out crew, but the men think they are traveling in style.

GUIDED READING

LITERAL QUESTIONS

1a. Why does the sled tip over? (It is overloaded and badly balanced, and Hal does not know how to steer it.)

2a. How does Mercedes react when the townspeople throw away her clothes? (She cries.)

INFERENTIAL QUESTIONS

1b. What type of conflict seems to be in the making between Buck and Hal? (Though Hal is a fool, Buck will have to take his orders.)

2b. Why do you think Mercedes is included in this group? (She adds another ridiculous figure to the little group—hers is a stereotypically weak and inappropriate presence.)

AT A GLANCE

- The group begins the trip to Dawson.
- The humans are unable to manage well.
- Food supplies dwindle; dogs begin to die.

1 POINT OF VIEW

Although the humans have provided the reader with amusement, from Buck's point of view the prospect of a repeat six-hundred-mile trip with them is discouraging.

2 CHARACTERIZATION

Hal's lack of foresight and common sense is startling. The dogs are vital to the success of Hal's adventure, but he has been fatally careless about providing for them.

3 STYLE: PARALLELISM

London drives home his point by balancing phrases that describe aspects of the humans' ignorance.

not drag one sled, and that was that one sled could not carry the food for fourteen dogs. But Charles and Hal did not know this. They had worked the trip out with a pencil, so much to a dog, so many dogs, so many days, Q.E.D.[7] Mercedes looked over their shoulders and nodded comprehensively, it was all so very simple.

Late next morning Buck led the long team up the street. There was nothing lively about it, no snap or go in him and his fellows. They were starting dead weary. Four times he had covered the distance between Salt Water and Dawson,
1 and the knowledge that, jaded and tired, he was facing the same trail once more, made him bitter. His heart was not in the work, nor was the heart of any dog. The Outsides were timid and frightened, the Insides without confidence in their masters.

Buck felt vaguely that there was no depending upon these two men and the woman. They did not know how to do anything, and as the days went by it became apparent that they could not learn. They were slack in all things, without order or discipline. It took them half the night to pitch a slovenly camp, and half the morning to break that camp and get the sled loaded in fashion so slovenly that for the rest of the day they were occupied in stopping and rearranging the load. Some days they did not make ten miles. On other days they were unable to get started at all. And on no day did they succeed in making more than half the distance used by the men as a basis in their dog-food computation.

It was inevitable that they should go short on dog food. But they hastened it by overfeeding, bringing the day nearer when underfeeding would commence. The Outside dogs, whose digestions had not been trained by chronic famine to make the most of little, had voracious appetites. And when, in addition to this, the worn-out huskies pulled weakly, Hal decided that the orthodox ration was too small. He doubled it. And to cap it all, when Mercedes, with tears in her pretty eyes and a quaver in her throat, could not cajole him into giving the dogs still more, she stole from the fish sacks and fed them slyly. But it was not food that Buck and the huskies needed, but rest. And though they were making poor time, the heavy load they dragged sapped their strength severely.

2 Then came the underfeeding. Hal awoke one day to the fact that his dog food was half gone and the distance only quarter covered; further, that for love or money no additional dog food was to be obtained. So he cut down even the orthodox ration and tried to increase the day's travel. His sister and brother-in-law seconded him; but they were frustrated by their heavy outfit and their own incompetence. It was a simple matter to give the dogs less food; but it was impossible to make the dogs travel faster, while their own ability to get under way earlier in the morning prevented them from traveling longer
3 hours. Not only did they not know how to work dogs, but they did not know how to work themselves.

The first to go was Dub. Poor blundering thief that he was, always getting caught and punished, he had none the less been a faithful worker. His wrenched shoulder blade, untreated and unrested, went from bad to worse, till finally Hal shot him with the big Colt's revolver. It is a saying of the country that an Outside dog starves to death on the ration of the husky, so the six Outside dogs under Buck could do no less than die on half the ration of the husky. The Newfoundland went first, followed by the three short-haired pointers, the two mongrels hanging more grittily on to life, but going in the end.

By this time all the amenities and gentlenesses of the Southland had fallen away from the three people. Shorn of its glamour and romance, Arctic travel became to them a reality too harsh for their manhood and womanhood. Mercedes ceased weeping over the dogs, being too occu-

7. **Q.E.D.**: abbreviation for *quod erat demonstrandum,* Latin for "that which must be proven or demonstrated."

GUIDED READING

LITERAL QUESTIONS

1a. What does Mercedes do when she cannot get the men to feed the dogs more? (steals from the fish sacks and secretly feeds the dogs)

2a. Which dog dies first? (Dub)

INFERENTIAL QUESTIONS

1b. What quality of the trio does her action reveal? (lack of discipline)

2b. How does Dub's death strike an ominous note in the tale? (Dub is a dog from the regular pack. He has been allowed to suffer and die, as any other veteran dog might be.)

pied with weeping over herself and with quarreling with her husband and brother. To quarrel was the one thing they were never too weary to do.

Charles and Hal wrangled whenever Mercedes gave them a chance. It was the cherished belief of each that he did more than his share of the work, and neither forbore to speak this belief at every opportunity. Sometimes Mercedes sided with her husband, sometimes with her brother. The result was a beautiful and unending family quarrel. Starting from a dispute as to which should chop a few sticks for the fire (a dispute which concerned only Charles and Hal), presently would be lugged in the rest of the family, fathers, mothers, uncles, cousins, people thousands of miles away, and some of them dead. That Hal's views on art, or the sort of society plays his mother's brother wrote, should have anything to do with the chopping of a few sticks of firewood, passes comprehension; nevertheless the quarrel was as likely to tend in that direction as in the direction of Charles's political prejudices. And that Charles's sister's talebearing tongue should be relevant to the building of a Yukon fire was apparent only to Mercedes, who disburdened herself of copious opinions upon that topic, and incidentally upon a few other traits unpleasantly peculiar to her husband's family. In the meantime the fire remained unbuilt, the camp half pitched, and the dogs unfed.

In the excess of their own misery they were callous to the suffering of their animals. Hal's theory, which he practiced on others, was that one must get hardened. He had started out preaching it to his sister and brother-in-law. Failing there, he hammered it into the dogs with a club. At the Five Fingers the dog food gave out, and a toothless old squaw offered to trade them a few pounds of frozen horse hide for the Colt's revolver that kept the big hunting knife company at Hal's hip. A poor substitute for food was this hide, just as it had been stripped from the starved horses of the cattlemen six months back. In its frozen state it was more like strips of galvanized iron, and when a dog wrestled it into his stomach it thawed into thin and innutritious leathery strings and into a mass of short hair, irritating and indigestible.

And through it all Buck staggered along at the head of the team as in a nightmare. He pulled when he could; when he could no longer pull, he fell down and remained down till blows from whip or club drove him to his feet again. All the stiffness and gloss had gone out of his beautiful
2 furry coat. The hair hung down, limp and draggled, or matted with dried blood where Hal's club had bruised him. His muscles had wasted away to knotty strings, and the flesh pads had disappeared, so that each rib and every bone in his frame were outlined cleanly through the loose hide that was wrinkled in folds of emptiness. It was heartbreaking, only Buck's heart was unbreakable. The man in the red sweater had proved that.

3 As it was with Buck, so was it with his mates. They were perambulating[8] skeletons. There were seven altogether, including him. In their very great misery they had become insensible to the bite of the lash or the bruise of the club. The pain of the beating was dull and distant, just as the things their eyes saw and their ears heard seemed dull and distant. They were not half living, or quarter living. They were simply so many bags of bones in which sparks of life fluttered faintly. When a halt was made, they dropped down in the traces like dead dogs, and the spark dimmed and paled and seemed to go out. And when the club or whip fell upon them, the spark fluttered feebly up, and they tottered to their feet and staggered on.

There came a day when Billee, the good-natured, fell and could not rise. Buck saw, and his mates saw, and they knew that this thing was very close to them. On the next day Koona

8. **perambulating** [pər am′byə lāt′ing]: walking.

AT A GLANCE

- The humans begin to quarrel.
- In desperation they feed the dogs horse hide.
- Buck's teammates begin to fail.

1 THEME

Civilization, which has weakened and debilitated these men, has also shaped their values. Art, drama, politics, and gossip are among the luxuries that these three ought to have left behind with the canned goods.

2 STYLE: DETAILS

Buck's coat, muscles, skeleton, and hide are described in vivid detail as he approaches his lowest point.

3 STYLE: METAPHOR

The exhausted, starving animals are vividly likened to walking skeletons.

GUIDED READING

LITERAL QUESTION

1a. What is "this thing" Buck and the other dogs see? (death)

INFERENTIAL QUESTION

1b. Why does London not use the word *death*? (This passage is reported from the point of view of the animals, who have no exact understanding of death; they possess, rather, an instinctual fear of it.)

AT A GLANCE

- As Buck and his teammates falter, spring arrives.
- The troop gains John Thornton's camp.
- Thornton advises them not to attempt to cross White River.

1 THEME: LOVE OF LABOR

Even in their weakness the dogs love their work and regret being unable to perform it properly.

2 STYLE: SENSORY LANGUAGE

The sounds of spring—*booming, knocking, chattering*—and the sense of movement are lyrically reported. Ironically, this renewal of life comes just when Buck is closest to giving up.

3 STYLE: DIALOGUE

The contrasting styles of speech mark Thornton as a laconic man of experience and Hal as a blind and proud man of little virtue.

went, and but five of them remained: Joe, too far gone to be malignant; Pike, crippled and limping, only half conscious and not conscious
1 enough longer to malinger; Sol-leks, the one-eyed, still faithful to the toil of trace and trail, and mournful in that he had so little strength with which to pull; Teek, who had not traveled so far that winter and who was now beaten more than the others because he was fresher; and Buck, still at the head of the team, but no longer enforcing discipline or striving to enforce it, blind with weakness half the time and keeping the trail by the loom of it and by the dim feel of his feet.

It was beautiful spring weather, but neither dogs nor humans were aware of it. Each day the sun rose earlier and set later. It was dawn by three in the morning, and twilight lingered till nine at night. The whole long day was a blaze of sunshine. The ghostly winter silence had given way to the great spring murmur of awakening life. This murmur arose from all the land, fraught with the joy of living. It came from the things that lived and moved again, things which had been as dead and which had not moved during the long months of frost. The sap was rising in the pines. The willows and aspens were bursting out in young buds. Shrubs and vines were
2 putting on fresh garbs of green. Crickets sang in the nights, and in the days all manner of creeping, crawling things rustled forth into the sun. Partridges and woodpeckers were booming and knocking in the forest. Squirrels were chattering, birds singing, and overhead honked the wild fowl driving up from the south in cunning wedges that split the air.

From every hill slope came the trickle of running water, the music of unseen fountains. All things were thawing, bending, snapping. The Yukon was straining to break loose the ice that bound it down. It ate away from beneath; the sun ate from above. Air holes formed, fissures sprang and spread apart, while thin sections of ice fell through bodily into the river. And amid all this bursting, rending, throbbing of awakening life, under the blazing sun and through the soft-sighing breezes, like wayfarers to death, staggered the two men, the woman, and the huskies.

With the dogs falling, Mercedes weeping and riding, Hal swearing innocuously, and Charles's eyes wistfully watering, they staggered into John Thornton's camp at the mouth of White River. When they halted, the dogs dropped down as though they had all been struck dead. Mercedes dried her eyes and looked at John Thornton. Charles sat down on a log to rest. He sat down very slowly and painstakingly what of his great stiffness. Hal did the talking. John Thornton was whittling the last touches on an ax handle he had made from a stick of birch. He whittled and listened, gave monosyllabic[9] replies, and, when it was asked, terse advice. He knew the breed, and he gave his advice in the certainty that it would not be followed.

"They told us up above that the bottom was dropping out of the trail and that the best thing for us to do was to lay over," Hal said in response to Thornton's warning to take no more chances on the rotten ice. "They told us we couldn't make White River, and here we are." This last with a sneering ring of triumph in it.

"And they told you true," John Thornton answered. "The bottom's likely to drop out at
3 any moment. Only fools, with the blind luck of fools, could have made it. I tell you straight, I wouldn't risk my carcass on that ice for all the gold in Alaska."

"That's because you're not a fool, I suppose," said Hal. "All the same, we'll go on to Dawson." He uncoiled his whip. "Get up there, Buck! Hi! Get up there! Mush on!"

Thornton went on whittling. It was idle, he knew, to get between a fool and his folly; while two or three fools more or less would not alter the scheme of things.

But the team did not get up at the command.

---

9. **monosyllabic** [mon′ə si lab′ik]: of one syllable, not communicative.

GUIDED READING

LITERAL QUESTION

1a. What melts the ice? (The sun melts it from above, and the Yukon melts it from underneath.)

INFERENTIAL QUESTION

1b. How does the description of thawing ice, *the unseen fountains,* help us understand Thornton's reference to "rotten ice"? (He describes ice that is thinner than it looks and no longer solid.)

It had long since passed into the stage where blows were required to rouse it. The whip flashed out, here and there, on its merciless errands. John Thornton compressed his lips. Sol-leks was the first to crawl to his feet. Teek followed. Joe came next, yelping with pain. Pike made painful efforts. Twice he fell over, when half up, and on the third attempt managed to rise. Buck made no effort. He lay quietly where he had fallen. The lash bit into him again and again, but he neither whined nor struggled. Several times Thornton started, as though to speak, but changed his mind. A moisture came into his eyes, and, as the whipping continued, he arose and walked irresolutely up and down.

This was the first time Buck had failed, in itself a sufficient reason to drive Hal into a rage. He exchanged the whip for the customary club. Buck refused to move under the rain of heavier blows which now fell upon him. Like his mates, he was barely able to get up, but, unlike them, he had made up his mind not to get up. He had a vague feeling of impending doom. This had been strong upon him when he pulled in to the bank, and it had not departed from him. What with the thin and rotten ice he had felt under his feet all day, it seemed that he sensed disaster close at hand, out there ahead on the ice where his master was trying to drive him. He refused to stir. So greatly had he suffered, and so far gone was he, that the blows did not hurt much. And as they continued to fall upon him, the spark of life within flickered and went down. It was nearly out. He felt strangely numb. As though from a great distance, he was aware that he was being beaten. The last sensations of pain left him. He no longer felt anything, though very faintly he could hear the impact of the club upon his body. But it was no longer his body, it seemed so far away.

And then, suddenly, without warning, uttering a cry that was inarticulate and more like the cry of an animal, John Thornton sprang upon the man who wielded the club. Hal was hurled backward, as though struck by a falling tree. Mercedes screamed. Charles looked on wistfully, wiped his watery eyes, but did not get up because of his stiffness.

John Thornton stood over Buck, struggling to control himself, too convulsed with rage to speak.

"If you strike that dog again, I'll kill you," he at last managed to say in a choking voice.

"It's my dog," Hal replied, wiping the blood from his mouth as he came back. "Get out of my way, or I'll fix you. I'm going to Dawson."

Thornton stood between him and Buck, and evinced no intention of getting out of the way. Then he stooped, and with two strokes cut Buck's traces.

Hal had no fight left in him. Besides, his hands were full with his sister, or his arms, rather; while Buck was too near dead to be of further use in hauling the sled. A few minutes later they pulled out from the bank and down the river. Buck heard them go and raised his head to see. Pike was leading, Sol-leks was at the wheel, and between were Joe and Teek. They were limping and staggering. Mercedes was riding the loaded sled. Hal guided at the gee pole, and Charles stumbled along in the rear.

As Buck watched them, Thornton knelt beside him and with rough, kindly hands searched for broken bones. By the time his search had disclosed nothing more than many bruises and a state of terrible starvation, the sled was a quarter of a mile away. Dog and man watched it crawling along over the ice. Suddenly, they saw its back end drop down, as into a rut, and the gee
2 pole, with Hal clinging to it, jerk into the air. Mercedes's scream came to their ears. They saw Charles turn and make one step to run back, and then a whole section of ice give way and dogs and humans disappear. A yawning hole was all that was to be seen. The bottom had dropped out of the trail.

John Thornton and Buck looked at each other.

"You poor devil," said John Thornton, and Buck licked his hand.

AT A GLANCE

- Though Hal beats him mercilessly, Buck refuses to get up.
- Thornton rescues the dog.
- The remaining team pulls the party onto the ice, which breaks; all of them drown.

1 CHARACTERIZATION

Thornton's stoicism and live-and-let-live attitude is tested by the sight of an ignorant, ruthless man beating a starved, exhausted, dying animal.

2 THEME

This accident (which other, wiser people foretold) is nature's revenge on the three "civilized" humans.

REFLECTING ON CHAPTERS 4–5

The last two chapters have ended with a death. How do they compare? (The death of Dave was an example of nature's taking its course; the second death scene is more vast, and it leaves Buck all alone.)

GUIDED READING

LITERAL QUESTIONS

1a. What reason does Hal give for telling Thornton not to interfere? ("It's my dog.")

2a. What does Thornton's "search" for Buck's broken bones disclose? (nothing more than bruises and starvation—no broken bones)

INFERENTIAL QUESTIONS

1b. What does London seem to think of this reasoning? (Hal has forfeited his right to Buck by his mistreatment of the dog and inability to survive in the wild.)

2b. What do the results of this search suggest? (Buck is indeed a "superior individual," who can withstand punishment.)

STUDY QUESTIONS

1. is good leader; keeps dogs in line with discipline
2.
   - dislikes their incompetence, feels he cannot rely on them
   - told to leave tent, that dogs need rest, not to go on river
3. is nearly dead, thin, unable to move
4.
   - threatens to kill Hal if he doesn't stop beating Buck
   - They leave him behind and drown when sled falls through ice.
5. He gave Buck his first lesson in survival; Buck's life with judge has no relation to new life.
6. They overload sled with luxuries, feed dogs irregularly, treat them poorly, travel on weak ice. Their desire for wealth leads them to push on despite warning not to.
7.
   - Setting is described in beautiful detail; thawing river represents danger.
   - Buck grows closer to death as spring brings new life.
8. *François, Perrault:* experienced, fair; *Scotsman:* competent, drove dogs too hard; *Hal, others:* cruel, incompetent; *Thornton:* saves Buck's life and Buck appreciates his fairness
9. Answers will vary.

LITERARY FOCUS

Characterization

1. *Charles:* middle-aged, with weak and watery eyes; *Hal:* callousness sheer and unutterable; *Mercedes:* dainty dismay
2. He does not want to interfere with Hal; knew his advice would not be heeded; defends Buck. Actions reveal he is experienced, kind, perceptive.

Plot

1. He is sick, needs rest; doing his job well is the only thing important to him.
2. Hal wants to drive team across river; ice gives way.
3. Hal wants Buck to continue away from Thornton's camp; Buck refuses to move.

STUDY QUESTIONS

Recalling

1. Briefly describe Buck's relationship with the other dogs while he is leader of the dog team in Chapter 4.
2. What is Buck's opinion of his new owners in Chapter 5? Find three examples of advice that Charles, Hal, and Mercedes receive from more experienced prospectors.
3. Describe Buck's physical condition by the end of Chapter 5.
4. Explain how John Thornton gets possession of Buck. What finally happens to Charles, Hal, and Mercedes?

Interpreting

5. In Chapter 4 why do you think Buck remembers the man in the red sweater more than he remembers the judge?
6. In what sense do Charles, Hal, and Mercedes fail because they are reluctant to leave civilization and to understand nature? In what sense do they fail because of a desire for wealth?
7. Once spring arrives in Chapter 5, explain how the setting represents both beauty and danger. Explain how the setting is used as a contrast to Buck's condition.
8. Compare Buck's various owners in the Klondike so far. What kinds of treatment does Buck appreciate most and least? Give examples from the novel to support your opinion.

Extending

9. From history or current events give an example of a catastrophe that occurred when people did not heed nature's warning.

LITERARY FOCUS

Characterization

Characterization is the personality of a character in a novel, short story, or play; it is also the method that an author uses to reveal this personality. Characterization can be **direct**—revealed through clear statements by the author—or **indirect**—revealed through the character's words and actions. We see the events of *The Call of the Wild* through Buck's eyes, and Buck judges people and other dogs by instinct and through their actions. As a result, the author tells us directly how Buck perceives characters. In addition, he tells us indirectly about some characters through their actions. Since the novel has little dialogue, we learn little about people from what they say.

Thinking About Characterization

1. Find three direct statements in Chapter 5 about the personalities of one or more of the following: Charles, Hal, and Mercedes.
2. In what way do his actions at the end of Chapter 5 reveal the personality of John Thornton?

Plot

Plot is the sequence of events in a novel, short story, or play, each event causing or leading to the next. Because of its greater length, a novel usually has a more complex plot than a short story or play. The plot of a novel usually includes a series of different situations and complications. For example, in *The Call of the Wild* Buck has a series of different owners and new experiences with each one. At the same time, however, Buck's efforts to survive the wilderness provide one central plot structure.

A novel usually contains a number of different conflicts. **Conflict**, a struggle between opposing forces, is especially important in an adventure novel like *The Call of the Wild*. As in a short story, a conflict may be **internal**, within a character, or **external**, between characters or between a character and nature, society, or fate.

Thinking About Plot

1. Explain Dave's internal conflict in Chapter 4.
2. Give one conflict between a human character and nature in Chapter 5.
3. Identify one conflict in which Buck is involved in Chapter 5.

AT A GLANCE

- Buck convalesces in Thornton's camp with Skeet and Nib, two other dogs.
- Buck rediscovers play.
- He experiences love for Thornton, who saved his life.

LITERARY OPTIONS

- plot
- sensory language
- the total effect

THEMATIC OPTIONS

- the bond between man and animal
- gratitude
- aspects of nature

1 CHARACTERIZATION

The love that Thornton awakens in Buck by saving the dog's life is as intense and overwhelming as Buck's hatred of Spitz or his pride in leading the pack.

6 For the Love of a Man

When John Thornton froze his feet in the previous December, his partners had made him comfortable and left him to get well, going on themselves up the river to get out a raft of saw logs for Dawson. He was still limping slightly at the time he rescued Buck, but with the continued warm weather even the slight limp left him. And here, lying by the river bank through the long spring days, watching the running water, listening lazily to the songs of birds and the hum of nature, Buck slowly won back his strength.

A rest comes very good after one has traveled three thousand miles, and it must be confessed that Buck waxed lazy as his wounds healed, his muscles swelled out, and the flesh came back to cover his bones. For that matter, they were all loafing—Buck, John Thornton, and Skeet and Nib—waiting for the raft to come that was to carry them down to Dawson. Skeet was a little Irish setter who early made friends with Buck, who, in a dying condition, was unable to resent her first advances. She had the doctor trait which some dogs possess; and as a mother cat washes her kittens, so she washed and cleansed Buck's wounds. Regularly, each morning after he had finished his breakfast, she performed her self-appointed task, till he came to look for her ministrations as much as he did for Thornton's. Nib, equally friendly, though less demonstrative, was half bloodhound and half deerhound, with eyes that laughed and a boundless good nature.

To Buck's surprise these dogs manifested no jealousy toward him. They seemed to share the kindliness and largeness of John Thornton. As Buck grew stronger they enticed him into all sorts of ridiculous games, in which Thornton
1 himself could not forbear to join; and in this fashion Buck romped through his convalescence and into a new existence. Love, genuine passionate love, was his for the first time. This he had never experienced at Judge Miller's down in the sun-kissed Santa Clara Valley. With the Judge's sons, hunting and tramping, it had been

GUIDED READING

LITERAL QUESTION

1a. What other dogs accompany Thornton? (Nib, half bloodhound and half deerhound; Skeet, a little female Irish setter)

INFERENTIAL QUESTION

1b. The dogs always seem to fit their masters. How do Thornton's dogs fit him? (They are good-natured, loyal, and kind.)

AT A GLANCE

- Thornton is the ideal master.
- Buck loves him completely.
- Love of Thornton does not snuff out his love of the wild.

1 THEME

Buck's gratitude to Thornton—both for saving his life and for being an ideal master—awakens a powerful love in Buck.

2 SENSORY LANGUAGE

This description of Buck's joy evokes a universal picture of the devotion of dogs to their masters.

3 CONFLICT

As Buck's love for Thornton (a soft, civilizing influence) grows, his love of the wild also increases.

a working partnership; with the Judge's grandsons, a sort of pompous guardianship; and with the Judge himself, a stately and dignified friendship. But love that was feverish and burning, that was adoration, that was madness, it had taken John Thornton to arouse.

1 This man had saved his life, which was something; but, further, he was the ideal master. Other men saw to the welfare of their dogs from a sense of duty and business expediency; he saw to the welfare of his as if they were his own children, because he could not help it. And he saw further. He never forgot a kindly greeting or a cheering word, and to sit down for a long talk with them (gas, he called it) was as much his delight as theirs. He had a way of taking Buck's head roughly between his hands, and resting his own head upon Buck's, of shaking him back and forth, the while calling him ill names that to Buck were love names. Buck knew no greater joy than that rough embrace and the sound of murmured oaths, and at each jerk back and forth it seemed that his heart would be shaken out of
2 his body so great was its ecstasy. And when, released, he sprang to his feet, his mouth laughing, his eyes eloquent, his throat vibrant with unuttered sound, and in that fashion remained without movement, John Thornton would reverently exclaim, "You can all but speak!"

Buck had a trick of love expression that was akin to hurt. He would often seize Thornton's hand in his mouth and close so fiercely that the flesh bore the impress of his teeth for some time afterward. And as Buck understood the oaths to be love words, so the man understood this feigned bite for a caress.

For the most part, however, Buck's love was expressed in adoration. While he went wild with happiness when Thornton touched him or spoke to him, he did not seek these tokens. Unlike Skeet, who was wont to shove her nose under Thornton's hand and nudge and nudge till petted, or Nib, who would stalk up and rest his great head on Thornton's knee, Buck was content to adore at a distance. He would lie by the hour, eager, alert, at Thornton's feet, looking up into his face, dwelling upon it, studying it, following with keenest interest each fleeting expression, every movement or change of feature. Or, as chance might have it, he would lie farther away, to the side or rear, watching the outlines of the man and the occasional movements of his body. And often, such was the communion in which they lived, the strength of Buck's gaze would draw John Thornton's head around, and he would return the gaze, without speech, his heart shining out of his eyes as Buck's heart shone out.

For a long time after his rescue, Buck did not like Thornton to get out of his sight. From the moment he left the tent to when he entered it again, Buck would follow at his heels. His transient masters since he had come into the Northland had bred in him a fear that no master could be permanent. He was afraid that Thornton would pass out of his life as Perrault and François and the Scotsman had passed out. Even in the night, in his dreams, he was haunted by this fear. At such times he would shake off sleep and creep through the chill to the flap of the tent, where he would stand and listen to the sound of his master's breathing.

3 But in spite of this great love he bore John Thornton, which seemed to bespeak the soft, civilizing influence, the strain of the primitive, which the Northland had aroused in him, remained alive and active. Faithfulness and devotion, things born of fire and roof, were his; yet he retained his wildness and wiliness. He was a thing of the wild, come in from the wild to sit by John Thornton's fire, rather than a dog of the soft Southland stamped with the marks of generations of civilization. Because of his very great love, he could not steal from this man, but from any other man, in any other camp, he did not hesitate an instant; while the cunning with which he stole enabled him to escape detection.

GUIDED READING

LITERAL QUESTIONS

1a. What is Buck's fear about Thornton, and how does it make him act? (He fears that Thornton will leave him; he listens to him breathing in his sleep.)

2a. How do Buck and Thornton express their love? (Thornton shakes Buck's head and calls him "ill names," while Buck takes Thornton's hand in his mouth and pretends to bite it.)

INFERENTIAL QUESTIONS

1b. What does this show about Buck's devotion? (He is willing to go to unusual and uncomfortable lengths to protect Thornton.)

2b. How do these exchanges of love seem appropriate for the two creatures? (They are examples of fierce instincts under control.)

His face and body were scored by the teeth of many dogs, and he fought as fiercely as ever and more shrewdly. Skeet and Nib were too good-natured for quarreling—besides, they belonged to John Thornton; but the strange dog, no matter what the breed or valor, swiftly acknowledged Buck's supremacy or found himself struggling for life with a terrible antagonist. And Buck was merciless. He had learned well the law of club and fang, and he never forwent an advantage or drew back from a foe he had started on the way to Death. He had lessoned from Spitz, and from the chief fighting dogs of the police and mail, and knew there was no middle course. He must master or be mastered; while to show mercy was a weakness. Mercy did not exist in the primordial life. It was misunderstood for fear, and such misunderstandings made for death. Kill or be killed, eat or be eaten, was the law; and this mandate he obeyed.

He was older than the days he had seen and the breaths he had drawn. He linked the past with the present, and the eternity behind him throbbed through him in a mighty rhythm to which he swayed as the tides and seasons swayed. He sat by John Thornton's fire, a broad-breasted dog, white-fanged and long-furred; but behind him were the shades of all manner of dogs, half wolves and wild wolves, urgent and prompting, tasting the savor of the meat he ate, thirsting for the water he drank, scenting the wind with him, listening with him and telling him the sounds made by the wild life in the forest, dictating his moods, directing his actions, lying down to sleep with him when he lay down, and dreaming with him and beyond him and becoming themselves the stuff of his dreams.

So peremptorily[1] did these shades beckon him, that each day mankind and the claims of mankind slipped farther from him. Deep in the forest a call was sounding, and as often as he heard this call, mysteriously thrilling and luring, he felt compelled to turn his back upon the fire and the beaten earth around it, and to plunge into the forest, and on and on, he knew not where or why; nor did he wonder where or why, the call sounding imperiously, deep in the forest. But as often as he gained the soft unbroken earth and the green shade, the love for John Thornton drew him back to the fire again.

Thornton alone held him. The rest of mankind was as nothing. Chance travelers might praise or pet him; but he was cold under it all, and from a too demonstrative man he would get up and walk away. When Thornton's partners, Hans and Pete, arrived on the long-expected raft, Buck refused to notice them till he learned they were close to Thornton; after that he tolerated them in a passive sort of way, accepting favors from them as though he favored them by accept-
2 ing. They were of the same large type as Thornton, living close to the earth, thinking simply and seeing clearly; and ere they swung the raft into the big eddy by the sawmill at Dawson, they understood Buck and his ways, and did not insist upon an intimacy such as obtained with Skeet and Nib.

For Thornton, however, his love seemed to grow and grow. He, alone among men, could put a pack upon Buck's back in the summer traveling. Nothing was too great for Buck to do, when Thornton commanded. One day (they had grubstaked[2] themselves from the proceeds of the raft and left Dawson for the headwaters of the
3 Tanana[3]) the men and dogs were sitting on the crest of a cliff which fell away, straight down, to naked bedrock three hundred feet below. John Thornton was sitting near the edge, Buck at his shoulder. A thoughtless whim seized Thornton, and he drew the attention of Hans and Pete to the experiment he had in mind.

1. **peremptorily** [pə remp′tər ə lē]: without question.

2. **grubstaked:** bought supplies.
3. **Tanana:** river in Alaska. Thornton and his companions are traveling west.

AT A GLANCE

- Buck hears "the call," which draws him away from the camp.
- Thornton decides to test Buck's love.

1 THEME

The wild animal's nature is detailed: its preference for meat got by its own efforts, its hunter's instincts and needs, which govern every moment of the day.

2 CHARACTERIZATION

Thornton's partners, Hans and Pete, are large, experienced men of the wild, who (like Buck) prefer to hunt their food and to live by their own abilities.

3 THEME

Both beauty and danger are in London's description of this majestic natural formation.

GUIDED READING

LITERAL QUESTION

1a. Why doesn't Buck fight with Nib and Skeet? (He recognizes that they are not fighting dogs.)

INFERENTIAL QUESTION

1b. How has Buck become a complex creature? (His behavior is based upon judgment and self-control; he is a wild dog who is able to live also in a civilized way.)

AT A GLANCE

- Thornton finds that he has power to command Buck.
- Buck defends Thornton in a Circle City bar.
- Thornton nearly drowns; Buck tries to save him.

1 THEME

When Thornton commands Buck to jump off the cliff, he discovers the tremendous power he exerts over the animal. His partners realize that Buck will protect Thornton's life at risk to his own.

2 PLOT: FORESHADOWING

Buck will experience three trials, which grow out of his love for Thornton. In this first one the man who shoved Thornton receives the full fury of the dog protecting his master.

3 STYLE: SENSORY LANGUAGE

London uses sensory language to describe the rushing water and convey the danger both man and dog sense.

1 "Jump, Buck!" he commanded, sweeping his arm out and over the chasm. The next instant he was grappling with Buck on the extreme edge, while Hans and Pete were dragging them back into safety.

"It's uncanny," Pete said, after it was over and they had caught their speech.

Thornton shook his head. "No, it is splendid, and it is terrible, too. Do you know, it sometimes makes me afraid."

"I'm not hankering to be the man that lays hands on you while he's around," Pete announced conclusively, nodding his head toward Buck.

"Py Jingo!" was Hans's contribution. "Not mineself either."

It was at Circle City,[4] ere the year was out, that Pete's apprehensions were realized. "Brick" Burton, a man evil-tempered and malicious, had been picking a quarrel with a tenderfoot at the bar, when Thornton stepped good-naturedly between. Buck, as was his custom, was lying in a corner, head on paws, watching his master's every action. Burton struck out, without warn-
2 ing, straight from the shoulder. Thornton was sent spinning, and saved himself from falling only by clutching the rail of the bar.

Those who were looking on heard what was neither bark nor yelp, but a something which is best described as a roar, and they saw Buck's body rise up in the air as he left the floor. The man saved his life by instinctively throwing out his arm, but was hurled backward to the floor with Buck on top of him. Then the crowd was upon Buck, and he was driven off; but while a surgeon checked the bleeding, he prowled up and down, growling furiously, attempting to rush in, and being forced back by an array of hostile clubs. A "miners' meeting," called on the spot, decided that the dog had sufficient provocation, and Buck was discharged. But his reputation was made, and from that day his name spread through every camp in Alaska.

Later on, in the fall of the year, he saved John Thornton's life in quite another fashion. The three partners were lining a long and narrow poling boat down a bad stretch of rapids on the Forty Mile Creek. Hans and Pete moved along the bank, snubbing with a thin Manila rope from tree to tree, while Thornton remained in the boat, helping its descent by means of a pole, and shouting directions to the shore. Buck, on the bank, worried and anxious, kept abreast of the boat, his eyes never off his master.

At a particularly bad spot, where a ledge of barely submerged rocks jutted out into the river, Hans cast off the rope, and, while Thornton poled the boat out into the stream, ran down the bank with the end in his hand to snub the boat when it had cleared the ledge. This it did, and was flying downstream in a current as swift as a millrace,[5] when Hans checked it with the rope and checked too suddenly. The boat flirted over and snubbed in to the bank bottom up, while Thornton, flung sheer out of it, was carried downstream toward the worst part of the rapids, a stretch of wild water in which no swimmer could live.

Buck had sprung in on the instant; and at the end of three hundred yards, amid a mad swirl of water, he overhauled Thornton. When he felt him grasp his tail, Buck headed for the bank, swimming with all his splendid strength. But the progress shoreward was slow, the progress
3 downstream amazingly rapid. From below came the fatal roaring where the wild current went wilder and was rent in shreds and spray by the rocks which thrust through like the teeth of an enormous comb. The suck of the water as it took the beginning of the last steep pitch was frightful, and Thornton knew that the shore was impossible. He scraped furiously over a rock, bruised across a second, and struck a third with crushing force. He clutched its slippery top with both hands, releasing Buck, and above the roar of the churning water shouted: "Go, Buck! Go!"

Buck could not hold his own, and swept on

4. **Circle City:** city on the Yukon River in eastern Alaska.

5. **millrace:** stream of water that turns a mill wheel.

GUIDED READING

LITERAL QUESTIONS

1a. What was Thornton doing with the boat on Forty Mile Creek? (He was trying to ease it down the rapids.)

2a. How was Thornton thrown out of the boat? (Hans pulled the rope too quickly, capsizing the boat.)

INFERENTIAL QUESTIONS

1b. How do man and animal seem different but equal in this passage? (Their abilities are different but of equal worth: The men know how to get a boat downstream; the dogs are stronger swimmers.)

2b. How does the author help us to feel the danger? (through sensory language: the roaring, shredding, sucking and spraying rapids, the scraping and brusing of man and dog)

downstream, struggling desperately, but unable to win back. When he heard Thornton's command repeated, he partly reared out of the water, throwing his head high, as though for a last look, then turned obediently toward the bank. He swam powerfully and was dragged ashore by Pete and Hans at the very point where swimming ceased to be possible and destruction began.

They knew that the time a man could cling to a slippery rock in the face of that driving current was a matter of minutes, and they ran as fast as they could up the bank to a point far above where Thornton was hanging on. They attached the line with which they had been snubbing the boat to Buck's neck and shoulders, being careful that it should neither strangle him nor impede his swimming, and launched him into the stream. He struck out boldly, but not straight enough into the stream. He discovered the mistake too late, when Thornton was abreast of him and a bare half-dozen strokes away while he was being carried helplessly past.

Hans promptly snubbed with the rope, as though Buck were a boat. The rope thus tightening on him in the sweep of the current, he was jerked under the surface, and under the surface he remained till his body struck against the bank and he was hauled out. He was half drowned, and Hans and Pete threw themselves upon him, pounding the breath into him and the water out of him. He staggered to his feet and fell down. The faint sound of Thornton's voice came to them, and though they could not make out the words of it, they knew that he was in his extremity. His master's voice acted on Buck like an electric shock. He sprang to his feet and ran up the bank ahead of the men to the point of his previous departure.

Again the rope was attached and he was launched, and again he struck out, but this time straight into the stream. He had miscalculated once, but he would not be guilty of it a second time. Hans paid out the rope, permitting no slack, while Pete kept it clear of coils. Buck held on till he was on a line straight above Thornton; then he turned, and with the speed of an express train headed down upon him. Thornton saw him coming, and, as Buck struck him like a battering ram, with the whole force of the current behind him, he reached up and closed with both arms around the shaggy neck. Hans snubbed the rope
2 around the tree, and Buck and Thornton were jerked under the water. Strangling, suffocating, sometimes one uppermost and sometimes the other, dragging over the jagged bottom, smashing against rocks and snags, they veered in to the bank.

Thornton came to, belly downward and being violently propelled back and forth across a drift log by Hans and Pete. His first glance was for Buck, over whose limp and apparently lifeless body Nib was setting up a howl, while Skeet
3 was licking the wet face and closed eyes. Thornton was himself bruised and battered, and he went carefully over Buck's body, when he had been brought around, finding three broken ribs.

"That settles it," he announced. "We camp right here." And camp they did, till Buck's ribs knitted and he was able to travel.

That winter, at Dawson, Buck performed another exploit, not so heroic, perhaps, but one that put his name many notches higher on the totem pole of Alaskan fame. This exploit was particularly gratifying to the three men; for they stood in need of the outfit which it furnished, and were enabled to make a long-desired trip into the virgin East, where miners had not yet appeared. It was brought about by a conversation in the Eldorado Saloon, in which men waxed boastful of their favorite dogs. Buck, because of his record, was the target for these men, and Thornton was driven stoutly to defend him. At the end of half an hour one man stated that his dog could start a sled with five hundred pounds and walk off with it; a second bragged six hundred for his dog; and a third, seven hundred.

"Pooh! pooh!" said John Thornton; "Buck can start a thousand pounds."

"And break it out! and walk off with it for a

AT A GLANCE

- Buck twice tries to reach Thornton with a rope.
- Thornton is saved; Buck breaks three ribs and nearly drowns.
- That winter at Dawson, Thornton wagers that Buck can start a load of a thousand pounds.

1 POINT OF VIEW

The dangers of the moment are seen through the eyes of Hans and Pete, who have experienced the strength of the wild river waters and can interpret them.

2 SENSORY LANGUAGE

The violence of the rescue is made vivid through vivid language: Buck and Thornton return *strangling, suffocating, dragging,* and *smashing* their way to shore.

3 THEME: GRATITUDE AND LOVE

Deeds like Thornton's examination continue to earn Buck's gratitude and strengthen his love for the man.

GUIDED READING

LITERAL QUESTIONS

1a. How does Buck try to save Thornton? (He has a rope tied around him with which he will swim out to his master.)

2a. Why does Buck have to make two tries at reaching Thornton? (He first misses his mark and winds up downstream of Thornton.)

INFERENTIAL QUESTIONS

1b. What other rivers have pitted people against nature? (François and Perrault made only thirty miles in six days because of the ice on Thirty Mile River; ice on White River ended the lives of the tenderfoots.)

2b. What makes this passage so exciting? (Vivid language captures the river's movement, the rocks' danger, and the creatures' difficulties.)

AT A GLANCE

- A sled is loaded with a thousand pounds of flour; its runners are frozen to the snow.
- Buck must break out the sled from a standstill.

1 POINT OF VIEW

The apprehension of the moment is registered from Thornton's point of view: He has spoken from faith and with bravado, but doesn't know if Buck can do it.

2 STYLE: DIALOGUE

Thornton borrows his part of the wager money from an Irishman. The various dialects throughout the story tell us that the miners were from many nations.

3 SETTING

London provides details about the environment—the 60° below zero temperature, the frozen runners, the crowd of onlookers—to show both natural and social pressures that Buck faces.

hundred yards?" demanded Matthewson, a Bonanza King, he of the seven hundred vaunt.

"And break it out, and walk off with it for a hundred yards." John Thornton said coolly.

"Well," Matthewson said, slowly and deliberately, so that all could hear, "I've got a thousand dollars that says he can't. And there it is." So saying, he slammed a sack of gold dust of the size of a bologna sausage down upon the bar.

1 Nobody spoke. Thornton's bluff, if bluff it was, had been called. He could feel a flush of warm blood creeping up his face. His tongue had tricked him. He did not know whether Buck could start a thousand pounds. Half a ton! The enormousness of it appalled him. He had great faith in Buck's strength and had often thought him capable of starting such a load; but never, as now, had he faced the possibility of it, the eyes of a dozen men fixed upon him, silent and waiting. Further, he had no thousand dollars; nor had Hans or Pete.

"I've got a sled standing outside now, with twenty fifty-pound sacks of flour on it," Matthewson went on with brutal directness; "so don't let that hinder you."

Thornton did not reply. He did not know what to say. He glanced from face to face in the absent way of a man who has lost the power of thought and is seeking somewhere to find the thing that will start it going again. The face of Jim O'Brien, a Mastodon King and old-time comrade, caught his eyes. It was as a cue to him, seeming to rouse him to do what he would never have dreamed of doing.

2 "Can you lend me a thousand?" he asked, almost in a whisper.

"Sure," answered O'Brien, thumping down a plethoric[6] sack by the side of Matthewson's. "Though it's little faith I'm having, John, that the beast can do the trick."

The Eldorado emptied its occupants into the street to see the test. The tables were deserted, and the dealers and gamekeepers came forth to see the outcome of the wager and to lay odds.

3 Several hundred men, furred and mittened, banked around the sled within easy distance. Matthewson's sled, loaded with a thousand pounds of flour, had been standing for a couple of hours, and in the intense cold (it was sixty below zero) the runners had frozen fast to the hard-packed snow. Men offered odds of two to one that Buck could not budge the sled. A quibble arose concerning the phrase "break out." O'Brien contended it was Thornton's privilege to knock the runners loose, leaving Buck to "break it out" from a dead standstill. Matthewson insisted that the phrase included breaking the runners from the frozen grip of the snow. A majority of the men who had witnessed the making of the bet decided in his favor, whereat the odds went up to three to one against Buck.

There were no takers. Not a man believed him capable of the feat. Thornton had been hurried into the wager, heavy with doubt; and now that he looked at the sled itself, the concrete fact, with the regular team of ten dogs curled up in the snow before it, the more impossible the task appeared. Matthewson waxed jubilant.

"Three to one!" he proclaimed. "I'll lay you another thousand at that figure, Thornton. What d'ye say?"

Thornton's doubt was strong in his face, but his fighting spirit was aroused—the fighting spirit that soars above odds, fails to recognize the impossible, and is deaf to all save the clamor for battle. He called Hans and Pete to him. Their sacks were slim, and with his own, the three partners could rake together only two hundred dollars. In the ebb of their fortunes, this sum was their total capital; yet they laid it unhesitatingly against Matthewson's six hundred.

The team of ten dogs was unhitched, and Buck, with his own harness, was put into the sled. He had caught the contagion of the excite-

6. **plethoric** [ple thôr′ik]: very full.

GUIDED READING

LITERAL QUESTION

1a. How much money does Thornton bet? ($1,000 of O'Brien's and $200 of his and his partners')

INFERENTIAL QUESTION

1b. How many trials has Buck faced with Thornton? (This is the third, after the incidents in the bar and on the river.)

AT A GLANCE

- Buck's splendid condition changes the odds.
- Thornton appeals to him to do his best in the name of love.

1 STYLE: DIALOGUE

The comic interjections of the "Skookum King" add color to the anticipation of the crowd. This third trial is climactic, and London has embroidered it with the greatest detail.

ment, and he felt that in some way he must do a great thing for John Thornton. Murmurs of admiration at his splendid appearance went up. He was in perfect condition, without an ounce of superfluous flesh, and the one hundred and fifty pounds that he weighed were so many pounds of grit and virility. His furry coat shone with the sheen of silk. Down the neck and across the shoulders, his mane, in repose as it was, half bristled and seemed to lift with every movement, as though excess of vigor made each particular hair alive and active. The great breast and heavy forelegs were no more than in proportion with the rest of the body, where the muscles showed in tight rolls underneath the skin. Men felt these muscles and proclaimed them hard as iron, and the odds went down to two to one.

"Gad, sir! Gad, sir!" stuttered a member of the latest dynasty, a king of the Skookum Benches. "I offer you eight hundred for him, sir, before the test, sir; eight hundred just as he stands."

Thornton shook his head and stepped to Buck's side.

"You must stand off from him," Matthewson protested. "Free play and plenty of room."

The crowd fell silent; only could be heard the voices of the gamblers vainly offering two to one. Everybody acknowledged Buck a magnificent animal, but twenty fifty-pound sacks of flour bulked too large in their eyes for them to loosen their pouch strings.

Thornton knelt down by Buck's side. He took his head in his two hands and rested cheek to cheek. He did not playfully shake him, as was his wont, or murmur soft love curses; but he whispered in his ear. "As you love me, Buck. As you love me," was what he whispered. Buck whined with suppressed eagerness.

GUIDED READING

LITERAL QUESTION

1a. What does Thornton say to Buck to get him to take the challenge? ("As you love me, Buck. As you love me.")

INFERENTIAL QUESTION

1b. How is this different from Thornton's earlier communications with Buck? (Today he doesn't "tease" Buck with love curses but appeals to him directly in full sincerity.)

AT A GLANCE

- Buck breaks out the sled and pulls it one hundred yards.
- Buck, Hans, Pete, and Thornton leave Dawson to look for a fabled lost mine.

1 STYLE: SENSORY LANGUAGE

Buck's violent effort is shown in the "writhing," "flying," "scarring," and "trembling" that take place as he tries to budge the sled.

2 POINT OF VIEW

The narrator draws back to show us the panorama of action: Buck's success is marked by the roaring of the crowd and the sight of hats and mittens in the air.

The crowd was watching curiously. The affair was growing mysterious. It seemed like a conjuration.[7] As Thornton got to his feet, Buck seized his mittened hand between his jaws, pressing in with his teeth and releasing slowly, half-reluctantly. It was the answer, in terms, not speech, but of love. Thornton stepped well back.

"Now, Buck," he said.

Buck tightened the traces, then slacked them for a matter of several inches. It was the way he had learned.

"Gee!" Thornton's voice rang out, sharp in the tense silence.

Buck swung to the right, ending the movement in a plunge that took up the slack and with a sudden jerk arrested his one hundred and fifty pounds. The load quivered, and from under the runners arose a crisp crackling.

"Haw!" Thornton commanded.

Buck duplicated the maneuver, this time to the left. The crackling turned into a snapping, the sled pivoting and the runners slipping and grating several inches to the side. The sled was broken out. Men were holding their breaths, intensely unconscious of the fact.

"Now, MUSH!"

Thornton's command cracked out like a pistol shot. Buck threw himself forward, tightening the traces with a jarring lunge. His whole 1 body was gathered compactly together in the tremendous effort, the muscles writhing and knotting like live things under the silky fur. His great chest was low to the ground, his head forward and down, while his feet were flying like mad, the claws scarring the hard-packed snow in parallel grooves. The sled swayed and trembled, half-started forward. One of his feet slipped, and one man groaned aloud. Then the sled lurched ahead in what appeared a rapid succession of jerks, though it never really came to a dead stop again . . . half an inch . . . an inch . . . two inches . . . . The jerks perceptibly diminished; as the sled gained momentum, he caught them up, till it was moving steadily along.

Men gasped and began to breathe again, unaware that for a moment they had ceased to breathe. Thornton was running behind, encouraging Buck with short, cheery words, The distance had been measured off, and as he neared the pile of firewood which marked the end of the hundred yards, a cheer began to grow 2 and grow, which burst into a roar as he passed the firewood and halted at command. Every man was tearing himself loose, even Matthewson. Hats and mittens were flying in the air. Men were shaking hands, it did not matter with whom, and bubbling over in a general incoherent babel.

But Thornton fell on his knees beside Buck. Head was against head, and he was shaking him back and forth. Those who hurried up heard him cursing Buck, and he cursed him long and fervently, and softly and lovingly.

"Gad, sir! Gad, sir!" spluttered the Skookum Bench king. "I'll give you a thousand for him, sir, a thousand, sir—twelve hundred, sir."

Thornton rose to his feet. His eyes were wet. The tears were streaming frankly down his cheeks.

Buck seized Thornton's hand in his teeth. Thornton shook him back and forth. As though animated by a common impulse, the onlookers drew back to a respectful distance; nor were they again indiscreet enough to interrupt.

7 The Sounding of the Call

When Buck earned sixteen hundred dollars in five minutes for John Thornton, he made it possible for his master to pay off certain debts and to journey with his partners into the East after a fabled lost mine, the history of which was as old as the history of the country. Many men had sought it; few had found it; and more

7. **conjuration:** making magic through words and gestures.

GUIDED READING

LITERAL QUESTION

1a. What does Thornton receive as a result of Buck's success? (Thornton receives $1,600.)

INFERENTIAL QUESTION

1b. How does this enable Thornton and his partners to search for the lost mine? (They pay off various debts and are free to leave Dawson.)

than a few there were who had never returned from the quest. This lost mine was steeped in tragedy and shrouded in mystery. No one knew of the first man. The oldest tradition stopped before it got back to him. From the beginning there had been an ancient and ramshackle cabin. Dying men had sworn to it, and to the mine the site of which it marked, clinching their testimony with nuggets that were unlike any known grade of gold in the Northland.

But no living man had looted this treasure house, and the dead were dead; wherefore John Thornton and Pete and Hans, with Buck and half a dozen other dogs, faced into the East on an unknown trail to achieve where men and dogs as good as themselves had failed. They sledded seventy miles up the Yukon, swung to the left into the Stewart River, passed the Mayo and the McQuestion, and held on until the Stewart itself became a streamlet, threading the upstanding peaks[1] which marked the backbone of the continent.

John Thornton asked little of man or nature. He was unafraid of the wild. With a handful of salt and a rifle he could plunge into the wilderness and fare wherever he pleased and as long as he pleased. Being in no haste, Indian fashion, he hunted his dinner in the course of the day's travel; and if he failed to find it, like the Indian, he kept on traveling, secure in the knowledge that sooner or later he would come to it. So, on this great journey into the East, straight meat was the bill of fare, ammunition and tools principally made up the load on the sled, and the time card was drawn upon the limitless future.

To Buck it was boundless delight, this hunting, fishing, and indefinite wandering through strange places. For weeks at a time they would hold on steadily, day after day; and for weeks upon end they would camp, here and there, the dogs loafing and the men burning holes through frozen muck and gravel and washing countless pans of dirt by the heat of the fire. Sometimes they went hungry, sometimes they feasted riotously, all according to the abundance of game and the fortune of hunting. Summer arrived, and dogs and men packed on their backs, rafted across blue mountain lakes, and descended or ascended unknown rivers in slender boats whipsawed from the standing forest.

The months came and went, and back and forth they twisted through the uncharted vastness, where no men were and yet where men had been if the Lost Cabin were true. They went across divides in summer blizzards, shivered under the midnight sun on naked mountains be-
3 tween the timber line and the eternal snows, dropped into summer valleys amid swarming gnats and flies, and in the shadows of glaciers picked strawberries and flowers as ripe and fair as any the Southland could boast. In the fall of the year they penetrated a weird lake country, sad and silent, where wild fowl had been, but where then there was no life nor sign of life—only the blowing of chill winds, the forming of ice in sheltered places, and the melancholy rippling of waves on lonely beaches.

And through another winter they wandered on the obliterated trails of men who had gone before. Once, they came upon a path blazed through the forest, an ancient path, and the Lost Cabin seemed very near. But the path began nowhere and ended nowhere, and it remained mystery, as the man who made it and the reason he made it remained mystery. Another time they chanced upon the time-graven wreckage of a hunting lodge, and amid the shreds of rotted blankets John Thornton found a long-barreled flintlock. He knew it for a Hudson Bay Company gun of the young days in the Northwest, when such a gun was worth its height in beaver skins packed flat. And that was all—no hint as to the man who in an early day had reared the lodge and left the gun among the blankets.

Spring came on once more, and at the end of

1. **They sledded . . . peaks:** They travel east along the Yukon and Stewart rivers to the Canadian Rockies.

AT A GLANCE

- The group heads east into the wilderness.
- Searching for the mine, they spend a summer and a winter living off the land.
- They find an abandoned hunting lodge.

1 FORESHADOWING

The travels of Buck and Thornton will take them out of the reach of even the tentative civilization of Dawson. The suggestion of mystery and tragedy, as well as the mention of the deaths of others, strikes an ominous note.

2 THEME

Buck's delight in this "natural" life—wandering without apparent goal, no pressures of time or money, living in harmony with nature—shows the intense joy possible in the wild.

3 THE TOTAL EFFECT

Images of seasons suggest aspects of Buck's development as well as various aspects of the natural world.

GUIDED READING

LITERAL QUESTIONS

1a. When Thornton plunges into the wilderness with "a handful of salt and a rifle," to whom does London compare him? (an Indian)

2a. What signs of previous mankind do the miners find? (a path that goes nowhere and an abandoned hunting lodge)

INFERENTIAL QUESTIONS

1b. Why does London compare Thornton to an Indian at this point in the story? (Previously Buck has been in the company of men who worked for money and for the government; now he enters an area where Indians still live.)

2b. What do the remnants of human life suggest about the area? (In this part of the world, death is always close.)

AT A GLANCE

- The men discover gold in a shallow creek.
- Buck enters the wild and meets a timber wolf.

1 CONFLICT

In this description of Buck's restlessness, we recognize his search for a thing that seems to call him further into this primeval land.

2 PLOT: RISING ACTION

At last, Buck sees "the real thing"—not a husky, but a timber wolf, exemplar of the fundamental stock from whom all dogs have sprung.

3 WORD CHOICE

London explicitly compares the wolf to Joe and to "all cornered husky dogs" so that we will see the direct link between wild and "civilized" dogs.

all their wandering they found, not the Lost Cabin, but a shallow placer[2] in a broad valley where the gold showed like yellow butter across the bottom of the washing pan. They sought no farther. Each day they worked earned them thousands of dollars in clean dust and nuggets, and they worked every day. The gold was sacked in moose-hide bags, fifty pounds to the bag, and piled like so much firewood outside the spruce-bough lodge. Like giants they toiled, days flashing on the heels of days like dreams as they heaped the treasure up.

There was nothing for the dogs to do, save the hauling in of meat now and again that Thornton killed, and Buck spent long hours musing by the fire.

1 Irresistible impulses seized him. He would be lying in camp, dozing lazily in the heat of the day, when suddenly his head would lift and his ears cock up, intent and listening, and he would spring to his feet and dash away, and on and on, for hours, through the forest aisles and across the open spaces. He loved to run down dry watercourses, and to creep and spy upon the bird life in the woods. For a day at a time he would lie in the underbrush where he could watch the partridges drumming and strutting up and down. But especially he loved to run in the dim twilight of the summer midnights, listening to the subdued and sleepy murmurs of the forest, reading signs and sounds as man may read a book, and seeking for the mysterious something that called—called, waking or sleeping, at all times, for him to come.

One night he sprang from sleep with a start, eager-eyed, nostrils quivering and scenting, his mane bristling in recurrent waves. From the forest came the call (or one note of it, for the call was many-noted), distinct and definite as never before—a long-drawn howl, like, yet unlike, any noise made by husky dog. And he knew it, in the old familiar way, as a sound heard before. He sprang through the sleeping camp and in swift silence dashed through the woods. As he drew closer to the cry he went more slowly, with cau-
2 tion in every movement, till he came to an open place among the trees, and looking out saw, erect on haunches, with nose pointed to the sky, a long, lean timber wolf.

He had made no noise, yet it ceased from its howling and tried to sense his presence. Buck stalked into the open, half-crouching, body gathered compactly together, tail straight and stiff, feet falling with unwonted care. Every movement advertised commingled threatening and overture of friendliness. It was the menacing truce that marks the meeting of wild beasts that prey. But the wolf fled at sight of him. He followed, with wild leapings, in a frenzy to overtake. He ran him into a blind channel, in the bed of the creek, where a timber jam barred the way.
3 The wolf whirled about, pivoting on his hind legs after the fashion of Joe and of all cornered husky dogs, snarling and bristling, clipping his teeth together in a continuous and rapid succession of snaps.

Buck did not attack, but circled him about and hedged him in with friendly advances. The wolf was suspicious and afraid; for Buck made three of him in weight, while his head barely reached Buck's shoulder. Watching his chance, he darted away, and the chase was resumed. Time and again he was cornered, and the thing repeated, though he was in poor condition, or Buck could not so easily have overtaken him. He would run till Buck's head was even with his flank, when he would whirl around at bay, only to dash away again at the first opportunity.

But in the end Buck's pertinacity[3] was rewarded; for the wolf, finding that no harm was intended, finally sniffed noses with him. Then they became friendly, and played about in the nervous, half-coy way with which fierce beasts belie their fierceness. After some time of this the

2. **placer:** field of sand mixed with gold.

3. **pertinacity** [purt′ən as′ə tē]: persistence.

GUIDED READING

LITERAL QUESTION

1a. How does the timber wolf react to Buck? (in fear)

INFERENTIAL QUESTION

1b. How does Buck convince the wolf that he is friendly? (Buck lets him know that he could overpower him but chooses not to.)

volf started off at an easy lope in a manner that lainly showed he was going somewhere. He nade it clear to Buck that he was to come, and hey ran side by side through the somber wilight, straight up the creek bed, into the orge from which it issued, and across the bleak ivide where it took its rise.

On the opposite slope of the watershed they ame down into a level country where were reat stretches of forest and many streams, and hrough these great stretches they ran steadily, nour after hour, the sun rising higher and the lay growing warmer. Buck was wildly glad. He new he was at last answering the call, running y the side of his wood brother toward the lace from where the call surely came. Old nemories were coming upon him fast, and he vas stirring to them as of old he stirred to the ealities of which they were the shadows. He nad done this thing before, somewhere in that other and dimly remembered world, and he was loing it again, now, running free in the open, he unpacked earth underfoot, the wide sky overhead.

They stopped by a running stream to drink, nd, stopping, Buck remembered John Thornon. He sat down. The wolf started on toward he place from where the call surely came, then eturned to him, sniffing noses and making acions as though to encourage him. But Buck urned about and started slowly on the back rack. For the better part of an hour the wild rother ran by his side, whining softly. Then he at down, pointed his nose upward, and nowled. It was a mournful howl, and as Buck eld steadily on his way he heard it grow faint nd fainter until it was lost in the distance.

John Thornton was eating dinner when Buck lashed into camp and sprang upon him in a frenzy of affection, overturning him, scrambling upon him, licking his face, biting his hand—'playing the general tomfool,'' as John Thornon characterized it, the while he shook Buck back and forth and cursed him lovingly.

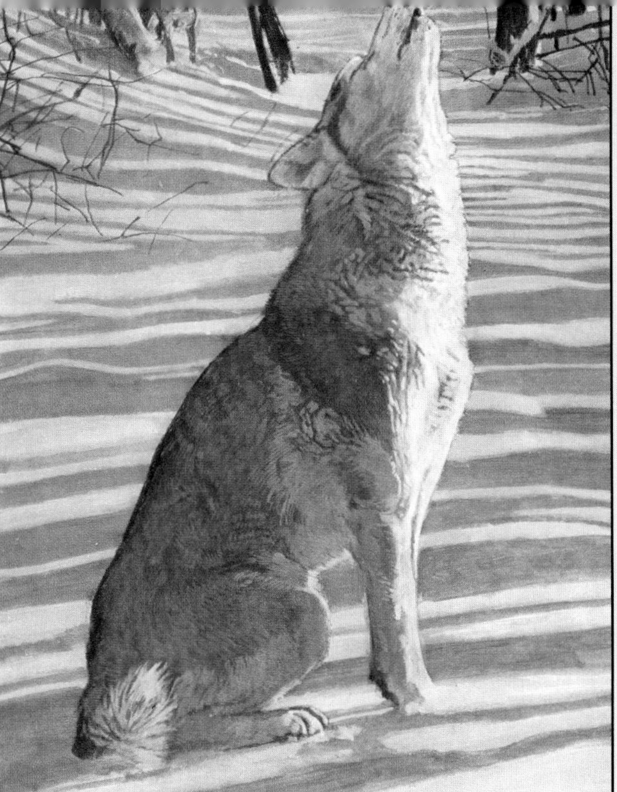

For two days and nights Buck never left camp, never let Thornton out of his sight. He followed him about at his work, watched him while he ate, saw him into his blankets at night and out of them in the morning. But after two days the call in the forest began to sound more imperiously than ever. Buck's restlessness came back on him, and he was haunted by recollections of the wild brother, and of the smiling land beyond the divide and the run side by side through the wide forest stretches. Once again he took to wandering in the woods, but the wild brother came no more; and though he listened through long vigils, the mournful howl was never raised.

He began to sleep out at night, staying away from camp for days at a time; and once he crossed the divide at the head of the creek and went down into the land of timber and streams. There

AT A GLANCE

- The timber wolf takes Buck for a long run.
- Buck remembers Thornton and goes back to camp, but not to stay.

1 THEME

Buck runs with the wolf and discovers a wild sense of joy; he is returning to a kind of home.

2 CONFLICT

Buck would suffer his severest trial if his love of the wild ever came into conflict with that of Thornton. Here his memory of the man draws him away from his new brother and back to camp.

GUIDED READING

LITERAL QUESTION

1a. How does Thornton greet Buck when he returns? (He shakes him and curses him lovingly.)

INFERENTIAL QUESTION

1b. In the friendliness of Thornton and the timber wolf toward Buck, what similarities do you note? (There is rough-and-tumble playfulness in the manners of both when they want to be friendly.)

AT A GLANCE

- Buck kills and eats a bear.
- He takes on the appearance of a gigantic wolf.
- He develops a taste for meat he has hunted himself.
- He finds a herd of moose.

1 THEME

Although Buck feels the call of the wild, he owes much to the inheritance of the "civilized" dogs who bore him, as well as to the men who schooled him "in the fiercest of schools."

2 THEME

London summarizes the life of a wild dog, stalking, striking, and savoring the fruit of the hunt.

he wandered for a week, seeking vainly for fresh sign of the wild brother, killing his meat as he traveled and traveling with the long, easy lope that seems never to tire. He fished for salmon in a broad stream that emptied somewhere into the sea, and by this stream he killed a large black bear, blinded by the mosquitoes while likewise fishing, and raging through the forest helpless and terrible. Even so, it was a hard fight, and it aroused the last latent remnants of Buck's ferocity. And two days later, when he returned to his kill and found a dozen wolverines quarreling over the spoil, he scattered them like chaff;[4] and those that fled left two behind who would quarrel no more.

Because of all this he became possessed of a great pride in himself, which communicated itself like a contagion to his physical being. It advertised itself in all his movements, was apparent in the play of every muscle, spoke plainly as speech in the way he carried himself, and made his glorious furry coat if anything more glorious. But for the stray brown on his muzzle and above his eyes, and for the splash of white hair that ran midmost down his chest, he might well have been mistaken for a gigantic wolf, larger than the largest of the breed. From his St. Bernard father he had inherited size and weight, but it was his shepherd mother who had given shape to that size and weight. His muzzle was the long wolf muzzle, save that it was larger than the muzzle of any wolf; and his head, somewhat broader, was the wolf head on a massive scale.

1 His cunning was wolf cunning, and wild cunning; his intelligence, shepherd intelligence and St. Bernard intelligence; and all this, plus an experience gained in the fiercest of schools, made him as formidable a creature as any that roamed the wild.

"Never was there such a dog," said John Thornton one day, as the partners watched Buck marching out of camp.

"When he was made, the mold was broke," said Pete.

"Py jingo! I t'ink so mineself," Hans affirmed.

They saw him marching out of camp, but they did not see the instant and terrible transformation which took place as soon as he was within the secrecy of the forest. He no longer marched. At once he became a thing of the wild,
2 stealing along softly, cat-footed, a passing shadow that appeared and disappeared among the shadows. He knew how to take advantage of every cover, to crawl on his belly like a snake, and like a snake to leap and strike. He could take a ptarmigan[5] from its nest, kill a rabbit as it slept, and snap in midair the little chipmunks fleeing a second too late for the trees. Fish, in open pools, were not too quick for him; nor were beaver, mending their dams, too wary. He killed to eat, not from wantonness; but he preferred to eat what he killed himself. So a lurking humor ran through his deeds, and it was his delight to steal upon the squirrels, and when he all but had them, to let them go, chattering in mortal fear to the treetops.

As the fall of the year came on, the moose appeared in greater abundance, moving slowly down to meet the winter in the lower and less rigorous valleys. Buck had already dragged down a stray part-grown calf; but he wished strongly for larger and more formidable quarry, and he came upon it one day on the divide at the head of the creek. A band of twenty moose had crossed over from the land of streams and timber, and chief among them was a great bull. He was in a savage temper, and, standing over six feet from the ground, was as formidable an antagonist as even Buck could desire. Back and forth the bull tossed his great palmated[6] antlers,

4. **chaff:** husks of grain plants after the seed has been removed.

5. **ptarmigan** [tär′mi gən]: wild bird of arctic regions.
6. **palmated:** branching.

GUIDED READING

LITERAL QUESTION

1a. What animals enter the valley and attract Buck's attention? (migrating herds of moose)

INFERENTIAL QUESTION

1b. How is Buck's wishing for "larger and more formidable quarry" related to his transformation? (He is developing into a killer and looks for ever greater challenges to his hunting ability.)

branching to fourteen points and embracing seven feet within the tips. His small eyes burned with a vicious and bitter light, while he roared with fury at sight of Buck.

From the bull's side, just forward of the flank, protruded a feathered arrow end, which accounted for his savageness. Guided by that instinct which came from the old hunting days of the primordial world, Buck proceeded to cut the bull out from the herd. It was no slight task. He would bark and dance about in front of the bull, just out of reach of the great antlers and of the terrible splay hoofs which could have stamped his life out with a single blow. Unable to turn his back on the fanged danger and go on, the bull would be driven into paroxysms[7] of rage. At such moments he charged Buck, who retreated craftily, luring him on by a simulated inability to escape. But when he was thus separated from his fellows, two or three of the younger bulls would charge back upon Buck and enable the wounded bull to rejoin the herd.

There is a patience of the wild—dogged, tireless, persistent as life itself—that holds motionless for endless hours the spider in its web, the snake in its coils, the panther in its ambuscade;[8] this patience belongs peculiarly to life when it hunts its living food; and it belonged to Buck as he clung to the flank of the herd, retarding its march, irritating the young bulls, worrying the cows with their half-grown calves, and driving the wounded bull mad with helpless rage. For half a day this continued. Buck multiplied himself, attacking from all sides, enveloping the herd in a whirlwind of menace, cutting out his victim as fast as it could rejoin its mates, wearing out the patience of creatures preyed upon, which is a lesser patience than that of creatures preying.

As the day wore along and the sun dropped to its bed in the northwest (the darkness had come back and the fall nights were six hours long), the young bulls retraced their steps more and more reluctantly to the aid of their beset leader. The downcoming winter was harrying them on to the lower levels, and it seemed they could never shake off this tireless creature that held them back. Besides, it was not the life of the herd, or of the young bulls, that was threatened. The life of only one member was demanded, which was a remoter interest than their lives, and in the end they were content to pay the toll.

As twilight fell the old bull stood with lowered head, watching his mates as they shambled on at a rapid pace through the fading light. He could not follow, for before his nose leaped the merciless fanged terror that would not let him go. Three hundredweight more than half a ton he weighed; he had lived a long, strong life, full of fight and struggle, and at the end he faced death at the teeth of a creature whose head did not reach beyond his great knuckled knees.

2 From then on, night and day, Buck never left his prey, never gave it a moment's rest, never permitted it to browse the leaves of trees or the shoots of young birch and willow. Nor did he give the wounded bull opportunity to slake his burning thirst in the slender trickling streams they crossed. Often, in desperation, he burst into long stretches of flight. At such times Buck did not attempt to stay him, but loped easily at his heels, satisfied with the way the game was played, lying down when the moose stood still, attacking him fiercely when he strove to eat or drink.

The great head drooped more and more under its tree of horns, and the shambling trot grew weak and weaker. He took to standing for long periods, with nose to the ground and dejected ears dropped limply; and Buck found more time in which to get water for himself and in which to rest. At such moments, panting with red lolling tongue and with eyes fixed upon the

7. **paroxysms** [par'ək siz'əmz]: outbursts.
8. **ambuscade** [am'bəs kād']: place of ambush.

AT A GLANCE

- An angry bull moose becomes Buck's prey.
- Buck cuts him out of the herd and weakens him.

1 STYLE: PARALLELISM

"Patience" is exemplified by the spider, the snake, and the panther, all described in parallel fashion using prepositional phrases.

2 CHARACTERIZATION

Buck's supreme patience and "doggedness" make him an excellent hunter. These same traits have made him superior at every other activity he has undertaken.

GUIDED READING

LITERAL QUESTIONS

1a. What season of the year is it? (autumn)

2a. What time of day is it when the moose is finally separated from the protection of the herd? (twilight)

INFERENTIAL QUESTIONS

1b. How does the season fit the action of the plot at this point? (Impending winter creates a proper setting for the impending death of the bull moose.)

2b. How is the death of the bull moose similar to the death of Dave earlier in the novella? (The moose is being abandoned by the herd; the dog train tried to leave Dave behind.)

AT A GLANCE

- Buck kills the moose.
- He returns to camp; Nib is dead and Indians are dancing by the wrecked lodge.

1 CHARACTERIZATION

There is no way for Buck to know about Indians; he feels only fear and a sense of calamity.

2 CHARACTERIZATION

In discovering the dead animals of Thornton's camp and sensing the danger to Thornton himself, Buck is overwhelmed by passion that overpowers reason.

3 BACKGROUND

London was somewhat ignorant of Indian civilization and culture. He portrays Indians as "uncivilized" rather than as having developed a civilization different from that of the European settlers.

big bull, it appeared to Buck that a change was coming over the face of things. He could feel a new stir in the land. As the moose were coming into the land, other kinds of life were coming in. Forest and stream and air seemed palpitant[9] with their presence. The news of it was borne in upon him, not by sight, or sound, or smell, but by some other and subtler sense. He heard nothing, saw nothing, yet knew that the land was somehow different; that through it strange things were afoot and ranging; and he resolved to investigate after he had finished the business in hand.

At last, at the end of the fourth day, he pulled the great moose down. For a day and a night he remained by the kill, eating and sleeping, turn and turn about. Then, rested, refreshed and strong, he turned his face toward camp and John Thornton. He broke into the long easy lope, and went on, hour after hour, never at loss for the tangled way, heading straight home through strange country with a certitude of direction that put man and his magnetic needle to shame.

1 As he held on he became more and more conscious of the new stir in the land. There was life abroad in it different from the life which had been there throughout the summer. No longer was this fact borne in upon him in some subtle, mysterious way. The birds talked of it, the squirrels chattered about it, the very breeze whispered of it. Several times he stopped and drew in the fresh morning air in great sniffs, reading a message which made him leap on with greater speed. He was oppressed with a sense of calamity happening, if it were not calamity already happened; and as he crossed the last watershed and dropped down into the valley toward camp, he proceeded with greater caution.

Three miles away he came upon a fresh trail that sent his neck hair rippling and bristling. It led straight toward camp and John Thornton. Buck hurried on, swiftly and stealthily, every nerve straining and tense, alert to the multitudinous details which told a story—all but the end. His nose gave him a varying description of the passage of the life on the heels of which he was traveling. He remarked the pregnant silence of the forest. The bird life had flitted. The squirrels were in hiding. One only he saw—a sleek gray fellow, flattened against a gray dead limb so that he seemed a part of it, a woody excrescence[10] upon the wood itself.

As Buck slid along with the obscureness of a gliding shadow, his nose was jerked suddenly to the side as though a positive force had gripped and pulled it. He followed the new scent into a thicket and found Nib. He was lying on his side, dead where he had dragged himself, an arrow protruding, head and feathers, from either side of his body.

A hundred yards farther on, Buck came upon one of the sled dogs Thornton had bought in Dawson. This dog was thrashing about in a death struggle, directly on the trail, and Buck passed around him without stopping. From the camp came the faint sound of many voices, rising and falling in a singsong chant. Bellying forward to the edge of the clearing, he found Hans, lying on his face, feathered with arrows like a porcupine. At the same instant Buck peered out where the spruce-bough lodge had been and saw what made his hair leap straight up on his
2 neck and shoulders. A gust of overpowering rage swept over him. He did not know that he growled, but he growled aloud with a terrible ferocity. For the last time in his life he allowed passion to usurp[11] cunning and reason, and it was because of his great love for John Thornton that he lost his head.

3 The Yeehats were dancing about the wreckage of the spruce-bough lodge when they heard a fearful roaring and saw rushing upon them an animal the like of which they had never seen

9. **palpitant:** throbbing, quivering.

10. **excrescence** [eks krēs′ǝns]: outgrowth.
11. **usurp** [ū surp′]: seize control.

GUIDED READING

LITERAL QUESTIONS

1a. What becomes of the bull moose? (Buck kills him on the fourth day and feasts for another day before returning to Thornton's camp.)

2a. How has Nib been killed? (by an arrow through his body)

INFERENTIAL QUESTIONS

1b. Why does Buck return to camp after the moose's death? (Although he is capable of surviving in the wild, he is still bound by love to Thornton and thus to civilization.)

2b. How has London prepared us for the presence of Indians in this climactic scene? (comparison of Thornton to an Indian, arrow protruding from the moose's side, the abandoned flintlock rifle)

efore. It was Buck, a live hurricane of fury, urling himself upon them in a frenzy to detroy. He sprang at the foremost man (it was the hief of the Yeehats). There was no withstandng him. He plunged about in their very midst, earing, rending, destroying, in constant and errific motion which defied the arrows they ischarged at him. In fact, so inconceivably apid were his movements, and so closely were he Indians tangled together, that they shot one nother with the arrows. Then a panic seized he Yeehats, and they fled in terror to the voods, proclaiming as they fled the advent of he Evil Spirit.

And truly Buck was the Fiend incarnate, ragng at their heels and dragging them down like eer as they raced through the trees. It was a ateful day for the Yeehats. They scattered far nd wide over the country, and it was not till a veek later that the last of the survivors gathered ogether in a lower valley and counted their osses. As for Buck, wearying of the pursuit, he eturned to the desolated camp. He found Pete vhere he had been killed in his blankets in the irst moment of surprise. Thornton's desperate truggle was fresh-written on the earth, and uck scented every detail of it down to the edge f a deep pool. By the edge, head and forefeet in he water, lay Skeet, faithful to the last. The ool itself, muddy and discolored from the luice boxes,[12] effectually hid what it contained, nd it contained John Thronton; for Buck folowed his trace into the water, from which no race led away.

All day Buck brooded by the pool or roamed estlessly about the camp. Death, as a cessation f movement, as a passing out and away from he lives of the living, he knew, and he knew ohn Thornton was dead. It left a great void in im, somewhat akin to hunger, but a void vhich ached and ached, and which food could not fill. At times, when he paused to contemplate the carcasses of the Yeehats, he forgot the pain of it; and at such times he was aware of a great pride in himself—a pride greater than any he had yet experienced.

Night came on, and a full moon rose high over the trees into the sky, lighting the land till it lay bathed in ghostly day. And with the coming of the night, brooding and mourning by the pool, Buck became alive to a stirring of the new life in the forest other than that which the Yeehats had made. He stood up, listening and scenting. From far away drifted a faint, sharp yelp, followed by a chorus of similar sharp yelps. As the moments passed the yelps grew closer and louder. Again Buck knew them as things heard in that other world which persisted in his memory. He walked to the center of the open space and listened. It was the call, the many-noted call, sounding more luringly and compellingly than ever before. And as never before, he was ready to obey. John Thornton was dead. The last tie was broken. Man and the claims of man no longer bound him.

Hunting their living meat, as the Yeehats were hunting it, on the flanks of the migrating moose, the wolf pack had at last crossed over from the land of streams and timber and invaded Buck's valley. Into the clearing where the moonlight streamed, they poured in a silvery flood; and in the center of the clearing stood Buck, motionless as a statue, waiting their coming. They were awed, so still and large he stood, and a moment's pause fell, till the boldest one leaped straight for him. Like a flash Buck struck. Then he stood, without movement, as before, the stricken wolf rolling in agony behind him. Three others tried it in sharp succession; and one after the other they drew back.

This was sufficient to fling the whole pack forward, pell-mell, crowded together, blocked and confused by its eagerness to pull down the prey. Buck's marvelous quickness and agility stood him in good stead. Pivoting on his hind

12. **sluice boxes:** long troughs through which water is run o extract the gold.

AT A GLANCE

- Buck attacks the entire war party of Yeehats.
- He discovers Thornton's trail to the pond.
- He experiences both loss and a great pride in surveying the Yeehat bodies.
- A wolf pack invades Buck's valley.

1 PLOT: CLIMAX

Buck attacks the Yeehat party and vanquishes it, killing many Indians and causing others to shoot one another.

2 CHARACTERIZATION

Although he loved Thornton intensely, Buck has reverted to the wild. He accepts the loss of Thornton as a fact of existence. He does not experience guilt or a sense of having failed his master.

GUIDED READING

LITERAL QUESTION

1a. What time of day does Buck become aware of the wolf pack? (night, under a full moon)

INFERENTIAL QUESTION

1b. How does the setting heighten the effect of this climactic moment? (Buck is like "a statue" in the moonlit clearing; the pack pours in "in a silvery flood.")

AT A GLANCE

- Buck fights the pack in a ritual of initiation.
- The wild brother recognizes him.
- Buck is accepted into the pack.

1 PLOT: FALLING ACTION

With the identification of the wild brother and the blessing of the old chief, Buck is invited to join in the wolf call. This act symbolizes his entrance into the world of the wild and the putting away of civilization and man forever.

legs, and snapping and gashing, he was everywhere at once, presenting a front which was apparently unbroken so swiftly did he whirl and guard from side to side. But to prevent them from getting behind him, he was forced back, down past the pool and into the creek bed, till he brought up against a high gravel bank. He worked along to a right angle in the bank which the men had made in the course of mining, and in this angle he came to bay, protected on three sides and with nothing to do but face the front.

And so well did he face it, that at the end of half an hour the wolves drew back discomfited. The tongues of all were out and lolling, the white fangs showing cruelly white in the moonlight. Some were lying down with heads raised and ears pricked forward; others stood on their feet, watching him; and still others were lapping water from the pool. One wolf, long and lean and gray, advanced cautiously, in a friendly manner, and Buck recognized the wild brother with whom he had run for a night and a day. He was whining softly, and, as Buck whined, they touched noses.

Then an old wolf, gaunt and battle-scarred, came forward. Buck writhed his lips into the preliminary of a snarl, but sniffed noses with him. Whereupon the old wolf sat down, pointed nose at the moon, and broke out the long wolf
1 howl. The others sat down and howled. And now the call came to Buck in unmistakable accents. He, too, sat down and howled. This over, he came out of his angle and the pack crowded around him, sniffing in half-friendly, half-savage manner. The leaders lifted the yelp of the pack and sprang away into the woods. The wolves swung in behind, yelping in chorus. And Buck ran with them, side by side with the wild brother, yelping as he ran.

And here may well end the story of Buck. The years were not many when the Yeehats noted a change in the breed of timber wolves; for some were seen with splashes of brown on head and muzzle, and with a rift of white centering down the chest. But more remarkable than this, the Yeehats tell of a Ghost Dog that runs at the head of the pack. They are afraid of

GUIDED READING

LITERAL QUESTION

1a. How is Buck welcomed into the pack? (The old wolf sniffs noses with him and invites him to howl.)

INFERENTIAL QUESTION

1b. How is this howling different from that of Buck and the huskies the night of the aurora borealis? (London emphasized the mournful quality of the previous howling. This seems to be joyful.)

this Ghost Dog, for it has cunning greater than they, stealing from their camps in fierce winters, robbing their traps, slaying their dogs, and defying their bravest hunters.

Each fall, when the Yeehats follow the movement of the moose, there is a certain valley which they never enter. And women there are who become sad when the word goes over the fire of how the Evil Spirit came to select that valley for an abiding place.

In the summers there is one visitor, however, to that valley, of which the Yeehats do not know. It is a great, gloriously coated wolf, like, and yet unlike, all other wolves. He crosses alone from the smiling timber land and comes 1 down into an open space among the trees. Here a yellow stream flows from rotted moose-hide sacks and sinks into the ground, with long grasses growing through it and vegetable mold overrunning it and hiding its yellow from the sun; and here he muses for a time, howling once, long and mournfully, ere he departs.

But he is not always alone. When the long winter nights come on and the wolves follow their meat into the lower valleys, he may be seen running at the head of the pack through the pale moonlight or glimmering borealis, leaping gigantic above his fellows, his great throat a-bellow as he sings a song of the younger world, which is the song of the pack.

STUDY QUESTIONS

Recalling

1. According to Chapter 6, what are Buck's feelings for Thornton? Explain briefly two things that Buck does to show his feelings for Thornton.
2. Describe the call that Buck hears in Chapter 6. What is Buck's reaction to this call? What holds him back?
3. Describe Thornton's method of traveling in the wild as it is pictured at the beginning of Chapter 7. What are Thornton and his partners searching for as they travel east? In what sense is the search successful?
4. Briefly describe two adventures that Buck has when he leaves camp alone. Describe the scene that Buck finds when he returns to camp after his hunt. What is his reaction?
5. What finally happens to Buck at the end of the novel? Describe the Ghost Dog of the Yeehats' legend.

Interpreting

6. In what sense does Thornton's personality affect Buck?
7. Using examples from the novel, explain Thornton's attitude toward nature.
8. Explain how the setting changes in Chapter 7. In what way does the change in setting reflect a change in Buck?
9. What proof does the novel give that Buck will survive? In what way does Buck continue to show his loyalty to humanity at the end of the novel?

Extending

10. Do you consider all of Buck's adventures realistic? Explain your opinion with examples from the novel.

VIEWPOINT

Writing about *The Call of the Wild*, one critic compares Buck to the heroes of myths and classical literature. The adventures of such heroes usually follow a pattern:

> The call to adventure, departure, initiation, the perilous journey...transformation, and apotheosis [becoming a glorified ideal]—these are the phases of the Myth....
>
> —E. Labor, *Jack London*

■ Explain how Buck's adventures follow the same pattern as adventures of mythical heroes.

AT A GLANCE

- In future years the Yeehats avoid the valley of the "Ghost Dog."
- The gold that Thornton harvested trickles back into the earth.

1 THE TOTAL EFFECT

The mention of the gold brings us back to Chapter 1, the yellow metal groped for in the Arctic darkness.

REFLECTING ON CHAPTERS 6–7

Did you find the novel's conclusion satisfying? (Students may express regret that Thornton and Buck could not continue together; most will probably emphasize that London has satisfied them by showing nature taking its course.)

STUDY QUESTIONS

1. loves him totally; gently bites his hand, stares at him
2. thrilling, "call of the wild"; is drawn; love for Thornton
3. travels with few provisions, hunts as he goes; lost gold mine; find rich gold deposit.
4. meets wolf, kills moose; dogs and men dead, camp ruined, Yeehats dancing; kills several Indians
5. joins wolf pack; has great cunning, steals from camps, robs traps, defies hunters
6. Kindness leads Buck to love him; ease in wilderness allows Buck to experience his freedom.
7. in tune with nature: settles in wilderness for winter; does not travel on thawing river; travels lightly
8. valley where Thornton makes camp wild but less harsh; represents Buck's comfort in the wild
9. wolves' acceptance, his traits are seen in new generations of wolves; revisits camp
10. Answers will vary.

VIEWPOINT

- Call to adventure: Buck sold
- Departure: travels many days
- Initiation: meets man in red sweater
- Journey: dangerous trips as sled dog
- Transformation: adapts as sled dog, loyal friend, wild dog
- Apotheosis: develops supernatural strength

LITERARY FOCUS

1. ▪ relates several adventures, spans many years, develops several relationships
   ▪ meeting with man in red sweater; fight with Spitz; trip with Hal; meeting with Thornton; Thornton's death
2. ▪ Buck's desire to return to the wild vs. hold of civilization
   ▪ After Thornton dies, Buck is free.
3. character vs. nature; Buck's learning to survive in wild
4. *cunning:* rebels against Spitz; *patient:* pursues moose for days; *brave:* risks life to save master; *proud:* refuses to let Sol-leks take lead; *loyal:* returns to camp
5. *judge:* civilized, trusts people; *Klondike:* learns cunning, force; *valley:* lives in harmony with wilderness
6. advantages: gives greater insight into Buck's feelings, actions; disadvantages: reveals less about human characters
7. ▪ Charles, others: treat dogs badly, carry unnecessary provisions; Thornton: treats dogs with kindness, travels with little
   ▪ People must live in harmony with nature or it will destroy them.
8. Nature can never be fully tamed.
9. ▪ gold found by Thornton at end
   ▪ He is killed by Indians.
   ▪ Greed for wealth may lead to disaster.
10. Buck's love for him pulls him back to camp; love is a powerful taming force.

LITERARY FOCUS

The Total Effect

The first four elements of the novel—plot, character, setting, and point of view—contribute to the **theme**, or main idea, of a novel. Because of its length, a novel often makes more than one general statement about life, has more than one theme. Theme, in turn, joins with the other elements to form the novel's total effect—its impact on the reader. Since a reader spends more time with a novel than with a short story, the total effect of a novel is usually deeper.

Thinking About Plot, Character, and Setting

1. In what sense is the plot of *The Call of the Wild* more complicated than the plot of a short story? What single incidents in the novel do you think would make good short stories? Why?
2. What do you think is the main internal conflict of the novel? What is its outcome?
3. What do you think is the main external conflict of the novel? What is its outcome?
4. Name at least three personality traits of Buck with an example from the novel for each.
5. Explain how each of the following settings from the novel represents a different stage in Buck's development: (a) the judge's place, (b) the frozen Klondike of Chapters 2 to 5, and (c) the spring and summer of Chapters 6 and 7.

Thinking About Point of View

6. What do you think are the advantages and disadvantages of seeing the events of the novel through Buck's eyes?

Thinking About Theme

7. Contrast Charles, Hal, and Mercedes with Thornton. Explain how they treat their dogs, how they travel in the wild. What theme does London imply about the relationship between humans and nature?
8. What theme about nature is implied by the savage weather and by the fact that Buck, a tame dog, joins a pack of wolves?
9. Although *The Call of the Wild* is about the Klondike Gold Rush, what is the only gold found in the novel? What is the aftermath of the discovery? What theme is implied about the effort to find sudden wealth?
10. Explain how Thornton counteracts the call of the wild for Buck. What theme is implied about the power of love?

COMPOSITION

Writing About the Total Effect

▪ Each element of the novel contributes to the story of Buck and his transformation at the end of the novel. Describe the total effect, the impact that *The Call of the Wild* had on you. Explain how London uses the following elements to achieve this effect: (a) plot, (b) character, (c) setting, (d) point of view, and (e) theme. *For help with this assignment, see Lesson 11 in the Writing About Literature Handbook at the back of this book.*

Writing About Theme

▪ Choose one of the themes of *The Call of the Wild*, and show how London illuminates that theme in the novel. First state the theme. Then tell which of the following elements help to reveal the theme and explain how: (a) plot, (b) character, (c) setting, (d) point of view, and (e) the title. *For help with this assignment, see Lesson 7 in the Writing About Literature Handbook at the back of this book.*

Writing an Animal Story

▪ Write a brief story about a common household pet that becomes free and has an adventure alone in the outside world. First explain how the animal gets loose. Then describe a setting that is foreign to the animal and the animal's reaction to the setting. Go on to describe one adventure that the animal has. Finally explain whether the animal remains free or becomes domesticated again.

COMPOSITION: GUIDELINES FOR EVALUATION

WRITING ABOUT THE TOTAL EFFECT

Objective

To convey the total effect novel has on reader

Guidelines for Evaluation

- suggested length: five to eight paragraphs
- should state impact of plot, character, point of view, setting, and theme
- should use example from novel to illustrate impact

WRITING ABOUT THEME

Objective

To illustrate how theme is developed in a novel

Guidelines for Evaluation

- suggested length: one to three paragraphs
- should state one theme from novel
- should explain which literary elements convey theme
- should contain details to support opinion

Guidelines continue on next page.

LITERARY FOCUS: Great Expectations

Charles Dickens (1812–1870) may be the best-remembered novelist who ever lived, and many people believe that *Great Expectations* is the best of all his works. The works include the classic tale *A Christmas Carol* (1843) and the well-loved novels *Oliver Twist* (1837–1839), *Nicholas Nickleby* (1838–1839), *David Copperfield* (1849–1850), and *A Tale of Two Cities* (1859).

Dickens wrote *Great Expectations* (1860–1861) toward the end of his long career, at a point when he could look back on the poverty of his boyhood while enjoying the fame and riches that his writing had brought him. The novel itself is about a blacksmith's apprentice, an orphan boy, who grows up to taste riches and to learn their value. As you read *Great Expectations,* therefore, you may want to remember certain facts about Dickens' early life.

Charles Dickens was born in England, in a coastal city, not far from London. His family moved to London when he was very young. When Dickens was twelve years old, his father, mother, and their younger children were forced to move into a London debtors' prison, and Charles had to find work.

He earned his own scanty living by pasting labels on boxes of shoe "blacking," or polish. He ate little, slept on the floor in tenement attics, and spent his nonworking hours with a rough crowd on the London

Dickens' Dream, R. W. Boss. The Dickens House. Charles Dickens is depicted in his study surrounded by many of the characters he created.

WRITING AN ANIMAL STORY

Objective

To write an animal story

Guidelines for Evaluation

- suggested length: four to six paragraphs
- should contain: how pet gets loose; foreign setting; an adventure; resolution
- should use concrete details to describe setting

streets. On Sundays he visited his family in their relatively comfortable prison.

An upturn in family fortunes permitted him to return briefly to school, but at fifteen he left school to work as a law clerk. He also taught himself shorthand, a skill that he later used as a reporter who specialized in covering debates in Parliament. At nineteen he was heartlessly rejected by a girl whom he loved. He later married the daughter of a fellow journalist; they eventually had ten children.

The Pickwick Papers (1836–1837), Dickens' first novel, was published when he was twenty-four. Like most of his novels, *Pickwick* was published serially, chapter by chapter, in a magazine. The novel made him famous, and Dickens enjoyed his success. This is how he described himself while writing his novel *Martin Chuzzlewit* (1843–1844): "In a baywindow . . . sits, from nine o'clock to one, a gentleman with rather long hair and no neckcloth, who writes and grins, as if he thought he was very funny indeed." He was, in fact, a happy, popular celebrity, making public appearance and lecture tours throughout England and the United States. The wonderland of scenes that he created and his gallery of characters—lovable or villainous, comic or sympathetic—keep Dickens' popularity alive today.

Great Expectations remains one of Dickens' most popular works. The title refers to the hopes for the future of Pip, the main character, who is not satisfied with his position as a blacksmith's apprentice. The background for the novel is the social structure of nineteenth-century England where a poor youth had little hope of getting an education and escaping a life of strenuous, poorly paid labor. *Great Expectations* illustrates vividly the reasons for Dickens' continued popularity. The novel contains some of his most colorful and sympathetic characters. It is warmed by some of his most cheerful humor, his most deeply felt sympathies, and his most startling surprises.

Key Ideas in *Great Expectations*

■ As you read *Great Expectations*, look for references to each of the following topics. If you keep track of what the novel says about each topic, you will begin to understand the major themes of *Great Expectations*.

- appearances and real happiness
- loyalty to friends and family
- sympathy toward the poor and victims of injustice
- criticism of educational and legal institutions
- the power of love
- the role of chance in life
- revenge

Charles Dickens

Great Expectations (abridged)

Chapter One

The time: The early 1800s. The place: A churchyard in a tiny village east of London.

My father's family name being Pirrip, and my Christian name Philip, my infant tongue could make of both names nothing longer or more explicit than Pip. So I called myself Pip, and came to be called Pip.

I give Pirrip as my father's family name on the authority of his tombstone and my sister—Mrs. Joe Gargery, who married the blacksmith. As I never saw my father or my mother, and never saw any likeness of either of them (for their days were long before the days of photographs), my first fancies regarding what they were like were unreasonably derived from their tombstones. The shape of the letters on my father's gave me an odd idea that he was a square, stout, dark man, with curly black hair. From the character and turn of the inscription, *"Also Georgiana Wife of the Above,"* I drew a childish conclusion that my mother was freckled

2 and sickly. To five little stone lozenges,[1] each about a foot and a half long, which were arranged in a neat row beside their grave, and were sacred to the memory of five little brothers of mine—who gave up trying to get a living exceedingly early in that universal struggle—I am indebted for a belief that they had all been born on their backs with their hands in their trousers pockets.

Ours was the marsh country, down by the river, within, as the river wound, twenty miles of the sea. My first most vivid and broad impression of the identity of things seems to me to have been gained on a memorable raw afternoon towards evening. At such a time I found out for certain that this bleak place overgrown with net-

1. **lozenges** [loz′inj iz]: diamond-shaped objects.

AT A GLANCE

- Pip introduces himself.
- He explains that his parents and brothers are dead.
- He describes the countryside in which he lives.

LITERARY OPTIONS

- point of view
- characterization
- style

THEMATIC OPTIONS

- appearance vs. reality
- freedom vs. imprisonment
- friendship

1 THEME: APPEARANCE VS. REALITY

Pip forms mental images of his parents according to their tombstones: Though imaginative, he is naive and has trouble seeing beyond the outer form to what is within.

2 BACKGROUND

In Pip's day, the early 1800s, it was not unusual for five children of a poor family to die young, since there was scant medical expertise to combat the many illnesses of the day.

SELECTION FOR PRACTICE IN ACTIVE READING
(TCR 5, p. 69)

GUIDED READING

LITERAL QUESTION

1a. Whose gravestones does Pip look at in the graveyard? (his parents' and five brothers')

INFERENTIAL QUESTION

1b. What does this tell you about his family situation? (He is an orphan.)

AT A GLANCE

- A man with an iron on his leg threatens Pip and takes bread from him.
- Pip explains to the man that he lives with his sister.
- The man learns that Pip's brother-in-law is a blacksmith.

1 SETTING

Words describing the graveyard and surrounding area (*dark flat, low leaden, distant savage*) lend a dim, threatening air to the place.

2 CHARACTERIZATION

Pip describes the man as "fearful," but he also notes that the man is "soaked, smothered, lamed, cut, and cold," showing a tendency toward sympathy for him.

3 CHARACTERIZATION

Though Pip is young and frightened, he refrains from crying and talks intelligently to the man, showing his courage in the face of danger.

1 tles was the churchyard; and that the dark flat wilderness beyond the churchyard was the marshes; and that the low leaden line beyond was the river; and that the distant savage lair from which the wind was rushing was the sea; and that the small bundle of shivers growing afraid of it all and beginning to cry was Pip.

"Hold your noise!" cried a terrible voice, as a man started up from among the graves at the side of the church porch. "Keep still, you little devil, or I'll cut your throat!"

2 A fearful man, all in coarse grey, with a great iron on his leg. A man with no hat, and with broken shoes, and with an old rag tied round his head. A man who had been soaked in water, and smothered in mud, and lamed by stones, and cut by flints, and stung by nettles, and torn by briars; who limped, and shivered, and glared, and growled; and whose teeth chattered in his head, as he seized me by the chin.

"Oh! Don't cut my throat sir," I pleaded in terror. "Pray don't do it, sir."

"Tell us your name!" said the man. "Quick!"

"Pip, sir."

"Once more," said the man, staring at me. "Give it mouth!"

"Pip. Pip, sir."

"Show us where you live," said the man. "Pint out the place!"

I pointed to where our village lay, on the flat in-shore among the alder-trees and pollards,[2] a mile or more from the church.

The man, after looking at me for a moment, turned me upside down, and emptied my pockets. There was nothing in them but a piece of bread. When the church came to itself—for he was so sudden and strong that he made it go head over heels before me, and I saw the steeple under my feet—when the church came to itself, I say, I was seated on a high tombstone, trembling, while he ate the bread ravenously.

2. **pollards:** trees with their branches cut back to the trunk.

"You young dog," said the man, licking his lips, "what fat cheeks you ha' got."

I believe they were fat, though I was at that time undersized, for my years, and not strong.

"Darn me if I couldn't eat 'em," said the man, with a threatening shake of his head, "and if I han't half a mind to't!"

3 I earnestly expressed my hope that he wouldn't, and held tighter to the tombstone on which he had put me; partly to keep myself upon it; partly to keep myself from crying.

"Now lookee here!" said the man. "Where's your mother?"

"There, sir!" said I.

He started, made a short run, and stopped and looked over his shoulder.

"There, sir!" I timidly explained. "Also Georgiana. That's my mother."

"Oh!" said he, coming back. "And is that your father alonger your mother?"

"Yes, sir," said I; "him, too; late of this parish."

"Ha!" he muttered then, considering. "Who d'ye live with—supposin' ye're kindly let to live, which I han't made up my mind about?"

"My sister, sir—Mrs. Joe Gargery—wife of Joe Gargery, the blacksmith, sir."

"Blacksmith, eh?" said he. And looked down at his leg.

After darkly looking at his leg and at me several times, he came closer to my tombstone, took me by both arms, and tilted me back as far as he could hold me, so that his eyes looked most powerfully down into mine, and mine looked most helplessly up into his.

"Now lookee here," he said, "the question being whether you're to be let to live. You know what a file is?"

"Yes, sir."

"And you know what wittles[3] is?"

"Yes, sir."

3. **wittles:** vittles, slang for "victuals," food. Some characters in the novel pronounce *v* as *w*.

GUIDED READING

LITERAL QUESTIONS

1a. What does the man wear around his legs? (an iron)

2a. With whom does Pip say he lives? (with his sister and her husband, the blacksmith)

INFERENTIAL QUESTIONS

1b. What does this suggest about him? (He may be an escaped convict.)

2b. Why do you think this information interests the man? (The blacksmith might be able to remove the iron on the man's leg.)

After each question he tilted me over a little nore, so as to give me a greater sense of helplessness and danger.

"You get me a file." He tilted me again. "And you get me wittles." He tilted me again. "You bring 'em both to me." He tilted me again. "Or I'll have your heart and liver out." He tilted me again.

I was dreadfully frightened, and so giddy[4] that I clung to him with both hands.

"You bring me, to-morrow morning early, that file and them wittles. You bring the lot to me at that old battery[5] over yonder. You do it, and you never dare to say a word or dare to make a sign concerning your having seen such a person as me, and you shall be let to live. You fail, or you go from my words in any partickler, no matter how small it is, and your heart and your liver shall be tore out, roasted, and ate."

I said that I would get him the file, and I would get him what broken bits of food I could, and I would come to him at the battery, early in the morning.

"Say, Lord strike you dead if you don't!" said the man.

I said so, and he took me down.

"Goo-good night, sir," I faltered.

"Much of that!" said he, glancing about him over the cold wet flat. "I wish I was a frog. Or a eel!"

At the same time, he hugged his shuddering body in both his arms—clasping himself, as if to hold himself together—and limped towards the low church wall.

When he came to the low church wall, he got over it like a man whose legs were numbed and stiff, and then turned round to look for me. When I saw him turning, I set my face towards home, and made the best use of my legs. But presently I looked over my shoulder, and saw him going on again towards the river, still hug-
3 ging himself in both arms, and picking his way with his sore feet among the great stones dropped into the marshes here and there for stepping-places when the rains were heavy, or the tide was in.

4. **giddy:** dizzy.
5. **battery:** mound of earth with mounted cannons.

Chapter Two

At home: We meet Joe Gargery, the blacksmith, and Mrs. Joe, Pip's sister.

My sister, Mrs. Joe Gargery, was more than twenty years older than I, and had established a great reputation with herself and the neighbors because she had brought me up "by hand."
4 Knowing her to have a hard and heavy hand, and to be much in the habit of laying it upon her husband as well as upon me, I supposed that Joe Gargery and I were both brought up by hand.

She was not a good-looking woman, my sister, and I had a general impression that she must have made Joe Gargery marry her by hand. Joe was a fair man, with curls of flaxen hair on each side of his smooth face, and with eyes of such a very undecided blue that they seemed to have somehow got mixed with their own whites. He was a mild, good-natured, sweet-tempered, easy-going, foolish, dear fellow.

Joe's forge[1] adjoined our house, which was a wooden house, as many of the dwellings in our country were—most of them, at that time. When I ran home from the churchyard, the forge was shut up, and Joe was sitting alone in the kitchen.
5 Joe and I being fellow-sufferers, and having confidences as such, Joe imparted a confidence to me the moment I raised the latch of the door and peeped in at him opposite to it, sitting in the chimney-corner.

"Mrs. Joe has been out a dozen times, looking for you, Pip. And she's out now, making it a baker's dozen."

1. **forge:** blacksmith's workshop and open furnace for heating metal.

AT A GLANCE

- The man tells Pip to bring him a file and food in the morning; Pip agrees.
- Pip returns home.
- Pip describes his home, his sister, and her husband, Joe Gargery.

1 STYLE: REPETITION

Dickens' repetition of the sentence "He tilted me again" adds a comic touch to the scene and reinforces the confusion and fear Pip feels.

2 POINT OF VIEW

Pip, the first-person narrator, notes that the man hugs himself and limps. The reader is allowed to know only as much as Pip can see and know about the world from his child's point of view.

3 SETTING

Pip's description of the inhospitable, wet marsh shows sympathy for the man with "sore feet" who must spend the night there.

4 CHARACTERIZATION

Pip reveals that his sister is strong, unattractive, and dominating, and that her husband, Joe, allows himself to be ruled by her.

5 THEME: FRIENDSHIP

Pip describes himself and Joe as "fellow-sufferers" and explains that their close and loving friendship is based partly on their similar treatment by Mrs. Joe.

GUIDED READING

LITERAL QUESTIONS

1a. What does the man insist Pip do? (bring him a file and food the next morning)

2a. What adjectives does Pip use to describe Joe? (*mild, good-natured, sweet-tempered, easy-going, foolish,* and *dear*)

INFERENTIAL QUESTIONS

1b. Why might Pip bring the food and file to him? (He is honest and feels sorry for the man; he is too fearful to defy him.)

2b. How does Pip seem to feel about Joe? (He seems to feel very fondly toward him.)

AT A GLANCE

- Mrs. Joe is outside hunting for Pip.
- When Mrs. Joe returns, she shouts at Pip and hits him.
- Mrs. Joe gives Joe and Pip food.
- As Joe eats, Pip hides his food for the man on the marshes.

1 CHARACTERIZATION

Pip reveals a certain snobbery by referring to Joe as "a larger species of child" and "no more than my equal."

2 THEME: APPEARANCE VS. REALITY

By insisting that she raised Pip "by hand," his sister strives to appear kindhearted and selfless; however, her actions and attitude suggest that she is a hard-hearted woman who had no choice in the matter.

3 CHARACTERIZATION

Pip's sister is presented as a dissatisfied, angry woman who lacks sensitivity and gratitude for that which she *does* have.

4 CHARACTERIZATION

Pip shows his loyalty to his word and his inventiveness when he sneaks food down the leg of his pants to save for the man in the marshes.

5 CHARACTERIZATION

Joe's honesty, concern, and slowness of wit are revealed when he stops eating and stares at Pip, trying to determine where Pip's bread-and-butter has gone.

"Is she?"

"Yes, Pip," said Joe; "and what's worse, she's got Tickler with her."

I twisted the only button on my waistcoat round and round, and looked in great depression at the fire. Tickler was a wax-ended piece of cane, worn smooth by collision with my tickled frame.

1 "Has she been gone long, Joe?" I always treated him as a larger species of child, and as no more than my equal.

"Well," said Joe, glancing up at the Dutch clock, "she's been on the ram-page,[2] this last spell, about five minutes, Pip. She's a-coming! Get behind the door."

I took the advice. My sister, Mrs. Joe, throwing the door wide open, and finding an obstruction behind it, immediately divined[3] the cause, and applied Tickler to its further investigation. She concluded by throwing me at Joe, who, glad to get hold of me on any terms, passed me on into the chimney and quietly fenced me up there with his great leg.

"Where have you been, you young monkey?" said Mrs. Joe, stamping her foot. "Tell me directly what you've been doing to wear me away with fret and fright and worrit, or I'd have you out of that corner if you was fifty Pips, and he was five hundred Gargerys."

"I have only been to the churchyard," said I from my stool, crying and rubbing myself.

2 "Churchyard!" repeated my sister. "If it warn't for me, you'd have been to the churchyard long ago, and stayed there. Who brought you up by hand?"

"You did," said I.

"And why did I do it, I should like to know?" exclaimed my sister.

I whimpered, "I don't know."

"I don't!" said my sister. "I'd never do it again! I know that. I may truly say I've never had
3 this apron of mine off, since born you were. It's bad enough to be a blacksmith's wife (and him a Gargery) without being your mother."

My thoughts strayed from that question as I looked disconsolately at the fire. For the fugitive out on the marshes with the ironed leg, the file, the food, and the dreadful pledge I was under to commit a larceny rose before me in the avenging coals.

My sister had a way of cutting our bread-and-butter for us that never varied. She took some butter (not too much) on a knife and spread it on the loaf, as if she were making a plaster—using both sides of the knife and trimming and moulding the butter off round the crust. Then she gave the knife a final smart wipe on the edge of the plaster, and then sawed a very thick round off the loaf; which she finally, before separating from the loaf, hewed into two halves, of which Joe got one, and I the other.

4 On the present occasion, though I was hungry, I dared not eat my slice. I felt that I must have something in reserve for my dreadful acquaintance. Therefore I resolved to put my hunk of bread-and-butter down the leg of my trousers. I took advantage of a moment when Joe had just looked at me, and got my bread-and-butter down my leg.

Joe was evidently made uncomfortable by what he supposed to be my loss of appetite, and took a thoughtful bite out of his slice, which he didn't seem to enjoy. He turned it about in his mouth much longer than usual, pondering over it a good deal, and after all gulped it down like a pill. He was about to take another bite when his eye fell on me, and he saw that my bread-and-butter was gone.

5 The wonder and consternation with which Joe stopped on the threshold of his bite and stared at me were too evident to escape my sister's observation.

"What's the matter now?" said she smartly, as she put down her cup.

"I say, you know!" muttered Joe, shaking his

2. **ram-page:** rampage, fit of anger.
3. **divined:** guessed.

GUIDED READING

LITERAL QUESTION

1a. How does Mrs. Joe prepare the bread-and-butter? (According to a method that never varies, she butters and cuts a thick slice, and slices that in two.)

INFERENTIAL QUESTION

1b. What does this tell you about Mrs. Joe? (She is methodical and devoted to carefully observed routines in her household duties; she is not generous with food.)

head at me in a very serious remonstrance. "Pip, old chap! You'll do yourself a mischief. It'll stick somewhere. You can't have chawed it, Pip."

"What's the matter *now*?" repeated my sister more sharply than before.

"You know, Pip," said Joe solemnly, with his last bite in his cheek, and speaking in a confidential voice, as if we two were quite alone, "you and me is always friends, and I'd be the last to tell upon you, any time. But such a"—he moved his chair, and looked about the floor between us, and then again at me—"such a most uncommon bolt as that!"

"Been bolting his food, has he?" cried my sister.

My sister made a dive at me, and fished me up by the hair: saying nothing more than the awful words, "You come along and be dosed."[4]

Conscience is a dreadful thing. The guilty knowledge that I was going to rob Mrs. Joe—I never thought I was going to rob Joe, for I never thought of any of the housekeeping property as his—almost drove me out of my mind. Then, as the marsh winds made the fire glow and flare, I thought I heard the voice outside of the man with the iron on his leg who had sworn me to secrecy.

It was Christmas Eve, and I had to stir the pudding for next day with a copper-stick, from seven to eight by the Dutch clock and found the tendency of exercise to bring the bread-and-butter out at my ankle quite unmanageable. Happily I slipped away, and deposited that part of my conscience in my garret[5] bedroom.

"Hark!" said I, when I had done my stirring, and was taking a final warm in the chimney-corner before being sent up to bed; "was that great guns, Joe?"

"Ah!" said Joe. "There's another conwict off."

"What does that mean, Joe?" said I.

Mrs. Joe, who always took explanations upon herself, said snappishly, "Escaped. Escaped."

While Mrs. Joe sat with her head bending over her needlework, I put my mouth into the forms of saying to Joe, "What's a convict?" Joe put ***his*** mouth into the forms of returning such a highly elaborate answer that I could make out nothing of it but the single word, "Pip."

"There was a conwict off last night," said Joe, aloud, "after sunset-gun. And they fired warning of him. And now it appears they're firing warning of another."

"***Who's*** firing?" said I.

"Drat that boy," interposed my sister, frowning at me over her work, "what a questioner he is." Joe opened his mouth very wide, and shook the form of a most emphatic word out of it. But I could make nothing of the word.

3 "Mrs. Joe," said I, as a last resort, "I should like to know—if you wouldn't much mind—where the firing comes from."

"Lord bless the boy!" exclaimed my sister, as if she didn't quite mean that, but rather the contrary. "From the Hulks!"

"Oh-h!" said I, looking at Joe. "Hulks!"

Joe gave a reproachful cough, as much as to say, "Well, I told you so."

"And please, what's Hulks?" said I.

"That's the way with this boy!" exclaimed my sister, pointing me out with her needle and thread, and shaking her head at me. "Answer him one question, and he'll ask you a dozen
4 directly. Hulks are prison-ships, right 'cross th' meshes." We always used that name for marshes in our country.

"I wonder who's put into prison-ships, and why they're put there?" said I, in a general way, and with quiet desperation.

It was too much for Mrs. Joe, who immediately rose. "I tell you what, young fellow," said she, "I didn't bring you up by hand to badger people's lives out. People are put in the Hulks because they murder, and because they rob, and

---

4. **dosed:** given medicine.
5. **garret:** attic.

AT A GLANCE

- Joe and Mrs. Joe think Pip has "bolted" his bread.
- Pip guiltily hides the bread.
- Guns are fired; Pip learns that a convict has escaped from the prison-ships.

1 CHARACTERIZATION

Pip's guilt over stealing food from his sister reveals both his strong ideas of right and wrong and his desire to keep his promise to the convict.

2 STYLE: HUMOR

Dickens uses the image of Pip's bread-and-butter coming "out at my ankle" as a humorous contrast to the grim household and Pip's guilty secret.

3 STYLE: DIALOGUE

Pip's conversation with his sister reveals his eager, inquiring mind as well as his sister's impatience and reluctance to speak to him.

4 BACKGROUND

In nineteenth-century England, convicts were often imprisoned on ships, as ships provided added security and other prisons were full.

GUIDED READING

LITERAL QUESTIONS

1a. What does Joe think Pip has done with his bread? (He thinks Pip has eaten it.)

2a. What does Pip ask Joe and his sister? (why guns sounded, what a convict is, where the firing comes from, why prisoners are kept in the Hulks)

INFERENTIAL QUESTIONS

1b. Why does Joe "tell on" Pip? (He is worried that "bolting" food might have a bad effect on Pip.)

2b. Why might Pip want this information? (He may sense that the man with the iron shackle is an escaped convict.)

AT A GLANCE

- Mrs. Joe sends Pip to bed.
- Before dawn Pip steals food and a file and heads for the marshes.
- In the churchyard Pip surprises another convict.
- He finds "his" convict; the convict devours the food.

1 MOOD

The creaking boards and Pip's vivid imagination work to build suspense and to create a mood of adventure and fear.

2 THEME: APPEARANCE VS. REALITY

The man whom Pip thought was "his" convict is actually another one, a surprise for the reader as well as for Pip.

3 READING SKILLS: COMPARISON AND CONTRAST

Pip compares and contrasts the two men: Both are dressed in coarse gray, wear leg irons, and are lame and cold; their faces, however, are different, and one man wears a hat.

4 CHARACTERIZATION

The fact that the convict leaves Pip right side up suggests that his earlier mishandling of the boy was due to hunger and desperation rather than to an innate cruelty.

5 DIALOGUE

Pip's view of the convict is increasingly sympathetic: He is less a fearsome character than a cold, sick man to be pitied.

forge, and do all sorts of bad; and they always begin by asking questions. Now you get along to bed!"

I was never allowed a candle to light me to bed, and, as I went upstairs in the dark, I felt fearfully that the Hulks were handy for me. I was clearly on my way there. I had begun by asking questions, and I was going to rob Mrs. Joe.

1 As soon as the great black velvet pall outside my little window was shot with grey, I got up and went downstairs; every board upon the way, and every crack in every board, calling after me, "Stop thief!" and "Get up, Mrs. Joe!" I stole some bread, some rind of cheese, about half a jar of mincemeat (which I tied up in my pocket-handkerchief with my last night's slice), some brandy from a stone bottle. I was tempted to mount upon a shelf, to look what it was that was put away so carefully in a covered earthenware dish in a corner, and I found it was a pie, and I took it, in the hope that it was not intended for early use, and would not be missed for some time.

There was a door in the kitchen communicating with the forge; I unlocked and unbolted that door, and got a file from among Joe's tools. Then I ran for the misty marshes.

Chapter Three

In the churchyard again: Pip delivers stolen goods.

I had just crossed a ditch which I knew to be very near the battery, and had just scrambled up the mound beyond the ditch, when I saw the man sitting before me. His back was towards me, and he had his arms folded, and was nodding forward, heavy with sleep.

2 I thought he would be more glad if I came upon him with his breakfast in that unexpected manner, so I went forward softly and touched him on the shoulder. He instantly jumped up, and it was not the same man, but another man!

3 And yet this man was dressed in coarse grey too, and had a great iron on his leg, and was lame, and hoarse, and cold, and was everything that the other man was; except that he had not the same face, and had a flat, broad-brimmed low-crowned felt hat on. All this I saw in a moment, for I had only a moment to see it in: he swore an oath at me, made a hit at me—it was a round, weak blow that missed me and almost knocked himself down, for it made him stumble—and then he ran into the mist, stumbling twice as he went, and I lost him.

I was soon at the battery, after that, and there was the right man—hugging himself and limping to and fro, as if he had never all night left off hugging and limping—waiting for me. He was awfully cold, to be sure. I half expected to see him drop down before my face and die of deadly cold. His eyes looked so awfully hungry, too, that when I handed him the file and he laid it down on the grass, it occurred to me he would have tried to eat it, if he had not seen my bundle.

4 He did not turn me upside down, this time, to get at what I had, but left me right side upwards while I opened the bundle and emptied my pockets.

"What's in the bottle, boy?" said he.

"Brandy," said I.

He was already handing mincement down his throat in the most curious manner—more like a man who was putting it away somewhere in a violent hurry, than a man who was eating it—but he left off to take some of the liquor. He shivered all the while so violently that it was quite as much as he could do to keep the neck of the bottle between his teeth, without biting it off.

5 "I think you have got the ague,"[1] said I.

"I'm much of your opinion, boy," said he.

"It's bad about here," I told him. "You've been lying out on the meshes."

"I'll eat my breakfast afore they're the death of me," said he. "I'd do that if I was going to be

1. **ague** [ā'gū]: chills and fever.

GUIDED READING

LITERAL QUESTION

1a. What difference is there in the way the two convicts treat Pip? (One tries to hit him; the other eats his food and speaks to Pip.)

INFERENTIAL QUESTION

1b. Why are their reactions different? (The first convict is either more brutal or frightened than the second; to the first man Pip is a total stranger, to the second he is a boy bringing aid.)

strung up to that there gallows as there is over there, directly arterwards. I'll beat the shivers so far, *I*'ll bet you."

He was gobbling mincemeat, meatbone, bread, cheese, and pork pie all at once, staring distrustfully while he did so at the mist all round us, and often stopping—even stopping his jaws—to listen. Some real or fancied sound, some clink upon the river or breathing of beast upon the marsh, now gave him a start, and he said suddenly:

"You're not a deceiving imp? You brought no one with you?"

"No, sir! No!"

"Nor giv' no one the office to follow you?"

"No!"

"Well," said he, "I believe you. You'd be but a fierce young hound indeed, if at your time of life you could help to hunt a wretched warmint,[2] hunted as near death as this poor wretched warmint is!"

Something clicked in his throat as if he had works in him like a clock, and was going to strike. And he smeared his ragged rough sleeve over his eyes.

Pitying his desolation, and watching him as he gradually settled down upon the pie, I made bold to say, "I am glad you enjoy it."

"Did you speak?"

"I said, I was glad you enjoyed it."

"Thankee, my boy. I do."

"I am afraid you won't leave any of it for him."

"Leave any for him? Who's him?" said my friend, stopping in his crunching of piecrust.

"Yonder," said I, pointing; "over there."

He held me by the collar and stared at me so that I began to think his first idea about cutting my throat had revived.

"Dressed like you, you know, only with a hat," I explained, trembling; "and—and"—I was very anxious to put this delicately—"and with—the same reason for wanting to borrow a file."

"This man, did you notice anything in him?"

"He had a badly bruised face," said I, recalling what I hardly knew I knew.

"Not here? exclaimed the man, striking his left cheek mercilessly with the flat of his hand.

"Yes, there!"

3 "Where is he?" He crammed what little food was left into the breast of his grey jacket. "Show me the way he went. I'll pull him down, like a bloodhound. Curse this iron on my sore leg! Give us hold of the file, boy."

I indicated in what direction the mist had shrouded the other man, and he looked up at it for an instant. But he was down on the rank wet grass, filing at his iron like a madman, and not minding me or minding his own leg, which had an old chafe[3] upon it, and was bloody.

I told him I must go, but he took no notice, so I thought the best thing I could do was to slip off. The last I saw of him, his head was bent over his knee and he was working hard at his fetter.[4] The last I heard of him, I stopped in the mist to listen, and the file was still going.

Chapter Four

At home: At Christmas dinner we meet Mr. Pumblechook, Mr. Wopsle, and the Hubbles.

I fully expected to find a constable[1] in the kitchen, waiting to take me up. But not only was there no constable there, but no discovery had yet been made of the robbery.

"And where the deuce[2] ha' *you* been?" was Mrs. Joe's Christmas salutation.[3]

I said I had been down to hear the carols. "Ah! well!" observed Mrs. Joe. "You might ha'

2. **warmint:** varmint, objectionable person.

3. **chafe:** soreness caused by friction.
4. **fetter:** chain or shackle; here, the convict's leg iron.
1. **constable** [kon'stə bəl]: police officer.
2. **deuce** [dōōs]: bad luck, a mild oath.
3. **salutation** [sal'yə tā'shən]: greeting.

AT A GLANCE

- The convict eats Pip's food.
- Pip tells him that there is another convict on the marsh.
- The first convict is furious; he starts to file his iron.
- Pip returns home and says he has been listening to carols.

1 PARAPHRASING

The convict would be surprised if a boy as young as Pip would help to hunt a man in as desperate circumstances as his.

2 STYLE: DIALOGUE

The discussion between Pip and the convict reveals Pip's concern and pity for the man and the convict's gratitude and growing feeling ("Thankee, my boy") for Pip.

3 CHARACTERIZATION

The convict's sudden fury indicates a deep-seated enmity between both convicts; "Pip's convict" has a temper and a streak of brutality despite his gentleness with Pip.

GUIDED READING

LITERAL QUESTIONS

INFERENTIAL QUESTIONS

AT A GLANCE

- Pip and Joe go to church, and company comes for Christmas dinner.
- Dinner is eaten, and Mrs. Joe prepares to serve the pork pie that Pip has stolen.
- Soldiers come to the door as she discovers that the pie is gone.

1 POINT OF VIEW

Pip's description of Joe reveals Pip's mixed opinion of the blacksmith: He anxiously makes fun of the way Joe looks in holiday clothes.

2 CHARACTERIZATION

Pip gives a clue to Pumblechook's character when Pip observes that he may not call him Uncle: Either Mrs. Joe or Pumblechook himself feels that he is too important to be claimed as Pip's relative.

3 STYLE: REPETITION

Dickens repeats the parallel phrases *I saw* and *I heard* to build suspense: Pip observes with enormous clarity every moment before the discovery of the missing pie.

done worse." Not a doubt of that, I thought.

We were to have a superb dinner, consisting of a leg of pickled pork and greens, and a pair of roast stuffed fowls. A handsome mince pie had been made yesterday morning (which accounted for the mincemeat not being missed), and the pudding was already on the boil.

My sister having so much to do, was going to church vicariously;[4] that is to say, Joe and I were
1 going. In his working clothes, Joe was a well-knit characteristic-looking blacksmith; in his holiday clothes, he was more like a scarecrow in good circumstances than anything else. Nothing that he wore fitted him or seemed to belong to him.

Mr. Wopsle, the clerk[5] at church, was to dine with us; and Mr. Hubble, the wheelwright,[6] and Mrs. Hubble; and Uncle Pumblechook (Joe's uncle, but Mrs. Joe appropriated[7] him), who was a well-to-do corn-chandler[8] in the nearest town, and drove his own chaise-cart.[9] The dinner hour was half-past one. When Joe and I got home, we found the table laid, and Mrs. Joe dressed, and the dinner dressing, and the front door unlocked (it never was at any other time) for the company to enter by, and everything most splendid. And still, not a word of the robbery.

The company came. Mr. Wopsle, united to a Roman nose and a large shining bald forehead, had a deep voice which he was uncommonly proud of. I opened the door first to Mr. Wopsle,
2 next to Mr. and Mrs. Hubble, and last of all to Uncle Pumblechook. N.B.[10] *I* was not allowed to call him uncle, under the severest penalties.

We dined on these occasions in the kitchen, and adjourned, for the nuts and oranges and apples, to the parlor. I remember Mrs. Hubble as a little curly sharp-edged person in sky-blue, Mr. Hubble as a tough high-shouldered stooping old man, of a sawdusty fragrance. I began to think I should get over the day, when my sister said to Joe, "Clean plates—cold."

I clutched the leg of the table immediately, and pressed it to my bosom. I foresaw what was coming, and I felt that this time I really was gone.

"You must taste," said my sister, addressing the guests with her best grace, "You must taste, to finish with, such a delightful and delicious present of Uncle Pumblechook's! It's a pie—a savory[11] pork pie."

3 My sister went out to get it. I heard her steps proceed to the pantry. I saw Mr. Pumblechook balance his knife. I saw reawakening appetite in the Roman nostrils of Mr. Wopsle. I heard Mr. Hubble remark that "a bit of savory pork pie would lay atop of anything you could mention, and do no harm," and I heard Joe say, "You shall have some, Pip." I have never been absolutely certain whether I uttered a shrill yell of terror, merely in spirit, or in the bodily hearing of the company. I felt that I could bear no more, and that I must run away. I released the leg of the table, and ran for my life.

But I ran no further than the house door, for there I ran head foremost into a party of soldiers with their muskets; one of whom held out a pair of handcuffs to me, saying, "Here you are, look sharp, come on!"

The apparition of a file of soldiers ringing down the butt-ends of their loaded muskets on our door-step caused the dinner-party to rise from table in confusion, and caused Mrs. Joe, re-entering the kitchen empty-handed, to stop short and stare, in her wondering lament of "Gracious goodness gracious me, what's gone—with the—pie!"

The sergeant and I were in the kitchen when

---

4. **vicariously** [vī kâr′ē əs lē]: by imaginary sharing in another's experience.
5. **clerk:** assistant to a parish priest.
6. **wheelwright** [hwēl′rīt]: one who makes wheels.
7. **appropriated** [ə prō′prē āt′id]: claimed as one's own.
8. **corn-chandler:** grain merchant.
9. **chaise-cart:** small carriage pulled by one horse.
10. **N.B.:** abbreviation for *nota bene*, Latin for "note well."
11. **savory** [sā′və rē]: appetizing, highly seasoned.

GUIDED READING

LITERAL QUESTIONS

1a. How is Uncle Pumblechook described? (He is well-to-do and has his own horse-drawn carriage.)

2a. What does the soldier at the door do to Pip? (He holds out handcuffs to him.)

INFERENTIAL QUESTIONS

1b. Why do you think Mrs. Joe has "appropriated" Uncle Pumblechook? (She may be impressed by his wealth and his belongings.)

2b. Do you think the soldier means to arrest Pip? Why or why not? (No; there is no way the soldier could know of Pip's thievery.)

Mrs. Joe stood staring; at which crisis I partially recovered the use of my senses. It was the sergeant who had spoken to me, and he was now looking round at the company, with his handcuffs invitingly extended towards them in his right hand, and his left on my shoulder.

"Excuse me, ladies and gentlemen," said the sergeant, "but as I have mentioned at the door to this smart young shaver"—which he hadn't—"I am on a chase in the name of the King, and I want the blacksmith."

"And pray, what might you want with *him*?" retorted my sister, quick to resent his being wanted at all.

"Missis," returned the gallant sergeant, "speaking for myself, I should reply, the honor and pleasure of his fine wife's acquaintance; speaking for the king, I answer, a little job done."

2 This was received as rather neat in the sergeant; insomuch that Mr. Pumblechook cried audibly, "Good again!"

"You see, blacksmith," said the sergeant, who had by this time picked out Joe with his eye, "we have had an accident with these, and I find the lock of one of 'em goes wrong, and the coupling don't act pretty. As they are wanted for immediate service, will you throw your eye over them?"

Joe threw his eye over them, and pronounced that the job would necessitate the lighting of his forge fire, and would take nearer two hours than one. "Will it? Then will you set about it at once, blacksmith?" said the off-hand sergeant, "as it's on his Majesty's service. And if my men can bear a hand anywhere, they'll make themselves useful." With that he called to his men, who came trooping into the kitchen one after

AT A GLANCE

- The soldiers announce they are on a chase.
- They request Joe's help in fixing the lock on their handcuffs, and Joe examines the cuffs.

1 CHARACTERIZATION

Pip reveals Mrs. Joe's selfishness and jealousy of others' recognition when he states that she resents the soldiers' need of her husband's services.

2 STYLE: HUMOR

The sergeant's speech is overblown and insincere, yet both Pumblechook and Mrs. Joe are comically shown to be impressed by the sergeant.

GUIDED READING

LITERAL QUESTION

1a. Why do the soldiers need the handcuffs fixed? (They are needed for "immediate service.")

INFERENTIAL QUESTION

1b. To what immediate service do you think the sergeant refers? (He must capture the convicts on the marsh.)

AT A GLANCE

- Pip realizes the soldiers are not after him.
- Joe fixes the handcuffs.
- Joe, Wopsle, and Pip join the soldiers in looking for the convicts.
- On the marsh they hear shouts.

1 PARAPHRASING

Pip is saying here that the soldiers have so attracted the company's attention that everyone has forgotten about the missing pie.

2 IRONY

Dickens uses dramatic irony to build suspense: Only the reader and Pip know that the boy has seen and spoken to the convicts on the marshes.

3 SETTING

Dickens' description of the "bitter sleet" provides a contrast between the convicts' plight and the warm Christmas celebration at the Gargerys.

4 STYLE: METAPHOR

The phrase *the wings of the wind and rain* is a metaphor that stresses the wild freedom of the weather; by contrast, the convicts are trapped.

another, and piled their arms in a corner. And then they stood about.

1 I saw that the handcuffs were not for me, and that the military had so far got the better of the pie as to put it in the background. I collected a little more of my scattered wits.

"Would you give me the time!" said the sergeant, addressing himself to Mr. Pumblechook.

"It's just gone half-past two."

"That's not so bad," said the sergeant, reflecting; "even if I was forced to halt here nigh two hours, that'll do. How far might you call yourselves from the marshes, hereabouts? Not above a mile, I reckon?"

"Just a mile," said Mrs. Joe.

"That'll do. We begin to close in upon 'em about dusk."

"Convicts, sergeant?" asked Mr. Wopsle, in a matter-of-course way.

"Aye!" returned the sergeant, "two. They're pretty well known to be out on the marshes still, and they won't try to get clear of 'em before
2 dusk. Anybody here seen anything of any such game?"

Everybody, myself excepted, said no, with confidence. Nobody thought of me.

"Well," said the sergeant, "they'll find themselves trapped in a circle, I expect, sooner than they count on. Now, blacksmith! If you're ready, his Majesty the King is."

Joe began to hammer and clink, hammer and clink, and we all looked on.

At last, Joe's job was done, and the ringing and roaring stopped. As Joe got on his coat, he mustered courage to propose that some of us should go down with the soldiers and see what came of the hunt. Mr. Pumblechook and Mr. Hubble declined, on the plea of a pipe and ladies' society; but Mr. Wopsle said he would go, if Joe would. Joe said he was agreeable, and would take me. The sergeant took a polite leave of the ladies. His men resumed their muskets and fell in. Mr. Wopsle, Joe, and I received strict charge to keep in the rear, and to speak no word after we reached the marshes. When we were all out in the raw air and were steadily moving towards our business, I treasonably whispered to Joe, "I hope, Joe, we sha'n't find them." And Joe whispered to me, "I'd give a shilling[12] if they had cut and run, Pip."

Chapter Five

On the marshes: Pursuit.

3 We struck out on the open marshes, through the gate at the side of the churchyard. A bitter sleet came rattling against us here on the east wind, and Joe took me on his back.

Now that we were out upon the dismal wilderness where they little thought I had been within eight or nine hours, and had seen both men hiding, I considered for the first time, with great dread, if we should come upon them, would my particular convict suppose that it was I who had brought the soldiers there?

It was of no use asking myself this question now. There I was, on Joe's back, and there was Joe beneath me, charging at the ditches like a hunter, and stimulating Mr. Wopsle not to tumble on his Roman nose, and to keep up with us. The soldiers were in front of us, extending into a pretty wide line with an interval between man and man.

With my heart thumping like a blacksmith at Joe's broad shoulder, I looked all about for any sign of the convicts. I could see none, I could hear none.

The soldiers were moving on in the direction of the old battery, and we were moving on a little way behind them, when, all of a sudden, we
4 all stopped. For, there had reached us, on the wings of the wind and rain, a long shout. It was repeated. It was at a distance towards the east, but it was long and loud. Nay, there seemed to be two or more shouts raised together. When it broke out again, the soldiers made for it at a greater rate than ever, and we after them. After a

12. **shilling:** British coin equivalent to a dime.

GUIDED READING

LITERAL QUESTIONS

1a. What does Joe whisper to Pip about the convicts? (He hopes they have escaped.)

2a. What does Pip realize the convicts might think if they see him? (that he has brought the soldiers to them)

INFERENTIAL QUESTIONS

1b. Why does Joe feel this way? (He seems to feel sorry for the hunted men.)

2b. Why does this realization cause him such dread? (He does not want "his" convict to think he has betrayed him.)

while, we had so run it down that we could hear one voice calling "Murder!" and another voice, "Convicts! Runaways! Guard! This way for the runaway convicts!" Then both voices would seem to be stifled in a struggle, and then would break out again. And when it had come to this, the soldiers ran like deer, and Joe too.

The sergeant ran in first, when we had run the noise quite down, and two of his men ran in close upon him.

"Here are both men!" panted the sergeant, struggling at the bottom of a ditch. "Surrender, you two! And confound you for two wild beasts!"

Water was splashing, and mud was flying, and oaths were being sworn, and blows were being struck, when some more men went down into the ditch to help the sergeant; and dragged out, separately, my convict and the other one. Both were bleeding and panting and execrating[1] and struggling.

1 "Mind!" said my convict, wiping blood from his face with his ragged sleeves, and shaking torn hair from his fingers; "*I* took him! *I* give him up to you! Mind that!"

"It's not much to be particular about," said the sergeant; "it'll do you small good, my man, being in the same plight yourself. Handcuffs there!"

"I don't expect it to do me any good. I don't want it to do me more good than it does now," said my convict, with a greedy laugh. "I took him. He knows it. That's enough for me."

The other convict was livid to look at, and, in addition to the old bruised left side of his face, seemed to be bruised and torn all over.

"Take notice, guard—he tried to murder me," were his first words.

2 "Tried to murder him?" said my convict disdainfully. "Try, and not do it? I took him, and giv' him up; that's what I done. I not only prevented him getting off the marshes, but I dragged him here—dragged him this far on his way back. He's a gentleman, if you please, this villain. Now, the Hulks has got its gentleman again, through me. Murder him? Worth my while, too, to murder him, when I could do worse and drag him back!"

The other one still gasped, "He tried—he tried—to—murder me. Bear—bear witness."

"Lookee here!" said my convict to the sergeant. "Single-handed I got clear of the prison-ship; I made a dash and I done it. I could ha' got clear of these death-cold flats likewise—look at my leg: you won't find much iron on it—if I hadn't made discovery that *he* was here. Let *him* go free? Let *him* profit by the means as I found out? Let *him* make a tool of me afresh and again? Once more? No, no, no."

The other fugitive, who was evidently in extreme horror of his companion, repeated, "He tried to murder me. I should have been a dead man if you had not come up."

3 "He lies!" said my convict, with fierce energy. "He's a liar born, and he'll die a liar. Look at his face; ain't it written there? Let him turn those eyes of his on me. I defy him to do it. Do you see those groveling and wandering eyes? That's how he looked when we were tried together. He never looked at me."

"Enough of this parley,"[2] said the sergeant. "Light those torches."

As one of the soldiers, who carried a basket in lieu[3] of a gun, went down on his knee to open it, my convict looked round him for the first time, and saw me. I had alighted from Joe's back on the brink of the ditch when we came up, and
4 had not moved since. I looked at him eagerly when he looked at me, and slightly moved my hands and shook my head. I had been waiting for him to see me, that I might try to assure him of my innocence. It was not at all expressed to me that he even comprehended my intention, for he gave me a look that I did not understand, and it all passed in a moment.

The soldier with the basket soon got a light,

---

1. **execrating** [ek'sə krāt'ing]: uttering curses.

2. **parley** [pär'lē]: conference.
3. **in lieu** [lo͞o]: instead.

AT A GLANCE

- The two convicts are discovered fighting.
- Pip's convict insists he captured the other man in order to hand him over to the soldiers.
- The convict looks at Pip, who tries to show that he didn't betray him.

1 THEME: FREEDOM VS. IMPRISONMENT

Although Pip's convict is no longer a free man, he disdains the other's similar state, a mark of the low state to which he has fallen.

2 CHARACTERIZATION

Although Pip's convict has been brought low, he still possesses enough pride to boast that he returned with the other convict rather than flee the marshes.

3 CHARACTERIZATION

By stating vehemently that the other convict is "a liar born," Pip's convict implies that *he* is not a liar.

4 POINT OF VIEW

To Pip, the most important factor in the capture is that the convict should know it is not Pip's fault, and therefore he does not understand (and, of course, relate) the convict's feelings.

GUIDED READING

LITERAL QUESTION

1a. What alerts the soldiers to the presence of the convicts? (shouting)

INFERENTIAL QUESTION

1b. Who is calling "This way for the runaway convicts!" to the soldiers? (Pip's convict)

AT A GLANCE

- The soldiers and convicts march back toward the Hulks.
- Pip's convict says that he stole food from the blacksmith.
- Joe expresses sympathy for the convict.

1 CHARACTERIZATION

To Pip the darkness of the marshes increases when the convicts are found, corresponding to a darkness he feels in his heart over the convict's capture.

2 THEME: FREEDOM VS. IMPRISONMENT

Although the convicts are now captured, their imprisonment is in a way a relief due to their weakened physical condition: Their freedom was an illusion.

3 CHARACTERIZATION

Pip's convict reveals that he is an honorable man by taking responsibility for the missing food, thus relieving Pip of the burden of his theft.

4 CHARACTERIZATION

Joe reveals the depths of his kindness and humility by telling the convict that he is welcome to the food he took and calling him a "fellow-creatur."

and lighted three or four torches, and took one
1 himself and distributed the others. It had been almost dark before, but now it seemed quite dark, and soon afterwards very dark. Before we departed from that spot, four soldiers standing in a ring fired twice into the air. Presently we saw other torches kindled at some distance behind us, and others on the marshes on the opposite bank of the river. "All right," said the sergeant. "March."

We had not gone far when three cannon were fired ahead of us with a sound that seemed to burst something inside my ear. "You are expected on board," said the sergeant to my convict; "they know you are coming. Don't straggle, my man. Close up here."

The two were kept apart, and each walked surrounded by a separate guard. I had hold of Joe's hand now, and Joe carried one of the
2 torches. Our lights warmed the air about us with their pitchy blaze, and the two prisoners seemed rather to like that, as they limped along in the midst of the muskets. We could not go fast because of their lameness; and they were so spent that two or three times we had to halt while they rested.

After an hour or so of this traveling, we came to a rough wooden hut and a landing-place. There was a guard in the hut, and they challenged, and the sergeant answered. Then, we went into the hut, where there was a smell of tobacco and whitewash, and a bright fire, and a lamp, and a stand of muskets, and a drum, and a low wooden bedstead. The sergeant made some kind of report, and some entry in a book, and then the convict whom I call the other convict was drafted off with his guard, to go on board first.

My convict never looked at me, except that once. While we stood in the hut, he stood before the fire looking thoughtfully at it, or putting up his feet by turns upon the hob,[4] and looking thoughtfully at them as if he pitied them for their recent adventures. Suddenly, he turned to the sergeant, and remarked:

"I wish to say something respecting this escape. It may prevent some persons laying under suspicion alonger me."

"You can say what you like," returned the sergeant, standing coolly looking at him, with his arms folded, "but you have no call to say it here. You'll have opportunity enough to say about it, and hear about it, before it's done with, you know."

"I know, but this is another pint, a separate
3 matter. A man can't starve; at least *I* can't. I took some wittles, up at the willage over yonder—where the church stands a'most out on the marshes."

"You mean stole," said the sergeant.

"And I'll tell you where from. From the blacksmith's."

"Halloa!" said the sergeant, staring at Joe.

"Halloa, Pip!" said Joe, staring at me.

"It was some broken wittles—that's what it was—and a dram of liquor, and a pie."

"Have you happened to miss such an article as a pie, blacksmith?" asked the sergeant confidentially.

"My wife did, at the very moment when you came in. Don't you know, Pip?"

"So," said my convict, turning his eyes on Joe in a moody manner, and without the least glance at me; "so you're the blacksmith, are you? Then I'm sorry to say I've eat your pie."

4 "God knows you're welcome to it—so far as it was ever mine," returned Joe, with a saving remembrance of Mrs. Joe. "We don't know what you have done, but we wouldn't have you starved to death for it, poor miserable fellow-creatur. Would us, Pip?"

The something that I had noticed before clicked in the man's throat again, and he turned his back. The boat had returned, and his guard were ready. Somebody in the boat growled as if to dogs, "Give way, you!" which was the signal for

4. **hob:** shelf inside a fireplace.

GUIDED READING

LITERAL QUESTIONS

1a. How does the convict treat Pip during the march to the ship? (He ignores Pip completely.)

2a. What does Joe say when the convict admits he stole food? (Joe says the convict is welcome to it.)

INFERENTIAL QUESTIONS

1b. Why do you think he behaves that way? (so Pip won't be implicated in his escape)

2b. How do you think this statement affects the convict? (He is probably touched by it.)

the dip of the oars. By the light of the torches, we saw the black Hulk lying out a little way from the mud of the shore. We saw the boat go alongside, and we saw him taken up the side and disappear. Then, the ends of the torches were flung hissing into the water, and went out, as if it were all over with him.

Chapter Six

At home: Pip receives an odd job.

At the time when I stood in the churchyard, reading the family tombstones, I had just enough learning to be able to spell them out. When I was old enough, I was to be apprenticed[1] to Joe. I was not only odd-boy about the forge, but if any neighbor happened to want an extra boy to frighten birds, or pick up stones, or do any such job, I was favored with the employment.

Mr. Wopsle's great-aunt kept an evening school in the village; that is to say, she was a ridiculous old woman of limited means who used to go to sleep from six to seven every evening in the society of youth who paid twopence[2] per week each for the improving opportunity of seeing her do it. She rented a small cottage, and Mr. Wopsle had the room upstairs, where we students used to overhear him reading aloud in a most dignified and terrific manner, and occasionally bumping on the ceiling. There was a fiction that Mr. Wopsle "examined"[3] the scholars once a quarter. What he did on those occasions was to turn up his cuffs, stick up his hair, and give us Mark Antony's oration over the body of Caesar.[4]

Mr. Wopsle's great-aunt, besides keeping this educational institution, kept in the same room—a little general shop. She had no idea what stock she had, or what the price of anything in it was; but there was a little greasy memorandum-book kept in a drawer which served as a catalogue of prices, and by this oracle[5] Biddy arranged all the shop transactions. Biddy was Mr. Wopsle's great-aunt's grand-daughter; I confess myself quite unequal to the working out of the problem, what relation she was to Mr. Wopsle. She was an orphan like myself; like me, too, had
3 been brought up by hand. She was most noticeable, I thought, in respect of her extremities; for her hair always wanted brushing, her hands always wanted washing, and her shoes always wanted mending and pulling up at heel.

Much of my unassisted self, and more by the help of Biddy than of Mr. Wopsle's great-aunt, I struggled through the alphabet as if it had been a bramble-bush, getting considerably worried and
4 scratched by every letter. After that, I fell among those thieves, the nine figures, who seemed every evening to do something new to disguise themselves and baffle recognition. But, at last I began to read, write, and cipher on the very smallest scale.

One night, I was sitting in the chimney-corner with my slate, expending great efforts on the production of a letter to Joe. I think it must have been a full year after our hunt upon the marshes, for it was a long time after, and it was winter and a hard frost. With an alphabet on the hearth[6] at my feet for reference, I contrived in an hour or two to print and smear this epistle:

"MI DEER JO i OPE U R KRWITE WELL i OPE i SHAL SON B HABELL 4 2 TEEDGE U JO AN THEN WE SHORL B SO GLODD AN WEN i M PRENGTD 2 U JO WOT LARX AN BLEVE ME INF XN PIP."

There was no necessity for my communicating with Joe by letter, inasmuch as he sat beside me and we were alone. But I delivered this written communication (slate and all) with my own

1. **apprenticed** [ə pren′tisd]: bound by indentures, or contract, to a master worker. The apprentice worked without payment and, in return, learned a trade.
2. **twopence:** two cents.
3. **examined:** tested.
4. **give us . . . Caesar:** recited for us Mark Antony's speech from William Shakespeare's *Julius Caesar.*
5. **oracle** [or′ə kəl]: wisdom, authority.
6. **hearth** [härth]: fireside.

AT A GLANCE

- The convict is taken aboard the Hulk.
- Pip describes his "school" and introduces Biddy, a relative of Wopsle.
- A year passes.
- Pip sits with Joe and writes a letter to him.

1 STYLE: IMAGERY

The image of the torches going out in the black water signifies the apparent end of hope for Pip's convict, who has returned to the prison ship.

2 TONE

Dickens uses the phrase "I was favored with the employment" sarcastically, since the neighbors actually take advantage of Pip.

3 THEME: APPEARANCE VS. REALITY

Pip's tendency to judge on appearances colors his opinion of Biddy: He dwells on her unkempt appearance rather than on those traits that they share.

4 STYLE: PERSONIFICATION

Pip refers to numbers as "those thieves," giving them unpleasant human characteristics to show how difficult he finds them.

GUIDED READING

LITERAL QUESTION

1a. What does Pip write in his letter about being apprenticed to Joe? ("wot larx")

INFERENTIAL QUESTION

1b. Why might he think this? (He will spend more time with Joe, whom he loves.)

AT A GLANCE

- Joe tries to read Pip's letter.
- Pip realizes Joe can only identify only letters from his own name.
- Joe tells Pip of his childhood.

1 POINT OF VIEW

In Pip's eyes Joe loses stature because he cannot read: Pip feels superior to him and acknowledges that he treats Joe "with modest patronage."

2 BACKGROUND

Dickens' reference to steam concerns the use of steam engines on the railroad, which came into use in the late 1820s. By the 1860s trains were becoming a popular mode of travel.

3 PARAPHRASING

Joe is explaining that his father became violent when drunk and abused both his mother and himself, while at the same time neglecting his trade as blacksmith.

4 STYLE: DIALOGUE

Joe's characterization of his father as "good in his hart" is transparent: The reader can see that his father was an abusive drunk.

5 CHARACTERIZATION

Joe insists his father was a good man and believes that he drank only because life was unjust; this reveals Joe's innocence and the goodness of his own heart.

hand, and Joe received it as a miracle of erudition.

"I say, Pip, old chap!" cried Joe, opening his blue eyes wide, "what a scholar you are! Ain't you?"

"I should like to be," said I, glancing at the slate as he held it—with a misgiving that the writing was rather hilly.

"Why, here's a J," said Joe, "and a O equal to anythink! Here's a J and a O, Pip, and a J-O, Joe."

I had never heard Joe read aloud to any greater extent than this monosyllable, and I had observed at church last Sunday, when I accidentally held our Prayer-book upside down, that it seemed to suit his convenience quite as well as if it had been all right. Wishing to embrace the present occasion of finding out whether, in teaching Joe, I should have to begin quite at the beginning, I said, "Ah! But read the rest, Joe."

"The rest, eh, Pip?" said Joe, looking at it with a slowly searching eye, "One, two, three. Why, here's three Js, and three Os and three J-O, Joes, in it, Pip!"

I leaned over Joe, and, with the aid of my forefinger, read him the whole letter.

"Astonishing!" said Joe, when I had finished.
1 "You ARE a scholar."

"How do you spell Gargery, Joe?" I asked him, with a modest patronage.[7]

"I don't spell it at all," said Joe.

"But supposing you did?"

"It *can't* be supposed," said Joe. "Tho' I'm oncommon fond of reading, too."

"Are you, Joe?"

"Oncommon. Give me," said Joe, "a good book, or a good newspaper, and sit me down afore a good fire, and I ask no better. Lord!" he continued, after rubbing his knees a little "when you *do* come to a J and a O, and says you, 'Here,
2 at last, is a J-O, Joe,' how interesting reading is!"

I derived from this last that Joe's education, like steam, was yet in its infancy.

"Didn't you ever go to school, Joe, when you were as little as me?"

"No, Pip."

"Why didn't you ever go to school, Joe, when you were as little as me?"

"Well, Pip," said Joe, taking up the poker, and settling himself to his usual occupation when he was thoughtful, of slowly raking the fire between the lower bars, "I'll tell you. My father, Pip, he were given to drink, and when he were overtook with drink, he hammered away
3 at my mother most onmerciful. It were a'most the only hammering he did, indeed, 'xcepting at myself. And he hammered at me with a wigor only to be equaled by the wigor with which he didn't hammer at his anwil.[8] You're a-listening and understanding, Pip?"

"Yes, Joe."

"'Consequence, my mother and me we ran away from my father several times; and then my mother she'd go out to work, and she'd say, 'Joe,' she'd say, 'now, please God, you shall have some schooling, child,' and she'd put me to
4 school. But my father were that good in his hart that he couldn't a-bear to be without us. So, he'd come with a most tremenjous crowd and make such a row at the doors of the houses where we was that they used to be obligated to have no more to do with us and to give us up to him. And then he took us home and hammered us. Which, you see, Pip," said Joe, pausing in his meditative raking of the fire, and looking at me, "were a drawback on my learning."

"Certainly, poor Joe!"

5 "Though mind you, Pip," said Joe, with a judicial touch or two of the poker on the top bar, "rendering unto all their doo, and maintaining equal justice betwixt man and man, my father were that good in his hart, don't you see?"

I didn't see, but I didn't say so.

"Well!" Joe pursued, "somebody must keep

7. **patronage** [pā′trə nij]: encouragement from a superior.

8. **anwil:** anvil, the iron block on which a blacksmith hammers metal.

GUIDED READING

LITERAL QUESTIONS

1a. What does Pip ask Joe to do with his letter? (He wants Joe to read it.)

2a. In what words does Joe describe his father? (He says that he was given to drink but was good in his heart.)

INFERENTIAL QUESTIONS

1b. Why does Pip want Joe to do this? (He is trying to find out if Joe can read.)

2b. Does Joe really believe what he says? (Possible answers: He is so kindhearted himself that he imagines everyone else is, too; Joe cannot easily admit what he knows is the truth—his father was flawed and cruel.)

the pot a-biling, Pip, or the pot won't bile, don't you know?"

I saw that, and said so.

"'Consequence, my father didn't make objections to my going to work; so I went to work at my present calling, which were his, too, if he would have followed it, and I worked tolerable hard, I assure *you*, Pip. In time I were able to keep him, and I kep him till he went off in a purple 'leptic fit."[9]

Joe's blue eyes turned a little watery.

"It were but lonesome then," said Joe, "living here alone, and I got acquainted with your sister. Now, Pip"—Joe looked firmly at me, as if he knew I was not going to agree with him—"your sister is a fine figure of a woman."

I could not help looking at the fire, in an obvious state of doubt.

"Whatever family opinions, or whatever the world's opinions, on that subject may be, Pip, your sister is"—Joe tapped the top bar with the poker after every word following—"a—fine—figure—of—a—woman!"

I could think of nothing better to say than, "I am glad you think so, Joe."

"So am I," returned Joe, catching me up. "*I* am glad I think so, Pip. And this I want to say very serous to you, old chap—I see so much in my poor mother, of a woman drudging and slaving that I'm dead afeerd of going wrong in the way of not doing what's right by a woman, and I'd fur rather of the two go wrong the t'other way, and be a little ill-conwenienced myself. I wish it was only me that got put out, Pip. I wish there warn't no Tickler for you, old chap. I wish I could take it all on myself; but this is the up-and-down-and-straight on it, Pip, and I hope you'll overlook shortcomings."

When I sat looking at Joe and thinking about him, I had a new sensation of feeling conscious that I was looking up to Joe in my heart.

---

9. **purple 'leptic fit:** Joe mispronounces "apoplectic [ap'ə plek'tik] fit," a stroke.

Mrs. Joe made occasional trips with Uncle Pumblechook on market-days, to assist him in buying such household stuffs and goods as required a woman's judgment; Uncle Pumblechook being a bachelor and reposing no confidences in his domestic servant. This was market-day, and Mrs. Joe was out on one of these expeditions.

3 "Here comes the mare," said Joe, "ringing like a peal of bells!"

The sound of her iron shoes upon the hard road was quite musical, as she came along at a much brisker trot than usual. Mrs. Joe was soon landed, and Uncle Pumblechook was soon down too, covering the mare with a cloth, and we were soon all in the kitchen.

"Now," said Mrs. Joe, unwrapping herself with haste and excitement, and throwing her bonnet back on her shoulders where it hung by the strings, "if this boy ain't grateful this night, he never will be!"

I looked as grateful as any boy possibly could who was wholly uninformed why he ought to assume that expression.

"Miss Havisham, up town, wants this boy to go and play there. And of course he's going. And he had better play there," said my sister, shaking her head at me, "or I'll work him."

4 I had heard of Miss Havisham—everybody for miles round, had heard of Miss Havisham—as an immensely rich and grim lady who lived in a large and dismal house barricaded against robbers.

"Well, to be sure!" said Joe, astounded. "I wonder how she comes to know Pip!"

"Noodle!" cried my sister. "Who said she knew him?"

"—Which some individual," Joe again politely hinted, "mentioned that she wanted him to go and play there."

"And couldn't she ask Uncle Pumblechook if he knew of a boy to go and play there? Isn't it just barely possible that Uncle Pumblechook may be a tenant of hers, and that he may some-

AT A GLANCE

- Joe explains why he went to work at a young age and that he admires Mrs. Joe.
- Mrs. Joe returns home with Uncle Pumblechook.
- Pip learns that Miss Havisham wants him to come and play at her house.

1 CHARACTERIZATION

Joe has an enormous sense of duty and responsibility: He worked to care for his abusive father, and he regards Pip's shrewish sister as a good woman.

2 THEME: APPEARANCE VS. REALITY

For the first time Pip has a sense of what Joe really is: He looks "up to Joe" in his heart and realizes that Joe is a good man.

3 READING SKILLS: INFERENCE

Joe's comparison of the sound of the mare's hooves to ringing bells reveals that—though he is uneducated—he is imaginative.

4 POINT OF VIEW

Pip's opinion of Miss Havisham is already formed: He sees her as "an immensely rich and grim lady" who is to be feared and treated with awe.

GUIDED READING

LITERAL QUESTIONS

1a. When speaking of his own childhood and family situation, what saying does Joe impart to Pip? (He says that someone must keep the pot boiling or the pot won't boil.)

2a. For what does Mrs. Joe say Pip should be grateful? (for Miss Havisham's request that he go and play at her house)

INFERENTIAL QUESTIONS

1b. What does Joe mean? (that someone had to work, or there would have been no food)

2b. Why does Mrs. Joe think Pip should be grateful for the invitation? (because Miss Havisham is rich and has shown an interest in Pip)

AT A GLANCE

- Pip is washed, combed, and sent home with Uncle Pumblechook.
- He spends the night at Mr. Pumblechook's; in the morning they go to Miss Havisham's.
- Pip is taken inside by a proud and very pretty young lady.

1 STYLE: SIMILE

Pip's comparison of his sister to an eagle pouncing suggests that he sees her as a scavenger who is willing to sacrifice him.

2 CHARACTERIZATION

Pip has never been away from Joe, and at first he is so upset that he cannot see through his tears; he is a rather sheltered and vulnerable boy.

3 VOCABULARY: CONNOTATION

Dickens describes Pumblechook's home as "peppercorny" and "farinaceous"—an unkempt house dusted with flour and sharply scented with pepper.

4 FORESHADOWING

Miss Havisham's home is described as having windows barred with iron—an image that foreshadows a link between the convict (iron shackles), Pip (the forge), and Miss Havisham.

times—we won't say quarterly or half-yearly, for that would be requiring too much of you—but sometimes—go there to pay his rent? And couldn't she then ask Uncle Pumblechook if he knew of a boy to go and play there? And couldn't Uncle Pumblechook, being always considerate and thoughtful for us—though you may not think it, Joseph," in a tone of the deepest reproach, as if he were the most callous of nephews, "then mention this boy, standing prancing here."—which I solemnly declare I was not doing.

"Good," cried Uncle Pumblechook. "Well put! Prettily pointed! Good indeed! Now, Joseph, you know the case."

"Uncle Pumblechook, being sensible that for anything we can tell, this boy's fortune may be made by his going to Miss Havisham's, has offered to take him into town to-night in his own chaise-cart, and to keep him to-night, and to take him with his own hands to Miss Havisham's to-morrow morning."

1 With that, she pounced on me, like an eagle on a lamb, and my face was squeezed into wooden bowls in sinks, and my head was put under taps of water-butts, and I was soaped, and kneaded, and toweled, and thumped, and harrowed, and rasped,[10] until I really was quite beside myself.

I was then delivered over to Mr. Pumblechook, who formally received me as if he were the sheriff, and who let off upon me the speech that I knew he had been dying to make all along: "Boy, be for ever grateful to all friends, but especially unto them which brought you up by hand!"

"Good-bye, Joe!"

"God bless you, Pip, old chap!"

2 I had never parted from him before, and what with my feelings and what with soap-suds, I could at first see no stars from the chaise-cart. But they twinkled out one by one, without throwing any light on the questions why on earth I was going to play at Miss Havisham's, and what on earth I was expected to play at.

Chapter Seven

At Miss Havisham's Satis House: We meet Miss Havisham and Estella.

3 Mr. Pumblechook's premises in the High Street of the market town were of a peppercorny and farinaceous character, as the premises of a corn-chandler and seedsman should be.

I was very glad when ten o'clock came and we started for Miss Havisham's; though I was not at all at my ease regarding the manner in which I should acquit[1] myself under that lady's roof.
4 Within a quarter of an hour we came to Miss Havisham's house, which was of old brick, and dismal, and had a great many iron bars to it. Some of the windows had been walled up. There was a court-yard in front, and that was barred; so, we had to wait, after ringing the bell. While we waited at the gate, I peeped in and saw that at the side of the house there was a large brewery. No brewing was going on in it, and none seemed to have gone on for a long time.

A window was raised, and a clear voice demanded "What name?" To which my conductor replied, "Pumblechook." The voice returned, "Quite right," and the window was shut again, and a young lady came across the court-yard, with keys in her hand.

"This," said Mr. Pumblechook, "is Pip."

"This is Pip, is it?" returned the young lady, who was very pretty and seemed very proud; "come in, Pip."

Mr. Pumblechook was coming in also, when she stopped him with the gate.

"Did you wish to see Miss Havisham?"

"If Miss Havisham wished to see me," returned Mr. Pumblechook, discomfited.

---

10. **harrowed and rasped:** distressed and scraped.

1. **acquit** [ə kwit′]: behave.

GUIDED READING

LITERAL QUESTIONS

1a. What does Mrs. Joe say might happen to Pip at Miss Havisham's? (She says his fortune might be made.)

2a. At Mr. Pumblechook's how does Pip feel when ten o'clock comes? (He is glad they are going to Miss Havisham's.)

INFERENTIAL QUESTIONS

1b. Why does Mrs. Joe think this? (The rich woman might bestow some wealth on Pip.)

2b. Why do you think Pip feels this way? (He is tired of being at Pumblechook's.)

"Ah!" said the girl; "but you see, she don't."

She said it so finally, and in such an undiscussible way, that Mr. Pumblechook, though in a condition of ruffled dignity, could not protest. But he eyed me severely—as if *I* had done anything to him!—and departed with the words reproachfully delivered: "Boy! Let your behavior here be a credit unto them which brought you up by hand!"

My young conductress locked the gate, and we went across the court-yard. It was paved and clean, but grass was growing in every crevice. The brewery buildings had a little lane of communication with it; and the wooden gates of that lane stood open, and all the brewery beyond stood open, away to the high enclosing wall; and all was empty and disused.

"What is the name of this house, miss?"

"It's name was Satis, which is Greek, or Latin, or Hebrew—or all one to me—for enough. But don't loiter, boy."

Though she called me "boy" so often, and with a carelessness that was far from complimentary, she was of about my own age. She seemed much older than I, of course, being a girl, and beautiful and self-possessed; and she was as scornful of me as if she had been one-and-twenty, and a queen.

We went into the house by a side door—the great front entrance had two chains across it outside—and the first thing I noticed was that the passages were all dark, and that she had left a candle burning there. She took it up, and we went through more passages and up a staircase, and still it was all dark, and only the candle lighted us.

At last we came to the door of a room, and she said, "Go in."

I answered, more in shyness than politeness, "After you, miss."

To this, she returned: "Don't be ridiculous, boy; I am not going in." And scornfully walked away, and—what was worse—took the candle with her.

3 This was very uncomfortable, and I was half-afraid. However, the only thing to be done being to knock at the door, I knocked, and was told from within to enter. I entered, therefore, and found myself in a pretty large room, well lighted with wax candles. No glimpse of daylight was to be seen in it. It was a dressing-room, as I supposed from the furniture, though much of it was of forms and uses then quite unknown to me. But prominent in it was a draped table with a gilded looking-glass, and that I made out at first sight to be a fine lady's dressing-table.

Whether I should have made out this object so soon if there had been no fine lady sitting at it, I cannot say. In an arm-chair, with an elbow resting on the table and her head leaning on that hand, sat the strangest lady I have ever seen, or shall ever see.

She was dressed in rich materials—satins, and lace, and silks—all of white. Her shoes were white. And she had a long white veil dependent from her hair, and she had bridal flowers in her hair, but her hair was white. Some bright jewels sparkled on her neck and on her hands, and some other jewels lay sparkling on the table. Dresses less splendid than the dress she wore, and half-packed trunks, were scattered about. She had not quite finished dressing, for she had but one shoe on—the other was on the table near her hand—her veil was but half arranged, her watch and chain were not put on, and some lace for her bosom lay with those trinkets, and with her handkerchief, and gloves, and some flowers, and a prayer-book, all confusedly heaped about the looking-glass.

4 I saw that everything within my view which ought to be white had lost its luster and was faded and yellow. I saw that the bride within the dress had withered like the dress.

"Who is it?" said the lady at the table.

"Pip, ma'am."

"Pip?"

"Pip, ma'am."

"Pip?"

AT A GLANCE

- Pip enters the house and is treated with disdain by the young lady.
- He goes into an old woman's room.
- He describes the woman and the candle-lighted room.

1 ATMOSPHERE

The details of the setting—grass growing between the paving stones, all appearing "empty and disused"—indicate a neglected, ruined house and an atmosphere of decay and despair.

2 CHARACTERIZATION

The details that Pip notices about the disdainful girl hint at their future relationship: She scornfully calls him "boy," and he is attracted to her beauty and self-possession.

3 CHARACTERIZATION

Though Pip is "half-afraid" to enter the room, he resolutely musters his courage and does "the only thing to be done."

4 THEME: APPEARANCE VS. REALITY

The woman appears to be a bride festooned for her wedding, but Pip notes that her attire has "lost its luster" and that the woman is "withered like the dress."

GUIDED READING

LITERAL QUESTIONS

1a. As Mr. Pumblechook departs, how does he look at Pip? (He stares at him severely.)

2a. What is the old woman wearing when Pip first sees her? (a faded wedding dress, a half-arranged veil, jewels, and one shoe)

INFERENTIAL QUESTIONS

1b. What is Mr. Pumblechook actually feeling? (He is angry and embarrassed.)

2b. What effect do these details have on her overall appearance? (She seems disheveled and distracted.)

AT A GLANCE

- Pip introduces himself to Miss Havisham.
- She commands him to play; Pip cannot.
- At Miss Havisham's insistence Pip calls Estella; she enters the room.

1 **POINT OF VIEW**

Pip's honesty as narrator is revealed when he admits that he told an "enormous lie" when he said he was not afraid of Miss Havisham.

2 **CHARACTERIZATION**

Miss Havisham's peculiarities begin to unfold as she proudly tells Pip that her heart is broken.

3 **STYLE: DIALOGUE**

Miss Havisham's bluntness elicits a string of nervous reactions from Pip: Her single-minded character and his naive, emotional one are emphasized by their spoken words.

"Mr. Pumblechook's boy, ma'am. Come—to play."

"Come nearer; let me look at you. Come close."

It was when I stood before her, avoiding her eyes, that I took note of the surrounding objects in detail, and saw that her watch had stopped at twenty minutes to nine, and that a clock in the room had stopped at twenty minutes to nine.

"Look at me," said Miss Havisham. "You are not afraid of a woman who has never seen the sun since you were born?"

1 I regret to state that I was not afraid of telling the enormous lie comprehended in the answer "No."

"Do you know what I touch here?" she said, laying her hands, one upon the other, on her left side.

"Yes, ma'am."

"What do I touch?"

2 "Your heart."

"Broken!"

She uttered the word with an eager look, and with strong emphasis, and with a weird smile that had a kind of boast in it. Afterwards, she kept her hands there for a little while, and slowly took them away as if they were heavy.

"I am tired," said Miss Havisham. "I want diversion, and I have done with men and women. Play."

I think it will be conceded by my most disputatious[2] reader that she could hardly have directed an unfortunate boy to do anything in the wide world more difficult to be done under the circumstances.

"I sometimes have sick fancies," she went on, "and I have a sick fancy that I want to see some play. There, there!" with an impatient movement of the fingers of her right hand; "play, play, play!"

For a moment, with the fear of my sister's working me before my eyes, I had a desperate idea of starting round the room in the assumed character of Mr. Pumblechook's chaise-cart. But I felt myself so unequal to the performance that I gave it up, and stood looking at Miss Havisham in what I suppose she took for a dogged[3] manner, inasmuch as she said, when we had taken a good look at each other:

3 "Are you sullen and obstinate?"

"No, ma'am, I am very sorry for you, and very sorry I can't play just now. If you complain of me I shall get into trouble with my sister, so I would do it if I could; but it's so new here, and so strange, and so fine—and melancholy—" I stopped, fearing I might say too much, or had already said it, and we took another look at each other.

Before she spoke again, she turned her eyes from me, and looked at the dress she wore, and at the dressing-table, and finally at herself in the looking-glass.

"So new to him," she muttered, "so old to me; so strange to him, so familiar to me; so melancholy to both of us! Call Estella."

As she was still looking at the reflection of herself, I thought she was still talking to herself, and kept quiet.

"Call Estella," she repeated, flashing a look at me. "You can do that. Call Estella. At the door."

To stand in the dark in a mysterious passage of an unknown house, bawling Estella to a scornful young lady neither visible nor responsive, and feeling it a dreadful liberty so to roar out her name, was almost as bad as playing to order. But she answered at last, and her light came along the dark passage like a star.

Miss Havisham beckoned her to come close, and took up a jewel from the table, and tried its effect upon her fair young bosom and against her pretty brown hair. "Your own, one day, my dear, and you will use it well. Let me see you play cards with this boy."

---

2. **disputatious** [dis′pyoo tā′shəs]: argumentative.

3. **dogged** [dô′gid]: stubborn.

GUIDED READING

LITERAL QUESTIONS

1a. What does Miss Havisham want Pip to do? (to play)

2a. In what words does Pip describe to Miss Havisham his feelings about the surroundings? (He says they are new, strange, fine, and melancholy.)

INFERENTIAL QUESTIONS

1b. Why is he unable to play? (He is scared, nervous, and self-conscious.)

2b. Why isn't Miss Havisham upset at this description? (She, too, finds the situation melancholy.)

"With this boy! Why, he is a common laboring-boy!"

1 I thought I overheard Miss Havisham answer—only it seemed so unlikely, "Well? You can break his heart."

"What do you play, boy?" asked Estella of myself, with the greatest disdain.

"Nothing but Beggar my Neighbor, miss."

"Beggar him," said Miss Havisham to Estella. So we sat down to cards.

It was then I began to understand that everything in the room had stopped, like the watch and the clock, a long time ago. I noticed that Miss Havisham put down the jewel exactly on the spot from which she had taken it up. As Estella dealt the cards, I glanced at the dressing-table again, and saw that the shoe upon it, once white, now yellow, had never been worn. I glanced down at the foot from which the shoe was absent, and saw that the silk stocking on it, once white, now yellow, had been trodden ragged. Miss Havisham sat, corpse-like, as we played at cards.

"He calls the knaves, jacks, this boy!" said Estella with disdain, before our first game was out. "And what coarse hands he has! And what thick boots!"

2 I had never thought of being ashamed of my hands before; but I began to consider them a very indifferent pair. Her contempt for me was so strong that it became infectious, and I caught it.

She won the game, and I dealt. I misdealt, as was only natural, when I knew she was lying in wait for me to do wrong; and she denounced me for a stupid, clumsy laboring-boy.

"You say nothing of her," remarked Miss Havisham to me, as she looked on. "She says

AT A GLANCE

- Estella and Pip play cards.
- Estella insults Pip and wins the card game.

1 FORESHADOWING

Miss Havisham's suggestion to Estella, "You can break his heart," is the first hint of a major plot development.

2 CHARACTERIZATION

Though he has felt disdainful of Pumblechook's pride, Pip reacts differently to Estella's: He becomes contemptuous of himself.

GUIDED READING

LITERAL QUESTION

1a. What is Pip ashamed of? (his hands)

INFERENTIAL QUESTION

1b. How might Pip's hands differ from Estella's? (His are probably rough and indelicate, as he spends time at the forge; hers are probably delicate and pretty.)

AT A GLANCE

- Pip tells Miss Havisham his opinion of Estella.
- Estella gives Pip food and leaves him in the yard.
- Pip cries with rage at Estella's insults.

1 DIALOGUE

Pip reveals his mixed feelings for Estella when he tells Miss Havisham that Estella is "proud," "pretty," and "insulting"; he does not seem to blame Estella for her scorn.

2 THEME: FREEDOM VS. IMPRISONMENT

When Pip leaves Miss Havisham's house, he is surprised that it is still daylight; the dark, prisonlike atmosphere has made him feel he has been incarcerated for much longer.

3 CHARACTERIZATION

Estella's pride is beginning to rub off on Pip: He admits to being ashamed of Joe and himself and to wishing that he had been "rather more genteely brought up."

4 CONFLICT

Pip finds himself in a battle of wills with Estella: She tries to hurt him as he tries to disguise his feelings of shame and hurt.

many hard things of you, yet you say nothing of her. What do you think of her?"

"I don't like to say," I stammered.

"Tell me in my ear," said Miss Havisham, bending down.

1 "I think she is very proud," I replied, in a whisper.

"Anything else?"

"I think she is very pretty."

"Anything else?"

"I think she is very insulting." (She was looking at me then with a look of supreme aversion.)

"Anything else?"

"I think I should like to go home."

"And never see her again, though she is so pretty?"

"I am not sure that I shouldn't like to see her again, but I should like to go home now."

"You shall go soon," said Miss Havisham aloud. "Play the game out."

I played the game to an end with Estella, and she beggared me. She threw the cards down on the table when she had won them all, as if she despised them for having been won of me.

"When shall I have you here again?" said Miss Havisham. "Let me think."

I was beginning to remind her that to-day was Wednesday when she checked me with her former impatient movement of the fingers of her right hand.

"There, there! I know nothing of days of the week; I know nothing of weeks of the year. Come again after six days, You hear?"

"Yes, ma'am."

"Estella, take him down. Let him have something to eat, and let him roam and look about him while he eats. Go, Pip."

I followed the candle down, as I had fol-
2 lowed the candle up. Until she opened the side entrance, I had fancied, without thinking about it, that it must necessarily be night-time. The rush of the daylight quite confounded me, and made me feel as if I had been in the candlelight of the strange room many hours.

"You are to wait here, you boy," said Estella, and disappeared and closed the door.

I took the opportunity of being alone in the court-yard to look at my coarse hands and my common boots. They had never troubled me be-
3 fore, but they troubled me now. I determined to ask Joe why he had ever taught me to call those picture-cards jacks which ought to be called knaves. I wished Joe had been rather more genteelly brought up, and then I should have been so, too.

She came back with some bread and meat and a little mug of beer. She put the mug down on the stones of the yard, and gave me the bread and meat without looking at me, as insolently as if I were a dog in disgrace. I was so humiliated, hurt, spurned, offended, angry, sorry—I cannot hit upon the right name for the smart—that tears
4 started to my eyes. The moment they sprang there, the girl looked at me with a quick delight in having been the cause of them. This gave me power to keep them back and to look at her. She—with a sense, I thought, of having made too sure that I was wounded—left me.

But, when she was gone, I looked about me for a place to hide my face in, and got behind one of the gates in the brewery-lane, and leaned my sleeve against the wall there, and leaned my forehead on it and cried. As I cried, I kicked the wall, and took a hard twist at my hair; so bitter were my feelings, and so sharp was the smart without a name.

I got rid of my injured feelings for the time by kicking them into the brewery-wall. Then I smoothed my face with my sleeve and came from behind the gate. The bread and meat were acceptable and I was soon in spirits to look about me.

Nothing less than the frosty light of the cheerful sky, the sight of people passing beyond the bars of the court-yard gate, and the reviving influence of the rest of the bread and meat could have brought me round. Even with those aids, I might not have come to myself as soon as I did

GUIDED READING

LITERAL QUESTION

1a. What does Miss Havisham say when Pip tries to tell her what day it is? (that she knows nothing of days or weeks)

INFERENTIAL QUESTION

1b. What does this reveal about her relation to time? (For Miss Havisham time has stopped.)

but that I saw Estella approaching with the keys, to let me out.

She opened the gate and stood holding it. I was passing out without looking at her, when she touched me with a taunting hand.

"Why don't you cry?"

"Because I don't want to."

"You do," said she. "You have been crying till you are half-blind, and you are near crying again now."

She laughed, pushed me out, and locked the gate upon me. I went straight to Mr. Pumblechook's, and was immensely relieved to find him not at home. So, leaving word with the shopman on what day I was wanted at Miss Havisham's again, I set off on the four-mile walk to our forge, pondering, as I went along, on all I had seen, and deeply revolving that I was a common laboring-boy; that my hands were coarse; that my boots were thick; that I was much more ignorant than I had considered myself last night; and generally that I was in a low-lived bad way.

Chapter Eight

At home: Pip reports on his visit with Miss Havisham.

When I reached home, my sister was very curious to know all about Miss Havisham's, and asked a number of questions. And I soon found myself getting heavily bumped from behind in the nape of the neck and the small of the back, and having my face shoved against the kitchen wall, because I did not answer those questions at sufficient length.

The worst of it was that that bullying old Pumblechook, preyed upon by a devouring curiosity to be informed of all I had seen and heard, came gaping over in his chaise-cart at tea-time to have the details divulged to him.

"Boy! What like is Miss Havisham?" Mr. Pumblechook began.

"Very tall and dark," I told him.

"Is she, Uncle?" asked my sister.

Mr. Pumblechook winked assent; from which I at once inferred that he had never seen Miss Havisham, for she was nothing of the kind.

"Good!" said Mr. Pumblechook conceitedly.

"Now, boy! What was she a-doing of, when you went in to-day?" asked Mr. Pumblechook.

"She was sitting," I answered, "in a black velvet coach."

Mr. Pumblechook and Mrs. Joe stared at one another—as they well might—and both
2 repeated, "In a black velvet coach?" "Yes," said I. "And Miss Estella—that's her niece, I think—handed her in cake and wine at the coach-window, on a gold plate. And we all had cake and wine on gold plates. And I got up behind the coach to eat mine, because she told me to."

"Was anybody else there?" asked Mr. Pumblechook.

"Four dogs," said I.

"Large or small?"

"Immense," said I. "And they fought for veal-cutlets out of a silver basket."

3 Mr. Pumblechook and Mrs. Joe stared at one another again, in utter amazement. I was perfectly frantic—a reckless witness under the torture—and would have told them anything.

"Where *was* this coach, in the name of gracious?" asked my sister.

"In Miss Havisham's room." They stared again. "But there weren't any horses to it." I added this saving clause, in the moment of rejecting four richly caparisoned coursers, which I had had wild thoughts of harnessing.

"Can this be possible, Uncle?" asked Mrs. Joe. "What can the boy mean?"

"I'll tell you, mum," said Mr. Pumblechook. "My opinion is, it's a sedan chair. She's flighty, you know—very flighty—quite flighty enough to pass her days in a sedan chair."

"Did you ever see her in it, Uncle?" asked Mrs. Joe.

"How could I," he returned, forced to the

AT A GLANCE

- Estella taunts Pip as he leaves Miss Havisham's.
- He returns home and is questioned by Mr. Pumblechook and Mrs. Joe.
- He makes up a fanciful story about his time at Miss Havisham's.

1 IRONY

Pip feels that he is seeing himself truly for the first time—as a "common laboring boy." He doesn't realize that this self-image is as false as the one that cast him as superior to Joe.

2 CHARACTERIZATION

Pip's imagination, which ranged so freely on the night of the convicts' capture, goes wild as he describes Miss Havisham.

3 RESPONSE JOURNAL

Have the students write in their journals an analysis of Pip's motivation to lie.

GUIDED READING

LITERAL QUESTION

1a. What does Pip think about himself as he walks home? (that he is common and ignorant)

INFERENTIAL QUESTION

1b. Why does he feel this way? (Estella's snobbery and Pip's feelings for her have made him ashamed of himself.)

AT A GLANCE

- Pip continues his lies about his day at Miss Havisham's.
- Mrs. Joe tells Joe the story.
- Pip admits to Joe he lied.

1 POINT OF VIEW

The narrator—the adult Pip—is able to look on his childish lies with both "amazement" and amusement.

2 THEME: FRIENDSHIP

Pip feels guilty for lying to Joe, the one friend he has; theirs is a friendship that Pip associates with honesty.

3 CHARACTERIZATION

Pip chooses to tell the truth to Joe: He does not want Joe to look foolish for believing him.

4 CHARACTERIZATION

Pip's experience at Miss Havisham's has confused him deeply. He knows only that he feels "miserable"; he doesn't know how to explain (even to himself) his strong reactions to the old woman and Estella.

admission, "when I never see her in my life? Never clapped eyes upon her!"

"Goodness, Uncle! And yet you have spoken to her?"

"Why, don't you know," said Mr. Pumblechook testily, "that when I have been there, I have been took up to the outside of her door, and the door has stood ajar, and she has spoken to me that way. Don't say you don't know *that*, mum. Howsever, the boy went there to play. What did you play at, boy?"

1 "We played with flags," I said. (I beg to observe that I think of myself with amazement when I recall the lies I told on this occasion.)

"Flags!" echoed my sister.

"Yes," said I. "Estella waved a blue flag, and I waved a red one, and Miss Havisham waved one sprinkled all over with little gold stars, out at the coach-window. And then we all waved our swords and hurrahed."

"Swords!" repeated my sister. "Where did you get swords from?"

"Out of a cupboard," said I. "And I saw pistols in it—and jam—and pills. And there was no daylight in the room, but it was all lighted up with candles."

"That's true, mum," said Mr. Pumblechook, with a grave nod. "That's the state of the case, for that much I've seen myself." And then they both stared at me, and I, with an obtrusive show of artlessness on my countenance, stared at them.

The subject still held them when Joe came in from his work to have a cup of tea—to whom my sister, more for the relief of her own mind than for the gratification of his, related my pretended experiences.

2 Now when I saw Joe open his blue eyes and roll them all round the kitchen in helpless amazement, I was overtaken by penitence.

After Mr. Pumblechook had driven off, and when my sister was washing up, I stole into the forge to Joe, and remained by him until he had done for the night. Then I said, "Before the fire goes out, Joe, I should like to tell you something."

"Should you, Pip?" said Joe, drawing his shoeing-stool near the forge. "Then tell us. What is it, Pip?"

3 "Joe," said I, taking hold of his rolled-up shirt-sleeve, and twisting it between my finger and thumb, "you remember all that about Miss Havisham's?"

"Remember?" said Joe. "I believe you! Wonderful!"

"It's a terrible thing, Joe; it ain't true."

"What are you telling of, Pip?" cried Joe, falling back in the greatest amazement. "You don't mean to say it's—"

"Yes, I do; it's lies, Joe."

"But not all of it? Why sure you don't mean to say, Pip, that there was no black welwet co—ch?" For, I stood shaking my head. "But at least there was dogs, Pip? Come, Pip," said Joe persuasively, "if there warn't no weal-cutlets, at least there was dogs?"

"No, Joe."

"A dog?" said Joe. "A puppy? Come!"

"No, Joe, there was nothing at all of the kind."

As I fixed my eyes hopelessly on Joe, Joe contemplated me in dismay. "Pip, old chap! This won't do, old fellow! I say! Where do you expect to go to?"

"It's terrible, Joe; ain't it?"

"Terrible?" cried Joe. "Awful! What possessed you?"

"I don't know what possessed me, Joe," I replied, letting his shirt-sleeve go, and sitting down in the ashes at his feet, hanging my head.

4 And then I told Joe that I felt very miserable, and that I hadn't been able to explain myself to Mrs. Joe and Pumblechook, who were so rude to me, and that there had been a beautiful young lady at Miss Havisham's who was dreadfully proud, and that she had said I was common, and that I knew I was common, and that I wished I was not common, and that the lies had come of it somehow, though I didn't know how.

GUIDED READING

LITERAL QUESTIONS

1a. What is Joe's response when Pip admits he lied? (He is aghast.)

2a. What reason does Pip give for lying? (He says he doesn't really know why he lied.)

INFERENTIAL QUESTIONS

1b. Why does Joe want to believe Pip's lies? (He is intrigued by the vision Pip has described; he does not want to believe that Pip is capable of lying.)

2b. Why do you think Pip lied? (He was confused, upset, and angry.)

"There's one thing you may be sure of, Pip," said Joe, after some rumination, "namely, that lies is lies. Howsever they come, they didn't ought to come. Don't you tell no more of 'em, Pip. *That* ain't the way to get out of being common, old chap. And as to being common, I don't make it out at all clear. You are oncommon in some things. You're oncommon small. Likewise you're a oncommon scholar."

"No, I am ignorant and backward, Joe."

"Why, see what a letter you wrote last night! Wrote in print even! I've seen letters—ah! and from gentlefolks!—that I'll swear weren't wrote in print," said Joe.

"I have learnt next to nothing, Joe. You think much of me. It's only that."

1 "Well, Pip," said Joe, "be it so, or be it son't, you must be a common scholar afore you can be a oncommon one."

"You are not angry with me, Joe?"

"No, old chap. That's all, old chap, and don't never do it no more."

STUDY QUESTIONS

Recalling

1. From the beginning of the novel, explain how the storyteller came to be called Pip.
2. According to Chapter 1, what does Pip know of his parents? With whom does he live?
3. What two items does the convict demand of Pip in Chapter 1? In Chapter 2 where does Pip get each of them?
4. In Chapter 5 why does Pip try to signal his convict when the convict is caught? What does the convict say about the items Pip took?
5. From Chapter 7 give three or four unusual details about Miss Havisham's appearance and three or four unusual details about her house.
6. Give three examples of Estella's rudeness to Pip. What three things does Pip say about Estella when Miss Havisham asks him what he thinks of her?
7. After returning from Miss Havisham's in Chapter 8, what opinion of himself does Pip share with Joe?

Interpreting

8. Describe Pip's relationship with his sister and his relationship with Joe.
9. In what ways is Pip's convict frightening? What details make him less frightening?
10. What do we learn about Pip's personality from his conversations with Miss Havisham and Estella in Chapter 7?
11. What has the novel shown so far about English education and transportation in Pip's day?

Extending

12. If you were Pip, would you have acted differently with the prisoner? With Estella? Explain how you would have acted, and why.

LITERARY FOCUS

Point of View

In novels just as in short stories, **point of view** is the relationship of the storyteller to the story. In a novel with **first-person point of view**, the story is told by one of the characters, referred to as "I." When an author uses a first-person storyteller, we see everything through that character's eyes. Therefore, we develop an interest in and a sympathy for that character. We are, however, told only what that character is experiencing or thinking. We cannot enter the minds of any other characters.

Thinking About Point of View

1. Give two examples of Pip's honesty and reliability as a storyteller.
2. Name two scenes in the novel so far in which we have more sympathy for Pip because he is telling his own story. Explain why.

AT A GLANCE

- Joe advises Pip to stop lying.
- Joe tells Pip that he is not angry.

1 THEME

Joe advises Pip to be responsible for himself: He warns Pip that he must make himself into someone of whom he can be proud.

REFLECTING ON CHAPTERS 1–8

The name of Miss Havisham's house is Satis, meaning "enough." Do any characters seem to feel they have enough? (Possible answer: Only Joe seems satisfied with his life; all others seem dissatisfied.)

STUDY QUESTIONS

1. His name is Phillip Pirrip; as a baby he pronounced it *Pip.*
2. nothing except what is written on tombstone; lives with sister and her husband
3. a file, food; steals food from sister's pantry, file from forge
4. Pip wants him to know he didn't bring soldiers; the convict says he stole items.
5. Havisham dressed in yellowed wedding gown, one shoe; house closed to daylight and lighted by candles, clocks stopped
6. She calls him "boy," says he is "common" and has "coarse hands" and "thick boots"; Pip says that she is proud, pretty, and insulting.
7. He is common, ignorant, backward.
8. *sister:* He is afraid, respectful; she beats him. *Joe:* They are friends.
9.
   - is desperate; has terrible voice, iron on leg; threatens to kill Pip
   - is pathetic, cold, hungry, sore; thanks Pip for food; diverts blame for theft
10. He is shy, polite, honest, compassionate, proud.
11. Education was not compulsory for lower classes; walking was most usual for lower classes.
12. Answers will vary, should establish Pip as calm and compassionate with convict, honest and polite with Estella.

LITERARY FOCUS

1. He accurately relates facts about his family to convict, is honest and direct with Miss Havisham, and includes details not flattering to himself.
2. He explains how fearful he is at stealing food, his humiliation at being common; his personal thoughts, feelings increase sympathy.

AT A GLANCE

- Pip asks Biddy to teach him all she knows.
- He goes to find Joe at a pub.
- Pip joins Joe and a stranger.

LITERARY OPTIONS

- conflict
- plot
- figurative language

THEMATIC OPTIONS

- time
- truth vs. hypocrisy
- manipulation

1 THEME

Pip decides that his aim in life is to be uncommon and asks Biddy to educate him; however, he takes advantage of her by not telling her of his true motives.

2 STYLE: SIMILE

The sinister, threatening aspect of the stranger is emphasized when Pip compares the stranger's squint to that of a man aiming a gun.

3 CHARACTERIZATION

Pip's description of the stranger as "odd" and "cunning" makes it clear that Pip sees the man as potentially threatening.

Chapter Nine

In the village: Biddy and a secret-looking stranger.

1 The idea occurred to me a morning or two later when I woke that the best step I could take towards making myself uncommon was to get out of Biddy everything she knew. I mentioned to Biddy when I went to Mr. Wopsle's great-aunt's at night that I had a particular reason for wishing to get on in life, and that I should feel very much obliged to her if she would impart all her learning to me. Biddy, who was the most obliging of girls, immediately said she would, and indeed began to carry out her promise within five minutes by imparting some information from her little catalogue of prices under the head of moist sugar, and lending me, to copy at home, a large old English D which she had imitated from the heading of some newspaper, and which I supposed, until she told me what it was, to be a design for a buckle.

Of course there was a public-house[1] in the village, and of course Joe liked sometimes to smoke his pipe there. I had received strict orders from my sister to call for him at the Three Jolly Bargemen that evening, on my way from school, and bring him home at my peril. To the Three Jolly Bargemen, therefore, I directed my steps.

I passed into the common-room[2] where there was a bright large kitchen fire, and where Joe was smoking his pipe in company with Mr. Wopsle and a stranger. Joe greeted me as usual with "Halloa, Pip, old chap!" and the moment he said that, the stranger turned his head and looked at me.

2 He was a secret-looking man whom I had never seen before. His head was all on one side, and one of his eyes was half-shut up, as if he were taking aim at something with an invisible gun. He had a pipe in his mouth, and he took it out, and, after slowly blowing all his smoke away and looking hard at me all the time, nodded. So, I nodded, and then he nodded again, and made room on the settle[3] beside him that I might sit down there.

But, as I was used to sit beside Joe whenever I entered that place of resort, I said "No, thank you, sir," and fell into the space Joe made for me. The strange man, after glancing at Joe, and seeing that his attention was otherwise engaged, nodded to me again when I had taken my seat, and then rubbed his leg—in a very odd way, as it struck me.

"You was saying," said the strange man, turning to Joe, "that you was a blacksmith."

"Yes. I said it, you know," said Joe.

The stranger, with a comfortable kind of grunt over his pipe, put his legs up on the settle that he had to himself. He wore a flapping broad-brimmed traveler's hat, and under it a handkerchief tied over his head in the manner of a cap, 3 so that he showed no hair. As he looked at the fire, I thought I saw a cunning expression, followed by a half-laugh, come into his face.

"I am not acquainted with this country, gentlemen, but it seems a solitary country towards the river."

"Most marshes is solitary," said Joe.

"No doubt, no doubt. Do you find any gypsies, now, or tramps, or vagrants of any sort, out there?"

"No," said Joe; "none but a runaway convict now and then. And we don't find *them*, easy. Eh, Mr. Wopsle?"

Mr. Wopsle, with a majestic remembrance of old discomfiture, assented, but not warmly.

"Seems you have been out after such?" asked the stranger.

"Once," returned Joe. "Not that we wanted to take them, you understand; we went out as lookers on; me and Mr. Wopsle, and Pip. Didn't us, Pip?"

1. **public-house:** tavern, pub.
2. **common-room:** public room.
3. **settle:** bench.

GUIDED READING

LITERAL QUESTIONS

1a. What reason does Pip give Biddy for wanting to learn? (He says only that he has a "particular reason" for wanting to get on in life.)

2a. What does the stranger ask about the marsh? (He wants to know if there are vagrants in the marsh.)

INFERENTIAL QUESTIONS

1b. What is Pip's real reason? (He wants to become Estella's equal.)

2b. Why do you think he asks this? (He seems to have some connection with the convicts in the marshes.)

"Yes, Joe."

The stranger looked at me again—still cocking his eye, as if he were expressly taking aim at me with his invisible gun—and said, "He's a likely young parcel of bones that. What is it you call him?"

"Pip," said Joe.

"Christened Pip?"

"No, not christened Pip."

"Surname Pip?"

"No," said Joe; "it's a kind of a family name what he gave himself when an infant, and is called by."

"Son of yours?"

"Well," said Joe meditatively—not, of course, that it could be in anywise necessary to consider about it, but because it was the way at the Jolly Bargemen to seem to consider deeply about everything that was discussed over pipes—"well, no. No, he ain't."

"Nevvy?"[4] said the strange man.

"Well," said Joe, with the same appearance of profound cogitation, "he is not—no, not to deceive you, he is *not*—my nevvy."

"What the blue blazes is he?" asked the stranger. Which appeared to me to be an inquiry of unnecessary strength.

Mr. Wopsle struck in upon that—as one who knew all about relationships, having professional occasion to bear in mind what female relations a man might not marry—and expounded the ties between me and Joe. Having his hand in, Mr. Wopsle finished off with a most terrifically snarling passage from ***Richard the Third***,[5] and seemed to think he had done quite enough to account for it when he added, "as the poet says."

All this while, the strange man looked at nobody but me, and looked at me as if he were determined to have a shot at me at last, and bring me down. But he said nothing until the glasses of rum-and-water were brought: and then he made his shot, and a most extraordinary shot it was.

3 It was not a remark, but a proceeding in dumb show, and was pointedly addressed to me. He stirred his rum-and-water pointedly at me, and he tasted his rum-and-water pointedly at me. And he stirred it and he tasted it: not with a spoon that was brought to him, but ***with a file.***

He did this so that nobody but I saw the file; and when he had done it, he wiped the file and
4 put it in a breast-pocket. I knew it to be Joe's file, and I knew that he knew my convict, the moment I saw the instrument. I sat gazing at him, spell-bound.

"Stop half a moment, Mr. Gargery," said the strange man. "I think I've got a bright new shilling somewhere in my pocket, and if I have, the boy shall have it."

He looked it out from a handful of small change, folded it in some crumpled paper, and gave it to me. "Yours!" said he. "Mind! Your own."

I thanked him, staring at him far beyond the bounds of good manners, and holding tight to Joe. He gave Joe good night, and he gave Mr. Wopsle good night (who went out with us), and he gave me only a look with his aiming eye.

My sister was not in a very bad temper when we presented ourselves in the kitchen, and Joe was encouraged to tell her about the bright shilling. "A bad un, I'll be bound," said Mrs. Joe triumphantly, "or he wouldn't have given it to the boy. Let's look at it."

I took it out of the paper, and it proved to be a good one. "But what's this?" said Mrs. Joe, throwing down the shilling and catching up the paper. "Two one-pound[6] notes?"

Nothing less than two fat sweltering one-pound notes that seemed to have been on terms of the warmest intimacy with all the cattle markets in the county. Joe caught up his hat again, and ran with them to the Jolly Bargemen

4. **Nevvy:** The stranger mispronounces ***nephew***.
5. ***Richard the Third:*** play by William Shakespeare.
6. **one-pound:** basic unit of British currency, each worth about five American dollars at the time of the novel.

AT A GLANCE

- The stranger asks questions about Pip.
- He stirs his drink with the file Pip gave to his convict.
- He gives Pip a shilling wrapped in two one-pound notes; Joe takes the notes back to the pub.

1 STYLE: DIALOGUE

Dickens contrasts Joe's slow deliberation with the stranger's peculiar, prying questions: The conversation is both funny and ominous.

2 BACKGROUND

Mr. Wopsle is a clergyman; through his acquaintance with church law he would know "what female relations a man might not marry."

3 STYLE: REPETITION

Dickens uses the phrase *pointedly at me* several times, heightening suspense by stressing the stranger's intense focus on Pip.

4 PLOT: RISING ACTION

The discovery that the stranger possesses the file advances the plot by reinforcing the link between Pip and the convict.

GUIDED READING

LITERAL QUESTIONS

1a. What does the stranger ask about Pip? (his name and his relation to Joe)

2a. What does the stranger give Pip? (a shilling wrapped in two one-pound notes)

INFERENTIAL QUESTIONS

1b. Do you think the stranger knows the answers? (Yes; he seems to know all about Pip, including his relationship with the convict.)

2b. Do you think he meant to give the notes? (Yes; he wanted Pip to have the money; he acted deliberately, and it is unlikely the notes would be a mistake.)

AT A GLANCE

- Joe tries to return the money, but the stranger has disappeared.
- Pip returns to Miss Havisham's.
- He meets relatives of Miss Havisham's: Camilla, Cousin Raymond, Sarah Pocket, and another lady.

1 THEME

Pip's fear and guilty conscience make the pound notes into a kind of punishment: Their presence is a constant reminder of his deception and theft.

2 SETTING

The description of the room—"gloomy," with a "low ceiling"—presents an oppressive atmosphere that sets the stage for the introduction of several unpleasant characters.

3 THEME

Camilla criticizes Tom for not trimming his children's mourning clothes, making it clear that she feels the clothing is more important than the fact that the children have lost their mother.

to restore them to their owner. While he was gone I sat down on my usual stool and looked vacantly at my sister, feeling pretty sure that the man would not be there.

Presently, Joe came back, saying that the man was gone, but that he, Joe, had left word at the Three Jolly Bargemen concerning the notes. Then my sister sealed them up in a piece of paper, and put them under some dried rose-leaves in an ornamental tea-pot on the top of a
1 press in the state parlor.[7] There they remained a nightmare to me many and many a night and day.

Chapter Ten

At Satis House: We meet the poor relations and a pale young gentleman.

At the appointed time I returned to Miss Havisham's, and my hesitating ring at the gate brought out Estella. She locked it after admitting me, as she had done before, and again preceded me into the dark passage where her candle stood. She took no notice of me until she had the candle in her hand, when she looked over her shoulder, superciliously[1] saying, "You are to come this way to-day," and took me to quite another part of the house.

2 We went in at the door, which stood open, and into a gloomy room with a low ceiling, on the ground floor at the back. There was some company in the room, and Estella said to me as she joined it, "You are to go and stand there, boy, till you are wanted." "There" being the window, I crossed to it, and stood "there" in a very uncomfortable state of mind, looking out.

There were three ladies in the room and one gentleman. Before I had been standing at the window five minutes, they somehow conveyed to me that they were all toadies and humbugs,[2] but that each of them pretended not to know that the others were toadies and humbugs, because the admission that he or she did know it would have made him or her out to be a toady and humbug. The most talkative of the ladies had to speak quite rigidly to suppress a yawn. This lady, whose name was Camilla, very much reminded me of my sister, with the difference that she was older.

"Poor dear soul!" said this lady, with an abruptness of manner quite my sister's. "Nobody's enemy but his own!"

"It would be much more commendable to be somebody else's enemy," said the gentleman; "far more natural."

"Cousin Raymond," observed another lady, "we are to love our neighbor."

"Sarah Pocket," returned Cousin Raymond, "if a man is not his own neighbor, who is?"

"Poor soul!" Camilla went on (I knew they had all been looking at me in the mean time), "he
3 is so very strange! Would any one believe that when Tom's wife died, he actually could not be induced to see the importance of the children's having the deepest of trimmings to their mourning? 'Good Lord!' says he, 'Camilla, what can it signify so long as the poor bereaved little things are in black?' So like Matthew! The idea!"

"Good points in him, good points in him," said Cousin Raymond; "Heaven forbid I should deny good points in him; but he never had, and he never will have, any sense of the proprieties."[3]

The ringing of a distant bell, combined with the echoing of some cry or call along the passage by which I had come, interrupted the conversation and caused Estella to say to me, "Now, boy!" On my turning round, they all looked at me with the utmost contempt, and, as I went

---

7. **press . . . parlor:** cabinet in the sitting room that is reserved for special occasions.
1. **superciliously** [sōō′pər sil′ē əs lē]: arrogantly.

2. **toadies and humbugs:** flatterers and people who pretend to be something they are not.
3. **proprieties** [prə prī′ə tēz]: socially accepted manners.

GUIDED READING

LITERAL QUESTIONS

1a. Of whom does Camilla remind Pip? (his sister)

2a. What do the relatives think of Tom? (They think he is strange and has no sense of propriety.)

INFERENTIAL QUESTIONS

1b. What does this imply about Pip's feelings for his sister? (He feels she is a "toady and a humbug.")

2b. Why do they think this? (They feel he failed to see the importance of appropriate mourning clothes.)

but, I heard Sarah Pocket say, "Well I am sure! What next!"

As we were going with our candle along the dark passage, Estella stopped all of a sudden, and, facing round, said in her taunting manner, with her face quite close to mine:

"Well?"

"Well, miss," I answered, almost falling over her and checking myself.

She stood looking at me, and of course I stood looking at her.

"Am I pretty?"

"Yes, I think you are very pretty."

"Am I insulting?"

"Not so much as you were last time," said I.

"Not so much so?"

"No."

She fired when she asked the last question, and she slapped my face with such force as she had, when I answered it.

"Now?" said she. "You little coarse monster, what do you think of me now?"

"I shall not tell you."

"Because you are going to tell upstairs. Is that it?"

"No," said I, "that's not it."

"Why don't you cry again, you little wretch?"

"Because I'll never cry for you again," said I. Which was, I suppose, as false a declaration as ever was made.

We went on our way upstairs after this episode, and as we were going up, we met a gentleman groping his way down.

"Whom have we here?" asked the gentleman, stopping and looking at me.

"A boy," said Estella.

He was a burly man of an exceedingly dark complexion, with an exceedingly large head and a corresponding large hand. He took my chin in his large hand and turned up my face to have a look at me by the light of the candle. He was prematurely bald on the top of his head, and had bushy black eyebrows that wouldn't lie down,

3 but stood up bristling. His eyes were set very deep in his head, and were disagreeably sharp and suspicious. He had a large watch-chain, and strong black dots where his beard and whiskers would have been if he had let them. He was nothing to me, and I could have had no foresight then that he ever would be anything to me, but it happened that I had this opportunity of observing him well.

"Boy of the neighborhood? Hey?" said he.

"Yes, sir," said I.

"How do *you* come here?"

"Miss Havisham sent for me, sir," I explained.

"Well! Behave yourself. I have a pretty large experience of boys, and you're a bad set of fellows. Now mind!" said he, biting the side of his great forefinger as he frowned at me, "you behave yourself!"

With these words he released me—which I was glad of, for his hand smelt of scented soap—and went his way downstairs.

We were soon in Miss Havisham's room.

4 "So!" she said, without being startled or surprised; "the days have worn away, have they?"

"Yes, ma'am. To-day is—"

"There, there, there!" with the impatient movement of her fingers. "I don't want to know. Are you ready to play?"

I was obliged to answer, in some confusion, "I don't think I am, ma'am."

"Not at cards again?" she demanded with a searching look.

"Yes, ma'am; I could do that, if I was wanted."

"Since this house strikes you old and grave, boy," said Miss Havisham impatiently, "and you are unwilling to play, are you willing to work?"

I said I was quite willing.

"Then go into that opposite room," said she, pointing at the door behind me with her withered hand, "and wait there till I come."

I crossed the staircase landing, and entered the room she indicated. From that room too, the

AT A GLANCE

- Estella slaps Pip.
- Pip meets a large, dark man.
- Miss Havisham asks Pip to "work."

1 CONFLICT

The conflict between Pip and Estella is defined: She wants him to suffer because of his feelings for her.

2 FORESHADOWING

Pip states that he will "never cry" for Estella again, but the adult narrator hints at a time in the future when Pip will shed many tears for her.

3 STYLE: DETAILS

The description of the man Pip meets on the stairs is so detailed that it suggests the man will appear again in Pip's life and have considerable impact on him.

4 THEME

Miss Havisham, speaking of time as having "worn away," reveals that she finds time an adversary, a force that, like a slow-moving glacier, carves out her life.

GUIDED READING

LITERAL QUESTIONS

1a. What does Estella do when Pip tells her she is not as insulting as before? (She slaps him.)

2a. Why does Pip say he is glad when the dark man lets go of him? (because the man's hand smelled of scented soap)

INFERENTIAL QUESTIONS

1b. Why do you think she does this? (She wants him to find her insulting.)

2b. What does this imply about the man? (that he is financially well-off)

AT A GLANCE

- Pip goes into a dark, cold room across the staircase landing.
- He sees a long table with an odd, cobweb-laden centerpiece and notices spiders, beetles, and mice.
- Miss Havisham says she will be placed on the table when she dies.

1 MOOD

The room Pip enters, described as "airless," "oppressive," dark, and cold, has an atmosphere of decay and morbidity.

1 daylight was completely excluded, and it had an airless smell that was oppressive. A fire had been lately kindled in the damp old-fashioned grate, and it was more disposed to go out than to burn up, and the reluctant smoke which hung in the room seemed colder than the clearer air—like our own marsh mist. Certain wintry branches of candles on the high chimney-piece faintly lighted the chamber, or, it would be more expressive to say, faintly troubled its darkness. It was spacious, and I dare say had once been handsome, but every discernible thing in it was covered with dust and mold, and dropping to pieces. The most prominent object was a long table with a table-cloth spread on it, as if a feast had been in preparation when the house and the clocks all stopped together. An épergne or center-piece of some kind was in the middle of this cloth; it was so heavily overhung with cobwebs that its form was quite undistinguishable; and, as I looked along the yellow expanse out of which I remember its seeming to grow, like a black fungus, I saw speckled-legged spiders with blotchy bodies running home to it, and running out from it, as if some circumstance of the greatest public importance had just transpired in the spider community.

I heard the mice too, rattling behind the panels, as if the same occurrence were important to their interests. But, the black beetles took no notice of the agitation, and groped about the hearth in a ponderous elderly way, as if they were short-sighted and hard of hearing, and not on terms with one another.

Miss Havisham laid a hand upon my shoulder. In her other hand she had a crutch-headed stick on which she leaned, and she looked like the witch of the place.

"This," said she, pointing to the long table with her stick, "is where I will be laid when I am dead. They shall come and look at me here."

"What do you think that is?" she asked me, again pointing with her stick; "that, where those cobwebs are?"

GUIDED READING

LITERAL QUESTION

1a. What is the most prominent object in the room? (a long table with a cloth spread on it)

INFERENTIAL QUESTION

1b. To what event to you think the table is connected? (to Miss Havisham's wedding day)

"I can't guess what it is, ma'am."

"It's a great cake. A bride-cake. Mine!"

She looked all round the room in a glaring manner, and then said, leaning on me while her hand twitched my shoulder, "Come, come, come! Walk me, walk me!"

I made out from this that the work I had to do was to walk Miss Havisham round and round the room. Accordingly, I started at once, and she leaned upon my shoulder.

She was not physically strong, and after a little time said, "Slower!" Still, we went at an impatient fitful speed, and as we went, she twitched the hand upon my shoulder, and worked her mouth, and led me to believe that we were going fast because her thoughts went fast. After a while she said, "Call Estella!" so I went out on the landing and roared that name as I had done on the previous occasion.

Estella brought with her the three ladies and the gentleman whom I had seen below.

"Dear Miss Havisham," said Miss Sarah Pocket. "How well you look!"

"I do not," returned Miss Havisham. "I am yellow skin and bone."

Camilla brightened when Miss Pocket met with this rebuff; and she murmured, as she plaintively contemplated Miss Havisham, "Poor dear soul! Certainly not to be expected to look well, poor thing. The idea!"

"And how are *you*?" said Miss Havisham to Camilla.

"Thank you, Miss Havisham," she returned, "I am as well as can be expected."

"Why, what's the matter with you?" asked Miss Havisham, with exceeding sharpness.

"Nothing worth mentioning," replied Camilla. "I don't wish to make a display of my feelings, but I have habitually thought of you more in the night than I am quite equal to."

"Then don't think of me," retorted Miss Havisham.

The gentleman present I understood to be Mr. Camilla. He said in a consolatory and complimentary voice, "Camilla, my dear, it is well known that your family feelings are gradually undermining you."

3 Miss Sarah Pocket I saw to be a little dry brown corrugated[4] old woman, with a small face that might have been made of walnut shells, and a large mouth like a cat's without the whiskers.

When Matthew was mentioned, Miss Havisham stopped me and herself, and stood looking at the speaker.

"Matthew will come and see me at last," said Miss Havisham sternly, "when I am laid on that table. That will be his place—there," striking the table with her stick, "at my head! And yours will be there! And your husband's there! And Sarah
4 Pocket's there! And Georgiana's there! Now you all know where to take your stations when you come to feast upon me.[5] And now go!"

At the mention of each name, she had struck the table with her stick in a new place. She now said, "Walk me, walk me!" and we went on again.

"I suppose there's nothing to be done," exclaimed Camilla, "but comply and depart. It's something to have seen the object of one's love and duty, even for so short a time. I wish Matthew could have that comfort."

While Estella was away lighting them down, Miss Havisham still walked with her hand on my shoulder, but more and more slowly. At last she stopped before the fire, and said, after muttering and looking at it some seconds:

"This is my birthday, Pip."

I was going to wish her many happy returns, when she lifted her stick.

"I don't suffer it to be spoken of. I don't suffer[6] those who were here just now, or any one, to speak of it. They come here on the day, but they dare not refer to it."

Of course *I* made no further effort to refer to it.

"On this day of the year, long before you

---

4. **corrugated** [kôr′ə gāt′id]: wrinkled.
5. **feast upon me:** claim their shares of her property after her death.
6. **suffer:** permit, tolerate.

AT A GLANCE

- The centerpiece is Miss Havisham's wedding cake.
- Pip walks Miss Havisham around the room.
- The relatives attempt to flatter Miss Havisham; she dismisses them.
- Miss Havisham tells Pip it is her birthday.

1 THEME

Sarah Pocket lies to Miss Havisham, telling her she looks well, but Miss Havisham's reply is direct and honest: She knows the relatives want to flatter her.

2 STYLE: SATIRE

Dickens, a master of social satire, mocks those who observe the "proprieties" at the expense of honesty when he has Camilla say to Miss Havisham, "I have habitually thought of you more in the night than I am quite equal to."

3 STYLE: FIGURATIVE LANGUAGE

Sarah Pocket is compared to a walnut and a cat, to show both how unpleasant and how sly she is.

4 STYLE: IMAGERY

Miss Havisham's accusation—that her relatives will "feast" upon her—presents an image of cannibalism that is both exaggerated and not entirely inaccurate.

GUIDED READING

LITERAL QUESTIONS

1a. Of what do the relatives try to convince Miss Havisham? (that they are concerned for her)

2a. What does Miss Havisham tell Pip about her birthday? (She won't allow anyone to speak of it.)

INFERENTIAL QUESTIONS

1b. Does Miss Havisham believe them? (No; she argues with them, speaks sharply to them, accuses them of feeding on her, and abruptly dismisses them.)

2b. How do you think she feels about her birthday and the passage of time? (She both resents time's passing and wishes it would pass faster.)

AT A GLANCE

- Estella and Pip play cards again.
- Pip meets a pale young man who challenges him to fight.

1 THEME

Miss Havisham compares time to the teeth of an animal; her tone suggests that she both fears and reviles time.

2 POINT OF VIEW

The adult narrator momentarily steps away from the scene to point out that he had had no choice but to fight the young man.

3 CONFLICT

The young man manufactures a conflict with Pip where none exists so that Pip will have reason to fight: He pulls Pip's hair and butts his head into Pip's stomach.

4 CHARACTERIZATION

By describing the young man as "lighthearted, business-like, and bloodthirsty," Pip reveals much about the character of a boy who may be important to the novel's plot.

were born, this heap of decay," stabbing with her crutched stick at the pile of cobwebs on the
1 table, but not touching it, "was brought here. It and I have worn away together. The mice have gnawed at it, and sharper teeth than teeth of mice have gnawed at me."

"When the ruin is complete," said she, with a ghastly look, "and when they lay me dead, in my bride's dress on the bride's table—which shall be done, and which will be the finished curse upon him—so much the better if it is done on this day!"

She stood looking at the table as if she stood looking at her own figure lying there. I remained quiet. Estella returned.

In an instant, Miss Havisham said, "Let me see you two play at cards; why have you not begun?" With that, we returned to her room, and sat down as before; I was beggared, as before; and again, as before, Miss Havisham watched us all the time. When we had played some half-dozen games, a day was appointed for my return, and I was taken down into the yard to be fed in the former dog-like manner. There, too, I was again left to wander about as I liked. I looked in at another window, and found myself, to my great surprise, exchanging a broad stare with a pale young gentleman with red eyelids and light hair.

"Halloa!" said he, "young fellow!"

Halloa being a general observation which I had usually observed to be best answered by itself, *I* said "Halloa!" politely omitting young fellow.

"Who let *you* in?" said he.

"Miss Estella."

"Who gave you leave to prowl about?"

"Miss Estella."

"Come and fight," said the pale young gentleman.

2 What could I do but follow him? I have often asked myself the question since; but what else could I do? His manner was so final, and I was so astonished, that I followed where he led, as if I had been under a spell.

"Stop a minute, though," he said, wheeling round before we had gone many paces. "I ought to give you a reason for fighting, too. There it
3 is!" In a most irritating manner he instantly slapped his hands against one another, flung one of his legs up behind him, pulled my hair, slapped his hands again, dipped his head, and butted it into my stomach.

The bull-like proceeding last mentioned was particularly disagreeable just after bread and meat. I therefore hit out at him, and was going to hit out again, when he said, "Aha! Would you?" and began dancing backwards and forwards in a manner quite unparalleled within my limited experience.

"Laws of the game!" said he. Here, he skipped from his left leg on to his right. "Regular rules!" Here, he skipped from his right leg on to his left. "Come to the ground, and go through the preliminaries!" Here, he dodged backwards and forwards, and did all sorts of things while I looked helplessly at him.

I was secretly afraid of him but I felt morally and physically convinced that his light head of hair could have had no business in the pit of my stomach. Therefore, I followed him, without a word, to a retired nook of the garden formed by the junction of two walls and screened by some rubbish. On his asking me if I was satisfied with the ground, and on my replying Yes, he begged my leave to absent himself for a moment, and quickly returned with a bottle of water and a sponge dipped in vinegar. "Available for both,"
4 he said, placing these against the wall. And then fell to pulling off, not only his jacket and waistcoat,[7] but his shirt too, in a manner at once lighthearted, business-like, and bloodthirsty.

Although he did not look very healthy, these dreadful preparations quite appalled me. I judged him to be about my own age, but he was much taller.

My heart failed me when I saw him squaring at me and eyeing my anatomy as if he were mi-

7. **waistcoat** [wes′kət]: vest.

GUIDED READING

LITERAL QUESTIONS

1a. What does Miss Havisham say will be the "finished curse upon him"? (when she is dead and laid out on the table)

2a. How does the young gentleman prepare for the fight? (He provokes Pip, gets water and a sponge, and takes off his jacket and shirt.)

INFERENTIAL QUESTIONS

1b. Who do you think is the "him" to whom she refers? (perhaps the betrothed lover who jilted her)

2b. Why do these preparations frighten Pip? (They make it seem as if the young gentleman is an experienced fighter.)

nutely choosing his bone. I never have been so surprised in my life as I was when I let out the first blow, and saw him lying on his back, looking up at me with a bloody nose and his face exceedingly foreshortened.

But, he was on his feet directly, and after sponging himself with a great show of dexterity, began squaring again. The second greatest surprise I have ever had in my life was seeing him on his back again, looking up at me out of a black eye.

His spirit inspired me with great respect. He seemed to have no strength, and he never once hit me hard, and he was always knocked down; but, he would be up again in a moment sponging himself or drinking out of the water bottle. He got heavily bruised, for I am sorry to record that the more I hit him, the harder I hit him; but, he
1 came up again and again and again, until at last he got a bad fall with the back of his head against the wall. He finally went on his knees to his sponge and threw it up, at the same time panting out, "That means you have won."

He seemed so brave and innocent that, although I had not proposed the contest, I felt but a gloomy satisfaction in my victory. I got dressed and said, "Can I help you?" and he said, "No thankee," and I said, "Good afternoon," and *he* said, "Same to you."

When I got into the court-yard, I found Estella waiting with the keys. But she neither asked me where I had been, nor why I had kept
2 her waiting; and there was a bright flush upon her face, as though something had happened to delight her. Instead of going straight to the gate too, she stepped back into the passage, and beckoned me.

"Come here! You may kiss me if you like."

I kissed her cheek as she turned it to me. I think I would have gone through a great deal to kiss her cheek. But I felt that the kiss was given to the coarse common boy as a piece of money

AT A GLANCE

- Pip beats the young man in the fight.
- Estella invites Pip to kiss her.

1 VOCABULARY: SYNTAX

Dickens chooses to write "he got a bad fall," rather than have Pip say "I gave him a bad fall," to hint that Pip feels guilty for beating the young man.

2 READING SKILLS: CAUSE AND EFFECT

Pip seems unaware that Estella lets him kiss her because he won the fight; she is "flushed" with delight that the boys fought over her.

GUIDED READING

LITERAL QUESTION

1a. How does Pip feel about the young gentleman by the end of the fight? (He respects him.)

INFERENTIAL QUESTION

1b. Why does he feel this way? (The young gentleman, though not physically strong, has shown great courage and perseverance.)

AT A GLANCE

- Pip feels that Estella's kiss is worth nothing.
- For the next eight months Pip visits Miss Havisham regularly.
- Miss Havisham demands to see Joe, thinking that Pip's apprenticeship should begin "at once."

1 THEME

Pip suffers guilt over having hurt the pale young gentleman and feels responsible for the fight, though it was the young man who initiated the confrontation.

2 THEME

Miss Havishman manipulates both Pip (by forcing him to admit his attraction to Estella) and Estella (by urging her to break Pip's heart).

3 POINT OF VIEW

The adult narrator thinks he knows why he could talk easily to Biddy, revealing that he and Biddy then possessed feelings they hadn't explored.

4 THEME

Miss Havisham is aware of the passage of time only because Pip is growing: She seems afraid and resentful of his entrance into manhood.

might have been, and that it was worth nothing.

What with the birthday visitors, and what with the cards, and what with the fight, my stay had lasted so long that, when I neared home, the light on the spit of sand off the point on the marshes was gleaming against a black night sky, and Joe's furnace was flinging a path of fire across the road.

Chapter Eleven

At Satis House: Pip is apprenticed to Joe.

1 My mind grew very uneasy on the subject of the pale young gentleman. The more I thought of the fight, and recalled the pale young gentleman on his back, the more certain it appeared that something would be done to me. I felt that the pale young gentleman's blood was on my head, and that the law would avenge it.

When the day came round for my return to the scene of the deed of violence, my terrors reached their height. However, go to Miss Havisham's I must, and go I did. And behold! nothing came of the late struggle. It was not alluded to in any way, and no pale young gentleman was to be discovered on the premises.

I am now going to sum up a period of at least eight or ten months. As we began to be more used to one another, Miss Havisham talked more to me, and asked me such questions as what was I going to be? I told her I was going to be apprenticed to Joe and I enlarged upon my knowing nothing and wanting to know everything.

Estella was always about, and always let me in and out, but never told me I might kiss her again. Miss Havisham would often ask me in a
2 whisper, or when we were alone, "Does she grow prettier and prettier, Pip?" And when I said Yes would seem to enjoy it greedily. Miss Havisham would embrace her with lavish fondness, murmuring something in her ear that sounded like, "Break their hearts, my pride and hope, break their hearts and have no mercy!"

Perhaps I might have told Joe about the pale young gentleman, if I had not previously been betrayed into those enormous inventions to which I had confessed. I said nothing of him, but
3 I told poor Biddy everything. Why it came natural for me to do so, and why Biddy had a deep concern in everything I told her, I did not know then, though I think I know now.

Meanwhile, councils went on in the kitchen at home. Pumblechook used often to come over of a night for the purpose of discussing my prospects with my sister. He and my sister would pair off in such nonsensical speculations about Miss Havisham, and about what she would do with me and for me, that I used to want—quite painfully—to burst into spiteful tears, fly at Pumblechook, and pummel[1] him all over. In these discussions, Joe bore no part.

We went on in this way for a long time, and it seemed likely that we should continue to go on
4 in this way for a long time, when, one day, Miss Havisham stopped short as she and I were walking—she leaning on my shoulder—and said, with some displeasure:

"You are growing tall, Pip! Tell me the name again of that blacksmith of yours."

"Joe Gargery, ma'am."

"Meaning the master you were to be apprenticed to?"

"Yes, Miss Havisham."

"You had better be apprenticed at once. Would Gargery come here with you, and bring your indentures,[2] do you think?"

I signified that I had no doubt he would take it as an honor to be asked.

"Then let him come."

"At any particular time, Miss Havisham?"

"There, there! I know nothing about times. Let him come soon, and come alone with you."

When I got home at night, and delivered this

1. **pummel:** strike repeatedly with fists.
2. **indentures:** contract that binds an apprentice to a master.

GUIDED READING

LITERAL QUESTION

1a. What does Miss Havisham tell Estella while embracing her? (to break men's hearts and have no mercy)

INFERENTIAL QUESTION

1b. Why does Miss Havisham say this to Estella? (She wants to use Estella to avenge her own broken heart.)

message for Joe, my sister "went on the rampage" in a more alarming degree than at any previous period. She asked me and Joe whether we supposed she was door-mats under our feet, and how we dared to use her so, and what company we graciously thought she *was* fit for? When she had exhausted a torrent of such inquiries, she threw a candlestick at Joe, burst into a loud sobbing, got out the dust-pan—which was always a very bad sign—put on her coarse apron, and began cleaning up to a terrible extent. Not satisfied with a dry cleaning, she took to a pail and scrubbing-brush, and cleaned us out of house and home, so that we stood shivering in the back-yard. It was ten o'clock at night before we ventured to creep in again.

It was a trial to my feelings, on the next day but one, to see Joe arraying himself in his Sunday clothes to accompany me to Miss Havisham's. I knew he made himself so dreadfully uncomfortable entirely on my account, and that it was for me he pulled up his shirt-collar so very high behind, that it made the hair on the crown of his head stand up like a tuft of feathers.

At breakfast-time, my sister declared her intention of going to town with us, and being left at Uncle Pumblechook's, and called for "when we had done with our fine ladies"—a way of putting the case from which Joe appeared inclined to augur[3] the worst. The forge was shut up for the day, and Joe inscribed in chalk upon the door (as it was his custom to do on the very rare occasions when he was not at work) the monosyllable HOUT,[4] accompanied by a sketch of an arrow supposed to be flying in the direction he had taken.

We walked to town, my sister leading the way in a very large beaver bonnet, and carrying a basket like the Great Seal of England in plaited straw, a pair of pattens,[5] a spare shawl, and an umbrella, though it was a fine bright day.

When we came to Pumblechook's, my sister bounced in and left us. As it was almost noon, Joe and I held straight on to Miss Havisham's house. Estella opened the gate as usual, and, the moment she appeared, Joe took his hat off and stood weighing it by the brim in both his hands, as if he had some urgent reason in his mind for being particular to half a quarter of an ounce.

Estella took no notice of either of us, but led us the way that I knew so well. I followed next
2 to her, and Joe came last. When I looked back at Joe in the long passage, he was still weighing his hat with the greatest care, and was coming after us in long strides on the tips of his toes.

Estella told me we were both to go in, so I took Joe by the coat-cuff and conducted him into Miss Havisham's presence. She was seated at her dressing-table, and looked round at us immediately.

"Oh!" said she to Joe. "You are the husband of the sister of this boy?"

3 I could hardly have imagined dear old Joe looking so unlike himself or so like some extraordinary bird, standing, as he did, speechless, with his tuft of feathers ruffled, and his mouth open as if he wanted a worm.

"You are the husband," repeated Miss Havisham, "of the sister of this boy?"

It was aggravating; but, throughout the interview, Joe persisted in addressing me instead of Miss Havisham.

"Which I meantersay, Pip," Joe now observed, in a manner that was at once expressive of forcible argumentation, strict confidence, and great politeness, "as I hup and married your sister, and I were at the time what you might call (if you was any ways inclined) a single man."

"Well!" said Miss Havisham. "And you have

---

3. **augur** [ô′gər]: predict.
4. HOUT: out. Some characters in the novel add an *h* sound to the beginning of words that begin with vowels.
5. **pattens:** clogs, or various kinds of shoes or sandals with thick wooden soles, worn to protect the feet from puddles or mud.

AT A GLANCE

- Pip delivers Miss Havisham's message; Mrs. Joe is greatly vexed.
- Joe accompanies Pip to Miss Havisham's.
- Miss Havisham asks Joe to define his relationship with Pip.

1 CHARACTERIZATION

Pip gives an honest report of Joe's appearance—his uncomfortable clothes, his hair standing straight up—but the reader can sense that he is ashamed of Joe.

2 READING SKILLS: INFERENCE

From Dickens' description of Joe "weighing his hat" and walking "on the tips of his toes," the reader can infer that Joe is tremendously nervous about visiting Miss Havisham.

3 STYLE: SIMILE

Pip compares Joe to a bird—"his tuft of feathers ruffled" and "his mouth open as if he wanted a worm"—a description that is both comic and revealing of Pip's embarrassment over Joe's appearance.

GUIDED READING

LITERAL QUESTIONS

1a. What does Mrs. Joe do when Pip tells her what Miss Havisham wants? (She goes "on the rampage.")

2a. What does Joe do when Miss Havisham asks him questions? (He directs his replies to Pip.)

INFERENTIAL QUESTIONS

1b. Why is she so angry? (She feels snubbed because she was not invited to Miss Havisham's.)

2b. Why does he do this? (He is too nervous to speak directly to Miss Havisham.)

AT A GLANCE

- Miss Havisham offers Joe a "premium" for taking Pip on as an apprentice.
- She says the fee is Pip's "reward" for his visits.

1 BACKGROUND

In the nineteenth century boys were often apprenticed to tradesmen: A boy was "indentured" to learn the trade in return for room and board, usually for a period of seven years.

2 CONFLICT

Pip experiences inner conflict when he realizes that Estella, whom he wants to impress, is scornful of Joe, whom he both loves and is ashamed of.

3 INTERPRETING

Pip feels "a sensation, first of burning, and then of freezing" when Joe calls him "old chap"; the sensation is really that of acute embarrassment at Joe's unfettered speech.

4 THEME

Miss Havisham further manipulates Pip by handing him over to Joe after she is done with him: Pip has no say in his own future.

reared the boy, with the intention of taking him for your apprentice; is that so, Mr. Gargery?"

"You know, Pip," replied Joe, "as you and me were ever friends, and it were looked for'ard to betwixt us, as being calc'lated to lead to larks.[6] Not but what, Pip, if you had ever made objections to the business."

"Has the boy," said Miss Havisham, "ever made any objection? Does he like the trade?"

"Which it is well beknown to yourself, Pip," returned Joe.

It was quite in vain for me to endeavor to make him sensible that he ought to speak to Miss Havisham. The more I made faces and gestures to him to do it, the more confidential, argumentative, and polite he persisted in being to me.

1 "Have you brought his indentures with you?" asked Miss Havisham.

"Well, Pip, you know," replied Joe, as if that were a little unreasonable, "you yourself see me put 'em in my 'at, and therefore you know as they are here." With which he took them out, and gave them, not to Miss Havisham, but to me.
2 I am afraid I was ashamed of the dear good fellow—I *know* I was ashamed of him—when I saw that Estella stood at the back of Miss Havisham's chair, and that her eyes laughed mischievously. I took the indentures out of his hand and gave them to Miss Havisham.

"You expected," said Miss Havisham, as she looked them over, "no premium[7] with the boy?"

"Joe!" I remonstrated; for he made no reply at all. "Why don't you answer—"

"Pip," returned Joe, cutting me short as if he were hurt, "which I meantersay that were not a question requiring a answer betwixt yourself and me, and which you know the answer to be full well No. You know it to be No, Pip, and wherefore should I say it?"

Miss Havisham glanced at him as if she understood and took up a little bag from the table beside her.

"Pip has earned a premium here," she said, "and here it is. There are five-and-twenty guineas[8] in this bag. Give it to your master, Pip."

As if he were absolutely out of his mind with the wonder awakened in him by her strange figure and the strange room, Joe, even at this pass, persisted in addressing me.

"This is very liberal on your part, Pip," said Joe, "and it is as such received and grateful welcome, though never looked for, far nor near
3 nor nowheres. And now, old chap," said Joe, conveying to me a sensation, first of burning and then of freezing, for I felt as if that familiar expression were applied to Miss Havisham; "and now, old chap, may we do our duty! May you and me do our duty, both on us by one and another, and by them which your liberal present—have—conweyed—to be—for the satisfaction of mind—of—them as never—" here Joe showed that he felt he had fallen into frightful difficulties, until he triumphantly rescued himself with the words, "and from myself far be it!" These words had such a round and convincing sound for him that he said them twice.

4 "Good-bye, Pip!" said Miss Havisham. "Let them out, Estella."

"Am I to come again, Miss Havisham?" I asked.

"No. Gargery is your master now. Gargery! One word!"

Thus calling him back as I went out of the door, I heard her say to Joe, in a distinct emphatic voice, "The boy has been a good boy here, and that is his reward. Of course, as an honest man, you will expect no other and no more."

How Joe got out of the room, I have never been able to determine, but I know that when he

---

6. **larks:** fun.
7. **premium:** fee that an apprentice pays to be accepted by a master.
8. **guineas** [gin'ēz]: gold coins—last minted in 1813—worth approximately one pound, or five dollars, each at the time the novel was written.

GUIDED READING

LITERAL QUESTIONS

1a. What are Pip's feelings toward Joe during the conversation with Miss Havisham? (shame and embarrassment)

2a. What does Joe reply when Miss Havisham asks if he expects a premium for Pip? (that he does not expect one)

INFERENTIAL QUESTIONS

1b. Why does he feel this way? (because Estella is watching and mocking Joe)

2b. Do you think Miss Havisham believes Joe? (Yes; she seems to understand the nature of Joe's discomfort and of his relationship with Pip.)

did get out, he was steadily proceeding upstairs instead of coming down. In another minute we were outside the gate, and it was locked, and Estella was gone. When we stood in the daylight alone again, Joe backed up against a wall, and
1 said to me, "Astonishing!" And there he remained so long, saying "Astonishing" at intervals so often that I began to think his senses were never coming back. At length, he prolonged his remark into "Pip, I do assure *you* this is as-TONishing!" and so, by degrees, became conversational and able to walk away.

I have reason to think that Joe's intellects were brightened by the encounter they had passed through, and that on our way to Pumblechook's, he invented a subtle and deep design. My reason is to be found in what took place in Mr. Pumblechook's parlor: where, on our presenting ourselves, my sister sat in conference with that detested seedsman.

"Well!" cried my sister, addressing us both at once. "And what's happened to *you*? I wonder you condescend to come back to such poor society as this, I am sure I do!"

"Miss Havisham," said Joe, with a fixed look at me, like an effort of remembrance, "made it wery partick'ler that we should give her—were it compliments or respects, Pip?"

"Compliments," I said.

"Which that were my own belief," answered Joe—"her compliments to Mrs. J. Gargery—"

"Much good they'll do me!" observed my sister, but rather gratified, too.

"And wishing," pursued Joe, with another fixed look at me, like another effort of remembrance, "that the state of Miss Havisham's 'elth were sitch as would have—allowed, were it, Pip?"

"Of her having the pleasure," I added.

"Of ladies' company," said Joe. And drew a long breath.

"Well!" cried my sister, with a mollified glance at Mr. Pumblechook. "She might have had the politeness to send that message at first, but it's better late than never. And what did she give young Rantipole[9] here?"

"She giv' him," said Joe, "nothing."

Mrs. Joe was going to break out, but Joe went on.

"What she giv'," said Joe, "she giv' to his friends. 'And by his friends,' were her explanation, 'I mean into the hands of his sister, Mrs. J. Gargery,' Them were her words, 'Mrs. J. Gargery.' She mayn't have know'd," added Joe, with an appearance of reflection, "whether it were Joe or Jorge."

My sister looked at Pumblechook, who smoothed the elbows of his wooden arm-chair, and nodded at her and at the fire, as if he had known all about it beforehand.

"And how much have you got?" asked my sister, laughing. Positively, laughing!

"What would present company say to ten pound?" demanded Joe.

"They'd say," returned my sister curtly, "pretty well. Not too much, but pretty well."

"It's more than that, then," said Joe.

2 That fearful imposter, Pumblechook, immediately nodded, and said, as he rubbed the arms of his chair: "It's more than that, mum."

"Why, you don't mean to say—" began my sister.

"Yes I do, mum," said Pumblechook; "but wait a bit. Go on, Joseph."

"What would present company say," proceeded Joe, "to twenty pound?"

"Handsome would be the word," returned my sister.

"Well, then," said Joe, "it's more than twenty pound."

That abject hypocrite, Pumblechook, nodded again, and said with a patronizing laugh, "It's more than that, mum. Good again! Follow her up, Joseph!"

"Then to make an end of it," said Joe,

9. **Rantipole** [ran'tē pōl]: wild, reckless, quarrelsome person.

AT A GLANCE

- Joe and Pip go to Mr. Pumblechook's.
- Joe lies about Miss Havisham's regards.
- Joe begins to reveal the amount of money Miss Havisham gave him.

1 STYLE: HUMOR

Joe's repetition of the word *astonishing* reveals how nervous and awed he was by Miss Havisham and, at the same time, makes his awe humorous and touching.

2 THEME

Though Joe has been fibbing, Pip perceives Joe as essentially honest but Mr. Pumblechook as pompous, deceptive, and dishonest.

GUIDED READING

LITERAL QUESTIONS

1a. What is the "subtle and deep design" that Joe invents on the way to Pumblechook's? (a series of compliments from Miss Havisham to Mrs. Joe)

2a. How does Joe tell Mrs. Joe about the money he received? (He hints at the amount, making it a little higher each time.)

INFERENTIAL QUESTIONS

1b. For what reason does Joe invent the "design"? (to keep Mrs. Joe from being angry)

2b. Why does he reveal the amount this way? (so that Mrs. Joe will appreciate the amount more)

AT A GLANCE

- Pip is apprenticed to Joe.
- Pip and Joe study together.
- Pip asks if he should visit Miss Havisham.

1 THEME

Pip's descriptions of Mr. Pumblechook grow harsher—from "imposter" to "hypocrite" to "swindler" to "diabolical." Pip is furious that he takes credit for getting the money from Miss Havisham.

2 THEME

Pip explains that his motives for educating Joe were less than pure: He wanted to make Joe "worthier" of his society.

3 THEME

Pip's memory of his time at Miss Havisham's is deceptive; rather than remembering the prisonlike atmosphere, he romanticizes it.

4 CHARACTERIZATION

Joe reveals his modesty and wisdom when he warns Pip that visiting Miss Havisham might leave Pip's motives open to misinterpretation: She might think Pip wants more money.

delightedly handing the bag to my sister; "it's five-and-twenty pound."

"It's five-and-twenty pound, mum," echoed that basest of swindlers, Pumblechook, rising to shake hands with her; "and it's no more than your merits."

"Goodness knows, Uncle Pumblechook," said my sister (grasping the money), "we're deeply beholden to you."

1 "Never mind me, mum," returned that diabolical corn-chandler. "A pleasure's a pleasure all the world over. But this boy, you know; we must have him bound. I said I'd see to it—to tell you the truth."

The justices were sitting in the Town Hall near at hand, and we at once went over to have me bound apprentice to Joe in the magisterial presence.

Finally, I remembered that when I got into my little bedroom, I was truly wretched, and had a strong conviction on me that I should never like Joe's trade. I had liked it once, but once was not now.

Chapter Twelve

At the forge: We meet Orlick.

As I was getting too big for Mr. Wopsle's great-aunt's room, my education under that preposterous female terminated. Not, however, until Biddy had imparted to me everything she knew, from the little catalogue of prices.

2 Whatever I acquired, I tried to impart to Joe. This statement sounds so well that I cannot in my conscience let it pass unexplained. I wanted to make Joe less ignorant and common, that he might be worthier of my society and less open to Estella's reproach.

The old battery out on the marshes was our place of study, and a broken slate and a short piece of slate pencil were our educational implements: to which Joe always added a pipe of tobacco. I never knew Joe to remember anything from one Sunday to another, or to acquire, under my tuition,[1] any piece of information whatever. Yet he would smoke his pipe at the battery with a far more sagacious air than anywhere else—even with a learned air—as if he considered himself to be advancing immensely. Dear fellow, I hope he did.

It was pleasant and quiet, out there with the sails on the river passing beyond the earthwork,[2] and sometimes, when the tide was low, looking as if they belonged to sunken ships that were still sailing on at the bottom of the water. Whenever I watched the vessels standing out to sea with their white sails spread, I somehow thought of Miss Havisham and Estella; and whenever the light struck aslant, afar off, upon a cloud or sail or green hillside or water-line, it was just the
3 same. Miss Havisham and Estella and the strange house and the strange life appeared to have something to do with everything that was picturesque.

One Sunday I resolved to mention a thought concerning them that had been much in my head.

"Joe," said I, "don't you think I ought to pay Miss Havisham a visit?"

"Well, Pip," returned Joe, slowly considering. "What for?"

"What for, Joe? What is any visit made for?"

4 "There is some wisits p'r'aps," said Joe, "as for ever remains open to the question, Pip. But in regard of wisiting Miss Havisham. She might think you wanted something—expected something of her."

"Don't you think I might say that I did not, Joe?"

"You might, old chap," said Joe. "And she might credit it. Similarly, she mightn't."

Joe felt, as I did, that he had made a point

1. **tuition:** tutoring.
2. **earthwork:** fortification made of earth.

GUIDED READING

LITERAL QUESTIONS

1a. How does Pip feel when he reaches his bedroom? (He is "wretched" and thinks he will never like Joe's trade.)

2a. What does Pip ask Joe? (if he should visit Miss Havisham)

INFERENTIAL QUESTIONS

1b. Why does he feel this way? (He feels that he has been sold into apprenticeship and will be stuck in a "common" trade for life.)

2b. Why do you think Pip wants to go? (to see Estella)

there, and he pulled hard at his pipe to keep himself from weakening it by repetition.

"You see, Pip," Joe pursued, as soon as he was past that danger, "Miss Havisham done the handsome thing by you. When Miss Havisham done the handsome thing by you, she called me back to say to me as that were all."

"Yes, Joe. I heard her."

"ALL," Joe repeated very emphatically.

"But, Joe."

"Yes, old chap."

"Here am I, getting on in the first year of my time, and, since the day of my being bound I have never thanked Miss Havisham, or asked after her, or shown that I remembered her."

"That's true, Pip; and unless you were to turn her out a set of shoes all four round—and which I meantersay as even a set of shoes all four round might not act acceptable as a present in a total wacancy of hoofs—"

"I don't mean that sort of remembrance, Joe; I don't mean a present."

But Joe had got the idea of a present in his head and must harp upon it. "Or even," said he, "if you was helped to knocking her up a new chain for the front door."

"My dear Joe," I cried in desperation, taking hold of his coat, "don't go on in that way. I never thought of making Miss Havisham any present."

"No, Pip," Joe assented, as if he had been contending for that all along, "and what I say to you is, you are right, Pip."

"Yes, Joe; but what I wanted to say was that, as we are rather slack just now, if you would give me a half-holiday to-morrow, I think I would go up town and make a call on Miss Est—Havisham."

"Which her name," said Joe gravely, "ain't Estavisham, Pip, unless she have been rechris' ended."

"I know, Joe, I know. It was a slip of mine. What do you think of it, Joe?"

In brief, Joe thought that if I thought well of it, he thought well of it.

Now Joe kept a journeyman[3] at weekly wages
3 whose name was Orlick. He was a broad-shouldered loose-limbed swarthy fellow of great strength, never in a hurry, and always slouching. He never even seemed to come to his work on purpose, but would slouch in as if by mere accident; and when he went to the Jolly Bargemen to eat his dinner, or went away at night, he would slouch out as if he had no idea where he was going, and no intention of ever coming back. He lodged at a sluice-keeper's[4] out on the marshes, and on working-days would come slouching from his hermitage,[5] with his hands in his pockets and his dinner loosely tied in a bundle round his neck and dangling on his back. On Sundays he mostly lay all day on sluice-gates, or stood against ricks[6] and barns. He always slouched with his eyes on the ground; and, when accosted or otherwise required to raise them, he looked up in a half-resentful, half-puzzled way.

The morose journeyman had no liking for me. When I became Joe's 'prentice, Orlick was perhaps confirmed in some suspicion that I should displace him.

Dolge Orlick was at work and present, next day, when I reminded Joe of my half-holiday. He said nothing at the moment, for he and Joe had just got a piece of hot iron between them, and I was at the bellows;[7] but by-and-by he said, leaning on his hammer:

4 "Now, master! Sure you're not a-going to favor only one of us. If young Pip has a half-holiday, do as much for Old Orlick." I suppose he was about five-and-twenty, but he usually spoke of himself as an ancient person.

---

3. **journeyman:** person who works for a master worker but is no longer an apprentice.
4. **sluice-keeper:** person who controls the drainage of water through an artificial channel with a series of gates.
5. **hermitage:** solitary, secluded home.
6. **ricks:** stacks of hay or grain.
7. **bellows:** device that blows air on a blacksmith's fire.

AT A GLANCE

- Pip decides to visit Miss Havisham.
- Orlick, Joe's journeyman, demands equal time off.

1 PARAPHRASING THE PASSAGE

The only present Pip could give Miss Havisham is a set of four horseshoes; even those would be impractical since she has no horses.

2 CHARACTERIZATION

Pip accidentally reveals his true reason for wanting to visit Miss Havisham: He hopes to see Estella when he is there.

3 CHARACTERIZATION

Dickens' first description of Orlick emphasizes his physical strength and cavalier bent.

4 THEME

Orlick tries to manipulate Joe into giving him a half-holiday by appealing to Joe's sense of fair play.

GUIDED READING

LITERAL QUESTION

1a. How does Orlick react when spoken to? (He looks at the speaker resentfully and with puzzlement.)

INFERENTIAL QUESTION

1b. What does this tell you about his character? (He is sullen and not very smart.)

AT A GLANCE

- Orlick argues with Joe.
- Joe accedes to Orlick's demand; Mrs. Joe criticizes her husband.
- Orlick insults Mrs. Joe.

1 CONFLICT

Joe wants to be fair but doesn't want Orlick to force him into a decision; Orlick's sullenness and temper ultimately get the best of Joe.

2 STYLE: DIALOGUE

Dickens places Joe's interruptions in parentheses to show how little effect they have on the strong clash of personalities between Orlick and Mrs. Joe.

"Why, what'll you do with a half-holiday, if you get it?" said Joe.

"What'll *I* do with it? What'll *he* do with it? I'll do as much with it as *him*," said Orlick.

"As to Pip, he's going up town," said Joe.

1 "Well, then, as to Old Orlick, *he's* a-going up town," retorted that worthy. "Two can go up town. Tain't only one wot can go up town."

"Don't lose your temper," said Joe.

"Shall if I like," growled Orlick. "Now, master! Come. No favoring in this shop. Be a man!"

The master refusing to entertain the subject until the journeyman was in a better temper, Orlick plunged at the furnace, drew out a red-hot bar, made at me with it as if he were going to run it through my body, whisked it round my head, laid it on the anvil, hammered it out—as if it were I, I thought, and the sparks were my spurting blood.

"Now, master!"

"Are you all right now?" demanded Joe.

"Ah! I am all right," said gruff Old Orlick.

"Then, as in general you stick to your work as well as most men," said Joe, "let it be a half-holiday for all."

My sister had been standing silent in the yard, within hearing—she was a most unscrupulous spy and listener—and she instantly looked in at one of the windows.

"Like you, you fool!" said she to Joe, "giving holidays to great idle hulkers like that. You are a rich man, upon my life, to waste wages in that way. I wish *I* was his master!"

2 "You'd be everybody's master if you durst," retorted Orlick, with an ill-favored grin.

("Let her alone," said Joe.)

"I'd be a match for all noodles and all rogues,"[8] returned my sister, beginning to work herself into a mighty rage.

"You're a foul shrew,[9] Mother Gargery," growled the journeyman.

---

8. **rogues** [rōgz]: dishonest, deceitful people.
9. **shrew**: bad-tempered, nagging woman.

GUIDED READING

LITERAL QUESTION

1a. How does Joe respond to Orlick's demand? (At first he won't answer; when Orlick cools down, Joe gives him the half-holiday.)

INFERENTIAL QUESTION

1b. Do you think that Joe's decision is entirely a result of Orlick's manipulation? (No; Joe let Orlick off because he found Orlick's work adequate and because he is fair.)

("Let her alone, will you?" said Joe.)

"What did you say?" cried my sister, beginning to scream. "What did you say? What did that fellow Orlick say to me, Pip? What did he call me, with my husband standing by? Oh! Oh! Oh!" Each of these exclamations was a shriek.

"Ah-h-h!" growled the journeyman, between his teeth, "I'd hold you, if you was my wife. I'd hold you under the pump, and choke it out of you."

("I tell you, let her alone," said Joe.)

"Oh! To hear him!" cried my sister, with a clap of her hands and a scream together—which was her next stage. "To hear the names he's giving me! That Orlick! In my own house! Me, a married woman! With my husband standing by! Oh! Oh!"

1 What could the wretched Joe do now, after his disregarded parenthetical interruptions, but stand up to his journeyman, and ask him what he meant by interfering betwixt himself and Mrs. Joe; and further, whether he was man enough to come on? Old Orlick felt that the situation admitted of nothing less than coming on, and was on his defense straightway, so, without so much as pulling off their singed and burnt aprons, they went at one another, like two giants. But if any man in that neighborhood could stand up long
2 against Joe, I never saw the man. Orlick, as if he had been of no more account than the pale young gentleman, was very soon among the coal dust, and in no hurry to come out of it. Then Joe unlocked the door and picked up my sister, who had dropped insensible at the window (but who had seen the fight first I think), and who was carried into the house and laid down, and who was recommended to revive.

I went upstairs to dress myself. When I came down again, I found Joe and Orlick sweeping up, without any other traces of discomposure than a slit in one of Orlick's nostrils, which was neither expressive nor ornamental.

With what absurd emotions (for we think the feelings that are very serious in a man quite comical in a boy) I found myself again going to Miss Havisham's matters little here.

Miss Sarah Pocket came to the gate. No Estella.

"How, then? You here again?" said Miss Pocket. "What do you want?"

When I said that I only came to see how Miss Havisham was, Sarah evidently deliberated whether or no she should send me about my business. But, unwilling to hazard the responsibility, she let me in, and presently brought the sharp message that I was to "come up."

Everything was unchanged, and Miss Havisham was alone. "Well!" said she, fixing her eyes upon me. "I hope you want nothing? You'll get nothing."

"No, indeed, Miss Havisham. I only wanted you to know that I am doing very well in my apprenticeship, and am always much obliged to you."

"There, there!" with the old restless fingers. "Come now and then; come on your birthday. Aye!" she cried suddenly, turning herself and her chair towards me, "You are looking round for Estella? Hey?"

I had been looking round—in fact, for Estella—and I stammered that I hoped she was well.

"Abroad," said Miss Havisham; "educating for a lady. Do you feel that you have lost her?"

There was such a malignant enjoyment in her utterance of the last words, and she broke into such a disagreeable laugh that I was at a loss what to say. She spared me the trouble of con-
3 sidering, by dismissing me. When the gate was closed upon me by Sarah of the walnut-shell countenance, I felt more than ever dissatisfied with my home and with my trade and with everything.

As I was loitering along the High Street, looking in disconsolately at the shop-windows, and thinking what I would buy if I were a gentleman, who should come out of the bookshop but Mr. Wopsle. Mr. Wopsle had in his hand the tragedy

AT A GLANCE

- Joe fights Orlick and wins.
- Pip goes to Miss Havisham's.
- Miss Havisham tells Pip that Estella is abroad.
- Pip wanders through town and sees Mr. Wopsle.

1 CONFLICT

Joe is forced into physical conflict with Orlick: Caught between his wife's hysterical demands and Orlick's fury, he has no choice but to fight.

2 READING SKILLS: COMPARISON AND CONTRAST

Pip compares Joe's and Orlick's fight with his own fight with the young gentleman. The outcome is the same, neither he nor Joe wanted to fight, and a woman plays a third part in each scene.

3 THEME

Because of his contact with Miss Havisham and Estella, Pip views his life (which had seemed full and satisfying) as a prison, too common to give him happiness.

GUIDED READING

LITERAL QUESTIONS

1a. What happens between Joe and Orlick? (They have a fight.)

2a. Where has Estella gone? Why? (abroad to learn to be a lady)

INFERENTIAL QUESTIONS

1b. Do you think Joe wanted to fight Orlick? (No; he tried to stop the argument with words but was forced to fight by the enmity between Mrs. Joe and Orlick.)

2b. Why does Miss Havisham enjoy telling Pip this? (She knows Pip misses Estella, and she is pleased that he is suffering.)

AT A GLANCE

- Mr. Wopsle reads aloud; Pip walks home from town with him.
- They meet Orlick, who says convicts have escaped.
- They learn that Mrs. Joe has been viciously attacked.

1 SETTING

The words *heavy, wet,* and *thick* create a sense of foreboding about Pip's journey.

2 STYLE: SATIRE

By mocking Mr. Wopsle, a minor clergyman who is "exalted" by his own reading, Dickens is satirizing those British clergy who preach only to hear themselves talk.

3 PLOT: NARRATIVE HOOK

Suspense has been building throughout Pip's homeward walk, and it peaks when Mr. Wopsle discovers that "there's something wrong" at the forge but cannot tell what.

4 BACKGROUND

The attack on Pip's sister is one of many crises in *Great Expectations:* Since the book was published a few chapters at a time, each group of chapters had to end with a miniclimax to maintain readers' interest in the next installment.

of George Barnwell, in which he had that moment invested sixpence, with the view of heaping every word of it on the head of Pumblechook, with whom he was going to drink tea. No sooner did he see me than he appeared to consider that a special Providence had put a 'prentice in his way to be read at. I don't know how long it may usually take; but I know very well that it took until half-past nine o'clock that night.

1 It was a very dark night when it was all over, and when I set out with Mr. Wopsle on the walk home. Beyond town, we found a heavy mist out, and it fell wet and thick. The turnpike[10] lamp was a blur. We were noticing this when we came upon a man, slouching under the lee[11] of the turnpike house.

''Halloa!'' we said, stopping. ''Orlick there?''

''Ah!'' he answered, slouching out. ''I was standing by, a minute, on the chance of company.''

''You are late,'' I remarked.

Orlick not unnaturally answered, ''Well? And *you*'re late.''

2 ''We have been,'' said Mr. Wopsle, exalted with his late performance, ''we have been indulging, Mr. Orlick, in an intellectual evening.''

Old Orlick growled, as if he had nothing to say about that, and we all went on together. I asked him presently whether he had been spending his half-holiday up and down town?

''Yes,'' said he, ''all of it. I come in behind yourself. I didn't see you, but I must have been pretty close behind you. By-the-bye, the guns is going again.''

''At the Hulks?'' said I.

''Aye! There's some of the birds flown from the cages. The guns have been going since dark, about. You'll hear one presently.''

Thus, we came to the village. The way by which we approached it took us past the Three Jolly Bargemen, which we were surprised to find—it being eleven o'clock—in a state of commotion, with the door wide open, and unwonted lights that had been hastily caught up and put down scattered about. Mr. Wopsle dropped in to ask what was the matter (surmising that a convict had been taken), but came running out in a great hurry.

3 ''There's something wrong,'' said he, without stopping, ''up at your place, Pip. Run all!''

''What is it?'' I asked, keeping up with him. So did Orlick, at my side.

''I can't quite understand. The house seems to have been violently entered when Joe Gargery was out. Supposed by convicts. Somebody has been attacked and hurt.''

We were running too fast to admit of more being said, and we made no stop until we got into our kitchen. It was full of people; the whole village was there, or in the yard; and there was a surgeon, and there was Joe, and there was a

4 group of women. I became aware of my sister—lying without sense or movement on the bare boards where she had been knocked down by a tremendous blow on the back of the head, dealt by some unknown hand when her face was turned towards the fire.

Chapter Thirteen

At home: After Mrs. Joe is struck down, Biddy takes over.

Joe had been at the Three Jolly Bargemen, smoking his pipe, from a quarter after eight o'clock to a quarter before ten. While he was there, my sister had been seen standing at the kitchen door and had exchanged good night with a farm-laborer going home. The man could not be more particular as to the time at which he saw her (he got into dense confusion when he tried to be) than that it must have been before nine. When Joe went home at five minutes

10. **turnpike:** road on which a toll must be paid.
11. **lee:** side that is protected from the wind.

GUIDED READING

LITERAL QUESTION

1a. What reason does Orlick give for waiting at the turnpike house? (He wanted company.)

INFERENTIAL QUESTION

1b. Why is this strange? (Orlick is usually solitary and avoids company.)

before ten, he found her struck down on the floor, and promptly called in assistance. The fire had not then burnt unusually low, nor was the snuff of the candle very long; the candle, however, had been blown out.

Nothing had been taken away from any part of the house. Neither, beyond the blowing out of the candle—which stood on a table between the door and my sister, and was behind her when she stood facing the fire and was struck—was there any disarrangement of the kitchen, excepting such as she herself had made, in falling and bleeding. But, there was one remarkable piece of evidence on the spot. She had been struck with something blunt and heavy, on the head and spine; after the blows were dealt, something heavy had been thrown down at her with con-
1 siderable violence, as she lay on her face. And on the ground beside her, when Joe picked her up, was a convict's leg-iron which had been filed asunder.

Now, Joe, examining this iron with a smith's eye, declared it to have been filed asunder some time ago. The hue and cry going off to the Hulks, and people coming thence to examine the iron, Joe's opinion was corroborated. They did not undertake to say when it had left the prison-ships to which it undoubtedly had once belonged, but they claimed to know for certain that that particular manacle had not been worn by either of two convicts who had escaped last night. Further, one of those two was already retaken, and had not freed himself of his iron.

Knowing what I knew, I set up an inference of my own here. I believed the iron to be my convict's iron—the iron I had seen and heard him filing at, on the marshes—but my mind did not accuse him of having put it to its latest use.
2 For, I believed one of two other persons to have become possessed of it, and to have turned it to this cruel account: either Orlick, or the strange man who had shown me the file.

Now, as to Orlick; he had gone to town exactly as he told us when we picked him up at the turnpike, he had been seen about town all the evening, he had been in divers[1] companies in several public-houses, and he had come back with myself and Mr. Wopsle. There was nothing against him, save the quarrel; and my sister had quarreled with him, and with everybody else about her, ten thousand times. As to the strange man, if he had come back for his two bank notes, there could have been no dispute about them, because my sister was fully prepared to restore them. Besides, there had been no altercation; the assailant had come in so suddenly that she had been felled before she could look round.

It was horrible to think that I had provided the weapon, however undesignedly, but I could
3 hardly think otherwise. I suffered unspeakable trouble while I considered and reconsidered whether I should at last dissolve that spell of my childhood and tell Joe all the story. For months afterwards, I every day settled the question finally in the negative. The secret was such an old one now that I could not tear it away.

4 The constables, and the Bow Street men from London—for, this happened in the days of the extinct red-waistcoated police—were about the house for a week or two, and did pretty much what I have heard and read of like authorities doing in other such cases.

My sister lay very ill in bed. Her sight was disturbed, so that she saw objects multiplied, and grasped at visionary tea-cups and wine-glasses instead of the realities; her hearing was greatly impaired; her memory also; and her speech was unintelligible. When, at last, she came round so far as to be helped downstairs, it was still necessary to keep my slate always by her, and she might indicate in writing what she could not indicate in speech. As she was (very bad handwriting apart) a more than indifferent speller, and as Joe was a more than indifferent reader, extraordinary complications arose between them, which I was always called in to

1. **divers** [dī′vərz]: various.

AT A GLANCE

- Mrs. Joe was struck with a convict's leg iron.
- Pip deduces that either Orlick or the strange man with the file did the deed.
- Mrs. Joe cannot see, speak, or move properly.

1 PLOT: RISING ACTION

The plot becomes yet more complicated when Pip learns of the leg iron that seems to link his convict to Mrs. Joe's assault and to Orlick.

2 RESPONSE JOURNAL

In their journals have the students write about who they think attacked Mrs. Joe. Encourage them to list all the evidence they can find that supports their choice.

3 CONFLICT

Pip realizes the weight of the secret he has kept for so many years about his convict and suffers "unspeakable trouble" in deciding if he should tell Joe about it.

4 IRONY

Dickens uses irony to describe the inefficiency of the police; by saying that they behave as others usually did in "such cases," he implicates a whole class of civil servants.

GUIDED READING

LITERAL QUESTIONS

1a. Does Pip believe his convict is guilty of hurting Mrs. Joe? (No)

2a. What does Pip decide about telling his secret to Joe? (He decides not to.)

INFERENTIAL QUESTIONS

1b. Why do you think he feels this way? (He trusts the convict, and he has two others to suspect.)

2b. Why does he make this decision? (The secret is so old he is almost comfortable with it; revealing it would create greater trouble than continuing to keep it to himself.)

AT A GLANCE

- Biddy moves in with the family.
- Mrs. Joe writes a sign on her slate; Biddy connects it with Orlick.
- Pip visits Miss Havisham again.

1 PARAPHRASING

When Pip says that Biddy's aunt "conquered a confirmed habit of living," he informs us that she died; Dickens uses this phraseology to make her death less solemn.

2 THEME

Joe's love is blind: His devotion to his wife is revealed when he mourns over the changes in her.

3 STYLE: REPETITION

Dickens repeats the phrase *Biddy looked thoughtfully* to emphasize the careful, intelligent consideration she gives to problems.

4 THEME

As Miss Havisham's life is marked by the passing of birthdays, so is Pip's; he looks forward to every birthday as a chance to visit Miss Havisham and hear news about Estella.

solve. The administration of mutton instead of medicine, the substitution of tea for Joe, and the baker for bacon, were among the mildest of my own mistakes.

However, her temper was greatly improved, and she was patient. A tremulous uncertainty of the action of all her limbs soon became a part of her regular state, and afterwards, at intervals of two or three months, she would often put her hands to her head, and would then remain for about a week at a time in some gloomy aberration[2] of mind. We were at a loss to find a suitable attendant for her, until a circumstance happened
1 conveniently to relieve us. Mr. Wopsle's great-aunt conquered a confirmed habit of living into which she had fallen, and Biddy became a part of our establishment.

It may have been about a month after my sister's reappearance in the kitchen when Biddy came to us with a small speckled box containing the whole of her worldly effects, and became a blessing to the household. Above all she was a
2 blessing to Joe, for the dear old fellow was sadly cut up by the constant contemplation of the wreck of his wife, and had been accustomed, while attending on her of an evening, to turn to me every now and then and say, with his blue eyes moistened, "Such a fine figure of a woman as she once were, Pip!" Biddy instantly taking the cleverest charge of her as though she had studied her from infancy, Joe became able in some sort to appreciate the greater quiet of his life, and to get down to the Jolly Bargemen now and then for a change that did him good.

Biddy's first triumph in her new office was to solve a difficulty that had completely vanquished me. I had tried hard at it, but had made nothing of it. Thus it was:

Again and again and again, my sister had traced upon the slate a character that looked like a curious T, and then with the utmost eagerness had called our attention to it as something she particularly wanted. I had in vain tried everything producible that began with a T, from tar to toast and tub. At length it had come into my head that the sign looked like a hammer, and on my lustily calling that word in my sister's ear, she had begun to hammer on the table and had expressed a qualified assent.

When my sister found that Biddy was very quick to understand her, this mysterious sign
3 reappeared on the slate. Biddy looked thoughtfully at it, heard my explanation, looked thoughtfully at my sister, looked thoughtfully at Joe (who was always represented on the slate by his initial letter), and ran into the forge, followed by Joe and me.

"Why, of course!" cried Biddy, with an exultant face. "Don't you see? It's *him!*"

Orlick, without a doubt! She had lost his name, and could only signify him by his hammer. We told him why we wanted him to come into the kitchen, and he slowly laid down his hammer, wiped his brow with his arm, took another wipe at it with his apron, and came slouching out.

I confess that I expected to see my sister denounce him, and that I was disappointed by the different result. She manifested the greatest anxiety to be on good terms with him, was evidently much pleased by his being at length produced, and motioned that she would have him given something to drink. After that day, a day rarely passed without her drawing the hammer on her slate, and without Orlick's slouching in and standing doggedly before her, as if he knew no more than I did what to make of it.

I now fell into a regular routine of apprenticeship life, which was varied, beyond the limits of the village and the marshes, by no more re-
4 markable circumstance than the arrival of my birthday and my paying another visit to Miss Havisham. I found Miss Sarah Pocket still on duty at the gate, I found Miss Havisham just as I

2. **aberration** [ab′ə rā′shən]: departure from the norm; here, mental lapse or disorder.

GUIDED READING

LITERAL QUESTIONS

1a. How has Mrs. Joe's temper changed as a result of the attack? (It is greatly improved.)

2a. How does Pip feel when Mrs. Joe confronts Orlick? (He is disappointed that she does not denounce or accuse.)

INFERENTIAL QUESTIONS

1b. Do you think Pip regrets these changes? (He probably feels both relief and guilt.)

2b. Why do you think Pip feels this way? (He is afraid of Orlick and considers him a suspect in the attack.)

had left her, and she spoke of Estella in the very same way, if not in the very same words. The interview lasted but a few minutes, and she gave me a guinea when I was going, and told me to come again on my next birthday. I may mention at once that this became an annual custom. I tried to decline taking the guinea on the first occasion, but with no better effect than causing her to ask me very angrily if I expected more? Then, and after that, I took it. So unchanging was the dull old house, it bewildered me, and under its influence I continued at heart to hate my trade and to be ashamed of home.

I became conscious of a change in Biddy, however. Her shoes came up at the heel, her hair grew bright and neat, her hands were always clean. She was not beautiful—she was common, and could not be like Estella—but she was pleasant and wholesome and sweet-tempered. I observed to myself one evening that she had curiously thoughtful and attentive eyes; eyes that were very pretty and very good.

It came of my lifting up my own eyes from a task I was poring at—writing some passages from a book, to improve myself in two ways at once by a sort of stratagem—and seeing Biddy observant of what I was about. I laid down my pen, and Biddy stopped in her needlework without laying it down.

"Biddy," said I, "how do you manage it? Either I am very stupid, or you are very clever."

"What is it that I manage? I don't know," returned Biddy, smiling.

She managed her whole domestic life, and wonderfully too; but I did not mean that, though that made what I did mean more surprising.

"How do you manage, Biddy," said I, "to learn everything that I learn, and always to keep up with me?" I was beginning to be rather vain of my knowledge, for I spent my birthday guineas on it, and set aside the greater part of my pocket-money for similar investment; though I have no doubt, now, that the little I knew was extremely dear at the price.

"I might as well ask you," said Biddy, "how *you* manage?"

"No; because when I come in from the forge of a night, any one can see me turning to at it. But you never turn to at it, Biddy."

"I suppose I must catch it—like a cough," said Biddy, quietly, and went on with her sewing.

Pursuing my idea as I leaned back in my wooden chair and looked at Biddy sewing away with her head on one side, I began to think her rather an extraordinary girl. For, I called to mind now that she was equally accomplished in the terms of our trade, and the names of our different sorts of work, and our various tools. In short, whatever I knew, Biddy knew. Theoretically, she was already as good a blacksmith as I, or better.

3 "You are one of those, Biddy," said I, "who make the most of every chance. You never had a chance before you came here, and see how improved you are!"

Biddy looked at me for an instant, and went on with her sewing. "I was your first teacher though, wasn't I?" said she, as she sewed.

"Biddy!" I exclaimed, in amazement. "Why, you are crying!"

"No I am not," said Biddy, looking up and laughing. "What put that in your head?"

What could have put it in my head but the glistening of a tear as it dropped on her work? I sat silent, recalling what a drudge[3] she had been until Mr. Wopsle's great-aunt successfully overcame that bad habit of living. I recalled the hopeless circumstances by which she had been surrounded in the miserable little shop and the miserable little noisy evening school, with that miserable old bundle of incompetence always to
4 be dragged and shouldered.

"Biddy," said I, after binding her to secrecy, "I want to be a gentleman."

---

3. **drudge** [drəj]: one who works hard at tedious and menial tasks.

AT A GLANCE

- Pip describes his annual visit to Miss Havisham's.
- He notices Biddy's looks and intelligence.
- He admits that he wants to be a gentleman.

1 THEME

Although he recognizes that she is "pleasant and wholesome and sweet-tempered," Pip labels Biddy "common" because she is not beautiful and is not like Estella; he does not understand the implications of her superiority to Estella.

2 POINT OF VIEW

The adult narrator admits that the knowledge he acquired was "extremely dear at the price"; he learned very little about what really matters, even though he spent all his pocket money on education.

3 STYLE: DIALOGUE

Pip's superior tone and words wound Biddy, who cares for him. His observation that she "never had a chance" before joining the family humiliates her.

4 BACKGROUND

Pip's goal is one that would be impossible in nineteenth-century English society under most circumstances: Social rank was determined by birth.

GUIDED READING

LITERAL QUESTIONS

1a. How does the visit to Miss Havisham affect Pip? (He is bewildered, ashamed of his home, and dissatisfied with his trade.)

2a. How does Biddy react to Pip telling her she has improved? (She cries.)

INFERENTIAL QUESTIONS

1b. Why is he affected this way? (He is still drawn to Estella and wants to fit into the world she represents.)

2b. Why does she cry? (She is hurt by his condescension.)

AT A GLANCE

- Pip admits that he wants to change for Estella's sake.
- Biddy is glad Pip can confide in her.
- Three years later, Pip notices a stranger in the pub.

1 THEME

Biddy, though uneducated, is aware that social status has little to do with happiness; she advises Pip to be content as he is.

2 CONFLICT

Pip identifies the conflict he feels within: He knows he should be content with Joe and Biddy, yet he is "dissatisfied and uncomfortable."

3 FORESHADOWING

Biddy predicts that if Pip were to become a gentleman he would no longer confide in her—a prediction that proves correct.

"Oh, I wouldn't, if I was you!" she returned. "I don't think it would answer."

1 "Biddy," said I, with some severity, "I have particular reasons for wanting to be a gentleman."

"You know best, Pip; but don't you think you are happier as you are?"

"Biddy," I exclaimed impatiently, "I am not at all happy as I am. I am disgusted with my calling and with my life. I have never taken to either since I was bound. Don't be absurd."

"Was I absurd?" said Biddy, quietly raising her eyebrows; "I am sorry for that; I didn't mean to be. I only want you to do well, and be comfortable."

"Well, then, understand once for all that I never shall or can be comfortable—or anything but miserable—there, Biddy!—unless I can lead a very different sort of life from the life I lead now."

"That's a pity!" said Biddy, shaking her head with a sorrowful air.

"If I could have settled down," I said, "and been but half as fond of the forge as I was when I was little, I know it would have been much better for me. You and I and Joe would have wanted nothing then, and Joe and I would perhaps have gone partners when I was out of my time, and I might even have grown up to keep company
2 with you. Instead of that, see how I am going on. Dissatisfied, and uncomfortable, and—what would it signify to me, being coarse and common, if nobody had told me so?"

"It was neither a very true nor a very polite thing to say," she remarked. "Who said it?"

I answered, "The beautiful young lady at Miss Havisham's, and she's more beautiful than anybody ever was, and I admire her dreadfully, and I want to be a gentleman on her account."

"Do you want to be a gentleman to spite her or to gain her over?" Biddy quietly asked me, after a pause.

"I don't know," I moodily answered.

"Because, if it is to spite her," Biddy pursued, "I should think—but you know best—that might be better and more independently done by caring nothing for her words. And if it is to gain her over, I should think—but you know best—she was not worth gaining over."

Exactly what I myself had thought, many times. Exactly what was perfectly manifest to me at the moment. But how could I, a poor dazed village lad, avoid that wonderful inconsistency into which the best and wisest of men fall every day?

"It may be all quite true," said I to Biddy, "but I admire her dreadfully."

"I am glad of one thing," said Biddy, "and that is that you have felt you could give me your confidence, Pip."

3 "Biddy," I cried, getting up, putting my arm around her neck, and giving her a kiss, "I shall always tell you everything."

"Till you're a gentleman," said Biddy.

Chapter Fourteen

In the village: Pip receives remarkable news.

It was in the fourth year of my apprenticeship to Joe, and it was a Saturday night. There was a group assembled round the fire at the Three Jolly Bargemen, attentive to Mr. Wopsle as he read the newspaper aloud. Of that group, I was one.

A highly popular murder had been committed, and Mr. Wopsle was imbrued in blood to the eyebrows. He gloated over every abhorrent adjective in the description, and identified himself with every witness at the inquest. He enjoyed himself thoroughly, and we all enjoyed ourselves, and were delightfully comfortable. In this cozy state of mind we came to the verdict of willful murder.

Then, and not sooner, I became aware of a strange gentleman leaning over the back of the settle opposite me, looking on.

GUIDED READING

LITERAL QUESTIONS

1a. What does Biddy say when Pip tells her he must lead a different life to be happy? (that it's a pity)

2a. How does Biddy react after Pip tells her that he admires Estella "dreadfully"? (She says she is glad Pip confides in her.)

INFERENTIAL QUESTIONS

1b. Why does she say this? (She believes Pip won't be truly happy and doesn't want to lose him.)

2b. How do you think she really feels? (She is probably hurt.)

The strange gentleman, with an air of authority not to be disputed, and with a manner expressive of knowing something secret about every one of us that would effectually do for each individual if he chose to disclose it, left the back of the settle, and came into the space between the two settles, in front of the fire, where he remained standing—his left hand in his pocket, and he biting the forefinger of his right.

"From information I have received," said he, looking round at us as we all quailed before him, "I have reason to believe there is a blacksmith among you, by name Joseph—or Joe—Gargery. Which is the man?"

"Here is the man," said Joe.

The strange gentleman beckoned him out of his place, and Joe went.

"You have an apprentice," pursued the stranger, "commonly known as Pip? Is he here?"

"I am here!" I cried.

The stranger did not recognize me, but I recognized him as the gentleman I had met on the stairs on the occasion of my second visit to Miss Havisham.

"I wish to have a private conference with you two," said he, when he had surveyed me at his leisure. "It will take a little time. Perhaps we had better go to your place of residence."

Amidst a wondering silence, we three walked out of the Jolly Bargemen, and in a wondering silence walked home.

2 It began with the strange gentleman's sitting down at the table, drawing the candle to him, and looking over some entries in his pocket-book. He then put up the pocket-book and set the candle a little aside, after peering round it into the darkness at Joe and me to ascertain which was which.

"My name," he said, "is Jaggers, and I am a lawyer in London. I am pretty well known. I have unusual business to transact with you, and I commence by explaining that it is not of my originating. If my advice had been asked, I should not have been here. It was not asked, and you see me here. What I have to do as the agent of another, I do. No less, no more."

"Now, Joseph Gargery, I am the bearer of an offer to relieve you of this young fellow, your

AT A GLANCE

- The stranger asks to speak to Pip and Joe at the forge.
- The stranger introduces himself as Jaggers, a London lawyer.
- Jaggers has an offer to "relieve" Joe of Pip.

1 PLOT: RISING ACTION

Pip's recognition of the stranger moves the plot forward by providing a link between past and present action.

2 MOOD

Dickens' description of the man's slow, deliberate movements and the candle in the darkness increases the scene's suspense.

GUIDED READING

LITERAL QUESTION

1a. What does Jaggers say about his part in the "unusual" business? (that he would not be there if his advice had been asked)

INFERENTIAL QUESTION

1b. What does he mean? (He seems not to approve of the "unusual business.")

AT A GLANCE

- Ascertaining that Joe will make no claims, Jaggers announces that Pip will come into property and must prepare to be a gentleman.
- Pip's benefactor is anonymous; Jaggers will be Pip's guardian.
- He informs Pip that he will be placed with a tutor.

1 PLOT: RISING ACTION

The suspense continues to mount as Pip learns that he may realize his dream. However, the source of his good fortune is still secret.

2 CONFLICT

Jaggers adds another secret to Pip's already heavy load: He is not to inquire about, nor to speculate upon, the name of the person who is his benefactor.

3 CHARACTERIZATION

Jaggers renders his services only because he is paid for them; he makes it clear that Pip is to do what he is told, and he changes the boy's whole life without any thought for Pip beyond that which he is paid to have.

apprentice. You would not object to cancel his indentures at his request and for his good? You would want nothing for so doing?''

''Lord forbid that I should want anything for not standing in Pip's way,'' said Joe, staring.

''Lord forbidding is pious, but not to the purpose,'' returned Mr. Jaggers. ''The question is, would you want anything? Do you want anything?''

''The answer is,'' returned Joe sternly, ''No.''

I thought Mr. Jaggers glanced at Joe as if he considered him a fool for his disinterestedness. But I was too much bewildered to be sure of it.

''Very well,'' said Mr. Jaggers. ''Recollect the admission you have made, and don't try to go from it presently.''

''Who's a-going to try?'' retorted Joe.

''I don't say anybody is. Do you keep a dog?''

''Yes, I do keep a dog.''

''Bear in mind then, that Brag is a good dog, but that Holdfast is a better. Bear that in mind, will you?'' repeated Mr. Jaggers, shutting his eyes and nodding his head at Joe, as if he were forgiving him something. ''Now, I return to this young fellow. And the communication I have got to make is that he has great expectations.''

Joe and I gasped, and looked at one another.

''I am instructed to communicate to him,'' said Mr. Jaggers, throwing his finger at me sideways, ''that he will come into a handsome property. Further, that it is the desire of the present possessor of that property that he be immediately removed from his present sphere of life and
1 from this place, and be brought up as a gentleman—in a word, as a young fellow of great expectations.''

My dream was out; my wild fancy was surpassed by sober reality; Miss Havisham was going to make my fortune on a grand scale.

''Now, Mr. Pip,'' pursued the lawyer, ''I address the rest of what I have to say to you. You are to understand, first, that it is the request of the person from whom I take my instructions that you always bear the name of Pip. You will have no objection, I dare say, to your great expectations being encumbered with that easy condition. But if you have any objection, this is the time to mention it.''

My heart was beating so fast, and there was such a singing in my ears, that I could scarcely stammer I had no objection.

''I should think not! Now you are to understand, secondly, Mr. Pip, that the name of the person who is your liberal benefactor remains a profound secret, until the person chooses to reveal it. I am empowered to mention that it is the intention of the person to reveal it at first hand by word of mouth to yourself. When or where that intention may be carried out, I can-
2 not say. It may be years hence. Now, you are distinctly to understand that you are most positively prohibited from making any inquiry. If you have a suspicion in your own breast, keep that suspicion in your own breast."

Once more, I stammered with difficulty that I had no objection.

''I should think not! Now, Mr. Pip, I have done with stipulations. We come next to mere details of arrangement. You must know that although I use the term 'expectations' more than once, you are not endowed with expectations only. There is already lodged in my hands a sum of money amply sufficient for your suitable education and maintenance. You will please consider me your guardian. Oh!'' for I was going to
3 thank him, ''I tell you at once, I am paid for my services, or I shouldn't render them. It is considered that you must be better educated, in accordance with your altered position, and that you will be alive to the importance and necessity of at once entering on that advantage.''

I said I had always longed for it.

''Never mind what you have always longed for, Mr. Pip,'' he retorted; ''keep to the record. If you long for it now, that's enough. Am I answered that you are ready to be placed at once under some proper tutor? Is that it?''

I stammered yes, that was it.

GUIDED READING

LITERAL QUESTIONS

1a. What does Mr. Jaggers say to Joe about dogs? (that Brag is a good dog but Holdfast is better)

2a. Whom does Pip believe has endowed him with his great expectations? (Miss Havisham)

INFERENTIAL QUESTIONS

1b. What does he mean? (He is telling Joe that actually sticking to one's position is of more value than speaking about one's intentions.)

2b. Why does he think this? (She is the only wealthy person he knows.)

"Good. Now, your inclinations are to be consulted. I don't think that wise, mind, but it's my trust. Have you ever heard of any tutor whom you would prefer to another?"

I had never heard of any tutor but Biddy, and Mr. Wopsle's great-aunt, so I replied in the negative.

"There is a certain tutor, of whom I have some knowledge, who I think might suit the purpose," said Mr. Jaggers. "I don't recommend him, observe; because I never recommend anybody. The gentleman I speak of is one Mr. Mathew Pocket."

Ah! I caught at the name directly. Miss Havisham's relation. The Matthew whom Mr. and Mrs. Camilla had spoken of. The Matthew whose place was to be at Miss Havisham's head, when she lay dead, in her bride's dress on the bride's table.

"You know the name?" said Mr. Jaggers, looking shrewdly at me, and then shutting up his eyes while he waited for my answer.

My answer was that I had heard of the name.

"Good. You had better try him in his own house. The way shall be prepared for you, and you can see his son first, who is in London. When will you come to London?"

I said (glancing at Joe, who stood looking on, motionless), that I supposed I could come directly.

"First," said Mr. Jaggers, "you should have some new clothes to come in, and they should not be working clothes. Say this day week.[1] You'll want some money. Shall I leave you twenty guineas?"

He produced a long purse, with the greatest coolness, and counted them out on the table and pushed them over to me. This was the first time he had taken his leg from the chair. He sat astride of the chair when he had pushed the money over, and sat swinging his purse and eyeing Joe.

"Well, Joseph Gargery? You look dumbfoundered!"

"I *am*!" said Joe, in very decided manner.

"It was understood that you wanted nothing for yourself, remember?"

"It were understood," said Joe. "And it are understood. And it ever will be similar according."

"But what," said Mr. Jaggers, swinging his purse, "what if it was in my instructions to make you a present, as compensation?"

"As compensation what for?" Joe demanded.

"For the loss of his services."

3 Joe laid his hand upon my shoulder. "Pip is that hearty welcome," said Joe, "to go free with his services, to honor and fortun', as no words can tell him. But if you think as money can make compensation to me for the loss of the little child—what come to the forge—and ever the best of friends!—"

Oh, dear good Joe, whom I was so ready to leave and so unthankful to, I see you again, with your muscular blacksmith's arm before your eyes, and your broad chest heaving, and your
4 voice dying away. Oh, dear good faithful tender Joe, I feel the loving tremble of your hand upon my arm, as solemnly this day as if it had been the rustle of an angel's wing!

Chapter Fifteen

At the scenes of his childhood: Pip says goodbye.

Putting on the best clothes I had, I went into town as early as I could hope to find the shops open, and presented myself before Mr. Trabb, the tailor, who was having his breakfast in the parlor behind his shop, and who did not think it worth his while to come out to me, but called me in to him.

"Well!" said Mr. Trabb, in a hail-fellow-well-met kind of way. "How are you, and what can I do for you?"

"Mr. Trabb," said I, "it's an unpleasant thing

---

1. **this day week:** one week from today; here, the following Saturday.

AT A GLANCE

- Jaggers recommends Mathew Pocket as a tutor.
- He gives Pip money for new clothes.
- Joe refuses compensation for Pip.
- Pip goes to the tailor.

1 CHARACTERIZATION

Jaggers doesn't think it wise that Pip is to be consulted about his future, revealing that he has his personal reservations about the way things are being handled.

2 THEME

Pip, who has been desperate for change for years, is ready to leave for London immediately; Joe, on the other hand, is "motionless," shocked by the speed of Pip's transformation.

3 THEME

Having been offered money by Jaggers, Joe claims that no amount can make up for the loss of Pip.

4 STYLE: FIGURATIVE LANGUAGE

Pip compares the touch of Joe's hand to the rustle of an angel's wing, a comparison that emphasizes the purity of Joe's spirit.

GUIDED READING

LITERAL QUESTIONS

1a. What does Jaggers think about consulting Pip's inclinations? (He thinks it is unwise.)

2a. How does Pip describe his feelings for Joe at the time? (He says he was ungrateful and ready to leave him.)

INFERENTIAL QUESTIONS

1b. Why does he think so? (He feels Pip does not know enough to make a judgment.)

2b. Why does he feel this way? (He is excited and eager to begin his new life in London.)

AT A GLANCE

- Pip orders clothes at Mr. Trabb's.
- Mr. Trabb fawns over Pip and abuses his assistant.
- Pip goes to Miss Havisham's to say good-by.

1 THEME

Mr. Trabb's treatment of Pip after learning of his expectations is hypocritical: He is respectful only because he thinks Pip is to become a gentleman. Pip, himself, seems to have adopted already a slightly pretentious attitude, as he "casually" shows his money.

2 THEME

Mr. Trabb abuses his assistant to make Pip feel respected; Trabb uses the boy in order to seem more important in Pip's eyes.

3 THEME

Pip gets his first taste of how money changes people's attitudes when he sees how Trabb's assistant is humiliated at his expense.

4 PLOT: FORESHADOWING

Pip's first purchase with his new wealth is a disappointment to him, foreshadowing his later feelings about money and other aspects of his "expectations."

to have to mention, because it looks like boasting, but I have come into a handsome property. I am going up to my guardian in London," said I, casually drawing some guineas out of my pocket and looking at them; "and I want a fashionable suit of clothes to go in. I wish to pay for them," I added—otherwise I thought he might only pretend to make them—"with ready money."

1 "My dear sir," said Mr. Trabb, as he respectfully bent his body, opened his arms, and took the liberty of touching me on the outside of each elbow, "don't hurt me by mentioning that. May I venture to congratulate you? Would you do me the favor of stepping into the shop?"

Mr. Trabb's boy was the most audacious boy in all that countryside. When I had entered he was sweeping the shop, and he had sweetened his labors by sweeping over me. He was still sweeping when I came out into the shop with Mr. Trabb, and he knocked the broom against all possible corners and obstacles to express (as I understood it) equality with any blacksmith, alive or dead.

"Hold that noise," said Mr. Trabb, with the greatest sternness, "or I'll knock your head off! Do me the favor to be seated, sir. Now, this," said Mr. Trabb, taking down a roll of cloth, and tiding it out in a flowing manner over the counter, preparatory to getting his hand under it to show the gloss, "is a very sweet article. I can recommend it for your purpose, sir, because it really is extra super. But you shall see some
2 others. Give me number four, you!" (To the boy, and with a dreadfully severe stare, foreseeing the danger of that miscreant's brushing me with it, or making some other sign of familiarity.)

Mr. Trabb never removed his stern eye from the boy until he had deposited number four on the counter and was at a safe distance again.

I selected the materials for a suit, with the assistance of Mr. Trabb's judgment, and re-entered the parlor to be measured. For, although Mr. Trabb had my measure already, and had previously been quite contented with it, he said apologetically that it "wouldn't do under existing circumstances, sir—wouldn't do at all." When he had at last done and had appointed to send the articles to Mr. Pumblechook's on the Thursday evening, he said, with his hand upon the parlor lock, "I know, sir, that London gentlemen cannot be expected to patronize local work, as a rule; but if you would give me a turn now and then in the quality of a townsman, I should greatly esteem it. Good morning, sir, much obliged. Door!"

3 The last word was flung at the boy, who had not the least notion what it meant. But I saw him collapse as his master rubbed me out with his hands, and my first decided experience of the stupendous power of money was that it had morally laid upon his back, Trabb's boy.

After this memorable event, I went to the hatter's, and the bootmaker's, and the hosier's. I also went to the coach-office and took my place for seven o'clock on Saturday morning.

So, Tuesday, Wednesday, and Thursday passed; and on Friday morning I went to Mr. Pumblechook's, to put on my new clothes and pay a visit to Miss Havisham. Mr. Pumblechook's own room was given up to me to dress in, and was decorated with clean towels expressly for the
4 event. My clothes were rather a disappointment, of course. Probably every new and eagerly expected garment ever put on since clothes came in fell a trifle short of the wearer's expectation.

I went circuitously to Miss Havisham's by all the back ways, and rang at the bell. Sarah Pocket came to the gate, and positively reeled back when she saw me so changed; her walnut-shell countenance likewise, turned from brown to green and yellow.

"You?" said she. "You? Good gracious! What do you want?"

"I am going to London, Miss Pocket," said I, "and want to say good-bye to Miss Havisham."

I was not expected, for she left me locked in the yard, while she went to ask if I were to be ad-

GUIDED READING

LITERAL QUESTIONS

1a. What does Trabb do after Pip chooses his suit materials? (He remeasures him.)

2a. How does Pip feel about his new clothes when he puts them on? (He is disappointed.)

INFERENTIAL QUESTIONS

1b. Why does he do this? (He finds old measurements good enough for a blacksmith's apprentice but believes new ones are necessary for a monied person.)

2b. Why does he feel this way? (They did not live up to his expectations.)

mitted. After a very short delay, she returned and took me up, staring at me all the way.

"I have come into such good fortune since I saw you last, Miss Havisham," I murmured. "And I am so grateful for it, Miss Havisham!"

"Aye, aye!" said she, looking at the discomfited and envious Sarah, with delight. "I have seen Mr. Jaggers. *I* have heard about it, Pip. So you go to-morrow?"

"Yes, Miss Havisham."

"And you are adopted by a rich person?"

"Yes, Miss Havisham."

"Not named?"

"No, Miss Havisham."

"And Mr. Jaggers is made your guardian?"

"Yes, Miss Havisham."

She quite gloated on these questions and answers, so keen was her enjoyment of Sarah Pocket's jealous dismay. "Well!" she went on; "you have a promising career before you. Be good—deserve it—and abide by Mr. Jaggers's instructions." She looked at me, and looked at Sarah, and Sarah's countenance wrung out of her watchful face a cruel smile. "Good-bye, Pip! You will always keep the name of Pip, you know."

Six days had run out fast and were gone. As the six evenings had dwindled away, I had become more and more appreciative of the society of Joe and Biddy. On this last evening, I dressed myself out in my new clothes for their delight. We were all very low, and none the higher for pretending to be in spirits.

Biddy was astir so early to get my breakfast that I smelt the smoke of the kitchen fire when I started up with a terrible idea that it must be late in the afternoon. But long after that, and long after I heard the clinking of the tea-cups and was quite ready, I wanted the resolution to go downstairs. After all, I remained up there, repeatedly unlocking and unstrapping my small portmanteau[1] and locking and strapping it up again, until Biddy called to me that I was late.

It was a hurried breakfast with no taste in it. I got up from the meal, saying with a sort of briskness, as if it had only just occurred to me, "Well! I suppose I must be off!" and then I kissed my sister, who was laughing, and nodding and shaking in her usual chair, and kissed Biddy, and threw my arms around Joe's neck. Then I took up my little portmanteau and walked out. The last I saw of them was when I presently heard a
3 scuffle behind me, and looking back, saw Joe throwing an old shoe after me and Biddy throwing another old shoe. I stopped then, to wave my hat, and dear old Joe waved his strong right arm above his head, crying huskily, "Hooroar!" and Biddy put her apron to her face.

The village was very peaceful and quiet, and the light mists were solemnly rising, as if to show me the world. In a moment with a strong heave and sob I broke into tears. It was by the finger-post at the end of the village, and I laid my hand upon it, and said, "Good-bye, O my dear, dear friend!"

So subdued I was by those tears that when I was on the coach, and it was clear of the town, I deliberated[2] with an aching heart whether I would not get down when we changed horses and walk back, and have another evening at home.

We changed again, and yet again, and it was now too late and too far to go back, and I went on. And the mists had all solemnly risen now, and the world lay spread before me.

This is the end of the first stage of Pip's expectations.

---

1. **portmanteau** [pôrt man′tō]: suitcase.
2. **deliberated** [di lib′ə rāt′id]: tried to decide.

AT A GLANCE

- Miss Havisham knows about his expectations.
- Pip prepares to leave home.
- Biddy and Joe bid him good-by; he leaves for London.

1 THEME

Miss Havisham uses Pip's good fortune to torture Sarah Pocket, who is disgruntled and jealous at the news.

2 CONFLICT

Pip feels the first pangs of loss as he prepares to go and has a brief desire to stay as he realizes what he is leaving behind.

3 THEME

Biddy and Joe reveal their true feelings for Pip when they bid him good-by and cheer his departure although they are saddened by his leaving.

REFLECTING ON CHAPTERS 9–15

Do you think Pip's tendency to look to the future is more likely to lead to happiness than Miss Havisham's tendency to live in the past? (Possible answers include: No, because expectations, as Pip has begun to learn, are rarely satisfied; Yes, because Pip can change, but Miss Havisham is trapped in her past.)

GUIDED READING

LITERAL QUESTIONS

1a. What does Pip say to Miss Havisham about his good fortune? (that he is grateful for it)

2a. How does Pip describe the rising mists? (He says the mists "were solemnly rising, as if to show me the world.")

INFERENTIAL QUESTIONS

1b. Why does he say this to her? (because he thinks she is the cause of his good fortune)

2b. What does he mean? (that the world is now spread before him; he feels he can do and be anything in the world now that he has money and "expectations")

STUDY QUESTIONS

1. long table covered with cloth; holds bridal cake covered with cobwebs, bugs, mice
2. Pip sees him through window, they box; Pip knocks him down, blackens his eye, wins fight; Pip offers help; boy leaves.
3. about Pip's being apprenticed; twenty-five guineas; as payment for his visits, as premium for taking Pip as apprentice
4.
   - Joe's journeyman
   - thinks he should be given one
   - Joe gives Orlick holiday, Orlick calls her "a foul shrew."
5. approached from behind, hit on head and spine; leg-iron; belonged to convict but used by Orlick
6. She is skeptical.
7. must always be called Pip; must not try to find out benefactor
8. is released from apprenticeship, acquires new clothes, moves to London
9. becomes dissatisfied with being blacksmith, embarrassed by Joe's ignorance and his own lack of education
10. He is honest, loves Pip, is shy and embarrassed with one from higher social class.
11.
    - He saw Mr. Jaggers at her house; she knows conditions of the arrangement.
    - They will be equal in station, may be intended to marry.
12. admires her wholesomeness, sweet temper, intelligence; thinks he would be better off in his own social class
13. Possible answers: should not be dissatisfied: has good home, loving friends, food, work; should be dissatisfied: has no opportunity for advancement or self-improvement

STUDY QUESTIONS

Recalling

1. Describe Miss Havisham's table and the objects on it in Chapter 10.
2. Describe Pip's encounter with the "pale young gentleman" in Chapter 10.
3. Why does Miss Havisham wish to see Joe in Chapter 11? What does she give him? Why?
4. According to Chapter 12, who is Orlick? Why is he upset at Pip's half-holiday? Why does Mrs. Joe become upset?
5. Describe the attack on Mrs. Joe in Chapter 13. What weapon was used? What does Pip imply about the weapon?
6. What is Biddy's reaction when Pip tells her that he wants to be a gentleman in Chapter 13?
7. Name two conditions attached to Pip's expectations in Chapter 14.
8. From Chapters 14 and 15 give two changes in Pip's life after he learns of his expectations.

Interpreting

9. In what ways does Pip's contact with Estella change his attitudes toward education, Joe, and being a blacksmith?
10. What do we learn about Joe's personality and his feelings for Pip from his meeting with Miss Havisham in Chapter 11?
11. Give two reasons that Pip assumes his new fortune comes from Miss Havisham. If he is correct about Miss Havisham, how may his relationship with Estella change?
12. How does Pip feel about Biddy? How does she feel about Pip and about his wanting to be a gentleman?

Extending

13. Do you think that Pip should be so dissatisfied with his life? Using Pip as an example, explain how such dissatisfaction can lead either to happiness or to misery.

LITERARY FOCUS

Plot and Conflict

At the heart of every plot is a **conflict**, or struggle between opposing forces. Conflicts can be internal or external. Since a novel is longer than a short story, a novel often has more than one plot and, therefore, more than one conflict. In addition to the main plot, a novel usually has at least one subplot. A **subplot** is a less important plot that is somehow related to the main action of a novel, story, or play. Each subplot is built around a conflict.

Thinking About Plot and Conflict

1. What is the main conflict within Pip so far in the novel?
2. Give one subplot in the novel so far. Identify the people or forces that are in conflict in this subplot.

LITERARY FOCUS

1. torn between his love for Joe and life he represents and the scorn he feels for same
2. relationship between Miss Havisham and relatives; feud between convicts; enmity between Mrs. Joe and Orlick

Chapter Sixteen

In London: We meet Jaggers again and Wemmick.

The journey from our town to the metropolis was a journey of about five hours. It was a little past midday when the four-horse stage-coach by which I was a passenger got into the ravel of traffic frayed out about the Cross Keys, Wood Street, Cheapside, London.

Mr. Jaggers had duly sent me his address; it was Little Britain, and he had written after it on his card, "just out of Smithfield, and close by the coach-office."

Mr. Jaggers's room was lighted by a skylight only, and was a most dismal place; the skylight, eccentrically patched like a broken head, and the distorted adjoining houses looking as if they had twisted themselves to peep down at me through it.

My guardian took me into his own room, and while he lunched, standing, from a sandwich-box and a pocket flask of sherry (he seemed to bully his very sandwich as he ate it), informed me what arrangements he had made for me. I was to go to "Barnard's Inn," to young Mr. Pocket's rooms, where a bed had been sent in for my accommodation; I was to remain with young Mr. Pocket until Monday; on Monday I was to go with him to his father's house on a visit, that I might try how I liked it. Also, I was told what my allowance was to be—it was a very liberal one—and had handed to me from one of my guardian's drawers the cards of certain tradesmen with whom I was to deal for all kinds of clothes, and such other things as I could in reason want.
2 "You will find your credit good, Mr. Pip," said my guardian. "Of course you'll go wrong somehow, but that's no fault of mine."

After I had pondered a little over this encouraging sentiment, I asked Mr. Jaggers if I could send for a coach. He said it was not worth

AT A GLANCE

- Pip visits Mr. Jaggers at his office in London.
- Mr. Jaggers gives Pip instructions on his new life.

LITERARY OPTIONS

- characterization
- setting
- dialogue

THEMATIC OPTIONS

- wealth and happiness
- secrecy
- self-awareness

1 SETTING

Mr. Jaggers' office, described as "dismal," and surrounded by "distorted" houses, reflects the lawyer's character: He has warped values and a distorted view of people.

2 PLOT: FORESHADOWING

While informing Pip that his credit will be honored, Mr. Jaggers predicts that Pip will "go wrong somehow," foreshadowing financial difficulties for Pip.

GUIDED READING

LITERAL QUESTION

1a. How does Pip describe the way Mr. Jaggers eats his sandwich? (He says Mr. Jaggers bullies his sandwich.)

INFERENTIAL QUESTION

1b. What does this tell you about Mr. Jaggers? (He seems to be a man who must be in control.)

AT A GLANCE

- Pip meets Mr. Wemmick, Jaggers' clerk.
- They journey to the younger Mr. Pocket's lodgings at Barnard's Inn.
- Wemmick leaves and Pip awaits Pocket's arrival.

1 READING SKILLS: DETAILS

The description of Mr. Wemmick ("dry," with a "square wooden face" and "glittering" eyes) is a study in contradictions and gives a clue to Wemmick's personality, which is equally contradictory.

2 STYLE: DIALOGUE

Mr. Wemmick's exclamation, "Rum to think of it now!" reveals a dissatisfaction with his present life and a willingness to open up to Pip, despite his dry talk and appearance.

3 THEME: WEALTH AND HAPPINESS

Pip is disappointed with his lodgings, and is beginning to learn that his expectations will not bring him everything he wants.

4 STYLE: DIALOGUE

Mr. Wemmick's confusion over shaking hands reveals that during his time in Mr. Jaggers' employ he has "got so out of" the habit of being friendly.

while, I was so near my destination; Wemmick should walk round with me, if I pleased.

I then found that Wemmick was the clerk[1] in the next room. Another clerk was rung down from upstairs to take his place while he was out, and I accompanied him into the street, after shaking hands with my guardian.

Casting my eyes on Mr. Wemmick as we went along, to see what he was like in the light of day,
1 I found him to be a dry man, rather short in stature, with a square wooden face, whose expression seemed to have been imperfectly chipped out with a dull-edged chisel. There were some marks in it that might have been dimples, if the material had been softer and the instrument finer. He had glittering eyes—small, keen, and black—and thin wide mottled lips. He had had them, to the best of my belief, from forty to fifty years.

"So you were never in London before?" said Mr. Wemmick to me.

"No," said I.

2 "*I* was new here once," said Mr. Wemmick. "Rum to think of now!"

"You are well acquainted with it now?"

"Why, yes," said Mr. Wemmick. "I know the moves of it."

"Is it a very wicked place?" I asked, more for the sake of saying something than for information.

"You may get cheated, robbed, and murdered in London. But there are plenty of people anywhere who'll do that for you."

"Do you know where Mr. Matthew Pocket lives?" I asked Mr. Wemmick.

"Yes," said he, nodding in the direction. "At Hammersmith, west of London."

"Is that far?"

"Well! Say five miles."

"Do you know him?"

"Yes, I know him. *I* know him!"

There was an air of toleration or depreciation about his utterance of these words that rather depressed me; and I was still looking sideways at his block of a face in search of any encouraging note when he said here we were at Barnard's Inn. I had supposed that establishment to be a hotel kept by Mr. Barnard, to which the Blue Boar in our town was a mere public-house. Whereas I now found his inn the dingiest collection of shabby buildings ever squeezed together in a rank corner.

3 So imperfect was this realization of the first of my great expectations that I looked in dismay at Mr. Wemmick. "Ah!" said he, mistaking me, "the retirement reminds you of the country. So it does me."

He led me into a corner and conducted me up a flight of stairs—which appeared to me to be slowly collapsing into sawdust, so that one of those days the upper lodgers would look out at their doors and find themselves without the means of coming down—to a set of chambers on the top floor. MR. POCKET, JUN., was painted on the door, and there was a label on the letter-box, "Return shortly."

"He hardly thought you'd come so soon," Mr. Wemmick explained. "You don't want me any more?"

"No, thank you," said I.

"As I keep the cash," Mr. Wemmick observed, "we shall most likely meet pretty often. Good day."

"Good day."

I put out my hand, and Mr. Wemmick at first looked at it as if he thought I wanted something. Then he looked at me, and said, correcting himself,

4 "To be sure! Yes. You're in the habit of shaking hands?"

I was rather confused, thinking it must be out of the London fashion, but said yes.

"I have got so out of it!" said Mr. Wemmick—"except at last. Very glad, I'm sure, to make your acquaintance. Good day!"

Mr. Pocket, Junior's, idea of shortly was not mine, for I had nearly maddened myself with

1. **clerk:** office worker who keeps records.

GUIDED READING

LITERAL QUESTIONS

1a. What does Mr. Wemmick say about Matthew Pocket? (He says, with an air of deprecation, that he knows him.)

2a. How does Pip feel about Barnard's Inn? (He is dismayed by its shabbiness.)

INFERENTIAL QUESTIONS

1b. Why does this depress Pip? (It implies that there is something wrong with Mr. Pocket.)

2b. Why does he feel this way? (He was expecting something grand and fine.)

looking out for half an hour, and had written my name with my finger several times in the dirt of every pane in the window, before I heard footsteps on the stairs. Gradually there arose before me the hat, head, neckcloth, waistcoat, trousers, boots, of a member of society of about my own standing. He had a paper bag under each arm and a pottle[2] of strawberries in one hand, and was out of breath.

"Mr. Pip?" said he.

"Mr. Pocket?" said I.

"Dear me!" he exclaimed. "I am extremely sorry; but I knew there was a coach from your part of the country at midday, and I thought you would come by that one. The fact is, I have been out on your account—not that that is any excuse—for I thought, coming from the country, you might like a little fruit after dinner, and I went to Covent Garden Market to get it good."

For a reason that I had, I felt as if my eyes would start out of my head. I acknowledged his attention incoherently, and began to think this was a dream.

As I stood opposite to Mr. Pocket, Junior, delivering him the bags, one, two, I saw the starting appearance come into his own eyes that I knew to be in mine, and he said, falling back:

"Lord bless me, you're the prowling boy!"

"And you," said I, "are the pale young gentleman!"

Chapter Seventeen

The first night in London: Pip finds a friend in Herbert Pocket and learns Miss Havisham's story.

The pale young gentleman and I stood contemplating one another until we both burst out laughing. "The idea of its being you!" said he. "The idea of its being *you!*" said I. And then we contemplated one another afresh, and laughed again. "Well!" said the pale young gentleman,

2 reaching out his hand good-humoredly, "it's all over now, I hope, and it will be magnanimous in you if you'll forgive me for having knocked you about so."

I derived from this speech that Mr. Herbert Pocket (for Herbert was the pale young gentleman's name) still rather confounded his intention with his execution.[1] But I made a modest reply, and we shook hands warmly.

"You hadn't come into your good fortune at that time?" said Herbert Pocket.

"No," said I.

"No," he acquiesced. "I heard it had happened very lately. *I* was rather on the lookout for good fortune then."

"Indeed?"

"Yes. Miss Havisham had sent for me, to see if she could take a fancy to me. But she couldn't—at all events, she didn't."

I thought it polite to remark that I was surprised to hear that.

3 "Bad taste," said Herbert, laughing. "but a fact. Yes, she had sent for me on a trial visit, and if I had come out of it successfully, I suppose I should have been provided for; perhaps I should have been what-you-may-called it to Estella."

"What's that?" I asked, with sudden gravity.

He was arranging his fruit in plates while we talked, which divided his attention, and was the cause of his having made this lapse of a word. "Affianced," he explained, still busy with the fruit. "Betrothed. Engaged. What's-his-named. Any word of that sort."

"How did you bear your disappointment?" I asked.

"Pooh!" said he, "I didn't care much for it. *She's* a Tartar."[2]

"Miss Havisham?"

"I don't say no to that, but I meant Estella. That girl's hard and haughty and capricious[3] to

---

2. **pottle:** pot that holds a half gallon.

1. **confounded . . . execution:** confused what he planned to do with what he actually did.
2. **Tartar** [tär′tər]: person who is not easily managed.
3. **haughty** [hô′tē] **and capricious** [kə prēsh′əs]: excessively proud and fickle.

AT A GLANCE

- Herbert Pocket returns; he is the "pale young gentleman."
- They apologize for their fight.
- Herbert explains he was at Miss Havisham's on a trial visit.

1 CHARACTERIZATION

On first meeting Pip, Herbert reveals that he has a thoughtful, generous nature; knowing Pip to be from the country, he has bought fruit to make him feel at home.

2 THEME: FRIENDSHIP

Pip and Herbert's friendship begins when Herbert offers to shake Pip's hand; Herbert is as open and sudden in friendship as he was in earlier conflict.

3 CHARACTERIZATION

Herbert's easygoing good nature is revealed when he speaks lightly of his failure to win Miss Havisham's approval and support.

GUIDED READING

LITERAL QUESTIONS

1a. Where has Herbert Pocket been while Pip was waiting? (to Covent Garden Market to find fresh fruit)

2a. How did Herbert react to being judged unacceptable for Estella? (He says he wasn't disappointed.)

INFERENTIAL QUESTIONS

1b. What does this tell you about Herbert? (that he is generous and thoughtful of others)

2b. Why was this Herbert's reaction? (He feels Estella is difficult and overly proud.)

AT A GLANCE

- Herbert hints at a dark secret in Miss Havisham's past.
- He tells Pip that Mr. Jaggers is Miss Havisham's lawyer.
- He explains his father's relationship to her.

1 STYLE: DIALOGUE

The conversation between Herbert and Pip about Miss Havisham hints at a secret in her past and builds suspense about her motivation for bringing up Estella as she did.

2 PLOT: CONFLICT

Although Pip wants to be open with Herbert, he must keep secret the subject of his guardianship, as promised.

the last degree, and has been brought up by Miss Havisham to wreak[4] revenge on all the male sex."

"What relation is she to Miss Havisham?"

"None," said he. "Only adopted."

1 "Why should she wreak revenge on all the male sex? What revenge?"

"Lord, Mr. Pip!" said he. "Don't you know?"

"No," said I.

"Dear me! It's quite a story, and shall be saved till dinner-time. And now let me take the liberty of asking you a question. How did you come there, that day?"

I told him, and he was attentive until I had finished, and then burst out laughing again, and asked me if I was sore afterwards? I didn't ask him if *he* was, for my conviction on that point was perfectly established.

"Mr. Jaggers is your guardian, I understand?" he went on.

"Yes."

"You know he is Miss Havisham's man of business and solicitor,[5] and has her confidence when nobody else has?"

2 This was bringing me (I felt) towards dangerous ground. I answered with a constraint I made no attempt to disguise, that I had seen Mr. Jaggers in Miss Havisham's house on the very day of our combat, but never at any other time, and that I believed he had no recollection of having ever seen me there.

"He was obliging as to suggest my father for your tutor, and he called on my father to propose it. Of course he knew about my father from his connection with Miss Havisham. My father is Miss Havisham's cousin; not that that implies familiar intercourse between them, for he is a bad courtier and will not propitiate her."[6]

Herbert Pocket had a frank and easy way with him that was very taking. I had never seen

4. **wreak** [rek]: inflict.

5. **solicitor** [sə lis′ə tər]: British lawyer who advises clients and presents cases in the lower courts.

6. **he is . . . her:** he is poor flatterer and will not try to win her approval.

GUIDED READING

LITERAL QUESTION

1a. Do Herbert's father and Miss Havisham have a warm relationship? (no)

INFERENTIAL QUESTION

1b. How do Pocket's feelings affect their relationship? (He is not willing to flatter Miss Havisham to earn her approval; thus, they have no contact.)

any one then, and I have never seen any one since, who more strongly expressed to me, in every look and tone, a natural incapacity[7] to do anything secret and mean. There was something wonderfully hopeful about his general air, and something that at the same time whispered to me he would never be very successful or rich. I don't know how this was.

"Will you do me the favor to begin at once to call me by my Christian name, Herbert?"

I thanked him, and said I would. I informed him in exchange that my Christian name was Philip.

"I don't take to Philip," said he, smiling. "Would you mind Handel[8] for a familiar name? There's a charming piece of music by Handel called 'The Harmonious Blacksmith.'"

"I should like it very much."

"Then, my dear Handel," said he, turning round as the door opened, "here is the dinner."

It was a nice little dinner—seemed to me then, a very Lord Mayor's Feast—with no old people by, and with London all around us.

We had made some progress in the dinner when I reminded Herbert of his promise to tell me about Miss Havisham.

"True," he replied. "I'll redeem it at once. Let me introduce the topic, Handel, by mentioning that in London it is not the custom to put the knife in the mouth—for fear of accidents—and that while the fork is reserved for that use, it is not put further in than necessary. It is scarcely worth mentioning, only it's as well to do as other people do. Also, the spoon is not generally used overhand, but under. This has two advantages. You get at your mouth better (which after all is the object), and you save a good deal of the attitude of opening oysters on the part of the right elbow."

He offered these friendly suggestions in such a lively way that we both laughed and I scarcely blushed.

"Now," he pursued, "concerning Miss Havisham. Miss Havisham, you must know, was a spoilt child. Her mother died when she was a baby, and her father denied her nothing. Her father was a country gentleman down in your part of the world. Mr. Havisham was very rich and very proud. So was his daughter."

"Miss Havisham was an only child?" I hazarded.

"Stop a moment, I am coming to that. No, she was not an only child; she had a half-brother. Her father privately married again—his cook, I rather think."

"I thought he was proud," said I.

"My good Handel, so he was. He married his second wife privately because he was proud, and in course of time *she* died. When she was dead, he first told his daughter what he had done, and then the son became a part of the family, residing in the house you are acquainted with. As the son grew, he turned out riotous, extravagant, undutiful—altogether bad. At last his father disinherited him; but he softened when he was dying, and left him well off, though not nearly so well off as Miss Havisham.

"Miss Havisham was now an heiress, and you may suppose was looked after as a great match.
2 Her half-brother had now ample means again, but with new madness, wasted them again. There were stronger differences between him and her than there had been between him and his father, and it is suspected that he cherished a deep and mortal grudge against her. Now, I come to the cruel part of the story.

"There appeared upon the scene—say at the races, or the public balls, or anywhere else you like—a certain man. I never saw him (for this happened five-and-twenty years ago, before you and I were, Handel), but I have heard my father mention that he was a showy man. This man

---

7. **incapacity** [in kə pas'ə tē]: inability.
8. **Handel** [hand'əl]: George Frederick Handel (1685–1759), German-born British composer.

AT A GLANCE

- Herbert gives Pip the nickname "Handel."
- Herbert advises Pip on his table manners.
- Herbert begins to tell Pip about Miss Havisham.

1 THEME: SELF-AWARENESS

Pip is given his first lesson in being a gentleman when Herbert gently advises him on the proper way to handle cutlery.

2 THEME: WEALTH AND HAPPINESS

Herbert's description of Miss Havisham's early life illustrates the fact that wealth does not lead to happiness: Miss Havisham was rich, but her doting father died and her half-brother hated her.

GUIDED READING

LITERAL QUESTIONS

1a. What nickname does Herbert give Pip? (Handel)

2a. How did Miss Havisham's brother feel toward her? (He carried "a deep and mortal grudge against her.")

INFERENTIAL QUESTIONS

1b. Why does he choose this name? (Handel wrote a piece of music called "The Harmonious Blacksmith," and Pip trained to be a blacksmith.)

2b. Why do you think he felt this way? (perhaps because she was her father's preferred child and inherited most of the money)

AT A GLANCE

- Miss Havisham loved a man who conspired with her brother.
- The man jilted her.
- Herbert explains that Estella is adopted.

1 THEME: PRIDE

Herbert's description of Miss Havisham as a woman "too haughty and too much in love to be advised by anyone" illustrates how her pride played a part in bringing about her downfall.

2 THEME: FREEDOM VS. IMPRISONMENT

The fact that Miss Havisham went into retirement at the moment she was jilted makes it clear that she is responsible for her own imprisonment in Satis House.

3 THEME: WEALTH AND HAPPINESS

It is thought that Miss Havisham's brother and lover conspired to cheat her out of a large amount of money. This conspiracy has wrought extreme emotional (as well as financial) trauma.

pursued Miss Havisham closely, and professed to be devoted to her. I believe she had not shown much susceptibility[9] up to that time, but all the susceptibility she possessed certainly came out then. There is no doubt that she idolized him.

"He got great sums of money from her, and he induced her to buy her brother out of a share in the brewery which had been left him by his father at an immense price, on the plea that when he was her husband he must hold and manage it
1 all. Your guardian was not at that time in Miss Havisham's councils, and she was too haughty and too much in love to be advised by any one. Her relations were poor and scheming, with the exception of my father. He was poor enough, but not time-serving or jealous. He warned her that she was doing too much for this man, and was placing herself unreservedly in his power. She took the first opportunity of angrily ordering my father out of the house, in his presence, and my father has never seen her since."

I thought of her having said, "Matthew will come and see me at last when I am laid dead upon that table."

"To return to the man, the marriage day was fixed, the wedding dresses were bought, the wedding tour was planned out, the wedding guests were invited. The day came, but not the bridegroom. He wrote a letter—"

"Which she received," I struck in, "when she was dressing for her marriage? At twenty minutes to nine?"

"At the hour and minute," said Herbert, nodding, "at which she afterwards stopped all the clocks. What was in it, further than that it most heartlessly broke the marriage off, I can't tell
2 you, because I don't know. When she recovered from a bad illness that she had, she laid the whole place waste, as you have seen it, and she has never since looked upon the light of day."

"Is that all the story?" I asked, after considering it.

3 "All I know of it. But I have forgotten one thing. It has been supposed that the man to whom she gave her misplaced confidence acted throughout in concert with her half-brother. It was a conspiracy between them; and they shared the profits."

"I wonder he didn't marry her and get all the property," said I.

"He may have been married already. Her cruel mortification[10] may have been a part of her half-brother's scheme," said Herbert. "Mind! I don't know that."

"What became of the two men?" I asked, after again considering the subject.

"They fell into deeper shame and degradation—if there can be deeper—and ruin."

"Are they alive now?"

"I don't know."

"You said just now that Estella was not related to Miss Havisham, but adopted. When adopted?"

Herbert shrugged his shoulders. "There has always been an Estella, since I have heard of a Miss Havisham. I know no more. And now, Handel," said he, finally throwing off the story as it were, "there is a perfectly open understanding between us. All I know about Miss Havisham, you know."

"And all I know," I retorted, "you know."

"I fully believe it. So there can be no competition or perplexity[11] between you and me. And as to the condition on which you hold your advancement in life—namely, that you are not to inquire or discuss to whom you owe it—you may be very sure that it will never be approached by me." He said it with so much meaning that I felt he as perfectly understood Miss Havisham to be my benefactress as I understood the fact myself.

I asked him, in the course of conversation, what he was? He replied, "A capitalist—an insurer of ships." I suppose he saw me glancing

9. **susceptibility** [sə sep′tə bil′ə tē]: ability to be affected or influenced.

10. **mortification** [môr tə fi kā′shən]: humiliation.

11. **perplexity** [pər plek′sə tē]: confusion, doubt.

GUIDED READING

LITERAL QUESTIONS

1a. What did Matthew Pocket tell Miss Havisham about her lover? (that she was doing too much for him and giving him too much power over her)

2a. Of what does Herbert assure Pip when they speak of Pip's benefactor? (that he will never inquire who it is)

INFERENTIAL QUESTIONS

1b. Why did Miss Havisham banish Matthew Pocket from her house? (She was proud and wanted no advice about her lover.)

2b. What does Pip infer from Herbert's assurance? (that Herbert knows Miss Havisham is his benefactor)

about the room in search of some tokens of shipping, or capital, for he added, "In the City."[12]

Again, there came upon me, for my relief, that odd impression that Herbert Pocket would never be very successful or rich.

"And the profits are large?" said I.

"Tremendous!" said he.

I wavered again, and began to think here were greater expectations than my own.

"I think I shall trade, also," said he, putting his thumbs in his waistcoat pockets, "to the West Indies, for sugar, tobacco, and rum. Also to Ceylon, especially for elephants' tusks."

"You will want a good many ships," said I.

"A perfect fleet," said he.

Quite overpowered by the magnificence of these transactions, I asked him where the ships he insured mostly traded to at present?

"I haven't begun insuring yet," he replied. "I am looking about me."

Somehow that pursuit seemed more in keeping with Barnard's Inn. I said (in a tone of conviction), "Ah-h!"

"Yes. I am in a counting-house,[13] and looking about me."

"Is a counting-house profitable?" I asked.

"To—do you mean to the young fellow who's in it?" he asked, in reply.

"Yes; to you."

"Why, n-no; not to me. But the thing is," said Herbert Pocket, "that you look about you. *That's* the grand thing. You are in a counting-house, you know, and you look about you."

Chapter Eighteen

Early days in London: We meet the rest of the Pocket family, Drummle, Startop, and the Aged Parent.

Mr. Pocket said he was glad to see me, and he hoped I was not sorry to see him. "For, I really am not," he added, with his son's smile, "an alarming personage." He was a young-looking
2 man, in spite of his very grey hair. There was something comic in his distraught way, as though it would have been downright ludicrous but for his own perception that it was very near being so. When he had talked with me a little, he said to Mrs. Pocket, with a rather anxious contraction of his eyebrows, which were black and handsome, "Belinda, I hope you have welcomed Mr. Pip?" And she looked up from her book, and said "Yes." She then smiled upon me in an absent state of mind, and asked me if I liked the taste of orange-flower water.

I found out within a few hours, and may mention at once, that Mrs. Pocket had grown up highly ornamental, but perfectly helpless and useless.

Mr. Pocket took me into the house and showed me my room; which was a pleasant one, and so furnished as that I could use it with comfort for my own private sitting-room. He then knocked at the doors of two other similar rooms, and introduced me to their occupants, by name Drummle and Startop. Drummle, and old-looking young man of a heavy order of architecture, was whistling. Startop, younger in years and appearance, was reading and holding his head, as if he thought himself in danger of exploding it with too strong a charge of knowledge.

In the evening there was rowing on the river. As Drummle and Startop had each a boat, I resolved to set up mine.

After two or three days, when I had established myself in my room and had gone backwards and forwards to London several times, and had ordered all I wanted of my tradesmen, Mr. Pocket and I had a long talk together. He knew more
3 of my intended career than I knew myself, for he referred to his having been told by Mr. Jaggers that I was not designed for any profession, and that I should be well enough educated for my destiny if I could "hold my own" with the

12. **the City:** downtown business district.
13. **counting-house:** accountant's office.

AT A GLANCE

- Herbert's ambition is to be an insurer of ships.
- Pip meets Matthew Pocket and his wife, and Drummle and Startop, two of the Pockets' lodgers.
- Pip moves into a room there.

1 CHARACTERIZATION

When Pip believes that Herbert will never succeed, he feels "relief," revealing an envious side of his nature.

2 THEME: SELF-AWARENESS

Pip describes Matthew Pocket as "comic," nearly "downright ludicrous," but since the man is aware of the figure he cuts, he avoids seeming ridiculous.

3 THEME: WEALTH AND HAPPINESS

Pip's expectations contain wealth enough so that he need not train for any specific profession; simply, he will receive enough education to "hold his own" in society.

GUIDED READING

LITERAL QUESTIONS

1a. What does Pip think of Herbert's business prospects? (that he will never be very rich or successful)

2a. What has Mr. Jaggers told Mr. Pocket about Pip's future? (that he is "not designed for any profession" but should be well educated)

INFERENTIAL QUESTIONS

1b. Why do you think Pip has this impression of Herbert? (Herbert seems more inclined to dream of success than to act.)

2b. What does this say about Mr. Jaggers' opinion of Pip? (that he doesn't feel Pip would perform well in a profession)

AT A GLANCE

- Pip decides to keep his room in Barnard's Inn.
- He asks Mr. Jaggers for money.
- Wemmick invites Pip to dine at his home.
- Pip describes Drummle and Startop.

1 STYLE: DIALOGUE

The conversation between Mr. Jaggers and Pip about money illustrates Pip's naiveté about financial matters.

2 THEME: MANIPULATION

Mr. Jaggers tries to confuse and fluster Pip by asking him, "What do you make of four times five?" and forcing him to answer before giving him money.

3 CHARACTERIZATION

Wemmick reveals that Mr. Jaggers likes to be thought of as contradictory and inscrutable, probably so he can keep clients nervous and afraid of him.

4 CHARACTERIZATION

In this description of Startop, Pip reveals his feelings about family life: He likes Startop because he is "devotedly attached" to his mother.

average of young men in prosperous circumstances.

When these points were settled, and so far carried out, it occurred to me that if I could retain my bedroom in Barnard's Inn, my life would be agreeably varied, while my manners would be none the worse for Herbert's society. Mr. Pocket did not object to this arrangement, but urged that before any step could possibly be taken in it, it must be submitted to my guardian. So I went off to Little Britain and imparted my wish to Mr. Jaggers.

"If I could buy the furniture now hired for me," said I, "and one or two other little things, I should be quite at home there."

"Go it!" said Mr. Jaggers, with a short laugh. "I told you you'd get on. Well! How much do you want?"

I said I didn't know how much.

1 "Come!" retorted Mr. Jaggers. "How much? Fifty pounds?"

"Oh, not nearly so much."

"Five pounds?" said Mr. Jaggers.

This was such a great fall that I said in discomfiture, "Oh! more than that."

"More than that, eh!" retorted Mr. Jaggers, lying in wait for me, with his hands in his pockets, his head on one side, and his eyes on the wall behind me; "how much more?"

"It is so difficult to fix a sum," said I, hesitating.

"Come!" said Mr. Jaggers. "Let's get at it. Twice five; will that do? Three times five; will that do? Four times five; will that do?"

I said I thought that would do handsomely.

"Four times five will do handsomely, will it?" said Mr. Jaggers, knitting his brows. "Now, what do you make of four times five?"

"What do I make of it!"

"Ah!" said Mr. Jaggers; "how much?"

"I suppose you make it twenty pounds," said I, smiling.

"Never mind what *I* make of it, my friend," observed Mr. Jaggers, with a knowing and con-
2 tradictory toss of the head. "I want to know what *you* make it."

"Twenty pounds, of course."

"Wemmick!" said Mr. Jaggers, opening his office door. "Take Mr. Pip's written order, and pay him twenty pounds."

As he happened to go out now, and as Wemmick was brisk and talkative, I said to Wemmick that I hardly knew what to make of Mr. Jaggers's manner.

3 "Tell him that, and he'll take it as a compliment," answered Wemmick; "he don't mean that you *should* know what to make of it."

He went on to say in a friendly manner:

"If at any odd time when you have nothing better to do, you wouldn't mind coming over to see me at Walworth, I could offer you a bed, and I should consider it an honor. I have not much to show you; but I have got a bit of garden and a summer-house."

I said I should be delighted to accept his hospitality.

Bentley Drummle, who was so sulky a fellow that he even took up a book as if its writer had done him an injury, did not take up an acquaintance in a more agreeable spirit. Heavy in figure, movement, and comprehension—in the sluggish complexion of his face, and in the large awkward tongue that seemed to loll about in his mouth as he himself lolled about in a room—he was idle, proud, and suspicious.

4 Startop had been spoiled by a weak mother, and kept at home when he ought to have been at school, but he was devotedly attached to her, and admired her beyond measure. He had a woman's delicacy of feature, and was—"as you may see, though you never saw her," said Herbert to me—"exactly like his mother." It was but natural that I should take to him much more kindly than to Drummle.

Herbert was my intimate companion and friend. I presented him with a half-share in my boat, which was the occasion of his often com-

GUIDED READING

LITERAL QUESTION

1a. How does Pip describe the way in which Mr. Jaggers questions him about money? (He says Jaggers was "lying in wait" for him.)

INFERENTIAL QUESTION

1b. What does Pip mean? (that Jaggers is like an animal ready to pounce; he was testing Pip)

ing down to Hammersmith; and my possession of a half-share in his chambers often took me up to London. We used to walk between the two places at all hours.

When I had been in Mr. Pocket's family a month or two, Mr. and Mrs. Camilla turned up. Camilla was Mr. Pocket's sister. Georgiana, whom I had seen at Miss Havisham's on the same occasion, also turned up. She was a cousin. These people hated me with the hatred of disappointment. As a matter of course, they fawned upon me in my prosperity with the basest meanness.

I had not seen Mr. Wemmick for some weeks, when I thought I would write him a note and propose to go home with him on a certain evening. He replied that it would give him much pleasure, and that he would expect me at the office at six o'clock. Thither I went, and there I found him, putting the key of his safe down his back as the clock struck.

"Did you think of walking down to Walworth?" said he.

"Certainly," said I, "if you approve."

"Very much," was Wemmick's reply, "for I have had my legs under the desk all day, and shall be glad to stretch them. Now I'll tell you what I've got for supper, Mr. Pip. I have got a stewed steak—which is of home preparation—and a cold roast fowl—which is from the cook's-shop. You don't object to an aged parent, I hope? Because I have got an aged parent at my place."

I then said what politeness required.

"So you haven't dined with Mr. Jaggers yet?" he pursued, as we walked along.

"Not yet."

"He told me so this afternoon when he heard you were coming. I expect you'll have an invitation to-morrow. He's going to ask your pals, too. Three of 'em; ain't there?"

Although I was not in the habit of counting Drummle as one of my intimate associates, I answered, "Yes."

With conversation Mr. Wemmick and I beguiled the time and the road, until he gave me to understand that we had arrived in the district of Walworth.

It appeared to be a collection of black lanes, ditches, and little gardens, and to present the aspect of a rather dull retirement. Wemmick's house was a little wooden cottage in the midst of plots of garden, and the top of it was cut out and painted like a battery mounted with guns.

"My own doing," said Wemmick. "Looks pretty, don't it?"

I highly commended it. I think it was the smallest house I ever saw, with the queerest Gothic[1] windows (by far the greater part of them sham), and a Gothic door, almost too small to get in at.

"That's a real flagstaff, you see," said Wemmick, "and on Sundays I run up a real flag. Then look here. After I have crossed this bridge, I hoist it up—so—and cut off the communication. You wouldn't mind being at once introduced to the Aged, would you? It wouldn't put you out?"

3 I expressed the readiness I felt, and we went into the castle. There, we found sitting by a fire, a very old man in a flannel coat—clean, cheerful, comfortable, and well cared for, but intensely deaf.

"Well, aged parent," said Wemmick, shaking hands with him in a cordial and jocose way, "how am you?"

"All right, John; all right!" replied the old man.

"Here's Mr. Pip, aged parent," said Wemmick, "and I wish you could hear his name. Nod away at him, Mr. Pip; that's what he likes. Nod away at him, if you please, like winking!"

"This is a fine place of my son's, sir," cried the old man, while I nodded as hard as I possibly could. "This is a pretty pleasure-ground, sir. This spot and these beautiful works upon it

1. **Gothic:** style of architecture characterized by pointed arches.

AT A GLANCE

- Pip meets Wemmick and walks home with him; Wemmick informs Pip that Mr. Jaggers will invite him to dine.
- Pip describes Wemmick's house and meets his father.

1 THEME: WEALTH AND HAPPINESS

Pip notes that Miss Havisham's relations, who were cruel to him when he lived with Joe, now fawn on him (though they hate and envy him, because of his new prosperity).

2 CHARACTERIZATION

Wemmick becomes more friendly and generous, pointing out that he has prepared steak and a fowl and talking about his aged parent, as soon as he is out of the office.

3 THEME: FAMILY

Pip describes the atmosphere of Wemmick's home by describing Wemmick's father: "clean, cheerful, comfortable, and well cared for"; again, he shows his inclination toward family life.

GUIDED READING

LITERAL QUESTION

1a. How do Miss Havisham's relatives now treat Pip? (They fawn on him.)

INFERENTIAL QUESTION

1b. Why do you behave this way? (because he is wealthy)

AT A GLANCE

- Pip and Wemmick dine, and Pip spends the night at Walworth.
- Mr. Jaggers invites Pip and his friends to dine.
- Mr. Jaggers immediately likes Drummle.
- Pip notes Mr. Jaggers' housekeeper.

1 THEME: SECRECY

Pip learns that the nature of Wemmick's home life is unknown to Mr. Jaggers; Wemmick asks Pip not to speak of it, adding another to Pip's list of secrets.

2 CHARACTERIZATION

The difference between Wemmick at home and Wemmick at the office is startling to Pip: At home Wemmick is warm, open, and loving, but as he walks to the office he gets progressively "dryer and harder."

3 READING SKILLS: COMPARISON AND CONTRAST

Mr. Jaggers' house, which is "dolefully in want of painting," reflects Jaggers' reluctance to pay for its upkeep; by contrast Wemmick's delightful home reflects its eccentric owner's pleasure in domesticity.

4 STYLE: DIALOGUE

Mr. Jaggers' and Pip's conversation, in which Mr. Jaggers says he likes Drummle, stresses Mr. Jaggers' contradictory nature: He likes a man whom he describes as "blotchy, sprawly, sulky."

ought to be kept together by the nation, after my son's time, for the people's enjoyment."

"Is it your own, Mr. Wemmick?"

"Oh, yes," said Wemmick, "I have got hold of it a bit at a time. It's a freehold,[2] by George!"

"Is it, indeed? I hope Mr. Jaggers admires it?"

"Never seen it," said Wemmick. "Never heard of it. Never seen the Aged. Never heard of
1 him. No; the office is one thing, and private life is another. When I go into the office, I leave the castle behind me, and when I come into the castle, I leave the office behind me. If it's not in any way disagreeable to you, you'll oblige me by doing the same. I don't wish it professionally spoken about."

There was a neat little girl in attendance, who looked after the Aged in the day. When she had laid the supper-cloth, the bridge was lowered to give her the means of egress, and she withdrew for the night. The supper was excellent.

Wemmick was up early in the morning, and I am afraid I heard him cleaning my boots. After that, he fell to gardening, and I saw him from my Gothic window pretending to employ the Aged, and nodding at him in a most devoted manner. Our breakfast was as good as the supper, and at half-past eight precisely we started for Little Bri-
2 tain. By degrees, Wemmick got dryer and harder as we went along, and his mouth tightened. At last, when we got to his place of business and he pulled out his key, he looked as unconscious of his Walworth property as if the castle and the drawbridge and the arbor and the lake and the fountain and the Aged had all been blown into space together.

Chapter Nineteen

London: At dinner with Mr. Jaggers, we meet Molly.

It fell out, as Wemmick had told me it would, that I had an early opportunity of comparing my guardian's establishment with that of his cashier and clerk. My guardian was in his room, washing his hands with his scented soap, when I went into the office from Walworth; and he called me to him, and gave me the invitation for myself and friends which Wemmick had prepared me to receive. "No ceremony," he stipulated, "and no dinner dress, and say tomorrow."

When I and my friends repaired[1] to him at six o'clock next day, he conducted us to Gerrard
3 Street, Soho, to a house on the south side of that street, rather a stately house of its kind, but dolefully in want of painting, and with dirty windows. He took out his key and opened the door, and we all went into a stone hall, bare, gloomy, and little used.

As he had scarcely seen my three companions until now—for he and I had walked together—he stood on the hearth-rug, after ringing the bell, and took a searching look at them. To my surprise, he seemed at once to be principally, if not solely, interested in Drummle.

"Pip," said he, putting his large hand on my shoulder and moving me to the window, "I don't know one from the other. Who's the spider?"

"The spider?" said I.

4 "The blotchy, sprawly, sulky fellow."

"That's Bentley Drummle," I replied; "the one with the delicate face in Startop."

Not making the least account of "the one with the delicate face," he returned, "Bentley Drummle is his name, is it? I like the look of that fellow."

He immediately began to talk to Drummle, not at all deterred by his replying in his heavy reticent way. I was looking at the two, when there came between me and them, the housekeeper, with the first dish for the table.

She was a woman of about forty, I supposed—but I may have thought her younger than she was. Rather tall, of a lithe nimble figure, ex-

2. **freehold:** land that can be left to heirs.

1. **repaired:** went.

GUIDED READING

LITERAL QUESTIONS

1a. How does Wemmick change as he reaches his office? (He becomes dry and hard.)

2a. How does Pip describe the hallway of Jaggers' house? (It is "a stone hall, bare, gloomy, and little used.")

INFERENTIAL QUESTIONS

1b. Why does he change? (He must be unemotional, impersonal, and hard in order to work for Jaggers.)

2b. What does this reveal about Mr. Jaggers? (that he seldom entertains and is neither hospitable nor inclined to think of others' comfort)

tremely pale, with large faded eyes, and a quantity of streaming hair. I cannot say whether any diseased affection of the heart caused her lips to be parted as if she were panting, and her face to bear a curious expression of suddenness and flutter.

She set the dish on, touched my guardian quietly on the arm with a finger to notify that dinner was ready, and vanished. I observed that whenever she was in the room, she kept her eyes attentively on my guardian, and that she would remove her hands from any dish she put before him, hesitatingly, as if she dreaded his calling her back. When we had got to the cheese, our conversation turned upon our rowing feats. The housekeeper was at that time clearing the table; my guardian, taking no heed of her, but with the side of his face turned from her, was leaning back in his chair, biting the side of his forefinger and showing an interest in Drummle that, to me, was quite inexplicable. Suddenly, he clapped his large hand on the housekeeper's, like a trap, as she stretched it across the table. So suddenly and smartly did he do this that we all stopped in our foolish contention.

"If you talk of strength," said Mr. Jaggers, "*I*'ll show you a wrist. Molly, let them see your wrist."

Her entrapped hand was on the table, but she had already put her other hand behind her waist: "Master," she said, in a low voice, with her eyes attentively and entreatingly fixed upon him, "don't."

"*I*'ll show you a wrist," repeated Mr. Jaggers, with an immovable determination to show it. "Molly, let them see your wrist."

"Master," she again murmured. "Please!"

"Molly," said Mr. Jaggers, not looking at her, but obstinately looking at the opposite side of the room, "let them see *both* your wrists. Show them. Come!"

He took his hand from hers, and turned that wrist up on the table. She brought her other hand from behind her, and held the two out side by side. The last wrist was much disfigured—
3 deeply scarred and scarred across and across. When she held her hands out, she took her eyes from Mr. Jaggers, and turned them watchfully on every one of the rest of us in succession.

"There's power here," said Mr. Jaggers, coolly tracing out the sinews with his forefinger. "Very few men have the power of wrist that this woman has. It's remarkable what mere force of grip there is in these hands."

While he said these words in a leisurely critical style, she continued to look at every one of us in regular succession as we sat. The moment he ceased, she looked at him again. "That'll do, Molly," said Mr. Jaggers, giving her a slight nod; "you have been admired, and can go."

Chapter Twenty

London: Joe pays Pip a visit.

MY DEAR MR. PIP,

I write this by request of Mr. Gargery, for to let you know that he is going to London in company with Mr. Wopsle and would be glad if agreeable to be allowed to see you. He would call at Barnard's Hotel Tuesday morning at nine o'clock, when if not agreeable please leave word. Your poor sister is much the same as when you left. We talk of you in the kitchen every night, and wonder what you
4 are saying and doing. If now considered in the light of a liberty, excuse it for the love of poor old days. No more, dear Mr. Pip, from

Your ever obliged, and affectionate servant,

BIDDY.

P.S. He wishes me most particular to write *what larks*. He says you will understand. I hope and do not doubt it will be agreeable to see him even though a gentleman, for you had ever a good heart, and he is a worthy worthy man. I

AT A GLANCE

- Mr. Jaggers forces Molly to show her scarred wrist.
- Biddy writes to tell Pip that Joe will visit London.

1 CHARACTERIZATION

The description of the housekeeper's uneasiness and hesitation before Mr. Jaggers makes it clear that she is terribly afraid of her employer.

2 THEME: MANIPULATION

Mr. Jaggers forces Molly to show her scarred wrist in order to humiliate and frighten her.

3 THEME: SECRECY

Although neither Mr. Jaggers nor Molly say anything revealing, it seems that the scars on Molly's wrists are part of a secret that she and Mr. Jaggers share.

4 THEME: WEALTH AND HAPPINESS

Biddy fears that her and Joe's nightly fond remembrances of Pip might be "considered in the light of a liberty," showing how their relationship with Pip has changed since he has come into money and has moved to London.

GUIDED READING

LITERAL QUESTIONS

1a. How does Molly's face look while she is serving dinner? (She parts her lips and has a nervous and fluttery expression.)

2a. What does Mr. Jaggers force Molly to do? (to show her scarred wrists to the dinner guests)

INFERENTIAL QUESTIONS

1b. What do you think makes Molly nervous? (the presence of Mr. Jaggers)

2b. Why do you think Mr. Jaggers does this? (He wants to humiliate and frighten her and to exercise control over her.)

AT A GLANCE

- Pip anticipates Joe's arrival with embarrassment.
- Joe visits Pip, who is ashamed.
- Joe explains that Wopsle has become an actor.
- Joe tells how Miss Havisham asked to speak to him.

1 CHARACTERIZATION

Pip's physical distance from Joe is accompanied by an emotional distance; he is now ashamed of Joe and "would have paid money" to avoid seeing him.

2 STYLE: SIMILE

Pip compares Joe shaking his hand to the priming of a pump, emphasizing Joe's country manners and roughness.

3 VOCABULARY: DIALECT

Joe says that Pip's friends are neither "backerder" nor "forarder," meaning that their health and fortunes have neither declined (moved backward) nor advanced (moved forward).

4 THEME: WEALTH AND HAPPINESS

Joe now calls Pip "sir," illustrating what a social and emotional wedge money has driven between two who were once equals.

have read him all excepting only the last little sentence, and he wishes me most particular to write again *what larks.*

I received this letter by post on Monday morning, and therefore its appointment was for next day. Let me confess exactly with what feelings I looked forward to Joe's coming.

1 Not with pleasure, though I was bound to him by so many ties; no; with considerable disturbance, some mortification. If I could have kept him away by paying money, I certainly would have paid money. As the time approached I should have liked to run away.

Presently I heard Joe on the staircase. I knew it was Joe by his clumsy manner of coming upstairs—his state boots being always too big for him—and by the time it took him to read the names on the other floors in the course of his ascent. When at last he stopped outside our door, I could hear his finger tracing over the painted letters of my name. I thought he never would have done wiping his feet, and that I must have gone out to lift him off the mat, but at last he came in.

"Joe, how are you, Joe?"

"Pip, how AIR you, Pip?"

2 With his good honest face all glowing and shining, and his hat put down on the floor between us, he caught both my hands and worked them straight up and down, as if I had been the last-patented pump.

"I am glad to see you, Joe. Give me your hat."

But Joe, taking it up carefully with both hands, like a bird's-nest with eggs in it, wouldn't hear of parting with that piece of property, and persisted in standing talking over it in a most uncomfortable way.

"Which you have that growed," said Joe, "and that swelled and that gentle-folked"—Joe considered a little before he discovered this word—"as to be sure you are a honor to your king and country."

"And you, Joe, look wonderfully well."

"Thank God," said Joe, "I'm ekerval to 3 most. And your sister, she's no worse than she were. And Biddy, she's ever right and ready. And all friends is no backerder, if not no forarder. 'Ceptin' Wopsle; he's had a drop."

All this time (still with both hands taking great care of the bird's-nest), Joe was rolling his eyes round and round the room, and round and round the flowered pattern of my dressing-gown.

"Had a drop, Joe?"

"Why, yes," said Joe, lowering his voice, "he's left the Church and went into the play-acting. Which the play-acting have likewise brought him to London along with me."

I took what Joe gave me, and found it to be the crumpled playbill of a small metropolitan theater, announcing the first appearance, in that very week, of "the celebrated provincial amateur, whose unique performance in the highest tragic walk of our national bard[1] has lately occasioned so great a sensation in local dramatic circles."

4 "Us two being alone, sir"—began Joe.

"Joe," I interrupted, pettishly, "how can you call me sir?"

"Well, sir," pursued Joe, "this is how it were. I were at the Bargemen t'other night, Pip, when there come up Pumblechook, and his word were, 'Joseph, Miss Havisham she wish to speak to you.' "

"Miss Havisham, Joe?"

" 'She wished,' were Pumblechook's word, 'to speak to you.' " Joe sat and rolled his eyes at the ceiling.

"Yes, Joe? Go on, please."

"Next day, sir," said Joe, looking at me as if I were a long way off, "having cleaned myself, I go and I see Miss A."[2]

"Miss A., Joe? Miss Havisham?"

"Which I say, sir," replied Joe, with an air of legal formality, as if he were making his will, "Miss A., or otherways Havisham. Her expres-

1. **our national bard:** William Shakespeare.
2. **Miss A:** Miss Havisham. Joe pronounces her name as "Avisham."

GUIDED READING

LITERAL QUESTIONS

1a. How does Pip feel when he learns Joe is coming to visit? (He is ashamed and displeased.)

2a. What does Joe do with his hat when Pip asks for it? (Joe insists on holding on to his hat while they talk.)

INFERENTIAL QUESTIONS

1b. Why does he feel this way? (He does not want his new friends to see Joe.)

2b. Why does Joe do this? (Pip is becoming a gentleman, and this makes Joe nervous.)

sion air then as follering: 'Mr. Gargery. You air in correspondence with Mr. Pip?' Having had a letter from you, I were able to say 'I am.' 'Would you tell him, then,' said she, 'that which Estella has come home, and would be glad to see him.' "

I felt my face fire up as I looked at Joe.

"Biddy," pursued Joe, "when I got home and asked her fur to write the message to you, a little hung back. Biddy says, 'I know he will be very glad to have it by word of mouth, it is holiday-time, you want to see him, go!' I have now concluded, sir," said Joe, rising from his chair, "and, Pip, I wish you ever well and ever prospering to a greater and greater height."

"But you are not going now, Joe?"

"Yes, I am," said Joe.

"But you are coming back to dinner, Joe?"

"No, I am not," said Joe.

Our eyes met, and all the "sir" melted out of that manly heart as he gave me his hand.

"Pip, dear old chap, life is made of ever so many partings welded together, as I may say, and one man's a blacksmith, and one's a whitesmith, and one's a goldsmith, and one's a coppersmith. Diwisions among such must come, and must be met as they come. If there's been any fault at all to-day, it's mine. You and me is not two figures to be together in London; nor yet anywheres else but what is private and understood among friends."

He touched me gently on the forehead, and went out. As soon as I could recover myself sufficiently, I hurried out after him and looked for him in the neighboring streets, but he was gone.

Chapter Twenty-one

A return to Satis House: Miss Havisham, Estella, and Orlick.

It was clear that I must repair to our town and in the first flow of my repentance it was equally clear that I must stay at Joe's. But when I had secured my box-place by to-morrow's coach, and had been down to Mr. Pocket's and back, I was not by any means convinced on the last point, and began to invent reasons and make
2 excuses for putting up at the Blue Boar. I should be an inconvenience at Joe's; I was not expected, and my bed would not be ready; I should be too far from Miss Havisham's, and she was exacting and mightn't like it. All other swindlers upon earth are nothing to the self-swindlers.

In the morning I was up and out. It was too early yet to go to Miss Havisham's, so I loitered into the country on Miss Havisham's side of town—which was not Joe's side.

I so shaped out my walk as to arrive at the gate at my old time. When I had rung at the bell with an unsteady hand, I turned my back upon the gate, while I tried to get my breath and keep the beating of my heart moderately quiet. I heard the side door open, and steps come across the court-yard; but I pretended not to hear, even when the gate swung on its rusty hinges.

Being at last touched on the shoulder, I started and turned. I started much more naturally, then, to find myself confronted by a man in a sober grey dress. The last man I should have expected to see in that place of porter at Miss Havisham's door.

"Orlick!"

"Ah, young master, there's more changes than yours. But come in, come in. It's opposed to my orders to hold the gate open."

I entered, and he swung it, and locked it, and took the key out. "Yes!" said he, facing round, after doggedly preceding me a few steps towards the house. "Here I am!"

"How did you come here?"

"I come here," he retorted, "on my legs. I had my box brought alongside me in a barrow."

"Are you here for good?"

"I ain't here for harm, I suppose."

I was not so sure of that. I had leisure to entertain the retort in my mind, while he slowly lifted his heavy glance from the pavement, up my legs and arms to my face.

AT A GLANCE

- Joe explains that Miss Havisham told him Estella has returned and wants to see Pip.
- Joe leaves Pip's house.
- Pip goes to see Estella.
- Orlick is now Miss Havisham's porter.

1 CHARACTERIZATION

Joe tells Pip that he and Pip are "not two figures to be together in London," showing that he is fully aware of the way in which Pip's wealth has changed their relationship.

2 POINT OF VIEW

Speaking from the distance of adulthood, Pip acknowledges that though he had excuses not to stay with Joe, he was nothing more than a "self-swindler" who was ashamed of his oldest friend.

GUIDED READING

LITERAL QUESTIONS

1a. What does Joe do after delivering his message? (He leaves Pip's rooms.)

2a. Where does Pip stay when he returns to visit Miss Havisham? (at the Blue Boar)

INFERENTIAL QUESTIONS

1b. Why doesn't Joe stay for dinner with Pip? (Joe feels that he should no longer keep friendly company with Pip.)

2b. Why does he stay there? (He doesn't want to stay at Joe's because he feels he has grown beyond it.)

AT A GLANCE

- Orlick explains how he came to work for Miss Havisham.
- Pip speaks briefly with Sarah Pocket.

1 **THEME: TIME**

Orlick reveals that he has fallen under the spell of Satis House when he says, "One day is so like another here"; like Miss Havisham, he is not aware of passing time.

2 **STYLE: DIALOGUE**

Sarah's words reveal that Matthew, who does not seek Miss Havisham's wealth, is well and happy; Sarah, who feels Matthew should fawn over Miss Havisham as she does, is "dismal."

"Then you have left the forge?" I said.

"Do this look like a forge?" replied Orlick, sending his glance all round him.

1 I asked him how long he had left Gargery's forge.

"One day is so like another here," he replied, "that I don't know without casting it up. It got about that there was no protection on the premises, and it come to be considered dangerous, with convicts and tag and rag and bobtail going up and down. And then I was recommended to the place as a man who could give another man as good as he brought, and I took it. It's easier than bellowsing and hammering."

"Well," said I, not desirous of more conversation, "shall I go up to Miss Havisham?"

"Burn me, if I know!" he retorted, "my orders ends here, young master. I give this here bell a rap with this here hammer, and you go on along the passage till you meet somebody."

At the end of the passage, while the bell was still reverberating, I found Sarah Pocket.

"Oh!" said she. "You, is it, Mr. Pip?"

2 "It is, Miss Pocket. I am glad to tell you that Mr. Pocket and family are all well."

"Are they any wiser?" said Sarah, with a dismal shake of the head; "they had better be wiser than well. Ah, Matthew, Matthew! You know your way, sir?"

I ascended now, in lighter boots than of yore, and tapped at the door of Miss Havisham's room. I heard her say immediately, "Come in, Pip."

She was in her chair near the old table, in the old dress, with her two hands crossed on her stick, her chin resting on them, and her eyes on the fire. Sitting near her, with the white shoe that had never been worn in her hand, and her head bent as she looked at it, was an elegant lady whom I had never seen.

GUIDED READING

LITERAL QUESTION

1a. Why did Orlick take the job at Miss Havisham's? (It gives him a chance to intimidate with his physical brawn and is easier than smithing.)

INFERENTIAL QUESTION

1b. What does this tell you about Orlick? (He is violent and lazy.)

"I heard, Miss Havisham," said I, rather at a loss, "that you were so kind as to wish me to come and see you, and I came directly."

"Well?"

The lady whom I had never seen before lifted up her eyes and looked archly at me, and then I saw that the eyes were Estella's eyes. But she was so much changed, was so much more beautiful that I slipped hopelessly back into the coarse and common boy again.

She gave me her hand. I stammered something about the pleasure I felt in seeing her again, and about my having looked forward to it for a long, long time.

"Do you find her much changed, Pip?" asked Miss Havisham, with her greedy look.

"When I came in, Miss Havisham, I thought there was nothing of Estella in the face or figure; but now it all settles down into the old—"

"What? You are not going to say into the old Estella?" Miss Havisham interrupted. "She was proud and insulting, and you wanted to go away from her. Don't you remember?"

I said confusedly that that was long ago, and that I knew no better then, and the like. Estella smiled with perfect composure, and said she had no doubt of my having been quite right, and of her having been very disagreeable.

"Is *he* changed?" Miss Havisham asked her.

"Very much," said Estella, looking at me.

"Less coarse and common?" said Miss Havisham, playing with Estella's hair.

Estella laughed, and looked at the shoe in her hand, and laughed again, and looked at me, and put the shoe down. She treated me as a boy still, but she lured me on.

It was settled that I should stay there all the rest of the day, and return to the hotel at night, and to London tomorrow. When we had conversed for a while, Miss Havisham sent us two out to walk in the neglected garden.

So Estella and I went out into the garden by the gate through which I had strayed to my encounter with the pale young gentleman, now Herbert; I, trembling in spirit and worshipping the very hem of her dress; she, quite composed and most decidedly not worshipping the hem of mine. As we drew near to the place of encounter, she stopped and said:

"I must have been a singular little creature to hide and see that fight that day—but I did, and I enjoyed it very much."

"You rewarded me very much."

"Did I?" she replied, in an incidental and forgetful way.

"He and I are great friends now."

"Are you? I think I recollect though, that you read with his father?"

"Yes."

"Since your change of fortune and prospects, you have changed your companions," said Estella.

"Naturally," said I.

"You had no idea of your impending good fortune in those times?" said Estella.

"Not the least."

"You must know," said Estella, condescending to me as a brilliant and beautiful woman
3 might, "that I have no heart—if that has anything to do with my memory. I am serious," she said, not so much with a frown (for her brow was smooth) as with a darkening of her face; "if we are to be thrown much together, you had better believe it at once."

There was no discrepancy of years between us to remove her far from me—we were of nearly the same age, but the air of inaccessibility which her beauty and her manner gave her tormented me in the midst of my delight.

At last we went back into the house, and there I heard, with surprise, that my guardian had come down to see Miss Havisham on business, and would come back to dinner. Estella left us to prepare herself.

Then, Estella being gone and we two left alone, she turned to me and said in a whisper:

"Is she beautiful, graceful, well-grown? Do you admire her?"

"Everybody must who sees her, Miss Havisham."

She drew an arm round my neck, and drew

AT A GLANCE

- Pip recognizes Estella.
- They walk in the garden; Estella warns him that she has no heart.
- Estella prepares herself for dinner.

1 CHARACTERIZATION

Pip's thin veneer of sophistication peels off, leaving him as tongue-tied as he was in his previous encounters with Estella.

2 STYLE: DIALOGUE

Miss Havisham's questions are part of her plan to have Pip love Estella and Estella break his heart.

3 THEME: SELF-KNOWLEDGE

Estella feels that she is heartless and warns Pip to "believe it at once," but, as the darkening of her face and her desire to warn him imply, she cares somewhat for Pip.

GUIDED READING

LITERAL QUESTIONS

1a. In what way has Estella changed? (She is older and more beautiful.)

2a. Of what does Estella warn Pip? (that she has no heart)

INFERENTIAL QUESTIONS

1b. In what way is she still the same? (She is still cold, unkind, and under Miss Havisham's control.)

2b. Do you think this is entirely true? (No; if it were, she would not feel compelled to warn him.)

AT A GLANCE

- Miss Havisham urges Pip to love Estella.
- Mr. Jaggers arrives at Satis House.
- Pip warns Mr. Jaggers that Orlick should not work for Miss Havisham; Mr. Jaggers agrees to fire Orlick.
- Pip returns to his rooms in London.

1 THEME: LOVE

In a "passionate whisper," Miss Havisham tells Pip her definition of love, which Pip takes to heart.

2 STYLE: DIALOGUE

Mr. Jaggers' conversation with Pip about Estella recalls their discussion of money: Again Mr. Jaggers is challenging Pip, trying to confuse him.

3 THEME: LOVE

When the action took place, Pip thought he experienced "high and great emotions" toward Estella; as an adult, Pip realizes that his love for Joe was a much nobler feeling and that his treatment of him was a great betrayal.

4 THEME: WEALTH AND HAPPINESS

Pip's ideas of friendship and loyalty have become corrupted, as illustrated by his sending Joe fish and oysters rather than visiting him.

my head close down to hers. "Love her, love
1 her, love her! I'll tell you," said she, in the same hurried passionate whisper, "what real love is. It is blind devotion, unquestioning self-humiliation, utter submission, trust and belief against yourself and against the whole world, giving up your whole heart and soul as I did!"

When she came to that, and to a wild cry that followed that, I caught her round the waist. For she rose up in the chair, in her shroud of a dress, and struck at the air as if she would as soon have struck herself against the wall and fallen dead.

All this passed in a few seconds. As I drew her down into her chair, I saw my guardian in the room.

Miss Havisham had seen him as soon as I, and was (like everybody else) afraid of him. She made a strong attempt to compose herself, and stammered that he was as punctual as ever.

"As punctual as ever," he repeated, coming up to us. "And so you are here, Pip?"

I told him when I had arrived, and how Miss Havisham wished me to come and see Estella. To which he replied, "Ah! Very fine young lady!" Then he pushed Miss Havisham in her chair before him, with one of his large hands, and put the other in his trousers-pocket as if the pocket were full of secrets.

2 "Well, Pip! How often have you seen Miss Estella before?" said he, when he came to a stop.

"How often?"

"Ah! How many times? Ten thousand times?"

"Oh! Certainly not so many."

"Twice?"

"Jaggers," interposed Miss Havisham, much to my relief, "leave my Pip alone, and go with him to your dinner."

He complied, and we groped our way down the dark stairs together.

"Pray, sir," said I, "may I ask you a question?"

"You may," said he, "and I may decline to answer it. Put your question."

"Estella's name, is it Havisham or—?" I had nothing to add.

"Or what?" said he.

"Is it Havisham?"

"It is Havisham."

At the Boar far into the night, Miss Havisham's words, "Love her, love her, love her!" sounded in my ears. I adapted them for my own repetition, and said to my pillow, "I love her, I love her, I love her!" hundreds of times.

3 I thought those were high and great emotions. But I never thought there was anything low and small in my keeping away from Joe, because I knew she would be contemptuous of him. It was but a day gone, and Joe had brought the tears into my eyes; they had soon dried—God forgive me!—soon dried.

After well considering the matter while I was dressing at the Blue Boar in the morning, I resolved to tell my guardian that I doubted Orlick's being the right sort of man to fill a post of trust at Miss Havisham's. "Why, of course he is not the right sort of man, Pip," said my guardian, comfortably satisfied beforehand on the general head, "because the man who fills the post of trust never is the right sort of man. Very good, Pip, I'll go round presently and pay our friend off." Rather alarmed by this summary action, I was for a little delay, and even hinted that our friend himself might be difficult to deal with. "Oh, no, he won't," said my guardian, "I should like to see him argue the question with *me.*"

The coach, with Mr. Jaggers inside, came up in due time, and I took my box-seat again, and arrived in London safe—but not sound, for my
4 heart was gone. As soon as I arrived, I sent a codfish and barrel of oysters to Joe (as reparation for not having gone myself), and then went on to Barnard's Inn. I found Herbert dining on cold meat, and delighted to welcome me back.

Dinner done, I said to Herbert, "My dear

GUIDED READING

LITERAL QUESTIONS

1a. With what words does Miss Havisham define love? (*blind devotion, unquestioning self-humiliation, utter submission, trust and belief against yourself and against the whole world*)

2a. How does Mr. Jaggers react to Pip's warning about Orlick? (He agrees.)

INFERENTIAL QUESTIONS

1b. What did this definition of love result in for Miss Havisham? (her present misery)

2b. What does Mr. Jaggers mean when he says, "the man who fills the post of trust never is the right sort of man"? (that he trusts no one)

Herbert, I have something very particular to tell you."

"My dear Handel," he returned, "I shall esteem and respect your confidence."

"It concerns myself, Herbert, and one other person. Herbert," said I, laying my hand upon his knee, "I love—I adore—Estella."

Instead of being transfixed, Herbert replied in an easy matter-of-course way, "Exactly. Well?"

"Well, Herbert. Is that all you say? Well?"

"What next, I mean?" said Herbert. "Of course I know *that*."

"How do you know it?" said I.

"How do I know it, Handel? Why, from you."

"I never told you."

"Told me! You have never told me when you have got your hair cut, but I have had senses to perceive it. You have always adored her, ever since I have known you."

I shook my head gloomily. "Oh! She is thousands of miles away from me," said I.

"Patience, my dear Handel—time enough, time enough. But you have something more to say?"

"I am ashamed to say it," I returned, "and yet it's no worse to say it than to think it. You call me a lucky fellow. Of course I am. I was a blacksmith's boy but yesterday; I am—what shall I say I am to-day? My dear Herbert, I cannot tell you how dependent and uncertain I feel, and how exposed to hundreds of chances and how unsatisfactory only to know so vaguely what they are!"

Chapter Twenty-two

London and its suburb Richmond: A visit with Estella.

One day when I was busy with my books and Mr. Pocket, I received a note by the post, the mere outside of which threw me into a great flutter; for though I had never seen the handwriting in which it was addressed, I divined whose hand it was. It had no set beginning, as Dear Mr. Pip, or Dear Pip, or Dear Sir, or Dear Anything, but ran thus:

> I am to come to London the day after to-morrow by the midday coach. I believe it was settled you should meet me? At all events Miss Havisham has that impression, and I write in obedience to it. She sends you her regard.
>
> —Yours, ESTELLA.

If there had been time, I should probably have ordered several suits of clothes for this occasion; but as there was not, I was fain to be content with those I had. My appetite vanished instantly, and I knew no peace or rest until the day arrived. Not that its arrival brought me either, for then I was worse than ever, and began haunting the coach-office in Wood Street, Cheapside, before the coach had left the Blue Boar in our town. For all that I knew this perfectly well, I still felt as if it were not safe to let the coach-office be out of my sight longer than five minutes at a time.

In her furred traveling-dress, Estella seemed more delicately beautiful than she had ever
3 seemed yet, even in my eyes. Her manner was more winning than she had cared to let it be to me before, and I thought I saw Miss Havisham's influence in the change.

We stood in the inn yard while she pointed out her luggage to me, and when it was all collected I remembered—having forgotten everything but herself in the meanwhile—that I knew nothing of her destination.

"I am going to Richmond," she told me. "Our lesson is that there are two Richmonds, one in Surrey and one in Yorkshire, and that

AT A GLANCE

- Pip admits his love for Estella to Herbert, who is not surprised.
- Pip receives a note from Estella saying she is coming to London.
- Estella arrives; Pip meets her.

1 STYLE: DIALOGUE

The conversation between Pip and Herbert, in which Herbert admits he is not surprised by Pip's love for Estella, reveals Herbert's sensitivity, intelligence, and powers of observation.

2 THEME: WEALTH AND HAPPINESS

Pip admits that his change of fortune leaves him feeling "dependent and uncertain"; he feels he is missing opportunities he doesn't recognize.

3 THEME: APPEARANCE VS. REALITY

Pip believes that Miss Havisham has Pip's best interests at heart and that she is working to promote a love match between himself and Estella.

GUIDED READING

LITERAL QUESTIONS

1a. What does Pip admit to Herbert? (that he loves Estella)

2a. At the end of Chapter Twenty-one, how does Pip say he feels? (dependent and uncertain)

INFERENTIAL QUESTIONS

1b. What does Pip mean when he says Estella is thousands of miles away from him? (both socially and emotionally Estella is inaccessible)

2b. Why does he feel this way? (He is not in control of his fate, and he doesn't know how he should act.)

AT A GLANCE

- Estella will live in Richmond, where she will be introduced into society.
- Estella reminds Pip of her warning not to love her but allows him to kiss her.
- Pip's extravagance begins to lead Herbert into debt.

1 THEME: MANIPULATION

Estella sees, as Pip does not yet, that they "have no choice . . . but to obey" those who control their lives and that they are constantly being manipulated.

2 STYLE: DIALOGUE

Estella says that their kiss was an instant of rebellion against the "fawners and plotters," not the romantic gesture that Pip supposed.

3 SETTING

The house at Richmond, described as *staid, ancient, formal and unnatural,* hints at the influence its inhabitants will have on Estella.

4 THEME: SELF-AWARENESS

Pip sees that his own extravagance has a negative effect on Herbert, who feels he must spend as lavishly as Pip does, though he cannot afford to.

mine is the Surrey Richmond. The distance is ten miles. I am to have a carriage, and you are to take me. This is my purse, and you are to pay my
1 charges out of it. Oh, you must take the purse! We have no choice, you and I, but to obey our instructions. We are not free to follow our own devices, you and I."

As she looked at me in giving me the purse, I hoped there was an inner meaning in her words. She said them slightingly, but not with displeasure.

"Where are you going to at Richmond?" I asked Estella.

"I am going to live," said she, "at a great expense, with a lady there, who has the power—or says she has—of taking me about, and introducing me, and showing people to me and showing me to people."

She gave me her hand playfully. I held it and put it to my lips.

"You ridiculous boy," said Estella, "will you
2 never take warning? Or do you kiss my hand in the same spirit in which I once let you kiss my cheek?"

"What spirit was that?" said I.

"I must think a moment. A spirit of contempt for the fawners and plotters."

"If I say yes, may I kiss the cheek again?"

"You should have asked before you touched the hand. But, yes, if you like."

I leaned down, and her calm face was like a statue's. "Now," said Estella, gliding away the instant I touched her cheek, "you are to take me to Richmond."

When we passed through Hammersmith, I showed her where Mr. Matthew Pocket lived, and said it was no great way from Richmond, and that I hoped I should see her sometimes.

"Oh, yes, you are to see me; you are to come when you think proper; you are to be mentioned to the family; indeed, you are already mentioned."

I inquired, was it a large household she was going to be a member of?

"No, there are only two; mother and daughter."

"I wonder Miss Havisham could part with you again so soon."

"It is a part of Miss Havisham's plans for me, Pip," said Estella, with a sigh, as if she were tired; "I am to write to her constantly and see her regularly, and report how I go on."

It was the first time she had ever called me by my name. Of course she did so purposely, and knew that I should treasure it up.

We came to Richmond all too soon, and our
3 destination there was a house by the green—a staid old house, where hoops and powder and patches, embroidered coats, rolled stockings, ruffles, and swords had had their court days many a time. Some ancient trees before the house were still cut into fashions as formal and unnatural as hoops and wigs and stiff skirts. A bell with an old voice sounded gravely in the moonlight. Estella gave me her hand and a smile, and said good night.

I got into the carriage to be taken back to Hammersmith, and I got in with a bad heart-ache, and I got out with a worse heart-ache.

Chapter Twenty-three

Back in the village: A sad occasion.

As I had grown accustomed to my expectations, I had insensibly begun to notice their effect upon myself and those around me. Their influence on my own character I disguised from my recognition as much as possible, but I knew
4 very well that it was not all good. Now, concerning the influence of my position on others, I was in no such difficulty, and so I perceived—though dimly enough perhaps—that it was not beneficial to anybody, and above all, that it was not beneficial to Herbert. My lavish habits led his easy nature into expenses that he could not afford, corrupted the simplicity of his life, and disturbed his peace with anxieties and regrets. I

GUIDED READING

LITERAL QUESTIONS

1a. According to Estella, why must she and Pip obey their instructions? (They have no choice: They are not free to follow their own devices.)

2a. What two unusual gratifications does Estella grant Pip? (She lets him kiss her, and she calls him by his name, Pip.)

INFERENTIAL QUESTIONS

1b. What "inner meaning" do you think Pip hopes Estella intends when she says this? (that love makes them captive)

2b. Why does she do this? (to bind him to her more closely)

began to contract a quantity of debt. I could hardly begin but Herbert must begin, too, so he soon followed.

At certain times I would say to Herbert, as if it were a remarkable discovery:

"My dear Herbert, we are getting on badly. Let us look into our affairs."

We shut our outer door on these solemn occasions in order that we might not be interrupted.

One evening, we heard a letter dropped through the slit in the said door and fall on the ground. "It's for you, Handel," said Herbert, going out and coming back with it, "and I hope there is nothing the matter." This was in allusion to its heavy black seal and border.

The letter was signed TRABB & CO., and its contents were simply that I was an honored sir, and that they begged to inform me that Mrs. J. Gargery had departed this life on Monday last at twenty minutes past six in the evening, and that my attendance was requested at the interment[1] on Monday next at three o'clock in the afternoon.

It was the first time that a grave had opened in my road of life, and the gap it made in the smooth ground was wonderful.[2] The figure of my sister in her chair by the kitchen fire haunted me night and day. That the place could possibly be without her was something my mind seemed unable to compass, and whereas she had seldom or never been in my thoughts of late, I had now the strangest idea that she was coming towards me in the street, or that she would presently knock at the door. In my rooms, too, with which she had never been at all associated, there was at once the blankness of death and a perpetual suggestion of the sound of her voice or the turn of her face or figure, as if she were still alive and had been often there.

1. **interment** [in tur'mənt]: burial.
2. **wonderful:** astonishing.

I could scarcely have recalled my sister with much tenderness. But I suppose there is a shock of regret which may exist without much tenderness. I was seized with a violent indignation against the assailant from whom she had suffered so much; and I felt that on sufficient proof I could have revengefully pursued Orlick, or any one else, to the last extremity.

Having written to Joe to offer him consolation, and to assure him that I would come to the funeral, I passed the intermediate days in the curious state of mind I have glanced at. I went down early in the morning, and alighted at the Blue Boar in good time to walk over to the forge.
3 It was fine summer weather again, and, as I walked along, the times when I was a little helpless creature, and my sister did not spare me, vividly returned. But they returned with a gentle tone upon them.

At last I came within sight of the house. Poor dear Joe was seated apart at the upper end of the room. When I bent down and said to him, "Dear Joe, how are you?" he said, "Pip, old chap, you know'd her when she were a fine figure of a—" and clasped my hand and said no more.

Biddy, looking very neat and modest in her black dress, went quietly here and there, and was very helpful. When I had spoken to Biddy, I went and sat down near Joe, and there began to wonder in what part of the house it—she—my sister—was. I became conscious of the servile Pumblechook in a black cloak and several yards of hatband. I then descried Mr. and Mrs. Hubble.

"Which I meantersay, Pip," Joe whispered me, "I would in preference have carried her to the church myself, along with three or four friendly ones wot come to it with willing harts and arms, but it were considered wot the neighbors would look down on such."

So, we all filed out two and two; Joe and I; Biddy and Pumblechook; Mr. and Mrs. Hubble.

And now the range of marshes lay clear before us, with the sails of the ships on the river growing out of it; and we went into the church-

AT A GLANCE

- A letter informs Pip that his sister has died.
- Pip returns home for the funeral.
- Biddy, Joe, the Hubbles, and Mr. Pumblechook are there.

1 STYLE: HUMOR

Although he is addressing a serious problem, Pip's recommendation that they look into their "affairs" is comic: Nothing ever comes of these overblown investigations.

2 THEME: LOSS

Pip finds himself oddly affected by his sister's death; he imagines her presence haunting him.

3 THEME: TIME

The years have cast Pip's memories in a more "gentle" light; although Mrs. Joe was truly wretched to him at times, he now thinks of her nostalgically.

GUIDED READING

LITERAL QUESTIONS

1a. How does Pip think and feel after his sister's death? (He imagines her haunting him; he feels a shock of regret and indignation against her attacker.)

2a. How did Joe want to bury Mrs. Joe? (by carrying her to the church with friends)

INFERENTIAL QUESTIONS

1b. Why do you think Pip's feelings are so strong? (He feels guilty for not loving his sister and regrets her injury and death.)

2b. Who do you think talked him out of it? Why? (probably Pumblechook, because he is obsessed with maintaining appearances and observing social proprieties)

AT A GLANCE

- Pip spends the night at his old home.
- Biddy will try to teach.
- She tells Pip she does not believe he will visit Joe.
- Pip returns to London.

1 CHARACTERIZATION

Pip now feels that he does a "great thing" by condescending to stay with Joe, a sentiment that underscores how his wealth has tapped an unpleasant part of his character.

2 STYLE: DIALOGUE

Biddy's flushed face and sudden outburst reveal that she resents Pip's condescension and wants to assure him that she can survive and prosper without his patronage.

3 THEME: TRUTH VS. HYPOCRISY

Pip finds he is "compelled to give up Biddy in despair" rather than face the unpleasant truth she has pointed out: She does not believe Pip will come to visit Joe.

REFLECTING ON CHAPTERS 16–23

In what ways has Pip changed since he was told of his "great expectations"? (Possible answer: He has become well mannered and educated, has neglected his old friends, and has become a snob.)

yard, close to the graves of my unknown parents, Philip Pirrip, Late of this Parish, and Also Georgiana, Wife of the Above. And there my sister was laid quietly in the earth while the larks sang high above it, and the light wind strewed it with beautiful shadows of clouds and trees.

When they were all gone, Biddy, Joe, and I had a cold dinner together. After dinner, I made him take his pipe, and I loitered with him about the forge, and we sat down together on the great
1 block of stone outside it. He was very much pleased by my asking if I might sleep in my own little room, and I, too, felt that I had done rather a great thing in making the request.

When the shadows of evening were closing in, I took an opportunity of getting into the garden with Biddy for a little talk.

"I suppose it will be difficult for you to remain here now, Biddy, dear?"

"Oh! I can't do so, Mr. Pip," said Biddy, in a tone of regret, but still of quiet conviction. "I have been speaking to Mrs. Hubble, and I am going to her to-morrow. I hope we shall be able to take some care of Mr. Gargery, together, until he settles down."

"How are you going to live, Biddy? If you want any mo—"

2 "How am I going to live?" repeated Biddy, striking in, with a momentary flush upon her face. "I'll tell you, Mr. Pip. I am going to try to get the place of mistress in the new school nearly finished here. I can be well recommended by all the neighbors, and I can be industrious and patient, and teach myself while I teach others."

"Biddy," said I, "I made a remark respecting my coming down here often, to see Joe, which you received with a marked silence. Have the goodness, Biddy, to tell me why."

"Are you quite sure, then, that you WILL come to see him often?" asked Biddy, stopping in the narrow garden walk, and looking at me under the stars with a clear and honest eye.

3 "Oh, dear me!" said I, as I found myself compelled to give up Biddy in despair. "This really is a very bad side of human nature! Don't say any more, if you please, Biddy. This shocks me very much."

Early in the morning, I was to go. Early in the morning, I was out, and looking in, unseen, at one of the wooden windows of the forge. There I stood for minutes looking at Joe, already at work with a glow of health and strength upon his face that made it show as if the bright sun of the life in store for him were shining on it.

"Good-bye, dear Joe! I shall be down soon and often."

"Never too soon, sir," said Joe, "and never too often, Pip!"

Biddy was waiting for me at the kitchen door, with a mug of new milk and a crust of bread. "Biddy," said I, when I gave her my hand at parting, "I am not angry, but I am hurt."

"No, don't be hurt," she pleaded, "let only me be hurt, if I have been ungenerous."

Once more, the mists were rising as I walked away. If they disclosed to me, as I suspect they did, that I should *not* come back, and that Biddy was quite right, all I can say is—they were quite right.

GUIDED READING

LITERAL QUESTION

1a. What are Biddy's plans for the future? (She will live with the Hubbles and try to get a position as a teacher in the new school.)

INFERENTIAL QUESTION

1b. Why is Biddy upset at Pip for asking how she will manage? (She feels Pip is being condescending and is implying that she cannot take care of herself.)

STUDY QUESTIONS

Recalling

1. According to Chapters 16 and 17, who is Herbert? When did Pip meet him before? How is he related to Miss Havisham and to Pip's tutor?
2. In Chapter 17 what explanation does Herbert give Pip about Miss Havisham's strange life? According to Herbert, what is Estella's role in life?
3. In Chapter 18 who are Drummle and Startop? What is Pip's opinion of each?
4. According to Chapter 18, who is Wemmick? Give two unusual details about his home. With whom does he live?
5. In Chapter 19 who is Molly? Give two unusual details about her.
6. Describe the contents of the three letters that Pip receives in Chapters 20, 22, and 23.
7. According to Chapter 21, what new job does Orlick have? What is Pip's reaction?
8. In Chapter 21 what warning does Estella give Pip about loving her?

Interpreting

9. To what extent do Pip's "great expectations" come true in London? Is Pip satisfied? Why or why not?
10. What new reasons does Pip have for thinking that Estella is intended for him? Do you agree with Pip? Why or why not?
11. In Chapter 23 why does Biddy doubt that Pip will visit? In what ways does Pip's behavior justify Biddy's opinion?

Extending

12. Mr. Pocket's aim is to educate Pip for no particular career but "to hold his own" in conversation with other young gentlemen. What do you think of this as an educational goal? What does this tell us about English society at the time?

LITERARY FOCUS

Characterization

Characterization is the personality of a character in a novel, short story, or play; it is also the method that an author uses to reveal this personality. Characterization can be **direct** – revealed through clear statements by the author – or **indirect** – revealed through the character's words and actions. Charles Dickens often indirectly reveals the personalities of characters in his novels by giving them names appropriate to their personalities or by using descriptive details that suggest personality. For example, Biddy's name suggests her good and simple nature, and Miss Havisham's wild appearance and the condition of her home make her eccentricity very clear.

Since a novel is longer than a short story, many characters in a novel will be **round characters,** characters who are complex, with many different personality traits. In addition, a good novelist does not present only **static characters**, characters who remain unchanged throughout the novel. Some characters in a good novel will change in the course of the novel; they are **dynamic characters**.

Thinking About Characterization

1. For each of the following characters, give one personality trait that we learn directly from Pip: Joe (Chapter 20), Biddy (Chapter 23), and Orlick (Chapter 21).
2. For each of the following, explain how we learn one personality trait from something the character says or does: Jaggers (Chapter 19), Estella (Chapter 22), and Wemmick (Chapter 18).
3. Explain how details of description reveal the personality of each of the following: the Aged Parent (Chapter 18), Drummle (Chapter 18), and Molly (Chapter 19).

STUDY QUESTIONS

1. Pip's roommate in London; as the pale young gentleman at Miss Havisham's; son of tutor, Miss Havisham's cousin
2. ■ She was swindled out of money and jilted by her fiancé; he sent letter as she was dressing for wedding; clocks were stopped the moment she received letter; her brother may have been involved.
   ■ Estella is to "wreak revenge on all the male sex."
3. Students of Matthew Pocket's; Drummle is disagreeable, Startop has delicate manner
4. Mr. Jagger's clerk and cashier; Gothic windows, door, flagpole, drawbridge; his father
5. Mr. Jagger's housekeeper; watches Jagger's nervously, has deeply scarred wrist
6. ■ Letter from Biddy says Joe is coming to London.
   ■ Estella says she is coming to London, and Pip is to meet her coach.
   ■ notice that Mrs. Joe has died
7. Havisham's gatekeeper; disturbed, as Orlick is not trustworthy
8. tells him she has no heart
9. has acquired the means by which he can become a gentleman; not really satisfied—wants better relationship with Estella and Joe, feels guilty
10. Miss Havisham tells him to love her, throws them together often; answers will vary.
11. realizes Pip is embarrassed by Joe; visits Miss Havisham, does not stop at forge
12. Dickens does not want readers to admire this goal; division between social classes was wide.

LITERARY FOCUS

1. *Joe:* honest; *Biddy:* neat, modest; *Orlick:* not trustworthy
2. *Jaggers:* can be cruel (forces Molly to show wrists); *Estella:* calculating (calls Pip by name, knowing how he will be affected); *Wemmick:* kind (looks after father)
3. *Aged Parent:* clean, cheerful, comfortable in appearance and disposition; *Drummle:* heavy in body and mind; *Molly:* pale, appears to be panting

AT A GLANCE

- Pip turns twenty-one and goes to see Mr. Jaggers.
- Mr. Jaggers informs Pip that he is in debt.
- Mr. Jaggers gives Pip a check for five hundred pounds, which will be the amount of Pip's annual maintenance.

LITERARY OPTIONS

- foreshadowing
- characterization
- irony

THEMATIC OPTIONS

- responsibility
- fortune and misfortune
- public institutions

1 CHARACTERIZATION

Mr. Jaggers again badgers Pip as if Pip were a witness. Mr. Jaggers is a character who remains static throughout the novel: manipulative, cold, and always "the lawyer."

2 STYLE: DIALOGUE

Mr. Jaggers, by forcing Pip to ask and answer questions, finally gets Pip to ask what Jaggers wants to reveal. Mr. Jaggers always manipulates to maintain control of the conversation.

3 BACKGROUND

Pip's check is for five hundred pounds, then the equivalent of about $2,500—at that time more than enough to live very comfortably for a year.

Chapter Twenty-four

London and Walworth: One expectation comes true and Pip helps Herbert.

Herbert and I went on from bad to worse, in the way of increasing our debts. But we had looked forward to my one-and-twentieth birthday for we had both considered that my guardian could hardly help saying something definite on that occasion.

I had taken care to have it well understood in Little Britain when my birthday was. On the day before it, I received an official note from Wemmick, informing me that Mr. Jaggers would be glad if I would call upon him at five in the afternoon of the auspicious[1] day. This convinced us that something great was to happen, and threw me into an unusual flutter when I repaired to my guardian's ofice.

In the outer office Wemmick offered me his congratulations, rubbed the side of his nose with a folded piece of paper that I liked the look of. It was November, and my guardian was standing before his fire leaning his back against the chimney-piece.

"Well, Pip," said he, "I must call you Mr. Pip to-day. Congratulations, Mr. Pip."

We shook hands—he was always a remarkably short shaker—and I thanked him.

1 "Now, my young friend," my guardian began, as if I were a witness in the box, "I am going to have a word or two with you."

"If you please, sir."

"What do you suppose you are living at the rate of?"

I confessed myself quite unable to answer the question. This reply seemed agreeable to Mr. Jaggers, who said, "I thought so!" and blew his nose with an air of satisfaction.

"Now, I have asked *you* a question, my friend," said Mr. Jaggers. "Have you anything to ask *me*?"

"Of course it would be a great relief to me to ask you several questions, sir; but I remember your prohibition."

"Ask one," said Mr. Jaggers.

"Is my benefactor to be made known to me to-day?"

"No. Ask another."

"Is that confidence to be imparted to me soon?"

2 "Waive that, a moment," said Mr. Jaggers, "and ask another."

I looked about me, but there appeared to be now no possible escape from the inquiry, "Have—I—anything to receive, sir?" On that, Mr. Jaggers said triumphantly, "I thought we should come to it!" and called to Wemmick to give him that piece of paper. Wemmick appeared, handed it in, and disappeared.

"Now, Mr. Pip," said Mr. Jaggers, "attend if you please. You have been drawing pretty freely here; your name occurs pretty often in Wemmick's cash-book: but you are in debt, of course?"

"I am afraid I must say yes, sir."

"You know you must say yes, don't you?" said Mr. Jaggers.

"Yes, sir."

"I don't ask you what you owe, because you don't know; and if you did know, you wouldn't tell me; you would say less. Yes, yes, my friend," cried Mr. Jaggers, waving his forefinger to stop me, as I made a show of protesting.

3 "This is a bank-note," said I, "for five hundred pounds."

"You consider it, undoubtedly, a handsome sum of money. Now, that handsome sum of money, Pip, is your own. It is a present to you on this day, in earnest of your expectations. And at the rate of that handsome sum of money per annum,[2] and at no higher rate, you are to live until the donor of the whole appears. That is to say, you will now take your money affairs entirely

1. **auspicious** [ôs pish′əs]: promising.

2. **per annum:** Latin for "yearly."

GUIDED READING

LITERAL QUESTIONS

1a. Why does Pip look forward to his twenty-first birthday? (He hopes Mr. Jaggers will "say something definite on that occasion.")

2a. How does Mr. Jaggers react when Pip admits he is in debt? (He seems pleased and satisfied.)

INFERENTIAL QUESTIONS

1b. What do you think Pip wants Mr. Jaggers to say? (He wants to learn for certain who his benefactor is.)

2b. Why does he react this way? (He wants people to conform to his ideas of them, and he has labeled Pip a spendthrift.)

1 into your own hands, and you will draw from Wemmick one hundred and twenty-five pounds per quarter, until you are in communication with the fountain-head,[3] and no longer with the mere agent."

I was beginning to express my gratitude to my benefactor for the great liberality with which I was treated, when Mr. Jaggers stopped me. "I am not paid, Pip," said he coolly, "to carry your words to any one."

I said, after hestitating, "that my patron, the fountain-head you have spoken of, Mr. Jaggers, will soon—" there I delicately stopped.

"Come!" said Mr. Jaggers. "That's a question I must not be asked. When that person discloses, you and that person will settle your own affairs."

We looked at one another until I withdrew my eyes, and looked thoughtfully at the floor. From this last speech I derived the notion that Miss Havisham, for some reason or no reason, had not taken him into her confidence as to her designing me for Estella.

"If that is all you have to say, sir," I remarked, "there can be nothing left for me to say."

I said I would go into the outer office and talk to Wemmick. The fact was that when the five hundred pounds had come into my pocket, a thought had come into my head which had been often there before; and it appeared to me that Wemmick was a good person to advise with, concerning such thought.

He had already locked up his safe, and made preparations for going home. He had left his desk, brought out his two greasy office candlesticks and stood them in line with the snuffers on a slab near the door, ready to be extinguished; he had raked his fire low, put his hat and great-coat ready.

2 "Mr. Wemmick," said I, "I want to ask your opinion. I am very desirous to serve a friend."

Wemmick shook his head, as if his opinion were dead against any fatal weakness of that sort.

3 "This friend," I pursued, "is trying to get on in commercial life but has no money, and finds it difficult and disheartening to make a beginning. Now, I want somehow to help him to a beginning."

"With money down?" said Wemmick, in a tone drier than any sawdust.

"With *some* money down," I replied, for an uneasy remembrance shot across me of that symmetrical bundle of papers at home; "with *some* money down, and perhaps some anticipation of my expectations."

"Mr. Pip," said Wemmick, "I should like just to run over with you on my fingers, if you please, the names of the various bridges up as high as Chelsea Reach. Let's see; there's London, one; Southwark, two; Blackfriars, three; Waterloo, four; Westminster, five; Vauxhall, six." He had checked off each bridge in its turn, with the handle of his safe-key on the palm of his hand. "There's as many as six, you see, to choose from."

"I don't understand you," said I.

"Choose your bridge, Mr. Pip," returned Wemmick, "and take a walk upon your bridge, and pitch your money into the Thames[4] over the center arch of your bridge, and you know the end of it. Serve a friend with it, and you may know the end of it, too—but it's a less pleasant and profitable end."

"This is very discouraging," said I.

"Meant to be so," said Wemmick.

"Then is it your opinion," I inquired, with some little indignation, "that a man should never—?"

"—Invest portable property in a friend?" said Wemmick. "Certainly he should not. Unless he wants to get rid of the friend—and then it becomes a question how much portable property it may be worth to get rid of him."

3. **fountain-head:** source.

4. **Thames** [temz]: river that flows through London.

AT A GLANCE

- Mr. Jaggers reiterates that Pip may not yet learn the identity of his benefactor.
- Pip asks Wemmick for advice.
- Wemmick advises against investing money in a friend.

1 THEME: RESPONSIBILITY

For the first time Pip is given the responsibility to handle a portion of his own life: He must control his finances.

2 CHARACTERIZATION

Pip shows a new aspect of his personality when he seriously considers using some of his money to help a friend.

3 THEME: WEALTH AND HAPPINESS

Pip is intrigued both by the opportunity to do good and to use the money to change the course of events by helping his friend make "a beginning."

GUIDED READING

LITERAL QUESTIONS

1a. Why does Pip say he wants to help a friend? (because the friend has no money and finds it difficult to set up in business)

2a. What does Wemmick advise Pip to do? (to throw his money off a bridge rather than help a friend)

INFERENTIAL QUESTIONS

1b. What friend do you think Pip wants to help? (Herbert)

2b. Why does Wemmick advise this? (He feels that one loses friends by giving them money.)

AT A GLANCE

- Pip realizes that Wemmick's attitude reflects the office's tone.
- At Walworth they arrange to start Herbert in business.
- Pip describes Estella's stay at Richmond.

1 CHARACTERIZATION

Wemmick reveals two distinct sides to his personality when he says "Walworth is one place, and this office is another"; Wemmick behaves differently in each setting.

2 THEME: SECRECY

For the first time Pip has a pleasant secret to keep, one that concerns his setting up Herbert in business.

3 THEME: WEALTH AND HAPPINESS

Pip is learning the power he has to do good and the positive feeling he gets from helping others.

4 CHARACTERIZATION

Estella's "sudden check" in her habitual uncaring tone toward Pip reveals her confusion over the role she has been playing.

"And that," said I, "is your deliberate opinion, Mr. Wemmick?"

"That," he returned, "is my deliberate opinion in this office."

"Ah!" said I, pressing him, for I thought I saw him near a loophole here. "But would that be your opinion at Walworth?"

1 "Mr. Pip, " he replied with gravity, "Walworth is one place, and this office is another. Much as the Aged is one person, and Mr. Jaggers is another. They must not be confounded together. My Walworth sentiments must be taken at Walworth; none but my official sentiments can be taken in this office."

"Very well," said I, much relieved, "then I shall look you up at Walworth, you may depend upon it."

"Mr. Pip," he returned, "you will be welcome there, in a private and personal capacity."

Before a week was out, I received a note from Wemmick, dated Walworth, stating that he hoped he had made some advance in that matter appertaining to our private and personal capacities, and that he would be glad if I could come and see him. So, I went out to Walworth. The upshot was that we found a worthy young merchant or shipping-broker, not long established in business, who wanted intelligent help, and who wanted capital, and who in due course of time
2 and receipt would want a partner. Between him and me, secret articles were signed of which Herbert was the subject, and I paid him half of my five hundred pounds down, and engaged for sundry other payments.

The whole business was so cleverly managed that Herbert had not the least suspicion of my hand being in it. I never shall forget the radiant face with which he came home one afternoon, and told me as a mighty piece of news, of his having fallen in with one Clarriker (the young merchant's name), and of Clarriker's having shown an extraordinary inclination towards him, and of his belief that the opening had come at last.

I had the greatest difficulty in restraining my tears of triumph when I saw him so happy.

At length, the thing being done, and he having that day entered Clarriker's House, and he having talked to me for a whole evening in a
3 flush of pleasure and success, I did really cry in good earnest when I went to bed, to think that my expectations had done some good to somebody.

Chapter Twenty-five

Richmond and Satis House: Miss Havisham, Estella, and Drummle.

A great event in my life, the turning point of my life, now opens on my view. But before I proceed to narrate it, and before I pass on to all the changes it involved, I must give one chapter to Estella. It is not much to give to the theme that so long filled my heart.

The lady with whom Estella was placed, Mrs. Brandley by name, was a widow, with one daughter several years older than Estella. They were in what is called a good position, and visited, and were visited by, numbers of people. Mrs. Brandley had been a friend of Miss Havisham's before the time of her seclusion.

In Mrs. Brandley's house and out of Mrs. Brandley's house, I suffered every kind and degree of torture that Estella could cause me. The nature of my relations with her, which placed me on terms of familiarity without placing me on terms of favor, conduced to my distraction.

I saw her often at Richmond. I heard of her often in town. I never had one hour's happiness in her society, and yet my mind all round the four-and-twenty hours was harping on the hap-
4 piness of having her with me unto death. She habitually reverted to that tone which expressed that our association was forced upon us. There were other times when she would come to a sudden check in this tone and in all her many tones, and would seem to pity me.

GUIDED READING

LITERAL QUESTIONS

1a. What are Wemmick's "Walworth sentiments" on Pip's proposal? (He is willing to help Pip aid Herbert.)

2a. What does Pip think about all day concerning Estella? (marrying her)

INFERENTIAL QUESTIONS

1b. Why doesn't Wemmick express those sentiments at the office? (He divides his life so firmly in two that he can only be generous and kind at home.)

2b. Do you believe, as he does, that this would make him happy? (Possible answer: no, for Estella has been taught not to love)

"Pip, Pip," she said one evening, coming to such a check, when we sat apart at a darkening window of the house in Richmond; "will you never take warning?"

"Of what?"

"Of me."

"Warning not to be attracted by you, do you mean, Estella?"

"Do I mean! If you don't know what I mean, you are blind."

1 "At any rate," said I, "I have no warning given me just now, for you wrote to me to come to you, this time."

"That's true," said Estella, with a cold careless smile that always chilled me.

After looking at the twilight without for a little while, she went on to say:

"The time has come round when Miss Havisham wishes to have me for a day at Satis. You are to take me there, and bring me back, if you will. She would rather I did not travel alone. Can you take me?"

"Can I take you, Estella!"

"You can then? The day after to-morrow, if you please. You are to pay all charges out of my purse. You hear the condition of your going?"

"And must obey," said I.

This was all the preparation I received for that visit, or for others like it: Miss Havisham never wrote to me, nor had I ever so much as seen her handwriting. We went down on the next day and we found her in the room where I had first beheld her, and it is needless to add there was no change in Satis House.

2 She was even more dreadfully fond of Estella than she had been when I last saw them together; I repeat the word advisedly, for there was something positively dreadful in the energy of her looks and embraces. She hung upon Estella's beauty, hung upon her words, hung upon her gestures, and sat mumbling her own trembling fingers while she looked at her, as though she were devouring the beautiful creature she had reared.

From Estella she looked at me, with a searching glance that seemed to pry into my heart and probe its wounds. "How does she use you, Pip, how does she use you?" she asked me again, with her witch-like eagerness, even in Estella's hearing.

3 I saw that Estella was set to wreak Miss Havisham's revenge on men and that she was not to be given to me until she had gratified it. I saw in this a reason for her being beforehand assigned to me.

We were seated by the fire, and Miss Havisham still had Estella's arm drawn through her own, and still clutched Estella's hand in hers, when Estella gradually began to detach herself.

"What!" said Miss Havisham, flashing her eyes upon her, "are you tired of me?"

"Only a little tired of myself," replied Estella, disengaging her arm, and moving to the great chimney-piece, where she stood looking down at the fire.

"Speak the truth, you ingrate!" cried Miss Havisham, passionately striking her stick upon the floor; "you are tired of me."

"You have been very good to me, and I owe everything to you. What would you have?"

"Love," replied the other.

"You have it."

"I have not," said Miss Havisham.

"Mother by adoption," retorted Estella, never departing from the easy grace of her attitude, "I have said that I owe everything to you. All that you have given me is at your command. Beyond that, I have nothing. And if you ask me to give you what you never gave me, my gratitude and duty cannot do impossibilities."

"So hard, so hard!" moaned Miss Havisham, with her former action.

"Who taught me to be hard?" returned Estella.

4 "But to be proud and hard to *me!*" Miss Havisham quite shrieked, as she stretched out her arms. "Estella, Estella, Estella, to be proud and hard to *me!*"

AT A GLANCE

- Estella reminds Pip not to be attracted to her; he is to take her to see Miss Havisham.
- Pip partially realizes that Miss Havisham is using Estella.
- Miss Havisham learns that Estella does not love her.

1 THEME: MANIPULATION

Estella, though she cares for Pip, cannot help using him: She continues to do what she has been trained to do—break hearts.

2 VOCABULARY: WORD CHOICE

Pip uses and remarks on the phrase "dreadfully fond" because he finds that Miss Havisham's fawning over Estella fills him with dread; it is both pathetic and frightening.

3 THEME: REVENGE

Pip finally sees that Miss Havisham plans to use Estella to wreak her revenge on men; he does not seem to have digested the fact that he is part of Miss Havisham's plan.

4 STYLE: IRONY

Miss Havisham's discovery of what the reader has always known is ironic: Estella is incapable of loving because of her long practice in calculation and indifference.

GUIDED READING

LITERAL QUESTIONS

1a. Of what does Estella keep warning Pip? (not to fall in love with her)

2a. What does Miss Havisham want from Estella? (her love)

INFERENTIAL QUESTIONS

1b. Why does she warn him? (She doesn't want to hurt him.)

2b. Why is Estella unable to give it? (Miss Havisham has trained Estella not to love.)

AT A GLANCE

- Pip spends the night at Satis House.
- He gets up and sees Miss Havisham walking and moaning.
- Pip goes to a ball at Richmond.
- He jealously confronts Estella.

1 MOOD

The strange atmosphere of Satis House surrounds Pip as he imagines ghosts and feels time slowing.

2 THEME: FREEDOM VS. IMPRISONMENT

Pip is trapped in the dark, unable to "get out and to go back," as surely as Miss Havisham is trapped in her own private darkness.

3 THEME: REVENGE

Estella, having made Pip fall in love with her, is furthering Miss Havisham's revenge by making Pip miserably jealous.

Estella looked at her for a moment with a kind of calm wonder. When the moment was past, she looked down at the fire again. When I left, Estella was yet standing by the great chimney-piece, just as she had stood through-
1 out. That was the first time I had ever lain down to rest in Satis House, and sleep refused to come near me. A thousand Miss Havishams haunted me.

When the night was slow to creep on towards two o'clock, I got up and put on my clothes, and went out across the yard into the long stone passage, to gain the outer court-yard and walk there for the relief of my mind. But, I was no sooner in the passage than I extinguished my candle, for I saw Miss Havisham going along in a ghostly manner, making a low cry. I followed her at a distance, and saw her go up the staircase. Standing at the bottom of the staircase, I felt the mildewed air of the feast-chamber, without seeing her open the door, and I heard her walking there, and so across into her own room, and so across again into that, never ceasing the low cry.
2 After a time, I tried in the dark both to get out and to go back, but I could do neither until some streaks of day strayed in and showed me where to lay my hands. During the whole interval, I heard her footsteps, saw her candle pass above, and heard her ceaseless low cry.

It is impossible to turn this leaf of my life without putting Bentley Drummle's name upon it; or I would, very gladly.

The Spider, as Mr. Jaggers had called him, was used to lying in wait. At a certain ball at Richmond, where Estella had outshone all other beauties, this blundering Drummle so hung about her, and with so much toleration on her part, that I resolved to speak to her concerning him. I took the next opportunity, which was when she was waiting for Mrs. Brandley to take her home, and was sitting apart among some flowers, ready to go.

"Are you tired, Estella?"

"Rather, Pip."

"You should be."

"Say, rather, I should not be, for I have my letter to Satis House to write before I go to sleep."

"Recounting to-night's triumph?" said I. "Surely a very poor one, Estella."

"What do you mean? I didn't know there had been any."

"Estella," said I, "do look at that fellow in the corner yonder who is looking over here at us."

"Why should I look at him?" returned Estella, with her eyes on me instead. "What is there in that fellow in the corner yonder—to use your words—that I need look at?"

"Indeed, that is the very question I want to ask you," said I. "For he has been hovering about you all night."

"Moths, and all sorts of ugly creatures," replied Estella, with a glance towards him, "hover about a lighted candle. Can the candle help it?"

"No," I returned: "but cannot the Estella help it?"

"Well!" said she, laughing after a moment, "perhaps. Yes. Anything you like."

3 "But, Estella, do hear me speak. It makes me wretched that you should encourage a man so generally despised as Drummle. You know he is despised."

"Well?" said she.

"You know he is as ungainly within as without. A deficient, ill-tempered, lowering, stupid fellow."

"Well?" said she.

"You know he has nothing to recommend him but money, and a ridiculous roll of addle-headed predecessors; now, don't you?"

"Well?" said she again; and each time she said it, she opened her lovely eyes the wider.

To overcome the difficulty of getting past that monosyllable, I took it from her, and said, repeating it with emphasis, "Well! Then, that is why it makes me wretched."

GUIDED READING

LITERAL QUESTIONS

1a. What does Pip see late at night at Satis House? (He sees Miss Havisham walking "in a ghostly manner" and moaning.)

2a. What upsets Pip during the ball at Richmond? (Estella has paid attention to Drummle.)

INFERENTIAL QUESTIONS

1b. Why do you think Miss Havisham is so distressed? (perhaps because she realizes that Estella doesn't love her)

2b. Do you think Estella would stop encouraging Drummle for Pip's sake? (No; she has been trained to toy with men.)

"Pip," said Estella, casting her glance over he room, "don't be foolish about its effect on ou. It may have its effect on others, and may be neant to have. It's not worth discussing."

"Do you deceive and entrap him, Estella?"

"Yes, and many others—all of them but you. Iere is Mrs. Brandley. I'll say no more."

hapter Twenty-six

)ne stormy evening in London: A long-awaited ppearance.

I was three-and-twenty years of age. Not nother word had I heard to enlighten me on the ubject of my expectations, and my twenty-third irthday was a week gone. We had left Barnard's nn more than a year, and lived in the Temple.[1] Our chambers were in Garden Court, down by he river. Business had taken Herbert on a ourney to Marseilles.[2] I was alone and had a dull ense of being alone.

It was wretched weather; stormy and wet; nud, mud, mud, deep in all the streets. Day after day, a vast heavy veil had been driving over London from the east in an eternity of cloud and wind. So furious had been the gusts that high buildings in town had had the lead stripped off their roofs; and in the country, trees had been torn up, and sails of windmills carried away; and gloomy accounts had come in from the coast of shipwreck and death.

I read with my watch upon the table, purposing to close my book at eleven o'clock. Saint Paul's, and all the many church-clocks in the City struck that hour when I heard a footstep on the stair.

I took up my reading-lamp and went out to the stair-head. Whoever was below had stopped on seeing my lamp, for all was quiet.

1. **Temple:** collection of apartment and office buildings.
2. **Marseilles** [mär sā']: port city in southern France.

"There is some one down there, is there not?" I called out, looking down.

"Yes," said a voice from the darkness beneath.

"What floor do you want?"

"The top. Mr. Pip."

"That is my name. There is nothing the matter?"

"Nothing the matter," returned the voice. And the man came on.

I stood with my lamp held out over the stair-
3 rail, and he came slowly within its light. He was in it for a mere instant, and then out of it. In the instant I had seen a face that was strange to me, looking up with an incomprehensible air of being touched and pleased by the sight of me.

Moving the lamp as the man moved, I made out that he was dressed like a voyager. That he had long iron-grey hair. That his age was about sixty. That he was a muscular man, strong on his legs, and that he was browned and hardened by exposure to weather. As he ascended the last stair or two, I saw, with a stupid kind of amazement, that he was holding out both his hands to me.

"Pray what is your business?" I asked him.

"My business?" he repeated, pausing. "Ah! Yes. I will explain my business, by your leave."

"Do you wish to come in?"

"Yes," he replied, "I wish to come in, master."

4 He looked about him with the strangest air—an air of wondering pleasure, as if he had some part in the things he admired. I saw him next moment, once more holding out both his hands to me.

"What do you mean?" said I, half-suspecting him to be mad.

He stopped in his looking at me, and slowly rubbed his right hand over his head. "It's disappointing to a man," he said, in a coarse broken voice, "arter having looked for'ard so distant, and come so fur; but you're not to blame for

AT A GLANCE

- Two years pass; Pip and Herbert live in another building in London.
- During a stormy night Pip hears footsteps on the stairs.
- A man whom Pip does not recognize enters the room.

1 CHARACTERIZATION

Estella's admission—that she deceives and entraps all men but Pip—reveals her complexity: She doesn't want to deceive Pip but seems powerless not to hurt him.

2 SETTING

The words used to describe the evening—*wretched, stormy and wet,* with *furious* gusts of wind and *an eternity of cloud and wind*—set the stage for the strange and frightening events that follow.

3 MOOD

Dickens creates suspense by making the stranger's face visible only for an instant and making his expression inexplicably "touched and pleased."

4 READING SKILLS: DETAILS

Dickens provides details about the man that add to the mystery of his identity: his air of "wondering pleasure" and his desire to touch Pip.

GUIDED READING

LITERAL QUESTION

1a. How is the stranger on the stairs described? (He is dressed like a voyager, has long iron-grey hair, is about sixty, muscular, brown, and weather-hardened.)

INFERENTIAL QUESTION

1b. Who do you think the man might be? (the convict)

AT A GLANCE

- Pip recognizes the stranger as his convict.
- The convict tells Pip he has been making his living in Australia.

1 THEME: TIME

Pip's memory, which is often faulty or overly romantic, is accurate when it comes to identifying the convict whom he helped more than a dozen years ago.

2 CHARACTERIZATION

Pip's attitude toward the convict has changed: He is no longer afraid of the man but is now repelled by him because of his own social status.

that—neither of us is to blame for that. I'll speak in half a minute. Give me half a minute, please."

He sat down on a chair that stood before the fire, and covered his forehead with his large brown veinous hands. I looked at him attentively then, and recoiled a little from him; but I did not know him.

"There's no one nigh," said he, looking over his shoulder, "is there?"

"Why do you, a stranger coming into my rooms at this time of the night, ask that question?" said I.

"You're a game one," he returned, shaking his head at me with a deliberate affection, at once most unintelligible and most exasperating; "I'm glad you've grow'd up a game one! But don't catch hold of me. You'd be sorry arterwards to have done it."

I relinquished the intention he had detected,
1 for I knew him! Even yet I could not recall a single feature, but I knew him! If the wind and the rain had driven away the intervening years, had swept us to the churchyard where we first stood face to face on such different levels, I could not have known my convict more distinctly than I knew him now, as he sat in the chair before the fire.

"You acted nobly, my boy," said he. "Noble Pip! And I have never forgot it!"

At a change in his manner as if he were even going to embrace me, I laid a hand upon his breast and put him away.

"Stay!" said I. "Keep off! If you are grateful to me for what I did when I was a little child, I hope you have shown your gratitude by mending your way of life. If you have come here to thank me, it was not necessary. Still, there must be something good in the feeling that has brought you here. I will not repulse you, but surely you must understand—I—"

The words died away on my tongue.

"You was a-saying," he observed, when we had confronted one another in silence, "surely I must understand. What must I understand?"

2 "That I cannot wish to renew that chance meeting with you of long ago. I am glad to believe you have repented and recovered yourself. I am glad to tell you so. But our ways are different ways. None the less, you are wet and you look weary. Will you drink something before you go?"

"I think," he answered, still observant of me, "that I *will* drink (I thank you) afore I go."

I saw with amazement that his eyes were full of tears.

Up to this time I had remained standing, not to disguise that I wished him gone. But I was softened by the softened aspect of the man, and felt a touch of reproach. "I hope," said I, hurriedly putting something into a glass for myself and drawing a chair to the table, "that you will not think I spoke harshly to you just now. I had no intention of doing it, and I am sorry for it if I did."

"How are you living?"

"I've been a sheep-farmer, stock-breeder, other trades besides, away in the New World," said he, "many a thousand mile of stormy water off from this."

"I hope you have done well."

"I've done wonderful well. There's others went out alonger me as has done well, too, but no man has done nigh as well as me. I'm famous for it."

"I am glad to hear it."

"I hope to hear you say so, my dear boy."

Without stopping to try to understand those words or the tone in which they were spoken, I turned off to a point that had just come into my mind.

"Have you ever seen a messenger you once sent to me," I inquired, "since he undertook that trust?"

"Never set eyes upon him. I warn't likely to it."

---

3. **New World:** Australia. At the time criminals were sent to colonize England's distant colonies in the territory of New South Wales.

GUIDED READING

LITERAL QUESTIONS

1a. What does Pip do when the convict tries to embrace him? (He pushes him away.)

2a. How does the convict react when Pip offers him a drink? (He accepts, and his eyes fill with tears.)

INFERENTIAL QUESTIONS

1b. Why does Pip behave that way? (He is repelled by a man who has disgraced himself and broken the law.)

2b. Why does he weep? (He is hurt at Pip's previous rejection of him.)

"He came faithfully, and he brought me the two one-pound notes. I was a poor boy then, as you know, and to a poor boy they were a little fortune. But, like you, I have done well since, and you must let me pay them back. You can put them to some other poor boy's use." I took out my purse.

He watched me as I laid my purse upon the table and opened it, and he watched me as I separated two one-pound notes from its contents. They were clean and new, and I spread them out and handed them over to him. Still watching me, he laid them one upon the other, folded them long-wise, gave them a twist, set fire to them at the lamp, and dropped the ashes into the tray.

"May I make so bold," he said then, with a smile that was like a frown, and with a frown that was like a smile, "as ask you *how* you have done well, since you and me was out on them lone shivering marshes?"

"How?"

"Ah!"

He emptied his glass, got up, and stood at the side of the fire, with his heavy brown hand on the mantelshelf. He put a foot up to the bars, to dry and warm it, but he neither looked at it, nor at the fire, but steadily looked at me. It was only now that I began to tremble.

When my lips had parted, and had shaped some words that were without sound, I forced myself to tell him (though I could not do it distinctly), that I had been chosen to succeed to some property.

"Might a mere warmint ask what property?" said he.

I faltered, "I don't know."

"Might a mere warmint ask whose property?" said he.

I faltered again, "I don't know."

"Could I make a guess, I wonder," said the convict, "at your income since you come of age! As to the first figure, now. Five?"

With my heart beating like a heavy hammer of disordered action, I rose out of my chair, and stood with my hand upon the back of it, looking wildly at him.

"Concerning a guardian," he went on. "There ought to have been some guardian or such-like, whiles you was a minor. Some lawyer, maybe. As to the first letter of that lawyer's name, now. Would it be J?"

3 All the truth of my position came flashing on me, and its disappointments, dangers, disgraces, consequences of all kinds rushed in in such a multitude that I was borne down by them and had to struggle for every breath I drew. "However, did I find you out? Why, I wrote from Portsmouth[4] to a person in London for particulars of your address. That person's name? Why, Wemmick."

I could not have spoken one word, though it had been to save my life. I stood, with a hand on the chair-back and a hand on my breast, where I seemed to be suffocating. He caught me, drew me to the sofa, put me up against the cushions, and bent on one knee before me, bringing the face that I now well remembered very near to mine.

"Yes, Pip, dear boy, I've made a gentleman on you! It's me wot has done it! I swore that time, sure as ever I earned a guinea, that guinea should go to you. I swore arterwards, sure as ever I spec'lated and got rich, you should get
4 rich. I lived rough, that you should live smooth; I worked hard that you should be above work. What odds, dear boy? Do I tell it fur you to feel a obligation? Not a bit. I tell it fur you to know as that there hunted dunghill dog wot you kep life in got his head so high that he could make a gentleman—and, Pip, you're him!"

The abhorrence in which I held the man, the dread I had of him, the repugnance with which I shrank from him could not have been exceeded if he had been some terrible beast.

---

4. **Portsmouth** [pôrt′sməth]: port city in southern England.

AT A GLANCE

- The convict asks how Pip came to be a gentleman.
- Pip realizes that the convict is his benefactor.
- Pip is horrified at the truth.

1 THEME: PRIDE

Pip wounds the convict's pride by offering him money to repay the gift of two pounds that the convict gave to Pip long ago out of gratitude.

2 STYLE: DIALOGUE

The convict's questions concerning Pip's "property" introduce a suspense that culminates in Pip's discovery that the convict is his benefactor.

3 PLOT: CLIMAX

Pip's discovery of his benefactor's identity is the central climax of the novel: For Pip, this revelation changes the meaning and value of everything in his life.

4 THEME: WEALTH AND HAPPINESS

In contrast to Pip's selfishness, the convict's sacrifices stand out as selfless and generous actions.

GUIDED READING

LITERAL QUESTIONS

1a. What does the convict do when Pip offers him money? (He burns it.)

2a. For what reason did the convict live rough and work hard? (so Pip could become a gentleman)

INFERENTIAL QUESTIONS

1b. Why does he do this? (He is offended by Pip's attempt to pay him back.)

2b. Why did the convict want to help Pip? (He was grateful for Pip's kindness on the marsh.)

AT A GLANCE

- The convict explains that he alone is responsible for Pip's expectations.
- Pip realizes that he was never intended to marry Estella.
- The convict asks to spend the night.

1 THEME: APPEARANCE VS. REALITY

Pip glimpses the full extent of Miss Havisham's revenge when he realizes that she never intended him to marry Estella; she planned for Estella to break his heart.

2 FORESHADOWING

The convict's emphasis on caution hints at possible future danger.

"Look'ee here, Pip. I'm your second father. You're my son—more to me nor any son. I've put away money, only for you to spend. When I was a hired-out shepherd in a solitary hut, not seeing no faces but faces of sheep till I half-forgot wot men's and women's faces wos like, I see yourn. I see you there a many times as plain as ever I see you on them misty marshes. Didn't you never think it might be me?"

"Oh, no, no, no," I returned. "Never, never!"

"Well, you see it *wos* me, and single-handed. Never a soul in it but my own self and Mr. Jaggers."

1 "Was there no one else?" I asked.

"No," said he, with a glance of surprise. "Who else should there be?"

O Estella, Estella!

"Where will you put me?" he asked presently. "I must be put somewheres, dear boy."

"To sleep?" said I.

"Yes. And to sleep long and sound," he answered, "for I've been sea-tossed and sea-washed, months and months."

"My friend and companion," said I, rising from the sofa, "is absent; you must have his room."

"He won't come back to-morrow, will he?"

"No," said I, answering almost mechanically, in spite of my utmost efforts, "not to-morrow."

2 "Because, look-ee here, dear boy," he said, dropping his voice, and laying a long finger on my breast in an impressive manner, "caution is necessary."

"How do you mean, caution?"

GUIDED READING

LITERAL QUESTION

1a. What does Pip say when the convict asks when Herbert will return? (that he won't come back the next day)

INFERENTIAL QUESTION

1b. Why must he work against his "utmost efforts" to answer? (He wants to lie to force the convict to leave, but cannot bring himself to do so.)

"It's death!"

"What's death?"

"I was sent for life. It's death to come back. There's been overmuch coming back of late years, and I should of a certainty be hanged if took."

Nothing was needed but this; the wretched man had risked his life to come to me, and I held it there in my keeping! My first care was to close the shutters, so that no light might be seen from without, and then to close and make fast the doors.

When I had gone into Herbert's room, and had shut off any other communication between it and the staircase than through the room in which our conversation had been held, I asked him if he would go to bed. He said yes, but asked me for some of my "gentleman's linen" to put on in the morning. I brought it out, and laid it ready for him, and my blood again ran cold when he again took me by both hands to give me good night.

I got away from him, without knowing how I did it, and mended the fire in the room where we had been together, and sat down by it, afraid to go to bed. For an hour or more, I remained too stunned to think; and it was not until I began to think that I began fully to know how wrecked I was, and how the ship in which I had sailed was gone to pieces.

Miss Havisham's intentions towards me, all a mere dream; Estella not designed for me; I only suffered in Satis House as a convenience, a sting for the greedy relations, a model with a mechanical heart to practice on when no other practice was at hand. Those were the first smarts I had.
2 But, sharpest and deepest pain of all—it was for the convict, guilty of I knew not what crimes, and liable to be hanged at the Old Bailey[5] door, that I had deserted Joe.

I would not have gone back to Joe now, I would not have gone back to Biddy now, for any
3 consideration—simply, I suppose, because my sense of my own worthless conduct to them was greater than every consideration. No wisdom on earth could have given me the comfort that I should have derived from their simplicity and fidelity; but I could never, never, never undo what I had done.

This is the end of the second stage of Pip's expectations.

Chapter Twenty-seven

London, the next day: Pip faces facts.

The impossibility of keeping my dreaded visitor concealed in the chambers was self-evident. It could not be done, and I resolved to announce in the morning that my uncle had unexpectedly come from the country.

This course I decided on while I was yet groping about in the darkness for the means of
4 getting a light. In groping my way down the black staircase, I fell over something, and that something was a man crouching in a corner.

As the man made no answer when I asked him what he did there, but eluded my touch in silence, I ran to the lodge and urged the watchman to come quickly, telling him of the incident on the way back. We examined the staircase from the bottom to the top and found no one there.

As there was full an hour and a half between me and daylight, I dozed again; now waking up uneasily, with prolix[1] conversations about nothing, in my ears; now making thunder of the wind in the chimney; at length falling off into a profound sleep from which the daylight woke me with a start.

By-and-by, his door opened and he came out. I could not bring myself to bear the sight of him, and I thought he had a worse look by daylight.

5. **Old Bailey:** Criminal court building in London.

1. **prolix** [prō′liks]: long and wordy.

AT A GLANCE

- Pip feels revolted and guilty about the convict.
- Pip mourns the loss of Joe and Biddy as friends.
- In the night Pip finds a man hiding on the stairs; the man flees.

1 BACKGROUND

In order to avoid the expense of keeping prisoners in English jails, authorities sent many to Australia to start new lives; although they could live freely there, they were barred from England under penalty of death.

2 THEME: SELF-KNOWLEDGE

For the first time Pip fully realizes how badly he has treated Joe and what a loving friendship he has squandered.

3 THEME: RESPONSIBILITY

Pip no longer blames Joe for his provincialism or Biddy for her criticism: He sees that his own conduct was "worthless."

4 FORESHADOWING

The man crouching in Pip's "black staircase" foreshadows later dangers that Pip and his convict will encounter—trouble rooted in the past.

GUIDED READING

LITERAL QUESTIONS

1a. What will happen to the convict if he is discovered in England? (He will be killed.)

2a. What does Pip regret most upon learning the convict is his benefactor? (Pip is most upset that he betrayed Joe for a convict.)

INFERENTIAL QUESTIONS

1b. What does this tell you about his character? (He is truly devoted to Pip.)

2b. Why does Pip feel he can't go back to Joe? (Pip is too ashamed of the way he has treated him.)

AT A GLANCE

- The convict, whose alias is Provis and real name is Abel Magwitch, says that Jaggers was his lawyer.
- Pip gets Magwitch a room.
- Pip goes to see Jaggers.

1 READING SKILLS: INFERENCE

From the convict's response to Pip's question, the reader can infer that he has been tried, and perhaps convicted, many times.

2 THEME: RESPONSIBILITY

Despite his feelings of revulsion, Pip knows that Magwitch's life is in his hands and arranges for a safe haven for him.

3 STYLE: IRONY

Magwitch's insistence that they make Herbert take an oath on the Bible is ironic in view of the fact that Magwitch is a convicted lawbreaker.

4 THEME: SECRECY

Mr. Jaggers is fearful of being implicated in illegal activities and shrinks from being told anything about Magwitch.

"I do not even know," said I, speaking low as he took his seat at the table, "by what name to call you. I have given out that you are my uncle."

"That's it, dear boy! Call me uncle."

"You assumed some name, I suppose, on board ship?"

"Yes, dear boy. I took the name of Provis."

"Do you mean to keep that name?"

"Why, yes, dear boy, it's as good as another—unless you'd like another."

"What is your real name?" I asked him in a whisper.

"Magwitch," he answered, in the same tone; "chrisen'd Abel."

"What were you brought up to be?"

"A warmint, dear boy."

He answered quite seriously, and used the words as if it denoted some profession.

"When you came into the Temple last night—" said I, pausing to wonder whether that could really have been last night, which seemed so long ago.

"Yes, dear boy?"

"When you came in at the gate and asked the watchman the way here, had you any one with you?"

"With me? No, dear boy."

"But there was some one there?"

"I didn't take particular notice," he said dubiously, "not knowing the ways of the place. But I think there *was* a person, too, come in alonger me."

"Are you known in London?"

"I hope not!" said he, giving his neck a jerk with his forefinger that made me turn hot and sick.

"Were you known in London, once?"

"Not over and above, dear boy. I was in the provinces mostly."

1 "Were you—tried—in London?"

"Which time?" said he, with a sharp look.

"The last time."

He nodded. "First knowed Mr. Jaggers that way. Jaggers was for me."

It was on my lips to ask him what he was tried for, but he took up a knife, gave it a flourish, and with the words, "And what I done is worked out and paid for!" fell to at his breakfast in a ravenous way that was very uncouth, noisy, and greedy.

2 It appeared to me that I could do no better than secure him some quiet lodging hard by, of which he might take possession when Herbert returned—whom I expected in two or three days. That the secret must be confided to Herbert as a matter of unavoidable necessity was by no means so plain to Mr. Provis (I resolved to call him by that name), who reserved his consent to Herbert's participation until he should have seen him and formed a favorable judgment of his
3 physiognomy.[2] "And even then, dear boy," said he, pulling a greasy little clasped black Testament out of his pocket, "we'll have him on his oath."

There being to my knowledge a respectable lodging-house in Essex Street, the back of which looked into the Temple, and was almost within hail of my windows, I first of all repaired to that house, and was so fortunate as to secure the second floor for my uncle, Mr. Provis. This business transacted, I turned my face, on my own account, to Little Britain. Mr. Jaggers was at his desk, but, seeing me enter, got up immediately and stood before his fire.

"Now, Pip," said he, "be careful."

"I will, sir," I returned. For coming along I had thought well of what I was going to say.

4 "Don't commit yourself," said Mr. Jaggers, "and don't commit any one. You understand—any one. Don't tell me anything; I don't want to know anything; I am not curious."

Of course I saw that he knew the man was come.

---

2. **physiognomy** [fiz′ē og′nə mē]: facial features.

GUIDED READING

LITERAL QUESTIONS

1a. What does Magwitch say he was raised to be? (a "warmint," or varmint)

2a. Of what does Mr. Jaggers warn Pip? (Mr. Jaggers warns Pip not to "commit himself" nor to tell him anything.)

INFERENTIAL QUESTIONS

1b. What does this tell you about his background? (that he never had the opportunity, through money, family, or education, to raise himself)

2b. Why does Mr. Jaggers give this warning? (He feels that admitting a knowledge of Magwitch is dangerous in some way.)

"I have been informed by a person named Abel Magwitch that he is the benefactor so long unknown to me."

"That is the man," said Mr. Jaggers, "—in New South Wales."

"And only he?" said I.

"And only he," said Mr. Jaggers.

"I am not so unreasonable, sir, as to think you at all responsible for my mistakes and wrong conclusions, but I always supposed it was Miss Havisham."

"As you say, Pip," returned Mr. Jaggers, turning his eyes upon me coolly, and taking a bite at his forefinger, "I am not at all responsible for that."

"And yet it looked so like it, sir," I pleaded with a downcast heart.

"Not a particle of evidence, Pip," said Mr. Jaggers, shaking his head.

"I have no more to say," said I, with a sigh, after standing silent for a little while.

"And Magwitch—in New South Wales—having at last disclosed himself," said Mr. Jaggers, "you will comprehend, Pip, how rigidly throughout my communication with you I have always adhered to the strict line of fact.

"I communicated to Magwitch—in New South Wales—when he first wrote to me—from New South Wales. He appeared to me to have obscurely hinted in his letter at some distant idea of seeing you in England here. I cautioned him that I must hear no more of that; that he was not at all likely to obtain a pardon; that he was expatriated[3] for the term of his natural life; and that his presenting himself in this country would be an act of felony,[4] rendering him liable to the extreme penalty of the law. I gave Magwitch that caution," said Mr. Jaggers, looking hard at me; "I wrote it to New South Wales. He guided himself by it, no doubt."

"No doubt," said I.

"I have been informed by Wemmick," pursued Mr. Jaggers, still looking hard at me, "that he has received a letter, under date Portsmouth, from a colonist of the name of Purvis, or—"

"Or Provis," I suggested.

"Or Provis—thank you, Pip. Perhaps it *is* Provis? Perhaps you know it's Provis?"

"Yes," said I.

"You know it's Provis. A letter, under date
3 Portsmouth, from a colonist of the name of Provis, asking for the particulars of your address, on behalf of Magwitch. Wemmick sent him the particulars, I understand, by return of post. Probably it is through Provis that you have received the explanation of Magwitch—in New South Wales?"

"It came through Provis," I replied.

"Good day, Pip," said Mr. Jaggers, offering his hand; "glad to have seen you. In writing by post to Magwitch—in New South Wales—or in communicating with him through Provis, have the goodness to mention that the particulars and vouchers[5] of our long account shall be sent to you, together with the balance; for there is still a balance remaining. Good day, Pip!"

At length, one evening when dinner was over and I had dropped into a slumber quite worn out, I was roused by the welcome footstep on the staircase. Provis, who had been asleep, too, staggered and in an instant I saw his jack-knife shining in his hand.

4 "Quiet! It's Herbert!" I said, and Herbert came bursting in, with the airy freshness of six hundred miles of France upon him.

"Handel, my dear fellow, how are you, and again how are you, and again how are you? I seem to have been gone a twelvemonth! Why, so I must have been, for you have grown quite thin and pale! Handel, my—Halloa! I beg your pardon."

3. **expatriated** [eks pā'trē āt id]: exiled.
4. **felony** [fel'ə nē]: serious crime.

5. **vouchers**: receipts.

AT A GLANCE

- Jaggers confirms that Pip's benefactor is Magwitch.
- Pip admits he had thought Miss Havisham his benefactor.
- Jaggers announces that his role in Pip's affairs is over.
- Herbert returns home from France.

1 THEME: SELF-DECEPTION

Pip still desperately wants to believe that Miss Havisham is involved in his expectations so he won't have to give up Estella, but Jaggers makes it obvious that Pip has been deceiving himself all along.

2 THEME: TRUTH VS. HYPOCRISY

Mr. Jaggers insists that he rigidly "adhered to the strict line of fact," but though it is true he never lied to Pip, he did allow Pip to believe something that was untrue.

3 INTERPRETING

Jaggers uses his legal skills to make it clear to Pip that he does not want to know Magwitch is in London. He speaks of "Provis," which is Magwitch's alias.

4 CHARACTERIZATION

Herbert, returning from France, brings "airy freshness" with him; he seems always positive, friendly, and cheerful.

GUIDED READING

LITERAL QUESTION

1a. What does Mr. Jaggers ask Pip to tell Magwitch? (that he is sending the vouchers, receipts, and balance of money to Pip)

INFERENTIAL QUESTION

1b. What does this mean regarding Jaggers' relationship with Pip? (It is over.)

AT A GLANCE

- Herbert meets Magwitch.
- Magwitch returns to his room.
- Pip tells Herbert that he cannot take more of Magwitch's money.
- Herbert advises Pip to get Magwitch out of the country.

1 THEME: FRIENDSHIP

Pip is learning the values of friendship—that one can depend on a friend to listen and help. Herbert's friendship helps Pip to be a better person himself.

2 THEME: WEALTH AND HAPPINESS

As suddenly as Pip's fortune was made, it is now lost, according to Pip. His enormous confusion about his worth and responsibility cause him to conclude (rather self-pityingly) that he is "fit for nothing."

He was stopped in his running on and in his shaking hands with me, by seeing Provis. Provis, regarding him with a fixed attention, was slowly putting up his jack-knife, and groping in another pocket for something else.

"Herbert, my dear friend," said I, shutting the double doors, while Herbert stood staring and wondering, "something very strange has happened. This is—a visitor of mine."

"It's all right, dear boy!" said Provis, coming forward, with his little clasped black book, and then addressing himself to Herbert. "Take it in your right hand. Lord strike you dead on the spot, if ever you split in any way sumever. Kiss it!"

"Do so, as he wishes it," I said to Herbert. So Herbert, looking at me with a friendly uneasiness and amazement, complied, and Provis immediately shaking hands with him, said, "Now, you're on your oath, you know."

We were anxious for the time when he would go to his lodging, and leave us together, but he was evidently jealous of leaving us together, and sat late. It was midnight before I took him round to Essex Street, and saw him safely in at his own
1 dark door. When it closed upon him, I experienced the first moment of relief I had known since the night of his arrival. I had never felt before so blessedly what it is to have a friend.

"What," said I to Herbert, "what is to be done?"

"My poor dear Handel," he replied, holding his head, "I am too stunned to think."

"So was I, Herbert, when the blow first fell. Still, something must be done. He is intent upon various new expenses—horses, and carriages, and lavish appearances of all kinds. He must be stopped somehow."

"You mean that you can't accept—"

"How can I?" I interposed, as Herbert paused. "Think of him! Look at him!"

An involuntary shudder passed over both of us.

"Yet I am afraid the dreadful truth is, Herbert, that he is attached to me, strongly attached to me. Was there ever such a fate!"

"My poor dear Handel," Herbert repeated.

2 "Then," said I, "after all, stopping short here, never taking another penny from him, think what I owe him already! Then again, I am heavily in debt—very heavily for me, who have now no expectations—and I have been bred to no calling, and I am fit for nothing."

"Well, well, well!" Herbert remonstrated. "Don't say fit for nothing."

"What am I fit for? I know only one thing that I am fit for, and that is to go for a soldier. And I might have gone, my dear Herbert, but for the prospect of taking counsel with your friendship."

"Anyhow, my dear Handel," said he presently, "soldiering won't do. You would be infinitely better in Clarriker's house, small as it is. I am working up towards a partnership, you know."

Poor fellow! He little suspected with whose money.

"But there is another question," said Herbert. "This is a man of a desperate and fierce character."

"I know he is," I returned. And I told him of that encounter with the other convict.

"See, then," said Herbert; "think of this! He comes here at the peril of his life for the realization of his fixed idea. In the moment of realization, after all his toil and waiting, you cut the ground from under his feet, destroy his idea, and make his gains worthless to him. Do you see nothing that he might do under the disappointment?"

"I have seen it, Herbert, and dreamed of it ever since the fatal night of his arrival."

"The first and the main thing to be done," said Herbert, "is to get him out of England. You will have to go with him, and then he may be induced to go."

"But get him where I will, could I prevent his coming back?"

GUIDED READING

LITERAL QUESTIONS

1a. How does Pip feel after he takes Magwitch back to his lodging and can talk to Herbert? (relieved)

2a. What does Pip decide about Magwitch's money? (that he will not accept more of it)

INFERENTIAL QUESTIONS

1b. Why does he feel this way? (In confiding in Herbert, Pip can relieve himself of part of the burden of knowing about Magwitch.)

2b. What does Herbert fear will result from Pip's decision? (that Magwitch may do something desperate or violent)

"Handel," said Herbert, stopping, "you feel convinced that you can take no further benefits from him, do you?"

"Fully. Surely you would, too, if you were in my place?"

"And you feel convinced that you must break with him?"

"Herbert, can you ask me?"

"Then you must get him out of England. That done, extricate yourself, in Heaven's name, and we'll see it out together."

Chapter Twenty-eight

London: Magwitch tells his story, and we learn about Compeyson and a man named Arthur.

"Dear boy and Pip's comrade. I am not a-going fur to tell you my life, like a song or a story-book. But to give it you short and handy, I'll put it at once into a mouthful of English. In jail and out of jail, in jail and out of jail, in jail and out of jail. There, you've got it. That's *my* life pretty much, down to such times as I got shipped off, arter Pip stood my friend.

"Tramping, begging, thieving, working sometimes when I could—though that warn't as often as you may think, till you put the question whether you would ha' been over-ready to give me work yourselves—a bit of a poacher,[1] a bit of a laborer, a bit of a waggoner, a bit of a haymaker, a bit of a hawker,[2] a bit of most things that don't pay and lead to trouble, I got to be a man.

"At Epsom races over twenty year ago, I got acquainted wi' a man whose skull I'd crack wi' this poker, like the claw of a lobster, if I'd got it on this hob. His right name was Compeyson; and that's the man, dear boy, what you see me a-pounding in the ditch.

"He set up fur a gentleman, this Compeyson, and he'd been to a public boarding-school and had learning. He was a smooth one to talk, and was a dab at the ways of gentlefolks. He was good-looking, too.

"Compeyson took me on to be his man and pardner. Compeyson's business was the swindling, handwriting forging, stolen bank-note passing, and such-like.

"There was another in with Compeyson, as was called Arthur—not as being so chrisen'd, but as a surname. He was in a decline, and was a
3 shadow to look at. Him and Compeyson had been in a bad thing with a rich lady some years afore, and they'd made a pot of money by it; but Compeyson betted and gamed, and he'd have run through the king's taxes. So Arthur was a-dying and a-dying poor and with the horrors on him, and Compeyson's wife (which Compeyson kicked mostly) was a-having pity on him when she could, and Compeyson was a-having pity on nothing and nobody.

"I mighta took warning by Arthur, but I didn't; and I won't pretend I was partick'ler—for where 'ud be the good on it, dear boy and comrade? So I begun wi' Compeyson, and a poor tool I was in his hands. Arthur lived at the top of Compeyson's house (over nigh Brentford, it was), and Compeyson kept a careful account agen him for board and lodging, in case he should ever get better to work it out. But Arthur soon settled the account. The second or third time as ever I see him, he come a-tearing down into Compeyson's parlor late at night, in only a flannel gown, with his hair all in a sweat. Then he lifted himself up hard, and was dead.

"Not to go into the things that Compeyson planned, and I done—which 'ud take a week—I'll simply say to you, dear boy, and Pip's com-
4 rade, that that man got me into such nets as made me his slave. I was always in debt to him, always under his thumb, always a-working, always a-getting into danger. He was younger than me, but he'd got craft, and he'd got learning, and he overmatched me five hundred times

1. **poacher** [pōch′ər]: one who hunts game or fishes illegally on the property of another.
2. **hawker:** peddler.

AT A GLANCE

- Herbert will help Pip face his problems.
- Magwitch fell into crime working with Compeyson.
- Arthur, a sickly man, worked with Compeyson.
- Compeyson forced Arthur and Magwitch to take risks and go to jail for him.

1 VOCABULARY: PARAPHRASING

Magwitch explains to Pip that he worked when he could, but he could not often find work because he looked so disreputable.

2 PLOT: FORESHADOWING

By mentioning Compeyson with reference to his previous appearance in Pip's life, Dickens subtly hints that he may appear again.

3 THEME

Magwitch tells how Compeyson lived well on the money he and Arthur got from "a rich lady," but through Compeyson's misuse their fortunes declined until Arthur became ill and died.

4 THEME

Magwitch describes how Compeyson manipulated him by getting him into debt and then forcing him to take illegal risks; Compeyson was the craftier man who took advantage of Magwitch.

GUIDED READING

LITERAL QUESTIONS

1a. What jobs did Magwitch have before he met Compeyson? (laborer, "waggoner," haymaker, peddler)

2a. Why did Magwitch agree to work with Compeyson? (He wanted to make money and was easily swayed by Compeyson's sophistication and "smooth" talk.)

INFERENTIAL QUESTIONS

1b. What do these jobs tell you about him? (that he was willing to work but undirected and not skilled enough to do what pays well)

2b. Why do you think Compeyson wanted to have Magwitch work with him? (He wanted someone whom he could manipulate.)

AT A GLANCE

- Magwitch and Compeyson were charged with a felony.
- The two were defended separately and received unequal sentences.
- Herbert tells Pip that Arthur was Miss Havisham's half-brother and Compeyson her lover.

1 THEME

Magwitch describes Compeyson's appearance (*what a gentleman . . .*) and his own (*a common sort of a wretch I looked*)—a difference that swayed the judge against Magwitch.

2 THEME

Magwitch began to realize that justice would not be done. Relying on deceptive appearances only, Compeyson's lawyer would make a convincing case that Magwitch had corrupted Compeyson and deserved the stiffer sentence.

3 PLOT: CLIMAX

Again, a coincidence of fate brings the plot to a climax: Herbert's realization that Magwitch, Compeyson, and Miss Havisham are linked provides a surprise ending to the chapter.

told and no mercy. My missis as I had the hard time wi'—Stop though! I ain't brought *her* in—"

"Did I tell you as I was tried, alone, for misdemeanor,[3] while with Compeyson?"

I answered, No.

"Well!" he said, "I *was*, and got convicted. As to took up[4] on suspicion, that was twice or three times in the four or five year that it lasted; but evidence was wanting. At last, me and Compeyson was both committed for felony—on a charge of putting stolen notes in circulation—and there was other charges behind. Compeyson says to me, 'Separate defenses, no communication,'[5] and that was all. And I was so miserable poor that I sold all the clothes I had, except what hung on my back, afore I could get Jaggers.

1 "When we was put in the dock,[6] I noticed first of all what a gentleman Compeyson looked, wi' his curly hair and his black clothes and his white pocket-handkercher, and what a common sort of a wretch I looked. When the evidence was giv in the box,[7] I noticed how it was always me that had come for'ard, and could be swore to, how it was always me that had seemed to work the thing and get the profit. But, when the defense come on, then I see the plan plainer; for, says the counselor for Compeyson, 'My lord and
2 gentlemen, here you has afore you, side by side, two persons as your eyes can separate wide; one, the younger, well brought up, one, the elder, ill brought up; one, the younger, seldom if ever seen in these here transactions; t'other, the elder, always seen in 'em and always wi' his guilt brought home.'

"And warn't it me as had been tried afore, and as had been know'd up hill and down dale? And when it come to speech-making, warn't it Compeyson as could speak to 'em wi' his face dropping every now and then into his white pocket-handkercher—ah! and wi' verses in his speech, too—and warn't it me as could only say, 'Gentlemen, this man at my side is a most precious rascal'? And when the verdict come, warn't it Compeyson as was recommended to mercy on account of good character and bad company, and giving up all the information he could agen me, and warn't it me as got never a word but guilty? And when I says to Compeyson, 'Once out of this court, I'll smash that face of yourn!' ain't it Compeyson as prays the judge to be protected? And when we're sentenced, ain't it him as gets seven year, and me fourteen?

"I was giv to understand as Compeyson was out on them marshes, too. 'And now,' says I, 'as the worst thing I can do, caring nothing for myself, I'll drag you back.' And I'd have swum off, towing him by the hair, if it had come to that, and I'd a-got him aboard without the soldiers."

"Is he dead?" I asked after a silence.

"Is who dead, dear boy?"

"Compeyson."

"He hopes *I* am, if he's alive, you may be sure," with a fierce look. "I never heard no more of him."

Herbert had been writing with his pencil in the cover of a book. He softly pushed the book over to me, as Provis stood smoking with his eyes on the fire, and I read in it:

3 Young Havisham's name was Arthur. Compeyson is the man who professed to be Miss Havisham's lover.

I shut the book and nodded slightly to Herbert, and put the book by; but we neither of us said anything, and both looked at Provis as he stood smoking by the fire.

---

3. **misdemeanor** [mis′di mē′nər]: illegal act punishable by fine or brief imprisonment.
4. **took up:** arrested.
5. **Separate . . . communication:** Each man would have his own lawyer and his own case, and each would not speak to the other before or during trial.
6. **dock:** place where the prisoner stands to face the court.
7. **box:** witness stand.

GUIDED READING

LITERAL QUESTIONS

1a. When they were convicted, what sentences were given to Magwitch and Compeyson? (seven years for Compeyson, fourteen years for Magwitch)

2a. What did Magwitch do when Compeyson escaped from prison and appeared on the marshes? (He determined to bring Compeyson back.)

INFERENTIAL QUESTIONS

1b. Why were the sentences different? (Compeyson's lawyer made the judge believe that Magwitch led Compeyson into crime.)

2b. Why did Magwitch do this? (because he hated what Compeyson had done to him and wanted him to suffer)

Chapter Twenty-nine

Richmond and Satis House: Estella's news.

A new fear had been engendered in my mind by his narrative. If Compeyson were alive and should discover his return, I could hardly doubt the consequence. Compeyson stood in mortal fear of him and would release himself for good from a dreaded enemy by the safe means of becoming an informer.

I said to Herbert that before I could go abroad, I must see both Estella and Miss Havisham. This was when we were left alone on the night of the day when Provis told us his story. I resolved to go out to Richmond next day.

On my presenting myself at Mrs. Brandley's, Estella's maid was called to tell me that Estella had gone into the country. Where? To Satis House, as usual. Not as usual, I said, for she had never yet gone there without me. I could make nothing of this, except that it was meant that I should make nothing of it, and I went home again in complete discomfiture.

Next day, I had the meanness to feign that I was under a binding promise to go down to Joe; but I was capable of almost any meanness towards Joe or his name. Provis was to be strictly careful while I was gone, and Herbert was to take charge of him.

Having thus cleared the way for my expedition to Miss Havisham's, I set off by the early morning coach before it was yet light, and was out in the open country-road when the day came creeping on, halting and whimpering and shivering, and wrapped in patches of cloud and rags of mist, like a beggar. When we drove up to the Blue Boar after a drizzly ride, whom should I see come out under the gateway, toothpick in hand, to look at the coach, but Bentley Drummle!

As he pretended not to see me, I pretended not to see him. It was a very lame pretense on both sides, the lamer because we both went into the coffee-room, where he had just finished his breakfast, and where I had ordered mine. It was
3 poisonous to me to see him in the town, for I very well knew why he had come there.

"Oh?" said I, "it's you, is it? Do you stay here long?"

"Can't say," answered Mr. Drummle. "Do you?"

"Can't say," said I.

Mr. Drummle looked at me, and then at my boots, and then said, "Oh!" and laughed.

"Are you amused, Mr. Drummle?"

"No," said he, "not particularly. I am going out for a ride in the saddle. I mean to explore those marshes for amusement. Out-of-the-way villages there, they tell me. Curious little public-houses—and smithies—and that. Waiter!"

"Yes, sir."

"Is that horse of mine ready?"

"Brought round to the door, sir."

"I say. Look here, you sir. The lady won't ride to-day; the weather won't do."

"Very good, sir."

"And I don't dine, because I am going to dine at the lady's."

"Very good, sir."

Then Drummle glanced at me, with an insolent triumph on his great-jowled face that cut me to the heart.

I saw him through the window, seizing his horse's mane, and mounting in his blundering brutal manner, and sidling and backing away. I thought he was gone, when he came back, calling for a light for the cigar in his mouth, which he had forgotten. A man in a dust-colored dress appeared with what was wanted, and as Drummle leaned down from the saddle and lighted his cigar and laughed with a jerk of his head towards
4 the coffee-room windows, the slouching shoulders, and ragged hair of this man, whose back was towards me, reminded me of Orlick.

Too heavily out of sorts to care much at the time whether it were he or no, or after all to touch the breakfast, I washed the weather and

AT A GLANCE

- Pip learns that Estella is with Miss Havisham.
- He travels to his home town and sees Bentley Drummle.
- Drummle will dine with Estella.

1 THEME

Pip fears for Magwitch's life (as well as for his own) and feels responsible for Magwitch's safety.

2 STYLE: FIGURATIVE LANGUAGE

Dickens compares the dawn to a beggar, "halting and whimpering and shivering," a reflection of Pip's helplessness before his impending visit to Miss Havisham and Estella.

3 STYLE: DIALOGUE

Pip's conversation with Drummle, innocuous as it seems, reveals their animosity: Each tries to find out how long the other is staying in order to know if his relationship with Estella may be threatened.

4 PLOT: FORESHADOWING

As Pip sees someone who looks like Orlick, Dickens hints that this character (whose role in the novel is still undefined) will appear again.

GUIDED READING

LITERAL QUESTION

1a. What does Drummle tell the waiter at the Blue Boar? (that he will not ride with "the lady" because of the bad weather and that he will dine with her)

INFERENTIAL QUESTION

1b. Why does he tell the waiter this? (to make it clear to Pip that Estella is receiving him)

AT A GLANCE

- Pip arrives at Miss Havisham's.
- He tells Miss Havisham and Estella that he knows his benefactor.
- He advises Miss Havisham that Matthew Pocket and his son are good and worthy people.

1 THEME

Pip imagines his relationship with Estella is so intimate that even the movement of her fingers on wool sends him a message.

2 THEME

Pip feels that he must tell Miss Havisham and Estella about his reverse in fortune: He has tired of deception and manipulation and is trying to control his life.

3 STYLE: DIALOGUE

As Miss Havisham admits her cruelty, Pip must confront the complete plan of her revenge: to lead Pip on by making him think he was meant for Estella.

4 THEME

Pip shows he has learned to be a true friend when he advises Miss Havisham that Matthew Pocket and his son Herbert are "generous, upright, open, and incapable of anything designing or mean."

the journey from my face and hands, and went out to the memorable old house that it would have been so much the better for me never to have entered, never to have seen.

In the room where the dressing-table stood, and where the wax candles burnt on the wall, I found Miss Havisham and Estella; Miss Havisham seated on a settee near the fire, and Estella on a cushion at her feet. Estella was knitting, and Miss Havisham was looking on. They both raised their eyes as I went in, and both saw an alteration in me. I derived that from the look they interchanged.

"And what wind," said Miss Havisham, "blows you here, Pip?"

Though she looked steadily at me, I saw that she was rather confused. Estella, pausing a moment in her knitting with her eyes upon me, and
1 then going on, I fancied that I read in the action of her fingers, as plainly as if she had told me in the dumb alphabet, that she perceived I had discovered my real benefactor.

"Miss Havisham," said I, "I went to Richmond yesterday, to speak to Estella; and finding that some wind had blown *her* here, I followed."

"What I had to say to Estella, Miss Havisham, I will say before you. It will not surprise you, it will not displease you. I am as unhappy as you can ever have meant me to be."

Miss Havisham continued to look steadily at me. I could see in the action of Estella's fingers as they worked that she attended to what I said—but she did not look up.

2 "I have found out who my patron is. It is not a fortunate discovery, and is not likely ever to enrich me in reputation, station, fortune, anything. There are reasons why I must say no more of that. It is not my secret, but another's."

As I was silent for a while, looking at Estella and considering how to go on, Miss Havisham repeated, "It is not your secret, but another's. Well?"

"When you first caused me to be brought here, Miss Havisham; when I belonged to the village over yonder, that I wish I had never left; I suppose I did really come here, as any other chance boy might have come—as a kind of servant, to gratify a want or a whim, and to be paid for it?"

"Aye, Pip," replied Miss Havisham, steadily nodding her head; "you did."

"And that Mr. Jaggers—"

"Mr. Jaggers," said Miss Havisham, taking me up in a firm tone, "had nothing to do with it, and knew nothing of it. His being my lawyer, and his being the lawyer of your patron, is a coincidence. He holds the same relation towards numbers of people, and it might easily arise. Be that as it may, it did arise, and was not brought about by any one."

Any one might have seen in her haggard face that there was no suppression or evasion so far.

3 "But when I fell into the mistake I have so long remained in, at least you led me on?" said I.

"Yes," she returned, again nodding steadily, "I let you go on."

"Was that kind?"

"Who am I," cried Miss Havisham, striking her stick upon the floor, and flashing into wrath so suddenly that Estella glanced up at her in surprise, "who am I, that I should be kind?"

Waiting until she was quiet again—for this, too, flashed out of her in a wild and sudden way—I went on.

"I have been thrown among one family of your relations, Miss Havisham, and have been constantly among them since I went to London. I know them to have been as honestly under my
4 delusion as I myself. And I should be false and base if I did not tell you that you deeply wrong both Mr. Matthew Pocket and his son Herbert, if you suppose them to be otherwise than generous, upright, open, and incapable of anything designing or mean."

"They are your friends," said Miss Havisham.

GUIDED READING

LITERAL QUESTIONS

1a. What is Miss Havisham's initial reaction to Pip's visit? (She is confused.)

2a. What does Pip say about Matthew Pocket and his son Herbert? (that they are kind and that Miss Havisham has wronged them)

INFERENTIAL QUESTIONS

1b. Why does she react this way? (She did not call for Pip.)

2b. Why do you think he speaks of them to Miss Havisham? (He may hope that Miss Havisham will help them financially.)

"They made themselves my friends," said I, "when they supposed me to have superseded them;[1] and when Sarah Pocket and Mistress Camilla were not my friends, I think."

This contrasting of them with the rest seemed, I was glad to see, to do them good with her. She looked at me keenly for a little while, and then said quietly:

"What do you want for them?"

"I am not so cunning, you see," I said, "as that I could hide from you that I do want something. Miss Havisham, if you could spare the money to do my friend Herbert a lasting service without his knowledge, I could show you how."

"Why must it be done without his knowledge?" she asked.

"Because," said I, "I began the service myself, more than two years ago, without his knowledge, and I don't want to be betrayed. Why I fail in my ability to finish it I cannot explain. It is a part of the secret."

She gradually withdrew her eyes from me, and turned them on the fire.

"Estella," said I turning to her now, and trying to command my trembling voice, "you know I love you. You know that I have loved you long and dearly."

She raised her eyes to my face and her fingers plied their work. I saw that Miss Havisham glanced from me to her and from her to me.

"I should have said this sooner, but for my long mistake. It induced me to hope that Miss Havisham meant us for one another. While I thought you could not help yourself, as it were, I refrained from saying it. But I must say it now."

With her fingers still going, Estella shook her head.

"I know," said I, in answer to that action; "I know. I have no hope that I shall ever call you mine, Estella. I am ignorant what may become of me very soon, how poor I may be, or where I may go. Still, I love you. I have loved you ever since I first saw you in this house."

Looking at me perfectly unmoved and with her fingers busy, she shook her head again.

"It would have been cruel in Miss Havisham, horribly cruel, to practice on the susceptibility of a poor boy, and to torture me through all these years with a vain hope and an idle pursuit, if she had reflected on the gravity of what she
3 did. But I think she did not. I think that in the endurance of her own trial, she forgot mine, Estella."

I saw Miss Havisham put her hand to her heart and hold it there, as she sat looking by turns at Estella and at me.

"It seems," said Estella very calmly, "that there are sentiments, fancies—I don't know how to call them—which I am not able to comprehend. When you say you love me, I know what you mean as a form of words, but nothing more. I don't care for what you say at all. I have tried to warn you of this, now, have I not?"

I said, in a miserable manner, "Yes."

"Yes. But you would not be warned, for you thought I did not mean it. Now, did you not think so?"

"I thought and hoped you could not mean it. Is it not true, that Bentley Drummle is in town here, and pursuing you?"

"It is quite true," she replied.

"That you encourage him, and ride out with him, and that he dines with you this very day?"

She seemed a little surprised but again replied, "Quite true."

4 "You cannot love him, Estella?"

Her fingers stopped for the first time.

"You would never marry him, Estella?"

She looked towards Miss Havisham. Then she said, "Why not tell you the truth? I am going to be married to him."

I dropped my face into my hands, but was able to control myself better than I could have expected, considering what agony it gave me to hear her say those words. When I raised my face

---

1. **superseded** [so͞o′pər sēd′id] **them:** replaced them in Miss Havisham's favor.

AT A GLANCE

- Pip asks Miss Havisham to help Herbert.
- Pip admits his love for Estella.
- Estella tells him she is going to marry Drummle.

1 THEME

Pip shows that (even though his own fortunes are reversed) he will now go to great lengths to see that his friend's opportunities are not ruined.

2 CHARACTERIZATION

Pip still possesses a fragile hope that Estella will respond to his declaration of love. Though his attitude has become more realistic, he still holds some romantic ideals.

3 THEME

By letting Miss Havisham know that he can forgive her cruelty, Pip forces her to realize the full extent of her responsibility for his heartbreak and Estella's heartlessness.

4 CHARACTERIZATION

The complexity of Estella's character is revealed when Pip asks if she loves Drummle: Her quiet fingers indicate that the question disturbs her, but she insists that she will marry him.

GUIDED READING

LITERAL QUESTIONS

1a. What excuse does Pip give for Miss Havisham's cruelty? (He says that in her own suffering she forgot his.)

2a. How does Estella react to Pip's declaration of love? (She says she does not comprehend it.)

INFERENTIAL QUESTIONS

1a. What effect does this statement have on Miss Havisham? (She realizes that others suffer as she does.)

2b. Why do you think Estella is going to marry Bentley Drummle, whom she clearly does not love? (She cannot love; she is coldly fulfilling the role for which she was trained.)

AT A GLANCE

- Pip begs Estella not to marry Drummle.
- She insists she will marry him and says Pip will soon forget her.
- Pip declares that his love for her will never die.

1 CHARACTERIZATION

Pip's character has broadened throughout the novel: By urging Estella to put him aside and give herself to a worthier man than Drummle, he shows his willingness to sacrifice his own for another's happiness.

2 RESPONSE JOURNAL

Have students write in their journals a description of the way in which Pip's feelings for Estella have changed over time.

again, there was such a ghastly look upon Miss Havisham's that it impressed me, even in my passionate hurry and grief.

1 "Estella, dearest, dearest Estella, do not let Miss Havisham lead you into this fatal step. Put me aside for ever—you have done so, I well know—but bestow yourself on some worthier person than Drummle. Miss Havisham gives you to him as the greatest slight and injury that could be done to the many far better men who admire you, and to the few who truly love you."

"I am going," she said again, in a gentler voice, "to be married to him. The preparations for my marriage are making, and I shall be married soon."

"Such a mean brute, such a stupid brute!" I urged in despair.

"Don't be afraid of my being a blessing to him," said Estella; "I shall not be that. Come! Here is my hand. Do we part on this, you visionary boy—or man?"

"Oh, Estella," I answered, as my bitter tears fell fast on her hand, do what I would to restrain them; "even if I remained in England and could hold my head up with the rest, how could I see you Drummle's wife?"

"Nonsense," she returned, "nonsense. This will pass in no time."

"Never, Estella!"

"You will get me out of your thoughts in a week."

"Out of my thoughts! You are part of my ex-
2 istence, part of myself. You have been in every line I have ever read, since I first came here, the rough common boy whose poor heart you wounded even then. You have been in every prospect I have ever seen since—on the river, on the sails of the ships, on the marshes, in the clouds, in the light, in the darkness, in the wind, in the woods, in the sea, in the streets. Estella, to the last hour of my life, you cannot choose but remain part of me. O God bless you, God forgive you!"

GUIDED READING

LITERAL QUESTION

1a. What does Estella say about how she will behave toward Drummle? (She says that she will not be a blessing to him.)

INFERENTIAL QUESTION

1b. What does she mean? (that her coldness and cruelty will make life miserable for Drummle)

I held her hand to my lips some lingering mo-
ents, and so I left her. But ever afterwards, I re-
embered that while Estella looked at me mere- with wonder, Miss Havisham, her hand still
overing her heart, seemed resolved into a ghast- stare of pity and remorse.

All done, all gone!

It was past midnight when I crossed London ridge. I was not expected till tomorrow, but I ad my keys, and, if Herbert were gone to bed, ould get to bed myself without disturbing him.

I came in at that Whitefriars gate and as I was ery muddy and weary, I did not take it ill that e night porter examined me with much atten- on as he held the gate a little way open for me pass in. To help his memory I mentioned my ame.

"I was not quite sure, sir, but I thought so. ere's a note, sir. The messenger that brought it id, Would you be so good as read it by my lan- rn?"

Much surprised by the request, I took the ote. It was directed to Philip Pip, Esquire,[2] and n the top were the words, "PLEASE READ THIS ERE." I opened it, the watchman holding up his ght, and read inside, in Wemmick's writing:

"DON'T GO HOME."

hapter Thirty

ondon and Walworth: Wemmick and Herbert ake action.

Turning from the Temple gate as soon as I ad read the warning, I made the best of my way Fleet Street, and there got a late hackney hariot[1] and drove to the Hummums in Covent arden. In those times a bed was always to be ot there at any hour of the night.

What a doleful night! How anxious, how dismal, how long! There was an inhospitable smell in the room of cold soot and hot dust.

DON'T GO HOME.

Whatever night-fancies and night-noises crowded on me, they never warded off this DON'T GO HOME.

I left directions that I was to be called at seven, for it was plain that I must see Wemmick before seeing any one else, and equally plain that this was a case in which his Walworth senti-
3 ments only could be taken. It was a relief to get out of the room where the night had been so miserable, and I needed no second knocking at the door to startle me from my uneasy bed.

The castle battlements arose upon my view at eight o'clock. The little servant happening to be entering the fortress with two hot rolls, I passed through the postern[2] and crossed the drawbridge in her company, and so came without announcement into the presence of Wemmick as he was making tea for himself and the Aged. An open door afforded a perspective view of the Aged in bed.

"Halloa, Mr. Pip!" said Wemmick. "You did come home, then?"

"Yes," I returned; "but I didn't go home."

"That's all right," said he, rubbing his hands. "I left a note for you at each of the Temple gates, on the chance. Which gate did you come to?"

I told him.

4 "I'll go round to the others in the course of the day and destroy the notes," said Wemmick. "*Would* you mind toasting this sausage for the Aged P.?"

I said I should be delighted to do it.

"Then you can go about your work, Mary Anne," said Wemmick to the little servant, "which leaves us to ourselves, don't you see, Mr. Pip?" he added, winking, as she disappeared.

I thanked him for his friendship and caution.

. **Esquire:** title of respect for a gentleman.
. **hackney chariot:** horse-drawn cab.

2. **postern:** back gate.

AT A GLANCE

- Pip returns to London and receives a note from Wemmick warning him not to go home.
- He spends the night at an inn.
- In the morning he goes to Walworth to see Wemmick.

1 IRONY

When at last Miss Havisham's revenge is realized, she discovers with "pity and remorse" that she really wants Pip and Estella to be together.

2 PLOT: NARRATIVE HOOK

Dickens again ends a chapter on a highly suspenseful note. Since Wemmick's warning says only *DON'T GO HOME,* the reader is as unsure of what danger awaits Pip as he is.

3 STYLE: PERSONIFICATION

Pip describes his bed as "uneasy," giving it the human characteristic that he himself possesses throughout the long night of waiting.

4 STYLE: HUMOR

Although the scene is one of mystery and tension, Dickens infuses it with humor by having Wemmick ask Pip to perform a task so ordinary that it appears amusing.

GUIDED READING

LITERAL QUESTIONS

1a. How does Miss Havisham look when Pip leaves? ("ghastly" and remorseful)

2a. Where does Pip plan to go to see Wemmick? (to Walworth)

INFERENTIAL QUESTIONS

1b. What do you think she is feeling? (She is sorry that she has ruined Pip's and Estella's relationship.)

2b. Why must he visit Wemmick there? (It seems that the message may concern Magwitch, which is a subject Wemmick could not approach officially.)

AT A GLANCE

- Wemmick explains that Pip and Magwitch have been watched.
- He hints that the watcher is Compeyson.
- At Herbert's suggestion, Magwitch was given a room in the house of Herbert's friend.

1 PARAPHRASING THE PASSAGE

Wemmick says (as indirectly as possible) that news of Magwitch's disappearance from Australia has led to potentially dangerous speculation on his present whereabouts.

2 READING SKILLS: INFERENCE

From the conversation between Wemmick and Pip, the reader can infer that Compeyson, who is in London, is watching Pip's rooms.

3 THEME

The concern that Wemmick and Herbert have for Pip has led them to devise a complex plan that will keep Pip safe and get Magwitch out of the country.

1 "Now, Mr. Pip, I accidentally heard, yesterday morning, that a certain person had made some little stir in a certain part of the world where a good many people go, by disappearing from such place, and being no more heard of thereabouts. From which," said Wemmick, "conjectures had been raised and theories formed. I also heard that you at your chambers in Garden Court, Temple, had been watched, and might be watched again."

"By whom?" said I.

"I wouldn't go into that," said Wemmick evasively; "it might clash with official responsibilities."

2 "You have heard of a man of bad character whose true name is Compeyson?"

He answered with a nod.

"Is he living?"

One other nod.

"Is he in London?"

He gave me one last nod, and went on with his breakfast.

"Now," said Wemmick, "questioning being over"—which he emphasized and repeated for my guidance—"I come to what I did, after hearing what I heard. I went to Garden Court to find you; not finding you, I went to Clarriker's to find Mr. Herbert."

"And him you found?" said I, with great anxiety.

"And him I found. Without mentioning any names or going into any details, I gave him to understand that if he was aware of anybody—Tom, Jack, or Richard—being about the chambers, or about the immediate neighborhood, he had better get Tom, Jack, or Richard out of the way while you were out of the way. Mr. Herbert, after being all of a heap for half an hour, struck out a plan. He mentioned to me as a secret that he is courting a young lady who has, as no doubt you are aware, a bedridden pa. Which pa, having been in the purser[3] line of life, lies a-bed in a bow-window where he can see the ships sail up and down the river. You are acquainted with the young lady, most probably?"

"Not personally," said I. The truth was that she had objected to me as an expensive companion.

"The house with the bow-window," said Wemmick, "being by the riverside, down the Pool there between Limehouse and Greenwich, and being kept, it seems, by a very respectable widow, who has a furnished upper floor to let, Mr. Herbert put it to me, what did I think of that as a temporary tenement for Tom, Jack, or Richard. Now, I thought very well of it, for three reasons I'll give you. That is to say, firstly, it's
3 altogether out of all your beats. Secondly, without going near it yourself, you could always hear of the safety of Tom, Jack, or Richard through Mr. Herbert. Thirdly, after a while, and when it might be prudent if you should want to slip Tom, Jack, or Richard on board a foreign packet-boat,[4] there he is—ready."

Much comforted by these considerations, I thanked Wemmick again and again, and begged him to proceed.

"Well, sir! Mr. Herbert threw himself into the business with a will, and by nine o'clock last night he housed Tom, Jack, or Richard—whichever it may be—you and I don't want to know—quite successfully. At the old lodgings it was understood that he was summoned to Dover, and in fact he was taken down the Dover road and cornered out of it. Now, another great advantage of all this is that it was done without you, and when, if any one was concerning himself about your movements, you must be known to be ever so many miles off, and quite otherwise engaged.

"And now, Mr. Pip," said he, "I have probably done the most I can do; but if I can ever do more—from a Walworth point of view, I shall be

3. **purser:** financial officer on a ship.

4. **packet-boat:** steamship that carries freight and passengers along a regular route.

GUIDED READING

LITERAL QUESTIONS

1a. By what names does Wemmick refer to Magwitch? ("Tom, Jack, or Richard")

2a. How do Herbert and Wemmick disguise Magwitch's move? (They say he was "summoned to Dover" and take him down the Dover Road.)

INFERENTIAL QUESTIONS

1b. Why doesn't he name Magwitch directly? (He is afraid of getting directly involved in illegal activities.)

2b. Why do they do this? (to confuse his pursuers)

glad to do it. Here's the address. There can be no harm in your going here to-night and seeing for yourself that all is well with Tom, Jack, or Richard before you go home.

"But after you have gone home, don't go back. Let me finally impress one important point upon you." He laid his hands upon my shoulders, and added in a solemn whisper: "Avail yourself of this evening to lay hold of his portable property. You don't know what may happen to him. Don't let anything happen to the portable property.

"Time's up," said Wemmick, "and I must be off. If you had nothing more pressing to do than to keep here till dark, that's what I should advise. You look very much worried, and it would do you good to have a perfectly quiet day with the Aged—he'll be up presently."

I soon fell asleep before Wemmick's fire, and the Aged and I enjoyed one another's society by falling asleep before it more or less all day. We had loin of pork for dinner, and greens grown on the estate, and I nodded at the Aged with a good intention whenever I failed to do it drowsily. When it was quite dark, I left the Aged preparing the fire for toast.

Eight o'clock had struck before I got into the air that was scented, not disagreeably, by the chips and shavings of the long-shore boat-builders. All that waterside region of the upper and lower Pool below the Bridge was unknown ground to me.

Selecting from the few queer houses upon Mill Pond Bank, a house with a wooden front and three stories of bow-window, I looked at the plate upon the door, and read there Mrs. Whimple. That being the name I wanted, I knocked, and an elderly woman of a pleasant and thriving appearance responded. She was immediately deposed, however, by Herbert, who silently led me into the parlor and shut the door. It was an odd sensation to see his very familiar face established quite at home in that very unfamiliar room and region.

AT A GLANCE

- Wemmick counsels Pip to take possession of Magwitch's "portable property."
- Wemmick leaves for work and Pip spends the day with the Aged.
- At nightfall, Pip goes to the lodging near the waterside to see Herbert and Magwitch.

1 PARAPHRASING THE PASSAGE

Wemmick advises Pip to take the remainder of his inheritance from Magwitch as soon as possible, as the convict may be recaptured or killed.

GUIDED READING

LITERAL QUESTION

1a. What advice does Wemmick give Pip concerning Magwitch? (to "lay hold of his portable property")

INFERENTIAL QUESTION

1b. Why does Wemmick advise this? (He is afraid Magwitch will be caught and his money confiscated.)

AT A GLANCE

- Herbert reassures Pip that all is well with Magwitch.
- Herbert and Pip plan to row up and down the Thames to disguise their real plans.

1 CHARACTERIZATION

Pip finds Magwitch "softened"—he is becoming gentler and more affectionate as he is exposed to Herbert's and Pip's kindness and aid.

2 THEME

Pip and Herbert plan to spend time rowing up and down the river so their pursuer will be fooled when they make their escape with Magwitch.

3 PLOT: FORESHADOWING

Magwitch says he doesn't like "good-bye," foreshadowing a later time when he and Pip may have to say "good-bye."

"All is well, Handel," said Herbert, "and he is quite satisfied, though eager to see you. My dear girl is with her father; and if you'll wait till she comes down, I'll make you known to her, and then we'll go upstairs. *That's* her father."

I had become aware of an alarming growling overhead, and had probably expressed the fact in my countenance.

"I am afraid he is a sad old rascal," said Herbert, smiling, "but I have never seen him."

While he thus spoke, the growling noise became a prolonged roar, and then died away.

"To have Provis for an upper lodger is quite a godsend to Mrs. Whimple," said Herbert, "for of course people in general won't stand that noise. Mrs. Whimple is the best of housewives, and I really do not know what my Clara would do without her motherly help. For Clara has no mother of her own, Handel, and no relation in the world but old Gruffandgrim."

In his two cabin rooms at the top of the
1 house, I found Provis comfortably settled. He expressed no alarm, and seemed to feel none that was worth mentioning, but it struck me that he was softened—indefinably. I asked him first of all whether he relied on Wemmick's judgment and sources of information.

"Aye, aye, dear boy!" he answered, with a grave nod, "Jaggers knows."

"Then, I have talked with Wemmick," said I, "and have come to tell you what caution he gave me and what advice."

I told him how Wemmick had heard, in Newgate prison[5] (whether from officers or prisoners I could not say), that he was under some suspicion, and that my chambers had been watched.

Herbert, who had been looking at the fire and pondering, here said that something had come into his thoughts arising out of Wemmick's suggestion. "We are both good watermen, Handel, and could take him down the river ourselves when the right time comes. No boat would then be hired for the purpose, and no boatmen; that would save at least a chance of suspicion, and any chance is worth saving. Don't
2 you think it might be a good thing if you began at once to keep a boat at the Temple stairs, and were in the habit of rowing up and down the river? You fall into that habit, and then who notices or minds? Do it twenty or fifty times, and there is nothing special in your doing it the twenty-first or fifty-first."

I liked this scheme, and Provis was quite elated by it. We agreed that it should be carried into execution, and that Provis should never recognize us if we came below Bridge and rowed past Mill Pond Bank. But we further agreed that he should pull down the blind in that part of his window which gave upon the east, whenever he saw us and all was right.

Everything arranged, I rose to go, remarking to Herbert that he and I had better not go home together, and that I would take half an hour's start of him. "I don't like to leave you here," I said to Provis, "though I cannot doubt your being safer here than near me. Good-bye!"

3 "Dear boy," he answered, clasping my hands, "I don't know when we may meet again, and I don't like good-bye. Say good night!"

"Good night! Herbert will go regularly between us, and when the time comes you may be certain I shall be ready. Good night, good night!"

All things were as quiet in the Temple as ever I had seen them. The windows of the rooms of that side lately occupied by Provis were dark and still, and there was no lounger in Garden Court.

Next day, I set myself to get the boat. It was soon done, and the boat was brought round to the Temple stairs, and lay where I could reach her within a minute or two. Then, I began to go

5. **Newgate prison:** prison in London. Wemmick's position as a law clerk would give him cause to visit prisoners.

GUIDED READING

LITERAL QUESTIONS

1a. How does Pip think Magwitch has changed? (He says Magwitch has "softened.")

2a. How does Pip feel about leaving Magwitch? (He doesn't want to leave him.)

INFERENTIAL QUESTIONS

1b. What do you think has caused the change? (Magwitch is aware that Pip and Herbert actually care about what happens to him.)

2b. Why does he feel this way? (He feels responsible for Magwitch and is beginning to be fond of him.)

out as for training and practice. At first, I kept above Blackfriars Bridge; but as the hours of the tide changed, I took towards London Bridge. Still, I knew that there was cause for alarm, and I could not get rid of the notion of being watched. I was always full of fears for the rash man who was in hiding.

Chapter Thirty-one

London, weeks later: Mr. Wopsle sees a ghost.

Some weeks passed without bringing any change. We waited for Wemmick, and he made no sign. If I had never enjoyed the privilege of being on a familiar footing at the castle, I might have doubted him; not so for a moment, knowing him as I did.

My worldly affairs began to wear a gloomy appearance, and I was pressed for money by more than one creditor. Even I myself began to know the want of money (I mean of ready money in my own pocket), and to relieve it by converting some easily spared articles of jewelry into cash. But I had quite determined that it would be a heartless fraud to take more money from my patron in the existing state of my uncertain thoughts and plans. I felt a kind of satisfaction in not having profited by his generosity since his revelation of himself.

As the time wore on, an impression settled heavily upon me that Estella was married. Fearful of having it confirmed, though it was all but a conviction, I avoided the newspapers, and begged Herbert (to whom I had confided the circumstances of our last interview) never to speak of her to me. Why I hoarded up this last wretched little rag of the robe of hope that was rent and given to the winds, how do I know?

It was an unhappy life that I lived. Condemned to inaction, I rowed about in my boat, and waited, waited, waited.

There were states of the tide when, having been down the river, I could not get back through the eddy-chafed arches and starlings of Old London Bridge; then I left my boat at a wharf near the Custom House. I was not averse to doing this, as it served to make me and my boat a commoner incident among the waterside people there. From this slight occasion sprang two meetings that I have now to tell of.

One afternoon, late in the month of February, I came ashore at the wharf at dusk. I had seen the signal in his window, All well. As it was a raw evening and I was cold, I thought I would comfort myself with dinner at once; I thought I would afterwards go to the play. The theater where Mr. Wopsle had achieved his questionable triumph was in that waterside neighborhood.

3 In the first scene it pained me to suspect that I detected Mr. Wopsle with red worsted legs under a highly magnified phosphoric countenance and a shock of red curtain-fringe for his hair, engaged in displaying great cowardice. And I observed with great surprise that he devoted it to staring in my direction as if he were lost in amazement.

There was something so remarkable in the increasing glare of Mr. Wopsle's eye that I could not make it out. I was still thinking of it when I came out of the theater an hour afterwards, and found him waiting for me near the door.

"How do you do?" said I, shaking hands with him as we turned down the street together. "I saw that you saw me."

4 "Saw you, Mr. Pip!" he returned. "Yes, of course I saw you. But who else was there?"

"Who else?"

"It is the strangest thing," said Mr. Wopsle.

Becoming alarmed, I entreated Mr. Wopsle to explain his meaning.

"Whether I should have noticed him at first but for your being there," said Mr. Wopsle, "I can't be positive."

Involuntarily I looked round me.

AT A GLANCE

- The next day Pip procures a boat and rows on the river.
- Pip waits for Wemmick to indicate the proper time for Magwitch's escape; he rows in the boat.
- He sees Mr. Wopsle perform.
- Mr. Wopsle saw someone with Pip.

1 THEME

Pip knows beyond doubt that Wemmick is a friend on whom he can depend, despite his dour office manner.

2 THEME

Pip desperately hopes that Estella might yet be his, although he knows it is impossible; so many of his dreams have been dashed that he feels he must cling to this deepest one.

3 STYLE: HUMOR

Dickens contrasts the past Wopsle—a pompous, proper man—and the present Wopsle "with red worsted legs . . . displaying great cowardice" to establish a humorous contradiction.

4 PLOT: NARRATIVE HOOK

With Wopsle's question Pip's short period of calm, inactive waiting is shattered; suspense builds once more as Pip realizes he is being followed.

GUIDED READING

LITERAL QUESTIONS

1a. What has happened to Pip's finances? (He is in debt and short of cash; he is "pressed for money by more than one creditor.")

2a. What does Pip do for the next several weeks? (He rows his boat and waits for a sign from Wemmick.)

INFERENTIAL QUESTIONS

1b. Why doesn't he want to take Magwitch's money? (He doesn't want to take advantage of him anymore.)

2b. Why does he call this "an unhappy life"? (He is nervous and afraid for Magwitch and for his own want of money, and he is depressed about Estella.)

AT A GLANCE

- From Mr. Wopsle's description Pip knows that the man following him is Compeyson.
- Pip writes to Wemmick to warn him of this turn of events.

1 STYLE: SIMILE

Wopsle compares the stranger to a ghost, a simile that echoes Compeyson's appearance on the marshes and the vague, threatening nature of his role in Pip's affairs.

2 THEME

Although Pip wants Wemmick to know what has happened, he is aware that Wemmick, too, is at risk. Pip acts responsibly by writing to Wemmick so he will not be implicated in Magwitch's doings.

REFLECTING ON CHAPTERS 24–31

How have Pip's feelings about his expectations changed since his arrival in London? (Possible answer: He no longer expects his dreams to come true through wealth and does not even want his "inheritance.")

"Oh! He can't be in sight," said Mr. Wopsle.
1 "He went out before I went off. I saw him go. I had a ridiculous fancy that he must be with you, Mr. Pip, till I saw that you were quite unconscious of him, sitting behind you there like a ghost."

My former chill crept over me again. Of course, I was perfectly sure and safe that Provis had not been there.

"I dare say you wonder at me, Mr. Pip; indeed, I see you do. But it is so very strange! You remember in old times a certain Christmas Day, when you were quite a child, and I dined at Gargery's, and some soldiers came to the door to get a pair of handcuffs mended?"

"I remember it very well."

"And you remember that there was a chase after two convicts, and that we joined in it, and that Gargery took you on his back? And you remember that we came up with the two in a ditch, and that there was a scuffle between them, and that one of them had been severely handled and much mauled about the face by the other?"

"I see it all before me."

"And that the soldiers lighted torches, and put the two in the center, and that we went on to see the last of them, over the black marshes, with the torchlight shining on their faces—I am particular about that—with the torchlight shining on their faces, when there was an outer ring of dark night all about us?"

"Yes," said I. "I remember all that."

"Then, Mr. Pip, one of those two prisoners sat behind you to-night. I saw him over your shoulder."

"Steady!" I thought. I asked him then, "Which of the two do you suppose you saw?"

"The one who had been mauled," he answered readily, "and I'll swear I saw him! The more I think of him, the more certain I am of him."

"This is very curious!" said I, with the best assumption I could put on of its being nothing more to me. "Very curious indeed!"

I cannot exaggerate the terror I felt at Compeyson's having been behind me "like a ghost." For if he had ever been out of my thoughts for a few moments together since the hiding had begun, it was in those very moments when he was closest to me; and to think that I should be so unconscious and off my guard after all my care. I could not doubt either that he was there, because I was there.

When Mr. Wopsle had imparted to me all that he could recall or I extract, and when I had treated him to a little refreshment after the fatigues of the evening, we parted. It was between twelve and one o'clock when I reached the Temple, and the gates were shut. No one was near me when I went in and went home.

Herbert had come in, and we held a very serious council by the fire. But there was nothing to be done, saving to communicate to Wemmick what I had that night found out, and
2 to remind him that we waited for his hint. As I thought that I might compromise him if I went too often to the castle, I made this communication by letter. I wrote it before I went to bed and went out and posted it; and again no one was near me. Herbert and I agreed that we could do nothing else but be very cautious.

GUIDED READING

LITERAL QUESTION

1a. What do Pip and Herbert agree must be the response to Compeyson's presence? (nothing can be done except communicate the information to Wemmick; they must continue to wait cautiously)

INFERENTIAL QUESTION

1b. Why must Pip wait? (If he takes action before Wemmick says the time is right, he might inadvertently betray Magwitch.)

STUDY QUESTIONS

Recalling

1. Describe Pip's plan for Herbert in Chapter 24.
2. According to Chapter 26, where has Magwitch been since Pip met him on the marshes? In what ways did he make his money? What risk does he take by returning to London?
3. According to Chapter 26, who is Pip's benefactor? In what way does knowing his benefactor change Pip's thinking about Estella? About Joe?
4. According to Chapter 28, what part has Compeyson played so far in the lives of Pip, Magwitch, and Miss Havisham?
5. What financial request does Pip make of Miss Havisham in Chapter 29?
6. What news does Pip learn about Estella and Drummle in Chapter 29?

Interpreting

7. Describe Pip's treatment of Magwitch in Chapter 26. Compare this to the way the younger Pip treated the convict on the marshes. In what ways has Pip changed?
8. Why does Pip vow to take no more money from Magwitch? What difficulties does this vow cause him?
9. Explain how Pip and Estella make Miss Havisham regret what she had planned for them.

Extending

10. In what way do you think Pip would define the word *gentleman*? How do you define the word? Do you think that Pip knows what a real gentleman is? Explain your opinion.

LITERARY FOCUS

Foreshadowing

Foreshadowing is the use of clues by the author to prepare readers for events that will happen later in a story, novel, or play. These clues appeal to our curiosity, increase our interest, and often build suspense. Dickens' novels often surprise readers with sudden reappearances of characters and with startling coincidences. Although these sudden revelations are meant to surprise, the reader must be given some warning or the events of the novel will not be believable.

Thinking About Foreshadowing

1. In what ways does Dickens use foreshadowing to prepare the reader for the return of Magwitch as Pip's benefactor?
2. Name two other characters from Pip's youth who have returned so far in the novel. What clues prepare us for these reappearances?
3. What startling coincidences have occurred so far in the novel? What warning was the reader given to make these coincidences more realistic and believable?

STUDY QUESTIONS

1. Pip secretly pays broker to take on Herbert with prospects of becoming partner.
2. in New South Wales; speculated with money earned as shepherd; risks death if caught
3. Magwitch; realizes Estella was never intended for him; regrets having abandoned Joe
4. was swindler involved with Magwitch; blamed him at trial; was second convict on marshes; was Miss Havisham's fiancé
5. to help Herbert by continuing payments to his company
6. They are to be married.
7. is aloof, coldly polite, judgmental; younger Pip more afraid but more compassionate; has changed from innocent boy into a gentleman and snob
8. thinks it wrong to be obligated to someone he detests; has no occupation and many debts
9. Estella says she cannot love Miss Havisham; Pip is unhappy about Estella's engagement; Havisham realizes she has caused others pain.
10.
- one who is educated, with correct social behavior
- Answers will vary.
- Pip is too caught up in appearances to know.

LITERARY FOCUS

1.
- *Chapter 9:* man in pub who stirs drink with file gives Pip money
- *Chapter 24:* infer benefactor is not in direct communication with Mr. Jaggers
- *Chapter 25:* Pip says he is approaching a turning point.

2.
- *Mr. Wopsle:* Joe told Pip he had gone to London to be an actor.
- *Compeyson:* Magwitch's tale, Wemmick's report that he is looking for Magwitch

3.
- Compeyson was Miss Havisham's fiancé, a swindler who worked with partner named Arthur; Miss Havisham's brother was named Arthur.
- Herbert Pocket is pale young gentleman; Pip is to be tutored by Matthew Pocket, a relative of Miss Havisham.

AT A GLANCE

- Pip and Wemmick dine with Jaggers.
- Jaggers gives Pip a note from Miss Havisham.
- Molly serves dinner, and Pip notes her resemblance to Estella.
- He believes that Molly is Estella's mother.

LITERARY OPTIONS

- the total effect
- conflict
- figurative language

THEMATIC OPTIONS

- revenge
- love
- guilt and forgiveness

1 CONFLICT

Pip's feelings for Mr. Jaggers are revealed in this conversation: He resents Jaggers' constant questioning and is "glad for once to get the better of him in cross-examination."

2 VOCABULARY: WORD CHOICE

Mr. Jaggers remarks that Drummle has "played his cards" and "won the pool," as if Pip's and Drummle's bid for Estella's hand were a game of chance.

Chapter Thirty-two

London: Dinner with Jaggers, more about Molly.

The second of the two meetings referred to in the last chapter occurred about a week after the first. I had strolled up into Cheapside, and was strolling along it, surely the most unsettled person in all the busy concourse, when a large hand was laid upon my shoulder by some one overtaking me. It was Mr. Jaggers's hand, and he passed it through my arm.

"As we were going in the same direction, Pip, we may walk together. Where are you bound for?"

"For the Temple, I think," said I.

1 "Don't you know?" said Mr. Jaggers.

"Well," I returned, glad for once to get the better of him in cross-examination, "I do *not* know, for I have not made up my mind."

"You are going to dine?" said Mr. Jaggers. "You don't mind admitting that, I suppose?"

"No," I returned, "I don't mind admitting that."

"And are not engaged?"

"I don't mind admitting also that I am not engaged."

"Then," said Mr. Jaggers, "come and dine with me."

I was going to excuse myself, when he added, "Wemmick's coming." So I changed my excuse into an acceptance.

We went to Gerrard Streeet, all three together, in a hackney-coach, and as soon as we got there, dinner was served.

"Did you send that note of Miss Havisham's to Mr. Pip, Wemmick?" Mr. Jaggers asked, soon after we began dinner.

"No, sir," returned Wemmick; "it was going by post, when you brought Mr. Pip into the office. Here it is." He handed it to his principal, instead of to me.

"It's a note of two lines, Pip," said Mr. Jaggers, handing it on, "sent up to me by Miss Havisham, on account of her not being sure of your address. She tells me that she wants to see you on a little matter of business you mentioned to her. You'll go down?"

"Yes," said I, casting my eyes over the note, which was exactly in those terms.

"When do you think of going down?"

"If Mr. Pip has the intention of going at once," said Wemmick to Mr. Jaggers, "he needn't write an answer, you know."

Receiving this as an intimation that it was best not to delay, I settled that I would go to-morrow, and said so.

2 "So, Pip! Our friend the Spider," said Mr. Jaggers, "has played his cards. He has won the pool."

It was as much as I could do to assent.

"So, here's to Mrs. Bentley Drummle," said Mr. Jaggers. "Now, Molly, Molly, Molly, Molly, how slow you are to-day!"

She was at his elbow when he addressed her, putting a dish upon the table. As she withdrew her hands from it, she fell back a step or two, nervously muttering some excuse. And a certain action of her fingers as she spoke arrested my attention. The action of her fingers was like the action of knitting. She stood looking at her master. Her look was very intent. Surely, I had seen exactly such eyes and such hands on a memorable occasion very lately!

He dismissed her, and she glided out of the room. But she remained before me, as plainly as if she were still there. I looked at those hands, I looked at those eyes, I looked at that flowing hair, and I compared them with other hands, other eyes, other hair, that I knew of, and with what those might be after twenty years of a brutal husband and a stormy life. I looked again at those hands and eyes of the housekeeper. I saw a face looking at me, and a hand waving to me from a stage-coach window; and how it had come back again and had flashed about me like lightning. And I felt absolutely certain that this woman was Estella's mother.

We took our leave early, and left together.

GUIDED READING

LITERAL QUESTION

1a. What does Pip deduce about Molly? (that she is Estella's mother)

INFERENTIAL QUESTION

1b. What effect do you think this knowledge would have on Estella? (It might shame her because she is so proud.)

"Well!" said Wemmick, "that's over!"

I asked him if he had ever seen Miss Havisham's adopted daughter, Mrs. Bentley Drummle? He said no.

"Wemmick," said I, "do you remember telling me, before I first went to Mr. Jaggers's private house, to notice that housekeeper?"

"Did I?" he replied. "Ah, I dare say I did."

"A wild beast tamed, you called her?"

"And what did *you* call her?"

"The same. How did Mr. Jaggers tame her, Wemmick?"

"That's his secret. She has been with him many a long year."

"I wish you would tell me her story. I feel a particular interest in being acquainted with it. You know that what is said between you and me goes no further."

"Well!" Wemmick replied, "I don't know her story—that is, I don't know all of it. But what I do know, I'll tell you. We are in our private and personal capacities, of course."

"Of course."

"A score[1] or so of years ago, that woman was tried at the Old Bailey for murder and was acquitted. She was a very handsome young woman.

"Mr. Jaggers was for her," pursued Wemmick, with a look full of meaning, "and worked the case in a way quite astonishing. It was a desperate case, and it was comparatively early days with him then, and he worked it to general admiration; in fact, it may almost be said to have made him.

"The murdered person was a woman; a woman, a good ten years older, very much larger, and very much stronger. It was a case of jealousy. This woman in Gerrard Street here had been married very young and was a perfect fury in point of jealousy. The murdered woman—more a match for the man, certainly, in point of years—was found dead in a barn near Hounslow Heath. There had been a violent struggle. She was bruised and scratched and torn, and had been held by the throat at last and choked. Now, there was no reasonable evidence to implicate any person but this woman, and, on the improbabilities of her having been able to do it, Mr. Jaggers principally rested his case. You may be sure," said Wemmick, touching me on the sleeve, "that he never dwelt upon the strength of her hands then, though he sometimes does now."

I had told Wemmick of his showing us her wrists that day of the dinner party.

"Well, sir!" Wemmick went on, "it hap-
2 pened— happened, don't you see?—that this woman was so very artfully dressed from the time of her apprehension[2] that she looked much slighter than she really was; in particular, her sleeves are always remembered to have been so skillfully contrived that her arms had quite a delicate look.

"It was attempted to be set up in proof of her jealousy that she was under strong suspicion of having, at about the time of the murder, frantically destroyed her child by this man—some three years old—to revenge herself upon him.

3 "To sum up, sir," said Wemmick, "Mr. Jaggers was altogether too many for the jury, and they gave in."

"Has she been in his service ever since?"

"Yes; but not only that," said Wemmick; "she went into his service immediately after her acquittal, tamed as she is now. She has since been taught one thing and another in the way of her duties, but she was tamed from the beginning."

4 "Do you remember the sex of the child?"

"Said to have been a girl."

"You have nothing more to say to me tonight?"

"Nothing. I got your letter and destroyed it. Nothing."

---

1. **score:** twenty.

2. **apprehension:** arrest.

AT A GLANCE

- After leaving Jaggers, Pip asks Wemmick about Molly.
- Molly was defended by Jaggers in a murder case; she was also suspected of killing her infant daughter.
- Jaggers won the case and Molly went to work for him.

1 STYLE: METAPHOR

Wemmick refers to Molly as "a wild beast tamed," implying that in the past she had the opposite of her present subservient demeanor.

2 THEME

Jaggers' case for Molly's defense was based on providing a deceptive appearance for the jury; he dressed her so she had a "delicate look," appearing too weak to commit a brutal murder.

3 THEME

Dickens again mocks the role of the court as Wemmick says that Jaggers was "altogether too many for the jury." Justice had no role in the jury's decision.

4 THE TOTAL EFFECT

Pip's idea about Estella's parentage is reinforced when Wemmick admits that Molly's child was a girl. Dickens intended that this subplot startle the reader and tie up many loose ends in the novel.

GUIDED READING

LITERAL QUESTIONS

1a. What does Wemmick tell Pip about Molly? (She was tried for murder, and Jaggers won her case.)

2a. What was Molly suspected of doing to her daughter? (destroying her to get revenge on the man she loved)

INFERENTIAL QUESTIONS

1b. Do you think she was guilty? (Perhaps; Jaggers now talks of the strength of her hands, and one wrist was badly scarred in a fight.)

2b. Do you think Wemmick knows Molly is Estella's mother? (Yes, Wemmick long ago warned Pip to look carefully at Molly.)

AT A GLANCE

- The next day, Pip goes to Satis House.
- Miss Havisham offers to give money to help Herbert.
- She asks if she can do anything to help Pip.

1 READING SKILLS: INFERENCE

Pip desires to "get into town quickly" and leave unnoticed; from this, the reader can infer that he does not want his presence known to Joe or Biddy.

2 VOCABULARY: WORD CHOICE

The use of the word *would* implies both that Miss Havisham will tolerate no expressions of pity and that Pip is too hurt by Estella's marriage to forgive Miss Havisham yet.

3 THEME

Pip collaborates in yet another secret when Miss Havisham asks him not to reveal that she has given him money for Herbert, but this time the need for secrecy is based on a plan established by him.

4 THE TOTAL EFFECT

Miss Havisham's change of heart reflects her realization that she destroyed Pip and Estella's happiness. Clearly Dickens means to move the reader.

We exchanged a cordial good night, and I went home, with new matter for my thoughts, though with no relief from the old.

Chapter Thirty-three

Satis House, the next day: Pip pays his last call on Miss Havisham.

Putting Miss Havisham's note in my pocket, that it might serve as my credentials for so soon reappearing at Satis House, in case her waywardness should lead her to express any surprise at seeing me, I went down again by the coach next
1 day. But I alighted at the Halfway House, and breakfasted there, and walked the rest of the distance, for I sought to get into the town quietly by the unfrequented ways, and to leave it in the same manner.

Miss Havisham was not in her own room, but was in the larger room across the landing. Looking in at the door, after knocking in vain, I saw her sitting on the hearth in a ragged chair, close before, and lost in the contemplation of, the ashy fire.

Doing as I had often done, I went in, and stood, touching the old chimney-piece, where
2 she could see me when she raised her eyes. There was an air of utter loneliness upon her that would have moved me to pity.

"It is I, Pip. Mr. Jaggers gave me your note yesterday, and I have lost no time."

"Thank you. Thank you."

As I brought another of the ragged chairs to the hearth and sat down, I remarked a new expression on her face, as if she were afraid of me.

"I want," she said, "to pursue that subject you mentioned to me when you were last here, and to show you that I am not all stone. But perhaps you can never believe, now, that there is anything human in my heart?"

When I said some reassuring words, she stretched out her tremulous right hand, as though she was going to touch me.

"You said, speaking for your friend, that you could tell me how to do something useful and good. Something that you would like done, is it not?"

"Something that I would like done very very much."

"What is it?"

I began explaining to her that secret history of the partnership.

"So!" said she, assenting with her head, but not looking at me. "And how much money is wanting to complete the purchase?"

I was rather afraid of stating it, for it sounded a large sum. "Nine hundred pounds."

3 "If I give you the money for this purpose, will you keep my secret as you have kept your own?"

"Quite as faithfully."

"And your mind will be more at rest?"

"Much more at rest."

"Are you very unhappy now?"

She asked this question, still without looking at me, but in an unwonted tone of sympathy. I could not reply at the moment, for my voice failed me. She put her left arm across the head of her stick, and softly laid her forehead on it.

"I am far from happy, Miss Havisham, but I have other causes of disquiet than any you know of. They are the secrets I have mentioned."

After a little while, she raised her head, and looked at the fire again.

"'Tis noble in you to tell me that you have other causes of unhappiness. Is it true?"

"Too true."

4 "Can I only serve you, Pip, by serving your friend? Regarding that as done, is there nothing I can do for you yourself?"

"Nothing. I thank you for the question. I thank you even more for the tone of the question. But there is nothing."

She presently rose from her seat, and looked about the blighted room for the means of writing. There were none there, and she took from her pocket a yellow set of ivory tablets, mounted

GUIDED READING

LITERAL QUESTIONS

1a. What does Miss Havisham say when Pip tells her he has "other" causes of disquiet? (that it is "noble" of him to say so)

2a. How does Pip respond when Miss Havisham asks if she can help him directly? (He thanks her for the question and its tone.)

INFERENTIAL QUESTIONS

1b. What does she mean? (She believes he is trying to help her feel better about making him lose Estella.)

2b. Why is he grateful for the tone of the question? (He sees that she is truly concerned about him.)

in tarnished gold, and wrote upon them with a pencil in a case of tarnished gold that hung from her neck.

"You are still on friendly terms with Mr. Jaggers?"

"Quite. I dined with him yesterday."

"This is an authority to him to pay you that money, to lay out at your irresponsible discretion for your friend. I keep no money here; but if you would rather Mr. Jaggers knew nothing of the matter, I will send it to you."

"Thank you, Miss Havisham; I have not the least objection to receiving it from him."

She read me what she had written, and it was direct and clear, and evidently intended to absolve me from any suspicion of profiting by the receipt of the money. I took the tablets from her hand.

"My name is on the first leaf. If you can ever write under my name, 'I forgive her,' though ever so long after my broken heart is dust, pray do it!"

"Oh, Miss Havisham," said I, "I can do it now. There have been sore mistakes; and my life has been a blind and thankless one; and I want forgiveness and direction far too much to be bitter with you."

She turned her face to me for the first time since she had averted it, and to my amazement, I may even add to my terror, dropped on her knees at my feet, with her folded hands.

To see her, with her white hair and her worn face, kneeling at my feet, gave me a shock through all my frame. I entreated her to rise, and got my arms about her to help her up, but she only pressed that hand of mine which was nearest to her grasp, and hung her head over it, and wept.

"Oh!" she cried, despairingly. "What have I done! What have I done!"

"If you mean, Miss Havisham, what have you done to injure me, let me answer. Very little. I should have loved her under any circumstances. Is she married?"

"Yes!"

It was a needless question, for a new desolation in the desolate house had told me so.

2 "What have I done! What have I done!" She wrung her hands, and crushed her white hair, and returned to this cry over and over again. "What have I done!"

"If you knew all my story," she pleaded, "you would have some compassion for me."

"Miss Havisham," I answered, as delicately as I could, "I believe I may say that I do know your story."

She was seated on the ground, with her arms on the ragged chair, and her head leaning on them.

"Whose child was Estella?"

She shook her head.

"You don't know?"

She shook her head again.

"But Mr. Jaggers brought her here, or sent her here?"

"Brought her here."

"Will you tell me how that came about?"

She answered in a low whisper and with cau-
3 tion: "I had been shut up in these rooms a long time (I don't know how long; you know what time the clocks keep here), when I told him that I wanted a little girl to rear and love, and save from my fate. He told me that he would look about him for such an orphan child. One night he brought her here asleep, and I called her Estella."

"Might I ask her age then?"

"Two or three. She herself knows nothing, but that she was left an orphan and I adopted her."

What more could I hope to do by prolonging the interview? I had succeeded on behalf of Herbert, Miss Havisham had told me all she knew of Estella, I had said and done what I could to ease her mind. We parted.

Taking the brewery on my way back, I raised the rusty latch of a little door at the garden end of it, and walked through. I was going out at the

AT A GLANCE

- Miss Havisham gives Pip written authority for Jaggers to give the money for Herbert.
- She asks Pip to forgive her and breaks down.
- Pip forgives her.
- He asks about Estella's parents.

1 THEME

As Miss Havisham repents her vengeance on Pip, she begs forgiveness; even Pip's forgiveness, however, is not enough to eliminate her guilt.

2 THE TOTAL EFFECT

The change in Miss Havisham's character reinforces a central theme of the novel: Wealth and power do not lead to happiness.

3 THEME

Miss Havisham reveals that her original reason for adopting Estella was to "rear and love" her and save the girl from her own fate—an unselfish motive that later becomes cruel and twisted.

GUIDED READING

LITERAL QUESTIONS

1a. How does Pip reply when Miss Havisham begs his forgiveness? (He forgives her.)

2a. What was Miss Havisham's original reason for taking Estella? (She wanted to have someone to love and to save a girl from her own fate.)

INFERENTIAL QUESTIONS

1b. What does he mean by saying that he wants forgiveness? (He has erred, too, in his poor treatment of Joe and Biddy.)

2b. Has Miss Havisham succeeded? (No; Estella is trapped in a loveless marriage.)

AT A GLANCE

- Pip has a strong premonition and goes back to check on Miss Havisham; her dress catches on fire.
- He puts the flames out, burning his own hands; a surgeon is summoned.

1 PLOT: FORESHADOWING

When Pip imagines that he sees Miss Havisham hanging from the beam, his imagination foretells a disaster that befalls her soon afterward.

2 THEME

The fire that envelops Miss Havisham destroys in a moment the timelessness she has sought for her entire life; the moment of rejection she preserved for decades is erased in an instant.

3 STYLE: SIMILE

Pip compares his rescue of Miss Havisham to the struggle of "desperate enemies," a simile that emphasizes his complex relationship with her: He considers her his enemy yet cares enough for her to risk his life to save her.

opposite door when I turned my head to look
1 back. A childish association revived with wonderful force in the moment of the slight action, and I fancied that I saw Miss Havisham hanging to the beam. So strong was the impression that I stood under the beam shuddering from head to foot before I knew it was a fancy.

I hesitated whether to call the woman to let me out at the locked gate, of which she had the key, or first go upstairs and assure myself that Miss Havisham was as safe and well as I had left her. I went up.

I looked into the room where I had left her, and I saw her seated in the ragged chair upon the hearth close to the fire, with her back towards
2 me. In the moment when I was withdrawing my head to go quietly away, I saw a great flaming light spring up. In the same moment I saw her running at me, shrieking, with a whirl of fire blazing all about her, and soaring at least as many feet above her head as she was high.

I had a double-caped great-coat[1] on, and over my arm another thick coat. That I got them off, closed with her, threw her down, and got them over her; that I dragged the great cloth from the table for the same purpose, and with it dragged down the heap of rottenness in the midst, and all
3 the ugly things that sheltered there; that we were on the ground struggling like desperate enemies, and that the closer I covered her, the more wildly she shrieked; that this occurred I knew through the result, but not through anything I thought or knew I did. I looked round and saw the disturbed beetles and spiders running away over the floor, and the servants coming in with breathless cries at the door.

She was insensible, and I was afraid to have her moved, or even touched. Assistance was sent for, and I held her until it came. When I got up, on the surgeon's coming to her with other aid, I was astonished to see that both my hands were burnt, for I had no knowledge of it through the sense of feeling.

On examination it was pronounced that she had received serious hurts, but that they of themselves were far from hopeless; the danger

1. **great-coat:** overcoat.

GUIDED READING

LITERAL QUESTION

1a. What happens when Pip tries to save Miss Havisham? (She struggles against him.)

INFERENTIAL QUESTION

1b. Why do you think she reacts this way? (She does not want to live.)

lay mainly in the nervous shock. By the surgeon's directions, her bed was carried into that room and laid upon the great table, which happened to be well suited to the dressing of her injuries. When I saw her again, an hour afterwards, she lay indeed where I had seen her strike her stick, and had heard her say she would lie one day.

Though every vestige of her dress was burnt, as they told me, she still had something of her old ghastly bridal appearance, for they had covered her to the throat with white cotton-wool, and as she lay with a white sheet loosely overlying that, the phantom air of something that had been was still upon her.

I found, on questioning the servants, that Estella was in Paris, and I got a promise from the surgeon that he would write by the next post. Miss Havisham's family I took upon myself, intending to communicate with Matthew Pocket only, and leave him to do as he liked about informing the rest.

2 Towards midnight she began to wander in her speech, and after that it gradually set in that she said innumerable times in a low solemn voice, "What have I done!" And then, "When she first came, I meant to save her from misery like mine." And then, "Take the pencil and write under my name, 'I forgive her!' "

Chapter Thirty-four

London: The truth about Estella is revealed.

My hands had been dressed twice or thrice in the night, and again in the morning. My left arm was a good deal burned to the elbow, and, less severely, as high as the shoulder; it was very painful, but the flames had set in that direction, and I felt thankful it was no worse.

Herbert was the kindest of nurses, and at stated times took off the bandages, and steeped them in the cooling liquid.

Neither of us spoke of the boat, but we both

3 thought of it. That was made apparent by our avoidance of the subject, and by our agreeing to make my recovery of the use of my hands a question of hours, not of weeks.

My first question when I saw Herbert had been, of course, whether all was well down the river. As he replied in the affirmative, with perfect confidence and cheerfulness, we did not resume the subject until the day was wearing away. But then, as Herbert changed the bandages, he went back to it spontaneously.

"I sat with Provis last night, Handel. He was very communicative last night, and told me more of his life. You remember his breaking off here about some woman that he had had great

4 trouble with. Did I hurt you?"

I had started, but not under his touch. His words had given me a start.

"It seems," said Herbert, "—there's a bandage off most charmingly, and now comes the cool one—makes you shrink at first, my poor dear fellow, don't it. It seems that the woman was a young woman, and a jealous woman, and a revengeful woman; revengeful, Handel, to the last degree."

"To what last degree?"

"Murder—does it strike too cold on that sensitive place?"

"I don't feel it. How did she murder? Whom did she murder?"

"Why, the deed may not have merited quite so terrible a name," said Herbert, "but she was tried for it, and Mr. Jaggers defended her, and the reputation of that defense first made his name known to Provis. It was another and a stronger woman who was the victim, and there had been a struggle—in a barn. She was acquitted. My poor Handel, I hurt you!"

"It is impossible to be gentler, Herbert. Yes? What else?"

"This acquitted young woman and Provis had a little child, a little child of whom Provis was exceedingly fond. On the evening of the very night when the object of her jealousy was

AT A GLANCE

- The surgeon tends to Miss Havisham as she lies on the table.
- Pip stays the night, then returns to London.
- Herbert relates that Magwitch told him of a woman who committed murder.

1 STYLE: IMAGERY

The image of Miss Havisham laid out on the dining table, introduced in Chapter 10, has become real, as Miss Havisham predicted.

2 THEME

Even as she is near death, Miss Havisham begs to be forgiven; she repents her earlier cruelty and longs to have her guilt assuaged.

3 THEME

Pip and Herbert are so attuned to each other that they communicate without speaking.

4 READING SKILLS: PREDICTING OUTCOMES

Pip's surprise indicates that another coincidence is about to be revealed.

GUIDED READING

LITERAL QUESTIONS

1a. What does Miss Havisham say in her delirium? (She begs forgiveness and says she meant to save Estella.)

2a. How does Herbert describe the woman with whom Magwitch was involved? (He says she was *young, jealous,* and *revengeful.*)

INFERENTIAL QUESTIONS

1b. What does this tell you about her state of mind? (She is obsessed over her role in destroying Pip and Estella's love; she has realized the extent of her guilt and wants to repent and be forgiven.)

2b. Who do you think the woman might be? (Molly)

AT A GLANCE

- Pip determines that Magwitch is Estella's father.
- He goes to Jaggers' office and gives him the note for money.
- Pip tells Jaggers and Wemmick that he knows the identities of Estella's mother and father.

1 THE TOTAL EFFECT

Pip tells Herbert that Magwitch is Estella's father, another surprising plot twist that helps tie the novel together. Dickens surely intended the revelation to shock and intrigue his readers.

2 INTERPRETING THE PASSAGE

Wemmick states that people's "business"—their attitudes and actions—is something they carry with them privately.

3 STYLE: DIALOGUE

This conversation between Pip and Jaggers stresses their new relationship: Since Pip is no longer dependent on Jaggers for money, he can play Jaggers' own questioning game.

strangled as I tell you, the young woman presented herself before Provis for one moment, and swore that she would destroy the child (which was in her possession), and he should never see it again. Then she vanished. . . ."

"Did the woman keep her oath?"

"Fearing he should be called upon to depose[1] about this destroyed child, he kept himself out of the way and out of the trial, and was only vaguely talked of as a certain man called Abel, out of whom the jealousy arose. After the acquittal she disappeared, and thus he lost the child and the child's mother. How old were you when you came upon him in the little churchyard?"

"I think in my seventh year."

"Aye. It had happened some three or four years, then, he said, and you brought into his mind the little girl so tragically lost, who would have been about your age."

"Herbert," said I, after a short silence, "you are not afraid that I am in any fever, or that my head is much disordered by the accident of last night?"

1 "N-no," said Herbert, after taking time to examine me.

"I know I am quite myself. And the man we have in hiding down the river is Estella's father."

Early next morning, I took my way to Little Britain.

There were periodical occasions when Mr. Jaggers and Mr. Wemmick went over the office accounts, and checked off the vouchers, and put all things straight. On these occasions Wemmick took his books and papers into Mr. Jaggers's room. I was not sorry to have Mr. Jaggers and Wemmick together, as Wemmick would then hear for himself that I said nothing to compromise him.

My appearance, with my arm bandaged and my coat loose over my shoulders, favored my object. While I described the disaster, Mr. Jaggers stood before the fire. Wemmick leaned back in his chair, staring at me, with his hands in the pockets of his trousers.

I then produced Miss Havisham's authority to receive the nine hundred pounds for Herbert. Mr. Jaggers's eyes retired a little deeper into his head when I handed him the tablets, but he presently handed them over to Wemmick, with instructions to draw the check for his signature. I looked on at Wemmick as he wrote, and Mr. Jaggers, poising and swaying himself on his well-polished boots, looked on at me. "I am sorry, Pip," said he, as I put the check in my pocket, when he had signed it, "that we do nothing for *you*."

"Miss Havisham was good enough to ask me," I returned, "whether she could do nothing for me, and I told her no."

2 "Everybody should know his own business," said Mr. Jaggers.

"Every man's business," said Wemmick, "is 'portable property.' "

"I did ask something of Miss Havisham, however, sir. I asked her to give me some information relative to her adopted daughter, and she gave me all she possessed."

"Did she?" said Mr. Jaggers.

"I know more of the history of Miss Havisham's adopted child than Miss Havisham herself does, sir. I know her mother."

Mr. Jaggers looked at me inquiringly, and repeated "Mother?"

"I have seen her mother within these three days."

3 "Yes?" said Mr. Jaggers.

"And so have you, sir. And you have seen her still more recently."

"Yes?" said Mr. Jaggers.

"Perhaps I know more of Estella's history than even you do," said I. "I know her father, too."

A certain stop that Mr. Jaggers came to in his manner assured me that he did not know who her father was. This I had strongly suspected from Provis's account which I pieced on to the

1. **depose:** testify.

GUIDED READING

LITERAL QUESTIONS

1a. What was Magwitch reminded of when he encountered Pip in the graveyard? (Pip reminded Magwitch of his lost little girl.)

2b. What does Pip say to Mr. Jaggers about Estella's father? (that he knows who he is)

INFERENTIAL QUESTIONS

1b. What does this tell you about Magwitch's character? (He loved his child; he is capable of an enduring love.)

2b. Why doesn't he tell Mr. Jaggers who it is outright? (Pip enjoys playing Jaggers' own game with him.)

fact that he himself was not Mr. Jaggers's client until some four years later, and when he could have no reason for claiming his identity.

"So! You know the young lady's father, Pip?" said Mr. Jaggers.

"Yes," I replied, "and his name is Provis—from New South Wales."

Even Mr. Jaggers started when I said those words.

"And on what evidence, Pip," asked Mr. Jaggers, very coolly, as he paused with his handkerchief half-way to his nose, "does Provis make this claim?"

"He does not make it," said I, "and has never made it, and has no knowledge or belief that his daughter is in existence."

My reply was so unexpected that Mr. Jaggers put the handkerchief back into his pocket, folded his arms, and looked with stern attention at me, though with an immovable face.

Then I told him all I knew.

Mr. Jaggers nodded his head two or three times, and actually drew a sigh. "Pip," said he, "we won't talk about 'poor dreams;' you know more about such things than I, having much fresher experience of that kind. I'll put a case to you. Mind! I admit nothing."

He waited for me to declare that I quite understood that he admitted nothing.

"Now, Pip," said Mr. Jaggers, "put this case. Put the case that a woman held her child concealed, and was obliged to communicate the fact to her legal adviser. Put the case that at the same time he held a trust to find a child for an eccentric rich lady to adopt and bring up."

"I follow you, sir."

"Put the case that he lived in an atmosphere of evil, that he often saw children solemnly tried at a criminal bar,[2] that he knew of their being imprisoned, whipped, transported, neglected, cast out."

"I follow you, sir."

"Put the case, Pip, that here was one pretty little child out of the heap who could be saved; whom the father believed dead, and dared make no stir about; as to whom, over the mother, the
2 legal adviser had this power: 'I know what you did, and how you did it. Give the child into my hands, and I will do my best to bring you off. If you are saved, your child will be saved, too; if you are lost, your child is still saved.' Put the case that this was done, and that the woman was cleared."

"I understand you perfectly."

"But that I make no admissions?"

"That you make no admissions." And Wemmick repeated, "No admissions."

"Put the case, Pip, that the terror of death had a little shaken the woman's intellects, and that when she was set at liberty, she was scared and went to him to be sheltered. Put the case that he took her in, and that he kept down the old wild violent nature, whenever he saw an inkling of its breaking out, by asserting his power over her in the old way. Do you comprehend the imaginary case?"

"Quite."

"Put the case that the child grew up and was married for money. That the mother was still living. That the father was still living. That the mother and father, unknown to one another, were dwelling within so many miles, furlongs, yards if you like, of one another. That the secret was still a secret, except that you had got wind of it. Put that last case to yourself very carefully."

"I do."

"I ask Wemmick to put it to *himself* very carefully."

And Wemmick said, "I do."

3 "For whose sake would you reveal the secret? For the father's? I think he would not be much the better for the mother. For the mother's? I think if she had done such a deed, she would be safer where she was. For the daughter's? I think it would hardly serve her to

2. bar: court.

AT A GLANCE

- Pip reveals that Magwitch is Estella's father.
- Mr. Jaggers indirectly relates the story of Magwitch, Estella, and Molly.
- Jaggers advises Pip to keep the information secret.

1 STYLE: DIALOGUE

Mr. Jaggers narrates the Molly-Estella story as a hypothetical case, speaking of himself in the third person to distance himself from his own actions.

2 THE TOTAL EFFECT

Mr. Jaggers reveals an unexpected side to his character when he admits that he was willing to save Estella. For the first time, Dickens portrays Jaggers as capable of human feeling.

3 THEME

Mr. Jaggers advises Pip to keep his knowledge of Estella's father a secret, revealing that he still possesses the kindness he displayed when Estella was a baby.

GUIDED READING

LITERAL QUESTIONS

1a. What is Mr. Jaggers' reaction to Pip's revelation about Estella's father? (He is surprised.)

2a. What does Mr. Jaggers advise Pip to do? (He wants Pip to keep the secret of Estella's parentage.)

INFERENTIAL QUESTIONS

1b. Why do you think Pip decides to tell Jaggers what he knows? (He isn't sure what he should do with the information.)

2b. Why does he advise this? (He feels revealing the secret would harm Estella, Molly, and Magwitch.)

AT A GLANCE

- Wemmick, Jaggers, and Pip agree to keep the secret.
- Wemmick writes that it is time for Magwitch to leave; Pip and Herbert enlist Startop's aid.
- Pip receives a note that beckons him to the marshes.

1 THEME

Pip confirms that he will go with Magwitch; Pip's sense of responsibility causes him to stick by the man who has risked his life for him.

2 BACKGROUND

In the 1800s, while the railroads were still young, much of the transport of goods occurred by ship. London, reached by the Thames River, was a great port, as were Hamburg, Rotterdam, and Antwerp.

establish her parentage for the information of her husband, and to drag her back to disgrace, after an escape of twenty years, pretty secure to last for life."

I looked at Wemmick, whose face was very grave. He gravely touched his lips with his forefinger. I did the same. Mr. Jaggers did the same. "Now, Wemmick," said the latter then, resuming his usual manner, "what item was it you were at when Mr. Pip came in?"

Chapter Thirty-five

Back on the marshes: A narrow escape.

On a Monday morning, when Herbert and I were at breakfast, I received the following letter from Wemmick by the post.

> Walworth. Burn this as soon as read. Early in the week, or say Wednesday, you might do what you know of, if you felt disposed to try it. Now, burn.

When I had shown this to Herbert and had put it in the fire—but not before we had both got it by heart—we considered what to do. For, of course, my being disabled could now be no longer kept out of view.

"I have thought it over, again and again," said Herbert, "and I think I know a better course then taking a Thames waterman. Take Startop. A good fellow, a skilled hand, fond of us, and enthusiastic and honorable."

I had thought of him more than once.

"But how much would you tell him, Herbert?"

"It is necessary to tell him very little. Let him suppose it a mere freak, but a secret one, until the morning comes—then let him know that there
1 is urgent reason for your getting Provis aboard and away. You go with him?"

"No doubt."

"Where?"

It had seemed to me, in the many anxious considerations I had given the point, almost in-
2 different what port we made for—Hamburg, Rotterdam, Antwerp[1]—the place signified little, so that he was out of England. Any foreign steamer that fell in our way and would take us up would do. As foreign steamers would leave London at about the time of high-water, our plan would be to get down the river by a previous ebb-tide, and lie by in some quiet spot until we could pull off to one. The time when one would be due where we lay could be calculated pretty nearly. Herbert assented to all this, and we went out immediately after breakfast to pursue our investigations.

We both did what we had to do without any hindrance, and when we met again at one o'clock reported it done. I, for my part, was prepared with passports; Herbert had seen Startop, and he was more than ready to join.

These precautions well understood by both of us, I went home.

On opening the outer door of our chambers with my key, I found a letter in the box, directed to me; a very dirty letter, though not ill-written. It had been delivered by hand (of course since I left home), and its contents were these.

> If you are not afraid to come to the old marshes to-night or to-morrow night at nine, and to come to the little sluice-house by the limekiln,[2] you had better come. If you want information regarding *your Uncle Provis,* you had much better come and tell no one and lose no time. *You must come alone.* Bring this with you.

I had had load enough upon my mind before the receipt of this strange letter. What to do now, I could not tell. And the worse was that I

1. **Hamburg, Rotterdam, Antwerp:** cities in Germany, Holland, and Belgium, respectively.
2. **limekiln:** furnace in which lime is made by burning limestone or shells.

GUIDED READING

LITERAL QUESTIONS

1a. Why do Pip and Herbert need another rower for their boat? (because Pip is "disabled"—his hands are burned)

2a. What does Pip reply when Herbert asks if he plans to go with Magwitch? (that he intends to do so)

INFERENTIAL QUESTIONS

1b. Why do you think they decide to take Startop? (They are afraid a hired boatman might betray them; they trust Startop.)

2b. Why do you think he has decided this? (He feels responsible for Magwitch's safety.)

must decide quickly, or I should miss the afternoon coach, which would take me down in time for to-night. To-morrow night I could not think of going, for it would be too close upon the time of the flight. And again, for anything I knew, the information might have some important bearing on the flight itself. I resolved to go. I should certainly not have gone but for the reference to my Uncle Provis. That, coming on Wemmick's letter, turned the scale.

It was dark before we got down, and the journey seemed long and dreary to me who could see little of it inside, and who could not go outside in my disabled state. Avoiding the Blue Boar, I put up at an inn of minor reputation down the town, and ordered some dinner. While it was preparing, I went to Satis House and inquired for Miss Havisham; she was still very ill, though considered something better.

My inn had once been a part of an ancient ecclesiastical[3] house, and I dined in a little octagonal common-room, like a font.[4] As I was not able to cut my dinner, the old landlord with a shining bald head did it for me. This bringing us into conversation, he was so good as to entertain me with my own story—of course with the popular feature that Pumblechook was my earliest benefactor and the founder of my fortunes.

I had never been struck at so keenly for my thanklessness to Joe, as through the brazen impostor Pumblechook. The falser he, the truer Joe; the meaner he, the nobler Joe.

My heart was deeply and most deservedly humbled as I mused over the fire for an hour or more. The striking of the clock aroused me, but not from my dejection or remorse, and I got up and had my coat fastened round my neck, and went out. I had previously sought in my pockets for the letter, that I might refer to it again, but I could not find it, and was uneasy to think that it must have been dropped in the straw of the coach. I knew very well, however, that the appointed place was the little sluice-house by the limekiln on the marshes, and the hour nine. Towards the marshes I now went straight, having no time to spare.

3 It was a dark night, though the full moon rose as I left the enclosed lands, and passed out upon the marshes. Beyond their dark line there was a ribbon of clear sky, hardly broad enough to hold the red large moon. There was a melancholy wind, and the marshes were very dismal.

The direction that I took was not that in which my old home lay, nor that in which we had pursued the convicts. My back was turned towards the distant Hulks as I walked on. I knew the limekiln as well as I knew the old battery, but they were miles apart, so that if a light had been burning at each point that night, there would have been a long strip of the blank horizon between the two bright specks.

It was another half-hour before I drew near to the kiln. The lime was burning with a sluggish stifling smell, but the fires were made up and left, and no workmen were visible. I saw a light in the old sluice-house. I quickened my pace,
4 and knocked at the door with my hand. Waiting for some reply, I looked about me, noticing how the sluice was abandoned and broken, and how the house—of wood with a tiled roof—would not be proof against the weather much longer. Still there was no answer, and I knocked again. No answer still, and I tried the latch.

It rose under my hand, and the door yielded. Looking in, I saw a lighted candle on a table, a bench, and a mattress on a truckle bedstead.[5] As there was a loft above, I called, "Is there any one here?" but no voice answered. Then, I looked at my watch, and, finding that it was past nine, called again, "Is there any one here?" There being still no answer, I went out at the door.

It was beginning to rain fast. Seeing nothing

---

3. **ecclesiastical** [i klē′zē as′ti kəl]: related to the church.
4. **font:** baptismal fountain.

5. **truckle bedstead:** bed on wheels.

AT A GLANCE

- Avoiding the Blue Boar, Pip goes to another, lesser inn near the marshes.
- He goes to the sluice-house near the limekiln, but finds no one there.

1 BACKGROUND

In the days when most overland travel was by stagecoach, a rider could travel inside the coach or outside with the driver, a more precarious seat that Pip cannot risk with his bandaged hands.

2 THEME

In comparing Joe and Pumblechook, Pip is struck anew by the depth of Joe's integrity.

3 ATMOSPHERE

Dickens creates an atmosphere on the marsh that mirrors the atmosphere of Pip's first encounter with Magwitch: The wind is "melancholy" and the marshes "dismal."

4 THE TOTAL EFFECT

As the sluice-house is nearing collapse, so the novel nears its end. Dickens returns the action to the place where it began to link the story's start and conclusion.

GUIDED READING

LITERAL QUESTIONS

1a. Where does Pip stay when he goes back home? (at "an inn of minor reputation")

2a. What does the landlord tell Pip? (He tells Pip's story.)

INFERENTIAL QUESTIONS

1b. Why doesn't he stay at the Blue Boar? (He wants no one, especially Joe and Biddy, to know he is there.)

2b. Why does this make Pip think of Joe? (The landlord's version features Pumblechook as Pip's benefactor, and Pip knows he owes more to Joe than to anyone.)

AT A GLANCE

- Pip is attacked and tied up.
- Orlick plans to kill Pip for causing him to lose his job.
- Pip worries about how he will be remembered.
- Orlick admits he attacked Mrs. Joe.

1 THE TOTAL EFFECT

Another plot thread is tied up as Orlick reenters the story. Again Dickens intends to startle the reader.

2 CONFLICT

A conflict that has fueled much of the action of the book is fully revealed as Orlick calls Pip his "enemy" and says that he hates Pip for causing him to lose his job.

3 THEME

As he thinks of his seemingly imminent death, Pip feels that his worst fate is "being misremembered after death." He longs to be forgiven by Joe and Biddy.

save what I had seen already, I turned back into the house, and stood just within the shelter of the doorway, looking out into the night.

The next thing I comprehended was that I had been caught in a strong running noose, thrown over my head from behind.

"Now," said a suppressed voice with an oath, "I've got you!"

"What is this?" I cried, struggling. "Who is it? Help, help, help!"

1 Not only were my arms pulled close to my sides, but the pressure on my bad arm caused me exquisite pain. A strong man's hand was against my mouth. Then a flare of light flashed up, and showed me Orlick.

Whom I had looked for, I don't know. I had not looked for him. Seeing him, I felt that I was in a dangerous strait indeed.

He lighted the candle with great deliberation, and dropped the match, and trod it out. Then, he put the candle away from him on the table, so that he could see me. I made out that I was fastened to a stout perpendicular ladder a few inches from the wall.

"Now," said he, when we had surveyed one another for some time, "I've got you."

"Unbind me. Let me go!"

"Ah!" he returned, "*I'll* let you go. I'll let you go to the moon, I'll let you go to the stars. All in good time."

"Why have you lured me here?"

"Don't you know?" said he, with a deadly look.

"Why have you set upon me in the dark?"

2 "Because I mean to do it all myself. One keeps a secret better than two. Oh, you enemy, you enemy!"

As I watched him in silence, he put his hand into the corner at his side, and took up a gun with a brassbound stock.

"You cost me that place.[6] You did. Speak!"

"What else could I do?"

"You did that, and that would be enough, without more. It was you as always give Old Orlick a bad name."

"What are you going to do to me?"

"I'm a-going," said he, bringing his fist down upon the table with a heavy blow, "I'm a-going to have your life!" He leaned forward, staring at me.

"More than that," said he, folding his arms on the table again, "I won't have a rag of you, I won't have a bone of you, left on earth. I'll put your body in the kiln."

My mind, with inconceivable rapidity, followed out all the consequences of such a death. Estella's father would believe I had deserted him, would be taken, would die accusing me. Even Herbert would doubt me. Joe and Biddy would never know how sorry I had been. The
3 death close before me was terrible, but far more terrible than death was the dread of being misremembered after death. And so quick were my thoughts that I saw myself despised by unborn generations—Estella's children, and their children—while the wretch's words were yet on his lips.

"Wolf!" said he, folding his arms again, "Old Orlick did for your shrew sister. I come upon her from behind, as I come upon you to-night."

"Wolf, I'll tell you something more. It was Old Orlick as you tumbled over on your stairs that night."

I saw the staircase with its extinguished lamps. I saw the shadows of the heavy stair-rails, thrown by the watchman's lantern on the wall. I saw the rooms that I was never to see again.

"And why was Old Orlick there? Old Orlick says to himself, 'Somehow or another I'll have him!' When I looks for you, I finds your Uncle Provis, eh? But when Old Orlick come for to hear that your Uncle Provis had mostlike wore the leg-iron wot Old Orlick had picked up, filed asunder, on these meshes ever so many year ago, and wot he kep by him till he dropped your sister with it—hey?—when he come for to hear that—hey?—"

In his savage taunting, he flared the candle so

6. **that place:** Orlick's job as Miss Havisham's gate keeper.

GUIDED READING

LITERAL QUESTIONS

1a. What does Orlick plan to do? (He plans to kill Pip.)

2a. What does Pip fear most about his situation? (being "misremembered" after his death)

INFERENTIAL QUESTIONS

1b. Why does Orlick hate Pip? (He blames Pip for his lost job and his bad name.)

2b. Why is he most afraid of this? (He doesn't want Herbert, Joe, and Biddy to think he has been ungrateful and false.)

close at me that I turned my face aside to save it from the flame.

"Old Orlick knowed you was a-smuggling your Uncle Provis away, Old Orlick's a match for you and know'd you'd come to-night! Now I'll tell you something more, wolf, and this ends it. There's them that's as good a match for your Uncle Provis. There's them that can't and that won't have Magwitch— yes, *I* know the name!—alive in the same land with them, and that's had such sure information of him when he was alive in another land, as that he couldn't and shouldn't leave it unbeknown and put them in danger."

He flared the candle at me again, smoking my face and hair, and for an instant blinding me, and turned his powerful back as he replaced the light on the table. I had thought a prayer, and had been with Joe and Biddy and Herbert, before he turned towards me again.

There was a clear space of a few feet between the table and the opposite wall. Within this space, he now slouched backwards and forwards. His great strength seemed to sit stronger upon him than ever before, as he did this with his hands hanging loose and heavy at his sides, and with his eyes scowling at me. I had no grain of hope left.

I shouted out with all my might, and struggled with all my might. It was only my head and my legs that I could move, but to that extent I struggled with all the force, until then unknown, that was within me. In the same instant I heard responsive shouts, saw figures and a gleam of light dash in at the door, heard voices and saw Orlick emerge from a struggle of men, clear the table at a leap, and fly out into the night!

After a blank, I found that I was lying unbound, on the floor, in the same place, with my head on some one's knee. Too indifferent at first even to look round and ascertain who supported me, I was lying looking at the ladder when there came between me and it, a face. The face of Trabb's boy!

"I think he's all right!" said Trabb's boy, in a sober voice, "but ain't he just pale though!"

At these words, the face of him who supported me looked over into mine, and I saw my supporter to be—

"Herbert! Great Heaven!"

"Softly," said Herbert, "Gently, Handel. Don't be too eager."

"And our old comrade, Startop!" I cried, as he too bent over me.

"Remember what he is going to assist us in," said Herbert, "and be calm."

The allusion made me spring up, though I dropped again from the pain in my arm. "The time has not gone by, Herbert, has it? What night is to-night? How long have I been here?" For, I had a strange and strong misgiving that I had been lying there a long time—a day and a night—two days and nights—more.

"The time has not gone by. It is still Monday night."

"Thank God!"

"And you have all to-morrow, Tuesday, to rest in," said Herbert.

I learnt that I had in my hurry dropped the letter, open, in our chambers, where he, coming home to bring with him Startop, found it very
3 soon after I was gone. Its tone made him uneasy, and the more so because of the inconsistency between it and the hasty letter I had left for him. His uneasiness increasing, he set off with Startop, who volunteered his company, to make inquiry when the next coach went down. So he and Startop arrived at the Blue Boar, fully expecting there to find me, or tidings of me but finding neither, went on to Miss Havisham's, where they lost me. Hereupon they went back to the hotel. Among the loungers under the Boar's archway happened to be Trabb's boy—true to his ancient habit of happening to be everywhere where he had no business—and Trabb's boy became their guide, and with him they went out to the sluice-house.

When I told Herbert what had passed within the house, he was for our immediately going before a magistrate in the town, late at night as it

AT A GLANCE

- Orlick has informed Compeyson about Magwitch.
- Pip and Orlick struggle.
- Pip is rescued, and Orlick flees.

1 PARAPHRASING THE PASSAGE

Orlick reveals that he has been in contact with Compeyson about Magwitch's whereabouts.

2 THEME

In what he believes are his last moments, Pip thinks of "Joe and Biddy and Herbert," the three people whom he considers his true friends.

3 CHARACTERIZATION

Herbert again proves the depths of his resourcefulness and caring nature when he sets off to rescue Pip.

GUIDED READING

LITERAL QUESTIONS

1a. Whose is the first face Pip sees when he awakens? (that of Trabb's boy)

2a. What does Pip ask Herbert when he regains consciousness? ("What night is to-night?")

INFERENTIAL QUESTIONS

1b. Why is this ironic? (In the past Pip's presence annoyed and alienated him.)

2b. Why is he concerned about this? (because he must take Magwitch to a steamer on Wednesday)

AT A GLANCE

- Pip, Herbert, and Startop return to London; Pip rests.
- On Wednesday they row down the Thames to Mill Pond.
- Magwitch boards the boat and expresses his gratitude.

1 STYLE: SIMILE

Pip compares the rising sun to a "marsh of fire," echoing both the fire that engulfed Miss Havisham and the marsh where Pip's story began.

2 STYLE: METAPHOR

Pip compares the veil of mist that rises from the river to a veil lifted from himself. The veil—one of fear and indecision—is removed, leaving his thoughts clear and his body "strong and well."

3 BACKGROUND

Pip, Herbert, and Startop row past several landmarks: London Bridge, which housed shops of all sorts, and the White Tower and Traitor's Gate of the Tower of London, where political prisoners were incarcerated.

was, and getting out a warrant. But I had already considered that such a course, by detaining us there, or binding us to come back, might be fatal to Provis. Wednesday being so close upon us, we determined to go back to London that night, three in the post-chaise.[7] It was daylight when we reached the Temple, and I went at once to bed, and lay in bed all day.

Wednesday morning was dawning when I
1 looked out of the window. The winking lights upon the bridges were already pale, the coming sun was like a marsh of fire on the horizon. The river, still dark and mysterious, was spanned by bridges that were turning coldly grey. As I looked along the clustered roofs, with church towers and spires shooting into the unusually
2 clear air, the sun rose up, and a veil seemed to be drawn from the river, and millions of sparkles burst out upon its waters. From me, too, a veil seemed to be drawn, and I felt strong and well.

Herbert lay asleep in his bed, and our old fellow-student lay asleep on the sofa. I could not dress myself without help, but I made up the fire which was still burning, and got some coffee ready for them. In good time they too started and we admitted the sharp morning air at the windows, and looked at the tide that was still flowing towards us.

"When it turns at nine o'clock," said Herbert cheerfully, "look out for us, and stand ready, you over there at Mill Pond Bank!"

Chapter Thirty-six

London, on the river: Escape.

It was one of those March days when the sun shines hot and the wind blows cold. We had our pea-coats[1] with us, and I took a bag. Of all my worldly possessions I took no more than the few necessaries that filled the bag. Where I might go, what I might do, or when I might return were questions utterly unknown to me.

We loitered down to the Temple stairs. Of course I had taken care that the boat should be ready, and everything in order. After a little show of indecision, we went on board and cast off. It was then about high-water—half-past eight.

Our plan was this. The tide beginning to run down at nine, and being with us until three, we intended still to creep on after it had turned, and row against it until dark. We should then be well in those long reaches below Gravesend.

There we meant to lie by all night. The steamer for Hamburg, and the steamer for Rotterdam, would start from London at about nine on Thursday morning. We should know at what time to expect them, according to where we were, and would hail the first, so that if by any accident we were not taken aboard, we should have another chance.

3 Old London Bridge was soon passed, and old Billingsgate market with its oyster-boats and Dutchmen, and the White Tower and Traitor's Gate, and we were in among the tiers of shipping and to the stern,[2] could see with a faster beating heart Mill Pond Bank and Mill Pond stairs.

"Is he there?" said Herbert.

"Not yet."

"Right! He was not to come down till he saw us. Can you see his signal?"

"Not well from here; but I think I see it. Now I see him! Pull both. Easy, Herbert. Oars!"

We touched the stairs lightly for a single moment, and he was on board and we were off again. He had a boat-cloak with him, and a black canvas bag, and he looked as like a river-pilot[3] as my heart could have wished.

"Dear boy!" he said, putting his arm on my shoulder, as he took his seat. "Faithful dear boy, well done. Thankye, thankye! If you knowed,

7. **post-chaise:** coach drawn by four horses that are replaced regularly to insure speed.
1. **pea-coats:** heavy woolen jackets often worn by sailors.
2. **stern:** rear of a boat.
3. **river-pilot:** person who guides a ship down river to open water.

GUIDED READING

LITERAL QUESTIONS

1a. How do the three young men act as they board the boat? (They loiter on the stairs and act indecisive about boarding.)

2a. How is Magwitch dressed? (He wears a boat-cloak and carries a black canvas bag.)

INFERENTIAL QUESTIONS

1b. Why do they act this way? (so they won't seem out of the ordinary)

2b. Why does he wear these clothes? (so he will look like a river-pilot and not arouse suspicion)

dear boy, what it is to sit here alonger my dear boy and have my smoke, arter having been day by day betwixt four walls, you'd envy me."

"If all goes well," said I, "you will be perfectly free and safe again, within a few hours."

"Well," he returned, drawing a long breath, "I hope so."

"And think so?"

He dipped his hand in the water over the boat's gunwale,[4] and said, smiling with that softened air upon him which was not new to me:

"Aye, I s'pose I think so, dear boy."

As the night was fast falling, and as the moon, being past the full, would not rise early, we held a little council—a short one, for clearly our course was to lie by at the first lonely tavern we could find. So they plied their oars once more, and I looked out for anything like a house. Thus we held on, speaking little, for four or five dull miles.

At this dismal time we were evidently all possessed by the idea that we were followed. As the tide made, it flapped heavily at irregular intervals against the shore. At length we descried a light and a roof, and presently afterwards ran alongside a little causeway[5] made of stones that had been picked up hard by. Leaving the rest in the boat, I stepped ashore, and found the light to be in the window of a public-house. A more solitary place we could not have found. We decided to remain there until near the steamer's time, which would be about one in the afternoon. Having settled this, we went to bed.

We were up early. We waited—sometimes lying on the bank wrapped in our coats, and sometimes moving about to warm ourselves—until we saw our boat coming round. We rowed out into the track of the steamer and we began to look out for her smoke.

It was half-past one before we saw her smoke, and soon after we saw behind it the smoke of another steamer. As they were coming on at full speed, we got the two bags ready, and took that opportunity of saying good-bye to Her-
2 bert and Startop. We had all shaken hands cordially, and neither Herbert's eyes nor mine were quite dry, when I saw a four-oared galley[6] shoot out from under the bank but a little way ahead of us, and row out into the same track.

A stretch of shore had been as yet between us and the steamer's smoke, by reason of the bend and wind of the river; but now she was visible coming head on. I called to Herbert and Startop to keep before the tide, that she might see us lying by for her, and adjured Provis to sit quite still, wrapped in his cloak. He answered cheerily, "Trust to me, dear boy," and sat like a statue. Meantime the galley, which was skillfully handled, had crossed us, let us come up with her, and fallen alongside. Leaving just room enough for the play of the oars, she kept alongside, drifting when we drifted, and pulling a stroke or two when we pulled. Of the two sitters, one held the rudder[7] lines, and looked at us attentively—as did all the rowers; the other sitter was wrapped up, much as Provis was, and seemed to shrink, and whisper some instruction to the steerer as he looked at us. Not a word was spoken in either boat.

Startop could make out, after a few minutes, which steamer was first, and gave me the word "Hamburg," in a low voice as we sat face to
3 face. She was nearing us very fast, and the beating of her paddles grew louder and louder. I felt as if her shadow were absolutely upon us, when the galley hailed us. I answered.

"You have a returned transport there," said the man who held the lines. "That's the man, wrapped in the cloak. His name is Abel Magwitch, otherwise Provis. I apprehend that man, and call upon him to surrender, and you to assist."

At the same moment, without giving any au-

4. **gunwale:** [gun′əl]: upper edge of the side of a boat.
5. **causeway:** raised path across wet ground.

6. **galley:** large rowboat.
7. **rudder:** boat's steering device.

AT A GLANCE

- The four passengers spend the night at a public house.
- The next afternoon the Hamburg steamer and a galley appear.
- A man from the galley calls on Magwitch to surrender.

1 PLOT: FORESHADOWING

Magwitch's hesitant answer when Pip asks him if he thinks he will soon be safe reveals his doubts about the plan and hints that it may not succeed.

2 THEME

Pip and Herbert's friendship is deep enough now to cause them both to weep when they are forced to part.

3 PLOT: RISING ACTION

The action moves suspensefully toward a crisis as the steamer and the galley both approach the rowboat.

GUIDED READING

LITERAL QUESTIONS

1a. What does Magwitch reply when Pip asks if he thinks he will be free and safe? (that he "supposes" he thinks so)

2a. How does Pip describe the people in the galley? (There are rowers and two sitters, one who holds the lines and one who is "wrapped up.")

INFERENTIAL QUESTIONS

1b. What does his reply tell you? (that he has some doubt that Pip's plan will succeed)

2b. Who do you think the covered man might be? (Compeyson)

AT A GLANCE

- It is Compeyson in the galley.
- Compeyson and Magwitch go overboard; Pip's boat capsizes and sinks.
- All but Compeyson are rescued.
- Magwitch, badly hurt, is taken prisoner.

1 THE TOTAL EFFECT

The revelation that Compeyson has at last caught up with Pip and Magwitch brings this subplot's action to a climax.

2 VOCABULARY: CONNOTATION

Pip describes the wake of the steamers as *troubled,* a word that reflects both the choppiness of the water and Pip's anxiety over the failure of his plan.

3 THEME

The hatred that has festered for so long between Magwitch and Compeyson reaches its climax as Magwitch attacks Compeyson and pulls him overboard; he gets his revenge on Compeyson but is injured and taken prisoner.

dible direction to his crew, he ran the galley aboard of us. They had pulled one sudden stroke ahead, had got their oars in, had run athwart[8] us, and were holding on to our gunwale, before we knew what they were doing. This caused great confusion on board of the steamer, and I heard them calling to us, and heard the order given to stop the paddles, and heard them stop, but felt her driving down upon us irresistibly. In the same moment, I saw the steersman of the galley lay his hand on his prisoner's shoulder, and saw that both boats were swinging round with the force of the tide, and saw that all hands on board the steamer were running forward quite frantically. Still in the same moment, I saw the prisoner start up, lean across his captor, and pull the cloak from the neck of the shrinking sitter in the
1 galley. Still in the same moment, I saw that the face disclosed was the face of the other convict of long ago. Still in the same moment, I saw the face tilt backward with a white terror on it that I shall never forget, and heard a great cry on board the steamer and a loud splash in the water, and felt the boat sink from under me.

It was but for an instant that I seemed to struggle with a thousand mill-weirs[9] and a thousand flashes of light; that instant passed, I was taken on board the galley. Herbert was there, and Startop was there, but our boat was gone, and the two convicts were gone.

What with the cries aboard the steamer, and the furious blowing off of her steam, I could not at first distinguish sky from water or shore from shore; but the crew of the galley righted her with great speed, and, pulling certain swift strong strokes ahead, lay upon their oars, every man looking silently and eagerly at the water astern. Presently a dark object was seen in it, bearing towards us on the tide. No man spoke, but the steersman held up his hand, and all softly backed water, and kept the boat straight and true before it. As it came nearer, I saw it to be Magwitch, swimming, but not swimming freely. He was taken on board, and instantly manacled at the wrists and ankles.

The galley was kept steady, and the silent eager look-out at the water was resumed. But the Rotterdam steamer now came up, and apparently not understanding what had happened, came
2 on at speed. By the time she had been hailed and stopped, both steamers were drifting away from us, and we were rising and falling in a troubled wake of water. The look-out was kept, long after all was still again and the two steamers were gone, but everybody knew it was hopeless.

At length we gave it up, and pulled under the shore towards the tavern we had lately left, where we were received with no little surprise. Here I was able to get some comforts for Magwitch— Provis no longer— who had received some very severe injury in the chest and a deep cut in the head.

He told me that he believed himself to have gone under the keel of the steamer, and to have been struck on the head in rising. The injury to his chest (which rendered his breathing extremely painful) he thought he had received against the side of the galley. He added that he did not pretend to say what he might or might not have done to Compeyson, but, that in the moment of his laying his hand on his cloak to identify him, that villain had staggered up and staggered back, and they had both gone overboard together; when the sudden wrenching of him (Magwitch) out of our boat, and the endeavor of his captor
3 to keep him in it, had capsized us. He told me in a whisper that they gone down, fiercely locked in each other's arms, and that there had been a struggle under water, and that he had disengaged himself, struck out, and swam away.

I never had any reason to doubt the exact truth of what he had told me. The officer who steered the galley gave the same account of their going overboard.

8. **athwart:** blocking the course.
9. **mill-weirs:** underwater fences used to catch fish or to measure the flow of water.

GUIDED READING

LITERAL QUESTION

1a. How does Pip react to Magwitch's version of what happened? (He says he had no reason to doubt it.)

INFERENTIAL QUESTION

1b. Do you think Magwitch's version is true and complete? (It is possible that Magwitch killed Compeyson underwater.)

When I asked this officer's permission to change the prisoner's wet clothes, he gave it readily, merely observing that he must take charge of everything his prisoner had about him. So the pocket-book which had once been in my hands passed into the officer's. He further gave me leave to accompany the prisoner to London.

When I took my place by Magwitch's side, I felt that that was my place henceforth while he lived. His breathing became more difficult and painful as the night drew on, and often he could not repress a groan. I tried to rest him on the arm I could use, in any easy position, but it was dreadful to think that I could not be sorry at heart for his being badly hurt, since it was unquestionably best that he should die.

I told him how grieved I was to think he had come home for my sake.

"Dear boy," he answered, "I'm quite content to take my chance. I've seen my boy, and he can be a gentleman without me."

No. I had thought about that while we had been there side by side. No. Apart from any inclinations of my own, I understand Wemmick's hint now. I foresaw that, being convicted, his possessions would be forfeited to the Crown.[10]

2 "I will never stir from your side," said I, "when I am suffered to be near you. Please God, I will be as true to you as you have been to me!"

I felt his hand tremble as it held mine, and he turned his face away as he lay in the bottom of the boat, and I heard that old sound in his throat—softened now, like all the rest of him. It was a good thing that he had touched this point, for it put into my mind what I might not otherwise have thought of until too late: that he need

---

10. **forfeited to the Crown:** seized by the government. Magwitch has lost his rights to his own possessions by returning to England.

AT A GLANCE

- Magwitch's personal property is handed over to the officer.
- Pip accompanies Magwitch to London.
- He tells Magwitch that he will stay by his side.

1 THEME

Knowing that he is indirectly responsible for Magwitch's capture and injuries and that he owes his loyalty to Magwitch, Pip decides he must stay by him "henceforth while he lives."

2 THEME

Pip realizes that Magwitch's love for him has been deep and true, even as Joe's was; Pip determines that he will be "true" to Magwitch as Magwitch has been to him.

GUIDED READING

LITERAL QUESTION

1a. How does Pip feel about Magwitch's injuries? (He is not sorry that Magwitch is badly hurt.)

INFERENTIAL QUESTION

1b. Why does he feel this way? (He prefers that Magwitch die naturally of his injuries rather than linger, suffer, and be executed.)

AT A GLANCE

- Pip goes to Mr. Jaggers to arrange Magwitch's defense.
- He tells Jaggers that Magwitch's money has been lost.
- Herbert says he must go to Cairo and offers Pip a position in his business.

1 THEME

The fairness of the British criminal justice system is questioned again as Jaggers tells Pip that "no power on earth" could prevent Magwitch from losing his case.

2 VOCABULARY: WORD CHOICE

As Pip states that his heart would be "sickened," he reveals that he would feel ashamed to attempt to take the money.

3 IRONY

Herbert's offer is ironic because it was Pip who secretly got Herbert his own position. Their fortunes have been reversed.

never know how his hopes of enriching me had perished.

Chapter Thirty-seven

London, later: Picking up the pieces.

He was taken to the police court next day, and would have been immediately committed for trial but that it was necessary to send down for an old officer of the prison-ship from which he had once escaped, to speak to his identity. Nobody doubted it; but Compeyson, who had meant to depose to it, was tumbling on the tides, dead, and it happened that there was not at that time any prison officer in London who could give the required evidence. I had gone direct to Mr. Jaggers at his private house, on my arrival over night, to retain his assistance, and Mr. Jaggers on the prisoner's behalf would admit noth-
1 ing. It was the sole resource, for he told me that the case must be over in five minutes when the witness was there, and that no power on earth could prevent its going against us.

I imparted to Mr. Jaggers my design of keeping him in ignorance of the fate of his wealth. Mr. Jaggers was angry with me for having "let it slip through my fingers," and said we must by-
2 and-by try for some of it. But I had no claim, and I finally resolved, and ever afterwards abided by the resolution, that my heart should never be sickened with the hopeless task of attempting to establish one.

There appeared to be reason for supposing that the drowned informer had hoped for a reward out of this forfeiture, and had obtained some accurate knowledge of Magwitch's affairs. When his body was found, many miles from the scene of his death, and so horribly disfigured that he was only recognizable by the contents of his pockets, notes were still legible, folded in a case he carried. Among these were the name of a banking-house in New South Wales where a sum of money was, and the designation of certain lands of considerable value. Both those heads of information were in a list that Magwitch, while in prison, gave to Mr. Jaggers, of the possessions he supposed I should inherit. His ignorance, poor fellow, at last served him; he never mistrusted but that my inheritance was quite safe with Mr. Jaggers's aid.

It was at this dark time of my life that Herbert returned home one evening, a good deal cast down, and said:

"My dear Handel, I fear I shall soon have to leave you."

His partner having prepared me for that, I was less surprised than he thought.

"We shall lose a fine opportunity if I put off going to Cairo,[1] and I am very much afraid I must go, Handel, when you most need me."

"Herbert, I shall always need you, because I shall always love you, but my need is no greater now than at another time."

"My dear fellow," said Herbert, "let the near prospect of our separation—for, it is very near—be my justification for troubling you about yourself. Have you thought of your future?"

"No, for I have been afraid to think of any future."

"But yours cannot be dismissed; indeed, my dear, dear Handel, it must not be dismissed. I wish you would enter on it now, as far as a few friendly words go, with me."

"I will," said I.

3 "In this branch-house of ours, Handel, we must have a—"

I saw that his delicacy was avoiding the right word, so I said, "A clerk."

"A clerk. And I hope it is not at all unlikely that he may expand (as a clerk of your acquaintance has expanded) into a partner. Now, Handel—in short, my dear boy, will you come to me?"

"If you thought, Herbert, that you could, without doing any injury to your business, leave

1. **Cairo:** capital city of Egypt.

GUIDED READING

LITERAL QUESTIONS

1a. What does Pip decide to do about Magwitch's money? (He decides never to try to establish a claim to it.)

2a. What does Herbert offer Pip? (a position as a clerk in his company)

INFERENTIAL QUESTIONS

1b. Why does he make this decision? (It would make him feel ashamed.)

2b. Why is Herbert hesitant about making the offer? (He doesn't want to embarrass Pip.)

the question open for a little while—''

"For any while," cried Herbert. "Six months, a year!"

"Not so long as that," said I. "Two or three months at most."

Herbert was highly delighted when we shook hands on this arrangement, and said he could now take courage to tell me that he believed he must go away at the end of the week.

"And Clara?" said I.

"The dear little thing," returned Herbert, "holds dutifully to her father as long as he lasts; but he won't last long. Mrs. Whimple confides to me that he is certainly going."

"Not to say an unfeeling thing," said I, "he cannot do better than go."

On the Saturday in that same week, I took my leave of Herbert—full of bright hope, but sad and sorry to leave me—as he sat on one of the seaport mail-coaches.

On the stairs I encountered Wemmick, who was coming down, after an unsuccessful application of his knuckles to my door. I had not seen him alone since the disastrous issue of the attempted flight, and he had come, in his private and personal capacity, to say a few words of explanation in the reference to that failure.

"The late Compeyson," said Wemmick, "had by little and little got at the bottom of half of the regular business now transacted, and it was from the talk of some of his people in trouble (some of his people being always in trouble) that I heard what I did. I kept my ears open, seeming to have them shut, until I heard that he was absent, and I thought that would be the best time for making the attempt. I can only suppose now that it was a part of his policy, as a very clever man, habitually to deceive his own instruments. You don't blame me, I hope. I tried to serve you, with all my heart."

"I am as sure of that, Wemmick, as you can be, and I thank you most earnestly for all your interest and friendship."

"Thank you, thank you very much. It's a bad job," said Wemmick, scratching his head, "and I assure you I haven't been so cut up for a long time. What I look at is the sacrifice of so much portable property. Dear me!"

"What *I* think of, Wemmick, is the poor owner of the property."

2 "Yes, to be sure," said Wemmick. "Of course there can be no objection to your being sorry for him. I do not think he could have been saved. Whereas the portable property certainly could have been saved. That's the difference between the property and the owner, don't you see?"

He lay in prison very ill, during the whole interval between his committal for trial, and the coming round of the sessions. He had broken two ribs, they had wounded one of his lungs, and he breathed with great pain and difficulty, which increased daily.

Being far too ill to remain in the common prison, he was removed, after the first day or so, into the infirmary. This gave me opportunities of being with him that I could not otherwise have had.

The trial was very short and very clear. Such
3 things as could be said for him were said—how he had taken to industrious habits, and had thriven lawfully and reputably. But nothing could unsay the fact that he had returned, and was there in presence of the judge and jury. It was impossible to try him for that, and do otherwise than find him guilty.

The daily visits I could make him were shortened now, and he was more strictly kept.

The number of the days had risen to ten, when I saw a greater change in him than I had seen yet. His eyes were turned towards the door, and lighted up as I entered.

'Dear boy," he said, as I sat down by his bed; "I thought you was late. But I knowed you couldn't be that."

"It is just the time," said I. "I waited for it at the gate."

AT A GLANCE

- Pip agrees to consider Herbert's offer; Herbert leaves.
- Wemmick explains how Compeyson fooled him.
- Magwitch is found guilty.

1 STYLE: IMAGERY

Wemmick speaks of Compeyson's underlings as *instruments*. With this image he characterizes a man who uses others as he would use tools.

2 CHARACTERIZATION

Wemmick's dual character merges here: While he is sympathetic to Pip's concern for Magwitch—a Walworth sentiment—he is also distressed about the loss of Magwitch's money, a sentiment appropriate for the office.

3 THEME

As expected, Magwitch is found guilty of returning to England; his "industrious habits" can hold no weight in court.

GUIDED READING

LITERAL QUESTIONS

1a. How did Wemmick hear about Compeyson's movements? (through Compeyson's own people)

2a. What upsets Wemmick about Magwitch's capture? (the loss of Magwitch's portable property)

INFERENTIAL QUESTIONS

1b. How does Compeyson manage to fool Wemmick? (He lies to his own people about being away, and Wemmick receives false information.)

2b. Do you think this is a purely coldhearted attitude on Wemmick's part? (No; Wemmick is trying to be practical on Pip's behalf.)

AT A GLANCE

- Pip visits Magwitch in the prison infirmary.
- Pip tells the dying Magwitch that he loves Magwitch's living daughter.
- After Magwitch's death, Pip gives notice to his chambers.

1 THEME

At last Pip can impart his greatest secret to Magwitch: the man's daughter is alive and Pip loves her. It is the only secret whose revelation can bring happiness.

2 THE TOTAL EFFECT

Magwitch's death concludes many subplots: those concerning Compeyson, Wemmick, Jaggers, and Molly. The moving scene shows how completely both Magwitch and Pip have learned the value of love and friendship.

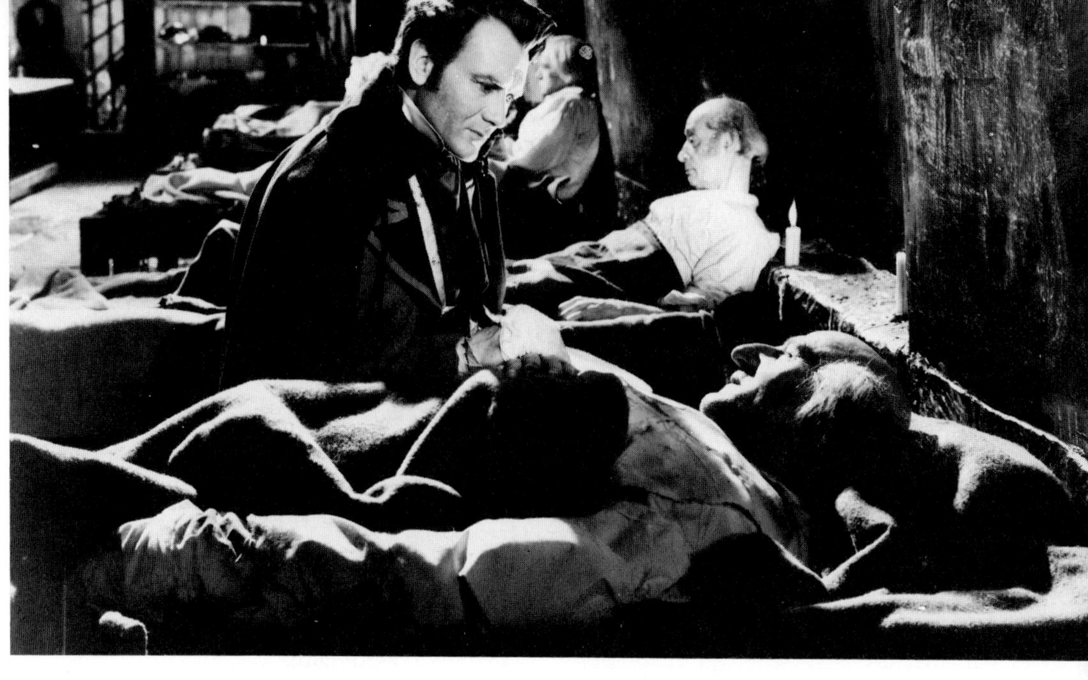

"You always waits at the gate, don't you, dear boy?"

"Yes. Not to lose a moment of the time."

"Thank'ee, dear boy, thank'ee. God bless you! You've never deserted me, dear boy."

I pressed his hand in silence, for I could not forget that I had once meant to desert him.

The allotted time ran out, while we were thus; but, looking round, I found the governor[2] of the prison standing near me, and he whispered, "You needn't go yet." I thanked him gratefully.

"Dear Magwitch, I must tell you, now at last. You understand what I say?"

A gentle pressure on my hand.

1 "You had a child once, whom you loved and lost."

A stronger pressure on my hand.

"She lived and found powerful friends. She is living now. She is a lady and very beautiful. And I love her!"

With a last faint effort, he raised my hand to
2 his lips. Then he gently let it sink upon his breast again, with his own hands lying on it. The placid look at the white ceiling came back, and passed away, and his head dropped quietly on his breast.

Chapter Thirty-eight

London: Pip has a kind nurse.

Now that I was left wholly to myself, I gave notice of my intention to quit the chambers in the Temple as soon as my tenancy could legally determine, and in the meanwhile to underlet them.[1] I was in debt, and had scarcely any money, and began to be seriously alarmed by the state of my affairs. Rather I should have been

2. **governor:** warden.

1. **to quit . . . underlet them:** to leave the apartment when the lease could be terminated, and in the meantime to sublet it.

GUIDED READING

LITERAL QUESTION

1a. What secret does Pip tell Magwitch? (that his daughter is alive)

INFERENTIAL QUESTION

1b. Why does Pip tell him? (to soothe Magwitch's last moments and to make up for his own unkindness)

alarmed if I had had energy enough to help me to the clear perception of any truth beyond the fact that I was falling very ill. The late stress upon me had enabled me to put off illness, but not to put it away; I knew that it was coming on me now, and I knew very little else.

For a day or two, I lay on the sofa, or on the floor—anywhere, according as I happened to sink down—with a heavy head and aching limbs, and no purpose, and no power. Then there came one night which appeared of great duration, and which teemed with anxiety and horror; and when in the morning I tried to sit up in my bed and think of it, I found I could not do so.

Whether I really had been down in Garden Court in the dead of the night, groping about for the boat that I supposed to be there; whether I had two or three times come to myself on the staircase with great terror, not knowing how I had got out of bed; whether I had been harassed by the distracted talking, laughing, and groaning of some one and had half-suspected those sounds to be of my own making; whether there had been a closed iron furnace in a dark corner of the room, and a voice had called out over and over again that Miss Havisham was within it; these were things that I tried to settle with myself and get into some order, as I lay on my bed.

"What do you want?" I asked, starting; "I don't know you."

"Well, sir," returned one of them, bending down and touching me on the shoulder, "this is a matter that you'll soon arrange, I dare say, but you're arrested."

"What is the debt?"

"Hundred and twenty-three pound, fifteen, six. Jeweler's account, I think."

"What is to be done?"

"You had better come to my house," said the man. "I keep a very nice house."

I made some attempt to get up and dress myself. When I next attended to them, they were standing a little off from the bed, looking at me. I still lay there.

"You see my state," said I. "I would come with you if I could; but indeed I am quite unable. If you take me from here, I think I shall die by the way."

Perhaps they replied, or argued the point, or tried to encourage me to believe that I was better than I thought. Forasmuch as they hang in my memory by only this one slender thread, I don't know what they did, except that they forbore to remove me.

That I had a fever and was avoided, that I suffered greatly, that I often lost my reason, that the time seemed interminable, that I sometimes struggled with real people, in the belief that they were murderers, and that I would all at once comprehend that they meant to do me good, and would then sink exhausted in their arms, and suffer them to lay me down, I also knew at the time. But, above all, I knew that there was a constant tendency in all these people—who, when I was very ill, would present all kinds of extraordinary transformations of the human face, and
2 would be much dilated in size—above all, I say, I knew that there was an extraordinary tendency in all these people, sooner or later, to settle down into the likeness of Joe.

After I had turned the worse point of my illness, I began to notice that while all its other features changed, this one consistent feature did not change. Whoever came about me, still settled down into Joe. I opened my eyes in the night, and I saw in the great chair at the bedside, Joe. I opened my eyes in the day, and, sitting on the window-seat, smoking his pipe in the shaded
3 open window, still I saw Joe. I asked for cooling drink, and the dear hand that gave it me was Joe's. I sank back on my pillow after drinking, and the face that looked so hopefully and tenderly upon me was the face of Joe.

At last, one day, I took courage, and said, "*Is* it Joe?"

AT A GLANCE

- Pip falls ill and becomes delirious.
- He is arrested for debt.
- He imagines he sees Joe constantly by his side.

1 CONFLICT

The internal conflicts that have plagued Pip throughout the novel—his desire for wealth and love, his guilt over Joe, his feeling of responsibility for Magwitch—are released in his delirium.

2 THEME

Pip's desperate desire to repent his selfishness and his overwhelming guilt combine with his illness to convince him that every face he sees resembles Joe's.

3 THEME

When Pip realizes that Joe is, in fact, at his side, he sees in Joe's "dear hand" and hopeful and tender face the truly selfless love that he has long been seeking.

GUIDED READING

LITERAL QUESTIONS

1a. What does Pip hear and see in his delirium? (He sees a boat and a furnace, and hears voices say that Miss Havisham is in the furnace.)

2a. Whom does Pip imagine is taking care of him? (He thinks it is Joe.)

INFERENTIAL QUESTIONS

1b. Why does he imagine those things? (He is confused and exhausted and his mind is overburdened with fear and guilt.)

2b. Why does Pip believe this? (He sees Joe's face, and the person is kind and caring, as Joe has always been.)

AT A GLANCE

- Pip realizes that Joe has been caring for him during his illness.
- Pip recovers slowly.
- Joe says that Miss Havisham is dead and has left money to Matthew Pocket.

1 THE TOTAL EFFECT

In a moment intended to move the reader emotionally, Pip learns that Joe—still constant, kind, and caring—has returned to him.

2 THEME

Pip's earlier thoughtful action sealed the fortunes of the Pockets, who have now received an inheritance of four thousand pounds.

3 THEME

Pip derives "great joy" from learning of Matthew Pocket's inheritance, a joy he was never able to feel when he had money himself.

1 And the dear old home-voice answered, "Which it air, old chap."

"Oh, Joe, you break my heart! Look angry at me, Joe. Strike me, Joe. Tell me of my ingratitude. Don't be so good to me!"

For Joe had actually laid his head down on the pillow at my side, and put his arm round my neck, in his joy that I knew him.

"Which dear old Pip, old chap," said Joe, "you and me was ever friends. And when you're well enough to go out for a ride—what larks!"

After which, Joe withdrew to the window, and stood with his back towards me, wiping his eyes. And as my extreme weakness prevented me from getting up and going to him, I lay there, whispering, "O God bless him! O God bless this gentle man!"

Joe's eyes were red when I next found him beside me, but I was holding his hand and we both felt happy.

"How long, dear Joe?"

"Which you meantersay, Pip, how long have your illness lasted, dear old chap?"

"Yes, Joe."

"It's the end of May, Pip. To-morrow is the first of June."

"And have you been here all the time, dear Joe?"

"Pretty nigh, old chap. For, as I says to Biddy when the news of your being ill were brought by letter, that how you might be amongst strangers, and that how you and me having been ever friends, a wisit at such a moment might not prove unacceptabobble. And Biddy, her word were, 'Go to him, without loss of time.' That," said Joe, summing up with his judicial air, "were the word of Biddy."

There Joe cut himself short, and informed me that I was to be talked to in great moderation, and that I was to take a little nourishment at stated frequent times, whether I felt inclined for it or not, and that I was to submit myself to all his orders. So I kissed his hand, and lay quiet, while he proceeded to indite a note to Biddy, with my love in it.

Evidently Biddy had taught Joe to write. As I lay in bed looking at him, it made me, in my weak state, cry again with pleasure to see the pride with which he set about his letter.

Not to make Joe uneasy by talking too much, even if I had been able to talk much, I deferred asking him about Miss Havisham until next day. He shook his head when I then asked him if she had recovered.

"Is she dead, Joe?"

"Why, you see, old chap," said Joe, "but she ain't—"

"Living, Joe?"

"That's nigher where it is," said Joe; "she ain't living."

"Dear Joe, have you heard what becomes of her property?"

"Well, old chap," said Joe, "it do appear that she had settled the most of it, which I meanter say tied it up, on Miss Estella. But she had wrote out a little coddleshell[2] in her own hand a day or two afore the accident, leaving a cool four thousand to Mr. Matthew Pocket. And why, do you suppose, above all things, Pip, she left that cool

2 four thousand unto him? 'Because of Pip's account of him the said Matthew.' I am told by Biddy that air the writing," said Joe, repeating the legal turn as if it did him infinite good, " 'account of him the said Matthew.' And a cool four thousand, Pip!"

I never discovered from whom Joe derived the conventional temperature of the four thousand pounds, but it appeared to make the sum of money more to him, and he had a manifest relish in insisting on its being cool.

3 This account gave me great joy, as it perfected the only good thing I had done.

"And now," said Joe, "you ain't that strong yet, old chap, that you can take in more nor one additional shovel-full to-day. Old Orlick he's been a-bustin' open a dwelling-'ouse."

2. **coddleshell:** Joe mispronounces "codicil" [kod′ə sil], an addition to a will to change, add, or delete a provision.

GUIDED READING

LITERAL QUESTIONS

1a. What is the first thing that Pip says to Joe? (He begs Joe to be angry and to admonish him for his ingratitude.)

2a. To whom did Miss Havisham leave four thousand pounds? (Matthew Pocket)

INFERENTIAL QUESTIONS

1b. Why does Pip say this? (He feels guilty and unworthy of Joe's kindness.)

2b. Why did she make this bequest? (because Pip assured her that Matthew was a good man)

"Whose?" said I.

"Not, I grant you, but what his manners is given to blusterous," said Joe apologetically; "still, a Englishman's 'ouse is his castle, and castles must not be busted 'cept when done in war-time. And wotsome'er the failings on his part, he were a corn and seedsman in his hart."

"Is it Pumblechook's house that has been broken into, then?"

"That's it, Pip," said Joe; "and they took his till, and they took his cash-box. But he knowed Orlick, and Orlick's in the county jail."

We looked forward to the day when I should go out for a ride, as we had once looked forward to the day of my apprenticeship. And when the day came, and an open carriage was got into the lane, Joe wrapped me up, got in beside me, and we drove away together into the country, where the rich summer growth was already on the trees and on the grass, and sweet summer scents filled all the air.

When we got back again and he lifted me out, and carried me—so easily!—across the court and up the stairs, I thought of that eventful Christmas Day when he had carried me over the marshes. We had not yet made any allusion to my change of fortune, nor did I know how much of my late history he was acquainted with. I was so doubtful of myself now, and put so much trust in him, that I could not satisfy myself whether I ought to refer to it when he did not.

"Have you heard, Joe," I asked him that evening, upon further consideration, as he smoked his pipe at the window, "who my patron was?"

"I heerd," returned Joe, "as it were not Miss Havisham, old chap."

"Did you hear who it was, Joe?"

"Well! I heerd as it were a person what sent the person what giv' you the bank-notes at the Jolly Bargemen, Pip."

"So it was."

"Astonishing!" said Joe, in the placidest way.

"Did you hear that he was dead, Joe?" I presently asked, with increasing diffidence.

"Which? Him as sent the bank-notes, Pip?"

"Yes."

"I think," said Joe, after meditating a long time, and looking rather evasively at the window-seat, "as I *did* hear tell that how he were something or another in a general way in that direction."

"Did you hear anything of his circumstances, Joe?"

"Not partickler, Pip."

"If you would like to hear, Joe—" I was beginning, when Joe got up and came to my sofa.

3 "Look'ee here, old chap," said Joe, bending over me. "Ever the best of friends; ain't us, Pip?"

I was ashamed to answer him.

"Werry good, then," said Joe, as if I *had* answered; "that's all right; that's agreed upon. Then why go into subjects, old chap, which as betwixt two sech must be for ever onnecessary?"

"I feel thankful that I have been ill, Joe," I said.

"Dear old Pip, old chap, you're a'most come round, sir."

"It has been a memorable time for me, Joe."

"Likeways for myself, sir," Joe returned.

"We have had a time together, Joe, that I can never forget. There were days once, I know, that I did for a while forget; but I never shall forget these."

"Pip," said Joe, appearing a little hurried and troubled, "there has been larks. And, dear sir, what have been betwixt us—have been."

At night, when I had gone to bed, Joe came into my room, as he had done all through my recovery. He asked me if I felt sure that I was as well as in the morning.

"Yes, dear Joe, quite."

"And are always a-getting stronger, old chap?"

"Yes, dear Joe, steadily."

Joe patted the coverlet on my shoulder with his great good hand, and said, in what I thought a husky voice, "Good night!"

AT A GLANCE

- Joe reports that Orlick robbed Pumblechook and is now in jail.
- Joe refuses to hear details about Magwitch.
- Pip and Joe reminisce as Pip recuperates.

1 THE TOTAL EFFECT

Orlick, as unsavory as ever, is put in jail—an action that Dickens used to satisfy the reader and conclude the subplot involving Orlick.

2 ATMOSPHERE

Now that Joe is with Pip and has forgiven him, the dark, gloomy atmosphere that has prevailed through most of the novel gives way to "rich summer growth" and "sweet summer scents."

3 THEME

As Joe reminds Pip that they are "ever the best of friends," he demonstrates again his ability to forgive and his unselfish love.

GUIDED READING

LITERAL QUESTIONS

1a. How does Joe change the subject from Magwitch? (He says, "Ever the best of friends.")

2a. What does Pip tell Joe about his illness? (Pip says he is thankful that he has been ill.)

INFERENTIAL QUESTIONS

1b. Why does he change the subject? (He does not want to discuss the time in which he and Pip were separated.)

2b. Why does he say this? (The illness has brought Joe back to him.)

AT A GLANCE

- Joe returns to the forge.
- Pip decides to go home and ask Biddy to marry him.
- He sleeps at the Blue Boar.

1 CHARACTERIZATION

Joe's sacrifices for Pip include paying Pip's debts; Joe shows his love with countless simple gestures and words.

2 THEME

Pip notices how rapidly and thoroughly attitudes toward him change: The innkeeper of the Blue Boar is now "exceedingly cool" and makes no attempt to please him.

3 THEME

Although he no longer has "expectations," Pip is as comfortable in his poor room "as in the most superior accommodation"; he has learned that his state of mind is more vital for happiness than his financial standing.

I got up in the morning, refreshed and stronger yet.

I hurried then to the breakfast-table, and on it found a letter. These were its brief contents.

> Not wishful to intrude I have departured fur you are well again dear Pip and will do better without Jo.
> P.S. Ever the best of friends.

Enclosed in the letter was a receipt for the debt and costs on which I had been arrested. Down to that moment I had vainly supposed that my creditor had withdrawn or suspended pro-
1 ceedings until I should be quite recovered. I had never dreamed of Joe's having paid the money; but Joe had paid it, and the receipt was in his name.

What remained for me now, but to follow him to the dear old forge, and to relieve my mind and heart.

I would go to Biddy. I would show her how humbled and repentant I came back. I would tell her how I had lost all I once hoped for, that I would remind her of our old confidences in my first unhappy time. Then, I would say to her, "Biddy, I think you once liked me very well, when my errant heart, even while it strayed away from you, was quieter and better with you than it ever has been since. If you can like me only half as well once more, if you can take me with all my faults and disappointments on my head, if you can receive me like a forgiven child, I hope I am a little worthier of you than I was—not much, but a little. And, Biddy, it shall rest with you to say whether I shall work at the forge with Joe, or whether I shall try for any different occupation down in this country, or whether we shall go away to a distant place where an opportunity awaits me which I set aside when it was offered, until I knew your answer. And now, dear Biddy, if you can tell me that you will go through the world with me, you will surely make it a better world for me, and me a bette man for it, and I will try hard to make it a bette world for you."

Such was my purpose.

Chapter Thirty-nine

Back at the forge: Biddy and Joe and Pip's pla to leave England.

The tidings of my high fortunes having had a heavy fall, had got down to my native place and its neighborhood before I got there. I found the Blue Boar in possession of the intelligence, and found that it made a great change in the Boar's
2 demeanor. Whereas the Boar had cultivated my good opinion with warm assiduity[1] when I was coming into property, the Boar was exceedingly cool on the subject now that I was going out of property.

It was evening when I arrived, much fatigued by the journey I had so often made so easily. The Boar could not put me into my usual bedroom, which was engaged (probably by some one who had expectations), and could only assign me a very indifferent chamber among the pigeons and
3 post-chaises up the yard. But I had as sound a sleep in that lodging as in the most superior accommodation the Boar could have given me, and the quality of my dreams was about the same as in the best bedroom.

Early in the morning while my breakfast was getting ready, I strolled round by Satis House. There were printed bills on the gate and on bits of carpet hanging out of the windows, announcing a sale by auction of the household furniture and effects, next week. The house itself was to be sold as old building materials, and pulled down.

When I got back to my breakfast in the Boar's coffee-room, I found Mr. Pumblechook convers-

1. **assiduity** [as′ə do͞o′ə tē]: diligence.

GUIDED READING

LITERAL QUESTIONS

1a. What does Pip plan to do when he goes home? (He plans to propose to Biddy.)

2a. How does the owner of the Blue Boar treat Pip? (He treats Pip cooly and gives him a poor room off the yard.)

INFERENTIAL QUESTIONS

1b. Why do you think he now wants to marry Biddy? (because he now recognizes what a good person she is)

2b. How does Pip feel about his treatment? (He is not bothered because he knows that his happiness is not founded on exterior things.)

ing with the landlord. Mr. Pumblechook was waiting for me, and addressed me in the following terms.

"Young man, I am sorry to see you brought low. But what else could be expected! What else could be expected!"

As he extended his hand with a magnificently forgiving air, and as I was broken by illness and unfit to quarrel, I took it.

It was pleasanter to turn to Biddy and to Joe. I went towards them slowly, for my limbs were weak, but with a sense of increasing relief as I drew nearer to them.

The June weather was delicious. The sky was blue, the larks were soaring high over the green corn, I thought all that country-side more beautiful and peaceful by far than I had ever known it to be yet.

The school-house where Biddy was mistress, I had never seen, but the little roundabout lane by which I entered the village for quietness' sake, took me past it. I was disappointed to find that the day was a holiday; no children were there, and Biddy's house was closed. Some hopeful notion of seeing her, busily engaged in her daily duties, before she saw me, had been in my mind and was defeated.

But the forge was a very short distance off, and I went towards it under the sweet green limes, listening for the clink of Joe's hammer. Long after I ought to have heard it, and long after I had fancied I heard it and found it but a fancy, all was still. The limes were there, and the white thorns were there, and the chestnut-trees were there, and their leaves rustled harmoniously when I stopped to listen, but the clink of Joe's hammer was not in the midsummer wind.

Almost fearing, without knowing why, to come in view of the forge, I saw it at last, and saw that it was closed. No gleam of fire, no glittering shower of sparks, no roar of bellows; all shut up, and still.

But the house was not deserted, and the best parlor seemed to be in use, for there were white curtains fluttering in its window, and the window was open and gay with flowers. I went softly towards it, meaning to peep over the flowers, when Joe and Biddy stood before me, arm in arm.

At first Biddy gave a cry, as if she thought it was my apparition, but in another moment she was in my embrace. I wept to see her, and she wept to see me; I because she looked so fresh and pleasant; she because I looked so worn and white.

"But, dear Biddy, how smart you are!"

"Yes, dear Pip."

"And Joe, how smart *you* are!"

"Yes, dear old Pip, old chap."

3 I looked at both of them, from one to the other, and then—

"It's my wedding-day," cried Biddy, in a burst of happiness, "and I am married to Joe!"

They had taken me into the kitchen, and I had laid my head down on the old deal table. Biddy held one of my hands to her lips, and Joe's restoring touch was on my shoulder. "Which he warn't strong enough, my dear, fur to be surprised," said Joe. And Biddy said, "I ought to have thought of it, dear Joe, but I was too
4 happy." They were both so overjoyed to see me, so proud to see me, so touched by my coming to them, so delighted that I should have come by accident to make their day complete!

My first thought was one of great thankfulness that I had never breathed this last baffled hope to Joe. How often, while he was with me in my illness, had it risen to my lips.

"Dear Biddy," said I, "you have the best husband in the whole world, and if you could have seen him by my bed you would have— But no, you couldn't love him better than you do."

"No, I couldn't indeed," said Biddy.

"And, dear Joe, you have the best wife in the whole world, and she will make you as happy as

AT A GLANCE

- Pumblechook extends his condolences to Pip.
- Pip arrives at his old house; Biddy and Joe have married that day.

1 CHARACTERIZATION

A flat character who is pompous and false, Pumblechook claims to be sorry for Pip's reversal, but he obviously feels that Pip never deserved his good fortune.

2 SETTING

The "delicious" and "peaceful" setting reflects Pip's happy, hopeful state of mind.

3 THE TOTAL EFFECT

Though Biddy's revelation destroys Pip's delicate happiness, it is news that does justice to the goodness of the two who are married.

4 IRONY

Joe and Biddy's happiness over seeing Pip, who has made their wedding day "complete," is ironic in light of Pip's intentions toward Biddy and his feelings about losing her.

GUIDED READING

LITERAL QUESTIONS

1a. What news does Biddy give Pip? (She tells him that she and Joe are married.)

2a. Of what is Pip thankful? (that he never told Joe he wanted to marry Biddy)

INFERENTIAL QUESTIONS

1b. How does Pip feel about this? (He is crushed because he wanted to marry Biddy, but happy because she and Joe are happy.)

2b. What might have happened if he had told Joe? (Joe might not have married her, and Pip would have felt responsible for this.)

AT A GLANCE

- Pip wishes Joe and Biddy happiness and leaves.
- He works in Cairo for Herbert's company.
- After many years he becomes a partner in the business.
- Eleven years pass; Pip returns to see Joe, Biddy, and their son.

1 THEME

Pip asks Joe not to tell his future children of Pip's thanklessness; thus, indirectly Pip admits his guilt and begs forgiveness for his former treatment of Joe and Biddy.

2 THEME

Pip is quietly happy in his new life, which was made possible partly through his own doing.

3 THEME

Pip returns to find a new Pip—Joe and Biddy's son—at his old home. Dickens has presented examples of time's passing—Joe's grey hair and Pip's nostalgic view of the scene—as well as an example of time's seemingly circular nature. The novel has moved from the child Pip to the adult Pip to another child.

even you deserve to be, dear, good, noble Joe!"

Joe looked at me with a quivering lip, and put his sleeve before his eyes.

"And Joe and Biddy both, as you have been to church to-day and are in charity and love with all mankind, receive my humble thanks for all you have done for me, and all I have so ill-repaid! And when I say that I am going away within the hour, for I am soon going abroad, and that I shall never rest until I have worked for the money with which you have kept me out of prison, and have sent it to you, don't think, dear Joe and Biddy, that if I could repay it a thousand times over, I suppose I could cancel a farthing[2] of the debt I owe you, or that I would do so if I could!"

They were both melted by these words, and both entreated me to say no more.

"But I must say more. Dear Joe, I hope you will have children to love, and that some little fellow will sit in this chimney-corner, of a winter night, who may remind you of another
1 little fellow gone out of it for ever. Don't tell him, Joe, that I was thankless; don't tell him, Biddy, that I was ungenerous and unjust; only tell him that I honored you both, because you were both so good and true, and that, as your child, I said it would be natural to him to grow up a much better man than I did."

"I ain't a-going," said Joe, from behind his sleeve, "to tell him nothink o' that natur, Pip. Nor Biddy ain't. Nor yet no one ain't."

I sold all I had and put aside as much as I could for my creditors—who gave me ample time to pay them in full—and I went out and joined Herbert. Within a month, I had quitted England, and within two months I was clerk to Clarriker & Co., and within four months I assumed my first undivided responsibility. For the beam across the parlor ceiling at Mill Pond Bank had then ceased to tremble under Clara's father's growls and was at peace, and Herbert had gone away to marry Clara, and I was left in sole charge of the Eastern branch until he brought her back.

2 Many a year went round, before I was a partner in the house; but I lived happily with Herbert and his wife, and lived frugally, and paid my debts, and maintained a constant correspondence with Biddy and Joe. It was not until I became third in the firm that Clarriker betrayed me to Herbert; but he then declared that the secret of Herbert's partnership had been long enough upon his conscience, and he must tell it. So, he told it, and Herbert was as much moved as amazed, and the dear fellow and I were not the worse friends for the long concealment. I must not leave it to be supposed that we were ever a great house, or that we made mints of money. We were not in a grand way of business, but we had a good name, and worked for our profits, and did very well.

Chapter Forty

Home again, eleven years later: A new Pip, a new Estella.

For eleven years I had not seen Joe nor Biddy with my bodily eyes—though they had both been often before my fancy in the East—when, upon an evening in December, an hour or two after dark, I laid my hand softly on the latch of the old kitchen door. I touched it so softly that I
3 was not heard, and I looked in unseen. There, smoking his pipe in the old place by the kitchen firelight, as hale and as strong as ever, though a little grey, sat Joe; and there, fenced into the corner with Joe's leg, and sitting on my own little stool looking at the fire, was—I again!

"We giv' him the name of Pip for your sake, dear old chap," said Joe, delighted when I took another stool by the child's side (but I did *not* rumple his hair), "and we hoped he might grow a little bit like you, and we think he do."

I thought so, too, and I took him out for a walk next morning, and we talked immensely, understanding one another to perfection. And I

2. **farthing:** British coin worth one quarter of a penny.

GUIDED READING

LITERAL QUESTIONS

1a. Where does Pip tell Biddy and Joe he is going? (abroad to work)

2a. How does Pip behave in his new position? (He is frugal, corresponds with Joe and Biddy, and is happy.)

INFERENTIAL QUESTIONS

1b. Why is he leaving? (There is nothing to keep him in England, and by going abroad and working for Herbert's company, he can pay Joe back.)

2b. What does this show about the way he has changed? (He has learned to be truly happy.)

ook him down to the churchyard, and set him on a certain tombstone there, and he showed me from that elevation which stone was sacred to the memory of Philip Pirrip, Late of this Parish, and Also Georgiana Wife of the Above.

"Biddy," said I, when I talked with her after dinner, as her little girl lay sleeping in her lap, 'you must give Pip to me, one of these days; or lend him, at all events."

"No, no," said Biddy gently. "You must marry."

"So Herbert and Clara say, but I don't think I shall, Biddy. I have so settled down in their home that it's not at all likely. I am already quite an old bachelor."

Biddy looked down at her child, and put its little hand to her lips, and then put the good matronly hand with which she had touched it into mine. There was something in the action and in the light pressure of Biddy's wedding ring that had a very pretty eloquence in it.

"Dear Pip," said Biddy, "you are sure you don't fret for her?"

"Oh, no—I think not, Biddy."

"Tell me as an old friend. Have you quite forgotten her?"

"My dear Biddy, I have forgotten nothing in my life that ever had a foremost place there, and little that ever had any place there. But that poor dream, as I once used to call it, has all gone by, Biddy, all gone by!"

Dickens originally added just two more paragraphs here to end the novel. Friends who were dissatisfied with that ending, however, convinced him to write a new, longer ending. The original ending is on page 667. What follows here is the new ending.

Nevertheless, I knew while I said those words that I secretly intended to revisit the sight of the old house that evening alone, for her sake. Yes, even so. For Estella's sake.

I had heard of her as leading a most unhappy life, and as being separated from her husband, who had used her with great cruelty, and who had become quite renowned as a compound of
2 pride, avarice, brutality, and meanness. And I had heard of the death of her husband from an accident consequent on his ill-treatment of a horse. This release had befallen her some two years before; for anything I knew, she was married again.

The early dinner-hour at Joe's left me abundance of time, without hurrying my talk with Biddy, to walk over to the old spot before dark. But what with loitering on the way to look at old objects and to think of old times, the day had quite declined when I came to the place.

3 There was no house now, no brewery, no building whatever left, but the wall of the old garden. The cleared space had been enclosed with a rough fence, and looking over it, I saw that some of the old ivy had struck root anew, and was growing green on low quiet mounds of ruin. A gate in the fence standing ajar, I pushed it open, and went in.

A cold silvery mist had veiled the afternoon, and the moon was not yet up to scatter it. But the stars were shining beyond the mist, and the moon was coming, and the evening was not dark. I could trace out where every part of the old house had been, and where the brewery had been, and where the gates, and where the casks. I had done so, and was looking along the desolate garden-walk, when I beheld a solitary figure in it.

The figure showed itself aware of me as I advanced. It had been moving towards me, but it stood still. As I drew nearer, I saw it to be the figure of a woman. As I drew nearer yet, it was about to turn away, when it stopped, and let me come up with it. Then it faltered as if much surprised, and uttered my name, and I cried out:

"Estella!"

"I am greatly changed. I wonder you know me."

The freshness of her beauty was indeed gone, but its indescribable majesty and its indescribable charm remained. Those attractions in it I

AT A GLANCE

- Pip and Biddy discuss Estella.
- In Dickens' second version, Pip goes to the site of Satis House.
- Estella speaks to him there.

1 THEME

Without words Biddy communicates her happiness and a sense of all that has happened (and not happened) between Pip and herself.

2 THEME

When Pip says that the death of Estella's husband was a "release" for her, he hints that Estella was imprisoned by her marriage, much as Miss Havisham was by her jilting.

3 THE TOTAL EFFECT

Dickens uses the setting—Satis House destroyed—to illustrate the result of misused wealth and power, but the description of ivy that has "struck root anew" echoes Pip's own hope for renewed life and love.

GUIDED READING

LITERAL QUESTION

1a. What has become of Satis House? (It is in ruins.)

INFERENTIAL QUESTION

1b. How does its present state reflect the conditions of its former inhabitants? (As the house is in ruins, Miss Havisham is dead, and Estella is unhappy.)

AT A GLANCE

- Pip and Estella speak of themselves.
- Pip says she still has a place in his heart.
- They vow to remain friends.

1 CHARACTERIZATION

Estella has completed a change that was only hinted at earlier in the novel: She is "saddened, softened," and unhappiness has humanized her.

2 THEME

Estella reminds Pip of his earlier unselfish parting from her; just as Joe's selfless love saved Pip, so Pip's love for Estella could help her.

1 had seen before; what I had never seen before was the saddened, softened light of the once proud eyes; what I had never felt before was the friendly touch of the once insensible hand.

We sat down on a bench that was near, and I said, "After so many years, it is strange that we should thus meet again, Estella, here where our first meeting was! Do you often come back?"

"I have never been here since."

"Nor I."

"And you," she said, in a voice of touching interest to a wanderer, "you live abroad still."

"Still."

"And do well, I am sure?"

"Yes, I do well!"

"I have often thought of you," said Estella.

"Have you?"

"Of late, very often. There was a long hard time when I kept far from me the remembrance of what I had thrown away when I was quite ignorant of its worth."

"You have always held your place in *my* heart," I answered.

And we were silent again until she spoke.

"I little thought," said Estella, "that I should take leave of you in taking leave of this spot. I am very glad to do so."

"Glad to part again, Estella? To me, parting is a painful thing. To me, the remembrance of our last parting has been ever mournful and painful."

2 "But you said to me," returned Estella very earnestly, " 'God bless you, God forgive you!' And if you could say that to me then, you will not hesitate to say that to me now. I have been bent and broken, but—I hope—into a better shape. Be as considerate and good to me as you were, and tell me we are friends."

"We are friends," said I, rising and bending over her, as she rose from the bench.

"And will continue friends apart," said Estella.

I took her hand in mine, and we went out of

GUIDED READING

LITERAL QUESTION

1a. What does Estella say has happened to her? (She has been "bent and broken" into what she hopes is a "better shape.")

INFERENTIAL QUESTION

1b. What does she mean? (that her suffering has made her into a better person)

the ruined place; and as the morning mists had risen long ago when I first left the forge, so the evening mists were rising now, and in all the broad expanse of tranquil light they showed to me, I saw no shadow of another parting from her.

The two paragraphs that follow make up Dickens' original ending to the novel and continue from page 665. This ending is no longer considered part of the novel. It is reprinted to provide an insight into Dickens' method of writing and editing his own work.

It was two years more before I saw herself. I had heard of her as leading a most unhappy life, and as being separated from her husband, who had used her with great cruelty, and who had become quite renowned as a compound of pride, brutality, and meanness. I had heard of the death of her husband from an accident consequent on ill-treating a horse, and of her being married again to a Shropshire doctor, who, against his interest, had once very manfully interposed on an occasion when he was in professional attendance upon Mr. Drummle, and had witnessed some outrageous treatment of her. I had heard that the Shropshire doctor was not rich, and that they lived on her own personal fortune. I was in England again—in London, and walking along Piccadilly with little Pip—when a servant came running after me to ask would I step back to a lady in a carriage who wished to speak to me. It was a little pony carriage which the lady was driving, and the lady and I looked sadly enough on one another.

"I am greatly changed, I know, but I thought you would like to shake hands with Estella, too, Pip. Lift up that pretty child and let me kiss it!" (She supposed the child, I think, to be my child.)
2 I was very glad afterwards, to have had the interview, for in her face and in her voice, and in her touch, she gave me assurance that suffering had been stronger than Miss Havisham's teaching, and had given her a heart to understand what my heart used to be.

STUDY QUESTIONS

Recalling

1. Describe the accident from which Pip saves Miss Havisham in Chapter 33. In what condition does each survive the accident?
2. What information about Estella do Jaggers and Pip exchange in Chapter 34?
3. Why does Orlick call Pip an enemy in Chapter 35? What two mysteries does Orlick clear up?
4. What steps are taken to get Magwitch out of England in Chapter 36? Explain how the plan fails. What is Magwitch's condition afterward?
5. What becomes of Magwitch's money in Chapter 36? What is Pip's financial condition?
6. What news does Joe give Pip about Miss Havisham in Chapter 38? About Orlick?
7. With what plans does Pip return to the forge at the end of Chapter 38? According to Chapter 39, why must he change his plans?
8. Where does Pip meet Estella again in Dickens' new ending? In the original ending?

Interpreting

9. Why does Pip begin to suspect that Estella is Molly's daughter? What support does he find for his suspicion?
10. Explain how Pip's feelings toward Magwitch have changed. Why does Pip tell Magwitch about loving Estella?
11. In what ways does the end of the novel remind us of the beginning?
12. Which of the two endings do you prefer? Explain your opinion.

AT A GLANCE

- As the second ending finishes, Pip and Estella walk off, hand in hand.
- In the original ending Pip learns that Estella's first husband died and she has remarried.
- He sees her as he walks in London with little Pip.

1 THE TOTAL EFFECT

The "tranquil light" of evening, Estella's peaceful new character, and Pip's new understanding of life and love combine to act as a quiet culmination to the novel's previous frenetic action.

2 THE TOTAL EFFECT

This sober ending upholds the dark and ironic tone of Pip's first-person narration throughout the novel by stressing that only Pip's good deeds and sentiments could bring him happiness.

REFLECTING ON CHAPTERS 32–40

Which ending do you think best fits the novel? Why? (Possible answers: the second is more sentimental and "happy"; the original is more consistent in tone and moral content.)

STUDY QUESTIONS

1. her dress catches fire; he rolls her in his coat; Havisham is badly burned, suffers from shock; Pip's hands and arms are burned
2. Jaggers admits Molly is her mother; Pip reveals Magwitch is her father.
3. got him fired; reveals he attacked Mrs. Joe; was hiding on stairs night Magwitch arrived
4. - smuggled into small boat, then to intercept steamer
   - Compeyson informs authorities; Magwitch is injured, apprehended.
5. It is forfeited to the crown; Pip loses inheritance.
6. She is dead; Orlick robbed Pumblechook, was caught and jailed.
7. He wants to ask Biddy to marry him; she has married Joe.
8. in Havisham's garden; London
9. Her eyes and hands remind him of Estella; Wemmick tells him she had a daughter who disappeared.
10. becomes grateful, begins to love him; wants to give him some happiness before he dies
11. Cemetery and Miss Havisham's house are similar; in the end Pip returns to where story began.
12. Some may prefer the original, as it is more realistic; others may enjoy the happy ending.

13. Possible answers: before he met Estella because he was content; after he leaves England to join Herbert; after he returns to find Estella

LITERARY FOCUS

1. *internal:* struggles to attain mature values, feels common, wants to be a gentleman; *person vs. person:* conflict with Estella throughout, Orlick; *person vs. society:* struggles to get Magwitch out of England, desires to become a gentleman

2. *Pip:* cruel, kind, deserts Joe, helps Magwitch; *Estella:* proud, heartless, avoids causing pain, warns Pip not to love her; *Wemmick:* tough professional at work, kindhearted at home, takes care of father, helps Herbert

3.
- Both grow and mature.
- *Joe* is static; *Biddy* changes from badly groomed, ignorant girl into neat, intelligent woman; *Miss Havisham* finally regrets the suffering she has caused; *Magwitch* changes from terrifying convict into loving father figure to Pip; *Jaggers* is static.

4.
- Possible answers: the forge, Miss Havisham's house, Pip's rooms in London
- Most actions can be depicted in these.

5. House represents the evil being plotted and reflects Miss Havisham herself.

6. Everything is gone but the garden wall; new ivy grows; both Estella and Pip have lost their previous lives.

7. Herbert tells Pip about Miss Havisham and Estella; Wemmick tells him Molly's history; Magwitch tells about Compeyson; Joe tells him of Miss Havisham's death and Orlick's arrest.

8. might reveal Estella's true feelings about Pip

9.
- *Biddy* happier, more understanding; *Estella* better dressed

Extending

13. At what time in his life do you think Pip is happiest? Why?

LITERARY FOCUS

The Total Effect

Charles Dickens earned his reputation as a great novelist in part because of his ability to create intricate, twisting plots with many vivid characters and a variety of settings, colorful and realistic. These elements, along with point of view, help him to illustrate his themes, many of them important social concerns that he held throughout his life. Dickens' works, therefore, demonstrate the fact that the elements of fiction—plot, character, setting, point of view, and theme—interact and create a total effect, an impact on the reader.

Thinking About Plot, Character, and Setting

1. Explain how Pip's adventures contain different types of conflict: internal conflict, person-against-person conflict, person-against-society conflict.
2. In what ways do the following round characters reveal more than one personality trait: Pip, Estella, Wemmick?
3. Why can Pip and Estella be considered dynamic characters? Explain whether you consider each of the following characters dynamic or static: Joe, Miss Havisham, Magwitch, and Jaggers.
4. If you were to adapt the novel into a play but could have only three scenes, which three settings would you choose as most important? Why?
5. Explain how setting creates atmosphere when Pip first goes to Miss Havisham's.
6. What changes does Pip see in his visit to Miss Havisham's at the end of the novel? What do the changes in the house tell us about changes in Miss Havisham, Estella, and Pip?

Thinking About Point of View

7. Since the novel is told in first-person point of view, we are told only what Pip knows. Certain incidents occurred in the past, and Pip must learn about such events from others. Name three characters who tell Pip about important events. What do we learn from each?
8. In what way might the new ending of the novel be different if the novel had an omniscient point of view?

Thinking About Theme

9. Compare the two characters in each of the following pairs. Which character presents a better appearance? Which character is a happier, kinder person? What is Dickens saying about appearances and real happiness?

   Biddy and Estella
   Drummle and Joe
   Magwitch and Compeyson

10. Find three characters in the novel who live to repay wrongs done to them in the past. What finally happens to each of them? What is Dickens saying about revenge?
11. What different kinds of love are shown by Miss Havisham, Estella, Magwitch, Pip, and Joe? What type of love does Dickens seem to respect?
12. Consider two characters in the novel who are wealthy—Miss Havisham and Estella—and two who are poor—Biddy and Herbert. What is the relationship between each character's happiness and the amount of money that the character has?
13. What criticism of English schools does Dickens imply in his description of Pip's education? What criticism of English legal institutions does Dickens imply with the story of Magwitch?

VIEWPOINT

Great Expectations belongs to a popular type of novel in which a young person grows to maturity. Two critics have called Pip's adventures

> a series of lessons learned the hard way. He finds in Joe Gargery that simplicity may conceal the highest understanding and wisdom.... In Estella, he finds that beauty is a shell when love does not inhabit it. In the great expectations that bring him [Pip] riches, he finds disillusion.
>
> —M. and M. Hardwick,
> *The Charles Dickens Companion*

- In what sense does Pip learn his lessons the hard way? Give two examples of Joe's wisdom. In what way is Estella a shell?

WRITING FROM A DIFFERENT POINT OF VIEW

Objective

To retell a story from an alternate point of view

Guidelines for Evaluation

- suggested length: four to five paragraphs
- should present point of view of narrator
- should adhere to character traits and speech patterns of narrator
- should include feelings of narrator

COMPOSITION

Writing About the Total Effect

■ Describe the total effect, the impact that *Great Expectations* had on you. Explain how Dickens used the following elements to achieve this effect: (a) plot, (b) character, (c) setting, (d) point of view, and (e) theme. *For help with this assignment, see Lesson 11 in the Writing About Literature Handbook at the back of this book.*

Writing About Characters

■ At the beginning of *Great Expectations*, Pip and Joe are quite alike. Later in the novel their differences help to keep them apart. Compare and contrast the characters of Pip and Joe. First describe the similarities that make them friends at the beginning of the novel. Secondly tell whether each character changes during the novel, and explain how he changes. Then describe the differences between them when they meet in London. Finally explain how alike or different they are at the end of the novel. *For help with this assignment, see Lesson 4 in the Writing About Literature Handbook at the back of this book.*

Writing from a Different Point of View

■ Rewrite a scene from *Great Expectations* from the first-person point of view of a character other than Pip. For each suggested scene below, the storyteller and a title are also listed. You may want to use one of these suggestions, or you may prefer to choose your own scene, storyteller, and title.

a. Scene: Pip meets Magwitch in the churchyard.
Storyteller: Magwitch
Title: "I Am Saved by a Boy"

b. Scene: Pip talks with Biddy about his future.
Storyteller: Biddy
Title: "Pip Wants to Be a Gentleman"

c. Scene: Joe visits Pip in London.
Storyteller: Joe
Title: "My Visit with Pip"

d. Scene: Pip visits Miss Havisham for the last time.
Storyteller: Miss Havisham
Title: "If I Could Do It Over Again"

COMPARING NOVELS

Buck in *The Call of the Wild* and Pip in *Great Expectations* must both adjust to new surroundings and change as a result. Compare the two novels. Why is each character faced with a new environment? What new skills or habits must each acquire in the new surroundings? What earlier traits does each character lose? To what extent is the adjustment that each character makes permanent? Is the change beneficial? Why or why not?

COMPOSITION: GUIDELINES FOR EVALUATION

WRITING ABOUT THE TOTAL EFFECT

Objective

To describe the total effect of a novel and explain how it is achieved

Guidelines for Evaluation

- suggested length: six to eight paragraphs
- should describe the impact of novel on writer
- should explain five elements' contribution
- should support opinions with details
- should show relationships between elements

WRITING ABOUT CHARACTERS

Objective

To compare and contrast two characters

Guidelines for Evaluation

- suggested length: three to four characters
- should tell how Pip and Joe are alike
- should explain how they become different
- should tell why differences keep them apart
- should explain how they are alike or different

- *Drummle* more education; *Joe* happier, kinder
- *Magwitch* appears hardened, a fugitive, dedicates life to helping Pip; *Compeyson* helps police, lives for revenge.
- Appearance has nothing to do with happiness.

10. ■ Miss Havisham alone, unhappy, regretful; Orlick arrested; Compeyson dies seeking revenge
- Revenge hurts its seeker.

11. ■ *Miss Havisham:* thwarted love turned into bitterness
- *Estella* cannot love.
- *Magwitch:* paternal love
- *Pip* loves Joe but is ashamed, is devoted to Estella, grows to love Magwitch.
- *Joe* gives selfless love.
- respects unselfish love

12. Miss Havisham and Estella, unhappy; Biddy and Herbert, happy; money and happiness not related

13. Education for poor was inferior; courts more concerned with letter of the law than with justice, mercy

VIEWPOINT

Pip suffers unrequited love for Estella and remorse for treatment of Joe and Magwitch before he learns how to love; Joe understands that Pip will grow away from him, tells Pip how his mother suffered with his father; Estella is beautiful but cannot feel love.

COMPARING NOVELS

- Buck: sold and shipped north; learns to survive on less food, toughen his body, cope with cold, defend himself; loses customs of civilization; will never revert to domestication; beneficial because he is stronger, more independent, or harmful because he is no longer safe, comfortable
- Pip: sent to London; learns social customs, distinction between appearances and gentlemanly conduct; loses innocence, simplicity; regains some childhood values but can never return to old life; beneficial because Pip matures

ACTIVE READING

Assign this essay after students have read the novels in the unit. After they have read the essay, ask them how each novel—*The Call of the Wild* and *Great Expectations*—is different from a short story. Encourage answers that lead to the idea that both novels record gradual changes in characters, changes that happen because of the passing of time and the changing of settings. Students may also mention that the novels feature more characters than short stories and inspire greater sympathy with characters because of the longer time spent with them.

Ask for scenes that students found memorable in each novel, and make a brief list of especially vivid scenes. Then ask for sensory details of the way different students imagine each of these scenes, encouraging them to disagree with each other. Try to create the impression that any scene in a novel will be imagined differently by each person who reads it.

You will find among the materials for this unit in your *Teacher's Classroom Resources* the related blackline master Participating in a Novel.

ACTIVE READING

Participating in a Novel

When true reading pleasure occurs, we enter the world of a piece of literature, we forget ourselves, and we almost forget that we are reading. This process can occur with any work of literature, but with a novel it can be unique. We allow the characters of a novel to live with us for a longer time than we spend with a poem or a short story. As a result, our involvement in a novel can be deeper and, perhaps, more meaningful.

The key to such reading pleasure is *participation*, a back-and-forth exchange between reader and novel. Each reader brings his or her own experience to a novel. Because we each have different memories and emotions, the reactions that a work of literature draws from each of us will differ. For example, in *Great Expectations* each reader will have a slightly different sense of what the marshes look and feel like, of what the convicts look and sound like. Every reader will take to heart in a different way the lessons that Pip learns about class, wealth, and loyalty. The words we read give us something, and we, in turn, give them something. From this interaction an experience takes place, a meaning arises.

With that sort of active exchange in reading, we are no longer just looking at Buck in *The Call of the Wild* when he is suddenly transported to the dark and frozen north. Rather, we are there sharing Buck's confusion and wonder. Each reader may have a slightly different conception of the Yukon's icy landscape. Each reader may have a slightly different reaction to Buck's expeditions into the wild. These differences arise because we all must complete London's words with material from our own memories and experiences.

Of course, to say that the reader supplies part of the meaning of a work is not to imply that we can say anything we want about the novel. The author's words place limits on our imaginations. We should not spin fanciful imaginative versions of a story that take us far away from the text.

Reading a novel with participation can result in pleasure so strong that we remember certain scenes many years after reading a book. If you read *The Call of the Wild* and *Great Expectations* with full participation, you may never forget Buck's first night in the snow or Miss Havisham's fire. You may never forget them because, to some extent, you helped to create them.

REVIEW:
THE NOVEL

Guide for Studying the Novel

As you read novels, review the following guide in order to appreciate how the author of a novel constructs a long story that invites you into a complete new world.

Plot

1. What is the main **plot** and central **conflict** of the novel?
2. What **subplots** does the novel have? What are their conflicts? In what way is each subplot related to the main plot?
3. In what ways does **foreshadowing** prepare us for events?

Character

1. Who is the main **character** of the novel? Of each subplot?
2. What personality traits of important characters does the author reveal through **direct characterization**?
3. What personality traits of important characters does the author reveal through **indirect characterization**?
4. What characters in the novel are **round**? **Flat**?
5. What characters are **dynamic characters**? **Static characters**?

Setting

1. Where and when does the novel take place? What changes occur in time and place during the novel?
2. Could the novel take place in any other time and place?
3. What **atmosphere** is created by the setting?
4. What do changes in setting tell us about changes in characters?

Point of View

1. Does the author use **first-person point of view**? If so, what other characters supply information to the storyteller?
2. Does the author use **limited third-person point of view**?
3. Does the author use **omniscient third-person point of view**?

Theme

1. What themes are directly **stated** by the author or by characters?
2. What themes are **implied** in the novel?
3. In what ways do subplots support the main theme or themes of the novel?

REVIEW

Familiarize students with the Review, Guide for Studying the Elements of the Novel, either before or after they have read the novels in this unit. As they read the novels, students can use the guide to help them keep track of events and focus on the most important elements, or they can use the guide afterwards as a review of the unit. Encourage them to use the guide as they read other novels as well in order that they may heighten their understanding and enjoyment.

The questions in the Guide for Studying the Elements of the Novel appear with write-on lines, in blackline master form, among the materials for this unit in your *Teacher's Classroom Resources*.

A major goal of this literature series is to help students become active, independent learners. Resources on the following pages are designed to help students develop and refine the skills that mature learners use constantly as they interact with literature. Such learners know how to manage their assignments by applying these skills:

- speaking and listening skills
- thinking skills
- reading and study skills
- writing skills

Students will be able to refer to these pages throughout the term—not just in connection with a single literary selection. In other words, students can use this easy-to-find reference and practice guide continually, as they experience all the literature they read. With outstanding literature, on the one hand, and a comprehensive resource guide, on the other, this literature series provides the means for you and your students to deal with both ideas and skills.

In addition, these pages also include the following elements, designed for successful teaching and learning:

- Literary Terms Handbook
- Glossary
- Vocabulary Review
- Index of Titles by Theme
- Index of Skills
- Index of Authors and Titles

STUDENT'S RESOURCES

LESSONS IN ACTIVE LEARNING

SPEAKING AND LISTENING HANDBOOK

THINKING SKILLS HANDBOOK

READING AND STUDY SKILLS HANDBOOK

WRITING ABOUT LITERATURE HANDBOOK

SPEAKING AND LISTENING HANDBOOK

This handbook enables students to practice and improve their speaking and listening skills while studying literature. The four lessons in the handbook cover a wide range of interrelated speaking and listening skills:

- public speaking
- listening / discussion
- oral interpretation of literature
- collaborative learning

Each literature-based lesson is set up in a step-by-step format so that students can easily work on the skill on their own. The final step in each lesson is a transfer activity in which the student is directed to apply the skill to a variety of selections in the anthology. In other words, the lessons are designed to be used or referred to many times—as often as you wish your students to work with a particular speaking or listening skill.

In addition to this handbook, speaking and listening skills are practiced in the Additional Projects in the unit booklets in your *Teacher's Classroom Resources*. The blackline masters Outline for Organizing a Speech About Literature and Questions for Evaluating an Oral Presentation (TCR 5, pages 33–34; Overhead Transparency 27) will prove helpful as your students work with the lessons in this handbook.

Lesson 1

The first lesson gives students an opportunity to work with public speaking—perhaps the activity they most often associate with speaking and listening. Here students practice techniques of preparing and delivering a speech and, at the same time, examine literature from new perspectives.

SPEAKING AND LISTENING HANDBOOK

LESSON 1: A Persuasive Speech About Literature

OVERVIEW

You will select an author of a work included in this anthology and read *another* work by him or her—one that is *not* included in this book. Then you will present a speech in which you will motivate your classmates to read that work. Your goal will be to "sell" a piece of literature; the number of students who do read it will be a measure of how persuasive you were.

PREPARING AND ORGANIZING THE SPEECH

1. **Select the right work of literature.**
   One way to find another work by an author is to read this book's biographical passage about the author. You may also use the library's catalog to see what other works the library has by him or her. Select a piece of literature that not only you like but that also is likely to have wide appeal to your audience.

2. **Think critically about the work.**
   To help you analyze and appreciate the work, consider using this book's Reviews, where you will find a guide that prompts you to see how the different literary elements create an affect. You'll find these guides on pages 159, 231, 291, 431, 489, 671.

3. **Plan your appeals to your audience, and organize your speech.**
   a. Appeal to emotions. Stress the feelings that the piece of literature brought out—e.g., compassion, anger, patriotism, romance, terror.

      Read a brief excerpt from the piece as part of your speech. If your classmates enjoy hearing this excerpt, they may want to read the entire work.

   b. Appeal to your audience through your character, reputation, credibility, sincerity, and knowledge of the work. To persuade your audience to believe in your taste in literature, you have to give them reason to trust you in general. Therefore, make sure that you know the work thoroughly—including its title, date, characters' names, setting, and so on.

   c. Appeal to your readers' intellect. For example, argue that by reading the piece they will have a greater grasp of the author and his or her concerns and style; as a result, you may argue, they will be better informed and perform better in literature classes.

SAMPLE SPEECH

Since there are two pieces by James Thurber in this anthology ("The Secret Life of Walter Mitty" and "The Spreading 'You Know' "), let us assume you want to read yet another piece by this famous humorist. According to the biographical notes in this book, he seems to have written a great deal.

Assume you have gone to a library, located several volumes by Thurber, and read a story here, an essay there. One in particular intrigued you, and you have decided that it will be of interest to your classmates too because of its subject matter. Its title is " 'There's Something Out There!' " and it is about the Loch Ness Monster.

Applying the Guide for Studying Nonfiction (page 291), you may come to your own conclusions about the essay. You might decide that it has characteristics of all kinds of essays: the narrative essay, the descriptive, the persuasive, and the expository.

Next, you would plan your appeals and outline your speech. Here is a sample outline:

I. Opening: Appeal to emotion

A. Intrigue audience with the idea of an essay about a monster.

B. Identify work, author, date of publication.

C. Quote from essay to show that it deals with *mystery* in a *humorous* way:

> Since the cry "There's something out there!" was first raised on the lochside in the troubled spring of 1933, the Thing in the Loch has bobbed up month after month . . . in the water and in the newspapers and periodicals of six continents.

II. Body: Appeal to intellect or logic

A. Thurber widely read and an influence on contemporary humorists

1. Wide range of interests

2. Worked in many media

3. Important to appreciate his style

B. Loch Ness still a "hot" issue, still in newspapers; important to be "up" on it

III. Conclusion: Appeal based on my sincerity

A. Other Thurber pieces I will read

B. My growing interest in his cartoons

DELIVERING THE SPEECH

1. Speak extemporaneously from a prepared outline. If you know your material, the words will come to you naturally.
2. Speak directly to your audience, making eye contact with individuals.
3. Print or type the excerpt clearly so that you will be able to say every word exactly as the author wrote it. Read the excerpt dynamically.
4. Sound enthusiastic.

ASSIGNMENT

Here are suggestions of other authors in this anthology whom you may want to explore further:

- Jessamyn West wrote a whole collection of stories about Cress Delahanty, the girl in the story on page 27.
- Marjorie Kinnan Rawlings wrote a Pulitzer Prize-winning novel, *The Yearling*, which if you haven't read before, you may want to now.
- Edgar Allan Poe wrote many, many short stories.
- Gordon Parks has written nonfiction as well as poetry.
- Horton Foote has published several screenplays.

Lesson 2

Listening and discussion skills form the second strand of the handbook. Listening is critical to clear communication; after all, listening is the first step in responding. Discussion is equally essential to the study of literature. Without developed discussion skills students' insights into and responses to literature can never be shared.

LESSON 2: *Evaluating Oral Presentations*

OVERVIEW

This lesson will guide you in the evaluation of speeches and oral interpretation of literature (see Lessons 1 and 3). The purpose of evaluating other students' presentations is to help them learn from their efforts so that they will improve in the future. You too will profit from the evaluation because you will learn what mistakes to avoid in your own presentations as well as what techniques to adopt for yourself. In addition, you will be practicing the important skill of listening closely.

GUIDELINES FOR EVALUATOR

1. Get ready to listen. Concentrate completely on the speaker, and give him or her your full attention. Sit up straight, and look at the speaker. Smile, appear friendly, and be open to anything the speaker may communicate. Try to become involved in the presentation.

2. If possible acquaint yourself beforehand with what the speaker will be presenting, especially the author or piece of literature on which the presentation is based. Then you will be more knowledgeable and better able to evaluate the speech or performance.

3. You may take notes during the presentation—not so many that you will distract the speaker or distract yourself from the rest of the presentation, but just enough to refresh your mind later when you fill out an evaluation form like the one on the opposite page or when you discuss the presentation.

4. As you listen, try to be fair. On the one hand, you want to listen sympathetically and supportively. On the other hand, you want to be objective, not overly influenced by what you think of the speaker personally. You must ask yourself, "Am I enjoying this? Am I involved?" If you are not, try to find out what the problem is, but withhold your final evaluation until the presentation is over.

5. Fill out an evaluation form like the one shown here. Note that some items on the form are more applicable to a speech and some to oral interpretation.

6. Make sure you focus on areas in which the speaker can improve as well as on areas in which he or she is already performing well. Students often learn from having their strengths pointed out to them.

7. You may want to compare your evaluation of the speaker with the evaluation given him or her by another student. Discuss any differences of perception, and try to account for them. How can you explain, back up, or support your evaluation in any particular category?

EVALUATING AN ORAL PRESENTATION

Speaker's Name ______________________

Title of Presentation ______________________

Audience ______________ Evaluator ______________

Content

1. a. What was the purpose of the presentation? ______________________

b. Did the speaker achieve that purpose? ______________________

2. Was the presentation appropriate for the audience? ______________________

3. Did the opening statement capture the audience's interest? ______________________

4. Were the speaker's explanations clear? ______________________

5. Did the speaker use interesting language? ______________________

6. Did the speaker connect ideas clearly and logically? ______________________

7. Did the ending *sound* like an ending? ______________________

8. Did the audience seem to like the presentation? ______________________

Delivery

9. Did the speaker use good posture and avoid fidgeting? ______________________

10. Did the speaker make eye contact while speaking? ______________________

11. Did the speaker speak distinctly? ______________________

12. Did the speaker vary his or her rate and volume? ______________________

13. Did the speaker avoid "uh," "and-a," "OK?" and "like"? ______________________

14. Was the speaker aware of the audience's reactions? ______________________

15. What were the strong points of the presentation? ______________________

16. In what ways could the presentation be improved? ______________________

Lesson 3

Oral interpretation—the performance of literature—is gaining increased attention as another avenue to the understanding and appreciation of literature. As students work on their oral presentation of poems, short stories, and so forth, they find themselves reading more closely and thinking about literature more critically than ever before.

LESSON 3: *Oral Interpretation of a Poem*

OVERVIEW

In this lesson you will learn how to read aloud a poem so that you reveal its meaning and feeling.

PREPARING AN ORAL INTERPRETATION

1. **Analyze the basic situation of the poem.**
   a. Who is speaking the poem?
   b. What is happening in the poem?
   c. What is the point of the poem?
   d. What is the most important part of the poem? (You will want to lead up to this part dramatically wherever possible.)
   e. Is the poem essentially a contemplative poem, in which the speaker is quietly remembering an experience (such as Millay's poem "The Courage That My Mother Had"), or is the poem basically an action poem, in which the speaker is describing something that is happening (such as "Casey at the Bat" and "The Base Stealer")? A contemplative poem may require a quieter and slower performance, while an action poem may require a loud, fast presentation.

2. **Pay attention to the sensory appeals and images in the poem.**
   See, hear, feel, even taste and smell what the speaker is experiencing as you prepare to speak the poem. You want to project to your audience the intensity of sensation that the speaker feels.

   Example: In "A Narrow Fellow in the Grass" (page 200) notice how the speaker pictures the snake. In the poem the snake divides the grass; you as the reader of the poem might look down as if you actually see the grass parting.

3. **Practice reading with great clarity.**
   Emphasize the sounds of individual words. Your audience must hear each word clearly because there are very few words in poems; if they lose one important word, the entire experience of the poem may be destroyed.

   Example: In Sandburg's poem "Lost" (page 226) let your audience sense aloneness by emphasizing the *o* vowel and by sustaining the *n* consonant.

4. **Constantly pay attention to the rhythm of the poem.**
   a. Notice which words and syllables should receive a primary stress and which should be unaccented.
   b. Read the poem line for line, but pay attention to the punctuation at the end of each line. A period means you should stop; a comma means you should pause a bit less; no punctuation means you should move right on to the next line.

NOTES FOR A SAMPLE ORAL INTERPRETATION

To illustrate what is involved in analyzing a poem and preparing to present an oral interpretation of it, consider the following notes for the poem "maggie and milly and molly and may" by E. E. Cummings (page 223). Taken together, the notes will help you figure out what to focus on for a performance of this poem.

1. The speaker describes the experiences of four young girls who visit the seaside. It is both an action poem and a contemplative poem; that is, the speaker describes both what they do and how they feel.

2. One of the most important features of the poem is its rhythm. It has a light, skipping rhythm, which mirrors the playfulness of the young girls. Each line has four major stresses, and the rhythm is very regular throughout the poem, even though some lines begin with a stress and some do not. Many lines have two unstressed syllables between the stressed ones, contributing to the skipping rhythm referred to above.

3. The two *and*'s at the ends of lines 4 and 8 can remind us of the breathless rush of young children telling a story.

4. The imagery changes for each girl, for each one's experience of the sea is different. Even with different experiences, however, all seem to have a remarkable time. The speaker says that all of us find ourselves at the sea. Perhaps he means that when we become engaged in something else we clear our heads and learn something about ourselves.

5. The sounds are important to consider for a performance of this poem. The alliteration of *m* in the girls' names shows how close they are; maybe all the names should be run together in reading the poem.

   Sounds and pacing also emphasize the difference in their experiences: The sounds in lines 7–8 (where Molly is being chased) encourage an explosive, fast reading, but the sounds in lines 9–10 (about May's gift from the sea) seem to demand a smooth, slow reading.

6. All the words in the poem are very simple, underscoring the childlike feel of the poem.

PERFORMANCE

1. Begin your presentation with a short introduction, in which you tell your audience the name of the poem and the poet and explain why you chose to present this poem. You may use notes during this explanation, but you should speak extemporaneously.

2. Because a poem can be so short, pause before you begin your oral interpretation of it. Think about the most important image of the poem. Focus on it. Then begin reading.

3. Pause again at the end of the poem. Hold your concentration for a moment on the final image of the poem before relaxing, or "breaking." Then return to your seat.

4. Maintain a high energy level during your short performance in order to communicate the intensity of the poem.

ASSIGNMENT

Using the notes provided here and any that you create based on your study of "maggie and millie and molly and may," rehearse and then present an oral interpretation of the poem. An alternative is to present an oral interpretation of any of the other poems in this anthology.

Lesson 4
Only by working together can students gain new and varied perspectives. Collaborative learning by its very nature is usually an oral language activity. Here students see how to work efficiently, imaginatively, and productively in small groups to explore literature in innovative ways.

LESSON 4: *Group Oral Interpretation (Fiction)*

OVERVIEW

Working with other students to present an oral reading of an excerpt from a short story or a novel, you will gain insights into the literature.

PREPARING AN ORAL PRESENTATION

1. **Decide upon an excerpt of the right length.**
   Your performance should last from eight to ten minutes.
2. **Prepare a script of the selection.**
   Divide the story up into parts so that each member can participate. Some general options:
   a. *Separate the narration from the dialogue.* One student (or a chorus of students) can read the narration; individual students can read each character. For example, in "The Gift of the Magi" one student can read the narration, one student can read Delia's dialogue, and one student can read Jim's.
   b. *Divide the narration among two or more students.* In a story with little dialogue (such as "The Son from America"), each student can take a part of the narration. A single sentence can be shared by two narrators.

   Example
   NARRATOR 1: The village of Lentshin was tiny—
   NARRATOR 2: a sandy marketplace where the peasants of the area met once a week.
3. **Think about "dialogue tags."**
   Many speeches contain a tag such as "she said" or "he exclaimed." You have to decide which of these tags can be dropped and how to treat the ones that remain. Will they be read by the student who reads the character's statement, or will they be read by a narrator? Should you pause before or after reading the tag, or should you run it right in with the character's statement?
4. **Assign lines.**
   After you distribute lines for a script, you have to decide who will read each part. Try to get vocal variety into the performance.
5. **Think about characterization.**
   If you are reading a particular character, think about his or her major traits, and try to convey those through voice and gestures.
6. **Consider the staging.**
   Where will the individual readers stand? Where will they look? As the group reads the story to the class, the narrator should look at the audience, and the individual characters should look at each other—or at the spot where the other character would be.
7. **Prepare an introduction.**
   One student should plan to tell the audience a little about the story—and perhaps why the group chose this story to perform.

ASSIGNMENT

Select another scene from "The Secret Life of Walter Mitty" (page 152), and script it as a continuation of the model script here. Alternatively, you may select a section of any other story or novel in this book.

MODEL SCRIPTING

Here is one of many possible script ideas for an excerpt from "The Secret Life of Walter Mitty" by James Thurber. This story moves back and forth between a fantasy life and a real life. This script features two narrators and two Walter Mittys, one of each for the fantasy world and one of each for the real world.

There is also a role for Mrs. Mitty. A chorus of three readers (chorus 1 is a male; chorus 2 is a male; chorus 3 is a female) will be, in turn or together, Lieutenant Berg, the crew, the nurse doctors, policeman, parking lot attendant, etc.; they can even play sound effects.

Here is a diagram of how readers can be positioned on the stage.

Chorus
(on stools;
stand when
speaking)
○ ○ ○
1 2 3

Real Narr. ○ (standing)
○ Fantasy Narr. (on stool)
Wife ○ (on chair)
○ Real Mitty (on chair)
○ Fantasy Mitty (standing)

FANTASY MITTY: We're going through!

FANTASY NARRATOR: The Commander's voice was like thin ice breaking. He wore his full-dress uniform, with the heavily braided white cap pulled down rakishly over one cold gray eye.

CHORUS 1: We can't make it, sir. It's spoiling for a hurricane, if you ask me.

FANTASY MITTY: I'm not asking you, Lieutenant Berg

FANTASY NARRATOR: said the Commander.

FANTASY MITTY: Throw on the power lights! Rev her up to 8,500! We're going through!

FANTASY NARRATOR: The pounding of the cylinders increased.

CHORUS 1, 2, 3: ta-pocketa-pocketa-pocketa-*pocketa-pocketa.*

FANTASY NARRATOR: The commander stared at the ice forming on the pilot window. He walked over and twisted a row of complicated dials.

FANTASY MITTY: Switch on No. 8 auxiliary!

FANTASY NARRATOR: he shouted.

CHORUS 1: Switch on No. 8 auxiliary!

FANTASY NARRATOR: repeated Lieutenant Berg.

FANTASY MITTY: Full strength in No. 3 turret!

FANTASY NARRATOR: shouted the Commander.

CHORUS 1: Full strength in No. 3 turret!

FANTASY NARRATOR: The crew, bending to their various tasks in the huge, hurtling eight-engined Navy hydroplane, looked at each other and grinned.

CHORUS 2: The Old Man'll get us through

FANTASY NARRATOR: they said to one another.

CHORUS 2: The Old Man ain't afraid of Hell! . . .

MRS. MITTY: Not so fast! You're driving too fast!

REAL NARRATOR: said Mrs. Mitty.

MRS. MITTY: What are you driving so fast for?

REAL MITTY: Hmmm?

REAL NARRATOR: said Walter Mitty. He looked at his wife, in the seat beside him, with shocked astonishment. She seemed grossly unfamiliar, like a strange woman who had yelled at him in a crowd.

MRS. MITTY: You were up to fifty-five. You know I don't like to go more than forty. You were up to fifty-five.

REAL NARRATOR: Walter Mitty drove on toward Waterbury in silence.

FANTASY NARRATOR: the roaring of the SN202 through the worst storm in twenty years of Navy flying fading in the remote, intimate airways of his mind.

MRS. MITTY: You're tensed up again

REAL NARRATOR: said Mrs. Mitty.

MRS. MITTY: It's one of your days. I wish you'd let Dr. Renshaw look you over.

REAL NARRATOR: Walter Mitty stopped the car in front of the building where his wife went to have her hair done.

THINKING SKILLS HANDBOOK

Each of the six lessons in this handbook serves to integrate a particular thinking skill with the experience of literature. Each lesson is literature-based and demonstrates to the student that the active reader is a thinking reader, that the results of thinking are both understanding and enjoyment. The step-by-step format of each lesson allows for either teacher involvement or student independence. Gradually, as students continue to use the procedures shown in the lessons, they can grow more and more independent as thinkers about literature and as confident, thinking young adults. Each lesson is structured in the following way:

- DEFINITION—A clear, jargon-free definition that expresses the thinking skill in a students' own terms
- EXAMPLE—A model of the thinking skill being applied in a literature-based situation. Each example emphasizes the students' own experience in using the skill.
- EXPLANATION—A detailed "walk-through" of the example, demonstrating and discussing each individual step in the application of the thinking skill.
- PROCEDURES—A list and summary of the individual steps used in the example and the explanation. Identifying procedures is an essential step in thinking about thinking and developing independence.

THINKING SKILLS HANDBOOK

LESSON 1: *Evaluation*

DEFINITION

Evaluation involves making judgments. Proper evaluation requires knowing how and when to select and apply appropriate criteria. **Criteria** are the standards, rules, or tests we use to make judgments.

EXAMPLE

Students are assigned to evaluate oral book reports. A group of students will make suggestions to the teacher as to how this evaluation can best be done.

EXPLANATION

Students will suggest criteria to be used in evaluating oral book reports. Criteria might include interest, organization, length of the report, choice of book, and quality of presentation. When students in the class evaluate oral book reports, they will be judging all the reports according to the same set of standards. This is essential for proper evaluation.

PROCEDURES

1. **Start with a reason or purpose** for evaluation.
2. **Identify the criteria**—the rules, tests, or standards you will use to judge an item.
3. **Apply the criteria.**
4. **Draw a conclusion.** What you decide will be your evaluation.

ACTIVITY I. DEVELOPING CRITERIA FOR EVALUATION OF SHORT STORIES

The purpose of this activity is to compare what you think is a great short story with one a classmate thinks is great.

1. **Select a story** in the Short Story unit in this book (pages 1–159) that you believe is a great story.
2. **Identify the individual elements** of the story that you think are great. The characters, the plot, the setting, or the theme may be especially appealing to you.
3. Based on your analysis, **write a set of criteria** you would use to evaluate another story for greatness.
4. **Compare your list** with a classmate's list. Discuss differences found on the lists.
5. **Show how your criteria can be applied** to the story your classmate chose.

ACTIVITY II. EXAMINING CRITERIA USED BY CHARACTERS

The purpose of this activity is to examine the evaluations that characters in a short story make. What seems to be important, and what seems to be unimportant?

1. **Select a short story** from the Short Story unit (pages 1–159) in which two characters have a disagreement about what is important.
2. For each of the two characters in the story, **make a list** of what things, ideas, or principles appear to be important or unimportant to the character.
3. **Compare the two lists.** Think about what criteria each character might be using to decide what is important or unimportant. Compare the criteria used by each character.
4. **Decide whether the criteria used by the two characters are related** to a conflict in the story. If

the criteria were changed, would the characters be able to resolve the conflict?

ACTIVITY III. EVALUATING YOUR OWN UNDERSTANDING OF A STORY

1. **Develop a set of criteria** you can use to evaluate your own understanding of a short story. By applying this set of rules to your own understanding, you will be able to decide whether or not you understand any story you read. You may want to consider such questions as, What do I need to know to understand the plot? and What do I need to know about the characters in order to be able to evaluate their actions?

2. Find a story you have not read. Read the story, and **apply the criteria** you have developed. Evaluate your understanding of the story.

3. **Prepare a brief oral report** on this experience. Share your experience with your classmates.

   Note: Most people tend to overestimate at first how well they think they know something. But by carefully establishing your criteria, you will make it easier to know what it is that you don't know.

- ACTIVITIES—All activities are literature-based. Those activities keyed to specific literary selections give the student an opportunity to follow the correct procedures in thinking about some aspect of the selection. Those activities not keyed to specific literary selections provide the opportunity to transfer the thinking skill to a new literary situation.

The detailed lessons in this handbook are not the only application of thinking skills in this literature series. Throughout each book students also practice and reinforce thinking skills through the following features:

- Purpose-setting questions
- Study Questions divided into Recalling, Interpreting, and Extending categories
- Thinking About . . . questions within Reading and Literary Focuses
- Models for Active Reading
- Thinking Skills blackline masters, TCR 5, pages 35–38
- Thinking Skills Overhead Transparency, TCR 5, pages 28–30

LESSON 2: Representation

DEFINITION

Representation involves changing the way that you perceive information. If the information is in words, making pictures or diagrams of the meaning is a different way of representing it. This is called *graphic* representation. If the information is in some type of picture or diagram, thinking about its meaning in words is another way of representing it. Representations are usually developed by asking yourself what the important elements are and how they are related. In making graphic representations, different shapes may be used to represent different ideas.

Graphic representations make it easier to *select* what is important, *integrate* and *organize* the different parts, and *summarize*.

EXAMPLE

Some of the poems in the Poetry unit of this book (pages 161–231) are narratives. They tell stories. "Casey at the Bat" (page 165) and "The Charge of the Light Brigade" (page 168) are examples.

Angelo found that he could easily see the sequence of events in "Casey at the Bat," so he did not need to make a graphic representation of the events in that poem. However, he had difficulty in understanding the order of events in "The Charge of the Light Brigade." To help himself figure out what was happening, he jotted down a summary of the events in each stanza and then tried to put them in the order in which they occurred. In this example the representation is the final set of events produced by Angelo through his self-questioning. This set might have been just a written list. Alternatively, he might have used a graphic representation, such as a sequence map.

EXPLANATION

Sequence maps are useful for understanding the order of events in a poem, a work of fiction, an autobiography or biography, or a historical narration such as "The Charge of the Light Brigade." They may also be used to represent the stages in a cycle, such as the "Seven Ages of Man" by Shakespeare (page 206).

Sequence maps may be formed in various ways. In the example below the events are written on lines, but they could just as well have been in a list or in the loops of a chain. In fact, mapping out the sequence of events is sometimes called *chaining*.

SITUATION ______________________

Event 1 ______________________

Event 2 ______________________

Event 3 ______________________

PROCEDURES

1. **Decide** whether the information you need to represent is a sequence of specific events or the stages in the development of something.
   a. If it is a simple sequence, place the name of the sequence after the word *situation*.
   b. If it is the stages of something, state the name of the "something" after the word *situation*.
2. **Identify the stages or specific events**, and place them on the lines for event 1, event 2, and so on. This step may involve some **brainstorming**, looking back at the information, and some figuring out to establish a meaningful order—especially if the author tells events out of order. Use the questions

below to help yourself in this process of identifying sequence.

a. When did this event occur?
b. What is the relationship between this event and other events?
c. How do I know? What proof or evidence do I have?

3. **Summarize the "essence" or "gist"** of the stage or event, and state that information in the appropriate box. This step is critical because it requires you to ask yourself:

a. What is *really* important about this stage or event?
b. How is it related to the previous events or stages? Does event 1 really lead to event 2?

ACTIVITY I. REPRESENTING INFORMATION IN A POEM

The purpose of this activity is to construct a sequence map representing the sequence of events in a particular poem.

1. **Read** William Shakespeare's "The Seven Ages of Man."
2. **Identify the general situation** or sequence of events being described in the poem.
3. **Construct a sequence map** like the one shown in the example, including boxes for seven separate events.
4. **Identify the seven separate events** described in the poem. Summarize each event, and state it in its appropriate box.

ACTIVITY II. REPRESENTING INFORMATION IN ANY LITERARY WORK

The purpose of this activity is to construct a sequence map representing the sequence of events in any literary selection you have read.

1. **Select a literary work** you like.
2. **Identify the general situation** or sequence of events being described in the work. You may have chosen a selection that includes a sequence of events, a sequence of places visited on a journey, a sequence of ideas, a sequence of emotions, or even a sequence of themes.
3. **Construct a sequence map** with boxes like the one in the example, or consider a list format or the loops of a chain.
4. **Identify the separate events** described in the work. Summarize each event, and state it in its appropriate box.

LESSON 3: Problem Solving

DEFINITION

Problem solving is a way of thinking. It requires two different kinds of knowledge—*what* the problem is made of and *how* to solve it. The first kind of knowledge (the what) is the basic information about the problem, specific facts about the subject. The second kind of knowledge (the how) is the procedures, or steps, of defining a problem, planning a solution, carrying out the plan, and checking the results.

EXAMPLE

In Maya Angelou's *I Know Why the Caged Bird Sings* (page 246), Mrs. Flowers faces a problem—to break Marguerite out of her silence.

EXPLANATION

Mrs. Flowers has acquired all the information, the specific facts, that she needs, and she follows problem-solving procedures. She knows Marguerite personally, she has talked with her family and has heard reports from her teachers, and she knows the problems faced by a girl of Marguerite's age. She identifies her **goal**—to make Marguerite aware that she is liked and respected for herself. These are the **givens** of the situation: Marguerite does excellent written school work but does not speak in school. This is the **obstacle**: How can she have a heart-to-heart conversation with someone who seems reluctant to speak? She then follows problem-solving procedures. She **plans** to overcome the obstacle by using someone else's words and building on Marguerite's love of literature. Talking about literature will give Marguerite confidence and help her grow into a mature person. She plans a cookies-and-lemonade talk with Marguerite and **carries out the plan**. She makes it possible to **check the results** of her solution by setting up a series of "lessons in living" for Marguerite.

PROCEDURES

1. **State a goal.**
   Identify what you want to do or achieve.
2. **List the givens.**
   What information is available to you as you start to think about reaching the goal?
3. **List the obstacles.**
   What will prevent you from reaching the goal? Obstacles may be easy to see and clearly stated. They may also be unstated or hidden. You may have to think very carefully to identify them.
4. **Identify the methods.**
   What will you do to reach a solution? What is your plan of attack? What steps will you follow to eliminate each obstacle?
5. **Carry out the plan.**
6. **Check the results.**
   Have you solved the problem? How will you be sure? Did you follow the best plan? Was there a better way to solve the problem?

ACTIVITY I. IDENTIFYING A PROBLEM-SOLVING STRATEGY

The purpose of this activity is to identify and describe the way a problem is solved in a particular work of nonfiction.

Read "Kilimanjaro!" by James Ramsey Ullman (page 264). Identify each step of the problem-solving process as it is described in this selection.

1. What is Ullman's **goal**?
2. What are the **givens** of his situation? What knowledge and information does he have?
3. What are the **obstacles**? Are all the obstacles obvious? Are some hidden?

4. What are his **methods**? In his plan what steps does he intend to follow and in what order?
5. Does he **carry out the plan**? Does he revise or change the plan in order to carry it out?
6. What are the **results**? Does he achieve his goal and solve the problem?

ACTIVITY II. DESCRIBING PROBLEM SOLVING IN ANY WORK OF NONFICTION

The purpose of this activity is to identify and describe the steps of the problem-solving process in any work of nonfiction in this book or any other work of nonfiction you have read.

1. Select a work of nonfiction—an essay, a biography, or an autobiography—and **state the writer's goal** or the goal of the person who is the subject of the biography.
2. **State the givens** in the situation.
3. **State the obstacles** to solving the problem.
4. **Identify the methods**, and the **plan** used to solve the problem.
5. **Tell whether the plan is carried out**.
6. **Check the results** by telling whether or not the problem is solved. If the problem is not solved, tell what change in the methods or plan you would make in order to solve it.

ACTIVITY III. WRITING A BRIEF BIOGRAPHICAL SKETCH ABOUT A PROBLEM SOLVER

The purpose of this activity is to describe in writing how someone used problem-solving procedures to reach a goal.

Select a person you have read about or someone you know who was faced with a problem to solve. The problem may have been a large and difficult one or a small and easy one. You may want to consider problems that are historical, political, military, scientific, literary, sports-related, or even problems of human relationships.

Make sure that your brief biographical sketch describes how each step of the problem-solving process was followed:

Stating the **goal**
Identifying the **givens**
Identifying the **obstacles**
Developing a **method**
Carrying out the plan
Checking the **results**

ACTIVITY IV. COMPARING SOLUTIONS

The purpose of this activity is for a group of students to define a problem and then plan individual solutions to the problem. Work in groups of three or four students.

1. As a group, brainstorm to make a list of problems that are of interest to each member of the group. Choose the one that the group would most like to solve.
2. As a group, identify the **goal**, the **givens**, and the **obstacles** to reaching the goal. Think carefully about the obstacles, describing as many as you can in detail.
3. As individuals, write a description of a **plan** to solve the problem. List the specific steps to be followed to overcome each obstacle.
4. When each group member has developed a plan, read each plan to the group. Discuss the advantages and the disadvantages of each plan. Do not forget to consider how you will check the **results** of your plan.
5. Vote on the best plan. You may want to consider using parts of different plans to develop another one. Present your group's problem and solution to the class.

LESSON 4: *Inductive Inquiry*

DEFINITION

Inductive inquiry is a way to *discover* meaning by observation. As you examine several examples of something, you begin to discover how the examples are alike. You discover what features the examples share—that is, what they have in common.

EXAMPLE

You have probably seen so many examples of drama on television that you have discovered, just by watching, that each program contains a number of separate scenes. You know that when a scene ends, some kind of break in the action occurs. Sometimes this break allows for a commercial announcement. At other times the break in the action simply divides a story or a program into several different but related parts. You recognize when a new scene has begun, and you have learned to distinguish a scene from a commercial. What is it that helps you recognize a scene and distinguish it from a commercial? To answer this question, you need to **inquire** into the idea of a scene.

EXPLANATION

In order to **inquire** into the special features of a scene, you first need to **find some examples** of scenes. Using television, movies, or plays you have seen or read, you might list three examples that you think are clearly defined scenes. Your next step is to **identify the general characteristics** of each of the scenes you have observed. Then, after you have identified the characteristics of *each* scene, you **identify which characteristics are common** to *all* of the scenes.

Making a chart to **display** all of the characteristics will help you to find the pattern you are looking for. A chart that displays the general characteristics of scenes might look something like this one:

Characteristics	Scene 1	Scene 2	Scene 3
Setting	+	+	+
Music	+	–	–
Characters	+	+	+
Action	+	+	+
Conflict	–	+	–
Dialogue	–	–	+

The plus and minus signs indicate whether or not a scene has (+) or does not have (–) that characteristic. Observing the chart, you see that three characteristics—setting, characters, and action—are common to all the examples you examined. Once you have identified common characteristics, you can more accurately and easily recognize any new example of a scene.

It is also useful to **test your findings** against examples that are not likely to share the characteristics. In this case, you might test your findings about scenes against an example of a commercial. Add one more column to your chart for a non-example (a commercial).

Characteristics	Scene 1	Scene 2	Scene 3	Non-example
Setting	+	+	+	–
Music	+	–	–	+
Characters	+	+	+	–
Action	+	+	+	–
Conflict	–	+	–	–
Dialogue	–	–	+	+

Observing this chart, you see that the non-example does share two characteristics of a scene—music and dialogue. But the chart shows that those two characteristics are not enough to make this particular commercial a scene. This non-example still does not share any of the other characteristics. You will want to expand your list of characteristics and add more examples and non-examples to make the basis of your inquiry stronger.

PROCEDURES

1. In order to inquire into a particular idea, first **examine several familiar examples** of the idea.
2. **List all the general characteristics** you can think of that are true of each of the examples.
3. **Display the list** in a way that helps you see the pattern of common characteristics.
4. **Identify the pattern** of common characteristics.
5. **Test your findings** by comparing what you found to be true of the idea with the characteristics of a closely related non-example. When you do this, you will find some combination of characteristics that is special to your idea and does not occur in the non-example.

ACTIVITY I. INQUIRING INTO THE IDEA OF A SCENE IN A PARTICULAR DRAMA

The purpose of this activity is to apply the steps of inductive inquiry to discover the common characteristics of scenes in Shakespeare's *Romeo and Juliet* (page 333).

1. **Identify five examples** of scenes in *Romeo and Juliet*, one from each act.
2. Look at each example separately, and **list all the general characteristics** of each scene. Do not forget to list some of the most obvious characteristics: place, time, characters, dialogue. How does the scene begin? How does the scene end? How long does it last?
3. **Display the list** in a way that helps you see the pattern of common characteristics. Use a chart, or invent another kind of display.
4. **Identify the pattern** of common characteristics.
5. **Test your findings** by comparing what you found to be true of the examples with the characteristics of a closely related non-example. (Consider as a non-example one particular speech, one act, or the entire play.)
6. **Write a brief summary** of the characteristics of a scene as you find it in *Romeo and Juliet*. Support your findings with specific examples.

ACTIVITY II. INQUIRING INTO AN IDEA IN A WORK OF LITERATURE

The purpose of this activity is to apply the steps of inductive inquiry to discover the common characteristics of love in *Romeo and Juliet* or in any other literary selection you have read.

Many characters in literature display love for someone or something. Each character may define love differently or use different words to describe it. Nevertheless, each character's sense of love has some characteristics that are shared by the others.

1. **Identify at least five examples** of characters in *Romeo and Juliet* or in any other work of literature. Tell whom or what each character loves.
2. **List all the general characteristics** of each example of love. For example, is the love hidden or open? Is the love expressed in words or in actions, or both? Does the love require a sacrifice? Does the love cause conflict? Is the love "blind"? Is it realistic?
3. **Display the list** in a way that helps you see the pattern of common characteristics.
4. **Identify the pattern** of common characteristics.
5. **Test your findings** by comparing what you found to be true of the examples with the characteristics of a closely related non-example. (Consider friendship or honor.)
6. **Write a brief summary** of the characteristics of the idea of love as you find it in literature. Support your findings with the specific examples you used as the basis for your inquiry.

LESSON 5: *Logical Reasoning*

DEFINITION

Logical reasoning is a way of explaining exactly why you believe that something is true. When you reason logically, you state the *necessary conditions* for the explanation to be true. Then you show that these necessary conditions do exist. When you reason logically, however, you must be sure that both you and your audience agree on the same set of assumptions. This means that you agree about what is important in the particular situation you are considering.

EXAMPLE

Some works of literature are called *epics*. In order to meet the definition of an epic, a literary work must fulfill certain necessary conditions. It must be a fairly long story or poem with larger-than-life superheroes who fight against almost overwhelming odds and are representative of their nation's values and ideals. If you want to convice someone that a work of literature is really an epic, you must assume that he or she agrees with your definition. What kind of evidence would be sufficient to support your position that a certain work is truly an epic?

EXPLANATION

In order to use logical reasoning to demonstrate that a work is an epic, you would have to show that the work is rather long and complicated and that the hero strives for a particular goal and represents a national ideal. You would also have to give sufficient examples of the hero's use of superhuman strength to overcome many obstacles and great enemies. Your explanation rests on the assumption that the examples you give will be accepted as evidence.

It will help you to make a chart to display the features of each example of a work of literature you are trying to classify as an epic. On this chart you can examine the features of each work to see whether they match the necessary conditions. Such a chart might look like this:

Features	Example 1	Example 2	Example 3
Long	+	+	+
Character is larger than life	+	+	–
Character overcomes enemies	+	+	+
Character represents national ideals	+	+	–

The chart reveals that example 3 does not fulfill all the necessary conditions and is therefore not an epic. As you consider each example, you engage in *logical reasoning*.

PROCEDURES

When you use logical reasoning to convice an audience that something is true or important, you will find the following steps helpful:

1. **State what you believe** to be true.
2. **Identify all of the conditions** that are necessary for the situation to be true.
3. Show how the necessary conditions have been met. **Give specific examples that constitute sufficient evidence** to support your position.
4. **Identify the important assumptions** your audience must share with you in order for your position to be convincing.

ACTIVITY I. REASONING LOGICALLY ABOUT AN EPIC HERO

Odysseus, hero of the *Odyssey* (page 438), has been described as an epic hero. The purpose of this activity is to demonstrate logically that Odysseus qualifies to be called an epic hero.

1. **List the necessary conditions** for an act to be considered heroic. You may want to use a chart.
2. Indicate how Odysseus meets these conditions. **Give a sufficient number of specific examples**, and enter the information on your chart. You may include details actually stated in the verse as well as those implied by the text.
3. **Identify the important assumptions** you and your audience share about an epic hero.
4. **Write a brief statement** in which you describe some of the conditions that allow Odysseus to qualify as an epic hero. Describe some other conditions where the same behavior would not be considered heroic.

ACTIVITY II. REASONING LOGICALLY ABOUT THE IDEA OF THE HERO

The purpose of this activity is to examine the idea of the hero as it applies to everyday life.

1. **Think of a situation** in ordinary, everyday life in which a person you know could perform some heroic action. **Describe the conditions** for the action to be considered heroic. Display them in chart form.
2. Describe one or more possible examples of actual heroic behavior in this situation. **Show how this behavior fits the necessary conditions** for heroism by representing it on the chart.
3. **Identify some of the assumptions** you are making about the causes of heroic behavior.
4. **Write a brief statement** in which you summarize your description of your hero.

LESSON 6: *Synthesis*

DEFINITION

Synthesis involves the creation of something new, a new pattern or a new perspective. Synthesis requires a complex combination of skills to organize ideas from different sources. This new pattern may be stated in various forms—as an essay, a definition, a point of view, a play or poem, a work of art.

Note: An essay on one perspective is not a synthesis because it represents only one point of view. A synthesis must contain elements from more than one source and/or point of view.

EXAMPLE

Lester's teacher has asked him to take the role of the teacher for the short story the class will read next. In order to do this, Lester will have to think hard about how to present the lesson from the perspective of the teacher and about his own interpretation of the story. He will also have to use information from a critical essay on that story. He will have to organize information from several sources into a cohesive statement.

EXPLANATION

The task is to combine information from several different sources and organize it into a new statement. In other words, it is a task of synthesis. The **purpose** is clear—to examine a topic or a situation and clarify it for an audience by presenting a conclusion. The thinker must **identify the elements** that contribute to the situation. The thinker must **state a relationship** between the elements—tell how they are related or opposed or associated in some way. The thinker must **construct an original product**—a conclusion that expresses the relationship. The conclusion is a synthesis, a combining of information into something that did not exist before. The most helpful synthesis will act as a jumping-off point for further thought.

PROCEDURES

1. **Establish a purpose** for the product. This step is given in the activities below.
2. **Identify the elements** to be combined.
3. **State a relationship** among the elements, and represent the statement in a graphic form if possible.
4. **Construct an original product** that expresses the relationship.

ACTIVITY I. DESCRIBING A SCENE FROM CONTRASTING LITERARY PERSPECTIVES

The purpose of this activity is to demonstrate how the same scene might differ markedly when viewed by different authors. Each description should be a **synthesis** of elements from a particular author.

1. Working in small groups, **select one of the following** authors and a work by him or her.
   - Edgar Allan Poe
   - Jesse Stuart
   - Jack London
   - Robert Burns
   - Alice Walker
   - Charles Dickens

   Note: If your favorite author is not listed, feel free to choose that author.
2. **Review the following elements** for the author and selection of your choice.
   - From what point of view is the selection written?
   - What is outstanding about the setting(s)?
   - How would you characterize the main characters in the selection?
   - What is the theme?

3. **Discuss how those elements would apply** to a description of a scene involving a family dinner.

4. **Develop a brief description** of a family dinner as it might be described by your chosen author. This activity may be done as an oral presentation or as an essay. In either case the presentation should be brief (a few minutes or a few paragraphs).

ACTIVITY II. INTEGRATING THEMES FROM DIFFERENT GENRES

People often refer to literature to help develop a point of view or conclusion about something. Write a brief essay on one of the following themes, using works from any genre in this book to support your point of view:

- Giving gifts is always a good thing to do.
- Everyone changes.
- Whether a person gets what he or she wants out of life depends on luck.
- Real heroism is still possible.
- A theme of your own choice

1. **Identify literary selections** from at least two different genres that relate to the theme. Jot down (in note form) what each selection seems to say about the theme.

2. **Select two contrasting points of view** for your essay. Label each point of view (for example, "for gift giving," "against gift giving").

3. **Construct a chart** with your labels as column headings. Make four rows. Label row 1 "author's point of view." Label row 2 "examples" (from the selection). Label row 3 "my evaluation" (of the author's viewpoint). Label row 4 "my examples/reasons."

4. **Plan and write your essay** in the following way:
   a. In paragraph 1 state a point of view (e.g., "for gift giving"), and support it by an example or examples from a selection of literature. Make a personal statement as to how this point of view relates to your knowledge and experience, giving examples that are similar to or disprove the point of view.
   b. In paragraph 2 state the second point of view (e.g., "against gift giving"), making sure to point out how it differs from the first. Support or explain this point of view by an example or examples from selections of literature. Relate this point of view to your own experience.
   c. In paragraph 3 develop statement that includes or refers to both points of view. State a preference for one view or the other, and give reasons for why you prefer it.

READING AND STUDY SKILLS HANDBOOK

Each of the four lessons in this handbook provides students with a direct instructional model of a reading skill or a study skill important for the active reading and study of literature. Each lesson is literature-based and emphasizes the application of a particular skill so that the student may more fully understand the ideas of a literary selection.

Each lesson is structured in the following way:

- EXPLANATION AND EXAMPLES—A definition of the reading or study skill, with clear examples drawn from students' own experiences. Each example is explained as the student is walked through each step in the application of the skill.
- PRACTICE—Literature-based activities for using the reading or study skill and examining how it is used.
- FURTHER ASSIGNMENTS—All assignments are literature-based. Those assignments keyed to specific literary selections give the students the opportunity to apply the skill. Those assignments not keyed to specific literary selections provide the opportunity to transfer the reading or study skill to any literary situation.

The detailed lessons in this handbook are not the only application of reading and study skills in this literature series. Throughout each book students also practice and reinforce reading and study skills through the following features:

- Purpose-setting questions
- Study Questions divided into Recalling, Interpreting, and Extending categories
- Reading and Literary Focuses
- Models for Active Reading
- Active Reading end-of-unit pages
- Reading and Study Skills blackline masters, TCR 5, pages 39–40
- Reading and Study Skills Overhead Transparency 31

READING AND STUDY SKILLS HANDBOOK

LESSON 1: *Distinguishing Between Fantasy and Reality*

EXPLANATION AND EXAMPLES

Distinguishing between fantasy and reality adds to a reader's enjoyment of a writer's skills. Basically, realistic fiction deals with events and situations that can indeed occur in the real world. In fantasy the characters will sometimes possess enormous strength or special powers. For instance, in the *Odyssey*, Polyphemus, a Cyclops, has enormous strength, and Circe can change men into swine.

All literature that contains elements of fantasy also has realistic components. The realistic elements provide a frame of reference for the more fantastic episodes or characters. If a selection were complete fantasy, the reader would reject it as impossible to understand or as too farfetched—*too* fantastic.

All of our myths, legends, and epics, and most folk tales, contain some fantasy. Paul Bunyan has enormous strength; Cupid has the ability to fly; dragons of old can breathe fire. Mixed in with these fantasy beings, however, are people to whom we can relate, people who have the same hopes and fears as we do. In fact, in many myths and epics, even the supernatural beings have human feelings and traits to which we can relate.

Read the passage below:

> Scott stared idly out the window, his history book opened in front of him.
>
> Scott's eyes were tiring of the window; the history book was beckoning. He glanced at the photograph of the ancient Greek vase that an archaeologist had dug up near Troy. Troy! The city of Homer's epics, the place of battle and heroism on the grandest scale! Then he saw the old green vase that had been in his room for as long as he could remember. His fingers examined the little ridges that circled the lower part of the base.
>
> Then suddenly, a strange vapor began to rise out of the vase. Mysteriously, it began to take shape—human shape. Scott sat transfixed.

As a reader, you can relate to this situation because you understand the elements of it: a boy, a window, a book, a vase. In the last paragraph, however, reality suddenly gives way to fantasy.

ASSIGNMENTS

1. Continue the story of Scott. As you develop the story, mix realistic elements with fantastic ones. You may want to tell the story from Scott's point of view. What questions would he ask as the story unfolds?

2. Look at Homer's *Odyssey*. Identify five of the fantastic characters or creatures. Describe the supernatural powers or features of each.

3. Review the short story "The Secret Life of Walter Mitty" by James Thurber (page 152). In this story Mitty becomes so involved with his fantasies that he often loses touch with reality. As you read the story,

however, *you* need to be aware of what is real and what is Mitty's fantasy. Choose a passage in the story and identify the specific clues in the story that tell you when fantasy has taken over in Mitty's mind. These clues may include:

- the names of characters who are not part of Mitty's real life (for example, "The Commander")
- scenes or situations that are not at all like Mitty's real life (for example, inside a Navy hydroplane)
- words spoken by Mitty that he would never say in his real life (for example, "Rev her up to 8500! We're going through!")
- comments by the author that reveal that Mitty has "changed" (for example, "He looked at his wife, in the seat beside him, with shocked astonishment.")

4. Choose any other work of literature that you have read and identify the elements of fantasy and the elements of reality in it. Identify clues the author provides to help you tell the difference between fantasy and reality.

LESSON 2: *Understanding Cause-and-Effect Relationships*

EXPLANATION AND EXAMPLES

Understanding cause-and-effect relationships is an important skill for critical reading. Stated most simply, an effect answers the question, "What happened?" A cause answers the question, "What made it happen?"

Look at the sentence below:

> *Since* he failed every one of the tests and rarely handed in his homework, John will definitely receive a failing grade for the report period.

Obviously, the effect is a failing grade. The causes are his failure to complete his homework and his poor test scores. Often in literature, however, causes and effects are not quite as apparent. An author expects the reader to infer causes or effects based on the situations described in the selection.

> *Example:* In the story "Raymond's Run" by Toni Cade Bambara (page 41), the main character, Squeaky, and her brother, Raymond, find themselves walking toward three of her former girlfriends on a street in Harlem, New York. Immediately, she thinks,
>
> > *So* they are steady coming up Broadway and I see right away that it's going to be one of these Dodge City scenes *cause* the street ain't that big and they're close to the buildings just as we are. [italics added]
>
> The effect in this piece is the confrontation ("those Dodge City scenes") that is going to take place between Squeaky and the condescending trio of girls she is about to meet. The stated immediate causes of this confrontation are the facts that "they are steady coming up Broadway," "the street ain't that big," and "they're close to the buildings just as we are." However, the reader must infer the more deep-seated cause of the confrontation—namely, that Squeaky dislikes these girls because of their condescending attitudes and their mocking taunts derected toward her brother.

Sometimes, authors use specific words that cue the reader to a cause-and-effect relationship. In the examples given above, the authors used the words *since* and [*be*]*cause*, which suggest a cause-and-effect relationship. Other words and phrases that can imply cause-and-effect relationships are *as a result, consequently, if, hence, then, therefore, thus,* and *when*. As you read, you should look to see if these words do suggest cause-and-effect relationships, but you should also be aware of inferences the authors wish you to make about such relationships.

Many times, cause-and-effect relationships are strings in a long series.

> *Example:* In an excerpt from her autobiography, *I Know Why the Caged Bird Sings,* Maya Angelou recounts such a series. Maya's mother is flattered (effect) when Mrs. Flowers, a prominent woman in the town, compliments her sewing (cause). Maya's mother then directs Maya to take off her dress (effect) so that Mrs. Flowers can see the French seams around the armholes (cause). The young Maya is understandably very embarrassed (effect) by having to take off her dress (cause). Notice that taking off the dress was the *effect* of one *cause* and the *cause* of another *effect*.

PRACTICE

1. Look at the items below. Each contains an implied cause-and-effect relationship. Rewrite each to make that relationship clear. Use one of the following signal words or phrases: *as a result, because, consequently, if, hence, since, so, then, therefore, thus, when.*

   a. The narrator in "The Tell-Tale Heart" paced nervously about the room. He thought he heard the old man's heart beating beneath the floor boards.
   b. Anne Frank and her family lived in a warehouse attic in Amsterdam for two years. The Nazis were herding all Jews into concentration camps.
   c. Romeo and Juliet's love was doomed from the start. Their families had been feuding for years.
   d. Pip's parents had supposedly died years ago. The young boy lived with his sister and her husband.

2. Read or reread the story "The Monkey's Paw" (page 2). Complete the cause-and-effect chain below.

Major Morris tells Mr. White the monkey's paw will grant three separate men each three wishes, but misfortune will also result from the wishes.

Mr. White becomes the owner of the monkey's paw.

↓

Mr. White wishes for two hundred pounds.

↓

Mr. White's son is killed.

↓

Mr. White receives two hundred pounds compensation for the death.

ASSIGNMENTS

1. Write a brief paragraph that has a series of cause-and-effect relationships. Draw arrows between the causes and the effects.

2. Read or reread Guy de Maupassant's story "The Necklace." Summarize the story in a series of sentences that express causes and effects. Try to use as many signal words as possible in your summary.

LESSON 3: *Taking a Test*

EXPLANATION AND EXAMPLES

Being able to take tests well is a crucial skill that you will use throughout your school career and beyond. For even after you are graduated from school, you will probably have to take some kind of tests. Many employers test applicants for jobs; the military tests prospective recruits; sometimes the federal, state, or local government requires that trainees take a test before entering a career path.

Of course, if the test is going to cover specific information, it is important that you study the material thoroughly before taking the test. Once the time for the test comes, however, there are simple guidelines that you should follow. Research has shown that by following these guidelines you can do better on tests.

1. **Have a good attitude about the test.**
   Be convinced that you can do well on a test before you begin. It is easier to have this attitude if you have studied the material thoroughly.
2. **Preview the test.**
   Quickly determine
   a. the kinds of questions on the test (multiple choice, matching, true/false, short answer, essay)
   b. the number of questions
   c. the points to be awarded for each question.
3. **Read the directions carefully.**
   Be alert for statements such as "Answer *three* of the following *five* questions."

   In standardized multiple-choice tests you may want to find out if there is any penalty for incorrect answers. Is it better to leave an item blank, or is it better to guess?
4. **If you are given options as to which questions to answer, choose the ones you are sure you can do.**
5. **Plan your time.**
   Decide how much time it should take you for each section of the test, and make sure you allocate enough time for your work.
6. **Answer the easy questions first.**
   Put a mark beside the questions that will require more careful thought.
7. **Work on the questions that are worth the greatest number of points.**
   Often, these are the essay questions.
8. **Go back, and answer the hard questions.**
9. **Leave time at the end to go over the entire test.**
   Check to make sure you have not inadvertently checked a wrong answer or misread a question.
10. **Make sure your name is on the test.**

SPECIAL HINTS

Short-answer tests

For questions on a true/false test, pay attention to words that may indicate under what *conditions* a statement may be true or false. Some of these words are *always, never, all, none, some, never, good, bad.*

In multiple-choice tests if you are not immediately sure of the correct answer, try to eliminate as many of the incorrect distractors. If you can bring your choice down to two possible answers, you can take a chance and guess at the right answer (assuming there is no penalty for incorrect answers).

Essay Questions

After reading the essay question carefully, jot down key facts and ideas required in your answer. Arrange your notes so that you have everything in a logical order.

After you have written your response, pay particular attention to any mistakes in spelling, grammar, or punctuation as well as to the overall clarity of what you have written.

PRACTICE

1. Look at these statements about test taking. Label them true (T) or false (F). Check your answers when you finish.

   a. When you get the test, start answering questions immediately.
   b. Do all the essay questions first.
   c. Read the directions carefully.
   d. Do the hard questions before the easy ones.
   e. In true and false tests pay attention to key words such as *always, never, all,* and *sometimes.*
   f. On standardized tests you should always guess when you don't know the answer.
   g. On essay tests, you should reread for punctuation, spelling, usage, and clarity.
   h. Do the essay questions first.

2. Look at the true/false items below. They are based on Anne Frank's *Diary of a Young Girl*. Mark *true* or *false* for each. Note the words in each item that helped you determine its truth or falseness.

   a. Anne Frank was always sad while she was confined to the attic.
   b. Anne's diary covers her life from the time she was six until her death before her sixteenth birthday.
   c. Sometimes Anne was melancholy.
   d. Sometimes Anne would read books from the library while the family was confined in the attic.
   e. Jews were only allowed to shop in stores that bore the placard "Jewish shop."

ASSIGNMENTS

1. Think of the last major test you took on literature. Describe what kind of test it was: objective (multiple choice, true and false, short answer), essay, or a combination. Discuss how you took the test. What could you have done to improve your test-taking abilities?

2. Skim one of the novels that you have already read: *The Call of the Wild* or *Great Expectations*. Also look over your notes. Make up a brief test with five multiple-choice items, five true/false items, and one essay question. Give your test to a partner. Ask him or her to describe how the test should be taken; ask him or her to evaluate the test.

LESSON 4: *Skimming and Scanning*

EXPLANATION AND EXAMPLES

Good readers vary their rates of reading according to the task at hand. **Skimming** is the label used for one specific rate of reading. When you skim, you want to find the main idea of a selection, the gist of an author's message, or some other idea about the selection. This advance information about the selection will help you comprehend the piece and will increase your speed of reading.

When you skim a selection in a literature anthology, you would probably want to

1. read the introductory note about the author
2. read the title
3. read the first few sentences in the selection
4. read any subtitles provided
5. look at the pictures throughout the selection
6. read any study questions that are provided at the end of the piece

> *Example:* If you were to skim Richard Connell's story "The Most Dangerous Game," you would do all the things listed above except read the subtitles since none are provided. The whole skimming process would take less than a minute. You would find that

1. the setting is Ship-Trap Island (from the first paragraphs and Study Questions)
2. there are two main characters: a man with a mustache and a white-haired man (from the pictures)
3. the names of the main characters are Rainsford and Zaroff (from the Study Questions)
4. the story has something to do with hunting (from the pictures and the Study Questions)
5. Rainsford and Zaroff are in conflict (from the Study Questions)
6. the story has an aura of danger (from the title and the Study Questions)

The skimming of any selection gives you a sketchy idea of the content. As you read, you fill in the details and the important plot elements.

Because literature varies so widely, it is not possible to give specific skimming directions that can be applied across all genres and all publishing formats. The preceding guidelines are for a piece in an anthology. For a novel published separately, the guidelines for skimming would be somewhat different. You would probably

1. look at the picture on the dust jacket
2. read the information on the dust jacket
3. read the first few paragraphs of the novel
4. read any information about the author and the kinds of novel he or she writes

Although the specific strategies for skimming differ according to the nature and format of the material, the basic purpose for skimming remains the same—to give the reader an overview of the selection to be read.

Scanning has a very different purpose. When you scan material, you are looking for a specific bit of information. Sometimes you scan a piece after you have already read it. For instance if you were writing about the characters in *Great Expectations*, you might want to find the last name of Pip's brother-in-law, Joe. You would want to quickly glance over the pages on which the name *Joe* appears and then look for other capitalized words on the page.

Sometimes, you might want to scan a document just to find a specific piece of information; you will have no intention of reading the whole selection. For instance, you might scan an entry in an encylopedia to find out when an author published a certain literary work. A table of contents or an index is often a tremendous asset when scanning for information.

PRACTICE

1. Read the following list of situations. Indicate whether you would *skim* or *scan* in that particular instance.

   a. to find out if you'd be interested in reading a newly published novel
   b. to find Gail Tallant's telephone number in the phone book
   c. to find when Marian Anderson first sang at the White House
   d. to look over a list to get an idea of the kind of information it contains
   e. to find out how many cups of breadcrumbs to put in the meat loaf
   f. to get an overview of the poem "Casey at the Bat"
   g. to find out what time the *Cosby Show* is on television
   h. to find a part-time job in a restaurant
   i. to prepare for reading the novel *Great Expectations*
   j. to get a general idea of John F. Kennedy's background and accomplishments from his autobiography

2. Using the nonfiction section of your book, *scan* for the following pieces of information. Write down the number of the page on which you located the information. Time yourself to see how long it takes you to find the information.

   a. the name of Seattle's most successful Japanese businessman in 1906
   b. the name of a theater in London during Shakespeare's time
   c. the century in which Kilamanjaro was discovered by the outside world
   d. the name of Anne Frank's sister
   e. the name of Ernesto Galarza's mother
   f. the Japanese word for *good-by*

ASSIGNMENTS

1. Look at the novel *Great Expectations* (beginning on page 541). Assume that you have three minutes to *skim* the selection. What information would you attend to? List these kinds of information in priority order.

2. Describe five specific situations in your own life when you have had to *scan* for information.

WRITING ABOUT LITERATURE HANDBOOK

The Writing About Literature Handbook guides students through the types of writing assignments that they are most likely to encounter in literature classes. Eleven lessons show students how to write analyses of literary works, each lesson focusing on a different aspect of literary criticism. The Handbook follows a writing-process approach to the various assignments, beginning with prewriting and continuing through writing and revising. Clearly sequenced instructions with specific examples reinforce students' familiarity with the writing process. Each lesson is cross-referenced to appropriate assignments throughout *Understanding Literature.* In addition, to help students complete their assignments, your *Teacher's Classroom Resources* contains Writing About Literature blackline masters corresponding to each lesson in this Handbook.

WRITING LITERARY ANALYSIS

Focusing on the task of responding to an essay question on a literary work, this first lesson introduces students to a writing-process approach to writing about literature. You may want to teach this lesson in conjunction with your first writing assignment on the material in the Short Story unit. Since the lesson uses examples from the story "The Monkey's Paw," you may want to assign that story before you teach this lesson. Under "Assignments" on the following page, you will find cross-references to appropriate Composition assignments throughout this textbook. In addition, in your *Teacher's Classroom Resources* you will find the Chart for Writing Literary Analysis (TCR 5, page 41; Overhead Transparency 32) and Checklist for Revising a Paper About a Literary Work (TCR 5, page 51).

WRITING ABOUT LITERATURE HANDBOOK

LESSON 1: *Writing Literary Analysis*

PREWRITING

Before you begin to write, apply these hints.

1. Read the assignment. Then reread it, and copy the **key words**, which tell you what is expected of your answer.

   Example: Write a brief essay in which you state your general reaction to the outcome of a short story. Specifically, explain whether you kept wondering how the story would end or whether you were easily able to predict its ending. Tell why, using examples.

2. Paraphrase the assignment to assure yourself that you know what is expected of you.

   Example: Tell what you think of how the short story ends. Were you in suspense, or did you guess the outcome? Why?

3. Sketch diagrams or charts, or prepare an outline that will help you organize your thoughts as you reread the literature with the essay question in mind. For example, the following chart will help you as you think about your reaction to a short story and the reasons for your reaction.

EVALUATION OF A STORY	
SELECTION: GENERAL REACTION:	
ELEMENTS OF SUSPENSE	CLUES TO ENDING

WRITING PARAGRAPH BY PARAGRAPH

1. Begin with an introductory paragraph that contains a thesis statement. A **thesis statement** addresses itself to the question that is implied in the assignment. It suggests an answer to the question—an answer that the rest of your essay will discuss. The thesis statement should be an exact summary of the topic sentences in the body of the essay. After filling in the chart in Prewriting Step 3 with your reaction to "The Monkey's Paw" by W. W. Jacobs, you might write a thesis statement as follows:

   Example: The conclusion of "The Monkey's Paw" by W. W. Jacobs is surprising even though some clues to the outcome become apparent on rereading.

2. Write the body of your essay, perhaps two or three paragraphs. It should be clear from the thesis statement how many paragraphs will follow the introductory paragraph. In each paragraph develop further one of the ideas from your thesis statement. Each of these paragraphs should provide proof that your thesis statement is valid. Each of these paragraphs should have its own **topic sentence**, which will state the main idea of that particular paragraph. The paragraph that comes after the introductory paragraph with the example thesis statement might begin with the following topic sentence:

   Example: Several clues to the outcome become apparent within the first few pages.

   Each subsequent sentence in the paragraph must support the topic sentence of that paragraph. The supporting sentences should be specific examples, quotations, or incidents that come from the literature you are analyzing.

3. Tie or hook your paragraphs together with transitions such as *then, although, however,* and *therefore*. The paragraph that might follow the paragraph begun in the previous step could begin as follows:

   Example: Although the clues to the story's outcome are always there, its ending is nevertheless surprising for a number of reasons.

4. Conclude your essay with a summary paragraph. Restate—in different words—the thesis statement from your introductory paragraph. Discuss the implications (the importance or the significance) of this statement. The opening sentence of the concluding paragraph for the example essay might be something like the following:

   Example: Recognizing the clues to the story's outcome enriches the reading experience, but the dominant reaction to its ending is, undeniably, surprise.

WRITING A ONE-PARAGRAPH ANSWER

All the preceding advice on structure applies as well to written responses that are only one paragraph long. If you are limited to one paragraph, begin with a strong topic sentence. Each of your following sentences should develop one aspect of the topic sentence. You will not have as much room for supporting details as in a five-paragraph essay, but you nevertheless must give evidence to support the topic sentence. For example, using the thesis statement from Step 1 in Writing Paragraph by Paragraph as a topic sentence, you could then devote a few sentences to the clues and a few sentences to the aspect of surprise. A final sentence can restate the topic sentence and act as a conclusion.

REVISING AND EDITING

Once you have finished the first draft, you must take time to polish it into an improved second draft.

1. Read your writing aloud.
2. Use the following checklist to revise your writing. If you can answer "yes" to each question on the list, you will submit an essay that your audience will find interesting and logical.

I. Organization
   a. Does your thesis statement in the introductory paragraph relate directly to the assignment?
   b. Are the ideas mentioned in the thesis statement then taken up in the following paragraphs with a topic sentence for each paragraph?
   c. Is there effective, clear movement from paragraph to paragraph by means of transitions?
   d. Does the final paragraph offer a restatement of the thesis statement?

II. Content
   a. Does the essay adequately answer the question posed in the assignment?
   b. Is each idea adequately developed with supporting details from the literature?

III. Grammar, Usage, Mechanics
   a. Is each sentence complete (no fragments, no run-ons)?
   b. Have you avoided errors in the use of verbs (especially, subject-verb agreement), pronouns, and modifiers?
   c. Have you correctly capitalized and punctuated all sentences?
   d. Are all words spelled correctly?

IV. Word Choice, Style
   a. Have you used words that are appropriate for your audience and your purpose?
   b. Have you avoided slang and clichés unless (and this should be rare) used for a very special purpose or effect?
   c. Have you eliminated wordiness and vagueness?
   d. Have you varied sentence length and structure while checking for parallelism?

ASSIGNMENTS

1. Use the preceding checklist to evaluate an essay that you have written. Revise the essay as necessary based on your answers to the questions on the preceding list.

2. Use the advice in this lesson to complete the assignment called "Writing About Your Reaction to a Story" on page 10.

WRITING ABOUT PLOT

This lesson guides students through the process of writing about the plot of a story. The lesson reinforces the textbook's teaching about plot structure and conflict. You may want to teach this lesson in conjunction with the first subunit in the Short Story unit in this textbook. Since the lesson uses examples from the story "The Monkey's Paw," you may want to assign that story before you teach this lesson. Under "Assignments" on the following page, you will find a cross-reference to a Composition assignment in this textbook that focuses on plot elements. In addition, in your *Teacher's Classroom Resources* you will find the Charts for Writing About Plot (TCR 5, page 42; Overhead Transparency 33) and Checklist for Revising a Paper About a Literary Work (TCR 5, page 51).

LESSON 2: *Writing About Plot*

The **plot** of a piece of literature is the sequence of events or actions. The plot is usually what you tell people about when you share a story or a movie with them. A plot usually involves one or more types of conflicts, or clashes. When you talk about plot, you tell about the specific problems the character faces. As you list the problems, you actually begin to identify the types of conflict that the character in the story experiences.

CONCEPTS TO REMEMBER

The character in a story may face many problems. Each problem may represent a different type of conflict, or all the problems may point to the same type of conflict. Here is a chart that will help you recognize the five types of conflict that can take place during a plot. Four types are external; one, internal.

TYPICAL ESSAY QUESTION

When asked to write about plot, you are often answering an essay question like this one:

> Identify the problems experienced by the character as the story unfolds. Then explain how these problems reveal the type of conflict experienced by the character. If there is more than one type of conflict, tell which dominates.

PREWRITING

Prepare a chart that allows you to focus on the most important parts of the essay assignment. Jot down notes about the character's problems, the character's reaction to the problems, and the type of conflict involved. For "The Monkey's Paw" (page 2) your chart might look like the one on the opposite page.

FIVE TYPES OF CONFLICT		
PROBLEM THAT ILLUSTRATES CONFLICT	**TYPE OF CONFLICT**	
One person prevents another from achieving a goal. One person exposes a flaw in another. One person takes something away from another.	person against person	EXTERNAL CONFLICT
A person is threatened by a dangerous animal or place.	person against nature	EXTERNAL CONFLICT
Society or tradition demands or prevents an action by a person. A person is ignorant of what society expects.	person against society	EXTERNAL CONFLICT
A person is frustrated by forces beyond his or her control.	person against fate	EXTERNAL CONFLICT
A person has a weakness that prevents him or her from doing the "right" thing. A person seeks an unrealistic goal. A person acts too hastily or has doubts about an action.	person against self	INTERNAL CONFLICT

ANALYSIS OF CONFLICT **SELECTION:** "The Monkey's Paw"		
PROBLEM	**CHARACTER'S REACTION**	**TYPE OF CONFLICT**
The Sergeant Major tries to burn the paw.	Mr. White rescues the paw from the fire.	person against person
Mr. White doubts whether he needs anything.	He wishes only for money to pay the mortgage.	person against self
The money is delivered as compensation for Herbert's death.	Mr. White realizes he should not have tampered with fate.	person against fate
Mrs. White wants to wish their son alive again.	Mr. White knows such a wish would be wrong.	person against person

WRITING PARAGRAPH BY PARAGRAPH

1. Begin the introductory paragraph with a thesis statement. The **thesis statement** should address the main point of the essay question by identifying the types of conflict in the story. Determine what the types of conflict are by studying the chart you prepared. Be sure to state which is the *main* conflict and which are secondary conflicts.

   Example: Mr. White in "The Monkey's Paw" experiences conflicts with other people and within himself, but his main conflict seems to be with fate.

2. In each of the following paragraphs, write about one of the specific problems you listed on the chart. Mention the problem, and tell about the character's reaction to the problem. Then explain how the specific incident is an example of one of the basic types of conflict.
3. In the last paragraph restate in other words the thesis statement from the introductory paragraph. Emphasize the similarity in all the problems described in the preceding paragraphs, and discuss how the character finally handles the conflict as the story ends.

REVISING AND EDITING

See Lesson 1 for detailed reminders about improving your writing.

ASSIGNMENTS

1. Use the chart for "The Monkey's Paw" to write about the conflicts in the plot. What problems does Mr. White face as the story unfolds? How do these problems reveal Mr. White's conflicts? Identify the type of each conflict.
2. Do the assignment called "Writing About Plot" on page 26, or select another story you have read in this book, and answer the following: Identify the problems experienced by the main character as the story unfolds. Then explain how these problems reveal the type of conflict experienced by the character. If there is more than one type of conflict, tell which dominates.

WRITING ABOUT CHARACTER

This lesson guides students through the process of comparing two fictional characters. The lesson reinforces the textbook's teaching about character traits, motivation, and change. You may want to teach this lesson in conjunction with the second subunit in the Short Story unit in this textbook. Since the lesson uses examples from "Sixteen," you may want to assign this story before you teach this lesson. Under "Assignments" on the following page, you will find cross-references to Composition assignments in this textbook that focus on characterization. In addition, in your *Teacher's Classroom Resources* you will find the Charts for Writing About Character (TCR 5, page 43, Overhead Transparency 34) and Checklist for Revising a Paper About a Literary Work (TCR 5, page 51).

LESSON 3: *Writing About Character*

A skilled writer creates characters so believable that we want to know how these imaginary people will act in various circumstances and why they act the way they do. A writer may directly offer an opinion about a character. More often, though, a writer allows characters to reveal themselves through their actions, thoughts, words, and feelings. When you are asked to write an essay about a character in a work of literature, examine what the writer of the work has shown you about the character's actions, thoughts, words, and feelings.

CONCEPT TO REMEMBER

An individual's actions, thoughts, words, and feelings add up to the individual's **key traits**, or most important characteristics. To write an effective essay you should mention at least two traits.

TYPICAL ESSAY QUESTION

When you are asked to write about a character in a piece of literature, you will often have to answer an essay question such as the following:

Describe the key traits of the character as revealed in what he or she does, thinks, says, and feels.

PREWRITING

As you read or reread a piece of literature, keep a list of what appear to be significant actions, comments, thoughts, or feelings by the character you are studying. Group together the actions, comments, and thoughts that add up to a particular key trait. You may have to read a selection more than once to recognize what is significant. Such a list for "Sixteen" (page 27) might look like the following:

ANALYSIS OF CHARACTER
SELECTION: "Sixteen"
CHARACTER: Cress

ACTIONS	COMMENTS	THOUGHTS	KEY TRAIT
Cress meets Edwin, as planned, in her green silk dress.	"He's an old man. . . . It's what we must expect when we grow old." "I'm not going home. . . . It's silly and useless."	"Why were they calling her home to watch grandpa die, she thought angrily and rebelliously. An old man past eighty." "But once on the train her resentment returned."	self-centeredness
Cress puts violets in grandfather's hand. Cress cries uncontrollably.	"Oh, Grandpa, I love you."	"The dikes about Cress's heart broke."	sensitivity to others

WRITING PARAGRAPH BY PARAGRAPH

1. Begin the introductory paragraph with a thesis statement that addresses the main ideas in the assignment. In this case the thesis statement should enumerate the character's key traits as summarized on the chart in Prewriting.

   Example: In "Sixteen" Cress, a self-centered young woman as the story begins, demonstrates through her actions, comments, thoughts, and feelings the key trait of sensitivity when she goes home to visit her dying grandfather.

2. In each of the following paragraphs concentrate on one particular key trait of the character's, and discuss the comments, actions, thoughts, or feelings that reveal that trait. For example, in an essay about the key traits of Cress in "Sixteen," devote one paragraph to her trait of self-centeredness and one paragraph to her trait of sensitivity.
3. In the concluding paragraph restate the thesis statement from the introductory paragraph. Here you can explain whether the various key traits seem related or contradictory. For example, in the final paragraph in an essay about Cress from "Sixteen," you could emphasize that Cress possesses the potential for sensitivity from the beginning but needs to relearn that feeling.

REVISING AND EDITING

See Lesson 1 for detailed reminders about improving your writing.

ASSIGNMENTS

1. Use the chart for "Sixteen" to write about characterization. Describe Cress's key traits, and explain how they are revealed in what she does, thinks, says, and feels.
2. Do an assignment called "Writing About Character" (pages 47, 429), or select a character from another story in this book, and answer the following question: Describe the key traits of the character as revealed in what he or she does, says, thinks, and feels.

COMPARING AND CONTRASTING CHARACTERS

This lesson guides students through the process of comparing and contrasting characters in a literary work. The lesson reinforces the textbook's teaching about flat, round, static, and dynamic characterization. You may want to teach this lesson in conjunction with the second subunit in the Short Story unit in this textbook. Since the lesson uses examples from "A Mother in Mannville," you may want to assign that story before you teach this lesson. Under "Assignments" on the following page, you will find cross-references to Composition assignments in this textbook that focus on comparing and contrasting characters. In addition, in your *Teacher's Classroom Resources* you will find the Charts for Writing About Character (TCR 5, page 43; Overhead Transparency 34) and Checklist for Revising a Paper About a Literary Work (TCR 5, page 51).

LESSON 4: Comparing and Contrasting Characters

Sometimes two characters in a work of literature are in conflict with each other. In other cases the two characters may parallel each other in several ways. Whether they are in conflict or in harmony, the two characters may reveal each other's nature simply by being put into the same work of literature. The best way to learn about one character may be to compare and contrast that character with another character in the selection.

CONCEPTS TO REMEMBER

1. In this lesson *to compare* means "to examine two or more things, ideas, people, and so on, for the purpose of noting similarities." *To contrast* means "to examine two or more things, ideas, people for the purpose of noting differences."
2. A character may be flat. A flat character's personality is dominated by a single trait. A character may be round. A round character displays many different traits, some of which may even appear contradictory.
3. A character may be static. A static character does not change from the beginning of the work of literature to the end. A character may be dynamic. A dynamic character changes in some way during the course of the work.

TYPICAL ESSAY QUESTION

When you are asked to compare and contrast characters in a selection, you will often have to answer an essay assignment such as the following:

Compare and contrast two characters within a piece of literature by showing how they are alike and different in their key traits.

PREWRITING

1. Select two characters to compare and contrast. Prepare a chart to fill in as you reread the piece of literature. The chart should allow you to itemize the actions, comments, thoughts, and feelings of each character so that you can determine his or her key traits and record similarities and differences between the two characters. You should use at least two traits for the characters.
2. Begin to fill in the chart by asking yourself the following questions and others as you reread the selection:
   a. What does each character say to indicate his or her goals?
   b. What does each character say to indicate his or her attitudes toward the conflicts in the selection?
   c. How does each character behave toward the other and toward other characters in the selection?
   d. What action does each take in response to the conflicts in the selection?
   e. Have the actions, comments, thoughts, and feelings of each character at the beginning of the selection remained the same, or have they changed?

For the story "A Mother in Mannville" (page 48) you could prepare a chart such as the one on the opposite page to help you compare and contrast Jerry and the narrator. The plus and minus signs indicate whether the two characters are similar (+) or different (−) on that characteristic.

WRITING PARAGRAPH BY PARAGRAPH

1. Begin your introductory paragraph with a thesis statement that addresses the main ideas of the essay assignment. In this case the thesis statement should clearly indicate that you intend to compare and contrast two characters from the same work. Be sure that your thesis statement includes information about how the characters are alike and how they are different.

   Example: In "A Mother in Mannville" Jerry, the young orphan, and the narrator share the key traits of generosity, fondness for nature, integrity, and rootlessness, but they differ in their response to their friendship and to their later parting.

You may fill in the rest of the introductory paragraph by providing some background for each character.

SIMILARITIES AND DIFFERENCES IN CHARACTERS **SELECTION:** "A Mother in Mannville"			
	1ST CHARACTER (Jerry)	**2ND CHARACTER** (Writer)	
ACTIONS	does extra tasks as a favor (for example, fixes the walk)	gives Jerry money, small gifts	⊕ –
	works hard for the writer and at the orphanage	dedicated to writing, follows schedule	⊕ –
	seeks companionship	seeks isolation	+ ⊖
COMMENTS	"It's pretty when the laurel blooms. . . . Some of it's pink and some of it's white."	"I was homesick, too, for the flaming maples of October, and for corn shocks and pumpkins."	⊕ –
	Speaking of the dog: "I wouldn't have let anything happen to him."	*Speaking of Jerry:* "It was none of my concern."	+ ⊖
THOUGHTS AND FEELINGS	alone, without roots, lives in an orphanage	travels (North Carolina, Mexico, Florida, Alaska)	⊕ –
	integrity—honesty and courage	admires integrity, a trait her father had	⊕ –
	upset when the writer leaves	feels relieved of her anxiety about Jerry when she leaves	+ ⊖

2. Use one of the following two options for organizing the body of the essay:

Option A
Introductory paragraph
Next paragraph: Describe one character.
Next paragraph: Describe the other character.
Next paragraph: Discuss similarities and differences between the two characters based on the preceding paragraphs.
Concluding paragraph

Option B
Introductory paragraph
Next paragraph: Note the similarities between the two characters.
Next paragraph: Note the differences between the two characters.
Concluding paragraph

3. In the concluding paragraph restate your thesis statement in different words. Focus on whether the two characters are more alike or different.

REVISING AND EDITING

See Lesson 1 for detailed reminders about improving your writing.

ASSIGNMENTS

1. Use the chart for "A Mother in Mannville" in Prewriting Step 2 to compare and contrast Jerry and the narrator in that story.
2. Do an assignment called "Writing About Character" (pages 63, 669), or select another story that you have read in this book, and answer the following question: Compare and contrast two characters from the story you have selected by showing how they are alike and different in their key traits.

WRITING ABOUT SETTING

This lesson guides students through the process of writing about the setting of a short story. The lesson reinforces the textbook's teaching about setting and atmosphere, as well as about the relationship between setting and character and plot. You may want to teach this lesson in conjunction with the third subunit in the Short Story unit in this textbook. Since the lesson uses examples from "A Day's Pleasure," you may want to assign this story before you teach this lesson. Under "Assignments" on the final page of this lesson, you will find a cross-reference to a Composition assignment in this textbook that focuses on setting. In addition, in your *Teacher's Classroom Resources* you will find the Charts for Writing About Setting (TCR 5, page 44; Overhead Transparency 35) and Checklist for Revising a Paper About a Literary Work (TCR 5, page 51).

LESSON 5: *Writing About Setting*

Setting anchors a story in time and space. Setting includes landscapes and buildings, weather, seasons, physical props, and the character's clothing, as well as the wider culture, working conditions, and traditions within which conflicts and action occur. When you talk about a work's setting, consider whether it is described clearly in the beginning of the work or if the setting emerges as the work unfolds—through events, through dialogue, or, in the case of drama, through stage directions.

Sometimes, if the author wants to focus on character or plot, setting serves as a backdrop for action; it will merely be the place or situation in which actions happen. At other times, however, the setting may be as important as any character, becoming a vital force overshadowing characters and plot.

CONCEPTS TO REMEMBER

Here is a way to remember the various aspects of setting that may occur in a work of literature.

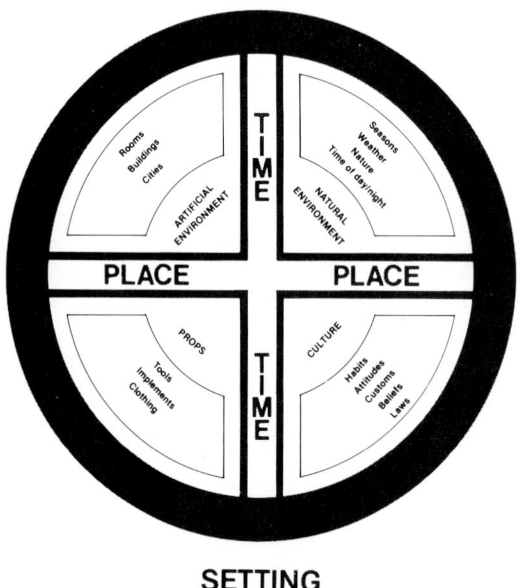

TYPICAL ESSAY QUESTION

When you are asked to write about the setting of a piece of literature, you are often answering a question such as the following:

> Select a piece of literature that you have read. How does the setting reveal a character in the selection? Discuss the significance of the author's choice of setting.

PREWRITING

1. Ask yourself questions such as the following as you think about the selection, its setting, and its characters:
   a. Is the environment (whether natural or artificial) customary or usual for the character? Or is the character in an unfamiliar set of surroundings?
   b. What props does the character use? What do the props tell you about the character's habits, customs, or ambitions?
   c. What does the clothing reveal about the character's social status and values?
   d. What is the attitude of the character toward the place? Specifically, is the character rebellious, rejecting the place? Does the character try to dominate the environment? Is the character threatened or protected by the environment? Is the character protective of the setting?
   e. Does the setting affect the character's view of himself or herself or of life?
   f. What do we learn about the character as a result of a change in setting?
   g. What details of the setting does the author choose to highlight?
2. Fill in a chart such as the following with details from the story. The following chart was prepared based on "A Day's Pleasure" by Hamlin Garland (page 34).

HOW SETTING REVEALS CHARACTER SELECTION: "A Day's Pleasure"		
ASPECT OF SETTING	**DETAILS OF SETTING**	**REVELATION ABOUT CHARACTER**
A. APPROPRIATENESS OF SETTING	barnyard, granary, dark, cold kitchen	Delia Markham seems typical of a character in this setting: hard-working, weary, poor, simple.
B. PROPS	wheat sacks, wood stove, hard limestone, water at sink	Delia is used to a primitive existence, makes her way from day to day through a life of drudgery.
C. CLOTHING	best dress "never a good fit," "hung in wrinkled folds everywhere"; "dusty clothes" of the baby	Delia seems starved, wan, pathetic.
D. ATTITUDE	toward farm	Delia has not been out of the house for six months and is eager to go into town.
E. EFFECT OF SETTING ON CHARACTER	demands of farm	Delia demonstrates "hopeless tragedy in her shambling walk and weak back."
F. EFFECT OF CHANGE OF SETTING	The Halls' home is attractive, dainty, and lovely with easy chair, piano, curtains.	Delia becomes faint and drowsy with pleasure and forgets her aches. She cries tears that "cooled her eyes and cleared her mind."

WRITING PARAGRAPH BY PARAGRAPH

1. In your introductory paragraph write a thesis statement in which you paraphrase the main ideas of the essay question.

   Example: In "A Day's Pleasure" the changing setting of the story reveals the loneliness and tragic emptiness of Delia Markham's existence.

2. In each of the following paragraphs, discuss a specific aspect of setting, and show how each reveals something about one or more characters.
3. In the concluding paragraph restate the thesis statement in different words. Summarize the importance of setting in the piece of literature.

REVISING AND EDITING

See Lesson 1 for detailed reminders about improving your writing.

ASSIGNMENTS

1. Use the chart for "A Day's Pleasure" to write about the setting. Identify the settings of the selection. What do the settings reveal about Delia Markham? That is, explain the effect that the settings have on the character.
2. Do an assignment called "Writing About Setting" (pages 69, 75), or select another story you have read in this book, and tell how the setting reveals a character in that selection. That is, explain the effect of the setting on the character.

WRITING ABOUT POINT OF VIEW

This lesson guides students through the process of writing about the point of view of a short story. The lesson reinforces the textbook's teaching about first-person, limited third-person, and omniscient narration. You may want to teach this lesson in conjunction with the fourth subunit in the Short Story unit in this textbook. Since the lesson uses examples from "Raymond's Run," you may want to assign this story before you teach this lesson. Under "Assignments" on the following page, you will find a cross-reference to a Composition assignment in this textbook that focuses on point of view. In addition, in your *Teacher's Classroom Resources* you will find the Chart for Writing About Point of View (TCR 5, page 45; Overhead Transparency 36) and Checklist for Revising a Paper About a Literary Work (TCR 5, page 51).

LESSON 6: *Writing About Point of View*

An author may choose to tell a story from the point of view of a character within the story or from the point of view of someone outside. We form our overall impression of a story on the basis of who narrates it. It is important when we read a story to ask, "Who is telling this to me?"

CONCEPTS TO REMEMBER

1. The narrator of a story may know everything about the characters and events in a story—or may not. It is important for you not only to determine what the narrator tells you but also to think about what the narrator does *not* tell you.
2. The author may select a narrator who uses a **first-person point of view.** This narrator uses "I" and other first-person pronouns. The important thing about a first-person narrator is that he or she cannot directly know what is going on in anyone else's mind or what is happening anywhere else.
3. The author may select the **omniscient point of view.** In this case the narrator knows about everything that is happening and knows what all the characters are thinking and feeling.
4. The author may select the **limited third-person point of view.** This narrator will report the *actions and words* of all characters but will reveal the *thoughts and feelings* of only one focal character.

TYPICAL ESSAY QUESTION

When you are asked to write about the point of view of a selection, you are often answering an essay question such as the following:

> What is the point of view of the selection? What is—and is *not*—revealed about characters and the events through the point of view?

PREWRITING

1. Determine the point of view by asking:
   a. Does the narrator use first-person pronouns or third-person pronouns?
   b. Does the narrator know about only the events that he or she is witness to, or does the narrator seem to know about everything?
2. Determine what is revealed about the characters by asking the following questions. Remember that in a story told by a first-person narrator the narrator is one of the characters.
   a. What is revealed about physical traits?
   b. What is revealed about the characters' key personality traits, motivations, and goals?
   c. In what ways do the characters change?
3. Determine what is revealed about the events by asking the following questions:
   a. What events do we learn about fully?
   b. What events are not described in detail?
4. Determine what this point of view does *not* reveal by asking the following questions:
   a. Can you trust everything the first-person narrator tells you?
   b. Are there any other characters whose thoughts and feelings are not known?
   c. Do you know more about any characters or events than the narrator does?
5. Prepare charts on which to record your answers to the questions in Prewriting Steps 1–4. The charts on the opposite page have been filled in based on "Raymond's Run" (page 41).

WRITING PARAGRAPH BY PARAGRAPH

1. Begin the introductory paragraph with a thesis statement stating the main idea of your essay.

   Example: In "Raymond's Run" all the characters and events are presented through the point of view of Squeaky in the first person, allowing us to learn about this young girl's goals and the race but forcing us to wonder about her self-image.
2. If the narrator is first person, discuss in the second paragraph what you learn about the narrator's appearance, personality, and goals. Tell whether the narrator changes or develops.
3. In the next paragraph discuss what is revealed about other characters by the narrator. Identify

WHAT THE POINT OF VIEW REVEALS

SELECTION: "Raymond's Run"

POINT OF VIEW: First person

CHARACTER TRAITS			
PHYSICAL TRAITS	**PERSONALITY TRAITS**	**MOTIVATIONS, GOALS**	**EVIDENCE OF CHANGE**
SQUEAKY: squeaky voice good runner good fighter	*brash:* "As anyone can tell you, I'm the fastest thing on two feet." *outspoken:* "I'm serious about my running, and I don't care who knows it." *caring, responsible:* "If anybody has. . . anything to say about his big head, they have to come by me."	to win May Day race and maintain reputation	without regret, considers possibility that she has lost the race considers Raymond's need for something to call his own manages to smile at Gretchen

EVENTS	
EVENTS WE WITNESS	**EVENTS NOT DESCRIBED IN DETAIL**
Squeaky confronts the girls on Broadway. Squeaky wins the race; Raymond runs beside her. Squeaky and Gretchen exchange smiles.	"I much rather just knock you down and take my chances. . . ." Squeaky and Mary Louise were friends at one time. The girls all hang out with Gretchen and talk about Squeaky. The Maypole dancing takes place before Squeaky arrives at the park.

QUESTIONS UNANSWERED BY THE STORY'S POINT OF VIEW
1. Is Squeaky really as tough as she wants us to believe? 2. Why have all the other girls gone over to Gretchen? 3. How do the girls really feel about Squeaky?

their physical traits, personality traits, motivations and goals, and any changes they undergo. (Characters other than the narrator are not represented on the sample chart).

4. In the next paragraph indicate what is revealed about events as filtered through the narrator. Focus on the narrator's view of the conflicts, climax, and falling action and resolution.
5. In the concluding paragraph mention what you do not learn about characters and events because of the choice of point of view. Then restate, in other words, the thesis statement from the introductory paragraph.

REVISING AND EDITING

See Lesson 1 for detailed reminders about improving your writing.

ASSIGNMENTS

1. Use the charts for "Raymond's Run" to write about point of view. What is the story's point of view? What is—and is *not*—revealed about character and events through the point of view?
2. Do the assignment called "Writing About Point of View" (page 85), or select another story, and answer the following: What is the point of view? What is—and is *not*—revealed?

WRITING ABOUT THEME

This lesson guides students through the process of writing about the theme of a fictional work. The lesson reinforces the textbook's teaching about stated and implied theme and about the way other fictional elements—plot, character, setting, and point of view—all help to illuminate the work's theme. You may want to teach this lesson in conjunction with the fifth subunit in the Short Story unit in this textbook. Since the lesson uses examples from "The Good Deed," you may want to assign this story before you teach this lesson. Under "Assignments" on the following page, you will find cross-references to Composition assignments in this textbook that focus on theme. In addition, in your *Teacher's Classroom Resources* you will find the Chart for Writing About Theme (TCR 5, page 46; Overhead Transparency 37) and Checklist for Revising a Paper About a Literary Work (TCR 5, page 51).

LESSON 7: *Writing About Theme*

A **theme** is a generalization about life that the author wants to communicate by writing a specific piece of literature. When you are asked what a story or novel "means," you usually respond by talking about its theme. True, you may talk in part about the work's plot – the work's events – but if you go a bit deeper, you will find yourself exploring the *thematic* element of the work.

The theme, or underlying meaning of a work of literature, is more than just its subject or topic. Rather, the theme involves an *opinion* about the subject or topic. For example, "poverty" may be the subject of a literary work, but the theme goes beyond a one-word subject by filling it out as a complete sentence that takes a particular stand regarding the subject: for example, "Poverty can open one's eyes to the real value of friendship." Therefore, when you write about a work's theme, you cannot just look for the work's subject. You must look at how other elements in the work contribute to forming the author's *opinion* about the subject.

CONCEPTS TO REMEMBER

1. A long work – for example, a lengthy, complex novel – may contain not just one theme but several.
2. Sometimes the theme may be clearly stated. More often, the theme is implied or suggested through other elements in the work. In fact, it is by looking closely at other elements that you can begin to determine the theme.

TYPICAL ESSAY QUESTION

When you are asked to write about the theme of a selection, you are often answering an essay assignment such as the following:

> Various themes in literature are:
>
> - Suffering may lead to novel action.
> - Ingratitude wounds more deeply than cruelty.
> - Power can corrupt those who abuse it.
> - Appearances are often misleading.
> - The only real love is selfless love.
>
> Select a piece of literature that presents one of these themes, or think of a story that reveals another truth about life. Write an essay in which you identify a piece of literature, state its theme, and then show how the author illuminates the theme through characterization, setting, and events.

PREWRITING

1. Identify the subject of a selection you have read. The selection may have more than one subject, but select only one. For example, the subject of "The Good Deed" (page 95) is learning to live in an alien culture.
2. Keeping the subject in mind, ask yourself the following questions so that you can get beyond the subject of the selection to its theme:

   a. What do the various characters (or the main character) think, say, and do regarding the subject?
   b. What are the characters' key traits? Does any character change at all during the course of the selection?
   c. How do the time, place, clothing, and other details of setting serve as a suitable background for the work's subject, or topic?
   d. What do the particular conflicts of the selection have to do with the selection's subject matter?
   e. What do the selection's climax and resolution have to say about the selection's subject matter?

3. Prepare a chart on which to record your answers to the questions in Prewriting Step 2. The chart on the opposite page is a sample prepared for "The Good Deed."
4. Examine the completed chart, and try to formulate a statement of the selection's theme. For example, for "The Good Deed" you might state the theme as follows: "When two different cultures clash, the best solution is a compromise that respects both."

ELEMENTS ILLUMINATING THEME **SELECTION:** "The Good Deed" **SUBJECT OF STORY:** Learning to live in another culture		
CHARACTERIZATION	**SETTING**	**EVENTS**
Old Mrs. Pan's key traits: leadership, determination, respect for tradition, loneliness, and a feeling of uselessness at first Mrs. Pan's mood changes by end.	contrast between quiet village in China and bustling New York Chinatown—Mrs. Pan seeks to recapture what she lost. *details:* China—water tastes of earth, not metal; children obedient; women polite; huge house; many relatives; New York—dirty; children bold; women aggressive; small rooms	Old Mrs. Pan misses home that she had to leave. Old Mrs. Pan disapproves of child rearing here and of Lili's remaining unmarried. At climax James Lim and Lili meet and like each other. Resolution indicates that arranging a marriage is "the best deed possible in the eyes of heaven."

WRITING PARAGRAPH BY PARAGRAPH

1. Begin your introductory paragraph with a thesis statement, which addresses the key points of the assignment. Indicate what the theme of the selection is, being certain to state the theme in terms of a generalization about human nature or experience. Then indicate that the theme is illuminated through characterization, setting, and events.

   Example: The theme of "The Good Deed" is that mutual respect and compromise are the best solution when two different cultures clash. All the elements in "The Good Deed" illuminate the truth of the theme: the characterization of Old Mrs. Pan, the two contrasting settings, and the events of Old Mrs. Pan's good deed.

2. In the next paragraph focus on how the characterization reveals the generalization that you feel the selection makes about life.
3. In the next paragraph focus on how the setting or settings illustrate the theme.
4. In the next paragraph focus on how the events clarify the theme.
5. In the concluding paragraph restate your thesis statement in other words. (You might explain whether the elements of the selection led you to understand a theme new to you or whether they helped renew an awareness that you had.)

REVISING AND EDITING

See Lesson 1 for detailed reminders about improving your writing.

ASSIGNMENTS

1. Use the chart for "The Good Deed" to write about the story's theme. How do characterization, setting, and events all illuminate the theme that compromise brings different cultures together?
2. Do an assignment called "Writing About Theme" (pages 114, 540), or select another story you have read in this book, and answer the following question: State the theme of the selection. Show how the author illuminates the theme through characterization, setting, and events.

WRITING ABOUT BIOGRAPHY, AUTOBIOGRAPHY

This lesson guides students through the process of writing about a biography or autobiography. The lesson reinforces the textbook's teaching about significant details and the author's purpose. You may want to teach this lesson in conjunction with the first subunit in the Nonfiction unit in this textbook. Since the lesson uses examples from the biography "Of Dry Goods and Black Bow Ties," you may want to assign that selection before you teach this lesson. Under "Assignments" on the following page, you will find cross-references to Composition assignments in this textbook that focus on writing about biography and autobiography. In addition, in your *Teacher's Classroom Resources* you will find the Charts for Writing About Biography, Autobiography, and the Essay (TCR 5, page 47, Overhead Transparency 38) and Checklist for Revising a Paper About a Literary Work (TCR 5, page 51).

LESSON 8: *Writing About Biography, Autobiography*

The author of a biography or autobiography wants to communicate the subject's general outlook on life and to make the reader *react* to the subject. To do so, the author of a biography or autobiography relies heavily on details. When you read and write about a biography or autobiography, your primary job is to pay attention to the details that the writer selects to present.

CONCEPTS TO REMEMBER

1. A **biography** is the story of a person's life told by someone other than that person. An **autobiography** is the story of a person's life told by the subject himself or herself.
2. The writer of a biography or autobiography can present a totally unbiased view of the subject. More often, however, the writer selects details that present a particular image of the subject—as generous, as forbidding, as brilliant, etc.
3. The **purpose** of a piece of nonfiction is the central idea, or general statement about life, that the author wants to make.

TYPICAL ESSAY QUESTION

When you are asked to write about a biography or an autobiography, you are often answering an essay question such as the following:

> Select a biography or an autobiography that you have read. How does the author's selection of details illustrate the subject's outlook on life? How do details support the author's purpose?

PREWRITING

Prepare a chart that allows you to focus on the most important parts of the essay assignment.

1. In the first column list significant details from the biography or autobiography relating to the subject's actions, words, and appearance.
2. In the second column note what these details tell you about the subject's outlook on life.
3. In the third column note what you think about the subject based on the data in the first two columns. For "Of Dry Goods and Black Bow Ties" (page 235) by Yoshiko Uchida, your chart might look like the one on the opposite page.

WRITING PARAGRAPH BY PARAGRAPH

1. Begin the introductory paragraph with a thesis statement. The thesis statement should answer the essay question in general terms by indicating how the details reveal the subject's outlook on life and serve the author's purpose.

   Example: In "Of Dry Goods and Black Bow Ties" the author's choice of details tells us about Shimada's outlook on life and inspires admiration for Shimada, whom the author wants us to see as a proud, brilliant entrepreneur who never lost his honesty or basic humanity despite the collapse of his business empire.

2. In the next paragraph emphasize how the actions of the subject reveal his or her outlook on life.

ANALYSIS OF BIOGRAPHY, AUTOBIOGRAPHY SELECTION: "Of Dry Goods and Black Bow Ties"		
SELECTION OF DETAILS	**SUBJECT'S OUTLOOK ON LIFE**	**READER'S JUDGMENT ABOUT SUBJECT (RELATES TO AUTHOR'S PURPOSE)**
ACTIONS abandoned job as laborer and began chain of stores and banks never forgot friends did not ask for help when banks failed	One must seize opportunity and welcome risk. One must hold on to values from the past. One must always try to be independent.	Uchida must want us to see Shimada as ambitious and humanitarian at the same time.
WORDS "One never knows when one might be indebted to even the lowliest of beggars." "I paid back every cent. . . . I owe nothing."	One must consider the future. One must value honesty and maintain a sense of pride.	Uchida must want us to see Shimada as humble in spite of success or failure.
APPEARANCE erect carriage, imposing spotless suit, immaculate white shirt and stiff collar (during successful days) faded morning coat, unpolished shoes, shabby black hat (after failure)	One must demonstrate a sense of self-worth and encourage others. See above. One must try to keep up one's standards even if it is hard to do so.	Uchida must want us to see Shimada as a man who will not give in to defeat. She may want us to feel sadness for his fate—but also admiration.

3. In the next paragraph emphasize how the words and appearance of the subject reveal his or her outlook on life.
4. In the next paragraph concentrate on the author's purpose. What does the author apparently want the reader to think about the subject based on the details supplied?
5. In the concluding paragraph restate in other words the thesis statement from the introductory paragraph.

REVISING AND EDITING

See Lesson 1 for detailed reminders about improving your writing.

ASSIGNMENTS

1. Use the chart for "Of Dry Goods and Black Bow Ties" to write about a biography. How does the selection of details reveal the outlook of Mr. Shimada? How do the details support the author's purpose?
2. Do the assignment called "Writing About a Biography" (page 245) or "Writing About an Autobiography" (page 257), or select another biography or autobiography in this book, and answer the following: How does the author's selection of details illustrate the subject's outlook on life? How do the details that are supplied support the author's purpose?

WRITING ABOUT THE ESSAY

This lesson guides students through the process of writing about an essay. The lesson reinforces the textbook's teaching about an essay's purpose and an author's techniques. You may want to teach this lesson in conjunction with the second subunit in the Nonfiction unit in this textbook. Since the lesson uses examples from the essay "Sayonara," you may want to assign that essay before you teach this lesson. Under "Assignments" on the following page, you will find cross-references to Composition assignments in this textbook that focus on writing about the essay. In addition, in your *Teacher's Classroom Resources* you will find the Charts for Writing About Biography, Autobiography, and the Essay (TCR 5, page 47; Overhead Transparency 38) and Checklist for Revising a Paper About a Literary Work (TCR 5, page 51).

LESSON 9: *Writing About the Essay*

When you analyze an essay, you have to concentrate on two things: (1) the content, especially the purpose, of the essay and (2) the techniques of the essay. You should discuss not only what the essayist says but also how he or she says it.

CONCEPTS TO REMEMBER

1. The **purpose** of an essay is the central idea, or general statement about life or about some situation or condition, that the author wants to make.
2. To communicate the purpose of the essay, the author uses various techniques such as sensory details, facts, statistics, examples, and opinions. Some authors rely on one technique more than on others, but some authors mix several techniques in one essay.

TYPICAL ESSAY QUESTION

When you are asked to write about an essay, you are often answering an assignment such as the following:

> An author always has a purpose for writing an essay. To accomplish this purpose, the author may use various techniques such as sensory details, facts, statistics, examples, and opinions. Select an essay that you have read. What is the purpose of the essay? Cite with examples the particular techniques that the author uses to accomplish this purpose.

PREWRITING

1. To determine the author's purpose in writing the essay, ask yourself the following questions:
   a. What, if anything, does the title suggest about the author's opinion of the subject?
   b. What opinion about life is suggested by the experiences that the author relates?
   c. What opinion about people in general is suggested by the details provided regarding specific people and their behavior? The details may include sensory details, facts, statistics, examples, and opinions.
   d. What ideas about the world in general are suggested by the details of setting?
   e. What attitude toward the subject is revealed by the author's style?
2. Based on your answers to the preceding questions, prepare a statement of the author's purpose, and prepare a chart such as the following one to record the techniques used to achieve that purpose. The filled-in chart on the opposite page represents an analysis of "Sayonara," the essay by Anne Morrow Lindbergh on page 274.

THE PURPOSE AND TECHNIQUES OF AN ESSAY

SELECTION: "Sayonara"

PURPOSE: To explain the suitability of the word *sayonara* as a way to say "good-by" and to arouse sympathy for a culture.

SENSORY DETAILS	FACTS	STATISTICS	EXAMPLES	OPINIONS
"clean, sharp . . . one cry" "clatter of wooden clogs" "flutter of kimonos" "brown faces hidden under enormous roof-like hats of straw" bright, fragile serpentine ribbons, linking those on shore with those leaving	*Literal translations of parting terms in various languages: Auf Wiedersehen* means "Till we meet again"; *Farewell* means ". . . do well"; *Good-by* and *Adios* mean "God be with you"; *Sayonara* means "Since it must be so."	NONE	*of what merits* sayonara: rice fields, thatched roofs, paper walls, little towns, blue paper umbrellas, little boys chasing dragonflies	*Sayonara* is the best good-by – doesn't say too much or too little (a simple acceptance of fact: It must be).

WRITING PARAGRAPH BY PARAGRAPH

1. Begin the introductory paragraph with a thesis statement, which should specify the author's purpose and state which techniques are used to achieve this purpose.

   Example: In "Sayonara," an essay by Anne Morrow Lindbergh recounting her farewell journey through Japan, the author explains the significance and suitability of the Japanese word for "good-by." By means of sensory details, facts, examples, and opinions, Lindbergh evokes sympathy for the Japanese culture, which quietly and with grave dignity accepts the inevitability of parting.

2. In each of the following paragraphs show how the author uses one technique to make the purpose of the essay clear.
3. In the concluding paragraph restate in other words the thesis statement from the introductory paragraph. Here you might give a brief personal reaction to the author's efforts.

REVISING AND EDITING

See Lesson 1 for detailed reminders about improving your writing.

ASSIGNMENTS

1. Use the chart for "Sayonara" (in Prewriting Step 2) to write an essay in which you discuss the author's purpose and techniques for achieving her purpose.
2. Do an assignment called "Writing About an Essay" (pages 277, 280, 285). What is the purpose of the essay you have selected to write about? Cite with examples the particular techniques that the author uses to accomplish the purpose.

WRITING ABOUT POETRY

This lesson guides students through the process of writing about a poem. The lesson reinforces the textbook's teaching about speaker, sound devices, imagery, and figurative language. You may want to teach this lesson in conjunction with the final subunit in the Poetry unit in this textbook. Since the lesson uses examples from the poem "The Base Stealer," you may want to assign that poem before you teach this lesson. Under "Assignments" on the following page, you will find cross-references to Composition assignments in this textbook that focus on writing about poetry. In addition, in your *Teacher's Classroom Resources* you will find the Chart for Writing About Poetry (TCR 5, page 48; Overhead Transparency 39), Questions to Explore a Literary Work (TCR 5, page 50), and Checklist for Revising a Paper About a Literary Work (TCR 5, page 51).

LESSON 10: *Writing About Poetry*

The meaning of a poem is revealed through highly compressed, musical language that evokes the reader's immediate emotional response—a response often followed by deeper, meditative reflections. As the poet Robert Frost said, "Poetry begins in delight and ends in wisdom." The pleasure experienced in listening to or reading poetry comes from sensing the interrelationship of *all* the literary elements that the poet uses to represent the "sense," or meaning: choice of speaker, sound, imagery, and figurative language.

CONCEPTS TO REMEMBER

1. The **speaker** of the poem is the voice of the poem. Sometimes the speaker is the poet himself or herself; sometimes the speaker is a character or thing created by the poet.
2. Among the sound devices that a poet may use are **onomatopoeia** (a word or phrase that actually imitates or suggests the sound of what it describes); **alliteration** (the repeating of initial consonant sounds); **consonance** (the repeating of similar consonant sounds preceded by different accented vowels); **assonance** (the repeating of vowel sounds).
3. Other aspects of sound in poetry are **rhyme** (the repeating at regular intervals of similar or identical sounds) and **rhythm** (the pattern created by arranging stressed and unstressed syllables).
4. A poem's images may appeal to one or more senses.
5. The most common kinds of figurative language available to a poet are metaphor, simile, and personification. (**Metaphor** is a figure of speech in which two unlike things are compared without the use of *like* or *as*; **simile** is a comparison using *like* or *as*; **personification** is a figure of speech in which an animal, object, or idea is described as having human form or characteristics.)

TYPICAL ESSAY QUESTION

When asked to write about poetry, you are often answering an assignment such as the following:

> Select a poem that you have read. What is the meaning of the poem? What techniques does the author use to reveal this meaning? Techniques to consider include the selection of speaker, sound, imagery, and figurative language.

PREWRITING

1. Use the following questions to help you determine the meaning of the poem.
   a. Does the poem focus on the actions of a character?
   b. Does the poem describe a person, place, or thing?
   c. Does the poem focus on an idea? A feeling?
   d. What emotional response does the poem seem to call up in you?
   e. After your immediate emotional response to the poem, on what does the poem cause you to reflect?
2. Prepare a chart on which to record your statement of the meaning of the poem and your observations about the techniques of the poem. The chart on the opposite page represents an analysis of "Base Stealer" by Robert Francis (page 180). Each column deals with one of the poetic techniques.

THE MEANING AND ANALYSIS OF A POEM SELECTION: "Base Stealer"			
SPEAKER	**SOUND**	**IMAGERY**	**FIGURATIVE LANGUAGE**
The speaker seems to be an observer in the ballpark, someone who seems to understand the base stealer, the crowd, and the opposing team. The speaker seems to appreciate the player's cleverness.	no predictable rhyme (mirrors unpredictable action) Alliteration and consonance with *p* sounds (lines 1–5) suggest character is like a motion. Assonance of long *e* and short *i* (line 7) and onomatopoeia of *scattering* suggest quickness, lightness. Repetition (*delicate*) suggests tension.	Besides clear visual image, poem uses words to create sound of fans ("come on, come on") and physical tension and release ("taut," "pointing," bouncing," "now!").	*similes:* "like a tightrope walker"; "like a dropped ball/Or a kid skipping rope"; "like an ecstatic bird" (suggest base stealer can be many different things)

WRITING PARAGRAPH BY PARAGRAPH

1. Begin your introductory paragraph with a thesis statement, which should address the main points of the assignment. Indicate that the various techniques used by the poet all serve to enhance and present effectively the underlying meaning of the poem.

   Example: In "The Base Stealer" the poet, Robert Francis, portrays the danger and risk taking of the baseball player who hovers on the brink of success or disaster as he attempts to steal a base. The poetic techniques of selection of speaker, sound, imagery, and figurative language all serve to present and enhance our appreciation of the base stealer's plunge toward success or failure.

2. In the next paragraph deal with at least two major techniques that the poet uses to underscore the poem's meaning—for example, selection of speaker and sound devices.
3. In the next paragraph deal with two other techniques that the poet uses to underscore the poem's meaning—for example, imagery and figurative language.
4. In the next paragraph develop the meaning and interpretation of the poem.
5. In the final paragraph restate your thesis statement in other words. Explain here the emotional impact the poem evokes as well as the ideas the poem leaves you with.

REVISING AND EDITING

See Lesson 1 for detailed reminders about improving your writing.

ASSIGNMENTS

1. Use the chart for "The Base Stealer" to write about the poem. What is the meaning of the poem? What techniques does the poet use to reveal this meaning? Techniques to consider include selection of speaker, sound devices, imagery, and figurative language.
2. Do an assignment called "Writing About Poetry" (pages 205, 212, 215), or select another poem you have read in this book and answer the following: "What is the meaning of the poem? What techniques does the author use to reveal this meaning? Techniques to consider include selection of speaker, sound, imagery, and figurative language.

WRITING ABOUT THE TOTAL EFFECT

This lesson guides students through the process of writing about the total effect of a fictional work. The lesson reinforces the textbook's teaching about how various literary elements interact in producing a particular impact on the reader. You may want to teach this lesson in conjunction with the final subunit in the Short Story unit in this textbook. Since the lesson uses examples from "The Necklace," you may want to assign that story before you teach this lesson. Under "Assignments" on the following page, you will find cross-references to Composition assignments in this textbook that focus on the total effect. In addition, in your *Teacher's Classroom Resources* you will find the Chart for Writing About the Total Effect (TCR 5, page 49; Overhead Transparency 40), Questions to Explore a Literary Work (TCR 5, page 50), and Checklist for Revising a Paper About a Literary Work (TCR 5, page 51).

LESSON 11: *Writing About the Total Effect*

The mark of any great work of art (whether it is a musical composition, a painting, or a piece of literature) is that all aspects of the work act together to produce a stirring, unified effect. Each element of the work seems inevitable; to change any aspect would be to alter the work's impact. You can explore the artistry involved in a piece of literature by writing about the total effect that the piece has on you. In doing so, you will write about many literary elements —plot, character, setting, point of view, and theme. The author uses all these elements to achieve a specific emotional response by the reader.

CONCEPTS TO REMEMBER

1. When discussing total effect, we often use the term *impact*. A selection makes an impact on a reader because of its theme and the skill with which all the other elements support the theme.
2. Review the definitions of the various literary elements (plot, character, setting, point of view, and theme) before proceeding to write about the total effect of a piece of literature. Remember that all the elements add up to form a whole.

TYPICAL ESSAY QUESTION

When you are asked to write about the total effect of a piece of literature, you are often answering an essay question such as the following:

> What is the total effect of the selection? That is, what is its impact on the reader? How does the author use the following literary elements to achieve this effect: plot, character, setting, point of view, and theme?

PREWRITING

1. Ask yourself the following questions.
   a. What is the impact of the work?
   b. Which literary element dominates?
   c. How do the other literary elements support or relate to the dominant element?
2. Prepare a chart on which to record your answers to the questions in Prewriting Step 1. This chart should have columns for the question, the answer, and the details that support your answer. Details may take the form of quotations from the selection. Keep in mind that more than one answer may be possible but any answer must be supported with details. For "The Necklace" (page 139) such a chart might look like the one on the opposite page.

WRITING PARAGRAPH BY PARAGRAPH

1. Begin the introductory paragraph with a thesis statement. The thesis statement should state the impact of the work on the reader and indicate that all the key literary elements work together to create this impact.

   Example: In "The Necklace" key literary elements contribute to the impact of the story on the reader: pity for Madame Loisel, who is blind to true worth because of her concern for appearances. A skillfully designed plot with an unexpected twist to the climax helps create this impact and provides the frame for the characters, setting, point of view, and theme, all of which contribute to the impact.

ANALYSIS OF THE TOTAL EFFECT **SELECTION:** "The Necklace"		
QUESTION	**ANSWER**	**DETAILS**
WHAT IS THE IMPACT OF THE WORK?	pity for the folly of Madame Loisel, who, through a twist of fate, loses true worth by pursuing mere appearances	*details arousing pity:* "What would have happened if she had not lost that necklace? Who knows? Who can say?... How little there is between happiness and misery!"
WHICH LITERARY ELEMENT DOMINATES?	*Plot:* Surprise ending focuses on what the Loisels mistakenly thought they had to do to replace the necklace.	*details of Loisels' actions:* "signed notes ...ran the whole gamut of moneylenders...compromised the rest of his life... risked his signature...terrified by the outlook for the future...blackness of despair...tortures of the spirit"
HOW DO THE OTHER LITERARY ELEMENTS SUPPORT THE DOMINANT ELEMENT?	*Character:* contrast between Madame Loisel at the beginning and at the end, contrast between Madame Loisel's values and her husband's	*at beginning:* vain, beautiful, never satisfied; dreamer ("dream of silent chambers...reception halls...fashionable dinner parties...delicious dishes") *at end:* a peasant woman ("heavy, rough, harsh...poor...voice shrill")
	Setting: contrast between Loisels' apartment and ball	*apartment:* shabby ("dinginess of the walls...worn-out appearance of the chairs...ugliness of the draperies") *party:* "prettiest one," "fashionable, gracious"
	Point of view: Third person with focus on Mathilde's thoughts and responses; we do not know until the end what Madame Forestier always knew.	Madame Forestier: "But mine was only paste. Why at most it was worth only five hundred francs!"
	Theme: Outward appearances are not reliable; true value is not always apparent.	The Loisels learn that their perception about the necklace was wrong.

2. In the next paragraph focus on the dominant element and how it contributes to the impact.
3. In the next paragraphs discuss the other elements and how each supports the dominant one.
4. In the concluding paragraph remind your audience that all the elements *work together* to produce the impact.

REVISING AND EDITING

See Lesson 1 for detailed reminders about improving your writing.

ASSIGNMENTS

1. Use the chart for "The Necklace" to write about its total effect. How does the author use the various elements to achieve this effect?
2. Do an assignment called "Writing About Total Effect" (pages 145, 429, 540, 669), or choose another selection you have read in this book, and answer the following: What is the total effect, or impact, of this selection? How does the author use the elements of plot, character, setting, point of view, and theme to achieve this effect?

LITERARY TERMS HANDBOOK

In this handbook you will find all of the reading and literary terms taught in this book. Each entry defines a term and then briefly discusses it, elaborating with examples from the selections. Each entry ends with a cross-reference to the pages that teach the literary term and, in some cases, to related entries in this handbook.

LITERARY TERMS HANDBOOK

ALLITERATION *The repeating of consonant sounds, most often at the beginnings of words.* For example, the *s* sound is repeated in this line from Wylie's "Velvet Shoes":

I shall go shod in silk

See page 195.

ALLUSION *A reference in a work of literature to a character, place, or situation from another work of literature, music, or art.* For example, an allusion to Shakespeare's murderous Lady Macbeth in "About Two Nice People" describes Ellen's anger.

See page 487.

ANECDOTE *A brief account of a true event, usually intended to entertain and to reveal personality through a person's actions.* In "Of Dry Goods and Black Bow Ties," for example, the anecdote about the party Mr. Shimada gave for his daughter reveals his acceptance of American customs.

See page 245.

ARGUMENT *That kind of writing that uses reason to affect people's opinions and actions.* In "The Spreading 'You Know'" Thurber's argument that clichés garble meaning is intended to inspire his readers to speak more carefully.

See page 280.
See also DESCRIPTION, PERSUASION.

ASIDE *In a play a character's comment that is heard by the audience but not by the other characters.* Asides reveal what a character is thinking and feeling, as in this example:

ROMEO: [*Aside.*] Shall I hear more, or shall I
speak at this?

See page 304.

ASSONANCE *The repeating of vowel sounds, especially in a line of poetry.* For example, the *i* sound is repeated in this line from Millay's "Courage That My Mother Had":

Now granite in a granite hill.

See page 195.

ATMOSPHERE *The emotional quality or mood of a story.* Atmosphere is created in part by setting, and it influences the attitudes of characters and the readers. The dreary atmosphere of the farm in "A Day's Pleasure," for example, saddens Delia.

See pages 75, 304.

AUTOBIOGRAPHY *The story of a person's life written by that person.* Angelou's *I Know Why the Caged Bird Sings* is an autobiography.

One form of autobiography is the **diary**, a day-by-day account of events in a person's life. See *Diary of a Young Girl.*

See pages 234, 251, 716.

BALLAD *A short, musical, narrative poem.* Ballads usually focus on a single situation that is a dramatic, often tragic episode about love, death, or physical courage. **Folk ballads** or **popular ballads**, such as "Lord Randal," were passed on by word of mouth for generations before being written down. **Literary ballads** are imitations of folk ballads.

See page 171.

BIOGRAPHY *The account of a person's life written by someone other than the subject.* Most biographies are book length, but biographical sketches present key events in a person's life. For example, Sandburg's *Abraham Lincoln: The Prairie Years* is the first of six volumes; Uchida's "Of Dry Goods and Black Bow Ties" is a biographical sketch.

See pages 234, 716.

BLANK VERSE *Poetry written in unrhymed iambic pentameter.* This is a **rhythm** made up of five feet to a line, each foot containing one unstressed and one stressed syllable. Shakespeare used blank verse for his plays, including *Romeo and Juliet*:

˘ ´ ˘ ´ ˘ ´ ˘ ´ ˘
But soft!/What light/through yon/der win/dow
´
breaks?

See page 356.

CHARACTER *A person in a story, play, or novel.* Characters who reveal only one personality trait are called **flat**. For example, in "The Secret Life of Walter Mitty" Mrs. Mitty is a flat character because we know only one aspect of her personality, her dominance of her husband.

Characters who show varied and sometimes contradictory traits are called **round**. For example, in "Split Cherry Tree" Pa is a round character because he is both tough and sensitive.

Stereotyped characters are common character types whose actions are predictable. They are often used for comic effect in farce. For example, in "The Secret Life of Walter Mitty" Mrs. Mitty is a stereotype of a domineering wife.

See pages 53, 63, 706, 708.
See also CHARACTERIZATION.

CHARACTERIZATION *The personality of a character and the method that an author uses to reveal this personality.* Through **direct characterization** the author directly states facts about a character's personality. For example, in "Sixteen" West says, "Being older suited Edwin."

With **indirect characterization** the author reveals a character's personality indirectly, through the character's words and actions, and through what other characters say and think about the character. In "Sixteen" Cress's refusal to return home and her parents' dismay over the change in her show her insensitivity.

See pages 40, 47, 522, 613.
See also CHARACTER.

CLIMAX *The point of our highest interest and greatest emotional involvement in a narrative.* At this point in a story, the outcome of the conflict becomes clear. For example, in "The Most Dangerous Game" the climax occurs when Rainsford defeats Zaroff. At the climax of a tragedy, the hero takes some action that will lead directly to a downfall. For example, in *Romeo and Juliet* the death of Tybalt in Act III dooms the young lovers.

See pages 10, 426.
See also PLOT.

COMEDY *A type of drama that is humorous and usually has a happy ending. A Sunny Morning* is a comedy.

See page 293.
See also FARCE, TRAGEDY.

CONCRETE LANGUAGE *Another name for* ***sensory language****, or words that appeal to the senses.*

See page 277.
See also SENSORY LANGUAGE.

CONFLICT *At the center of a plot, the struggle between two opposing forces.* An **external conflict** exists when a character struggles against some outside force, such as another person, nature, society, or fate. The argument between Pa and Professor Herbert in "Split Cherry Tree" is an external conflict. An **internal conflict**, a conflict of person against self, exists within a character. The character may struggle to reach a decision, to make a moral choice, or to attain a personal goal. Pa in "Split Cherry Tree" also wrestles with an internal conflict while trying to reconcile his background with a new approach to education.

See pages 26, 33.
See also PLOT.

CONNOTATION *The unspoken or unwritten meanings associated with a word beyond its dictionary definition or* ***denotation.*** In "Knoxville, Tennessee" Nikki Giovanni speaks of being "warm all the time." The denotation of *warm* relates to temperature. Its connotations, however, convey feelings of comfort, security, confidence, and happiness.

See page 213.

COUPLET *Two consecutive lines in a poem or play that rhyme.* For example:

> For never was a story of more woe
> Than this of Juliet and her Romeo
>
> —*Romeo and Juliet*

See page 356.
See also RHYME, REPETITION.

DENOTATION *The literal or dictionary meaning of a word.* Literal language conveys denotation, or exact meaning.

See page 213.
See also CONNOTATION.

DESCRIPTION *Any careful detailing of a person, place, thing, or event.* While description can be the writer's primary aim in the descriptive essay, this kind of writing is used in stories, biography, and other forms of essays.

See pages 240, 277.
See also NARRATION, EXPOSITION, PERSUASION.

DIALECT *A variation of a language, sometimes spoken by a particular group but most often associated with a particular region.* Dialects differ from standard language because they contain different sounds, forms, and meanings. For example, Robert Burns's "My Love Is Like a Red Red Rose" illustrates the Scottish dialect. The conversational language in the short story "A Day's Pleasure" shows the dialect of the midwestern farmer of the early twentieth century.

See pages 126, 210.

DIALOGUE *Conversation between characters in a story, work of nonfiction, novel, play, or dramatic poem.* Dialogue can advance plot and reveal characters' personalities.

See pages 33, 293.
See also ASIDE, DRAMA, DRAMATIC POETRY, MONOLOGUE, SOLILOQUY.

DIARY *A day-by-day account of events in a person's life.* Diary is a form of autobiography. See *Diary of a Young Girl.*

See pages 234, 261.
See also AUTOBIOGRAPHY, BIOGRAPHY.

DRAMA *A play or story meant to be performed before an audience.* Drama can be divided into two types: **tragedy**, such as Shakespeare's *Romeo and Juliet*, and **comedy**, such as the Quinteros' *A Sunny Morning*. The two basic parts of a drama are script and staging. Script includes dialogue and stage directions, or instructions for performance.

See page 293.

DRAMATIC CONVENTION *A device that a playwright uses to present a story on stage and that the audience accepts as realistic.* Shakespeare's audience, for example, accepted the convention of boys playing the roles of women in plays. Today's audiences accept the conventions of music, lighting, and the quick passage of time.

See page 375.

DRAMATIC POETRY *Poetry in which one or more characters speak,* such as "Lord Randal," which takes the form of a dialogue between mother and son:

"O where hae ye been, my handsome young man?"
"I hae been to the wild wood; mother, make my bed soon."

See also BALLAD, NARRATIVE POETRY.

EPIC *A long narrative poem that traces the adventures of a hero.* Epics intertwine myths, legends, and history and reflect the values of the societies in which they originate. Gods and goddesses often intervene in the affairs of humans. The mood of the epic is serious; its language, elevated. Two of the most famous epics are Homer's *Illiad* and *Odyssey.* Many epics were first recited or sung. They were passed on orally before they were collected and written down.

See pages 433, 690.
See also EPIC HERO.

EPIC HERO *A legendary figure of almost superhuman qualities whose adventures form the core of the epic poem.* The hero embodies the goals and virtues of an entire nation or culture. For example, Odysseus, the hero of Homer's *Odyssey*, personifies his country's values of loyalty to family, love of home, hospitality, and courage.

See pages 433, 467.
See also EPIC.

EPITHET *A descriptive word or phrase attached to the name of a person or thing, usually stressing a particular characteristic.* The hero of the *Odyssey* is often described with an epithet as "*crafty* Odysseus."

See page 480.

ESSAY *A short piece of nonfiction writing on any topic.* The **formal essay** was popular during the eighteenth and nineteenth centuries because of its serious and impersonal style. The **informal essay**, which is more popular today, entertains while it informs and usually displays a light approach and conversational style. The personality of the author often shines through the informal essay. Thurber's "Spreading 'You Know'" is an informal essay.

Narrative essays ("Kilimanjaro!") recount true events. **Descriptive essays** ("Sayonara") describe actual people, places, or things. **Persuasive essays** ("The Spreading 'You Know'") aim to convince the reader of an opinion or to rouse the reader to action. **Expository essays** (the excerpt from *Shakespeare of London*) present information and explain ideas.

See pages 263, 273, 277, 280, 285, 718.

EXPOSITION *An introduction to people, places, and situations that are important to the plot of a story, novel, or play.* For example, in "A Day's Pleasure" the exposition quickly reveals the hardship of Delia's life. The term also refers to the **expository essay**, such as the excerpt from *Shakespeare of London*, which presents facts or explains ideas.

See pages 10, 285.

FABLE *A very brief story told to teach a lesson.* Fables such as Aesop's usually have stated themes.

See page 114.
See also THEME.

FALLING ACTION *In a play or story the action that is the result of the climax.* In *Romeo and Juliet*, for instance, the relationship of the two lovers declines after the deaths in Act III.

See pages 10, 427.
See also PLOT.

FARCE *A type of comedy that presents stereotyped characters in improbable situations.* In addition, exaggeration, fast physical action, and coarse wit set farce apart from other forms of comedy.

See also COMEDY, CHARACTER.

FICTION *A prose narrative work of the imagination including novels and short stories.* Fiction may be based on fact or experience, such as London's use of the Gold Rush in *The Call of the Wild.*

See pages 1, 491.

FIGURATIVE LANGUAGE *Language used for descriptive effect.* For example, a character in "A Slander" by Chekhov uses figurative language to say that he has been slandered: "Why did you smear me with mud?"

See pages 63, 196.
See also LITERAL LANGUAGE, FIGURE OF SPEECH, METAPHOR, PERSONIFICATION, SIMILE.

FIGURE OF SPEECH *A specific device or kind of figurative language, such as a **simile** or **metaphor**.*

See page 196.
See also LITERAL LANGUAGE, SIMILE, METAPHOR, PERSONIFICATION.

FLASHBACK *A scene in a narrative that breaks the normal time sequence of the plot to narrate events that happened earlier.* The flashback usually provides necessary background information. Much of the *Odyssey* is told in flashback as Odysseus narrates to the court of King Alcinous the events that brought him there.

See page 480.
See also IN MEDIAS RES.

FOOT *The basic unit of measurement in rhythm.* A foot usually contains one accented syllable and one or more unaccented syllables. For example, the following line from "The Secret Heart" contains four feet:

◡ ´ ◡ ´ ◡ ´ ◡ ´
Acróss/the yéars/he cóuld/recáll

See page 185.
See also METER, RHYTHM.

FORESHADOWING *The use of clues by an author to prepare readers for events that will happen later in a story.* For example, in "The Monkey's Paw" Herbert says, "I don't see the money.... and I bet I never shall." The comment hints at his death the next day.

See page 26.

FRAME STORY *A story structure that includes the telling of a story within a story.* The **frame** is the outer story, usually before and after the inner and more important story. The frame usually echoes the theme of the inner story. "The Heyday of the Blood" is a frame story.

See page 126.

FREE VERSE *Poetry that has no fixed meter or pattern.* Walt Whitman, for example, uses free verse in "I Hear America Singing."

See also RHYTHM.

FULL-LENGTH PLAY *A drama that usually has several major characters and a complicated plot and is usually divided into acts and scenes. Romeo and Juliet* is a full-length play.

See page 294.
See also DRAMA, ONE-ACT PLAY.

HAIKU *A three-line poem, usually about nature, often with a suggestion of deeper meaning.* The form of the traditional haiku requires seventeen syllables — five in the first line, seven in the second, and five in the third. For example,

Within plum orchard,
sturdy oak takes no notice
of flowering blooms.
—*Bashō*

See page 199.

HOMERIC SIMILE *An extended comparison also called **epic simile.*** The Homeric simile gets its name from Homer, the Greek poet who used these lengthy comparisons in the epics *Iliad* and

Here is a definition of *genre,* the term that identifies the unit organization of the student anthology. You may wish to draw special attention to this term with some of your students.

GENRE *A type or category of literature.* The term may refer to a broad literary category, such as the short story, poetry, or nonfiction, or to a specific literary type, such as the haiku or the narrative essay.

See pages 1 (short story), 161 (poetry), 233 (nonfiction), 199 (haiku), 264 (narrative essay).

Odyssey. For example, in comparing Penelope's slain suitors to a catch of fish, Homer extends the comparison for seven lines.

See page 487.
See also SIMILE.

IMAGE *A picture or likeness made with words to help the reader of a poem or story form a mental portrait.* Poetic images are usually visual, but a poet may use images that convey sound, smell, taste, and touch. Note the images of sight, touch, and sound in these lines from "Sea Fever":

And the wheel's kick and the wind's song and the white sail's shaking,
And a gray mist on the sea's face and a gray dawn breaking.

See page 199.
See also IMAGERY, FIGURATIVE LANGUAGE.

IMAGERY *The collection of sense images in a poem or a story.*

See page 199.
See also IMAGE, FIGURATIVE LANGUAGE.

IN MEDIAS RES *A Latin term meaning "in the middle of things."* Epic poems usually begin *in medias res*, after much of the action has already happened. In the *Odyssey*, for instance, Odysseus has already struggled for many years before the story opens. He tells of those struggles in a flashback.

See page 480.

IRONY *A term used to talk about a contrast between reality and what seems to be real.* **Situational irony** exists when what actually happens in a situation is the opposite of what we expect to happen. For example, "The Interlopers" is ironic because the two main characters become trapped on the land that has been the subject of their feud. **Verbal irony** exists when a person says one thing and means another. For example, in "The Gift of the Magi" O. Henry wants readers to admire the selflessness of his characters, but he calls them "two foolish children in a flat who most unwisely sacrificed for each other. . . ." **Dramatic irony** occurs when the audience has important information that characters in the play do not have. For example, in *A Sunny Morning* the audience knows that the former lovers recognize each other, but each of them believes that the other is unaware.

See pages 145, 428.

JARGON *Slang that is associated with a particular career or activity.* In "Casey at the Bat," for instance, expressions such as "tore the cover off the ball" are the jargon of baseball.

See page 181.
See also WORD CHOICE.

LITERAL LANGUAGE *The ordinary language of everyday speech that states facts or ideas directly.*

See pages 63, 196.
See also FIGURATIVE LANGUAGE.

LOCAL COLOR *Literature with local color is tied in location and topic to one section of the country.* It includes the language, customs, and geography of the area. For example, Jack London uses local color of the Yukon in *The Call of the Wild.*

See page 40.

LYRIC POETRY *Poetry that expresses a speaker's personal thoughts and feelings.* Lyric poems are usually short and musical. For example, Langston Hughes expresses personal thoughts in "Dreams."

See page 208.
See also NARRATIVE POETRY.

METAPHOR *A figure of speech that makes a comparison between two seemingly unlike things.* For example, "The rhododendron was . . . a carpet of color . . ." ("A Mother in Mannville") is a metaphor.

See pages 63, 203.
See also FIGURATIVE LANGUAGE, SIMILE.

METER *A regular pattern of stressed and unstressed syllables giving a line of poetry its rhythm.* Notice the pattern of one stressed and two unstressed syllables forming the meter in this line from "The Runaway":

Ońce when the/snów of the/yéar was be/gínning
to/fáll.

See page 185.
See also RHYTHM, FOOT.

MONOLOGUE *A long speech by a character in a play,* such as Juliet's speech to Romeo in *Romeo and Juliet*, Act II, Scene ii.

See page 399.
See also SOLILOQUY.

MOOD *The emotional quality of a story—and especially of a story's setting—that influences the attitudes of characters and the readers.*

See pages 75, 304.
See also ATMOSPHERE.

NARRATION *The kind of writing or speaking that tells a story.* Narration includes novels, short stories, and narrative poetry. Narration can also be an element in biography and the essay.

See also DESCRIPTION, EXPOSITION, PERSUASION.

NARRATIVE HOOK *The point in a story, novel, or play at which the author catches reader attention by presenting an interesting problem or situation that begins the conflict.* For example, in "Beware of the Dog" the conflict begins when Williamson hears planes that he recognizes as German.

See page 10.
See also PLOT.

NARRATOR *The person who tells a story.* Sometimes the narrator is a character in the story, such as Squeaky in "Raymond's Run." Sometimes the narrator is a third-person storyteller who is not involved in the action, such as the narrator in "The Secret Life of Walter Mitty."

See also POINT OF VIEW.

NONFICTION *Factual prose writing.* Nonfiction deals with real people and experiences. It is divided into two main types: (1) the **essay**, and (2) **biography** and **autobiography**. Thurber's "Spreading 'You Know'" is an essay. Galarza's *Barrio Boy* is an autobiography.

See page 233.
See also FICTION.

NOVEL *A long work of narrative prose fiction.* The novel is almost limitless in terms of plot, character, setting, and theme. *Great Expectations* is a novel of many characters set in various parts of nineteenth-century England.

See page 491.
See also SHORT STORY, FICTION.

ONE-ACT PLAY *A drama that usually has few characters, a simple plot, and only one or a few scenes. A Sunny Morning* is a one-act play.

See page 294.
See also FULL-LENGTH PLAY.

ONOMATOPOEIA *The use of a word or phrase that actually imitates or suggests the sound of what it describes.* For example, Poe uses onomatopoeia in "The Bells":

From the jingling and the tinkling of the bells

See page 188.
See also SENSORY LANGUAGE.

PARABLE *A simple story from which a lesson should be drawn.* The biblical story of "The Prodigal Son" is an example of a parable.

See page 492.

PARALLELISM *The repeating of phrases or sentences so that the repeated parts are alike in structure or in meaning.* For example, many lines in "Knoxville, Tennessee" contain only two words, the first of which is *and.*

See page 195.
See also ALLITERATION, REPETITION, REFRAIN.

PARAPHRASE *A summary in the reader's own words of a piece of literature.* It tells briefly what the selection is about.

See page 225.
See also LITERAL LANGUAGE.

PERSONIFICATION *A figure of speech in which an animal, object, or idea is described as having human form or characteristics.* Sandburg uses personification in "Lost" when he says that the boat's whistle "Calls and cries unendingly."

See page 201.
See also FIGURATIVE LANGUAGE.

PERSUASION *A type of writing that aims to convince the reader of the author's opinion and perhaps to rouse the reader to action.* Persuasion is often found in essays—for example, in "The Spreading 'You Know.'"

See pages 263, 280.
See also ARGUMENT, DESCRIPTION, EXPOSITION, NARRATION.

PLOT *The sequence of events in a story, novel, or play, each event causing or leading to the next.* The plot begins with **exposition**, which is an introduction to characters, setting, and situations, and then catches reader attention with the **narrative**

hook. The **rising action** adds complications to the conflict and leads to the **climax**, or point of highest emotional involvement. The **falling action** presents the results of the climax, and the **resolution** gives the final outcome.

See pages 10, 273, 427, 522, 704.

POETRY *A special kind of writing in which language, imagery, and sound combine to create a special emotional effect. Poetry is usually arranged in lines, frequently has regular rhythm, and sometimes rhyme.* Types of poetry include **narrative**, **dramatic**, and **lyric**.

See pages 161, 720.
See also EPIC.

POINT OF VIEW *The relationship of the storyteller to the story.* In a story with **first-person point of view**, the story is told by one of the characters, referred to as *I*. Pip in *Great Expectations*, for instance, is a first-person narrator.

In a story with **limited third-person point of view**, the narrator tells the story from the limited viewpoint of only one character, speaking of the character as *he* or *she*. Jack London uses this point of view in *The Call of the Wild*, showing all action through Buck's eyes.

In a story with **omniscient point of view**, the author acts as an omniscient narrator who stands outside the story. Garland's "Day's Pleasure" has an omniscient narrator.

See pages 85, 94, 109, 509, 565, 712.
See also NARRATOR.

PUN *A joke based on words with several meanings, or on words that sound alike but have different meanings.* Shakespeare uses puns in *Romeo and Juliet:*

You have dancing shoes
With nimble soles; I have a soul of lead
So stakes me to the ground I cannot move.

See pages 428–429.

REPETITION *The repeating of sounds, letters, words, or lines, which helps give poetry its meaning, form, and sound.* Common forms of repetition are **alliteration, rhyme,** and **refrain.**

See page 195.

RESOLUTION *The part of a plot that ends the falling action by telling or implying the final outcome.* For example, in "Split Cherry Tree" the resolution occurs when Pa tells Mom about his day at Dave's school.

See pages 10, 426.
See also PLOT.

RHYME *The repetition of accented vowel sounds and all succeeding consonant sounds.* Rhyme occurring at the ends of lines is called **end rhyme.** Rhyme occurring within lines is called **internal rhyme.** Both are seen in Merriam's "Onomatopoeia":

gushes rushes splashes
clear water dashes

See page 187.
See also COUPLET, REPETITION, RHYME SCHEME.

RHYME SCHEME *The pattern of rhymes formed by the end rhyme in a poem.* Rhyme scheme is indicated by assigning a different letter of the alphabet to each new rhyme. For instance, the rhyme scheme for Booth's "Ego" is *ababa:*

When I was on Night Line, *a*
flying my hands to park *b*
a big-bird B-29, *a*
I used to command the dark: *b*
four engines were mine *a*

See page 187.

RHYTHM *The pattern created by arranging stressed and unstressed syllables, particularly in poetry.* Rhythm gives poetry its musical sound to help convey its meaning. Rhythm can be regular or irregular. Listen to the regular pattern of stressed and unstressed syllables in these lines from Shakespeare's "Seven Ages of Man":

All/the world's/a stage
and all/the men/and wo/men mere/ly play/ers;
They have/their ex/its and/their en/trances

See page 185.
See also FOOT, METER, BLANK VERSE.

RISING ACTION *That part of a story's plot that adds complications to the problems and increases reader interest.* For example, in "The Necklace" the action rises as the Loisels attempt to find the lost jewels and then to pay for their replacement.

See pages 10, 427.
See also PLOT.

SENSORY LANGUAGE *Language that appeals to the senses and represents concrete objects, people, or events.* Sensory language enables the reader to picture what happens in a poem or story. For example, Yeats uses sensory language in "The Song of Wandering Aengus":

And when white moths were on the wing,
And moth-like stars were flickering out.

See page 185.
See also CONCRETE LANGUAGE, FIGURATIVE LANGUAGE.

SETTING *The place and time in which a story, play, or novel happens.* In some stories the setting helps create an atmosphere, or mood, that can influence the reader as well as the characters. The dark jungle setting of "The Most Dangerous Game," for instance, heightens the tension for both character and reader.

See pages 69, 75, 304, 509, 710.

SHORT STORY *A brief fictional narrative in prose.* Elements of the short story are **plot, characterization, setting, point of view,** and **theme.**

SIMILE *A figure of speech that directly compares two seemingly unlike things using a comparing word such as* like *or* as. For example, "... holding up their bare feet from the cold floor, *like* chickens in new-fallen snow" is a simile from "A Day's Pleasure."

See pages 63, 202.
See also FIGURATIVE LANGUAGE, METAPHOR.

SOLILOQUY *In a play a long speech spoken by a character who is alone on stage.* This speech usually reveals the personal thoughts and emotions of the character. In *Romeo and Juliet* Juliet's "farewell" speech before her death is a soliloquy.

See page 399.
See also MONOLOGUE.

SPEAKER *The voice of a poem, or the role that the poet plays in a poem.* The speaker in "Sea Fever," for instance, is a sailor.

See pages 175, 177.

STAGE DIRECTIONS *Instructions for staging a play and descriptions of setting, characters, and actions.*

See pages 293, 304, 312, 327.
See also DRAMA.

STANZA *A group of lines forming a unit in a poem.* Wylie's "Velvet Shoes," for example, has four stanzas organized in the same pattern.

Let us walk in the white snow
    In a soundless space;
With footsteps quiet and slow,
    At a tranquil pace,
    Under veils of white lace.

See page 161.

STYLE *An author's choice and arrangement of words in any kind of writing.* Style often reveals the author's personality and the theme or purpose of the writing.

See page 277.

THEME *The main idea of a story, poem, novel, or play, usually expressed as a general statement about life.* The theme of "A Day's Pleasure," for example, is that life can be more pleasant when human sympathy is exchanged. Some stories have **stated themes**, which are announced directly. Most stories have **implied themes**, which are revealed gradually through the unfolding of the story, as in "Sixteen."

See pages 114, 118, 126, 327, 540.

TRAGEDY *A play in which a main character suffers a major downfall.* That character often is a person of dignified or heroic stature. The downfall may result from outside forces or from a weakness within the character. *Romeo and Juliet* is a tragedy.

See page 293.
See also DRAMA, COMEDY.

WORD CHOICE *The selection of words in a piece of literature to convey meaning, suggest attitude, and create images.* For example, "Base Stealer" uses words that capture the tension of a dramatic moment in a baseball game.

See pages 175, 181.

GLOSSARY

The following Glossary lists words that are from the selections but may be unfamiliar to you. Although many of the words have several different meanings, they are defined only as they are used in the selections. Some words may be familiar to you in other contexts but may have unusual meanings in the text.

Each Glossary entry contains a pronunciation, a part of speech, and a definition. Some words are used in more than one way in the textbook and therefore have more than one definition and occasionally more than one part of speech. Related words are often combined in one entry: The main form (for example, the adjective *callow*) is defined, and another form (for example, the noun *callowness*) is run on after the main definition. Adverbs ending in *-ly* are usually run on after the definition of the adjective form.

Some unusual words or meanings of words are labeled ARCHAIC (old-fashioned), OBSOLETE (no longer in use), RARE, or POETIC. Other special usage labels include COLLOQUIAL, SLANG, CHIEFLY BRITISH, MILITARY, and so on. Occasionally an unfamiliar idiomatic expression is used within a selection; in such cases the main word of the expression is listed, followed by a definition of the idiom.

The following abbreviations are used in this Glossary:

n.	noun	*conj.*	conjunction
v.	verb	*prep.*	preposition
adj.	adjective	*interj.*	interjection
adv.	adverb	*pl.*	plural
pron.	pronoun	*n.pl.*	plural noun

A key to pronunciations may be found in the lower right-hand corner of each right-hand page of the Glossary.

A

abash [ə bash′] *v.* to make embarrassed and ashamed.
abdicate [ab′də kāt′] *v.* to give up a high office or throne.
abstracted [ab strak′tid] *adj.* preoccupied.
abyss [ə bis′] *n.* a bottomless depth; the ocean.
accost [ə kost′] *v.* to approach and greet.
acquiesce [ak′wē es′] *v.* to agree or accept quietly. **– acquiescence,** *n.*
acute [ə kūt′] *adj.* **1.** very serious; critical. **2.** sharp; sensitive.
adjure [e joor′] *v.* to order solemnly.
admonish [ad mon′ish] *v.* to warn. **– admonition** [ad′mə nish′ən], *n.*
adornment [ə dôrn′mənt] *n.* a decoration or ornament.
adulation [aj′ə lā′shən] *n.* lavish praise or flattery.
advent [ad′vent] *n.* arrival.
adversary [ad′vər ser′ē] *n.* opponent; enemy.
affable [af′ə bəl] *adj.* pleasant; friendly.
afflict [ə flict′] *v.* to cause suffering to.
affray [ə frā′] *n.* a noisy quarrel or public fight.
affright [ə frīt′] *n.* ARCHAIC. terror.
aghast [ə gast′] *adj.* horrified.
agile [aj′əl] *adj.* moving with ease and speed.
agitation [aj′ə tā′shən] *n.* violent motion.
akin [ə kin′] *adj.* similar.
albeit [ôl bē′it] *conj.* although.
albino [al bī′nō] *n.* an animal that is white because it lacks normal coloring.
allude [ə lo͞od′] *v.* to refer in a casual or indirect way. **– allusion,** *n.*
alluring [ə loor′ing] *adj.* tempting.
amble [am′bəl] *v.* to walk in a slow, leisurely way.
amenity [ə men′ə tē, ə mē′nə-] *n.pl.* something that adds to people's comfort.
amidships [ə mid′ships′] *adv.* in or toward the middle of a ship.
amorous [am′ər əs] *adj.* in love.
analytical [an′əl it′i kəl] *adj.* examining things in detail.
anesthetizer [ə nes′thə tī′zər] *n.* a device for giving a drug or gas to make a person unconscious.
animated [an′ə mā′tid] *adj.* lively.
apathy [ap′ə thē] *n.* lack of interest.
apex [ā′peks] *n.* the highest point.
appall [ə pôl′] *v.* to fill with horror.
apparition [ap′ə rish′ən] *n.* something that comes into view unexpectedly.
appease [ə pēz′] *v.* to gain someone's favor by pleasing acts. **– appeasingly,** *adv.* **– appeasement,** *n.*
appertain [ap′ər tān′] *v.* to belong as a part; pertain.
appointments [ə point′mənts] *n.pl.* equipment.
apprehend [ap′ri hend′] *v.* capture; arrest.
appropriate [ə prō′prē āt′] *v.* to take for one's own use without permission.
ardent [ärd′ənt] *adj.* intense; glowing.
ardor [är′dər] *n.* passion; emotional warmth.
arena [ə rē′nə] *n.* a place for public meetings or entertainment.
artless [ärt′lis] *adj.* simple; innocent. **– artlessness,** *n.*
ascertain [as′ər tān′] *v.* to find out.
askew [ə skū′] *adj.* twisted to one side.
aspire [əs pīr′] *v.* to have an ambition to achieve something.
assent [ə sent′] *n.* agreement.
assertion [ə sur′shən] *n.* a statement; declaration.
assess [ə ses′] *v.* to judge the worth of.
assessor [ə ses′ər] *n.* a person who judges the value of property to be taxed.
athwart [ə thwort′] *prep.* across.
attain [ə tān′] *v.* **1.** to gain or achieve through effort. **2.** to reach; arrive at.
attribute [ə trib′ūt] *v.* to think of as caused by.
audacious [ô dā′shəs] *adj.* bold; fearless; daring. **– audacity** [ô das′ə tē], *n.*
audible [o′də bəl] *adj.* loud enough to be heard. **– audibly,** *adv.*

at; āpe; cär; end; mē; it; īce; hot; ōld; fôrk; wood; fo͞ol; oil; out; up; ūse; turn; ə in ago, taken, pencil, lemon, circus; bat; chin; dear; five; game; hit; hw in white; joke; kit; lid; man; not; singer; pail; ride; sat; shoe; tag; thin; this; very; wet; yes; zoo; zh in treasure; KH in loch, German ach; N in French bon; œ in French feu, German schön

GLOSSARY

In the Glossary you will find the more difficult words in the selection, along with pronunciations and definitions of the words as they are used in the selections. In addition, you will find the Glossary words for each selection listed in the teacher's materials for that selection in your *Teacher's Resource Book*.

aura [ôr′ə] *n.* a certain quality or atmosphere that surrounds a person or thing.
auxiliary [ôg zil′yər ē, -zil′ər ē] *n.* a thing that gives help or support.
avail [ə vāl′] *v.* to be of use to. **— avail oneself of** to take advantage of.
avaricious [av′ə rish′əs] *adj.* greedy.
aversion [ə vur′zhən, -shən] *n.* a strong dislike.
avert [ə vurt′] *v.* to turn away.
avowal [ə vou′əl] *n.* an open declaration or admission.

B

barbaric [bär bar′ik] *adj.* rough; savage; uncivilized.
battery [bat′ər ē] MILITARY. *n.* **1.** a group of heavy guns operating as a unit. **2.** a fort or other safe position.
bedlam [bed′ləm] *n.* noise and confusion.
beguile [bi gīl′] *v.* to pass (time) pleasantly.
beholden [bi hōl′dən] *adj.* owing thanks.
belie [bi lī′] *v.* to disguise; give a false impression of.
bemuse [bi mūz′] *v.* to confuse; bewilder.
benediction [ben′ə dik′shən] *n.* a blessing.
benign [bi nīn′] *adj.* kindly; gracious.
bestir [bi stur′] *v.* to rouse to action.
bestow [bi stō′] *v.* to present as a gift.
bicarbonate [bī kär′bə nit, -nāt′] **of soda** *n.* a white substance taken for stomach problems.
bicker [bik′ər] *v.* to quarrel; squabble.
blanch [blanch] *v.* to turn white or pale.
bland [bland] *adj.* dull; mildly pleasant. **— blandly,** *adv.*
blight [blīt] *n.* something that damages or destroys.
boggle [bog′əl] *v.* to be stunned or overwhelmed.
boring [bôr′ing] *n.* a hole made as if by drilling.
boutonnier [bo͞o′tən yār′] *n.* a flower or bunch of flowers worn in a buttonhole.
brazen [brā′zən] *adj.* made of or like brass.
breach [brēch] *n.* a gap; opening.
brine [brīn] *n.* sea water.
broach [brōch] *v.* to bring up; begin a discussion of.
buffet [buf′it] *v.* to hit repeatedly; knock about.
buoy [bo͞o′ē, boi] *n.* a floating object used as a marker.
buoyant [boi′ənt, bo͞o′yənt] *adj.* able to float.

C

cajole [kə jōl′] *v.* to persuade by flattery; coax.
callous [kal′əs] *adj.* unfeeling.
callow [kal′ō] *adj.* immature; inexperienced. **— callowness,** *n.*
candid [kan′did] *adj.* honest; frank. **— candidly,** *adv.*
capacious [kə pā′shəs] *adj.* roomy.
caper [kā′pər] *v.* to jump or skip around playfully.
Carborundum [kär′bə run′dəm] *n.* TRADEMARK. a very hard substance used for grinding or polishing.
carcass [kär′kəs] *n.* the dead body of an animal.
caricature [kar′ə kə chər, -choor′] *v.* to imitate.
cascade [kas kād′] *n.* a waterfall.
caterer [kā′tər ər] *n.* a person who provides food for parties.
celerity [sə ler′ə tē] *n.* speed.
censure [sen′shər] *n.* strong disapproval.
certitude [sur′tə to͞od′, -tūd′] *n.* sureness; confidence.
cessation [se sā′shən] *n.* a stopping.
chant [chant] *n.* a repetitive song or way of speaking.
chaste [chāst] *adj.* simple; not ornate.
chloroform [klôr′ə fôrm′] *n.* a liquid used to make a person or animal unconscious. *— v.* to make unconscious or kill with chloroform.
chorister [kôr′is tər, kor′-] *n.* a singer in a choir.
chronic [kron′ik] *adj.* constant.
chronicle [kron′i kəl] *n.* a record of events in time order; story.
cipher [sī′fər] *v.* to do arithmetic.
circuitous [sər kū′ə təs] *adj.* roundabout; not direct. **— circuitously,** *adv.*
clamber [klam′bər, klam′ər] *v.* to climb clumsily.
clamor [klam′ər] *v.* to make a loud noise.
clangor [klang′gər, klang′ər] *n.* loud ringing; clanging.
clarion [klar′ē ən] *adj.* clear and ringing.
clot [klot] *v.* to form into or fill with lumps; thicken.
collateral [kə lat′ər əl] *n.* something that guarantees that a debt will be paid.
collective [kə lek′tiv] *adj.* belonging to a group; shared.
commendable [kə men′də bəl] *adj.* worthy of praise.
commingle [kə ming′gəl] *v.* to mix together.
commotion [kə mō′shən] *n.* noisy confusion.
commute [kə mūt′] *v.* to change (a punishment) to a lighter one.
compel [kəm pel′] *v.* to force.
compensation [kom′pən sā′shən] *n.* something given to make up for a loss, damage, etc.
competent [kom′pət ənt] *adj.* capable. **— competently,** *adv.*
complacent [kəm plā′sənt] *adj.* satisfied. **— complacently,** *adv.*
comply [kəm plī′] *v.* to agree to; follow (a request or order).
compromise [kom′prə mīz′] *v.* to endanger the interests or reputation of.
compunction [kəm pungk′shən] *n.* sense of guilt.
conclusive [kən klo͞o′siv] *adj.* final; decisive. **— conclusively,** *adv.*
concurrence [kən kur′əns] *n.* agreement; approval.
condole [kən dōl′] *v.* to show sympathy. **— condolence,** *n.*
condone [kən dōn′] *v.* to overlook or excuse.
conduce [kən do͞os′, -dūs′] *v.* to lead to or help bring about.
confer [kən fur′] *v.* to give or grant.
confidante [kon′fə dant′, -dänt′, kon′fə dant′, -dänt′] *n.* a person to whom one reveals private thoughts and secrets.
confines [kon′fīnz] *n.pl.* borders; territory.
confirmation [kon′fər mā′shən] *n.* proof.
confiscate [kon′fis kāt′] *v.* to seize by authority or for public use.
confound [kən found′, kon-] *v.* to mix up; confuse.
confront [kən frunt′] *v.* to meet; face.
conglomerate [kən glom′ər it] *adj.* made up of various parts.
conjecture [kən jek′chər] *n.* a conclusion based on guesswork; a guess.
conscientious [kon′shē en′shəs] *adj.* doing what is right; honest; careful.
conservative [kən sur′və tiv] *adj.* traditional.
consignment [kən sīn′mənt] *n.* shipment.
consistent [kən sis′tənt] *adj.* not varying; uniform.
consternation [kon′stər nā′shən] *n.* shock or dismay that leads to confusion.
constraint [kən strānt′] *n.* a holding back of true feelings.

contemplative [kon'təm plā'tiv, kən tem'plə-] *adj.* thoughtful. **– contemplatively,** *adv.*
contemptible [kən temp'tə bəl] *adj.* deserving to be despised; worthless.
contend [kən tend'] *v.* to fight; compete.
contentious [kən ten'shəs] *adj.* tending to argue; quarrelsome.
contour [kon'toor] *n.* outline.
convention [kən ven'shən] *n.* a custom.
copious [kō'pē əs] *adj.* numerous.
corroborate [kə rob'ə rāt'] *v.* to support or confirm.
couch [kouch] *v.* express.
countenance [koun'tə nəns] *n.* a person's face.
coupling [kup'ling] *n.* a device for joining parts of machinery together.
courtier [kôr'tē ər] *n.* a person who attends a royal court.
covert [kuv'ərt, kō'vərt] *adj.* secret; disguised.
covet [kuv'it] *v.* to want; long for.
cranium [krā'nē əm] *n.* skull.
craven [krā'vən] *adj.* cowardly.
credulity [kri dōō'li tē, -dū'-] *n.* willingness to believe too easily.
crevice [krev'is] *n.* a narrow crack.
crystalline [krist'əl in, -īn'] *adj.* clear; transparent.
cur [kur] *n.* a mean, cowardly person.
curio [kyoor'ē ō'] *n.* an unusual object.
cynicism [sin'ə siz'əm] *n.* belief that people act for reasons of selfishness.

D

dab [dab] *n.* BRITISH COLLOQUIAL. an expert.
dainty [dān'tē] *n.* a delicious food; delicacy.
damsel [dam'zəl] *n.* ARCHAIC. a young, unmarried woman.
dank [dangk] *adj.* unpleasantly damp.
dappled [dap'əld] *adj.* spotted.
dauntless [dônt'lis] *adj.* fearless.
decree [di krē'] *n.* an official order.
degenerate [di jen'ə rāt'] *v.* to fall to a lower condition.
deign [dān] *v.* to consider something good enough for oneself.
dejected [di jek'tid] *adj.* sad; depressed.
delirious [di lēr'ē əs] *adj.* in a state of mental confusion; imagining things.
denounce [di nouns'] *v.* to attack; criticize.
deplorable [di plôr'ə bəl] *adj.* that should be disapproved of.
depreciate [di prē'shē āt'] *v.* to make seem of less value.
depute [di pūt'] *v.* to give authority.
deride [di rīd'] *v.* to laugh at; make fun of. **– derision** [di rizh'ən], *n.* **– derisive** [di rī'siv], *adj.*
derive [di rīv'] *v.* to figure out; conclude.
descry [di skrī'] *v.* to catch sight of.
designing [di zī'ning] *adj.* sly and scheming.
desolate [des'ə lit] *adj.* lonely; forlorn. **– desolately,** *adv.*
deter [di tur'] *v.* to discourage or prevent from doing something.
devious [dē'vē əs] *adj.* not honest or direct.
dexterity [deks ter'ə tē] *n.* skill in using the hands or body.
dictation [dik tā'shən] *n.* the act of saying or reading something for another person to write down.
didactic [dī dak'tik] *adj.* instructive; informative.
disarming [dis är'ming] *adj.* reducing distrust or hostility.
discern [di surn', -zurn'] *v.* to perceive; detect; make out. **– discernible,** *adj.*
discompose [dis'kəm pōz'] *v.* to make uneasy or nervous. **– discomposure** [-pō'zhər], *n.*
disconsolate [dis kon'sə lit] *adj.* unable to be comforted; hopelessly sad.
discreet [dis krēt'] *adj.* showing good judgment in what one says and does.
discrepancy [dis krep'ən sē] *n.* difference.
disintegrate [dis in'tə grāt'] *v.* to break into parts.
disinterested [dis in'tris tid, -in'tər is-, -in'tə res'-] *adj.* not having selfish motives. **– disinterestedness,** *n.*
dismember [dis mem'bər] *v.* to cut or tear off the limbs of.
dispatch [dis pach'] *v.* to finish quickly. *– n.* a message.
dispossess [dis'pə zes'] *v.* to take away one's property.
dissect [di sekt', dī-] *v.* to cut up into parts.
dissemble [di sem'bəl] *v.* to disguise true facts or feelings.
dissimulation [di sim'yə lā'shən] *n.* the disguising of one's feelings or intentions.
distracted [dis trak'tid] *adj.* confused; worried.
distraught [dis trôt'] *adj.* very troubled.
diverting [di vur'ting, dī-] *adj.* amusing; entertaining.
divide [di vīd'] *v.* a ridge.
divine [di vīn'] *v.* to guess.
dogged [dô'gid] *adj.* determined; stubborn.
doleful [dōl'fəl] *adj.* sad; mournful.
domination [dom'ə nā'shən] *n.* control; rule.
dowry [dour'ē] *n.* the money or property that a woman brings to her marriage.
draggle [drag'əl] *v.* to make wet and dirty by dragging on the ground.
drastic [dras'tik] *adj.* severe; extreme.
drear [drēr] *adj.* POETIC. dreary; gloomy.
droll [drōl] *adj.* amusing in an odd way.
drop [drop] *n.* **– to have the drop on** SLANG. to have an advantage over.
drove [drōv] *n.* herd; flock; crowd.
dung [dung] *n.* manure.

E

egress [ē'gres] *n.* exit.
elate [i lāt'] *v.* to make proud or joyful.
eloquence [el'ə kwəns] *n.* forceful, persuasive speech.
encumber [en kum'bər] *v.* to hold back; hinder; burden.
engender [en jen'dər] *v.* to cause to grow.
enhance [en hans'] *v.* to make better or greater.
enigmatic [en'ig mat'ik, ē'nig-] *adj.* mysterious; puzzling.
ennui [än wē'] *n.* a feeling of weariness and boredom.
enterprising [en'tər prī'zing] *adj.* full of energy and ambition.
entrails [en'trālz, -trəlz] *n.pl.* the organs inside the body.
entreat [en trēt'] *v.* to beg.

at; āpe; cär; end; mē; it; īce; hot; ōld; fôrk; wood; fōōl; oil; out; up; ūse; turn; ə in ago, taken, pencil, lemon, circus; bat; chin; dear; five; game; hit; hw in white; joke; kit; lid; man; not; singer; pail; ride; sat; shoe; tag; thin; this; very; wet; yes; zoo; zh in treasure; KH in loch, German ach; N in French bon; œ in French feu, German schön

enunciation [i nun'sē ā'shən] *n.* clarity of pronunciation.
epic [ep'ik] *adj.* like a long poem about the adventures of a hero; heroic; impressive.
essence [es'əns] *n.* the basic nature of something.
evade [i vād'] *v.* to avoid or escape.
evoke [i vōk'] *v.* to call forth; bring out.
exhilarate [ig zil'ə rāt'] *v.* to make lively or excited.
exorbitant [ig zôr'bə tənt] *adj.* higher or greater than is reasonable.
expedient [iks pē'dē ənt] *adj.* **1.** based on selfish interests. **2.** useful for achieving a purpose; convenient. **— expediency,** *n.*
expound [iks pound'] *v.* to state or explain in detail.
expressly [iks pres'lē] *adv.* for a certain purpose; specifically.
extremity [iks trem'ə tē] *n.* the greatest or highest degree.
extricate [eks'trə kāt'] *v.* to set free; remove.
exult [ig zult'] *v.* to be joyful; rejoice.

F

faculty [fak'əl tē] *n.* a power of the mind.
fain [fān] *adj.* ARCHAIC. glad; willing.
fancy [fan'sē] *v.* to imagine; suppose.
fare [fār] *v.* to get along; manage.
farinaceous [far'ə nā'shəs] *adj.* like flour; mealy.
fastidious [fas tid'ē əs] *adj.* difficult to please; critical. **— fastidiousness,** *n.*
feign [fān] *v.* to pretend.
finagle [fi nā'gəl] *v.* COLLOQUIAL. to use trickery or craftiness to get something.
fissure [fish'ər] *n.* a deep crack.
flighty [flī'tē] *adj.* silly; slightly crazy.
florid [flôr'id, flor'-] *adj.* showy; ornate.
flush [flush] *v.* to drive from cover. *—adv.* squarely; directly.
forfeiture [fôr'fi chər] *n.* the act of giving something up.
formidable [fôr'mi də bəl] *adj.* causing fear or awe.
founder [foun'dər] *v.* to sink.
fraught [frôt] *adj.* filled.
frigid [frij'id] *adj.* cold; formal.
frivolous [friv'ə ləs] *adj.* unimportant; trivial.
froth [frôth] *v.* to foam.
fuddle [fud'əl] *n.* confusion.
fugitive [fū'jə tiv] *n.* a person who flees from justice.
futile [fū'til, -tīl] *adj.* useless; hopeless. **— futilely,** *adv.* **— futility** [fū til'ə tē], *n.*
furl [furl] *v.* to roll up.

G

gabble [gab'əl] *v.* to chatter.
gad [gad] *v.* to wander around.
gallivant [gal'ə vant'] *v.* to roam around in search of excitement.
gamut [gam'ət] *n.* the entire range.
garble [gär'bəl] *v.* to mix up; distort.
gesticulation [jes tik'yə lā'shən] *n.* a gesture.
giddy [gid'ē] *adj.* causing dizziness.
girdler [gur'dlər] *n.* a person or thing that surrounds.
glut [glut] *n.* a supply greater than required; excess.
gnarled [närld] *adj.* twisted and lumpy.
gondola [gon'də lə] *n.* a railroad freight car with low sides and no top.
grapple [grap'əl] *v.* a hand-to-hand fight.
gringo [gring'gō] *n.* in Latin America a foreigner, especially when American or English.
guile [gīl] *n.* slyness; craftiness; deceit.
gut [gut] *n.* cord made from animal intestines, used for strings on musical instruments.

H

haggard [hag'ərd] *adj.* looking wasted and worn.
hale [hāl] *adj.* free of defects; sound.
hapless [hap'lis] *adj.* unlucky.
harry [har'ē] *v.* to torment; trouble.
haversack [hav'ər sak'] *n.* a canvas bag for carrying provisions.
hawker [hô'kər] *n.* a peddlar.
hearken [här'kən] *v.* to listen; pay attention.
heft [heft] *n.* weight; heaviness.
hew [hū] *v.* to cut with blows from a knife or ax.
heyday [hā'dā'] *n.* the period of greatest strength or prosperity.
hinder [hin'dər] *adj.* back; rear.
hinterland [hin'tər land'] *n.* a region far from cities or towns.
hulk [hulk] *n.* a ship.
hurtle [hurt'əl] *v.* to move quickly and with great force or noise.

I

ignominious [ig'nə min'ē əs] *adj.* shameful; disgraceful. **— ignominiously,** *adv.*
imbrue [im bro͞o'] *v.* to soak or stain.
immaculate [i mak'yə lit] *adj.* completely clean; spotless.
impact [im'pakt] *n.* force; power.
impair [im pār'] *v.* to damage; weaken.
impart [im pärt'] *v.* to give; tell; reveal.
impartial [im pär'shəl] *adj.* not favoring one more than another; fair.
impassioned [im pash'ənd] *adj.* filled with strong feeling.
impediment [im ped'ə mənt] *n.* something that blocks or delays.
impel [im pel'] *v.* to force; urge.
impending [im pen'ding] *adj.* about to happen; threatening.
imperative [im per'ə tiv] *adj.* urgent; necessary.
imperial [im pēr'ē əl] *adj.* majestic.
imperious [im pēr'ē əs] *adj.* ruling over others; overly proud; scornful.
implant [im plant'] *v.* to set firmly or deeply.
imposing [im pō'zing] *adj.* causing awe because of great size or dignity.
impress [im pres'] *v.* to mark by pressing.
inaccessible [in'ək ses'ə bəl] *adj.* not able to be approached or talked to. **— inaccessibility** [in'ək ses'ə bil'ə tē], *n.*
inarticulate [in'är tik'yə lit] *adj.* not understandable.
inaudible [in ô'də bəl] *adj.* not loud enough to be heard. **— inaudibility,** *n.*
incalculable [in kal'kyə lə bəl] *adj.* too great to be counted.
incarnation [in'kär nā'shən] *n.* the visible form of a quality or idea.
incessant [in ses'ənt] *adj.* never stopping; constant. **— incessantly,** *adv.*

inclusive [in klo͞o'siv] *adj.* including or covering everything. **—inclusively,** *adv.*
incoherent [in'kō hēr'ənt, -her'-] *adj.* not connected or ordered; confused. **—incoherently,** *adv.*
inconsequential [in kon'sə kwen'chəl] *adj.* unimportant.
inconsistency [in'kən sis'tən sē] *n.* lack of agreement.
incorrigible [in kôr'ə jə bəl, -kor'-] *adj.* not capable of being changed or corrected.
incorruptible [in'kə rup'tə bəl] *adj.* that cannot be bribed or made immoral.
incubator [ing'kyə bā'tər, in'-] *n.* a container for growing bacteria, etc.
indolent [ind'əl ənt] *adj.* lazy. **—indolently,** *adv.*
induce [in do͞os', -dūs'] *v.* persuade.
ineffectual [in'i fek'cho͞o əl] *adj.* not getting the desired result. **—ineffectually,** *adv.*
inexplicable [in'iks plik'ə bəl, in eks'pli kə-] *adj.* not explainable or understandable.
inextricable [in eks'tri kə bəl, -iks trik'ə bəl] *adj.* that cannot be untangled, untied, or solved. **—inextricably,** *adv.*
infuse [in fūz'] *v.* to fill; inspire.
initiative [i nish'ə tiv] *n.* the ability to take the lead in ideas and actions.
innards [in'ərdz] *n.pl.* the organs inside the body.
innocuous [i nok'ū əs] *adj.* harmless; not offensive. **—innocuously,** *adv.*
inscrutable [in skro͞o'tə bəl] *adj.* difficult to understand; mysterious.
insensible [in sen'sə bəl] *adj.* unconscious.
inseparable [in sep'ər ə bəl, -sep'rə-] *adj.* not able to be separated.
insidious [in sid'ē əs] *adj.* working in a slow, subtle, and harmful way.
insinuate [in sin'ū āt'] *v.* to hint; suggest. **—insinuatingly,** *adv.*
insolent [in'sə lənt] *adj.* bold; arrogant.
instantaneous [in'stən tā'nē əs] *adj.* happening without delay; immediate.
instigate [in'stə gāt'] *v.* **1.** to urge on. **2.** to cause. **—instigation** [in'stə gā'shən], *n.*
instinctive [in stingk'tiv] *adj.* natural; automatic.
insubordination [in'sə bôrd'ən ā'shən] *n.* disobedience.
insufferable [in suf'ər ə bəl] *adj.* unbearable.
insular [in'sə lər, ins'yə-] *adj.* cut off; isolated.
integrity [in teg'rə tē] *n.* honesty; sincerity.
intellectual [int'əl ek'cho͞o əl] *adj.* appealing to the mind or reason.
intent [in tent'] *adj.* firmly fixed.
interloper [in'tər lo'pər] *n.* someone who meddles in other people's business.
interminable [in tur'mi nə bəl] *adj.* endless.
interpose [in'tər pōz'] *v.* to come between; step in.
intimate [in'tə māt'] *v.* to hint; suggest.
intolerant [in tol'ər ənt] *adj.* not willing to endure.
intoxication [in tok'sə kā'shən] *n.* great excitement or joy.
intricate [in'tri kit] *adj.* full of detail; complicated. **—intricately,** *adv.*
invariable [in vār'ē ə bəl] *adj.* not changing; always the same. **—invariably,** *adv.*
invocation [in'və kā'shən] *n.* a call or prayer for support or inspiration.
involuntary [in vol'ən ter'ē] *adj.* done without choice or control. **—involuntarily,** *adv.*
irresolute [i rez'ə lo͞ot'] *adj.* uncertain how to act; wavering. **—irresolutely,** *adv.*

J

jocose [jō kōs'] *adj.* joking; playful; merry.
justify [jus'tə fī'] *v.* to prove to be just or right. **—justification** [jus'tə fə kā' shən], *n.*

K

ken [ken] *n.* RARE. range of vision.

L

lacerate [las'ə rāt'] *v.* to tear jaggedly.
languor [lang'gər] *n.* tiredness; weakness.
lapse [laps] *v.* to slip or fall.
larceny [lär'sə nē] *n.* theft; robbery.
larder [lär'dər] *n.* a place where food is stored; pantry.
latent [lāt'ənt] *adj.* present but not visible or developed.
lavish [lav'ish] *adj.* overly generous.
legitimate [li jit'ə mit] *adj.* having just cause; reasonable. **—legitimately,** *adv.*
liability [lī'ə bil'ə tē] *n.* legal obligation; responsibility.
liberal [lib'ər əl, lib'rəl] *adj.* large; ample.
limbo [lim'bō] *n.* a condition of forgetfulness or neglect.
lingo [ling'gō] *n.* SLANG. language.
lithe [līth] *adj.* bending and moving easily.
livid [liv'id] *adj.* discolored; black-and-blue.
loam [lōm] *n.* a rich soil.
loll [lol] *v.* to hang loosely; droop.
lotus [lō'təs] *n.* a water lily.
lout [lout] *n.* a clumsy person.
ludicrous [lo͞o'də krəs] *adj.* ridiculous.
lull [lul] *v.* to calm; soothe. *n.* a period of quiet or calm.

M

magistrate [maj'is trāt', -trit] *n.* a local judge. **—magisterial** [maj'is tēr'ē əl], *adj.*
magnetize [mag'nə tīz'] *v.* to charm; hypnotize.
malign [mə līn'] *v.* to speak badly of; give false reports about.
malignant [mə lig'nənt] *adj.* wishing evil or harm.
malingerer [mə ling'gər ər] *n.* a person who pretends to be sick to avoid work.
mandate [man'dāt] *n.* an official order.
manifest [man'ə fest'] *adj.* clear; obvious.
marauder [mə rô'dər] *n.* someone who roams around raiding and looting.
marrowbone [mar'ō bōn'] *n.* a bone containing soft, fatty tissue.
maudlin [môd'lin] *adj.* foolishly sentimental.

at; āpe; cär; end; mē; it; īce; hot; ōld; fôrk; wood; fo͞ol; oil; out; up; ūse; turn; ə in ago, taken, pencil, lemon, circus; bat; chin; dear; five; game; hit; hw in white; joke; kit; lid; man; not; singer; pail; ride; sat; shoe; tag; thin; this; very; wet; yes; zoo; zh in treasure; KH in loch, German ach; N in French bon; œ in French feu, German schön

melancholy [mel'ən kol'ē] *n.* sad; gloomy.
merge [murj] *v.* to combine.
millet [mil'it] *n.* a kind of grain.
mimicry [mim'ik rē] *n.* the act of copying or imitating.
ministration [min'is trā'shən] *n.* the act of giving help or care.
miscreant [mis'krē ənt] *n.* a criminal; villain.
misdemeanor [mis'di mē'nər] *n.* a minor crime.
mission [mish'ən] *n.* a special purpose in life.
mollify [mol'ə fī'] *v.* to soften the anger of.
molten [mōlt'ən] *adj.* melted; liquified.
moor[1] [moor] *v.* to tie or anchor (a ship) in place.
moor[2] [moor] *n.* an area of open, wild land, often marshy. **—moorlike,** *adj.*
mottled [mot'əld] *adj.* spotted or streaked with color.
multihued [mul'ti hūd'] *adj.* having many colors.
multitudinous [mul'tə to͞od'ən əs, -tūd'-] *adj.* numerous.
muster [mus'tər] *v.* to gather; summon up.
mutilate [mūt'əl āt'] *v.* to cut off or destroy a limb or other part of a person.
mutual [mū'cho͞o əl] *adj.* felt by two people toward each other.

N

nettle [net'əl] *n.* a plant with stinging hairs.
newfangled [no͞o'fang'gəld, nū'-] *adj.* new in style; modern.
nicety [nī'sə tē] *n.* something elegant or refined.
nigh [nī] *adv.* ARCHAIC. nearly.
nimble [nim'bəl] *adj.* moving quickly and lightly.

O

obscure [əb skyoor'] *adj.* not well-known.
obsession [əb sesh'ən] *n.* an idea that greatly occupies or haunts the mind.
obstruction [əb struk'shən] *n.* something that blocks the way; obstacle.
obtrusive [əb tro͞o'siv] *adj.* very noticeable in an annoying way.
odyssey [od'ə sē] *n.* a long wandering or journey.
offing [ô'fing, of'ing] *n.* the distant part of the sea seen from the shore.
ominous [om'ə nəs] *adj.* suggesting future evil; threatening **—ominously,** *adv.*
onslaught [ôn'slôt', on'-] *n.* an attack.
opaqueness [ō pāk'nis] *n.* darkness.
opiate [ō'pē it, -āt'] *n.* something that quiets or soothes.
opulence [op'yə ləns] *n.* wealth; luxury.
ordain [ôr dān'] *v.* to order; decree.
overture [ō'vər choor', -chər] *n.* an offer to begin something.

P

palate [pal'it] *n.* **1.** the roof of the mouth. **2.** the sense of taste.
palatial [pə lā'shəl] *adj.* like a palace; large and stately.
pall [pôl] *n.* a dark covering.
palpable [pal'pə bəl] *adj.* able to be felt.
palpitate [pal'pə tāt'] *v.* to beat rapidly.
pandemonium [pan'də mō'nē əm] *n.* wild uproar or confusion.
panorama [pan'ə ram'ə, -rä'mə] *n.* a complete view in all directions.
par [pär] *n.* the average amount.
parapet [par'ə pit, -pet'] *n.* a railing.
partition [pär tish'ən] *n.* a wall or other divider.
passive [pas'iv] *adj.* not active; lacking in energy. **—passiveness,** *n.*
patent [pat'ənt, pāt'ənt] *adj.* obvious.
pauper [pô'pər] *n.* a very poor person.
peaked [pēkt, pē'kid] *adj.* having a peak; pointed.
pending [pen'ding] *adj.* about to happen.
pent [pent] *adj.* kept in; shut up.
perception [pər sep'shən] *n.* understanding; insight.
perfunctory [pər fungk'tər ē] *adj.* routine; superficial; mechanical. **—perfunctorily,** *adv.*
perpetual [pər pech'o͞o əl] *adj.* constant; continual; eternal. **—perpetually,** *adv.*
pervade [pər vād'] *v.* to spread throughout.
pestilential [pes'tə len'shəl] *adj.* annoying; harmful.
phenomenal [fə nom'ən əl] *adj.* extraordinary.
phosphoric [fos fôr'ik, -for'-] *adj.* shining; glowing.
pike [pīk] *n.* a sharp point.
pillage [pil'ij] *v.* to rob by violence; loot.
pinion [pin'yən] *v.* to tie or hold firmly.
placate [plā'kāt, plak'āt] *v.* to soothe the anger of; give in to. **—placatingly,** *adv.*
platoon [plə toon'] *n.* a small unit in an army, etc.
pliant [plī'ənt] *adj.* easily bent; flexible.
plight [plīt] *n.* condition; situation.
plumb [plum] *adv.* exactly.
plunder [plun'dər] *v.* to rob by force, especially in war.
plush [plush] *n.* a soft, thick fabric, similar to velvet, often used for upholstery.
ply [plī] *v.* to perform or work at steadily.
point-blank [point'blangk'] *adv.* directly; bluntly.
pointed [poin'tid] *adj.* obvious; emphasized. **—pointedly,** *adv.*
poise [poiz] *n.* dignity and relaxed self-confidence.
ponder [pon'dər] *v.* to think deeply.
ponderous [pon'dər əs] *adj.* extremely heavy.
precarious [pri kār'ē əs] *adj.* not stable or secure. **—precariously,** *adv.*
precedence [pres'ə dəns, pri sēd'əns] *n.* the right to go before in order or importance.
precipitate [pri sip'ə tāt'] *v.* to cause.
precipitous [pri sip'ə təs] *adj.* containing precipices or cliffs.
predicate [pred'i kāt'] *v.* to base on something.
predominate [pri dom'ə nāt'] *v.* to be greater in number or strength.
preeminent [prē em'ə nənt] *adj.* surpassing others; outstanding. **—preeminently,** *adv.*
preoccupation [prē ok'yə pā'shən] *n.* the state of being completely occupied or absorbed.
presumable [pri zo͞o'mə bəl] *adj.* capable of being taken for granted; probable. **—presumably,** *adv.*
presumptuous [pri zump'cho͞o əs, -shəs] *adj.* overly bold or confident.
primeval [prī'mē vəl] *adj.* of the earliest time.
privation [prī vā'shən] *n.* lack of basic necessities or comforts.
proclaim [prə klām'] *v.* to announce.
procure [prə kyoor'] *v.* to get; obtain.

prodigious [prə dij'əs] *adj.* enormous.
prodigy [prod'ə jē] *n.* an unusually talented child.
profess [prə fes'] *v.* to work at as a profession.
proffer [prof'ər] *v.* to offer.
profound [prə found'] *adj.* having deep understanding or insight.
profusion [prə fū'zhən] *n.* plentiful supply; abundance.
prosaic [prō zā'ik] *adj.* ordinary; commonplace.
prostrate [pros'trāt] *adj.* lying flat.
protozoa [prō'tə zō'ə] *n.pl.* single-celled microscopic animals.
provident [prov'ə dənt] *adj.* providing for the future.
provocation [prov'ə kā'shən] *n.* cause for an action or feeling.
prowess [prou'is] *n.* extraordinary ability or skill.
prudent [pro͞od'ənt] *adj.* careful; cautious. **–prudence,** *n.*
pulsate [pul'sāt] *v.* to beat or move rhythmically.
purl [purl] *v.* to ripple; move with a murmuring sound.

Q

quality [kwol'ə tē] *n.* position or role.
quarry [kwôr'ē, kwor'ē] *v.* to dig out.
quest [kwest] *v.* to search for.

R

radical [rad'i kəl] *adj.* extreme.
rail [rāl] *v.* to complain bitterly.
raillery [rā'lər ē] *n.* good-natured teasing.
rakish [rā'kish] *adj.* carelessly stylish; dashing. **–rakishly,** *adv.*
rampant [ram'pənt] *adj.* wild; not controlled.
rank and file *n.* the ordinary members of a group, rather than the leaders. **–rank-and-file,** *adj.*
ravage [rav'ij] *n.* damage; destruction.
rebuff [ri buf'] *n.* a cold refusal of an offer of help or friendship.
rebuke [ri būk'] *v.* to scold sharply.
recede [ri sēd'] *v.* to move back or away.
rectitude [rek'tə to͞od', -tūd'] *n.* correctness.
recurrent [ri kur'ənt] *adj.* occurring repeatedly.
refectory [ri fek'tər ē] *n.* the dining hall of a school, monastery, etc.
referendum [ref'ə ren'dəm] *n.* a vote on a law.
regale [ri gāl'] *v.* to entertain.
reiteration [rē it'ə rā'shən] *n.* repetition.
reminiscence [rem'ə nis'əns] *n.* a memory; recollection.
renowned [ri nound'] *adj.* famous.
rent [rent] *n.* a hole or tear.
reparation [rep'ə rā'shən] *n.* a making up for something.
repel [ri pel'] *v.* to disgust.
replenish [ri plen'ish] *v.* to fill or supply again.
repose [ri pōz'] *v.* to place.
repository [ri poz'ə tôr'e] *n.* a place or container for storing things safely.
representative [rep'ri zen'tə tiv] *adj.* being a typical example.
repress [ri pres'] *v.* to hold in or keep down.
repugnance [ri pug'nəns] *n.* strong dislike or distaste.
repulsive [ri pul'siv] *adj.* disgusting.
resolute [rez'ə lo͞ot'] *adj.* decided; resolved; determined.
resolution [rez'ə lo͞o'shən] *n.* determination; resolve.
resort [ri zôrt'] *n.* a person who is turned to for help.
respite [res'pit] *n.* a period of rest or relief.
restitution [res'tə to͞o'shən, -tū'-] *n.* replacement or repayment.
restraint [ri strānt'] *n.* a holding back; control.
retaliate [ri tal'ē āt'] *v.* to repay an injury or wrong with the same.
reticent [ret'ə sənt] *adj.* reluctant to speak; reserved.
rev [rev] *v.* to speed up (an engine).
revelation [rev'ə lā'shən] *n.* something remarkable that is made known.
reverberate [ri vur'bə rāt'] *v.* to echo repeatedly; resound.
revere [ri vēr'] *v.* to feel deep respect and love for.
revival [ri vī'vəl] *n.* a coming back into being or use.
rhetoric [ret'ər ik] *n.* showy language.
rigorous [rig'ər əs] *adj.* harsh; strict.
ritual [rich'o͞o əl] *adj.* relating to a religious ceremony.
rivet [riv'it] *n.* a metal bolt.
rosette [rō zet'] *n.* an ornament resembling a rose.
rowdy [rou'dē] *n.* a rough, disorderly person.
ruction [ruk'shən] *n.* COLLOQUIAL. an uproar; disturbance.
ruddy [rud'ē] *adj.* having a healthy reddish color.
rude [ro͞od] *adj.* roughly made or done.
rueful [ro͞o'fəl] *adj.* regretful. **–ruefully,** *adv.*
ruminate [ro͞o'mə nāt'] *v.* to go over something in the mind; ponder. **–rumination,** *n.*
ruse [ro͞oz] *n.* a trick.
russet [rus'it] *adj.* yellowish- or reddish-brown.

S

Sabbath [sab'əth] *n.* the day of the week set aside for rest and worship.
sacrilegious [sak'rə lij'əs, -lē'jəs] *adj.* showing disrespect toward God or religion.
sagacious [sə gā'shəs] *adj.* having sound judgment; clever. **–sagacity** [sə gas'ə tē], *n.*
sage [sāj] *adj.* wise.
salient [sāl'yənt, sā'lē ənt] *adj.* noticeable; striking.
sate [sāt] *v.* to make tired or disgusted by giving more than enough.
scourge [skurj] *v.* to cause suffering to or punish.
scrollwork [skrōl'wurk'] *n.* ornamental work containing shapes like loosely rolled sheets of paper.
scruple [skro͞o'pəl] *n.* a hesitation about doing something that may be wrong.
scrutiny [skro͞ot'ən ē] *n.* a careful study or examination.
seamark [sē'märk'] *n.* an object that serves as a guide for ships.
season [sē'zən] *v.* to become ready for use; age or dry out.
seasonal [sē'zə nəl] *adj.* happening in a certain season.
sedative [sed'ə tiv] *n.* something that reduces nervousness.
semblance [sem'bləns] *n.* appearance; form.

at; āpe; cär; end; mē; it; īce; hot; ōld; fôrk; wood; fo͞ol; oil; out; up; ūse; turn; ə in ago, taken, pencil, lemon, circus; bat; chin; dear; five; game; hit; hw in white; joke; kit; lid; man; not; singer; pail; ride; sat; shoe; tag; thin; this; very; wet; yes; zoo; zh in treasure; KH in loch, German ach; N in French bon; œ in French feu, German schön

sensuous [sen'sho͞o əs] *adj.* appealing to the senses.
servile [sur'vil, -vīl] *adj.* lacking self-respect; timid and obedient.
shank [shangk] *n.* the straight, narrow part of something.
shaver [shā'vər] *n.* COLLOQUIAL. a boy.
sheathe [shēth] *v.* to pull back or in; cover.
shipwright [ship'rīt'] *n.* a person who builds and repairs ships.
shroud [shroud] *n.* a cloth for wrapping a body for burial.
shun [shun] *v.* to stay away from; avoid.
singularity [sing'gyə lar'ə tē] *n.* uniqueness.
sinker [sing'kər] *n.* a weight used in fishing.
slander [slan'dər] *n.* a false and harmful statement made about a person. —*v.* to say something false and harmful about.
slaver [slav'ər] *v.* to slobber or drool.
slink [slingk] *v.* to sneak.
smite [smīt] *v.* to hit hard.
smolder [smōl'dər] *v.* to exist while being held back or stifled.
smote [smōt] past tense of **smite**.
sociological [sō'sē ə loj'i kəl, sō'shē-] *adj.* having to do with society.
solicitous [sə lis'ə təs] *adj.* showing concern. —**solicitously,** *adv.*
sorrel [sor'əl, sor'-] *adj.* reddish-brown.
sound [sound] *adj.* sensible.
souse [sous] *v.* to plunge.
span [span] *v.* to reach across.
spare [spār] *adj.* thin.
spasm [spaz'əm] *n.* a sudden, violent movement or activity.
specter [spek'tər] *n.* a ghost. —**spectral,** *adj.*
spectrum [spek'trəm] *n.* the bands of color that make up white light.
speculative [spek'yə lā'tiv, -lə tiv] *adj.* pondering; reflective. —**speculatively,** *adv.*
spellbound [spel'bound'] *adj.* entranced; fascinated.
spindly [spind'lē] *adj.* tall and very thin.
spume [spūm] *n.* foam.
spurn [spurn] *v.* to reject scornfully.
squadron [skwod'rən] *n.* a unit in an air force, navy, etc.
squalid [skwol'id] *adj.* filthy; miserable.
staccato [stə kä'tō] *adj.* made up of abrupt, separate sounds.
staff [staf] *n.* a pole.
stain [stān] *v.* to spoil; disgrace.
static [stat'ik] *adj.* at rest; not moving.
steadfast [sted'fast', -fəst] *adj.* firm; fixed. —**steadfastly,** *adv.*
stealthy [stel'thē] *adj.* secret; sly; sneaky. —**stealthily,** *adv.*
stifle [stī'fəl] *v.* to hold back or cut off; smother; muffle.
stimulate [stim'yə lāt'] *v.* to cause to act; spur on.
stipulation [stip'yə lā'shən] *n.* a point or condition of an agreement.
strait [strāt] *n.* **1.** a narrow passage between two large bodies of water. **2.** a difficult or upsetting situation.
stratagem [strat'ə jəm] *n.* a clever plan or trick for achieving something.
stricken [strik'ən] *adj.* overwhelmed by sorrow or distress.
stronghold [strông'hōld'] *n.* a place strengthened against attack; fortress.
stupendous [sto͞o pen'dəs, stū-] *adj.* amazingly large.
submission [səb mish'ən] *n.* a giving in to the power or control of another.
subordinate [sə bôr'də nit] *adj.* below another in rank.
subside [səb sīd'] *v.* to sink.
subterfuge [sub'tər fūj'] *n.* a plan or trick used to hide or avoid something.
succor [suk'ər] *n.* help or relief.
suffice [sə fīs'] *v.* to be enough.
suffuse [sə fūz'] *v.* to spread over and fill (with light or liquid, etc.).
sullen [sul'ən] *adj.* gloomy and bad-tempered.
summary [sum'ər ē] *adj.* prompt; hasty.
sump [sump] *n.* a pit for storing liquids.
sunder [sun'dər] *v.* to break apart; separate.
sundry [sun'drē] *adj.* various.
superficial [so͞o'pər fish'əl] *adj.* on the surface; obvious; apparent.
superfluous [soo pur'flo͞o əs] *adj.* unnecessary; extra.
suppliant [sup'lē ənt] *n.* one who asks humbly.
supposition [sup'ə zish'ən] *n.* something that is believed or imagined.
surcharge [sur chärj', sur'chärj'] *v.* to fill or load beyond normal.
surf-cast [surf'kast'] *v.* to fish from or near the seashore.
surfeit [sur'fit] *v.* to supply more than enough.
surmise [sər mīz'] *v.* to guess; imagine.
surpass [sər pas'] *v.* to be greater or better than.
surreptitious [sur'əp tish'əs] *adj.* secret; sneaking. —**surreptitiously,** *adv.*
susceptible [sə sep'tə bəl] *adj.* easily affected or influenced; sensitive. —**susceptibility,** *n.*
suspend [sə spend'] *v.* to stop or put off.
sustain [sə stān'] *v.* to support; nourish.
symmetrical [si met'ri kəl] *adj.* having sides or parts that match in form; even.

T

tallow [tal'ō] *n.* a fat from animals, used for making candles.
tally [tal'ē] *v.* to count.
talon [tal'ən] *n.* a claw.
tangible [tan'jə bəl] *adj.* capable of being touched.
tapestry [tap'is trē] *n.* a heavy woven cloth used as a wall hanging.
tartar [tär'tər] *n.* a hard deposit on teeth.
tattoo [ta to͞o'] *n.* a drumming sound.
taunt [tônt, tänt] *v.* to jeer at; insult or make fun of.
taut [tôt] *adj.* **1.** pulled or stretched tightly. **2.** trim.
teem [tēm] *v.* to be full or overflowing.
tempered [tem'pərd] *adj.* having been brought to the desired hardness.
thrive [thrīv] *v.* to be successful.
thriven past participle of **thrive**.
throes [thrōz] *n.pl.* a condition of pain or struggle.
throttle [throt'əl] *v.* to slow down (a vehicle) by pulling a lever that reduces the flow of fuel vapor.
till [til] *v.* to prepare and use (land) for raising crops.
tissue [tish'o͞o] *n.* a web; mesh.
titanic [tī tan'ik] *adj.* very powerful.
tithe [tīth] *n.* a tax.

transaction [tran sak'shən, -zak'-] *n.* a business dealing.
transient [tran'shənt] *adj.* staying for a short time; temporary.
transpire [tran spīr'] *v.* to happen.
travail [trə vāl', trav'āl] *n.* great pain; agony.
trek [trek] *n.* a journey or part of a journey.
tremulous [trem'yə ləs] *adj.* trembling; shaking.
tresses [tres'iz] *n.pl.* long hair.
trigger [trig'ər] *v.* to set off; start.
truant [trōō'ənt] *adj.* staying out of school without permission.
truncated [trung'kā tid] *adj.* cut short; having the top cut off.
tumult [tōō'məlt, tū'-] *n.* **1.** the loud, confusing noise of a crowd. **2.** violent motion.
tumultuous [too mul'chōō əs, tyoo-] *adj.* wild and noisy. **—tumultuously,** *adv.*
turbulency [tur'byə lən sē] *n.* wild motion or noisy confusion.
tureen [too rēn', tyoo-] *n.* a deep, covered serving dish.
turret [tur'it] *n.* **1.** a small tower, often at the corner of a building. **2.** a towerlike, usually revolving structure for guns on a ship, airplane, or tank.
tycoon [tī kōōn'] *n.* a wealthy and powerful businessman.

U

unassuming [un'ə sōō'ming] *adj.* not proud or showy; modest.
unbosom [un booz'əm, -bōō'zəm] *v.* to reveal one's feelings.
unbridled [un brīd'əld] *adj.* not held back; uncontrolled.
uncowed [un koud'] *adj.* not timid or afraid.
undermine [un'dər mīn'] *v.* to weaken or injure.
undesignedly [un'di zī'nid lē] *adv.* not purposely.
undoing [un dōō'ing] *n.* the cause of ruin or downfall.
undulate [un'je lāt', -dyə-] *v.* to move in waves.
unfilial [un fil'ē əl] *adj.* not like a loving son or daughter.
unfledged [un flejd'] *adj.* lacking experience; immature.
unflesh [un flesh'] *v.* to take away the flesh of.
unimpaired [un'im pārd'] *v.* not reduced or damaged.
unkempt [un kempt'] *adj.* messy; not combed. **—unkemptly,** *adv.*
unperceived [un'pər sēvd'] *adj.* not seen, heard, etc.
unwonted [un wôn'tid, -wōn'-] *adj.* not common or usual.
uppish [up'ish] *adj.* haughty; snobbish.

V

valor [val'ər] *n.* great courage or bravery.
varmint [vär'mənt] *n.* a bothersome animal; pest.
vaunt [vônt, vänt] *n.* a boast.
vehement [vē'ə mənt] *adj.* having great force or feeling. **—vehemently,** *adv.*
vendor [ven'dər] *n.* a person who sells.
verdant [vurd'ənt] *adj.* green.
verify [ver'ə fī'] *v.* to prove to be true.
vermilion [vər mil'yən] *adj.* bright red.
vex [veks] *v.* to annoy or disturb. **—vexation,** *n.*
visionary [vizh'ə ner'ē] *adj.* not real; imaginary.
visor [vī'zər] *n.* a brim on the front of a cap that shades the eyes.
voluminous [və lōō'mə nəs] *adj.* of great bulk or volume; large. **—voluminously,** *adv.*
voracious [vô rā'shəs, və-] *adj.* eating or wanting large amounts of food.

W

waive [wāv] *v.* to put off; postpone.
wane [wān] *v.* to approach the end.
wanton [wont'ən] *adj.* without cause; senseless. **—wantonness,** *n.*
warrant [wôr'ənt, wor'-] *n.* an order for an arrest.
wary [wār'ē] *adj.* guarding against danger; cautious; alert.
waver [wā'vər] *v.* **1.** to swing back and forth. **2.** to have trouble deciding; show doubt. **—waveringly,** *adv.*
wax [waks] *v.* to become; grow.
weazened [wē'zənd] *adj.* a variation of **wizened.**
well [wel] *v.* to spring or flow upward; gush.
wend [wend] *v.* to go on (one's way).
whelm [hwelm, welm] *v.* to cover; bury.
whimsical [hwim'zi kəl, wim'-] *adj.* making sudden changes; unpredictable.
wiliness [wī'lē nis] *n.* craftiness; slyness.
wizened [wiz'ənd] dried out; shriveled.
wont [wōnt, wônt, wunt] *adj.* accustomed; used.
writhe [rīth] *v.* to twist; turn; squirm.

at; āpe; cär; end; mē; it; īce; hot; ōld; fôrk; wood; fōōl; oil; out; up; ūse; turn; ə in ago, taken, pencil, lemon, circus; bat; chin; dear; five; game; hit; hw in white; joke; kit; lid; man; not; singer; pail; ride; sat; shoe; tag; thin; this; very; wet; yes; zoo; zh in treasure; KH in loch, German ach; N in French bon; œ in French feu, German schön

VOCABULARY REVIEW

In addition to the words listed in the Glossary and the words covered in the word study sections throughout this book, each of the following words is presented to help you prepare for standardized tests of verbal skills. The page numbers at the right tell where you can find these words treated in *Understanding Literature.*

acquiescence	40
acute	85
agile	114
alluring	40
apex	273
athwart	273
capacious	273
capitulation	262
censure	245
condoling	10
condone	26
confiscated	245
credulity	10
crevice	85
deigned	273
deplorable	26
depreciate	114
desolately	40
devious	245
distraught	157
dogged	40
enhance	262
hurtling	157
impact	262
inconsequential	114
inscrutable	157
insolent	157
instigates	114
invariably	26
maligned	10
melancholy	262
precariously	26
presumptuous	10
radical	10
rebuked	245
receding	26
resolute	40
rev	157
sagacity	85
scrutiny	114
stifled	85
stimulates	85
superficial	262
trek	273
valor	245

INDEX OF TITLES BY THEMES

MYSTERY AND ADVENTURE

HOPES AND IDEALS

RELATIONSHIPS BETWEEN GENERATIONS

QUALITIES OF LEADERSHIP

IDENTITY AND SELF-RESPECT

UNDERSTANDING DIFFERENT LIFE STYLES

INDEX OF TITLES BY THEME

This index groups all of the selections according to the themes that they address. Every selection is listed at least once; many are listed more than once. You may want to use this index to help students examine the presentation of a particular theme in different selections.

COPING WITH LOSS

FRIENDSHIP AND LOVE

RESPONDING TO NATURE

METHODS OF COMMUNICATION

INDEX OF SKILLS

Page numbers in boldface italics indicate entries in the Writing About Literature Handbook. Page numbers in italics indicate entries in the Literary Terms Handbook.

See the Table of Contents for list of complete *lessons* on Speaking and Listening Skills, Thinking Skills, Reading and Study Skills, and Writing Skills.

LITERARY SKILLS

INDEX OF SKILLS

This index lists the skills covered under the following heads in the postselection study aids: Literary Focus, Composition, Vocabulary. The index identifies the pages on which the skills are taught or reinforced. For example, every Composition assignment is listed in the Composition Skills section of this index. Page numbers in boldface indicate entries in the Writing About Literature Handbook. Page numbers in italics indicate entries in the Literary Terms Handbook.

COMPOSITION SKILLS

ANALYTICAL
Writing *about* the following:

CREATIVE
Writing the following:

VOCABULARY SKILLS

TEST-TAKING SKILLS

WORD STUDY

Continued from page v

Little, Brown and Company

MAY SWENSON: "Water Picture" from *New & Selected Things Taking Place.* First appeared in *The New Yorker.* Copyright © 1956 by May Swenson.

DAVID WAGONER: "Lament for the Non-Swimmers" from *In Broken Country: Poems.* Copyright © 1979 by David Wagoner.

The preceding selections were reprinted by permission of Little, Brown and Company in association with the Atlantic Monthly Press.

Macmillan Publishing Company

HAMLIN GARLAND: From pp. 68–75 in *A Son of the Middle Border.* Copyright 1917 by Hamlin Garland, renewed 1945 by Mary I. Lord and Constance G. Williams.

JOHN MASEFIELD: "Sea Fever" from *Poems.* Copyright 1953 by Macmillan Publishing Co., Inc.

MARJORIE KINNAN RAWLINGS: "A Mother in Mannville" from *When the Whippoorwill...* Copyright 1940 by Marjorie Kinnan Rawlings, copyright renewed © 1968 by Norton Baskin. Reprinted with the permission of Charles Scribner's Sons, an imprint of Macmillan Publishing Company.

WILLIAM BUTLER YEATS: "The Song of Wandering Aengus" from *Collected Poems of William Butler Yeats.*

The preceding selections were reprinted by permission of Macmillan Publishing Co., Inc.

Harold Matson Company, Inc.

JAMES RAMSEY ULLMAN: "Kilimanjaro!" Copyright © 1958 by James Ramsey Ullman. Reprinted by permission of the Harold Matson Company, Inc.

N. Scott Momaday

N. SCOTT MOMADAY: "To a Child Running with Outstretched Arms in Canyon de Chelly" from *Carriers of the Dream Wheel: Contemporary Native American Poetry,* edited by Duane Niatum. Copyright © 1975 by N. Scott Momaday. Reprinted by permission of N. Scott Momaday.

William Morrow & Company

NIKKI GIOVANNI: "Knoxville, Tennessee" from *Black Feeling, Black Talk, Black Judgment.* Copyright 1968, 1970 by Nikki Giovanni. Reprinted by permission of William Morrow & Company.

The New Yorker Magazine, Inc.

WILLIAM MAXWELL: "The Patterns of Love." Copyright 1945, © 1973 by The New Yorker Magazine, Inc. Reprinted by permission of The New Yorker Magazine, Inc.

Random House, Inc.

MAYA ANGELOU: From *I Know Why the Caged Bird Sings.* Copyright © 1969 by Maya Angelou.

TONI CADE BAMBARA: "Raymond's Run" from *Gorilla, My Love.* Copyright © 1970 by Toni Cade Bambara.

LANGSTON HUGHES: "Dreams" from *The Dream Keeper and Other Poems.* Copyright 1932 by Alfred A. Knopf, Inc. and renewed 1960 by Langston Hughes.

ELINOR WYLIE: "Velvet Shoes" from *Collected Poems of Elinor Wylie.* Copyright 1921 by Alfred A. Knopf, Inc. and renewed 1949 by William Rose Benét.

The preceding selections were reprinted by permission of the publisher and Random House, Inc.

Marian Reiner

EVE MERRIAM: "Onomatopoeia" from *It Doesn't Have to Rhyme.* Copyright © 1964 by Eve Merriam. Reprinted by permission of Marian Reiner for the author.

The Society of Authors

WALTER DE LA MARE: "Silver" from *Collected Poems.* The Literary Trustees of Walter de la Mare and The Society of Authors as their representative.

W. W. JACOBS: "The Monkey's Paw."

JOHN MASEFIELD: "Sea-Fever" from *Salt Water Poems and Ballads.*

The preceding selections were reprinted by permission of The Society of Authors as the literary representative of the authors, their estates and trustees.

The Jesse Stuart Foundation

JESSE STUART: "Split Cherry Tree" from *Esquire* Magazine, January 1939. Copyright © 1938 by Esquire, Inc. Reprinted by permission of The Jesse Stuart Foundation and its agents, Raines & Raines.

Rosemary Thurber

JAMES THURBER: "The Secret Life of Walter Mitty" from *My World and Welcome to It.* Copyright © 1942 by James Thurber, © 1970 by Helen Thurber. Published by Harcourt Brace Jovanovich. "The Spreading 'You Know' " from *Lanterns and Lances.* Copyright © 1961 by James Thurber. Published by Harper & Row.

The preceding selections were reprinted by permission of Rosemary Thurber.

Twayne Publishers, Inc.

CLAUDE MC KAY: "The Tropics in New York" from *Selected Poems by Claude McKay.* Copyright © 1910 and reprinted with the permission of Twayne Publishers, Inc., a division of G. K. Hall & Co., Boston.

Yoshiko Uchida

YOSHIKO UCHIDA: "Of Dry Goods and Black Bow Ties." Copyright by Yoshiko Uchida. Reprinted by permission of the author.

The University of Notre Dame Press
ERNESTO GALARZA: "North From Mexico" as edited from pp. 183–191 in *Barrio Boy.* Copyright © 1971 by The University of Notre Dame Press. Reprinted by permission of The University of Notre Dame Press.

Viking Penguin, Inc.
PHILIP BOOTH: "Ego" from *Letter from a Distant Land.* Originally published in *The New Yorker.* Copyright © 1956 by Philip Booth.
GORDON PARKS: "The Funeral" from *Whispers of Intimate Things.* Copyright © 1971 by Gordon Parks.
SAKI (H.H. MUNRO): "The Interlopers" from *The Complete Short Stories of Saki (H. H. Munro).* Copyright 1930 by The Viking Press, Inc. Copyright renewed 1958 by The Viking Press, Inc.
The preceding selections were reprinted by permission of Viking Penguin, Inc.

Watkins, Loomis Agency, Inc.
ROALD DAHL: "Beware of the Dog" from *Over to You.* Copyright 1946 by Roald Dahl. Reprinted by permission of A. Watkins, Inc.

A. P. Watt Ltd., Literary Agents
WILLIAM BUTLER YEATS: "Song of Wandering Aengus" from *Collected Poems.* Reprinted by permission of M. B. Yeats, Anne Yeats and Macmillan London Limited.

Wesleyan University Press
ROBERT FRANCIS: "The Base Stealer" from *The Orb Weaver.* Copyright © 1948 by Robert Francis. Reprinted by permission of Wesleyan University Press.

CREDITS

Illustration Credits:
Cover: David Frampton.
Lynn Adams, 4. Jan Brett, 282, 283. David Chestnutt, 148, 149, 150. Donna Diamond, 36, 38. Leo and Diane Dillon, cover, 432–433, 438–439, 440–441, 442–443, 445, 448–449, 454–455, 460–461, 462–463, 464–465, 468–469, 470, 474–475, 478–479, 482–483, 484–485. Dan Fione, 90–91. John Freas, 96, 103, 107. Eva Fuka, 191, 192, 193, 194. Jeff Lieppman, 154–155. Bob LoGrippo, xiv–1, 123. Ed Martinez, 56, 60. Bob Masheris, cover, 292–293, 295, 301. Sal Murdocca, 13, 14, 19, 22. Ivan Powell, 305, 307, 310. John Thompson, 490–491, 493, 497, 507, 510, 515, 523, 529, 533, 538. Arthur Tress, 117. Richard Williams, 134

Photo Credits: © Paul Agresti, 214–5. © Ann Atwood, 160T, 184, 186–7, 198, 203. Art Resources: © Museum of Modern Art, 72; © Musee des Augustins, 113; © SEF, 434L; © Scala, New York/ Florence, 437R; © Saskia/Kunsthistorisches Museum, Vienna, 78; © Zurich Museum, 210. Courtesy of the Bancroft Library, University of California, 255. © Jerry Bauer, 86. © The Bettmann Archive, 164. © BBC Hulton Picture Library, 541. Black Star: © Mark Morrow, 54; © Norman Myers, 232–3, 266, 270; © John Rees, 321T; © Werner Wolff, 128. California Historical Society Library, 232–3B, 236, 238, 239. © Colour Library International USA Ltd., 160–161, 226. © Culver Pictures, Inc., 34, 81, 95, 110, 115, 119, 139, 152, 162B, 163, 182T, 183B, 196T, C, B, 208T, C, 220T, 221B, 232–3, 242, 243, 274, 287, 316, 490–1, 543, 551, 561, 570, 573, 580, 587, 593, 596, 606, 622, 632, 635, 644, 655, 658, 666. By Kind Permission of The Dickens House, 541. © Bay Ellis, 172–3, 214–5. Mary Evans Picture Library, 169. By permission of the Folger Shakespeare Library, 197B, 329. The Folger Shakespeare Theatre: © Joan Marcus, 292–3, 353T, R, C, 339, 345, 349, 355, 359, 369, 374, 381, 389, 396, 402, 407, 411, 420, 425. © George Fry, Addison-Wesley, 235. The Granger Collection, 76, 183T, 197T, 220C, 258, 264, 328. Guildhall Art Gallery, City of London, 141. The Image Bank: © Murray Alcosser, 217; © Jan Cobb, 216. International Museum of Photography at George Eastman House: detail of Lewis W. Hine photo, 218–219T, B. © Courtesy Lucy Kroll Agency, 209C. Lescher & Lescher Ltd. N.Y.: private collection, 50. Magnum Photos: © Cornell Eapa, 313; © Elliott Erwitt, 306; © Burt Glinn, 175B; © Erich Lessing, 434, 435, 436L, R, 437R; © Dennis Stock, 275C, R. Courtesy of Marlborough Fine Art, London: private collection, 82. © Lawrence Migdale, 42,43. The Museum of Modern Art: Film Stills Archive, Courtesy of United Artists, 330. The New York Public Library Picture Collection: 2, 11, 86, 146, 176, 196T, 295; Rare Book Division, Astor, Lenox and Tilden Foundations, 189; Schomburg Collection, 209T. © The New York Times, 48, 182B, 220B, 241. © Perry Pictures, 182C, 208C. Photo Researchers, Inc.: © Ken Brate, 1C, 29R; © Bob Fearon, 29L; © Davis/Gillete, 66; © Chester Higgins, Jr., 175T; © George Holton, 490–1; © William Katz, 436R; © Russ Kinne, 160–1C, 224–5; © Bernard P. Wolff, 201. The Pierpont Morgan Library, © Birgit Pohl, 204–5. © P. H. Polk, 248. Kay Reese & Associates: Berlitz, 180. © San Jose Mercury & News, 252. © Maurice Segoura Gallery, N. Y.: Photo by Bruce C. Jones, 228–9. Shostal Associates: © Eddie Stangler, 275T. The Stock Market: Greg Davis, 275B; © Luis Villota, 275C, L. © Time Inc., Hank Walker, 309B. © Photo by Arthur Tress, 117. United Press International, 64, 197C. 287, 309T, 317. © U.S. Navy, 179. Courtesy Victoria and Albert Museum: Photo by Eileen Tweedy, 207. © Evangelina Vigil-Piñon, 209C. © Patt Wagoner, 221T. © Wide World Photos, 260, 321B, 492. Woodfin Camp & Associates: © Adam Woolfitt, cover, 171.

INDEX OF AUTHORS AND TITLES

Page numbers in italics indicate biographical material.

INDEX OF AUTHORS AND TITLES

This index is an alphabetical listing of all the selections and authors included in this textbook. Page numbers in italics indicate biographical information.

TEACHER'S PERSONAL RECORD

Most Successful Assignments and Projects

Page Notes

TEACHER'S PERSONAL RECORD

Most Successful Pairings or Groupings of Selections

TEACHER'S PERSONAL RECORD

Most Successful Pairings or Groupings of Selections

TEACHER'S PERSONAL RECORD

Original Assignments and Projects

Literary work being taught	My original assignment or project

TEACHER'S PERSONAL RECORD

Original Assignments and Projects

Literary work being taught	My original assignment or project

TEACHER'S PERSONAL RECORD

Additional Resources

Literary work being taught	Title and location of article, illustration, recording, film, etc.

TEACHER'S PERSONAL RECORD

Additional Resources

Literary work being taught	Title and location of article, illustration, recording, film, etc.

E. Dickinson William Faulkner Tom Wolfe

Gerard M. Hopkins S.J. Mark Twain Rudyard Kipling

Gwendolyn Brooks Randall Jarrell Joseph Conrad.

Stephen Spender R M Rilke C Brontë Virginia Woolf

John Keats Arthur Conan Doyle Sidney Lanier

Fr Kafka Robert Graves A Bradstreet William [illegible]

A Lincoln Henry W. Longfellow Marianne Moore

James Joyce Fred'k Douglass W Blake J. Austen

Wallace Stevens Robert Graves Phillis Wheatley Walt Whitman

C Brontë [illegible] F Scott Fitzgerald